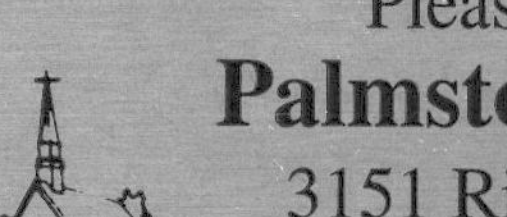

The Complete

BIBLICAL LIBRARY

The Complete
BIBLICAL LIBRARY

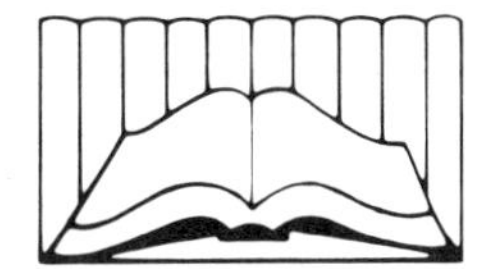

THE NEW TESTAMENT GREEK-ENGLISH DICTIONARY

Sigma–Omega

Word Numbers
4375–5457

The Complete
BIBLICAL LIBRARY

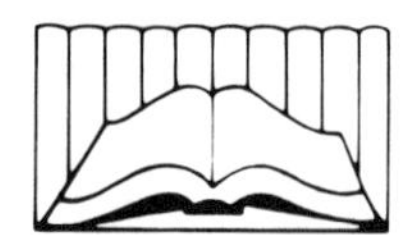

The Complete Biblical Library, part 1, a 16-volume study series on the New Testament. Volume 16: GREEK-ENGLISH DICTIONARY, SIGMA—OMEGA, Word Numbers 4375–5457.

Printed in the United States of America 1991 by R.R. Donnelley and Sons Company, Chicago, Illinois 60606. Library of Congress Catalog Card Number 90-85592 International Standard Book Number 0-88243-376-8.

THE COMPLETE BIBLICAL LIBRARY
International and Interdenominational Bible Study System

THE NEW TESTAMENT
Study Bible, Greek-English Dictionary, Harmony of the Gospels

THE OLD TESTAMENT
Study Bible, Hebrew-English Dictionary

THE BIBLE ENCYCLOPEDIA

THE NEW TESTAMENT GREEK-ENGLISH DICTIONARY

Sigma–Omega

Word Numbers
4375–5457

THE COMPLETE BIBLICAL LIBRARY
Springfield, Missouri, U.S.A.

Table of Contents

INTERNATIONAL EDITOR
Thoralf Gilbrant

Executive Editor: Ralph W. Harris, M.A.

National Editor: Stanley M. Horton, Th.D.

Managing Editor: Gayle A. Seaver, J.D.

Greek-English Dictionary Editor: Denis W. Vinyard, M.Div.

Greek-English Dictionary Associate Editor: Donald F. Williams, M.Div.

BOARD OF REVIEW

John D. Bechtle, D.Min.
Daniel L. Black, Th.D.
David Alan Black, D.Theol.
David R. Bundrick, Th.M.
Vernon D. Doerksen, Th.D.
Thomas E. Friskney, B.D.
Timothy P. Jenney, M.A.
Fred R. Johnson, Ph.D.
Erich H. Kiehl, Th.D.
Oliver McMahan, D.Min.
Siegfried S. Schatzmann, Ph.D.
Virgil Warren, Ph.D.
William C. Williams, Ph.D.
Barney D. Wimer, Ph.D.

STAFF

Senior Editors: Gary L. Leggett, M.A.; Dorothy B. Morris

Editorial Team: Paul S. Ash, M.A., GED Technical Editor; David A. Baca, B.A.; Patti J. Christensen; Faye Faucett; Charlotte L. Gribben; Susan Hall; Melvin M.S. Ho, M.Div.; Gilberto Huerta, M.A.; Carlos E. Johnson, Jr., M.A., GED Background Research; Debra K. King, B.A.; Robert F. Land, B.A., GED Background Research; Gregory A. Lint, M.Div., Septuagint Research; Charles F. Lynch, M.Div., GED Technical Editor; Paul J. Martin, M.A.; Michael Ritchie, M.Div.; Marietta L. Vinyard; Karen D. Wuertz, M.Div.

Production Coordinator, Study Bible, and GED Layout Artist: Cynthia D. Riemenschneider

Art Director: Terry Van Someren, B.F.A.

Word Processing and Secretarial: Sonja Jensen; Rochelle L. Holman; Therese Ritchie; Rachel Wisehart Harvey, B.A.

Volume 16 Contributors

The following writers contributed research and original manuscripts for the word studies in Volume 16.

Paul S. Ash, M.A.

Carolyn D. Baker, M.Div.

Timothy B. Cargal, M.A.

Wilber T. Dayton, Th.D.

David A. Dean, Th.D.

Steve D. Eutsler, M.A.

Carlos E. Johnson, Jr., M.A.

Erich H. Kiehl, Th.D.

Byron D. Klaus, D.Min.

Richard A. Koffarnus, M.Div.

Robert F. Land, M.Div.

Gregory A. Lint, M.Div.

A. Wayne Lowen, Ph.D.

Howard Lucas, M.Div.

M. Robert Mansfield, Ph.D.

Paul R. McReynolds, Ph.D.

Johnny V. Miller, Th.D.

Bernard Rossier, Ph.D.

Siegfried S. Schatzmann, Ph.D.

Gayle Garrity Seaver, J.D.

Stan J. Tharp, M.A.

Francis C. R. Thee, Ph.D.

Robert E. Tourville, M.A.

Denis W. Vinyard, M.Div.

Paul Walker, Ph.D.

Donald F. Williams, M.Div.

Paul O. Wright, Th.D.

Richard A. Young, Ph.D.

Greek and Hebrew Alphabets

Greek

Α	α	alpha	a	(f<u>a</u>ther)
Β	β	beta	b	
Γ	γ	gamma	g	(got)
Δ	δ	delta	d	
Ε	ε	epsilon	e	(g<u>e</u>t)
Ζ	ζ	zeta	z	dz (lea<u>ds</u>)
Η	η	eta	ē	(<u>a</u>te)
Θ	θ	theta	th	(<u>th</u>in)
Ι	ι	iota	i	(s<u>i</u>n or mach<u>i</u>ne)
Κ	κ	kappa	k	
Λ	λ	lambda	l	
Μ	μ	mu	m	
Ν	ν	nu	n	
Ξ	ξ	xi	x	
Ο	ο	omicron	o	(l<u>o</u>t)
Π	π	pi	p	
Ρ	ϱ	rho	r	
Σ	σ,ς[1]	sigma	s	
Τ	τ	tau	t	
Υ	υ	upsilon	u	German ü
Φ	φ	phi	ph	(<u>ph</u>ilosophy)
Χ	χ	chi	ch	(<u>ch</u>aos)
Ψ	ψ	psi	ps	(li<u>ps</u>)
Ω	ω	omega	ō	(<u>o</u>cean)

Hebrew

א		aleph	’[2]	
בּ, ב		beth	b, v	
גּ, ג		gimel	g, gh	
דּ, ד		daleth	d, dh	(<u>th</u>ey)[3]
ה		he	h	
ו		waw	w	
ז		zayin	z	
ח		heth	ch	(kh)
ט		teth	<u>t</u>	
י		yodh	y	
כּ, כ	ך	kaph	k, kh	
ל		lamedh	l	
מ	ם	mem	m	
נ	ן	nun	n	
ס		samekh	<u>s</u>	
ע		ayin	‘	
פּ, פ	ף	pe	p, ph	
צ	ץ	sadhe	ts	
ק		qoph	q	
ר		resh	r	
שׂ		sin	s	
שׁ		shin	sh	
תּ, ת		taw	t, th	(<u>th</u>ing)[3]

Hebrew Vowels

ָ	ā	father	ֻ	u	rule	ֵי	ê	they
ַ	a	dam	ֹ	ō	role	ָה	âh	ah
ֶ	e	men	וּ	û	tune	ֲ	ă	hat
ֵ	ē	they	וֹ	ô	hole	ֱ	ĕ	met
ִ	i	pin	ִי	î	machine	ְ	ᵉ	av<u>e</u>rage
ָ	o	roll	ֶי	ê	they	ֳ	ŏ	not

Greek Pronunciation Rules

Before another *g*, or before a *k* or a *ch*, *g* is pronounced and spelled with an *n*, in the transliteration of the Greek word.

In the Greek, ς is written at the end of a word, elsewhere it appears as σ. The rough breathing mark (‛) indicates that an *h*-sound is to be pronounced before the initial vowel or diphthong. The smooth breathing mark (’) indicates that no such *h*-sound is to be pronounced.

There are three accents, the acute (—́), the circumflex (—̂) and the grave (—̀). These stand over a vowel and indicate that stress in pronunciation is to be placed on the syllable having any one of the accents.

Pronouncing Diphthongs

ai is pronounced like *ai* in aisle
ei is pronounced like *ei* in eight
oi is pronounced like *oi* in oil
au is pronounced like *ow* in cow
eu is pronounced like *eu* in feud
ou is pronounced like *oo* in food
ui is pronounced like *ui* in suite (sweet)

1. Where two forms of a letter are given, the one at the right is used at the end of a word.
2. Not represented in transliteration when the initial letter.
3. Letters underscored represent pronunciation of the second form only.

4375. σαβαχθανί sabachthani verb

Sabachthani; "You have forsaken me."

1. σαβαχθανί sabachthani 2sing
2. σαβαχθανι sabachthani 2sing

2 saying, Eli, Eli, lama **sabachthani?** .... Matt 27:46
1 saying, Eloi, Eloi, lama **sabachthani?** .... Mark 15:34

This word is a Greek transliteration of the Aramaic term *shᵉvaqᵉtanî,* which is part of the last seven expressions uttered by Jesus on the cross just before His death: "*Eloi, Eloi* (Hebrew: *'Eli, Elî*), *lama sabachthani* . . . My God, my God, why hast thou forsaken me?" (Mark 15:34; cf. Matthew 27:46).

The variations in the words used for "my God" in Matthew and Mark seem to indicate some uncertainty whether Jesus cried out in Hebrew or Aramaic. In either language the first two words are so similar that the crowd thought Jesus was calling out for Elias (Elijah; cf. Matthew 27:47; Mark 15:35).

In any case, the expression, which is a quotation of the opening words of Psalm 22:1 in Aramaic (the Hebrew is *'azavtānî*), is full of overwhelming emotion. Jesus' sense of abandonment by God reflects the intensity of His suffering yet does not imply any lack of trust in God for deliverance. There are other instances where the Gospel writers compare the suffering of Christ with that of the Psalmist in Psalm 22 (cf. Mark 15:29 and Psalm 22:7; Matthew 27:43 and Psalm 22:8; Matthew 27:35/Mark 15:24 and Psalm 22:18). Finally, as Psalm 22 ends with a proclamation of thanksgiving to God for His deliverance, Christ's crucifixion ended with His glorious resurrection.

Strong 4518, Bauer 738.

4376. Σαβαώθ Sabaōth name

Armies, hosts.

צְבָא tsāvā' (6893), Hosts, Almighty (1 Sm 1:3, Is 5:7, 22:14f.).

1. Σαβαώθ Sabaōth masc

1 Except the Lord **of Sabaoth** had left us a seed,...... Rom 9:29
1 are entered into the ears of the Lord of **sabaoth**...... Jas 5:4

Septuagint Usage

This noun is a Greek transliteration of the Hebrew term *tsᵉvā'ôth* (a plural form of *tsāvā',* "army") which means "armies, hosts." It appears in the Septuagint as part of a compound that includes the divine name of God, "Lord of the *Armies,* Lord of *Hosts*" (cf. *Bauer*). This title for God does not occur in the Pentateuch but can be found occasionally in the books of 1 and 2 Samuel (LXX 1 and 2 Kings), 1 and 2 Kings (LXX 3 and 4 Kings), 1 and 2 Chronicles, and the Psalms. It also occurs frequently in the Prophets, especially Isaiah, Jeremiah, Haggai, Zechariah, and Malachi (cf. Walker, "God, Names of," *International Standard Bible Encyclopedia,* 2:507). In 1 Samuel 17:45 (LXX 1 Kings 17:45) the "hosts" refer to the armies of Israel. However, in the prophetic literature *Sabaōth* is used in nonmilitary contexts, perhaps referring to supernatural beings (Isaiah 40:26). In either case it is clear that its usage with the divine name of God indicates that He is sovereignly all-powerful over all created beings both human and supernatural.

New Testament Usage

In the New Testament *Sabaōth* is used only twice, once each by Paul and James. In Romans 9:29 Paul used the term to introduce the doctrine of the faithful "remnant" (further discussed in Romans 11:1-10). The "Lord of *Hosts*" is both free and able to preserve a "remnant" from His chosen people and also include Gentiles in His salvation. In James 5:4 it is used in a manner similar to the Septuagint where the "Lord of *Hosts*" is a descriptive title of God's omnipotence. James warned those who use their wealth to oppress the poor that an all-powerful God knows of such injustice and will vindicate their victims.

Strong 4519, Bauer 738, Moulton-Milligan 567.

4377. σαββατισμός sabbatismos noun

Keeping the sabbath, sabbath rest.

Cross-Reference:

σάββατον sabbaton (4378)

1. σαββατισμός sabbatismos nom sing masc

1 remaineth therefore **a rest** to the people of God. . . . . Heb 4:9

This noun is related to the verb *sabbatizō*, "to keep the sabbath," and means "a sabbath keeping" or "sabbath rest." It is used only once in the New Testament, at Hebrews 4:9. There the "rest" reserved for God's people is called a "sabbath rest" because it marks ceasing from works done for oneself and giving attention to the work God has for us. When God completed His creative work He "rested," that is, "ceased" His work of creation and gave himself to work in behalf of His creation. He offers the same promise to those who remain faithful to Him (verse 10).

Strong 4520, Bauer 739, Moulton-Milligan 567, Kittel 7:34-35, Liddell-Scott 1579, Colin Brown 3:411.

4378. σάββατον sabbaton noun

Sabbath, a period of 7 days.

Cognates:

προσάββατον prosabbaton (4173)
σαββατισμός sabbatismos (4377)

שַׁבָּת shabbāth (8141), Sabbath (Lv 23:3, Neh 9:14, Ez 20:12f.).

שַׁבָּתוֹן shabbāthôn (8142), Sabbath (Ex 16:23).

1. σάββατον sabbaton nom/acc sing neu
2. σαββάτου sabbatou gen sing neu
3. σαββάτῳ sabbatō dat sing neu
4. σαββάτων sabbatōn gen pl neu
5. σάββασιν sabbasin dat pl neu
6. σάββατα sabbata nom/acc pl neu
7. σαββάτοις sabbatois dat pl neu

5 Jesus went on the **sabbath** day through the corn; . . . Matt 12:1
3 which is not lawful to do upon the **sabbath day**. 12:2
5 how that on the **sabbath days** the priests 12:5
1 the priests in the temple profane the **sabbath**, ... 12:5
2 the Son of man is Lord even of the **sabbath day**. 12:8
5 saying, Is it lawful to heal on the **sabbath days**? 12:10
5 and if it fall into a pit on the **sabbath day**, ... 12:11
5 it is lawful to do well on the **sabbath days**. 12:12
3 your flight be not ... neither on the **sabbath day**: 24:20
4 In the end **of the sabbath**, as it began to dawn 28:1
4 it began to dawn toward the first day **of the week**, ... 28:1
5 on the **sabbath day** he entered into the synagogue, . . Mark 1:21
5 went through the corn fields on the **sabbath day**; 2:23
5 Behold, why do they on the **sabbath day** 2:24
1 The **sabbath** was made for man, and not man for 2:27
1 was made for man, and not man for the **sabbath**: 2:27
2 the Son of man is Lord also of the **sabbath**. 2:28
5 whether he would heal him on the **sabbath day**; 3:2
5 Is it lawful to do good on the **sabbath days**, ... 3:4
2 And when the **sabbath day** was come, ... 6:2
2 And when the **sabbath** was past, Mary Magdalene, Mark 16:1
4 very early in the morning the first day **of the week**, ... 16:2
2 Jesus was risen early the first day **of the week**, ... 16:9
4 he went into the synagogue on the **sabbath** day, ... Luke 4:16
5 of Galilee, and taught them on the **sabbath days**. 4:31
3 came to pass on the second **sabbath** after the first, ... 6:1
5 that which is not lawful to do on the **sabbath days**? 6:2
2 That the Son of man is Lord also of the **sabbath**. 6:5
3 And it came to pass also on another **sabbath**, ... 6:6
3 whether he would heal on the **sabbath day**; 6:7
5 Is it lawful on the **sabbath days** to do good, ... 6:9
5 teaching in one of the synagogues on the **sabbath**. 13:10
3 because that Jesus had healed on the **sabbath day**, ... 13:14
2 come and be healed, and not on the **sabbath** day. 13:14
3 on the **sabbath** loose his ox or his ass from the stall, . . . 13:15
2 be loosed from this bond on the **sabbath** day? 13:16
3 eat bread **on the sabbath day**, ... they watched him. 14:1
3 Is it lawful to heal on the **sabbath day**? 14:3
2 not straightway pull him out on the **sabbath** day? 14:5
2 I fast twice in the **week**, I give tithes of all 18:12
1 day was the preparation, and the **sabbath** drew on. 23:54
1 and rested the **sabbath** day 23:56
4 Now upon the first day of the **week**, ... 24:1
1 and on the same day was the **sabbath**. . . . . John 5:9
1 It is the **sabbath** day: it is not lawful for thee 5:10
3 he had done these things on the **sabbath day**. 5:16
1 because he not only had broken the **sabbath**, ... 5:18
3 and ye on the **sabbath** day circumcise a man. 7:22
3 If a man on the **sabbath day** receive circumcision, ... 7:23
3 made a man every whit whole on the **sabbath day**? 7:23
1 it was the **sabbath** day when Jesus made the clay, ... 9:14
1 because he keepeth not the **sabbath day**. 9:16
3 not remain upon the cross on the **sabbath** day, ... 19:31
2 for that **sabbath day** was an high day, ... 19:31
4 The first day of the **week** cometh Mary Magdalene 20:1
4 being the first day of the **week**, ... 20:19
2 which is from Jerusalem a **sabbath day's** journey. . . . . Acts 1:12
4 and went into the synagogue on the **sabbath** day, ... 13:14
1 the prophets which are read every **sabbath day**, ... 13:27
1 might be preached to them the next **sabbath**. 13:42
3 the next **sabbath day** came almost the whole city 13:44
1 being read in the synagogues every **sabbath day**. 15:21
4 And on the **sabbath** we went out of the city 16:13
6 and three **sabbath days** reasoned with them 17:2
1 And he reasoned in the synagogue every **sabbath**, ... 18:4
4 And upon the first day of the **week**, ... 20:7
4 Upon the first day of the **week** let every one of you 1 Co 16:2
4 or of the new moon, or of the **sabbath days**: . . . . Col 2:16

Old Testament Background

This noun is a Greek transliteration of the Hebrew term *shabbāth*, which was probably derived from the verb *sāvath*, "to cease." "Sabbath" referred to the day when all work ceased (cf. Leviticus 23:32; 2 Chronicles 36:21). After God established a covenantal relationship with Israel, He instituted a sabbath-day observance among the Jews that was to serve as a memorial of the Exodus (Deuteronomy 5:15). Exodus 20 shows that the *way* Israel was to observe the Sabbath was analogous to God's rest (cf. Genesis 2:3): no work on the seventh day of each week (verses 8-11). The Israelite sabbath was a unique institution in the ancient Near East that testified to the covenant relationship between God and His people (Exodus 31:12-17; Jeremiah 17:19-27; Ezekiel 20:12-21).

In the Old Testament the Hebrew term *shabbāth* is used most frequently to designate observance of the seventh day by ceasing from work and participating in cultic activity (Exodus 16:29; 20:8-11; 31:15; Leviticus 23:3). The "sabbath" also came to be used to designate certain feast days. In Leviticus 16:31 (cf. 23:32) it is used of the Day of Atonement, and it can also be found in reference to the Feast of Trumpets (first day of the seventh month, 23:24) and to the first and last days of the Feast of Booths (23:39). In Leviticus 25:2,4 *shabbāth* is used for the sabbatical year which included the idea of a "sabbath rest" for the land (leaving it fallow, 25:6).

The command to cease from work had a humanitarian as well as religious purpose. Its observance made provision so "thine ox and thine ass may rest, and the son of thy handmaid, and the stranger, may be refreshed" (Exodus 23:12). However, it is somewhat difficult to specify the exact nature of this cessation from work. For example, it did not apply to guard duty (2 Kings 11:4-12).

By the end of the Old Testament period the emphasis on observing the Sabbath as a day of cessation from work and participation in corporate religious activity also came to include a time of theological reflection (cf. McCann, "Sabbath," *International Standard Bible Encyclopedia*, 4:250). The prophet Jeremiah exhorted the Israelites to "hallow the sabbath day" (Jeremiah 17:27). Ezekiel echoed this emphasis by saying that such observance would be a "sign" that the people know God (Ezekiel 20:12,20). From the Exodus to the period of the exile, the Sabbath was to be positively observed, remembered, and hallowed as a witness to God's saving activity in both creation and in deliverance from captivity (ibid.).

Intertestamental Period

In the period between 400 B.C. and the First Century A.D. the Sabbath became an even greater distinctive of the Jewish faith. The conquest of foreign nations and the Dispersion seemed to intensify the efforts of the Jews to preserve their distinctiveness. The Sabbath was one such institution that lent itself well to such a purpose. A faithful Jew could continue its observance in any location. As the Sabbath became a central element in Judaism there was more pressure to define exactly how it should be observed.

Perhaps the most prominent Jewish party by the First Century A.D. was the Pharisees. While they were not the strictest of Jewish parties, they did attempt to interpret the Law concerning the Sabbath so that it could be obeyed by ordinary people of that day (ibid., 4:251). In the Mishnah tractate *Shabbath* 7.2, there is a list of 39 prohibitions for the Sabbath including all types of agricultural work, textile manufacturing, hunting, building, writing letters, and even making or extinguishing fires. In addition, other prohibitive lists were developed along with their possible exceptions (cf. McCann, "Sabbath," *International Standard Bible Encyclopedia*, 4:251). For example, the Sabbath prohibitions did not have to be obeyed if one's life was in danger. Also, by depositing food prior to the Sabbath at the allowed sabbath travel distance, one could extend the "legal" limit set for sabbath travel. Perhaps initially the Pharisees saw their efforts as making it easier to obey sabbath law, but they were very strict with regard to demanding the death penalty for intentional violations (ibid., cf. the Book of Jubilees 2:18-33; 50:6-13).

New Testament Usage

In the New Testament *sabbaton* is used only by the Gospel writers and Paul. All of the occurrences in the Gospels concern Jesus and His ministry. In one respect Jesus faithfully observed the Sabbath by attending activities in the synagogue and temple and on occasion by teaching there (Mark 1:21; 6:2; Luke 4:16,31). However, as far as the Pharisees were concerned Jesus was far from being a model Jew. In Mark 2:23-28 the Pharisees accused Jesus of violating their sabbath regulations by reaping ("plucking grain"). Jesus responded in good Pharisaic fashion by citing Scripture. He reminded them of how David "broke" the law when he ate the bread of Presence (1 Samuel 21:1-6), suggesting that it was necessary for survival. Then Jesus concluded that "the *sabbath* was made for man, and not man for the *sabbath*" (Mark 2:27), and furthermore, "the Son of man is Lord also of the *sabbath*" (verse 28). Christ's insight into Scripture may have humbled and embarrassed the Pharisees, but His claim of authority over the Sabbath angered them (parallel passage in Matthew 12:1-12; cf. Hosea 6:6).

In Mark 3:1-6 (cf. Matthew 12:9-14) the Pharisees accused Jesus of another violation by healing a man's withered hand on the Sabbath. Perhaps if the man's life was in danger the Pharisees would not have been disturbed. Jesus responded by saying that any good act could be done on the Sabbath (Mark 3:4) and that the Pharisees themselves would do the same if such an act were of personal importance to them (cf. Matthew 12:1f.). Luke also included two instances of Jesus healing on the Sabbath (Luke 13:10-17; 14:1-6), and in both Jesus responded in a manner similar to that recorded in Mark and Matthew.

These conflicts over sabbath regulations did not involve any violation of the Mosaic law. Jesus never violated the Torah. He did, however, take exception to the Pharisaic interpretations and applications of the sabbath regulations.

Paul, like Jesus, continued to observe the Sabbath even after his conversion. Luke recorded Paul's practice of evangelistic preaching in synagogues wherever he went (Acts 13:14,42,44; 17:2; 18:4). Paul later urged the Colossians not to let anyone judge them "in respect of a holy-day . . . or of the *sabbath* days" (Colossians 2:16). This seems to refer to the shift in the Gentile churches from observance of the Jewish Sabbath Day (Saturday) to worshiping on the Lord's Day (Sunday) (cf. Acts 20:7; 1 Corinthians 16:2; Revelation 1:10). Because of the redemptive work of Christ, a prescribed observance of the Jewish sabbath is no longer required for righteousness in God's eyes (McCann, "Sabbath," *International Standard Bible Encyclopedia*, 4:252). Thus, the importance of the Resurrection in the Christian faith caused the day Jesus rose from the dead to be considered the "Lord's Day," the first day of the week (cf. John 20:1,19).

Later, by the Fourth Century A.D., the Lord's Day began to acquire sabbath characteristics when Constantine prohibited certain kinds of work from being done on Sunday (ibid.). Today many Christians continue to set aside Sunday as a day of worship and rest, while some, like the Seventh-Day Adventists, practice a more literal seventh-day sabbath. In spite of their differences, both practices hold that the present observance of a "sabbath rest" is also a look to the future when Christ will usher believers into an eternal sabbath.

STRONG 4521, BAUER 739, MOULTON-MILLIGAN 567, KITTEL 7:1-34, LIDDELL-SCOTT 1579, COLIN BROWN 3:405.

4379. σαγήνη sagēnē noun

Dragnet.

חֵרֶם chērem (2870), Net (Eccl 7:26 [7:27], Ez 26:5, 47:10).

מִכְמֶרֶת mikhmereth (4503I), Fishing net (Hb 1:15).

מִכְמֹרֶת mikhmōreth (4503II) Net (Is 19:8).

1. σαγήνῃ sagēnē dat sing fem

1 the kingdom of heaven is like unto a net,..........Matt 13:47

The dragnet was a large net used for fishing. The word occurs only in Matthew 13:47, but the same kind of net may have been in use on the occasion of the miraculous "draught" recorded in Luke 5:7-9. The dragnet was an expensive piece of equipment, sometimes immense in size. It was used in two different ways. It could be stretched between two boats and then dragged through the water, or it may have been weighted on one side to hold it on the bottom of the lake while the other side was held at the surface by floats. A single boat could then drag it along, pushing everything ahead of the vertical wall thus formed. In either usage, fish of any size were trapped in this net.

STRONG 4522, BAUER 739, MOULTON-MILLIGAN 567, LIDDELL-SCOTT 1580.

4380. Σαδδουκαῖος

Saddoukaios name

Sadducee (always plural in the New Testament, referring to members of the "party of the Sadducees").

1. Σαδδουκαῖοι Saddoukaioi nom pl masc

2. Σαδδουκαίων Saddoukaiōn gen pl masc

3. Σαδδουκαίους Saddoukaious acc pl masc

2 many of the Pharisees and **Sadducees** come.........Matt 3:7
1 The Pharisees also with the **Sadducees** came,.......... 16:1
2 the leaven of the Pharisees and of the **Sadducees**...... 16:6
2 the leaven of the Pharisees and of the **Sadducees**?..... 16:11
2 the doctrine of the Pharisees and of the **Sadducees**..... 16:12
1 The same day came to him the **Sadducees**,............ 22:23
3 heard that he had put the **Sadducees** to silence,....... 22:34
1 Then come unto him the **Sadducees**,..............Mark 12:18
2 Then came to him certain of the **Sadducees**,.......Luke 20:27
1 and the **Sadducees**, came upon them,...............Acts 4:1
2 which is the sect of the **Sadducees**,.................... 5:17
2 one part were **Sadducees**, and the other Pharisees,..... 23:6
2 between the Pharisees and the **Sadducees**:............. 23:7
1 For the **Sadducees** say that there is no resurrection,.... 23:8

The Sadducees were a socioreligious party centered in Jerusalem and composed primarily of priests who were part of the Jewish aristocracy in Palestine (cf. Acts 5:17). As priests their primary concerns were for the operation of the temple and the interpretation of the Law. While various theories regarding the origin of the name *Sadducees* have been offered, "(n)one of the . . . suggested etymologies is entirely satisfactory" (Moulder, "Sadducees," *International Standard Bible Encyclopedia*, 4:278). The most likely explanation is that it is derived from the Hebrew name "Zadok," and thus represents the attempt by these priests to identify themselves as legitimate members of the "Zadokite priesthood" (when, in fact, most of them were not of Zadokite lineage [Reicke, *New Testament Era*, p.153]). Zadok served as priest with Abiathar during David's reign and was appointed high priest in Abiathar's stead by Solomon; the descendants of Zadok held a special prominence among the priests (cf. Ezekiel 40:45f.).

The earliest mentions of this Sadducean party come from the Maccabean period (mid-Second Century B.C.), though an exact point of origin has not been isolated. However, the transfer of allegiance from the Pharisees to the Sadducees by John Hyrcanus (134–104 B.C.) established the association between them and the Hasmonean high priests that ensured their prominence. This lasted until the destruction of the temple in the Jewish War of A.D. 70. The Sadducees rejected belief in angels and spirits and promoted "this-worldly" positions both in sociopolitical and religious issues in order to protect their economic interests and to hold theological innovations in check (see Jagersma, *A History of Israel from Alexander the Great to Bar Kochba*, pp.69,70). Consequently, they opposed apocalyptic and messianic movements in general and not just Christianity in particular.

The little that is known about the Sadducees has been reported by their opponents. Even Josephus, originally a member of the Sadducees by his birth into an aristocratic priestly family, had already joined the rival party of the Pharisees before writing any of his accounts about the group. His portrayal of the Sadducees is clearly biased against them (see Sundberg, "Sadducees," *Interpreter's Dictionary of the Bible*, 4:161f.). Likewise, since the Pharisaic rabbis largely controlled the development of Judaism following the destruction of the temple, most references to the Sadducees within rabbinic literature have a decidedly polemical tone.

The close association between the Sadducees and the Pharisees implied by Matthew 3:7 and 16:1-12 was certainly not the normal state of affairs, but it shows how great their opposition to Jesus had become. Deep theological divisions existed between the two groups, as is evidenced by Paul's use of their differing views regarding the resurrection of the dead to divide the Pharisaic and Sadducean elements within the Sanhedrin (Acts 23:6-9). It is their lack of belief in the resurrection of the dead or of any type of life after death which is perhaps their most widely attested theological position (cf. Matthew 22:23; Mark 12:18; Luke 20:27, and *Antiquities* 13.4.6).

The basis for these disagreements seems to lie in the unique authority which the Sadducees ascribed to the Torah, the first five books of the Old Testament. While the Sadducees apparently recognized the Prophets and other writings of the Old Testament, they did not feel these books provided an authoritative interpretation of the Law. Consequently, any doctrine that could not be directly substantiated from the Torah was rejected by them. Since the Pharisees maintained there was an "Oral Torah" that had been handed down in the "traditions of the fathers" that interpreted the "Written Torah," these two groups were constantly in conflict (cf. Koester, *History, Culture and Religion of the Hellenistic Age*, p.230).

STRONG 4523, BAUER 739, KITTEL 7:35-54, LIDDELL-SCOTT 1580, COLIN BROWN 3:439.

4381. Σαδώκ Sadōk name

Zadok.

1. Σαδώκ Sadōk masc

1 And Azor begat Sadoc; and Sadoc begat Achim;....Matt 1:14
1 And Azor begat Sadoc; and Sadoc begat Achim;....... 1:14

A name in Matthew's genealogy of Jesus (1:14). (Another Zadok, the priest under David, was the one who anointed Solomon king [see 1 Kings 1].)

4382. σαίνομαι sainomai verb

Move, shake, disturb, agitate.

1. σαίνεσθαι sainesthai inf pres mid

1 That no man should be moved by these afflictions:...1 Th 3:3

Classical Greek

This verb in its active form (*sainō*) can be found in classical Greek from the Eighth Century B.C. meaning "wag the tail" when used of dogs. When used metaphorically of persons it means "fawn, gladden, flatter." In its passive form it can mean "beguile, deceive" (*Liddell-Scott*). It is probably related to the verb *seiō* (4434), "shake, agitate," and is used in this manner in Christian literature (cf. *Bauer*).

New Testament Usage

The Septuagint does not use *sainomai*, and it occurs only once in the New Testament, at 1

Thessalonians 3:3. Beginning at 1 Thessalonians 2:17 Paul recounted the events that transpired since he left this newborn church in order to explain why he sent Timothy to them (3:2). Paul wanted the Thessalonians to know that "afflictions" are inevitable for the Christian and are to be considered evidence of the genuineness of one's faith. Therefore, no one should be "moved" or "shaken" when affliction comes. This does not ignore or lessen the difficulty experienced in affliction but rather offers encouragement in light of vicarious empathy with Christ's suffering (cf. John 15:20; 16:33; Romans 5:3).

STRONG 4525, BAUER 740 (see "sainō"), MOULTON-MILLIGAN 567 (see "sainō"), KITTEL 7:54-56 (see "sainō"), LIDDELL-SCOTT 1580 (see "sainō").

4383. σάκκος sakkos noun

Sackcloth.

שַׂק saq (8012), Sack (Gn 42:35); sackcloth (Est 4:1-4, Jer 49:3 [30:3]).

1. **σάκκος sakkos** nom sing masc
2. **σάκκῳ sakkō** dat sing masc
3. **σάκκους sakkous** acc pl masc

2 they would have repented long ago in **sackcloth**.... Matt 11:21
2 while ago repented, sitting in **sackcloth** and ashes... Luke 10:13
1 and the sun became black as **sackcloth** of hair,....... Rev 6:12
3 and they shall prophesy ... clothed in **sackcloth**........ 11:3

Sackcloth was a rough-textured, dark material (Revelation 6:12) woven from the long, dark hair of the goat or camel. It gave its name (Hebrew *saq*) to both the material and the things made from it. It was used to make sacks for carrying grain (Genesis 42:25) and for the general transporting of goods (Joshua 9:4). It was made especially in Cilicia which exported large quantities for tent making (cf. Stahlin, "sakkos," *Kittel*, 7:57).

Old Testament Background

Both the color and the constitution of the material made it especially adaptable for symbolic use to represent grief and repentance, and that is its primary function in the Old Testament and its only function in the New Testament. It was worn both as an outer garment (Isaiah 50:3) and undergarment (2 Kings 6:30 [LXX 4 Kings 6:30]). In the Old Testament the wearing of sackcloth is especially associated with the act of fasting (1 Kings 21:27 [LXX 3 Kings 20:27]; Nehemiah 9:1; Daniel 9:3; Jonah 3:5). The sackcloth garment signified the mourning and self-abasement of the individual who fasted in penitence. In a similar vein, wearing sackcloth was accompanied by sprinkling ashes on oneself to evidence mourning or disgrace (Esther 4:1,3; Isaiah 58:5; Jeremiah 6:26). It may be that since the theme of prophetic preaching was so often a call to repentance, sackcloth was the prophet's standard garb (Isaiah 20:2; Zechariah 13:4), a badge of his profession (ibid., 7:63).

Sackcloth also signified deep distress and commitment to prayer. The Psalmist wore it when he interceded for his sick companions (Psalm 35:13 [LXX 34:13]). Kings wore it to express feelings of despondency (1 Kings 21:27 [LXX 3 Kings 20:27]) and of distress, rebuke, and rejection (2 Kings 19:1-3 [LXX 4 Kings 19:1-3]). Answers to prayer called for the casting off of sackcloth and for girding with gladness (Psalm 30:11 [LXX 29:11]).

New Testament Usage

New Testament references to sackcloth are completely consistent with Old Testament customs. John the Baptist was apparently dressed in sackcloth as a prophet (Matthew 3:4). So also will be the two witnesses who prophesy in the latter days (Revelation 11:3). The Lord Jesus alluded to its use as a symbol of repentance when He chided two Jewish cities by saying that Tyre and Sidon would have repented in "sackcloth and ashes" if they had been privileged to see the Lord's wonders (Matthew 11:21).

STRONG 4526, BAUER 740, MOULTON-MILLIGAN 567-68, KITTEL 7:56-64, LIDDELL-SCOTT 1581.

4384. Σαλά Sala name

Shelah.

1. **Σαλά Sala** masc

1 the son of **Sala** (NASB, margin).................. Luke 3:32
1 which was the son of **Sala**,.......................... 3:35

The name appears twice in the genealogy of Jesus at Luke 3:32, where the more usual form of the name is Salmon (cf. Luke 3:35).

4385. Σαλαθιήλ Salathiēl name

Shealtiel.

1. **Σαλαθιήλ Salathiēl** masc

1 Jechonias begat **Salathiel**;......................... Matt 1:12
1 and **Salathiel** begat Zorobabel;........................ 1:12
1 which was the son of **Salathiel**,..................... Luke 3:27

The father of Zerubbabel in the genealogy of Jesus (Matthew 1:12; Luke 3:27).

4386. Σαλαμίς Salamis name

Salamis.

1. Σαλαμῖνι Salamini dat fem

1 And when they were at **Salamis**, ... Acts 13:5

This important city on the east coast of Cyprus was the first place Paul preached on his first missionary journey. He was accompanied by Barnabas who was from Cyprus (Acts 13:5).

4387. Σαλείμ Saleim name

Salim.

1. Σαλείμ Saleim neu
2. Σαλίμ Salim neu

1 John also was baptizing in Aenon near to **Salim**, ... John 3:23

A place near Aenon where John the Baptist baptized (John 3:23). There are several possible locations for the site, the most likely of which is 12 kilometers south of Beisan (Bethshan-Scythopolis).

4388. σαλεύω saleuō verb

Shake, totter.

COGNATES:
ἀσάλευτος asaleutos (755)
σάλος salos (4392)

SYNONYMS:
ἀνασείω anaseiō (381)
σείω seiō (4434)
τρέμω tremō (4981)

גָּעַשׁ gāʻash (1649), Qal: shake (Ps 18:7 [17:7]); hithpael: tremble (Ps 18:7 [17:7]).

זוּעַ zûaʻ (2194), Tremble (Eccl 12:3).

זָלַל zālal (2236), Niphal: quake (Jgs 5:5).

חִיל chîl (2523), Writhe; tremble (Pss 96:9 [95:9], 97:4 [96:4], 114:7 [113:7]).

חָפַז chāphaz (2753), Niphal: flee (Ps 48:5 [47:4]).

לֶכֶד lekhedh (4059), Catching (Prv 3:26).

מוּג mûgh (4265), Qal: melt (Ps 46:6 [45:6], Am 9:5); hithpolel: melt away (Na 1:5).

מוּד mûdh (4266), Polel: shake (Hb 3:6).

מוֹט môṭ (4267), Totter, waver; qal: slip (Pss 38:16 [37:16], 94:18 [93:18]); niphal: be moved, be shaken (1 Chr 16:30, Pss 13:4 [12:4], 16:8 [15:8]).

מָסַס māṣaṣ (4701), Niphal: melt (Mi 1:4).

מָעַד māʻadh (4726), Slip (2 Sm 22:37).

נוּד nûdh (5290), Wander, sway; hiphil: make wander (2 Kgs 21:8).

נוּט nûṭ (5302), Shake (Ps 99:1 [98:1]).

נוּעַ nûaʻ (5309), Qal: stagger, wander (Pss 107:27 [106:27], 109:10 [108:10], Lam 4:14f.); niphal: be shaken (Na 3:12); hiphil: shake (Ps 109:25 [108:25]).

נָטָה nāṭâh (5371), Spread out, extend; stumble (Ps 73:2 [72:2]).

סוּר ṣûr (5681), Turn aside, stop; hiphil: remove (2 Chr 33:8).

עָנָה ʻānâh (6257), Answer; piel: afflict (2 Kgs 17:20).

פָּלַץ pālats (6670), Hithpael: shake (Jb 9:6).

צָעַן tsāʻan (7090), Be moved (Is 33:20—only some Alexandrinus texts).

רָגַז rāghaz (7553), Tremble (Ps 77:18 [76:18]).

רָחַף rāchaph (7646), Tremble (Jer 23:9).

רַעַל raʻal (7766), Reeling (Zec 12:2).

רָעַם rāʻam (7769), Roar, resound (Pss 96:11 [95:11], 98:7 [97:7]).

1. σαλεύοντες saleuontes nom pl masc part pres act
2. ἐσάλευσεν esaleusen 3sing indic aor act
3. σαλεῦσαι saleusai inf aor act
4. σαλευόμενον saleuomenon acc sing masc part pres mid
5. σαλευόμενα saleuomena nom/acc pl neu part pres mid
6. σαλευομένων saleuomenōn gen pl neu part pres mid
7. ἐσαλεύθη esaleuthē 3sing indic aor pass
8. σαλευθῶ saleuthō 1sing subj aor pass
9. σαλευθῆναι saleuthēnai inf aor pass
10. σεσαλευμένον sesaleumenon nom/acc sing neu part perf mid
11. σαλευθήσονται saleuthēsontai 3pl indic fut pass

4 A reed **shaken** with the wind? .... Matt 11:7
11 and the powers of the heavens **shall be shaken**: 24:29
11 and the powers that are in heaven **shall be shaken**. Mark 13:25
10 good measure, pressed down, and **shaken together**, Luke 6:38
3 could not **shake** it: for it was founded upon a rock..... 6:48
4 to see? A reed **shaken** with the wind? 7:24
11 for the powers of heaven **shall be shaken**. 21:26
8 that I **should not be moved**: .... Acts 2:25
7 the place **was shaken** where they were assembled 4:31
9 so that the foundations of the prison **were shaken**: 16:26
1 they came thither also, and **stirred up** the people...... 17:13
9 That ye **be** not soon **shaken** in mind, ... 2 Th 2:2
2 Whose voice then **shook** the earth: .... Heb 12:26
6 the removing of those things that **are shaken**, ... 12:27
5 those things which cannot **be shaken** may remain...... 12:27

The verb *saleuō* refers to various types of shaking, such as the motion of a wave or an earthquake, which results in a to-and-fro movement or in tottering. Figuratively it means to produce instability or agitation within a person or a nation and thus denotes temporariness in contrast to something unshakable or permanent.

Classical Greek

In classical Greek the verb occurs in its literal sense to describe the tossing of the sea or an earthquake. Figuratively it refers to the vacillations of human nature, to political unrest, and to the disruptions of normal life and beliefs (cf. Bertram, "saleuō," *Kittel*, 7:65).

Septuagint Usage

In the canonical text of the Septuagint there are about 60 occurrences representing 23 different roots, most frequent of which is *môṭ*, a common term for "shaking" or figuratively for great insecurity (Kaiser, "môṭ," *Theological Wordbook of the Old Testament*, 1:493). The world, under God's sovereign control, has been so established that "it be not moved" (1 Chronicles 16:30; Psalm 96:10 [LXX 95:10]). Likewise, the obedient child of God is secure within God's control and will never be shaken (Psalms 15:5 [LXX 14:5]; 16:8 [15:8]; Proverbs 10:30; 12:3). In contrast, the foot of the ungodly will slip (Deuteronomy 32:35) despite his determination to stand on his own (Psalm 10:6 [LXX 9:27]). In the latter days God will violently shake everything (Isaiah 24:19), knocking over and doing away with everything temporal in order to make room for His personal and permanent kingdom.

New Testament Usage

The verb occurs 15 times in the New Testament. With the literal sense at the forefront, Jesus contrasted John the Baptist to a "reed shaken with the wind" (Matthew 11:7; Luke 7:24), indicating John's sturdiness in the face of opposition. It was an earthquake that shook the foundation of the prison at Philippi, jarring doors open and rattling chains from their moorings (Acts 16:26). The presence of God at Sinai, with the cyclonic winds and trumpeting voice, shook that mountain (Hebrews 12:26,27). But not even a great flood will shake the foundation of the house—figurative for a person's life—built upon hearing and heeding God's Word (Luke 6:48). Finally, the return on a believer's financial investment to God's program will be packed down and running over, as cereal that has been shaken to allow settling (Luke 6:38).

Figuratively the verb is used twice of agitation in a negative sense. The Thessalonian Jews followed Paul to Beroea, agitating the crowd to produce a riot (Acts 17:13). Significantly, Paul prayed that the Thessalonian believers might not be easily agitated by the spread of the false teaching that Christ already had returned (2 Thessalonians 2:2).

Such shaking or agitation can produce disruption and dislodging (cf. *Moulton-Milligan*). That will be the effect of the Lord's return. He will shake the powers of the heavens, dislodging their authority and rendering them powerless before himself (Matthew 24:29; Mark 13:25; Luke 21:26; in contrast to Acts 2:25). God's presence can also produce a positive shaking. As the saints prayed in unity, their meetingplace shook to demonstrate God's power which is available through prayer on behalf of His persecuted people (Acts 4:31).

Strong 4531, Bauer 740, Moulton-Milligan 568, Kittel 7:65-70, Liddell-Scott 1581, Colin Brown 3:558-60.

4389. Σαλήμ Salēm name

Salem.

1. Σαλήμ Salēm fem

1 **For this Melchisedec, king of Salem,** .... **Heb 7:1**
1 **and after that also King of Salem,** **7:2**

Hebrews 7:1f., following Genesis 14:18, calls Melchizedek king of Salem and interprets it "king of peace" (from Hebrew *shalom*). Of several possibilities, the identification with Jerusalem is the most likely.

4390. Σαλμών Salmōn name

Salmon.

1. Σαλμών Salmōn masc

1 **and Naasson begat Salmon;** .... **Matt 1:4**
1 **And Salmon begat Booz of Rachab;** **1:5**
1 **which was the son of Salmon,** .... **Luke 3:32**

The father of Boaz in the genealogy of Jesus (Matthew 1:4f.; Luke 3:32; cf. Ruth 4:20f.).

4391. Σαλμώνη Salmōnē name

Salmone.

1. Σαλμώνην Salmōnēn acc fem

1 **we sailed under Crete, over against Salmone;** .... **Acts 27:7**

A headland which forms the eastern tip of Crete, the modern Cape Sidheros. Paul sailed past it en route to Rome (Acts 27:7).

4392. σάλος salos noun

Waves, sea swells; restlessness.

Cross-Reference:

σαλεύω saleuō (4388)

זַעַף za'aph (2281), Raging (Jon 1:15).

מוֹט môṭ (4267), Be moved, let slip (Pss 55:22 [54:22], 66:9 [65:9], 121:3 [120:3]).

נִידָה nîdhāh (5393), An unclean thing (Lam 1:8).

נָשָׂא nāsâ' (5558), Rise (Ps 89:9 [88:9]).

סְעָרָה ṣeʿārāh (5788), Windstorm (Zec 9:14).

1. σάλου salou gen sing masc

1 distress of nations, ... sea and the **waves** roaring; . . . Luke 21:25

Classical Greek and Septuagint Usage

This term refers literally to the rolling, surging motion of the waves of a rough sea, or some similar swelling or tossing such as might accompany an earthquake (Jonah 1:15). Figuratively it describes the restless tossing of the nations or of a person's inner being.

New Testament Usage

It occurs in the New Testament only at Luke 21:25 where it refers to the signs of the end times. The roaring waves may be extraordinary tossings of a literal ocean, but more likely they symbolize the extreme unrest of the Gentile nations at the uncertainties surrounding them.

STRONG 4535, BAUER 741, MOULTON-MILLIGAN 568, KITTEL 7:65-70, LIDDELL-SCOTT 1582, COLIN BROWN 3:558-61.

4393. σάλπιγξ salpinx noun

Trumpet.

COGNATES:

σαλπίζω salpizō (4394)
σαλπιστής salpistēs (4395)

חֲצֹצְרָה chătsōtsrāh (2792), Trumpet (Nm 10:2, 1 Chr 15:24, 2 Chr 20:28).

יוֹבֵל yôvēl (3207), Ram (Ex 19:13).

קֶרֶן qeren (A7452), Horn (Dn 3:5,7,10,15—Aramaic).

שׁוֹפָר shôphār (8223), Trumpet, ram's horn (Lv 25:9, Jos 6:13, Jer 4:19).

תָּקוֹעַ tāqôaʿ (8955), Trumpet (Ez 7:14).

תְּרוּעָה teruʿāh (8980), Trumpet blast (Lv 23:24).

1. σάλπιγξ salpinx nom sing fem
2. σάλπιγγος salpingos gen sing fem
3. σάλπιγγι salpingi dat sing fem
4. σάλπιγγα salpinga acc sing fem
5. σάλπιγγες salpinges nom pl fem
6. σάλπιγγας salpingas acc pl fem

2 send his angels with a great sound **of a trumpet**, ... Matt 24:31
1 For if the **trumpet** give an uncertain sound, ... 1 Co 14:8
3 at the last **trump**: for the trumpet shall sound, ... 15:52
3 voice of the archangel, and with the **trump** of God: 1 Th 4:16
2 the sound of a **trumpet**, and the voice of words; . . . . Heb 12:19
2 heard behind me a great voice, as **of a trumpet**, ... Rev 1:10
2 was as it were **of a trumpet** talking with me; 4:1
5 and to them were given seven **trumpets**. 8:2
6 the seven angels which had the seven **trumpets** 8:6
2 other voices of the **trumpet** of the three angels, ... Rev 8:13
4 Saying to the sixth angel which had the **trumpet**, ... 9:14

Classical Greek

The origin of the trumpet seems to be Oriental, a conclusion based on drawings found on the Mari Temple which date to 2700 B.C. The trumpet was made from a number of materials including bone, shell, bronze, iron, or copper. Its limited range (two or three notes) suggests it was not used as a musical instrument or in conjunction with other instruments. Rather, its use was limited to that of signals such as military signals, signals to call a civic or religious assembly, or a signal used to call sheep (Friedrich, "salpinx," *Kittel*, 7:73-76).

Old Testament Background

The Hebrews used two major kinds of trumpets. The *shôphār*, made originally from a curved ram's horn, was blown at Sinai to signal Israel to approach (Exodus 19:16). It also announced the arrival of the new moon and the new year (Psalm 81:3 [LXX 80:3]), and the enthronement of a new king (1 Kings 1:34 [LXX 3 Kings 1:34]; 2 Kings 9:13 [4 Kings 9:13]). It was also sounded in the temple to accompany the expressions of praise (Psalms 98:6 [LXX 97:6]; 150:3). Militarily it gave the signal for battle (Judges 3:27; 2 Samuel 20:1 [LXX 2 Kings 20:1]) and was instrumental in Joshua's victory at Jericho (Joshua 6) and Gideon's victory over the Midianites (Judges 7). Figuratively the prophet was called a *shôphār* as God's instrument to signal Israel, calling them to worship and warning of danger (Ezekiel 33:3-6; Isaiah 58:1; Jeremiah 6:17).

The *shôphār* was possibly supplanted to a large degree by the *chatsōtsrāh*, a tube of straight narrow bore, often made of metal (cf. 2 Kings 11:14 [LXX 4 Kings 11:14]/2 Chronicles 23:13; 2 Samuel 6:15 [LXX 2 Kings 6:15]/1 Chronicles 13:8; ibid., 7:77). It produced only two or three pitches and was used primarily for religious purposes. A third term of significance for trumpet, although translated *salpinx* only once in the Old Testament (Exodus 19:13), is *yôvēl* which means "ram." It gave its name to both an instrument and to a year whose beginning it signaled, Jubilee.

New Testament Usage

In the New Testament the trumpet is used chiefly to signal. Such a signal had to be blown clearly if it was to have meaning for its intended audience. This idea served as a standard for the use of tongues in the public assembly (1 Corinthians 14:8). In addition, the blast of a trumpet will signal the Second Coming (1 Corinthians 15:52; 1 Thessalonians 4:16) and the gathering of the elect (Matthew 24:31). It also signals the second round of judgments (Revelation 8:2,6,13; 9:14). These blasts probably represent a military clarion. Finally, the forceful voice of the Saviour is said to trumpet (Revelation 1:10; 4:1), perhaps a reminder of God's voice at Sinai (Hebrews 12:19).

STRONG 4536, BAUER 741, MOULTON-MILLIGAN 568, KITTEL 7:71-88, LIDDELL-SCOTT 1582, COLIN BROWN 3:873-74.

4394. σαλπίζω salpizō verb

To trumpet, blow a bugle.

CROSS-REFERENCE:
σάλπιγξ salpinx (4393)

חצצר chtstsr (2791), Blow, sound (1 Chr 15:24, 2 Chr 5:12f., 29:28).

רוּעַ rûaʿ (7607), Hiphil: shout (Is 44:23).

תָּקַע tāqaʿ (8965), Qal: blow, sound (Nm 10:4-8, 2 Sm 20:1, Jl 2:1); niphal: be blown (Is 27:13).

1. **σαλπίζειν salpizein** inf pres act
2. **ἐσάλπισεν esalpisen** 3sing indic aor act
3. **σαλπίσῃς salpisēs** 2sing subj aor act
4. **σαλπίσωσιν salpisōsin** 3pl subj aor act
5. **σαλπίσει salpisei** 3sing indic fut act

3 do not **sound a trumpet** before thee, ... Matt 6:2
5 at the last trump: for the **trumpet shall sound,** ...... 1 Co 15:52
4 the seven angels ... prepared themselves to **sound.** .... Rev 8:6
2 The first angel **sounded,** and there followed hail 8:7
2 And the second angel **sounded,** 8:8
2 And the third angel **sounded,** 8:10
2 And the fourth angel **sounded,** 8:12
1 of the three angels, which are yet to **sound!** 8:13
2 And the fifth angel **sounded,** and I saw a star fall 9:1
2 And the sixth angel **sounded,** and I heard a voice 9:13
1 the seventh angel, when he shall begin to **sound,** 10:7
2 And the seventh angel **sounded;** 11:15

Since the trumpet was not a musical instrument but a tool for signaling, the verb does not mean to "play" the instrument in the modern sense but, rather, to skillfully coax from it the available two or three notes used to signal large gatherings or military maneuvers.

New Testament Usage

All of the literal New Testament uses of the verb entail the blast of the trumpet within eschatological contexts (1 Corinthians 15:52; Revelation 8–11). The trumpet blast will signal the Lord's return and the unfolding of the end time, militantly announcing God's unfolding battle plan against the unrepentant world of the Antichrist.

Figuratively in Matthew 6:2 the verb clearly indicates drawing attention to oneself, i.e., "trumpeting one's own deeds," specifically in the act of almsgiving. Exactly what practice was behind the Lord's prohibition is not clear, but the point is obvious: give quietly and secretly, not ostentatiously.

STRONG 4537, BAUER 741, MOULTON-MILLIGAN 568, KITTEL 7:71-88, LIDDELL-SCOTT 1582, COLIN BROWN 3:873-74.

4395. σαλπιστής salpistēs noun

Trumpeter.

CROSS-REFERENCE:
σαλπιστής salpistēs (4395)

1. **σαλπιστῶν salpistōn** gen pl masc

1 and musicians, and of pipers, and **trumpeters,** .... Rev 18:22

This word refers to the person who sounded the trumpet to signal national or religious gatherings or military maneuvers. Its only use in the New Testament is at Revelation 18:22. Since the trumpeter is included within a list of musicians, this may be the only reference in the New Testament to the use of the trumpet as a musical instrument (cf. Friedrich, "salpinx," *Kittel,* 7:88). It is more likely that the blasts of the trumpet punctuated musical celebrations.

STRONG 4538, BAUER 741, MOULTON-MILLIGAN 568, KITTEL 7:71-88, LIDDELL-SCOTT 1582, COLIN BROWN 3:874.

4396. Σαλώμη Salōmē name

Salome.

1. **Σαλώμη Salōmē** nom fem

1 mother of James the less and of Joses, and **Salome;** Mark 15:40
1 and Mary the mother of James, and **Salome,** 16:1

The wife of Zebedee and the mother of James and John (cf. Mark 15:40; 16:1).

4397. Σαμάρεια Samareia name

Samaria.

1. **Σαμάρεια Samareia** nom fem
2. **Σαμαρείας Samareias** gen fem
3. **Σαμαρείᾳ Samareia** dat fem
4. **Σαμάρειαν Samareian** acc fem

2 passed through the midst **of Samaria** and Galilee... Luke 17:11
2 And he must needs go through **Samaria.** .... John 4:4
2 Then cometh he to a city **of Samaria,** 4:5
2 There cometh a woman of **Samaria** to draw water: 4:7
3 in Jerusalem, and in all Judaea, and in **Samaria,** ..... Acts 1:8
2 regions of Judaea and **Samaria,** except the apostles...... 8:1

2 Then Philip went down to the city **of Samaria**, ... Acts 8:5
2 and bewitched the people **of Samaria**, ... 8:9
1 heard that **Samaria** had received the word of God, ... 8:14
2 throughout all Judaea and Galilee and **Samaria**, ... 9:31
4 they passed through Phenice and **Samaria**, ... 15:3

The name originally applied to a city in the northern kingdom of Israel, but by New Testament times applied instead to the region. The area was home to the Samaritans who had intermarried with non-Jews during the time of the exile in the Sixth Century B.C. and had mixed other beliefs and practices with their Jewish faith. The Jews, therefore, despised them and avoided entering Samaria. Jesus, by contrast, associated with them (see John 4), and the Early Church followed His example. The result was the early establishment of a church in Samaria (Acts 8:1-25).

4398. Σαμαρείτης Samareitēs name

Samaritan.

1. **Σαμαρείτης Samareitēs** nom sing masc
2. **Σαμαρεῖται Samareitai** nom pl masc
3. **Σαμαρειτῶν Samareitōn** gen pl masc
4. **Σαμαρείταις Samareitais** dat pl masc
5. **Σαμαρίτης Samaritēs** nom sing masc
6. **Σαμαρῖται Samaritai** nom pl masc
7. **Σαμαριτῶν Samaritōn** gen pl masc
8. **Σαμαρίταις Samaritais** dat pl masc

3 and into any city **of the Samaritans** enter ye not: ... Matt 10:5
3 and entered into a village of the **Samaritans**, ... Luke 9:52
1 But a certain **Samaritan**, as he journeyed, ... 10:33
5 giving him thanks: and he was **a Samaritan**. 17:16
4 for the Jews have no dealings with the **Samaritans**. .. John 4:9
3 And many of the **Samaritans** of that city believed 4:39
2 So when the **Samaritans** were come unto him, ... 4:40
1 Say we not well that thou art **a Samaritan**, ... 8:48
3 the gospel in many villages of the **Samaritans**. .... Acts 8:25

Samareitēs is the designation for a member of an ethnoreligious group that seems to have originated sometime during the Persian occupation of Palestine. This group continues in existence, in very limited numbers, to the present. *Samareitēs* designates male members of the group in the singular and the group as a whole in the plural. It is to be distinguished from *Samareitis* (John 4:9), which designates a female member of the group. These spellings evidence the substitution of the diphthong *ei* for the simple vowel *i*; thus the spelling *Samaritēs* is probably to be preferred (see Blass and DeBrunner, *Greek Grammar of the New Testament*, pp.20,21).

Deep-seated animosity existed between the Jews and the Samaritans during Biblical times. The origins of these prejudices probably date back to the conflicts between Judah and the 10 northern tribes of Israel that resulted in the division of the monarchy following the death of Solomon. According to Jewish tradition, the Samaritans were descended from the colonists brought into Israel by the Assyrian king Shalmaneser following the conquest of the northern tribes and the deportation of their populations (see 2 Kings 17). The Samaritans, however, claimed to be the legitimate descendants of the tribes of Ephraim and Manasseh since only a small portion of the population was actually deported. The historical reality is probably somewhere between these two traditions. It is more likely that the Samaritans were composed of a mixture of native Israelites, probably of the lower socioeconomic groups who were not deported, and foreign colonists who had been settled into the area (see Gaster, "Samaritans," *Interpreter's Dictionary of the Bible*, 4:191f.; and Anderson, "Samaritans," *International Standard Bible Encyclopedia*, 4:303).

The tensions between the two groups continued to mount during the Persian and Hasmonean periods (in addition to Gaster and Anderson, see Jeremias, "samareia," *Kittel*, 7:90). The Samaritans opposed the reconstruction of the temple in Jerusalem by the Jews who returned from the Babylonian captivity (about 538 B.C.; cf. Ezra 4). The Samaritans themselves constructed a temple on Mount Gerizim around the time of Alexander the Great (about 332 B.C.). This Samaritan temple was destroyed by the Maccabean ruler John Hyrcanus (about 128 B.C.). Later, the Samaritans defiled the Jerusalem temple by scattering human bones within it (about A.D. 6–9; see Josephus *Antiquities* 18.2.2).

It was such disagreements about temple worship that were the most divisive between the Jews and the Samaritans. Against the Zion theology (see "Siōn" [4477]) of Judaism, the Samaritans believed that Eli had corrupted the temple system when he established the cultic center at Shiloh (cf. 1 Samuel 1:3). Consequently, they maintained that the Solomonic temple, erected in Jerusalem and related historically to the tabernacle at Shiloh, was an apostate temple. The true site for temple worship, they argued, was Mount Gerizim which they identified as the "navel" (i.e., central point) of the universe and as the site of the first sacrifice by Abel, of Abraham's "sacrifice" of Isaac, and of other significant events (see Gaster, *Interpreter's Dictionary of the Bible*, 4:194). This dispute between the Jews and Samaritans played an important role in Jesus' discussion with the

Samaritan woman (John 4:20). Jesus instructed her that in the "hour" of salvation "true worship" would not be identified by where it occurred but rather by the attitude of the worshipers ("in spirit and in truth," John 4:21-24).

Related to the issue of temple worship was the rejection by the Samaritans of all the books of the Old Testament except the Pentateuch. They argued that the Prophets and the Writings (as divisions of the Jewish canon) supported the "apostate" temple worship in Jerusalem. Thus their messianic expectations (cf. John 4:25) were based on the "prophet like Moses" in Deuteronomy 18:15-19 rather than a view of the Messiah as a "Son of David" (see Jeremias, "samareia," *Kittel*, 7:89). Additionally, the Samaritan Pentateuch differs from its Hebrew counterpart at some 6,000 points (ibid.). Other religious beliefs characteristic of modern Samaritans may have been influenced by Christianity and Islam (cf. Anderson, *International Standard Bible Encyclopedia*, 4:307f. and Gaster, *Interpreter's Dictionary of the Bible*, 4:193-195) and so may not have been true of first-century Samaritans.

The prejudice between Jews and Samaritans is a constant feature in the use of the term *Samaritēs* in the New Testament. In the commissioning of the disciples, Jesus told them to go only "to the lost sheep of the house of Israel," and not to the Samaritans or the Gentiles (Matthew 10:5). "The Jews" (John 8:31) used the name *Samaritan* as a term of derision against Jesus and associated it with demonic possession (John 8:48). The prejudices of the Samaritans are evidenced in Luke 9:52f. where they denied hospitality to Jesus because He was en route to the Jerusalem temple.

The most "positive" attitudes toward the Samaritans are found in Luke—Acts. Luke recorded Jesus' rebuke of the disciples' hatred for the Samaritans (Luke 9:51-56) and used Samaritans as positive examples (cf. the "Good Samaritan" of Luke 10:25-37 and the one "thankful leper" of Luke 17:11-19). The Samaritans also played an important transitional role in the spread of the gospel among all people: "Ye shall be witnesses unto me both in Jerusalem, and in all Judea (i.e., the Jews), and in Samaria (i.e., the Samaritans), and unto the uttermost part of the earth" (i.e., the Gentiles) (Acts 1:8).

STRONG 4541, BAUER 741 (see "Samaritēs"), MOULTON-MILLIGAN 568, KITTEL 7:88-94 (see "Samaritēs"), LIDDELL-SCOTT 1582 (see "Samaritēs"), COLIN BROWN 3:449-66.

4399. Σαμαρεῖτις Samareitis name

Samaritan woman.

1. **Σαμαρεῖτις Samareitis** nom sing fem
2. **Σαμαρείτιδος Samareitidos** gen sing fem
3. **Σαμαρῖτις Samaritis** nom sing fem
4. **Σαμαρίτιδος Samaritidos** gen sing fem

1 Then saith the woman **of Samaria** unto him, ... John 4:9
2 askest drink of me, which am a woman **of Samaria**? 4:9

Jesus met and evangelized a Samaritan woman, so described in John 4:9.

4400. Σαμοθρᾴκη Samothrakē name

Samothracia.

1. **Σαμοθρᾴκην Samothrakēn** acc fem

1 we came with a straight course to **Samothracia**, ... Acts 16:11

An island in the northern Aegean Sea. It was a stepping-stone in Paul's voyage from Troas in Asia to Europe (Acts 16:11).

4401. Σάμος Samos name

Samos.

1. **Σάμον Samon** acc fem

1 and the next day we arrived at **Samos**, ... Acts 20:15

Paul passed through this island of the eastern Aegean en route to Jerusalem (Acts 20:15).

4402. Σαμουήλ Samouēl name

Samuel.

1. **Σαμουήλ Samouēl** masc

1 Yea, and all the prophets from **Samuel** .... Acts 3:24
1 until **Samuel** the prophet. 13:20
1 of David also, and **Samuel**, and of the prophets: .... Heb 11:32

A famous prophet and leader of Old Testament Israel. In the New Testament he is named as the last in the line of the judges (Acts 13:20) and the first in the line of the prophets (Acts 3:24).

4403. Σαμψών Sampsōn name

Samson.

1. **Σαμψών Sampsōn** masc

1 and of Barak, and of **Samson**, and of Jephthae; .... Heb 11:32

An Israelite leader of legendary strength (Judges 13—16) who is listed among the heroes of faith at Hebrews 11:32.

4404. σανδάλιον sandalion noun

Sandal.

נַעַל na'al (5458), Sandal (Jos 9:5).

1. σανδάλια sandalia nom/acc pl neu

1 be shod with **sandals**; and not put on two coats..... Mark 6:9
1 Gird thyself, and bind on thy **sandals**.............. Acts 12:8

The sandal was the common warm weather footwear of the Palestinian. It had a flat sole made usually of wood or leather but sometimes even of dried grass (Bouquet, *Everyday Life In New Testament Times*, p.65). It was bound on the foot with leather thongs. The sandal protected only the soles and sides of feet.

New Testament Usage

The word *sandalion* occurs only twice in the New Testament. In Mark 6:9 (cf. Matthew 10:10) Jesus told His disciples to provide for themselves only one pair of sandals for their evangelistic trips, trusting God to provide further (cf. Deuteronomy 29:5). The angel commanded Peter to put on his sandals as he escaped jail (Acts 12:8). (See the related word *hupodēma* [5104].)

Strong 4547, Bauer 742, Moulton-Milligan 568, Kittel 5:310-12, Liddell-Scott 1582.

4405. σανίς sanis noun

Board, plank.

דֶּלֶת deleth (1878), Lid (2 Kgs 12:9—Sixtine Edition only).

לוּחַ lûach (4008), Board (S/S 8:9).

1. σανίσιν sanisin dat pl fem

1 And the rest, some on **boards**,.................... Acts 27:44

The word denotes a piece of wood and refers to anything from a small scrap used for writing purposes, to a wooden bench used to sit on, to larger pieces which might be used for construction (*Liddell-Scott*). It occurs only once in the New Testament, Acts 27:44, where it refers to the lifesaving pieces of flotsam which contributed to Paul's survival of shipwreck. *Bauer* suggests that it was "perhaps boards or planks that were used to hold the cargo of grain in place," but it is also plausible that they were pieces from the wreckage or loose boards that had been on the ship.

Strong 4548, Bauer 742, Moulton-Milligan 568, Liddell-Scott 1583.

4406. Σαούλ Saoul name

Saul.

1. Σαούλ Saoul masc

1 **Saul**, Saul, why persecutest thou me?............... Acts 9:4
1 Saul, **Saul**, why persecutest thou me?.................. 9:4
1 and putting his hands on him said, Brother **Saul**,....... 9:17
1 and God gave unto them **Saul** the son of Cis,......... 13:21
1 and heard a voice saying unto me, **Saul**, Saul,......... 22:7
1 and heard a voice saying unto me, Saul, **Saul**,......... 22:7
1 and said unto me, Brother **Saul**, receive thy sight...... 22:13
1 and saying in the Hebrew tongue, **Saul**, Saul,.......... 26:14
1 Saul, **Saul**, why persecutest thou me?................. 26:14

The name *Saoul* refers to two people in the New Testament: the first king of Israel, Paul mentioned in Acts 13:21f.; the Hebrew name of the apostle Paul. It is used in Acts in early references to him and later in the accounts which recall his conversion.

4407. σαπρός sapros adj

Rotten, useless, unsound.

1. σαπρόν sapron nom/acc sing masc/neu
2. σαπρός sapros nom sing masc
3. σαπρά sapra nom/acc pl neu

1 but a **corrupt** tree bringeth forth evil fruit........... Matt 7:17
1 neither can a **corrupt** tree bring forth good fruit......... 7:18
1 else make the tree **corrupt**, and his fruit corrupt:...... 12:33
1 else make the tree corrupt, and his fruit **corrupt**:...... 12:33
3 gathered the good ... but cast the **bad** away............ 13:48
1 For a good tree bringeth not forth **corrupt** fruit;.... Luke 6:43
1 neither doth a **corrupt** tree bring forth good fruit........ 6:43
2 Let no **corrupt** communication proceed.............. Eph 4:29

Commentators and translators differ on the primary meaning of *sapros* in the New Testament with the majority restricting it to the original root meaning of "corrupt" or "rotten." As such it refers to decaying trees and their bad fruit (Matthew 7:17,18; 12:33; Luke 6:43), spoiled fish (Matthew 13:48), and foul speech (Ephesians 4:29).

However, others point out that in secular usage the word came to have the more general meaning of "unfit for use, worthless." For example, an old person could be called *sapros* as could stale drugs and worn-out articles of clothing (*Liddell-Scott*). If this broader meaning is the sense of the word in the New Testament, then the contrast of Matthew 7:17,18 is not between healthy and decaying trees but between trees of an excellent variety and trees of a worthless kind. In their biological condition they are the same, but the fruit produced reveals the worth of each. Similarly, the fish of Matthew 13:48 may be quite normal biologically but are not good as food.

The same sense of unprofitableness could be applied to the use of *sapros* in Ephesians 4:29, a meaning that seems to be reinforced by the antithesis "good." Added support comes from the use of the word to describe unpleasant or offensive sounds, such as dissonant and clangorous music. If the broader use of *sapros* is to be understood in Ephesians 4:29, then it includes all empty or reproachful speech. Its positive counterpart is found in Colossians 4:6 which calls for graceful speech "seasoned with salt."

Apparently the idea of worthlessness is prominent in the uses of the word in the New Testament, but the root meaning must always be considered. The word is used to designate something that is disgusting and offensive.

STRONG 4550, BAUER 742, MOULTON-MILLIGAN 569, KITTEL 7:94-97, LIDDELL-SCOTT 1583.

4408. Σάπφειρα Sappheira name

Sapphira.

1. **Σαπφείρῃ Sappheirē** dat fem
2. **Σαπφίρῃ Sapphirē** dat fem

1 Ananias, with **Sapphira** his wife, sold a possession, .. Acts 5:1

Sapphira and her husband were early members of the church. They both died suddenly after lying about the extent of their generosity (Acts 5:1).

4409. σάπφειρος sappheiros noun

Sapphire.

סַפִּיר ṣappîr (5800), Sapphire (Ex 28:18, Jb 28:6, Ez 28:13).

1. **σάπφειρος sappheiros** nom sing fem
2. **σάπφιρος sapphiros** nom sing fem

1 first foundation was jasper; the second, **sapphire**; . . . .Rev 21:19

This stone is found in the New Testament only in Revelation 21:19 where it is one of the precious gems adorning the foundation stones of the heavenly New Jerusalem. The word occurs in the Septuagint in Exodus 24:10 as part of a vision of God's throne. Of its four uses in Ezekiel, it is translated *lapis lazuli* in 1:26 and 28:13 in the New American Standard Bible. It was most certainly a beautiful blue stone.

STRONG 4552, BAUER 742 (see "sapphiros"), MOULTON-MILLIGAN 569, LIDDELL-SCOTT 1583, COLIN BROWN 3:396-97.

4410. σαργάνη sarganē noun

Braided rope, rope basket, hamper.

1. **σαργάνῃ sarganē** dat sing fem

1 And through a window in a **basket** was I let down 2 Co 11:33

The basket in which Paul escaped over the wall of Damascus is called *sarganē* in 2 Corinthians 11:33, its only New Testament usage. It is similar in meaning to the term *spuris* (4562), Acts 9:25, the kind of basket used to collect the fragments from the feeding of the 4,000 (Matthew 15:37). It was a large basket, braided probably of rope but possibly of reeds (cf. *Bauer*).

STRONG 4553, BAUER 742, MOULTON-MILLIGAN 569, LIDDELL-SCOTT 1584.

4411. Σάρδεις Sardeis name

Sardis.

1. **Σάρδεις Sardeis** nom/acc pl fem
2. **Σάρδεσιν Sardesin** dat pl fem

1 and unto Thyatira, and unto **Sardis**, ... Rev 1:11
2 And unto the angel of the church in **Sardis** write; 3:1
2 Thou hast a few names even in **Sardis** 3:4

The ancient capital of Lydia in the west of Asia Minor but, in New Testament times, a city of past glory. The church in Sardis is addressed in one of the seven letters of Revelation (1:11; 3:1-6). The call to "wake up" (3:2) and the threat that God will "come like a thief" recall history: twice its mighty acropolis (hill fortress) had been captured by an enemy trick made possible by the inattention of the defenders. It seems the warnings were heeded, for the city long remained home to a flourishing church.

4412. σάρδινος sardinos noun

Sardius.

1. **σαρδίνῳ sardinō** dat sing masc

1 was to look upon like a jasper and a **sardine** stone: .. Rev 4:3

Sardinos is a variant form (found in the Received text) of *sardion*, "sardius." See the word study at number 4412B.

4412B. σάρδιον sardion noun

Carnelian, sardius.

אֹדֶם 'ōdhem (122), Ruby (Ex 28:17, 39:10 [36:17], Ez 28:13).

שֹׁהַם shōham (8172), Onyx (Ex 25:7 [25:6], 35:9 [35:8]).

1. **σάρδιον sardion** nom/acc sing neu
2. **σαρδίῳ sardiō** dat sing neu

1 the fifth, sardonyx; the sixth, **sardius**; (NASB)...... Rev 21:20

Sardion, also spelled *sardinos* (4412) or *sardius* (4413), is the designation of a reddish stone, perhaps of the deep orange-red chalcedony or of the carnelian type (Achtemeier, "sardius," *Harper's Bible Dictionary*). It occurs in writings as early as Aristophanes (Fifth Century B.C.) and Plato (Fourth Century B.C.). The sardius stone is found on the breastplate of the priest described in Exodus 28:17. In the New Testament is used twice in Revelation. In 4:3 *sardion* describes one facet of the splendor of the One who sits on the throne; God's radiance is described using this term. In Revelation 21:20 the *sardion* is one of the precious stones adorning the foundation of the walls of the New Jerusalem.

STRONG 4556, BAUER 742, MOULTON-MILLIGAN 569, LIDDELL-SCOTT 1584, COLIN BROWN 3:396-98.

4413. σάρδιος sardios noun

Sardius.

1. σάρδιος sardios nom sing masc

1 The fifth, sardonyx; the sixth, **sardius**;.............. Rev 21:20

Sardios is a variant spelling of the term *sardion* which occurs in a few Byzantine texts. See the word study at number 4412B.

4414. σαρδόνυξ sardonux noun

Sardonyx.

1. σαρδόνυξ sardonux nom sing masc

1 The fifth, **sardonyx**; the sixth, sardius;.............. Rev 21:20

The sardonyx is a precious stone, a yellow or red-brown variety of chalcedony (Bullard, "Stones, precious," *International Standard Bible Encyclopedia*, 4:626; cf. also Robertson, *Word Pictures in the New Testament*, 6:475, who says that it is a red [sard] and white [onyx] layered stone). *Bauer* proposes that it is a variety of agate. It is to be one of the gems adorning the foundation stones of the New Jerusalem (Revelation 21:20).

STRONG 4557, BAUER 742, MOULTON-MILLIGAN 569, LIDDELL-SCOTT 1584, COLIN BROWN 3:396-97.

4415. Σάρεπτα Sarepta name

Zarephath.

1. Σάρεπτα Sarepta nom/acc pl neu

2. Σάρεφθα Sarephtha nom/acc neu

1 unto none ... was Elias sent, save unto **Sarepta**,..... Luke 4:26

A city on the Phoenician coast south of Sidon. Jesus reminded His hearers that it was in Zarephath that Elijah survived the great famine (Luke 4:26).

4416. σαρκικός sarkikos adj

Fleshly, in the manner of the flesh, belonging to the realm of the flesh, material.

COGNATE:

σάρξ sarx (4418)

1. σαρκικοῖς sarkikois dat pl masc/neu

2. σαρκικός sarkikos nom sing masc

3. σαρκικοί sarkikoi nom pl masc

4. σαρκικῆς sarkikēs gen sing fem

5. σαρκικῇ sarkikē dat sing fem

6. σαρκικῶν sarkikōn gen pl fem

7. σαρκικά sarkika nom/acc pl neu

2 but I am **carnal**, sold under sin..................... Rom 7:14
1 duty is also to minister unto them in **carnal** things..... 15:27
1 but as **unto carnal**, even as unto babes in Christ..... 1 Co 3:1
3 For ye are yet **carnal**: ... is among you envying,......... 3:3
3 and divisions, are ye not **carnal**, and walk as men?..... 3:3
3 and another, I am of Apollos; are ye not **carnal?**....... 3:4
7 a great thing if we shall reap your **carnal things?**....... 9:11
5 not with **fleshly** wisdom, but by the grace of God,... 2 Co 1:12
7 For the weapons of our warfare are not **carnal**,........ 10:4
4 not after the law of a **carnal** commandment,......... Heb 7:16
6 I beseech you ... abstain from **fleshly** lusts,.......... 1 Pt 2:11

Classical Greek

Known at least since the Fourth Century B.C. (e.g., Aristotle), *sarkikos* means "belonging to the flesh" (cf. *sarkinos* [4417] which means "composed of flesh, fleshly"; *Bauer*). *Sarkikos* has no inherently negative aspect in classical Greek. That changes to some extent in the New Testament. *Sarkikos* and *sarkinos* are used interchangeably in our literature (ibid.), but only *sarkinos* appears in the Septuagint.

New Testament Usage

Essentially *sarkikos* has either a neutral or a negative connotation in the New Testament. When it is contrasted with *pneumatikos* (4012), "spiritual," it should often be read in terms of "belonging to the sinful nature, the flesh" (cf. Romans 7:14). Otherwise it can simply represent the earthly, material realm, without prejudice.

We have examples of the former understanding in the New Testament where, except for one use in 1 Peter 2:11 and one in Hebrews 7:16, *sarkikos* is a uniquely Pauline term. In reference to the Corinthians' spiritual condition Paul said they were "worldly" (NIV). The implication is that they were immature, they were quarreling among themselves, and they were continuing to be ruled by their sinful nature rather than by Christ (1 Corinthians 3:3). Perhaps the same connotation is intended in 2 Corinthians 1:12. Paul's conduct was governed by grace rather than by "worldly (*sarkikos*) wisdom (*sophia*)" (cf. 2 Corinthians 10:4). As well, Paul sought to fight the good fight of faith with weapons that are not carnal, i.e., human reasoning and power which are of no effect in the spiritual struggle (2 Corinthians 10:4).

In a more neutral sense Paul spoke of receiving a "material" (NIV, i.e., "tangible") harvest from spiritual sowing (1 Corinthians 9:11). This same neutral usage is attested in early Christian literature. Ignatius spoke of Jesus as *sarkikos te kai pneumatikos* (*To the Ephesians* 7:2). Here we have a clear indication that *sarkikos* does not necessarily imply the sinful nature. Such a thought would have appalled Ignatius (cf. Ignatius *To the Smyrnaeans* 3:3; cf. *Bauer*).

Picking up on the link between *sarkikos* and the sinful nature, Peter warned the Gentiles to "abstain from *sinful desires*" (*tōn sarkikōn epithumiōn*; 1 Peter 2:11, NIV). Peter was not simply speaking of sexual desires here as the translation "fleshly lusts" implies. Rather, Peter was referring to every kind of expression of the sinful nature (see e.g., Romans 8, and see the article on *sarx*). As with Paul in Galatians 5:17, there is no indication here of a platonic dualism. Rather, the apostles were simply warning their readers against allowing themselves to become slaves to what are very often normal desires.

STRONG 4559, BAUER 742-43, MOULTON-MILLIGAN 569, KITTEL 7:98-151, LIDDELL-SCOTT 1584, COLIN BROWN 1:671,674,677,682.

4417. σάρκινος sarkinos adj

Fleshy, made of flesh.

CROSS-REFERENCE:
σάρξ sarx (4418)

בָּשָׂר bāsār (1340), Flesh (2 Chr 32:8, Ez 11:19, 36:26).

1. **σαρκίναις sarkinais** dat pl fem
2. **σαρκίνοις sarkinois** dat pl masc/neu
3. **σάρκινος sarkinos** nom sing masc
4. **σαρκίνης sarkinēs** gen sing fem

3 I am of flesh, sold into bondage to sin. (NASB) . . . . . Rom 7:14
2 but as to men of flesh, as to babes (NASB) . . . . 1 Co 3:1
1 in tables of stone, but in fleshly tables of the heart. 2 Co 3:3
4 not on the basis of physical requirement, (NASB) . . . . Heb 7:16

This adjective is related to *sarx* (4418), "flesh," and can have either the literal or metaphoric sense of that term. *Sarkinos* occurs only once in the Received text of the New Testament, 2 Corinthians 3:3. Here the tablets of stone inscribed with the Ten Commandments are contrasted with the hearts of flesh on which the new covenant is written. In this sense flesh is a positive symbol of something living and sensitive. In modern critical texts *sarkinos* is found instead of *sarkikos* (4416) in Romans 7:14, 1 Corinthians 3:1, and Hebrews 7:16.

STRONG 4560, BAUER 743, MOULTON-MILLIGAN 569, KITTEL 7:98-151, LIDDELL-SCOTT 1584, COLIN BROWN 1:671,674,682.

4418. σάρξ sarx noun

Flesh, human, mortal nature, physical life.

COGNATES:
σαρκικός sarkikos (4416)
σάρκινος sarkinos (4417)

בָּשָׂר bāsār (1340), Flesh (Gn 2:23f., Jb 33:21, Ez 21:4f.).

בְּשַׂר b^esar (A1341), Flesh (Dn 2:11, 7:5—Aramaic).

חַי chay (2508), Life, people; flesh (Sir 44:24).

לְחוּם l^echûm (4028), Flesh (Zep 1:17).

שְׁאֵר sh^e'ēr (8083), Flesh (Mi 3:2f.).

1. **σάρξ sarx** nom sing fem
2. **σαρκός sarkos** gen sing fem
3. **σαρκί sarki** dat sing fem
4. **σάρκα sarka** acc sing fem
5. **σαρκῶν sarkōn** gen pl fem
6. **σάρκας sarkas** acc pl fem

1 for flesh and blood hath not revealed it unto thee, Matt 16:17
4 and they twain shall be one flesh? 19:5
1 Wherefore they are no more twain, but one flesh. 19:6
1 there should no flesh be saved: 24:22
1 the spirit indeed is willing, but the flesh is weak. 26:41
4 And they twain shall be one flesh: . . . . Mark 10:8
1 so then they are no more twain, but one flesh. 10:8
1 no flesh should be saved: but for the elect's sake, ... 13:20
1 The spirit truly is ready, but the flesh is weak. 14:38
1 And all flesh shall see the salvation of God. . . . . Luke 3:6
4 and see; for a spirit hath not flesh and bones, ... 24:39
2 not of blood, nor of the will of the flesh, ... John 1:13
1 the Word was made flesh, and dwelt among us, ... 1:14
2 That which is born of the flesh is flesh; 3:6
1 That which is born of the flesh is flesh; 3:6
1 and the bread that I will give is my flesh, ... 6:51
4 How can this man give us his flesh to eat? 6:52
4 Except ye eat the flesh of the Son of man, ... 6:53
4 Whoso eateth my flesh, and drinketh my blood, ... 6:54
1 For my flesh is meat indeed, ... 6:55
4 He that eateth my flesh, and drinketh my blood, ... 6:56
1 spirit that quickeneth; the flesh profiteth nothing: 6:63
4 Ye judge after the flesh; I judge no man. 8:15
2 As thou hast given him power over all flesh, ... 17:2
4 I will pour out of my Spirit upon all flesh: . . . . Acts 2:17
1 moreover also my flesh shall rest in hope: 2:26
4 that of the fruit of his loins, according to the flesh, ... 2:30
1 neither his flesh did see corruption. 2:31
4 made of the seed of David according to the flesh; . . . Rom 1:3
3 circumcision, which is outward in the flesh: 2:28
1 there shall no flesh be justified in his sight: 3:20

4 as pertaining to the **flesh**, hath found? ... Rom 4:1
2 because of the infirmity of your **flesh**: ... 6:19
3 For when we were in the **flesh**, the motions of sins, ... 7:5
3 For I know that in me that is, in my **flesh**, ... 7:18
3 but with the **flesh** the law of sin. ... 7:25
4 who walk not after the **flesh**, but after the Spirit. ... 8:1
2 in that it was weak through the **flesh**, ... 8:3
2 sending his own Son in the likeness of sinful **flesh**, ... 8:3
3 and for sin, condemned sin in the **flesh**: ... 8:3
4 who walk not after the **flesh**, but after the Spirit. ... 8:4
4 are after the **flesh** do mind the things of the flesh; ... 8:5
2 are after the flesh do mind the things of the **flesh**; ... 8:5
2 For to be **carnally** minded is death; ... 8:6
2 Because the **carnal** mind is enmity against God: ... 8:7
3 then they that are in the **flesh** cannot please God. ... 8:8
3 But ye are not in the **flesh**, but in the Spirit, ... 8:9
3 not to the **flesh**, to live after the flesh. ... 8:12
4 not to the flesh, to live after the **flesh**. ... 8:12
4 For if ye live after the **flesh**, ye shall die: ... 8:13
4 my brethren, my kinsmen according to the **flesh**: ... 9:3
4 and of whom as concerning the **flesh** Christ came, ... 9:5
2 That is, They which are the children of the **flesh**, ... 9:8
4 provoke to emulation them which are my **flesh**, ... 11:14
2 and make not provision for the **flesh**, ... 13:14
4 how that not many wise men after the **flesh**, ... 1 Co 1:26
1 That no **flesh** should glory in his presence. ... 1:29
2 unto Satan for the destruction of the **flesh**, ... 5:5
4 for two, saith he, shall be one **flesh**. ... 6:16
3 Nevertheless such shall have trouble in the **flesh**: ... 7:28
4 Behold Israel after the **flesh**: ... 10:18
1 All **flesh** is not the same flesh: ... 15:39
1 All flesh is not the same **flesh**: ... 15:39
1 but there is one kind of **flesh** of men, ... 15:39
1 another **flesh** of beasts, another of fishes, ... 15:39
1 that **flesh** and blood cannot inherit the kingdom ... 15:50
4 do I purpose according to the **flesh**, ... 2 Co 1:17
3 Jesus might be made manifest in our mortal **flesh**. ... 4:11
4 henceforth know we no man after the **flesh**: ... 5:16
4 yea, though we have known Christ after the **flesh**, ... 5:16
2 from all filthiness of the **flesh** and spirit, ... 7:1
1 were come into Macedonia, our **flesh** had no rest, ... 7:5
4 think of us as if we walked according to the **flesh**. ... 10:2
3 For though we walk in the **flesh**, ... 10:3
4 we do not war after the **flesh**: ... 10:3
4 that many glory after the **flesh**, I will glory also. ... 11:18
3 there was given to me a thorn in the **flesh**, ... 12:7
3 immediately I conferred not with **flesh** and blood: ... Gal 1:16
1 by the works of the law shall no **flesh** be justified. ... 2:16
3 and the life which I now live in the **flesh** ... 2:20
3 are ye now made perfect by the **flesh**? ... 3:3
2 how through infirmity of the **flesh** I preached ... 4:13
3 temptation which was in my **flesh** ye despised not, ... 4:14
4 was of the bondwoman was born after the **flesh**; ... 4:23
4 But as then he that was born after the **flesh** ... 4:29
3 only use not liberty for an occasion to the **flesh**, ... 5:13
2 and ye shall not fulfil the lust of the **flesh**. ... 5:16
1 For the **flesh** lusteth against the Spirit, ... 5:17
2 and the Spirit against the **flesh**: ... 5:17
2 Now the works of the **flesh** are manifest, ... 5:19
4 And they that are Christ's have crucified the **flesh** ... 5:24
4 For he that soweth to his **flesh** ... 6:8
2 shall of the **flesh** reap corruption; ... 6:8
3 As many as desire to make a fair show in the **flesh**, ... 6:12
3 you circumcised, that they may glory in your **flesh**. ... 6:13
2 in times past in the lusts of our **flesh**, ... Eph 2:3
2 fulfilling the desires of the **flesh** and of the mind; ... 2:3
3 that ye being in time past Gentiles in the **flesh**, ... 2:11
3 the Circumcision in the **flesh** made by hands; ... 2:11
3 Having abolished in his **flesh** the enmity, ... 2:15
4 For no man ever yet hated his own **flesh**; ... 5:29
2 For we are members of his body, of his **flesh**, ... 5:30
4 unto his wife, and they two shall be one **flesh**. ... 5:31
4 them that are your masters according to the **flesh**, ... 6:5
4 For we wrestle not against **flesh** and blood, ... 6:12
3 if I live in the **flesh**, this is the fruit of my labour: .. Phlp 1:22
3 to abide in the **flesh** is more needful for you. ... 1:24
3 and have no confidence in the **flesh**. ... 3:3
3 Though I might also have confidence in the **flesh**. ... Phlp 3:4
3 If any ... might trust in the **flesh**, I more: ... 3:4
2 In the body of his **flesh** through death, ... Col 1:22
3 afflictions of Christ in my **flesh** for his body's sake, ... 1:24
3 for as many as have not seen my face in the **flesh**; ... 2:1
3 absent in the **flesh**, yet am I with you in the spirit, ... 2:5
2 in putting off the body of the sins of the **flesh** ... 2:11
2 in your sins and the uncircumcision of your **flesh**, ... 2:13
2 vainly puffed up by his **fleshly** mind, ... 2:18
2 not in any honour to the satisfying of the **flesh**. ... 2:23
4 your masters according to the **flesh**; ... 3:22
3 God was manifest in the **flesh**, ... 1 Tm 3:16
3 more unto thee, both in the **flesh**, and in the Lord? Phlm 1:16
2 as the children are partakers of **flesh** and blood, ... Heb 2:14
2 Who in the days of his **flesh**, ... 5:7
2 and divers washings, and **carnal** ordinances, ... 9:10
2 sanctifieth to the purifying of the **flesh**: ... 9:13
2 that is to say, his **flesh**; ... 10:20
2 have had fathers of our **flesh** which corrected us, ... 12:9
6 and shall eat your **flesh** as it were fire. ... Jas 5:3
1 For all **flesh** is as grass, ... 1 Pt 1:24
3 being put to death in the **flesh**, ... 3:18
2 not the putting away of the filth of the **flesh**, ... 3:21
3 as Christ hath suffered for us in the **flesh**, ... 4:1
3 as Christ hath suffered for us in the **flesh**, ... 4:1
3 the rest of his time in the **flesh** to the lusts of men, ... 4:2
3 might be judged according to men in the **flesh**, ... 4:6
2 that walk after the **flesh** in the lust of uncleanness, .. 2 Pt 2:10
2 they allure through the lusts of the **flesh**, ... 2:18
2 For all that is in the world, the lust of the **flesh**, ... 1 Jn 2:16
3 that Jesus Christ is come in the **flesh** is of God: ... 4:2
3 confesseth not that Jesus Christ is come in the **flesh** ... 4:3
3 confess not that Jesus Christ is come in the **flesh**. ... 2 Jn 1:7
2 over to fornication, and going after strange **flesh**, ... Jude 1:7
4 Likewise also these filthy dreamers defile the **flesh**, ... 1:8
2 hating even the garment spotted by the **flesh**. ... 1:23
6 and shall eat her **flesh**, and burn her with fire. ... Rev 17:16
6 the **flesh** of kings, and the flesh of captains, ... 19:18
6 the flesh of kings, and the **flesh** of captains, ... 19:18
6 the flesh of captains, and the **flesh** of mighty men, ... 19:18
6 the flesh of mighty men, and the **flesh** of horses, ... 19:18
6 and the **flesh** of all men, both free and bond, ... 19:18
5 and all the fowls were filled with their **flesh**. ... 19:21

In secular Greek *sarx* primarily denotes the flesh and muscle of a body as over against the bones. Later, in addition to being used of human flesh, *sarx* describes the flesh of animals, fish, or even fruit. At times flesh (*sarx*) represents the entire body (cf. *sōma* [4835]; Seabass, "Flesh," *Colin Brown*, 1:671).

Classical Greek

Hellenism's dualistic concept of mankind led to a sharp distinction between flesh (*sarx*) and soul (*psuchē* [5425]) (cf. *nous* [3426], "mind"). Hellenistic philosophy not only separated the spiritual from the physical, the material from the immaterial, it also made the material (*sarx*) inferior to the spiritual. Thus it was common to believe that one's body/flesh was merely a "robe" or even a "prison" of the real person that was believed to be solely the spirit.

Septuagint Usage

Sarx translates the Hebrew term *bāsār* more than any other expression in the Septuagint (approximately 140 times). About 80 times *bāsār* is rendered *kreas.* Usually *kreas* denotes flesh as in "food, meat." The term sh^{e}'ēr (four times) is also translated by *sarx*.

Old Testament Background

In the Old Testament *bāsār* can denote the flesh, the physical makeup of men and animals (Deuteronomy 12:15; 1 Samuel 2:15). It can also denote the human body in its entirety (1 Kings 12:27; Job 4:15; Psalm 63:2; ibid., 1:672).

Contrasting "flesh" is "spirit." The contrast highlights that man is a perishable, earthly, powerless being in comparison with God who is exalted above all His creation (Psalm 78:39; Isaiah 31:3; 40:6). Because of the weak and rebellious nature of man as a perishable, mortal being, "flesh" can represent the sinful condition (cf. Job 4:17; Psalm 51:5).

The difference between Greek and Hebrew anthropology is that the Greeks used "flesh" to describe the physical body whereas the Hebrews used it to denote man as a whole (ibid.). This is demonstrated in the fact that the hope of the Old Testament centers on a resurrected body, whereas the Greeks looked for a spiritual immortality that had no need (or desire) of a body. Some Old Testament texts anticipate the resurrection of the flesh (Psalm 16:9; cf. Acts 2:26). David declared that his "flesh" would rest in hope. Job testified that he and his "flesh" would see God (Job 19:26). Reading Job's comment at face value (all historical-critical arguments that Job could not have known of a resurrection aside) we have evidence of a typical Hebrew anthropology.

New Testament Usage

The Old Testament word *bāsār* provides most of the backdrop for understanding *sarx* in the New Testament. At the same time *sarx* in the New Testament is even more richly developed than in the Old. *Sarx* denotes the body, the entire person, the individual. It portrays man in his earthly state. Moreover, one of the chief meanings of *sarx* is "sinful nature," the unregenerate dimension of humanity, mankind's fallen nature. We can see a regular contrast drawn between flesh and spirit in a wide variety of overlapping meanings.

The literal understanding of *sarx* is relatively rare in comparison to its figurative instances. *Sarx* is an extremely important theological term in the Greek New Testament. As such, "flesh" is an altogether inadequate translation if one desires to give a translation with any preciseness.

Sarx occurs approximately 150 times in the New Testament. Of these about 90 are credited to Paul, especially being prevalent in his letters to the Romans and Galatians. Paul added new dimensions to *sarx* not previously present. His understanding can only be appreciated in light of his juxtaposing "flesh" with "spirit." "Flesh" is the rule of the Old Age; "spirit," the New. Believers are to be guided by the Spirit, but the natural man is under the control of his "sinful nature"; he is ruled by sin rather than by God. Thus "flesh" depicts an entire aspect of life. Either it is earthly in contrast to the heavenly, or it is the sinful in contrast to the life in Christ.

Therefore, *sarx* signifies man's sinful nature, the seat of sinful desires and passions. In this sense "flesh" includes not only the physical body but the spiritual side as well (Romans 7:18; 8:3,12; Galatians 5:13,19; Ephesians 2:3). The sinful nature is corrupt (Romans 7:18); it resists the Spirit of God (Galatians 5:17). It becomes expressed overtly in behavior (Galatians 5:19f.; 1 Corinthians 3:3). Fundamentally the sinful nature is at enmity with God (Romans 8:7); its consequence is death (Romans 8:6).

Any believer who lives according to the sinful nature is abusing his freedom in Christ (Galatians 5:13). Unbelievers live according to their sinful nature; believers are cautioned against doing so (Ephesians 2:3). Those living according to their sinful nature will find it impossible to please God (Romans 8:8). They are His enemies (Romans 8:7) and will not inherit the kingdom of God (1 Corinthians 15:50; Galatians 5:21). Sinful behavior is contagious; it affects others and tries to drag them down too (2 Peter 2:18f.). The final outcome of "living according to the *flesh*" is condemnation and death (Romans 8:13; 2 Peter 2:19,20).

Those who belong to Christ are not controlled by the sinful nature (*sarx*) (Romans 8:12); consequently, they are not to live as if they were. Believers fulfill God's will by living not according to the sinful nature but according to the Spirit (Galatians 5:16; Romans 8:4,9). The believer has died to the sinful nature; he has "crucified the *flesh*" (Galatians 5:24).

Sarx has another, nonpejorative meaning when it denotes the "flesh" of a man, i.e., his body or personality. *Sarx* in this capacity is a key Christological expression for describing the person and work of Jesus Christ. In this second sense *sarx* is especially used in reference to the incarnation of Christ: "The Word was made *flesh*" (*sarx*) (John 1:14); "Christ is come in the *flesh*"

(1 John 4:2); God sent His Son "in the likeness of sinful *flesh*" (Romans 8:3); He partook of "*flesh* and blood" (Hebrews 2:14). In addition, the human ancestry (*kata sarxa*) of Christ can be traced back to the patriarchs (Romans 9:5) from the seed (genealogy) of David (Romans 1:3).

Furthermore, *sarx* also plays an important role in the redemptive work of Christ. Jesus himself declared that He would give His "flesh" (*sarx* = person) "for the life of the world" (John 6:51). Through the blood of Jesus the veil has been opened, granting access to the Most High God. The writer of Hebrews (10:20) equates the "veil" (NIV, "curtain") with Christ's "flesh" (NIV, "body"). At the cross Christ broke down the middle barrier separating Jews and Gentiles, "having abolished in his *flesh* the enmity, even the law of commandments contained in ordinances" (Ephesians 2:14-16). He partook of "*flesh* and blood" so through His death He might destroy the power of the devil (Hebrews 2:14).

These Scripture references are central to the entire Christian faith. Paul stressed that the atonement made by Christ took place *en tō sōmati tēs sarkos autou*, "in the body of his *flesh*" (Colossians 1:22). In this text we see that *sōma* ("body") and *sarx* ("flesh") are used together in order to indicate the reality of Christ's incarnation. He did not have only an apparent body without any actual physical elements, such as the Docetists taught He did. He was truly man. Christ did not reconcile us to God by offering himself in a "spiritual body"; instead, He offered the "body of his flesh."

It should also be observed that in the prologue to John's Gospel the word *anthrōpos* (442), "man," does not occur. Instead, John uses *sarx*, "flesh" (e.g., John 1:14). This observation is of great import because it expresses a thought traceable throughout the New Testament: the true bodily nature of Jesus as God the Son incarnate is indispensable and nonnegotiable. Many respected theologians point to the significance that *sarx* is the term employed here.

Jesus' true humanity and the genuineness of His physical body, as emphasized in the statement "the Word became flesh," are unmatched. No other statement penetrates any deeper into the mystery of the Incarnation than John 1:14. When one recognizes the tremendous space devoted to the proclamation of Jesus "come in the flesh" in the New Testament, one cannot deny that the powerful and majestic declaration "the Word became flesh" expresses one of the most vital truths of the gospel.

STRONG 4561, BAUER 743-44, MOULTON-MILLIGAN 569, KITTEL 7:98-151, LIDDELL-SCOTT 1585, COLIN BROWN 1:671-72,674-82.

4419. Σαρούχ Sarouch name

Serug.

1. **Σαρούχ Sarouch** masc
2. **Σερούχ Serouch** masc

1 Which was the son of **Saruch**, ... Luke 3:35

A character in the genealogy of Jesus (Luke 3:35).

4420. σαρόω saroō verb

Sweep.

1. **σαροῖ saroi** 3sing indic pres act
2. **σεσαρωμένον sesarōmenon** acc sing masc part perf mid

2 and when he is come, he findeth it empty, **swept**, .. Matt 12:44
2 he cometh, he findeth it **swept** and garnished. ...... Luke 11:25
1 doth not light a candle, and **sweep** the house, ... 15:8

Except for a metaphoric meaning in classical Greek of "exhausted," *saroō* means to "sweep" or "sweep clean" (*Liddell-Scott*). This word occurs three times in the New Testament—once in Matthew and twice in Luke.

In Matthew 12:44 and Luke 11:25 the word is used metaphorically by Jesus to describe a house cleaned and decorated, but empty. In a parable about the wicked generation Jesus lived in, He described the Pharisee who was seeking for a sign as a demon-possessed person who experiences a temporary cessation from demonic influence in his life but does not subsequently repent. Such a person is void of any protection against demonic activity. In Luke 15:8 the literal meaning "sweep" appears in the Parable of the Lost Coin.

STRONG 4563, BAUER 744, MOULTON-MILLIGAN 569-70, LIDDELL-SCOTT 1585.

4421. Σάῤῥα Sarrha name

Sarah.

1. **Σάῤῥα Sarrha** nom fem
2. **Σάῤῥας Sarrhas** gen fem
3. **Σάῤῥᾳ Sarrha** dat fem

2 neither yet the deadness of **Sarah's** womb: .... Rom 4:19
3 this time will I come, and **Sarah** shall have a son. 9:9
1 Through faith also **Sara** herself received strength .... Heb 11:11
1 Even as **Sara** obeyed Abraham, calling him lord: .... 1 Pt 3:6

Sarah was the wife of Abraham and mother of Isaac. She is commended in the New Testament for her husband's faith (Romans 4:19) and her own (Hebrews 11:11), and as a properly submissive wife (1 Peter 3:6). She is also recalled as the mother of the child of promise (Romans 9:9; cf. Galatians 4:21-31).

4422. Σαρών Sarōn name

Sharon.

1. Σαρῶνα Sarōna acc masc
2. Σαρωνᾶν Sarōnan acc masc

2 And all that dwelt at Lydda and **Saron** saw him,.... Acts 9:35

Sharon, or The Sharon, was the name of the coastal plain which stretches from Mount Carmel southward to Jaffa, the site of ancient Joppa. Many of its residents turned to the Lord through Peter's ministry (Acts 9:35).

4423. σατανᾶς satanas noun

Satan.

שָׂטָן sāṭān (7931), Adversary (1 Kgs 11:14).

1. σατανᾶς satanas nom sing masc
2. σατανᾶ satana gen/voc sing masc
3. σατανᾷ satana dat sing masc
4. σατανᾶν satanan acc sing masc
5. σατᾶν satan sing masc

2 Then saith Jesus unto him, Get thee hence, **Satan**:.. Matt 4:10
1 And if **Satan** cast out Satan, he is divided............ 12:26
4 And if Satan cast out **Satan**, he is divided............ 12:26
2 said unto Peter, Get thee behind me, **Satan**:.......... 16:23
2 in the wilderness forty days, tempted of **Satan**;..... Mark 1:13
1 said ... in parables, How can **Satan** cast out Satan?..... 3:23
4 said ... in parables, How can Satan cast out **Satan**?..... 3:23
1 if **Satan** rise up against himself, and be divided,........ 3:26
1 when they have heard, **Satan** cometh immediately,...... 4:15
2 rebuked Peter, saying, Get thee behind me, **Satan**:...... 8:33
2 Get thee behind me, **Satan**: for it is written,........ Luke 4:8
4 I beheld **Satan** as lightning fall from heaven.......... 10:18
1 If **Satan** also be divided against himself,.............. 11:18
1 a daughter of Abraham, whom **Satan** hath bound,..... 13:16
1 Then entered **Satan** into Judas surnamed Iscariot,...... 22:3
1 Simon, behold, **Satan** hath desired to have you,....... 22:31
1 And after the sop **Satan** entered into him.......... John 13:27
1 Ananias, why hath **Satan** filled thine heart.......... Acts 5:3
2 and from the power of **Satan** unto God,............... 26:18
4 shall bruise **Satan** under your feet shortly.......... Rom 16:20
3 unto **Satan** for the destruction of the flesh,......... 1 Co 5:5
1 that **Satan** tempt you not for your incontinency......... 7:5
2 Lest **Satan** should get an advantage of us:.......... 2 Co 2:11
1 **Satan** himself is transformed into an angel of light..... 11:14
5 the messenger of **Satan** to buffet me,................ 12:7
1 come unto you, ... but **Satan** hindered us............ 1 Th 2:18
2 him, whose coming is after the working of **Satan**.... 2 Th 2:9
3 and Alexander; whom I have delivered unto **Satan**, 1 Tm 1:20
2 For some are already turned aside after **Satan**.......... 5:15
2 and are not, but are the synagogue of **Satan**.......... Rev 2:9
2 where thou dwellest, even where **Satan's** seat is:........ 2:13
1 who was slain among you, where **Satan** dwelleth..... Rev 2:13
2 and which have not known the depths of **Satan**,........ 2:24
2 I will make them of the synagogue of **Satan**,........... 3:9
1 that old serpent, called the Devil, and **Satan**,.......... 12:9
1 and **Satan**, and bound him a thousand years,.......... 20:2
1 **Satan** shall be loosed out of his prison,............... 20:7

Both the Greek word *satanas* and its English derivative *Satan* are simply transliterations of the Hebrew word *sāṭān* and the Aramaic *sāṭānâ*, both of which mean "adversary" as nouns. *Moulton-Milligan* adds that the Aramaic verb meant originally "one lying in ambush for."

Old Testament Background

In the Old Testament the Hebrew word *sāṭān* is widely used in its common sense of "adversary" and only in four books to refer to the prince of evil. In the general sense, the Angel of Jehovah is described as the *sāṭān* of Balaam when the latter went with the princes of Moab defying the will of God: "The angel of the LORD stood in the way for an adversary against him" (Numbers 22:22; cf. also verse 32 where the verb form is translated "withstand"). David referred to Abishai as his adversary (2 Samuel 19:22), as well as anyone who rendered evil for good (Psalm 38:20). Likewise, the political opponents of Solomon were his adversaries (1 Kings 11:14,23,25).

Of the 31 uses of the noun and verb forms of the Hebrew word, 17 are references to the devil. These are found in Job (12 times in chapters 1 and 2), Zechariah (3 references, 3:1,2), Psalm 109:6, and 1 Chronicles 21:1 which J. Barton Payne cites as "perhaps the only use of the proper noun in the Old Testament" ("sāṭān," *Theological Wordbook of the Old Testament*, 2:875). In these references the Septuagint uniformly translated the Hebrew *sāṭān* with the Greek word *diabolos*, the root of our English word *devil*. Thus the interchangeableness of the two terms *Satan* and *devil* find their origin in the Greek translation of the Old Testament.

New Testament Usage

The identity of Satan with the devil is also clear in the New Testament. Revelation 12:9 says: "And *the great dragon* was cast out, that *old serpent*, called *the Devil*, and *Satan*, which deceiveth the whole world." Further, Matthew says that Jesus was tempted by the devil (Matthew 4:1), the same one to whom Jesus commanded, "Begone, Satan!" (Matthew 4:10, RSV; cf. also Mark 1:13; Luke 4:2). Other titles by which Satan is known in the New Testament include: "Abaddon" and "Apollyon" (Revelation 9:11), both meaning "the destroyer"; "the accuser of our brethren" (Revelation 12:10); "adversary" (*antidikos* [473], 1 Peter 5:8); "Beelzebub" (Matthew 12:24, on which also cf. Brown, "Satan," *Colin Brown*, 3:472f.); "Belial" (2 Corinthians 6:15); "an enemy" (Matthew 13:28, 39); "the wicked one" (Matthew 13:19,38); "a murderer . . . a liar, and the father of it" (John 8:44); "the god of this world" (2 Corinthians 4:4); "the prince of the power of the air" (Ephesians 2:2); "the prince of this world" (John 12:31; 14:30; 16:11); "the tempter" (Matthew 4:3; 1 Thessalonians 3:5).

Satan is a created being and therefore is subordinate to the Creator (John 1:3; Colossians 1:16). He is not divine even though he is supernatural. He was probably present with God and the angelic host at the creation of the physical world (Job 38:7; cf. "sons of God," Job 1:6). If so, then his rebellion would have followed the creation. If he is to be identified with the king of Tyre (Ezekiel 28:12-19, cf. Payne, "śāṯān," *Theological Wordbook of the Old Testament*, 2:875), then his primordial splendor shows both the beauty with which he was gifted by God and also part of the reason that Adam and Eve could so easily have been deluded by him. There is no clear explanation in the Bible as to why Satan rebelled against God, simply that "unrighteousness" was found in him (Ezekiel 28:15; although verse 17 indicates pride was the major factor).

Since the Fall, he has been the adversary of God and therefore of God's family. It was to discredit God that Satan sought permission to attack Job, wanting to demonstrate that Job would not be loyal to God if stripped of his family, wealth, and health (Job 1—2). Satan stood before the Lord to directly accuse Joshua the high priest (Zechariah 3:1,2). He led David into the sin of pride in order to bring destruction on the nation of Israel (1 Chronicles 21:1). Such power was, and is, limited by the greater sovereignty of God. Satan gains access to a believer only with the permission of God (Job 1:12; 2:6; cf. Luke 22:31) or through the sin of the believer. Thus the Lord taught His disciples to pray, "Deliver us from (the) evil (one)" (Matthew 6:13).

The sin of Adam and Eve presented Satan a limited dominion over the earthly realm, limited both in time and authority. Satan is the ruler of this world (John 14:30; cf. 12:31). As such, he is the "prince of the power of the air, the spirit that now worketh in the children of disobedience" (Ephesians 2:2). To retain his followers, he tries to oppose every sowing of the gospel seed lest someone believe and be saved (Matthew 13:19); furthermore, he sows counterfeit Christians to confuse the world as to what true Christianity looks like (Matthew 13:36-43). When a person is born again, he is transferred from Satan's dominion to God's (Acts 26:18).

Satan wars against the children of God to cause them to defect from God or to distract them from faithful service. Peter warned that the devil is on the prowl as a hungry lion seeking to devour God's children (1 Peter 5:8). He can cause illness (Luke 13:16; cf. 2 Corinthians 12:7), although not all illness is attributed directly to him. He can also thwart the believer's service (1 Thessalonians 2:18).

But the devil is probably most active and effective in his role as tempter (1 Thessalonians 3:5). He thus lures people into sin through the cravings of the flesh, the eyes, and the ego, and renders them unfit for service (2 Timothy 2:21). He uses sexual urges to trap the incontinent (1 Corinthians 7:5). He uses hypocrisy that is intent on making a good appearance without underlying reality (Acts 5:3). He uses division within the ranks of Christians to weaken their united stand (2 Corinthians 2:11). He uses idleness and gossip (1 Timothy 5:15). He is so effective because he is able to transform himself into an angel of light (2 Corinthians 11:14), not only making evil look appealing but actually making it seem to be good.

The Lord Jesus confronted Satan, showing the believer how to withstand personal temptation, and secured for the believer the final victory over Satan by His resurrection from the dead. Jesus cast out Satan as a demonstration of the superior power of His superior kingdom (Matthew 12:26-30). He rejected Satan's every temptation and chose to suffer physical discomfort in order to obey the Father, to wait for the cross instead of taking a shortcut to glory (cf. Matthew 16:23), and to worship God instead of the material things and their glory which Satan offered (Luke 4:1-13). In all this the Lord showed every Christian how to resist Satan.

When the enemy could not lure the Saviour into sin, Satan attacked directly, taking possession of a cooperative Judas to perform the heinous betrayal of Christ (Luke 22:3; John 13:27). But even this fit God's sovereign plan, setting the stage for Christ's substitutionary death and resurrection which canceled the accuser's grounds for indictment and released the Christian both from the threat and the fear of death (Hebrews 2:14,15).

God's sovereign plan has also determined the eventual defeat of Satan. Jesus foresaw it in the powerful works of the 70 evangelists (Luke 10:18), prefiguring a final fall of Satan parallel to his original casting down (cf. Isaiah 14:12). Elsewhere, the apostle Paul foretold the devil's defeat in his letter to the Romans (16:20). It is worked out in history in the latter days when Satan and his angels are cast down from heaven to earth by God's forces (Revelation 12:7-9). He will engage in battle with God through the personage of the Antichrist (2 Thessalonians 2:9), but the personal return of Christ will squash this rebellion (Revelation 19), and Satan will be locked away for the duration of the Millennium (Revelation 20:2). At the end of the Millennium he is allowed one more opportunity to deceive the world, which climaxes in God's final victory and Satan's final doom in the lake of fire (Revelation 20:7-10).

Until this final defeat, the Christian can be certain of ongoing warfare against Satan (Ephesians 6:12). The Christian's protection comes from two directions. First, the Lord prays for the believer (Luke 22:32). Secondly, the believer has been provided with a panoply of armor with which to protect himself (Ephesians 6:13-18). The supreme weapon is his own prayers to God for moral and spiritual protection (Jude 20,21), buttressed by a holy life that gives the enemy no further grounds for accusation.

STRONG 4567, BAUER 744-45, MOULTON-MILLIGAN 570, KITTEL 7:151-65, LIDDELL-SCOTT 1585, COLIN BROWN 3:468-70.

4424. σάτον saton noun

Seah.

SYNONYMS:
κόρος koros (2857)
μέτρον metron (3228)
χοῖνιξ choinix (5354)

1. σάτα sata nom/acc pl neu

1 leaven, ... and hid in three measures of meal, ... Matt 13:33
1 a woman took and hid in three measures of meal, .. Luke 13:21

The *saton* (Hebrew *s^e'āh*, Aramaic *sā'thā'*) is a measure for grain, one-third of an ephah or bath, which is 22 liters. However, the imprecise nature of weights and measures in the ancient world has resulted in several different computations (see Carson, *The Expositor's Bible Commentary*, 8:319, note 33). In Jesus' Parable of the Leaven (Matthew 13:33; Luke 13:21) it was into three *sata* of meal that the woman hid the leaven. This appears to be the proper amount of dough to use when preparing bread for a family or larger group; it is the same amount prepared by Sarah in Genesis 18:6 (ibid.). The relative amount of leaven to dough was very small.

STRONG 4568, BAUER 745, MOULTON-MILLIGAN 570, LIDDELL-SCOTT 1585.

4425. Σαῦλος Saulos name

Saul.

1. Σαῦλος Saulos nom masc
2. Σαύλου Saulou gen masc
3. Σαύλῳ Saulō dat masc
4. Σαῦλον Saulon acc masc

2 at a young man's feet, whose name was Saul. .... Acts 7:58
1 And Saul was consenting unto his death. 8:1
1 As for Saul, he made havock of the church, ... 8:3
1 And Saul, yet breathing out threatenings 9:1
1 And Saul arose from the earth; 9:8
4 inquire in the house of Judas for one called Saul, ... 9:11
1 Then was Saul certain days with the disciples 9:19
1 But Saul increased the more in strength, ... 9:22
3 But their laying await was known of Saul. 9:24
1 And when Saul was come to Jerusalem, ... 9:26
4 departed Barnabas to Tarsus, for to seek Saul: 11:25
2 to the elders by the hands of Barnabas and Saul. 11:30
1 And Barnabas and Saul returned from Jerusalem, ... 12:25
1 brought up with Herod the tetrarch, and Saul. 13:1
4 Separate me Barnabas and Saul for the work 13:2
4 who called for Barnabas and Saul, ... 13:7
1 Then Saul, who also is called Paul, ... 13:9

A hellenized form of the Hebrew name *Saul*. (See "Saoul" [4406], the transliterated form of the name.)

4426. σβέννυμι sbennumi verb

To extinguish or quench; to suppress, subdue, stifle.

COGNATES:
ἄσβεστος asbestos (756)
σεβάζομαι sebazomai (4428)
σέβασμα sebasma (4429)

דָּעַךְ dā'akh (1906), Be put out, be snuffed out (Jb 18:5f., Prv 13:9, 24:20).

כָּבָה kāvâh (3637), Qal: go out, be quench (Lv 6:12f., 2 Chr 34:25, Jer 17:27); piel: extinguish, quench (2 Sm 14:7, /S 8:7, Is 42:3).

נָכָא nākhâ' (5404), Niphal: be scourged out (Jb 30:8).

1. σβέννυτε sbennute 2pl impr pres act
2. ἔσβεσαν esbesan 3pl indic aor act
3. σβέσαι sbesai inf aor act

4. σβέσει sbesei 3sing indic fut act
5. σβέννυται sbennutai 3sing indic pres mid
6. σβέννυνται sbennuntai 3pl indic pres mid

4 and smoking flax **shall he not quench**,............. Matt 12:20
6 Give us of your oil; for our lamps **are gone out**........ 25:8
5 worm dieth not, and the fire **is not quenched**....... Mark 9:44
5 worm dieth not, and the fire **is not quenched**........... 9:46
5 worm dieth not, and the fire **is not quenched**.......... 9:48
3 be able **to quench** all the fiery darts of the wicked....Eph 6:16
1 **Quench** not the Spirit.............................. 1 Th 5:19
2 **Quenched** the violence of fire,...................... Heb 11:34

Classical Greek

This verb is used in three primary ways in classical literature. Literally it is used of extinguishing a fire. Similarly it is used of liquids that "dry up." As a figure of speech *sbennumi* can be used of anything that is checked, quenched, or quelled (*Liddell-Scott*).

Septuagint Usage

The verb is used frequently in the Septuagint continuing the uses seen in classical literature. Literally it refers to the fire on the sacrificial altar which was never to be quenched (Leviticus 6:9, etc.). Unquenchable fire was seen as the tool of God's judgment on both Edom (Isaiah 34:10) and the Negev (Ezekiel 20:47 [LXX 21:3]). Figuratively *sbennumi* is used of the ending of a life (2 Samuel 21:17 [LXX 2 Kings 21:17]), of a family line (2 Samuel 14:7 [2 Kings 14:7]), of love (Song of Solomon 8:7), and of fury (Jeremiah 4:4). Four times the reader is warned that the lamp of the wicked will be extinguished (Job 18:5,6; 21:17; Proverbs 13:9; 24:20).

New Testament Usage

Sbennumi occurs eight times in the New Testament. Seven occurrences refer to literal fire. The Messiah's restraint is shown by the statement He was not to quench smoldering flax (Isaiah 42:3; Matthew 12:20). The lamps of the foolish virgins went out because they had not properly provided oil ahead of time (Matthew 25:8). Hell (Gehenna [see 1060]) is a place of unquenchable fire, unrelieved by death (Mark 9:44,46,48; some Greek texts contain *sbennumi* in verse 48 only), probably taking its earthly counterpart in the smoldering refuse heap in the Valley of Hinnom. The "shield of faith," spiritual counterpart to the leather-covered *thureos* (2352) of the Roman soldier, is able to deflect and quench the fiery darts of Satan (Ephesians 6:16). Finally, Hebrews 11:34 alludes to the exploit of Shadrach, Meshach, and Abednego, the heroes of faith who "*quenched* the violence of fire."

The lone figurative use of *sbennumi* in the New Testament is 1 Thessalonians 5:19: "*Quench* not the Spirit." The Spirit is associated with fire several times: Matthew 3:11; Acts 2:3; and by allusion, 2 Timothy 1:6. Resistance to His ministry in or through another believer (such as despising prophecy, 1 Thessalonians 5:20) can snuff out His influence, halting a genuine working of God's Holy Spirit. Believers are instructed to test the spirits and not to naively accept everything that purports to be of the Holy Spirit. But such testing must be with humble yieldedness to welcome and obey that which is truly from the Holy Spirit.

Strong 4570, Bauer 745, Moulton-Milligan 570, Kittel 7:165-68, Liddell-Scott 1587, Colin Brown 3:109-10.

4427. σεαυτοῦ seautou prs-pron

Yourself, of yourself.

1. σεαυτοῦ seautou gen sing masc
2. σεαυτῷ seautō dat sing masc
3. σαυτόν sauton acc sing masc
4. σεαυτόν seauton acc sing masc

4 cast **thyself** down: for it is written,................. Matt 4:6
4 See thou tell no man; but go **thy** way,.................. 8:4
4 Thou shalt love thy neighbour as **thyself**.............. 19:19
4 Thou shalt love thy neighbour as **thyself**.............. 22:39
4 save **thyself**. If thou be the Son of God,.............. 27:40
4 but go thy way, show **thyself** to the priest,..........Mark 1:44
4 Thou shalt love thy neighbour as **thyself**.............. 12:31
4 Save **thyself**, and come down from the cross........... 15:30
4 If thou be the Son of God, cast **thyself** down....... Luke 4:9
4 say unto me this proverb, Physician, heal **thyself**:....... 4:23
4 but go, and show **thyself** to the priest,................. 5:14
4 shalt love the Lord ... and thy neighbour as **thyself**..... 10:27
4 saying, If thou be the king of the Jews, save **thyself**.... 23:37
4 saying, If thou be Christ, save **thyself** and us........... 23:39
1 What sayest thou of **thyself**?....................... John 1:22
4 If thou do these things, show **thyself** to the world....... 7:4
1 Thou bearest record of **thyself**;....................... 8:13
4 the prophets are dead: whom makest thou **thyself**?...... 8:53
4 that thou, being a man, makest **thyself** God........... 10:33
4 how is it that thou wilt manifest **thyself** unto us,....... 14:22
2 glorify thou me with **thine own self** with the glory...... 17:5
1 saying this on **your own** initiative, (NASB)............ 18:34
4 When thou wast young, thou girdedst **thyself**,........... 21:18
2 arise, and make **thy** bed........................... Acts 9:34
2 Do **thyself** no harm: for we are all here.............. 16:28
1 Thou art permitted to speak for **thyself**............... 26:1
4 judgest another, thou condemnest **thyself**;........... Rom 2:1
2 **unto thyself** wrath against the day of wrath............. 2:5
4 confident that thou **thyself** art a guide of the blind,..... 2:19
4 which teachest another, teachest thou not **thyself**?....... 2:21
4 YOUR NEIGHBOR AS **YOURSELF**." (NASB)....... 13:9
3 Hast thou faith? have it to **thyself** before God.......... 14:22
4 YOUR NEIGHBOR AS **YOURSELF**." (NASB)......Gal 5:14
4 considering **thyself**, lest thou also be tempted.......... 6:1
4 and exercise **thyself** rather unto godliness.......... 1 Tm 4:7
2 Take heed **unto thyself**, and unto the doctrine;.......... 4:16
4 shalt both save **thyself**, and them that hear thee......... 4:16
4 keep **thyself** pure.................................... 5:22
4 Study to show **thyself** approved unto God,..........2 Tm 2:15
1 Take Mark, and bring him with **thee**:.................. 4:11
4 showing **thyself** a pattern of good works:............. Tit 2:7
4 thou owest unto me even **thine own self** besides..... Phlm 1:19
4 Thou shalt love thy neighbour as **thyself**,............ Jas 2:8

This is the second person singular form of the reflexive pronoun which is used only in the genitive, dative, and accusative cases (*Bauer*). It does not occur in the nominative case because it is never appositive to the subject or used as a subject (Robertson, *A Grammar of the Greek New Testament*, p.688).

STRONG 4572, BAUER 745, MOULTON-MILLIGAN 570, LIDDELL-SCOTT 1587.

4428. σεβάζομαι sebazomai verb

To worship, honor, revere.

COGNATES:

σβέννυμι sbennumi (4426)
σέβομαι sebomai (4431)

SYNONYM:

σέβομαι sebomai (4431)

1. ἐσεβάσθησαν esebasthēsan 3pl indic aor pass

1 and **worshipped** and served the creature more than .. Rom 1:25

Sebazomai's single New Testament occurrence is in Romans 1:25. Here it describes the rebellious elevation of the creature to the place of reverence that belongs solely to the Creator. This is not simply a pious reverence but an act (or acts) of worship (Foerster, "sebazomai," *Kittel*, 7:173).

STRONG 4573, BAUER 745, MOULTON-MILLIGAN 570, KITTEL 7:172-73, LIDDELL-SCOTT 1587, COLIN BROWN 2:91-93.

4429. σέβασμα sebasma noun

Object of worship, place of worship.

COGNATES:

σβέννυμι sbennumi (4426)
σέβομαι sebomai (4431)

1. σέβασμα sebasma nom/acc sing neu
2. σεβάσματα sebasmata nom/acc pl neu

2 For as I passed by, and beheld your **devotions**, ... Acts 17:23
1 above all that is called God, or that is **worshipped**; .. 2 Th 2:4

This noun refers to those objects and places (idols and shrines) that are granted the religious honor indicated in the verb *sebazomai* (4428). In the New Testament these include objects of heathen devotion. Paul used this term to refer to the many idols crowding the marketplace of Athens (Acts 17:23, "your devotions"), including the one dedicated to the Unknown God. In another New Testament usage the apostle characterized the Antichrist as one who will elevate himself above all other deities or objects of worship (2 Thessalonians 2:4), appropriating to himself all religious obeisance.

STRONG 4574, BAUER 745, MOULTON-MILLIGAN 570, KITTEL 7:173-74, LIDDELL-SCOTT 1587, COLIN BROWN 2:91-93.

4430. Σεβαστός Sebastos name-adj

Worthy of reverence.

1. Σεβαστοῦ Sebastou gen sing masc
2. Σεβαστόν Sebaston acc sing masc
3. Σεβαστῆς Sebastēs gen sing fem

1 to be reserved unto the hearing of **Augustus**, ... Acts 25:21
2 and that he himself hath appealed to **Augustus**, ... 25:25
3 one named Julius, a centurion of **Augustus'** band. 27:1

This adjective translates into Greek the Latin *Augustus*, and is used as a title for the emperor. In the New Testament it is variously translated "honored," or (of Nero, Acts 25:21,25; especially 26) "His Majesty," or (of a cohort of soldiers, Acts 27:1) "Imperial."

4431. σέβομαι sebomai verb

Worship.

COGNATES:

ἀσέβεια asebeia (757)
ἀσεβέω asebeō (758)
ἀσεβής asebēs (759)
εὐσέβεια eusebeia (2131)
εὐσεβέω eusebeō (2132)
εὐσεβής eusebēs (2133)
εὐσεβῶς eusebōs (2134)
θεοσέβεια theosebeia (2293)
θεοσεβής theosebēs (2294)
σεβάζομαι sebazomai (4428)
σέβασμα sebasma (4429)
σεμνός semnos (4441)
σεμνότης semnotēs (4442)

SYNONYM:

εὐλαβέομαι eulabeomai (2106)

יָרֵא yārē' (3486), Fear (Jos 4:24, 22:25).

יָרֵא yārē' (3487), Be fearful (Jb 1:9).

יִרְאָה yir'āh (3488), Fear (Is 29:13).

עֶבֶד 'evedh (5860), Servant (Is 66:14).

1. σέβεται sebetai 3sing indic pres mid
2. σέβονται sebontai 3pl indic pres mid
3. σεβομένου sebomenou gen sing masc part pres mid
4. σεβομένων sebomenōn gen pl masc part pres mid
5. σεβομένοις sebomenois dat pl masc part pres mid
6. σεβομένη sebomenē nom sing fem part pres mid
7. σεβομένας sebomenas acc pl fem part pres mid
8. σέβεσθαι sebesthai inf pres mid

2 But in vain they do **worship** me, ... Matt 15:9
2 Howbeit in vain do they **worship** me, ... Mark 7:7
4 **religious** proselytes followed Paul and Barnabas: ... Acts 13:43
7 But the Jews stirred up the **devout** ... women, ... 13:50
6 which **worshipped** God, heard us: 16:14
4 and of the **devout** Greeks a great multitude, ... 17:4

5 **with the Jews, and with the devout persons,** .... Acts 17:17
3 **named Justus, one that worshipped God,** 18:7
8 **to worship God contrary to the law** 18:13
1 **whom all Asia and the world worshippeth** 19:27

Classical Greek

In both the active and middle forms this verb denotes the act of "worshiping, revering," or "the sense of awe, fear," usually in a religious sense. Nonetheless, it is also applied to esteemed persons such as parents (*Liddell-Scott*). Essentially, though, the middle form means "to worship, fear" when directed to a deity or "to revere, respect, honor" when directed to an individual (ibid.). The religious connotations tend to dominate.

Septuagint Usage

In the Septuagint *sebomai* usually translates the verb *yārē'* ("to fear, worship, revere"), although *yārē'* is not exclusively equated with *sebomai* (e.g., see *phobeō* [5236]). Frequently it is God who is to be revered instead of idols (Joshua 4:24; cf. 22:5; Job 1:9; Jonah 1:9). False "reverence," even when directed to God, is despised (Isaiah 29:13), but those who "fear" Him will rejoice at His coming (Isaiah 66:14).

Use of *sebomai* in the apocryphal literature corresponds with what we have encountered elsewhere—it functions primarily in a religious capacity. This is most clearly illustrated in the interesting account in Bel and the Dragon (verses 2-4,26) where the entire issue centers around "worship." The Babylonians worshiped the idol Bel and a great dragon (verses 3,23, RSV). Daniel destroyed Bel (verse 22), and when the king tried to get him to worship the dragon Daniel replied, "I will *worship* the Lord my God, for he is the living God." Then, "without sword or club" Daniel slew the dragon (verse 21ff., RSV).

New Testament Usage

Sebomai occurs 10 times in the New Testament: once in Mark (7:7), a citation of Isaiah 29:13; again in the parallel text in Matthew 15:9; and 8 times in Acts.

The Book of Acts reveals a unique, virtually technical understanding of *sebomai*. The substantive use (e.g., 13:43; 17:17), i.e., the "God-fearers," refers to those pagans who had attached themselves to Judaism but who had not taken every necessary step toward becoming full-fledged converts (cf. *Bauer*). Papyri evidence interestingly suggests that others may have used the term substantivally to refer to Jews (*Moulton-Milligan*). The same understanding is reflected in the adjectival usage as well. Lydia was a God-fearing woman (Acts 16:14; cf. 18:7, of Titius Justus). On one occasion (Acts 19:27) *sebomai* refers to pagan worship practice. The goddess Artemis is worshiped throughout all of Asia according to some Ephesians.

Strong 4576, Bauer 746 (see "sebō"), Moulton-Milligan 570-71, Kittel 7:169-72, Liddell-Scott 1588, Colin Brown 2:90-95.

4432. σειρά seira noun

Cord, rope, chain.

Synonym:

ἅλυσις halusis (252)

חֶבֶל chevel (2346), Cord (Prv 5:22).

מַחְלָפוֹת machlāphôth (4389), Lock of hair (Jgs 16:13).

1. σειραῖς seirais dat pl fem

1 **and delivered them into chains of darkness,** .... 2 Pt 2:4

This word refers to a cord or rope used especially to snare or bind an enemy. In classical Greek *seira* refers to a rope with a noose, like a lasso, which was used to capture and drag away an enemy (see *Liddell-Scott*).

Second Peter 2:4 uses *seira* in the sense of a chain, i.e., the "chains of darkness" with which the fallen angels are bound until the time of judgment. If in fact *seirais*, "chains," is the correct reading in this verse, the writer of 2 Peter apparently interpreted *desmois*, "chains," in Jude 6 metaphorically (Bauckham, *Word Biblical Commentary*, 50:249). Thus these chains are the darkness of the underworld. Such a description of "chains of darkness" is also seen in Wisdom of Solomon 17:16 where the phrase describes the Egyptian plague of darkness. If, however, the correct reading is *seirois*, "pits," then one must suppose Peter had independent knowledge of a tradition found in 1 Enoch called "the fall of the Watchers." Here it speaks of valleys (1 Enoch 10:12) or the abyss (1 Enoch 18:11; 21:7) that served as a dungeon for the fallen angels (ibid.). Both readings must be viewed as highly possible.

Strong 4577, Bauer 746, Moulton-Milligan 571, Liddell-Scott 1588.

4433. σεισμός seismos noun

Shaking, earthquake, commotion, storm.

Cross-Reference:

σείω seiō (4434)

סְעָרָה seʻārāh (5788), Storm (Jer 23:19).

רַעַשׁ ra'ash (7783), Rattling, rumbling (Jb 41:29 [41:20], Ez 3:12f.); earthquake (Am 1:1).

1. **σεισμός seismos** nom sing masc
2. **σεισμῷ seismō** dat sing masc
3. **σεισμόν seismon** acc sing masc
4. **σεισμοί seismoi** nom pl masc

1 And, behold, there arose a great **tempest** in the sea, Matt 8:24
4 pestilences, and **earthquakes**, in divers places.......... 24:7
3 saw the **earthquake**, and those things ... were done,.... 27:54
1 And, behold, there was a great **earthquake**:........... 28:2
4 and there shall be **earthquakes** in divers places,....Mark 13:8
4 And great **earthquakes** shall be in divers places,....Luke 21:11
1 And suddenly there was a great **earthquake**,........Acts 16:26
1 and, lo, there was a great **earthquake**;..............Rev 6:12
1 thunderings, and lightnings, and **an earthquake**.......... 8:5
1 And the same hour was there a great **earthquake**,..... 11:13
2 in the **earthquake** were slain ... seven thousand:....... 11:13
1 thunderings, and **an earthquake**, and great hail......... 11:19
1 and lightnings; and there was a great **earthquake**,...... 16:18
1 so mighty **an earthquake**, and so great................ 16:18

Classical Greek

The noun *seismos* is related to the verb *seiō* (4434), "to shake" or "quake." In the papyri it is used metaphorically of extortion (*Moulton-Milligan*), but such usage is foreign to Biblical literature.

Septuagint Usage

Seismos occurs 15 times in the Septuagint. It is used literally of the rattling of bones as they come together (Ezekiel 37:7), and of earthquakes (Amos 1:1; Zechariah 14:5). It refers to the "rumbling" (NASB) that accompanied the movement of God's chariot (Ezekiel 3:12,13). It is also prominent in apocalyptic vision: Isaiah prophesied Jerusalem's judgment would include an earthquake (Isaiah 29:6), and Ezekiel foresaw a "great shaking" of Israel at the invasion of Gog (Ezekiel 38:19).

New Testament Usage

New Testament usage reflects that of the Septuagint. It refers once to the shaking of the sea, creating "a great tempest" which the Lord Jesus quelled with a command (Matthew 8:24f.). There are three references to historical earthquakes: the response of the Father to His Son's crucifixion (Matthew 27:54); the opening of the tomb to expose the Resurrection (Matthew 28:2); and the prying open of the Philippian jail to release Paul and Silas (Acts 16:26).

The remainder of the earthquakes in the New Testament are directly related to apocalyptic images. The Lord promised that "famines, and pestilences, and earthquakes" would accompany the latter days (Matthew 24:7; parallel Mark 13:8; Luke 21:11), and such is the scene in the Book of Revelation. The breaking of the sixth seal of judgment (6:12), preparations for the seven trumpet judgments (8:5), destruction of a tenth of Jerusalem (11:13), and the exposure of God's temple in heaven (11:19) are all marked by devastating earthquakes. But the greatest one of all history is poured out in the seventh bowl judgment which shakes all the world powers, including the apostate Babylon (16:18-21). Such shaking symbolizes God's sovereign power over world politics as well as over global geology. He is able at will to knock down any or all existing structures in order to prepare the earth for reconstruction with His divine kingdom. As at Sinai (Exodus 19:18), when God visits, the earth quakes.

STRONG 4578, BAUER 746, MOULTON-MILLIGAN 571, KITTEL 7:196-200, LIDDELL-SCOTT 1589, COLIN BROWN 3:556-58.

4434. σείω seiō verb

Shake, tremble, quake, move.

COGNATES:
ἀνασείω anaseiō (381)
διασείω diaseiō (1280)
κατασείω kataseiō (2648)
σεισμός seismos (4433)

SYNONYMS:
ἀνασείω anaseiō (381)
σαλεύω saleuō (4388)
τρέμω tremō (4981)

נוּד nûdh (5290), Hithpael: sway (Is 24:20).

נוּעַ nûa' (5309), Tremble (Is 19:1).

סָעַר ṣā'ar (5786), Storm in (Hb 3:14).

צָעַן tsā'an (7090), Be moved (Is 33:20).

רָגַז rāghaz (7553), Qal: tremble (Prv 30:21); hiphil: make tremble (Jb 9:6).

רָעַשׁ rā'ash (7782), Qal: quake, shake (2 Sm 22:8, Ez 26:10, Am 9:1); niphal: tremble (Jer 50:46 [27:46]); hiphil: make tremble (Is 14:16, Ez 31:16, Hg 2:6 [2:7]).

תָּעָה tā'âh (8912), Stagger (Is 28:7).

1. **σείω seiō** 1sing indic pres act
2. **σειομένη seiomenē** nom sing fem part pres mid
3. **ἐσείσθη eseisthē** 3sing indic aor pass
4. **ἐσείσθησαν eseisthēsan** 3pl indic aor pass
5. **σείσω seisō** 1sing indic fut act

3 all the city **was moved**, saying, Who is this?........Matt 21:10
3 and the earth **did quake**, and the rocks rent;.......... 27:51
4 And for fear of him the keepers **did shake**,............ 28:4
1 Yet once more I **shake** not the earth only,.........Heb 12:26
2 when she **is shaken** of a mighty wind...............Rev 6:13

Classical Greek

This is a verb which means "to shake, to move back and forth," especially in a violent manner.

In classical Greek *seiō* is used both in a literal as well as in a figurative sense. Homer, Sophocles, and others used the word to denote the literal shaking of a spear, a door, the reins, a mane, a head, or the earth itself in the form of an earthquake or a similar cosmic disturbance. Figuratively *seiō* denoted the emotional disturbance of the heart through fear and the upsetting of governmental affairs (see Bornkamm, "seiō," *Kittel*, 7:196f.).

Septuagint Usage

The usage of *seiō* in the Septuagint is plentiful, for it is found in the historical, poetical, and prophetic books. It is commonly used to denote the trembling or shaking of the earth at the judgments or the wrath of God (cf. Judges 5:4; 2 Samuel 22:8 [LXX 2 Kings 22:8]; Job 9:6; Isaiah 13:13; Ezekiel 38:20; Joel 2:10; Haggai 2:6). It seems to be a theme of the Old Testament to show a connection between the appearance of God on the scene and the shaking of the heavens and the earth (cf. Exodus 19:18; 1 Kings 19:11 [LXX 3 Kings 19:11]; Psalm 68:8 [LXX 67:8]).

New Testament Usage

Five instances of *seiō* are recorded in the New Testament. In two places *seiō* is used literally of the earth: (1) when it shook at the death of Christ (Matthew 27:51); and (2) when both it and the heavens undergo the eschatological shaking of God's judgment (Hebrews 12:26). Judgment is the theme again in the occurrence of *seiō* in Revelation 6:13 where the symbolism of a fig tree being shaken by a mighty wind is used. According to Vine, *seiō* is also used metaphorically to denote the stirring up or agitation of a crowd (Matthew 21:10) and the result of fear (Matthew 28:4) (*Expository Dictionary*, "Move").

STRONG 4579, BAUER 746, MOULTON-MILLIGAN 571, KITTEL 7:196-200, LIDDELL-SCOTT 1589, COLIN BROWN 3:556-57.

4435. Σεκοῦνδος Sekoundos name

Secundus.

1. Σεκοῦνδος Sekoundos nom masc

1 of the Thessalonians, Aristarchus and **Secundus**; .... Acts 20:4

A Christian of Thessalonica who accompanied Paul on his journey to Jerusalem (Acts 20:4).

4436. Σελεύκεια Seleukeia name

Seleucia.

1. Σελεύκειαν Seleukeian acc fem

1 forth by the Holy Ghost, departed unto **Seleucia**; ... Acts 13:4

The port city of Antioch in Syria from which Paul and Barnabas started their missionary travels (Acts 13:4).

4437. σελήνη selēnē noun

Moon.

יָרֵחַ yārēach (3507), Moon (Dt 17:3, Ps 104:19 [103:19], Jl 2:10).

לְבָנָה levānāh (3970), Moon (S/S 6:10 [6:9], Is 30:26).

1. σελήνη selēnē nom sing fem
2. σελήνης selēnēs gen sing fem
3. σελήνῃ selēnē dat sing fem

1 and the **moon** shall not give her light, ... Matt 24:29
1 and the **moon** shall not give her light, ... Mark 13:24
3 signs in the sun, and in the **moon**, and in the stars; Luke 21:25
1 sun ... into darkness, and the **moon** into blood, ... Acts 2:20
2 and another glory of the **moon**, ... 1 Co 15:41
1 and the **moon** became as blood; .... Rev 6:12
2 and the third part of the **moon**, ... 8:12
1 clothed with the sun, and the **moon** under her feet, ... 12:1
2 city had no need of the sun, neither of the **moon**, ... 21:23

Classical Greek

This term, which is related to *selas*, "brightness," has several usages in Greek literature. In addition to "moon," it can denote "month, a moon-shaped wheat cake, a round table, a tripod," or the name of a plant. As a feminine proper noun *Selēnē* refers to the goddess of the moon (*Liddell-Scott*).

Septuagint Usage

Like classical Greek, the Septuagint primarily uses *selēnē* literally to denote the moon. Often reference is made to the use of the phases of the moon to mark time and the Jewish religious festivals (Sirach 43:6-8). A few metaphoric uses are also found (Sirach 27:11; 50:6; Hagner, "Sun," *Colin Brown*, 3:733).

New Testament Usage

In the New Testament *selēnē* is always used in conjunction with *hēlios* (2229), "sun," and in all but two occurrences (1 Corinthians 15:41; Revelation 12:1) is apocalyptic in tone (cf. Matthew 24:29; Mark 13:24; Luke 21:25; Acts 2:20; Revelation 6:12; 8:12; 21:23). Vine suggests that the usage of *selēnē* in Revelation 6:12 and 12:1 refers symbolically to derived authority in contrast to the supreme authority represented by the sun ("Moon," *Expository Dictionary*).

Strong 4582, Bauer 746, Moulton-Milligan 571, Liddell-Scott 1590, Colin Brown 3:733-34.

4438. σεληνιάζομαι
selēniazomai verb

To be epileptic, lunatic.

1. σεληνιάζεται selēniazetai 3sing indic pres mid
2. σεληνιαζομένους selēniazomenous acc pl masc part pres mid

2 and those which were **lunatic,** .... Matt 4:24
1 for he is a **lunatic,** and sore vexed: 17:15

This verb literally means "to be moonstruck" and is not found prior to the New Testament. A common ancient belief linked certain phases of the moon with various irrational actions and central nervous system disorders including epilepsy.

New Testament Usage

Selēniazomai occurs twice in the New Testament, both times in the Gospel of Matthew. In Matthew 4:24 *selēniazomai* occurs in a list of four different kinds of sick people healed or delivered by Jesus during His great Galilean ministry. Included in the list are: (1) those who suffered from "divers diseases and torments"; (2) those who were "possessed with devils"; (3) those who were "lunatic" (*selēniazomai*); and (4) those "that had the palsy." Here the word *selēniazomai* is especially distinguished from *daimonizomai*, "demon possessed." By this distinction Matthew clearly showed that epilepsy and demonic possession are not one and the same. Although similar convulsions may be manifested in each, the cause is definitely different. *Selēniazomai* is a purely physical disorder, while *daimonizomai* finds its source in demons.

The other New Testament occurrence of *selēniazomai* is in Matthew 17:15. It is obvious in this passage that the boy who was brought to Jesus and said to be *selēniazomai*, "lunatic," was in reality demon possessed (cf. Matthew 17:18). Matthew did not try to correct the mistake by using the word *daimonizomai* but simply quoted the boy's father, who used the word *selēniazomai*. Although the father of the boy did not understand the difference between *selēniazomai* and *daimonizomai*, Jesus certainly did. In the parallel passages Mark (9:14-27) provides an accurate picture of "idiopathic epilepsy," while Luke (9:37-42) employs the term *sparassō*, "convulse," a technical medical term employed by Hippocrates and others (Harrison, "Epilepsy," *Interpreter's Dictionary of the Bible*, 2:123).

Strong 4583, Bauer 746, Moulton-Milligan 571, Liddell-Scott 1590, Colin Brown 3:733-34.

4439. Σεμεΐ Semei name

Semei.

1. Σεμεΐ Semei masc
2. Σεμεΐν Semein masc

1 which was the son of **Semei,** .... Luke 3:26

A figure in the genealogy of Jesus (Luke 3:26).

4440. σεμίδαλις semidalis noun

Flour.

סֹלֶת ṣōleth (5755), Fine flour (Lv 2:1f., Nm 28:12f., Ez 16:13).

קֶמַח qemach (7343), Flour (1 Sm 1:24).

1. σεμίδαλιν semidalin acc sing fem

1 and frankincense, and wine, and oil, and **fine flour,** Rev 18:13

This word denotes a fine flour made from wheat. It was used in the baking of bread, especially by the upper classes. *Semidalis* occurs only once in the New Testament, in Revelation 18:13. There it appears in a list of valuable commodity items traded by the world's merchants. It would seem to be a rather expensive item, based on its appearance in this list, its very fine quality, and the fact the poorer people usually ate bread made from barley rather than wheat (see Wight, *Manners and Customs of Bible Lands*, p.45).

Strong 4585, Bauer 746, Moulton-Milligan 572, Liddell-Scott 1590.

4441. σεμνός semnos adj

Worthy of respect, dignified, holy, honorable.

Cognate:
σέβομαι sebomai (4431)

Synonyms:
ἅγιος hagios (39)
ἁγνός hagnos (52)
ἱερός hieros (2393)
ὅσιος hosios (3603)

נָגִיד nāghîdh (5233), Leader; something noble (Prv 8:6).

נֹעַם nōʻam (5461), Something pleasant (Prv 15:26).

1. σεμνούς semnous acc pl masc
2. σεμνάς semnas acc pl fem
3. σεμνά semna nom/acc pl neu

3 whatsoever things are **honest,** .... Phlp 4:8
1 Likewise must the deacons be **grave,** .... 1 Tm 3:8
2 Even so must their wives be **grave,** not slanderers, ... 3:11
1 That the aged men be sober, **grave,** temperate, ... Tit 2:2

Classical Greek

The adjective *semnos* (compare the verb *sebomai* [4431]) especially describes deities as "revered, holy, august" (*Liddell-Scott*) in classical Greek. As well, *semnos* can be applied to things divine, persons or objects, with a partial supernatural character (ibid.). Finally, *semnos* can describe humans or their endeavors (especially seen on tombstones or sepulchers, *Moulton-Milligan*). Foerster notes that when used of persons *semnos* "is that which . . . calls forth *sebesthai* (to revere something) from others" ("semnos," *Kittel*, p.193). Describing objects, *semnos*'s emphasis often falls upon the visible greatness (e.g., of a city; ibid., 7:191). One might be "worthy of respect, honored," or "noble in character." In a negative sense it is used of those who are proud or pompous (*Liddell-Scott*).

Septuagint Usage

Only two canonical instances of *semnos* are found in the Septuagint, both in Proverbs. Elsewhere it occurs in the Septuagintal addition to Proverbs 6:8 and in the apocryphal 2 and 4 Maccabees. The Proverbs texts speak of "worthy" (perhaps "noble" or "holy") words of Wisdom (8:6) and "noble, honorable," or "holy" words which please the Lord (15:26). Second Maccabees relates the "sacredness" of the Sabbath to those Jews who died because of their unwillingness to defend themselves and "that most holy day" (6:11, RSV). Through giving his life Eleazar hoped to leave the young a "noble example of how to die a good death willingly and nobly for the revered and holy laws" (6:28, RSV). Here we see strong evidence supporting Foerster's contention that a primary feature is its exemplary nature (see above; cf. 4 Maccabees 5:36; 7:15; 17:5). In the Maccabean writings it is particularly the example of the old to the young.

New Testament Usage

Semnos occurs four times in the New Testament (cf. the related word *semnotēs* [4442], 1 Timothy 2:2; 3:4; Titus 2:7), all of which are attributed to Paul. *Semnos* falls in a list of "suitable thoughts" for the believer in Philippians 4:8. It joins the elite company of such qualities as "true" (*alēthēs* [225]), "just" (*dikaios* [1335B]), and "holy, pure" (*hagnos* [52]). Paul associated these abstract qualities with concrete behavior; he expected these to be "put . . . into practice" (Philippians 4:9, NIV).

The circumstances of the use of *semnos* in the Pastoral Epistles is slightly different. Instead of being tied to requirements for leaders in the sense they are to be "serious and worthy," *semnos* must also be understood in the same ethical terms presupposed by Paul in Philippians 4:8. *Semnos* has to do with conduct as well as character, especially since it was the *misconduct* of the false teacher/elders in Crete which prompted Paul to advise about how to replace them (cf. Titus 2:1,2).

Church leadership ("deacons" is perhaps too strong, since it is doubtful that Paul saw positions of leadership as "offices") must be *semnos*, both men and women. They must model good conduct and godliness (*eusebeia* [2131]). We can see that this concern occupies a major place in Paul's reason for writing in 1 Timothy 3:14f.: "I am writing you these instructions so that . . . people in God's household might know how to conduct their lives" (author's translation; note: the NIV's translation misses the point and interprets Paul's letter as a guideline for church order; on the situation and circumstance of the Pastoral Epistles see Fee, *Good News Commentary, 1 and 2 Timothy, Titus*).

Strong 4586, Bauer 746-47, Moulton-Milligan 572, Kittel 7:191-96, Liddell-Scott 1591, Colin Brown 2:91-93.

4442. σεμνότης semnotēs noun

Dignity, honorableness, nobility, propriety.

Cross-Reference:

σέβομαι sebomai (4431)

1. **σεμνότητος semnotētos** gen sing fem
2. **σεμνότητι semnotēti** dat sing fem
3. **σεμνότητα semnotēta** acc sing fem

2 peaceable life in all godliness and honesty.......... 1 Tm 2:2
1 having his children in subjection with all gravity;........ 3:4
3 in doctrine showing uncorruptness, gravity,........... Tit 2:7

Classical Greek and Septuagint Usage

This noun is related to the verb *sebomai* (4431), "to reverence." It is used in classical Greek as an honorable attribute of the gods and to describe a person's deportment that commands respect. In the Septuagint it is used to describe the reverence and respect due to the temple (2 Maccabees 3:12).

New Testament Usage

In the New Testament *semnotēs* is found only three times, all in the Pastoral Epistles. In 1 Timothy 2:2 it describes the conduct of Christian citizens. In 1 Timothy 3:4 it is presented as a necessary characteristic of a bishop in his household. Paul used the word in Titus 2:7 to characterize how Titus was to conduct himself as a teacher.

Semnotēs is difficult to translate into English. The King James Version renders it both as "honesty" and "gravity," while various other versions use additional words suggestive of a propriety of demeanor which is worthy of respect. The word "venerable" would be an excellent translation if its meaning could be restricted to its original sense of "worthy of reverence," without any implication of age.

Strong 4587, Bauer 747, Moulton-Milligan 572, Kittel 7:191-96, Liddell-Scott 1591, Colin Brown 2:91-93.

4443. Σέργιος Sergios name

Sergius.

1. Σεργίῳ Sergiō dat masc

1 **Sergius Paulus, a prudent man;.................. Acts 13:7**

The family name of Sergius Paulus. He was the Roman governor of Cyprus and was converted during Paul's visit (Acts 13:7).

4444. Σήθ Sēth name

Seth.

1. Σήθ Sēth masc

1 **which was the son of Seth,......................... Luke 3:38**

The son of Adam and Eve listed in Luke's genealogy of Jesus (Luke 3:38).

4445. Σήμ Sēm name

Shem.

1. Σήμ Sēm masc

1 **which was the son of Sem,......................... Luke 3:36**

The son of Noah listed in Luke's genealogy of Jesus (Luke 3:36).

4446. σημαίνω sēmainō verb

To signify, to give a sign, to indicate.

Cognates:

ἄσημος asēmos (761)
ἐπίσημος episēmos (1962)
εὔσημος eusēmos (2135)
παράσημος parasēmos (3763)
σημεῖον sēmeion (4447)
σημειόομαι sēmeioomai (4448)
σύσσημος syssēmos (4805)

זָהַר zāhar (2178), Hiphil: warn (Ez 33:3).

יָדַע yādha' (3156), Know; hiphil: teach (Ex 18:20).

יְדַע y^{e}dha' (A3157), Know; haphel: inform, make known (Dn 2:15,23,30,45— Aramaic).

מָלַל mālal (4589), Speak; signal (Prv 6:13).

נָגַד nāghadh (5222), Hiphil: tell (Est 2:22).

רוּעַ rûa' (7607), Hiphil: cry out (Jgs 7:21).

תָּקַע tāqa' (8965), Blow (Jos 6:7, Jer 4:5).

1. σημαίνων sēmainōn nom sing masc part pres act
2. ἐσήμανεν esēmanen 3sing indic aor act
3. σημᾶναι sēmanai inf aor act
4. ἐσήμαινεν esēmainen 3sing indic imperf act

1 **This he said, signifying what death he should die... John 12:33**
1 **signifying what death he should die.................. 18:32**
1 **signifying by what death he should glorify God........ 21:19**
2 **and signified by the Spirit that there should be..... Acts 11:28**
3 **not withal to signify the crimes laid against him........ 25:27**
2 **signified it by his angel unto his servant John:....... Rev 1:1**

Classical Greek

The verb *sēmainō* is related to the noun *sēma*, "a sign." *Sēmainō* carries such meanings as "to give a sign, to indicate," and "to signify," especially with the purpose of revealing, explaining, or interpreting something that was before unclear. It does not carry any specific religious sense in and of itself, even though it is at times used in connection with religious or divine actions (Rengstorf, "sēmainō," *Kittel*, 7:262).

Frequent usage of *sēmainō* is found in classical Greek literature beginning with the writings of Homer. There "sign" and "command" bear a close relationship. *Sēmainō* is thus used in connection with the giving of specific orders or commands, such as, "to give a signal for battle, to signal retreat," or "to reinforce a command" (ibid.).

Philo used *sēmainō* in the sense of "to represent" or "to mean." Often in his exposition of Scripture he used *sēmainō* to refer to the hidden meaning of a word or passage he was attempting to explain.

Josephus' usage includes the basic meanings of *sēmainō* already expressed. However, his writings show an extended meaning, "to seal," in reference to a royal document. Josephus also used *sēmainō* in the sense of God revealing or making known His will to man (ibid., 7:263).

Septuagint Usage

The Septuagint occurrences of *sēmainō* are frequent, translating a variety of Hebrew words. It is used in the sense of giving a warning or signaling an alarm, especially through the blowing of a trumpet (Numbers 10:9; 2 Chronicles 13:12;

Jeremiah 4:5). *Sēmainō* also translates other Hebrew terms in such senses as "to show the way" (Exodus 18:20) and "to make known" through explanation (Daniel 2:15) or by a dream (Daniel 2:45). The idea of interpreting or giving the clear meaning of something is seen throughout (ibid., 7:262f.).

New Testament Usage

The New Testament records six instances of *sēmainō*. Three of these instances are found in the Gospel of John (12:33; 18:32; 21:19). Each of the usages in the Fourth Gospel occurs in a parenthetic note included by John to explain a statement of Jesus concerning the manner of someone's death. In John 12:33 and 18:32 it is Jesus' own death that is in reference. *Sēmainō* is used in the sense of "signifying" that Jesus' death will be by crucifixion. In John 21:19 the "signifying" of the manner of Peter's death is indicated. These instances in John provide further evidence for the deity of Jesus Christ, since only God knows the time or manner of any man's death beforehand.

Two other occurrences of *sēmainō* are found in Acts (11:28; 25:27). In the latter passage Festus spoke of examining Paul in order "to signify" or "to show" the accusations made against him. Agabus the prophet, in Acts 11:28, "signified" through the agency of the Holy Spirit that a famine was coming. Agabus simply showed or indicated what the Spirit revealed to him.

The final New Testament occurrence is in Revelation 1:1. There Jesus "signified" (indicated or declared) to John through His angel the things which would occur in the future.

Strong 4591, Bauer 747, Moulton-Milligan 572, Kittel 7:262-65, Liddell-Scott 1592-93.

4447. σημεῖον sēmeion noun

Sign, token, signal, miracle, portent.

Cross-Reference:

σημειόομαι sēmeioomai (4448)

אוֹת 'ôth (225), Sign (Dt 11:18, 1 Sm 10:7, Is 7:11).

אָת 'āth (A880), Sign (Dn 4:2 [3:32]—Aramaic).

מוֹעֵד mô'ēdh (4287), Appointed signal (Jgs 20:38).

מוֹפֵת môphēth (4295), Miracle, wonder (Ex 7:9, 11:9, 2 Chr 32:24).

מַשְׂאֵת mas'ēth (5020), Tax, something that rises; fire signal (Jer 6:1).

נֵס nēs (5438), Pole, mast (Nm 21:8f., Is 33:23); standard (Jer 51:12 [28:12]).

צִיּוּן tsîyûn (6996), Marker (Ez 39:15).

תָּו tāw (8750), Mark (Ez 9:4,6).

תִּקְוָה tiqwāh (8950), Cord (Jos 2:18).

1. **σημεῖον** sēmeion nom/acc sing neu
2. **σημεῖα** sēmeia nom/acc pl neu
3. **σημείων** sēmeiōn gen pl neu
4. **σημείοις** sēmeiois dat pl neu

1 saying, Master, we would see **a sign** from thee...... Matt 12:38
1 evil and adulterous generation seeketh after **a sign**;.... 12:39
1 and there shall no **sign** be given to it,................ 12:39
1 no sign be given to it, but the **sign** of ... Jonas:....... 12:39
1 that he would show them **a sign** from heaven.......... 16:1
2 but can ye not discern the **signs** of the times?......... 16:3
1 and adulterous generation seeketh after **a sign**;........ 16:4
1 and there shall no **sign** be given unto it,.............. 16:4
1 no sign ... but the **sign** of the prophet Jonas........... 16:4
1 and what shall be the **sign** of thy coming,............. 24:3
2 and shall show great **signs** and wonders;.............. 24:24
1 shall appear the **sign** of the Son of man in heaven:.... 24:30
1 Now he that betrayed him gave them **a sign**,.......... 26:48
1 seeking of him **a sign** from heaven, tempting him.... Mark 8:11
1 Why doth this generation seek after **a sign**?............ 8:12
1 There shall no **sign** be given unto this generation....... 8:12
1 be the **sign** when all these things shall be fulfilled?.... 13:4
2 For false Christs ... shall show **signs** and wonders,...... 13:22
2 And these **signs** shall follow them that believe;....... 16:17
3 confirming the word with **signs** following. Amen....... 16:20
1 And this shall be a **sign** unto you;................. Luke 2:12
1 and for **a sign** which shall be spoken against;........... 2:34
1 tempting him, sought of him **a sign** from heaven....... 11:16
1 This is an evil generation: they seek **a sign**;........... 11:29
1 This is an evil generation: they seek a **sign**;........... 11:29
1 but the **sign** of Jonas the prophet.................... 11:29
1 For as Jonas was **a sign** unto the Ninevites,........... 11:30
1 what **sign** ... when these things shall come to pass?.... 21:7
2 and fearful sights and great **signs** shall there be........ 21:11
2 **signs** in the sun, and in the moon, and in the stars;.... 21:25
1 he hoped to have seen some **miracle** done by him..... 23:8
3 This beginning of **miracles** did Jesus in Cana........ John 2:11
1 What **sign** showest thou unto us,....................... 2:18
2 when they saw the **miracles** which he did............... 2:23
2 for no man can do these **miracles** that thou doest,...... 3:2
2 Except ye see **signs** and wonders, ye ... not believe...... 4:48
1 This is again the second **miracle** that Jesus did,......... 4:54
2 followed him, because they saw his **miracles**............ 6:2
1 when they had seen the **miracle** that Jesus did,......... 6:14
2 Ye seek me, not because ye saw the **miracles**,.......... 6:26
1 What **sign** showest thou then, that we may see,......... 6:30
2 Christ ... will he do more **miracles** than these.......... 7:31
2 How can a man that is a sinner do such **miracles**?...... 9:16
1 John did no **miracle**: but all things ... were true........ 10:41
2 What do we? for this man doeth many **miracles**........ 11:47
1 for that they heard that he had done this **miracle**...... 12:18
2 though he had done so many **miracles** before them,.... 12:37
2 And many other **signs** truly did Jesus................. 20:30
2 wonders in heaven ... **signs** in the earth beneath;.... Acts 2:19
4 approved ... by miracles and wonders and **signs**,........ 2:22
2 wonders and **signs** were done by the apostles........... 2:43
1 for that indeed a notable **miracle** hath been done....... 4:16
1 on whom this **miracle** of healing was showed........... 4:22
2 and that **signs** and wonders may be done.............. 4:30
2 And by the hands of the apostles were many **signs**...... 5:12
2 did great wonders and **miracles** among the people....... 6:8
2 showed wonders and **signs** in the land of Egypt,........ 7:36
2 hearing and seeing the **miracles** which he did........... 8:6
2 beholding the miracles and **signs** which were done....... 8:13
2 **signs** and wonders to be done by their hands.......... 14:3
2 declaring what **miracles** and wonders God had......... 15:12
1 And he received the **sign** of circumcision,........... Rom 4:11
3 Through mighty **signs** and wonders,.................. 15:19
1 For the Jews require **a sign**,...................... 1 Co 1:22
1 tongues are for **a sign**, not to them that believe,....... 14:22
2 Truly the **signs** of an apostle were wrought........ 2 Co 12:12

4 in **signs,** and wonders, and mighty deeds........... 2 Co 12:12
4 with all power and **signs** and lying wonders,........ 2 Th 2:9
1 which is the **token** in every epistle: so I write........... 3:17
4 witness, both **with signs** and wonders,............... Heb 2:4
1 And there appeared a great **wonder** in heaven;..... Rev 12:1
1 And there appeared another **wonder** in heaven;........ 12:3
2 great **wonders,** so that he maketh fire come down...... 13:13
2 deceiveth them ... by the means of those **miracles**...... 13:14
1 saw another **sign** in heaven, great and marvellous,..... 15:1
2 For they are the spirits of devils, working **miracles,**.... 16:14
2 false prophet that wrought **miracles** before him,....... 19:20

Classical Greek

At the most basic level *sēmeion* (a noun related to *sēma*) denotes the "mark" by which something is known, a "sign," especially in the sense of a sign of what will happen in the future. Thus *sēmeion* might be a "sign from the gods, an omen." *Sēmeion* often includes a supernatural or wondrous dimension, and it might be described as a miracle (*Liddell-Scott*).

Nonreligious usages include a "signal," a "boundary" or "limit," the "signet of a ring," and a "birthmark." Much of *sēmeion*, therefore, concerns its being a visual sign by which something is distinguished (ibid.). In the language of logic and reasoning a *sēmeion* is a "proof," something which could probably be regarded as certain. Medically a *sēmeion* is a "symptom" (ibid.; cf. Rengstorf, *Kittel*, 7:200-207).

Septuagint Usage

The translators of the Septuagint predominantly recognized *sēmeion* as the equivalent of the Hebrew term *'ôth* (in various forms), a "sign, mark" (e.g., Genesis 1:14, the sun and the moon are "signs" for marking seasons; Genesis 4:15, the "mark" of Cain). Of theological import is the *sēmeion* of the covenant with Abraham—"circumcision" (Genesis 17:11), or the sign of the covenant with Noah—the rainbow (Genesis 9:12,13,17). God regularly offered signs as signifiers and reminders of His covenantal promises. This may involve a future circumstance (Exodus 3:12) or a supernatural event calling for belief (Exodus 4:8,9), or a reminder (Exodus 31:13; Numbers 17:10).

God empowers His servants to perform signs (Exodus 4:17,28,30) with the result and intent that people can turn to God (Exodus 4:30; Numbers 14:11). But signs are no guarantee that belief will follow (Exodus 7:3,9ff.; 8:23f.; Numbers 14:22; Deuteronomy 29:3). In fact, disbelief or stubbornness may stimulate signs by God (Exodus 10:1; 11:9f.). "Signs" in and of themselves, however, are no guarantee of the reliability of a prophet or seer (Deuteronomy 13:1ff.).

Signs are future oriented, and they are often supernatural (e.g., Isaiah 38:7; Joel 2:30). The prophet Samuel told Saul of certain "signs" he would experience which would be a "signal" that God was with him (1 Samuel 10:1,7,9 [LXX 1 Kings 10:1,7,9]; cf. 14:10). The Lord's signs were carried out by the prophets (2 Kings 20:8,9ff. [LXX 4 Kings 20:8,9ff.]; cf. Psalm 105:27 [LXX 104:27]).

Of the Prophets, the Book of Isaiah has the most instances of *sēmeion* (15 times). Apparently, asking God for a sign came to be regarded as "testing God" (Isaiah 7:12; cf. Matthew 4:7; 1 Corinthians 1:22). But God gave signs anyway (Isaiah 7:13ff.), sometimes to His enemies for war and judgment ("banner," NIV; Isaiah 11:12; 13:2; 18:3; 19:20). The prophet Isaiah acted out God's sign against Egypt and Cush (20:3).

Apocryphal writers stressed that God alone is the worker of miracles (Letter of Jeremiah 67; 3 Maccabees 6:32; Sirach 36:6). God is best known for His "signs" (usually "and wonders," *sēmeia kai terasi*) worked during the exodus from Egypt (Baruch 2:11; cf. Joshua 24:5; Psalm 78:43 [LXX 77:43]).

New Testament Usage

Sēmeion occurs around 75 times in the Greek New Testament. If one accepts the readings of some manuscripts then Matthew 16:3 (parallel Matthew 12:39) contains two other instances. Mark 16 (verses 17,20) also attests to two readings whose authenticity is disputed. The Gospels and Acts are the dominant sites of usage, although Paul used *sēmeion* eight times and John's Revelation seven times; Hebrews (2:4) is the only other document reading *sēmeion*.

The Synoptic Gospels

Rengstorf observes that in the Synoptics *sēmeion* is not used to describe Jesus' miraculous works of healings, exorcisms, or miracles of nature. Rather, *dunamis* (1405), "miracle," answers that call ("sēmeion," *Kittel*, 7:235). He asserts the miracles prompt the demand for *sēmeia*, "signs." What is at stake here is the rabbinic aversion to anything that even hinted at sorcery. They desired "proof" of Jesus' identity because "miracles" were no guarantee of "orthodoxy." They were seeking confirmation that it was God's power at work and not human or demonic forces (ibid.; cf. the debate in Mark 3:22ff.).

Jesus denied their challenge to confirm himself on their terms (Matthew 12:38ff., with parallels Mark 8:11; Matthew 16:1; Luke 23:8); instead, the "sign" of the Cross and Resurrection would be the ultimate confirmation (cf. the sign of Jonah). But it was not the kind of sign they were looking for; they wanted Messiah to overthrow Rome and to set up His world rule.

Elsewhere in the Synoptics Luke, at 2:12 in typical Septuagintal style (e.g., Exodus 3:12; 1 Samuel 2:34; 14:10; 2 Kings 19:29; ibid., 7:231), used *sēmeion* in the sense of a "proof" or "confirmation, indication." The baby wrapped in clothes and lying in a manger was the "confirmation" of the angelic testimony about the good news of the Saviour's birth. In a more secular understanding Judas gave the religious leaders the "signal" (distinguishing sign) by kissing Jesus on the cheek (Matthew 26:48). Elsewhere, Jesus' words about the end time and His return prompted the disciples to ask what the "sign" would be (Matthew 24:3; Mark 13:4; Luke 21:7). He reported that cataclysmic celestial "signs" would herald those events (Luke 21:11,25; ibid.).

Gospel of John

Whereas the Synoptic writers use *sēmeion* in an essentially negative sense (e.g., the evil and adulterous generation seeks a sign)—a sense which is also attested in John (e.g., 2:18; 6:30)—John saw *sēmeion* in a favorable light for the most part. Signs can lead men and women to faith, but they are not always an adequate basis for continuing trust (e.g., 2:23ff.; 4:48; 6:26). Faith produced by Jesus' signs indicates some recognition of His divine authorization, but such faith is still not satisfactory (see Brown, *The Anchor Bible*, 29:127).

Jesus' signs in John's Gospel point to a significance beyond themselves. They positively outline Jesus' ministry. For example, John marked time with the first sign (Cana, 2:11) or the second sign (healing at Capernaum, 4:54). Indeed, the positive place of signs is so pronounced in John's Gospel that scholars have come to label chapters 1–12 as the "Book of Signs." Interestingly, the only other instance of *sēmeion* apart from these chapters is 20:30—a verse telling that Jesus did many other signs, bearing witness that He is the Son of God. Signs are typically miraculous, and there is little indication that a superficially normal event was actually a disguised sign.

Acts Account

When turning to examine *sēmeion* in Acts we encounter the striking phenomenon of the recurrence of the stock phrase (especially in the Septuagint)—usually a reference to the Exodus miracles (e.g., Acts 7:36)—"signs and wonders" (*sēmeia kai terata*, or vice versa; see e.g., Acts 2:43; 4:30; 5:12; 6:8; 7:36; 14:3; 15:12; cf. 2:19). It is particularly striking since Luke did not use it in his Gospel; it occurs only twice in connection with false prophets in the Synoptics (Matthew 24:24; Mark 13:22) and once in John, which is probably referring to the Septuagintal usage (John 4:48).

First, but not primarily, signs and wonders are eschatological portents that the new age has dawned (Acts 2:19; cf. Joel 2:28; see also Revelation 12:1; 15:1). Second, they are "proofs" of Jesus' divine authority (Acts 2:22). Third, and most significantly, signs and wonders—including at least healings and exorcisms (cf. Acts 8:6,13)—were carried out by the apostles (and others, cf. 6:8) as they were enabled by God (2:43; 4:30; 5:12). The signs "confirm" God's activity among the Gentiles (15:12). They signal the age of the Spirit; the new covenant sign is given.

Pauline Epistles

The eight Pauline usages of *sēmeion* are of less import theologically than those in the Gospels and Acts; nonetheless, they mirror the general views found in them. In Old Testament language "circumcision" is the "sign" of God's covenant with Abraham (Genesis 17:11; cf. Romans 4:11). But from the New Testament perspective signs (and wonders) confirm the gospel message (Romans 15:19; cf. Hebrews 2:4) and the apostolic calling (2 Corinthians 12:22).

Paul also revealed an understanding of signs shared by the Gospel writers: signs and miracles would be performed in the last days by false prophets through the power of Satan (2 Thessalonians 2:9). Jesus warned of this impending deception in His speech on the Mount of Olives (Matthew 24:24; Mark 13:22). John wrote in the Book of Revelation of evil spirits coming out of the mouths of the dragon, beast, and false prophet. These evil spirits work counterfeit miraculous signs all over the earth and deceive many (Revelation 16:14; cf. 13:13,14; 19:20).

Here we see clearly the paradox of *sēmeion* in the New Testament. "Signs" in and of themselves confirm God's miraculous power and summon faith in Him. At the same time, however, "signs"—counterfeit—are a trick of the enemy to lead believers astray. In the final analysis, Christians are not to put their faith in signs themselves. Although signs can lead people to faith and confirm the truth of the gospel, they are only a starting point for true faith. Any sign pointing away from Christ or pointing toward a human being is not of God. "Sign-seekers" still belong to the "evil and adulterous generation."

STRONG 4592, BAUER 747-48, MOULTON-MILLIGAN 572, KITTEL 7:200-61, LIDDELL-SCOTT 1593, COLIN BROWN 2:626-27,629.

4448. σημειόομαι sēmeioomai verb

To mark for oneself, to note for oneself.

נָשָׂא nāsâ' (5558), Lift up (Ps 4:6).

1. σημειοῦσθε sēmeiousthe 2pl impr pres mid

1 **note that man, and have no company with him,..... 2 Th 3:14**

This is the middle voice form of the verb *sēmeioō* which, like *sēmainō* (4446), carries such meanings as "to denote, to seal," or "to signal." The middle form adds a subjective tendency to the verb. *Sēmeioomai* thus means "to mark for oneself" or "to note for oneself" (see Rengstorf, "sēmeioō," *Kittel*, 7:265).

Classical Greek

In classical Greek literature *sēmeioomai* is rather common. Polybius (ca. Second Century B.C.) used the term in its basic meaning. Strabo, however, extended its meaning to include "to take something as a sign" (*sēmeion* [4447]). The word is also used in a medical context with the meaning "to diagnose something on the basis of symptoms" (*sēmeia*). When employed in relation to documents *sēmeioomai* denotes "signing in one's own hand" (*Liddell-Scott*).

Philo used only the middle voice form *sēmeioomai*. Such meanings as "to characterize, to show, to signify," or "to get proof" are carried by his use of the word. Josephus also used *sēmeioomai* in the sense of "to note" (see Rengstorf, "sēmeioō," *Kittel*, 7:266).

New Testament Usage

The only New Testament occurrence of *sēmeioomai* is in 2 Thessalonians 3:14. There Paul admonished the believers to "note" for themselves any man who refused to obey the instructions he gave in the epistle. The immediate context reveals that Paul was instructing the church about those who refused to work but instead went around as idle busybodies causing disorder in the church (cf. 2 Thessalonians 3:11). The disciplinary action intended in Paul's use of *sēmeioomai* was not necessarily that a public identification of such disobedient individuals be made. Rather, he probably meant that the faithful believers were to stop associating with these busybodies in worship and other Christian activities. The purpose of such discipline was to cause the wrongdoer to realize his sin, to repent, and to be drawn back into the full fellowship of Christ and the church (ibid., cf. 2 Thessalonians 3:15).

STRONG 4593, BAUER 748 (see "sēmeioō"), MOULTON-MILLIGAN 573 (see "sēmeioō"), KITTEL 7:265-66 (see "sēmeioō"), LIDDELL-SCOTT 1593-94 (see "sēmeioō").

4449. σήμερον sēmeron adv

Today.

1. σήμερον sēmeron

1 Give us **this day** our daily bread.................... Matt 6:11
1 which **to day** is, ... to morrow is cast into the oven,..... 6:30
1 in Sodom, it would have remained until **this day**....... 11:23
1 It will be foul weather **to day**:....................... 16:3
1 and said, Son, go work **to day** in my vineyard.......... 21:28
1 field was called, The field of blood, unto **this day**...... 27:8
1 I have suffered many things **this day** in a dream....... 27:19
1 commonly reported among the Jews until **this day**...... 28:15
1 That **this day**, even in this night, before the cock .. Mark 14:30
1 is born **this day** in the city of David a Saviour,...... Luke 2:11
1 **This day** is this scripture fulfilled in your ears.......... 4:21
1 saying, We have seen strange things **to day**............. 5:26
1 God so clothe the grass, which is **to day** in the field,... 12:28
1 and I do cures **to day** and to morrow,................. 13:32
1 Nevertheless I must walk **to day**, and to morrow,...... 13:33
1 come down; for **to day** I must abide at thy house...... 19:5
1 **This day** is salvation come to this house,............. 19:9
1 Peter, the cock shall not crow **this day**,............... 22:34
1 "Before a cock crows **today**, (NASB)................. 22:61
1 **To day** shalt thou be with me in paradise.............. 23:43
1 to day is the third day since these ... were done........ 24:21
1 If we **this day** be examined of the good deed........ Acts 4:9
1 Thou art my Son, **this day** have I begotten thee........ 13:33
1 to be called in question for this **day's** uproar,.......... 19:40
1 Wherefore I take you to record **this** day,.............. 20:26
1 and was zealous toward God, as ye all are **this day**..... 22:3
1 I am called in question by you **this day**................ 24:21
1 because I shall answer for myself **this day**............ 26:2
1 but also all that hear me **this day**,.................... 26:29
1 **This day** is the fourteenth day that ye have tarried..... 27:33
1 and ears that they should not hear; unto this **day**... Rom 11:8
1 for until **this day** remaineth the same veil untaken ... 2 Co 3:14
1 But even unto **this day**, when Moses is read,........... 3:15
1 Thou art my Son, **this day** have I begotten thee?..... Heb 1:5
1 Holy Ghost saith, **To day** if ye will hear his voice,...... 3:7
1 exhort one another daily, while it is called **To day**;...... 3:13
1 While it is said, **To day** if ye will hear his voice,........ 3:15
1 **To day**, after so long a time; as it is said,.............. 4:7
1 as it is said, **To day** if ye will hear his voice,........... 4:7
1 Thou art my Son, **to day** have I begotten thee.......... 5:5
1 the same yesterday, and **to day**, and for ever........... 13:8
1 **To day** or to morrow we will go into such a city,..... Jas 4:13

Classical Greek

Related to *hē*, *sēmeron*, meaning "today," is found in classical Greek literature beginning with Homer. It is used to refer to the period of man's activity in a day up until evening, the period of time man presently has at his disposal. It could possibly be the final time he has (see Fuchs, "sēmeron," *Kittel*, 7:269f.).

Septuagint Usage

The Septuagint is replete with usages of *sēmeron*. However, the meaning there often contrasts with its usage in classical literature. Rather than basically referring to the present time at man's disposal, *sēmeron* primarily represents the temporary period in which man may receive or respond to the blessings of God (Exodus 32:29; Deuteronomy 6:24), or else encounter His wrath (Deuteronomy 4:26; Joshua 7:25). Used in this manner *sēmeron* is the actual time of decision between God and His people which determines their relationship to each other (Deuteronomy 11:26; 26:17-19; ibid., 7:270f.).

Although not its primary meaning, *sēmeron* does have a secular usage in the Septuagint that bears close resemblance to its usage in classical literature. Man's dealings with man are usually referred to when *sēmeron* is so used (Genesis 30:32; 42:13,32) (ibid.).

Sēmeron appears in the writings of both Philo and Josephus. Their usage of the term was almost always in relation to quotations from the Septuagint, although some secular uses were made. Josephus did add a new emphasis to *sēmeron*. Based on the Old Testament, he indicated that the proclamation of God's will was to take place "today," thus enabling God's revelation to be expressed as Israel's history (ibid.).

New Testament Usage

In the New Testament *sēmeron* continues to be used in both secular and theological ways. Each of these finds numerous examples. The secular or ordinary usage of *sēmeron* finds expression in such instances as Matthew 27:19, where the term actually means "this night" (last night); in Matthew 6:11, where God's children are to ask Him "this day" (each and every "today") for their daily bread; and in Acts 4:9, where Peter referred to the present day ("this day") in which he was on trial. The usage of *sēmeron* in the Book of Acts often refers to the present day in which the speaker is making his address (cf. Acts 19:40; 20:26; 22:3; 24:21; 26:2,29; 27:33). Jesus used *sēmeron* to refer to the present day in His statement in Luke 23:43 to the penitent thief while on the cross.

Sēmeron carries theological significance beyond ordinary reference to "today" as the present day in a number of New Testament passages. In Hebrews 13:8 *sēmeron* means the continuing present time, not just the day the writer wrote the statement. The oft recurring phrase "unto (or until) this day" (cf. Matthew 11:23; 27:8; 28:15; Romans 11:8; 2 Corinthians 3:14) denotes a promise, usually its fulfillment. Fulfilled promise is also the theme in other passages where *sēmeron* is used (cf. Luke 2:11; 4:21; Acts 13:33). Christ himself is seen to be the fulfillment of these promises. This is also true in Hebrews 1:5; 3:13; 4:7; and 5:5 where the context makes it clear that the *sēmeron* referred to is made available to those who place their faith in and hold fast to Jesus Christ (cf. Hebrews 4:3,14).

Strong 4594, Bauer 749, Moulton-Milligan 573, Kittel 7:269-75, Liddell-Scott 1594, Colin Brown 3:833-34,837,841.

4450. σήπω sēpō verb

To corrupt, rot.

כָּלָה kālâh (3735), Be at an end, be complete; waste away (Jb 33:21).

מָקַק māqaq (4905), Niphal: fester (Ps 38:5 [37:5]).

רָקֵב rāqēv (7830), Rot (Sir 14:19).

1. σέσηπεν sesēpen 3sing indic perf act

1 Your riches are corrupted,.......................... Jas 5:2

This is a verb that means "to make corrupt, rotten, putrid." In classical literature Aeschylus (ca. Sixth Century B.C.) used the term to refer to the festering action caused by a serpent's poison (*Liddell-Scott*). Primarily it appears in the passive form and is used of dead bodies that have begun to "rot," the mortification of live flesh, and of water or food that is rejected after digestion (ibid.).

Sēpō appears in the New Testament in James 5:2. There it is used figuratively to denote the perishing or wasting of the wealth of the rich because they have defrauded laborers of their fair wages.

Strong 4595, Bauer 749, Moulton-Milligan 573, Kittel 7:94-97, Liddell-Scott 1594.

4451. σηρικός sērikos adj

Silken, silk.

1. σηρικοῦ sērikou gen sing neu

1 and fine linen, and purple, and silk, and scarlet,.... Rev 18:12

This term is used as an adjective and as a noun. As an adjective *sērikos* means "silken." It is derived from a tribe of people either in India or China from whom silk was first obtained (*Moulton-Milligan*).

As a noun *sērikos* is translated "silk" and denotes fabric made of silk. It is so used in Revelation 18:12 (*Textus Receptus*), its only New Testament occurrence. There *sērikos* appears in a list of marketable commodities which, according to Vine, were sold prior to the fall of the symbolic Babylon (*Expository Dictionary*, "silk"). See also the word study at *sirikos* (4472B), a later variant spelling of *sērikos*.

STRONG 4596, BAUER 751 (see "sirikos"), MOULTON-MILLIGAN 575 (see "sirikos"), LIDDELL-SCOTT 1594.

4452. σής sēs noun

Moth.

סָס sās (5775), Moth (Is 51:8).

עָשׁ 'āsh (6468), Moth (Jb 4:19).

רָקָב rāqāv (7831), Rottenness (Prv 14:30).

1. σής sēs nom sing masc

1 **earth, where moth and rust doth corrupt,** .... **Matt 6:19**
1 **where neither moth nor rust doth corrupt,** **6:20**
1 **no thief approacheth, neither moth corrupteth.** ...... **Luke 12:33**

Classical Greek

This term occurs in Greek literature since Pindar (Fifth Century B.C.), where gold is referred to as that which neither moth nor anything else consumes (Fragment 222).

Septuagint Usage

In the Septuagint the term occurs 12 times: once for the Hebrew noun *sās*, which denotes "moth" (see Isaiah 51:8); 3 times for the Hebrew verb *'āsh*, which also denotes "moth" (see Job 4:19; 27:18; and Isaiah 50:9); once for the Hebrew verb *rāqāv* which means to "rot" or "become worm-eaten" (see Proverbs 14:30); and 7 times with no Hebrew counterpart (Job 27:20; 32:22; Proverbs 25:20; Micah 7:4; Isaiah 33:1; Sirach 19:3; and 42:13).

New Testament Usage

In the New Testament *sēs* occurs only three times, being used in such a way as to show the transitory nature of material possessions. It is used twice at Matthew 6:19,20 where Jesus instructed His audience, "Lay not up for yourselves treasures upon earth, where *moth* and rust doth corrupt, and where thieves break through and steal: but lay up for yourselves treasures in heaven, where neither *moth* nor rust doth corrupt, and where thieves do not break through nor steal." It is used once again at Luke 12:33 where a similar reading occurs.

STRONG 4597, BAUER 749, MOULTON-MILLIGAN 573, KITTEL 7:275-78, LIDDELL-SCOTT 1594.

4453. σητόβρωτος sētobrōtos adj

Moth-eaten.

1. σητόβρωτα sētobrōta nom/acc pl neu

1 **and your garments are motheaten.** .... **Jas 5:2**

Classical Greek

This adjective is a compound from the noun for moth, *sēs* (4452), and the verb *bibrōskō* (970), "to eat." It is found only one time in secular Greek literature, in the *Sybilline Oracles*. There it describes wooden idols that have been damaged or destroyed by moths (*Moulton-Milligan*).

Septuagint Usage

Its only occurrence in the Septuagint is in Job 13:28. There *sētobrōtos* refers to a "moth-eaten" garment.

New Testament Usage

In the New Testament *sētobrōtos* occurs only once, in James 5:2. It denotes the "moth-eaten" garments of the wealthy that will have been destroyed along with their other material possessions because of their greed and injustice to their hired laborers. The connection here is at the same time both literal and figurative. The destruction of the garments and possessions of the rich oppressors is certain. However, the implication seems to be that all earthly wealth is at best only temporal, especially in light of coming judgment. Those who base their security upon their possessions will find that they cannot make those possessions last forever despite their efforts to do so (cf. Bauerfeind, "sētobrōtos," *Kittel*, 7:277f.).

STRONG 4598, BAUER 749, MOULTON-MILLIGAN 573, KITTEL 7:275-78, LIDDELL-SCOTT 1595.

4454. σθενόω sthenoō verb

To strengthen, to make strong.

SYNONYMS:

βεβαιόω bebaioō (943)
δυναμόω dunamoō (1406)
ἐνδυναμόω endunamoō (1727)
ἐνισχύω enischuō (1749)
ἐπιστηρίζω epistērizō (1975)
κυρόω kuroō (2937)

σερεόω stereoō (4583)
στηρίζω stērizō (4592)

1. σθενώσαι sthenōsai 3sing opt aor act
2. σθενώσει sthenōsei 3sing indic fut act

1 make you perfect, stablish, **strengthen**, settle you..... 1 Pt 5:10

Sthenoō is a verb related to the noun *sthenos*, "strength." It means "to make strong, to strengthen." The only New Testament occurrence of *sthenoō* is in 1 Peter 5:10 where it is used in the future tense. Peter wrote that God will "strengthen" the faithful believers after a period of suffering. According to Vine it is their spiritual condition or their faith that is the object of God's strengthening (*Expository Dictionary*, "Strength").

Strong 4599, Bauer 749, Moulton-Milligan 573, Liddell-Scott 1595.

4455. σιαγών siagōn noun

Cheek, jaw.

לְחִי lechî (4029), Jawbone (Jgs 15:15ff.); cheek (S/S 1:10, Lam 1:2).

לְחִי lechî (4030), Lehi (Jgs 15:14).

פֶּה peh (6552), Mouth (Jb 21:5).

1. σιαγόνα siagona acc sing fem

1 but whosoever shall smite thee on thy right **cheek**,.. Matt 5:39
1 And unto him that smiteth thee on the one **cheek**... Luke 6:29

Siagōn is a noun that means "jaw" or "jawbone." It is used to refer to the "cheek." Its first appearance is in the classical writings of Sophocles (ca. Fifth Century B.C.).

There are two New Testament occurrences of *siagōn* (Matthew 5:39; Luke 6:29). Both passages record the same statement of Jesus about turning the other "cheek" to one who strikes you in the face, instead of taking revenge. This does not prohibit defending others, but it illustrates the principle of nonresistance to wrongs that are done to oneself. A disciple of Jesus must not resist wrongs done to him or her and must be ready to give rather than demand restitution.

Strong 4600, Bauer 749, Moulton-Milligan 573-74, Liddell-Scott 1595.

4456. σιγάω sigaō verb

Be silent, keep still, say nothing, stop speaking, hold one's peace, conceal, silence.

Cognate:
σιγή sigē (4457)
Synonyms:
ἡσυχάζω hēsuchazō (2248)
σιωπάω siōpaō (4478)

דָּמָה dāmâh (1880), Be like; cease (Lam 3:49).

הַס has̱ (2085), Hush! (Am 6:10 [6:11]).

חָרַשׁ chārash (2896), Qal: hold one's peace (Ps 83:1 [82:1]); hiphil: keep silent (Pss 32:3 [31:3], 50:21 [49:21]).

חָשָׁה chāshāh (2924), Qal: be hushed, be silent (Ps 107:29 [106:29], Eccl 3:7); hiphil: refrain (Ps 39:2 [38:2]).

סָכַת s̱ākhath (5728), Niphal: keep silent (Sir 13:23).

1. σιγάτω sigatō 3sing impr pres act
2. σιγάτωσαν sigatōsan 3pl impr pres act
3. σιγᾶν sigan inf pres act
4. ἐσίγησεν esigēsen 3sing indic aor act
5. ἐσίγησαν esigēsan 3pl indic aor act
6. σιγῆσαι sigēsai inf aor act
7. σεσιγημένου sesigēmenou gen sing neu part perf mid
8. σιγήσῃ sigēsē 3sing subj aor act

5 they **kept it close**, and told no man in those days.... Luke 9:36
8 were sternly telling him to **be quiet**; (NASB).......... 18:39
5 they marvelled at his answer, and **held their peace**..... 20:26
3 beckoning unto them with ... to **hold their peace**,... Acts 12:17
4 Then all the multitude **kept silence**,.................. 15:12
6 after they **had held their peace**, James answered,....... 15:13
7 which was **kept secret** since the world began,....... Rom 16:25
1 let him **keep silence** in the church;............... 1 Co 14:28
1 let the first **hold his peace**........................ 14:30
2 Let your women **keep silence** in the churches:......... 14:34

Classical Greek

The verb *sigaō* means "to be silent, quiet" among classical authors. A frequent use is the imperative "be quiet, be still" (e.g., Homer uses it exclusively in the imperative, cf. *Liddell-Scott*). There are indications that "secrecy" ("to be secret") was understood in certain contexts.

Septuagint Usage

Sigaō is not widely employed in the Septuagint, but it does occur in 10 canonical texts and in 9 texts which are either apocryphal or without a Hebrew original. Two Hebrew words—*chārash*, "be deaf, be still, silent," and *chāshāh*, "to command silence, be silent"—are translated by *sigaō*. To be "still" is perhaps the best translation in Exodus 14:14. Israel was to let God work His deliverance without interference. The five instances in Psalms show the range of meaning. God can "quiet" a storm (Psalm 107:29 [LXX 106:29]); or the Psalmist could plead with God not to be "silent" when it came to delivering him from his enemies (Psalm 83:1 [82:1]). "Silence" from God symbolizes His patience that will give way to wrath and judgment (Psalm 50:21 [LXX

49:21]; cf. Isaiah 42:14) or salvation (Isaiah 62:1), which are typically "not silent" (cf. Psalm 50:3; Isaiah 57:11).

New Testament Usage

Sigaō (cf. the noun *sigē* [4457]) occurs nine times in the New Testament. The disciples accompanying Jesus on the Mount of Transfiguration "kept silence and told no one in those days anything of what they had seen" (Luke 9:36, RSV). The blind beggar at Jericho could not keep "quiet" when he heard that Jesus was approaching.

In Acts *sigaō* suggests more than simply an absence of speech or noise. Peter asked everyone to "be quiet" so he could explain how the angel had delivered him from prison (Acts 12:17). A cessation from activity as well as speech is implied (cf. Acts 15:12ff.).

This may shed some light on the difficult passage in 1 Corinthians 14:34: "Let the women/wives be silent in the church." The context is charismatic worship and more specifically prophecy (verse 29ff.). Since we know that women/wives were praying and prophesying in Corinth (11:5), this need not be interpreted as some eternal instruction forbidding women to speak in the church. Rather, the issue may refer to women who were asking questions at the wrong time, thereby disrupting the service. They should be quiet (not "remain silent," NIV) during the exercise of the gifts by others, then they are free to participate. The emphasis falls upon their being quiet, not upon their not speaking. Their questions should be deferred until a more appropriate time and setting. The similar commands in 14:28 and 30 to other (obviously male) participants—"Let (the one speaking in a tongue) keep silence"; "Let the first (prophet) hold his peace"—are never interpreted as eternal commands forbidding speech.

Romans 16:25 gives us a different perspective on *sigaō*. Here Paul used it to mean "having been kept a secret" (*sesigēmenou*, perfect passive participle). This is the only transitive use of *sigaō* in the New Testament. The "hidden" nature of the gospel is not that it was totally unknown; after all, the prophets' having foretold the event is central to New Testament theology. What is at stake here is similar to what we encounter in 1 Corinthians 2:6-10 (cf. 2 Timothy 1:9f.; 1 Peter 1:20). God has fully disclosed the gospel in Jesus Christ and in the proclamation of the gospel by the apostles.

STRONG 4601, BAUER 749, MOULTON-MILLIGAN 574, LIDDELL-SCOTT 1596.

4457. σιγή sigē noun

Silence, quietness.

CROSS-REFERENCE:
σιγάω sigaō (4456)

1. σιγή sigē nom sing fem
2. σιγῆς sigēs gen sing fem

2 And when there was made a great silence, ... Acts 21:40
1 silence in heaven about the space of half an hour. .... Rev 8:1

Classical Greek and Septuagint Usage

This term occurs in Greek literature from the classical Greek period through the Koine or New Testament Greek period. In the classical period the term was used both as a noun and as an adverb. As a noun it generally meant "silence." As an adverb it could mean "silently" or "quietly, secretly." In the Septuagint the term occurs only twice, both times in the apocryphal books (Wisdom 18:14; 3 Maccabees 3:23). In both references *sigē* means "silence."

New Testament Usage

In the New Testament, as in the Septuagint, the term occurs only twice. In Acts 21:40 it describes the setting in which Paul presented his defense before the Jewish crowd: "Paul stood on the stairs, and beckoned with the hand unto the people. And when there was made a great *silence*, he spake unto them in the Hebrew tongue." In Revelation 8:1 it describes heaven after the seventh seal was opened: "And when he had opened the seventh seal, there was *silence* in heaven about the space of half an hour."

STRONG 4602, BAUER 749-50, MOULTON-MILLIGAN 574, LIDDELL-SCOTT 1596.

4458. σιδήρεος sidēreos adj

Made of iron.

בַּרְזֶל barzel (1298), Iron (Dt 28:23, 2 Chr 18:10, Jer 11:4).

פַּרְזֶל parzel (A6774), Iron (Dn 2:33f.,42, 7:7,19—Aramaic).

1. σιδηροῦς sidērous acc pl masc
2. σιδηρᾷ sidēra dat sing fem
3. σιδηρᾶν sidēran acc sing fem

3 came unto the iron gate that leadeth unto the city; Acts 12:10
2 And he shall rule them with a rod of iron; .... Rev 2:27
1 had breastplates, as it were breastplates of iron; 9:9
2 who was to rule all nations with a rod of iron: 12:5
2 nations: and he shall rule them with a rod of iron: 19:15

Classical Greek

In Greek literature from the time of Homer (Eighth Century B.C.) this adjective (also spelled *sidērous*) occurs with the literal meaning "made of iron" or "steel." In classical Greek literature it is used both literally and figuratively. Literally it describes such things as the sky, which many ancient peoples believed to be made of metal (*Odyssey* 15.329). Figuratively it describes individuals as being "ironhearted."

Septuagint Usage

In the Septuagint the term was also used both literally and figuratively. It translated the Hebrew noun *barzel* and the Aramaic noun *parzel*, both meaning "iron." It appears in Deuteronomy 3:11 which speaks of the "*iron* bedstead" belonging to Og the king of Bashan. Other examples are Judges 4:3,13 ("*iron* chariots") and Amos 1:3 ("*iron* saws"). Its figurative usage is manifold. In Leviticus 26:19 *sidēreos* speaks of the heavens being "iron"; in Deuteronomy 4:20 it describes a furnace which symbolizes "bondage"; in Deuteronomy 28:23 it is a metaphor for "unwatered earth"; in Psalm 2:9 it describes "power"; in Isaiah 45:2 it portrays "oppression"; and in Isaiah 48:4 it suggests "stubbornness."

New Testament Usage

Although *sidēreos* occurs only 5 times in the New Testament (compared with more than 40 times in the Septuagint), it still follows suit with both the classical and Septuagintal meanings. Its only literal usage is found in Acts 12:10 where it describes the *iron* gate of a prison. The remaining four occurrences are in Revelation where it was used in a figurative sense (with the possible exception at 9:9). At 2:27 the Revelator spoke of the rod which when coupled with the adjective *sidēreos* (4458) denotes "might" or "power." "And he shall rule them with a rod of *iron*." (See also 12:5 and 19:15 for similar usages.) At 9:9 the writer described the breastplates of the locusts which came up out of the bottomless pit: "And they had breastplates, as it were breastplates of *iron*."

STRONG 4603, BAUER 750, MOULTON-MILLIGAN 574, LIDDELL-SCOTT 1597, COLIN BROWN 2:97 (see "sidērous").

4459. σίδηρος sidēros noun

Iron.

בַּרְזֶל barzel (1298), Iron (Nm 31:22, 1 Chr 22:3, Ez 22:18).

גַּרְזֶן garzen (1676), Axe (Dt 20:19).

חֶרֶב cherev (2820), Sword (Jb 5:20).

מוֹרָה môrāh (4311), Razor (Jgs 13:5, 1 Sm 1:11).

פַּרְזֶל parzel (A6774), Iron (Dn 2:33,35,40f.,43,45—Aramaic).

1. σιδήρου sidērou gen sing masc

1 precious wood, and of brass, and iron, and marble, Rev 18:12

Classical Greek

This substantive occurs in Greek literature from the time of Homer (Eighth Century B.C.) onward. Its literal meaning is "iron," but it is also used in a figurative sense to denote "hardness" or "stubborn force" (*Liddell-Scott*). In addition, it denotes anything made of iron such as an iron tool, ax head, sword, or fetters (ibid.). It could also refer to "a place for selling iron," such as a smithy or cutler's shop.

Man's use of iron has a long and involved history. Archaeology has uncovered some articles made of iron in the period generally called the Bronze Age (ca. 3000–1200 B.C.), and even before. These objects were almost entirely for ceremonial and ritual use (Muhly, *The Bronze Age Setting*, p.50). Iron did not become the predominant metal for agricultural tools or weapons in the Eastern Mediterranean until about 900 B.C. (Waldbaum, *First Archaeological Appearance of Iron*, p.87). Some of these Bronze Age articles had been smelted (the rest were cold-hammered from iron derived from meteors), but it is difficult to know if these pieces were deliberately smelted (ibid., p.73).

The accelerated use of iron for tools and weapons appears to have been the result of the breakdown of trade in copper and tin (used to make bronze) around 1200 B.C., caused perhaps by the Sea Peoples (Muhly, *The Bronze Age Setting*, p.47). Until then, iron remained very rare and very valuable (ibid., pp.36f.). It is generally assumed that ironworking began with the Hittites (Winnett, "Iron," *Interpreter's Dictionary of the Bible*, 2:725), but evidence is lacking for this assertion. The Hittites may have made quicker progress in its use, however (Muhly, p.50; Snodgrass, p.357).

In Palestine iron weapons have been found in graves from the 12th Century B.C., but bronze materials still predominate (Waldbaum, *First Archaeological Appearance of Iron*, p.83). Iron use grew through the 11th Century until it became the predominant metal in the 10th Century B.C.

Septuagint Usage

Many of these meanings are evidenced in the Septuagint where *sidēros* translates a number of Hebrew terms, namely, *barzel*, "iron" (Genesis 4:22); *garzen*, "ax" (Deuteronomy 20:19);

cherev, "sword" (Job 5:20); and *môrāh*, "razor" (1 Samuel 1:11 [LXX 1 Kings 1:11]). It also translates one Aramaic word: *parzel*, "iron" (Daniel 2:33).

New Testament Usage

Unlike its frequent usage in the Septuagint, *sidēros* occurs only once in the New Testament. At Revelation 18:12 it occurs in a literal sense with a list of products no longer purchased in Babylon.

Strong 4604, Bauer 750, Moulton-Milligan 574, Liddell-Scott 1597, Colin Brown 2:97.

4460. Σιδών Sidōn name

Sidon.

1. **Σιδῶνος Sidōnos** gen fem
2. **Σιδῶνι Sidōni** dat fem
3. **Σιδῶνα Sidōna** acc fem

2 done in you, had been done in Tyre and **Sidon**, ... Matt 11:21
2 It shall be more tolerable for Tyre and **Sidon** 11:22
1 and departed into the coasts of Tyre and **Sidon**. 15:21
3 beyond Jordan; and they about Tyre and **Sidon**, ... Mark 3:8
1 and went into the borders of Tyre and **Sidon**, ... 7:24
1 departing from the coasts of Tyre and **Sidon**, ... 7:31
1 a city of **Sidon**, unto a woman that was a widow..... Luke 4:26
1 and from the sea coast of Tyre and **Sidon**, ... 6:17
2 mighty works had been done in Tyre and **Sidon**, ... 10:13
2 But it shall be more tolerable for Tyre and **Sidon** 10:14
3 And the next day we touched at **Sidon**. .... Acts 27:3

Sidon was an ancient city-state on the Phoenician coast, the modern Saida. It is recorded as the scene of ministry among Gentiles by Jesus (Matthew 15:21; Mark 7:24,31), and people from there came to hear Him (Mark 3:8; Luke 6:17). Paul passed through on his way to Rome (Acts 27:3).

4461. Σιδώνιος Sidōnios name-adj

Sidonian.

1. **Σιδωνίοις Sidōniois** dat pl masc
2. **Σιδωνίας Sidōnias** gen sing fem

2 in the land of **Sidon**, to a woman (NASB) .... Luke 4:26
1 highly displeased with them of Tyre and **Sidon**: .... Acts 12:20

The word is an adjective used as a noun to signify the area around Sidon (Luke 4:26); it refers to the Sidonians (Acts 12:20).

4462. σικάριος sikarios noun

Dagger carrier, assassin.

Synonym:

ἀνθρωποκτόνος anthrōpoktonos (441)

1. **σικαρίων sikariōn** gen pl masc

1 four thousand men that were **murderers**? .... Acts 21:38

This Greek transliteration of the Latin word *sicarius* literally denotes a "dagger carrier" and by extension an "assassin" or "murderer." It is derived from the Latin *sica*, a curved dagger. It is not found in Greek literature before the New Testament, where it occurs only once. In Acts 21:38 the chief captain asked Paul, "Art not thou that Egyptian, which before these days madest an uproar, and leddest out into the wilderness four thousand men that were *murderers* (*sikariōn*)?" The Sicarii were a fanatical group of Zealots who used murder and assassination to achieve their goals. They appeared during the Jewish war (A.D. 66–70). Josephus noted that these men committed murders in broad daylight, especially at festivals (*Wars of the Jews* 2.13.3).

Strong 4607, Bauer 750, Moulton-Milligan 574, Kittel 7:278-82, Liddell-Scott 1598.

4463. σίκερα sikera noun

Strong drink.

שֵׁכָר shākhar (8335), Strong drink (Nm 6:3, Dt 29:6, Is 5:11).

1. **σίκερα sikera** neu

1 and shall drink neither wine nor **strong drink**; .... Luke 1:15

Sikera is a loanword from Aramaic (*shikh*[e]*rā'*). It is cognate with Hebrew *shākhār* and Akkadian *shikaru*. The exact range of meaning for the Hebrew term *shākhār* is not specifically elucidated in Scripture, but from the several passages in which it is coupled with *yayin*, "wine," it evidently refers to all alcoholic beverages not made from grapes. Thus, when the Nazarite was forbidden to drink "wine and strong drink," all alcoholic beverages are in view (Numbers 6:3).

The Akkadian word *shikaru* originally meant "beer," a beverage made from grain, but by 700 B.C. date wine was also called *shikaru* (Forbes, *Studies in Ancient Technology*, 3:82). According to Forbes, Hebrew *shākhar* included "strong drinks . . . brewn not only from dates, but also from apples and even from barley" (ibid., 3:64). Beer, however, was the most common form since it was the drink preferred by the Philistines.

Septuagint Usage

In the Septuagint, Hebrew *shākhar* is generally translated *sikera*. Occasionally *shēkhār* is translated *methē* (3149) or *methusma*, both of which can mean "strong drink." According to

Walters *methē* and *methusma* represent "later stages" of translation "which avoided such patent Aramaisms" as *sikera* (*Text of the Septuagint*, p.170). He believes that the use of *sikera* points "to an old and primitive stratum of the LXX, when the translators in an unreflecting and spontaneous way incorporated into their translation what may well have been modes of expression used in the vernacular Greek of the Egyptian Jews" (ibid.).

The range of meaning of *sidera* is the same as that of *shākhar*. Greek *oinos* (3494), which translates Hebrew *yayin*, referred to "fermented beverages made from the juice of grapes" (Louw and Nida, *Greek-English Lexicon*, 1:77). Thus, *sikera* includes all other fermented drinks. Jerome translated *shākhar* as "all which is able to inebriate" (Leviticus 10:9, Vulgate).

Sikera is generally viewed in a highly unfavorable light in the Septuagint. It destroys judgment (Isaiah 28:7), leads to drunkenness, and is associated with revelry (Isaiah 5:11,12). Nazarites were forbidden to drink it (Numbers 6:3; Judges 13:4,7,14, Codex A). Priests were not to drink *sikera* while ministering (Leviticus 10:9). However, it was used for certain types of libations (Numbers 28:7), and it was not strictly forbidden to all Israelites. They were permitted to buy *sikera* with the silver derived from their tithes (Deuteronomy 14:26).

New Testament Usage

Sikera appears only once in the New Testament. John the Baptist was forbidden to drink *oinos* or *sikera*. It is evident from its connection with *oinos* that *sikera* retains its Septuagintal meaning. It is not just "beer" that is in mind. John was not allowed to drink *any* alcoholic beverages.

Strong 4608, Bauer 750, Moulton-Milligan 574, Liddell-Scott 1598.

4464. Σίλας Silas name

Silas.

1. Σίλας Silas nom masc
2. Σίλᾳ Sila dat masc
3. Σίλαν Silan acc masc

3 namely, Judas surnamed Barsabas, and **Silas**,.......Acts 15:22
3 We have sent therefore Judas and **Silas**,.............. 15:27
1 Judas and **Silas**, being prophets also themselves,....... 15:32
2 Notwithstanding it pleased **Silas** to abide there still.... 15:34
3 And Paul chose **Silas**, and departed,.................. 15:40
3 they caught Paul and **Silas**,.......................... 16:19
1 Paul and **Silas** prayed, and sang praises unto God:.... 16:25
2 and fell down before Paul and **Silas**,.................. 16:29
2 and consorted with Paul and **Silas**;.................. 17:4
3 sent away Paul and **Silas** by night unto Berea:........ 17:10
1 but **Silas** and Timotheus abode there still............. 17:14
3 and receiving a commandment unto **Silas**.......... Acts 17:15
1 **Silas** and Timotheus were come from Macedonia,...... 18:5

Silas was an early Christian leader who became a missionary colleague of Paul. His name appears as Silas in Acts but in the Latin form Silvanus in the letters of Paul and Peter. Like Paul, he was a Jew with the privilege of Roman citizenship (Acts 16:37).

He was chosen with Judas Barsabas to carry and interpret the decisions of the Council of Jerusalem to the church in Antioch (Acts 15:22,27), and he exercised a ministry of prophecy there (15:32).

After Paul's split from Barnabas, Paul chose Silas as his main companion for his second missionary journey, and he is mentioned frequently in Acts 15—18 and at 2 Corinthians 1:19.

He is associated with Paul and Timothy in the sending of the two letters to the Thessalonians, which were written on that journey. He may well have been the secretary of those letters and also for 1 Peter. The Silvanus named in 1 Peter 5:12 is almost certainly the same man.

4465. Σιλουανός Silouanos name

Silvanus.

1. Σιλουανός Silouanos nom masc
2. Σιλουανοῦ Silouanou gen masc

2 even by me and **Silvanus** and Timotheus,........... 2 Co 1:19
1 Paul, and **Silvanus**, and Timotheus,................. 1 Th 1:1
1 Paul, and **Silvanus**, and Timotheus,................. 2 Th 1:1
2 By **Silvanus**, a faithful brother unto you,........... 1 Pt 5:12

The Latin form of the name Silas used in the New Testament letters. See *Silas* (4464).

4466. Σιλωάμ Silōam name

Siloam.

1. Σιλωάμ Silōam masc

1 eighteen, upon whom the tower in **Siloam** fell,..... Luke 13:4
1 wash in the pool of **Siloam**,........................ John 9:7
1 and said unto me, Go to the pool of **Siloam**,........... 9:11

In New Testament times Siloam referred to a pool in the southeast of Jerusalem. The pool received the water from the spring Gihon, which was led by an underground aqueduct into the city. Jesus ordered the blind man to wash in Siloam after He anointed his eyes with clay. As the man did so, he received his sight (John 9:7,11). Siloam also denoted the area of the city near the pool. The tower Jesus mentioned in Luke 13:4 may have been situated on the Ophel ridge above the pool (Josephus *Wars of the Jews* 5.4.2).

4467. σιμικίνθιον simikinthion noun

An apron.

1. σιμικίνθια simikinthia nom/acc pl neu

1 brought unto the sick handkerchiefs or **aprons**,..... Acts 19:12

This term, a transliteration of the Latin term *semicinctium*, is not found in Greek literature before its occurrence in the New Testament, where it occurs only once. At Acts 19:12 it is used in conjunction with *soudarion* (4529), "handkerchief": "From his (Paul's) body were brought unto the sick handkerchiefs or *aprons*, and the diseases departed from them." Due to the lack of certainty concerning its exact meaning, some take *simikinthion* to denote a "bandage," a "handkerchief" (Bauer), or a "piece of clothing worn next to the apostle's skin" (*Moulton-Milligan*). Most, however, take it to refer to an "apron" like that worn by a workman, possibly a tentmaker. (See Acts 18:3 where Paul is referred to as a tentmaker.)

STRONG 4612, BAUER 751, MOULTON-MILLIGAN 575, LIDDELL-SCOTT 1599.

4468. Σίμων Simōn name

Simon.

1. Σίμων Simōn nom masc
2. Σίμωνος Simōnos gen masc
3. Σίμωνι Simōni dat masc
4. Σίμωνα Simōna acc masc

4 saw two brethren, **Simon** called Peter, and Andrew ..Matt 4:18
1 The first, **Simon**, who is called Peter,................. 10:2
1 **Simon** the Canaanite, and Judas Iscariot,............. 10:4
1 brethren, James, and Joses, and **Simon**, and Judas?.... 13:55
1 And **Simon** Peter answered and said,................ 16:16
1 Blessed art thou, **Simon** Barjona:.................... 16:17
1 Jesus ... saying, What thinkest thou, **Simon**?........... 17:25
2 in Bethany, in the house **of Simon** the leper,.......... 26:6
4 they found a man of Cyrene, **Simon** by name:......... 27:32
4 he saw **Simon** and Andrew his brother............. Mark 1:16
2 Andrew, the brother **of Simon**, (NASB)............... 1:16
2 they entered into the house **of Simon** and Andrew,..... 1:29
2 But **Simon's** wife's mother lay sick of a fever,.......... 1:30
1 And **Simon** and they that were with him followed...... 1:36
3 And **Simon** he surnamed Peter;...................... 3:16
4 and Thaddaeus, and **Simon** the Canaanite,............ 3:18
2 of James, and Joses, and of Juda, and **Simon?**.......... 6:3
2 being in Bethany in the house **of Simon** the leper,..... 14:3
1 and saith unto Peter, **Simon**, sleepest thou?........... 14:37
4 And they compel one **Simon** a Cyrenian,.............. 15:21
2 and entered into **Simon's** house.................... Luke 4:38
2 **Simon's** wife's mother was taken with a ... fever;....... 4:38
2 entered into one of the ships, which was **Simon's**,....... 5:3
4 when he had left speaking, he said unto **Simon**,........ 5:4
1 And **Simon** answering said unto him, Master,........... 5:5
1 **Simon** Peter saw it, he fell down at Jesus' knees,....... 5:8
3 sons of Zebedee, which were partners **with Simon**....... 5:10
4 And Jesus said unto **Simon**, Fear not;................. 5:10
4 **Simon**, whom he also named Peter, and Andrew....... 6:14
4 the son of Alphaeus, and **Simon** called Zelotes,......... 6:15
1 And Jesus answering said unto him, **Simon**,............ 7:40
1 **Simon** answered and said, I suppose that he,........Luke 7:43
3 he turned to the woman, and said **unto Simon**,......... 7:44
1 **Simon**, Simon, behold, Satan hath desired............. 22:31
1 **Simon**, behold, Satan hath desired to have you,....... 22:31
2 they laid hold upon one **Simon**, a Cyrenian,........... 23:26
3 Lord is risen indeed, and hath appeared **to Simon**...... 24:34
2 followed him, was Andrew, **Simon** Peter's brother... John 1:40
4 He first findeth his own brother **Simon**,................ 1:41
1 Thou art **Simon** the son of Jona:...................... 1:42
2 Andrew, **Simon** Peter's brother, saith unto him,........ 6:8
1 Then **Simon** Peter answered him,..................... 6:68
2 He spake of Judas Iscariot the son of **Simon**:........... 6:71
2 Judas Iscariot, **Simon's** son,......................... 12:4
2 Judas Iscariot, **Simon's** son, to betray him;............ 13:2
4 Then cometh he to **Simon** Peter:..................... 13:6
1 **Simon** Peter saith unto him, Lord,..................... 13:9
1 **Simon** Peter therefore beckoned to him,.............. 13:24
2 he gave it to Judas Iscariot, the son of **Simon**.......... 13:26
1 **Simon** Peter said unto him, Lord,.................... 13:36
1 Then **Simon** Peter having a sword drew it,............ 18:10
1 And **Simon** Peter followed Jesus,..................... 18:15
1 And **Simon** Peter stood and warmed himself........... 18:25
4 Then she runneth, and cometh to **Simon** Peter,........ 20:2
1 Then cometh **Simon** Peter following him,............. 20:6
1 There were together **Simon** Peter, and Thomas........ 21:2
1 **Simon** Peter saith unto them, I go a fishing........... 21:3
1 Now when **Simon** Peter heard that it was the Lord,.... 21:7
1 **Simon** Peter went up, and drew the net to land....... 21:11
3 Jesus saith **to Simon** Peter,.......................... 21:15
1 **Simon**, son of Jonas, lovest thou me more........... 21:15
1 **Simon**, son of Jonas, lovest thou me?................. 21:16
1 **Simon**, son of Jonas, lovest thou me?................. 21:17
1 **Simon** Zelotes, and Judas the brother of James...... Acts 1:13
1 But there was a certain man, called **Simon**,............. 8:9
1 Then **Simon** himself believed also:..................... 8:13
1 And when **Simon** saw that through laying on........... 8:18
1 answered **Simon**, and said, Pray ye to the Lord......... 8:24
3 many days in Joppa with one **Simon** a tanner........... 9:43
4 and call for one **Simon**, whose surname is Peter:...... 10:5
3 He lodgeth with one **Simon** a tanner,................. 10:6
2 had made inquiry for **Simon's** house,................. 10:17
1 asked whether **Simon**, which was surnamed Peter,..... 10:18
4 Send therefore to Joppa, and call hither **Simon**,....... 10:32
2 in the house **of one Simon** a tanner by the sea side:... 10:32
4 Send men to Joppa, and call for **Simon**,............... 11:13

Simon is the Greek name of nine New Testament characters. (See also *Sumeōn* [4677], "Simeon," a Hebrew name often used as an equivalent.) There are two apostles called Simon: Simon Peter, also called the "rock," one of the three closest to Jesus (see *petros* [3935]); and Simon the Canaanite or Zealot (cf. Matthew 10:4; Mark 3:18). The word "Cananaean" itself means "Zealot," and Luke rightly translated it thus in his references to Simon (Luke 6:15; Acts 1:13). The Zealots were a Jewish nationalist group dedicated to the overthrow of Roman rule. They "insisted that political submission to Rome was a denial of God's lordship" (Schreiner, "Zealot," *International Standard Bible Encyclopedia*, 4:515).

Three other Simons are linked with Jesus' circle in the Gospels. First there was Simon, a brother of Jesus (Matthew 13:55; Mark 6:3). Secondly there was Simon the leper. The anointing of Jesus took place in his house in Bethany according to Matthew 26:6 and Mark 14:3. (John 12:1-8 has a similar account but does not mention Simon the leper.) Lastly there was Simon Iscariot, the father of Judas Iscariot, who betrayed Jesus (cf. John 6:71; 12:4; 13:2,26).

Two other Simons appear in the Gospels: first, Simon the Pharisee—Jesus dined in his house and unfavorably contrasted his cold politeness with the saving love of the sinful woman (Luke 7:36-50). Second, Simon of Cyrene—this Simon was compelled to carry Jesus' cross on the way to His crucifixion (Matthew 27:32; Mark 15:21; Luke 23:26). Mark's mention of his sons Alexander and Rufus suggests they became Christians and were known to the church in Rome (cf. Mark 15:21; Romans 16:13 for Rufus).

Lastly, two Simons appear in Acts: Simon the sorcerer, a worker of magic in Samaria who made claims of messiahship or divinity. He was converted by the ministry of Philip, the deacon and evangelist. When he saw the dramatic results of the gift of the Holy Spirit mediated by the laying on of the apostles' hands, he attempted to buy the same power. Peter roundly condemned him, and he humbly repented (cf. Acts 8:9-24). Supposed followers of Simon were well-known in the first centuries of the Church, and many legends grew up around his name. (To separate fact from fiction, see McCasland, "Simon Magus," *Interpreter's Dictionary of the Bible*, 4:358-360.) Simon gave his name to the sin of simony, the attempt to buy offices in the church.

Finally, the New Testament speaks of Simon the tanner. Peter lodged with this Simon at Joppa (Acts 9:43; 10:6,17,32). Tanning was not only a malodorous trade, but also to the Jews an unclean one (see Leviticus 11:39f.); hence his isolation.

4469. Σινᾶ Sina name

Sinai.

1. Σινᾶ Sina neu

1 in the wilderness of mount Sina an angel .... **Acts 7:30**
1 the angel which spake to him in the mount Sina, ... **7:38**
1 the one from the mount Sinai, ... **Gal 4:24**
1 For this Agar is mount Sinai in Arabia, ... **4:25**

The place named *Sinai* refers most specifically to a mountain (part of the Horeb range) located on the peninsula bounded on the west by the Gulf of Suez and on the east by the Gulf of Aqaba and the Negev, to which it lends its name. "Sinai" can also designate the "wilderness" area immediately surrounding this mountain (see Acts 7:30). There is considerable uncertainty as to which peak among the mountains on this peninsula should be identified as Mount Sinai (cf. Wright, "Sinai," *Interpreter's Dictionary of the Bible*, 4:376-378), but one of the more likely candidates is Jebel Musa near the southern tip of the Sinai peninsula. Mount Sinai was also known as Mount Horeb (see Stephen's substitution in Acts 7:30 of "Sinai" for "Horeb" in referring to Exodus 3:1 and the consistent use of "Horeb" for "Sinai" in Deuteronomy).

The importance of Mount Sinai in the Judeo-Christian tradition derives from its being the site where God revealed the Law to Moses and where the Israelites entered into covenant with God. There are, however, two strikingly different assessments of this event in the New Testament. Stephen described the Law given to their ancestors at Sinai as "lively (better, 'living') oracles" (Acts 7:38). But Paul, in the Hagar and Sarah allegory of Galatians 4:21 to 5:1, identified Hagar, Sinai, and the "Jerusalem which now is" (see "Hierousalēm" [2395]) with those who are enslaved under the power of the Law. These are contrasted to those who, by faith in Christ, are no longer enslaved to the Law; they have become "children of the free woman" (Sarah) and are like Isaac, "the children of promise." Judaizers from Jerusalem totally misunderstood the role of grace. Like their ancestors they made the "grace event" at Mount Sinai into a "law event." In their minds salvation involved circumcision and adherence to the Law. But as Lohse points out, "There is a break with Jewish tradition and the Law of Sinai is superseded; for Christ is the end of the Law, R(omans) 10:4" (Lohse, "Sina," *Kittel*, 7:286).

The covenant made at Sinai is also contrasted in Hebrews 12:18-24 with the new covenant mediated by Christ; here the comparison is between Mount Sinai (though the name itself does not appear), which symbolizes the old covenant of the Law, and Mount Zion, which symbolizes the new covenant of Christ.

Strong 4614, Bauer 751, Kittel 7:282-87, Colin Brown 3:1013-14.

4470. σίναπι sinapi noun

Mustard.

1. σινάπεως sinapeōs gen sing neu

1 The kingdom ... is like to a grain of mustard seed, **Matt 13:31**
1 If ye have faith as a grain of mustard seed, ... **17:20**
1 It is like a grain of mustard seed, ... **Mark 4:31**
1 It is like a grain of mustard seed, ... **Luke 13:19**
1 If ye had faith as a grain of mustard seed, ... **17:6**

This is a borrowed word of unknown origin (possibly Egyptian) used both in literary and nonliterary (e.g., papyri) Greek writings. In the New Testament it is found in the phrase "mustard seed" (*kokkos sinapeōs*). Here it is used as an analogy by Jesus Christ to teach about the kingdom of God. His kingdom starts as an apparently insignificant force in the world but has an amazing power that dominates all others as it brings protection and relief to those who rely upon it (cf. Matthew 13:31; Mark 4:31; Luke 13:19). Jesus also used the same word picture to show that exercising even the smallest faith will have great results (cf. Matthew 17:20; Luke 17:6).

STRONG 4615, BAUER 751, MOULTON-MILLIGAN 575, KITTEL 7:287-91, LIDDELL-SCOTT 1599.

4471. σινδών sindōn noun

Linen, cloth.

SYNONYMS:

βύσσινος bussinos (1032)
βύσσος bussos (1033)
λίνον linon (3017)

סָדִין ṣādhîn (5650), Linen undergarment, linen garment (Jgs 14:12, Prv 31:24).

1. σινδόνι sindoni dat sing fem
2. σινδόνα sindona acc sing fem

1 the body, he wrapped it in a clean linen cloth,..... Matt 27:59
2 having a linen cloth cast about his naked body;.... Mark 14:51
2 he left the linen cloth, and fled from them naked...... 14:52
2 And he bought fine linen, and took him down,........ 15:46
1 and took him down, and wrapped him in the linen,.... 15:46
1 And he took it down, and wrapped it in linen,..... Luke 23:53

Classical Greek

The word *sindōn* is used in classical Greek referring to a fine cloth, a piece of cambric or muslin (i.e., a plain-woven sheer to coarse cotton fabric). The term *sindōn boosinē* was used by Sophocles and Thucydides (Fifth Century B.C.) to denote a mummy cloth (*Liddell-Scott*). In the papyri this term is used when referring to wrapping the dead for burial (Tebtunis papyri) during the Third to First Century B.C. (cf. *Moulton-Milligan*). Some believe this word has a Semitic origin while others see it deriving from India, *Indos*, where similar fine fabrics are used for wrapping the dead.

Septuagint Usage

The Septuagint translates this word from the Hebrew (*ṣādhîn*). In Judges 14:12,13 Samson offered 30 sheets of fine linen to those whom he challenged with his riddle. One quality of a woman with noble character is her ability to provide this fabric for her family (cf. Proverbs 31:24). Here we see its high quality.

New Testament Usage

Othonion (3470) is used with parallel meaning to *sindōn* in the Gospels (see Luke 24:12; John 19:40; 20:5-7). Mark used this term to describe the only clothing worn by a young man who was following Jesus after His arrest (Mark 14:51,52).

Three times the New Testament uses this term in plural form to describe Jesus' burial garments (Matthew 27:59; Mark 15:46; Luke 23:53). As such it gives evidence that Christ did indeed die, for only the dead were wrapped with burial linens. Peter and John's subsequent visit to the tomb of Jesus showed that the linens that once contained His dead body no longer did so, for later they saw, as did so many others, that He had risen!

STRONG 4616, BAUER 751, MOULTON-MILLIGAN 575, LIDDELL-SCOTT 1600.

4472. σινιάζω siniazō verb

Sift.

1. σινιάσαι siniasai inf aor act

1 that he may sift you as wheat:.................... Luke 22:31

This verb is derived from the earlier word *sethō* (*Bauer*) and means "sift, winnow." In the New Testament this word is used only once (Luke 22:31). Here it occurs figuratively as an infinitive, *siniasai* (i.e., "to sift, shake in a sieve"). Satan wanted to "sift," that is, to put the apostle Peter and the rest of the disciples through a severe trial (see Schneider, "Tempt," *Colin Brown*, 3:804). In verse 31 the Greek word for "you" (*humas*) is plural, indicating that Satan intended to tempt Peter and all Christ's disciples in order to lead them into apostasy. When Jesus responded (verse 32) He spoke to Peter ("you" is singular in the Greek). However, the context shows His comments were applicable to all the disciples.

STRONG 4617, BAUER 751, MOULTON-MILLIGAN 575, KITTEL 7:291-92, LIDDELL-SCOTT 1600.

4472B. σιρικός sirikos noun

Silken, made of silk.

1. σιρικοῦ sirikou gen sing neu

1 and fine linen, and purple, and silk, and scarlet,.... Rev 18:12

Sirikos (in nonbiblical writings the spelling is *sērikos*) is an adjective which denotes something made of or having the quality of silk. *Sirikos* may have derived from the *Sēres*, the name of an oriental people who produced and marketed silk in antiquity. There is only scant evidence of the term's usage in the classical Greek period, but it seems to have been common in first-century Rome. Josephus pointed to Vespasian and Titus who, in their triumphal march, were clothed *en esthēsin sērikais*, "in silken robes" (*Wars of the Jews* 7.5.4). In the New Testament *sirikos* occurs only in Revelation 18:12 where it describes one of the items of luxury which the merchants of apocalyptic Babylon are no longer able to trade and thus lament their losses. (Cf. *sērikos* [4451].)

Bauer 751, Moulton-Milligan 575, Liddell-Scott 1594 (see "sērikos").

4472C. σιρός siros adj

Pit, cave.

1. σιροῖς sirois dat pl masc

2. σειροῖς seirois dat pl masc

1 and committed them to pits of darkness, (NASB)....2 Pt 2:4
2 and delivered them into chains of darkness,............ 2:4

This noun (also spelled *seiros*) is used in classical Greek generally meaning "pit" (e.g., a "pit" for keeping corn; cf. *Liddell-Scott*). It does not appear in the Septuagint and is used only once in the New Testament. In 2 Peter 2:4 it sits in apposition to hell or Tartarus, describing this place of confinement as "pits of nether gloom" (RSV). The New American Standard Bible translates, "For . . . God did not spare angels when they sinned, but cast them into hell and committed them to pits of darkness, reserved for judgment." Here the writer of 2 Peter alludes to the interpretation of Genesis 6:1-4 as found in Jude 6 and 1 Enoch. The "pits" mentioned here could refer to the "valleys of the earth" (1 Enoch 10:12) or the "abyss" (1 Enoch 18:11; 21:7; 88:1,3) that served as a dungeon for the fallen angels (Bauckham, *Word Biblical Commentary*, 50:249).

Strong 4577, Bauer 751-52, Moulton-Milligan 575, Liddell-Scott 1600.

4473. σιτευτός siteutos adj

Fed, fatted, fattened.

Cross-Reference:
σῖτος sitos (4476)

אָבַס 'āvas̱ (70), Something fattened (1 Kgs 4:23).

מַרְבֵּק marbēq (4932), Fattened animal (Jer 46:21 [26:21]).

שׁוֹר shôr (8228), Bull (Jgs 6:25—Codex Alexandrinus only).

שֵׁנִי shēnî (8529), Second (Jgs 6:28—Codex Alexandrinus only).

1. σιτευτόν siteuton acc sing masc

1 And bring hither the fatted calf, and kill it;........Luke 15:23
1 and thy father hath killed the fatted calf,.............. 15:27
1 thou hast killed for him the fatted calf................ 15:30

Classical Greek

This adjective is related to the word *sitos* (4476) meaning "corn, wheat," or "grain." It is used in both literary (e.g., Xenophon) and nonliterary (papyri) Greek documents. Here *siteutos* refers to the fattening of oxen, cattle, sheep, or even children.

Septuagint Usage

The Septuagint translates several Hebrew words (*'āvas̱, marbēq, shôr, shēnî*) with *siteutos*. Both literal and figurative uses are evident. An example of its literal use occurs in 1 Kings 4:23 (LXX 3 Kings 4:23) which states that Solomon's provision of food for one day (i.e., food consumed by servants, family, etc.) included: "ten choice calves, and twenty pastured oxen, and a hundred sheep, besides stags and choice fatted does" (Benton translation). In a figurative use of the term Jeremiah 46:21 (LXX 26:21) says that the paid mercenaries of Egypt "are like fattened calves" (NASB), i.e., they are on the verge of being slaughtered.

New Testament Usage

Siteutos occurs only three times in the New Testament (Luke 15:23,27,30). It appears in the Parable of the Prodigal Son to help describe the foods prepared for sacrificial religious or festive occasions of celebration. The "fattened calf" (literally "calf of the stall") was raised with special care specifically for consumption at feasts (cf. Cobern, "Calf," *International Standard Bible Encyclopedia*, 1:579).

Strong 4618, Bauer 752, Moulton-Milligan 575, Liddell-Scott 1601.

4473B. σιτίον sition noun

Grain, food.

Cross-Reference:
σῖτος sitos (4476)

אֹכֶל 'ōkhel (406), Food (Jb 12:11, 38:41, 39:29).

בַּר bar (1277), Grain (Gn 41:35, Prv 11:26, Jer 23:28).

דָּגָן dāghān (1765), Grain (Dt 11:14, Neh 5:2f., Hos 14:7 [14:8]).

חִטָּה chiṭṭāh (2498), Wheat (1 Chr 21:23, S/S 7:2, Ez 27:17).

לֶחֶם lechem (4035), Food, bread (Gn 47:12f., Jb 6:7, Prv 4:17).

עָבוּר ʿāvûr (5878), Produce (Jos 5:11f.).

עֲרִיסָה ʿărîṣāh (6420), Dough (Neh 10:37).

שֶׁבֶר shever (8134), Grain (Gn 42:26, 43:2, 44:2).

1. σιτία sitia nom/acc pl neu

1 THERE WAS GRAIN IN EGYPT, (NASB) .... Acts 7:12

Foodstuffs made from grain were called *sition.* This neuter noun can also denote "wheat." The King James Version translates it "corn" in its only occurrence in the New Testament. There it is found in Stephen's speech to the Sanhedrin (Acts 7:12). He reminded them by way of Old Testament quotation that "when Jacob heard that there was grain in Egypt, he sent our fathers there the first time" (NASB).

STRONG 4621, BAUER 752, MOULTON-MILLIGAN 575, LIDDELL-SCOTT 1601.

4474. σιτιστός sitistos adj

Fatted, fattened; a fatling.

CROSS-REFERENCE:
σῖτος sitos (4476)

1. σιτιστά sitista nom/acc pl neu

1 my oxen and my **fatlings** are killed, ... Matt 22:4

Classical Greek

Sitistos denotes an animal that has been fattened (see *siteutos* [4473]). It is rarely found in Greek literature (Josephus) and nonliterary writings (papyri) (cf. *Liddell-Scott*). This term is related to the verb *sitizō,* "to fatten," and the noun *sitos* (4476), which refers to "grain" or "wheat." The fattened cattle were sacrificed for festive banquets or special religious ceremonies.

New Testament Usage

The sole occurrence of *sitistos* in the New Testament is found in Matthew 22:4. The kingdom of heaven has been offered to many but rejected by those first invited. The fattened livestock (*ta sitista*), symbolic of the joyous wedding banquet soon to occur, are prepared for the feast.

STRONG 4619, BAUER 752, MOULTON-MILLIGAN 576, LIDDELL-SCOTT 1601.

4475. σιτομέτριον sitometrion noun

Ration of grain.

CROSS-REFERENCE:
μετρέω metreō (3224)

1. σιτομέτριον sitometrion nom/acc sing neu

1 to give them their **portion of meat** in due season? .. Luke 12:42

This word refers to a certain measure of grain given to slaves as a food allowance. *Sitometrion* comes from two words: *sitos* (4476), "wheat," and *metreō* (3224), "to measure." The verb form translates the Hebrew *kûl* found in the Septuagint at Genesis 47:12,14 where Joseph provided grain for his father and brothers. The New Testament shows only one occurrence, in Luke 12:42. Here Jesus Christ used the analogy of the faithful and wise manager (believer in Christ) faithfully giving the servants (fellow believers) their food allowance (using his gifts to minister to others).

STRONG 4620, BAUER 752, MOULTON-MILLIGAN 576, LIDDELL-SCOTT 1602.

4476. σῖτος sitos noun

Wheat, grain.

COGNATES:
ἀσιτία asitia (770)
ἄσιτος asitos (771)
ἐπισιτισμός episitismos (1963)
σιτευτός siteutos (4473)
σιτίον sition (4473B)
σιτιστός sitistos (4474)
σιτομέτριον sitometrion (4475)

SYNONYM:
κόκκος kokkos (2821)

1. σίτου sitou gen sing masc
2. σῖτον siton acc sing masc
3. σῖτα sita nom/acc pl neu
4. σῖτος sitos nom/acc sing neu

2 and gather his **wheat** into the garner; .... Matt 3:12
1 his enemy came and sowed tares among the **wheat**, ... 13:25
2 up the tares, ye root up also the **wheat** with them. 13:29
2 but gather the **wheat** into my barn. 13:30
2 then the ear, after that the full **corn** in the ear. ..... Mark 4:28
2 and will gather the **wheat** into his garner; .... Luke 3:17
2 I will store all my **grain** (NASB) 12:18
1 And he said, An hundred measures **of wheat**. 16:7
2 that he may sift you as **wheat**: 22:31
1 Except a corn of **wheat** fall into ... ground and die, John 12:24
3 when Jacob heard that there was **corn** in Egypt, ... Acts 7:12
2 and cast out the **wheat** into the sea. 27:38
1 it may chance **of wheat**, or of some other grain: .... 1 Co 15:37
1 A measure **of wheat** for a penny, ... Rev 6:6
2 and **wheat**, and beasts, and sheep, and horses, ... 18:13

This word is used in classical (Homer), literary (Philo, Josephus), and nonliterary (papyri) Greek writings as a general term for "grain" (e.g., wheat, barley; cf. *Liddell-Scott*). In both the Septuagint and the New Testament *sitos* denotes "wheat" or "grain" ("corn" in the KJV means "grain" or "wheat") in its literal sense (Genesis 30:14;

Psalm 81:16 [LXX 80:16]; Luke 16:7). Often it is used symbolically for the life of a righteous person (versus the unrighteous) who at death will be rewarded by God with a new, resurrected life (cf. 1 Corinthians 15:37; John 12:24) in heaven with God (cf. Matthew 3:12; 13:25,29). *Sitos* is also used figuratively to denote a severe test (Luke 22:31) or the Word of God which comes to fruition on its own accord (Mark 4:28).

STRONG 4621, BAUER 752, MOULTON-MILLIGAN 576, LIDDELL-SCOTT 1602.

4477. Σιών Siōn name

Zion.

1. Σιών Siōn fem

1 **Tell ye the daughter of Sion,** .... **Matt 21:5**
1 **Fear not, daughter of Sion:** .... **John 12:15**
1 **I lay in Sion a stumblingstone and rock of offence:** ..**Rom 9:33**
1 **There shall come out of Sion the Deliverer,** **11:26**
1 **But ye are come unto mount Sion,** .... **Heb 12:22**
1 **Behold, I lay in Sion a chief corner stone,** .... **1 Pt 2:6**
1 **and, lo, a Lamb stood on the mount Sion,** .... **Rev 14:1**

Zion was originally the name applied to the hill where the ancient Jebusite city of Jerusalem was located. After this city was conquered by David sometime around 1000 B.C., he had a tabernacle built and the ark of the covenant moved there. As a result, Zion was associated with the "temple mount," even after the ark was moved to the temple constructed by Solomon on Mount Moriah, a neighboring hill. Ultimately, the use of "Zion" was extended to include the entire city of Jerusalem as well as its inhabitants (cf. Rainey, "Zion," *International Standard Bible Encyclopedia*, 4:1198).

The fact that God manifested His presence in the Jerusalem temple (specifically, over the mercy seat of the ark of the covenant in the Holy of Holies) contributed to the development of an elaborate "Zion theology." This theology included several major components. God was "enthroned" on Mount Zion, believed to be the most important of all mountains and the very "navel" (or center) of the universe (Isaiah 2:2; Ezekiel 38:12; Micah 4:1). From the millennial temple will flow a river of life and blessing that brings joy and healing to the people of God (Ezekiel 47:1-12; cf. the river in Revelation 22:1,2). God did protect this holy city by destroying its enemies in Isaiah's day. All enemies must ultimately admit God's sovereignty and come to Jerusalem to worship (Isaiah 18:1-7). The prophets also foretold judgment because of the sins of the people and prophesied future messianic and eschatological salvation. For a more extended treatment of this "Zion theology," see Roberts, "Zion tradition," *Interpreter's Dictionary of the Bible*, 5:985-987.

Of the seven occurrences of "Zion" in the New Testament, all but two of them are found in citations from the Old Testament. Zechariah 9:9 is cited in both Matthew 21:5 and John 12:15. The expression *thugatēr Siōn* (Hebrew *bath-Tsîyōn*), usually translated "daughter of Zion," does not imply an idea like "offspring of Zion." Rather, the use of the word *daughter* here is a term of endearment, and so the idiom would be better translated "darling Zion" (see Stinespring, "Zion, daughter of," *Interpreter's Dictionary of the Bible*, 5:985). This personification of Jerusalem is used to refer to the inhabitants of that city.

Isaiah 28:16 is cited in both 1 Peter 2:6 and Romans 9:33, but with very different effects. Peter cited all of Isaiah 28:16 so what is laid in Zion is "a chief corner stone (i.e., a 'head of the corner' stone), elect, precious: and he that believeth on him shall not be confounded." However, Paul conflated the text of Isaiah 28:16 with Isaiah 8:14f., so what is laid in Zion is "a stumblingstone and a rock of offense" for the Jews who would not accept the gospel. In both 1 Peter and Romans 9, however, "Zion" includes not only the inhabitants of Jerusalem but also the people of Israel in general. The same is probably also true of the prophecy cited in Romans 11:26 that "there shall come out of Zion the Deliverer" (cf. Isaiah 59:20f.).

All of these citations from the Old Testament reflect the association between Zion and the hoped for eschatological salvation. The same theological setting lies behind the two New Testament uses of "Zion" not drawn directly from the Old Testament. In Hebrews 12:22 Mount Zion is identified with the "heavenly Jerusalem," itself an ultimate home for those enjoying the eschatological salvation brought by the new covenant mediated by Jesus. Mount Zion is the gathering place of "the Lamb" and the "hundred forty and four thousand" during the messianic reign according to Revelation 14:1.

Strong 4622, BAUER 752, MOULTON-MILLIGAN 576, KITTEL 7:292-338, COLIN BROWN 2:324,326,330.

4478. σιωπάω siōpaō verb

Be silent.

SYNONYMS:
ἡσυχάζω hēsuchazō (2248)
σιγάω sigaō (4456)

אָלַם 'ālam (487), Niphal: be speechless (Dn 10:15).

דָּמָה dāmâh (1880), Be like; cease (Lam 3:49—Codex Alexandrinus only).

דָּמַם dāmam (1887), Keep silent, be silent (Jb 29:21, Lam 2:10, 3:28).

הַס haṣ (2085), Silence! Be still! (Jgs 3:19, Neh 8:11).

חָדַל chādhal (2403), Stop, refrain (2 Chr 25:16, Jb 16:6 [16:7]).

חָרַשׁ chārash (2896), Hiphil: say nothing, keep silent (Nm 30:14 [30:15], Jb 41:12 [41:3], Jer 4:19).

חָשָׁה chāshāh (2924), Be silent, keep silent (Is 62:6, 64:12); hiphil: do nothing, hold one's peace (1 Kgs 22:3, 2 Kgs 2:3,5, 7:9).

סָכַת ṣākhath (5728), Hiphil: be silent (Dt 27:9).

1. **σιώπα siōpa** 2sing impr pres act
2. **σιωπῶν siōpōn** nom sing masc part pres act
3. **σιωπήσῃς siōpēsēs** 2sing subj aor act
4. **σιωπήσῃ siōpēsē** 3sing subj aor act
5. **σιωπήσωσιν siōpēsōsin** 3pl subj aor act
6. **ἐσιώπα esiōpa** 3sing indic imperf act
7. **ἐσιώπων esiōpōn** 3pl indic imperf act
8. **σιωπήσουσιν siōpēsousin** 3pl indic fut act

5 because they **should hold their peace:** .... Matt 20:31
6 But Jesus **held his peace** 26:63
7 to save life, or to kill? But they **held their peace** .... Mark 3:4
1 and said unto the sea, **Peace**, be still. 4:39
7 But they **held their peace:** 9:34
4 many charged him that he **should hold his peace:** 10:48
6 But he **held his peace**, and answered nothing. 14:61
2 behold, thou shalt be **dumb**, and not able to speak, ..Luke 1:20
4 rebuked him, that he **should hold** his **peace:** 18:39
5 if these **should hold** their **peace**, the stones would 19:40
3 Be not afraid, but speak, and **hold** not thy **peace:** ...Acts 18:9

Classical Greek and Septuagint Usage

This verb is found in Greek literature from the time of Homer when it was used as a command to "be silent" (*Iliad* 23.568; *Odyssey* 17.513; cf. *Liddell-Scott*). In the Septuagint the word has a variety of translations. In Deuteronomy 27:9 Moses and the priests told the people to "take heed" (KJV) or "be silent" (NASB, NIV). Lamentations 2:18 reads, "Let not the apple of thine eye *cease*" (KJV); "Give . . . your eyes no *rest*" (NIV); "Let your eyes have no *rest*" (NASB).

New Testament Usage

Siōpaō is found 11 times in the New Testament. All but one of these appearances refer to human beings. The most common translation has to do with holding one's peace. This translation is found nine times ranging from a statement of fact, "Jesus held his peace" (Matthew 26:63), to an exhortation to hold one's peace (Luke 18:39). When Zechariah doubted the message brought to him by Gabriel, he was told, "Thou shalt *be dumb*" (Luke 1:20). In a figurative sense Jesus "said unto the sea, Peace, *be still*" (Mark 4:39).

STRONG 4623, BAUER 752, MOULTON-MILLIGAN 576, LIDDELL-SCOTT 1603.

4479. σκανδαλίζω skandalizō verb

To put a stumbling block in the way, cause to be caught (or) to fall, cause to fall away, be led into sin, offend, anger, shock.

COGNATE:
σκάνδαλον skandalon (4480)

כָּשַׁל kāshal (3911), Niphal: fall (Dn 11:41).

1. **σκανδαλίζει skandalizei** 3sing indic pres act
2. **σκανδαλίζῃ skandalizē** 3sing subj pres act
3. **σκανδαλίσω skandalisō** 1sing subj aor act
4. **σκανδαλίσῃ skandalisē** 3sing subj aor act
5. **σκανδαλίσωμεν skandalisōmen** 1pl subj aor act
6. **σκανδαλίζεται skandalizetai** 3sing indic pres mid
7. **σκανδαλίζονται skandalizontai** 3pl indic pres mid
8. **ἐσκανδαλίσθησαν eskandalisthēsan** 3pl indic aor pass
9. **σκανδαλισθῇ skandalisthē** 3sing subj aor pass
10. **σκανδαλισθῆτε skandalisthēte** 2pl subj aor pass
11. **σκανδαλισθήσομαι skandalisthēsomai** 1sing indic fut pass
12. **σκανδαλισθήσεσθε skandalisthēsesthe** 2pl indic fut pass
13. **σκανδαλισθήσονται skandalisthēsontai** 3pl indic fut pass
14. **ἐσκανδαλίζοντο eskandalizonto** 3pl indic imperf pass
15. **σκανδαλίζωμεν skandalizōmen** 1pl subj pres act

1 And if thy right eye **offend** thee, pluck it out, ... Matt 5:29
1 And if thy right hand **offend** thee, cut it off, ... 5:30
9 blessed ... whosoever shall not **be offended** in me. 11:6
6 persecution ariseth ... by and by he **is offended**. 13:21
14 And they **were offended** in him. 13:57
8 Knowest thou that the Pharisees **were offended**, ... 15:12
5 Notwithstanding, lest we **should offend** them, ... 17:27
4 But whoso **shall offend** one of these little ones 18:6
1 Wherefore if thy hand or thy foot **offend** thee, ... 18:8
1 And if thine eye **offend** thee, pluck it out, ... 18:9
13 And then shall many **be offended**, ... 24:10
12 All ye **shall be offended** because of me this night: 26:31
13 Though all men **shall be offended** because of thee, ... 26:33
11 Peter answered ... yet will I never **be offended**. 26:33
7 immediately they **are offended**. .... Mark 4:17
14 And they **were offended** at him. 6:3
4 And whosoever **shall offend** one of these little ones 9:42
2 And if thy hand **offend** thee, cut it off: 9:43
2 And if thy foot **offend** thee, cut it off: 9:45
2 And if thine eye **offend** thee, pluck it out: 9:47
12 All ye **shall be offended** because of me this night: 14:27
13 Although all **shall be offended**, yet will not I. 14:29
9 And blessed is he, whosoever **shall not be offended** Luke 7:23
4 than that he **should offend** one of these little ones. 17:2
1 he said unto them, Doth this **offend** you? .... John 6:61
10 that ye **should not be offended**. 16:1

6 **brother stumbleth, or is offended, or is made weak.Rom 14:21**
1 **Wherefore, if meat make my brother to offend,.....1 Co 8:13**
3 **lest I make my brother to offend....................... 8:13**
6 **who is offended, and I burn not?.................2 Co 11:29**

Classical Greek

No examples of *skandalizō*—apart from those influenced by the Bible—appear in Greek writings. It is related to the rare noun *skandalon* (4480), a "trap," specifically the "stick" of a trap to which bait was attached. In classical Greek the noun functions literally, but related terms do have metaphoric meanings related to the idea of "trap, snare" (cf. Stahlin, "skandalizō," *Kittel*, 7:339; *Moulton-Milligan*).

Septuagint Usage

Whereas the noun *skandalon* occurs in 14 canonical texts of the Septuagint (e.g., Leviticus 19:14; Joshua 23:13; 1 Kings 18:21 [LXX 3 Kings 18:21]), the verb appears in only one canonical text, Daniel 11:41, a reference to a military "defeat" (NIV, "fall"; Hebrew *kāshal*). Three texts in the apocryphal Sirach read *skandalizō*. These reveal that the classical sense of "trap, snare" (metaphorically) continue to be linked to the verb (Sirach 9:5, cf. verse 4 of the "trap" of sexual desires; 23:8, of the difficulties [i.e., "snare"] of wealth). The link between hypocrisy and spiritual stumbling appears in Sirach 32:15 (LXX 35:15). Idolatry is regarded as a "snare" of sorts (Judges 2:3; 8:27; Psalm 106:36 [LXX 105:36]; cf. Psalm 69:22 [68:22], of idolatrous meals?). Thus the idea of "apostasy" as well as the deceptive (trap) nature of idols is brought together. The ultimate outcome of *skandalizō* is ruin, and the image is usually tragic and violent (Stahlin, "skandalizō," *Kittel*, 7:342).

New Testament Usage

To fully understand the meaning of *skandalizō* in the New Testament one must address the background of the term in the Old Testament (e.g., as reflected in Romans 9:33; 11:9, citations of Isaiah 8:14; 28:16; and Psalm 69:22 respectively). *Skandalizō* involves not so much setting a trap, although that may be an intrinsic part of the term (*Moulton-Milligan*); instead, it concerns "causing offense, causing stumbling." Stumbling directly corresponds to a relationship with God. Thus "to stumble" is to resist coming to faith or to fall from faith.

Matthew's Gospel uses the *skandalizō* word group more than any other writer (9 times). Ten instances of the word appear in Pauline literature. The gospel message does one of two things: (1) men and women repent and are saved; or (2) men and women stumble and perish. This double-edged quality resembles the effect of a sign (see *sēmeion* [4447]). The issue of "offense" centers around Jesus and His message. Stumbling can be a form of apostasy in the face of tribulation or persecution (e.g., Mark 4:17; cf. Matthew 11:6). Jesus' somber call to a new morality based on the inner law of the Spirit must either be wholeheartedly accepted or rejected. While Jesus' example in Matthew 5:29 and 18:8 should not be taken literally, it does reflect the seriousness and extent of His call for obedience. This is possible only through the combined work of the Spirit and Word in the heart. Total participation in the life of Jesus is the only alternative (John 6:61). This includes loving others, a point of stumbling for some (1 John 2:10). Despite the seriousness of Jesus' call, He does not expect believers to follow Him without help. The Holy Spirit works in them to prevent and keep them from "stumbling" (John 16:1).

The idea of a "crucified Messiah," like a "triumphant loser," is so paradoxical as to seem absurd. To the Jews it is a "stumbling block" (1 Corinthians 1:23; cf. Romans 9:33; *skandalon*) that Jesus, the Messiah, the deliverer of Israel, should himself die the ignominious death of a state criminal. In the light of Deuteronomy 21:22,23, God's curse rested on one condemned and executed for blasphemy. Such a condition captures the essence of the *skandalizō* word group when applied to Jesus or the gospel message. The grace of the Cross, which ignores any human effort or work, causes the self-centered to stumble (Matthew 15:12; Luke 7:23).

In contrast to the stumbling effect Jesus and the gospel have upon individuals (keeping in mind the double-edged nature), believers must be careful not to cause a brother or sister to stumble and fall (i.e., "to sin"). This especially applies to children and those who are young in the Faith (Matthew 18:6; Mark 9:42; cf. Romans 14:21; 1 Corinthians 8:13; 2 Corinthians 11:29). This should not be confused with the scandal of the Cross whose offense cannot and should not be removed.

Strong 4624, Bauer 752-53, Moulton-Milligan 576, Kittel 7:339-58, Liddell-Scott 1604, Colin Brown 2:707-10.

4480. σκάνδαλον skandalon noun

Offense, stumbling block, snare.

Cross-Reference:
σκανδαλίζω skandalizō (4479)

דֳּפִי dŏphî (1908), Slander (Ps 50:20 [49:20]).

כֶּסֶל keṣel (3815), Foolish confidence (Ps 49:13 [48:13]).

מוֹקֵשׁ môqēsh (4305), Snare (Jos 23:13, Jgs 2:3, Ps 106:36 [105:36]).

מִכְשֹׁל mikhshōl (4520I), Stumbling block (Lv 19:14).

מִכְשׁוֹל mikhshôl (4520II) Offense (1 Sm 25:31).

1. **σκάνδαλον skandalon** nom/acc sing neu
2. **σκανδάλου skandalou** gen sing neu
3. **σκανδάλων skandalōn** gen pl neu
4. **σκάνδαλα skandala** nom/acc pl neu

4 out of his kingdom all things **that offend**, ... Matt 13:41
1 behind me, Satan: thou art **an offence** unto me: 16:23
3 Woe unto the world because of **offences**! 18:7
4 for it must needs be that **offences** come; 18:7
1 but woe to that man by whom the **offence** cometh! 18:7
4 It is impossible but that **offences** will come: .... Luke 17:1
2 I lay in Sion a stumblingstone and rock **of offence**: .. Rom 9:33
1 a **stumblingblock**, and a recompense unto them: 11:9
1 or an **occasion to fall** in his brother's way. 14:13
4 mark them which cause divisions and **offences** 16:17
1 unto the Jews a **stumblingblock**, ... 1 Co 1:23
1 then is the **offence** of the cross ceased. .... Gal 5:11
2 And a stone of stumbling, and a rock **of offence**, ... 1 Pt 2:8
1 and there is none **occasion of stumbling** in him. ...... 1 Jn 2:10
1 cast a **stumblingblock** before the children of Israel, ... Rev 2:14

Septuagint Usage

Although *skandalon* is not found in classical Greek, it is found frequently in both the Septuagint and the New Testament. In the Septuagint it is used to translate the Hebrew words *môqēsh*, "bait, lure" (figuratively, "snare"), and *mikhshōl*, "stumbling block," both meaning "cause of ruin"; the sense of a stumbling block (Leviticus 19:14) or trap (Psalm 141:9 [LXX 140:9]) is present in certain contexts. The primary meaning of the term in the Septuagint is simply "cause of ruin." In this sense it refers more to the basis for divine punishment of sin than to the "occasion of sinning."

New Testament Usage

The New Testament use of *skandalon* is a carryover of the thought pattern of the Old Testament (Stählin, "skandalon," *Kittel*, 7:344). In the New Testament *skandalon* describes something that would entice one from the Faith. Matthew 16:23 records Jesus' rebuke to Peter, "Get thee behind me, Satan: thou art an offense unto me." One could interpret this as "you are tempting Me to sin." These enticements come from outside; they are put in the path of someone by another (Matthew 18:7; Romans 16:17).

The New Testament uses *skandalon* on three occasions to describe something that causes revulsion or anger. Romans 9:33; Galatians 5:11; and 1 Peter 2:8 call attention to the fact that Jesus and His cross are a "rock of offense," a "stumbling block" (NASB) to Jews and unbelievers. Stählin states "the *skandalon* is an obstacle in coming to faith and a cause of going astray in it" (ibid.). John wrote that there is no occasion of stumbling in the one who loves his brother (1 John 2:10).

Strong 4625, Bauer 753, Moulton-Milligan 576, Kittel 7:339-58, Liddell-Scott 1604, Colin Brown 2:707-10.

4481. σκάπτω skaptō verb

Dig, dig up.

Cognates:
κατασκάπτω kataskaptō (2649)
σκάφη skaphē (4482)

Synonym:
ὀρύσσω orussō (3599)

עָדַר ʿādhar (5952), Help, hoe; niphal: be hoed (Is 5:6).

1. **σκάπτειν skaptein** inf pres act
2. **ἔσκαψεν eskapsen** 3sing indic aor act
3. **σκάψω skapsō** 1sing subj aor act

2 a man which built an house, and **digged** deep, ... Luke 6:48
3 let it alone this year also, till I **shall dig** about it, ... 13:8
1 I cannot **dig**; to beg I am ashamed. 16:3

Skaptō is an ancient Greek word referring to digging up the ground for cultivation, to plant seed or flowers. It is used in both literary (Hippocrates) and nonliterary (papyri) Greek documents (cf. *Moulton-Milligan*). Digging was thought to be one of the hardest lines of work (*Bauer*). In the New Testament the term is used literally, meaning "to dig" (Luke 16:3). There are also figurative uses: building one's life solely upon Christ and His Word, a life that will stand up to life's pressures (Luke 6:48); and God's loving care and provision for His vineyard, Israel (Isaiah 5:6; Luke 13:8).

Strong 4626, Bauer 753, Moulton-Milligan 576, Liddell-Scott 1604.

4482. σκάφη skaphē noun

A small boat.

Cognate:
σκάπτω skaptō (4481)

Synonyms:
πλοιάριον ploiarion (4002)
πλοῖον ploion (4003)

1. **σκάφης skaphēs** gen sing fem
2. **σκάφην skaphēn** acc sing fem

1 we had much work to come by the **boat**: .... Acts 27:16
2 when they had let down the **boat** into the sea, ... 27:30
1 Then the soldiers cut off the ropes of the **boat**, ... 27:32

This is a word with a general meaning for anything that is dug out, excavated, or hollowed out. Thus, the developed usage for "small boat" or "skiff," *skaphē*, occurs in classical (Aeschylus, Herodotus) and New Testament contemporary Greek literature (Josephus) as well as nonliterary papyri (cf. *Bauer*). According to Louw and Nida, this small vessel (roughly equivalent to a rowboat) was kept on board a ship and was used for placing anchors, repairing the ship, or for saving lives in case of a storm (*Greek-English Lexicon*, 1:59). The only New Testament occurrences of the word are in Acts (27:16,30,32). In these instances it refers to a small lifeboat on board the ship.

STRONG 4627, BAUER 753, MOULTON-MILLIGAN 576, LIDDELL-SCOTT 1605.

4483. σκέλος skelos noun

Leg.

יָרֵךְ yārēkh (3525), Thigh (Ex 24:4).

כְּרָעַיִם kᵉrāʿayim (3896), Jointed legs, legs (Lv 11:21, Am 3:12).

קַרְסֹל qarṣōl (7457), Ankle; foot (2 Sm 22:37).

רֶגֶל reghel (7559), Leg, sole (1 Sm 17:6, Ez 1:7, 16:25).

שׁוֹק shôq (8225), Leg (Prv 26:7).

שָׁק shāq (A8612), Leg (Dn 2:33—Aramaic).

1. σκέλη skelē nom/acc pl neu

1 besought Pilate that their **legs** might be broken,.... John 19:31
1 came the soldiers, and brake the **legs** of the first,...... 19:32
1 came to Jesus, ... they brake not his **legs**:............ 19:33

Skelos appears in the classics from Homer on. In the Septuagint it is the translation of several different Hebrew words. Literally *skelos* denotes the "leg" (from the hip on down, including the toes). Metaphorically it can refer to such diverse things as walls connecting buildings and tails of a headdress. In the New Testament the term appears three times and that in one setting. The soldiers broke the "legs" of the two men who had been crucified on either side of Christ (John 19:31-33).

STRONG 4628, BAUER 753, MOULTON-MILLIGAN 576-77, LIDDELL-SCOTT 1606.

4484. σκέπασμα skepasma noun

A covering, protection, clothing.

SYNONYMS:
ἔνδυμα enduma (1726)
ἐσθής esthēs (2049B)
ἱμάτιον himation (2416)
ἱματισμός himatismos (2417)
χιτών chitōn (5345)

1. σκεπάσματα skepasmata nom/acc pl neu

1 food and raiment let us be therewith content........ 1 Tm 6:8

The noun *skepasma*, used from Plato (Fourth Century B.C.) on, is related to the verb *skepazō*, "to cover, shelter." Literally *skepasma* denotes "a covering," hence anything that serves as a covering for protection. It came to refer chiefly to clothing. The one New Testament usage is 1 Timothy 6:8. The believer should be content if he has food and "clothing" (perhaps the idea is "protection" from the elements).

STRONG 4629, BAUER 753, MOULTON-MILLIGAN 577, LIDDELL-SCOTT 1606.

4485. Σκευᾶς Skeuas name

Sceva.

1. Σκευᾶ Skeua gen masc

1 And there were seven sons of one **Sceva**, a Jew,... Acts 19:14

A "high priest" whose seven sons were exorcists in Ephesus (Acts 19:14).

4486. σκευή skeuē noun

Equipment, gear, furnishing, rigging, apparel.

CROSS-REFERENCE:
κατασκευάζω kataskeuazō (2650)

1. σκευήν skeuēn acc sing fem

1 third day we cast out ... the **tackling** of the ship.... Acts 27:19

Used from Pindar (Fifth Century B.C.) on, the noun *skeuē* occurs only once in the Septuagint (3 Maccabees 5:45). The term could be used of the "outfit, dress" of an actor or singer, of the "uniform" of a priest or public servant, and of the "tackle, rigging, gear" of a ship (*Liddell-Scott*). Its only appearance in the New Testament is Acts 27:19. During Paul's shipwreck the ship's tackle was thrown overboard. *Skeuos* (4487), "vessel, utensil, tackle," is a synonymous term.

STRONG 4631, BAUER 754, MOULTON-MILLIGAN 577, LIDDELL-SCOTT 1607.

4487. σκεῦος skeuos noun

A vessel, implement, or utensil used for a variety of purposes.

COGNATE:
κατασκευάζω kataskeuazō (2650)

כְּלִי kᵉlî (3747), Article, vessel (Nm 31:50f., 2 Chr 36:18f., Jer 27:16 [34:16]).

מָאן mā'n (A4127), Vessel (Ezr 5:15, 7:19, Dn 5:2,23—Aramaic).

1. **σκεῦος skeuos** nom/acc sing neu
2. **σκεύει skeuei** dat sing neu
3. **σκεύη skeuē** nom/acc pl neu
4. **σκεύεσιν skeuesin** dat pl neu

3 into a strong man's house, and spoil his **goods**,.... Matt 12:29
3 into a strong man's house, and spoil his **goods**,..... Mark 3:27
1 man should carry any **vessel** through the temple........ 11:16
2 covereth it **with a vessel**, or putteth it under a bed;.. Luke 8:16
3 be upon the housetop, and his **stuff** in the house,...... 17:31
1 Now there was set **a vessel** full of vinegar:......... John 19:29
1 for he is a chosen **vessel** unto me,.................. Acts 9:15
1 and a certain **vessel** descending unto him,............. 10:11
1 and the **vessel** was received up again into heaven...... 10:16
1 A certain **vessel** descend,............................ 11:5
1 struck **sail**, and so were driven....................... 27:17
1 of the same lump to make one **vessel** unto honour,.. Rom 9:21
3 the **vessels** of wrath fitted to destruction:.............. 9:22
3 the riches of his glory on the **vessels** of mercy,.......... 9:23
4 But we have this treasure in earthen **vessels**,........ 2 Co 4:7
1 to possess his **vessel** in sanctification and honour;... 1 Th 4:4
3 there are not only **vessels** of gold and of silver,..... 2 Tm 2:20
1 he shall be **a vessel** unto honour, sanctified,............ 2:21
3 the tabernacle, and all the **vessels** of the ministry.....Heb 9:21
2 honour unto the wife, as unto the weaker **vessel**,.... 1 Pt 3:7
3 **vessels** of a potter shall they be broken to shivers:... Rev 2:27
1 and all manner **vessels** of ivory,...................... 18:12
1 and all manner **vessels** of most precious wood,......... 18:12

Classical Greek

The noun *skeuos* can denote a wide range of items. In classical Greek it is used to mean an object such as a dish, jar, or vessel used for any purpose at all (*Bauer*).

Septuagint Usage

In the Septuagint this word displays many meanings. Rendering the Hebrew stem (*kᵉlî*) it is translated as jewels (Genesis 24:53), ordinary or religious vessels (Exodus 27:3; 1 Kings 10:21 [LXX 3 Kings 10:21]), and as weapons of war (Ecclesiastes 9:18). It also may refer to furniture (Genesis 31:37), one's goods (Isaiah 10:28), or a vessel used for other purposes (Zechariah 11:15; Ezekiel 40:42).

A distinguishing figurative use occurring in the Bible represents man in his finite weakness, fragile morality, and brevity upon the earth (cf. Maurer, "skeuos," *Kittel*, 7:358). God's infinite superiority is often in view here (Jeremiah 22:28; Psalm 31:12 [LXX 30:12]; Hosea 8:8), as the potter is superior to the clay. Literary and nonliterary papyri give a similar variety of applications, e.g., furniture, movables, utensils, anchors, or holy objects (Josephus, Philo; cf. *Bauer*).

New Testament Usage

The Gospels, Revelation, and most of Acts continue to use *skeuos* in its similar multiplicity of uses. This term may denote one's "goods," meaning the possessions stored in vessels (Matthew 12:29; Luke 17:31).

Paul's writings and the Epistle of Peter further develop the Old Testament figurative sense, referring to the vessel as the place of a person's soul. The Lord may use man as an instrument of honor or destruction (Romans 9:21-23).

Christ's glorious presence in the believer's soul is likened to an immense treasure placed in a clay pot (2 Corinthians 4:7). The believer who cleanses his life from wickedness will be useful to his Master and prepared for every work (2 Timothy 2:21). All men should strive to "possess his *vessel* in sanctification," that is, have an honorable marriage; not one based on inordinate lust (1 Thessalonians 4:4,5 [1 Thessalonians 4:4 may also refer to learning to control one's sexual passions]). Instead, husbands are exhorted to live in an understanding way with their precious wives ("weaker vessels"—1 Peter 3:7), honoring them so their prayers will not be hindered.

STRONG 4632, BAUER 754, MOULTON-MILLIGAN 577, KITTEL 7:358-67, LIDDELL-SCOTT 1607.

4488. σκηνή skēnē noun

Tent, booth, dwelling.

COGNATE:

σκηνόω skēnoō (4492)

SYNONYMS:

κατοικητήριον katoikētērion (2702)
κατοικία katoikia (2703)
οἰκητήριον oikētērion (3476)

אֹהֶל 'ōhel (164), Tent, tabernacle (Ex 33:7-11, Nm 4:37,39, Jer 10:20).

חָצֵר chātsēr (2793), Villages, tabernacle (Gn 25:16, Ex 38:31 [39:9]).

מִשְׁכָּן mishkān (5088), Tabernacle, dwelling place (Ex 26:6f., Nm 1:50f., 2 Chr 29:6).

סָךְ ṣākh (5710), Multitude (Ps 42:4 [41:4]).

סֻכָּה ṣukkāh (5712), Booth, hut (Lv 23:42, 2 Sm 11:11, Is 1:8).

סֻכּוֹת ṣukkôth (5713), Succoth (Gn 33:17).

סִכּוּת ṣikkûth (5714), Sikkuth? shrine? (Am 5:26).

1. **σκηνή skēnē** nom sing fem
2. **σκηνῆς skēnēs** gen sing fem
3. **σκηνῇ skēnē** dat sing fem
4. **σκηνήν skēnēn** acc sing fem
5. **σκηναῖς skēnais** dat pl fem
6. **σκηνάς skēnas** acc pl fem

6 if thou wilt, let us make here three **tabernacles**;.... Matt 17:4
6 and let us make three **tabernacles**; one for thee,.... Mark 9:5
6 and let us make three **tabernacles**; one for thee,.....Luke 9:33
6 they may receive you into everlasting **habitations**....... 16:9

4 Yea, ye took up the **tabernacle** of Moloch, ... Acts 7:43
1 Our fathers had the **tabernacle** 7:44
4 and will build again the **tabernacle** of David, ... 15:16
2 and of the true **tabernacle**, which the Lord pitched, .. Heb 8:2
4 when he was about to make the **tabernacle**: 8:5
1 Then verily the first **covenant** had also ordinances 9:1
1 For there was a **tabernacle** made; the first, ... 9:2
1 the **tabernacle** which is called the Holiest of all; 9:3
4 the priests went always into the first **tabernacle**, ... 9:6
2 while as the first **tabernacle** was yet standing: 9:8
2 by a greater and more perfect **tabernacle**, ... 9:11
4 he sprinkled with blood both the **tabernacle**, ... 9:21
5 dwelling in **tabernacles** with Isaac and Jacob, ... 11:9
3 have no right to eat which serve the **tabernacle**. 13:10
4 to blaspheme his name, and his **tabernacle**, ... Rev 13:6
2 **tabernacle** of the testimony in heaven was opened: 15:5
1 Behold, the **tabernacle** of God is with men, ... 21:3

Classical Greek

In classical Greek *skēnē* denotes a "tent, dwelling, abode" (cf. the related word *skēnos* [4491] that was frequently a figurative expression for the body). Pictured here is a lodging (usually in the open and portable) constructed with branches, poles, or planks covered with cloth, straw, or animal skin. In its most basic use a *skēnē* is a "cover" (Michaelis, "skēnē," *Kittel*, 7:368).

Septuagint Usage

Skēnē translates four Hebrew terms in the Septuagint (*'ōhel*, *chātsēr* [rarely], *mishkān*, and various forms of *ṣukkāh/ṣikkûth*). A majority of its appearances occur in the Pentateuch, especially in Exodus, Leviticus, and Numbers. A *skēnē* is the place of dwelling for the bedouin-like Israelites and their ancestors (Genesis 12:8; 13:3; 33:17ff.) prior to entering the Promised Land. But *skēnē* continued in use even after Israel settled; it simply meant "dwelling, home" (e.g., 1 Kings 8:66 [LXX 3 Kings 8:66]; Isaiah 38:12).

Just as God's people inhabit tents, God accommodated himself to dwell in the tabernacle (*skēnē*) He instructed them to build (Exodus 25:8; 26:1-36; both *'ōhel* and *mishakān*/[from *shākhan*], "to dwell"). The Israelites were told to build a tabernacle, and they received the plans from God (Exodus 26). The essential materials—precious metals, colorful materials, fine linens, animal hides, and acacia wood—were donated by the people (Exodus 25:1ff.; 25:8; 29:45) for God's "sanctuary." (For a more thorough discussion on the tabernacle see: Davis, "Tabernacle," *Interpreter's Dictionary of the Bible*, 4:498-506; Gooding, "Tabernacle," *New Bible Dictionary*, pp.1231-34.)

Primarily the tabernacle served as the Tent of Meeting (or "Witness"; *skēnē marturiou*, Exodus 29:4,10,11ff.) where God met with His people. Additionally, the tabernacle housed the covenant tablets in the ark (chest) within the Holy of Holies. Other articles furnishing the tabernacle included: the table of the bread of Presence, the altar of incense, the golden lampstand, the laver, and the altar of burnt offering. Thus the tabernacle was the site of Israel's formal worship of God. Israel transported the tabernacle throughout the wilderness experience, and even kept it after it entered the Promised Land (Joshua 18:1; 1 Samuel 21 [LXX 1 Kings 21]; 2 Chronicles 1:3-6).

A second interesting role played by *skēnē* is the usage in association with the Feast of Booths/ Tabernacles (*skēnai*; Hebrew *ṣikkûth*), one of Israel's three great pilgrimage feasts (Passover and Feast of Weeks [Pentecost] are the other two). Also known as the "Feast of the Ingathering," the Feast of Booths occurred at the end of harvest. During the celebrations every Israelite was required to live in a tent for 7 days (Leviticus 23:42f.) as a reminder of the days of wandering and living in tents after the Exodus. The feast remained integral to Israelite religion during Solomon's time (2 Chronicles 8:13), following the Exile (Ezra 3:4 [LXX 2 Esdras 3:4]; Zechariah 14:16,18), and continuing into the New Testament period (e.g., John 7:2f.; cf. Freeman, "Tabernacles, Feast of," *New Bible Dictionary*, pp.1234f.).

New Testament Usage

Skēnē occurs over 20 times in the Greek New Testament, half of which belong to Hebrews. Four references occur in the Synoptics, three in Acts, and three in Revelation. There are no instances in Paul and, surprisingly—given John's interest in the festival system of Judaism—none in Johannine literature outside of Revelation.

The Synoptic texts (excluding Luke 16:9, see below) are parallel accounts of Peter's request to build three *skēnas* ("shelters," NIV), one each for Moses, Elijah, and Jesus on the Mount of Transfiguration (Mark 9:5; Matthew 17:4; Luke 9:33). It is possible that the practice of temporarily dwelling in tents during the Feast of Tabernacles is implicit in the background of Peter's request (as reflected in such Old Testament expectations as Joel 3:21; Zechariah 2:10f.; 8:3; 14:16,19; cf. John 7:2ff.).

The use of *skēnē* for an "eternal dwelling" in Luke 16:9 reflects a more Hellenistic understanding (see above). Elsewhere in Luke's writings *skēnē* does not refer to the "eternal home" of believers, thus it is unwise to invest this occurrence (16:9) with any theological import (cf. Acts 7:43/Amos 5:26 of the "shrine" of Moloch).

In a different usage the *skēnē* of David, i.e., his "household," is for all peoples (Acts 15:16). Stephen argues in his speech that possession of the tabernacle did not insure the patriarch's "possession" of God. Even when the temple was erected God chose not to live in houses made with human hands (Acts 7:48). Rather, His dwelling place is with (*meta* [3196]) men (Revelation 21:3).

The Book of Hebrews uses *skēnē* 11 times. The earthly "tabernacle," like so many other Old Testament images, merely anticipated (as a "copy") the "true tabernacle" established by Christ in heaven (Hebrews 8:2,5). *Skēnē* depicts the inner tabernacle (the Holy of Holies) as the heavenly site of Christ's entering by His own blood in order to secure atonement for sin once and for all. By entering the "heavenly, more perfect tabernacle," Christ's sacrifice occurred on a plane beyond simple earthly sacrifice.

Strong 4633, Bauer 754, Moulton-Milligan 577, Kittel 7:368-81, Liddell-Scott 1608, Colin Brown 3:811-14.

4489. σκηνοπηγία skēnopēgia noun

Setting up of tents, Feast of Tabernacles.

Cross-References:

πήγνυμι pēgnumi (3939)
σκηνόω skēnoō (4492)

סֻכָּה ṣukkāh (5712), Tabernacle (Dt 16:16, 31:10, Zec 14:18f.).

1. σκηνοπηγία skēnopēgia nom sing fem

1 Now the Jews' feast of tabernacles was at hand......John 7:2

Classical Greek

Skēnopēgia is a combination of the two Greek words *skēnos* (4491), "tent," and *pegnumi*, "to pitch or set up." In classical Greek Aristotle used this term to refer to the nest building of swallows (ca. Fourth Century B.C.). Two centuries later a Coan (from the Island of Cos) religious inscription used this word as it instructs its followers to erect a booth (see *Moulton-Milligan*).

Septuagint Usage

The Septuagint uses this word nine times (including the Apocrypha) translating the Hebrew word *ṣukkāh*. Here, with the Greek *heortē* (1844), "feast," it refers to the Feast of Tabernacles or Booths. This festival is celebrated over an 8-day period starting on the 15th of the month of Tishri (7 days of dwelling in booths). Booths were made of tree branches, and the feast was observed outdoors when possible (see Leviticus 23:39-41). The historian Josephus in his *Antiquities* considered this as the most important of the Hebrew holidays (*Bauer*). In modern Israel there is a celebration of Succoth that includes "camping out."

The Feast of Tabernacles was instituted by the Lord for Israel to keep as a thanksgiving for the harvest and in memory of their 40 years of wandering in the desert under Moses' leadership before being given their new land. During that time of wandering they had no permanent home but had to live as nomads in tents. Even their Lord had no permanent place but a mobile Tent of Meeting where He tabernacled (i.e., dwelt) among them. Here the Israelites enjoyed all the remarkable privileges of the God of creation living in their midst and anticipated the time when the Lord would always dwell with them.

New Testament Usage

The only occurrence of this word in the New Testament is found in John 7:2 with *heortē* and again refers to the Feast of Tabernacles. Here Jesus went up to the feast in Jerusalem. He pointed to himself as the ultimate purpose of all their feasts.

During their feast, water from the pool of Siloam was apparently used in their holy rituals (see Brown, "Feast," *Colin Brown*, 3:814). Jesus directed all who thirsted (for everlasting life) to believe in Him in order to receive the life-giving Holy Spirit. Likewise, they used great lamps in their celebration. Jesus was probably referring to these lamps when He called himself the true light which guides every man's life (John 8:12).

As God dwelt among His people in the wilderness, so again He came to them as God incarnate and tabernacled among them for a short while (John 1:14). Now He ministers before God in the true tabernacle in heaven, of which the earthly sanctuary was only a shadow (Hebrews 8:1,2,5), and dwells among all believers through God's Holy Spirit (John 14:16,18). Jesus Christ is himself the feast that all Christians celebrate (1 Corinthians 5:7).

Strong 4634, Bauer 754-55, Moulton-Milligan 577, Kittel 7:390-92; Liddell-Scott 1608, Colin Brown 3:813.

4490. σκηνοποιός skēnopoios noun

Tentmaker, leather worker.

CROSS-REFERENCES:
ποιέω poieō (4020)
σκηνόω skēnoō (4492)

1. σκηνοποιοί skēnopoioi nom pl masc

1 for by their occupation they were **tentmakers**....... Acts 18:3

Classical Greek

This is a word of rare occurrence outside the Bible and Christian literature. It combines the Greek words *skēne* (4488), "tent," and *poieō* (4020), "to make." In classical Greek it exhibits a great deal of overlap with *mechanopoios* (i.e., a stagehand who made and moved the stage props) used by Aristophanes (ca. Fifth to Fourth Century B.C., according to Pollux; *Bauer*). But because the Jews thought theatrical production improper, the word *skēnopoios* was given an added meaning (ibid.).

There is no occurrence of this word in the Septuagint. However, the verb form *skēnopoieō* is found, which refers to the pitching of tents (cf. Isaiah 13:20; 22:15).

In the writings of Hermes during the time of Imperial Rome this term was used to describe the production of a dwelling appropriate for the soul (ibid.).

New Testament Usage

This term appears in the New Testament only in Acts 18:3. It describes the trade of Paul, Aquila, and Priscilla. Here it is usually translated as "tentmaker." Some believe, however, that tentmaking was too menial a profession for a young Jewish scholar like Paul, because tents were often woven from a coarse fabric made of goat's hair (Michaelis, "skēnē," *Kittel*, 7:368). Therefore, some think that they were more probably leather workers. Others believe that many tents were in fact made of leather at that time which afforded Paul the leather worker the title of tentmaker as well (see Harris, "Tent," *Colin Brown*, 3:812). As such, Paul maintained a marketable trade which helped support his God-given calling to take the gospel to both the Jews and the Gentiles.

STRONG 4635, BAUER 755, MOULTON-MILLIGAN 577, KITTEL 7:393-94, LIDDELL-SCOTT 1608, COLIN BROWN 3:811-12.

4491. σκῆνος skēnos noun

Tabernacle, tent.

CROSS-REFERENCE:
σκηνόω skēnoō (4492)

1. σκήνους skēnous gen sing neu
2. σκήνει skēnei dat sing neu

1 earthly house of this **tabernacle** were dissolved,...... 2 Co 5:1
2 For we that are in this **tabernacle** do groan,............ 5:4

Though used from Hippocrates (Fifth Century B.C.) on, *skēnos* occurs only once in the Septuagint (Wisdom of Solomon 9:15). And though the word properly means "tent, lodging," it is only used metaphorically of the human body; i.e., the soul dwells in the tent of the body. If one is in his "tent," he is alive physically. In the two occurrences of *skēnos* in the New Testament, Paul used the term to describe dwelling in the earthly "tent," that is, in the physical, biological body, the house of the soul (2 Corinthians 5:1,4).

STRONG 4636, BAUER 755, MOULTON-MILLIGAN 577, KITTEL 7:381-83, LIDDELL-SCOTT 1608, COLIN BROWN 3:811,814.

4492. σκηνόω skēnoō verb

To live, dwell, tabernacle.

COGNATES:
ἐπισκηνόω episkēnoō (1965)
κατασκηνόω kataskēnoō (2651)
κατασκήνωσις kataskēnōsis (2652)
σκηνή skēnē (4488)
σκηνοπηγία skēnopēgia (4489)
σκηνοποιός skēnopoios (4490)
σκῆνος skēnos (4491)
σκήνωμα skēnōma (4493)

SYNONYMS:
αὐλίζομαι aulizomai (829)
καθίζω kathizō (2495)
καταμένω katamenō (2620)
κατασκηνόω kataskēnoō (2651)
κατοικέω katoikeō (2700)
μένω menō (3176)
οἰκέω oikeō (3474)

אָהַל 'āhal (163), Pitch a tent (Gn 13:12—Sixtine Edition only).

שָׁכַן shākhan (8331), Stay, dwell (Jgs 5:17, 8:11).

1. σκηνοῦντας skēnountas acc pl masc part pres act
2. σκηνοῦντες skēnountes nom pl masc part pres act
3. ἐσκήνωσεν eskēnōsen 3sing indic aor act
4. σκηνώσει skēnōsei 3sing indic fut act

3 the Word was made flesh, and **dwelt** among us,..... John 1:14
4 that sitteth on the throne shall **dwell** among them.....Rev 7:15
2 rejoice, ye heavens, and ye that **dwell** in them......... 12:12
1 and his tabernacle, and them that **dwell** in heaven...... 13:6
4 will **dwell** with them, and they shall be his people,..... 21:3

Classical Greek and Septuagint Usage

Used from Xenophon (Fourth Century B.C.) on, the verb *skēnoō* appears several times in the Septuagint, both as a translation of *'āhal*, "to move, pitch a tent" (Genesis 13:12), and *shākhan*, "to abide, settle down" (Judges 5:17). The verb carries the idea of pitching a tent and dwelling in it. The noun *skēnos* (4491) denotes "a tabernacle, tent," sometimes used metaphorically of the body as a tent for the soul (2 Corinthians 5:4). The verb may, but not necessarily, include the thought of being nonpermanent or temporary. Often there is emphasis on shelter and security.

New Testament Usage

In the New Testament *skēnoō* is used only by John; once in the Gospel and four times in Revelation. John used this graphic verb when he wrote of the incarnation of Jesus; Jesus became flesh and "tabernacled, pitched tent" among us (John 1:14). The verb may suggest a temporary sojourn on earth, but more probably the emphasis is on the dwelling of God with His people. He is Immanuel, "God with us" (Isaiah 7:14; Matthew 1:23). John 1:14 has echoes of Psalm 85:9,10: "Surely his salvation is nigh them that fear him; that glory may dwell (*kataskēnoō* [2651], 'to abide, fix one's tent') in our land. Mercy and truth are met together; righteousness and peace have kissed each other." The truth of Christ's dwelling among His people would be a reminder to Jewish believers of the Hebrew concept, *Shekinah*, "that which dwells, presence."

In the Book of Revelation *skēnoō* is always used of dwelling in heaven. God "spreads His tent" over those delivered out of the Great Tribulation (7:15). Heavenly inhabitants are spoken of as those who "dwell" there (12:12; 13:6). The great truth of the ages is that God will "dwell, tent" among His people (21:3). Through the Incarnation, when Jesus tabernacled with man, true believers were able to behold the divine glory; so also in heaven as the Lord tabernacles with His own, they will behold the glory of God.

Episkēnoō (1965), "to fix a tent upon, rest on" (2 Corinthians 12:9), and *kataskēnoō*, "to fix one's abode, nest" (Matthew 13:32; Acts 2:26), are compounds formed from *skēnoō*.

Strong 4637, Bauer 755, Moulton-Milligan 578, Kittel 7:385-86, Liddell-Scott 1608, Colin Brown 3:811,813.

4493. σκήνωμα skēnōma noun

Tent, lodging, dwelling place, quarters.

Cross-Reference:

σκηνόω skēnoō (4492)

אֹהֶל 'ōhel (164), Tent (Dt 33:18, 2 Chr 10:16, Ps 91:10 [90:10]).

מִסְכְּנוֹת miskenôth (4694), Stores (1 Kgs 9:19—Codex Alexandrinus only).

מִשְׁכָּן mishkān (5088), Dwelling place (Jb 21:28, Ps 43:3 [42:3], Hb 1:6).

סֻכָּה sukkāh (5712), Succoth (Ps 108:7 [107:7]—Codex Sinaiticus only).

שׂךְ sōkh (7950), Garden? (Lam 2:6).

1. **σκηνώματος skēnōmatos** gen sing neu
2. **σκηνώματι skēnōmati** dat sing neu
3. **σκήνωμα skēnōma** nom/acc sing neu

3 desired to find a **tabernacle** for the God of Jacob.... Acts 7:46
2 I think it meet, as long as I am in this **tabernacle**,... 2 Pt 1:13
1 that shortly I must put off this my **tabernacle**,.......... 1:14

Classical Greek and Septuagint Usage

Skēnōma is a noun found in classical Greek literature from Euripides (Fifth Century B.C.) on, generally referring to "quarters, hut, tent." It appears in the Septuagint numerous times and as a translation of several Hebrew words. The noun literally denotes a "tent, dwelling," hence soldiers' "quarters" (1 Samuel 4:10 [LXX 1 Kings 4:10]), and metaphorically it is used of the human body as a "dwelling" for the soul (cf. *skēnos* in 2 Corinthians 5:1,4). In the Septuagint it is often used of the dwelling of God, the tabernacle (1 Kings 2:28 [LXX 3 Kings 2:28]; Psalms 15:1 [LXX 14:1]; 26:8 [25:8]).

New Testament Usage

Skēnōma occurs three times in the New Testament. Stephen used the term for the dwelling place for the Lord that David desired to build (Acts 7:46). Peter used the term figuratively of the earthly body in which the human soul is resident (2 Peter 1:13,14). He portrayed the physical body as the tent for the true self. At death the earthly dwelling is cast aside. It is interesting that Peter, like Paul (2 Corinthians 5:1,4), mixed the metaphors of tent and garment.

Strong 4638, Bauer 755, Moulton-Milligan 578, Kittel 7:383-84, Liddell-Scott 1608-9, Colin Brown 3:811,815.

4494. σκιά skia noun

Shade, shadow.

Cognates:

ἀποσκίασμα aposkiasma (638)
ἐπισκιάζω episkiazō (1966)
κατασκιάζω kataskiazō (2653)

צֵל tsēl (7009), Shadow, shade (2 Kgs 20:9ff., S/S 2:3, Ez 17:23).

צַלְמָוֶת tsalmāweth (7024), Darkness (Am 5:8).

1. **σκιά skia** nom sing fem
2. **σκιᾷ skia** dat sing fem
3. **σκιάν skian** acc sing fem

2 them which sat in the region and **shadow** of death . . . Matt 4:16
3 fowls of the air may lodge under the **shadow** of it. . . Mark 4:32
2 that sit in darkness and in the **shadow** of death, ... Luke 1:79
1 that at the least the **shadow** of Peter . . . . Acts 5:15
1 Which are **a shadow** of things to come; . . . . Col 2:17
2 unto the example and **shadow** of heavenly things, ... Heb 8:5
3 the law having **a shadow** of good things to come, ... 10:1

Classical Greek

Skia is a noun denoting "shade, shadow" and appears from Homer on. *Skia* can be used both literally and figuratively. Literally it refers to a "shadow" or "shade," particularly "that offered by trees or rocks" (Schulz, "skia," *Kittel*, 7:394). Figuratively *skia* can denote "the unreality of an object," that which is unstable or fleeting, and even the phantom of a dead person (ibid., p.395).

Septuagint Usage

In the Septuagint it is a translation of two different Hebrew words: *tsēl*: "shade, protection, shelter," or *tsalmāweth*, "deep shadow, death-like shadow." It is used both literally and figuratively in this book also. It can refer to the shade of trees (Jonah 4:6) or a sundial (2 Kings 20:9-11 [LXX 4 Kings 20:9-11]). Figurative uses abound. Great trials are indicated by the phrase "the valley of thc *shadow* of death" (Psalm 23:4 [LXX 22:4]). Protection is in view in Psalm 57:1 (LXX 56:1): "I will take refuge in the *shadow* of your wings" (NIV).

New Testament Usage

In the New Testament *skia* has a variety of nuances. Literally it is used of "shadow, shade," that is, the interception of light (Mark 4:32; Acts 5:15). In Matthew 4:16 (quoted from Isaiah 9:2) and Luke 1:79 *skia* is used of the "shadow" of death and is almost synonymous with sitting in "darkness" (*skotos* [4510]; see also Psalm 23:4 [LXX 22:4]).

In the three remaining New Testament uses *skia* is used of a foreshadowing, a shadow of the real. The Old Testament system was a shadow, a portrayal of the real (*sōma* [4835], "body") which was to come in Christ (Colossians 2:17). The Old Testament tabernacle and the Levitical system were shadows, cast images that resembled or outlined the genuine (Hebrews 8:5; 10:1). *Skia* is the opposite of *eikōn* (1494), "exact image, very form" (Hebrews 10:1). The cognate *aposkiasma* (638), "a shadow upon" something, is used in James 1:17.

STRONG 4639, BAUER 755, MOULTON-MILLIGAN 578, KITTEL 7:394-98, LIDDELL-SCOTT 1609, COLIN BROWN 3:553-56.

4495. σκιρτάω skirtaō verb

Leap, jump joyously, gambol.

SYNONYMS:
ἅλλομαι hallomai (240)
ἀναπηδάω anapēdaō (374B)

פּוּשׁ pûsh (6578), Frolic (Jer 50:11 [27:11]).

רָצַץ rātsats (7827), Crush, abuse; hithpolel: struggle with one another (Gn 25:22).

רָקַד rāqadh (7833), Skip (Ps 114:4,6 [113:4,6]).

1. **ἐσκίρτησεν eskirtēsen** 3sing indic aor act
2. **σκιρτήσατε skirtēsate** 2pl impr aor act

1 the babe **leaped** in her womb; . . . . Luke 1:41
1 salutation ... the babe **leaped** in my womb for joy. 1:44
2 Rejoice ye in that day, and **leap for joy**: 6:23

Septuagint Usage

The word first appears in Genesis 25:22 describing the twins Jacob and Esau "jostling" each other for position to be born first. Rabbis believed that the twins were already manifesting their destiny as founders of nations, particularly Jacob ("Israel"). Jeremiah prophesied (50:11 [LXX 27:11]) that Babylonian invaders would express their sadistic glee when they "frolic like a heifer" (NIV) as they plundered others. In Malachi 4:2 a very different joy is expressed by the righteous when the judgment of God comes upon evildoers: they will "go out and leap like calves released from the stall" (NIV). This leaping is a characteristic of the last days with the appearance of "Elijah" as an end-time witness.

New Testament Usage

The appearance of *skirtaō* in Luke 1:41,44 suggests the destiny of the new Elijah (John the Baptist) "leaping" in response to the voice of "the mother of my Lord." This is the eschatological joy precipitated by the coming of divine judgment against an evil world. Similarly, in Luke 6:23 those who are experiencing persecution should "rejoice in that day and leap for joy" (RSV), because persecution is a sign of God's impending judgment and vindication of His servants. Causing the lame to leap (and healing generally) is also a sign of the kingdom of God breaking into this age (Isaiah 35:6 fulfilled in Luke 7:22; Acts 3:28).

STRONG 4640, BAUER 755-56, MOULTON-MILLIGAN 578, KITTEL 7:401-2, LIDDELL-SCOTT 1611.

4496. σκληροκαρδία

sklērokardia noun

Spiritual insensitivity or hostility toward God's revelation, "hardness of heart."

Cross-References:

καρδία kardia (2559)
σκληρύνω sklērunō (4500)

1. σκληροκαρδίαν sklērokardian acc sing fem

1 Moses because of the hardness of your hearts...... Matt 19:8
1 For the hardness of your heart he wrote you this...Mark 10:5
1 with their unbelief and hardness of heart,............. 16:14

Septuagint Usage

This is a distinctively Old Testament term combining "hardness" and "heart" and used as a parallel with "stiffnecked" (Deuteronomy 10:16). The "heart" in ancient semitic thought was not simply, as is usually preached today, "the center of the emotions," but rather the center of thought, planning, feeling, and above all, spiritual perception and responsiveness (cf. Burke, "Heart," *International Standard Bible Encyclopedia*, 2:650f.). "Hardness of heart," then, means the whole internal thought and motivational processes are resistant to change from the outside—almost always from God.

The classic text for understanding the concept "hardness of heart" appears in Exodus 4 through 14 where Pharaoh's heart hardened repeatedly because of the warnings, signs, and wonders. The actual word *sklērokardia*, however, appears in the Septuagint of Deuteronomy 10:16 and of Jeremiah 4:4 to translate a metaphoric use of the Hebrew phrase, "the foreskin of the heart."

New Testament Usage

Its appearance in the New Testament occurs in Mark 10:5 (parallel Matthew 19:8) in which Jesus said that the law of Moses permitted divorce because of the "stubborn unwillingness" to accept God's plan for marriage, preferring to dissolve what God had joined. This is an interesting note on progressive revelation, allowing under the Law (divorce) what is no longer permitted between those in Christ whose hearts are no longer hard against God's will. Christians are those of a new covenant whose hearts are no longer hard as stone but have become hearts of flesh (Ezekiel 36:26) on which the law of God is now written (2 Corinthians 3:3-15). No longer is the will of God forced onto one's hard heart from the outside; in the believer God's will is internalized and freely active.

Strong 4641, Bauer 756, Kittel 3:613-14, Liddell-Scott 1612, Colin Brown 2:153,156,180,184.

4497. σκληρός sklēros adj

Hard, harsh, bitter, unpleasant, rough, strong, stern, cruel.

Cross-Reference:

σκληρύνω sklērunō (4500)

אַמִּיץ 'ammîts (541), Strong (Is 28:2).

עֹז 'ōz (6010), Strong; fierce (Is 19:4).

פָּרִיץ pārîts (6782), Violent person (Ps 17:4 [16:4]).

קָשָׁה qāshâh (7481), Qal: be heavy (1 Sm 5:7); niphal: be distressed (Is 8:21); hiphil: harden (Prv 28:14).

קָשֶׁה qāsheh (7482), Hard, fierce (Ex 1:14, 1 Kgs 12:4, Is 27:8).

רָשָׁע rāshā' (7857), Condemned (Nm 16:26).

1. σκληρῶν sklērōn gen pl masc/neu
2. σκληρός sklēros nom sing masc
3. σκληρόν sklēron nom/acc sing neu

2 Lord, I knew thee that thou art an hard man,......Matt 25:24
2 This is an hard saying; who can hear it?............John 6:60
3 it is hard for thee to kick against the pricks......... Acts 9:5
3 it is hard for thee to kick against the pricks........... 26:14
1 also the ships, ... and are driven of fierce winds,..... Jas 3:4
1 ungodly deeds ... and of all their hard speeches..... Jude 1:15

Classical Greek

The versatile adjective *sklēros* means "hard, dry, rough" (cf. the verb *sklērunō* [4500] and the noun *sklērotēs* [4498]), but these extend to a wide range of contexts. Objects can be "hard" to the touch; sounds "harsh" to the ears; tastes "bitter" to the tongue. Figuratively, *sklēros* can describe individuals as "stubborn, cruel, unkind, merciless."

Septuagint Usage

Sklēros occurs around 35 times in the canonical material of the Septuagint with a Hebrew counterpart. There are 14 instances in which there is either no Hebrew parallel (e.g., 1 Kings 12:24 [LXX 3 Kings 12:24]; Proverbs 17:27) or no certain Hebrew term behind it (e.g., Genesis 49:3; Psalm 17:4 [LXX 16:4]; Isaiah 8:12). *Qāsheh* ("hard, difficult, severe") in various forms is the most frequently replaced by *sklēros* (of "harsh" speech, Genesis 42:7,30; of "hard" labor, Exodus 1:14; 6:9).

The link between *sklēros* and a "stubborn" spiritual condition ("hard heart") occurs in Proverbs 28:14 and in Proverbs 29:19 (no Hebrew) where the Septuagint qualifies a servant who cannot be corrected simply with words as *sklēros*.

Of the prophets, Isaiah's work contains the most instances of *sklēros*. He hinted at the figurative/spiritual understanding in 8:21, and in 48:4 he equated it with being "stiff-necked" (cf.

sklērotrachēlos [4499], "stiff-necked," Exodus 33:3,5; 34:9; Deuteronomy 9:6,13; Baruch 2:30, of the people of Israel; cf. Deuteronomy 10:16; Nehemiah 9:16f.; cf. also the verb *sklērunō*, which occurs regularly in connection with *kardia* [2559], "heart," e.g., Exodus 4:21; 7:3 etc. of Pharaoh's heart; 2 Chronicles 30:8; Psalm 95:8 [LXX 94:8]). The author of Sirach makes the same connection (3:26,27, RSV reads *kardia* as "mind"; Sirach 30:8-12).

New Testament Usage

Sklēros is found in the New Testament only six times. It typically reflects the diversity of meaning encountered in classical Greek, although other members of the word group function in conjunction with the concept of spiritual hardness.

The sense of "severe, harsh" is implied in Matthew's single usage in the Parable of the Talents. The servant regarded the master as "severe" (Matthew 25:24; cf. the "parallel" in Luke 19:21, *austēros* [834], "severe"). Jesus' words in John 6:60 are "difficult," that is, "hard to accept" as well as "difficult" to obey. In a related but distinct sense the "harsh" words of evil men are "cruel" and evil, being spoken against the Lord (Jude 15). James speaks of "strong" winds that carry ships along (3:4).

STRONG 4642, BAUER 756, MOULTON-MILLIGAN 578, KITTEL 5:1022-24,1028, LIDDELL-SCOTT 1612, COLIN BROWN 2:153-56.

4498. σκληρότης sklērotēs noun

Hardness; resistance to movement or change, stubbornness.

CROSS-REFERENCE:
σκληρύνω sklērunō (4500)

חָרוּץ chārûts (2844), Threshing-sledge (Is 28:27).

מוֹקֵשׁ môqēsh (4305), Snare (2 Sm 22:6).

קְשִׁי qeshî (7487), Stubbornness (Dt 9:27).

1. σκληρότητα sklērotēta acc sing fem

1 But after thy hardness and impenitent heart ....Rom 2:5

Sklērotēs is a noun related to *skellō*, "dry, hard, rough." It appears in parallel with "impenitent heart" in its only New Testament appearance, Romans 2:5. One is "hard" when one judges another, particularly as that person characteristically commits the same sins for which he is judging others.

STRONG 4643, BAUER 756, MOULTON-MILLIGAN 578, KITTEL 5:1022-24,1028-29, LIDDELL-SCOTT 1612, COLIN BROWN 2:153,155.

4499. σκληροτράχηλος sklērotrachēlos adj

Stiffnecked.

CROSS-REFERENCE:
σκληρύνω sklērunō (4500)

1. σκληροτράχηλοι sklērotrachēloi nom pl masc

1 Ye stiffnecked and uncircumcised in heart ....Acts 7:51

Classical Greek and Septuagint Usage

In classical Greek and the Septuagint, the term *sklērotrachēlos* vividly describes one whose jaws and neck are rigid from angrily resisting argument or counsel (Exodus 33:3, "hard in neck," also 33:5; 34:9; Deuteronomy 9:6; 31:27; 2 Kings 17:14; 2 Chronicles 30:8; 36:13; Nehemiah 9:16,17; Jeremiah 7:26; 17:23).

New Testament Usage

Sklērotrachēlos appears only once in the New Testament. In Acts 7:51 Stephen characterized the Jews as those who "resist the Holy Spirit." This was manifested in being "uncircumcised in heart and ears"; that is, though they were visibly circumcised and in covenant with God, their real covenant was against God, and they refused to hear anything from Him. Similarly, they showed their hostile reaction to God by hardening their necks and clenching their teeth (verse 54) in rage against the word of the Spirit.

STRONG 4644, BAUER 756, MOULTON-MILLIGAN 578, KITTEL 5:1022-24,1029, LIDDELL-SCOTT 1612, COLIN BROWN 2:153,155.

4500. σκληρύνω sklērunō verb

To make hard, stubborn, or resistant to movement or change.

COGNATES:
σκληροκαρδία sklērokardia (4496)
σκληρός sklēros (4497)
σκληρότης sklērotēs (4498)
σκληροτράχηλος sklērotrachēlos (4499)

SYNONYM:
πωρόω pōroō (4313)

חָזַק chāzaq (2480), Qal: be hardened (Ex 8:19, 9:35); piel: harden (Ex 4:21, 10:20, 14:4).

כָּבֵד kāvēdh (3632), Be heavy; hiphil: harden (Ex 10:1).

קָשָׁה qāshāh (7481), Qal: be fierce, be harsh (Gn 49:7, 2 Sm 19:43); hiphil: harden, stiffen (Ex 7:3, Jer 17:23); ask for a difficult thing (2 Kgs 2:10).

קָשֶׁה qāsheh (7482), Stranger (Jgs 4:24).

קָשַׁח qāshach (7483), Hiphil: harden (Is 63:17).

1. σκληρύνει sklērunei 3sing indic pres act
2. σκληρύνητε sklērunēte 2pl subj aor act

3. σκληρυνθῇ sklērunthē 3sing subj aor pass
4. ἐσκληρύνοντο esklērunonto 3pl indic imperf pass

4 But when divers were **hardened**, and believed not,.. Acts 19:9
1 and whom he will he **hardeneth**.................... Rom 9:18
2 **Harden** not your hearts, as in the provocation,....... Heb 3:8
3 be **hardened** through the deceitfulness of sin........... 3:13
2 **harden** not your hearts, as in the provocation.......... 3:15
2 if ye will hear his voice, **harden** not your hearts......... 4:7

Classical Greek and Septuagint Usage

In classical literature *sklērunō* usually carries a literal sense of dry, stiff, rough, or hard. It first appears as a medical term in the works of the classical Greek physician Hippocrates (cf. *Bauer*). In the Old Testament, hardening "results from men's persistence in shutting themselves to God's call and command. A state then arises in which a man is no longer able to hear and in which he is irretrievably enslaved. Alternatively, God makes the hardening final, so that the people affected by it cannot escape from it" (Becker, "Hard," *Colin Brown*, 2:154). God hardened not only the heart of Pharaoh but the enemies of Israel as well "in order that they should be utterly destroyed" (Joshua 11:20, RSV).

New Testament Usage

God's divine sovereignty in hardening men is precisely congruent with man's responsibility for this hardening, hence, Psalm 95:7,8 (LXX 94:7,8) can urge, "O that today you would hearken to his voice! Harden not your hearts." This verse is cited three times in Hebrews (3:8,15; 4:7). The "deceitfulness of sin" generates a divine hardening (Hebrews 3:13, RSV) as is illustrated by the Jews who heard Paul's message in Acts 19:9. Paul commented on the general condition of the Jews as an expression of God's freedom to do as He wills, even to harden someone in unbelief (Romans 9:18), though it is man's reaction that causes the hardening. The same sun that melts wax hardens clay.

STRONG 4645, BAUER 756, MOULTON-MILLIGAN 578, KITTEL 5:1022-24,1030-31, LIDDELL-SCOTT 1612, COLIN BROWN 2:153,155.

4501. σκολιός skolios adj

Crooked, full of obstacles, disorganized, devious, corrupt, evil, unjust.

הֲפַכְפַּךְ hăphakhpakh (2092), Crooked (Prv 21:8).
מַעֲקַשִּׁים maʿăqashshîm (4787), Rugged place (Is 42:16).
סָרַר sārar (5842), Stubborn person (Ps 78:8 [77:8]).
עָקֹב ʿāqōv (6359), Rough ground (Is 40:4).
עֲקַלָּתוֹן ʿăqallāthôn (6367), Twisting (Is 27;1).
עִקֵּשׁ ʿiqqēsh (6379), Perverse, devious (Dt 32:5, Prv 2:15, 22:5).
עִקְּשׁוּת ʿiqshûth (6381), Deceitful thing (Prv 4:24).
פָּתַל pāthal (6871), Niphal: be crooked (Prv 8:8).
תָּהֳלָה tāhŏlāh (8746), Error (Jb 4:18).
תַּהְפֻּכָה tahpukhāh (8749), Perverse person (Prv 16:28).

1. σκολιοῖς skoliois dat pl masc
2. σκολιᾶς skolias gen sing fem
3. σκολιά skolia nom/acc pl neu

3 and the **crooked** shall be made straight,............. Luke 3:5
2 Save yourselves from this **untoward** generation....... Acts 2:40
2 in the midst of a **crooked** and perverse nation,...... Phlp 2:15
1 not only to the good ... but also to the **froward**...... 1 Pt 2:18

Classical Greek

In classical Greek *skolios* is generally used of rivers and roads, and by extension refers to something difficult to travel, such as the obstacle-ridden path to knowledge (Bertram, "skolios," *Kittel*, 7:403). It is also used of the twisting appearance and movements of snakes and dragons. In a figurative sense, *skolios* is used of a rebellious, disorderly, or evil state. For example, one horse in a team is straight and orderly while the other is *skolios*.

Septuagint Usage

In the Septuagint *skolios* refers to the twisting, coiled snake, symbolic of its crookedness and evil (Isaiah 27:1). The Lord's "way" or "road" may be crooked (rough and full of obstacles) but must be made straight (Isaiah 40:3-5) by studying and receiving the law of God. A prophet can encounter stumbling blocks to his ministry laid by evildoers (Hosea 9:8). Not only can the evildoer walk on a crooked road (Proverbs 2:15; 14:2; 28:18), but he can also have a crooked heart (cf. Jeremiah 17:9) or be essentially crooked as a person (Proverbs 16:28; Ezekiel 16:5). To speak crookedly is to gossip maliciously.

New Testament Usage

Isaiah 40:3-5 is cited in Luke 3:4-6, where at the coming of the Messiah the paths shall be made straight and smooth, even to the point of leveling mountains and filling valleys. In other words, through repentance and forgiveness of sins (verse 3), "all flesh shall see the salvation of God." Acts 2:40 and Philippians 2:15 refer to a "crooked generation" (see Mark 9:19 and parallels). They are characterized as being hardhearted, mockers, and corrupt. In 1 Peter 2:18 the Christian employee is told to serve submissively even for a "harsh" (literally, "crooked") employer who continually causes suffering by creating evil and destructive obstacles to a moral and godly path.

Strong 4646, Bauer 756, Moulton-Milligan 578, Kittel 7:403-8, Liddell-Scott 1613.

4502. σκόλοψ skolops noun

Sharp stake, thorn, splinter, sliver.

סִיר sîr (5708), Thorns (Hos 2:6).

סִלּוֹן sillôn (5738), Brier (Ez 28:24).

שֵׂךְ sēkh (7949), Barb (Nm 33:55).

1. σκόλοψ skolops nom sing masc

1 there was given to me a thorn in the flesh,........ 2 Co 12:7

Classical Greek

In classical Greek *skolops* was first used to describe pointed stakes that were arranged around fortifications to impale attackers or were hidden at the bottom of covered pits. They also were used to protect vineyards against thieves. The severed head of an enemy was often hoisted upon a *skolops* as a sign of triumph. Impaling on a *skolops* was a means of execution, originally distinct from crucifying, but later, in many cases, identical with it.

Septuagint Usage

In the Septuagint *skolops* does not refer to a stake but means "sliver" or "thorn." Gentiles who caused suffering among the Israelites are described as a "splinter" in the eye (Numbers 33:55) or as a "pricking brier" or a "painful thorn" (Ezekiel 28:24).

New Testament Usage

Skolops in the New Testament appears only in 2 Corinthians 12:7 as Paul's famous "thorn in the flesh." Unfortunately, the context does not specifically identify whether the "thorn" is small or large, physical, mental, or spiritual. Scholars have often debated what was meant by the "thorn." Tertullian thought it was an earache; Chrysostom, a headache; and Augustine saw it as a general term for all of Paul's physical sufferings. Others have thought it was an affliction of the eyes. Still others, because of the phrase "messenger of Satan" found in this verse, think the thorn was a false prophet at Corinth who tried to refute the message which Paul preached. Whatever the thorn was, it affected Paul's work, and he prayed for its removal three times (2 Corinthians 12:8). However, Paul soon learned that it was to be permanent and that God could still bless him through it (verses 9f.,12; 13:3). (See also Pinnock, "Thorn in the Flesh," *International Standard Bible Encyclopedia*, 4:843.)

Strong 4647, Bauer 756, Moulton-Milligan 578-79, Kittel 7:409-13, Liddell-Scott 1613, Colin Brown 1:726-27.

4503. σκοπέω skopeō verb

Look at, examine carefully; hold something as a goal or model.

Cognates:

κατασκοπέω kataskopeō (2654)
κατάσκοπος kataskopos (2655)
σκοπός skopos (4504)

Synonyms:

ἀτενίζω atenizō (810)
βλέπω blepō (984)
ἐποπτεύω epopteuō (2013)
θεάομαι theaomai (2277)
θεωρέω theōreō (2311)
καταμανθάνω katamanthanō (2618)
κατανοέω katanoeō (2627)
ὁράω horaō (3571)

1. σκόπει skopei 2sing impr pres act
2. σκοπεῖτε skopeite 2pl impr pres act
3. σκοπῶν skopōn nom sing masc part pres act
4. σκοπούντων skopountōn gen pl masc part pres act
5. σκοπεῖν skopein inf pres act
6. σκοποῦντες skopountes nom pl masc part pres act

1 Take heed therefore that the light which is in thee Luke 11:35
5 mark them which cause divisions and offences......Rom 16:17
4 While we look not at the things which are seen,.....2 Co 4:18
3 considering thyself, lest thou also be tempted.........Gal 6:1
2 Look not every man on his own things,............. Phlp 2:4
2 mark them which walk so as ... us for an ensample...... 3:17

Classical Greek

In secular Greek *skopeō* is used in the sense of "examine carefully" either as a judge, a philosopher (the "skeptics" were a school of philosophers), or as a historian. An actor "reads his audience" and performs accordingly. *Skopeō* is also used to describe an inspection of evidence for determining the right time or circumstances for action to accomplish a purpose. *Skopeō* can also mean "to hold something as a model (or goal) before one's eyes" (Fuchs, "skopeō," *Kittel*, 7:414-415).

Septuagint Usage

In the Septuagint *skopeō* and its closely related cognate, *skopeuō*, appear nine times, in each case with the meaning "to keep a watchful eye on" something (cf. Esther 8:13; 2 Maccabees 4:5).

New Testament Usage

Luke 11:35 urges that people "*take heed* therefore, that the *light* which is in thee be not darkness." Jesus exhorted His hearers to be sure that what they accept as "light" (truth) was really true "light" and not "darkness" (deception). Only those who are full of true "light" will be able to "illuminate" (help) others (verse 36); cf. Matthew 6:22f. The ethical responsibility of believers is also discussed in Galatians 6:1 where Paul said "*considering* thyself"; one should have a compassionate, nonjudgmental attitude. In Philippians 2:4 Paul encouraged his readers to "*look* not only" to their own interests (needs), "but also to the interests of others" (RSV). The proper motivation for being "others-centered" is that believers should "*look* not *at* the things which are seen, but at the things which are not seen: for the things which are seen are temporal; but the things which are not seen are eternal" (2 Corinthians 4:18).

STRONG 4648, BAUER 756, MOULTON-MILLIGAN 579, KITTEL 7:414-16, LIDDELL-SCOTT 1613-14.

4504. σκοπός skopos noun

Goal, objective, finish line.

CROSS-REFERENCE:

σκοπέω skopeō (4503)

מַטָּרָה maṯṯārāh (4446), Target (Jb 16:12 [16:13], Lam 3:12).

מַשְׂכִּית maskîth (5031), Something carved (Lv 26:1).

צָפָה tsāphâh (7099), Qal: watchman (2 Sm 18:24-27, 2 Kgs 9:17f., Ez 33:6f.); piel: lookout (Is 21:6).

1. σκοπόν skopon acc sing masc

1 I press toward the mark for the prize .... Phlp 3:14

Classical Greek

The meaning of *skopos* in the classical Greek refers either to someone who casts a watchful eye (that is, a watchman, guard, scout), to a supervisor, or to a target for arrows. Metaphorically it can mean a goal which controls a man's whole life (Fuchs, "skopos," *Kittel*, 7:413).

Septuagint Usage

The Septuagint shares two of the above meanings. The first refers to a "watchman" on the wall (1 Samuel 14:16 [LXX 1 Kings 14:16]) or to a prophet who "watches" over the people (Jeremiah 6:17; Ezekiel 3:17; 33:2). In a second usage, one can become a "target" for God's wrath (Job 16:12 [LXX 16:13]; Lamentations 3:12).

New Testament Usage

The New Testament uses *skopos* in the second sense where Paul, and all Christians, must forget the part of the race already run and "press on toward the *goal* for the prize of the upward call of God in Christ Jesus" (Philippians 3:14, RSV). This "goal" of obeying Christ is to control a person's life.

STRONG 4649, BAUER 756-57, MOULTON-MILLIGAN 579, KITTEL 7:413-14, LIDDELL-SCOTT 1614.

4505. σκορπίζω skorpizō verb

Scatter, disperse; scatter abroad, dissipate.

COGNATES:

διασκορπίζω diaskorpizō (1281)
σκορπίος skorpios (4506)

זוּר zûr (2197), Crush (Jb 39:15).

זָרָה zārâh (2306), Piel: spread (Mal 2:3).

נַעַר na'ar (5470), Young one (Zec 11:16).

פּוּץ pûts (6571), Hiphil: scatter (2 Sm 22:15, Pss 18:14 [17:14], 144:6 [143:6]).

פָּזַר pāzar (6582), Piel: distribute (Ps 112:9 [111:9]).

פָּרַד pāradh (6754), Niphal: separate (Neh 4:19).

1. σκορπίζει skorpizei 3sing indic pres act
2. ἐσκόρπισεν eskorpisen 3sing indic aor act
3. σκορπισθῆτε skorpisthēte 2pl subj aor pass

1 he that gathereth not with me **scattereth abroad**.... Matt 12:30
1 and he that gathereth not with me **scattereth**....... Luke 11:23
1 the wolf catcheth them, and **scattereth** the sheep... John 10:12
3 that ye **shall be scattered**, every man to his own,....... 16:32
2 As it is written, He **hath dispersed abroad**;.......... 2 Co 9:9

Classical Greek

In classical Greek literature *skorpizō* is rare, meaning "divide, scatter, disperse." In Hellenistic Greek *skorpizō* is used in one case to describe the scattering of materials hastily built into a dam which was struck by a violent flood (Polybius 27:2; cf. Michel, "skorpizō," *Kittel*, 7:418).

Septuagint Usage

In the Septuagint *skorpizō* translates several different Hebrew terms. David sang his "Song of Deliverance," recalling how God "scattered" (*pûts*) his enemies (cf. Psalms 18:14 [LXX 17:14]; 144:6 [143:6]). In Psalm 112:9 (LXX 111:9) the Psalmist praised God for "dispersing" (*pāzar*) His prosperity. When Nehemiah was rebuilding the walls of Jerusalem, he was concerned for the safety of the workers because they were "separated" (*pāradh*) (Nehemiah 4:19).

New Testament Usage

The New Testament uses *skorpizō* in the first sense mentioned above, in 2 Corinthians 9:9. Here the believer is urged to imitate God by dispersing generosity abroad, as in sowing seed. In doing so believers are promised that they will be "enriched in everything for all liberality." In parallel passages (Matthew 12:30 and Luke 11:23) Jesus castigates those who are not committed to Him and His mission: "He who does not gather with Me, scatters" (NASB). This is closely associated with the use of *diaskorpizō* in Matthew 26:31 and Mark 14:27 which cite Zechariah 13:7. Closely related is John 10:12 and 16:32, though the former speaks of "hired pastors" who abandon the sheep to the wolf, as in Ezekiel 34.

STRONG 4650, BAUER 757, MOULTON-MILLIGAN 579, KITTEL 7:418-22, LIDDELL-SCOTT 1614, COLIN BROWN 2:33-34.

4506. σκορπίος skorpios noun

Scorpion.

COGNATE:

σκορπίζω skorpizō (4505)

עַקְרָב ʿaqrāv (6375), Scorpion (Dt 8:15, 2 Chr 10:14, Ez 2:6).

1. **σκορπίου skorpiou** gen sing masc
2. **σκορπίον skorpion** acc sing masc
3. **σκορπίοι skorpioi** nom pl masc
4. **σκορπίων skorpiōn** gen pl masc
5. **σκορπίοις skorpiois** dat pl masc

4 unto you power to tread on serpents and scorpions, Luke 10:19
2 if he shall ask an egg, will he offer him a scorpion?.... 11:12
3 as the scorpions of the earth have power............Rev 9:3
1 and their torment was as the torment of a scorpion,..... 9:5
5 And they had tails like unto scorpions,................ 9:10

Classical Greek and Septuagint Usage

Skorpios, "skorpion," refers to a species of arachnid, about 4 or 5 inches long at maturity, which has an extremely dangerous and poisonous sting in its tail (cf. *Bauer*). Many ancient references in the classical period and in the Septuagint are metaphoric, referring to extreme danger. For example, it describes prostitutes, evil persons, or stinging words or looks (Ezekiel 2:6).

New Testament Usage

Jesus gave authority to His disciples, and by extension to all who believe in Him, to "tread on serpents and *scorpions*" (Luke 10:19). This is likely a reference to the extremely dangerous demonic powers which are both spiritually and physically poisonous (cf. Revelation 9:3,5,10). The "all authority . . . given to Me . . . " in the Great Commission (Matthew 28:19,20, NASB) includes authority over the demonic powers of sin, sickness, etc. In a completely different context, the Father is good, not evil, and will not give His children a "scorpion" when they ask for food (Luke 11:12).

STRONG 4651, BAUER 757, MOULTON-MILLIGAN 579, LIDDELL-SCOTT 1615, COLIN BROWN 1:510.

4507. σκοτεινός skoteinos adj

Darkness.

COGNATE:

σκοτόω skotoō (4511)

SYNONYM:

αὐχμηρός auchmēros (843)

חֹשֶׁךְ chōshekh (2932), Darkness, dark places (Jb 10:21, 15:23, Is 45:19).

חֲשֵׁכָה chăshēkhāh (2934), Darkness, something dark (Gn 15:12, Ps 18:11 [17:11]).

מַחְשָׁךְ machshākh (4423), Dark place, darkness (Pss 88:6 [87:6], 143:3 [142:3]).

נֶשֶׁף nesheph (5582), Darkening area (Jer 13:16).

סְתַר sᵉthar (A5850), Pael: hidden things (Dn 2:22—Aramaic).

1. **σκοτεινόν skoteinon** nom/acc sing neu

1 thy whole body shall be full of darkness........... Matt 6:23
1 thy body also is full of darkness.................. Luke 11:34
1 be full of light, having no part dark,................. 11:36

Classical Greek and Septuagint Usage

In classical Greek usage this noun denotes "darkness." It describes the state of things that are difficult to see and the results of such a state (e.g., perilous movement, a kind of paralysis, danger, and fear). To be locked outside the city gates after dark was to be at the mercy of vicious bandits and wild animals. Darkness also signifies ignorance, obscurity, deception, or even the inability to "see," that is, to learn anything new. Hence, darkness can refer to all that is dangerous or evil (Psalm 69:23 [LXX 68:23]), including captivity (Psalm 107:10 [LXX 106:10]), sin (Psalm 74:20 [LXX 73:20]), and sorrow (Lamentations 5:17). Darkness is also the condition of death and the underworld (Job 10:20-22; Psalm 88:6 [LXX 87:6]; Ezekiel 32:17-32). The evil person is "darkened" (spiritually blinded), but the godly man can have faith even in a condition of "darkness" (suffering, lack of understanding the situation) (Psalms 97:11 [LXX 96:11]; 112:4 [111:4]).

New Testament Usage

Skoteinos appears in a saying of Jesus recorded in Matthew 6:23 and Luke 11:34,36. The saying is placed in teaching on the "darkness" of greed and materialism. One should not be "laying up treasures on earth," because one's "heart" identifies with one's "treasure" (Matthew 6:19-21). The passage is followed by the inability to "serve God and mammon (money)" in verse 24. If one is not generous with his wealth and ignores the needs of others, even though he thinks he is a good or religious person, he is deceived: his "whole body (self) shall be full of darkness" (i.e., greed, deception, danger, death [verse 23]; cf. James 1:27-2:16).

Luke 11:35 uses the saying to illustrate the suppression of truth, specifically the truth of generosity: the light one has should not be hidden but put to good use (11:33). Verses 34 and 35 refer to the same principle as Matthew and continue with the self-deception of the Pharisees who are "religious" but self-deceived, "full of greed and wickedness" (verse 39, NIV).

STRONG 4652, BAUER 757, MOULTON-MILLIGAN 579, KITTEL 7:423-45, LIDDELL-SCOTT 1615, COLIN BROWN 1:421-23.

4508. σκοτία skotia noun

Dark, darkness, gloom.

COGNATE:

σκοτόω skotoō (4511)

SYNONYMS:

γνόφος gnophos (1099)
ζόφος zophos (2200)
σκότος skotos (4510)

אֹפֶל 'ōphel (669), Darkness (Jb 28:3).

חָשַׁךְ chāshakh (2931), Be dark (Mi 3:6).

1. **σκοτία skotia** nom sing fem
2. **σκοτίας skotias** gen sing fem
3. **σκοτίᾳ skotia** dat sing fem

3 SITTING IN DARKNESS SAW (NASB) .... Matt 4:16
3 What I tell you in darkness, that speak ye in light: 10:27
3 Therefore whatsoever ye have spoken in darkness .. Luke 12:3
3 And the light shineth in darkness; .... John 1:5
1 and the darkness comprehended it not. 1:5
1 And it was now dark, ... 6:17
3 he that followeth me shall not walk in darkness, ... 8:12
1 lest darkness come upon you: 12:35
3 for he that walketh in darkness knoweth not 12:35
3 believeth on me should not abide in darkness. 12:46
2 early, when it was yet dark, unto the sepulchre, ... 20:1
1 that God is light, and in him is no darkness at all... 1 Jn 1:5
1 darkness is past, and the true light now shineth. 2:8
3 hateth his brother, is in darkness even until now. 2:9
3 But he that hateth his brother is in darkness, ... 2:11
3 is in darkness, and walketh in darkness, ... 2:11
1 because that darkness hath blinded his eyes. 2:11

This noun is related to *skotos* (4510) and denotes "darkness, gloom" (*Liddell-Scott*). In classical Greek *skotia* is used both literally and figuratively, especially as a symbol for death (cf. *Bauer*). In the Septuagint the word is associated with death (Job 28:3), grief (Isaiah 16:3), and lack of spiritual understanding (Micah 3:6).

New Testament Usage

While most New Testament writers use *skotos*, John's writings show a preference for *skotia* with 14 of its 16 occurrences in his Gospel and Epistles. The word is used literally in reference to the time of day in John 6:17 and 20:1. It is used figuratively in Matthew 10:27 and Luke 12:3 where it denotes spiritual or moral darkness (cf. John 1:5; 8:12; 12:35,46; 1 John 1:5; 2:8,9,11). In expressing spiritual ignorance or moral depravity, *skotia* signifies more than the mere absence of light. It is a wicked and hostile system that utterly opposes divine light; its result is a ruinous state of misery characterized not only by spiritual blindness but by uncertainty, furtiveness, and anxiety.

STRONG 4653, BAUER 757, KITTEL 7:423-45, LIDDELL-SCOTT 1615, COLIN BROWN 1:421-25.

4509. σκοτίζομαι skotizomai verb

To be darkened.

CROSS-REFERENCE:

σκοτόω skotoō (4511)

חָשַׁךְ chāshakh (2931), Qal: be darkened (Ps 69:23 [68:23], Eccl 12:2); hiphil: be dark (Ps 139:12 [138:12]).

מַחְשָׁךְ machshākh (4423), Dark place (74:20 [73:20]—only Codex Sinaiticus and some Vaticanus texts).

1. **ἐσκοτίσθη eskotisthē** 3sing indic aor pass
2. **σκοτισθῇ skotisthē** 3sing subj aor pass
3. **σκοτισθήτωσαν skotisthētōsan** 3pl impr aor pass
4. **ἐσκοτισμένοι eskotismenoi** nom pl masc part perf mid
5. **σκοτισθήσεται skotisthēsetai** 3sing indic fut pass

5 after the tribulation ... shall the sun be darkened, ... Matt 24:29
5 after that tribulation, the sun shall be darkened, ... Mark 13:24
1 the sun was darkened, and the veil of the temple ... Luke 23:45
1 and their foolish heart was darkened. .... Rom 1:21
3 Let their eyes be darkened that they may not see, ... 11:10
4 Having the understanding darkened, ... Eph 4:18
2 stars; so as the third part of them was darkened, ... Rev 8:12
1 were darkened by reason of the smoke of the pit. 9:2

Classical Greek and Septuagint Usage

This verb is related to *skotos* (4510) and can be found in classical Greek meaning "to be darkened, to be blinded" (*Liddell-Scott*). In the Septuagint the word is used both in the literal sense for the darkening of heavenly bodies (Psalm 139:12 [LXX 138:12]; Ecclesiastes 12:2; Isaiah 13:10) and metaphorically for spiritual blindness (Psalms 69:23 [LXX 68:23]; 74:20 [73:20]).

New Testament Usage

The word is used literally and prophetically in the apocalyptic passages of Matthew 24:29 and Mark 13:24 where the darkening of the sun and the moon presages the end of the age (see Revelation 8:12; 9:2). Similar apocalyptic occurrences are found in Ecclesiastes 12:2 and Isaiah 13:10.

The New Testament also employs *skotizomai* in a figurative sense to describe the mental and spiritual incapacity of perverse people to understand divine truth (Romans 1:21; 11:10; Ephesians 4:18). This obtuseness is caused by a deliberate rejection of the truth in favor of an earthly system characterized by immorality and deception. The result is that the ability to discern between truth and error, or good and evil, is lost. People in that condition are not merely *in* darkness; they *are* darkness.

STRONG 4654, BAUER 757 (see "skotizō"), MOULTON-MILLIGAN 579 (see "skotizō"), KITTEL 7:423-45 (see "skotizō"), LIDDELL-SCOTT 1615 (see "skotizō"), COLIN BROWN 1:421,423 (see "skotizō").

4510. σκότος skotos noun

Dark, darkness, gloom.

COGNATE:

σκοτόω skotoō (4511)

SYNONYMS:

γνόφος gnophos (1099)
ζόφος zophos (2200)
σκοτία skotia (4508)

אֹפֶל 'ōphel (669), Darkness (Jb 3:6).

אֲפֵלָה 'ăphēlāh (671), Darkness (Dt 28:29).

חָשַׁךְ chāshakh (2931), Be dark (Jb 18:6).

חֹשֶׁךְ chōshekh (2932), Darkness (Gn 1:2, Jb 12:22, Am 5:18).

חֲשֵׁכָה chăshēkhāh (2934), Darkness (Ps 82:5 [81:5]).

מַחְשָׁךְ machshākh (4423), Darkness (Is 29:15).

נֶשֶׁף nesheph (5582), Twilight (2 Kgs 7:5, Jb 24:15, Prv 7:9 [7:8]).

עָנָן 'ānān (6281), Clouds (Ex 14:20, Dt 5:22).

עֲרָפֶל 'ărāphel (6441), Darkness (Jer 13:16).

קַדְרוּת qadhrûth (7225), Blackness (Is 50:3).

1. σκότος skotos nom/acc sing masc/neu
2. σκότῳ skotō dat sing masc
3. σκότους skotous gen sing neu
4. σκότει skotei dat sing neu

4 The people which sat in **darkness** saw great light; ... Matt 4:16
1 If therefore the light that is in thee be **darkness**, ... 6:23
1 the light ... be darkness, how great is that **darkness**! 6:23
1 shall be cast out into outer **darkness**: 8:12
1 and cast him into outer **darkness**; 22:13
1 cast ye ... unprofitable servant into outer **darkness**: 25:30
1 Now from the sixth hour there was **darkness** 27:45
1 **darkness** over the whole land until the ninth hour. Mark 15:33
4 To give light to them that sit in **darkness** .... Luke 1:79
1 that the light which is in thee be not **darkness**. 11:35
3 but this is your hour, and the power of **darkness**. 22:53
1 a **darkness** over all the earth until the ninth hour. 23:44
1 and men loved **darkness** rather than light, ... John 3:19
1 The sun shall be turned into **darkness**, ... Acts 2:20
1 there fell on him a mist and a **darkness**; 13:11
3 and to turn them from **darkness** to light, ... 26:18
4 a light of them which are in **darkness**, ... Rom 2:19
3 let us therefore cast off the works of **darkness**, ... 13:12
3 will bring to light the hidden things of **darkness**, ... 1 Co 4:5
3 who commanded the light to shine out of **darkness**, .. 2 Co 4:6
1 and what communion hath light with **darkness**? 6:14
1 For ye were sometimes **darkness**, ... Eph 5:8
3 the unfruitful works of **darkness**, ... 5:11
3 against the rulers of the **darkness** of this world, ... 6:12
3 hath delivered us from the power of **darkness**, ... Col 1:13
4 But ye, brethren, are not in **darkness**, ... 1 Th 5:4
3 we are not of the night, nor of **darkness**. 5:5
2 nor unto blackness, and **darkness**, and tempest, ... Heb 12:18
3 out of **darkness** into his marvellous light: .... 1 Pt 2:9
3 to whom the mist of **darkness** is reserved for ever. ... 2 Pt 2:17
4 and walk in **darkness**, we lie, and do not the truth: .. 1 Jn 1:6
3 is reserved the blackness of **darkness** for ever. .... Jude 1:13

Classical Greek

Skotos (cf. the Hellenistic feminine form *skotia* [4508] which is identical in meaning) denotes the absence of light in the strictest sense. In classical writings darkness typically implied the inability to see and thus the inability to know how to walk. From this, "darkness" implied a sense of anxiety or apprehension of what lay ahead. Therefore, darkness and its "ominous character" became linked to the ultimate anxiety—death (always used this way in Homer's *Iliad*; cf. *Liddell-Scott*). Darkness became synonymous with Hades (the place of the dead) (Hahn, "Darkness," *Colin Brown*, 1:421).

Metaphorically "darkness" denotes "ignorance" or "obscurity," and it has come to describe the human condition or behavior. Later, in Gnostic discussions darkness acquired a more specialized character. Darkness equaled the earthly realm; light, acquired through *gnōsis* (1102), "knowledge," provided the only means of escape from darkness (ibid., 1:422).

Septuagint Usage

Nine Hebrew words as well as other related forms are translated by *skotos* in the Septuagint. The most frequent Hebrew counterpart is a form of *chōshekh*, "darkness." This can be the cosmic darkness before Creation (Genesis 1:2,4,5; cf. Isaiah 45:7) which became separated from the light to give us the night and day (Genesis 1:18; cf. Job 37:15). The plague of darkness covered Egypt, but the Israelites had light within their dwellings (Exodus 10:21f.; cf. 14:20). But "deep darkness" is also the source of God's voice (Deuteronomy 4:11; 5:22; cf. Psalm 18:11 [LXX 17:11]). Typically speaking, however, light is better than darkness (Ecclesiastes 2:13).

"Darkness" symbolizes the distress and affliction (i.e., judgment) Israel (and the nations) incurred because of disobedience (Deuteronomy 28:29ff.; of the Day of the Lord, Joel 2:2; Amos 5:18,20; cf. Zephaniah 1:15). Disobedience separates one from the light of God (Psalms 105:28 [LXX 104:28]; 107:10-14 [106:10-14]).

Darkness thus can denote a spiritual condition closely akin to "blindness" (*tuphlos* [5026]; e.g., Isaiah 59:9ff.; Jeremiah 13:16). In both cases, when one cannot see, one risks the chance of falling. "Darkness" is furthermore connected to death (Lamentations 3:6, the verb *skoteō*; Epistle of Jeremiah 71). Nevertheless, darkness and its threats are overcome by God's light (Psalm 18:28 [LXX 17:28]; cf. Psalm 23 [22]; Isaiah 5:20; 29:15; Lamentations 3:1ff.).

New Testament Usage

In the New Testament *skotos* is used over 30 times to figuratively depict an unalterable reality. Evil is real and has power, and "darkness" is often used to depict this (Luke 22:53). All men are being influenced by the principalities, the rulers of "darkness" (Ephesians 6:12). The effects of darkness on men take different forms. In Romans 2:19 *skotos* is used of intellectual "darkness," but usually it refers to moral or spiritual "darkness" (Luke 1:79; 11:35; John 3:19; Acts 26:18; 2 Corinthians 6:14; Colossians 1:13; 1 Thessalonians 5:4,5; 1 Peter 2:9; and 1 John 1:6). In Matthew 6:22ff. Jesus taught that the "sound (*haplous* [568]) eye" permits light's entrance (*phōteinos* [5296]), but the "evil eye" (*ponēros* [4050]) makes the whole body "darkness." Here, the contrast is intentionally shown between "darkness" as evil and "sound" as light (good). In Ephesians 5:8 Paul spoke of those who were in "darkness" before but now are "light."

"Darkness" is the domain of death (Matthew 22:13; 25:30; cf. Luke 1:79) that rules the world. Closely connected to the death of Jesus, darkness—in apparently symbolic action of victory—covers the earth (Matthew 27:45; Mark 15:33; Luke 23:44). But with the light of the first Easter morning's sun, the reign of darkness (Luke 22:53) was broken through the power of the Resurrection.

Darkness ruled until Jesus, but as Isaiah prophesied, "The people living in *darkness* have seen a great light" (Matthew 4:16, NIV; Isaiah 9:2). John particularly developed the theme that the realm of Jesus is the light, but the world and its ways are darkness (*skotia*, e.g., John 1:5; 8:12; 12:35). The gospel summons men and women (especially used of Gentiles in the Biblical texts) to turn from darkness and Satan's power to the light (Acts 26:18; cf. Ephesians 5:8; 6:12; Colossians 1:13; 1 Peter 2:9). Those in the light have nothing in common with those living in darkness (2 Corinthians 6:14; Ephesians 5:11; 1 Thessalonians 5:4). Ultimately, darkness will be the punishment of the wicked, that is, separation from God (2 Peter 2:17; Jude 13), and in that place of punishment there will be "weeping and gnashing of teeth" (Matthew 8:12). But those whose names are written in the Book of Life will live where there is no "night" (Revelation 21:25; 22:5). There the influences and effects of "darkness" are forever conquered by the Lamb who is the "light" of the city (Revelation 21:23), and His glory will shine over His redeemed (Revelation 22:5).

STRONG 4655, BAUER 757-58, MOULTON-MILLIGAN 579, KITTEL 7:423-45, LIDDELL-SCOTT 1615, COLIN BROWN 1:420-21,423,425.

4511. σκοτόω skotoō verb

To darken.

COGNATES:

σκοτεινός skoteinos (4507)
σκοτία skotia (4508)
σκοτίζομαι skotizomai (4509)
σκότος skotos (4510)

חָשַׁךְ chāshakh (2931), Become dark (Jb 3:9).

מַחְשָׁךְ machshākh (4423), Dark place (Ps 74:20 [73:20]—Sixtine Edition and some Vaticanus texts only).

רָמָתִי rāmāthî (7722), Be wounded, be in mourning (Jer 8:21, 14:2).

שָׁחַר shāchar (8264), Be black (Jb 30:30).

1. ἐσκοτωμένη eskotōmenē nom sing fem part perf mid
2. ἐσκοτώθη eskotōthē 3sing indic aor pass
3. ἐσκοτωμένοι eskotōmenoi nom pl masc part perf mid

3 being darkened in their understanding, (NASB) ...... Eph 4:18
2 were darkened by the smoke of the pit. (NASB) ..... Rev 9:2
1 of the beast; and his kingdom was full of darkness; 16:10

Classical Greek and Septuagint Usage

This word can be found in classical Greek from the Fifth Century B.C. meaning "darken, blind, stupefy" (*Liddell-Scott*). However in the Septuagint and New Testament it can only be found in the passive voice, "to be darkened." In Job 3:9 it is used of the stars becoming literally dark. Jeremiah used it in reference to physical injury evidenced by a "darkening" of the skin (Jeremiah 8:21).

New Testament Usage

In the New Testament, Ephesians 4:17,18 (NIV) notes that "Gentiles" (those outside of God's covenant) are characterized by "the futility (uselessness, lack of direction, ineffectiveness) of their thinking," because they "are darkened (God's action on them) due to the hardening of their hearts" (their own action). This results in: (1) "ignorance" and losing "all sensitivity"; (2) becoming addicted to "sensuality" and "every kind of impurity" (verse 19, NIV); and (3) being destined for death ("alienated from the life of God" [KJV]).

Ultimately, the "sun and the air" will be "darkened by reason of the smoke of the pit" (Revelation 9:2). As judgment for deceiving the earth, the kingdom of the beast will become "full of darkness" because of the vial that the fifth angel will pour upon his throne (Revelation 16:10).

Strong 4656, Bauer 758, Moulton-Milligan 579, Kittel 7:423-45, Liddell-Scott 1616, Colin Brown 1:421,423.

4512. σκύβαλον skubalon noun

Table scraps, trash, garbage, sewage, manure, excrement.

Synonyms:

περικάθαρμα perikatharma (3890)
περίψημα peripsēma (3927)
ῥύπος rhupos (4366)

1. σκύβαλα skubala nom/acc pl neu

1 do count them but dung, that I may win Christ,..... Phlp 3:8

Classical Greek

The Greek world used *skubalon* essentially as "something to be thrown out or disposed of," such as food leftovers to the dogs, or sweepings, sewage, muck, or dung. Hence, it connoted something disgusting, filthy, abhorrent, that which was to be rejected or thrown out. It can also refer to "pitiful or horrible remains" as a rotting corpse partly eaten by fish (Lang, "skubalon," *Kittel*, 7:445). In Gnostic thought, the human body is *skubalon* in contrast to the soul—a view not shared by the Bible.

New Testament Usage

This word is not found in the Septuagint and occurs only once in the New Testament. In Philippians 3:8 Paul listed all his achievements: his Hebrew birth and his keeping the Law according to the highest standards of the day (i.e., as a Pharisee). But all this was a prideful "righteousness" highly regarded only by humans and not by God. As Paul came to see it all from God's point of view, this righteousness was as *skubalon* and was to be replaced by "the righteousness which is of God by faith" (verse 9).

Strong 4657, Bauer 758, Moulton-Milligan 579-80, Kittel 7:445-47, Liddell-Scott 1616, Colin Brown 1:480.

4513. Σκύθης Skuthēs name

Scythian.

1. Σκύθης Skuthēs nom sing masc

1 Barbarian, Scythian, bond nor free:................. Col 3:11

The Scythians were a nomadic Indo-European people who originated in what is now southern Russia (Central Asia). They moved into the ancient Near East by crossing the Caucasus Mountains in the Eighth Century B.C. where they were initially resisted by the Assyrians but later were enlisted by them against the Medes. The Scythians led a major military "raid" into Palestine about 630 B.C.; their advance was only stopped when Pharaoh Psammetichus "paid them off." This military incursion may have been the "foe from the north" mentioned in Jeremiah and Zephaniah, though there is some question as to whether it was severe enough to coincide with the descriptions by these prophets (cf. Millard, "Scythians," *International Standard Bible Encyclopedia*, 4:365). The Scythians are referred to by the name *Ashkenaz* in the Old Testament (e.g., in Jeremiah 51:27). When the Assyrian empire began to collapse under the pressure from the Medes and the Babylonians, the Scythians withdrew across the Caucasus and established settlements along the northern shore of the Black Sea.

Although the Scythians left no written records, a good deal is known about them from archaeological discoveries and references to them in ancient literature (more than half of Book IV of Herodotus' *History* is devoted to them). They were accomplished artisans and equestrians, but they were most noted in antiquity for the savagery of their military exploits. According to Greek legend, this people received their name from Scythes, the son of the hero Hercules and Echidna, who became their leader (Herodotus *History* 4.8-10). The Scythians were noted by the Greeks for "their crudity, excess and ferocity" (Michel, "skuthēs," *Kittel* 7:448). The Greeks even coined the verb *skuthizein* to refer to their military practice of scalping enemies killed in battle as well as to their excessive drinking. The Scythians were the "barbarian(s) or savage(s) 'par excellence' " (*Bauer*) in the Hellenistic world.

The Scythians are mentioned only once in the New Testament. In Colossians 3:11 when Paul endeavored to show the all-inclusiveness and unity of the community "in Christ," he wrote, "There is neither Greek nor Jew, circumcision nor uncircumcision, Barbarian, Scythian, bond *nor* free." The fact that three of these couplets involve antithetical pairs (Greek/Jew, circumcision/uncircumcision, slave/free person) has led some to propose that some distinction is being made between "barbarian" and "Scythian" (see Windisch, "barbaros," *Kittel*, 1:552f. for possibilities). However, most scholars now agree that both these terms stand as another contrast to "Greek"; "Greeks" being civilized Gentiles, the elite, and "barbarians and Scythians" being the most uncivilized of Gentiles (cf. ibid.; Lohse, *Hermenia, Colossians and Philemon*, p.144). "The obvious meaning is that even the offence which a Scythian must give to natural sensitivity is overcome by the baptism of the Messiah Jesus" (Michel, "skuthēs," *Kittel*, 7:450).

STRONG 4658, BAUER 758, MOULTON-MILLIGAN 580, KITTEL 7:447-50, LIDDELL-SCOTT 1616.

4514. σκυθρωπός skuthrōpos adj

A sad, depressed, or sullen appearance.

רַע raʿ (7737II) Sad (Gn 40:7).

1. σκυθρωποί skuthrōpoi nom pl masc

1 be not, as the hypocrites, of a sad countenance:...... Matt 6:16
1 ye have one to another, as ye walk, and are sad? .. Luke 24:17

The adjective *skuthrōpos* is formed by *skuthros*, "serious, sad," and *ōps*, "eye, face," and appears twice in the New Testament. In Matthew 6:16 Jesus described the Pharisees as putting on "a gloomy face" (NASB) to broadcast their fasting. In Luke 24:17 Jesus described the two disciples on the way to Emmaus as "sad" or "depressed" because they believed in the hopelessness of Jesus' crucifixion rather than believing in "all that the prophets have spoken" (verse 25).

STRONG 4659, BAUER 758, MOULTON-MILLIGAN 580, KITTEL 7:450-51, LIDDELL-SCOTT 1616.

4515. σκύλλω skullō verb

Wear out, exhaust or harass (someone); passive: to be troubled, agitated.

SYNONYMS:
θορυβέω thorubeō (2327)
τυρβάζω turbazō (5023)

1. σκύλλεις skulleis 2sing indic pres act
2. σκύλλε skulle 2sing impr pres act
3. σκύλλου skullou 2sing impr pres mid
4. ἐσκυλμένοι eskulmenoi nom pl masc part perf mid

4 because they were distressed and downcast (NASB) .. Matt 9:36
1 why troublest thou the Master any further? .... Mark 5:35
3 Lord, trouble not thyself: for I am not worthy ...... Luke 7:6
2 Thy daughter is dead; trouble not the Master. 8:49

Classical Greek

In classical literature, e.g., Aeschylus, *skullō* could mean "to flay, skin," or "to tear" or "mangle." Metaphorically it came to mean "to trouble" or "annoy," while in the passive voice it could mean "trouble oneself" or "be distressed" (see *Liddell-Scott*). While *skullō* does not appear in the Septuagint, certainly the concept of "troubling" someone (1 Kings 18:17 [LXX 3 Kings 18:17]) or being "troubled" in one's mind (1 Samuel 1:15 [LXX 1 Kings 1:15]; Psalm 6:3) occurs often.

New Testament Usage

In the New Testament *skullō* appears three times. In Mark 5:35 and the parallel passage in Luke 8:49 *skullō* illustrates the lack of faith among the household of a Jewish religious leader; they did not believe that Jesus could raise a young girl from the dead. The ruler said, "Do not trouble (bother, harass) the Teacher any more" (RSV). The false implication is that death is beyond the power of Jesus. In Luke 7:6,7 an opposite attitude is displayed: a pagan soldier did not want to "trouble" Jesus to travel for the healing of his servant. All he wanted was for Jesus to "say the word" (NIV). Jesus' response was that "even in Israel," including the religious leaders present, Jesus had "not found such great faith" (verse 9, NIV).

STRONG 4660, BAUER 758, MOULTON-MILLIGAN 580, LIDDELL-SCOTT 1617.

4516. σκῦλον skulon noun

Spoils, loot, booty.

בַּז baz (993), Baz, spoils (Is 8:1).

בִּזָּה bizzāh (996), Plunder, spoils of war (2 Chr 14:14, 25:13, Ez 29:19).

מַלְקוֹחַ malqôach (4596), Spoils, plunder (Nm 31:11f.,26f., Is 49:24f.).

שָׁלָל shālāl (8395), Spoils, plunder (Dt 3:7, 1 Sm 30:19f., Zec 14:1).

1. σκῦλα skula nom/acc pl neu

1 armour wherein he trusted, and divideth his spoils. Luke 11:22

Early in classical Greek usage *ta skula* (plural: "looted things") referred to armor and weapons stripped from the slain enemy after a battle. By the time of its single appearance in the New Testament (Luke 11:22) *skulon* was generalized to refer to anything taken from its owner after a violent struggle for it. Hence in the warfare against demonic powers, Satan's "palace" is invaded by "a stronger than he" (in this case, Christ). He takes the "armor wherein he trusted" (completely disarms him) and "divideth his spoils" (the people under Satan's control in demonic possession, and sickness). This concept is paraphrased in Psalm 68 and in Ephesians 4 where the "gifts" (the spoils from the enemy) are now God's "captives" who serve one another by means of spiritual ministries and charismata. "Divideth" implies that other believers share in the benefits of Christ's victory.

Strong 4661, Bauer 758, Moulton-Milligan 580, Liddell-Scott 1617.

4517. σκωληκόβρωτος skōlēkobrōtos adj

Eaten by worms.

1. σκωληκόβρωτος **skōlēkobrōtos** nom sing masc

1 **and he was eaten of worms, and gave up the ghost.** Acts 12:23

In classical Greek this adjective means "worm-eaten" and can be found in reference to both trees and men that have been eaten by worms. It is not used in the Septuagint but does occur once in the New Testament at Acts 12:23. There it refers to the death of Herod who was killed by an angel for failing to give God glory for divine provision. Herod, when dressed in brilliant clothes, accepted his audience's claim that he was a god, that is, ready for a high place in the afterlife. Instead, he was struck down by God and "eaten of worms." This perhaps is an echo of Jesus' description of Gehenna in Mark 9:44.

Strong 4662, Bauer 758, Moulton-Milligan 580, Kittel 7:456-57, Liddell-Scott 1618.

4518. σκώληξ skōlēx noun

Worm, maggot.

רִמָּה rimmāh (7704), Maggot, worm (Ex 16:24, Jb 7:5).

תּוֹלֵעָה tôlēʿāh (8770), Maggot, worm (Ex 16:20, Jb 25:6, Is 14:11).

תּוֹלַעַת tôlaʿath (8772), Worm (Dt 28:39, Ps 22:6 [21:6], Jon 4:7).

1. σκώληξ **skōlēx** nom sing masc

1 **Where their worm dieth not,** .... Mark 9:44
1 **Where their worm dieth not,** 9:46
1 **Where their worm dieth not,** 9:48

Classical Greek and Septuagint Usage

In classical Greek this noun is used as the general word for "worm," especially the "earthworm," but can also denote "grubs" or "larvae" (cf. *Liddell-Scott*). In Old Testament times a worm was regarded as the most loathsome and disgusting creature, and this is reflected in the Septuagint as well: "I am a worm, and no man; a reproach of men, and despised of the people" (Psalm 22:6 [LXX 21:6]). The idea is developed in Isaiah 66:24 where transgressors against God are eternally eaten by gnawing worms and fire. These will be an abhorrence to everyone.

New Testament Usage

Jesus picked up this verse in describing Gehenna (Jerusalem's garbage dump where bodies of indigents, criminals, and animals were sometimes thrown, and by extension, "hell"). This quotation appears three times in parallel passages (Mark 9:44,46,48; though some ancient manuscripts lack verses 44 and 46). In these bodies, and other garbage, the smoky fires burned continuously, and the maggots were never without food. Jesus was saying, however, that unlike the corpses, those in hell who are burned with unquenchable fire and eaten by eternal worms are eternally conscious of their condition.

Strong 4663, Bauer 758, Moulton-Milligan 580, Kittel 7:452-56, Liddell-Scott 1618.

4519. σμαράγδινος smaragdinos adj

Of emerald, made of emerald, emerald-green.

1. σμαραγδίνῳ **smaragdinō** dat sing masc
2. σμαραγδίνων **smaragdinōn** gen pl masc

1 **in sight like unto an emerald.** .... Rev 4:3

This adjective is related to the noun *smaragdos* (4520), a precious stone usually rendered "emerald." It occurs in the New Testament only in Revelation 4:3. There the rainbow (or halo) that John saw encircling God's throne was in appearance "like unto an emerald." Probably, the characteristic color of this bow was green, although Flinders Petrie argued that the *smaragdos* was "rock crystal" (Hastings, *Dictionary of the Bible*, p.466). If so, there might have been a true rainbow of color as thrown by a hexagonal prism of crystal.

This rainbow has been variously regarded as a symbol of life, hope, mercy, or covenant: "hope based on the faithfulness of a covenant-making God" (Summers, *Worthy Is the Lamb*, p.131).

Strong 4664, Bauer 758, Moulton-Milligan 580, Liddell-Scott 1619.

4520. σμάραγδος smaragdos noun

Emerald.

בַּהַט bahaṭ (960), Porphyry (Est 1:6—Codex Alexandrinus only).

בָּרֶקֶת bāreqeth (1330II) Emerald (Ex 28:17, 39:10 [36;17]).

יַהֲלֹם yahălōm (3198II) Diamond? emerald? (Ez 28:13).

שֹׁהַם shōham (8172), Onyx (Ex 35:27, 39:6 [36:13]).

1. σμάραγδος smaragdos nom sing masc

1 the third, a chalcedony; the fourth, an emerald; ..... Rev 21:19

This noun appears once in the New Testament (Revelation 21:19) as the fourth of 12 different kinds of jewels that adorned the foundations of the wall of the New Jerusalem. Most versions render it "emerald," a transparent, brilliant green, precious stone. Charles shows that a wide range of green gemstones might be included under the name *smaragdos* (*International Critical Commentary, Revelation,* 1:115). (See the discussion of the adjective *smaragdinos* [4519].)

The Septuagint used this word for the third jewel in the first row of the high priest's breastplate (Exodus 28:17, translating the Hebrew *bāreqeth*). The KJV translates it as "carbuncle" (cf. NIV, "beryl"; NASB, "emerald"). Some suggest an intentional comparison: "What the old covenant confined to the high priest is now a privilege extended to the whole people of God (cf. ver. 22)" (Moffatt, *Expositor's Greek Testament, Revelation,* 5:484).

Strong 4665, Bauer 758, Moulton-Milligan 580-81, Liddell-Scott 1619, Colin Brown 3:396-97.

4521. σμύρνα smurna noun

Myrrh.

Cross-Reference:

μύρον muron (3326)

מֹר mōr (4915), Myrrh (Ex 30:23, S/S 4:6, 5:1).

1. σμύρνης smurnēs gen sing fem

2. σμύρναν smurnan acc sing fem

2 gold, and frankincense, and myrrh. .... Matt 2:11
1 and brought a mixture of myrrh and aloes, ... John 19:39

This noun occurs twice in the New Testament and denotes "myrrh." Myrrh is a valuable tree extract of bitter gum that yields a costly perfume. The variety of uses is illustrated in the Bible: an ingredient in the holy anointing oil (Exodus 30:23); perfume (Psalm 45:8 [LXX 44:8]; Song of Solomon 3:6); in women's purification/ beautification rites (Esther 2:12); and in "embalming" (John 19:39).

Because of its great value, myrrh was a suitable gift for the Eastern magi to present to the infant Jesus, along with gold and frankincense (Matthew 2:11). Traditionally this gift has been regarded as foreshadowing the death of Jesus. Myrrh was one of the substances used at His burial (John 19:39). The myrrh and aloes (cf. Psalm 45:8) were "laid in pulverized form between the clothes in which the body of Jesus was wrapped" (Michaelis, "smurna," *Kittel,* 7:458). The purpose was to protect against rapid decomposition. In doing this, the followers of Jesus revealed that they did not expect Him to rise again (Brown, "Incense," *Colin Brown,* 2:295).

Smurna (Smyrna [see 4522]) was also the name of a city (now Izmir) in the province of Asia. It was one of the seven churches addressed in the Revelation (1:11; 2:8).

Strong 4666, Bauer 758, Moulton-Milligan 581, Kittel 7:457-58, Liddell-Scott 1620, Colin Brown 2:294-95.

4522. Σμύρνα Smurna name

Smyrna.

1. Σμύρναν Smurnan acc fem

2. Σμύρνῃ Smurnē dat fem

1 and unto Smyrna, and unto Pergamos, ... Rev 1:11
2 to the angel of the church in Smyrna (NASB) 2:8

A wealthy trading and port city on the west coast of Asia Minor, now the city of Izmir. The church there received one of the seven letters in Revelation (1:11; 2:8-11); it is one of the only two which received unqualified praise. The church was of major importance in the Second Century A.D.

4523. Σμυρναῖος Smurnaios name

Smyrnaean.

1. Σμυρναίων Smurnaiōn gen pl masc

1 And unto the angel of the church in Smyrna write; .. Rev 2:8

An adjective used as a noun at Revelation 2:8 in reference "to the church in Smyrna."

4524. σμυρνίζω smurnizō verb

To mix or flavor with myrrh.

1. ἐσμυρνισμένον esmurnismenon
acc sing masc part perf mid

1 they gave him to drink wine **mingled with myrrh:**.. Mark 15:23

The verb is related to the noun *smurna* (4521), "myrrh." It is used in the New Testament only once, in Mark 15:23. There, some at the Crucifixion (the soldiers, apparently) offered Jesus "wine mingled with myrrh." He refused the drink.

Michaelis ("smurnizō," *Kittel*, 7:458) indicates that the spicing of wine with myrrh is known from other ancient sources. The result was "a spiced wine which was a special fancy," one regarded by the Romans as not very intoxicating (ibid., note 2). This raises the question whether its purpose was to dull one's senses and if Jesus refused it for that reason—a common view. "Jesus was resolved to taste death at its bitterest and to go to God with open eyes" (Barclay, *Daily Study Bible, Mark*, p.362). One should compare Matthew 27:34 where the wine is described as mixed with "gall" (*cholē* [5357]).

STRONG 4669, BAUER 759, KITTEL 7:458-59, LIDDELL-SCOTT 1620, COLIN BROWN 2:295.

4525. Σόδομα Sodoma name

Sodom.

1. **Σόδομα Sodoma** nom/acc pl neu
2. **Σοδόμων Sodomōn** gen pl neu
3. **Σοδόμοις Sodomois** dat pl neu

2 It shall be more tolerable for the land **of Sodom**... Matt 10:15
3 if the mighty works, ... had been done in **Sodom**,...... 11:23
2 it shall be more tolerable for the land **of Sodom**....... 11:24
3 shall be more tolerable **for Sodom** and Gomorrha...Mark 6:11
3 it shall be more tolerable in that day **for Sodom**,...Luke 10:12
2 But the same day that Lot went out of **Sodom**........ 17:29
1 we had been as **Sodoma**, ... like unto Gomorrha.....Rom 9:29
2 And turning ... **Sodom** and Gomorrha into ashes.... 2 Pt 2:6
1 Even as **Sodom** and Gomorrha, and the cities.......Jude 1:7
1 city, which spiritually is called **Sodom** and Egypt,... Rev 11:8

Sodom was the most prominent of the five ancient Canaanite "cities of the plain" (RSV and others read "valley" for Hebrew *kikār*, literally "a round district") that were destroyed by God "because their sin (was) very grievous" (Genesis 18:20). Some disagreement now exists as to the location of these cities. The earlier consensus was that the cities had been located in the area which now is submerged under the waters of the Dead Sea south of the Lisan (the "tongue-shaped" peninsula extending into the Dead Sea from the east). This location was theorized in part because of the shallowness of the southern sections of the sea—approximately 18 feet as compared to 1200 feet for the northern waters (cf. Harland, "Sodom," *Interpreter's Dictionary of the Bible*, 4:396). More recently it has been suggested that the cities were located on the Lisan itself as well as the eastern shore of the Dead Sea (Dearman, "Sodom," *Harper's Bible Dictionary*, p.974).

The extent of the wickedness of these cities along with the magnitude of the divine judgment against them gave proverbial status to the cities of Sodom and Gomorrah as symbolic of extreme sinfulness and the certainty of God's punishment (Luke 17:29; 2 Peter 2:6; Jude 7). Even so, those cities that rejected Jesus' emissaries (Matthew 10:15; Luke 10:12) or failed to repent after seeing the manifestation of the kingdom of God (Matthew 11:20-24) would find the "day of judgment" less "tolerable" than it was for Sodom. The symbolic use of "Sodom" in Revelation 11:8 is a reference to Jerusalem ("spiritually [allegorically; RSV] . . . called Sodom and Egypt") and should be understood in the same manner. In Romans 9:29 (citing Isaiah 1:9) Sodom and Gomorrah symbolize the fiery judgment of those who come under the wrath of God.

STRONG 4670, BAUER 759, MOULTON-MILLIGAN 581.

4526. Σολομών Solomōn name

Solomon.

1. **Σολομών Solomōn** nom masc
2. **Σολομῶντος Solomōntos** gen masc
3. **Σολομῶντα Solomōnta** acc masc
4. **Σολομῶνος Solomōnos** gen masc
5. **Σολομῶνα Solomōna** acc masc

3 and David the king begat **Solomon**................Matt 1:6
1 And **Solomon** begat Roboam;......................... 1:7
1 That even **Solomon** in all his glory..................... 6:29
2 for she came ... to hear the wisdom **of Solomon**;....... 12:42
2 and, behold, a greater than **Solomon** is here........... 12:42
2 she came ... to hear the wisdom **of Solomon**;.......Luke 11:31
2 and, behold, a greater **than Solomon** is here........... 11:31
1 that **Solomon** in all his glory was not arrayed like..... 12:27
2 Jesus walked in the temple in **Solomon's** porch.....John 10:23
2 unto them in the porch that is called **Solomon's**,.....Acts 3:11
2 they were all with one accord in **Solomon's** porch....... 5:12
1 But **Solomon** built him an house....................... 7:47

A son of David and his successor as king of Israel. He is listed in the genealogy of Jesus (Matthew 1:6f.). Jesus spoke of his legendary fine clothing (Matthew 6:29; Luke 12:27) and wisdom (Matthew 12:42; Luke 11:31), but only to contrast them respectively with God's provision for the wild lilies and with the wisdom He had brought. Stephen remembered him as chosen to build the temple (Acts 7:47). A colonnade in Herod's temple was named for him (John 10:23; Acts 3:11; 5:12).

4527. σορός soros noun

Funeral couch, bier, coffin.

אֲרוֹן 'ărôn (751), Coffin (Gn 50:26).

1. σοροῦ sorou gen sing fem

1 And he came and touched the bier: .... Luke 7:14

This noun appears in the New Testament only in Luke 7:14. There it refers to the "bier" (KJV; "coffin," NIV, NASB) upon which lay the dead son of the widow of Nain. Jesus touched the *soros* and restored the young man to life.

Originally *soros* was an urn or receptacle for keeping the bones of the dead (see Genesis 50:26). By New Testament times it included (as here) a coffin or according to Vine "the funeral-couch or bier on which the Jews bore their dead to burial" (*Expository Dictionary*, "Bier"). The one in Luke 7:14 may have been an open "coffin" (perhaps of wicker) or stretcherlike wooden slab (cf. *Zondervan Pictorial Encyclopedia*, 1:610). For details about the incident and customs involved, see Edersheim, *Life and Times of Jesus the Messiah*, 1:552-558.

Strong 4673, Bauer 759, Moulton-Milligan 581, Liddell-Scott 1621.

4528. σός sos adj

Your (thy).

1. σῷ sō dat 2sing masc/neu
2. σός sos nom 2sing masc
3. σοί soi nom 2pl masc
4. σούς sous acc 2pl masc
5. σῆς sēs gen 2sing fem
6. σῇ sē dat 2sing fem
7. σήν sēn acc 2sing fem
8. σόν son nom/acc 2sing neu
9. σά sa nom/acc 2pl neu

1 considerest not the beam that is in **thine** own eye? .. Matt 7:3
1 have we not prophesied in **thy** name? 7:22
1 and in **thy** name have cast out devils? 7:22
1 and in **thy** name done many wonderful works? 7:22
1 didst not thou sow good seed in **thy** field? 13:27
8 Take that **thine** is, and go thy way: 20:14
5 and what shall be the sign of **thy** coming, ... 24:3
8 afraid, ... lo, there thou hast that is **thine**. 25:25
3 the Pharisees fast, but **thy** disciples fast not? .... Mark 2:18
4 Go home to **thy** friends, and tell them how great 5:19
3 disciples of the Pharisees; but **thine** eat and drink? .. Luke 5:33
9 that taketh away **thy goods** ask them not again...... Luke 6:30
9 thou art ever with me, and all that I have is **thine**..... 15:31
8 nevertheless not my will, but **thine**, be done........... 22:42
7 Now we believe, not because of **thy** saying: .... John 4:42
9 And all mine are **thine**, and thine are mine; 17:10
9 And all mine are thine, and **thine** are mine; 17:10
2 Sanctify them through thy truth: **thy** word is truth...... 17:17
8 **Thine** own nation and the chief priests 18:35
6 after it was sold, was it not in **thine own** power? ..... Acts 5:4
5 deeds are done unto this nation by **thy** providence, ... 24:2
6 wouldest hear us of **thy** clemency a few words......... 24:4
6 through **thy** knowledge ... the weak brother perish, .. 1 Co 8:11
6 the unlearned say Amen at **thy** giving of thanks, ... 14:16
5 But without **thy** mind would I do nothing; .... Phlm 1:14

Sos is equivalent to the English second person singular possessive pronoun *your* (KJV, "thy"). In Greek form and syntax it is strictly an adjective. It is used only about two dozen times in the New Testament, since the possessive is much more commonly expressed by the genitive of the personal pronoun. Therefore, when it is used it tends to call more attention to the possessor thus identified, often in contrast. Robertson (*Grammar of the Greek New Testament*, p.684) observes that when the possessive adjectives are used for emphasis.

The following examples demonstrate this emphasis: Matthew 7:3, "the beam that is in *thine own* eye"; 7:22, "in *thy* name"; Mark 2:18, "*thy* disciples"; Luke 6:30, "*thy* goods"; 15:31, "all that I have is *thine*"; 22:42, "not my will, but *thine*, be done."

Strong 4674, Bauer 759, Moulton-Milligan 581, Liddell-Scott 1621.

4529. σουδάριον soudarion noun

Handkerchief, sweatcloth, facecloth.

1. σουδαρίῳ soudariō dat sing neu
2. σουδάριον soudarion nom/acc sing neu
3. σουδάρια soudaria nom/acc pl neu

1 thy pound, which I have kept laid up in a **napkin**: ..Luke 19:20
1 and his face was bound about **with a napkin**........John 11:44
2 And the **napkin**, that was about his head, ... 20:7
3 brought unto the sick **handkerchiefs** or aprons, ... Acts 19:12

This noun is a Latin loanword (*sudarium*, from *sudor*, "sweat") denoting small cloths used by the Romans for wiping the hands and face (*Illustrated Bible Dictionary*, "Handkerchief," 2:608).

The word appears four times in the New Testament. In the Parable of the Pounds, one servant kept his pound in a "napkin" (Luke 19:20, KJV; NASB, "handkerchief"; NIV, "piece of cloth"). In Acts 19:12 the sweatcloths ("handkerchiefs," KJV, NIV, NASB) Paul apparently tied around his head while making tents were taken to heal the sick (Bruce, *New International*

Commentary on the New Testament, Acts, p.384). In John 11:44 and 20:7 such "cloths" were used, according to Jewish custom, to cover the faces of the corpses of Lazarus and Jesus.

Strong 4676, Bauer 759, Moulton-Milligan 581, Liddell-Scott 1621.

4530. Σουσάννα Sousanna name

Susanna.

1. Σουσάννα Sousanna nom fem

1 the wife of Chuza Herod's steward, and **Susanna,**... Luke 8:3

One of several women who were healed by Jesus. They accompanied Him and the Twelve on their travels and helped meet the group's expenses (Luke 8:3).

4531. σοφία sophia noun

Skill, wisdom.

Cognates:
- ἄσοφος asophos (775)
- κατασοφίζομαι katasophizomai (2656)
- σοφίζω sophizō (4532)
- σοφός sophos (4533)
- φιλοσοφία philosophia (5221)
- φιλόσοφος philosophos (5222)

בִּינָה bînāh (1035), Insight, understanding (Prv 2:3, 3:5).

דַּעַת da'ath (1907), Knowledge (Prv 1:7).

חָכְמָה chokhmāh (2551), Skill, wisdom (Ex 36:1, Jb 12:13, Jer 10:12).

חָכְמָה chokhmāh (A2552), Wisdom (Dn 2:20f.,23,30—Aramaic).

מוּסָד mûşādh (4280), Instruction (Prv 8:33—Codex Alexandrinus only).

מַחֲשֶׁבֶת machăsheveth (4422II) Something inventive or artistic (Ex 35:33).

שֵׂכֶל sēkhel (7961I), Discretion (1 Chr 22:12).

תְּבוּנָה t^evûnāh (8722), Understanding (Prv 18:2).

1. σοφία sophia nom sing fem
2. σοφίας sophias gen sing fem
3. σοφίᾳ sophia dat sing fem
4. σοφίαν sophian acc sing fem

1 But **wisdom** is justified of her children............ Matt 11:19
4 for she came ... to hear the **wisdom** of Solomon;........ 12:42
1 Whence hath this man this **wisdom,**................. 13:54
1 and what **wisdom** is this which is given unto him,... Mark 6:2
2 and waxed strong in spirit, filled **with wisdom:**...... Luke 2:40
3 And Jesus increased in **wisdom** and stature,........... 2:52
1 But **wisdom** is justified of all her children.............. 7:35
4 she came ... to hear the **wisdom** of Solomon;.......... 11:31
1 Therefore also said the **wisdom** of God,.............. 11:49
4 For I will give you a mouth and **wisdom,**............. 21:15
2 seven men ... full of the Holy Ghost and **wisdom,**....Acts 6:3
3 resist the **wisdom** and the spirit by which he spake...... 6:10
4 and gave him favour and **wisdom**.................. Acts 7:10
3 And Moses was learned in all the **wisdom**............. 7:22
2 riches both of the **wisdom** and knowledge of God! Rom 11:33
3 to preach the gospel: not with **wisdom** of words,.... 1 Co 1:17
4 I will destroy the **wisdom** of the wise,................. 1:19
4 not God made foolish the **wisdom** of this world?........ 1:20
3 For after that in the **wisdom** of God.................. 1:21
2 the world by **wisdom** knew not God,.................. 1:21
4 and the Greeks seek after **wisdom:**.................... 1:22
4 Christ the power of God, and the **wisdom** of God....... 1:24
1 who of God is made unto us **wisdom,**................. 1:30
2 came not with excellency of speech or of **wisdom,**....... 2:1
2 not with enticing words of man's **wisdom,**............. 2:4
3 your faith should not stand in the **wisdom** of men,...... 2:5
4 we speak **wisdom** among them that are perfect:......... 2:6
4 yet not the **wisdom** of this world,..................... 2:6
4 But we speak the **wisdom** of God in a mystery,......... 2:7
2 not in the words which man's **wisdom** teacheth,......... 2:13
1 the **wisdom** of this world is foolishness with God........ 3:19
2 to one is given by the Spirit the word **of wisdom;**...... 12:8
3 not with fleshly **wisdom,** but by the grace of God,... 2 Co 1:12
3 abounded toward us in all **wisdom** and prudence;.... Eph 1:8
2 may give unto you the spirit **of wisdom**................ 1:17
1 known by the church the manifold **wisdom** of God,...... 3:10
3 his will in all **wisdom** and spiritual understanding;.... Col 1:9
3 and teaching every man in all **wisdom;**................ 1:28
2 In whom are hid all the treasures of **wisdom**............ 2:3
2 have indeed a show **of wisdom** in will worship,......... 2:23
3 Let the word ... dwell in you richly in all **wisdom;**...... 3:16
3 Walk in **wisdom** toward them that are without,......... 4:5
2 If any of you lack **wisdom,** let him ask of God,...... Jas 1:5
2 show out ... his works with meekness **of wisdom.**........ 3:13
1 This **wisdom** descendeth not from above,............... 3:15
1 But the **wisdom** that is from above is first pure,........ 3:17
4 also according to the **wisdom** given unto him........ 2 Pt 3:15
4 to receive power, and riches, and **wisdom,**........... Rev 5:12
1 Saying, Amen: Blessing, and glory, and **wisdom,**....... 7:12
1 Here is **wisdom.** Let him that hath understanding...... 13:18
4 And here is the mind which hath **wisdom.**............. 17:9

Classical Greek

In its earliest occurrences *sophia* was used to mean "cleverness" or "skill" in any kind of handicraft, art, or knowledge; later, however, the term was used exclusively in philosophical discussions (cf. *Liddell-Scott*). There it acquired various shades of meaning including "insight, sound judgment, and practical wisdom" regarding matters of common life (ibid.). It could also mean "speculative wisdom" when used of the complexities of life and existence, and theoretical knowledge.

Septuagint Usage

Sophia primarily replaces the Hebrew word *chokhmāh,* although it translates other terms as well. Besides the noun *chokhām,* the adjective *chokhmāh* is often used substantively ("wise man"). The Aramaic *chokhmāh* occurs in the plural in this way in Daniel also. All of these Semitic words for wisdom have different shades of meaning in the Old Testament, but include the common element of practical wisdom or skill.

Like the earliest meaning of *sophia* in Greek, *chokhmāh* may describe "skill" or "expertise" in some practical matter or task. The construction and interior design (artistic) of the tabernacle was carried out by men chosen and equipped by God with knowledge and *skill* for the various tasks (Exodus 31:2-6; 35:30f.; 36:1f.). The garments of Aaron the high priest were made by men having skill in such matters. God gave them "wisdom" to do this (Exodus 28:3). "Skilled" women spun the yarn for the tabernacle curtains (Exodus 35:25f.).

The same circumstances surround the building and adornment of the Temple of Solomon. Solomon had at his disposal people skilled in the necessary crafts (1 Chronicles 28:21). Furthermore, he himself had the wisdom and understanding needed to oversee the building of the temple as well as his palace (2 Chronicles 2:12 [LXX 2:11]). His own skilled craftsmen joined with the skilled workers of King Hiram from Tyre to create artistic metal works of gold, silver, copper, and iron (1 Kings 7:13-46 [LXX 3 Kings 7:13-46]; 2 Chronicles 2:7 [LXX 2:6]).

Outside of Israel, Gentile artisans used their "skill" and knowledge to produce worthless idols (Isaiah 40:20; Jeremiah 10:8,9). The king of Tyre misused the wisdom and understanding given him to increase his wealth (Isaiah 28:4).

The ability to lead groups of men (either small or large) is termed *chokhmāh*, "wisdom." This kind of wisdom was a requirement for any king of the land (2 Chronicles 1:10). Those who administered the kingdom with the authority of the king needed wisdom (Genesis 41:33-40). Those administering justice needed wisdom (1 Kings 3:28; cf. Deuteronomy 1:13). Wisdom is not the exclusive possession of the old or wealthy, however. The poorest of men or even the very young may be endowed with wisdom to lead (Ecclesiastes 4:13). Within the unique structure of a household, parental wisdom is of critical importance (Proverbs 24:3; 31:26 [LXX 31:27]).

Especially in those books commonly known as Wisdom literature (Job, Proverbs, some Psalms [19, 37, 104, 107, 147, 148], Ecclesiastes), *chokhmāh* means "judgment, insight, wisdom." Here "wisdom" concerns wisdom for living; wisdom affords one guidance in the complex situations of life (cf. Ecclesiastes 10:10: "skill will bring success" [NIV]). This involves not only practical issues of life, but wisdom above all guides one in moral and ethical decisions. A wise heart delivers one from the evil ways of sexual immorality (Proverbs 2:10f.; 5:1f.; 7:4f.) and drunkenness (Proverbs 20:1; 23:19-21). Greed makes the wise person a fool (Ecclesiastes 7:7 [LXX 7:8]). The wisdom of the wise is best expressed in discernment of the proper way of life (Proverbs 14:8). The seat of understanding life's nature is the heart, the center of the personality (Proverbs 16:23). The righteous one speaks wisdom (Psalm 37:30 [LXX 36:30]), and anyone desirous of this "wisdom" must be willing to make the necessary sacrifices (Proverbs 23:23).

Here is seen the unique character of wisdom in the Old Testament: Wisdom and piety are inseparable; in fact, they might be considered interchangable at times. The avenue to true wisdom is through a relationship with God. "The fear of the LORD is the beginning of wisdom" (Psalm 111:10 [LXX 110:10]; Proverbs 9:10). "The fear of the LORD is the instruction of wisdom" (Proverbs 15:33 [LXX 16:4]). "Behold, the fear of the Lord, that is wisdom" (Job 28:28). To listen to the teachings of devout wise men strengthens trust in God (Proverbs 22:17-19). An awareness of life's fleeting nature promotes dependence upon God and the desire for more of His wisdom (Psalm 90:12 [LXX 89:12]). The repentant sinner prays for "wisdom in the inmost place" (Psalm 51:6, NIV [LXX 50:6]). To humble oneself before God is in and of itself an act of wisdom (Proverbs 11:2); likewise, accepting God's commands (10:8) and His guidance (13:10) is wise. The wise listen to God's Word through the prophets (Hosea 14:9 [LXX 14:10]). They discern God's mercy or judgment in the lives of individuals and nations (Deuteronomy 32:19-42; Psalm 107 [LXX 106]). But the foolish ignore and reject God's grace, choosing instead to become enslaved to the forces of evil (Deuteronomy 32:5-18).

All wisdom originates with God and is in God. "With him is wisdom and strength, he hath counsel and understanding" (Job 12:13). God is mighty in wisdom (Isaiah 28:29). Those resisting His wisdom will not prosper (Job 9:4; Proverbs 21:30). Even the greatest human wisdom turns into folly in the presence of God's wisdom (Isaiah 19:11f.), and it is destroyed (Isaiah 29:14). By His wisdom God directs all creation toward His divine purpose, as determined by His holy love, both for the individual and the entire world.

The Lord reveals His wisdom in His creation (Psalm 104:24 [LXX 103:24]; Proverbs 3:19f.; Isaiah 40:13f.; Jeremiah 10:12; 51:15 [LXX 28:15]). The laws governing the universe were determined by His wisdom (Job 37:16; 38:36f.), but they do not in any way restrict His power (Job 9:4f.).

God demonstrates His wisdom by guiding persons as well as nations (Job 11:5f.). He sovereignly governs the affairs of nations and their leaders with divine wisdom (Job 12:16-25; Daniel 2:19-22). Through the coming of the Messiah, on whom the Spirit of wisdom and understanding would rest, God would fulfill His salvation promises to Israel and to all of humanity (Isaiah 11:1f.; 33:6).

Wisdom acquires a very unique understanding in Proverbs 8:12-36 where it is personified almost beyond figurative limits as a description of God. Wisdom is personified in this context. It describes God's nature, character, His gifts, as well as His relationship to man's moral, religious, and social life (verses 12-21). Furthermore, wisdom is portrayed as being with God from eternity, before creation; wisdom was the master builder with God in creation. The New Testament texts referring to Christ's preexistence (John 1:1; Colossians 1:15) and His participation in creation (Colossians 1:16,17; Hebrews 1:2) are apparently Biblically connected to this personification of God's wisdom in Proverbs 8. Remarkably, Christian tradition since the time of Justin Martyr (Second Century A.D.) has seen in Proverbs 8 "wisdom" as being an expression of Christ in His preincarnate form.

New Testament Usage

Sophia's usage in the New Testament cannot be understood apart from the background of the Old Testament. *Sophia* occurs 14 times in the Synoptic Gospels and Acts; 5 times in the General Epistles; and 4 times in Revelation. Elsewhere *sophia* appears exclusively in Paul (28 times). No less than 15 instances occur in the first 3 chapters of 1 Corinthians.

The New Testament applies *sophia* exclusively to God and righteous men; rarely, in an ironic fashion, is it applied to others (e.g., the "wisdom" of the world, 1 Corinthians 1:20; fleshly wisdom, 2 Corinthians 1:12). The children of this age are never referred to as "wise" unless it is with explicit or implicit sarcasm (Luke 10:21), although they might boast of wisdom themselves (Romans 1:22). It is in contexts such as these that wisdom should be interpreted from its Hellenistic perspective. No true wisdom can exist apart from godliness. The opposite of *sophos* (4533), "wise," is thus *anoētos* (451), "unwise" (Romans 1:14), a word which may also suggest moral deficiency.

God's saving grace is extended to all men and women having understanding and wisdom (Ephesians 1:8). The gospel is divine wisdom and power, not human "wisdom" (1 Corinthians 1:17 to 3:20). The focus of God's wisdom is Christ crucified, to the Jews a "stumbling block" and to the Greek "foolishness," but to those who are called it is wisdom and power from God. In view of the gospel all human wisdom is foolishness (1 Corinthians 3:18-23). Human wisdom must give place to God's.

The success of apostolic preaching does not depend upon human wisdom for either its form or content (1 Corinthians 2:1-5). The gospel has a wisdom of its own, but it is not of this world. Human faculties cannot grasp or perceive the gospel; only the Spirit can reveal it to the willing heart (1 Corinthians 2:6-12). To share in this wisdom one must give up the wisdom of this world which is folly to God (1 Corinthians 3:18-21). The Holy Scriptures—in both the old and new covenants—make one wise unto salvation (2 Timothy 3:15).

The heralds of the gospel are equipped with divine wisdom for preaching (Colossians 1:28) and for building the church of God (1 Corinthians 3:10). Before their accusers they will be given divine wisdom against which none of their opponents can resist or dispute (Luke 21:12f.). Stephen is a classic example of this gift (Acts 6:10).

The image of God in the New Testament focuses largely upon His wisdom. He is the only wise one (Romans 16:27). His salvation in both scope and plan reveals a supernatural, eternal wisdom for which He will receive worship and honor from the redeemed and the angels in the consummation of the ages (Revelation 7:12). His wisdom is demonstrated in salvation history because Israel and the Gentile nations are united into a single people of God. The Church proclaims His manifold wisdom to the heavenly powers and authorities (Ephesians 3:10).

New Testament Christology also includes the quality of wisdom. As the true man, the Christ child experienced mental, spiritual, and physical development in keeping with His humanity. He grew and increased in wisdom (Luke 2:40-52). The wisdom of Jesus marked all of His teaching and ministry, and it created much astonishment among the people (Matthew 13:54).

The Johannine prologue with its *logos* (3030) terminology is perhaps related to Proverbs 8:12ff.

(see above). Paul also perceived Christ as the expression of personified wisdom as seen in Proverbs (cf. Colossians 1:15ff.). All the treasures of wisdom and knowledge are hidden in Christ (Colossians 2:2,3). He himself is the power and wisdom of God (1 Corinthians 1:24); for the believer He is the wisdom of God (1:30). At the consummation of the ages He, like the Father, will be worshiped: "Worthy is the Lamb . . . to receive power, and riches, and wisdom" (Revelation 5:12).

Strong 4678, Bauer 759-60, Moulton-Milligan 581, Kittel 7:465-526, Liddell-Scott 1621-22, Colin Brown 3:1026-28,1030-32.

4532. σοφίζω sophizō verb

To make wise, instruct.

Cross-Reference:
σοφία sophia (4531)

בִּין bîn (1032), Perceive (1 Sm 3:8).

חָכַם chākham (2549), Qal: be wise (1 Kgs 4:31, Eccl 2:15, 7:23 [7:24]); piel: teach wisdom, make wise (Pss 105:22 [104:22], 119:98 [118:98]); hiphil: make wise (Ps 19:7 [18:7]); hithpael: be wise (Eccl 7:16 [7:17]).

1. σοφίσαι sophisai inf aor act
2. σεσοφισμένοις sesophismenois dat pl masc part perf mid

1 **which are able to make thee wise unto salvation.... 2 Tm 3:15**
2 **For we have not followed cunningly devised fables,.. 2 Pt 1:16**

Classical Greek

This verb is related to *sophos* (4533), "wise," and *sophia* (4531), "wisdom," and is found in classical Greek meaning "make wise, instruct." The Septuagint usage of *sophizō* is best illustrated by two locations in the Psalms: 19:7 and 119:98 (18:8, 118:98 in the Septuagint). Here, it is the law of the Lord that "makes wise" those who learn from it. This wisdom has more than mere intellectual dimensions; it is founded on "the fear of the Lord." (See the word study on *sophia*.)

New Testament Usage

This is the background for 2 Timothy 3:15. There Paul urged Timothy to stay with the Scriptures, which are able to "make wise" unto salvation. This is "traditional Jewish usage according to which the knowledge of the Law makes men wise," and, in verses 16 and 17, "this wisdom is expounded as the morally blameless conduct of the man of God" (Wilckens, "sophos," *Kittel*, 7:527). (Cf. Exodus 7:11 where the term is used of Pharaoh's "wise" men.)

While the active voice of the verb does not occur before the Septuagint, the middle and passive forms do. In such usage the verb meant to possess wisdom or understand something. But it can also mean to "reason out, concoct subtly," or "devise craftily."

This usage provides the background for 2 Peter 1:16. Peter denied that he had followed "cunningly devised fables" (Greek *muthos* [3316], "myths"). Apparently the enemies of the Cross accused the apostles of this, that the gospel teaching was "clever fabrication" (see Bauckham, *Word Biblical Commentary*, 50:213f.). Others think Peter was implying that the false teachers followed such "sly concoctions." Either way, the word is derogatory, a usage also found in the papyri and the Epistle of Barnabas.

Strong 4679, Bauer 760, Moulton-Milligan 582, Kittel 7:527-28, Liddell-Scott 1622, Colin Brown 3:1026,1028,1033.

4533. σοφός sophos adj

Wise, clever, skillful.

Cross-Reference:
σοφία sophia (4531)

בִּין bîn (1032), Niphal: be prudent (1 Sm 16:18).

חַכִּים chakkîm (A2545), Wise men (Dn 2:12,21,27—Aramaic).

חָכָם chākhām (2550), Wise (Dt 1:13, Prv 14:1, Jer 8:8f.).

חַרְטֹם charṭōm (A2852), Magician (Dn 2:10—Aramaic).

נָכֹחַ nākhōach (5416), Right (Prv 24:26 [24:41]).

1. σοφός sophos nom sing masc
2. σοφῷ sophō dat sing masc
3. σοφοί sophoi nom pl masc
4. σοφῶν sophōn gen pl masc
5. σοφοῖς sophois dat pl masc
6. σοφούς sophous acc pl masc
7. σοφώτερον sophōteron comp nom/acc sing neu

4 **because thou hast hid these things from the wise ... Matt 11:25**
6 **prophets, and wise men, and scribes: 23:34**
4 **hast hid these things from the wise and prudent, ... Luke 10:21**
5 **both to the wise, and to the unwise................. Rom 1:14**
3 **Professing themselves to be wise, ... became fools,...... 1:22**
6 **yet I would have you wise unto that which is good,.... 16:19**
2 **To God only wise, be glory through Jesus Christ...... 16:27**
4 **I will destroy the wisdom of the wise,.............. 1 Co 1:19**
1 **Where is the wise? where is the scribe?................ 1:20**
7 **Because the foolishness of God is wiser than men;...... 1:25**
3 **how that not many wise men after the flesh,............ 1:26**
6 **foolish things of the world to confound the wise;....... 1:27**
1 **as a wise masterbuilder, I have laid the foundation,..... 3:10**
1 **If any man among you seemeth to be wise............. 3:18**
1 **let him become a fool, that he may be wise............ 3:18**
6 **He taketh the wise in their own craftiness............. 3:19**
4 **again, The Lord knoweth the thoughts of the wise,...... 3:20**
1 **Is it so, that there is not a wise man among you?....... 6:5**
3 **walk circumspectly, not as fools, but as wise,........ Eph 5:15**

2 the only wise God, be honour and glory for ever... 1 Tm 1:17
1 Who is a wise man and endued with knowledge...... Jas 3:13
2 To the only wise God our Saviour,................. Jude 1:25

Classical Greek

This adjective, translated "wise," is related to the noun for wisdom (see *sophia* [4531]). According to Wilckens ("sophos," *Kittel*, 7:465-528) the Greeks conceived this "wisdom" as an attribute or quality, not as activity. It describes any person with a well-developed, practical skill. During the classical period it was more narrowly used for theoretical, intellectual skill. Then, among the later Greek philosophers (the Stoics, for example), "wise" described the man in whom was the ideal combination of practical skill and theoretical knowledge. In its broadest sense it might mean "clever, learned, subtle, ingenious, shrewd," or "worldly-wise" (see *Liddell-Scott*).

Septuagint Usage

Both the noun and the adjective are common in the Septuagint, especially in the Wisdom books. They usually represent the Hebrew root *chākhām*. While there is a broad variety of meaning, the dominant usage is different from the secular Greek. The truly wise man is the one who fears God (cf. Proverbs 1:7, *sophia*). Such wisdom is spiritual, a gift of God (cf. Proverbs 2:6 which uses *sophia*). It is the opposite of being "wise" in one's own eyes (Proverbs 3:7). It issues both in righteous living (Proverbs 2:7-9) and in practical wisdom (Proverbs 6:6).

New Testament Usage

New Testament usage reflects both the Greek and the Jewish backgrounds. Thus, when men like Jesus (Luke 2:40,52) and Stephen (Acts 6:3,10) were described as possessing wisdom, the Old Testament sense of the word prevailed (cf. James 3:13). But the word can also be used in the classical Greek sense to refer to the "worldly-wise" as in Matthew 11:25 (parallel, Luke 10:21). In addition, it could be used in a nontechnical sense, as in 1 Corinthians 3:10, referring to a "wise" ("skillful") master builder.

Half of the New Testament appearances of *sophos* are found in 1 Corinthians 1—3. In 1:19,20,26,27 and in 3:18,19,20 Paul spoke of "worldly wisdom" (cf. Romans 1:14,22). These "worldly-wise" were those who utilized human thinking rather than accepting God's revelation. In contrast to this worldly wisdom is true wisdom, referred to in 2:6,7 (*sophia*) and 3:18 (*sophos*) (see also Romans 16:19).

One should also note that only God himself is wise in the absolute sense of the word (cf. Romans 16:27; 1 Timothy 1:17 in the Received text; see also Revelation 5:12 and 7:12 where the noun appears.) Finally, the Old Testament tendency to personify Wisdom (Proverbs 8, 9) probably led to the identification of Jesus Christ, the Word of God, as the *Wisdom* of God (1 Corinthians 1:24,30). But this relates to the usage of the noun, not the adjective.

STRONG 4680, BAUER 760, MOULTON-MILLIGAN 582, KITTEL 7:465-526, LIDDELL-SCOTT 1622, COLIN BROWN 3:1026-28.

4534. Σπανία Spania name

Spain.

1. Σπανίαν Spanian acc fem

1 Whensoever I take my journey into Spain,......... Rom 15:24
1 I will come by you into Spain........................ 15:28

A major peninsula of southwest Europe, comprising the modern nations of Portugal and Spain. Paul planned to evangelize Spain (Romans 15:24,28). It is not known whether he regained his freedom after his trial in Rome and thus was able to do so.

4535. σπαράσσω sparassō verb

To tear, convulse, throw into a (violent) spasm.

COGNATE:
συσπαράσσω susparassō (4804)

SYNONYMS:
διαῤῥήσσω diarrhēssō (1278)
ῥήγνυμι rhēgnumi (4342)
συσπαράσσω susparassō (4804)
σχίζω schizō (4829)

גָּעַשׁ gā'ash (1649), Hithpael: shake (2 Sm 22:8).

הָמָה hāmâh (2064), Pound (Jer 4:19).

שָׁלַךְ shālakh (8390), Hiphil: cast down (Dn 8:7).

1. σπαράσσει sparassei 3sing indic pres act
2. ἐσπάραξεν esparaxen 3sing indic aor act
3. σπαράξαν sparaxan nom/acc sing neu part aor act
4. σπαράξας sparaxas nom sing masc part aor act

3 And when the unclean spirit had torn him,......... Mark 1:26
2 when he saw him, straightway the spirit tare him;....... 9:20
3 and rent him sore, and came out of him:............... 9:26
1 and it teareth him that he foameth again,........... Luke 9:39

This verb is used in the New Testament, only in Mark and Luke, to describe the "convulsion" of demoniacs as they encountered Jesus. The KJV translates *sparassō* "tear" or "rend." The NASB consistently renders it "throw into a convulsion," and the NIV, "shake violently, throw into a convulsion," or "convulse violently."

In nonbiblical usage the word can mean "to tear, maul," or "rend asunder (as by violent animals), to attack violently, to retch in spasms" (*Liddell-Scott*). The New Testament usage is best understood as a violent, thrashing spasm. In each instance the demon produced the phenomenon.

Strong 4682, Bauer 760, Moulton-Milligan 582, Liddell-Scott 1624.

4536. σπαργανόω sparganoō verb

To wrap in swaddling cloths, swathe.

חָתַל chāthal (2961), Pual: be wrapped in cloths (Ez 16:4).

חֲתֻלָּה chăthullāh (2962), Swaddling band (Jb 38:9).

1. ἐσπαργάνωσεν esparganōsen 3sing indic aor act
2. ἐσπαργανωμένον esparganōmenon nom/acc sing neu part perf mid

1 and **wrapped** him **in swaddling clothes,** .... Luke 2:7
2 shall find the babe **wrapped in swaddling clothes,** 2:12

Classical Greek

This verb means "to wrap in *spargana*," wrapping cloths or bands: "strips of cloth like bandages, wrapped around young infants to keep their limbs straight" (Marshall, *New International Greek Testament Commentary, Luke* p.106). The word is especially associated with the wrapping of the newborn, both in Biblical usage and in other Greek sources.

Septuagint Usage

In the Septuagint the word occurs just twice, both times metaphorically. In Ezekiel 16:4 wicked Jerusalem is compared to a newborn; uncared for, cast out, not wrapped in swaddling clothes. In Job 38:9 the Lord speaks of His creation of the sea as though it were a newborn which He wrapped in the swaddling clothes of the mist.

New Testament Usage

In the New Testament *sparganoō* appears only in Luke 2:7,12 referring to the newborn Jesus whom Mary wrapped in swaddling cloths. In light of the Old Testament usage this probably carries the unspoken implication that the baby thus treated was loved and properly cared for. In New Testament times the baby was wrapped in a large square of cloth, and strips of cloth were tied around the square to keep it in place.

Strong 4683, Bauer 760-61, Moulton-Milligan 582, Liddell-Scott 1624.

4537. σπαταλάω spatalaō verb

To live luxuriously, live in indulgence, give oneself to pleasure.

Synonyms:
στρηνιάω strēniaō (4614)
τρυφάω truphaō (5012)

שָׁקַט shāqaṭ (8618), Hiphil: careless ease (Ez 16:49).

1. σπαταλῶσα spatalōsa nom sing fem part pres act
2. ἐσπαταλήσατε espatalēsate 2pl indic aor act

1 she that **liveth in pleasure** is dead while she liveth... 1 Tm 5:6
2 **lived in pleasure** on the earth, and been wanton; ...... Jas 5:5

Classical Greek and Septuagint Usage

This verb can be found in classical Greek from the Second Century B.C. and means "to live in excess comfort or indulgence" (cf. *Liddell-Scott*). The word appears in the Septuagint in Ezekiel 16:49 where Sodom's indulgence is compared to that of the idle rich (cf. similar usage in Sirach 21:15).

New Testament Usage

This verb appears twice in the New Testament, translated in the King James Version "liveth in pleasure" (1 Timothy 5:6) and "be wanton" (James 5:5). The meaning suggests a luxurious self-indulgence. Trench (*Synonyms of the New Testament*, pp.201f.) notes that it also includes the "notion of wastefulness"; he sees the Prodigal Son, who "scattered his substance in riotous living," as an example.

In 1 Timothy 5:6 Paul instructed Timothy to exclude from the roll of widows (those to be supported by the church) any who lived in such excess "pleasure." James 5:5 rebuked the self-indulgent rich, with *spatalaō* closely linked with *truphaō* (5012) (as in other Greek sources), a near synonym suggesting wanton carousing. "This is precisely the life-style of the rich man in the parable" in Luke 16 (Davids, *New International Greek Testament Commentary, James*, p.178).

Strong 4684, Bauer 761, Moulton-Milligan 582, Liddell-Scott 1624-25.

4538. σπάω spaō verb

To draw (as a sword).

Cognates:
διασπάω diaspaō (1282)
διασπορά diaspora (1284)
ἐπισπάω epispaō (1970)
περισπάω perispaō (3912)

Synonyms:
ἀντλέω antleō (498)
ἀποσπάω apospaō (639)

ἑλκύω helkuō (1657)
σύρω surō (4803)

מָרַט mārat (4965), Be polished (Ez 21:28).

נָתַק nāthaq (5607), Tear away; piel: snap (Jgs (16:12—Codex Alexandrinus only).

עוּר 'āwar (5996), Stir, awaken; polel: raise, take in hand (1 Chr 11:11,20).

פָּתַח pāthach (6858), Open; draw (Ps 37:14 [36:14], Ez 21:28).

שָׁלַף shālaph (8418), Draw (Nm 22:23, 2 Sm 24:9, 1 Chr 21:16).

1. σπασάμενος spasamenos nom sing masc part aor mid

1 **And one of them that stood by drew a sword,..... Mark 14:47**
1 **drew out his sword, and would have killed himself, Acts 16:27**

This verb has a variety of meanings in classical Greek: "draw, pull (apart), snatch, drag, derive," etc. (cf. *Liddell-Scott*). But in the Bible it is used only to mean "to draw" a sword from its scabbard, ready to fight. In the Septuagint it is used with this meaning some two dozen times, often when the expression "those that draw a sword" identifies warriors.

In the New Testament *spaō* appears just twice. In Mark 14:47 Peter "drew" his sword when Jesus was being arrested in Gethsemane. In Acts 16:27 the Philippian jailer "drew" his sword to kill himself, assuming that his prisoners had escaped.

Strong 4685, Bauer 761, Moulton-Milligan 582, Liddell-Scott 1625.

4539. σπεῖρα speira noun

Band, cohort.

Cross-Reference:
σπείρω speirō (4540)

1. σπεῖρα speira nom sing fem
2. σπείρης speirēs gen sing fem
3. σπεῖραν speiran acc sing fem

3 **and gathered unto him the whole band of soldiers. Matt 27:27**
3 **and they call together the whole band............. Mark 15:16**
3 **having received a band of men and officers........ John 18:3**
1 **Then the band and the captain and officers............ 18:12**
2 **a centurion of the band called the Italian band,.... Acts 10:1**
2 **tidings came unto the chief captain of the band,....... 21:31**
2 **one named Julius, a centurion of Augustus' band....... 27:1**

In its earliest occurrences in classical Greek *speira* described anything "twisted or wound around or together" (*Liddell-Scott*). Thus it could be used of a "band" of men, a tactical unit of soldiers. In classical usage it can also denote the coils of a serpent, a mode of hairdressing, a knot in wood, etc. However, a "cohort" is its only meaning in the New Testament, a translation of the Latin *cohors*. (In other Greek literature *speira* also represents *manipulus*, one-third of a cohort.) The "cohort" in the regular Roman legions typically had 600 men but could number as many as 1,000 in the auxiliary forces (all New Testament references, apparently; see Bruce, *New International Commentary on the New Testament, Acts*, p.202).

One "cohort" was stationed in Jerusalem while Judea was a Roman province. This cohort was active in the arrest of Jesus (John 18:3,12), in His crucifixion (Matthew 27:27; Mark 15:16), and in the arrest of Paul (Acts 21:31).

Two other "cohorts" are mentioned by name: one originally made up of volunteers recruited in Italy (Acts 10:1), the other (Acts 27:1) wearing the name of Emperor Augustus, "a title of honor bestowed on select cohorts of auxiliary troops" (ibid., p.477).

Strong 4686, Bauer 761, Moulton-Milligan 582, Liddell-Scott 1625.

4540. σπείρω speirō verb

To sow (as seed), scatter, spread, disperse.

Cognates:
ἐπισπείρω epispeirō (1970B)
σπεῖρα speira (4539)
σπέρμα sperma (4543)
σπερμολόγος spermologos (4544)
σπορά spora (4554)
σπόριμος sporimos (4555)
σπόρος sporos (4556)

זָרָה zārâh (2306), Scatter (Nm 16:37).

זָרַע zāra' (2319), Qal: sow (Lv 25:3f., Ps 107:37 [106:37], Jer 35:7 [42:7]); niphal: be sown, be perpetuated (Lv 11:37, Dt 21:4, Na 1:14); pual: be sown (Is 40:24); hiphil: yield seed (Gn 1:11f.).

זֶרַע zera' (2320), Descendant, seed (Prv 11:21, Is 5:10).

מִזְרָע mizrā' (4352), A sown field (Is 19:7).

נָדַח nādhach (5258), Niphal: an outcast (Jer 30:17 [37:17]).

פּוּץ pûts (6571), Qal: dispersed people (Zep 3:10—only some Sinaiticus texts); hiphil: sow (Is 28:25).

פָּזַר pāzar (6582), Scatter, disperse; piel: give freely (Prv 11:24).

1. σπείρῃ speirē 3sing subj pres/aor act
2. σπείρεις speireis 2sing indic pres act
3. σπείρει speirei 3sing indic pres act
4. σπείρουσιν speirousin 3pl indic pres act
5. σπείρων speirōn nom sing masc part pres act
6. σπείροντος speirontos gen sing masc part pres act

7. σπείροντι speironti dat sing masc part pres act
8. σπείρειν speirein inf pres act
9. ἔσπειρα espeira 1sing indic aor act
10. ἔσπειρας espeiras 2sing indic aor act
11. ἔσπειρεν espeiren 3sing indic aor act
12. ἐσπείραμεν espeiramen 1pl indic aor act
13. σπείρας speiras nom sing masc part aor act
14. σπεῖραι speirai inf aor act
15. σπείρεται speiretai 3sing indic pres mid
16. σπειρόμενοι speiromenoi nom pl masc part pres mid
17. σπαρῇ sparē 3sing subj aor pass
18. σπαρείς spareis nom sing masc part aor pass
19. σπαρέντες sparentes nom pl masc part aor pass
20. ἐσπαρμένον esparmenon nom/acc sing masc/neu part perf mid
21. σπείραντος speirantos gen sing masc part aor act
22. σπείραντι speiranti dat sing masc part aor act
23. ἔσπειρες espeires 2sing indic imperf act

4	for they sow not, neither do they reap,	Matt 6:26
5	saying, Behold, a sower went forth to sow;	13:3
8	saying, Behold, a sower went forth to sow;	13:3
8	when he sowed, some seeds fell by the way side,	13:4
6	Hear ye therefore the parable of the sower.	13:18
20	catcheth away that which was sown in his heart.	13:19
18	This is he which received seed by the way side.	13:19
18	But he that received the seed into stony places,	13:20
18	He also that received seed among the thorns	13:22
18	But he that received seed into the good ground	13:23
7	a man which sowed good seed in his field:	13:24
11	his enemy came and sowed tares among the wheat,	13:25
10	didst not thou sow good seed in thy field?	13:27
11	seed, which a man took, and sowed in his field:	13:31
5	He that soweth the good seed is the Son of man;	13:37
13	The enemy that sowed them is the devil;	13:39
10	hard man, reaping where thou hast not sown,	25:24
9	thou knewest that I reap where I sowed not,	25:26
5	Hearken; Behold, there went out a sower to sow:	Mark 4:3
14	Hearken; Behold, there went out a sower to sow:	4:3
8	as he sowed, some fell by the way side,	4:4
5	The sower soweth the word.	4:14
3	The sower soweth the word.	4:14
15	they by the way side, where the word is sown;	4:15
20	Satan ... and taketh away the word that was sown	4:15
16	they likewise which are sown on stony ground;	4:16
16	And these are they which are sown among thorns;	4:18
19	And these are they which are sown on good ground;	4:20
17	which, when it is sown in the earth,	4:31
17	But when it is sown, it groweth up,	4:32
5	A sower went out to sow his seed: and as he sowed,	Luke 8:5
14	A sower went out to sow his seed: and as he sowed,	8:5
8	A sower went out to sow his seed: and as he sowed,	8:5
4	Consider the ravens: ... they neither sow nor reap;	12:24
10	and reapest that thou didst not sow.	19:21
9	Thou knewest ... and reaping that I did not sow:	19:22
5	that both he that soweth and he that reapeth	John 4:36
5	One soweth, and another reapeth.	4:37
12	If we have sown unto you spiritual things,	1 Co 9:11
2	which thou sowest is not quickened, except it die:	15:36
2	And that which thou sowest,	15:37
2	sowest not that body that shall be, but bare grain,	15:37
15	is sown in corruption; it is raised in incorruption:	15:42
15	It is sown in dishonour; it is raised in glory:	15:43
15	it is sown in weakness; it is raised in power:	15:43
15	It is sown a natural body;	15:44
5	which soweth sparingly shall reap also sparingly;	2 Co 9:6
5	soweth bountifully shall reap also bountifully.	9:6
7	Now he that ministereth seed to the sower	9:10
1	whatsoever a man soweth, that shall he also reap.	Gal 6:7
5	For he that soweth to his flesh	Gal 6:8
5	but he that soweth to the Spirit	6:8
15	And the fruit of righteousness is sown in peace	Jas 3:18

Classical Greek

This verb means "to sow", especially to sow seed in planting; see also the related noun *sperma* (4543), "seed". In classical Greek usage *speirō* can mean "to sow" or "plant" seed, "to sow" ideas, "to scatter" or "disperse" things or people, and even "to beget" (Schulz, "speirō," *Kittel*, 7:537). The ancient method of sowing was to scatter the seed onto fertile ground; hence *speirō* can mean "scatter."

Septuagint Usage

Speirō appears more than 50 times in the Septuagint, mostly for sowing the seed of plants, as in Genesis 47:23; Exodus 23:10; etc. It is also used metaphorically, as to "sow" righteousness in Proverbs 11:21 (where the Septuagint has "the one sowing righteousness" [participle] instead of "the seed of the righteous"). See also Proverbs 11:24 where generous persons are (literally) "they who sow (or disperse) their own things" (cf. Jeremiah 4:3). In Hosea 2:23 (LXX 2:25) Israel was "sown" in Canaan; in Zechariah 10:9 Israel was "sown/scattered" among the nations.

New Testament Usage

In the New Testament *speirō* appears some 50 times, in two main categories of meaning. Half of these occur in the two parables about sowing in Matthew 13 (and parallels in Mark 4 and Luke 8). In the parables the seed of plants was sown, representing—in the interpretation—the Word as "seed." In Matthew 6:26; 25:24,26; Luke 19:21,22; and 1 Corinthians 15:36,37 *speirō* also refers to the sowing of the seed of plants.

The other uses of *speirō* are more or less metaphoric. All of them, directly or implicitly, involve correspondence between sowing and reaping. In John 4:36,37 an aphorism about sowing and reaping was applied by Jesus to the sowing and reaping of a spiritual harvest. In 1 Corinthians 9:11 Paul presented his preaching/teaching of the Word of God as a sowing of spiritual things. In 1 Corinthians 15:42-44 he presented resurrection truth in these terms. The burial of the body is, by analogy, like the planting of seed; it must decay before it brings forth new, incorruptible life. In 2 Corinthians 9:6,10 Paul used the law of sowing and reaping as a thinly veiled analogy for liberal giving. In Galatians 6:7,8 he used that same law as an analogy for "sowing" to the Spirit (rather than the flesh) and reaping eternal reward. Sowing to/for the flesh is "practicing such things as are included among the works of the flesh," while sowing to/ for the Spirit is "to cultivate the fruit of the Spirit" as in Galatians 5:19-23 (Bruce, *New International Greek Testament Commentary, Galatians*, p.265). Finally, in James 3:18 those who make peace are represented as sowing that which will yield the fruit of righteousness as reward.

STRONG 4687, BAUER 761, MOULTON-MILLIGAN 582, KITTEL 7:536-47, LIDDELL-SCOTT 1625-26, COLIN BROWN 3:521-22,525.

4541. σπεκουλάτωρ

spekoulatōr noun

Spy, courier, bodyguard, executioner.

1. σπεκουλάτωρα spekoulatōra acc sing masc
2. σπεκουλάτορα spekoulatora acc sing masc

1 And immediately the king sent an executioner,..... Mark 6:27

This noun is a Latin loanword, *speculator*, denoting "an observer, spy, scout, sentinel." A.B. Bruce notes that in the Roman world it came to mean "a military official . . . who acted partly as courier, partly as police officer, partly as an executioner" (*Expositor's Greek Testament, Synoptic Gospels*, 1:382).

Spekoulatōr appears in the New Testament just once, in Mark 6:27, referring to the "executioner" whom Herod sent to behead John the Baptist. This man did as charged and brought John's head to Salome for Herodias.

STRONG 4688, BAUER 761, MOULTON-MILLIGAN 582, LIDDELL-SCOTT 1626.

4542. σπένδω spendō verb

Offer a libation or drink offering, pour out, offer.

נָסַךְ nāṣakh (5445), Qal: pour out (Hos 9:4); piel: pour out as an offering (1 Chr 11:18); hiphil: pour out a drink offering or libation (Gn 35:14, Nm 28:7, Jer 44:19 [51:19]); hophal: have drink offerings be poured out (Ex 37:16 [38:12]).

נֶסֶךְ neṣekh (5447II) Drink offering (Nm 4:7).

1. σπένδομαι spendomai 1sing indic pres mid

1 Yea, and if I be offered upon the sacrifice.......... Phlp 2:17
1 For I am now ready to be offered,................. 2 Tm 4:6

Classical Greek

This verb can be found in classical Greek from the Eighth Century B.C. and means "make or pour out a drink offering," rarely without a religious sense (cf. *Liddell-Scott*). In the Greek religions libations were considered as important as animal sacrifices. Libation offerings were performed at the forming of an oath, to appease gods, to drive away demons, as rituals for the dead, etc.

Septuagint Usage

The Septuagint uses the verb 20 times from Genesis to Hosea, normally of a sacrificial act, especially the offering of wine. It became the technical term for the act. The drink offering played an important part in fertility cults. Israel offered libations to other deities during the Monarchy while they engaged in their idolatry. The libation offering could be independent or an extension of the main offering.

New Testament Usage

Spendō is found twice in the New Testament, both times in Paul's writings (Philippians 2:17; 2 Timothy 4:6). In the passive voice and figurative sense it means "to be offered up." Paul compared his ensuing death to a drink offering "poured out" before God. It would be pleasing to the Almighty because it was offered according to His will, yet it would be of no further value to the human agent who offered it. His death would not atone for any of his own sins, rather it was a means of completely dedicating himself to God.

STRONG 4689, BAUER 761, MOULTON-MILLIGAN 583, KITTEL 7:528-36 (see "spendomai"), LIDDELL-SCOTT 1626, COLIN BROWN 2:853-55.

4543. σπέρμα sperma noun

Seed, offspring, posterity.

COGNATE:
σπείρω speirō (4540)
SYNONYM:
σπόρος sporos (4556)

אַחֲרִית 'achărîth (321), End (Nm 24:20).

בֵּן bēn (1158), Son (Dt 25:5).

זֵרוּעַ zērûa' (2308), Something sown (Is 61:11).

זָרַע zāra' (2319), Sow (Prv 11:18); sower (Jer 50:16 [27:16]).

זֶרַע zera' (2320), Descendant, offspring (Gn 17:7-10, 1 Kgs 2:33, Is 14:20); seed (Gn 1:11f.).

נִין nîn (5397), Descendant (Gn 21:23).

1. σπέρμα sperma nom/acc sing neu
2. σπέρματος spermatos gen sing neu
3. σπέρματι spermati dat sing neu
4. σπερμάτων spermatōn gen pl neu
5. σπέρμασιν spermasin dat pl neu

1 a man which sowed good seed in his field:.........Matt 13:24
1 didst not thou sow good seed in thy field?........... 13:27

4 Which indeed is the least of all seeds:............ Matt 13:32
1 He that soweth the good seed is the Son of man;...... 13:37
1 the good seed are the children of the kingdom;........ 13:38
1 marry his wife, and raise up seed unto his brother..... 22:24
1 married a wife, deceased, and, having no issue,........ 22:25
4 is less than all the seeds that be in the earth:....... Mark 4:31
1 take his wife, and raise up seed unto his brother....... 12:19
1 and the first took a wife, and dying left no seed....... 12:20
1 neither left he any seed: and the third likewise......... 12:21
1 And the seven had her, and left no seed:............. 12:22
3 our fathers, to Abraham, and to his seed for ever.... Luke 1:55
1 and raise up seed unto his brother.................... 20:28
2 That Christ cometh of the seed of David,........... John 7:42
1 They answered him, We be Abraham's seed,........... 8:33
1 I know that ye are Abraham's seed;................... 8:37
3 And in thy seed shall all the kindreds ... be blessed. Acts 3:25
3 for a possession, and to his seed after him,............. 7:5
1 That his seed should sojourn in a strange land;......... 7:6
2 Of this man's seed hath God ... raised unto Israel..... 13:23
2 our Lord, which was made of the seed of David..... Rom 1:3
3 not to Abraham, or to his seed, through the law,....... 4:13
3 the end the promise might be sure to all the seed;...... 4:16
1 So shall thy seed be.................................. 4:18
1 Neither, because they are the seed of Abraham,........ 9:7
1 but, In Isaac shall thy seed be called.................. 9:7
1 children of the promise are counted for the seed........ 9:8
1 Except the Lord of Sabaoth had left us a seed,......... 9:29
2 For I also am an Israelite, of the seed of Abraham,.... 11:1
4 and to every seed his own body.................. 1 Co 15:38
1 Now he that ministereth seed to the sower.......... 2 Co 9:10
1 Are they the seed of Abraham? so am I.............. 11:22
3 to Abraham and his seed were the promises made.... Gal 3:16
5 He saith not, And to seeds, as of many;............... 3:16
3 but as of one, And to thy seed, which is Christ......... 3:16
1 seed should come to whom the promise was made;..... 3:19
1 And if ye be Christ's, then are ye Abraham's seed,..... 3:29
2 Remember that Jesus Christ of the seed of David... 2 Tm 2:8
2 but he took on him the seed of Abraham............ Heb 2:16
2 Sara herself received strength to conceive seed,........ 11:11
1 That in Isaac shall thy seed be called:................. 11:18
1 for his seed remaineth in him: and he cannot sin,.... 1 Jn 3:9
2 went to make war with the remnant of her seed,.... Rev 12:17

Classical Greek

The noun *sperma* means "seed"; see the related verb *speirō* (4540), "to sow." In classical Greek *sperma* can refer to the seed of plants or animals, to the basic element of anything, to one's immediate children or further progeny, and to anything that has life-giving force (Schulz, "sperma," *Kittel*, 7:536f.).

In other Greek literature *sperma* has breadth of usage similar to that of the classical period. Philo, for example, used the word both literally and metaphorically, the latter sometimes approaching our use of "germ" (as in the germ of life). As well, he used *sperma* of the starting point of the universe.

Septuagint Usage

Sperma appears over 200 times in the Septuagint with a similar variety of meanings including (occasionally) the male "sperm" (semen), as in Leviticus 15:16 for humans and Jeremiah 31:27 (LXX 38:27) for animals.

One of the most common uses of *sperma* in the Septuagint is for the seed of plants described in the creation narrative (Genesis 1:11,12,29). Growing out of this, apparently, the Old Testament cultivates a sense of respect and care for seed as God-given and containing a precious, life-giving force (see Leviticus 11:37,38; 26:16; 27:30).

Just as seed produces the plant, and the plant produces seed, so a person's immediate offspring or subsequent lineage are his "seed" (posterity). This explains the other most common use of *sperma* in the Septuagint in reference to the seed of Abraham (Isaiah 41:8), seed of Aaron, seed of David, seed of Jacob (Isaiah 45:19), etc. Again, implicit in this is the sense of a God-given, life-giving force that is kept alive from one generation to another and represents its progenitor. Thus the ancients despaired if they had no "seed" (Genesis 15:3). This gives a reason for God's provision for levirate marriage (Genesis 38:9; cf. 19:32,34) and the seriousness of a judgment that "cut off" one's seed (1 Samuel 24:21 [LXX 1 Kings 24:22]).

New Testament Usage

In the New Testament *sperma* also has a variety of meanings. In Matthew 13:24ff. it refers to the seed of plants (cf. 1 Corinthians 15:38, of kernels of grain; 2 Corinthians 9:10, etc.). In Hebrews 11:11 the word denotes the male sperm. Here the phrase "to conceive seed" (KJV) apparently is "the standard and technical term for the projection or deposition of the *semen virile* into the womb" (Lenski, *Epistles to the Hebrews and James*, p.393). Elsewhere *sperma* refers to natural posterity (Matthew 22:24,25, "seed" and "issue" in the KJV; John 7:42; 8:33,37; Hebrews 11:18) or spiritual posterity (Romans 4:16,18; 9:8; cf. Revelation 12:17).

The usage in Galatians 3:16,29 is significant. In 3:16 Paul cited the Abrahamic covenant (Genesis 13:15; 17:7,8) to make a point that Jesus, in the truest sense, is the (singular) "seed"—posterity—promised to Abraham. Then, in 3:29, he affirmed that all who are in Christ are therefore Abraham's "seed." (Compare Psalm 22:30 where *sperma* identifies the spiritual "progeny" of the Messiah.)

The meaning of 1 John 3:9—"his seed remaineth in him"—is debatable. It might mean that God's children, *His* "seed," abide in Him. More likely it means that the "germ" of spiritual life implanted in the believer remains in that one as a child of God. "*Sperma* signifies the divine principle of life (the Spirit?) in the believer, which renders continuance in sin incongruous" (Demarest, "Seed," *Colin Brown*, 2:524). Weiss believes it is the Word of God (cf. *Bauer*). (For a full discussion see Smalley, *Word Biblical Commentary*, 51:172-175.) Romans 9:29 (quoting Isaiah 1:9) describes survivors from which grow a new nation. Lastly, Jesus identified *sperma* with the Word of God, which served as a symbolic proclamation of the arrival of the Kingdom. Many of the New Testament uses are in parables of Jesus using this comparison.

STRONG 4690, BAUER 761-62, MOULTON-MILLIGAN 583, KITTEL 7:536-47, LIDDELL-SCOTT 1626, COLIN BROWN 3:521-24.

4544. σπερμολόγος spermologos adj

Seed picker, one who picks up scraps, gossiper, babbler.

CROSS-REFERENCES:
λόγος logos (3030)
σπείρω speirō (4540)

1. σπερμολόγος spermologos nom sing masc

1 What will this **babbler** say? .... Acts 17:18

Classical Greek

This adjective is a compound of *sperma* (4543), "seed," and *legō* (2978), "to pick up, gather." It is most frequently used as a substantive: "one who picks up seeds." Its classical use often applied this to a bird, thus it could denote a rook or crow or other small bird. Another usage is illustrated by Eustathius in Homer's *Odyssey* (5.490): "a man hanging about the shops and the markets, picking up scraps which fell from the loads and thus gaining a livelihood" (cf. Knowling, *Expositor's Greek Testament*, *Acts*, 2:367)—what we might call a "ragpicker."

It was easy, then, for the word to be used metaphorically of those who picked up scraps of information here and there and passed them on to others, making what capital they could from them (Bruce, *New International Commentary on the New Testament*, *Acts*, p.351). The implication is that such a person delighted to hear and then spread about bits and pieces of the ideas of others as though they were his own: thus, according to Vine, he was a "plagiarist, or of those who make a show, in unscientific style, of knowledge obtained from misunderstanding lectures" (*Expository Dictionary*, "Babbler").

New Testament Usage

This is the sense of the word in its only appearance in the New Testament. In Acts 17:18 some of the Athenian philosophers thought Paul was such a person (KJV: "babbler"). "The Athenian philosophers, in calling Paul a *spermologos*, or 'ignorant plagiarist,' meant that he retailed odds and ends of knowledge which he had picked up from others, without possessing himself any system of thought or skill of language, i.e., without culture" (Rees, "Babbler," *International Standard Bible Encyclopedia*, 1:382). A single English word hardly translates the variety of ideas implicit in the word: idleness, plagiarism, living off others' efforts, failure to understand ideas used or to put them together in a meaningful way, thus having nothing worth listening to and being the object of ridicule.

STRONG 4691, BAUER 762, MOULTON-MILLIGAN 583, LIDDELL-SCOTT 1627, COLIN BROWN 3:525.

4545. σπεύδω speudō verb

To hurry, hasten, desire earnestly, strive (for).

אָמֵץ 'āmēts (563), Be strong; hithpael: make haste (2 Chr 10:18).

בָּהַל bāhal (963), Niphal: hasten (Prv 28:22); piel: be hasty, be eager (Eccl 5:2 [5:1], 7:9 [7:10]).

בְּהַל b^ehal (A964), Hithpeel: hurry (Dn 3:24—Aramaic).

דָּחַף dāchaph (1821), Qal: hasten (Est 3:15); niphal: hasten (2 Chr 26:20).

חוּשׁ chûsh (2456), Go quickly! (1 Sm 20:38).

חָפַז chāphaz (2753), Hurry to flee (2 Sm 4:4).

מָהִיר māhîr (4248), Prompt (Is 16:5).

מָהַר māhar (4257), Piel: do something quickly, hurry (Gn 24:18, 1 Sm 25:18, Na 2:5).

1. σπεύδοντας speudontas acc pl masc part pres act
2. σπεῦσον speuson 2sing impr aor act
3. σπεύσας speusas nom sing masc part aor act
4. σπεύσαντες speusantes nom pl masc part aor act
5. ἔσπευδεν espeuden 3sing indic imperf act

4 And they came **with haste,** and found Mary, ... Luke 2:16
3 Zacchaeus, **make haste,** and come down; for to day 19:5
3 he **made haste,** and came down, and received him 19:6
5 he would not spend the time in Asia: for he **hasted,** Acts 20:16
2 And saw him saying unto me, **Make haste,** 22:18
1 and **hasting** unto the coming of the day of God, ... 2 Pt 3:12

Classical Greek

This verb is used in classical Greek with a variety of related meanings: "get going, urge or press on, hasten, seek eagerly, strive after, further zealously, be eager (to do something), show eagerness (for something), be anxious (that something be done)," etc. (cf. *Liddell-Scott*). It is almost always used in a literal sense to describe the movement of people or animals.

Septuagint Usage

Speudō appears some 50 times in the Septuagint most frequently to mean "make haste." Even so, various shades of meaning are implicit: (1) to move with fear, as in 2 Chronicles 10:18 when Rehoboam "made haste" to flee; (2) to move quickly to obey, as in 2 Chronicles 24:5 when Joash commanded the priests to "make haste" to gather taxes for repairs to the temple; (3) to respond without delay, with alacrity, as in 2 Kings 9:13 (LXX 4 Kings 9:13) when they "made haste" to put their garments under Jehu at the top of the stairs; (4) to strive zealously, as in Proverbs 28:22 of one who "makes haste" to be rich; (5) to be hasty, as in Ecclesiastes 5:1 of one who is "hasty" with the mouth (cf. Ecclesiastes 7:9 [LXX 7:10]); and (6) to hasten, as in Isaiah 16:5 where the prophet held out the prospect of "hastening" righteousness.

Thus both transitive meanings (a desire or effort to bring something about) and intransitive meanings (one's own sense of urgency or haste) accrue to *speudō*, a fact illustrated in the papyri of the New Testament period also. (See *Moulton-Milligan.*)

New Testament Usage

In the New Testament, except for 2 Peter 3:12, *speudō* was used exclusively by Luke. The meaning in each of these is rather ordinary, indicating (intransitively) that one hurried or made haste. But perhaps the Septuagint usage discussed above should cause us to see in most of these instances a sense of moving with alacrity or quickness to obey. At the least, the idea is to "waste no time" (Marshall, *New International Greek New Testament, Luke*, p.697).

The meaning in 2 Peter 3:12 is more debatable: "Those who wait are at one and the same time the *speudontes*, which some interpret as those who strive and are zealous, some as those who hasten the day through their holy conduct" (Hoffman, "Hope," *Colin Brown*, 2:245). Thus some interpreters defend an intransitive meaning: "being eager for" (Lenski, *Epistles of St. Peter's Epistles*, p.348). Others defend a transitive meaning: "The Jewish background is decisive in favor of 'hastening' .... Clearly this idea of hastening the End is the corollary of the explanation (verse 9) that God defers the Parousia because he desires Christians to repent. Their repentance and holy living may therefore, from the human standpoint, hasten its coming" (Bauckham, *Word Biblical Commentary*, 50:325). Perhaps this is "reminiscent of the Jewish belief that absolutely faithful observance of the Torah for one day would bring the Messianic age" (Sidebottom, *New Century Bible, James, Jude, 2 Peter*, p.124).

Strong 4692, Bauer 762, Moulton-Milligan 583, Liddell-Scott 1627.

4546. σπήλαιον spēlaion noun

Cave, den.

מְעוֹר mā'ôr (4742), Nakedness (Hb 2:15).

מוֹעֵצָה mô'ētsāh (4292), Cave (Gn 49:29f., 1 Sm 24:3 [24:4], Ez 33:27).

נָצַר nātsar (5526), Keep watch, observe, guard; secret place (Is 65:4).

סָעִיף sā'îph (5780), Cleft (Jgs 15:8—Codex Alexandrinus only).

1. σπήλαιον spēlaion nom/acc sing neu
2. σπηλαίοις spēlaiois dat pl neu
3. σπήλαια spēlaia nom/acc pl neu

1 but ye have made it a **den** of thieves.............. Matt 21:13
1 but ye have made it a **den** of thieves.............. Mark 11:17
1 but ye have made it a **den** of thieves.............. Luke 19:46
1 It was a **cave**, and a stone lay upon it............. John 11:38
2 in mountains, and in **dens** and caves of the earth.... Heb 11:38
3 hid themselves in the **dens** and in the rocks.......... Rev 6:15

This noun can refer to a natural or man-made "cave." It appears six times in the New Testament, all but one of these refer to a "cave" or "den" as a place of hiding or refuge. Papyri usage also supports the idea that the word identifies a cave, especially, as inhabited (*Moulton-Milligan*).

In Matthew 21:13 (also Mark 11:17; Luke 19:46) Jesus accused the traders and money changers of making the temple precincts a "den" of robbers. Thus what should have been a place of refuge for prayer by the Gentiles (the outer court) was instead a place of refuge for robbers. Jesus' words came from Jeremiah 7:11 where the Septuagint has the same Greek. (The word appears elsewhere in the Septuagint as a place of refuge [Genesis 19:30] or a tomb [Genesis 23:9]; Hillyer, "Cave," *Colin Brown*, 3:380).

In Hebrews 11:38 (KJV, "dens"; NIV, "caves") *spēlaion* provided a place of hiding for the godly (in Old Testament times), taking refuge from persecution or want. Revelation 6:15 looks to the time when the ungodly will seek hiding in caves from the wrath of God.

Finally, since the ancients often used caves for the bodies of the dead, Lazarus' tomb "was a cave" (John 11:38).

Strong 4693, Bauer 762, Moulton-Milligan 583, Liddell-Scott 1627, Colin Brown 3:380-81.

4547. σπιλάς spilas noun

(Dangerous) rock, reef; spot, stain.

SYNONYM:
σπίλος spilos (4548)

1. σπιλάδες spilades nom pl fem

1 These are **spots** in your feasts of charity, ... Jude 1:12

This noun appears once in the New Testament (Jude 12) where there is considerable debate about its meaning. Primarily the debate is whether Jude 12 used it to mean "spot, stain" or a "dangerous rock, reef."

The greater part of classical usage would call for the meaning "rock over which the sea dashes," although it can also denote a "slab" or other exposed, land-based rock (*Liddell-Scott*). Except for Jude 12 there is but one instance of the word referring to a "spot" in Greek literature—in a Fourth Century A.D. document. (For a defense of the view that Jude intended "dangerous reefs" and a good discussion of all possibilities, see Bauckham, *Word Biblical Commentary*, 52:85.) Not only does this fit the most well-attested usage of the word, it also "makes excellent sense. In context the word should indicate the danger which the false teachers present to Jude's readers . . . . (They) are like dangerous reefs; close contact with them will result in shipwreck" (ibid.).

Bigg is typical of many who interpret *spilas* as "spot, blemish" in Jude 12, regarding the word as "merely a variant for the *spiloi* of 2 Peter" (*International Critical Commentary, Jude*, p.333). In this case, Jude regarded the false teachers, tolerated in the church's fellowship meals, as a "disgrace, actual eyesore" (Lenski, *Interpretation of the Epistles of St. Peter*, p.635). This meaning can be supported by appeal to the parallel in 2 Peter 2:13, and such a usage might have resulted from confusion with *spilos*. In this case, one should compare the use of the cognate verb *spiloō* (4549) in Jude 23.

Theoretically, two other meanings are possible: "storm, squall" (*Liddell-Scott*) or "dirty, foul (wind)" (cf. *Moulton-Milligan*). Neither of these has found much favor among the interpreters of Jude.

STRONG 4694, BAUER 762, MOULTON-MILLIGAN 583-84, LIDDELL-SCOTT 1628.

4548. σπίλος spilos noun

Spot, stain, fault, blemish.

SYNONYM:
σπιλάς spilas (4547)

1. σπίλον spilon acc sing masc
2. σπίλοι spiloi nom pl masc

1 not having **spot**, or wrinkle, or any such thing; .... Eph 5:27
2 **Spots** they are and blemishes, ... 2 Pt 2:13

Classical Greek

Spilos, denoting a "spot, stain," is found in later Greek writers who used the word in the sense of "a spot on the skin" or in a general way to refer to a "spot" or "stain." It is also used in a figurative sense meaning "impurity, vice," or "moral fault"; it was so used by the rhetorician Dionysius of Halicarnassus in speaking of people, their vices and moral impurities (cf. *Bauer*). *Spilos* does not appear in the Septuagint.

New Testament Usage

It occurs only twice in the New Testament. In Ephesians 5:27 Paul used the noun in its figurative sense of "moral blemish." He wrote in the context of presenting the Church, glorious and "not having spot," i.e., a Church without moral blemish.

Peter used the noun a bit differently. In 2 Peter 2:1, and in the context of the entire chapter, he wrote that "there shall be false teachers among you." After a rather lengthy description of their kind, and of what happened to their kind in Old Testament times, verse 13 begins a sort of summary in which the apostle described the kind of people these false teachers were. He used a number of adjectives to depict such people; one of which is *spilos*, "moral blemishes."

STRONG 4696, BAUER 762, MOULTON-MILLIGAN 584, LIDDELL-SCOTT 1628.

4549. σπιλόω spiloō verb

To stain, soil, defile.

SYNONYMS:
κοινόω koinoō (2813)
μιαίνω miainō (3256)
μολύνω molunō (3298)

1. σπιλοῦσα spilousa nom sing fem part pres act
2. ἐσπιλωμένον espilōmenon acc sing masc part perf mid

1 the tongue ... that it **defileth** the whole body, ... Jas 3:6
2 hating even the garment **spotted** by the flesh. .... Jude 1:23

This verb is cognate with *spilos* (4548), "spot, stain." According to Vine it means "to make a stain or spot, and so to defile" (*Expository Dictionary*, "Defile"). *Spiloō* appears in the New Testament only twice. James 3:6 states that the tongue "defiles" the whole body. Here the body stands for "the whole person . . . morally tarred with the brush of the tongue" (Davids, *New International Greek Testament Commentary, James,* p.143). It stains the person "because it formulates desires and designs which may be evil" (Sidebottom, *New Century Bible, James, Jude, 2 Peter,* p.47). (Compare Mark 7:15.)

In Jude 23 the believer is exhorted to rescue those who fall into sin, hating even the clothing "spotted" by the flesh. Apparently Jude alluded to Zechariah 3:3,4 where Joshua was seen as clothed with filthy garments, and interpreted this to mean clothes "soiled by the body"—a picture "which Jude uses to suggest that whatever comes into contact with these people is contaminated by their sins" (Bauckham, *Word Biblical Commentary,* 52:116).

Strong 4695, Bauer 762, Moulton-Milligan 584, Liddell-Scott 1628.

4550. σπλαγχνίζομαι

splanchnizomai verb

Have compassion, feel sympathy, have mercy.

Cognates:

εὔσπλαγχνος eusplanchnos (2136)
πολύσπλαγχνος polusplanchnos (4043)
σπλάγχνον splanchnon (4551)

Synonyms:

ἐλεέω eleeō (1640)
οἰκτείρω oikteirō (3489)
συμπαθέω sumpatheō (4685)

1. **σπλαγχνίζομαι splanchnizomai** 1sing indic pres mid
2. **ἐσπλαγχνίσθη esplanchnisthē** 3sing indic aor pass
3. **σπλαγχνισθείς splanchnistheis** nom sing masc part aor pass

2 **he was moved with compassion** on them, ... Matt 9:36
2 and **was moved with compassion** toward them, ... 14:14
1 **I have compassion** on the multitude, ... 15:32
3 lord of that servant **was moved with compassion,** 18:27
3 So Jesus **had compassion** on them, ... 20:34
3 **moved with compassion,** put forth his hand, ... Mark 1:41
2 and **was moved with compassion** toward them, ... 6:34
1 **I have compassion** on the multitude, ... 8:2
3 if thou canst do any thing, **have compassion** on us, ... 9:22
2 when the Lord saw her, he **had compassion** on her, .. Luke 7:13
2 and when he saw him, he **had compassion** on him, ... 10:33
2 his father saw him, and **had compassion,** and ran, ... 15:20

Classical Greek

Often appearing as *splancheuō* in classical literature (in the active form *splanchnizō*), this term depicts the act of eating the internal organs (*splanchna* [see 4551]) of a sacrifice (cf. *Liddell-Scott*). The middle form *splanchnizomai* means "to feel compassion, pity, mercy." The *splanchna* (plural of *splanchnon*) are the internal organs of an animal or person, such as the heart, liver, or lungs. The "inner parts" were regarded by the ancient Greeks as the site of emotions, thus the verb form emerged. The "inner parts" were especially seen as the source of the emotions of anger and anxiety but also of pity and mercy (ibid.).

Septuagint Usage

In the Septuagint the middle form (perhaps *episplanchnizomai,* as other manuscripts read) is used in Proverbs 17:5, a text lacking a Hebrew original. The thought, however, illustrates the relationship between pity/mercy and *splanchnizomai.* The statement, "Those being compassionate will be shown mercy," stands in antithesis to the Hebrew verse, "Whoever gloats over disaster will not go unpunished" (Proverbs 17:5, NIV) (cf. the use of the noun in Proverbs 12:10; 4 Maccabees 14:13). The infinitive usage in 2 Maccabees 6:8 reflects the classical understanding of *splanchnizō* as partaking of the sacrifice's internal organs (cf. the noun use in the Septuagint).

New Testament Usage

Splanchnizomai occurs only in the Synoptic Gospels in the New Testament (cf. the noun in Paul [e.g., 2 Corinthians 6:12; 7:15; Philippians 1:8, of Christ]; and 1 John 3:17). Matthew and Luke use the term independently of Mark (e.g., Matthew 18:27; Luke 15:20). They do not follow Mark (cf. Mark 1:41 with Matthew 8:3; Luke 5:13), omitting the reference to Jesus' compassion. However, apart from three uses in the parables (Matthew 18:27; Luke 10:33; 15:20), they share one common feature: "The showing of compassion" is typical of Jesus' response, whether to crowds (e.g., Matthew 9:36; 14:14) or to individuals (Luke 7:13). He is willing to extend His merciful touch to all.

Here we see the compassionate character of our Lord most clearly illustrated. God in Christ is moved with compassion and pity to act on behalf of a lost and dying world. At the heart of this compassion is His great love for all mankind (John 3:16).

Strong 4697, Bauer 762, Moulton-Milligan 584, Kittel 7:548-59, Liddell-Scott 1628 (see "splanchnizō"), Colin Brown 2:599-600.

4551. σπλάγχνον splanchnon noun

Inward parts, intestines; heart, affections.

Cross-Reference:

σπλαγχνίζομαι splanchnizomai (4550)

1. σπλάγχνα splanchna nom/acc pl neu
2. σπλάγχνοις splanchnois dat pl neu

1 Through the tender mercy of our God; (NT)........Luke 1:78
1 and all his **bowels** gushed out.......................Acts 1:18
2 but ye are straitened in your own **bowels**............2 Co 6:12
1 his **inward affection** is more abundant toward you,...... 7:15
2 I long after you all in the **bowels** of Jesus Christ.....Phlp 1:8
1 fellowship of the Spirit, if any **bowels** and mercies,...... 2:1
1 **bowels** of mercies, kindness, humbleness of mind,.... Col 3:12
1 because the **bowels** of the saints are refreshed...... Phlm 1:7
1 therefore receive him, that is, mine own **bowels**:......... 1:12
1 Yea, brother, ... refresh my **bowels** in the Lord.......... 1:20
1 shutteth up his **bowels** of compassion from him,..... 1 Jn 3:17

Classical Greek and Septuagint Usage

Occurring as early as Homer in classical writings, *splanchnon* denotes the internal organs, such as the heart, lungs, or liver. It especially refers to the inner parts of sacrificial animals that were removed, prepared, and eaten following the sacrifice (cf. *Liddell-Scott*). A *splanchnon*, therefore, signifies the meal itself. Several instances are attested in the Septuagint (Proverbs 12:10; 26:22).

Metaphorically the inward parts were considered the seat of all emotions. *Splanchnon* came to describe the emotions themselves. Greek poets employed *splanchnon* for anger or anxiety. The "bowels" (cf. the KJV) were regarded as the source of the most ardent passions, such as anger or love. Jewish understanding believed that the "bowels" were the source of compassion and pity, of mercy and kindness.

New Testament Usage

Splanchnon refers to "tender mercy" (of God, Luke 1:78; of Christ, Philippians 1:8), "affection" (2 Corinthians 6:12), the "heart" (Philemon 12), "pity" (1 John 3:17), and other emotions (e.g., 2 Corinthians 7:15; Colossians 3:12). The literal sense occurs in Acts 1:18 where we read that Judas' "intestines" (NIV) spilled out.

STRONG 4698, BAUER 763, MOULTON-MILLIGAN 584, KITTEL 7:548-59, LIDDELL-SCOTT 1628, COLIN BROWN 2:599-600.

4552. σπόγγος spongos noun

Sponge.

1. σπόγγον spongon acc sing masc

1 straightway one of them ran, and took a **sponge**,... Matt 27:48
1 And one ran and filled a **sponge** full of vinegar,... Mark 15:36
1 and they filled a **sponge** with vinegar,............. John 19:29

This noun, denoting a "sponge," originally referred to the true marine sponge, but later it came to be used for "any spongy substance" such as might be used for bathing, wiping, or cleaning (*Liddell-Scott*).

In the New Testament *spongos* appears only in the parallel passages of Matthew 27:48, Mark 15:36, and John 19:29. There a "sponge" soaked in vinegar was used to offer Jesus a drink on the cross. "According to Pliny it was standard practice for Roman soldiers to carry a piece of sponge for use as a drinking vessel, precisely as described in the gospels" (Cansdale, "Sponge," *Zondervan Pictorial Encyclopedia of the Bible*, 5:510).

STRONG 4699, BAUER 763, MOULTON-MILLIGAN 584, LIDDELL-SCOTT 1628.

4553. σποδός spodos noun

Ashes, wood ashes, embers.

אֵפֶר 'ēpher (684), Ashes (Nm 19:9, Jb 30:19, Mal 4:3).
דֶּשֶׁן deshen (1942), Fat; ashes (Lv 1:16).

1. σποδός spodos nom sing fem
2. σποδῷ spodō dat sing fem

2 have repented long ago in sackcloth and **ashes**......Matt 11:21
2 while ago repented, sitting in sackcloth and **ashes**...Luke 10:13
1 and the **ashes** of an heifer sprinkling the unclean,....Heb 9:13

Spodos denotes "wood ashes" or "embers" and was so used as early as the Greek poet Homer (Eighth Century B.C.). Secondary meanings are "dust, dust of ashes," and in terms of metals, "oxides" and "lava." The noun occurs over 25 times in the Septuagint.

In the New Testament it occurs twice in the Gospels and once in Hebrews. In both of the Gospels occurrences (Matthew 11:21 and Luke 10:13) *spodos* is used in the Old Testament formula "repent in sackcloth and ashes." In Hebrews 9:13 it is used with a qualifier: "ashes of a heifer."

STRONG 4700, BAUER 763, MOULTON-MILLIGAN 584, LIDDELL-SCOTT 1629.

4554. σπορά spora noun

Sowing of seed, seed.

COGNATE:
σπείρω speirō (4540)
SYNONYM:
σπόρος sporos (4556)

זָרַע zāra' (2319), Sow (2 Kgs 19:29).

1. σπορᾶς sporas gen sing fem

1 Being born again, not of corruptible **seed**,...........1 Pt 1:23

Classical Greek and Septuagint Usage

Spora is a noun which means "sowing." Used rather frequently in classical and Koine Greek, it is found only twice in the Septuagint and once in the New Testament. The noun is used literally in reference to "sowing seeds" for crops and figuratively of "seed," meaning "offspring" from procreation. Other meanings denoted by this term included "birth, origin, posterity, race," and "generation." In the Septuagint it occurs in 2 Kings 19:29 (LXX 4 Kings 19:29) where it means "that which is sown" or, simply put, "seed" (cf. a similar usage in 1 Maccabees 10:30).

New Testament Usage

In its only occurrence in the New Testament (1 Peter 1:23) the apostle used the noun in a collective sense of "those born from incorruptible seed," i.e., "being born anew, from above" as distinguished from "born of human (corruptible) seed." (The apostle perhaps was alluding to Christ's meeting with Nicodemus; see John 3.) Peter explained more precisely the origin of this "new birth" stating we are "born again, not of corruptible seed, but of incorruptible, by the word of God." *Alford's Greek Testament* (4:343) makes an interesting observation relative to *spora*: in brief, and without spiritualizing *spora*, it states: "As the grain is the vehicle of the mysterious germinating power, so the word of God is not the begetting principle itself but only that by which the principle (*spora*: seed) works."

Strong 4701, Bauer 763, Moulton-Milligan 584, Kittel 7:536-47, Liddell-Scott 1629.

4555. σπόριμος sporimos adj

Sown.

Cross-Reference:
σπείρω speirō (4540)

זֵרוּעַ zērûa' (2308), Something sown (Lv 11:37).

זָרַע zāra' (2319), Yield seed (Gn 1:29).

1. σποριμων sporimōn gen pl neu

1 Jesus went on the sabbath day through the corn; ... Matt 12:1
1 went through the corn fields on the sabbath day; .... Mark 2:23
1 that he went through the corn fields; .... Luke 6:1

Classical Greek and Septuagint Usage

Sporimos is related to the verb *speirō* (4540), "to sow," and means "sown." Used in reference to fields it is translated "to be sown" or "fit for sowing." In the Septuagint it means "bearing seed" (Genesis 1:29).

New Testament Usage

In the New Testament both Matthew and Mark used the plural form to denote "cornfields," which is rendered more accurately "the fields sown with grain" (Matthew 12:1). In Mark's account (2:23) Jesus "went through the corn fields." It should be noted that *sporimos* does not refer to "corn" as we in the Western world understand its usage; rather the word simply denotes a field "sown" and by extension in its plural form, "seed sown" or "fields sown with grain" without mention of the species of grain (usually wheat or barley).

Strong 4702, Bauer 763, Moulton-Milligan 584, Kittel 7:536-47, Liddell-Scott 1630.

4556. σπόρος sporos noun

Sowing.

Cognate:
σπείρω speirō (4540)

Synonyms:
σπέρμα sperma (4543)
σπορά spora (4554)

זָרַע zāra' (2319), Plant (Is 28:24).

זֶרַע zera' (2320), Sowing time, seed (Lv 26:5, Dt 11:10, Am 9:13).

חָרִישׁ chārîsh (2863), Plowing time (Ex 34:21).

יְבוּל yevûl (3090), Crops (Lv 26:20).

שָׂדֶה sādheh (7898), Field of grain (Sir 40:22).

1. σπόρος sporos nom sing masc
2. σπόρον sporon acc sing masc

2 as if a man should cast seed into the ground; .... Mark 4:26
1 and the seed should spring and grow up, ... 4:27
2 A sower went out to sow his seed: and as he sowed, Luke 8:5
1 the parable is this: The seed is the word of God. 8:11
2 Now He who supplies seed to the sower (NASB) .... 2 Co 9:10
2 and multiply your seed sown, ... 9:10

Classical Greek and Septuagint Usage

Sporos, "sowing," is related to the verb *speirō* (4540), "to sow." In classical and late Greek it also refers to "seedtime, seed, harvest, crop," and "offspring." It is used in the Septuagint about 10 times in a manner similar to that in classical Greek (cf. Exodus 34:21; Leviticus 26:5,20).

New Testament Usage

In the New Testament, Mark used the noun in the sense of "seed" to convey the meaning that the "seed" of the gospel is sown (Mark 4:26). Luke 8:5,11 also uses the noun in the sense of the "seed" of the gospel. Paul, in 2 Corinthians 9:10, used *sporos* in the sense of "seed": "He who ministers seed to the sower . . . will in return supply your *seed*" (free translation), i.e., the means by which you will have resources to help others, as verse 11 explains. (This passage is not a sound basis for the popular "seed-faith" doctrine. The context says nothing about faith.)

Strong 4703, Bauer 763, Moulton-Milligan

584-85, Kittel 7:536-47, Liddell-Scott 1630, Colin Brown 3:521,523.

4557. σπουδάζω spoudazō verb

Hasten, do one's best, be eager or diligent.

Cognates:
σπουδαῖος spoudaios (4558)
σπουδαιότερος spoudaioteros (4559)
σπουδαίως spoudaiōs (4560)
σπουδή spoudē (4561)

אוּץ 'ûts (211), Hurry; hiphil: urge someone (Gn 19:15—Sixtine Edition only).

בָּהַל bāhal (963), Niphal: be terrified (Jb 21:6); piel: terrify (Jb 22:10); hiphil: terrify (Jb 23:16).

חוּשׁ chûsh (2456), Hurry (Jb 31:5).

1. **σπουδάζοντες spoudazontes** nom pl masc part pres act
2. **ἐσπούδασα espoudasa** 1sing indic aor act
3. **ἐσπουδάσαμεν espoudasamen** 1pl indic aor act
4. **σπουδάσωμεν spoudasōmen** 1pl subj aor act
5. **σπούδασον spoudason** 2sing impr aor act
6. **σπουδάσατε spoudasate** 2pl impr aor act
7. **σπουδάσω spoudasō** 1sing indic fut act

2 the same which I also **was forward** to do............. Gal 2:10
1 **Endeavouring** to keep the unity of the Spirit......... Eph 4:3
3 **endeavoured** the more abundantly to see your face...1 Th 2:17
5 **Study** to show thyself approved unto God,......... 2 Tm 2:15
5 **Do thy diligence** to come shortly unto me:............ 4:9
5 **Do thy diligence** to come before winter................. 4:21
5 **be diligent** to come unto me to Nicopolis:............ Tit 3:12
4 Let us **labour** therefore to enter into that rest,....... Heb 4:11
6 **give diligence** to make your ... election sure:........ 2 Pt 1:10
7 Moreover I **will endeavour** that ye may be able......... 1:15
6 **be diligent** that ye may be found of him in peace,....... 3:14

Classical Greek and Septuagint Usage

Spoudazō is a common verb occurring in Greek literature from the time of Plato (Fourth Century B.C.). It most generally means "to make haste." This is often extended to the ideas of being eager about doing something or applying oneself to a task with diligence. This core of meanings lends itself to a variety of nuances. In classical Greek it is used of doing something hastily, of being serious about something, of being busy at doing something, of paying attention to a person, of being zealous, and of being eager.

The most common meaning in the Septuagint is "to hurry." For example, in Genesis 19:15 the angels "hastened Lot" to leave Sodom. Josephus used it of doing one's best. Archelaus wanted to make every effort to show himself kinder to the Jews than his father (Herod) had been (*Antiquities* 17.8.4). The word can even mean "study." Philostratus (Third to Second Century B.C.) wrote that Dio of Prusa "did not neglect the study of letters, but sustained himself with two books" (*Lives of the Sophists* 1.7.2; cf. *Liddell-Scott*).

New Testament Usage

The word occurs 11 times in the New Testament. The exact shade of meaning is not always discernible. It can mean "to do quickly." For example, Paul told Titus, "Be diligent to come unto me to Nicopolis" (Titus 3:12). This could mean "quickly come to me" or "do your best to come to me." But the most common meaning in the New Testament is "to do one's best," as in 2 Peter 1:10. Associated expressions include "to make every effort, to endeavor, to give diligence," or "to work hard." For example, "Do your best to preserve the unity of the Spirit" (free translation, Ephesians 4:3) and, "Do your best to show yourself approved unto God" (free translation, 2 Timothy 2:15). Although *spoudazō* can mean "to study" as noted above, the idea in this latter passage is most likely "to be diligent." The word *study* meant "to exercise oneself" or "to endeavor" when the KJV was translated. Another possibility is that *spoudazō* could simply mean "to be eager" as in Galatians 2:10 where Paul wrote that remembering the poor was the very thing he had been eager or anxious to do. The second meaning would also make good sense, "This was the very thing I have worked hard to do" (free translation).

Strong 4704, Bauer 763, Moulton-Milligan 585, Kittel 7:559-68, Liddell-Scott 1630, Colin Brown 3:1168-69.

4558. σπουδαῖος spoudaios adj

Haste, speed; active, zealous, eager, diligent, earnest.

Cross-Reference:
σπουδάζω spoudazō (4557)

1. **σπουδαῖον spoudaion** acc sing masc

1 we have oftentimes proved **diligent** in many things,..2 Co 8:22

Classical Greek

The adjective *spoudaios* comes from the noun *spoudē* (4561) and denotes "haste" or "speed." It is commonly used in classical Greek. *Spoudaios* can also be found meaning "eager, zealous, earnest," or "diligent" depending on the context. The word is used only once in the Septuagint at Ezekiel 41:25.

New Testament Usage

Paul is the only New Testament writer who employed the adjective, twice in its comparative form (2 Corinthians 8:17,22) and once in its positive form (2 Corinthians 8:17). In 2 Corinthians 8:16-22 the apostle thanked God who gave to the heart of Titus the "same earnest care (*spoudēn*) . . . for you." Paul explained this in verse 17 by saying, "For not only did Titus accept our exhortation but was *very eager* (comparative of *spoudaios*) to do so" (free translation). In verse 22 Paul again used the comparative degree but this time also employed the positive degree of the adjective when speaking of the great zeal of a brother whom he did not name, " . . . whom we have proved *zealous* in many ways, but now even *more zealous*" (free translation). In both cases the translation could well be "eager" and "more eager" or "diligent" and "more diligent" respectively.

STRONG 4705, BAUER 763, MOULTON-MILLIGAN 585, KITTEL 7:559-68, LIDDELL-SCOTT 1630, COLIN BROWN 3:1168-69.

4559. σπουδαιότερος spoudaioteros adj

In haste, quicker.

CROSS-REFERENCE:
σπουδάζω spoudazō (4557)

1. σπουδαιότερον spoudaioteron comp nom/acc sing masc/neu
2. σπουδαιότερος spoudaioteros comp nom sing masc

2 but being **more forward,** of his own accord he went . . 2 Co 8:17
1 but now much **more diligent,** 8:22
1 he sought me out **very diligently,** and found me. . . . . 2 Tm 1:17

This word is the comparative form of the adjective *spoudaios*. It is used in a superlative sense in 2 Corinthians 8:17,22. See the word study at number 4558.

4560. σπουδαίως spoudaiōs adv

Hastily, zealously, earnestly.

COGNATE:
σπουδάζω spoudazō (4557)

SYNONYMS:
ἀκριβῶς akribōs (197)
ἐπιμελῶς epimelōs (1945)

1. σπουδαίως spoudaiōs
2. σπουδαιοτέρως spoudaioterōs comp

1 they came to Jesus, they besought him **instantly,** . . . . Luke 7:4
2 I sent him therefore the **more carefully,** . . . . Phlp 2:28
1 he **eagerly** searched for me, and found me (NASB) 2 Tm 1:17
1 and Apollos on their journey **diligently,** . . . . Tit 3:13

Spoudaiōs is an adverb formed from the adjective *spoudaios* (4558). Of the gospel writers, Luke is the only one who employed the adverb. In Luke 7:4 the term carries the idea of "concern." Paul used the comparative form in Philippians 2:28 where it has the force of a superlative adverb, i.e., "most quickly," with a strong nuance of "concern." In 2 Timothy 1:17 and Titus 3:13 the adverb indicates "carefully, with concern."

STRONG 4709, BAUER 763, MOULTON-MILLIGAN 585, LIDDELL-SCOTT 1630.

4561. σπουδή spoudē noun

Haste, speed, zeal, effort, earnestness, diligence.

CROSS-REFERENCE:
σπουδάζω spoudazō (4557)

בָּהַל bāhal (963), Niphal: something sudden (Zep 1:18).
בְּהַל b^ehal (A964), Hithpeel: do in a hurry (Dn 2:25—Aramaic).
בֶּהָלָה behālāh (965), Terror (Ps 78:33 [77:33], Jer 15:8).
בְּעָתָה b^eʿāthāh (1228), Terror (Jer 8:15).
חִפָּזוֹן chippāzôn (2754), Haste (Ex 12:11, Dt 16:3).
מָהַר māhar (4257), Piel: hurry (Ex 12:33).
נָחַץ nāchats (5350), Urgent (1 Sm 21:8).
רֶגַע regha' (7569), Moment (Lam 4:6).

1. σπουδῆς spoudēs gen sing fem
2. σπουδῇ spoudē dat sing fem
3. σπουδήν spoudēn acc sing fem

1 she came in straightway with **haste** unto the king, . . . Mark 6:25
1 and went into the hill country with **haste,** . . . . Luke 1:39
2 he that ruleth, with **diligence;** . . . . Rom 12:8
2 Not slothful in **business;** fervent in spirit; 12:11
3 what **carefulness** it wrought in you, ... 2 Co 7:11
3 our **care** for you in the sight of God might appear 7:12
2 and in all **diligence,** and in your love to us, ... 8:7
1 but by occasion of the **forwardness** of others, ... 8:8
3 which put the same **earnest care** into the heart 8:16
3 that every one of you do show the same **diligence** . . . Heb 6:11
3 And beside this, giving all **diligence,** . . . . 2 Pt 1:5
3 when I gave all **diligence** to write unto you . . . . . . Jude 1:3

The noun *spoudē* and other members of the same word group are related to the verb *speudō*, "to be eager, to hasten, to hurry" (cf. the New Testament verb *spoudazō* [4557]; the adverb *spoudaiōs* [4560], "more eagerly"; and the adjective *spoudaioteros* [4559], "more eager"). The noun denotes "eagerness, zeal, haste, speed."

Classical Greek

The word group generally describes external action, "to hurry" or "to be quick" to fulfill a task. But it can also describe an internal attitude or response: "to be eager, earnest, diligent." This may contrast diligence with laziness, or it may indicate earnestness versus apathy or frivolousness.

Spoudē was regarded as a virtue in Greek philosophy. Being "earnest" denotes moral integrity and a concern for becoming perfect. *Spoudē* might suggest "willingness" and "goodwill." In a religious context *spoudē* and its companions can express "sincerity, commitment."

Septuagint Usage

Finding any directly corresponding Hebrew word poses problems. The association in the apocryphal writings is with "zeal." Elsewhere *spoudē* means "hurry"; Lot was urged by the angels to "hurry" and leave Sodom (Genesis 19:15). The people of Israel were forced to leave Egypt in "haste" on Passover (Exodus 12:11; cf. verse 33).

New Testament Usage

The word group continues to mean "eagerness, earnestness, diligence," and "haste" in the New Testament. *Spoudē* is even used to portray the kind of commitment expected of all Christians in virtually every aspect of their lives (e.g., Romans 12:11 of business). More importantly, believers must be eager to maintain the unity of the Spirit in the body (Ephesians 4:3). They are to be eager to maintain fellowship with one another (1 Thessalonians 2:17; 2 Timothy 4:9,21; Titus 3:12). Believers are earnestly and diligently to help those in need (Galatians 2:10). An overseer of the church must perform his "duties" responsibly and with all earnestness (Romans 12:8). A commitment to remind the church of the truth of the gospel is expected of all (2 Peter 1:15). Even discipline in the church should be carried out diligently (2 Corinthians 7:11).

One's personal life before God must display *spoudē*. He or she must be diligent in the quest for eternal rest (Hebrews 4:11). He or she must *earnestly* strive to make his or her calling certain (2 Peter 1:10) and to insure that Christ will find them "spotless and blameless" at His coming (2 Peter 3:14, NASB).

STRONG 4710, BAUER 763-64, MOULTON-MILLIGAN 585-86, KITTEL 7:559-68, LIDDELL-SCOTT 1630-31, COLIN BROWN 3:1168-69.

4562. σπυρίς spuris noun

Large basket, wicker basket.

SYNONYM:
κόφινος kophinos (2867)

1. **σπυρίδι spuridi** dat sing fem
2. **σπυρίδων spuridōn** gen pl fem
3. **σπυρίδας spuridas** acc pl fem
4. **σφυρίδας sphuridas** acc pl fem

3 of the broken meat that was left seven **baskets** full. Matt 15:37
3 and how many **baskets** ye took up? 16:10
3 of the broken meat that was left seven **baskets**...... Mark 8:8
2 how many **baskets** full of fragments took ye up? 8:20
1 and let him down by the wall in a **basket**........... Acts 9:25

This noun is found in classical and Koine Greek where it denotes a "large basket" that would hold money or food (cf. *Liddell-Scott*). It is used four times in the Gospels: twice by Matthew and twice by Mark. In each of these four occurrences *spuris* (also spelled *sphuris*) is used for the baskets of food which were taken up. In Acts 9:25 the word refers to the basket Paul was placed in when he was lowered from the wall of Damascus. The meaning is simply "large basket."

STRONG 4711, BAUER 764, MOULTON-MILLIGAN 618 (see "sphuris"), LIDDELL-SCOTT 1631.

4563. στάδιον stadion noun

Stade, furlong, stadium, race-course.

1. **σταδίῳ stadiō** dat sing masc/neu
2. **σταδίων stadiōn** gen pl masc/neu
3. **σταδίους stadious** acc pl masc
4. **στάδια stadia** nom/acc pl neu

3 boat was already many **stadia** away (NASB) .... Matt 14:24
3 was from Jerusalem about threescore **furlongs**...... Luke 24:13
3 rowed about five and twenty or thirty **furlongs**,..... John 6:19
2 nigh unto Jerusalem, about fifteen **furlongs** off: 11:18
1 Know ye not that they which run in a **race** run all, .. 1 Co 9:24
2 the space of a thousand and six hundred **furlongs**... Rev 14:20
2 he measured the city ... twelve thousand **furlongs**...... 21:16

Classical Greek

In early Greek literature *stadion* can be found denoting a "stade," which was a unit of measure equivalent to about one-eighth of a Roman mile (607 English feet, 192 meters). Because of its application to the Olympia, which was exactly one stade in length, the noun came to denote "race course," then "race," then the building itself, i.e., the "amphitheater." It also came to be used for any area designated for an activity such as dancing; it also describes a board for playing games like backgammon (*Liddell-Scott*). It is not found in the canonical Septuagint.

New Testament Usage

Stadion occurs seven times in the New Testament. In the Gospels (Luke 24:13; John 6:19; 11:18) the noun is used in its normal sense of "stade" or a "measure" of distance. Paul used *stadion* in 1 Corinthians 9:24 to refer to the Isthmian games so well known to the Corinthians. From this picture he made this comparison, particularly important in light of the undisciplined spirit of the Corinthian assembly: "Those who run in the stadium (race course), all run . . . but only one receives the prize" (author's translation). Thus

Paul alluded to the Corinthian Christians' need for self-discipline as practiced by the Greek runners. Its two occurrences in Revelation (14:20 and 21:16) indicate a measurement of "stades."

STRONG 4712, BAUER 764, MOULTON-MILLIGAN 586, LIDDELL-SCOTT 1631.

4564. στάμνος stamnos noun

Clay jar, wine jar.

בַּקְבֻּק baqbuq (1254), Jar (1 Kgs 14:3—Codex Alexandrinus only).

צִנְצֶנֶת tsintseneth (7079), Jar (Ex 16:33).

1. στάμνος stamnos nom sing fem

1 wherein was the golden pot that had manna,........ Heb 9:4

According to various Greek authors and the papyri, *stamnos* denotes either "a clay jar for wine, a container to hold money, a ballot urn, a jar to hold figs," or an "oil jar" (cf. *Liddell-Scott*). Its only occurrence in the New Testament is Hebrews 9:4 where it is translated as the "jar" or "container" in which the manna was kept.

STRONG 4713, BAUER 764, MOULTON-MILLIGAN 586, LIDDELL-SCOTT 1633.

4564B. στασιαστής stasiastēs noun

A rebel, insurrectionist, revolutionary.

CROSS-REFERENCE:
ἵστημι histēmi (2449)

1. στασιαστῶν stasiastōn gen pl masc

1 imprisoned with the insurrectionists (NASB).......Mark 15:7

This first declension masculine noun, which occurs only once in the New Testament, is given two meanings in Greek literature. It can denote "one who stirs up sedition," or it can denote a "weigher" in a wool factory (cf. *Liddell-Scott*).

In Mark 15:7 the plural form of *stasiastēs* is used to describe certain ones who had been imprisoned for crimes committed against the state. One member's name in the band is given, Barabbas. He, instead of Jesus, was delivered to the people. Barabbas, in addition to being an insurrectionist, was also accused of murder.

BAUER 764, MOULTON-MILLIGAN 586, LIDDELL-SCOTT 1633.

4565. στάσις stasis noun

Placing, setting, standing, existing; sedition, insurrection, strife.

COGNATE:
ἵστημι histēmi (2449)

SYNONYMS:
ἐριθεία eritheia (2036)
ἔρις eris (2038)
μάχη machē (3135)
φιλονεικία philoneikia (5216)

הֲדֹם hădhōm (1986), Footstool (1 Chr 28:2).

מָנוֹחַ mānôach (4638), Resting place (Dt 28:65).

מָעוֹז mā'ôz (4735), Refuge (Na 3:11).

מַעֲמָד ma'ămādh (4771), Attendance (1 Kgs 10:5, 2 Chr 9:4): position (Is 22:19).

מַצֵּבָה matstsēvāh (4838), Pillar (Jgs 9:6).

מַתְכֹּנֶת mathkōneth (5147), Original design (2 Chr 24:13).

עָמַד 'āmadh (6198), Stand (Jos 10:13).

עֹמֶד 'ōmedh (6199), Station, place (2 Chr 30:16, 35:10).

עַמּוּד 'ammûdh (6204), Pillar (2 Chr 23:13).

קְיָם q^eyām (A7292), Statute (Dn 6:7—Aramaic).

רִיב rîv (7663), Dispute (Prv 17:14).

1. στάσις stasis nom sing fem
2. στάσεως staseōs gen sing fem
3. στάσει stasei dat sing fem
4. στάσιν stasin acc sing fem
5. στάσεις staseis acc pl fem

3 who had committed murder in the insurrection.....Mark 15:7
4 Who for a certain sedition made in the city,....... Luke 23:19
4 that for sedition and murder was cast into prison,...... 23:25
2 no small dissension and disputation with them,..... Acts 15:2
2 to be called in question for this day's uproar,......... 19:40
1 And when he had so said, there arose a dissension..... 23:7
2 And when there arose a great dissension,............. 23:10
4 and a mover of sedition among all the Jews........... 24:5
4 while as the first tabernacle was yet standing:........Heb 9:8

Classical Greek

Stasis is an important noun in classical Greek literature. Not only does the substantive have the meanings "placing, standing, sedition, strife," but it contains numerous overtones and metaphors. For example, depending on the context, it means "standing still," hence "pillar" or "statue"; "the place in which one stands," hence "position" or "posture"; "the arrangement of horses or soldiers," hence "state of affairs, condition of people" (*Liddell-Scott*). The noun was employed as early as Herodotus (Fifth Century B.C.) to denote "parties, bands," or "factions" particularly in a seditious sense (ibid.).

Septuagint Usage

In the Septuagint *stasis* has the basic ideas listed above, but also (as in Daniel 6:7) the word refers to a "decree" or "statue." In Proverbs 17:14 it can be translated as a "hot argument, dissension."

New Testament Usage

Stasis occurs nine times in the New Testament. Luke used the noun seven times, Mark once, and the author of Hebrews once. In Mark 15:7 it is used in the sense of an insurrection, as is the case in Luke 23:19, 25. In Acts 15:2 *stasis* means "disagreement" or "holding a firm position." In Acts 19:40 the idea is not so much that of "sedition" as it is of a "riot" of the people. In Acts 23:7, 10 the thought is that of "riot" resulting from the position taken by the Sadducees against the Pharisees (see verses 8,9); in Acts 24:5 the idea is one of sedition: "a mover of *sedition* among all the Jews."

The writer to the Hebrews at 9:8 employed *stasis* in the sense of "existing" or "standing" with the idea of "in effect." He wrote, "The way into the holiest of all was not yet made manifest, while as the first tabernacle was yet standing (*echousēs stasin*)," i.e., "in effect."

Strong 4714, Bauer 764, Moulton-Milligan 586, Kittel 7:568-71, Liddell-Scott 1634.

4566. στατήρ statēr noun

Weight, standard coin.

1. στατῆρα statēra acc sing masc

1 thou shalt find a piece of money:.................. Matt 17:27

Statēr, meaning "weight," also came to denote "money" or a "standard coin." In late Greek the noun is transliterated "stater," a silver coin worth about four drachmas. It is used once in the New Testament, by Matthew only: at 17:27 where it is translated "shekel" (RSV) or "piece of money" (KJV).

Strong 4715, Bauer 764, Moulton-Milligan 586, Liddell-Scott 1634, Colin Brown 2:851; 3:752-53.

4567. σταυρός stauros noun

A cross.

Cognates:

ἀνασταυρόω anastauroō (386)
σταυρόω stauroō (4568)
συσταυρόω sustauroō (4809)

Synonym:

ξύλον xulon (3448)

1. σταυρός stauros nom sing masc
2. σταυροῦ staurou gen sing masc
3. σταυρῷ staurō dat sing masc
4. σταυρόν stauron acc sing masc

4 he that taketh not his cross, and followeth after me,Matt 10:38
4 deny himself, and take up his cross, and follow me.... 16:24
4 him they compelled to bear his cross.................. 27:32
2 If ... be the Son of God, come down from the cross.... 27:40
2 let him now come down from the cross,............... 27:42
4 let him deny himself, and take up his cross,........ Mark 8:34
4 and come, take up the cross, and follow me........... 10:21
4 father of Alexander and Rufus, to bear his cross....... 15:21
2 Save thyself, and come down from the cross....... Mark 15:30
2 Let Christ the King ... descend now from the cross,.... 15:32
4 and take up his cross daily, and follow me.......... Luke 9:23
4 whosoever doth not bear his cross, and come after..... 14:27
4 Simon, a Cyrenian, ... on him they laid the cross,...... 23:26
4 And he bearing his cross went forth...............John 19:17
2 And Pilate wrote a title, and put it on the cross....... 19:19
3 Now there stood by the cross of Jesus his mother,..... 19:25
2 that the bodies should not remain upon the cross...... 19:31
1 lest the cross ... should be made of none effect...... 1 Co 1:17
2 the cross is to them that perish foolishness;............ 1:18
2 then is the offence of the cross ceased............... Gal 5:11
3 should suffer persecution for the cross of Christ......... 6:12
3 glory, save in the cross of our Lord Jesus Christ,....... 6:14
2 reconcile both unto God in one body by the cross,... Eph 2:16
2 obedient unto death, even the death of the cross.....Phlp 2:8
2 that they are the enemies of the cross of Christ:........ 3:18
2 having made peace through the blood of his cross,... Col 1:20
3 and took it out of the way, nailing it to his cross;...... 2:14
4 endured the cross, despising the shame,............ Heb 12:2

In secular Greek *stauros* denotes a "pole," or a "pile," such as is used in foundations. The term is also used of a "fence, stake," or a "tent peg"; however, it also refers to a "cross" upon which criminals were executed (cf. *Liddell-Scott*). This is its use in the New Testament. The noun does not occur in the Septuagint, although the verb, *stauroō* (4568), does occur in Esther (7:9) where it means to hang on a pole.

Execution by means of crucifixion was employed in Greece, but the practice did not originate there. In all likelihood the Persians invented this means of torture and execution. Later, Alexander the Great, the Phoenicians, and the Carthaginians used this method of punishment. The Romans adopted it from the Carthaginians; however, except in rare cases they seldom executed Roman citizens by crucifixion. Usually only slaves and the most serious criminals, e.g., traitors, perjurers, etc. were crucified.

Felix the governor (see Acts 23 and 24) ordered many insurrectionists crucified during his administration. During the destruction of Jerusalem more than 500 Jews were crucified each day during one particular period. At one point the Romans lacked the wood necessary to crucify all those they had sentenced to die.

Although Jews did not commonly employ crucifixion, they nonetheless hung up the corpses of those stoned for idolatry or blasphemy. These were thus branded as cursed by God in accordance with Deuteronomy 21:23: "Anyone who is hung on a tree is under God's curse" (NIV; cf. Galatians 3:13).

Crucifixion was regarded as the most humiliating and ignominious punishment of all. Josephus termed it "the most wretched of deaths" (*Wars of the Jews* 7.6.4); Tacitus the historian described it as "the most pitiful of all means of death" (cf.

Brandenburger, "Cross," *Colin Brown*, 1:392). The one to be crucified experienced the ridicule and mockery of his executioners; onlookers participated in this too, as did the judges (Matthew 27:27-31,39-44; Mark 15:16-20,29-32; Luke 23:35-39). The site of execution, outside the town gate, was itself a place of disgrace (Hebrews 13:12,13). Because of this understanding, a crucified Messiah caused many Jews to disbelieve (1 Corinthians 1:23).

After sentencing, the criminal was scourged, itself a punishment so painful and horribly debilitating that some died from it. This took place either immediately after the sentence was pronounced or en route to the execution site. In Jesus' case the scourging probably took place before He was sentenced, perhaps in the hope that the crowds might have compassion on the exhausted, bleeding Man from Galilee and ask Pilate to release Him (Luke 23:16; John 19:1f.). That His punishment was so severe may explain why Jesus did not have to bear the cross the last steps to Golgotha (Matthew 27:32).

Ordinarily the criminal was forced to carry the crossbeam all the way to the execution site; the upright beam was usually left in place at the crucifixion site. Once there, the criminal was stripped (Matthew 27:35; John 19:23f.), and his shoulders and outstretched arms were extended above the crosspiece as he lay on his back. After the criminal was tied or nailed—Jesus was nailed—to the crosspiece (John 20:25), the body was lifted up and the beam set on the already erected pole. The feet were then bound or nailed to the pole (cf. the prophecy of Psalm 22:16).

The charge was displayed above the criminal on a board in black or red letters. On the way from the trial to the site of execution the criminal either wore the board with the charge around his neck or someone else carried it in front of him. At the execution site it was fastened to the top of the stake so its inscription might be clearly read at a distance (cf. Matthew 27:37; Mark 15:26; Luke 23:38; John 19:19). In Jesus' case the charge was written in three languages: the language of Palestine, Hebrew; the language of the occupying forces from Rome, Latin; and the common language of the day, Greek.

To die upon a cross meant excruciating pain. The searing wounds, the agonizing thirst and hunger, the hemorrhaging of the blood vessels in the head and heart, the scorching heat of the sun by day or the cold of the nights gradually robbed the victim of all strength. He became insane from the pain. Death came slowly. Medical studies show that death itself was caused by asphyxiation. Jewish women often offered the doomed man a narcotic-like concoction of wine and myrrh in accordance with the directive of Proverbs 31:6: "Give strong drink unto him that is ready to perish." Jesus did not accept this drink, choosing instead to suffer all the pain of death (Mark 15:23).

The condition of the criminal's body played an important role in the effects of crucifixion. Ordinarily the crucified person lived for some time, frequently lasting more than 24 hours and sometimes as long as 48 hours. Some records exist of crucifixions lasting from 3 to 6 days. At times the legs of the victim were broken to put an end to the suffering of the victim (John 19:32). Thus Pilate was surprised when he was told that Jesus died within 6 hours (Mark 15:44f.).

The words of the Apostles' Creed, "suffered under Pontius Pilate, was crucified, dead, and buried," emphasize the historicity of the event. The gospel is more than a timeless philosophy. Rather, the gospel is grounded in an historically verifiable setting. The same holds true for Christ's death. It should not be interpreted "spiritually" or "figuratively." It was the "body of his flesh" that died (Colossians 1:22); He was "put to death in the flesh" (1 Peter 3:18). "For this thing was not done in a corner" (Acts 26:26); instead, it was publicly witnessed on Calvary's hill. Christ's death on the cross was well known by His first-century contemporaries. Jewish rabbis, many of whom bitterly opposed Christianity, mocked Christ as "the hanged one," a reference to His death on the cross. The Roman historian Tacitus wrote: "Christ, from whom the Christians have taken their name, was executed during the reign of Tiberius by the procurator Pontius Pilate" (Annals 15.44).

Jesus forewarned His disciples that His impending mode of death in Jerusalem would not be stoning by the Jews but by the Roman death penalty of crucifixion (Matthew 20:19). Under Roman occupation the Jews did not have the authority to carry out capital punishment except for certain cases of sacrilege. Jesus also knew that the Jewish leaders would sentence their Messiah to death and hand Him over to the Gentiles to be crucified (Matthew 20:18f.).

The crowds demanded His crucifixion from Pilate as they cried, "Crucify him!" (Matthew

27:22). Jesus himself declared that the one who delivered Him to the Roman governor (Pilate), Caiphas, had "greater sin" than Pilate (John 19:11). And in his sermon on the Day of Pentecost, Peter stressed how grievous to God was the Jewish manipulation of the Roman government to destroy Jesus. He said, "Ye have taken, and by wicked hands have crucified and slain" Jesus (Acts 2:23). Such action was treason against God (Acts 3:13f.).

Nevertheless, while this magnifies the guilt of the Jewish leaders for Jesus' death, it also leads to the fact that the Gentiles must assume their share of the responsibility. Everyone conspired against the "holy child Jesus." Pontius Pilate, together with the Gentiles and the nation of Israel, were guilty of the ultimate act of sin and cruelty: the crucifixion of the beloved and only Son of God (Acts 4:27).

In the New Testament the term *stauros* is employed generally in three ways: literally, symbolically or figuratively, and theologically. The literal use of the term may be found throughout the New Testament. At Matthew 27:32 Simon of Cyrene is described as being conscripted to bear the cross for Jesus: "Him they compelled to bear his cross" (cf. the parallels at Mark 15:21; Luke 23:26). The chief priests, scribes, and elders mocked Christ while He was on the cross: "If he be the King of Israel, let him now come down from the cross" (Matthew 27:42; cf. verse 40; Mark 15:30,32). At John 19:17 Christ's journey to Golgotha is described: "And he bearing his cross went forth into a place called *the place* of a skull." Pilate is described as putting an inscription on the cross: "And Pilate wrote a title, and put *it* on the cross" (John 19:19). Jesus' mother is said to have stood by the cross: "Now there stood by the cross of Jesus his mother" (John 19:25). At John 19:31 the victims are said to be on the cross: "The bodies should not remain upon the cross on the sabbath day." Paul referred to Christ's death on the cross: "And being found in fashion as a man, he humbled himself, and became obedient unto death, even the death of the cross" (Philippians 2:8). Paul spoke of reconciliation made because of Jesus' blood shed on the cross: " . . . and, having made peace through the blood of his cross" (Colossians 1:20). The writer of Hebrews spoke of Christ's enduring the cross: "Looking unto Jesus the author and finisher of *our* faith; who for the joy that was set before him endured the cross" (Hebrews 12:2).

Although the above passages refer to the cross in literal terms, the word itself may also be used in a symbolic way. The cross symbolizes the suffering and crucifixion of Jesus. Hebrews 12:2 shows this clearly: Christ "endured the cross," which speaks of every aspect surrounding that event. The cross was the climax of Christ's suffering, and it symbolizes the penalty for sin.

The Gospels are the account of His suffering with detailed introductory remarks. But the recollection of His suffering is in no way elaborated upon or embellished. There is no attempt to evoke sympathy or pity. The entire portrait focuses upon the silent dignity of that Just One before the unjust judges (Matthew 26:62f.; 27:14; Luke 23:9). He does not ask for sympathy; He even discourages the tears of the "daughters of Jerusalem" (Luke 23:28).

The cross stands as a symbol of the humiliation and disgrace that Christ willingly endured. The New Testament highlights this aspect of the cross more than the physical suffering it caused. Permeating the passion narrative are accounts of the scorn and mockery by the onlookers and the humiliation Jesus endured. The cross symbolizes the suffering, disgrace, and humiliation experienced by Jesus; nevertheless, this "tree of shame and curse," through the death of Jesus Christ, became the sign of victory to all who believe in Him.

In Matthew 10:38 the writer used the term *stauros* figuratively of Jesus when He said to His disciples, "He that taketh not his cross, and followeth after me, is not worthy of me" (cf. parallels at Mark 8:34; Luke 9:23). The suffering and humiliation endured by Christ serve as an example to every believer today: "Let this mind be in you, which was also in Christ Jesus: who, being in the form of God, thought it not robbery to be equal with God: but made himself of no reputation, and took upon him the form of a servant, and was made in the likeness of men: and being found in fashion as a man, he humbled himself, and became obedient unto death, even the death of the cross (*stauros*)" (Philippians 2:5-8).

As a theological term the cross summarizes the gospel, the message of salvation, in the New Testament. The cross assumes a central role in the drama of salvation; consequently, the preaching of the apostles also focused upon the cross. Paul described the gospel as "the preaching of the cross" (1 Corinthians 1:18). This is the only true gospel, thus Paul declared: "For I determined not to know any thing among you, save Jesus Christ, and him crucified" (1 Corinthians 2:2). The preaching of the cross is the power of God unto salvation (1 Corinthians 1:18; cf. Romans 1:16).

The saving effect of the cross is concealed in the mystery that the death of Christ has atoning power. He offered himself as our perfect substitute, the sacrifice for our sins. He thus experienced the judgment of God, the penalty of sin (death), on our behalf. Jesus endured the hardship of the cross and placed himself under the curse of the law; because He experienced God's wrath, we can escape it.

Jesus understood that His punishment would come from God himself. Quoting the words of the prophet Zechariah He said, "I (God) will smite the shepherd" (Matthew 26:31; cf. Zechariah 13:17). In the Garden of Gethsemane Jesus implied that it was God who would give Him the "cup of suffering." This recalls the words of Isaiah 53:10: "It pleased the LORD to bruise him." He came "under the curse" of the law; He was "made a curse for us" (Galatians 3:10,13).

At the cross mankind is reconciled with God (Ephesians 2:16). Through Christ's blood on the cross God made peace with us (Colossians 1:20). At the point of the supreme act of human cruelty and rebellion God demonstrated His love for us and His unsurpassed grace, for "God demonstrates his own love for us in this: While we were still sinners, Christ died for us" (Romans 5:8, NIV). Furthermore, we are told "who his own self bare our sins in his own body on the tree" (1 Peter 2:24). Through the cross everyone who believes receives the forgiveness of sins (Ephesians 1:7; Colossians 1:14).

The cross also signifies the believer's union with Christ in His death. This is depicted in two slightly different ways. First, the cross is an example to all believers. Whoever wants to follow Christ must take up his or her own cross (Matthew 16:24). Everyone in Jesus' day knew that the one sentenced to be crucified had to carry his cross. Moreover, they knew that from the moment the crossbeam was placed upon the shoulders, death was inescapable. Thus when Jesus utilized this imagery He intended for His listeners to realize that to become His disciple meant to give up everything, even one's own life (Matthew 10:37-39; Luke 14:26,27). Here Jesus is the ultimate example of the true disciple (1 Peter 2:21-24; cf. Philippians 2:5-8).

In addition to the concept that the disciple must imitate Christ in taking up the cross, note also that the believer's sinful nature has been crucified with Christ (Romans 6:6,10,11; Galatians 5:24; 1 Peter 2:24; cf. Romans 7:4; Galatians 2:19,20; 6:14). The issue here is not some psychological manipulation by Christ's example; rather, the shift takes place because of the fellowship shared with the Risen One. Consequently, every aspect of life—ethical, social, economic—comes under the rule of God. The believer not only imitates Christ, he has been "united with Him in the likeness of His death" (Romans 6:5, NASB); he is "dead with Christ" (6:8); he has been "buried with him by baptism into death" (6:4). Moreover, he or she has "risen with Christ" (Colossians 3:1). Thus "cross" carries significant Christological and soteriological implications.

Finally, the cross has universal and cosmic implications. Through the power of the cross the "middle wall of partition," the enmity between Jews and Gentiles, is broken down because the Old Testament covenant is abolished (Ephesians 2:14-16). God also intends that His divided creation is to be reunited in Christ (Ephesians 1:10). " . . . And through him (Christ) to reconcile to himself all things, whether things on earth or things in heaven, by making peace through his blood, shed on the cross" (Colossians 1:20, NIV). Through Christ's work on the cross the evil spirits were conquered: "And having spoiled principalities and powers, he made a show of them openly, triumphing over them in it" (Colossians 2:15; cf. John 12:31,32).

STRONG 4716, BAUER 764-65, MOULTON-MILLIGAN 586, KITTEL 7:572-80, LIDDELL-SCOTT 1635, COLIN BROWN 1:391-99,403-4.

4568. σταυρόω stauroō verb

To fence with stakes, to fix to a cross, crucify.

COGNATE:

σταυρός stauros (4567)

SYNONYM:

προσπήγνυμι prospēgnumi (4220)

תָּלָה tālâh (8847), Hang (Ext 7:9).

1. **σταυροῦσιν staurousin** 3pl indic pres act
2. **ἐσταυρώσατε estaurōsate** 2pl indic aor act
3. **ἐσταύρωσαν estaurōsan** 3pl indic aor act
4. **σταυρώσω staurōsō** 1sing subj aor act
5. **σταυρώσωσιν staurōsōsin** 3pl subj aor act

6. **σταύρωσον stauröson** 2sing impr aor act
7. **σταυρώσατε staurösate** 2pl impr aor act
8. **σταυρώσαντες staurösantes** nom pl masc part aor act
9. **σταυρῶσαι staurōsai** inf aor act
10. **σταυρώσετε staurōsete** 2pl indic fut act
11. **σταυροῦνται staurountai** 3pl indic pres mid
12. **ἐσταυρώθη estaurōthē** 3sing indic aor pass
13. **σταυρωθῇ staurōthē** 3sing subj aor pass
14. **σταυρωθήτω staurōthētō** 3sing impr aor pass
15. **σταυρωθῆναι staurōthēnai** inf aor pass
16. **ἐσταύρωται estaurōtai** 3sing indic perf mid
17. **ἐσταυρωμένος estaurōmenos** nom sing masc part perf mid
18. **ἐσταυρωμένον estaurōmenon** acc sing masc part perf mid
19. **σταύρου staurou** 2sing impr pres act
20. **σταυρώσουσιν staurōsousin** 3pl indic fut act

9 to mock, and to scourge, and **to crucify him:** ...... Matt 20:19
10 and some of them ye shall kill and **crucify;** 23:34
15 and the Son of man is betrayed **to be crucified.** 26:2
14 They all say unto him, Let him **be crucified.** 27:22
14 they cried out the more, ... Let him **be crucified.** 27:23
13 he delivered him **to be crucified.** 27:26
9 and led him away **to crucify him.** 27:31
8 And they **crucified him,** and parted his garments, ... 27:35
11 Then were there two thieves **crucified** with him, ... 27:38
18 for I know that ye seek Jesus, **which was crucified.** 28:5
6 And they cried out again, **Crucify him.** .... Mark 15:13
6 they cried out the more exceedingly, **Crucify him.** 15:14
13 and delivered Jesus, ... **to be crucified.** 15:15
5 and led him out **to crucify him.** 15:20
8 And when they **had crucified him,** 15:24
3 And it was the third hour, and **they crucified him.** 15:25
1 And with him **they crucify** two thieves; 15:27
18 Ye seek Jesus of Nazareth, **which was crucified:** 16:6
6 But they cried, saying, **Crucify him,** crucify him... Luke 23:21
6 But they cried, saying, Crucify him, **crucify him.** 23:21
15 requiring that he **might be crucified.** 23:23
3 there they **crucified** him, and the malefactors, ... 23:33
15 and **be crucified,** and the third day rise again. 24:7
3 to be condemned to death, and **have crucified him.** ... 24:20
6 they cried out, saying, **Crucify him,** crucify him.... John 19:6
6 they cried out, saying, Crucify him, **crucify him.** 19:6
7 and **crucify** him: for I find no fault in him. 19:6
9 knowest thou not that I have power **to crucify thee,** .. 19:10
6 Away with him, away with him, **crucify him.** 19:15
4 Pilate saith unto them, **Shall I crucify** your King? 19:15
13 delivered he him ... unto them **to be crucified.** 19:16
3 Where they **crucified him,** and two others 19:18
12 where Jesus **was crucified** was nigh to the city: 19:20
3 Then the soldiers, when they **had crucified Jesus,** 19:23
12 place where he **was crucified** there was a garden; 19:41
2 whom ye have **crucified,** both Lord and Christ. ..... Acts 2:36
2 Jesus Christ of Nazareth, whom ye **crucified,** 4:10
12 Is Christ divided? **was Paul crucified** for you? ...... 1 Co 1:13
18 But we preach Christ **crucified,** 1:23
18 save Jesus Christ, and him **crucified.** 2:2
3 they **would** not **have** crucified the Lord of glory. 2:8
12 For though he **was crucified** through weakness, ... 2 Co 13:4
17 evidently set forth, **crucified** among you? .... Gal 3:1
3 And they that are Christ's have **crucified** the flesh 5:24
16 cross ... by whom the world **is crucified** unto me, ... 6:14
12 where also our Lord **was crucified.** .... Rev 11:8

Classical Greek and Septuagint Usage

Staurō̄ is a common verb in Greek literature. The noun form *stauros* (4567) was used to denote a "cross" as an instrument of torture or crucifixion, and the verb form *stauroō* was used to mean "to crucify," (ca. Second Century B.C.). In the Septuagint the noun is found once (Esther 7:9) where it refers to a pale (stake) on which an individual was impaled. That was a common means of torture and execution in the Persian Empire.

New Testament Usage

In the New Testament the verb is used in both literally and figuratively. Matthew 20:19 employs the term literally to mean "to crucify on a cross" or "to put to death on a cross." The verb's occurrence in the other Gospels is translated in the same way. In Galatians 5:24 and 6:14 Paul employed *stauroō* as a picture of his high standard of personal holiness: "My desire for the things of the world has been crucified," or "The power of such has been destroyed, put to death" (author's translations). In 6:14 Paul made an appeal to those who would futilely try to "glory" in the Law, to embrace "the cross of . . . Christ," as he had done (verse 14), and to glory in the victory of the Cross by means of which the power of the world has been destroyed.

STRONG 4717, BAUER 765, MOULTON-MILLIGAN 586-87, KITTEL 7:581-83, LIDDELL-SCOTT 1635, COLIN BROWN 1:391,393-94,397,399.

4569. σταφυλή staphulē noun

Bunch of grapes, grape.

עֵנָב ʿēnāv (6252), Grapes (Nm 6:3, Neh 13:15, Hos 9:10).

1. **σταφυλήν staphulēn** acc sing fem
2. **σταφυλαί staphulai** nom pl fem
3. **σταφυλή staphulē** nom sing fem
4. **σταφυλάς staphulas** acc pl fem

1 Do men gather **grapes** of thorns, or figs of thistles? Matt 7:16
1 nor of a bramble bush gather they **grapes.** .... Luke 6:44
2 clusters of the vine ... for her **grapes** are fully ripe. Rev 14:18

This noun is commonly found in classical Greek denoting a "bunch of grapes." It is used similarly in the Septuagint. In the New Testament it is used three times, twice in the Gospels and once in Revelation. In Matthew 7:16 and Luke 6:44 it refers to "grape(s)." In Revelation 14:18 John used it metaphorically; here the comparison is between a ripe bunch of grapes ready for the harvest and destined to be pressed, and the nations of the world "fully ripe" for the judgment of God.

Strong 4718, Bauer 765, Moulton-Milligan 587, Liddell-Scott 1635.

4570. στάχυς stachus noun

Stalks of grain, ear of grain (corn).

מְלִילָה mᵉlîlāh (4564), Head of grain (Dt 23:25 [24:1]).

קָמָה qāmāh (7339), Standing grain (Jgs 15:5).

שִׁבֹּלֶת shibbōleth (8119), Head of grain, ear of grain [not corn] (Gn 41:22ff., Ru 2:2, Is 17:5).

1. στάχυϊ stachui dat sing masc

2. στάχυν stachun acc sing masc

3. στάχυας stachuas acc pl masc

3 his disciples ... and began to pluck the **ears of corn**, Matt 12:1
3 his disciples began, ... to pluck the **ears of corn**..... Mark 2:23
2 first the blade, then the **ear**, after that the full corn..... 4:28
1 then the **ear**, after that the full corn in the **ear**.......... 4:28
3 his disciples plucked the **ears of corn**, and did eat,...Luke 6:1

This noun is frequently used in the Septuagint and in Greek literature denoting an "ear of corn (grain)." *Stachus* occurs five times in the New Testament. Each occurrence relates that while Christ and His disciples were traversing the fields, being hungry, they picked the *stachus*, "heads of grain," (i.e., wheat or barley or some other cereal grain) and ate it. "Corn" was the old English word for wheat or grain.

Strong 4719, Bauer 765, Moulton-Milligan 587, Liddell-Scott 1635.

4571. Στάχυς Stachus name

Stachys.

1. Στάχυν Stachun acc masc

1 our helper in Christ, and **Stachys** my beloved...... Rom 16:9

A "dear friend" of Paul whom he greeted in Romans 16:9.

4572. στέγη stegē noun

Roof, house.

מִכְסֶה mikhṣeh (4510), Covering (Gn 8:13).

צֵל tsēl (7009), Shelter (Gn 19:8—Codex Alexandrinus only).

1. στέγην stegēn acc sing fem

1 that thou shouldest come under my **roof**:........... Matt 8:8
1 they uncovered the **roof** where he was:.............Mark 2:4
1 worthy that thou shouldest enter under my **roof**:.... Luke 7:6

This is a common noun found in both classical Greek literature and the Septuagint denoting a "roof." It occurs three times in the New Testament where its precise use is determined by the context. For example, in Mark 2:4 it refers to a "roof." In Matthew 8:8 and Luke 7:6 the phrase "to come under my *roof*" means "to enter my house."

Strong 4721, Bauer 765, Moulton-Milligan 587, Liddell-Scott 1636.

4573. στέγω stegō verb

Cover, cover closely, shelter, protect, sustain.

Synonyms:
ἀνέχομαι anechomai (428)
καρτερέω kartereō (2565)
ὑπομένω hupomenō (5116)
ὑποφέρω hupopherō (5135)
φέρω pherō (5179)

1. στέγει stegei 3sing indic pres act

2. στέγομεν stegomen 1pl indic pres act

3. στέγων stegōn nom sing masc part pres act

4. στέγοντες stegontes nom pl masc part pres act

2 we have not used this power; but **suffer** all things,...1 Co 9:12
1 **Beareth** all things, believeth all things,................ 13:7
4 Wherefore when we could no longer **forbear**,........1 Th 3:1
3 For this cause, when I could no longer **forbear**,......... 3:5

Classical Greek

Stegō appears in early Greek literature to describe the act of "covering closely" in order to keep a liquid within a container or from coming into a container; hence, "watertight, repel"; and in later Greek, "to ward off, to bear up, sustain," and thence "to endure" or "to resist" (*Liddell-Scott*). This verb form is not found in the Septuagint. However, its noun form *stegē* (4572), "roof," and another verb form, *stegadeō*, "to cover," are used.

New Testament Usage

The four occurrences of *stegō* in the New Testament appear in the writings of Paul. In 1 Corinthians 9:12 the King James Version has translated the noun as "suffer" which in A.D. 1611 meant what "endure" or "bear" mean today; thus, "but we *bear/endure* all things in order not to impede the progress of the gospel." In 1 Corinthians 13:7 the idea is also "endure, bear up," or "resist"; thus, "love resists all attempts against it" or "endures all onslaughts." In his first letter to the Thessalonians (3:1) the nuance of *stegō* would be more like our phrase "could not stand it any longer," which would give a translation something like, "Since we could not stand it any longer . . . " and in verse 5, "For this reason when I couldn't stand it any longer, I made inquiry as to where you stand in the Lord."

Strong 4722, Bauer 765-66, Moulton-Milligan 587, Kittel 7:585-87, Liddell-Scott 1636.

4574. στεῖρος steiros adj

Barren, sterile.

עָקָר ʿāqār (6371), Barren (Gn 11:30, Jgs 13:2f., Is 54:1).

1. στεῖρα steira nom sing fem

2. στείρᾳ steira dat sing fem

3. στεῖραι steirai nom pl fem

1 no child, because that Elisabeth was barren,......... Luke 1:7
2 is the sixth month with her, who was called barren...... 1:36
3 Blessed are the barren,............................... 23:29
1 Rejoice, thou barren that bearest not;............... Gal 4:27
1 and Sarah herself was barren--was enabled (NIV)... Heb 11:11

Steiros occurs four times in the New Testament always referring to an inability to biologically reproduce. Luke used the substantive to explain why Elisabeth had not borne children: she was sterile (1:7). Thus two miracles were wrought by the Lord: (1) she bore a son in her old age, and (2) she was healed of sterility, which was her lot from youth. In Galatians 4:27 the idea is sterility and quotes Isaiah 54:1 from the Septuagint.

Strong 4723, Moulton-Milligan 587, Liddell-Scott 1637.

4575. στέλλομαι stellomai verb

Set, place, get ready, send, furl a sail, restrict.

Cognates:

ἀποστέλλω apostellō (643)
διαστέλλω diastellō (1285)
διαστολή diastolē (1287)
ἐπιστέλλω epistellō (1973)
καταστέλλω katastellō (2657)
καταστολή katastolē (2659)
συστέλλω sustellō (4810)
ὑποστέλλω hupostellō (5126)
ὑποστολή hupostolē (5127)
ὑποστρέφω hupostrephō (5128)

Synonyms:

ἐκκλίνω ekklinō (1565)
ἐκτρέπω ektrepō (1610)
περιΐστημι periistēmi (3889)
φεύγω pheugō (5180)

חָתַת chāthath (2973), Niphal: stand in awe (Mal 2:5).

1. στελλόμενοι stellomenoi nom pl masc part pres mid

2. στέλλεσθαι stellesthai inf pres mid

1 Avoiding this, that no man should blame us......... 2 Co 8:20
2 withdraw yourselves from every brother that........ 2 Th 3:6

Classical Greek and Septuagint Usage

Stellomai is a rather common verb in Greek generally meaning "make ready." It is the middle form of the verb *stellō* meaning "set, place," or "send." As early as Herodotus we find the meanings "make ready, prepare, furnish with" and the passive meanings "prepare oneself, to set out, to summon" (cf. *Liddell-Scott*). With reference to ships it can mean "to furl a sail, shifting a sail to avoid enemy contact," or "make compact." Its medical use is "to restrict one's diet," hence the idea "to withdraw, shrink," or "restrict oneself from someone or something" (ibid.). Of the seven occurrences in the Septuagint, Malachi 2:5 uses the idea of withdrawing in fear: " . . . to shrink (withdraw) in fear from His name" (author's translation).

New Testament Usage

The verb occurs twice in the New Testament. In 2 Corinthians 8:20 *stellomai* means "avoiding"; thus Paul wrote, "We do not want anyone to blame us in the matter of the contribution of money which we administer, but provide all things honest . . . in the sight of the Lord . . . and in the sight of men" (author's translation). In its second occurrence (2 Thessalonians 3:6) the meaning is not unlike that of "avoid," i.e., "Avoid those who walk in a disorderly fashion"; more precisely, "withdraw yourself from" (author's translations). The verse indicates that a Christian has an obligation to withdraw from a brother whose behavior is characterized by insistent idleness and rejection of the clear teaching of Christ and the apostles.

Strong 4724, Bauer 766 (see "stellō"), Moulton-Milligan 587-88 (see "stellō"), Kittel 7:588-90, Liddell-Scott 1637-38 (see "stellō").

4576. στέμμα stemma noun

Wreath of flowers.

Synonym:

στέφανος stephanos (4586)

1. στέμματα stemmata nom/acc pl neu

1 brought oxen and garlands unto the gates,......... Acts 14:13

This noun is related to the verb *stephō*, "to surround, to crown, to bind around." (Cf. *stephanoō* [4588].) A *stemma* is a wreath or garland of flowers (*Bauer*). The word appears only once in the New Testament, in Acts 14:13. The heathen priests of Jupiter in Lystra brought oxen along with garlands; these garlands adorned animals which soon would be sacrificed. The priests intended to honor Paul and Barnabas with a sacrifice, thinking that they were gods.

Strong 4725, Bauer 766, Moulton-Milligan 588, Liddell-Scott 1638, Colin Brown 1:405.

4577. στεναγμός stenagmos noun

Sigh, groan, groaning.

Cross-Reference:
στενάζω stenazō (4578)

אֲנָחָה 'ănāchāh (599), Sighing, groaning (Jb 3:24, Ps 102:5 [101:5], Lam 1:22).

אֲנָקָה 'ănāqāh (617), Groan (Ps 102:20 [101:20], Mal 2:13).

הֵרָיוֹן hērāyôn (2112), Childbearing (Gn 3:16 [3:17]).

נְאָקָה ne'āqāh (5184), Groaning (Ex 2:24, 6:5, Jgs 2:18).

נְהָמָה nehāmāh (5279), Groan (Ps 38:8 [37:8]).

צָרָה tsārāh (7150), Anguish (Jer 4:31).

1. στεναγμοῦ stenagmou gen sing masc
2. στεναγμοῖς stenagmois dat pl masc

1 and I have heard their **groaning,** .... Acts 7:34
2 for us with **groanings** which cannot be uttered....... Rom 8:26

Classical Greek and Septuagint Usage

This noun can be found in classical Greek from the Fifth Century B.C. and means "sighing" or "groaning." It is also used in the Septuagint to translate several different Hebrew terms. In Genesis 3:16 it describes the "groanings" of the pain of childbirth that all women experience as a result of Eve's sin. In Exodus 2:24 God heard the "groaning" of His people enslaved in Egypt. In all of its Septuagint occurrences *stenagmos* is associated with pain or sorrow.

New Testament Usage

This term appears only twice in the New Testament. In Acts 7:34 Stephen recalled how God heard the "groaning" of His people in Egypt (cf. Exodus 2:24; 3:7). Paul also used *stenagmos* in his epistle to the Romans (8:26). There Paul stated that the Holy Spirit would help believers pray in their weakness with "*groanings* which cannot be uttered." Through divine intercession the believer's longings are uttered in expressions that cannot be put into words. In addition, Christians have the assurance that whatever the Spirit prays through them will be in perfect harmony with God's will (verse 27; cf. Carlson, *Complete Biblical Library, Romans*, p.133).

Strong 4726, Bauer 766, Moulton-Milligan 588, Kittel 7:600-603, Liddell-Scott 1638, Colin Brown 2:423-24.

4578. στενάζω stenazō verb

Grieve, groan, sigh.

Cognates:
ἀναστενάζω anastenazō (387)
στεναγμός stenagmos (4577)
στενός stenos (4579)
στενοχωρέω stenochōreō (4580)
στενοχωρία stenochōria (4581)
συστενάζω sustenazō (4811)

אָבַל 'āval (57), Lament (Is 19:8).

אָנָה 'ānāh (589), Mourn (Is 19:8).

אָנַח 'ānach (598), Niphal: sigh, groan (Is 24:7, Lam 1:21, Ez 21:6).

אָנַק 'ānaq (616), Groan (Ez 26:15).

אַשְׁמַנִּים 'ashmannîm (848), Vigorous or strong person (Is 59:10).

זָעַק zā'aq (2283), Cry out (Jb 31:38).

נוד nûdh (5290), Bemoan (Na 3:7).

עָגַם 'āgham (5909), Grieve (Jb 30:25).

שָׁוַע shāwa' (8209), Piel: cry out (Jb 24:12).

1. στενάζομεν stenazomen 1pl indic pres act
2. στενάζετε stenazete 2pl impr pres act
3. στενάζοντες stenazontes nom pl masc part pres act
4. ἐστέναξεν estenaxen 3sing indic aor act

4 And looking up to heaven, he **sighed,** .... Mark 7:34
1 even we ourselves **groan** within ourselves,........... Rom 8:23
1 in this we **groan,** earnestly desiring to be clothed.... 2 Co 5:2
1 For we that are in this tabernacle **do groan,** 5:4
3 that they may do it with joy, and not **with grief:**.... Heb 13:17
2 **Grudge** not one against another, brethren,........... Jas 5:9

Classical Greek and Septuagint Usage

This verb is used in classical Greek to express intense inward feelings of heaviness, anxiety, or sorrow, depending on context (cf. *Liddell-Scott*). The Septuagint uses the word in Lamentations 1:8 to describe the calamity that befell Jerusalem when the city and the temple were destroyed in the year 586 B.C. In the desolation that followed it is said that her priests "groan," conveying intensity of sorrow.

New Testament Usage

One of the best known passages where the word occurs is Romans 8:23 which speaks of the Spirit interceding for believers with sighs too deep for utterance. The same word is used in Mark 7:34 describing Jesus' healing of the boy with a hearing and speech impediment. Jesus "sighed" in the process of healing him.

The word is used by Paul to express the deep longing of believers to enter into "a building of God . . . eternal in the heavens," while in their present state they "groan" and long to put on their heavenly dwelling (2 Corinthians 5:1,2,4). The passage expresses a positive attitude toward death as a gateway to being present with the Lord.

Believers are urged to submit to those who bear responsibility for the care of their souls so pastors may carry out their duties joyfully without grieving (Hebrews 13:17).

The word is graphically used of the universe in concert with mankind (*sustenazei*) awaiting with intense anxiety their future redemption (Romans 8:22).

In all of these instances the word *stenazō* expresses intensity of feeling, usually anxiety or grief.

Strong 4727, Bauer 766, Moulton-Milligan 588, Kittel 7:600-603, Liddell-Scott 1638, Colin Brown 2:423-24.

4579. στενός stenos adj

Narrow.

Cross-Reference:

στενάζω stenazō (4578)

לַחַץ lachats (4041), Affliction (Is 30:20).

מְצָד m^e^tsādh (4841), Stronghold (1 Sm 23:14,19,29 [24:1]).

מְצוּדָה m^e^tsûdhāh (4849), Stronghold (1 Sm 24:22 [24:23]).

צַר tsar (7140), Narrow, small (Nm 22:26, 2 Kgs 6:1).

צַר tsar (7141), Affliction, distress (1 Chr 21:13, Zec 10:11).

1. στενή stenē nom sing fem
2. στενῆς stenēs gen sing fem

2 Enter ye in at the strait gate: for wide is the gate,.. Matt 7:13
1 Because strait is the gate, and narrow is the way,....... 7:14
2 Strive to enter in at the strait gate:............... Luke 13:24

Classical Greek and Septuagint Usage

The adjective *stenos* ("narrow") conveys the idea of "narrowness" either literally or figuratively. In classical Greek it denotes a narrow space, for example, the "straits" of a sea or a "narrow" strip of land. Figuratively it can refer to narrow-mindedness or narrowness of options as when one is driven into a corner. When used of sound or style it can denote something hard to pronounce or something thin or meager (cf. *Liddell-Scott*). Both literal and figurative uses can also be found in the Septuagint. In Numbers 22:26 the angel of the Lord "stood in the *narrow* place," blocking the path of Balaam and his donkey. The writer of Proverbs warned that a prostitute is a "*narrow* pit" (23:27), meaning that going to one is like falling into an inescapable trap.

New Testament Usage

Stenos appears only three times in the New Testament, and all three occurrences refer figuratively to Jesus as the "*narrow* gate" through which one must pass to enter His kingdom (Matthew 7:13,14; Luke 13:24). The "*narrow* gate" is contrasted with the "broad way . . . that leadeth to destruction," implying that the "*narrow* way" is more difficult now but leads to eternal life in the future.

Strong 4728, Bauer 766, Moulton-Milligan 588, Kittel 7:604-8, Liddell-Scott 1638.

4580. στενοχωρέω stenochōreō verb

To confine, compress, cramp, press closely.

Cognates:

στενάζω stenazō (4578)
στενοχωρία stenochōria (4581)
χωρέω chōreō (5397)

Synonyms:

θλίβω thlibō (2323)
συνέχω sunechō (4762)
συνθλίβω sunthlibō (4768)

אוּץ 'ûts (211), Be too narrow (Jos 17:15).

אָלַץ 'ālats (516), Piel: press daily or continually (Jgs 16:16).

צָרַר tsārar (7173), Be too narrow (Is 49:19).

קָצַר qātsar (7403), Be short (Is 28:20 [28:19]).

1. στενοχωρεῖσθε stenochōreisthe 2pl indic pres mid
2. στενοχωρούμενοι stenochōroumenoi nom pl masc part pres mid

2 We are troubled on every side, yet not distressed;... 2 Co 4:8
1 Ye are not straitened in us,......................... 6:12
1 but ye are straitened in your own bowels.............. 6:12

Classical Greek

Stenochōreō is a verb meaning "to cram or press into a narrow place" or "to compress into a confined space." *Stenochōreō* can be found used of pressing a ship through a narrow waterway, or traveling through a narrow ravine or gorge such as the Cilician Gates, the famous pass through the steep mountains near Paul's native Tarsus.

Septuagint Usage

In the Septuagint the word is used of the topography of the boundary of Ephraim (Joshua 17:15), while in Judges it is figuratively used of Delilah's blandishing pressures upon Samson to force him to reveal the secret of his strength (Judges 16:16). The word is translated in Isaiah 28:20 (LXX 28:19) of a bed that is too narrow or too short to stretch oneself upon in a word of condemnation to the scoffers in Jerusalem.

New Testament Usage

Stenochōreō finds figurative expression in Paul's writings to denote difficult circumstances he experienced in the course of his ministry. "We are troubled on every side, yet not *distressed*" (2 Corinthians 4:8).

The only other occurrences of *stenochōreō* are in 2 Corinthians 6:12: "Ye are not *straitened* in us, but ye are *straitened* in your own bowels." Paul used *stenochōreō* in these verses to give the Corinthians a word picture. Paul was not shutting the Corinthians out by "squeezing" them out of his heart. But rather, if there was any shortage of space for affection, it was in their "bowels," meaning that their hearts had no room to respond with affection towards him.

Strong 4729, Bauer 766, Moulton-Milligan 588, Kittel 7:604-8, Liddell-Scott 1639.

4581. στενοχωρία stenochōria noun

Narrowness of space, confined space; affliction, distress, anguish.

Cognates:

στενάζω stenazō (4578)
στενοχωρέω stenochōreō (4580)

מָצוֹר mātsôr (4856), Suffering (Dt 28:53,55).

מָצוֹר mātsôr (4857), Siege (Dt 28:57).

צוּקָה tsûqāh (6960), Distress (Is 8:22).

צֹרֶךְ tsōrekh (7163), Need, distress (Sir 10:26).

1. **στενοχωρία stenochōria** nom sing fem
2. **στενοχωρίαις stenochōriais** dat pl fem

1 Tribulation and anguish, ... Rom 2:9
1 shall tribulation, or distress, or persecution, ... 8:35
2 in afflictions, in necessities, in distresses, ... 2 Co 6:4
2 in persecutions, in distresses for Christ's sake: 12:10

Classical Greek

Related to the verb *stenochōreō* (4580) ("to be confined"; metaphorically, "to be anxious"), the noun *stenochōria* literally means "a lack of space, absence of room, a limited time (remaining)." Metaphorically it means "difficulty, distress" (cf. *Liddell-Scott*).

Septuagint Usage

There are six canonical occurrences of the noun *stenochōria* in the Septuagint. The Hebrew behind it varies, but the essential idea is "distress" since *stenochōria* is almost invariably united with *thlipsis* (2324), "tribulation." Deuteronomy links it to the kind of extreme "distress and suffering" one might experience during a military siege (Deuteronomy 28:53,55,57; cf. 1 Maccabees 13:3; *Bauer*). A sense of "panic" might be included in the term, because there is seemingly no escape for those under "distress" (Isaiah 8:22; cf. 8:20). Also implied may be the kind of "anxiety" that comes from a lack of something, such as food (Deuteronomy 28:53ff.; Isaiah 8:21f.; cf. Sirach 10:26); nonetheless, the more general sense of "distress, difficulty, anguish" dominates.

New Testament Usage

Stenochōria occurs only four times in the New Testament, all of which are used by Paul. In Paul's discussion on his "thorn in the flesh" he said he experienced infirmities, reproaches, necessities, persecution, and *distresses* "for Christ's sake" (2 Corinthians 12:7-10). Paul knew that when he was weak, God would make him strong.

Paul used the same word to express a sense of *distress* ("anguish," KJV) and tribulation evildoers will experience (Romans 2:9). Believers will also experience *distress* and tribulation in this present life, yet they are strengthened by the knowledge that nothing can separate them from the love of God (Romans 8:35f.).

Strong 4730, Bauer 766, Moulton-Milligan 588, Kittel 7:604-8, Liddell-Scott 1639, Colin Brown 2:807-8.

4582. στερεός stereos adj

Firm, solid, strong.

Cross-Reference:

στερεόω stereoō (4583)

אַדִּיר 'addîr (116), Mighty (1 Sm 4:8).

אַכְזָרִי 'akhzārî (400), Cruel (Jer 30:14 [37:14]).

אָנַשׁ 'ānash (619), Be incurable (Jer 15:18).

חָזָק chāzāq (2481), Strong (Jer 31:11 [38:11]).

חַלָּמִישׁ challāmîsh (2597), Flint (Dt 32:13).

מִקְשָׁה miqshāh (4911), A hammered metal work (Ex 37:17,22 [38:14,16], Nm 8:4).

1. **στερεός stereos** nom sing masc
2. **στερεοί stereoi** nom pl masc
3. **στερεά sterea** nom sing fem
4. **στερεᾶς stereas** gen sing fem

1 Nevertheless the foundation of God standeth sure, .. 2 Tm 2:19
4 such as have need of milk, and not of strong meat... Heb 5:12
3 strong meat belongeth to them that are of full age, ... 5:14
2 Whom resist stedfast in the faith, ... 1 Pt 5:9

This descriptive adjective means "firm, hard, strong." Though related to *stereoō* (4583), "confine, contract," *stereos* did not assume the strong sacred meaning associated with the verb. In a positive sense it means "firm, rigid, solid, hard, strong." In a negative sense it could mean "cruel, stubborn, unyielding" (Bertram, "stereos," *Kittel*, 7:609).

In the New Testament *stereos* is found four times and is used only with a positive meaning. Second Timothy 2:19 assures believers that the Word of the Lord is "sure"; Hebrews 5:12,14 refers to "*strong* meat" (solid food) which is the food of the spiritually mature (as opposed to the "milk" of a child). And finally, 1 Peter 5:9 admonishes Christians to resist the devil "*steadfast* in the faith."

STRONG 4731, BAUER 766, MOULTON-MILLIGAN 588, KITTEL 7:609-14, LIDDELL-SCOTT 1640.

4583. στερεόω stereoō verb

To make strong, establish, strengthen.

COGNATES:
- στερεός stereos (4582)
- στερέωμα stereōma (4584)

SYNONYMS:
- βεβαιόω bebaioō (943)
- δυναμόω dunamoō (1406)
- ἐνδυναμόω endunamoō (1727)
- ἐνισχύω enischuō (1749)
- ἐπιστηρίζω epistērizō (1975)
- κυρόω kuroō (2937)
- σθενόω sthenoō (4454)
- στηρίζω stērizō (4592)

אָמֵץ 'āmēts (563), Be strong (Ps 18:17 [17:7]).

חָזַק chāzaq (2480), Be strong; be severe (Jer 52:6); piel: fasten (Jer 10:4).

טָפַח ṭāphach (3055), Piel: spread out (Is 48:13).

כּוּן kûn (3679), Niphal: be established (Ps 93:1 [92:1]).

מִבְצָר mivtsār (4152), Fortified place (1 Sm 6:18).

נָטָה nāṭâh (5371), Stretch out (Is 45:12).

נָצַב nātsav (5507), Niphal: set (Lam 2:4).

עָלַץ 'ālats (6192), Rejoice (1 Sm 2:1).

עָצֹם 'ātsōm (6343), Be mighty (Dn 8:24).

עָשָׂה 'āsâh (6449), Do, make; niphal: be made (Ps 33:6 [32:6]).

רָקַע rāqa' (7847), Qal: stretch out (Ps 136:6 [135:6], Is 42:5, 44:24); hiphil: spread out (Jb 37:18).

תָּכַן tākhan (8834), Piel: keep steady (Ps 75:3 [74:3]).

1. ἐστερέωσεν estereōsen 3sing indic aor act
2. ἐστερεώθησαν estereōthēsan 3pl indic aor pass
3. ἐστερεοῦντο estereounto 3pl indic imperf pass

2 his feet and ankle bones **received strength**........... Acts 3:7
1 faith in his name hath **made** this man **strong**,........... 3:16
3 And so were the churches **established** in the faith,..... 16:5

Classical Greek and Septuagint Usage

In classical Greek this verb means literally "to confine, contract," or metaphorically "to be in difficulty" (*Liddell-Scott*). It also includes the meanings of "hard, obstinate, firm, true, healthy, ripe (as grain)."

The New Testament use of the term was strongly influenced by *stereōma* (4584), a noun related to the verb *stereoō*; the noun is used to translate "firmament" in the Septuagint creation account in Genesis 1. The ancients thought of the firmament as an inverted bowl, solid and strong. (See Bertram, "stereos," *Kittel*, 7:609f.) In this context the Old Testament writers pictured the heavens as an impregnable fortress, a safe retreat. It is here that God dwells, and all who dwell with Him enjoy perfect safety and security. The verb *stereoō* then logically conveyed the meaning "to establish" or "to make strong." The Septuagint translators of the Psalms used *stereoō* in two contexts: by the Lord the heavens were "made" (Psalm 33:6 [LXX 32:6]), and by the Lord of majesty "the world also is stablished" so "it cannot be moved" (Psalm 93:1 [LXX 92:1]).

New Testament Usage

Stereoō is used in only two passages in the New Testament. In Acts 3:7,16 Peter and John spoke a word of healing to the lame beggar at the Beautiful Gate, and his feet and ankle bones "were strengthened" so he went walking and leaping into the temple. One would expect Luke the physician to use a term of this nature to describe the miraculous healing of a lame man, but the word is not really a medical term. Rather, consistent with its use in the Old Testament, it conveys the idea of creative power. The second use of the word is in Acts 16:5 which states that the assemblies "were strengthened" in the Faith. The growth and maturity of the Church was a spiritual work of creative grace evidenced in the fellowship of obedient disciples.

STRONG 4732, BAUER 766, MOULTON-MILLIGAN 588, KITTEL 7:609-14, LIDDELL-SCOTT 1640.

4584. στερέωμα stereōma noun

Firmness, steadfastness, solidness.

סֶלַע sela' (5748), Rock (Ps 18:2 [17:2], 71:3 [70:3]).

רָקִיעַ rāqîa' (7842), Expanse, firmament (Gn 1:6ff., Ps 150:1, Ez 1:22f.).

שַׁחַק shachaq (8263), Clouds (Dt 33:26).

1. στερέωμα stereōma nom/acc sing neu

1 and the **stedfastness** of your faith in Christ........... Col 2:5

Classical Greek

The main emphasis of *stereōma* and its cognates is "firmness" or "solidity" (*Liddell-Scott*). Other uses appearing in classical Greek include "what is made firm or thick, basis, foundation, solid body, support," and "firmament" (Bertram, "stereos," *Kittel*, 7:609).

Septuagint Usage

"Firmament" is the most frequently used meaning in the Septuagint. *Stereōma* usually translates the Hebrew word *rāqîa'* whose root *rāqa'* means "to stamp down" or "to spread out." *Stereōma* occurs nine times in the creation account of Genesis 1 and four times in the record of Ezekiel's call in Ezekiel 1. Each time the translation is "firmament." The idea here is the expanse of the sky over the earth.

New Testament Usage

Stereōma occurs only once in the New Testament, in Colossians 2:5. In this paragraph (2:1-5) the Colossians are warned against persuasive but false arguments. After this warning Paul commended the believers for the "steadfastness" of their faith. He rejoiced that he could say this about them. The use of *stereōma* could refer in a military sense to drawing up in solid ranks for battle, or perhaps to a castle or bulwark being solid and somewhat impregnable (Bertram, "stereos," *Kittel*, 7:614). The Colossians could continue in their strong faith in Jesus with a little instruction from Paul.

STRONG 4733, BAUER 766-67, MOULTON-MILLIGAN 588, KITTEL 7:609-14, LIDDELL-SCOTT 1640.

4585. Στεφανᾶς Stephanas name

Stephanas.

1. Στεφανᾶ Stephana gen masc

1 And I baptized also the household of Stephanas:.... 1 Co 1:16
1 brethren, ye know the house of Stephanas,............ 16:15
1 I am glad of the coming of Stephanas................. 16:17

Stephanas and his extended family were among the earliest Christians at Corinth and were baptized by Paul himself. Paul commended his dedication in "serving the saints," which made him a model of Christian leadership. With two others he visited Paul at Ephesus on behalf of the Corinthian church (cf. 1 Corinthians 1:16; 16:15-17).

4586. στέφανος stephanos noun

Wreath, crown, reward.

COGNATE:
στεφανόω stephanoō (4588)

SYNONYMS:
διάδημα diadēma (1232)
στέμμα stemma (4576)

אַבְנֵט 'avnēṯ (68), Sash (Is 22:21).

כָּלִיל kālîl (3752), Perfect (Ez 28:12).

לִוְיָה liwyāh (4017), Garland (Prv 1:9).

עֲטָרָה 'ăṭārāh (6065), Crown (1 Chr 20:2, Prv 14:24, Is 28:1).

צִיץ tsîts (7001), Crown (Sir 40:4).

1. στέφανος stephanos nom sing masc
2. στέφανον stephanon acc sing masc
3. στέφανοι stephanoi nom pl masc
4. στεφάνους stephanous acc pl masc

2 And when they had platted a crown of thorns,..... Matt 27:29
2 and platted a crown of thorns,.................... Mark 15:17
2 And the soldiers platted a crown of thorns,........ John 19:2
2 wearing the crown of thorns, and the purple robe...... 19:5
2 Now they do it to obtain a corruptible crown;....... 1 Co 9:25
1 dearly beloved and longed for, my joy and crown,... Phlp 4:1
1 For what is our hope, or joy, or crown of rejoicing? 1 Th 2:19
1 there is laid up for me a crown of righteousness,.... 2 Tm 4:8
2 when he is tried, he shall receive the crown of life,... Jas 1:12
2 receive a crown of glory that fadeth not away........ 1 Pt 5:4
2 and I will give thee a crown of life................. Rev 2:10
2 fast which thou hast, that no man take thy crown....... 3:11
4 and they had on their heads crowns of gold............ 4:4
4 cast their crowns before the throne, saying,............. 4:10
1 and a crown was given unto him:...................... 6:2
3 on their heads were as it were crowns like gold,........ 9:7
1 and upon her head a crown of twelve stars:........... 12:1
2 Son of man, having on his head a golden crown,...... 14:14

Classical Greek

Normally in secular Greek *stephanos* denotes a "wreath" or "crown," especially in reference to the victor's crown awarded to the winning participant in the Greek athletic games. The victor's wreath was constructed of leaves, often of laurel. A golden crown might be awarded by the Greek state to special citizens as a high mark of honor (Hemer, "Crown," *Colin Brown*, 1:405).

Septuagint Usage

Stephanos ordinarily translates the Hebrew word *'ăṭārāh* in the Septuagint where it is used of a king's crown (e.g., 2 Samuel 12:30 [LXX 1 Kings 12:30]; 1 Chronicles 20:2) or of the multiple royal crowns placed on the head of the priest as a typology showing the Messiah ("the Branch") must first do His priestly work and then reign. The background of the Septuagint should be taken into consideration when evaluating the term's meaning in the New Testament.

New Testament Usage

Stephanos occurs 18 times in the New Testament where it often denotes the crown of victory; in fact, some texts are direct allusions to the "crowns" of victory awarded at the athletic games (e.g., 1 Corinthians 9:25; 2 Timothy 4:8). It would be an error to assert that *stephanos* never stands for the kingly crown or for what the royal crown symbolizes.

When the soldiers placed the "crown" (*stephanos*) of thorns upon Jesus' head, it was not because they were mocking Him as any kind of "victor." Rather, they mocked Him as "King of the Jews" (Matthew 27:29; Mark 15:18; John 19:2,5). These Gospel texts read *stephanos* instead of *diadēma* (1232), "crown." Such an observation's significance should not be explained away by suggesting that the thorns more closely resemble the laurel of the victor's crown rather than the gold of the king (cf. Revelation 9:7 where *stephanos* means a crown like gold).

STRONG 4735, BAUER 767, MOULTON-MILLIGAN 589, KITTEL 7:615-36, LIDDELL-SCOTT 1642, COLIN BROWN 1:405-6.

4587. Στέφανος Stephanos name

Stephen.

1. **Στέφανος Stephanos** nom masc
2. **Στεφάνου Stephanou** gen masc
3. **Στεφάνῳ Stephanō** dat masc
4. **Στέφανον Stephanon** acc masc

4 and they chose **Stephen,** a man full of faith .... Acts 6:5
1 And **Stephen,** full of faith and power, ... 6:8
3 of Cilicia and of Asia, disputing with **Stephen.** 6:9
4 And they stoned **Stephen,** calling upon God, ... 7:59
4 And devout men carried **Stephen** to his burial, ... 8:2
3 upon the persecution that arose about **Stephen** 11:19
2 when the blood of thy martyr **Stephen** was shed, ... 22:20

Stephen was one of the seven men chosen from among the Hellenistic (i.e., Greek-speaking) Jews in the Early Church to supervise the daily distribution of food to those in need. Luke named him first in the list (Acts 6:5), and he rapidly stood out by his grace, miracles, and wisdom in speaking, and by the Holy Spirit's presence in him.

D.A. Hagner says he "made his mark through his pathbreaking understanding of the inherent newness of Christianity over against Judaism" ("Stephen," *International Standard Bible Encyclopedia*, pp.615-617). Opposition from other Hellenists rapidly developed, and Stephen was brought to trial before the Sanhedrin. Luke, in recording the trial, included a long speech by Stephen. The major theme of this speech is that God's people have always rejected those He has sent, and the murder of Christ had climaxed this rejection. Luke's account then recalls in several ways the end of the trial of Stephen. After he spoke of seeing the Son of Man (Jesus) glorified, Stephen was condemned and put to death. At the end, he prayed for Jesus to receive his spirit and forgive his executioners. See Acts 6:1 to 8:1.

4588. στεφανόω stephanoō verb

To crown, wreathe, adorn.

CROSS-REFERENCE:
στέφανος stephanos (4586)

עָטַר ʿāṭar (6064), Qal: surround with favor (Ps 5:12); piel: crown (Pss 8:5, 103:4 [102:4], S/S 3:11).

1. **ἐστεφάνωσας estephanōsas** 2sing indic aor act
2. **στεφανοῦται stephanoutai** 3sing indic pres mid
3. **ἐστεφανωμένον estephanōmenon** acc sing masc part perf mid

2 yet is he not **crowned,** except he strive lawfully..... 2 Tm 2:5
1 thou **crownedst** him with glory and honour, ... Heb 2:7
3 we see Jesus, ... **crowned** with glory and honour; 2:9

This verb is derived from the root *stepho-* meaning "to enclose" or "encircle." According to Thayer *stephanoō* means "to encircle with a crown"; "to crown, to adorn, to honor" (*Greek-English Lexicon*).

Classical Greek

Trench (*Synonyms of the New Testament*, p.74f.) notes that the Greek language provides two different words for "crown," each with clearly discernible differences. A *diadēma* was a crown of royalty worn only by kings. A *stephanos* was a wreath made from the branches of certain plants or trees. In ancient Greece and Rome they were worn by victors in athletic contests or military battles, honored principals in a procession such as a wedding, respected governmental officials, or participants in a religious rite (usually a sacrifice). It signified honor, protection, joy, or (in the case of newly married couples) hope of fertility.

Septuagint Usage

Septuagint translators avoided using the term in ways that suggested heathen religious practices or values but did use the word in other contexts, usually meaning "to surround." In Psalm 5:12 the writer declared that the Lord "with favor wilt . . . compass him (the righteous) as with a shield." (See Grundmann, "stephanos," *Kittel*, 7:624.)

New Testament Usage

In the New Testament Paul used *stephanoō* to depict the crowning of a victorious athlete as an example of one who "strives lawfully" (competes according to the rules) and wins (2 Timothy 2:5). The writer of Hebrews described the ascended Jesus as being crowned "with glory and honor" (Hebrews 2:7,9), a messianic reference to Psalm 8:5.

STRONG 4737, BAUER 767, MOULTON-MILLIGAN 589, KITTEL 7:615-36, LIDDELL-SCOTT 1642, COLIN BROWN 1:405.

4589. στῆθος stēthos noun

Breast.

גָּחוֹן gāchôn (1543), Belly (Gn 3:14 [3:15).

חֲדֵה chădhēh (A2398), Chest (Dn 2:32—Aramaic).

לֵב lēv (3949), Heart (Ex 28:29f. [28:23,26]).

1. στῆθος stēthos nom/acc sing neu

2. στήθη stēthē nom/acc pl neu

1 **but smote upon his breast, saying, God be merciful Luke 18:13**
2 **all the people ... smote their breasts, and returned..... 23:48**
1 **He then lying on Jesus' breast saith unto him,..... John 13:25**
1 **which also leaned on his breast at supper,............. 21:20**
2 **having their breasts girded with golden girdles...... Rev 15:6**

This noun is related to the verb *histēmi* (2449), "to stand," and denotes "that which stands out, is prominent." It is an anatomical term uniformly translated "breast" (of both sexes) in the New Testament but it also generally refers to the "chest" as the "seat of the heart" (cf. *Liddell-Scott*). The *stēthos* was struck to express repentance (Luke 18:13) and sorrow (Luke 23:48). It was upon the *stēthos* of Jesus where the "beloved disciple" leaned when inquiring about the identity of the Lord's betrayer (John 13:25; 21:20). And finally, the breasts of the seven plague-bearing angels were girded with golden girdles (Revelation 15:6).

Strong 4738, Bauer 767, Moulton-Milligan 589, Liddell-Scott 1643.

4590. στήκω stēkō verb

Stand, stand still, stand firm, persevere.

יָצַב yātsav (3429), Hithpael: stand firm (Ex 14:13—Codex Alexandrinus only).

כּוּן kûn (3679), Niphal: rest on (Jgs 16:26—Codex Vaticanus only).

עָמַד ʿāmadh (6198), Stand (1 Kgs 8:11).

1. στήκετε stēkete 2pl indic/impr pres act

2. στήκει stēkei 3sing indic pres act

3. στήκητε stēkēte 2pl subj pres act

4. στήκοντες stēkontes nom pl masc part pres act

4 **standing outside they sent word (NASB)........... Mark 3:31**
3 **And when ye stand praying, forgive,.................. 11:25**
2 **but among you stands One (NASB)................ John 1:26**
2 **to his own master he standeth or falleth...........Rom 14:4**
1 **stand fast in the faith, quit you like men, be strong. 1 Co 16:13**
1 **Stand fast therefore in the liberty.................. Gal 5:1**
1 **hear of your affairs, that ye stand fast in one spirit, ..Phlp 1:27**
1 **so stand fast in the Lord, my dearly beloved........... 4:1**
3 **For now we live, if ye stand fast in the Lord........ 1 Th 3:8**
1 **Therefore, brethren, stand fast,..................... 2 Th 2:15**

Classical Greek and Septuagint Usage

Stēkō is a verb related to *estēka*, the perfect stem of *histēmi* (2449), "to stand." *Histēmi* expresses a broad spectrum of meanings, such as "to cause to stand still; to stop; to set upright, raise up, erect; to appoint, institute, make." *Stēkō*, however, is strongly influenced by the force of the perfect tense, which denotes a present condition resulting from a past act. Thus it means "to stand, to stand still, to persist, to persevere." (Cf. Grundmann, "stēkō," *Kittel*, 7:636f.) The Septuagint uses *stēkō* only three times in two texts, none of which were used by the KJV.

New Testament Usage

Except for Mark 11:25 all New Testament uses of *stēkō* are in the epistles of Paul. He especially used this verb instead of *histēmi* in commands or hortatory conditional clauses when he urged believers to "*stand fast* in the faith" (1 Corinthians 16:13), "*stand fast* therefore in the liberty wherewith Christ hath made us free" (Galatians 5:1), "*stand fast* in one spirit" (Philippians 1:27), or "*stand fast* in the Lord" (Philippians 4:1; 1 Thessalonians 3:8). Perhaps Paul used the latter verb because of its perfect tense implications. In his writings faith and stability are inseparable partners. As Isaiah had written, "If ye will not believe, surely ye shall not be established" (Isaiah 7:9).

Grundmann (ibid., 7:637) observes: "In faith man attains to the position which allows him to stand firm. This standing does not result from secular securities such as health, power, property, or connections. It is based on the transcendent God on Whose promise faith is fixed."

More specifically, to stand in faith (1 Corinthians 16:13) is to "stand fast in the Lord" (Philippians 4:1), for faith is not so much a substance to be possessed or an action to be practiced as it is a living relationship to be cultivated. Faith does not focus on itself, but it ushers the believer into personal acquaintance with the living Christ. We know Him; we fellowship with Him; we trust Him; and we commit ourselves without hesitation and without reservation to His lordship. It is this unconditional resolution to remain with Him that makes us "steadfast, unmovable, always abounding in the work of the Lord" (1 Corinthians 15:58).

Our "standing fast in the Lord" gives special meaning to Paul's admonition to "stand fast therefore in the liberty wherewith Christ hath made us free" (Galatians 5:1). It is Christ in us (not our own will or ability) that gives us freedom over the flesh, temptation, and sin. As we stand in Christ, we stand with one another "in one spirit" (Philippians 1:27), for in sharing His life and love we discover a unity with other believers that will withstand any social and antagonistic spiritual pressures that would attempt to disrupt it.

STRONG 4739, BAUER 767-68, MOULTON-MILLIGAN 589, KITTEL 7:636-38, LIDDELL-SCOTT 1643.

4591. στηριγμός stērigmos noun

Perseverance; steadfastness.

COGNATE:
στηρίζω stērizō (4592)

SYNONYM:
στερέωμα stereōma (4584)

1. στηριγμοῦ stērigmou gen sing masc

1 being led away ... fall from your own **stedfastness**.... 2 Pt 3:17

According to Thayer this noun, related to *stereoō* (4583), means "firm condition, steadfastness" (*Greek-English Lexicon*). Its only appearance in the New Testament is in 2 Peter 3:17, "Beware lest ye . . . fall from your own steadfastness." It denotes "perseverance" in the true teachings that were handed down. This *stērigmos* is threatened when believers are carried away by "lawless error" (*athesmōn planē*).

STRONG 4740, BAUER 768, MOULTON-MILLIGAN 589, KITTEL 7:653-57, LIDDELL-SCOTT 1644.

4592. στηρίζω stērizō verb

Fix, set firmly, establish; support, confirm, strengthen.

COGNATES:
ἐπιστηρίζω epistērizō (1975)
στηριγμός stērigmos (4591)

SYNONYMS:
βεβαιόω bebaioō (943)
δυναμόω dunamoō (1406)
ἐνδυναμόω endunamoō (1727)
ἐνισχύω enischuō (1749)
ἐπιστηρίζω epistērizō (1975)
κυρόω kuroō (2937)
σθενόω sthenoō (4454)
στερεόω stereoō (4583)

אֱמוּנָה 'ĕmûnāh (536), Steady (Ex 17:12).

אָמְנָה 'ōmnāh (559), Gold overlay (2 Kgs 18:16).

נְטַר neṯar (A5388), Keep (Dn 7:28—Aramaic).

נָפַל nāphal (5489), Fall; hiphil: look at in anger (Jer 3:12).

נָצַב nātsav (5507), Stand; hiphil: establish (Prv 15:25); hophal: be set (Gn 28:12).

נָתַן nāthan (5598), Give; set (Ez 14:8).

סָמַךְ ṣāmakh (5759), Qal: sustain, be steadfast (Gn 27:37, Ps 111:8 [110:8], Is 59:16); niphal: lean on (2 Kgs 18:21); piel: sustain (S/S 2:5).

סָעַד ṣā'adh (5777), Strengthen oneself, sustain (Jgs 19:5,8, Ps 104:15 [103:15]).

סָפַח ṣāphach (5794), Hithpael: share with (1 Sm 26:19).

שִׂים sîm (7947), Set (Jer 24:6, Ez 6:2, Am 9:4).

תָּמַךְ tāmakh (8881), Hold up (Ex 17:12).

תָּקַע tāqa' (8965), Drive (Is 22:25).

1. ἐστήριξεν estērixen 3sing indic aor act
2. στηρίξαι stērixai 3sing opt/inf aor act
3. στηρίξατε stērixate 2pl impr aor act
4. στήριξον stērixon 2sing impr aor act
5. στηρίξει stērixei 3sing indic fut act
6. στηριχθῆναι stērichthēnai inf aor pass
7. ἐστήρικται estēriktai 3sing indic perf mid
8. ἐστηριγμένους estērigmenous acc pl masc part perf mid
9. στηρίζων stērizōn nom sing masc part pres act
10. ἐστήρισεν estērisen 3sing indic aor act
11. στήρισον stērison 2sing impr aor act

1 he **stedfastly set** his face to go to Jerusalem,........ Luke 9:51
7 between us and you there is a great gulf **fixed**:........ 16:26
4 when thou art converted, **strengthen** thy brethren...... 22:32
9 **strengthening** all the disciples. (NASB)............ Acts 18:23
6 spiritual gift, to the end ye **may be established**;...... Rom 1:11
2 is of power **to stablish** you according to my gospel,.... 16:25
2 sent Timotheus, our brother, ... to **establish** you,.... 1 Th 3:2
2 To the end he **may stablish** your hearts................ 3:13
2 and **stablish** you in every good word and work...... 2 Th 2:17
5 who **shall stablish** you, and keep you from evil.......... 3:3
3 Be ye also patient; **stablish** your hearts:..............Jas 5:8
2 make you perfect, **stablish**, strengthen, settle you.....1 Pt 5:10
8 and **be established** in the present truth...............2 Pt 1:12
4 watchful, and **strengthen** the things which remain,.... Rev 3:2

Classical Greek

In classical writings *stērizō* means "to secure, establish; make fast, firm." It could be used literally, such as for "setting" a stone "fast" in the ground (*Liddell-Scott*), or metaphorically for "grounding" or "establishing" someone, i.e., "to confirm" someone, "to encourage, strengthen" (ibid.; cf. *Bauer*).

Septuagint Usage

Stērizō translates 11 Hebrew words. Of these, two are equated with *stērizō* more often, although *stērizō* may not be the chief term used to replace the Hebrew: *ṣāmakh*, "to support (something)" (in the qal, e.g., Genesis 27:37), "to support oneself" (in the niphal, e.g., 2 Kings 18:21 [LXX 4 Kings 18:21]), "to refresh" (in the piel, e.g., Song of Solomon 2:5; cf. Judges 19:5,8); and on other occasions *sîm*, "to set, place, fix, appoint" (e.g., Amos 9:4, of "fixed" eyes).

To "set one's face" (imperative from God, *stērison to prosōpon sou*) or the setting of God's own face toward a particular person or object signals judgment against it. Ezekiel especially makes use of this idiom (Ezekiel 6:2; 13:17; 21:2, and throughout; Jeremiah 21:10; cf. Ezekiel 14:8; 15:7).

The sense of "to confirm, to establish, to secure" is also known. A righteous man can be "secure" in his heart, having no fear (Psalm 112:8 [LXX 111:8]). Here *stērizō* joins the company of such terms as "steadfast" (verse 7) or "he will never be shaken" (verse 6, NASB). Other positive meanings include the ability of something, like bread or God's Spirit, to "sustain" the individual (e.g., Psalms 51:12 [LXX 50:12]; 104:15 [103:15]; cf. Sirach 3:9: "a father's blessing *strengthens* the houses of the children" [RSV]; or the invitation to "be refreshed," Judges 19:5,8 [NIV]).

New Testament Usage

Stērizō occurs only in Luke among the Gospels. He employed it three times, none of which have a corresponding Synoptic parallel. He used it literally of the "fixed" gulf between Lazarus and the rich man (Luke 16:26). Metaphorically, Peter was instructed that he was to "strengthen" his brothers following his denial of Jesus (Luke 22:32). And perhaps echoing the Old Testament idiom of the prophet's "setting his face" to prophesy against something or someone, Jesus himself "steadfastly set his face" (*autos to prosōpon autou estērixen*) against (*eis* [1506B], or "toward") Jerusalem (Luke 9:51, "resolutely set out," NIV). Certainly the image reflects Jesus' resolve to reach Jerusalem (cf. Luke 13:33), but it may also suggest that Jesus is the eschatological prophet pronouncing judgment against Jerusalem (cf. Acts 3:22).

Paul's writings contain six occurrences of *stērizō*. Elsewhere James, 1 and 2 Peter, and Revelation each have it one time. Like Luke they may use it of "strengthening" disciples (Romans 1:11; 1 Thessalonians 3:2; cf. Revelation 3:2). However, implicit in this is that the believer will stand more firmly in the Faith (Romans 16:25; 2 Thessalonians 3:3; cf. 1 Peter 5:10; 2 Peter 1:12, cf. verse 10).

STRONG 4741, BAUER 768, MOULTON-MILLIGAN 589, KITTEL 7:653-57, LIDDELL-SCOTT 1644.

4592B. στιβάς stibas noun

Bed of straw or leaves; leafy branches, foliage.

1. στιβάδας stibadas acc pl fem

1 and others spread leafy branches (NASB)......... Mark 11:8

This term, also spelled *stoibas*, is related to *steibō*, "tread underfoot," and has a variety of usages in Greek literature. It can refer to a "bed of straw," the "straw scattered at a sacrifice," a "mattress," a "bed," a "nest," or a "grave."

The only occurrence of this term in the New Testament is found in conjunction with the account of the Triumphal Entry (Mark 11:8) where it refers to "leaves" or "leafy branches." Several people "cut down branches off the trees, and strewed them in the way" (Mark 11:8). John, inspired by the Spirit and an eyewitness, specifies that the leaves were taken from palm trees (John 12:13).

BAUER 768, MOULTON-MILLIGAN 589-90, LIDDELL-SCOTT 1645.

4593. στίγμα stigma noun

Mark, brand, tattoo.

SYNONYM:

χάραγμα charagma (5316)

נְקֻדָּה nequddāh (5534), Silver studding on jewelry (S/S 1:11).

1. στίγματα stigmata nom/acc pl neu

1 for I bear in my body the marks of the Lord Jesus... Gal 6:17

Classical Greek

A *stigma* is a mark or tattoo pricked or branded upon the body as a means of identification (cf. *Liddell-Scott*). The idea of a mark or brand on the body for identification is almost as old as civilization. The ancient Babylonians and Egyptians marked cattle with a symbol identifying ownership. Slaves also bore a physical mark signifying their status and the name of their owner. Later marks were placed on those who, by reason of some unacceptable social behavior, were considered unworthy of social freedom. Among those so marked were rebellious concubines, sons who mistreated their widowed mothers, or adopted sons who denied their fathers.

In a less negative sense, Egyptians marked themselves with symbols denoting membership in a particular tribe or religious cult. A man so marked was acknowledged as a servant of his chosen deity and thereby protected by the god (Betz, "stigma," *Kittel*, 7:660).

The Greeks and Romans adopted the practice of marking domestic animals and slaves but expanded it to include criminals and soldiers as well. At first the mark on humans was a sign of dishonor. A slave was marked for running away, stealing, or failing in his duties. A soldier was marked for cowardice or disrespect to a superior. The mark labeled him as "good for nothing." Many attempted, by various means, to remove the mark, but to no avail. It usually persisted for life. In later times, new recruits in the Roman army received a tattoo (usually in their palms) of an abbreviation of their emperor's name.

Septuagint Usage
The Septuagint uses the word *stigma* only once, in Song of Solomon 1:11. Here it refers not to a mark on the skin but to a tiny ball or point on a piece of jewelry (ibid.).

Though the word *stigma*, in its accustomed meaning, is not found in the Old Testament, the idea of identification marks in the body was not unknown among the Jews. In the Mosaic ordinances concerning slavery (Exodus 21:1-6) a man bore the mark of a pierced ear to denote his deliberate, free choice of lifelong servitude. A Hebrew could be held as a slave only for a maximum of 6 years for a debt that he could not pay. In the seventh year his debt was paid, and he was free. If, during his period of servitude, he married one of his master's female slaves, she could not go free with him when he was released. If he chose to remain with his master and his wife and children, he would publicly renounce his freedom before the council of elders and allow his earlobe to be pierced as a sign of his voluntary life of slavery.

The Levitical code prohibited the Jews from cutting or otherwise disfiguring their bodies as a sign of grief for the dead, after the custom of their heathen neighbors (Leviticus 19:28). However, they did adopt the practice and continued it until the captivity (ibid., 7:660f.). (See Jeremiah 16:6; 41:4,5.)

New Testament Usage
Stigma appears only once in the New Testament. Paul wrote to the Galatians (6:17), "From henceforth let no man trouble me: for I bear in my body the *marks* of the Lord Jesus." He doubtless was thinking of the prevailing custom of branding one's body with the identifying mark of ownership (as a slave) or of devotion to deity (as a worshiper), but the marks that he bore were not self-inflicted tattoos or mutilations. They were the marks of physical suffering, torture, persecution, and privation he had endured for Christ.

According to Christian tradition, certain holy men—noted for their piety, self-denial, and humility—are said to have borne the physical marks of Jesus' cross (also known as the *stigmata*): nailprints in their hands and feet, wounds in their sides, or marks duplicating the crown of thorns or scourging. The Roman Catholic Church recognizes about 300 such occurrences. Many of those reputed to have borne these marks were later canonized or beatified by the church as saints (ibid., 7:664).

STRONG 4742, BAUER 768, MOULTON-MILLIGAN 590, KITTEL 7:657-64, LIDDELL-SCOTT 1645, COLIN BROWN 2:572,575.

4594. στιγμή stigmē noun

A point, a moment of time, an instant.

פֶּתַע petha' (6875), Instantly (Is 29:5).

1. στιγμῇ stigmē dat sing fem

1 all the kingdoms of the world in a moment of time. Luke 4:5

The word originally meant "a point." Later it assumed the meaning "an insignificant thing," and finally, "a moment of time" (*Bauer*). Luke used the word to describe how Satan showed Jesus all the kingdoms of the world "in a moment of time" (Luke 4:5).

STRONG 4743, BAUER 768, MOULTON-MILLIGAN 590, LIDDELL-SCOTT 1645.

4595. στίλβω stilbō verb

To shine, be radiant, glisten.

לַהַב lahav (3987), Flashing (Na 3:3).

צָהֵב tsāhēv (6932), Hophal: be shiny (Ezr 8:27).

1. στίλβοντα stilbonta nom/acc pl neu part pres act

1 raiment became shining, exceeding white as snow; .. Mark 9:3

The Septuagint uses *stilbō* to express the shining of stars or glistening of metals (for example, the brightness of a sword, Nahum 3:3). In the New Testament Mark noted that Jesus' robe "became shining" at His transfiguration (Mark 9:3). Oepke states that the shining garments of Christ are "the heavenly confirmation of the Messianic confession" ("stilbō," *Kittel*, 4:25).

STRONG 4744, BAUER 768, MOULTON-MILLIGAN 590, KITTEL 7:665-66, LIDDELL-SCOTT 1645-46.

4596. στοά stoa noun

Porch, portico.

אַתִּיק 'attîq (893), Story (Ez 42:3).

מְזוּזָה m^{e}zûzāh (4331), Doorpost (1 Kgs 6:33 [6:31]).

רִצְפָּה rits^{e}phāh (7826), Pavement (Ez 40:18).

1. στοᾷ stoa dat sing fem

2. στοάς stoas acc pl fem

2 Bethesda, having five porches...................... John 5:2
1 Jesus walked in the temple in Solomon's porch........ 10:23

1 all the people ran together unto them in the **porch**.. Acts 3:11
1 they were all with one accord in Solomon's **porch**....... 5:12

The word *stoa* refers to a roofed colonnade, porch, or cloister. The most familiar *stoa* in the New Testament was Solomon's Porch, a roofed colonnade on the east side of the temple in Jerusalem. Left intact by the Babylonians when they razed the temple, it was incorporated into Herod's rebuilt temple which existed in the time of Jesus. It was here that Jesus debated with the Jews concerning His sonship (John 10:23ff.) and Peter and John healed the lame man (Acts 3:11).

The only other *stoa* mentioned in the New Testament was at the Pool of Bethesda in Jerusalem. According to John's description it was surrounded by five "porches" (John 5:2), which has been verified in recent archaeological excavations near St. Stephen's Gate and the Church of St. Anne (cf. Wilkinson, *Jerusalem as Jesus Knew It*).

STRONG 4745, BAUER 768, MOULTON-MILLIGAN 590, LIDDELL-SCOTT 1647, COLIN BROWN 1:68.

4597. στοιβάς stoibas noun

Bed made of straw or leaves.

1. στοιβάδας stoibadas acc pl fem

1 and others cut down **branches** off the trees,....... Mark 11:8

This is an alternate spelling of *stibas*. See the word study at number 4592B.

4598. στοιχεῖον stoicheion noun

Elements, rudiments, fundamental principles; letters of the alphabet; heavenly bodies.

COGNATES:

στοιχέω stoicheō (4599)
συστοιχέω sustoicheō (4812)

1. στοιχεῖα stoicheia nom/acc pl neu
2. στοιχείων stoicheiōn gen pl neu

1 were in bondage under the **elements** of the world:....Gal 4:3
1 turn ye again to the weak and beggarly **elements**,....... 4:9
1 tradition of men, after the **rudiments** of the world,... Col 2:8
2 dead with Christ from the **rudiments** of the world,...... 2:20
1 the first **principles** of the oracles of God;...........Heb 5:12
1 and the **elements** shall melt with fervent heat,....... 2 Pt 3:10
1 and the **elements** shall melt with fervent heat?.......... 3:12

Classical Greek

The substantive *stoicheion*, which means "what belongs in a series," has several usages. In classical Greek it was used (1) in the naming of the shadow of the gnomon (the length of which indicated the time of day, e.g., sundial) and (2) in reference to an element, the simplest part of a whole (*Liddell-Scott*).

Plato (late Fifth, early Fourth Century B.C.) used the term to denote a simple sound of speech, like the first component of a syllable (*Liddell-Scott*). He also used it when referring to the components into which matter was ultimately divisible. Xenophon (contemporary of Plato) used the term when referring to the elementary or fundamental principles (*Bauer*). Aristotle (Fourth Century B.C.) used the term when referring to the elements of proof in general reasoning (*Liddell-Scott*). Manetho (Fourth Century A.D.) used the term with reference to the stars. Along this same line it was used in reference to planets and as a sign of the zodiac (*Bauer*).

Septuagint Usage

Stoicheion appears only three times in the Septuagint and that only in the apocryphal books. It is used to depict the basic elements that make up the physical world (Wisdom of Solomon 7:17; 19:18) and to refer to that which constitutes man himself (4 Maccabees 12:13).

New Testament Usage

In the New Testament *stoicheion* appears seven times (Galatians 4:3,9; Colossians 2:8,20; Hebrews 5:12; 2 Peter 3:10,12). In Galatians 4:3 Paul used the term in the phrase *stoicheia tou kosmou*, "elements of the world." There has been much debate over Paul's meaning for the term here as well as his use of the same phrase in Colossians 2:8,20. Ernest De Witt Burton (*International Critical Commentary*, *Galatians*, p.515f.) outlines four various interpretations given to *stoicheion* as used in this phrase: (1) the physical elements of the universe, (2) the heavenly bodies, (3) spirits, and (4) elements of religious knowledge.

Taking a cue from more recent interpretations one might be inclined to conclude that the expression plays upon the ancient belief that the elements of the universe and the planets and stars contain the fundamental creative/controlling forces of the world. These were regarded as the abode of demonic forces who rule all of humanity. In support of this thesis it is pointed out that the context of Galatians warns against turning back to those "which by nature are no gods" with its resultant enslavement (Galatians 4:8,9).

The context of Colossians 2:8-23 is concerned with the worship of angels and Christ's victory over "principalities and powers" (2:15-18). In both instances the issue is whether Jewish ritual is to be followed. There is apparently some relationship between that and the Gentile and pre-Gnostic belief that the heavenly bodies control such cycles. By submitting to the ordinances concerning these festivals, believers would once again be enslaved by the demonic forces who ruled them in their Gentile (or Jewish) past.

Against this view it is objected that it would be unreasonable and out of character for Paul to have regarded the Jewish people, whose lives were governed by the Law, as under the control of demonic forces. Equally unreasonable is the thought that Paul would call these powerful world rulers "weak and poor." Those unwilling to accept that *stoicheia* can refer to spiritual powers contend that outside evidence of *stoicheia*'s usage in this way is absent, therefore such an interpretation is unparalleled. For, although *stoicheia* does refer to the elements and heavenly bodies, it is never associated with spiritual powers or demons.

Consequently, the most natural way of interpreting the expression is identical to the normal interpretation of the verbal forms (see above). Just as there is "instruction" about Christ consisting of the "elementary truths of God's word" (Hebrews 5:12, NIV), in the same way there is a "worldly doctrine." To the Jews the law of Sinai was the fundamental revelation of God. Likewise, using the imagery of childhood, Paul stated that the Gentiles were "in slavery under the basic principles of the world" (Galatians 4:3, NIV).

The Gentile bondage to these principles of the world, as is particularly expressed in philosophy, do not, like the Law, point to Christ. But, like the Jewish "elementary principles," the Gentile "principles of the world" are "weak and beggarly" (Galatians 4:9, KJV) or "miserable" (NIV) when compared with the glorious gospel of Christ.

To turn away from Christ—either as a Jew or a Gentile—is to return to the bondage of the "elementary principles," either the principle of the Law which cannot be obeyed or the spiritual bondage of demonic forces. Paul was explicit here. Both paths are paths of destruction and enslavement.

In Hebrews 5:12 there seems to be little doubt that the writer is using *stoicheion* with reference to the elements of learning: "For though by this time you ought to be teachers, you have need again for some one to teach you the elementary (literally, *elements* of the beginning) principles of the oracles of God" (NASB).

In 2 Peter 3:10 *stoicheion* takes on the sense of that which constitutes the world, the elemental substances or basic elements from which everything in the natural world is made: "But the day of the Lord will come like a thief, in which the heavens will pass away with a roar and the *elements* will be destroyed with intense heat" (NASB [see verse 12]).

STRONG 4747, BAUER 768-69, MOULTON-MILLIGAN 591, KITTEL 7:670-87, LIDDELL-SCOTT 1647.

4599. στοιχέω stoicheō verb

To proceed in a row, to walk by rule, to walk in a rule (of life).

CROSS-REFERENCE:

στοιχεῖον stoicheion (4598)

כָּשֵׁר kāshēr (3916), Succeed (Eccl 11:6).

1. **στοιχεῖς stoicheis** 2sing indic pres act
2. **στοιχῶμεν stoichōmen** 1pl subj pres act
3. **στοιχοῦσιν stoichousin** dat pl masc indic/part pres act
4. **στοιχεῖν stoichein** inf pres act
5. **στοιχήσουσιν stoichēsousin** 3pl indic fut act

1 but that thou thyself also walkest orderly,.......... Acts 21:24
3 but who also walk in the steps of that faith......... Rom 4:12
2 let us also walk in the Spirit........................ Gal 5:25
5 And as many as walk according to this rule,............ 6:16
4 let us walk by the same rule,........................Phlp 3:16

Classical Greek

The verb *stoicheō* means "to be drawn up in a line." This idea is extended to mean "to be in line with, to hold to, to agree, to follow" (*Bauer*). The ancient Greeks first used the word to refer to military troops who were arranged behind one another (*Liddell-Scott*). The term then acquired an abstract meaning "to agree, to be in harmony with," or, consistent with the figure of a military parade, "to stay in the series" of what went before (Delling, "stoicheō," *Kittel*, 7:666).

Septuagint Usage

Stoicheō appears only once in the Septuagint. Ecclesiastes 11:6 reads, "In the morning sow thy seed, and in the evening withhold not thine hand: for thou knowest not . . . whether they both shall be *alike good* (will be agreeable with me, will satisfy me)" (ibid., 7:667).

New Testament Usage

Since the time of Jerome, many New Testament translators have considered *stoicheō* to be a synonym of *peripateō* (3906) or *poreuomai* (4057), "to walk." If the New Testament writers used *stoicheō* this way, they stood alone in giving it this meaning. Delling suggests (ibid.) that a careful analysis of the etymology and grammatical usage of the words reveals a qualitative difference between *peripateō* and *poreuomai*, "walk; be in agreement with," and *stoicheō*, "follow the leader or example." In *peripateō* and *poreuomai* the spatial connotation seems to be "abreast of" or "side by side." In *stoicheō*, however, the idea becomes "follow behind" the precedent or pattern.

Consider this shade of meaning in Romans 4:12: Abraham has become "the father of circumcision to them who are not of the circumcision only, but who also walk (*stoicheō*) in the steps of that faith of our father Abraham, which he had being yet uncircumcised." (See also Galatians 5:25: "If we live in the Spirit, let us also *walk in* [literally, 'follow the leading of'] the Spirit.")

Galatians 6:16 states, "As many as *walk according to* ('follow,' NASB margin, *stoichēsousin*) this rule, peace be on them, and mercy." "This rule" is the life of freedom inherent in Paul's principal theme in Galatians, " . . . knowing that a man is not justified by the works of the law, but by the faith of Jesus Christ . . . for by the works of the law shall no flesh be justified" (Galatians 2:16).

Another example of its use is seen at Philippians 3:16: "Whereto we have already attained, let us *walk* by the same rule." Hence Paul's "rule" is the example of Christ in the humiliation of His self-emptying (Philippians 2:5-7) when He divested himself of His divine rights and prerogatives (but not His essential deity) having become a man.

Strong 4748, Bauer 769, Moulton-Milligan 591, Kittel 7:666-69, Liddell-Scott 1647-48, Colin Brown 2:451-52,454.

4600. στολή stolē noun

Flowing robe, festal robe.

אַדֶּרֶת 'addereth (152), Robe (Jon 3:6).

אֵפוֹד 'ēphôdh (661), Ephod (2 Sm 6:14, 1 Chr 15:27).

בֶּגֶד beghedh (933), Garment, clothing (Ex 28:2ff., 2 Kgs 5:5, Ez 44:19).

חֲלִיפָה chălîphāh (2588), Change (Jgs 14:12).

חֲלִיצָה chălîtsāh (2589), A set of clothes (Jgs 14:19—Codex Alexandrinus only).

כֻּתֹּנֶת kuttōneth (3930I), Robe (Is 22:21).

לְבוּשׁ l^evûsh (3961), Garment (Gn 49:11, Is 63:1); royal garments (Est 6:8,11, 8:15).

מְעִיל m^e'îl (4752), Robe (1 Chr 15:27, Jb 2:12).

עֵרֶךְ 'ērekh (6425), Suit (Jgs 17:10).

שַׂלְמָה salmāh (7969), Clothes (Jb 9:31).

שִׂמְלָה simlāh (7980), Garment, clothes (Gn 35:2, 41:14, 45:22, Dt 22:5).

1. **στολήν stolēn** acc sing fem
2. **στολαί stolai** nom pl fem
3. **στολαῖς stolais** dat pl fem
4. **στολάς stolas** acc pl fem
5. **στολή stolē** nom sing fem

3 the scribes, which love to go in **long clothing**, ... Mark 12:38
1 on the right side, clothed in a long white **garment**; 16:5
1 Bring forth the best **robe**, and put it on him; ...... Luke 15:22
3 the scribes, which desire to walk in **long robes**, ... 20:46
2 white **robes** were given unto every one of them; ..... Rev 6:11
4 before the Lamb, clothed with white **robes**, ... 7:9
4 What are these which are arrayed in white **robes**? 7:13
4 of great tribulation, and have washed their **robes**, ... 7:14
4 and have washed their **robes**, ... 7:14
4 Blessed are those who wash their **robes**, (NASB) 22:14

A *stolē* is a long flowing robe worn as an outer garment. Distinguished from *himation* (2416) (any ordinary article of clothing, or more explicitly an outer cloak or mantle), a *stolē* is a stately robe reaching to the feet or sometimes sweeping the ground like a train. It was a fine garment of special solemnity, beauty, or richness commonly associated with priests in their sacerdotal duties in the sanctuary. Such garments were also worn by men who were afforded special dignity or honor (Trench, *Synonyms of the New Testament*, p.175).

The joyous father dressed the returned prodigal in a *stolē* to celebrate the return of his "dead" son to "life" (Luke 15:22). The angel who announced Christ's resurrection was dressed in a *stolē*, befitting one who delivers a message from deity (Mark 16:5). The glorified believers in Revelation 6:11; 7:9; and 7:13f. are so clothed to signify the glory of their salvation and the splendor of their eschatological reward. Jesus rebuked the Pharisees, priests, and scribes who habitually wore such robes, because their intent was to draw attention to their piety or status, gratifying their own inflated egos with the honor and esteem of the common people (Mark 12:38; Luke 20:46).

Strong 4749, Bauer 769, Moulton-Milligan 591, Kittel 7:687-91, Liddell-Scott 1648.

4601. στόμα stoma noun

Mouth.

COGNATES:
δίστομος distomos (1359)
ἐπιστομίζω epistomizō (1977)
στόμαχος stomachos (4602)

חֵךְ chēkh (2541), Palate, mouth (Sir 49:1).

פֶּה peh (6552), Mouth (Gn 29:2f., Prv 10:6, Jer 44:25f. [51:25f.]).

פֻּם pum (A6677), Mouth (Dn 4:31 [4:28], 6:17, 7:5—Aramaic).

שָׂפָה sāphāh (8004), Lips (Lv 13:45, Ez 24:22).

1. στόμα stoma nom/acc sing neu
2. στόματος stomatos gen sing neu
3. στόματι stomati dat sing neu
4. στομάτων stomatōn gen pl neu
5. στόματα stomata nom/acc pl neu

2 word that proceedeth out of the **mouth** of God...... Matt 4:4
1 And he opened his **mouth,** and taught them,........... 5:2
1 of the abundance of the heart the **mouth** speaketh..... 12:34
1 saying, I will open my **mouth** in parables;............. 13:35
3 people draweth nigh unto me with their **mouth,**......... 15:8
1 Not ... which goeth into the **mouth** defileth a man;.... 15:11
2 but that which cometh out of the **mouth,**.............. 15:11
1 entereth in at the **mouth** goeth into the belly,......... 15:17
2 But those things which proceed out of the **mouth**...... 15:18
1 and when thou hast opened his **mouth,**................ 17:27
2 that in the **mouth** of two or three witnesses........... 18:16
2 Out of the **mouth** of babes and sucklings.............. 21:16
1 And his **mouth** was opened immediately,........... Luke 1:64
2 As he spake by the **mouth** of his holy prophets,........ 1:70
2 gracious words which proceeded out of his **mouth.**...... 4:22
1 of the abundance of the heart his **mouth** speaketh....... 6:45
2 and seeking to catch something out of his **mouth,**...... 11:54
2 Out of thine own **mouth** will I judge thee,............ 19:22
1 For I will give you **a mouth** and wisdom,.............. 21:15
3 And they shall fall **by the edge** of the sword,.......... 21:24
2 for we ourselves have heard of his own **mouth.**........ 22:71
3 and put it upon hyssop, and put it to his **mouth.**... John 19:29
2 which the Holy Ghost by the **mouth** of David....... Acts 1:16
2 had showed by the **mouth** of all his prophets,........... 3:18
2 which God hath spoken by the **mouth** ... prophets...... 3:21
2 Who by the **mouth** of thy servant David hast said,...... 4:25
1 so opened he not his **mouth:**......................... 8:32
1 Then Philip opened his **mouth,**........................ 8:35
1 Then Peter opened his **mouth,** and said,............. 10:34
1 unclean hath at any time entered into my **mouth.**....... 11:8
2 by my **mouth** should hear the word of the gospel,..... 15:7
1 And when Paul was now about to open his **mouth,**.... 18:14
2 and shouldest hear the voice of his **mouth.**............ 22:14
1 them that stood by him to smite him on the **mouth.**... 23:2
1 Whose **mouth** is full of cursing and bitterness:....... Rom 3:14
1 that every **mouth** may be stopped,..................... 3:19
3 The word is nigh thee, even in thy **mouth,**............ 10:8
3 That if thou shalt confess with thy **mouth** the Lord.... 10:9
3 with the **mouth** confession is made unto salvation...... 10:10
3 ye may with one mind and one **mouth** glorify God,.... 15:6
1 our **mouth** is open unto you, our heart is enlarged... 2 Co 6:11
2 In the **mouth** of two or three witnesses.............. 13:1
2 communication proceed out of your **mouth,**.......... Eph 4:29
2 that I may open my **mouth** boldly,..................... 6:19
2 filthy communication out of your **mouth.**............ Col 3:8
2 Lord shall consume with the spirit of his **mouth,**.... 2 Th 2:8
2 and I was delivered out of the **mouth** of the lion.... 2 Tm 4:17
5 obtained promises, stopped the **mouths** of lions,.... Heb 11:33
5 escaped the **edge** of the sword,....................... 11:34
5 Behold, we put bits in the horses' **mouths,**........... Jas 3:3
2 Out of ... **mouth** proceedeth blessing and cursing........ 3:10
3 neither was guile found in his **mouth:**............... 1 Pt 2:22
1 I trust to come unto you, and speak **face** to face,.... 2 Jn 1:12
1 I trust to come unto you, and speak face to **face,**....... 1:12
1 shortly see thee, and we shall speak **face** to face..... 3 Jn 1:14
1 shortly see thee, and we shall speak face to **face.**.... 3 Jn 1:14
1 and their **mouth** speaketh great swelling words,...... Jude 1:16
2 out of his **mouth** went a sharp twoedged sword:...... Rev 1:16
2 fight against them with the sword of my **mouth.**........ 2:16
2 art lukewarm, ... I will spue thee out of my **mouth.**..... 3:16
4 and out of their **mouths** issued fire and smoke.......... 9:17
4 the brimstone, which issued out of their **mouths.**........ 9:18
3 their power is in their **mouth,** and in their tails:........ 9:19
3 but it shall be in thy **mouth** sweet as honey........... 10:9
3 and it was in my **mouth** sweet as honey:.............. 10:10
2 will hurt them, fire proceedeth out of their **mouth,**..... 11:5
2 out of his **mouth** water as a flood after the woman,.... 12:15
1 the earth opened her **mouth,** and swallowed up........ 12:16
2 the flood which the dragon cast out of his **mouth.**..... 12:16
1 and his **mouth** as the mouth of a lion:................ 13:2
1 and his mouth as the **mouth** of a lion:................ 13:2
1 **a mouth** speaking great things and blasphemies;....... 13:5
1 he opened his **mouth** in blasphemy against God,....... 13:6
3 And in their **mouth** was found no guile:.............. 14:5
2 like frogs come out of the **mouth** of the dragon,....... 16:13
2 of the dragon, and out of the **mouth** of the beast,..... 16:13
2 and out of the **mouth** of the false prophet............ 16:13
2 And out of his **mouth** goeth a sharp sword,........... 19:15
2 which sword proceeded out of his **mouth:**............ 19:21

Classical Greek

The common Greek word for "mouth," *stoma* refers to the opening in the face of a human or animal, the human organ of speech, the opening or entrance of a house, or the beginning or end of a river or highway. From the idea of a mouth being the front of the face, *stoma* may mean "front" or "front side." Extending the idea of the mouth as the organ of speech, *stoma* may refer to the speech itself or the person speaking (Weiss, "stoma," *Kittel,* 7:693f.).

Ancient religions viewed spirit and life as coming from deity through a life-giving word. Thus it was natural to refer anthropomorphically to the "mouth" of deity from which the breath or word comes. From this divine mouth proceeds life—whether of men or of the earth—and divine blessing. All that is good or that provides and ensures life is from the "mouth of God" (ibid.).

Septuagint Usage

In the Septuagint the Greek term *stoma* translates the Hebrew word *peh.* It is variously translated by the KJV as "mouth, speech, edge, portion," or "side." In Hebrew idioms it may mean "eat, edge (of a sword), entry, end, mind, part, portion, spoken, talk, wish," or "word."

When referring to God's mouth, *peh* almost always refers to His speech. Old Testament writers declared that from the mouth of God proceeds the creative word (Psalm 33:6 [LXX 32:6]), good and evil as the destiny that overtakes man (Lamentations 3:38), law, teaching, and wisdom (Job 22:22; 23:12; Psalms 105:5 [LXX 104:5]; 119:13,72,88 [118:13,72,88]; Proverbs 2:6).

God transfers His word into the mouth of the prophets and priests, making them for the moment the mouth of God (1 Kings 17:24 [LXX 3 Kings 17:24]; 2 Chronicles 36:12f.; Malachi 2:7). Even the heathen Pharaoh Necho of Egypt was made to speak the words of God (2 Chronicles 35:22).

New Testament Usage

New Testament writers follow the pattern of ancient Greeks and Old Testament writers in their use of *stoma* but add some significant ideas. In the apocalyptic imagery of Revelation, that which issues from the mouth is often judgment and destruction. Fire proceeds from the mouth of the two witnesses to burn up their enemies (Revelation 11:5); the scourging armies from the east (9:17-19) ride horses from whose mouths issue fire, smoke, and brimstone; the dragon (serpent) sends forth a stream of water from his mouth to drown the woman giving birth (12:15); and from the mouth of the unholy trinity (dragon, beast, and false prophet) proceed unclean demonic spirits in the form of frogs (16:13).

Because of the power and authority of words that proceed from their mouths, New Testament writers repeatedly urged Christians to keep their mouths pure from all immoral or unchristian speech and to speak only that which would uplift Christ and advance the cause of the Christian faith. (See Ephesians 4:29; Colossians 3:8; 1 Peter 3:10.) James maintained that the pure praises of God and the destructive curses of men cannot proceed from the same mouth (James 3:10-12). Jesus declared that a man's purity of character can be detected by the purity of his speech (Luke 6:45; cf. ibid., 7:695-701.) Lastly, the phrase "mouth to mouth" is used to mean "face to face" (2 John 12; 3 John 14), and in Luke 21:24 and Hebrews 11:34 the "mouth" of the sword means the edge of the sword.

Strong 4750, Bauer 769-70, Moulton-Milligan 592, Kittel 7:692-701, Liddell-Scott 1648-49.

4602. στόμαχος stomachos noun

Stomach.

Cross-Reference:
στόμα stoma (4601)

1. στόμαχον stomachon acc sing masc

1 but use a little wine for thy stomach's sake......... 1 Tm 5:23

This term is related to the noun *stoma* (4601), "mouth." In classical Greek *stomachos* refers to the "throat" or "gullet." As well, it can also denote the neck, such as the neck of a bladder or the neck of the uterus. It later referred to the "orifice of the stomach," then simply "stomach," its meaning in the New Testament. The word appears only once in the New Testament. In 1 Timothy 5:23 Paul encouraged young Timothy, "Use a little wine for thy *stomach's* sake." Paul knew of Timothy's weak health and of the possible ill-effects of exclusively drinking water that may be contaminated, so he reminded Timothy of the medicinal value of a "little wine."

Strong 4751, Bauer 770, Liddell-Scott 1649.

4603. στρατεία strateia noun

Military expedition or campaign, warfare.

Cross-Reference:
στρατεύομαι strateuomai (4605)

1. στρατείας strateias gen sing fem

2. στρατείαν strateian acc sing fem

1 For the weapons of our warfare are not carnal,.... 2 Co 10:4
2 that thou by them mightest war a good warfare;.... 1 Tm 1:18

Classical Greek

In classical Greek *strateia* is related to *strateuō*, "to war, serve as soldier," and denotes a "campaign, expedition," especially in a military sense. It only rarely describes the "army" itself (*Liddell-Scott*, cf. *stratia* [4607]). A more general definition of "military service" is also widely attested. Furthermore, a metaphoric application of *strateia* to "life" (either *bios* [972] or *zōē* [2205]) is known (*Moulton-Milligan*).

Septuagint Usage

By the time of the Septuagint there was little difference in usage between *strateia* and *stratia*. The Hebrew term *chayil* (e.g., Exodus 14:4,9) along with *memshālāh* (only 2 Chronicles 32:9) and *maṣṣa'* (Numbers 10:28) infrequently become *strateia* in the Septuagint. Ordinarily *tsāvā'*, "military forces, campaigns, troops," stands behind *strateia*.

Figuratively, the "starry host" (NIV) of the heavens may speak of the immense number of the stars; however, this is more likely an allusion to the "cosmic forces" (either "good" or "bad"; 1 Kings 22:19 [LXX 3 Kings 22:19]) which are not to be worshiped (2 Chronicles 33:3,5; Jeremiah 7:18 [no Hebrew]; 8:2; 19:13; Zephaniah 1:5). But it is God who has made these powers, and He rules over them (Nehemiah 9:6; Hosea 13:4, Septuagint). (Cf. the cosmic imagery of 4 Maccabees 4:10.)

New Testament Usage

The connection between *strateia* and *stratia* continues into the New Testament (see e.g.,

2 Corinthians 10:4). Probably there are two readings of *strateia* (2 Corinthians 10:4; 1 Timothy 1:18) and two of *stratia* (Luke 2:13; Acts 7:42). (See the word study on *stratia* [4607].) Although the terms are formally different, they tend to share the same definition under many circumstances (see Bauerfeind, "strateia," *Kittel*, 7:702).

Paul's usage in 2 Corinthians 10:4 is in keeping with the primary definition of "campaign": "the weapons of our *campaign* are not earthly" (author's translation) but the divine power of God. Since the context is not cosmic (cf. Ephesians 6:12), it is unnecessary to read into *strateia* any cosmic sense. The same holds true for 1 Timothy 1:18. As he elsewhere used military imagery (e.g., 2 Timothy 2:3), Paul was merely reminding Timothy to "wage the good campaign" (not "fight the good fight," a more athletic-sounding image [NIV]).

STRONG 4752, BAUER 770, MOULTON-MILLIGAN 592, KITTEL 7:701-13, LIDDELL-SCOTT 1651, COLIN BROWN 3:958,963.

4604. στράτευμα strateuma noun

Army, soldiers, a company of soldiers.

CROSS-REFERENCE:

στρατεύομαι strateuomai (4605)

1. **στρατεύματος strateumatos** gen sing neu
2. **στρατεύματι strateumati** dat sing neu
3. **στράτευμα strateuma** nom/acc sing neu
4. **στρατεύματα strateumata** nom/acc pl neu
5. **στρατευμάτων strateumatōn** gen pl neu
6. **στρατεύμασιν strateumasin** dat pl neu

4 and he sent forth his **armies**, ... Matt 22:7
6 And Herod with his **men of war** set him at nought, Luke 23:11
3 commanded the **soldiers** to go down, ... Acts 23:10
2 then came I with an **army**, and rescued him, ... 23:27
5 And the number of the **army** of the horsemen were .. Rev 9:16
4 the **armies** which were in heaven followed him 19:14
4 and the kings of the earth, and their **armies**, ... 19:19
1 him that sat on the horse, and against his **army**........ 19:19

This word denotes an army, a detachment of soldiers, or a troop (*Bauer*). Even though the military forces represented a heathen, often oppressive, ruling nation, the New Testament Church did not view them as their enemies as did the Jews. The New Testament writers even viewed them with some admiration, often referring to them as examples of unconditional obedience (Matthew 8:5-13) and discipline (2 Timothy 2:4). They are depicted as extensions and executors of governmental authority (Acts 23:10,27). Although they were participants in the crucifixion of Jesus, they were not described in ways to imply their personal guilt; rather, they were simply servants of the state in carrying out the government's directive. At worst, they are depicted as ignorant and uncaring bystanders making sport of the tragedy, unaware of the miscarriage of justice or the sacredness of the occasion. (See Matthew 27:27ff.; Mark 15:16ff.; Luke 23:36f.; John 19:2ff.)

STRONG 4753, BAUER 770, MOULTON-MILLIGAN 592, KITTEL 7:701-13, LIDDELL-SCOTT 1651, COLIN BROWN 3:958,964.

4605. στρατεύομαι strateuomai verb

Serve as a soldier, serve in the army.

COGNATES:

ἀντιστρατεύομαι antistrateuomai (494)
στρατεία strateia (4603)
στράτευμα strateuma (4604)
στρατεύομαι strateuomai (4605)
στρατηγός stratēgos (4606)
στρατιά stratia (4607)
στρατιώτης stratiōtēs (4608)
στρατολογέω stratologeō (4609)
στρατοπεδάρχης stratopedarchēs (4610)
στρατόπεδον stratopedon (4611)
συστρατιώτης sustratiōtēs (4813)

יָצָא yātsâ' (3428), Go out; march (Prv 30:27 [24:62]).
מָהַהּ māhahh (4244), Hithpalpel: wait (2 Sm 15:28).
צָבָא tsāvâ' (6892), Fight (Is 29:7).

1. **στρατεύεται strateuetai** 3sing indic pres mid
2. **στρατευόμεθα strateuometha** 1pl indic pres mid
3. **στρατεύονται strateuontai** 3pl indic pres mid
4. **στρατεύῃ strateuē** 2sing subj pres mid
5. **στρατευόμενος strateuomenos** nom sing masc part pres mid
6. **στρατευόμενοι strateuomenoi** nom pl masc part pres mid
7. **στρατευομένων strateuomenōn** gen pl fem part pres mid
8. **στρατεύσῃ strateusē** 2sing indic fut act

6 And the **soldiers** likewise demanded of him, saying, Luke 3:14
1 Who **goeth a warfare** any time at his own charges? .. 1 Co 9:7
2 we **do not war** after the flesh: .... 2 Co 10:3
4 that thou by them **mightest war** a good warfare; .... 1 Tm 1:18
5 No man that **warreth** entangleth himself with .... 2 Tm 2:4
7 even of your lusts that **war** in your members? .... Jas 4:1
3 from fleshly lusts, which **war** against the soul; .... 1 Pt 2:11

Classical Greek

The term *strateuomai* is a verb that means "serve as a soldier, serve in the army," or "do military service." Related nouns denote "campaign, warfare, army division, troops, soldier, fellow soldier, camp military leader, chief magistrate, captain." The verb appears in an active form (*strateuō*) in Homer's *Iliad* (ca. Eighth Century

B.C.) and is also found in the writings of Aeschylus and Herodotus (Fifth Century B.C.; Kittel, "strateia," *Kittel*, 7:701-705; cf. *Bauer*).

Septuagint Usage

Instances of the verb and word group related to *strateuomai* are not as numerous in the Septuagint. *Strateuō* occurs only in Judges 19:8; 2 Samuel 15:28 (LXX 2 Kings 15:28); and Isaiah 29:7 in reference perhaps to "holy wars or campaigns" directed by God. (*Stratia* or *strateia* are used less than 30 times.)

New Testament Usage

Although the word group appears frequently in the New Testament, forms of the verb *strateuomai* occur only seven times. The single instance in Luke 3:14 is a participle that functions as a noun and refers to Roman soldiers.

In the Epistles Paul drafted the originally secular term into the service of the gospel. He used it to describe the Christian's life as a soldier with supreme allegiance to Jesus Christ who is engaged in divine warfare. In 1 Corinthians 9:7 Paul noted by a rhetorical question that he should not be expected to work for nothing any more than one would expect a soldier to.

The verb is used twice in the General Epistles: James 4:1; 1 Peter 2:11. In both passages the term refers to inner lusts that seek to destroy the soul.

Strong 4754, Bauer 770 (see "strateuō"), Moulton-Milligan 592, Kittel 7:701-13, Liddell-Scott 1651 (see "strateuō"), Colin Brown 1:646.

4606. στρατηγός stratēgos noun

Commander of an army; governor, magistrate.

Cross-Reference:

στρατεύομαι strateuomai (4605)

אֲחַשְׁדַּרְפְּנִים 'ăchashdarpᵉnîm (325), Satrap (Est 3:12).

מֶלֶךְ melekh (4567), King (Jb 15:24, Dn 10:13).

סָגָן sāghān (5644I), Official, commander (Jer 51:23,28 [28:23,28], Ez 23:6,12).

סְגַן sᵉghan (A5645), Prefect, counselor (Dn 3:2f.—Aramaic).

סֶרֶן seren (5837), Leader (1 Chr 12:19).

שַׂר sar (8015), Commander, officer (1 Sm 29:3f., 2 Chr 32:21); prince, demonic leader (Dn 10:13).

1. στρατηγός stratēgos nom sing masc
2. στρατηγοί stratēgoi nom pl masc
3. στρατηγοῖς stratēgois dat pl masc
4. στρατηγούς stratēgous acc pl masc

3 and communed with the chief priests and **captains**, Luke 22:4
4 chief priests, and **captains** of the temple, ... 22:52
1 the priests, and the **captain** of the temple, ...Acts 4:1
1 Now when the high priest and the **captain** 5:24
1 Then went the **captain** with the officers, ... 5:26
3 And brought them to the **magistrates**, saying, ... 16:20
2 and the **magistrates** rent off their clothes, ... 16:22
2 when it was day, the **magistrates** sent the serjeants, ... 16:35
2 The **magistrates** have sent to let you go: 16:36
3 the serjeants told these words unto the **magistrates**: 16:38

In the strictest sense a *stratēgos* denotes a military leader. In the New Testament, however, the word is used with two technical meanings. First, a *stratēgos* was the "captain of the temple." Called the "man of the Temple Mount" in Jewish writings, he was a priest who served as chief superintendent of the Levites and priests who stood guard at the temple. He occupied a place of dignity second only to the high priest (Luke 22:4,52; Acts 4:1; 5:24,26) (Knowling, *Expositor's Greek Testament*, 2:122).

Second, *stratēgos* refers to a chief magistrate or highest official of the Roman Empire in certain provinces such as Philippi (Acts 16:20,22,35,36,38).

Strong 4755, Bauer 770, Moulton-Milligan 592-93, Kittel 7:701-13, Liddell-Scott 1652, Colin Brown 3:958,964.

4607. στρατιά stratia noun

Army, host.

Cross-Reference:

στρατεύομαι strateuomai (4605)

חַיִל chayil (2524), Army (Ex 14:4,9,17).

מֶמְשָׁלָה memshālāh (4617), Forces (2 Chr 32:9).

מַסַּע massa' (4702), Order of march (Nm 10:28).

צָבָא tsāvā' (6893), Army (2 Sm 3:23, 1 Chr 12:14); host (Zep 1:5).

1. στρατιᾶς stratias gen sing fem
2. στρατιᾷ stratia dat sing fem

1 a multitude of the heavenly **host** praising God, ... Luke 2:13
2 and gave them up to worship the **host** of heaven; .... Acts 7:42

The noun *stratia* commonly means "army" in classical Greek literature and the papyri. It appears only twice in the New Testament. In Luke 2:13 the term refers to the army or host of heaven that accompanied the angel who appeared to the shepherds. The only other occurrence of the word in the New Testament is in Acts 7:42 where Stephen designated the *stratia* as the idolatrous host of heaven worshiped by Israel.

Strong 4756, Bauer 770, Moulton-Milligan 593, Kittel 7:701-13, Liddell-Scott 1652, Colin Brown 3:958,964.

4608. στρατιώτης stratiōtēs noun

Soldier, mercenary.

Cross-Reference:
 στρατεύομαι strateuomai (4605)

1. **στρατιώτης stratiōtēs** nom sing masc
2. **στρατιώτῃ stratiōtē** dat sing masc
3. **στρατιώτην stratiōtēn** acc sing masc
4. **στρατιῶται stratiōtai** nom pl masc
5. **στρατιωτῶν stratiōtōn** gen pl masc
6. **στρατιώταις stratiōtais** dat pl masc
7. **στρατιώτας stratiōtas** acc pl masc

7 a man under authority, having **soldiers** under me:... Matt 8:9
4 Then the **soldiers** of the governor took Jesus 27:27
6 they gave large money unto the **soldiers**,............... 28:12
4 And the **soldiers** led him away into the hall,...... Mark 15:16
7 under authority, having under me **soldiers**,.......... Luke 7:8
4 And the **soldiers** also mocked him,.................. 23:36
4 And the **soldiers** platted a crown of thorns,......... John 19:2
4 Then the **soldiers**, when they had crucified Jesus,...... 19:23
2 and made four parts, to every **soldier** a part;.......... 19:23
4 These things therefore the **soldiers** did............... 19:24
4 came the **soldiers**, and brake the legs of the first,...... 19:32
5 one of the **soldiers** with a spear pierced his side,...... 19:34
3 and a devout **soldier** of them that waited on him... Acts 10:7
5 and delivered him to four quaternions of **soldiers**...... 12:4
5 Peter was sleeping between two **soldiers**,............. 12:6
6 there was no small stir among the **soldiers**,........... 12:18
7 Who immediately took **soldiers** and centurions,........ 21:32
7 when they saw the chief captain and the **soldiers**,...... 21:32
5 that he was borne of the **soldiers** for the violence...... 21:35
7 Make ready two hundred **soldiers**.................... 23:23
4 Then the **soldiers**, as it was commanded them,......... 23:31
6 Paul said to the centurion and to the **soldiers**,......... 27:31
4 Then the **soldiers** cut off the ropes of the boat,........ 27:32
5 And the **soldiers'** counsel was to kill the prisoners,.... 27:42
2 to dwell by himself with a **soldier** that kept him........ 28:16
1 endure hardness, as a good **soldier** of Jesus Christ... 2 Tm 2:3

The term *stratiōtēs* appears frequently in classical Greek literature and the Greek papyri from the Fifth Century B.C. to the Christian Era (*Bauer*), as well as in the Septuagint, generally denoting "soldier." A "soldier" was anyone who served in a war. Only later did the idea of a "professional soldier" (*misthophoros*) develop (*Liddell-Scott*), denoting one who was trained and paid regardless of whether or not there was a war to fight in.

In the four Gospels and Acts the word occurs 25 times and is used exclusively in the literal sense to refer to Roman (and perhaps temple) soldiers. The only other occurrence is in 2 Timothy 2:3. In this verse Paul gave the term a new, figurative connotation by encouraging Timothy to be "a good soldier of Jesus Christ."

Strong 4757, Bauer 770, Moulton-Milligan 593, Kittel 7:701-13, Liddell-Scott 1653, Colin Brown 3:958,964.

4609. στρατολογέω stratologeō verb

Enlist soldiers, to recruit an army.

Cross-References:
 λόγος logos (3030)
 στρατεύομαι strateuomai (4605)

1. **στρατολογήσαντι stratologēsanti** dat sing masc part aor act

1 please him who **hath chosen him to be a soldier**..... 2 Tm 2:4

This verb can be found in the writings of Roman historians from the First Century B.C. to express the act of enlisting for military service (Kittel, "stratologeō," *Kittel*, 7:705). Since it was a relatively new word in the Koine language, it does not appear in the Septuagint.

The term is used in 2 Timothy 2:4 where it appears in a military analogy constructed by Paul. Paul instructed Timothy to set aside his own desires in order to give full attention to pleasing his "commander," the one "*who hath chosen* him *to be a soldier.*"

Strong 4758, Bauer 770, Moulton-Milligan 593, Kittel 7:701-13, Liddell-Scott 1653, Colin Brown 3:958,964.

4610. στρατοπεδάρχης stratopedarchēs noun

Military commander, captain of the guard.

Cross-Reference:
 στρατεύομαι strateuomai (4605)

1. **στρατοπεδάρχῃ stratopedarchē** dat sing masc

1 delivered the prisoners to the **captain of the guard**:..Acts 28:16

This word is attested in the writings of Roman historians from the First Century B.C. and denotes a "military commander, commandant of a camp" (*Bauer*). A relatively new (Koine) word, it does not appear in the Septuagint.

The term occurs only once in the New Testament and refers to the military commander to whom Paul was delivered (Acts 28:16). Here it means either the commander of the headquarters of legionary officers on furlough in Rome or, more likely, the captain of the Roman praetorian guard who was named Afranius Burrus (Longenecker, *Expositor's Bible Commentary*, 9:568).

Strong 4759, Bauer 771, Moulton-Milligan 593, Liddell-Scott 1653, Colin Brown 3:958,964.

4611. στρατόπεδον

stratopedon noun

Army, troops.

Cross-Reference:

στρατεύομαι strateuomai (4605)

חַיִל chayil (2524), Army (Jer 34:1 [41:1]).

1. στρατοπέδων stratopedōn gen pl neu

1 ye shall see Jerusalem compassed with armies,..... Luke 21:20

The compound noun *stratopedon* refers to a "camp" or "soldiers in a camp." It also denotes a "body of troops" or an "army," and may be used when referring to an army "legion." In the New Testament the word is used only once, in Luke 21:20, where it is part of a prophecy that saved the lives of many Christians. When those believers, who were in or near Jerusalem, saw the city encircled by "armies," they fled. In A.D. 70 the Jews who remained and ignored the prophecy were destroyed along with the entire city and temple.

Strong 4760, Bauer 771, Moulton-Milligan 593, Kittel 7:701-13, Liddell-Scott 1653, Colin Brown 3:958,964.

4612. στρεβλόω strebloō verb

Wrest, twist, pervert, torture, torment.

פָּתַל pāthal (6871), Twist; hithpael: show oneself to be astute (2 Sm 22:27).

1. στρεβλοῦσιν streblousin 3pl indic pres act

1 which they that are unlearned and unstable wrest,... 2 Pt 3:16

Classical Greek

The verb *strebloō* can be found in classical Greek meaning "to hoist or to tighten with a windlass or screw." In the writings of Herodotus and Aristophanes (ca. Fifth Century B.C.) the noun designates an instrument of torture in which the limbs of a victim were "twisted" or dislocated on a rack (Vincent, *Word Studies in the New Testament*, 1:708; cf. *Moulton-Milligan*). Hence, stemming from these usages in the early Greek sources, the verb was commonly applied to wrenching the joints and came to mean "to torture, to torment" (*Liddell-Scott*).

Septuagint Usage

The verb *strebloō* occurs six times in the Septuagint but only in one passage in the Old Testament canon: 2 Samuel 22:27 (LXX 2 Kings 22:27). Here the verb is used in a figurative sense to express God's displeasure or punishment upon the froward or perverse. In 4 Maccabees (e.g., 9:17) and in Josephus (*Wars of the Jews* 5.5.2) the term means "to torture" or "torment." Numenius of Apamea, Second Century A.D., also used the verb in the figurative sense, "to twist or to distort . . . so that a false meaning results" (*Bauer*).

New Testament Usage

This vivid figurative meaning of *strebloō* is employed in 2 Peter 3:16, the only verse in the New Testament in which the verb occurs. Here the term describes the wresting or twisting of portions of Scripture by the "unlearned and unstable." These heretics distorted the Scriptures as torturously as the hated rack twisted and dislocated the joints and limbs of its victim. "It is a singularly graphic word applied to the perversion of Scripture" (Vincent, *Word Studies in the New Testament*, 1:708).

Strong 4761, Bauer 771, Moulton-Milligan 593, Liddell-Scott 1653.

4613. στρέφω strephō verb

Turn, return, change.

Cognates:

ἀναστρέφω anastrephō (388)
ἀποστρέφω apostrephō (648)
διαστρέφω diastrephō (1288)
ἐκστρέφω ekstrephō (1599)
ἐπιστρέφω epistrephō (1978)
καταστρέφω katastrephō (2660)
καταστροφή katastrophē (2662)
μεταστρέφω metastrephō (3214)
συστρέφω sustrephō (4814)

Synonyms:

ἀλλάσσω allassō (234)
ἀποστρέφω apostrephō (648)
διαστρέφω diastrephō (1288)
ἐκτρέπω ektrepō (1610)
ἐπανέρχομαι epanerchomai (1865)
ἐπιστρέφω epistrephō (1978)
κομίζω komizō (2837)
μεταστρέφω metastrephō (3214)
μετασχηματίζω metaschēmatizō (3215)
μετατίθημι metatithēmi (3216)
στρέφω strephō (4613)
ὑποστρέφω hupostrephō (5128)

גָּלִיל gālîl (1591), Something that turns (1 Kgs 6:34).

גָּרַר gārar (1688), Drag; hithpolel: whirl (Jer 30:23 [37:23]).

הָפַךְ hāphakh (2089), Qal: overthrow, turn back (Jb 34:25, Ps 78:9 [77:9], Prv 12:7); niphal: be changed (Ex 7:15); be exhausted, be disturbed (Ps 32:4 [31:4],

Lam 1:20); hithpael: turn in every direction (Gn 3:24 [3:25]).

סָבַב sâvav (5621), Qal: turn about, turn back (1 Kgs 2:15, Ps 114:3 [113:3]); hiphil: turn back (1 Kgs 18:37).

פָּנָה pānâh (6680), Qal: turn (Jer 2:27); hiphil: turn (Jer 48:39 [31:39]).

שֵׂת sēth (8051), Raising up (Jb 41:25 [41:16]).

שׁוּב shûv (8178), Return; qal: restore (Zep 3:20—only some Vaticanus texts); hiphil: make go back (Is 38:8).

1. **στρέφειν strephein** inf pres act
2. **ἔστρεψεν estrepsen** 3sing indic aor act
3. **στρέψον strepson** 2sing impr aor act
4. **στρεφόμεθα strephometha** 1pl indic pres mid
5. **ἐστράφη estraphē** 3sing indic aor pass
6. **ἐστράφησαν estraphēsan** 3pl indic aor pass
7. **στραφῆτε straphēte** 2pl subj aor pass
8. **στραφείς strapheis** nom sing masc part aor pass
9. **στραφέντες straphentes** nom pl masc part aor pass
10. **στραφεῖσα strapheisa** nom sing fem part aor pass
11. **στραφῶσιν straphōsin** 3pl subj aor pass

3 on thy right cheek, **turn** to him the other also...... Matt 5:39
9 and **turn** again and rend you........................ 7:6
8 But Jesus **turning** and seeing her said, (NASB)........ 9:22
8 But he **turned**, and said unto Peter,................. 16:23
7 Except **ye be converted**, and become as ... children,... 18:3
2 and **returned** the thirty pieces of silver (NASB)...... 27:3
8 he marvelled at him, and **turned** him about,....... Luke 7:9
8 he **turned** to the woman, and said unto Simon,........ 7:44
8 But he **turned**, and rebuked them, and said,........... 9:55
8 **turned** him unto his disciples, and said privately,..... 10:23
8 multitudes ... and he **turned**, and said unto them,..... 14:25
8 And the Lord **turned**, and looked upon Peter......... 22:61
8 **turning** unto them said, Daughters of Jerusalem,...... 23:28
8 Then Jesus **turned**, and saw them following,....... John 1:38
11 PERCEIVE ... , AND **BE CONVERTED**, (NASB).... 12:40
5 she **turned** herself back, and saw Jesus standing,...... 20:14
10 She **turned herself**, and saith unto him, Rabboni;..... 20:16
6 and in their hearts **turned back again** into Egypt,... Acts 7:39
2 Then God **turned**, and gave them up to worship....... 7:42
4 lo, **we turn** to the Gentiles.......................... 13:46
1 and have power over waters **to turn** them to blood, Rev 11:6

Classical Greek

In classical Greek this term means "turn, turn aside, turn about, change." Compounds of this word relate to the scriptural idea of conversion (*Moulton-Milligan*). Other usages of this word include "cause to rotate, sprain, dislocate," and "twist" or "plait" the hair. Figuratively it can mean "return, consider" (turn over in one's mind), and "give back" (*Liddell-Scott*).

Septuagint Usage

Strephō is used 50 times in the Septuagint. Twenty-three times it translates the word *hāphakh*, "turn, change, pervert, overturn," etc. For example, in 1 Samuel 10:6 Saul was changed into another man when God appointed him as king over Israel. Lamentations 1:10 speaks of inner torment caused by circumstances. Changing a curse into a blessing is indicated in Esther 9:22 and Psalms 30:11 (LXX 29:11) and 114:8 (LXX 113:8).

Five times *strephō* translates the Hebrew word *sāvav*. Several examples may be cited: the heart of the people is "turned back" to the Lord (1 Kings 18:37 [LXX 3 Kings 18:37]); the flow of the Jordan is "driven back," i.e., the direction was changed when Israel crossed it into the Promised Land (Psalm 114:3,5 [LXX 113:3,5]); and Proverbs 26:14 speaks of a door "turning" on its hinges as picturing a slothful person on his bed.

New Testament Usage

In the New Testament *strephō* carries many of the same meanings as in classical and especially Septuagintal Greek. Most references mean "turn to or toward" or "turn around" (Matthew 7:6; Luke 7:9,44; 9:55; 14:25; 22:61; John 1:38; 20:14,16).

This word is used figuratively in Acts 13:46 of Paul's decision to stop trying to evangelize the Jews as a general rule. Because of the hardness of their hearts, Paul stated, "We turn to the Gentiles." In Revelation 11:6 the two witnesses have the power to change water to blood. In Luke 10:23 Jesus stated that all power had been "given" to the Son by the Father.

Another concept related by *strephō* in the New Testament is repentance. In Matthew 18:3 Jesus taught His disciples that they would not enter the kingdom of heaven unless they "be converted, and become as little children." Finally, in Acts 7:39 Stephen said that the fathers of Israel as a whole did not have their hearts "turned back." As a result, God "turned" against them (7:42).

STRONG 4762, BAUER 771, MOULTON-MILLIGAN 593, KITTEL 7:714-15, LIDDELL-SCOTT 1654, COLIN BROWN 1:354-55.

4614. στρηνιάω strēniaō verb

Live luxuriously, wax wanton, run riot.

COGNATE:

καταστρηνιάω katastrēniaō (2661)

SYNONYMS:

σπαταλάω spatalaō (4537)
τρυφάω truphaō (5012)

1. **ἐστρηνίασεν estrēniasen** 3sing indic aor act
2. **στρηνιάσαντες strēniasantes** nom pl masc part aor act

1 she hath glorified herself, and **lived deliciously**,...... Rev 18:7
2 the kings ... and **lived deliciously** with her,............ 18:9

The verb *strēniaō*, meaning "run riot" or "growing unrestraint," is related to the adjective *strēnēs*, "rough" or "harsh" (especially of sounds). In literature from the Fifth Century B.C. the term denotes a sensual life-style and later was even applied to "bulls running wild" (*Bauer*). The verb occurs in the New Testament at Revelation 18:7,9 and describes a sensual, luxurious way of living that displeases God.

Strong 4763, Bauer 771, Moulton-Milligan 593, Liddell-Scott 1654.

4615. στρῆνος strēnos noun

Luxury, sensuality.

שַׁאֲנָן sha'ănān (8077), Arrogance (2 Kgs 19:28).

1. στρήνους strēnous gen sing neu

1 rich through the abundance of her **delicacies**........ Rev 18:3

The noun *strēnos* means "insolent luxury, wantonness, sensuality." In Greek literature from the Fourth Century B.C. the term denotes luxury with an air of "insolence or arrogance" (cf. *Liddell-Scott*). The term appears in the New Testament only at Revelation 18:3. The King James Version translates it "delicacies," perhaps because "delicacy" is defined in the *Oxford English Dictionary* as "the quality of being addicted to pleasure or sensuous delights" (Earle, *Word Meanings in the New Testament*, 6:159).

Strong 4764, Bauer 771, Moulton-Milligan 594, Liddell-Scott 1654.

4616. στρουθίον strouthion noun

Sparrow.

יָעֵן yā'ēn (3392), Ostrich (Lam 4:3).

עָגוּר 'āghûr (5900), Thrush (Jer 8:7).

צִפּוֹר tsippôr (7109), Sparrow, bird (Pss 84:3 [83:3], 104:17 [103:17], Eccl 12:4).

1. στρουθία strouthia nom/acc pl neu

2. στρουθίων strouthiōn gen pl neu

1 Are not two **sparrows** sold for a farthing?......... Matt 10:29
2 ye are of more value than many **sparrows**............ 10:31
1 Are not five **sparrows** sold for two farthings,.......Luke 12:6
2 ye are of more value than many **sparrows**............ 12:7

The substantive *strouthion* is the diminutive form of *strouthos*, denoting "sparrow," a small bird considered to be of little value. Hence the term *strouthion* was used metaphorically by writers from Aristotle to Josephus to designate various articles having little value. Both the literal and the metaphoric meanings of the term are employed in Jesus' sayings in Matthew 10:29,31 and Luke 12:6,7 where Jesus contrasted the earth's value system with God's. Judging by their purchase price, "sparrows" are worth next to nothing here, yet not one of them can die without God knowing about it. If this is how God values and cares for sparrows, how much more does He care for people?

Strong 4765, Bauer 771, Moulton-Milligan 594, Kittel 7:730-32, Liddell-Scott 1655.

4617. στρώννυμι strōnnumi verb

Spread, strew; furnished.

Cognates:
καταστρώννυμι katastrōnnumi (2662B)
ὑποστρώννυμι hupostrōnnumi (5129)

חָלַל chālal (2591), Piel: defile (Ez 28:7).

יָצַע yātsa' (3440), Spread out; hophal: be spread out (Is 14:11).

כָּבוֹד kāvôdh (3638), Elegant (Ez 23:41).

מָחַץ māchats (4410), Smite (Jb 26:12).

מְשֻׂכָה m^esukhāh (5029), Hedge of thorns (Prv 15:19).

פָּלַשׁ pālash (6672), Hithpael: wallow (Ez 27:30).

רָפַד rāphadh (7790), Piel: spread out (Jb 17:13).

1. ἔστρωσαν estrōsan 3pl indic aor act

2. στρῶσον strōson 2sing impr aor act

3. ἐστρώννυον estrōnnuon 3pl indic imperf act

4. ἐστρωμένον estrōmenon nom/acc sing neu part perf mid

1 great multitude **spread** their garments in the way;.. Matt 21:8
3 cut ... branches ... and **strowed** them in the way........ 21:8
1 And many **spread** their garments in the way:...... Mark 11:8
3 branches off ... trees, and **strowed** them in the way..... 11:8
4 a large upper room **furnished** and prepared:........... 14:15
4 he shall show you a large upper room **furnished**:... Luke 22:12
2 arise, and **make** thy bed........................... Acts 9:34

Classical Greek

The verb *strōnnumi*, also spelled *stornumi* and *strōnnuō*, can be found in classical Greek meaning "spread" (e.g., "to *spread* the clothes over a bed," *Liddell-Scott*). It was used through classical Greek and the papyri generally to mean "spread, strew"; however, it also had a third meaning when used in the passive voice: "to be furnished with" (ibid.).

Septuagint Usage

Strōnnumi appears only eight times in the canonical portions of the Septuagint. In Job 17:13 it is used of "making" a bed (cover with a spread) (cf. Proverbs 7:16). In Proverbs 15:19 it is used figuratively to describe how "the way of the righteous is *made plain*" (spread smooth), while "the way of the slothful man is as a hedge of thorns."

New Testament Usage

In a manner similar to classical Greek, the New Testament uses *strōnnumi* in the general sense of "spread, strew." In Matthew 21:8 (cf. Mark 11:8) "a very great multitude *spread* their garments in the way" of Jesus as He entered Jerusalem on a donkey. In Acts 9:34 Peter proclaimed to Aeneas, "Jesus Christ maketh thee whole: arise, and *make thy bed*." A third usage can be found at Mark 14:15 (cf. Luke 22:12) where Jesus described the Upper Room where they would celebrate Passover as "*furnished* and prepared." This means that the room was already spread out with carpets and places to recline and dine.

STRONG 4766, BAUER 771, MOULTON-MILLIGAN 594, LIDDELL-SCOTT 1656.

4618. στυγητός stugētos adj

Hated, hateful.

COGNATE:

θεοστυγής theostugēs (2295)

1. στυγητοί stugētoi nom pl masc

1 **hateful, and hating one another**...................... Tit 3:3

The word *stugētos* is an adjective that means "hated, hateful, abominated" (*Liddell-Scott*). Although the term is attested in literature from the Fifth Century B.C. (e.g., Aeschylus), it appears only in Titus 3:3 in the New Testament (*Bauer*). In this verse it is uncertain whether the term means "hated" by others or being "hateful" ourselves; both renderings are possible. Both meanings of *stugētos* are also found in the writings of Philo (cf. *Moulton-Milligan*).

STRONG 4767, BAUER 771, MOULTON-MILLIGAN 594, LIDDELL-SCOTT 1657.

4619. στυγνάζω stugnazō verb

Be shocked; become sorrowful, gloomy, lowering.

שָׁמֵם shāmēm (8460), Qal: be appalled (Ez 27:35); hiphil: cause to be appalled (Ez 32:10).

1. στυγνάζων stugnazōn nom sing masc part pres act

2. στυγνάσας stugnasas nom sing masc part aor act

1 **foul weather ... for the sky is red and lowering**..... Matt 16:3
2 **he was sad at that saying, and went away grieved:** Mark 10:22

In classical Greek and the Septuagint this verb means "to have a gloomy (dark) look" (cf. *Liddell-Scott*). In the New Testament it has two usages. In Mark 10:22 the rich man could have left Jesus having been "shocked" or "appalled." Secondly, the term expresses a state of becoming "gloomy" or "dark." This latter meaning can be used in two ways: in reference to man or to the appearance of the sky. It is this latter sense that Jesus used in Matthew 16:3 in the expression "foul weather" (*stugnazōn ho ouranos*).

STRONG 4768, BAUER 771, MOULTON-MILLIGAN 594, LIDDELL-SCOTT 1657.

4620. στῦλος stulos noun

Pillar, column.

אֶדֶן 'edhen (132), Base (Jb 38:6—Codex Alexandrinus only).

כֹּתֶרֶת kōthereth (3934), Capital of a column (1 Kgs 7:41).

מַצֵּבָה matstsēvāh (4838), Obelisk (Jer 43:13 [50:13]).

עֹמֶד 'ōmedh (6199), Place (2 Chr 34:31).

עַמּוּד 'ammûdh (6204), Pillar (Ex 27:11f., 1 Kgs 7:16f., Ez 42:6).

קֶרֶשׁ qeresh (7468), Board for framing (Ex 26:15-23).

1. στῦλος stulos nom sing masc

2. στῦλον stulon acc sing masc

3. στῦλοι stuloi nom pl masc

3 **Cephas, and John, who seemed to be pillars,**.........Gal 2:9
1 **the pillar and ground of the truth**.................. 1 Tm 3:15
2 **will I make a pillar in the temple of my God,**........Rev 3:12
3 **face was as ... the sun, and his feet as pillars of fire:**.. 10:1

Classical Greek and Septuagint Usage

The noun *stulos* is a common term in classical Greek for many kinds of pillars, columns, and other architectural supports. In the Septuagint the Greek term *stulos* is used to translate five Hebrew words, of which the terms for pillars (e.g., Exodus 27:10-17; 36:36 [LXX 37:4]; 1 Kings 7:41-45 [3 Kings 7:41-45]) and column, an upright board or studding in the tabernacle (e.g., Exodus 26:15-29), are the most prominent (Madvig, "Temple," *Colin Brown*, 3:795). However, the term is also employed in a more metaphoric, cosmological sense to refer to God's shaking the "foundations" of earth (Job 9:6) or of heaven (Job 26:11). The underlying idea is that God, the master architect, has constructed the created order as His dwelling place (Wilckens, "stulos," *Kittel*, 7:733).

New Testament Usage

The term *stulos* is used exclusively in a metaphoric or quasimetaphoric, cosmological sense in its four appearances in the New Testament. In Revelation 3:12 the overcomer is told by the Spirit that he will become a pillar in the temple of God.

The reference likely pertains to the pillars which adorned the porch of Solomon's Temple (Madvig, "Temple," *Colin Brown*, 3:795). In Revelation 10:1 the angel from heaven is described as having feet like "pillars of fire," a metaphoric reference to the Old Testament theophanies in which God appeared in this manner in towering glory to Israel.

In 1 Timothy 3:15 the Church of the living God is called the pillar and ground of the truth. The Church is viewed as the house of God, which God has constructed to support and to conserve this truth. The architectural metaphor is pronounced, although here *stulos* refers more to the support and foundation provided by the columns than the columns per se.

In Galatians 2:9 Paul referred to James, Cephas, and John, leaders of the Jerusalem church, as ones "who seemed to be pillars." Paul conceived of the Church as God's temple, and in this striking metaphor he viewed these leaders as basic pillars. Upon them rested the authority and responsibility to provide guidance for the Jerusalem church.

In all four instances the term *stulos* is based on either the design of the temple or the concept of the earth as God's building. Within this framework, the term is used metaphorically to refer to angels, leaders, and the Church.

Strong 4769, Bauer 772, Moulton-Milligan 594, Kittel 7:732-36, Liddell-Scott 1657, Colin Brown 3:795.

4621. Στωϊκός Stōikos name-adj

Stoic.

1. Στωϊκῶν Stōikōn gen pl masc

2. Στοϊκῶν Stoikōn gen pl masc

1 philosophers of the Epicureans, and of the **Stoicks**, Acts 17:18

Stoicism was a Greek school of thought that originated in Athens with the teaching of the Phoenician merchant Zeno (approximately 335–260 B.C.). It was named for the portico (*stoa*) where Zeno taught (Bromiley, "Stoics," *International Standard Bible Encyclopedia*, 4:621). Briefly stated, Stoics held that "the wise man would be indifferent to pain and pleasure, to wealth and poverty, to success and misfortune" (Beare, "Stoics," *Interpreter's Dictionary of the Bible*, 4:444). In addition, virtue was defined "living conformably to nature . . . , for virtue is the goal toward which nature leads us" (ibid.).

Its spiritual basis was monistic or pantheistic; i.e., everything contains God, including man himself who is a "fragment of divinity" (Glover, *The Conflict of Religions*, p.36). Like most pantheists, the Stoics were also fatalists, believing in divine determinism.

In light of that, human happiness is to be found in disinterested virtue. "To be godlike, a man had to suppress his affections just as he suppressed his own sensations of pain and hunger" (ibid., p.66). The goal for man is to align himself with the inherent reason of the universe (personalized as the *Logos* [see 3030]) and to want nothing more than what is. This means eliminating passion and desire from life.

It was followers of such a school of thought, modified most probably by the doctrines of Platonism, who were present with the Epicureans, another Greek school of philosophy, when Paul preached on Mars' hill (Acts 17:18).

Strong 4770, Bauer 768 (see "Stoikos"), Moulton-Milligan 590 (see "Stoikos"), Liddell-Scott 1658.

4622. σύ su prs-pron

You, thou.

1. σύ su nom 2sing

2. σού sou gen 2sing

3. σοί soi dat 2sing

4. σέ se acc 2sing

2 for out **of thee** shall come a Governor, ... Matt 2:6
3 for it is profitable **for thee** that one of thy members 5:29
3 one **for thee**, and one for Moses, and one for Elias..... 17:4
3 and who gave **thee** this authority? 21:23
4 Lord, when saw we **thee** an hungered, or athirst, ... 25:44
3 or in prison, and did not minister **unto thee**? 25:44
3 Where ... we prepare **for thee** to eat the passover? 26:17
1 Master, is it I? He said unto him, **Thou** hast said...... 26:25
1 nevertheless not as I will, but as **thou** wilt............ 26:39
2 not pass away ... except I drink it, **thy** will be done.... 26:42
1 Art **thou** the King of the Jews? 27:11
1 And Jesus said unto him, **Thou** sayest................. 27:11
2 he saith unto the man, Stretch forth **thine** hand..... Mark 3:5
1 and cried, saying, **Thou** art the Son of God............ 3:11
3 What have I to do **with thee**, Jesus, thou Son 5:7
3 And he asked him, What is **thy** name? 5:9
4 and hath had compassion **on thee**...................... 5:19
3 one **for thee**, and one for Moses, and one for Elias...... 9:5
3 What wilt thou that I should do **unto thee**? 10:51
3 thou art true, and carest for no man: (NT) 12:14
4 If I should die with thee, I will not deny **thee** 14:31
3 Abba, Father, all things are possible **unto thee**;........ 14:36

The word *su* is the ordinary personal pronoun, second person singular, meaning "you" or "thou." The pronoun appears often in all types of Greek literature from the earliest period. In the New Testament it is used about 180 times with over 60 of the instances occurring in the Gospel of

John. In most cases *su* adds emphasis, intensity, or clarity.

Strong 4771, Bauer 772, Moulton-Milligan 594-95, Liddell-Scott 1658-59.

4623. συγγένεια sungeneia noun

Relatives, kindred.

Cross-Reference:

γένος genos (1079)

דּוֹדָה dôdhāh (1787), Aunt (Lv 20:20).

טַף ṭaph (3054), Little ones, children (Gn 50:8).

יָנָה yānāh (3347), Subdue (Ps 74:8 [73:8]).

מוֹלֶדֶת môledheth (4274), Relatives (Gn 12:1).

מִשְׁפָּחָה mishpāchāh (5121), Family, clan (Ex 6:14, Jgs 9:1, Jb 32:2).

תּוֹלְדוֹת tôlēdhôth (8765), Generation, descendant (Ex 6:16, Nm 1:20,22,24).

1. **συγγενείας sungeneias** gen sing fem
2. **συγγενείᾳ sungeneia** dat sing fem
3. **συγγένειαν sungeneian** acc sing fem

2 none of thy **kindred** that is called by this name...... Luke 1:61
1 Get thee out of thy country, and from thy **kindred**,.. Acts 7:3
3 called his father Jacob to him, and all his **kindred**,...... 7:14

The term *sungeneia* is the noun form of the adjective *sungenēs* (4624), "related," and correspondingly means "relationship," or more concretely, "kinship" or "relatives." The word occurs three times in the New Testament. In Luke 1:61 it designates the relatives or kindred of Zechariah and Elisabeth. In Acts 7:3 and 7:14 the term refers to relatives in the extended families of Abraham and Joseph respectively.

Strong 4772, Bauer 772, Moulton-Milligan 595, Kittel 7:736-42, Liddell-Scott 1659.

4624. συγγενής sungenēs adj

Related, relative.

Cross-Reference:

γένος genos (1079)

דּוֹד dôdh (1782), Uncle (Lv 20:20—only some Vaticanus texts).

דּוֹדָה dôdhāh (1787), Aunt (Lv 18:14).

מִשְׁפָּחָה mishpāchāh (5121), Family (Lv 25:45).

רֵעַ rēa' (7739), Kinsman (Sir 41:21).

1. **συγγενής sungenēs** nom sing masc/fem
2. **συγγενῆ sungenē** acc sing masc
3. **συγγενεῖς sungeneis** nom/acc pl masc
4. **συγγενῶν sungenōn** gen pl masc
5. **συγγενέσιν sungenesin** dat pl masc
6. **συγγενεῦσιν sungeneusin** dat pl masc

5 and among his own **kin**, and in his own house...... Mark 6:4
1 And, behold, thy **cousin** Elisabeth, she hath also.... Luke 1:36
3 And her neighbours and her **cousins** heard............ 1:58
5 sought him among their **kinsfolk** and acquaintance....... 2:44
3 neither thy **kinsmen**, nor thy rich neighbours;.......... 14:12
4 parents, and brethren, and **kinsfolks**, and friends;...... 21:16
1 being his **kinsman** whose ear Peter cut off,........ John 18:26
3 had called together his **kinsmen** and near friends....Acts 10:24
4 my brethren, my **kinsmen** according to the flesh:.... Rom 9:3
3 Salute Andronicus and Junia, my **kinsmen**,............ 16:7
2 Salute Herodion my **kinsman**......................... 16:11
3 and Jason, and Sosipater, my **kinsmen**, salute you...... 16:21

Classical Greek and Septuagint Usage

The term *sungenēs* is an adjective, but in Greek literature it usually functions as a noun. The primary meaning is "related by blood," that is, "relative"; however, it is sometimes used in a broader sense to mean "fellow-countrymen" (Vincent, *Word Studies in the New Testament*, 3:180).

This dual meaning of *sungenēs* is reflected in earlier works from Pindar and Aeschylus (Fifth Century B.C.;cf. *Bauer*). The word means "of common origin," and thus was applied to members of the same family or race, or to persons related by political or sacral bonds (Michaelis, "sungenēs," *Kittel*, 7:736f.). In the Septuagint the term usually means "relative" in the narrower family sense, although in a few instances it is a title of honor for one related to the king in a special way. Philo (First Century A.D.) employed *sungenēs* over 160 times in the sense of "related, belonging, corresponding," most often in describing the relationship between the soul, body, and mind (ibid., 7:739).

New Testament Usage

In the New Testament Luke used the term four times in his Gospel (1:58; 2:44; 14:12; 21:16) and once in Acts (10:24). John also used it once (18:26). These instances demonstrate that the word was used to mean either relatives in a family or friends related by broader bonds. Paul employed the term in the primary sense at Romans 9:3 in describing his Jewish kinsmen to whom he was related by blood and race. However, he likely used it in the narrower, secondary sense at Romans 16:7 in referring to Andronicus and Junias as members of his extended family (see also 16:11,21).

Strong 4773, Bauer 772, Moulton-Milligan 595, Kittel 7:736-42, Liddell-Scott 1659.

4624B. συγγενίς sungenis noun

Kinswoman, female relative.

Cross-Reference:
γένος genos (1079)

1. συγγενίς sungenis nom sing fem

Only once does this noun, denoting a female relative, appear in the New Testament. However, it was a common word despite its being an unusual spelling of *sungenēs* (4624) (*Liddell-Scott*). Mary was informed by the angel Gabriel, "Thy *cousin* Elisabeth, she hath also conceived a son in her old age" (Luke 1:36). This miracle served as encouragement to Mary that she also, a virgin, could bear a child.

Bauer 772, Moulton-Milligan 595, Liddell-Scott 1660.

4625. συγγνώμη sungnōmē noun

Concession.

Cross-Reference:
γνώμη gnōmē (1100)

1. συγγνώμην sungnōmēn acc sing fem

1 But I speak this by permission,....................1 Co 7:6

Classical Greek and Septuagint Usage

In classical Greek this compound, formed by the word *gnōmē* (1100), "mind" or "means of knowing," and the preposition *sun* (4713), "with," contains the idea of "forbearance, allowance." With the verb *echō* (2174), "to have," *sungnōmē* is used in the sense of "pardon" or "forgiveness" both in the classical usage and in the papyri (see *Moulton-Milligan*). The word is not used in the Septuagint except in the apocryphal books. In Sirach 3:13 it expresses the idea of a son showing understanding and leniency to his father, "Even if he is lacking in understanding, *show forbearance*; in all your strength do not despise him" (RSV). It is also found in 2 Maccabees 14:20.

New Testament Usage

Sungnōmē occurs only once in the New Testament, in 1 Corinthians 7:6. Here Paul contrasted it with the word *epitage* or "command." That is, Paul allowed married couples to practice abstinence from sexual relations for a short time as a spiritual discipline, but this should not be interpreted as a command for such activities. Rather, it is an act of forbearance or tolerance on the part of Paul to agree to such disciplines. There is a sense of reluctant agreement in the word that suggests an act of tolerant concession rather than wholehearted endorsement. The basic idea is that of "permission."

Strong 4774, Bauer 773, Moulton-Milligan 595, Kittel 1:716-17, Liddell-Scott 1660.

4626. συγκάθημαι sunkathēmai verb

To sit with (someone).

Cross-Reference:
κάθημαι kathēmai (2493)

יָשַׁב yāshav (3553), Dwell (Ps 101:6 [100:6]).

1. συγκαθήμενος sunkathēmenos nom sing masc part pres mid

2. συγκαθήμενοι sunkathēmenoi nom pl masc part pres mid

3. συνκαθήμενος sunkathēmenos nom sing masc part mid

1 and he sat with the servants, and warmed himself..Mark 14:54
2 and Bernice, and they that sat with them:..........Acts 26:30

Sunkathēmai (also spelled with a *nu* in place of the *gamma*) is a compound made up of the verb *kathēmai* (2493), "to sit," and the preposition *sun* (4713), "with." In classical literature the word is used to indicate people sitting *by* one another, or in larger groups of people the idea of gathering together in a conclave or assembly (cf. *Liddell-Scott*). In the papyri it is used to indicate official sessions where people are convened for specific purposes (*Moulton-Milligan*). The latter sense is implied in the use of *sunkathēmai* in Acts 26:30 where the word denotes the court of Agrippa. In Mark 14:54 the word simply suggests that Peter sat with the servants in the courtyard as Jesus was questioned by the high priest.

Strong 4775, Bauer 773, Moulton-Milligan 608 (see "sunkathēmai"), Liddell-Scott 1661.

4627. συγκαθίζω sunkathizō verb

Sit down with, to make to sit together with.

Cross-Reference:
καθίζω kathizō (2495)

יָשַׁב yāshav (3553), Sit (Ex 18:13).

רָבַץ rāvats (7547), Lay down (Nm 22:27).

1. συνεκάθισεν sunekathisen 3sing indic aor act

2. συγκαθισάντων sunkathisantōn gen pl masc part aor act

3. συνκαθισάντων sunkathisantōn gen pl masc/neu part aor act

2 and were set down together, Peter sat down among Luke 22:55
1 made us sit together in heavenly places in Christ.....Eph 2:6

Classical Greek

The term *sunkathizō* is a compound of the Greek verb *kathizō* (2495), "to sit down," and the prepositional prefix *sun* (4713), "with." Hence the usual definition of the intransitive verb is "to sit down with" or "to sit together."

This form of the word was rarely used before the Hellenistic era. It is a later development of the older form *sunkathēmai* (4626) which also means "to sit with." This form appears in the works of Herodotus (Fifth Century B.C.) and in the Zenon Papyri (258–257 B.C.; cf. *Liddell-Scott*). Josephus (*Antiquities* 16.11.2) shows that this form of the word continued to be used even after the development of the alternative term *sunkathizō* (*Bauer*).

Septuagint Usage

Most of the earliest references to *sunkathizō* are found in the Septuagint (Genesis 15:11; Exodus 18:13; 1 Esdras 9:6). In these passages the verb is used in a transitive sense to mean "sit down with" someone else.

New Testament Usage

The New Testament records two instances of use of the verb in this sense. Luke 22:55 states that "Peter sat down among them" and Paul said that all who are raised in Christ will "sit together" in heavenly places with Him (Ephesians 2:6). The unique feature of *sunkathizō* is the intensive transitive meaning given to the term: "to cause someone to sit down with, to make persons sit together." This is likely the reason for the development of the word from the older intransitive form. The single outstanding passage in the New Testament which contains this use of *sunkathizō* is Ephesians 2:6. Paul stated that God "hath . . . made us sit together in heavenly places in Christ Jesus"; or, possibly "made us sit down with (Christ) in heaven" (ibid.). The transitive verb denotes that "us" is the object and that God has *made* or *caused us* to sit down in heaven.

Strong 4776, Bauer 773, Kittel 7:766-97, Liddell-Scott 1662.

4628. συγκακοπαθέω

sunkakopatheō verb

Suffer together with, endure hardship with.

Cross-Reference:

πάθος pathos (3669)

1. συγκακοπάθησον sunkakopathēson 2sing impr aor act

1 but be thou partaker of the afflictions of the gospel . . 2 Tm 1:8
1 Suffer hardship with me, (NASB) 2:3

Classical Greek

The word *sunkakopatheō* is made up of the Greek verb *kakopatheō* (2524), "to suffer misfortune," and the prepositional prefix *sun* (4713), "with." Hence the compound verb means "to suffer misfortune with," or simply "to suffer with." The compound form does not appear in classical Greek literature prior to the New Testament.

New Testament Usage

The New Testament has only two verses in which the compound verb is used, although the simple verb and noun occur in several other passages. In 2 Timothy 1:8 the term means "share afflictions with me for the gospel" (Vincent, *Word Studies in the New Testament*, 4:290) or "be thou partaker of the afflictions of the gospel."

In 2 Timothy 2:3 Paul urged Timothy "to endure hardness (suffer hardship, *kakopathēson* [see 2524], *Textus Receptus*), as a good soldier of Jesus Christ." The term does not imply that they will be overcome by the hardships and sufferings, but rather that they must endure sufferings and ill treatment with the implicit expectation of ultimate victory.

Strong 4777, Bauer 773, Kittel 5:936-38, Liddell-Scott 1662, Colin Brown 3:719,722 (see "sunkakopatheō").

4629. συγκακουχέομαι

sunkakoucheomai verb

To suffer with, endure adversity with.

Cross-Reference:

ἔχω echō (2174)

1. συγκακουχεῖσθαι sunkakoucheisthai inf pres mid

1 rather to suffer affliction with the people of God, . . . Heb 11:25

The word occurs only in Hebrews 11:25 in the New Testament and is unknown outside of this one citation. The noun form, *kakouchia*, is known outside the New Testament meaning "ill-treatment" or "ill-conduct." In Hebrews 11:25 the context is Moses' willingness to reject the fleeting pleasures of sin in order to identify with the sufferings of his people as a sign of his faith.

Strong 4778 (see "sunkakoucheō"), Bauer 773, Moulton-Milligan 608 (see "sunkakoucheō"), Liddell-Scott 1662.

4630. συγκαλέω sunkaleō verb

To call together.

Cognate:

καλέω kaleō (2535)

Synonyms:

ἐπικαλέω epikaleō (1926)
καλέω kaleō (2535)
μετακαλέομαι metakaleomai (3203)
μεταπέμπομαι metapempomai (3213)
παρακαλέω parakaleō (3731)
προσκαλέομαι proskaleomai (4200)

συγκαλέω sunkaleō (4630)
φωνέω phōneō (5291)

קָרָא qārâ' (7410), Qal: call, summon (Ex 7:11, Jos 9:22); invite (Zec 3:10 [3:11]); niphal: be called (Is 62:12—only some Sinaiticus texts).

1. συγκαλεῖ sunkalei 3sing indic pres act
2. συγκαλοῦσιν sunkalousin 3pl indic pres act
3. συνεκάλεσαν sunekalesan 3pl indic aor act
4. συγκαλεῖται sunkaleitai 3sing indic pres mid
5. συγκαλεσάμενος sunkalesamenos nom sing masc part aor mid
6. συγκαλέσασθαι sunkalesasthai inf aor mid
7. συνκαλεῖ sunkalei 3sing indic pres act
8. συνκαλεσάμενος sunkalesamenos nom sing masc part aor mid

2 and **they call together** the whole band............ Mark 15:16
5 Then he **called** his twelve disciples **together**,........ Luke 9:1
1 he **calleth together** his friends and neighbours,......... 15:6
4 she **calleth** her friends and her neighbours **together**,.... 15:9
5 Pilate, when he **had called together** the ... priests...... 23:13
3 and **called** the council **together**,..................... Acts 5:21
5 **had called together** his kinsmen and near friends....... 10:24
6 Paul **called** the chief of the Jews **together**:............. 28:17

Classical Greek

Sunkaleō (sometimes spelled with a *nu* in place of the *gamma*, a common change in consonants in Greek) is a compound of *sun* (4713), "with," and *kaleō* (2535), "to call." As such, the word has the idea of "calling together" a group or a meeting. In classical Greek the word generally suggests "to call to council" or "convene" and occasionally, "to invite" (*Liddell-Scott*).

Septuagint Usage

In the Septuagint the word appears some 15 times and normally replaces the Hebrew word which means "to call." It is used almost exclusively in connection with large assemblies. Pharaoh "called together" the magicians of Egypt, and Joshua "called together" the people of Israel (Joshua 9:22; 10:24; 22:1; 23:2; 24:1). In this sense the Septuagint uses the word to mean "summon" or "assemble." When not used by a leadership figure, the term can have a gentler tone, such as in Zechariah 3:10 (LXX 3:11) when the same word is translated: "In that day, says the Lord of hosts, every one of you will *invite* his neighbor under his vine and under his fig tree" (RSV).

New Testament Usage

Sunkaleō appears eight times in the New Testament. Most of these reflect an informal "calling together" of friends in informal occasions or for celebration. In the Parable of the Lost Sheep and the Parable of the Lost Coin, the finder "calls together" friends and neighbors to celebrate the discovery of what had been lost (Luke 15:6,9). In other contexts the setting is more formal, suggesting a convening of a specific group such as the Sanhedrin (Acts 5:21), the 12 disciples (Luke 9:1), or the mustering of a company of soldiers (Mark 15:16).

STRONG 4779, BAUER 773, MOULTON-MILLIGAN 608-9 (see "sunkaleō"), KITTEL 3:496, LIDDELL-SCOTT 1662.

4631. συγκαλύπτω sunkaluptō verb

To cover completely.

COGNATE:
καλύπτω kaluptō (2543)

SYNONYMS:
ἀποκρύπτω apokruptō (607)
ἐπικαλύπτω epikaluptō (1928)
καλύπτω kaluptō (2543)
κατακαλύπτω katakaluptō (2589)
κρύπτω kruptō (2900)
λανθάνω lanthanō (2963)
παρακαλύπτω parakaluptō (3732)
περικαλύπτω perikaluptō (3891)
περικρύπτω perikruptō (3895)

גָּהַר gāhar (1487), Stretch oneself out (2 Kgs 4:35—Codex Alexandrinus only).

חָפַשׂ chāphas (2769), Look for, search; hithpael: disguise oneself (2 Chr 18:29).

כָּסָה kāsâh (3803), Piel: cover (Gn 9:23, 2 Chr 4:12, Ez 12:6).

סָבַב sāvav (5621), Turn; hiphil: turn away (1 Kgs 21:4 [20:4]).

סָרַח sārach (5831), Hang over (Ex 26:13).

1. συγκεκαλυμμένον sunkekalummenon nom/acc sing neu part perf mid

1 is nothing **covered**, that shall not be revealed;...... Luke 12:2

A somewhat more emphatic verb than the simpler form, *kaluptō* (2543), *sunkaluptō* has the idea of completely covering an object. In the Old Testament it is occasionally used to indicate that someone covers himself in a disguise (1 Kings 22:30 [LXX 3 Kings 22:30]; 2 Chronicles 18:29). The word is also used in actions where the face or head is covered as a sign of shame or anger (1 Kings 21:4 [LXX 3 Kings 20:4]).

The idea of secrecy and disguise certainly is suggested in the one New Testament use of the word, Luke 12:2. There Jesus promised that everything which is "covered over," i.e., whatever someone is tempted to hide or disguise, will finally be revealed. (See Marshall, *New International Greek Testament Commentary, Luke*, p.512.)

STRONG 4780, BAUER 773, MOULTON-MILLIGAN 609 (see "sunkaluptō"), KITTEL 7:743, LIDDELL-SCOTT 1662.

4632. **συγκάμπτω** sunkamptō verb

Cause to bend, to oppress.

Cognate:

κάμπτω kamptō (2549)

Synonyms:

κάμπτω kamptō (2549)
κλίνω klinō (2800)

גָּהַר gāhar (1487), Stretch oneself out (2 Kgs 4:35).

כָּרַע kāra' (3895), Sink down (Jgs 5:27—Codex Alexandrinus only).

מָעַד mā'adh (4726), Shake; hiphil: cause to shake (Ps 69:23 [68:23]).

1. σύγκαμψον sunkampson 2sing impr aor act

1 and bow down their back alway....................Rom 11:10

This rare word is found only once in the New Testament. Romans 11:10 is a quotation of Psalm 69:23 (LXX 68:23). According to Louw and Nida the word is an idiom meaning "to undergo particularly difficult hardships, possibly implying forced labor" (*Greek-English Lexicon*, 1:288). The bending of a back pictures one who is being forced to carry a heavy load. The passage in Romans indicates that the oppression and trouble Israel experienced was a result of her unbelief.

Strong 4781, Bauer 773, Moulton-Milligan 609 (see "sunkamptō"), Liddell-Scott 1662.

4633. **συγκαταβαίνω** sunkatabainō verb

Go down with, to descend.

Cross-Reference:

ὑπερβαίνω huperbainō (5070)

יָרַד yāradh (3495), Descend (Ps 49:17 [48:17]).

1. συγκαταβάντες sunkatabantes nom pl masc part aor act

1 which among you are able, go down with me,...... Acts 25:5

Sunkatabainō occurs only once in the New Testament. In Acts 25:5 Festus called for the influential men of the province to "go down with" him to accuse Paul if he was guilty of any wrongdoing. The word means physically traveling with someone to another geographical location.

Strong 4782, Bauer 773, Moulton-Milligan 609 (see "sunkatabainō"), Liddell-Scott 1662.

4634. **συγκατάθεσις** sunkatathesis noun

Agreement, approval.

Cross-Reference:

τίθημι tithēmi (4935)

1. συγκατάθεσις sunkatathesis nom sing fem

1 what agreement hath the temple of God with idols? 2 Co 6:16

Classical Greek

This word is a double compound comprised of *sun* (4713), "with," *kata* (2567), "down, according to," and *thesis*, "thesis, position." The resultant form means "to set down a position with (someone)," hence, "an agreement." In the philosophy of the Stoics *sunkatathesis* meant the "assent given by the mind to its perceptions" (*Liddell-Scott*). This term is not found in the Septuagint.

New Testament Usage

The only usage of this noun in the New Testament is found in 2 Corinthians 6:16 where the word is found parallel with the noun *sumphōnēsis* (4708), "agreement." (This latter word forms the basis of our English word *symphony*, which suggests things that move in harmony together.) *Sunkatathesis* is meant to have a similar force in verse 16. In 2 Corinthians 6:14-18 Paul compared a list of opposites (light/dark, righteousness/iniquity, Christ/Belial) in order to emphasize the impossibility of *sunkatathesis*, that is, "concord" or "agreement" between those who belong to Christ and those who do not.

Strong 4783, Bauer 773, Moulton-Milligan 609 (see "sunkatathesis"), Liddell-Scott 1662.

4635. **συγκατατίθημι** sunkatatithēmi verb

To agree with, consent to.

Cognate:

τίθημι tithēmi (4935)

Synonyms:

ἐπινεύω epineuō (1947)
συνευδοκέω suneudokeō (4759)

כָּרַת kārath (3901), Cut; make (Ex 23:32).

1. συγκατατεθειμένος sunkatatetheimenos nom sing masc part perf mid

2. συνκατατιθέμενος sunkatatithemenos nom sing masc part pres mid

1 The same had not consented to the counsel........ Luke 23:51

The word is found twice in the Septuagint where it translates the expression "to join hands with" (Exodus 23:1, RSV) and "to make a covenant with" (Exodus 23:32). In both places the Law forbade the people of Israel to make agreements or act together with unrighteous people or with other gods. The idea of "agreement" in these passages does not suggest casual actions but the idea of deliberate, contractual agreements.

The lone New Testament usage of the word (Luke 23:51) has a similar meaning. Here the verse notes that Joseph of Arimathea, although a member of the Sanhedrin, was not one who cast his vote with the Sanhedrin against Jesus (see Marshall, *New International Greek Testament Commentary, Luke*, p.879). The suggestion is that Joseph not only disagreed with the verdict against Jesus, but voted in opposition to the council's decision.

STRONG 4784 (see "sunkatatithēmi"), BAUER 773, MOULTON-MILLIGAN 609 (see "sunkatatithēmi"), LIDDELL-SCOTT 1663.

4636. συγκαταψηφίζω

sunkatapsēphizō verb

To be counted or reckoned with.

CROSS-REFERENCE:
ψηφίζω psēphizō (5420)

1. συγκατεψηφίσθη **sunkatepsēphisthē**
3sing indic aor pass

1 and he was numbered with the eleven apostles....... Acts 1:26

This compound verb is made up of the prepositions *sun* (4713), "with," *kata* (2567), "alongside of," and the verb *psēphizō* (5420), "to count or reckon with." The full compound is found in Plutarch where the verb is in the middle voice and has the sense of "join in a vote of condemnation" (cf. *Bauer*). This term is not found in the Septuagint.

New Testament Usage

In the New Testament the verb *sunkatapsēphizō* is found only in Acts 1:26 which says that "the lot fell upon Matthias; and he was *numbered* with the eleven apostles." Barclay emphasizes the underlying idea of voting in the verb *sunkatapsēphizō* when he translates the phrase as "he was *elected to be along with* the twelve disciples." This may imply a tie vote before the lot was cast (*Daily Study Bible, Acts*, p.10).

STRONG 4785, BAUER 773 , MOULTON-MILLIGAN 609 (see "sunkatapsēphizō"), KITTEL 9:604-7, LIDDELL-SCOTT 1664.

4637. συγκεράννυμι

sunkerannumi verb

To mix or mingle.

CROSS-REFERENCE:
κεράννυμι kerannumi (2738)

עֲרַב ʿărav (A6387), Hithpaal: mix (Dn 2:43—Aramaic).

1. συνεκέρασεν **sunekerasen** 3sing indic aor act
2. συγκεκραμένος **sunkekramenos**
nom sing masc part perf mid
3. συγκεκερασμένος **sunkekerasmenos**
nom sing masc part perf mid
4. συγκεκραμένους **sunkekramenous**
acc pl masc part perf mid
5. συγκεκερασμένους **sunkekerasmenous**
acc pl masc part perf mid

1 but God hath tempered the body together,......... 1 Co 12:24
2 not being mixed with faith in them that heard it...... Heb 4:2

Classical Greek

The meaning of *sunkerannumi* is "to mix together with" or "to mingle." In classical usage the word is used to indicate when two things are mixed or blended together. The word is sometimes applied in connection with relationships between people suggesting close friendship or personal attachment. Xenophon used the word to suggest that one has become deeply involved in a situation (*Liddell-Scott*).

The papyri use the word similarly. One document uses the word in connection with people joining together in a wedding. Another document uses it in the context of the "mixing of souls" in friendship (*Moulton-Milligan*). In both cases the idea suggests an intimate joining together of people in love or friendship.

Septuagint Usage

Sunkerannumi occurs only twice in the Septuagint, once to refer to the mixing of metals in an earthen pot (Daniel 2:43, LXX only), and once in the noncanonical book of 2 Maccabees where there is a reference to the mixing of water and wine (2 Maccabees 15:39).

New Testament Usage

The word is used only twice in the New Testament. The first is in 1 Corinthians 12:24 where Paul developed the metaphor of the Church as the body of Christ. The idea here is that God has "compounded" or "put together" the Body in such a way as to help create peace in the Body. The word pictures God as a craftsman, structuring the Church intentionally and carefully, and mixing the gifts and personalities of the believers like a metallurgist mixes metals to give strength to the final product.

The second use of the word is found in Hebrews 4:2. Here *sunkerannumi* describes the interrelationship between the preaching of the word of the gospel and the reception of the Word in the hearer. In Hebrews 4:2 it suggests that there must be a mixing or a joining of faith (that is, faith-obedience) in the hearer with the preached word. We can translate the phrase in Hebrews 4:2 something like this, "For the word which they heard did not benefit them, because it was not mingled with faith in the ones that heard it" (see also Hagner, *Good News Commentary, Hebrews,* p.49).

STRONG 4786, BAUER 773, MOULTON-MILLIGAN 609 (see "sunkerannumi"), LIDDELL-SCOTT 1664.

4638. συγκινέω sunkineō verb

To arouse or stir up.

CROSS-REFERENCE:
κινέω kineō (2767)

1. συνεκίνησαν sunekinēsan 3pl indic aor act

1 And they **stirred up** the people, and the elders,...... Acts 6:12

This compound verb is formed by *sun* (4713), "with," and *kineō* (2767), "to cause to move," and means "to arouse or stir up" (*Liddell-Scott*). In the New Testament the word occurs only in Acts 6:12 where it appears in the context of the orchestrated action against Stephen. Here Luke recorded that those who were spreading false allegations against Stephen "*stirred up* the people, and the elders, and the scribes" to seize Stephen and drag him before the council for trial (6:12ff.). Acts 6:11 uses *hupebalon* (see 5098), "instigate (secretly)," in parallel with *sunekinēsan* in 6:12 emphasizing that the whole action was a coordinated plot against Stephen and not just a happenstance reaction to his ministry.

STRONG 4787, BAUER 773, MOULTON-MILLIGAN 609 (see "sunkineō"), LIDDELL-SCOTT 1665.

4639. συγκλείω sunkleiō verb

Enclose, imprison, consign.

CROSS-REFERENCE:
κλείω kleiō (2781)

אָלַם 'ālam (487), Niphal: be speechless (Ez 33:22—Codex Alexandrinus only).

סָגַר ṣāghar (5646), Qal: shut in, shut (Ex 14:3, Jb 3:10, Mal 1:10); niphal: be shut (Is 45:1); pual: be shut up (Jer 13:19); hiphil: deliver, hand over (Jos 20:5, Ps 31:8 [30:8], Ob 14).

מַסְגֵּר masgēr (4674), Smith (2 Kgs 24:14,16).

סָכַךְ ṣākhakh (5718), Hiphil: hedge in (Jb 3:23).

עָצַר 'ātsar (6352), Prevent (Gn 16:2).

פָּצַח pātsach (6723), Piel: break (Mi 3:3).

צוּר tsûr (6961), Besiege (Jer 21:9, Ez 4:3).

צָרַר tsārar (7173), Be hampered (Prv 4:12).

1. συνέκλεισεν sunekleisen 3sing indic aor act

2. συνέκλεισαν sunekleisan 3pl indic aor act

3. συγκεκλεισμένοι sunkekleismenoi nom pl masc part perf mid

4. συγκλειόμενοι sunkleiomenoi nom pl masc part pres mid

2 they **enclosed** a great multitude of fishes:........... Luke 5:6
1 For God **hath concluded** them all in unbelief,...... Rom 11:32
1 But the scripture **hath concluded** all under sin,....... Gal 3:22
3 **shut up** unto the faith which should ... be revealed...... 3:23

Classical Greek

Sunkleiō is used to mean "close up" or "enclose," in classical literature (see *Liddell-Scott*). In military contexts the word is employed to mean "closing up" the ranks. It is similarly used in Polybius to indicate the imprisonment or the "locking up" of people (Michel, "sunkleiō," *Kittel,* 7:744). These same meanings are found in the papyri (*Moulton-Milligan*).

Septuagint Usage

In the Septuagint *sunkleiō* is usually found translating the Hebrew verb *ṣāghar,* "to encircle, enclose, imprison" (see 1 Kings 11:27 [LXX 3 Kings 11:27]; 1 Samuel 1:6 [1 Kings 1:6]). In certain cases the verb has the idea of "deliver up" (as for imprisonment or capture) as in Joshua 20:5 where provisions for the cities of refuge are discussed: "If the avenger of blood pursues him, they shall not *give up* the slayer into his hand" (RSV) (cf. also Psalm 31:8 [LXX 30:8]). This is most clearly seen in Psalm 78:61,62 (LXX 77:61,62) where *sunkleiō* is used in parallel with *paradidōmi* (3722), "to turn over or deliver": He "*delivered* (*paredōken*) his power to captivity . . . He *gave* his people *over* (*sunekleisen*) to the sword" (RSV).

New Testament Usage

Sunkleiō occurs four times in the New Testament. In Luke 5:6 the word refers to Peter's catch of fish, indicating that many were captured in the net. Paul used the word three times. In Romans 11:32 the idea is that the disobedience infecting all people is a result of God's decision. The RSV translates this verse as follows: "For God has *consigned* all men to disobedience, that he may have mercy upon all." Paul's discussion of the fate of Israel in the midst of the mission to the Gentiles (Romans 9–11) seems to be implying that Israel's disobedience, for the time, is decreed by God to allow an opportunity to show His mercy through Christ to all people. The symbolism of "imprisonment" seems natural since God is coming as "Deliverer" (Romans 11:26).

A similar idea is expressed in Galatians 3:22,23. Here Paul pointed out that though the Law is in itself unable to create life in people (3:21), this does not mean that the Law acts against God's purposes. The purpose of the Law is restraint (3:23) until the revelation of faith. In this sense the Law "imprisons" us in an awareness of sin without deliverance from sin, until the message of faith in Jesus Christ is received and understood (3:22).

STRONG 4788, BAUER 774, MOULTON-MILLIGAN 609 (see "sunkleiō"), KITTEL 7:744-47, LIDDELL-SCOTT 1665.

4640. συγκληρονόμος

sunklēronomos adj

Fellow or joint heir.

COGNATES:

κληρόω klēroō (2793)
νόμος nomos (3414)

1. **συγκληρονόμοι sunklēronomoi** nom pl masc
2. **συγκληρονόμων sunklēronomōn** gen pl masc
3. **συγκληρονόμα sunklēronoma** nom/acc pl neu
4. **συγκληρονόμοις sunklēronomois** dat pl masc

1 heirs of God, and **joint-heirs** with Christ; .... Rom 8:17
3 That the Gentiles should be **fellowheirs**, ... Eph 3:6
2 and Jacob, the **heirs with** him of the same promise: Heb 11:9
1 and as being **heirs together** of the grace of life; ...... 1 Pt 3:7

Sunklēronomos is a compound of the word *klēronomos* (2791), "one who has been given an inheritance," and the preposition *sun* (4713), "with." The meaning of the word in the New Testament always suggests a joint or common inheritance between two people or two groups of people. In addition there is always an eschatological sense to the use of the word in the New Testament: the inheritance at stake is not material goods but the inheritance of God's promises (see Mundle, "Inheritance," *Colin Brown*, 2:300). The word is normally followed by a reference either to the coheir or to the things that are shared in the inheritance. In Romans 8:17 the point is that Christians are "joint heirs" with Christ in terms of their hope for heavenly glory. The possession of the Spirit (Romans 8:12-18) confirms that they, like Christ, have become God's children.

In Ephesians 3:6 the emphasis changes. Now both Jews and Gentiles are noted as "fellow heirs." Both share in the promise of Christ and are therefore now "one body." The promise motif is also picked up in Hebrews 11:9 where the writer showed that Abraham was a "fellow heir" with Jacob and Isaac of the covenant promise.

First Peter 3:7 applies the word to the husband/wife relationship. Peter warned husbands that wives are their "joint heirs" of the grace of God and therefore must be treated with respect and integrity or God would not hear their prayers. Far from accepting the social standards that see women as the "weaker sex," Peter was in fact overturning the social order that perceives women as inferiors. *Sunklēronomos* emphasizes the equality of men and women in God's eyes—an equality that men disregard at their own risk.

STRONG 4789, BAUER 774, MOULTON-MILLIGAN 609 (see "sunklēronomos"), KITTEL 3:767-85; 7:766-97, LIDDELL-SCOTT 1665, COLIN BROWN 2:295-96 (see "sunklēronomos").

4641. συγκοινωνέω

sunkoinōneō verb

To participate, to share with.

CROSS-REFERENCE:

κοινόω koinoō (2813)

1. **συγκοινωνεῖτε sunkoinōneite** 2pl impr pres act
2. **συγκοινωνήσητε sunkoinōnēsēte** 2pl subj aor act
3. **συγκοινωνήσαντες sunkoinōnēsantes** nom pl masc part aor act

1 And **have no fellowship with** the unfruitful works ..... Eph 5:11
3 that ye **did communicate with** my affliction.......... Phlp 4:14
2 Come out ... that ye **be not partakers** of her sins, ... Rev 18:4

Sunkoinōneō is a compound form of the term *koinōneō* (2814), "to share or participate in something." The noun form *koinōnia* (2815), often used by Paul, indicates the common brotherhood or participation that Christians share in the gospel (see Schattenmann, "Fellowship," *Colin Brown*, 1:639-644).

Sunkoinōneō occurs in two Pauline passages and in Revelation 18:4. In Philippians 4:14 Paul thanked the Philippians for "sharing" in his tribulations. By sending aid and a fellow worker, the Philippians showed a personal and active interest in Paul's needs. This is the essence of the meaning of *sunkoinōneō*. In contrast, in Ephesians 5:11 Paul urged the church *not* to participate in works which are fruitless and come from darkness. He had already listed a catalog of acts and attitudes to avoid (5:3-8), and expected Christians to avoid both participating or associating with people who do ungodly things, or to participate in those deeds themselves. Similarly, in Revelation 18:4 a voice from heaven commanded the people of God to "come out" and to dissociate from "Babylon" and her sinful activities.

STRONG 4790, BAUER 774, KITTEL 3:797,809, LIDDELL-SCOTT 1666, COLIN BROWN 1:639,642,644 (see "sunkoinōneō").

4642. συγκοινωνός

sunkoinōnos noun

Partnership, fellow sharer.

COGNATE:

κοινόω koinoō (2813)

SYNONYMS:

κοινωνός koinōnos (2817)
μέτοχος metochos (3223)

1. συγκοινωνός sunkoinōnos nom sing masc
2. συγκοινωνούς sunkoinōnous acc pl masc

1 and with them **partakest** of the root............... Rom 11:17
1 that I might be **partaker** thereof with you........... 1 Co 9:23
2 ye all are **partakers** of my grace.................... Phlp 1:7
1 your brother, and **companion** in tribulation,.......... Rev 1:9

Classical Greek

Sunkoinōnos is a member of the word group built on the more familiar term *koinōnia* (2815). "Fellowship" or *koinōnia* was an important concept both in the secular and sacred life of the ancient Greek world. *Koinōnia* implied not only participation in another person's life in friendship (or some other close relationship), but the term was a basic description of an ideal society which shared for the common good all things. The Stoic philosophers and Plato used the word to describe society working for the common good and sharing the basic needs of all among all (see Schattenmann, "Fellowship," *Colin Brown*, 1:640). Similarly, in religious contexts the word expressed the idea of union between man and the gods (see Hauck, "koinonos," *Kittel*, 3:799). In the papyri *sunkoinōnos* seems to be in a business context suggesting the word "partner(ship)" (cf. *Moulton-Milligan*). It does not occur in the Septuagint.

New Testament Usage

The New Testament uses of *sunkoinōnos* are found in Paul's writings (Romans 11:17; 1 Corinthians 9:23; Philippians 1:7) and in the Book of Revelation (1:9). In Romans 11:17 the Gentile Christians are portrayed as wild olive vines grafted into the cultivated vine of Israel and thereby sharing or participating in the benefits and blessings of Israel. Here, *sunkoinōnos* indicates that the Gentile Christians are now *people who partake* in the kindness of God (11:22) through their faith in Jesus Christ (cf. Cranfield, *International Critical Commentary, Romans*, 2:567). The same basic idea is visible in 1 Corinthians 9:23 where Paul described his ministry as something he did in the hope of becoming a *sunkoinōnos* in the gospel. Paul looked forward to sharing in the benefits of the gospel through his ministry to others (cf. Barrett, *Harper's New Testament Commentaries, First Corinthians*, p.216). In Philippians 1:7 Paul pictured the church of Philippi as *sunkoinōnous* with Paul in grace and in his ministry of the gospel. Here the word seems to suggest both the Philippians' partnership with Paul in ministry (cf. 1:5) and their sharing with Paul in the benefits of God's grace through Jesus Christ.

The final use of the word in Revelation 1:9 is consistent with the last idea. Here John pictured himself as a "brother and companion (*sunkoinōnos*) in tribulation, and in the kingdom and patience of Jesus Christ." That is, John saw himself with others as one who shared both the joys of the Kingdom in Jesus Christ and the cost of being faithful to that kingdom.

STRONG 4791, BAUER 774, MOULTON-MILLIGAN 609 (see "sunkoinōnos"), KITTEL 3:797-809, LIDDELL-SCOTT 1666, COLIN BROWN 1:639,642,644 (see "sunkoinōnos").

4643. συγκομίζω sunkomizō verb

To help to bury (someone).

COGNATE:

κομίζω komizō (2837)

SYNONYMS:

ἐνταφιάζω entaphiazō (1763)
θάπτω thaptō (2267)

עָלָה 'ālâh (6148), Go up (Jb 5:26).

1. συνεκόμισαν sunekomisan 3pl indic aor act

1 And devout men carried Stephen to his **burial**,...... Acts 8:2

Sunkomizō appears only in Acts 8:2 where it refers to the burial of Stephen by unnamed devout men. This usage is well known in classical sources and in the papyri, though the word is more frequently used in terms of "bringing in" or "gathering" the harvest (see *Liddell-Scott*). In Luke 7:12 *ekkomizō* (1567), a similar form of the root verb *komizō* (2837), is used to describe the crowd "carrying out" the body of the widow's son for burial. It may be that the occurrence in Acts 8:2 refers not only to the burial of the body, but also to collecting the body of Stephen from outside the city and carrying it to a place of burial (cf. *Moulton-Milligan*).

Strong 4792, Bauer 774, Moulton-Milligan 609 (see "sunkomizō"), Liddell-Scott 1666.

4644. συγκρίνω sunkrinō verb

Join together, compare, interpret, evaluate.

Cross-Reference:

κρίνω krinō (2892)

פָּרַשׁ pārash (6817), Pual: be declared (Nm 15:34).

פָּתַר pāthar (6876), Interpret (Gn 40:8,16, 41:12f.).

1. συγκρίνοντες sunkrinontes nom pl masc part pres act

2. συγκρῖναι sunkrinai inf aor act

1 **comparing** spiritual things with spiritual............ 1 Co 2:13
2 or **compare** ourselves with some that commend..... 2 Co 10:12
1 and **comparing** themselves among themselves,.......... 10:12

Classical Greek

Sunkrinō is found frequently in classical literature meaning "to combine or bring into combination, to compare," and rarely, "to interpret." The former meaning is found in Aristotle's *Metaphysics* in terms of the combination of the basic elements. The second meaning is also found in Aristotle, among others, and has more of the suggestion of comparing things nearly equal (so also Büchsel, "sunkrinō," *Kittel*, 3:953). In the papyri the word is preserved mainly in judicial documents where *sunkrinō* basically has the idea of "to decide" (cf. *Moulton-Milligan*) in terms of giving a decision to a case.

Septuagint Usage

The translation "to interpret" occurs in the Septuagint where *sunkrinō* is used to translate the Hebrew *pāthar*, "to interpret" or "to solve." This meaning is found primarily in the Joseph narrative in Genesis (40:8,16,22; 41:12,13,15) and in Daniel (5:7, there translating the Aramaic form of the verb, *p[e]shar*). In Genesis 40 and 41 Joseph interpreted a series of dreams first for his fellow prisoners and then for Pharaoh. In Daniel 5:7 King Belshazzar asked his court magicians to interpret the writing on the wall. They were unable to do so, but recommended Daniel as one known for his "interpretations" (Daniel 5:12, *sunkrimata*).

In the apocryphal books *sunkrinō* occurs in Wisdom of Solomon 7:29; 15:18; and 1 Maccabees 10:71. In Wisdom 7:29 wisdom is "compared" to the sun and found superior. In 15:18 the word is translated in the RSV as "judged," but carries a sense of comparison (and the results found wanting). Similarly, in 1 Maccabees 10:71 the governor, Apollonius, challenges Jonathan, the Jewish leader, to "match" forces in open battle. Again, the sense of comparison remains.

New Testament Usage

This latter sense is clearly the point in 2 Corinthians 10:12. Paul here used *enkrinein* (see 1462) and *sunkrinein* together. The former has the idea of "classing someone with someone." In the second part of the verse *metrountes* (see 3224) and *sunkrinontes* are used in parallel—meaning "measuring" and "comparing." The point is that Paul did not want to "class" or "measure" himself by his rival's standards for themselves. They, indeed, "compared" themselves to themselves and had scope for boasting, while Paul measured himself according to the limits God had set for him, and preferred to talk about his hope for God's commendation (2 Corinthians 10:13ff.).

The other New Testament occurrence of *sunkrinō* is not nearly so clear. In 1 Corinthians 2:13 Paul contrasted the wisdom and knowledge given by the Spirit with wisdom gained through human teachings and logic. He described this Spirit-taught wisdom as *pneumatikois pneumatika sunkrinontes*. Two problems exist here—the meaning of *pneumatikois* (either "with spiritual things" or "to spiritual men") and the meaning of the participle *sunkrinontes* (either "interpreting" or "comparing"). The verse could be read "interpreting spiritual things to spiritual people" or "comparing spiritual things with spiritual." Because the constant emphasis in 1 Corinthians 1 and 2 is the distinction between the world of human wisdom and thinking, the idea of "comparing" is certainly possible. Still, the emphasis on teaching and understanding what is taught in 1 Corinthians 2:1-12 probably best supports the RSV translation, "interpreting spiritual truths to those who possess the Spirit" (see Barrett, *Harper's New Testament Commentaries, First Corinthians*, p.76).

Strong 4793, Bauer 774, Moulton-Milligan 610 (see "sunkrinō"), Kittel 3:953-54, Liddell-Scott 1667.

4645. συγκύπτω sunkuptō verb

To be bent over, bent double, bowed down.

Cross-Reference:

κύπτω kuptō (2928)

נָחֵת nācheth (5365), Crouch (Sir 12:11).

עָזַב ʻāzav (6013), Leave (Jb 9:27).

1. **συγκύπτουσα** **sunkuptousa** nom sing fem part pres act
2. **συνκύπτουσα** **sunkuptousa** nom sing fem part pres act

1 infirmity eighteen years, and was **bowed together**,.. Luke 13:11

The word appears in Luke 13:11 where it describes the condition of the woman whom Jesus healed on the Sabbath. The term is used in contrast to *anakuptō* (350), "to stand straight" or "stand erect." In this context *sunkuptō* emphasizes that the woman was bent over due to some sort of affliction. Whether the more vivid translation "bent over double" is justified depends not on the meaning of *sunkuptō*, but on the phrase *eis to panteles*. This phrase can mean "completely" (hence, "she was not able to straighten up completely") or "at all" ("she was not able at all to straighten up"—a more severe description of the ailment). Either, however, is consistent with the basic meaning of the word.

STRONG 4794, BAUER 775, LIDDELL-SCOTT 1668.

4646. συγκυρία sunkuria noun

By chance, coincidence.

1. **συγκυρίαν** **sunkurian** acc sing fem

1 And by **chance** there came down a certain priest... Luke 10:31

Sunkuria occurs only once in the New Testament. In the Parable of the Good Samaritan (Luke 10:31) it refers to the priest's passing by the wounded traveler. The word probably reflects the Hebraism of Old Testament phrases translated as "and it came to pass" or "and it happened." Therefore, it happened "by chance" may simply mean that the priest was traveling on the same road where the incident had occurred.

STRONG 4795, BAUER 775, LIDDELL-SCOTT 1668.

4647. συγχαίρω sunchairō verb

Rejoice with; congratulate.

CROSS-REFERENCE:
χαίρω chairō (5299)

צָחַק tsāchaq (6978), Laugh (Gn 21:6).

1. **συγχαίρω** **sunchairō** 1sing indic pres act
2. **συγχαίρει** **sunchairei** 3sing indic pres act
3. **συγχαίρετε** **sunchairete** 2pl impr pres act
4. **συνέχαιρον** **sunechairon** 3pl indic imperf act
5. **συγχάρητε** **suncharēte** 2pl impr aor pass
6. **συνχάρητε** **suncharēte** 2pl impr aor pass

4 great mercy upon her; and they **rejoiced with** her.... Luke 1:58
5 saying unto them, **Rejoice with** me; 15:6
5 saying, **Rejoice with** me; for I have found the piece.... 15:9
2 all the members **rejoice with** it.................... 1 Co 12:26
2 not in iniquity, but **rejoiceth** in the truth;............ 13:6
1 if I be offered ... I joy, and **rejoice with** you all......Phlp 2:17
3 the same cause also do ye joy, and **rejoice with** me...... 2:18

Sunchairō is related to of *chairō* (5299), the common Greek verb meaning "to rejoice" or "to be merry." When the preposition *sun* (4713), "with," is added to *chairō*, the resulting word *sunchairō* means "to rejoice with." At times the compounded term takes the same meaning as the root verb (i.e., simply "to rejoice") and at times the only difference between the simple and compounded form is that the meaning of the compound is intensified.

Classical Greek and Septuagint Usage

The term is first found in the writings of classical Greek authors Aeschylus and Xenophon (ca. Fifth and Fourth Centuries B.C.) with the meaning "to rejoice with." Aeschines 2:45 (ca. Fourth Century B.C.) establishes an additional meaning when used with a person's name and a reason for rejoicing, i.e., "to congratulate" (*Bauer*).

Both meanings of *sunchairō* ("rejoice [with]" and "congratulate") are found in ancient inscriptions and in the papyri (ibid.). One papyrus text contains a message of congratulations from a father to his son on his happy marriage (see *Moulton-Milligan*). It appears only twice in the Septuagint. At Genesis 21:6 it is used of the rejoicing ("laughing") of Sarah when Isaac was born.

In Josephus' *Antiquities of the Jews* (15.7.2) the compound verb *sunchairō* takes the same meaning as the simple verb, "to rejoice," and in 8.2.5 it means "to congratulate" (*Bauer*). In early Christian literature *sunchairō* appears in the writings of the Apostolic Fathers in Ignatius' *Letter to the Trallians* 1:1 ("I rejoiced with you from the bottom of my heart"), and in Polycarp 1:1 it is used with the Greek word *hoti* (3617), "because," and includes the reason for rejoicing (*Bauer*).

New Testament Usage

In the New Testament the term occurs in Luke 15:6 and 9, the parables of the Lost Sheep and the Lost Coin. It is possible that in Luke 1:58 and perhaps in Philippians 2:17,18 the meaning "to congratulate" may be appropriate. In 1 Corinthians 12:26, though the term is used without the dative, it is easily supplied—rejoice *with* the member who is honored. In 1 Corinthians

13:6 *sunchairō* has the same meaning as the simple, uncompounded verb *chairō*, "rejoice": "(Charity) rejoiceth not in iniquity, but rejoiceth in the truth."

Strong 4796, Bauer 775, Moulton-Milligan 616 (see "sunchairō"), Kittel 9:359-72, Liddell-Scott 1668.

4648. συγχέω suncheō verb

To stir up, incite, confuse.

Cognate:

ἐκχύνω ekchunō (1619)

Synonyms:

ἀνασείω anaseiō (381)
ἐπεγείρω epegeirō (1877)
παροτρύνω parotrunō (3813)

בָּלַל bālal (1140), Confuse (Gn 11:7,9).

הָלַל hālal (2054), Praise; hithpoel: race madly (Na 2:4).

הָמַם hāmam (2072), Throw into confusion (1 Sm 7:10—Codex Vaticanus only).

חָרָה chārâh (2835), Become angry (Jon 4:1).

נָכָה nākhâh (5409), Hiphil: smite (Am 3:15).

נָקַר nāqar (5548), Piel: pierce (Jb 30:17).

סַר ṣar (5821), Sullen (1 Kgs 20:43 [21:43]).

עָצַר 'ātsar (6352), Slave (2 Kgs 14:26—Codex Alexandrinus only).

רָגַז rāghaz (7553), Quake, tremble (Jl 2:10, Mi 7:17).

1. **συνέχυνεν sunechunen** 3sing indic imperf act
2. **συνέχεον sunecheon** 3pl indic imperf act
3. **συνεχύθη sunechuthē** 3sing indic aor pass
4. **συγκέχυται sunkechutai** 3sing indic perf mid
5. **συγκεχυμένη sunkechumenē** nom sing fem part perf mid
6. **συνέχυννεν sunechunnen** 3sing indic imperf act
7. **συγχύννεται sunchunnetai** 3sing indic pres mid

3 multitude came together, and **were confounded,** ...... Acts 2:6
1 and **confounded** the Jews which dwelt at Damascus, ... 9:22
5 and some another: for the assembly **was confused;** 19:32
2 **stirred up** all the people, and laid hands on him, ... 21:27
4 that all Jerusalem **was in an uproar** 21:31

The basic meaning of the verb in most of classical literature is to "pour together, commingle," or "confound," although in Polybius *suncheō* is used in the sense of "stirring up" or "inciting" war (*Liddell-Scott*). It is this latter sense which is clearly the meaning in Acts 21:27. "Jews from Asia" made charges against Paul and led a lynch mob against him. A Roman cohort saved him from the crowd. In verse 31 the passive form of the word is used to suggest that the whole city of Jerusalem was thrown into disarray or was in a state of confusion.

Strong 4797, Bauer 775, Moulton-Milligan 616 (see "suncheō"), Liddell-Scott 1668.

4649. συγχράομαι sunchraomai verb

To use with, to associate with.

Cross-Reference:

χράομαι chraomai (5366)

1. **συγχρῶνται sunchrōntai** 3pl indic pres mid

1 for the Jews have no **dealings** with the Samaritans... John 4:9

Classical Greek

The sole occurrence of this word in the New Testament is found in John 4:9 where the RSV translates it, "The Samaritan woman said to him, 'How is it that you, a Jew, ask a drink of me, a woman of Samaria?' For Jews *have no dealings* with Samaritans." The primary meaning of the word *chraomai* (5366) is "to use," although *Liddell-Scott* gives instances in Xenophon and classical literature that mean "to be intimate with." *Moulton-Milligan* offers evidence in the papyri that the word can mean "to associate" or have dealings with, but David Daube casts doubt on this in his article on the word and this passage ("Jesus and the Samaritan Woman," p.142f.).

New Testament Usage

The concern for ritual purity among the Pharisees and in later rabbinic writings is well known (see, for example, Luke 7:36-50 where Simon the Pharisee's inhospitality may reflect his own hesitancy about Jesus' ritual purity). To touch instruments or people who were ritually unclean made one unclean. Since saliva was considered a prime carrier of ritual impurity, Jesus' willingness to take a drink from the Samaritan woman perhaps indicated a willingness to share her unclean state (ibid., p.137ff.). Following Daube's recommendation, therefore, Raymond Brown translates the word as follows: "Jews, you remember, *use nothing in common with* Samaritans" (see *Anchor Bible*, 29:166f.).

Strong 4798, Bauer 775, Moulton-Milligan 616 (see "sunchraomai"), Liddell-Scott 1668.

4650. σύγχυσις sunchusis noun

Confusion, tumult, disturbance.

Cross-Reference:

ἐκχύνω ekchunō (1619)

בָּבֶל bāvel (928), Babel (Gn 11:9).

מְהוּמָה m^ehûmāh (4245), Confusion (1 Sm 14:20).

1. **συγχύσεως sunchuseōs** gen sing fem

1 And the whole city was filled with **confusion:** .... Acts 19:29

This noun is found in the New Testament only in Acts 19:29. Here it describes the mob scene stirred up by Demetrius against the Ephesian

Christians. The word emphasizes the riotous, but uncertain, confusion of the crowd. The verbal form of the word is repeated in 19:32 where it is reported that "most of them did not know why they had come together" (RSV). The noun form indicates the *resulting* confusion, disorder, and anger that accompanied the mob scene.

STRONG 4799, BAUER 775, LIDDELL-SCOTT 1669.

4651. συζάω suzaō verb

To live with (someone).

CROSS-REFERENCE:
ζάω zaō (2180)

1. συζῆν suzēn inf pres act
2. συζήσομεν suzēsomen 1pl indic fut act

2 we believe that we **shall also live with him:** .... Rom 6:8
1 that ye are in our hearts to die and **live with** you.... 2 Co 7:3
2 be dead with him, we shall also **live with him:** ...... 2 Tm 2:11

Suzaō (also spelled *sunzaō*) is found three times in the New Testament, all in the Pauline epistles (Romans 6:8; 2 Corinthians 7:3; 2 Timothy 2:11). The word is made up of the preposition *sun* (4713), "with," and the verb *zaō* (2180), "to live." The normal translation of the term is "to live with." But Paul never used the verb in the simple sense of "living with" another person; instead, he used it as a metaphor. In all three cases Paul connected "living with" someone to "dying with" the same person. In Romans 6:8 and 2 Timothy 2:11 that person is Christ. In Romans 6 Paul drew a parallel between the meaning of baptism and the reality of the Christian life: as the believer "dies with" Christ in baptism, he now "lives with" Christ as a matter of his own will (verse 11). Ultimately, Christians "live with" Jesus by living the life of faith through the Holy Spirit both now and, more perfectly, later at the end of the age (Romans 8; see Cranfield, *International Critical Commentary*, *Romans*, 1:312f.). Second Timothy 2:11 emphasizes the future aspects of "living with" Christ: believers shall fully experience salvation if they are faithful to what they have received.

In 2 Corinthians 7:3 the same formula is applied to the relationship between Paul and the Corinthians: "For I said before that you are in our hearts, to die together and to live together" (RSV). Paul in this sense emphasized the commitment he felt toward the Corinthians and he believed they felt toward him. Paul used the phrase in order to place his criticism of the Corinthians and his exhortations to reform their lives in the context of his real and permanent commitment to them. Perhaps he also wished to emphasize their common destiny "in Christ" and the resurrection.

STRONG 4800, BAUER 775, MOULTON-MILLIGAN 607 (see "sunzaō"), KITTEL 7:766,783,787, LIDDELL-SCOTT 1669.

4652. συζεύγνυμι suzeugnumi verb

To yoke or join together; to pair.

CROSS-REFERENCE:
ζυγός zugos (2201)

חָבַר chāvar (2357), Touch (Ez 1:11).

1. συνέζευξεν sunezeuxen 3sing indic aor act

1 What therefore God hath **joined together,** .... Matt 19:6
1 What therefore God **hath joined together,** .... Mark 10:9

Classical Greek and Septuagint Usage

Suzeugnumi is a compound verb meaning "to yoke together." In the Septuagint rendering of Ezekiel 1:11 the verb is used to describe the "joining together" of the wings of the creatures the prophet saw in a vision. It translates the Hebrew verb *chāvar*, "to bind, entwine, touch."

The term appears in secular Greek literature and the writings of Josephus with reference to marriage (see Link, "Yoke," *Colin Brown*, 3:1164).

New Testament Usage

The only New Testament occurrences of *suzeugnumi* are in parallel passages in Matthew 19:6 and Mark 10:9: "Therefore what God has *joined together*, let man not separate" (NIV). The use of *suzeugnumi* is emphasized by the contrasting term "separate." As used in these two passages, the word signifies the "one flesh" relationship between husband and wife that God creates when the two leave their former relationships and unite together (see Brown, "Separate," *Colin Brown*, 3:539).

STRONG 4801, BAUER 775, MOULTON-MILLIGAN 607 (see "sunzeugnumi"), LIDDELL-SCOTT 1669, COLIN BROWN 3:1160,1162,1164.

4653. συζητέω suzēteō verb

To discuss, dispute.

COGNATE:
ζητέω zēteō (2195)

SYNONYMS:
διακρίνω diakrinō (1246)
διαλέγομαι dialegomai (1250)
συμβάλλω sumballō (4671)

בָּקַשׁ bāqash (1272), Piel: request (Neh 2:4).

1. **συζητεῖτε suzēteite** 2pl indic pres act
2. **συζητοῦντες suzētountes** nom pl masc part pres act
3. **συζητούντων suzētountōn** gen pl masc part pres act
4. **συζητοῦντας suzētountas** acc pl masc part pres act
5. **συζητεῖν suzētein** inf pres act
6. **συνεζήτει sunezētei** 3sing indic imperf act
7. **συνζητεῖν sunzētein** inf pres act
8. **συνζητοῦντες sunzētountes** nom pl masc part pres act
9. **συνζητοῦντας sunzētountas** acc pl masc part pres act
10. **συνζητεῖτε sunzēteite** 2pl indic pres act
11. **συνζητούντων sunzētountōn** gen pl masc part pres act

5 insomuch that they **questioned** among themselves, ... Mark 1:27
5 came forth, and began **to question with** him, ... 8:11
2 **questioning** one with another what the rising 9:10
4 and the scribes **questioning** with them. 9:14
1 he asked the scribes, What **question** ye with them? 9:16
3 and having heard them **reasoning together**, ... 12:28
5 And they began **to inquire** among themselves, ... Luke 22:23
5 while they communed together and **reasoned**, ... 24:15
2 of Cilicia and of Asia, **disputing** with Stephen. .... Acts 6:9
6 and **disputed** against the Grecians: 9:29

Classical Greek and Septuagint Usage

The verb *suzēteō* carries the sense of "discuss, carry on a discussion," from which then develop the meanings "to dispute, debate, argue." It is the root from which the nouns *suzētēsis* (4654), "dispute, quarrel," and *suzētētēs* (4655), "debater, disputant," are derived. In the works of Plato (ca. 375 B.C.) *suzēteō* means "to examine together" (*Cratylus* 384c; *Meno* 90b; cf. *Bauer*). Though absent from the Septuagint, the verb occurs in Nehemiah 2:4 (LXX 2 Esdras 12:4), where it is sometimes translated "prying into."

Sources outside the New Testament during the First and Second Centuries attest similar meanings. The *Oxyrhynchus Papyri* (ca. Second Century A.D.) yield the sense "to dispute" and "to strive" (cf. *Moulton-Milligan*). The Epistle of Barnabas 4:10 uses *suzēteō* to mean "discuss," while other documents from the period use it to mean "dispute" or "ponder" (Schneider, "suzēteō," *Kittel,* 7:748). The word is common in the writings of Justin Martyr (died ca. A.D. 165), who used it along with *punthanomai* (4299) to refer to the disputes between Jesus and the Pharisees (e.g., *Dialogue* 64:2; cf. *Bauer*).

New Testament Usage

New Testament usage is limited to 10 occurrences, all in the writings of Mark and Luke. In Mark 1:27 the term describes the activity of the people who stood amazed at Jesus' exorcism of an evil spirit. Likewise, in Mark 9:10, after Jesus informed the disciples that He would have to die but then would rise again, the disciples kept *discussing* this "rising from the dead." *Suzēteō* also describes the discussion of the two disciples on the road to Emmaus in Luke 24:15.

Four additional occurrences of *suzēteō* appear in Mark and three in Luke's writings. The four in Mark are all used in the context of controversy and confrontation. Mark 8:11 uses the verb to describe the manner in which the Pharisees *challenged* Jesus on points of belief and doctrine. Two occurrences in Mark 9 depict an argument between the teachers of the Law and Jesus' disciples. Mark 12:28 uses *suzēteō* to describe a debate scene.

The three additional occurrences of the term in Luke's writings are similar. When Jesus announced at the Last Supper that one of the Twelve would betray Him, they began *arguing* among themselves who the traitor might be (Luke 22:23). In Acts 6:9 *suzēteō* describes the negative reaction of men to the ministry and message of Stephen: they *argued* with him. Acts 9:29 uses *suzēteō* to depict an important aspect in Saul's (Paul's) early ministry. He *debated* with the Hellenistic Jews.

Strong 4802, Bauer 775, Moulton-Milligan 607 (see "sunzēteō"), Kittel 7:747-48, Liddell-Scott 1670.

4654. συζήτησις suzētēsis noun

Dispute, discussion.

Cognate:
ζητέω zēteō (2195)

Synonyms:
διάκρισις diakrisis (1247)
διαλογισμός dialogismos (1255)

1. **συζητήσεως suzētēseōs** gen sing fem
2. **συζήτησιν suzētēsin** acc sing fem

1 no small dissension and **disputation** with them, ... Acts 15:2
1 And when there had been much **disputing**, ... 15:7
2 and had great **reasoning** among themselves. 28:29

Classical Greek

Suzētēsis means "discussion, quarrel, investigation." It does not appear in the Septuagint and is rare in early Greek literature. Philo's writings attest its usage in pre-New Testament times (see Schneider, "suzētēsis," *Kittel,* 7:748).

New Testament Usage

The term appears three times in the New Testament, but only in the *Textus Receptus* (Acts

15:2,7; 28:29). Many early as well as many later Greek texts omit Acts 28:29 altogether, and *zētēsis* (2197) replaces *suzētēsis* in Acts 15:2,7 (see, for example, the appropriate passages in *Nestle-Aland 26th* or *UBS 3rd*).

The occurrences in Acts 15:2,7 involve the sharp discussions that arose in response to the circumcision issue in the Early Church. Paul and Barnabas engaged in *pointed debate* with those who claimed circumcision as necessary for salvation. The *Textus Receptus* in Acts 28:29 uses *suzētēsis* to describe the quarreling of the Jews among themselves in response to Paul's claim that God's salvation has been delivered to the Gentiles.

STRONG 4803, BAUER 775, MOULTON-MILLIGAN 607 (see "sunzētēsis"), KITTEL 7:748, LIDDELL-SCOTT 1670.

4655. συζητητής suzētētēs noun

Disputer, debater.

CROSS-REFERENCE:
ζητέω zēteō (2195)

1. συζητητής suzētētēs nom sing masc

1 where is the **disputer** of this world? .... 1 Co 1:20

Suzētētēs, not attested outside the New Testament, describes "one who disputes with" or "a person who investigates with." The only New Testament occurrence is in 1 Corinthians 1:20 where, in a series of rhetorical questions, the apostle Paul asks, "Where is the philosopher of this age?" (NIV). "Philosopher" translates *suzētētēs.*

Given the nature and the reputation of the "philosopher" in ancient times, this is probably an accurate rendering of *suzētētēs* (see Fee, *New International Commentary on the New Testament, First Corinthians,* p.71). It signifies the person who investigates, questions, even disputes accepted traditional ideas, understandings, and norms. The term does not carry an inherently negative connotation, but the way Paul used it gave it negative overtones from the Christian perspective.

STRONG 4804, BAUER 775, KITTEL 7:748, LIDDELL-SCOTT 1670.

4656. σύζυγος suzugos adj

Comrade, yokefellow, companion.

CROSS-REFERENCE:
ζυγός zugos (2201)

1. σύζυγε suzuge voc sing masc

1 And I entreat thee also, true **yokefellow**, ... Phlp 4:3

Classical Greek

This term can be found in classical Greek meaning "yoked together, paired, united" (*Liddell-Scott*). Frequently it is used concerning marriage, but it can also be found of things and animals that are paired (cf. ibid.). *Suzugos* can refer to a "spouse" (Euripides *Alcestis* 314) and to "pairs" (Delling, "suzugos," *Kittel,* 7:748f.).

Suzugos does not occur in the Septuagint. However, in Aquila's translation of the Old Testament into Greek (ca. A.D. 130–150), a form of *suzugos* is used to denote a "yoking together" or "coupling" of the Israelites with the Egyptians in Ezekiel 23:21.

New Testament Usage

Suzugos occurs only in Philippians 4:3 in the New Testament, but the term has spawned a long-running discussion. The issue concerns whether the word is used as a common noun or a proper name. Philippians 4:3 reads, in part: "Now I ask you, loyal companion, help these ladies . . . " (author's translation). "Companion" is the translation of *suzugos* that occurs here. Whether the term is taken as a common noun or a proper name, it denotes a "yokefellow" or "comrade." Paul addressed this individual as one who had served well as a comrade in the cause of the gospel and now must help to assuage the dissension between Euodia and Syntyche.

Most translations render *suzugos* as a common noun (e.g., KJV, RSV, NASB, NIV, NEB). Several commentators, however, opt to understand it as a proper name (e.g., Vincent, *International Critical Commentary, Philippians and Philemon,* p.131; Hendriksen, *New Testament Commentary, Philippians,* p.191). The "proper name" understanding is complicated by the term "loyal/true" that qualifies *suzugos* in Philippians 4:3. For the modifier to make sense in relation to *suzugos* as a proper name, the combination could be understood as a play on words: you are "rightly named *Suzugos* (comrade)," implying Paul's confidence that the situation would be cared for by this individual. "In all probability," writes Hendriksen, "the apostle is making use here of a play on a name, for Syzygus means yoke-fellow, a person who pulls well in a harness for two, and Paul is saying that Syzygus was true to his name" (ibid.).

Majority opinion opposes understanding *suzugos* as a proper name. The name has been nowhere else attested, and the usage of the qualifier, "loyal/true," militates against such an interpretation (see Delling, "suzogos," *Kittel*, 7:749). The identity of the "comrade" remains unknown, theories suggesting individuals such as Timothy, Silas, Syntyche, and even Paul's own wife are pure speculation.

STRONG 4805, BAUER 775-76, MOULTON-MILLIGAN 607 (see "sunzugos"), KITTEL 7:748-50, LIDDELL-SCOTT 1670, COLIN BROWN 3:1160,1164.

4657. συζωοποιέω suzōopoieō verb

To make alive together with.

COGNATES:

ζάω zaō (2180)
ποιέω poieō (4020)

1. συνεζωοποίησεν sunezōopoiēsen 3sing indic aor act

2. συνεζωποίησεν sunezōpoiēsen 3sing indic aor act

1 hath quickened us together with Christ, ... Eph 2:5
2 hath he quickened together with him, ... Col 2:13

Suzōopoieō is a compound verb comprised of three elements: the preposition *sun* (4713), "with/together with," a form of the root *zōē* (2205), "life" or "alive," and the verb *poieō* (4020), "to make." The term is attested only in two New Testament occurrences, both times bearing a significant spiritual or soteriological sense.

In Colossians 2 Paul declared that all the fullness of the Deity dwells in Jesus Christ in bodily form. Through spiritual circumcision, the believer's sinful nature has been put off, and through baptism, burial to the old life and resurrection to the new life have occurred. Through this process the believer is "made alive with" Christ (2:13) by the power of God. Those who were dead outside of Christ are made alive with Him through the remission of sins; they are removed from the dominion of all other powers and authorities.

Ephesians 2 echoes similar ideas. Because all have sinned, the sentence of death has been passed upon all (cf. Romans 3:23; 6:23). But because of His great love, God has rescinded His wrath and "made us alive with Christ" (NIV). This affirms His grace toward those who believe on Jesus Christ. This new life results in a new position ("God . . . seated us with [Christ] in the heavenly realms," Ephesians 2:6, NIV) and a new purpose ("that . . . he might show the incomparable riches of his grace, expressed in his kindness to us . . . ," verse 7, NIV) (see Grundmann, "suzōopoieō," *Kittel*, 7:792f.).

STRONG 4806, BAUER 776, KITTEL 7:766-97, LIDDELL-SCOTT 1670.

4658. συκάμινος sukaminos noun

Mulberry tree.

שִׁקְמָה shiqmāh (8622), Sycamore-fig tree (1 Kgs 10:27, 1 Chr 27:28, Is 9:10).

1. συκαμίνῳ sukaminō dat sing fem

1 ye might say unto this sycamine tree, ... Luke 17:6

Sukaminos denotes a sycamine tree (most likely a mulberry tree) that grew to a height of 10 to 20 feet, with a broad crown, and large lobed leaves. The female head ripens to a fleshy fruit that is eaten fresh or cooked (Zohary, "Flora," *Interpreter's Dictionary of the Bible*, 2:287). In other Greek literature *sukaminos* sometimes refers not only to the mulberry tree but also to the sycamore fig (e.g., Amos 7:14; cf. Hunzinger, "sukaminos," *Kittel*, 7:758).

Luke 17:6 is the only New Testament usage of *sukaminos*. Jesus appealed to the "mulberry tree" to illustrate the power of a minute particle of faith. Even such a strong, deeply-rooted obstacle as the *sukaminos* was no match for a "mustard seed" of faith properly deployed. The tree could be uprooted and planted in the heart of the sea.

STRONG 4807, BAUER 776, MOULTON-MILLIGAN 595-96, KITTEL 7:758, LIDDELL-SCOTT 1670.

4659. συκῆ sukē noun

Fig tree.

COGNATES:

συκομορέα sukomorea (4659B)
συκομωραία sukomōraia (4660)
σῦκον sukon (4661)
συκοφαντέω sukophanteō (4662)

תְּאֵנָה te'ēnāh (8711), Fig (Nm 20:5, S/S 2:13, Hg 2:19 [2:20]).

1. συκῆ sukē nom sing fem

2. συκῆς sukēs gen sing fem

3. συκῇ sukē dat sing fem

4. συκῆν sukēn acc sing fem

4 when he saw a fig tree in the way, he came to it, .. Matt 21:19
1 And presently the fig tree withered away. 21:19
1 How soon is the fig tree withered away! 21:20
2 not only do this which is done to the fig tree, ... 21:21
2 Now learn a parable of the fig tree; 24:32
4 And seeing a fig tree afar off having leaves, ... Mark 11:13

4 they saw the fig tree dried up from the roots...... Mark 11:20
1 the fig tree which thou cursedst is withered away....... 11:21
2 Now learn a parable of the fig tree;.................. 13:28
4 certain man had a fig tree planted in his vineyard; Luke 13:6
3 three years I come seeking fruit on this fig tree,....... 13:7
4 he spake to them a parable; Behold the fig tree,....... 21:29
4 when thou wast under the fig tree, I saw thee....... John 1:48
2 I saw thee under the fig tree, believest thou?........... 1:50
1 Can the fig tree, my brethren, bear olive berries?.....Jas 3:12
1 even as a fig tree casteth her untimely figs,.......... Rev 6:13

Sukē refers to the fruit-producing tree that was common throughout the area of Palestine. Testimony from as early as the third millennium B.C. attests its presence in this region. The fig tree is mentioned often in the Old Testament (e.g., Judges 9:7-15; Isaiah 34:4; Jeremiah 8:13; 24:1-10; etc.) and thrives in Israel even today (Hunzinger, "sukē," *Kittel*, 7:752f.). It can grow to the size of a tree or may spread out in the form of a shrub, its size being dependent on soil and location. Two crops of figs are usually produced each year. The tree's leaves appear in the spring, after the blooms (see Matthew 24:32). Unless a fig tree has young fruit along with its leaves, it will be barren for the season (Harrison, "Fig," *International Standard Bible Encyclopedia*, 2:301f.).

The fig tree is mentioned frequently in the New Testament, most often in the Synoptic Gospels. Jesus cursed the fig tree in Mark 11:13,14 because of the absence of any fruit.

STRONG 4808, BAUER 776, MOULTON-MILLIGAN 596, KITTEL 7:751-57, LIDDELL-SCOTT 1670 (see "sukea"), COLIN BROWN 1:723-25.

4659B. συκομορέα sukomorea noun

Sycamore fig tree.

CROSS-REFERENCE:
συκῆ sukē (4659)

1. συκομορέαν sukomorean acc sing fem

1 and climbed up into a sycamore tree (NASB)...... Luke 19:4

This noun, also spelled *sukomōraia* (4660), is synonymous with *sukomoros* and means "sycamore fig," but it can also refer to the "tree." It is found only once in the New Testament, at Luke 19:4.

4660. συκομωραία sukomōraia noun

Sycamore fig, fig-mulberry tree.

CROSS-REFERENCE:
συκῆ sukē (4659)

1. συκομωραίαν sukomōraian acc sing fem

1 and climbed up into a sycamore tree to see him:... Luke 19:4

Sukomōraia is the sycamore fig tree, a large evergreen tree attaining heights of 40 to 50 feet, with trunk circumferences of over 12 feet. The tree's leaves were heart-shaped, its fruit similar in appearance but smaller and inferior in quality to the true fig. Sycamore fig trees could not tolerate cold climates; they generally grew on the plains (1 Kings 10:27 [LXX 3 Kings 10:27]).

Luke 19:4, the only New Testament usage of *sukomōraia*, describes the tree Zacchaeus climbed in order to gain a better point of vantage from which to see Jesus.

The form *sukomōraia* occurs only in the *Textus Receptus*. Other Greek texts have *sukomorea* (4659B) or *sukomōros* instead. Some ambiguity existed in the meaning and usage of *sukomōraia* and *sukaminos* (4658) in the ancient Near East (see Hunzinger, "sukomōraia," *Kittel*, 7:758). The New Testament does not help to resolve this ambiguity, since both *sukomōraia* and *sukaminos* occur only one time each (Luke 19:4 and Luke 17:6 respectively).

STRONG 4809, BAUER 776 (see "sukomorea"), MOULTON-MILLIGAN 596 (see "sukomorea"), KITTEL 7:758 (see "sukomorea"), LIDDELL-SCOTT 1670.

4661. σῦκον sukon noun

Fig.

CROSS-REFERENCE:
συκῆ sukē (4659)

תְּאֵנָה teʾēnāh (8711), Fig (Neh 13:15, Is 38:21, Jer 24:1f.).

1. σύκων sukōn gen pl neu

2. σῦκα suka nom/acc pl neu

2 Do men gather grapes of thorns, or figs of thistles? Matt 7:16
1 for the time of figs was not yet.................. Mark 11:13
2 For of thorns men do not gather figs,............. Luke 6:44
2 bear olive berries? either a vine, figs?............... Jas 3:12

Classical Greek and Septuagint Usage

Sukon is the fruit of the fig tree, especially the ripe fig. Figs were very common in the area of Palestine. Old Testament references indicate they were eaten fresh (2 Kings 18:31 [LXX 4 Kings 18:31]), made into cakes (1 Samuel 25:18 [LXX 1 Kings 25:18]), or could even be pressed into a poultice and used for medicinal purposes (Isaiah 38:21).

New Testament Usage

Sukon appears four times in the New Testament: Matthew 7:16; Mark 11:13; Luke 6:44; and James 3:12. With the exception of Mark 11:13, the fig is used in the context of discussions about discerning the true nature of people by observing the fruit they produce. For example, Matthew 7:16 says, "By their fruit you will recognize them. Do people pick grapes from thornbushes, or figs from thistles?" (NIV). In Mark 11:13 the reference to figs occurs in the context of Jesus' cursing the fig tree.

STRONG 4810, BAUER 776, MOULTON-MILLIGAN 596, KITTEL 7:751-57, LIDDELL-SCOTT 1670-71.

4662. συκοφαντέω sukophanteō verb

Accuse falsely, defraud, slander, blackmail, extort.

CROSS-REFERENCES:
συκῆ sukē (4659)
φαίνω phainō (5154)

גָּלַל gālal (1597), Roll; hithpolel: fall on (Gn 43:18).

עֲשׁוּקִים 'ăshûqîm (6471), Oppression (Jb 35:9).

עָשַׁק 'āshaq (6479), Oppress (Ps 119:22 [118:22]).

שָׁקַר shāqar (8631), Piel: deceive (Lv 19:11).

1. ἐσυκοφάντησα esukophantēsa 1sing indic aor act
2. συκοφαντήσητε sukophantēsēte 2pl subj aor act

2 Do violence to no man, neither **accuse** any **falsely**; .. Luke 3:14
1 taken any thing from any man **by false accusation**, ... 19:8

Classical Greek

This verb appears in classical Greek from the Fifth Century B.C. with the meaning "accuse falsely, defraud, slander." Frequently such action was done in the form of "blackmail" by public officials (cf. *Liddell-Scott*), but it could refer to any effort by a person who seeks to oppress or exhort someone with false charges or threats.

Septuagint Usage

It is used occasionally in the Septuagint in a similar manner. In Job 35:9 Elihu spoke of how "the multitude of *oppressions* . . . make the oppressed to cry." In Psalm 119:122 (LXX 118:22) the Psalmist entreated God saying: "Be surety for thy servant for good: let not the proud *oppress* me." An underlying principle throughout the Old Testament is whoever "oppresses" the poor brings reproach on their Creator (cf. Proverbs 14:31; 22:16).

New Testament Usage

In the New Testament *sukophanteō* is used only twice, both times by Luke. John the Baptist instructed soldiers who came to him under conviction from his preaching to "do violence to no man, neither *accuse* any *falsely*; and be content with your wages" (Luke 3:14). Later, in a different setting, Zaccheus said to Jesus, "Behold, Lord, the half of my goods I give to the poor; and if I have *taken* any thing from any man *by false accusation*, I restore him fourfold" (Luke 19:8). Jesus responded by declaring that salvation had come to this man who had recognized his sins, had repented of them, and would make restitution for them (verses 9,10).

STRONG 4811, BAUER 776, MOULTON-MILLIGAN 596, KITTEL 7:759, LIDDELL-SCOTT 1671.

4663. συλαγωγέω sulagōgeō verb

To carry off booty, to lead captive, to rob.

CROSS-REFERENCE:
συλάω sulaō (4664)

1. συλαγωγῶν sulagōgōn nom sing masc part pres act

1 Beware lest any man **spoil** you through philosophy ... Col 2:8

Sulagōgeō is not attested in Greek literature prior to the New Testament, but in later literature it is used to mean "kidnap" (McDonald, *Commentary on Colossians and Philemon*, p.76). It appears in contexts that mean to carry off a man's daughter, to plunder a house, and to seduce a maiden (see Lohse, *Hermenia, Colossians and Philemon*, p.94).

New Testament Usage

Its only New Testament occurrence is in Colossians 2:8. In the midst of Paul's discussion of the false teaching that was infiltrating the Colossian congregation, he warned them not to let anyone "rob" or "make spoil of" them. The apostle's concern is apparent: someone was waging an assault on the Colossian church, not so much with the intent of robbing it of its saints, but rather to lead them away captive from the freedom of truth to the slavery of error. Paul warned them to beware. (See Hillyer, "Rob," *Colin Brown*, 3:379.)

STRONG 4812, BAUER 776, MOULTON-MILLIGAN 596, LIDDELL-SCOTT 1671, COLIN BROWN 3:379.

4664. συλάω sulaō verb

To plunder, rob.

COGNATE:
συλαγωγέω sulagōgeō (4663)

SYNONYM:
ἀποστερέω apostereō (644)

1. ἐσύλησα esulēsa 1sing indic aor act

1 I **robbed** other churches, taking wages of them, ... 2 Co 11:8

Classical Greek and Septuagint Usage

The word *sulaō* means "to plunder" or "to rob." The term sometimes depicts the stripping of armaments from a defeated army, or the sudden unsheathing of a weapon of war. It can even carry the connotation of "cheating" (*Liddell-Scott*). It occurs in the Septuagint in the Epistle of Jeremy 18, part of the apocryphal Book of Baruch, where it refers to burglary. Fearful of being robbed, the priests fortified their temples.

New Testament Usage

Second Corinthians 11:8 is the only occurrence of *sulaō* in the New Testament. Paul used the term in a powerful, ironic fashion while explaining his rationale for not accepting remuneration from the Corinthian congregation. Through this strong military metaphor, the apostle underscored the point that his ministry at Corinth cost the Corinthians nothing. Instead, he had "plundered" other churches by accepting their support, their "ration-money," rather than burdening the Corinthian congregation (Hillyer, "Rob," *Colin Brown*, 3:379).

Strong 4813, Bauer 776, Moulton-Milligan 596, Liddell-Scott 1671, Colin Brown 3:379.

4665. συλλαλέω sullaleō verb

Talk, discuss, converse with.

Cognate:
λαλέω laleō (2953)

Synonym:
συνομιλέω sunomileō (4777)

דָּבַר dāvar (1744), Piel: speak (Ex 34:35).

שִׂיחַ sîach (7943), Talk (Prv 6:22).

1. **συλλαλοῦντες sullalountes** nom pl masc part pres act
2. **συνελάλησεν sunelalēsen** 3sing indic aor act
3. **συλλαλήσας sullalēsas** nom sing masc part aor act
4. **συνελάλουν sunelaloun** 3pl indic imperf act
5. **συνλαλοῦντες sunlalountes** nom pl masc part pres act

1 appeared ... Moses and Elias **talking with him**...... Matt 17:3
1 Elias with Moses: and they were **talking with Jesus**. Mark 9:4
4 were all amazed, and **spake among** themselves,...... Luke 4:36
4 And, behold, there **talked with** him two men,........... 9:30
2 and **communed with** the chief priests and captains,..... 22:4
3 Festus, when he had **conferred with** the council,.... Acts 25:12

Classical Greek and Septuagint Usage

A compound verb, *sullaleō* is composed of the verbal root *laleō* (2953), "to speak," and the preposition *sun* (4713), "with, together." In extra-Biblical literature prior to the New Testament it can mean "to talk together with" or "to carry on a conversation with" (*Moulton-Milligan*; cf. *Bauer*). The word appears in the Septuagint in passages such as Exodus 34:35, of Moses talking with God; Proverbs 6:22, of the commandments talking with an individual; and Isaiah 7:6, of men conferring together.

New Testament Usage

Sullaleō appears six times in the New Testament. In Matthew 17:3; Mark 9:4; and Luke 9:30, the word describes the conversation among Jesus, Moses, and Elijah on the Mount of Transfiguration. Luke 4:36 uses the term to describe the discussion among the crowd in response to Jesus' exorcism of an evil spirit. The treacherous plotting between Judas and the chief priests is described by *sullaleō* in Luke 22:4. Acts 25:12 employs the term to depict Festus' consultation with his advisers concerning Paul's declaration, "I appeal to Caesar" (cf. verse 11).

Strong 4814, Bauer 776, Moulton-Milligan 610 (see "sunlaleo"), Liddell-Scott 1672.

4666. συλλαμβάνω sullambanō verb

Seize; conceive; assist, take hold of together.

Cognate:
λαμβάνω lambanō (2956)

Synonyms:
ἀντιλαμβάνομαι antilambanomai (479)
ἁρπάζω harpazō (720)
βοηθέω boētheō (990)
δράσσομαι drassomai (1399)
ἐπιλαμβάνομαι epilambanomai (1934)
ἔχω echō (2174)
καταλαμβάνω katalambanō (2608)
κρατέω krateō (2875)
λαμβάνω lambanō (2956)
πιάζω piazō (3945)
συμβάλλω sumballō (4671)
συναντιλαμβάνομαι sunantilambanomai (4729)
συναρπάζω sunarpazō (4734B)

הָרָה hārâh (2106), Be pregnant (Gn 29:32f., 1 Sm 1:20, Hos 1:3).

הָרָה hārāh (2107), Pregnant (1 Sm 4:19).

חִיל chîl (2523), Polel: bear a child (Ps 51:5 [50:5]).

לָכַד lākhadh (4058), Qal: capture, catch (Jgs 7:25, Ps 35:8 [34:8], Jer 37:8 [44:8]); niphal: be captured, be caught (2 Kgs 18:10, Ps 9:15, Jer 38:28 [45:28]).

לָקַח lāqach (4089), Take, seize (Ex 12:4, Jer 36:26 [43:26]).

נָקַשׁ nāqash (5550), Niphal: be snared (Ps 9:16).

קָמַט qāmaṭ (7344), Seize; pual: be snatched away (Jb 22:16).

תָּפַשׂ tāphas (8945), Qal: take, capture (Jos 8:23, 2 Kgs 14:7, Jer 52:9); niphal: be caught, be trapped (Nm 5:13, Ps 10:2 [9:23], Ez 19:4).

1. **συνέλαβον sunelabon** 1/3sing/pl indic aor act
2. **συνέλαβεν sunelaben** 3sing indic aor act

3. **συλλαβόντες** sullabontes nom pl masc part aor act
4. **συλλαβοῦσιν** sullabousin dat pl masc part aor act
5. **συλλαβοῦσα** sullabousa nom sing fem part aor act
6. **συλλαβεῖν** sullabein inf aor act
7. **συνειληφυῖα** suneilēphuia nom sing fem part perf act
8. **συλλαμβάνου** sullambanou 2sing impr pres mid
9. **συλληφθέντα** sullēphthenta acc sing masc part aor pass
10. **συλλαβόμενοι** sullabomenoi nom pl masc part aor mid
11. **συλληφθῆναι** sullēphthēnai inf aor pass
12. **συλλαβέσθαι** sullabesthai inf aor mid
13. **συλλήψῃ** sullēpsē 2sing indic fut mid
14. **συνείληφεν** suneilēphen 3sing indic perf act
15. **συλλημφθέντα** sullēmphthenta acc sing masc part aor pass
16. **συλλημφθῆναι** sullēmphthēnai inf aor pass
17. **συλλήμψῃ** sullēmpsē 2sing indic fut mid

6 with swords and staves for to **take** me?........... Matt 26:55
6 with swords and with staves to **take** me?......... Mark 14:48
2 And after those days his wife Elisabeth **conceived**, .. Luke 1:24
17 And, behold, thou **shalt conceive** in thy womb,........ 1:31
7 she **hath** also **conceived** a son in her old age:.......... 1:36
11 of the angel before he **was conceived** in the womb...... 2:21
12 that they **should** come and **help** them.................. 5:7
1 at the draught of the fishes which they **had taken**:..... 5:9
3 Then **took** they him, and led him,.................. 22:54
1 the captain and officers of the Jews **took** Jesus,... John 18:12
4 which was guide to them **that took** Jesus........... Acts 1:16
6 he proceeded further to **take** Peter also............... 12:3
9 This man **was taken** of the Jews,.................... 23:27
10 For these causes the Jews **caught** me in the temple,... 26:21
8 **help** those women which laboured with me......... Phlp 4:3
5 when lust **hath conceived**, it bringeth forth sin:...... Jas 1:15

Classical Greek

Sullambanō consists of a combination of the verb *lambanō* (2956), "to take," and the preposition *sun* (4713), "with, together." Secular Greek writers employ the term to mean "put together, bring together, to gather, assemble, acquire," as well as related ideas, such as "to seize, to grasp, apprehend." "To conceive" or "to become pregnant" is a frequently found usage of the word in the writings of Aristotle and later writers (cf. Delling, "sullambanō," *Kittel*, 7:759.)

Septuagint Usage

In the Septuagint *sullambanō* translates several Hebrew words that convey the sense "to seize" or "to capture": *tāphas, lākhadh, qāmaṯ,* and *lāqach* (see Exodus 12:4; Numbers 5:13; Judges 15:4; Job 22:16; Psalm 10:2 [LXX 9:23]; Jeremiah 36:26 [43:26]; Ezekiel 19:4,8). *Sullambanō* can describe the capture of cities by military force, the arrest of an individual, the catching of an animal, or even the snatching away of sinners by God's judgment (Psalm 9:16). It can also mean "to get hold of someone" or "to seize or surprise someone."

The Jewish historian Josephus (ca. A.D. 37–100) used *sullambanō* to mean "assist," but this meaning is not attested in the Septuagint (cf. *Bauer*). However, it is used frequently to translate the Hebrew *hārāh*, "to conceive, become pregnant." In Genesis 4:1 *sullambanō* describes the literal conception of Cain (see also Genesis 4:17; 1 Samuel 1:20 [LXX 1 Kings 1:20]). Psalm 7:14 uses the term figuratively: "He who is pregnant with evil and *conceives* trouble gives birth to disillusionment" (NIV).

New Testament Usage

Three distinct nuances are discernible among the 16 occurrences of *sullambanō* in the New Testament. First, it means "to take, to seize, to capture," or "to arrest" in a number of passages. Luke 5:9 employs the term to describe a huge catch of fish "taken" in a net. Jesus' arrest in the Garden of Gethsemane is described by *sullambanō* in all four Gospels (Matthew 26:55; Mark 14:48; Luke 22:54; John 18:12), as well as by Luke, quoting Peter, in Acts 1:16. Peter and Paul experienced treatment like that of Jesus (Acts 12:3; 23:27).

A second nuance of the word can be seen in the opening chapters of Luke's Gospel where *sullambanō* means "to conceive, become pregnant." In his account of the births of John the Baptist and Jesus, Luke referred to both the pregnancy of Elisabeth (Luke 1:24,36) and of Mary (Luke 1:31). James 1:15 falls into this same range of meanings, though in a figurative sense. James described the person pregnant with illicit desires—desires that will give birth to sin and ultimately to death. The text makes it clear that only good comes from God (cf. 1:17); sin is never caused by God.

A third sense is conveyed by *sullambanō* in the two cases where it appears in the middle voice in the New Testament. Luke 5:7 employs *sullambanō* to mean "help," when another boat and additional fishermen were needed to assist with a miraculous catch of fish. Paul used *sullambanō* in Philippians 4:3 when he appealed to a member of that congregation to "help" resolve the differences between Euodia and Syntyche. (See Field, "Conceive," *Colin Brown*, 1:343f.)

STRONG 4815, BAUER 776-77, MOULTON-MILLIGAN 597, KITTEL 7:759-62, LIDDELL-SCOTT 1672, COLIN BROWN 1:343-44.

4667. συλλέγω sullegō verb

Collect, gather.

Cognate:
λέγω legō (2978)
Synonyms:
ἀθροίζω athroizō (119B)
ἐπισυνάγω episunagō (1980)
συνάγω sunagō (4714)
συναθροίζω sunathroizō (4718)
συστρέφω sustrephō (4814)
τρυγάω trugaō (5007)

אָסַף 'āsaph (636), Gather (1 Kgs 10:26—Codex Alexandrinus only).

לָקַח lāqach (4089), Take, get (Gn 31:46, Ex 5:11, 16:16).

לָקַט lāqaṭ (4092), Qal: gather (Ex 16:4, Nm 11:8, Ps 104:28 [103:28]); piel: gather, glean (Lv 19:10, Ru 2:15-19, 2 Kgs 4:39); hithpael: gather oneself (Jgs 11:3—Codex Alexandrinus only).

קָטַף qāṭaph (7280), Pick (Dt 23:25 [24:1]).

קָשַׁשׁ qāshash (7492), Polel: gather (Nm 15:32, 1 Kgs 17:10,12).

1. **συλλέγουσιν** **sullegousin** 3pl indic pres act
2. **συλλέγοντες** **sullegontes** nom pl masc part pres act
3. **συνέλεξαν** **sunelexan** 3pl indic aor act
4. **συλλέξωμεν** **sullexōmen** 1pl subj aor act
5. **συλλέξατε** **sullexate** 2pl impr aor act
6. **συλλέξουσιν** **sullexousin** 3pl indic fut act
7. **συλλέγεται** **sullegetai** 3sing indic pres mid

1 Do men **gather** grapes of thorns, or figs of thistles? Matt 7:16
4 Wilt thou then that we go and **gather** them up? 13:28
2 But he said, Nay; lest while ye **gather** up the tares, ... 13:29
5 **Gather** ye together first the tares, ... 13:30
7 the tares **are gathered** and burned in the fire; 13:40
6 and they **shall gather** out of his kingdom all things 13:41
3 and sat down, and **gathered** the good into vessels, ... 13:48
1 For of thorns men **do** not **gather** figs, ... Luke 6:44

In the Septuagint this word usually translates the Hebrew verb *lāqaṭ*, "to gather, pick up" or even "to glean" (see Genesis 31:46; Ruth 2:8). *Sullegō* appears only in Matthew and Luke in the New Testament, always with the sense of "collecting" or "gathering." It is used in Matthew 7:16 and Luke 6:44 for gathering grapes; in Matthew 13:48 for collecting fish in a dragnet; and several times in Matthew 13:28-41 for gathering up the tares for destruction (Trites, "Gather," *Colin Brown*, 2:31). The various occurrences of *sullegō* all appear in contexts involving the separation of the good from the bad.

Strong 4816, Bauer 777, Moulton-Milligan 597, Liddell-Scott 1672, Colin Brown 2:33.

4668. συλλογίζομαι sullogizomai verb

To reckon, reason; discuss.
Cross-Reference:
λογίζομαι logizomai (3023)

בִּין bîn (1032), Discern, understand; hithpalpel: consider (Is 43:18).

חָשַׁב chāshav (2913), Piel: calculate (Lv 25:27,50,52); hithpael: be considered (Nm 23:9).

1. **συνελογίσαντο** **sunelogisanto** 3pl indic aor mid

1 And they **reasoned** with themselves, saying, ... Luke 20:5

Classical Greek and Septuagint Usage

In extra-Biblical sources, both before and after the New Testament period, *sullogizomai* conveys the meaning "compute, infer, conclude from premises, reckon," etc. (*Moulton-Milligan*). Septuagintal occurrences of *sullogizomai* usually translate the Hebrew verb *chāshav*, "to think, reckon, account."

New Testament Usage

Luke 20:5 preserves the only usage of *sullogizomai* in the New Testament. The chief priests and teachers of the Law questioned Jesus about His authority, about His right to do the things He did. Jesus responded with a question of His own about the authority of John's baptism. In response to Jesus' question, all the people *discussed* or *debated* the matter among themselves.

Strong 4817, Bauer 777, Moulton-Milligan 597, Liddell-Scott 1673.

4669. συλλυπέω sullupeō verb

Hurt, grieve.
Cross-Reference:
λυπέω lupeō (3048)

נוּד nûdh (5290), Have sympathy, comfort (Ps 69:20 [68:20], Is 51:19).

1. **συλλυπούμενος** **sullupoumenos** nom sing masc part pres mid
2. **συνλυπούμενος** **sunlupoumenos** nom sing masc part pres mid

1 **being grieved** for the hardness of their hearts, ... Mark 3:5

Classical Greek and Septuagint Usage

Sullupeō is a compound composed of the preposition *sun* (4713), "with," and the verb *lupeō* (3048), "to grieve, distress, cause pain." It can be found in classical Greek meaning "hurt together, share in grief" (*Liddell-Scott*). In the Septuagint Psalm 69:20 (LXX 68:20) conveys the idea of "sympathy," or "grieving with," the parallel term often being translated "comfort." Isaiah 51:19 is similar, the Hebrew word underlying *sullupeō* being rendered "to comfort" or "to console."

New Testament Usage

Mark 3:5 is the only New Testament usage of *sullupeō*. Here it describes the emotion of Jesus in response to the stubbornness and hardheartedness of the people of His day. The religious leaders thought their sabbath laws were more important than helping the man with a withered hand. By His sympathy for the man Jesus showed He was grieved at their hardness.

STRONG 4818, BAUER 777, KITTEL 4:323-24 (see "sullupeomai"), LIDDELL-SCOTT 1673.

4670. συμβαίνω sumbainō verb

To happen, come about, occur.

COGNATE:

ὑπερβαίνω huperbainō (5070)

SYNONYMS:

γίνομαι ginomai (1090)
συναντάω sunantaō (4727)

בּוֹא bô' (971), Come, go; happen (Dt 18:22).

הָיָה hāyâh (2030), Be (Gn 41:13).

מָצָא mātsâ' (4834), Happen (Jos 2:23).

עָשָׂה 'āsâh (6449), Qal: do (Ex 3:16); niphal: be done (Is 3:11).

קָרָא qārâ' (7410), Call; qal: happen (Gn 42:4, Lv 10:19).

קָרָה qārâh (7424), Happen (Gn 44:29, Est 6:13, Is 41:22).

1. **συμβαίνοντος sumbainontos** gen sing neu part pres act
2. **συμβαίνειν sumbainein** inf pres act
3. **συνέβη sunebē** 3sing indic aor act
4. **συμβάντων sumbantōn** gen pl masc part aor act
5. **συμβέβηκεν sumbebēken** 3sing indic perf act
6. **συμβεβηκότι sumbebēkoti** dat sing neu part perf act
7. **συμβεβηκότων sumbebēkotōn** gen pl neu part perf act
8. **συνέβαινον sunebainon** 3pl indic imperf act
9. **συνέβαινεν sunebainen** 3sing indic imperf act

2 and began to tell them what things should **happen** Mark 10:32
7 talked ... of all these things which **had happened**.... Luke 24:14
6 amazement at that which **had happened** unto him..... Acts 3:10
4 which **befell** me by the lying in wait of the Jews:...... 20:19
3 And when he came upon the stairs, so **it was**,......... 21:35
8 these things **happened** unto them for ensamples:.... 1 Co 10:11
1 as though some strange thing **happened** unto you:.... 1 Pt 4:12
5 But it **is happened** unto them according to.......... 2 Pt 2:22

Classical Greek and Septuagint Usage

Sumbainō is attested in numerous works prior to and contemporary with the New Testament (see *Liddell-Scott*). Etymologically the word is compounded from the preposition *sun* (4713), "with/together," and the verb *bainō*, "to go/come." According to Vine the combination conveys the sense "to go/come together," indicative of a converging of circumstances or events to yield a particular occurrence (*Expository Dictionary*, "Happen"). In the Septuagint *sumbainō* is used most frequently to mean "befall," in the sense of something that will "happen to" someone (cf. Genesis 42:4,38) or something that is "done to" someone (Exodus 3:16; Isaiah 3:11).

Various shades of meaning are conveyed by *sumbainō* in ancient inscriptions and papyri. The term can refer to the fall of a house *occurring*, to an engagement *happening*, or even to a person's death *coming about* (*Moulton-Milligan*).

New Testament Usage

The word occurs eight times in the New Testament. Its usage, however, seems to convey a sense of significance or severity concerning the circumstances or events it describes. In Mark 10:32, for example, the word is used in the context of Jesus' taking His disciples aside and telling them what was going to *happen* to Him. He then went on to foretell His death in Jerusalem. In Acts 20:19 and 21:35 *sumbainō* is used to depict difficult and dangerous events in the ministry of the apostle Paul. Likewise, 1 Peter 4:12 uses the word in the midst of a discussion about the suffering taking place among God's people; and 1 Corinthians 10:11 uses it in a passage which looked back on the difficulties endured by the people of the Old Testament. Similarly, Luke 24:14 employs the term to describe the conversation of the two disciples on the Emmaus Road who discussed "everything that had happened" (NIV).

Acts 3:10 reports the bewilderment of the crowds over what *had happened* to the crippled beggar healed through the ministry of Peter and John. And 2 Peter 2:22 employs *sumbainō* to describe how it always happens that certain evil people inevitably return to their sinful ways.

STRONG 4819, BAUER 777, MOULTON-MILLIGAN 597, LIDDELL-SCOTT 1673-74.

4671. συμβάλλω sumballō verb

To confer, dispute, ponder, converse.

COGNATE:

βάλλω ballō (900)

SYNONYMS:

ἀναλογίζω analogizō (355)
ἀντιλαμβάνομαι antilambanomai (479)
βοηθέω boētheō (990)
βουλεύομαι bouleuomai (1003)
διαλογίζομαι dialogizomai (1254)
δοκέω dokeō (1374)
εἶδον eidon (1481)
ἐνθυμέομαι enthumeomai (1744)

ἐπιβλέπω epiblepō (1899)
ἔχω echō (2174)
ἡγέομαι hēgeomai (2216)
κατανοέω katanoeō (2627)
κρίνω krinō (2892)
λογίζομαι logizomai (3023)
νοέω noeō (3401)
νομίζω nomizō (3406)
ὁμιλέω homileō (3519)
συζητέω suzēteō (4653)
συλλαμβάνω sullambanō (4666)
συμβουλεύω sumbouleuō (4674)
συναντιλαμβάνομαι sunantilambanomai (4729)

גָּרָה gārâh (1667), Hithpael: provoke trouble (2 Chr 25:19).

זוּל zûl (2189), Pour out (Is 46:6).

סוּת sûth (5684), Hiphil: incite (Jer 43:3 [50:3]).

1. συμβάλλουσα sumballousa nom sing fem part pres act
2. συνέβαλεν sunebalen 3sing indic aor act
3. συνέβαλον sunebalon 3pl indic aor act
4. συμβαλεῖν sumbalein inf aor act
5. συνέβαλλον suneballon 3pl indic imperf act
6. συνεβάλετο sunebaleto 3sing indic aor mid
7. συνβάλλουσα sunballousa nom sing fem part pres act
8. συνέβαλλεν suneballen 3sing indic imperf act

1 Mary kept all ... and **pondered** them in her heart.... Luke 2:19
4 what king, going to **make war** against another king,.... 14:31
3 they **conferred** among themselves,.................. Acts 4:15
5 of the Stoicks, **encountered** him. And some said,....... 17:18
6 **helped** them ... which had believed through grace:..... 18:27
2 And when he **met with** us at Assos, we took him in,... 20:14

Classical Greek

Sumballō is a combination of the preposition *sun* (4713), "with, together," and the verb *ballō* (900), "to throw, cast." It can mean "to converse, to carry on a discussion," or "to consider carefully and draw conclusions" about a certain matter. Other meanings include "to dispute" or "quarrel" with someone, even to the point of engaging in a fight. It can even mean "to offer help" to someone.

Septuagint Usage

This term is used in the Septuagint with a variety of usages similar to classical Greek usage. In 2 Chronicles 25:19 it is translated "meddle" (KJV), meaning "dispute," and in Isaiah 46:6 it means "offer help."

New Testament Usage

These various connotations appear in the New Testament usages of the verb *sumballō*, all of which occur in the writings of Luke. Acts 4:15 and 17:18 employ the word to mean "converse" or "confer." Luke 2:19 uses it in the related sense of "ponder" or "consider" to describe the reaction of Mary to the astounding events surrounding the birth of Jesus. These are transitive forms of the verb. The intransitive forms in Acts 20:14 and Luke 14:31 convey the idea of "meeting" or "falling in with," the latter even connoting the idea of engaging in combat. A variant reading of Luke 11:53 employs *sumballō* in a manner similar to Luke 14:31. Acts 18:27 uses the middle voice of *sumballō* with the sense of "help, be of assistance."

Strong 4820, Bauer 777, Moulton-Milligan 603 (see "sunballō"), Liddell-Scott 1674-75.

4672. συμβασιλεύω sumbasileuō verb

To reign (as king) with, share the rule.

Cross-Reference:
βασιλεία basileia (926)

1. συμβασιλεύσωμεν sumbasileusōmen 1pl subj aor act
2. συμβασιλεύσομεν sumbasileusomen 1pl indic fut act

1 that we also **might reign with** you.................. 1 Co 4:8
2 If we suffer, we **shall** also **reign with** him:.......... 2 Tm 2:12

The verb *sumbasileuō* is formed by *basileuō* (929), "to rule (as king)," and *sun* (4713), "with, together with." It occurs as early as the Second Century B.C. (Polybius) meaning "rule or reign together with" (*Liddell-Scott*).

New Testament Usage

The word occurs twice in the New Testament, both times in the Pauline literature. In 1 Corinthians 4:8 Paul employed the term ironically, mocking the bold claims of the Corinthian Christians to have attained lofty levels of spirituality. He addressed them as if they were already reigning as kings with the Lord. The apostle wished that were true; then he too, rather than being miserable, would be reigning with them.

In 2 Timothy 2:12 *sumbasileuō* depicts the eschatological status of Christians, sharing the kingship and ruling with Christ himself. This rule involves patience, obedience, and service (Schmidt, "sumbasileuō," *Kittel*, 1:591). It is based on a willingness to endure in the Faith.

Strong 4821, Bauer 777, Kittel 1:591; 7:766-97, Liddell-Scott 1675, Colin Brown 2:372-73.

4673. συμβιβάζω sumbibazō verb

To unite, bring together, prove, conclude, teach, instruct.

COGNATE:
ἐπιβιβάζω epibibazō (1898)
SYNONYMS:
διδάσκω didaskō (1315)
κατηχέω katēcheō (2697)
μαθητεύω mathēteuō (3072)
παιδεύω paideuō (3674)
παραδίδωμι paradidōmi (3722)

בִּין bîn (1032), Discern, understand; hiphil: instruct (Is 40:14).

יָדַע yādha' (3156), Know; hiphil: make known, teach (Ex 18:16, Dt 4:9).

יָרָה yārâh (3498), Throw, shoot; hiphil: teach (Ex 4:12, Lv 10:11, Ps 32:8 [31:8]).

1. **συμβιβάζων** **sumbibazōn** nom sing masc part pres act
2. **συμβιβάζοντες** **sumbibazontes** nom pl masc part pres act
3. **συμβιβάσει** **sumbibasei** 3sing indic fut act
4. **συμβιβαζόμενον** **sumbibazomenon** nom/acc sing neu part pres mid
5. **συμβιβασθέντων** **sumbibasthentōn** gen pl masc part aor pass
6. **συνεβίβασαν** **sunebibasan** 3pl indic aor act
7. **συμβιβασθέντες** **sumbibasthentes** nom pl masc part aor pass

1 proving that this is very Christ. .... Acts 9:22
2 assuredly gathering that the Lord had called us 16:10
6 the crowd shouted instructions to him. (NIV) 19:33
3 the mind of the Lord, that he may instruct him? .... 1 Co 2:16
4 compacted by that which every joint supplieth, ... Eph 4:16
5 might be comforted, being knit together in love, ... Col 2:2
4 having nourishment ministered, and knit together, ... 2:19

Classical Greek and Septuagint Usage

Used widely in extra-Biblical Greek, *sumbibazō* means "to cause to stride together" (Delling, "sumbibazō," *Kittel*, 7:763) and includes various connotations, such as, "to bring together, to reconcile, to conclude, to unite," and even "to teach" (see *Bauer*). It is with this latter sense alone, "to instruct," that *sumbibazō* occurs in the Septuagint. It is always used to translate Hebrew verbs in the hiphil stem with the meaning "to teach someone something" or "to instruct about something" (see, for example, Exodus 4:12,15; Leviticus 10:11; Deuteronomy 4:9; Judges 13:8; Isaiah 40:13,14).

New Testament Usage

New Testament usages of *sumbibazō* fall in line with those of other sources. In Colossians 2:2,19 and Ephesians 4:16 it means "unite" or "hold together." The stress in these passages lies on the unity of the Christian community, the body held together by Jesus Christ, the Head.

The typical Septuagint force of *sumbibazō* occurs in 1 Corinthians 2:16 where Paul quoted Isaiah 40:13: "Who has understood the mind of the LORD, or *instructed* him as his counselor?" (NIV). In Acts 9:22 *sumbibazō* is taken a step further. Here it means not simply "to instruct" but "to prove" conclusively. The passage summarizes the early stage of Paul's ministry and affirms that he baffled many Jews in Damascus "by *proving conclusively* that Jesus is the Christ" (author's translation). This was proof that rested on the authority of Scripture, not simply personal observation or experience (Delling, "sumbibazō," *Kittel*, 7:764ff.). In Acts 16:10 it means to "consider" or "conclude" (as in the NIV). There Paul believed the vision he received was all the instruction he needed to take the gospel to Macedonia.

STRONG 4822, BAUER 777, KITTEL 7:763-66, LIDDELL-SCOTT 1675.

4674. συμβουλεύω sumbouleuō verb

Give (take) advice, recommend, deliberate.

COGNATES:
βούλομαι boulomai (1007)
συμβούλιον sumboulion (4675)
σύμβουλος sumboulos (4676)
SYNONYMS:
ἀναλογίζω analogizō (355)
βουλεύομαι bouleuomai (1003)
διαλογίζομαι dialogizomai (1254)
δοκέω dokeō (1374)
εἶδον eidon (1481)
ἐνθυμέομαι enthumeomai (1744)
ἐπιβλέπω epiblepō (1899)
ἔχω echō (2174)
ἡγέομαι hēgeomai (2216)
κατανοέω katanoeō (2627)
κρίνω krinō (2892)
λογίζομαι logizomai (3023)
νοέω noeō (3401)
νομίζω nomizō (3406)
παραινέω paraineō (3728)
προτρέπομαι protrepomai (4247)
συμβάλλω sumballō (4671)

יָעַץ yā'ats (3398), Qal: advise, give counsel (Nm 24:14, 1 Kgs 1:12, Jer 38:15 [45:15]); niphal: consult (Is 40:14).

סוּת sûth (5684), Hiphil: persuade (Jos 15:18).

שָׁקַל shāqal (8620), Count (Is 33:18).

1. **συμβουλεύω** **sumbouleuō** 1sing indic pres act
2. **συμβουλεύσας** **sumbouleusas** nom sing masc part aor act
3. **συνεβουλεύσαντο** **sunebouleusanto** 3pl indic aor mid

3 consulted that they might take Jesus by subtlety, ... Matt 26:4
3 they took counsel together for to put him to death. John 11:53
2 Caiaphas was he, which gave counsel to the Jews, ... 18:14
3 the Jews took counsel to kill him: .... Acts 9:23
1 I counsel thee to buy of me gold tried in the fire, ... Rev 3:18

Classical Greek

Sumbouleuō is a combination of the preposition, *sun* (4713), "with," and the verb *bouleuō* (see 1003), "take counsel," and means "to give (take) counsel"; "to deliberate, recommend," or "determine action." It can be found in classical Greek since the Fifth Century B.C. meaning (in the active voice) "advise one to do" and (in the middle voice) "consult with" (*Liddell-Scott*). *Sumbouleuō* is also found in the Greek tragedies. Josephus used *sumbouleuō* in both the *Antiquities of the Jews* and *Wars of the Jews*, but there is no difference in meaning in his use of this word (cf. *Bauer*). The word is found in other nonbiblical writings and inscriptions from the First Century B.C. through the Third Century A.D. (cf. *Moulton-Milligan*).

Septuagint Usage

In the Septuagint *sumbouleuō* occurs mainly in the Pentateuch and the historical books. In all but two occurrences this word translates the Hebrew word *yāʿats.* While the basic meaning remains the same as in classical Greek, other shades of meaning include "to allow oneself to be advised, take counsel together," or "advise after consultation." The only two verses that use this word differently are Joshua 15:18 ("she *moved* him to ask . . . ") and Isaiah 33:18 ("where is the *receiver*?"). In Joshua the Hebrew term (*sûth* ["entice, stir up"]) carries an insistent overtone; that is, Caleb's daughter provoked or incited her husband to ask Caleb for the inheritance. The usage in Isaiah refers to a receiver (*shāqal*) of goods who weighs out each item carefully.

New Testament Usage

The New Testament usage of this word concurs with the nonbiblical meanings. In all but one of its occurrences it refers to the actions of the Sanhedrin (Matthew 26:4; John 11:53; 18:14; Acts 9:23). In each of these verses *sumbouleuō* is used to describe the Sanhedrin's attempts to arrest and/or kill Jesus. Only Revelation 3:18 uses it differently. Here it refers to Jesus' advising the Laodicean church. (In some manuscripts John 11:53 uses *bouleuomai*, omitting the attached preposition *sun.*)

Strong 4823, Bauer 777-78, Moulton-Milligan 597, Liddell-Scott 1677, Colin Brown 1:362-63.

4675. συμβούλιον sumboulion noun

A council, counsel.

Cognate:

συμβουλεύω sumbouleuō (4674)

Synonyms:

βουλή boulē (1005)

συνέδριον sunedrion (4742)

1. συμβουλίου sumbouliou gen sing neu

2. συμβούλιον sumboulion nom/acc sing neu

2 and held **a council** against him, ... Matt 12:14
2 Then went the Pharisees, and took **counsel** 22:15
2 took **counsel** against Jesus to put him to death: 27:1
2 And they took **counsel**, and bought with them 27:7
2 assembled with the elders, and had taken **counsel**, ... 28:12
2 and straightway took **counsel** with the Herodians .... Mark 3:6
2 the chief priests held a **consultation** with the elders 15:1
1 Festus, when he had conferred with the **council**, ... Acts 25:12

Classical Greek and Septuagint Usage

This noun refers to a council with the emphasis placed on the result of the council's deliberations. The word occurs quite often from the classical period onward. Plutarch used it to refer to a council of advisors or with the idea of convening a council (*Bauer*). It was also used in inscriptions of the Second Century B.C. (cf. *Moulton-Milligan*). *Sumboulion* occurs only at 4 Maccabees 17:17 in some manuscripts of the Septuagint.

New Testament Usage

In the New Testament each occurrence of *sumboulion* emphasizes the gathering together of a group for the specific purpose of determining or confirming a plan of action. While most of these consultations have a deceitful intent, this is not inherent to the word itself. Matthew used *sumboulion* to refer to the Pharisees' actions of taking counsel (12:14; 22:15), as well as to those of the full Sanhedrin (27:1,7), identified as the chief priests and the elders. Mark used it in a similar fashion (cf. 3:6; 15:1). Only Luke used this word in a non-Jewish context. In Acts 25:12 *sumboulion* refers to the advisory council of Festus.

Strong 4824, Bauer 778, Moulton-Milligan 597, Liddell-Scott 1677, Colin Brown 1:362-63.

4676. σύμβουλος sumboulos noun

Adviser, counselor.

Cross-Reference:

συμβουλεύω sumbouleuō (4674)

יְעַט yeʿaṭ (A3378), Counselor (Ezr 7:14f.—Aramaic).

יָעַץ yāʿats (3398), Counsclor (1 Chr 27:32f., 2 Chr 22:3f., Is 3:3).

1. σύμβουλος sumboulos nom sing masc

1 or who hath been his **counsellor**? .... Rom 11:34

Classical Greek and Septuagint Usage

Sumboulos is related to the verb *sumbouleuō* (4674), "to advise, give advice." The noun occurs frequently in noncanonical material from around the New Testament period (see *Bauer*). It refers to one who gives advice, an adviser or counselor, and can even refer to public officials. In the Septuagint *sumboulos* appears in Isaiah 40:13 where it refers to a person attempting to counsel God, as ridiculous as that might be (see Marshall, "Council," *Colin Brown*, 1:362).

New Testament Usage

Romans 11:34, the only New Testament usage of *sumboulos*, is a quotation of Isaiah 40:13. The rhetorical question in which it is set stresses the absurdity of anyone trying to advise God, thereby extolling the wonder of God's wisdom and ways.

STRONG 4825, BAUER 778, MOULTON-MILLIGAN 597-98, LIDDELL-SCOTT 1677, COLIN BROWN 1:362-63.

4677. Συμεών Sumeōn name

Simeon.

1. Συμεών **Sumeōn** masc

1 a man in Jerusalem, whose name was **Simeon**;...... Luke 2:25
1 And **Simeon** blessed them,............................ 2:34
1 Which was the son **of Simeon**,........................ 3:30
1 as Barnabas, and **Simeon** that was called Niger,.... Acts 13:1
1 **Simeon** hath declared how God at the first............ 15:14
1 **Simon** Peter, a servant and an apostle of Jesus...... 2 Pt 1:1
1 tribe **of Simeon** were sealed twelve thousand......... Rev 7:7

Five individuals in the New Testament bear this Hebrew name (see also *Simōn* [4468], a Greek name often used as an equivalent): Simeon the patriarch who was a son of Jacob by Leah and ancestor of one of the 12 tribes of Israel (Revelation 7:7); Simeon, a figure in the genealogy of Jesus (Luke 3:30). In addition, the name of the apostle Peter appears twice as Simeon (Acts 15:14; 2 Peter 1:1, "Simon Peter").

A fourth Simeon was a righteous and holy man who met Mary and Joseph in the temple and praised God for sending the infant Jesus (Luke 2:25-34). The words the Spirit gave him have been handed down as the early Christian hymn known as the "Nunc Dimittis" (Luke 2:29-32). Lastly, Simeon surnamed Niger was a prophet and teacher in the church at Antioch. He was among those who set apart and prayed for Paul and Barnabas as they started their missionary journeys.

4678. συμμαθητής summathētēs noun

Fellow disciple.

CROSS-REFERENCE:
μανθάνω manthanō (3101)

1. συμμαθηταῖς **summathētais** dat pl masc
2. συνμαθηταῖς **sunmathētais** dat pl masc

1 Then said Thomas, ... unto his **fellow disciples**,..... John 11:16

This noun combines the preposition *sun* (4713), "with," and the noun *mathētēs* (3073), "disciple, student," yielding the concept of "fellow disciple." It occurs only once in the New Testament (John 11:16). In this verse Thomas encouraged his "fellow disciples" to return to Judea with Jesus at the time of the death of Lazarus. There is a shared identification expressed here that indicates the special relationship among the disciples.

Just as *summathētēs* is used only once in the New Testament, it is also rarely found in nonbiblical writings. However, it does occur in the last sentence of the *Martyrdom of Polycarp* 17:3 (written about A.D. 155). This passage is almost a prayer that the Smyrneans (to whom the document is addressed) would become fellow disciples with the earlier disciples and martyrs of the Church. As in John, the implication of the word is one of a shared special relationship with the other disciples.

STRONG 4827, BAUER 778, MOULTON-MILLIGAN 610 (see "sunmathētēs"), KITTEL 4:460, LIDDELL-SCOTT 1677.

4679. συμμαρτυρέω summartureō verb

Testify with, bear witness with.

CROSS-REFERENCE:
μαρτυρέω martureō (3113)

1. συμμαρτυρεῖ **summarturei** 3sing indic pres act
2. συμμαρτυρούσης **summarturousēs** gen sing fem part pres act
3. συμμαρτυροῦμαι **summarturoumai** 1sing indic pres mid

2 their conscience also **bearing witness**,............... Rom 2:15
1 The Spirit itself **beareth witness with** our spirit,......... 8:16
2 I lie not, my conscience also **bearing me witness**........ 9:1
3 I **testify** unto every man that heareth the words..... Rev 22:18

Classical Greek

This verb is composed of the preposition *sun* (4713), "with," and the verb *martureō* (3113), "testify." It can mean to "bear witness with," and can also express the idea of confirming, supporting, and attesting something or someone as genuine.

In the classical period Ptolemy used this word to describe a configuration of planets

(*Liddell-Scott*). *Summartureō* is not found in the Septuagint, although Josephus did use it (cf. *Bauer*). In a document from A.D. 155 the name of each of the attesting witnesses of a transaction was followed by the term *sunmarturō*, a different form of this same word (*Moulton-Milligan*).

New Testament Usage

In the New Testament *summartureō* occurs three times in Romans. In 2:15 Paul used this verb to describe the confirming witness of the Gentiles' conscience that the work of the Law truly was written in their hearts. It is the witness of the Holy Spirit together with the Christians' spirits that confirms they are God's children (8:16). Lastly, Romans 9:1 indicates that the Holy Spirit confirmed Paul's words as truth. In each case there is a strong, positive connotation to the word. It gives surety to the declarations attached to its usage.

Summartureō also appears in some manuscripts in Revelation 22:18, although others use the verb *martureō* without the attached preposition. In this instance Jesus is declaring the certainty of the prophecies of the Book of Revelation, confirming them as true.

STRONG 4828, BAUER 778, MOULTON-MILLIGAN 610 (see "sunmartureō"), KITTEL 4:508-10, LIDDELL-SCOTT 1677, COLIN BROWN 3:1038-39,1042.

4680. συμμερίζω summerizō verb

To divide with, share in or with someone or something.

CROSS-REFERENCE:

μερίζω merizō (3177)

חָלַק chālaq (2606), Be a partner (Prv 29:24—only some Sinaiticus texts).

1. συμμερίζονται summerizontai 3pl indic pres mid

1 which wait at the altar are **partakers** with the altar? 1 Co 9:13

This compound verb consists of the preposition *sun* (4713), "with," and the verb *merizō* (3177), "distribute," and means "to share with or in." It occurs once in the New Testament (1 Corinthians 9:13). In this verse Paul used the middle voice of the verb to show that ministers have a right to share in offerings given to God. He drew the parallel from the Old Testament practice that allowed the priests to eat portions of the animals and other foodstuffs offered to God on the altar in the tabernacle (Numbers 18:24 and Deuteronomy 18:1-8, for example).

STRONG 4829, BAUER 778, MOULTON-MILLIGAN 610 (see "sunmerizō"), LIDDELL-SCOTT 1678.

4681. συμμέτοχος summetochos adj

Partaker, sharer.

CROSS-REFERENCE:

μετέχω metechō (3218)

1. συμμέτοχοι summetochoi nom pl masc

2. συμμέτοχα summetocha nom/acc pl neu

2 **partakers** of his promise in Christ by the gospel: ..... Eph 3:6
1 Be not ye therefore **partakers** with them. 5:7

This compound adjective, which functions as a noun, means "partaker" or "sharer." It occurs only twice in the New Testament (Ephesians 3:6; 5:7), but it was also used by Josephus (*Wars of the Jews* 1.24.6). While the base noun *metochos* (3223) means "sharer," the addition of the preposition *sun* (4713), "with," in Ephesians is significant. In 3:6 Paul emphasized that the Gentiles were partakers, or sharers, *with* the Jews in the promised salvation through Christ.

In Ephesians 5:7 Paul again emphasized the sharing *with* some group in something. However, this time he admonished the Ephesians *not* to be partakers with the "children of disobedience" (verse 6) in their practices and the associated guilt for their evil actions. *Bauer* indicates that the usage in 5:7 might be translated "(not) casting one's lot with them."

STRONG 4830, BAUER 778, MOULTON-MILLIGAN 610 (see "sunmetochos"), KITTEL 2:830-32, LIDDELL-SCOTT 1679.

4682. συμμιμητής summimētēs noun

Fellow imitator.

CROSS-REFERENCE:

μιμέομαι mimeomai (3265)

1. συμμιμηταί summimētai nom pl masc

1 Brethren, be **followers together** of me, ... Phlp 3:17

Summimētēs is a compound noun made up of the preposition *sun* (4713), "with," and the noun *mimētēs* (3266), "imitator." This compound form is rarely found in any Greek literature. While Plato used its verb form, the noun form does not occur in the Septuagint or other Greek literature before the New Testament period.

New Testament Usage

Summimētēs is found only in Philippians 3:17, "Brethren, be *followers together* of me." This common theme of Paul is seen also in 1 Corinthians 4:16 and 11:1. However, only in

Philippians is the preposition *sun* attached. This is a significant addition.

While the "with" here could imply "with Paul," the context seems to indicate another emphasis. Paul was encouraging the Philippians, as a group, to be imitators together of his example. This is borne out by his comments in the rest of the verse as he told the Philippians to take note of the ones who were following his example (see *tupos* [5020]). A further explanation is found in verse 18 where Paul gave the counterexample, that of the "enemies of the cross of Christ."

Wilhelm Michaelis sees this usage as a call to obedience on the part of the Philippians. According to Michaelis, Paul was asserting his apostolic authority and calling on the Philippians to recognize this and be obedient to what he said throughout this entire section of the book ("mimētēs," *Kittel*, 4:668).

Strong 4831, Bauer 778, Moulton-Milligan 610 (see "sunmimētēs"), Kittel 4:659-74, Liddell-Scott 1679, Colin Brown 1:490-91.

4682B. συμμορφίζω

summorphizō verb

Give the same form, conform.

Cross-Reference:
μορφόω morphoō (3308)

1. συμμορφιζόμενος summorphizomenos nom sing masc part pres mid

1 **being conformed to His death; (NASB)** .... **Phlp 3:10**

In the passive voice this verb means "be conformed to, take on the same form as." It appears in the New Testament only in Philippians 3:10 where Paul expressed his desire to be made conformable unto Christ's death.

The word may have been first used by the apostle Paul as he shared his insight from the Holy Spirit. Romans 8:29 and Philippians 3:21 are parallel passages that clarify Paul's meaning (see *summorphos* [4683]). As Christ died on the cross *for* sin, believers must die *to* sin. (Some manuscripts use this term to replace *summorphoō* [4684].)

Bauer 778, Moulton-Milligan 598, Kittel 7:766-97, Liddell-Scott 1680, Colin Brown 1:705,707.

4683. σύμμορφος summorphos adj

Being conformed, having the same form.

Cross-Reference:
μορφόω morphoō (3308)

1. συμμόρφους summorphous acc pl masc
2. σύμμορφον summorphon nom/acc sing neu

1 to be **conformed** to the image of his Son, ... **Rom 8:29**
2 it may be **fashioned** like unto his glorious body, ... **Phlp 3:21**

Summorphos, a compound adjective being used as a noun, occurs twice in the New Testament (Romans 8:29; Philippians 3:21). This type of structure is somewhat common with Paul; for example, see *summetochos* (4681). The common English translation of "being conformed to" is accurate in its implication.

In Romans 8:29 Paul used *summorphos* to indicate that God has already determined that those who become His sons will be changed to be like Christ, i.e., "*conformed* to the image" of Jesus. This same concept is repeated in Philippians 3:21 where God again is the One doing the work. In this verse Paul said that God would change the mortal body of the Christian "that it may be fashioned like unto his glorious body." Both instances indicate the goal of becoming Christlike, of having His image.

Strong 4832, Bauer 778, Kittel 7:787, Liddell-Scott 1680, Colin Brown 1:705,707.

4684. συμμορφόω summorphoō verb

Give/take the same form.

Cross-Reference:
μορφόω morphoō (3308)

1. συμμορφούμενος summorphoumenos nom sing masc part pres mid

1 **being made conformable unto his death;** .... **Phlp 3:10**

Summorphoō, a combination of the preposition *sun* (4713), "with," and the verb *morphoō* (3308), "to form," is found in only one verse in the New Testament, Philippians 3:10. Even here, some manuscripts have a related verb, *summorphizō* (4682B). Both verbs have the same basic meaning of taking, giving, or granting the same form as something or someone. The verb does not occur in the Septuagint. While *summorphizō* is found only in Christian writings, the specific form *summorphoō* is found in both Christian and secular literature.

In Philippians 3 Paul described his determination to do whatever was necessary in order to become like Christ. In verse 10 he specifically referred to Christ's sufferings and death, seeing his own identification with (i.e., "taking the same form as") them as another step in his becoming like Christ. He wanted to become like Christ, even to the point of sharing the experience of His sufferings and death.

Strong 4833, Bauer 778, Liddell-Scott 1680 (see "summorphoomai"), Colin Brown 1:705 (see "summorphoomai").

4685. συμπαθέω sumpatheō verb

Sympathize with, feel for, have compassion on.

Cross-Reference:
πάθος pathos (3669)

1. συνεπαθήσατε sunepathēsate 2pl indic aor act
2. συμπαθῆσαι sumpathēsai inf aor act

2 **be touched with the feeling of our infirmities;** .... Heb 4:15
1 For ye **had compassion** of me in my bonds, ... 10:34

Sumpatheō is a verb meaning "sympathize with" or "have compassion on." It is found from the classical through the New Testament periods in both religious and secular contexts.

In the New Testament it is found only in Hebrews 4:15 and 10:34. In 4:15 it is used to describe Christ, our High Priest, who "feels with us" in our weaknesses or infirmities. In 10:34 the writer referred to the sympathetic concern of the Hebrews for his bonds, even to the point of taking part in them. The Hebrews even lost their own possessions because of their sharing in his troubles. In both of these verses a deep emotional commitment is expressed, not merely a superficial emotional feeling.

Strong 4834, Bauer 778-79, Moulton-Milligan 611, Kittel 5:935-36, Liddell-Scott 1680, Colin Brown 3:719,722,724.

4686. συμπαθής sumpathēs adj

Sympathetic, affected by like feelings.

Cross-Reference:
πάθος pathos (3669)
אָבַל 'āval (57), Mourner (Jb 29:25—Codex Alexandrinus only).

1. συμπαθεῖς sumpatheis nom pl masc

1 **having compassion** one of another, ... 1 Pt 3:8

An adjective related to the verb *sumpatheō* (4685), *sumpathēs* means to be "sympathetic" or "affected by like feelings." It occurs in the Septuagint, and both Philo and Josephus used it with the meaning of "fellow feeling" or "participation with" (Michaelis, "sumpatheō," *Kittel*, 5:935).

In the New Testament *sumpathēs* occurs only in 1 Peter 3:8 where it means "having compassion one of another." Peter included it in a list of admonitions to his audience, along with their being one-minded, courteous, pitiful, etc. In both the Biblical and nonbiblical usages of *sumpathēs* there is an emphasis on a committed relationship and participation in the lives of others.

Strong 4835, Bauer 779, Moulton-Milligan 598, Kittel 5:935-36, Liddell-Scott 1680.

4687. συμπαραγίνομαι sumparaginomai verb

Come together; stand by someone, help.

Cross-Reference:
γίνομαι ginomai (1090)
לָוָה lāwâh (4004), Niphal: join (Ps 83:8 [82:8]).

1. συμπαρεγένετο sumparegeneto 3sing indic aor mid
2. συμπαραγενόμενοι sumparagenomenoi nom pl masc part aor mid
3. συνπαραγενόμενοι sunparagenomenoi nom pl masc part aor mid

2 And all the people **that came together** to that sight, Luke 23:48
1 At my first answer no man **stood with** me, ... 2 Tm 4:16

This compound verb is formed by two prepositions, *sun* (4713), "with," and *para* (3706), "beside," and the verb *ginomai* (1090), "become," and means "come together" or "come to the assistance/aid of." It is found in the Septuagint in Psalm 83:8 (LXX 82:8) "Assur also is *joined with* them." In the New Testament it is found in Luke 23:48 and (in some manuscripts) in 2 Timothy 4:16. In this latter text, other manuscripts use a similar verb without the first preposition *sun*, i.e., *paraginomai* (3716), "stand beside."

In Luke 23:48 this word simply describes the people who came together to see the Crucifixion. The passage in 2 Timothy has a different meaning. Here Paul stated that no one came to his assistance in his first defense at Rome; he had been left to stand alone before his accusers.

Strong 4836, Bauer 779, Moulton-Milligan 611 (see "sunparaginomai"), Liddell-Scott 1680 (see "sumparagignomai").

4688. συμπαρακαλέω sumparakaleō verb

Comfort together.

Cross-Reference:
παρακαλέω parakaleō (3731)

1. συμπαρακληθῆναι sumparaklēthēnai inf aor pass

1 That is, that I may be comforted together with you . . . Rom 1:12

Sumparakaleō is a compound verb in which the preposition *sun* (4713), "with," is attached to the verb *parakaleō* (3731), "comfort, exhort, summon to one's side," etc. In this combination the common meaning is "to comfort together/with." While it was used during the classical period by Plato and others (cf. *Liddell-Scott*), there is no example of it found in the Septuagint or in other Greek literature of the period.

In the New Testament it occurs only in Romans 1:12. Here Paul used it to express this common meaning, "That I may be comforted together with you . . . . " Since this example is in the passive voice, it could be translated "that I may receive comfort (or strength) together with you."

Strong 4837, Bauer 779, Liddell-Scott 1680.

4689. συμπαραλαμβάνω

sumparalambanō verb

Take (someone) with.

Cross-Reference:
λαμβάνω lambanō (2956)

סָפָה sāphâh (5793), Take away, sweep away; niphal: be swept away (Gn 19:17).

1. συμπαραλαβών sumparalabōn nom sing masc part aor act
2. συμπαραλαβόντες sumparalabontes nom pl masc part aor act
3. συμπαραλαβεῖν sumparalabein inf aor act
4. συμπαραλαμβάνειν sumparalambanein inf pres act

2 took with them John, whose surname was Mark. . . . . Acts 12:25
3 And Barnabas determined to take with them John, ... 15:37
3 But Paul thought not good to take him with them, ... 15:38
1 with Barnabas, and took Titus with me also. . . . . Gal 2:1

Classical Greek and Septuagint Usage

This compound verb is formed by the prepositions *sun* (4713), "with," and *para* (3706), "beside," and the verb *lambanō* (2956), "give, take, receive." Its basic meaning is "to take with." Referring to a person it means to "take in as an adjunct or assistant" (*Liddell-Scott*). In Genesis 19:17 it is used of the angels who "brought them (Lot and his family) forth" before destroying Sodom and Gomorrah.

New Testament Usage

In the New Testament it appears four times (Acts 12:25; 15:37,38; Galatians 2:1). In all three examples from Acts, John Mark was the person being taken with (or going with) Paul and Barnabas. In Galatians, Paul took Titus with him. In each case the person being taken was a servant, minister, or assistant who was going to help in the mission of the person taking him.

Strong 4838, Bauer 779, Moulton-Milligan 611 (see "sunparalambanō"), Liddell-Scott 1680-81.

4690. συμπαραμένω

sumparamenō verb

Continue with.

Cross-Reference:
μένω menō (3176)

1. συμπαραμένω sumparamenō 1sing indic pres act

1 I know that I shall abide and continue with you all . . Phlp 1:25

Sumparamenō—a compound verb formed by the prepositions *sun* (4713), "with," and *para* (3706), "beside," with the verb *menō* (3176), "stay, remain"—means "to remain, stay, continue with." It was used in the classical period, and it is found in Psalm 72:5 (LXX 71:5) in the Septuagint: "as long as the sun and moon *endure*."

In the New Testament it occurs only once in some manuscripts (Philippians 1:25). In this verse Paul used both *menō*, "remain," and *sumparamenō*, "continue with," to express the internal tension he felt between his desire to leave this world and be with Christ or stay and be with the Philippians. In other manuscripts the verb *paramenō* (3748) is used instead of *sumparamenō*. This shorter verb (without the preposition *sun*) is nearly synonymous with the longer word.

Strong 4839, Bauer 779, Liddell-Scott 1681.

4691. συμπάρειμι sumpareimi verb

Be present with.

Cross-Reference:
παρουσία parousia (3814)

1. συμπαρόντες sumparontes nom pl masc part pres act

1 and all men which are here present with us, ... Acts 25:24

Classical Greek and Septuagint Usage

Sumpareimi is a compound verb containing the prepositions *sun* (4713), "with," and *para* (3706), "beside," with the verb *eimi* (1498), "be," and means "to be present with (beside)." In classical Greek and frequently in the papyri it can be found meaning "to be present also or at the same time" in reference to human desires (*Liddell-Scott*). It is also used figuratively of "Wisdom" who "was there" with God during creation (Proverbs 8:27).

New Testament Usage

In the New Testament *sumpareimi* occurs only once (Acts 25:24). When Festus was addressing Agrippa and his entourage, he alluded to the others who were present by using the participial form of this verb; that is, "the ones who are present with us." While this is the only place where this particular form is used, there are numerous instances in which the related verb *pareimi* (3780) is used.

STRONG 4840, BAUER 779, MOULTON-MILLIGAN 611 (see "sunpareimi"), LIDDELL-SCOTT 1681.

4692. συμπάσχω sumpaschō verb

Suffer with, suffer like.

CROSS-REFERENCE:

πάσχω paschō (3819)

1. συμπάσχει sumpaschei 3sing indic pres act

2. συμπάσχομεν sumpaschomen 1pl indic pres act

2 if so be that we **suffer with** him, ... Rom 8:17
1 all the members **suffer with** it; .... 1 Co 12:26

Classical Greek

The verb *sumpaschō* is formed by the preposition *sun* (4713), "with," and *paschō* (3819), "suffer," and means "suffer with" or "suffer like/just as." In the classical period writers such as Aristotle, Plutarch, and Solon used it to mean "suffer with." Plato used it to mean "to suffer at the same time" (Michaelis, "paschō," *Kittel*, 5:926). *Sumpaschō* is not found in the Septuagint.

In nonbiblical writings of the New Testament period, including those of the church fathers, *sumpaschō* was used with at least three different meanings. In addition to the one mentioned above, both Ignatius (*To Polycarp* 6:1) and Clement (2 Clement 4:3) used this word to mean "have sympathy with." Both Polycarp (9:2) and Ignatius used it to refer to death (Michaelis, "paschō," *Kittel*, 5:926).

New Testament Usage

Sumpaschō occurs twice in the New Testament (Romans 8:17; 1 Corinthians 12:26). In both cases Paul used it to mean suffering with someone else. In Romans, believers suffer with Christ so they may become glorified with Him. This may be the source of the meaning found in both Polycarp and Ignatius, identifying "suffering" with death. In 1 Corinthians all of the members of the body of Christ suffer when one member suffers. While this might imply literal suffering, it could also mean an empathetic or sympathetic sharing in the one member's suffering.

STRONG 4841, BAUER 779, MOULTON-MILLIGAN 612 (see "sunpaschō"), KITTEL 5:925-26; 7:766-97, LIDDELL-SCOTT 1681, COLIN BROWN 3:719,722,724.

4693. συμπέμπω sumpempō verb

Send with.

COGNATE:

πέμπω pempō (3854)

SYNONYM:

συναποστέλλω sunapostellō (4733)

1. συνεπέμψαμεν sunepempsamen 1pl indic aor act

1 And we **have sent with** him the brother, ... 2 Co 8:18
1 And we **have sent with** them our brother, ... 8:22

In classical Greek *sumpempō*—which is formed by the preposition *sun* (4713), "with," and the verb *pempō* (3854), "send"—means "send with." It is not found in the Septuagint. In the New Testament the compound occurs only twice (2 Corinthians 8:18,22). In both cases Paul used this verb to describe his sending "the brother" with Titus to the Corinthians. This brother was probably Timothy (see 2 Corinthians 1:1).

STRONG 4842, BAUER 779, MOULTON-MILLIGAN 612 (see "sunpempō"), LIDDELL-SCOTT 1682.

4694. συμπεριλαμβάνω sumperilambanō verb

Embrace.

CROSS-REFERENCE:

λαμβάνω lambanō (2956)

צָרַר tsārar (7173), Bind (Ez 5:3).

1. συμπεριλαβών sumperilabōn nom sing masc part aor act

1 and **embracing** him said, Trouble not yourselves; ... Acts 20:10

This verb is formed by *sun* (4713), "with"; *peri* (3875), "around"; and *lambanō* (2956), "throw," and means "embrace" or "throw one's arms around" (*Bauer*). It is found at Ezekiel 5:3 in the Septuagint where it describes how Ezekiel was directed to "bind" some of his hair and burn it in a fire to depict the judgment that was about to come upon Israel.

In the New Testament it occurs only in Acts 20:10. This verse describes Paul's actions when he went downstairs to where Eutychus had fallen. He "went down, and fell on him, and *embracing* him said . . . . "

STRONG 4843, BAUER 779, MOULTON-MILLIGAN 612 (see "sunperilambanō"), LIDDELL-SCOTT 1682.

4695. συμπίνω sumpinō verb

Drink with.

CROSS-REFERENCE:
πίνω pinō (3956)

1. συνεπίομεν sunepiomen 1pl indic aor act

1 even to us, who did eat and drink with him .... Acts 10:41

In classical Greek and the Septuagint this verb means "to drink with" (cf. *Liddell-Scott*; Esther 7:1). It appears only once in the New Testament, at Acts 10:41. Here Peter was preaching to the household of Cornelius in Caesarea when he used this word to describe how Jesus ate and drank with him and other disciples after His resurrection.

STRONG 4844, BAUER 779, LIDDELL-SCOTT 1683.

4695B. συμπίπτω sumpiptō verb

Fall together, collapse, fall.

CROSS-REFERENCE:
πίπτω piptō (3959)

הָרַס hāraṣ (2117), Break down, destroy; niphal: be torn down (Ez 30:4).

יָרַד yāradh (3495), Go down, come down; fall (Is 34:7).

נָגַשׂ nāghas (5241), Oppress, drive, exact; niphal: be oppressed (Is 3:5).

נָטַשׁ nāṭash (5389), Abandon, leave; niphal: spread out (2 Sm 5:18,22).

נָפַל nāphal (5489), Fall, fail (Gn 4:5f., 1 Sm 17:32).

פָּחַד pāchadh (6585), Tremble; hiphil: cause to shake (Jb 4:14—only some Alexandrinus only).

פָּשַׁט pāshaṭ (6838), Raid (1 Chr 14:13).

1. συνέπεσεν sunepesen 3sing indic aor act

1 and immediately it collapsed, (NASB) .... Luke 6:49

Classical Greek and Septuagint Usage

This term takes its meaning from the preposition *sun* (4713), "together," and the verb *piptō* (3959), "fall down." Many nuances of meaning are associated with this term in Greek literature: "fall in with" (especially with accidents or misfortunes); "fall upon" (of accidents); "happen to" or "occur"; "coincide with"; "fall in" or "collapse" (especially of buildings); and "fall together into the same line" or "impinge" (cf. *Liddell-Scott*). Figuratively, in the Septuagint and the Apocrypha, it is used of the collapse of a person's emotional state.

New Testament Usage

The only New Testament occurrence of this term is in some manuscripts at Luke 6:49 (the *Textus Receptus* has *epesen* [see *piptō*] here). In the Parable of the Two Houses, one built on the rock and the other on the sand; the latter is said to have fallen because of the flood.

BAUER 779, LIDDELL-SCOTT 1683.

4696. συμπληρόω sumplēroō verb

Fill completely, become entirely full, complete.

COGNATE:
πληρόω plēroō (3997)

SYNONYMS:
ἀνταναπληρόω antanaplēroō (463)
γεμίζω gemizō (1065)
ἐμπίμπλημι empimplēmi (1689)
κορέννυμι korennumi (2853)
μεστόω mestoō (3195)
πληρόω plēroō (3997)

מָלֵא mālē' (4527), Be completed (Jer 25:12—Codex Alexandrinus only).

1. συμπληροῦσθαι sumplērousthai inf pres mid
2. συνεπληροῦντο suneplērounto 3pl indic imperf pass

2 they were filled with water, and were in jeopardy.... Luke 8:23
1 the time was come that he should be received up,....... 9:51
1 And when the day of Pentecost was fully come,......Acts 2:1

Classical Greek and Septuagint Usage

Sumplēroō is formed by the preposition *sun* (4713), "with," and the verb *plēroō* (3997), "fill, fulfill," and can be found in classical Greek meaning "to completely fill, to complete" (cf. *Liddell-Scott*). Both Philo and Josephus used it in the sense of "become complete" or "come to an end" (*Bauer*). This meaning is also found in a variant reading of Jeremiah 25:12 in the Septuagint. When the 70-year period was "completed" God promised to perpetually "punish the king of Babylon . . . and the land of the Chaldeans."

New Testament Usage

Luke is the only New Testament writer who used this word (Luke 8:23; 9:51; Acts 2:1) and always in the passive voice. Luke 8:23 demonstrates the literal meaning of *sumplēroō*. Here Luke used an idiomatic expression by saying that the disciples were "*filled* with water." Not only was the boat taking on water because of the storm, but the disciples were also in danger of drowning.

In both Luke 9:51 and Acts 2:1 the word is used figuratively with reference to time. In 9:51 it refers to the time of Jesus' departure to heaven. The specific form used here indicates that the time was then being completed, not that it was already full. This actually occurred within the last 6 months of Jesus' life. Acts 2:1 uses the same expression, but here the context indicates that the time (the Day of Pentecost) was full or "fully come." The implication here is that the outpouring of the Holy Spirit occurred in the morning of that day, not during the evening or night before, since the Jewish day began at sundown the day before.

STRONG 4845, BAUER 779, MOULTON-MILLIGAN 612, KITTEL 6:308-9, LIDDELL-SCOTT 1684.

4697. συμπνίγω sumpnigō verb

Choke together, press together.

COGNATE:
πνίγω pnigō (4015)

SYNONYMS:
θλίβω thlibō (2323)
συνθλίβω sunthlibō (4768)

1. **συμπνίγει sumpnigei** 3sing indic pres act
2. **συμπνίγουσιν sumpnigousin** 3pl indic pres act
3. **συνέπνιξαν sunepnixan** 3pl indic aor act
4. **συνέπνιγον sunepnigon** 3pl indic imperf act
5. **συμπνίγονται sumpnigontai** 3pl indic pres mid
6. **συνπνίγονται sunpnigontai** 3pl indic pres mid
7. **συνπνίγουσιν sunpnigousin** 3pl indic pres act
8. **συνπνίγει sunpnigei** 3sing indic pres act

1 choke the word, and he becometh unfruitful........ Matt 13:22
3 and the thorns grew up, and choked it,............. Mark 4:7
2 choke the word, and it becometh unfruitful............ 4:19
5 and are choked with cares and riches and pleasures.. Luke 8:14
4 But as he went the people thronged him................ 8:42

This verb is formed by the preposition *sun* (4713), "with," and the verb *pnigō* (4015), "choke, strangle," and means to "press closely together, choke." While there are few classical references using it, it was more common by New Testament times.

New Testament Usage

Four of the five New Testament uses of *sumpnigō* are in conjunction with parallel accounts of the Parable of the Sower (Matthew 13:22; Mark 4:7,19; Luke 8:14). Mark 4:7 refers to the parable itself, with the seed being choked by the thorns. The other three references refer to the interpretation of the parable which Jesus gave to the disciples later. In each case the idea is that the thorns crowd around the seedling, choking it out.

The last example (Luke 8:42) shows the usage of *sumpnigō* in a figurative manner. Here the situation is Jesus' going to the house of Jairus to heal his daughter. After having explained who Jairus was and the situation concerning his daughter, Luke recorded by means of a very emphatic form, "But as he (Jesus) went the people *thronged* him," i.e., they crowded around Him to the point that He found it hard to breathe (Louw and Nida, *Greek-English Lexicon*, 1:227).

STRONG 4846, BAUER 779, KITTEL 6:455-58, LIDDELL-SCOTT 1685, COLIN BROWN 1:226.

4698. συμπολίτης sumpolitēs noun

Fellow citizen.

CROSS-REFERENCE:
πόλις polis (4032)

1. **συμπολῖται sumpolitai** nom pl masc

1 but fellow citizens with the saints,................... Eph 2:19

Sumpolitēs is a noun that means "citizen with," hence, "fellow citizen." It can be found in classical Greek from the Fifth Century B.C. but is not found in the Septuagint. *Sumpolitēs* is found only once in the New Testament, in Ephesians 2:19. Here Paul wrote to the Ephesians that they were truly members of God's kingdom. He told them they were fellow citizens with the saints and the household of God. This idea of citizenship is seen in other Pauline writings; for example, Philippians 3:20. In other passages the noun (without the preposition *sun* [4713] attached) *politēs* (4037) is also used to mean "fellow citizen."

STRONG 4847, BAUER 780, MOULTON-MILLIGAN 612 (see "sunpolitēs"), LIDDELL-SCOTT 1685.

4699. συμπορεύομαι sumporeuomai verb

Go with, come together, assemble.

COGNATE:
πορεύομαι poreuomai (4057)

SYNONYM:
συνέρχομαι sunerchomai (4755)

בּוֹא bô' (971), Qal: come (Dt 31:11); hiphil: bring (Dn 11:6).

הָלַךְ hālakh (2050), Go (Gn 14:24, Nm 22:35, Jb 1:4).

מָבוֹא māvô' (4136), Coming (Ez 33:31).

פָּעַם pā'am (6717), Stir (Jgs 13:25—Codex Alexandrinus only).

רָעָה rā'âh (7749), Shepherd, graze; be a companion (Prv 13:20).

1. **συμπορεύονται** **sumporeuontai** 3pl indic pres mid
2. **συνεπορεύετο** **suneporeueto** 3sing indic imperf mid
3. **συνεπορεύοντο** **suneporeuonto** 3pl indic imperf mid
4. **συνπορεύονται** **sunporeuontai** 3pl indic pres act

1 and the people **resort** unto him again; .... Mark 10:1
3 and many of his disciples **went with** him, ... Luke 7:11
3 And there **went** great multitudes **with** him: 14:25
2 Jesus himself drew near, and **went with** them. 24:15

Classical Greek
Sumporeuomai is formed by the preposition *sun* (4713), "with," and the verb *poreuomai* (4057), "go," and means "to go with." In classical Greek it is used of simply two people who "proceed together" with the implication that such action is advantageous for both (*Liddell-Scott*). It is also used of the "assembling" of the Senate or even a worker's guild (ibid.).

Septuagint Usage
This word appears repeatedly in the Septuagint. In most cases it translates the Hebrew root *hālakh*, again meaning "go, walk, bring, get," etc. For example, in Genesis 13:5 "Lot . . . *went with* Abram." Similarly, in Exodus 33:15,16 Moses prayed that Jehovah would go with Israel to the Promised Land. In other passages it translates *bô'*, "come, follow."

New Testament Usage
In the New Testament *sumporeuomai* occurs four times (Mark 10:1; Luke 7:11; 14:25; 24:15). The first three passages describe situations in which the multitudes or disciples went with Jesus. In Mark 10:1 the implication is that the people flocked to Jesus (*Bauer*). The same connotation may be present in Luke 14:25.

Luke 7:11 describes an occasion where the people were "going with" Jesus as He entered Nain, and Luke 24:15 describes the two disciples "going" from Jerusalem to Emmaus. As they were going along, "Jesus himself drew near, and went with them." In each example of its use, *sumporeuomai* carries the same meaning; namely, a "going to or with" someone.

STRONG 4848, BAUER 780, MOULTON-MILLIGAN 612 (see "sunporeuomai"), LIDDELL-SCOTT 1685.

4700. συμπόσιον sumposion noun

Group, company, party.

CROSS-REFERENCE:
πίνω pinō (3956)

1. **συμπόσια** **sumposia** nom/acc pl neu

1 sit down by **companies** upon the green grass. .... Mark 6:39
1 sit down by **companies** upon the green grass. 6:39

Classical Greek and Septuagint Usage
This noun can be found in classical Greek from the Sixth Century B.C. meaning "drinking party." Occasionally it is used for the "room in which such parties were given" (*Liddell-Scott*). Similar usage can also be found in the Septuagint, although such parties were not limited to just drinking. In Esther 7:2 the king and Haman were invited to a "banquet of wine." Throughout classical Greek and the Septuagint the inference is that such parties were composed of small groups of people.

New Testament Usage
Sumposion occurs only at Mark 6:39 in the New Testament where it is used twice: *sumposia sumposia*, "group by group." Here the word is used in the general sense of "small groups" who arrived together and would naturally sit together. These groups were probably made up of families and friends as opposed to a division of a crowd into groups of people that did not know each other. The implication of close fellowship is intentional with regards to Jesus' subsequent actions of giving thanks, breaking bread, and then distributing the food so that all ate their fill (verses 41f.).

STRONG 4849, BAUER 780, MOULTON-MILLIGAN 598, LIDDELL-SCOTT 1685.

4701. συμπρεσβύτερος sumpresbuteros noun

Fellow elder, fellow minister, copastor.

CROSS-REFERENCE:
πρεσβύτερος presbuteros (4104)

1. **συμπρεσβύτερος** **sumpresbuteros** nom sing masc

1 who am **also an elder**, and a witness .... 1 Pt 5:1

This noun can only be found in Christian literature (*Bauer*) and means "fellow elder" or "church leader." In classical Greek the related word *sumpresbeutēs*, "fellow ambassador," appears much more frequently. In the New Testament *sumpresbuteros* occurs only in 1 Peter 5:1. Peter's context and the reference in 5:2 to "shepherd and oversee" (*poimanate . . . episkopountes*) describes the work of pastor and bishop and points to the ministry of "copastor" (see *Bauer*). His self-designation as *ho sumpresbuteros* ("fellow elder," NIV) lends dignity and honor to the ones bearing the title of *presbuteros* (4104). "It is true that the apostle is here setting himself alongside the presbyters with emphatic modesty. It is also true, however, that he is setting them alongside himself" (Bornkamm, "presbus," *Kittel*, 6:666).

STRONG 4850, BAUER 780, KITTEL 6:651-80, LIDDELL-SCOTT 1686.

4702. συμφέρω sumpherō verb

To be good or best, advantageous, profitable, expedient.

COGNATE:
- φέρω pherō (5179)

SYNONYMS:
- ἀμύνομαι amunomai (290)
- ἀντέχομαι antechomai (469)
- ἀντιλαμβάνομαι antilambanomai (479)
- βοηθέω boētheō (990)
- ἐλεέω eleeō (1640)
- παραγίνομαι paraginomai (3716)
- συλλαμβάνω sullambanō (4666)
- συμβάλλω sumballō (4671)
- συμφέρω sumpherō (4702)
- συναντιλαμβάνομαι sunantilambanomai (4729)
- ὠφελέω ōpheleō (5456)

טוֹב ṭôv (3005), Good (Jer 26:14 [33:14]).

טוֹבָה ṭôvāh (3009B), Prosperity (Dt 23:6).

נָאוֶה nā'weh (5173), Be fitting (Prv 19:10).

שָׁוָה shāwâh (8187), Be in one's best interest (Est 3:8).

1. συμφέρει sumpherei 3sing indic pres act

2. συμφέρον sumpheron nom/acc sing neu part pres act

3. συμφερόντων sumpherontōn gen pl neu part pres act

4. συνενέγκαντες sunenenkantes nom pl masc part aor act

1 for it is profitable for thee that one of thy members Matt 5:29
1 for it is profitable for thee that one of thy members 5:30
1 it were better for him that a millstone were hanged 18:6
1 the case of the man be so ... it is not good to marry... 19:10
1 Nor consider that it is expedient for us,............John 11:50
1 It is expedient for you that I go away: 16:7
1 that it was expedient that one man should die 18:14
4 used curious arts brought their books together,..... Acts 19:19
3 I kept back nothing that was profitable unto you,...... 20:20
1 but all things are not expedient:................... 1 Co 6:12
2 And this I speak for your own profit;................. 7:35
1 but all things are not expedient:..................... 10:23
2 not seeking mine own profit,......................... 10:33
2 the Spirit is given to every man to profit withal........ 12:7
1 this is expedient for you, who have begun before,... 2 Co 8:10
2 It is not expedient for me doubtless to glory........... 12:1
2 a few days chastened us ... but he for our profit,... Heb 12:10

Classical Greek

Sumpherō is a compound of the preposition *sun* (4713), "with," and the verb *pherō* (5179), "to bring" or "bear." It can be found in classical Greek with the transitive meaning "to bring together," the intransitive meaning "to be profitable," and the passive meaning "to come together" or "meet" (cf. *Liddell-Scott*).

Septuagint Usage

The Septuagint uses *sumpherō* to translate such Hebrew terms as *ṭôv* ("good"), *nā'weh* ("fitting"), and *shāwâh* ("suitable"). The Septuagint uses the word 13 times, 9 of which are exclusively Greek compositions. The Greek papyri also use *sumpherō* in ways similar to all the early classical denotations (*Moulton-Milligan*). It is the New Testament which uses *sumpherō* in an exclusively spiritual realm.

New Testament Usage

Sumpherō occurs 17 times in the New Testament and refers to the ultimate good and not necessarily the good of the present situation. To pluck out an eye or cut off an arm or jump in the river with a millstone tied around the neck is not good for the present, but it would be good if it was the only way to avoid going to hell (Matthew 5:29,30). (Jesus was not recommending these actions.) Celibacy would not be pleasing to most, but it might bring the "highest good" to some. The crucifixion of Christ was not a pleasant experience, and Peter suggested to the Lord that He should avoid it (Matthew 16:22). One might even say Jesus had to deal with the horror of His approaching death in the Garden, but Calvary was for the "highest good" of all (John 11:50; 16:7).

For the apostle Paul the spiritual benefit became the touchstone for all experience (1 Corinthians 6:12; 10:23). Whether it was knowledge, divine discipline, teaching and preaching, or gifts of the Spirit, it was all for the "highest good," not for temporal powers or favors (Acts 20:20; 1 Corinthians 12:7; 2 Corinthians 8:10; Hebrews 12:10).

STRONG 4851, BAUER 780, MOULTON-MILLIGAN 598, KITTEL 9:69-78, LIDDELL-SCOTT 1686-87.

4703. σύμφημι sumphēmi verb

Agree with, consent to.

CROSS-REFERENCE:
- φημί phēmi (5183)

1. σύμφημι sumphēmi 1sing indic pres act

1 I consent unto the law that it is good.............. Rom 7:16

This term is formed by *sun* (4713), "with," and *phēmi* (5183), "to speak" or "say," and means "agree, consent." It does not occur in the Septuagint, although it occasionally appears in classical literature. Paul used the word once, in Romans 7:16 which reads, "I *consent* unto the law that it is good." In this context the apostle expressed the view that although a man sins, it is not because his conscience opposes the law of God. On the contrary, the conscience, even of the sinner, is in "full agreement" with the Law. It is sin which is the opposing evil power, not man's conscience.

STRONG 4852, BAUER 780, LIDDELL-SCOTT 1687.

4703B. σύμφορος sumphoros adj

Profitable, beneficial, useful, advantageous.

CROSS-REFERENCE:

φέρω pherō (5179)

1. σύμφορον sumphoron nom/acc sing masc/neu

1 **And this I say for your own benefit; (NASB)** .... **1 Co 7:35**
1 **not seeking my own profit, (NASB)** **10:33**

Classical Greek

This adjective, a composite of the preposition *sun* (4713), "together," and the verb *pherō* (5179), "bear" or "carry," has two primary uses in Greek literature prior to the New Testament: (1) "accompanying" (e.g., "hunger is the sluggard's companion") and (2) "suitable, useful, profitable" (cf. *Liddell-Scott*). By New Testament times this latter usage predominated. It is used in the Septuagint in 2 Maccabees 4:5.

New Testament Usage

This second declension adjective is used substantivally in both of its two occurrences in the New Testament. The apostle Paul pointed out to the Corinthians, "I speak for your own *profit*" and "not seeking mine own *profit*, but the *profit* of many . . . " (1 Corinthians 7:35; cf. 10:33). The second "profit" found in the latter reference is in italics in the KJV; this usually means the translator added it to help make the meaning clear. It does not appear in the earliest manuscripts.

BAUER 780, MOULTON-MILLIGAN 598, KITTEL 9:69-78, LIDDELL-SCOTT 1688.

4704. συμφυλέτης sumphuletēs noun

Fellow countryman.

CROSS-REFERENCE:

φυλή phulē (5279)

1. συμφυλετῶν sumphuletōn gen pl masc

1 **have suffered like things of your own countrymen,** ... **1 Th 2:14**

Sumphuletēs is a compound of *sun* (4713), "with," and *phulē* (5279), "race" or "tribe," and denotes a "fellow countryman" (*Liddell-Scott*). *Sumphuletēs* can also refer to close national ties, as expressed in 1 Thessalonians 2:14, "For ye also have suffered like things of your own *countrymen*." In this single New Testament occurrence *sumphuletēs* refers to those who were of the same religion.

STRONG 4853, BAUER 780, MOULTON-MILLIGAN 598, LIDDELL-SCOTT 1688.

4705. σύμφυτος sumphutos adj

Planted, grow up with.

CROSS-REFERENCE:

φύω phuō (5289)

בָּצוּר bātsiwr (1232), Impenetrable? thick? (Zec 11:2).

מוּג mûgh (4265), Hithpolel: melt (Am 9:13).

1. σύμφυτοι sumphutoi nom pl masc

1 **been planted together in the likeness of his death,** ... **Rom 6:5**

The verbal adjective *sumphutos* appears only once in the New Testament (Romans 6:5) but is present in the contemporary literature of the First Century (*Bauer*). The term carries the primary sense of being "born with one, congenital," or "innate," hence, "to be grown together" or "united" (cf. *Liddell-Scott*). Unlike the King James translation, "planted together" (which would be the correct translation of *sumphuteuō*, not *sumphutos*), the meaning of this adjective carries the sense of being "grown together" or "united." Thus the NIV correctly renders the sense, "If we have been *united* with him . . . . "

STRONG 4854, BAUER 780, MOULTON-MILLIGAN 598, KITTEL 7:766-97, LIDDELL-SCOTT 1689.

4706. συμφύω sumphuō verb

Grow together, spring up.

CROSS-REFERENCE:

φύω phuō (5289)

1. συμφυεῖσαι sumphueisai nom pl fem part aor pass

2. συνφυεῖσαι sunphueisai nom pl fem part aor pass

1 **and the thorns sprang up with it, and choked it.** ..... **Luke 8:7**

The verb *sumphuō* can be found in classical Greek literature meaning "make to grow together" (*Liddell-Scott*). It is also used in medical references to "unite" a wound, broken bones, etc. (ibid.). Only Luke, the beloved physician, used this word in the New Testament: "And some fell among thorns; and the thorns *sprang up with it*, and choked it" (Luke 8:7). The implication is that as both "grow with each other," they will compete for space and nutrients to the detriment of the wheat.

STRONG 4855, BAUER 780, LIDDELL-SCOTT 1689.

4707. συμφωνέω sumphōneō verb

Agree, make a deal, be in alliance with.

COGNATES:
ἀσύμφωνος asumphōnos (794)
συμφώνησις sumphōnēsis (4708)
συμφωνία sumphōnia (4709)
σύμφωνος sumphōnos (4710)
φωνέω phōneō (5291)

SYNONYMS:
συγκατατίθημαι sunkatatithēmai (4635)
συνευδοκέω suneudokeō (4759)

אוּת 'ûth (224), Niphal: agree (2 Kgs 12:8).
חָבַר chāvar (2357), Join forces (Gn 14:3).
נוּחַ nûach (5299), Encamp (Is 7:2).

1. **συμφωνεῖ sumphōnei** 3sing indic pres act
2. **συμφωνοῦσιν sumphōnousin** 3pl indic pres act
3. **συνεφώνησας sunephōnēsas** 2sing indic aor act
4. **συμφωνήσωσιν sumphōnēsōsin** 3pl subj aor act
5. **συμφωνήσας sumphōnēsas** nom sing masc part aor act
6. **συνεφωνήθη sunephōnēthē** 3sing indic aor pass
7. **συμφωνήσει sumphōnēsei** 3sing indic fut act
8. **συμφωνήσουσιν sumphōnēsousin** 3pl indic fut act

4 That if two of you **shall agree** on earth as touching Matt 18:19
5 And when he **had agreed** with the labourers 20:2
3 didst not thou **agree** with me for a penny? 20:13
1 was taken out of the new **agreeth** not with the old...Luke 5:36
6 **agreed together** to tempt the Spirit of the Lord? ..... Acts 5:9
2 And to this **agree** the words of the prophets; 15:15

Classical Greek

Sumphōneō is a compound of *sun* (4713), "with, together," and *phōneō* (5291), "make a sound, speak." *Sumphōneō* and its cognates appear in Greek literature from the time of Plato meaning "sound together, be in harmony or unison" (*Liddell-Scott*). In a more general sense it can also mean "to agree." The word carried the musical connotation of "harmonize."

Septuagint Usage

Sumphōneō occurs four times in the Septuagint, usually denoting common action and planning. It describes the conspiracy among the kings in the Siddim Valley (Genesis 14:3) and between the armies of Syria and Ephraim (Isaiah 7:2). It also refers to the general acceptance of a royal decree in 2 Kings 12:8 (LXX 4 Kings 12:8). And lastly, *sumphōneō* indicates a common acceptance and readiness for martyrdom (4 Maccabees 14:6).

New Testament Usage

Sumphōneō occurs six times in the New Testament. In Matthew 20:2,13 there is an employer-employee agreement on wages. In the case of Ananias and Sapphira they "*agreed together* to tempt the Spirit of the Lord" (Acts 5:9). This was a fiscal agreement: a deal the two made to lie and cheat.

In Acts 15:15 the prophets of the Old Testament and the apostles are in agreement concerning the conversion of the Gentiles. In Matthew 18:19 two believers may insure an answer to their prayers by being in alliance on the matter. Finally, Luke used *sumphōneō* with the negative particle *ou* (3620) in the Parable of New Wine and Old Wineskins. A new patch cannot be put on an old garment, for the new will cause the old to rip; they are not "compatible" (5:36). Mark's Gospel, relating this parable (2:21), says the two pieces of cloth "pull away" (*airō*, NIV) from one another.

STRONG 4856, BAUER 780-81, MOULTON-MILLIGAN 598-99, KITTEL 9:304-9, LIDDELL-SCOTT 1689-90.

4708. συμφώνησις sumphōnēsis noun

Agreement, concord.

CROSS-REFERENCE:
συμφωνέω sumphōneō (4707)

1. **συμφώνησις sumphōnēsis** nom sing fem

1 And what **concord** hath Christ with Belial? .... 2 Co 6:15

This noun rarely occurs in all of Greek literature but can be found meaning "agreement." One reference in the papyri concerning the settling of accounts and 2 Corinthians 6:15 are the only extant occurrences (*Moulton-Milligan*). Paul stated with his well-known rhetoric, "What *concord* hath Christ with Belial?" Simply put, Christ and the devil can make no deal, settle no account, and can come to no agreement!

STRONG 4857, BAUER 781, MOULTON-MILLIGAN 599, KITTEL 9:304-9, LIDDELL-SCOTT 1689.

4709. συμφωνία sumphōnia noun

Music.

CROSS-REFERENCE:
συμφωνέω sumphōneō (4707)

סוּמְפֹּנְיָה ṣûmpônyāh (A5666), Bagpipes (Dn 3:5,15—Aramaic).

1. **συμφωνίας sumphōnias** gen sing fem

1 nigh to the house, he heard **music** and dancing..... Luke 15:25

In classical Greek this noun means "concord or unison of sound" (*Liddell-Scott*). Frequently this idea of "harmonious union" is applied to music, but it is not limited to that. The term is transliterated into Aramaic characters in Daniel 3:5,10,15 and refers to the ensemble playing of several instruments (Werner, "Musical

Instruments," *Interpreter's Dictionary of the Bible*, 3:476). In its only use in the New Testament the prodigal's elder brother heard the "music and dancing," a party going on to celebrate the return of a lost son (Luke 15:25). In agreement with Jewish customs of the First Century A.D., there would be wind instruments (flute, cornet), string instruments (lyre, harp), and percussion (hand drum, cymbal, tambourine). Good food, good music, and dancing made for a festive occasion (see *New Standard Jewish Encyclopedia*, "Music").

STRONG 4858, BAUER 781, MOULTON-MILLIGAN 599, KITTEL 9:304-9, LIDDELL-SCOTT 1689.

4710. σύμφωνος sumphōnos adj

Mutual agreement, consent.

CROSS-REFERENCE:

συμφωνέω sumphōneō (4707)

1. συμφώνου sumphōnou gen sing neu

1 except it be with consent for a time,................1 Co 7:5

Sumphōnos occurs in classical Greek and the Septuagint meaning "harmonious, unison of sounds." From its musical context comes a general usage that means "agreement." In its only New Testament appearance Paul instructed couples not to deny one another sexual obligations unless there is mutual consent and agreement (1 Corinthians 7:5). To abstain from sexual relations is never to be the decision of one partner in the marriage relationship. It must be agreed upon by both parties. Such sexual obligation was a divine institution in the Mosaic covenant (Exodus 21:10).

STRONG 4859, BAUER 781, MOULTON-MILLIGAN 599, KITTEL 9:304-9, LIDDELL-SCOTT 1689-90.

4711. συμψηφίζω sumpsēphizō verb

Count up, tally up, compute.

COGNATE:

ψηφίζω psēphizō (5420)

1. συνεψήφισαν sunepsēphisan 3pl indic aor act

1 and they counted the price of them,............... Acts 19:19

Sumpsēphizō rarely occurs in all Greek literature but can be found meaning "count up." It only appears in Acts 19:19 in the New Testament. Certain Ephesians, who before their conversion had studied and practiced sorcery, burned their books. When "they *counted* the price of them" it equaled "fifty thousand pieces of silver."

STRONG 4860, BAUER 781, MOULTON-MILLIGAN 599, KITTEL 9:604-7, LIDDELL-SCOTT 1690.

4712. σύμψυχος sumpsuchos adj

United in soul, of one accord, at unity.

CROSS-REFERENCE:

ψυχή psuchē (5425)

1. σύμψυχοι sumpsuchoi nom pl masc

1 being of one accord, of one mind................... Phlp 2:2

The adjective *sumpsuchos* appears rarely in all of Greek literature but can be found meaning "of one mind, united in soul" (cf. *Liddell-Scott*). Philippians 2:2 is its only occurrence in the New Testament. It is a singular word for a singular historical event: the *kenosis* of God's Son. If Christians see how Christ humbled himself by becoming a servant and by putting himself on man's level, they should do the same. This is the meaning of *sumpsuchos*: having the same desires and passions, "united in soul and mind."

STRONG 4861, BAUER 781, LIDDELL-SCOTT 1690, COLIN BROWN 3:687.

4713. σύν sun prep

With, together with, besides.

1. σύν sun

1 I should have received mine own with usury........Matt 25:27
1 Though I should die with thee, yet will I not deny..... 26:35
1 Then were there two thieves crucified with him,....... 27:38
1 who had been crucified with him (NASB)............. 27:44
1 and gave also to them which were with him?....... Mark 2:26
1 they ... with the twelve asked of him the parable........ 4:10
1 called the people unto him with his disciples also,...... 8:34
1 And there appeared unto them Elias with Moses:....... 9:4
1 And with him they crucify two thieves;............... 15:27
1 who were crucified with Him (NASB)................ 15:32
1 And Mary abode with her about three months,......Luke 1:56
1 To be taxed with Mary his espoused wife,.............. 2:5
1 And suddenly there was with the angel a multitude..... 2:13
1 For he was astonished, and all that were with him,..... 5:9
1 and let him down through the tiling with his couch..... 5:19
1 Then Jesus went with them.......................... 7:6
1 and much people of the city was with her............... 7:12
1 preaching ... and the twelve were with him,............. 8:1
1 man ... besought him that he might be with him:....... 8:38
1 did not allow anyone to enter with Him, (NASB)....... 8:51
1 they that were with him were heavy with sleep:......... 9:32
1 I might have required mine own with usury?.......... 19:23
1 and the scribes came upon him with the elders,........ 20:1
1 he sat down, and the twelve apostles with him......... 22:14
1 maid beheld him ... This man was also with him....... 22:56
1 And Herod with his men of war set him at nought,.... 23:11
1 malefactors, led with him to be put to death.......... 23:32
1 And the rulers also with them derided him, saying,.... 23:35
1 they had prepared, and certain others with them....... 24:1
1 and other women that were with them,............... 24:10
1 and beside all this, to day is the third day............ 24:21
1 of them which were with us went to the sepulchre,..... 24:24
1 And he went in to tarry with them.................... 24:29

1 found the eleven ... and them that were with them, Luke 24:33
1 I spake unto you, while I was yet with you, ... 24:44
1 those reclining at the table with him. (NASB) ..... John 12:2
1 he went forth with his disciples 18:1
1 They say unto him, We also go with thee. 21:3
1 with the women, and Mary the mother of Jesus, ... Acts 1:14
1 Mary the mother of Jesus, and with his brethren. 1:14
1 For he was numbered with us, ... 1:17
1 to be a witness with us of his resurrection. 1:22
1 But Peter, standing up with the eleven, ... 2:14
1 Peter, fastening his eyes upon him with John, said, ... 3:4
1 and entered with them into the temple, ... 3:8
1 that they had been with Jesus. 4:13
1 the man which was healed standing with them, ... 4:14
1 both Herod, and Pontius Pilate, with the Gentiles, ... 4:27
1 Ananias, with Sapphira his wife, sold a possession, ... 5:1
1 and all they that were with him, ... 5:17
1 the high priest came, and they that were with him, ... 5:21
1 Then went the captain with the officers, ... 5:26
1 and a deliverer with the help of the angel (NASB) 7:35
1 Peter said unto him, Thy money perish with thee, ... 8:20
1 Philip that he would come up and sit with him. 8:31
1 and one that feared God with all his house, ... 10:2
1 and get thee down, and go with them, ... 10:20
1 And on the morrow Peter went away with them, ... 10:23
1 Moreover these six brethren accompanied me, (NT) 11:12
1 Which was with the deputy of the country, ... 13:7
1 part held with the Jews, and part with the apostles. 14:4
1 part held with the Jews, and part with the apostles. 14:4
1 and also of the Jews with their rulers, ... 14:5
1 and would have done sacrifice with the people. 14:13
1 the next day he departed with Barnabas to Derbe. 14:20
1 And there they abode long time with the disciples. 14:28
1 the apostles and elders, with the whole church, ... 15:22
1 to Antioch with Paul and Barnabas; 15:22
1 with our beloved Barnabas and Paul, ... 15:25
1 Him would Paul have to go forth with him; 16:3
1 together with all who were in his house. (NASB) 16:32
1 a woman named Damaris, and others with them. 17:34
1 Crispus, ... believed on the Lord with all his house; 18:8
1 and with him Priscilla and Aquila; 18:18
1 Demetrius, and the craftsmen which are with him, ... 19:38
1 he kneeled down, and prayed with them all. 20:36
1 brought us on our way, with wives and children, ... 21:5
1 with us also certain of the disciples of Caesarea, ... 21:16
1 the day following Paul went in with us unto James; 21:18
1 Them take, and purify thyself with them, ... 21:24
1 and the next day purifying himself with them 21:26
1 with him in the city Trophimus an Ephesian, ... 21:29
1 And they that were with me saw indeed the light, ... 22:9
1 ye with the council signify to the chief captain 23:15
1 then came I with an army, and rescued him, ... 23:27
1 the morrow they left the horsemen to go with him, ... 23:32
1 when Felix came with his wife Drusilla, ... 24:24
1 with the chief captains, and principal men 25:23
1 about me and them which journeyed with me. 26:13
1 a Macedonian of Thessalonica, being with us. 27:2
1 to dwell by himself with a soldier that kept him. 28:16
1 Now if we be dead with Christ, ... Rom 6:8
1 shall he not with him also freely give us all things? 8:32
1 Hermes, and the brethren which are with them. 16:14
1 Olympas, and all the saints which are with them. 16:15
1 with all that in every place call upon the name ...... 1 Co 1:2
1 with the power of our Lord Jesus Christ, ... 5:4
1 will with the temptation also make a way to escape, ... 10:13
1 that we should not be condemned with the world. 11:32
1 yet not I, but the grace of God which was with me. ... 15:10
1 if it be meet that I go also, they shall go with me. 16:4
1 with the church that is in their house. 16:19
1 with all the saints which are in all Achaia: .... 2 Co 1:1
1 Now he which stablisheth us with you in Christ, ... 1:21
1 will raise us also with Jesus (NASB) 4:14
1 us also by Jesus, and shall present us with you. 4:14
1 also chosen ... to travel with us with this grace, ... 8:19
1 Lest haply if they of Macedonia come with me, ... 9:4
1 but we shall live with him by the power of God 13:4
1 And all the brethren which are with me, ... Gal 1:2
1 neither Titus, who was with me, being a Greek, ... Gal 2:3
1 of faith are blessed with faithful Abraham. 3:9
1 crucified the flesh with the affections and lusts. 5:24
1 May be able to comprehend with all saints .... Eph 3:18
1 be put away from you, with all malice: 4:31
1 to all the saints ... with the bishops and deacons: .... Phlp 1:1
1 having a desire to depart, and to be with Christ; 1:23
1 he hath served with me in the gospel. 2:22
1 The brethren which are with me greet you. 4:21
1 absent in the flesh, yet am I with you in the spirit, ... Col 2:5
1 hath he quickened together with him, ... 2:13
1 dead with Christ from the rudiments of the world, ... 2:20
1 and your life is hid with Christ in God. 3:3
1 then shall ye also appear with him in glory. 3:4
1 ye have put off the old man with his deeds; 3:9
1 With Onesimus, a faithful and beloved brother, ... 4:9
1 which sleep in Jesus will God bring with him. .... 1 Th 4:14
1 caught up together with them in the clouds, ... 4:17
1 and so shall we ever be with the Lord. 4:17
1 we should live together with him. 5:10
1 For the sun is no sooner risen with a burning heat, ... Jas 1:11
1 when we were with him in the holy mount. .... 2 Pt 1:18

Sun is a preposition, and when used with the dative case it provides the sense of association, companionship, fellowship, accompaniment, inclusion, by the aid of, or in accordance with. In composition or with compound words *sun* means "with, together, altogether." The word is common in Greek literature. The preposition also occurs in the cognate language Latin as *cum* with the same range of meanings. In the Attic dialect of the Greek language *sun* appears as *xun*, but this morphology is completely absent from Koine and New Testament Greek.

Classical Greek

In classical Greek *sun* is mainly used in poetry, infrequently appearing in Attic prose with the exception of Xenophon. In its poetic context *sun* expresses the meaning of "along with," as one being joined by another, hence its meaning "with the help of" when used in conjunction with *theos* (2292B) or *theois*. *Sun tois theois* was a common oath for the Greek world: "with the help of the gods." The same has traveled three millennia to the 20th Century as "by the help of God" or "by God." This is a very ancient petition.

Septuagint Usage

In the Septuagint *sun* occurs with the genitive case in the phrase *sun tou andros tou penētos*, "with the poor man" (Ecclesiastes 9:15), and with the accusative case in the phrase *sun ton hēlion*, "with the sun" (Ecclesiastes 11:7). Although *sun* occurs in the Septuagint only once with the genitive, it occurs with the accusative throughout Ecclesiastes and seven other times in the historical books. It also occurs with the accusative case in other Greek versions of the Old Testament: Aquila, about 50 times; Theodotion, 6 times; Symmachus, 4 times. It is interesting that in Isaiah *sun* does not occur as a translation of the

Immanuel phrases but rather *meta* (3196): *meth hēmōn ho theos*, "God with us" (Isaiah 8:8). *Sun* occurs by far more frequently with the dative: about 200 times in the Septuagint.

New Testament Usage

By the time of the New Testament the use of *sun* in prose is "much less restricted" (*Liddell-Scott*). Matthew, Mark, and John together used the word 10 times. Luke–Acts uses *sun* 73 times. This may be attributed to Luke's style as a historian. Of course, Luke used some of the most literary Greek of the New Testament, and his own literary style is a study in itself. Paul used *sun* 38 times, but this is dispersed throughout 8 epistles.

Theological significance is given to *sun* in Paul's use of the expression *sun Christō*, "together with Christ." This expression—plus the equivalent phrases *sun autō*, "together with Him," and *sun Kuriō*, "together with the Lord"—may be seen throughout Paul's writings. For instance, *sun Christō* is found at Romans 6:8, Philippians 1:23, Colossians 3:3; *sun autō* is found at Romans 8:32, Colossians 2:13 and 3:4, 1 Thessalonians 4:14 and 5:10; and *sun Kuriō* is found at 1 Thessalonians 4:17. Paul never used *sun Christō* to describe the believer's relationship with Christ before the resurrection or death of that believer. Being "together with Christ" occurs for the Christian after this earthly existence.

Strong 4862, Bauer 781-82, Moulton-Milligan 599-600, Kittel 7:766-97, Liddell-Scott 1690-91, Colin Brown 3:1172-73,1190,1201,1206-7.

4714. συνάγω sunagō verb

To gather together, meet together.

Cognates:
- ἄγω agō (70)
- ἐπισυνάγω episunagō (1980)
- ἐπισυναγωγή episunagōgē (1981)
- συναγωγή sunagōgē (4715)

Synonyms:
- ἀθροίζω athroizō (119B)
- ἐπισυνάγω episunagō (1980)
- συλλέγω sullegō (4667)
- συναθροίζω sunathroizō (4718)
- συστρέφω sustrephō (4814)
- τρυγάω trugaō (5007)

אָסַף 'āṣaph (636), Qal: gather (Nm 11:32, 2 Sm 12:28f., Jer 10:17); niphal: be gathered, gather (Gn 29:7f., 1 Sm 17:1f., Ps 35:15 [34:15]); piel: take in as a guest, gather (Jgs 19:18, Jer 9:22); pual: be gathered (Ez 38:12, Hos 10:10, Zec 14:14); hithpael: assemble oneself together (Dt 33:5).

אָסֹף 'āṣōph (638), Storeroom (Neh 12:25).

אֹסֶף 'ōṣeph (639), Gleaming (Mi 7:1).

אָצַר 'ātsar (709), Lay up in store (Is 39:6).

אָתָה 'āthâh (885), Come (Dt 33:21).

בּוֹא bô' (971), Go, come; hiphil: bring (2 Kgs 19:25).

בָּלַע bāla' (1142), Swallow (Jb 20:15).

דָּגַר dāghar (1766), Hatch (Jer 17:11).

חוּשׁ chûsh (2456), Hiphil: hasten (Is 60:22).

חָטַב chāṭav (2497), Cut (Dt 19:5).

חָשַׂךְ chāsakh (2910), Withhold (Prv 11:24).

יָסַד yāṣadh (3354), Lay a foundation; niphal: counsel together (Ps 2:2).

יָסַף yāṣaph (3362), Hiphil: do again (2 Sm 3:34).

יָעַד yā'adh (3366), Niphal: assemble, meet together (Nm 10:3, Neh 6:2); join forces (Ps 48:4 [47:4]).

יָצָא yātsâ' (3428), Go out, come out; hiphil: bring out (2 Sm 10:16).

יָצַב yātsav (3429), Station oneself, stand; hithpael: pledge one's allegiance (2 Chr 11:13).

כָּמַס kāmaṣ (3769), Lay in store (Dt 32:34).

כָּנַס kānaṣ (3788), Qal: gather (1 Chr 22:2, Neh 12:44, Eccl 3:5); hithpael: wrap oneself up (Is 28:20).

כְּנַשׁ k^enash (A3798), Hithpaal: assemble, gather (Dn 3:3,27—Aramaic).

לָקַט lāqaṭ (4092), Qal: gather (Ex 16:16); piel: gather, glean (Gn 47:14, Ru 2:2, Is 17:5); pual: be gathered (Is 27:12).

מָנַע māna' (4661), Keep (Jb 20:13).

מִקְוֶה miqweh (4884), Hope (Jer 50:7 [27:7]).

נָגַע nāgha' (5236), Hiphil: come (Dn 12:12).

נָהַר nāhar (5281), Stream (Jer 51:44 [28:44]).

נוּחַ nûach (5299), Rest, settle; hiphil: lay (Ez 22:20).

נוּס nûṣ (5308), Flee, escape; hiphil: cause to flee (Ex 9:20).

נָצַל nātsal (5522), Be saved; hiphil: deliver (Ez 34:12—Codex Alexandrinus only).

נָקַב nāqav (5529), Curse, pierce, designate; niphal: be designated (Ezr 8:20).

נָתַן nāthan (5598), Give, put; cause (Prv 10:10).

סָפַר ṣāphar (5807), Assign (2 Chr 2:2); number (2 Chr 2:17).

עוּז 'ûz (5974), Go into refuge; hiphil: bring into shelter (Ex 9:19).

עָלָה 'ālâh (6148), Go up; hiphil: make to come up (Ex 8:5—Codex Alexandrinus only).

עָמַד 'āmadh (6198), Stand; hiphil: muster (Dn 11:13).

פָּדָה pādhâh (6540), Ransomed (Is 35:10).

צָבַר tsāvar (6914), Store up, pile, heap up (Gn 41:49, Ex 8:14, Jb 27:16).

צָעַק tsā'aq (7094), Cry out; niphal: be summoned (Jgs 12:1—Codex Alexandrinus only).

קָבַץ qāvats (7192), Qal: gather, assemble (Gn 41:48, Dt 13:16, 2 Chr 18:5); niphal: gather together, assemble together (Gn 49:2, Jos 10:6, Is 60:4); piel; gather (Dt 30:3f., Neh 1:9, Is 56:8); pual: be gathered (Ez 38:8); hithpael: gather together (Jgs 9:47, 1 Sm 22:2, Is 44:11).

קָהַל qāhal (7234), Niphal: assemble (Est 9:15,18); hiphil: assemble, convene (Nm 8:9, 10:7, Ez 38:13).

קָוָה qāwâh (7245), Wait; niphal: be gathered (Gn 1:9, Jer 3:17); piel: wait for (Mi 5:7).

קָטַף qāṭaph (7280), Pick (Dt 23:25 [24:1]—only some Alexandrinus texts).

קָפַץ qāphats (7376), Shut (Is 52:15—Codex Alexandrinus only).

קָצִיר qātsîr (7392), Harvest (Jb 5:5).

קָרֵב qārēv (7414), Niphal: come near (Jos 7:14); hiphil: bring near (Jer 30:21 [37:21]).

קָשַׁר qāshar (7489), Conspire together (Neh 4:8).

קָשַׁשׁ qāshash (7492), Polel: gather (Ex 5:7,12); hithpolel: gather oneself (Zep 2:1).

רָגַז rāghaz (7553), Tremble (Jl 2:1—Codex Alexandrinus only).

שָׂכַר sākhar (7963), Hire; hithpael: earn wages (Hg 1:6).

שׁוּב shûv (8178), Return; polel: bring back (Is 49:5).

שָׁמַר shāmar (8490), Keep (Gn 41:35—Codex Alexandrinus only).

1. **συνάγω sunagō** 1sing indic pres act
2. **συνάγει sunagei** 3sing indic pres act
3. **συνάγουσιν sunagousin** 3pl indic pres act
4. **συνάγων sunagōn** nom sing masc part pres act
5. **συνήγαγεν sunēgagen** 3sing indic aor act
6. **συνηγάγομεν sunēgagomen** 1pl indic aor act
7. **συνηγάγετε sunēgagete** 2pl indic aor act
8. **συνήγαγον sunēgagon** 3pl indic aor act
9. **συναγάγῃ sunagagē** 3sing subj aor act
10. **συναγάγετε sunagagete** 2pl impr aor act
11. **συναγαγών sunagagōn** nom sing masc part aor act
12. **συναγαγόντες sunagagontes** nom pl masc part aor act
13. **συναγαγούσῃ sunagagousē** dat sing fem part aor act
14. **συναγαγεῖν sunagagein** inf aor act
15. **συνάξω sunaxō** 1sing indic fut act
16. **συνάξει sunaxei** 3sing indic fut act
17. **συνάγονται sunagontai** 3pl indic pres mid
18. **συνάγεσθε sunagesthe** 2pl indic/impr pres mid
19. **συνήχθη sunēchthē** 3sing indic aor pass
20. **συνήχθησαν sunēchthēsan** 3pl indic aor pass
21. **συναχθέντες sunachthentes** nom pl masc part aor pass
22. **συναχθέντων sunachthentōn** gen pl masc part aor pass
23. **συναχθῆναι sunachthēnai** inf aor pass
24. **συνηγμένοι sunēgmenoi** nom pl masc part perf mid
25. **συνηγμένων sunēgmenōn** gen pl masc part perf mid
26. **συνηγμένα sunēgmena** nom/acc pl neu part perf mid
27. **συναχθήσεται sunachthēsetai** 3sing indic fut pass
28. **συναχθήσονται sunachthēsontai** 3pl indic fut pass
29. **συνάγεται sunagetai** 3sing indic pres mid
30. **συνάχθητε sunachthēte** 2pl impr aor pass
31. **συνάγετε sunagete** 2pl impr pres act

11 And when he **had gathered** all the chief priests..... Matt 2:4
16 and **gather** his wheat into the garner;................. 3:12
3 neither do they reap, nor **gather** into barns;........... 6:26
4 he that **gathereth** not with me scattereth abroad...... 12:30
20 great multitudes **were gathered together** unto him,.... 13:2
10 but **gather** the wheat into my barn.................. 13:30
13 was cast into the sea, and **gathered** of every kind:.... 13:47
24 two or three are **gathered together** in my name,...... 18:20
8 and **gathered together** all as many as they found,..... 22:10
20 Sadducees to silence, they **were gathered together**..... 22:34
25 While the Pharisees **were gathered together**,.......... 22:41
28 there **will** the eagles **be gathered together**............. 24:28
4 and **gathering** where thou hast not strowed:.......... 25:24
1 and **gather** where I have not strowed:................ 25:26
27 And before him **shall be gathered** all nations:........ 25:32
7 I was a stranger, and ye **took** me **in**:................ 25:35
6 When saw we thee a stranger, and **took** thee **in**?..... 25:38
7 I was a stranger, and ye **took** me not **in**:............ 25:43
20 Then **assembled together** the chief priests,............ 26:3
20 where the scribes and the elders **were assembled**...... 26:57
25 Therefore when they **were gathered together**,......... 27:17
8 and **gathered** unto him the whole band of soldiers.... 27:27
20 priests and Pharisees **came together** unto Pilate,...... 27:62
21 And when they **were assembled** with the elders,...... 28:12
20 And straightway many **were gathered together**,..... Mark 2:2
19 and there **was gathered** unto him a great multitude,.... 4:1
19 much people **gathered** unto him:..................... 5:21
17 apostles **gathered themselves together** unto Jesus,....... 6:30
17 Then **came together** unto him the Pharisees,........... 7:1
16 and **will gather** the wheat into his garner;.......... Luke 3:17
4 and he that **gathereth** not with me scattereth......... 11:23
15 because I have no room where **to bestow** my fruits?.. 12:17
15 and there **will I bestow** all my fruits and my goods.... 12:18
11 the younger son **gathered** all together,............... 15:13
28 thither **will** the eagles **be gathered together**........... 17:37
19 and the chief priests and the scribes **came together**,... 22:66
2 and **gathereth** fruit unto life eternal:.............. John 4:36
10 **Gather up** the fragments that remain,................ 6:12
8 Therefore they **gathered** them **together**,............... 6:13
8 Then **gathered** the chief priests and the Pharisees..... 11:47
9 but that also he **should gather together** in one........ 11:52
3 and men **gather** them, and cast them into the fire,.... 15:6
19 Jesus ofttimes **resorted** thither with his disciples....... 18:2
24 the disciples were **assembled** for fear of the Jews,..... 20:19
20 the rulers **were gathered** together against the Lord, Acts 4:26
20 and the people of Israel, **were gathered together**,....... 4:27
24 was shaken where they were **assembled together**;....... 4:31
23 year they **assembled themselves** with the church,...... 11:26
19 the whole city **together** to hear the word of God...... 13:44
12 and **had gathered** the church **together**,.............. 14:27
20 And the apostles and elders **came together**........... 15:6
12 when they **had gathered** the multitude **together**,....... 15:30
25 when the disciples **came together** to break bread,..... 20:7
24 where they were **gathered together**.................. 20:8
22 when ye **are gathered together**, and my spirit,...... 1 Co 5:4
2 that **leadeth** into captivity shall go into captivity:... Rev 13:10
14 **to gather** them to the battle of that great day........ 16:14
5 he **gathered** them **together** into ... Armageddon....... 16:16

18 Come and gather yourselves together .... Rev 19:17
26 and their armies, gathered together to make war 19:19
14 Gog and Magog, to gather them together to battle: ... 20:8

Classical Greek

Sunagō is a common word occurring in classical Greek from the time of Homer (ca. Eighth Century B.C.). In classical usage it usually conveys the meaning of "to gather together" persons or things for any of several reasons: worship, deliberation, festivity, battle, work, hospitality, or reconciliation (*Liddell-Scott*).

The nonliterary papyri offer an illustration of *sunagō* in relationship to money or goods. "The verb is frequently used of the total amount, the full sum, received by sale or by purchase" (*Moulton-Milligan*). For example, in the Parable of the Prodigal Son (Luke 15:11-32) it is possible that the "prodigal converted his goods into money, sold all off and realized their full value, rather than that he 'gathered all together' to take with him" (ibid.).

Septuagint Usage

Sunagō occurs about 350 times in the Septuagint and translates 50 different Hebrew words, the most frequent being *'āsaph*, "gather," and *qāvats*, "assemble."

New Testament Usage

One can divide New Testament occurrences into two general categories: gathering things and gathering persons (*Bauer*). Matthew uses *sunagō* for the "assembling" of the religious leaders, usually against Jesus (26:3,57); for the "gathering together" of people which came to hear Jesus (13:2); and a cryptic reference to "gathering together" of birds of prey (24:28). An interesting reference to the classical usage as "hospitality" occurs in the Olivet discourse: "I was a stranger, and ye took me in," that is, you showed Me hospitality (Matthew 25:35,38,43).

Mark always uses *sunagō* for the "gathering together" of people: crowds, apostles, or Pharisees (2:2; 4:1; 5:21; 6:30; 7:1). Luke and John also use the word with the two basic ideas of "gathering people and things." Luke 15:13 is the only exception (see reference to *Moulton-Milligan* above). Beginning with Acts 4:31 Luke used the word exclusively to denote the assembly of the Church (Acts 4:31; 11:26; 13:44; 14:27) as did Paul in his only reference to the word (1 Corinthians 5:4).

The Book of Revelation employs *sunagō* to indicate the "gathering together" for the purpose of war (13:10; 16:14,16; 19:19; 20:8) and the assembling of the birds for the great supper of God (19:17).

Strong 4863, Bauer 782, Moulton-Milligan 600, Liddell-Scott 1691-92, Colin Brown 2:31-33.

4715. συναγωγή sunagōgē noun

Place of assembly, synagogue, a congregation.

Cognate:

συνάγω sunagō (4714)

Synonym:

ἐκκλησία ekklēsia (1564)

אָסִיף 'āsîph (628), Ingathering (Ex 34:22—Codex Vaticanus only).

אָסַף 'āsaph (636), Gather (Ex 23:16).

בַּיִת bayith (1041), House (1 Kgs 12:21).

בֵּן bēn (1158), Children (Lv 22:18).

גַּל gal (1569), Pile (Jb 8:17).

הָמוֹן hāmôn (2066), Army (Dn 11:10-13).

חַיִל chayil (2524), Army (Ez 37:10).

מָחוֹל māchôl (4369), Dance (Jer 31:4,13 [38:4,13]).

מַחֲנֶה machăneh (4402), Camp (Nm 5:2—Codex Alexandrinus only).

מִקְוֶה miqweh (4885), Collecting (Lv 11:36).

מָקוֹם māqôm (4887), Place (Gn 1:9).

מִשְׁכָּן mishkān (5088), Dwelling (Nm 16:24).

סוֹד sôdh (5660), Gathering (Jer 6:11).

עֵדָה 'ēdhāh (5920), Congregation, company (Nm 16:21f., Jos 22:16f., Ps 106:17 [105:17]).

עָם 'ām (6194II) People (Lv 10:3, Nm 32:15).

קָבַץ qāvats (7192), Gather, collect; niphal: be gathered (Is 56:8).

קָהָל qāhāl (7235), Assembly, congregation (Lv 4:13f., Ps 40:10 [39:10], Ez 32:22f.).

קְהִלָּה qᵉhillāh (7236), Assembly (Dt 33:4).

תִּקְוָה tiqwāh (8951), Hope (Zec 9:12).

1. **συναγωγή sunagōgē** nom sing fem
2. **συναγωγῆς sunagōgēs** gen sing fem
3. **συναγωγῇ sunagōgē** dat sing fem
4. **συναγωγήν sunagōgēn** acc sing fem
5. **συναγωγῶν sunagōgōn** gen pl fem
6. **συναγωγαῖς sunagōgais** dat pl fem
7. **συναγωγάς sunagōgas** acc pl fem

6 Jesus went about ... teaching in their synagogues, ... Matt 4:23
6 hypocrites do in the synagogues and in the streets, ... 6:2
6 for they love to pray standing in the synagogues 6:5
6 teaching in their synagogues, and preaching 9:35
6 and they will scourge you in their synagogues; 10:17
4 he went into their synagogue: 12:9
3 he taught them in their synagogue, ... 13:54
6 and the chief seats in the synagogues, ... 23:6
6 some of them shall ye scourge in your synagogues, ... 23:34
4 on the sabbath day he entered into the synagogue, .. Mark 1:21
3 in their synagogue a man with an unclean spirit; 1:23

2 when they were come out of the **synagogue**, ... Mark 1:29
6 And he preached in their **synagogues** 1:39
4 And he entered again into the **synagogue**; 3:1
3 he began to teach in the **synagogue**: 6:2
6 And the chief seats in the **synagogues**, ... 12:39
7 and in the **synagogues** ye shall be beaten: 13:9
6 taught in their **synagogues**, being glorified of all..... Luke 4:15
4 he went into the **synagogue** on the sabbath day, ... 4:16
3 the eyes of all them that were in the **synagogue** 4:20
3 all they in the **synagogue**, when they heard these 4:28
3 And in the **synagogue** there was a man, ... 4:33
2 And he arose out of the **synagogue**, ... 4:38
6 And he preached in the **synagogues** of Galilee.......... 4:44
4 that he entered into the **synagogue** and taught: 6:6
4 and he hath built us a **synagogue**. 7:5
2 Jairus, and he was a ruler of the **synagogue**: 8:41
6 for ye love the uppermost seats in the **synagogues**, ... 11:43
7 And when they bring you unto the **synagogues**, ... 12:11
5 And he was teaching in one of the **synagogues** 13:10
6 and the highest seats in the **synagogues**, ... 20:46
7 persecute ... delivering you up to the **synagogues**, ... 21:12
3 These things said he in the **synagogue**, ... John 6:59
3 I ever taught in the **synagogue**, and in the temple, ... 18:20
2 Then there arose certain of the **synagogue**, ... Acts 6:9
7 of him letters to Damascus to the **synagogues**, ... 9:2
6 straightway he preached Christ in the **synagogues**, ... 9:20
6 they preached the word of God in the **synagogues** 13:5
4 and went into the **synagogue** on the sabbath day, ... 13:14
2 when the Jews were gone out of the **synagogue**, ... 13:42
2 Now when the **congregation** was broken up, ... 13:43
4 that they went both together into the **synagogue** 14:1
6 being read in the **synagogues** every sabbath day........ 15:21
1 Thessalonica, where was a **synagogue** of the Jews: 17:1
4 went into the **synagogue** of the Jews. 17:10
3 disputed he in the **synagogue** with the Jews, ... 17:17
3 And he reasoned in the **synagogue** every sabbath, ... 18:4
3 whose house joined hard to the **synagogue**. 18:7
4 but he himself entered into the **synagogue**, ... 18:19
3 And he began to speak boldly in the **synagogue**: 18:26
4 And he went into the **synagogue**, ... 19:8
7 in every **synagogue** them that believed on thee: 22:19
6 neither in the **synagogues**, nor in the city: 24:12
7 And I punished them oft in every **synagogue**, ... 26:11
4 For if there come unto your **assembly** a man .... Jas 2:2
1 and are not, but are the **synagogue** of Satan. .... Rev 2:9
2 I will make them of the **synagogue** of Satan, ... 3:9

Classical Greek

Sunagōgē, "synagogue," is related to the verb *sunagō* (4714), "to bring together." This might be a gathering of either objects or persons. Later, *sunagō* came to be associated with cultic feasts (cf. *Liddell-Scott*; Schrage, "sunagōgē," *Kittel*, 7:800).

Septuagint Usage

The Hebrew terms *ʿēdhāh* and *qāhāl*, both used of meetings or gatherings of the people of Israel, stand behind *sunagōgē* in the Septuagint. Whereas *ʿēdhāh* consistently depicts the gathering of Israel, *qāhāl* tends to be reserved for describing the cultic gathering of the community under special circumstances (ibid., 7:802). Later Judaism adopted the idea of the institutional gathering, as reflected by *ʿēdhah*, in its naming of the synagogue. Thus the thought behind *synagogue* is the "gathering of the people" of Israel rather than a meeting for some special purpose (ibid., 7:804f.).

Intertestamental Period

Insufficient evidence exists to know for certain when the synagogue came into being. We can be sure that it dates back to the Babylonian captivity; however, it is entirely possible that the initial trend to meet in synagogues developed inside Israel, perhaps even occurring within Jerusalem (as well as outside). Possibly they originated some time before the destruction of Solomon's Temple (586 B.C.). Local worship services other than in the temple or tabernacle, such as new moon festivals and sabbaths, were conducted at a very early date.

During the exile in Babylon and in those lands of the Dispersion the synagogue grew rapidly. Since the temple was destroyed, there was no temple worship. The synagogue in one way substituted for this lack. When the temple was rebuilt the synagogue service, whose main focus was prayer and the reading of Scripture, became the complement to the sacrificial service of the temple.

Thus the synagogue is not in contrast to the temple service. In the Diaspora (regions of the Dispersion), where regular temple attendance was impossible, the synagogue in one sense replaced the temple. By participating in the synagogue service one indirectly shared in the temple rituals. This relationship between the two is reflected by such similarities as location: both were situated on the highest ground; and position: all synagogues faced Jerusalem (Sonne, "Synagogue," *Interpreter's Dictionary of the Bible*, 4:485). Thus we note that in Mesopotamia the synagogues face the west; in Greece and Italy they face the east; in Galilee they point to the south.

Jerusalem itself contained a rather large number of synagogues. According to Jewish tradition—however unreliable—there were as many as 480 synagogues of varying sizes in the Holy City. This indicates that the synagogue not only substituted for the temple, it was the chief expression of and site of worship among the common people of God in that time.

New Testament Usage

Jesus showed the same attitude toward the synagogue as did the common people. He went "as his custom was" to the synagogue, and He evidently endorsed it as being ordained by God (Luke 4:16; cf. Matthew 4:23; 9:35; John 6:59; 18:20). Although Jesus condemned the Pharisaic legalism, He never criticized the synagogue service. Undoubtedly this comes from the fact that the synagogue service had remained relatively uninfluenced by the Pharisaic philosophy and practice that had contaminated Judaism on so many other fronts.

The earliest Christians also maintained a close relationship with the synagogue whenever they could. On his missionary journeys Paul never neglected to visit the synagogue of the city. There he participated in the service and even had the opportunity to preach the gospel (Acts 13:14; 14:1; 17:1,10; 18:4; 19:8). Paul did not discourage participation in the synagogue service until some started to speak "evil of that way (of Christianity)" (Acts 19:9). Under some circumstances Jewish Christians continued to worship in the synagogue as late as A.D. 100 when the legal experts of rabbinic Judaism added the so-called Eighteenth Benediction to the synagogue prayer. This prayer invoked a curse upon the "heretical" Christians.

The synagogue gathering was not only a religious phenomenon, it also functioned socially and legally. Synagogues afforded relief to the poor; their leaders were authorized to judge legal matters. According to the Talmud there were as many as 168 violations of the Law which could be punished by scourging. Such a penalty was determined by the body of elders of a synagogue, and it was administered by the attendant of the synagogue (Matthew 10:17). In accordance with the law of Moses, no more than 40 strokes were given (cf. Deuteronomy 25:3). An even more serious punishment was to be excommunicated from the synagogue. This isolated an individual from his own people; he could have no contact with orthodox Jews whatsoever.

The synagogues also became places of instruction and training in the Law. Besides the place of assembly there were rooms for education and for the administration of the affairs of the synagogue. Furthermore, several rooms were set aside as places of lodging for travelers.

The style of service in the synagogue consisted of prayer and the reading of Scripture with comments upon it. There were alternate readings between the "angel/messenger of the church/assembly" (cf. Revelation 1:20) and the gathering itself. Scripture was read verbatim, quoted from memory, paraphrased and explained, and set in poetic form. Scripture thus became the focal point of every service. The form of earliest Christian worship was influenced by and patterned after the synagogue service.

Strong 4864, Bauer 782, Moulton-Milligan 600-601, Kittel 7:798-841, Liddell-Scott 1692, Colin Brown 1:291-93,295-97,307.

4716. συναγωνίζομαι
sunagōnizomai verb

Share in a contest, strive together.

Cross-Reference:
ἀγωνίζομαι agōnizomai (74)

1. συναγωνίσασθαι sunagōnisasthai inf aor mid

1 **that ye strive together with me in your prayers** ..... **Rom 15:30**

This verb can be found in classical Greek from the time of Plato meaning "contend along with, share in a contest" (*Liddell-Scott*). In its single New Testament occurrence Paul urged his hearers to "*join* me *in* my *struggle* by praying to God for me" (Romans 15:30, NIV). Paul was concerned about the successful distribution of money collected in Jerusalem (cf. verses 31f.).

Strong 4865, Bauer 783, Moulton-Milligan 601, Liddell-Scott 1692, Colin Brown 1:645,647-48.

4717. συναθλέω sunathleō verb

Struggle together, strive together.

Cross-Reference:
ἀθλέω athleō (118)

1. συναθλοῦντες sunathlountes nom pl masc part pres act

2. συνήθλησαν sunēthlēsan 3pl indic aor act

1 **with one mind striving together for the faith** .... **Phlp 1:27**
2 **help those women which laboured with me** **4:3**

This verb overlaps in meaning with *sunagōnizomai* (4716) and means "struggle together" (cf. *Liddell-Scott*). It appears only twice in the New Testament, both times in Paul's letter to the Philippians. In 1:27 Paul exhorted the Philippians to "strive together," that is, "stand and contend in unity," especially whenever the gospel is under attack. Paul also used their "contending together" for the gospel as a basis for encouraging reconciliation between Euodias and Syntyche (4:3).

Strong 4866, Bauer 783, Kittel 1:167-68, Liddell-Scott 1692.

4718. συναθροίζω sunathroizō verb

Assemble, gather together, call together.

Synonyms:
ἀθροίζω athroizō (119B)
ἐπισυνάγω episunagō (1980)

συλλέγω sullegō (4667)
συνάγω sunagō (4714)
συστρέφω sustrephō (4814)
τρυγάω trugaō (5007)

הוּן hûn (2018), Hiphil: think something to be easy (Dt 1:41).

יָעַד yāʿadh (3366), Niphal: be gathered together (Nm 16:11).

מָגוֹר māghôr (4171), Terror (Jer 20:10).

נוּעַ nûaʿ (5309), Stagger (Am 4:8).

עוּשׁ ʿûsh (6002), Hurry (Jl 3:11).

קָבַץ qāvats (7192), Qal: gather (1 Sm 28:1, 2 Sm 3:21, 1 Kgs 18:19); niphal: be gathered, gather (1 Sm 25:1, 28:4); hithpael: gather, assemble (1 Sm 7:7, 8:4, 2 Sm 2:25).

קָהַל qāhal (7234), Niphal: gather (Jos 22:12); hiphil: assemble (Ex 35:1).

1. συναθροίσας sunathroisas nom sing masc part aor act
2. συνηθροισμένοι sunēthroismenoi nom pl masc part perf mid
3. συνηθροισμένους sunēthroismenous acc pl masc part perf mid

3 and found the eleven **gathered together,** .... Luke 24:33
2 where many were **gathered together** praying......... Acts 12:12
1 Whom he **called together** with the workmen 19:25

Classical Greek

In classical Greek this verb can be found meaning "gather together." Greek historians often used *sunathroizō* of assembling soldiers (cf. *Liddell-Scott*).

Septuagint Usage

In the papyri *sunathroizō* occurs in a military context stating that the military commanders had assembled the public magistrates in rank with themselves (*Moulton-Milligan*). The word occurs in the Septuagint over 30 times, translating some 7 different Hebrew words. Some of the most familiar Hebrew terminology are *qāvats* (compare *kibbuts*) and *qāhal.* The majority of Septuagint references are in Samuel and Kings where leaders assemble the men or tribes of Israel. Reasons for assembling were war, conference, or religious purposes. A typical example is at 2 Samuel 3:21 (LXX 2 Kings 3:21): "And Abner said unto David, I will arise and go, and will gather all Israel unto my lord the king." *Sunathroizō* is usually, as in this instance, assembly under leadership for a definite purpose (see Exodus 35:1; Numbers 20:2).

New Testament Usage

The New Testament uses *sunathroizō* in three passages: Luke 24:33; Acts 12:12; 19:25. In the Gospel of Luke *sunathroizō* is a textual variant with *athroizō* (119B). The majority of manuscripts support the Received text in contrast to modern critical texts and the Egyptian texts. The compound is a Lucan word, and no doubt the Eleven did gather under some leadership of one of the apostles.

Luke again used *sunathroizō* in Acts. In these two remaining New Testament contexts one can see two opposing groups assembled: one for prayer (12:12), one for greed and opposition (19:25). Both groups were under spiritual leadership: believers under the Holy Spirit and the others under the demonic seduction of the goddess Diana. Both assemblies were under direction, and both had purpose: the one for good and the other for evil.

Strong 4867, Bauer 783, Moulton-Milligan 601, Liddell-Scott 1692.

4719. συναίρω sunairō verb

Settle accounts, take up together.

Cross-Reference:
αἴρω airō (142)

עָזַב ʿāzav (6013), Leave (Ex 23:5).

1. συναίρει sunairei 3sing indic pres act
2. συναίρειν sunairein inf pres act
3. συνᾶραι sunarai inf aor act

3 king, which would **take account** of his servants..... Matt 18:23
2 And when he had begun to **reckon,**.................... 18:24
1 the lord ... cometh, and **reckoneth** with them.......... 25:19

Sunairō appears in classical Greek from the Eighth Century B.C. and means "take up together." The word occurs three times in two passages in the New Testament: both times in stewardship parables of Jesus and both written by a former accountant (Matthew 18:23,24; 25:19). How man deals with man has a direct relationship to how God deals with man. The first parable deals with mercy in settling accounts; the second deals with faithfulness. When the Christian "settles accounts" with others, he should show mercy and compassion if he expects God to be merciful toward him on judgment day. When the Christian is dealing with his own obligations, he must be faithful—planning a very strict "settling of accounts."

Strong 4868, Bauer 783, Moulton-Milligan 601, Liddell-Scott 1693.

4720. συναιχμάλωτος sunaichmalōtos noun

Fellow prisoner.

CROSS-REFERENCE:
αἰχμαλωτίζω aichmalōtizō (161)

1. συναιχμάλωτος **sunaichmalōtos** nom sing masc
2. συναιχμαλώτους **sunaichmalōtous** acc pl masc

2 **And Junia, my kinsmen, and my fellow prisoners,** . . . **Rom 16:7**
1 **Aristarchus my fellow prisoner saluteth you,** . . . . **Col 4:10**
1 **Epaphras, my fellow prisoner in Christ Jesus;** . . . . **Phlm 1:23**

Sunaichmalōtos rarely occurs in Greek literature but can be found denoting a "fellow prisoner." This compound occurs three times in the New Testament, each time from the mouth of an experienced prisoner himself, the apostle Paul. In every instance of *sunaichmalōtos* one of Paul's prison mates sends greetings to the church. The *sunaichmalōtoi*, or "fellow prisoners," were Andronicus, Junia, Aristarchus, and Epaphras (Romans 16:7; Colossians 4:10; Philemon 23). All of these men were in jail for the gospel, and several of them became significant contributors to the kingdom of God.

STRONG 4869, BAUER 783, MOULTON-MILLIGAN 601, KITTEL 1:195-97, LIDDELL-SCOTT 1693.

4721. συνακολουθέω

sunakoloutheō verb

Accompany someone, follow.

COGNATE:
ἀκολουθέω akoloutheō (188)

SYNONYMS:
ἀκολουθέω akoloutheō (188)
ἐξακολουθέω exakoloutheō (1795)
ἐπακολουθέω epakoloutheō (1857)
κατακολουθέω katakoloutheō (2598)
μιμέομαι mimeomai (3265)
παρακολουθέω parakoloutheō (3738)

1. συνακολουθήσασαι **sunakolouthēsasai** nom pl fem part aor act
2. συνακολουθῆσαι **sunakolouthēsai** inf aor act
3. συνακολουθοῦσαι **sunakolouthousai** nom pl fem part pres act
4. συνηκολούθει **sunēkolouthei** 3sing indic imperf act

2 **And he suffered no man to follow him,** . . . . **Mark 5:37**
4 **young man was following Him, (NASB)** **14:51**
1 **and the women that followed him from Galilee,** . . . . **Luke 23:49**

This verb can be found in classical Greek from the Fifth Century B.C. and means "follow along with or closely" (*Liddell-Scott*). Both New Testament occurrences of *sunakoloutheō* appear in Mark and Luke, with Jesus being the object of the verb in all cases. In Mark 5:37 only the men of the inner circle (Peter, James, and John) were permitted to accompany Jesus to raise Jairus' daughter. In the Passion narrative, mention is made of the women from Galilee who accompanied Jesus (Luke 23:49). Luke gave the names of some of the women as Mary, Joanna, Susanna, and others (Luke 8:2,3). Some have promoted the idea that *sunakoloutheō* carries the connotation "to be a disciple," but from its only uses in the New Testament one can see that the emphasis is on companionship rather than discipleship.

STRONG 4870, BAUER 783, MOULTON-MILLIGAN 601, KITTEL 1:216, LIDDELL-SCOTT 1693, COLIN BROWN 1:480-81.

4722. συναλίζω sunalizō verb

Assemble, eat with, dwell with.

CROSS-REFERENCE:
ἁλίζω halizō (231)

1. συναλιζόμενος **sunalizomenos** nom sing masc part pres mid

1 **And, being assembled together with them,** . . . . **Acts 1:4**

Classical Greek

Sunalizō is a difficult compound to interpret, having no clear references in the papyri or Septuagint (*Moulton-Milligan*). The term does occur in classical literature, but the root (spelled *halizō*) form represents two different words: one means "to assemble" and the other (see 231), "to salt." To further complicate the matter, several ancient manuscripts and versions consider *sunalizō* to be a variant spelling for *sunaulizō*, "to have dealings with, congregate, spend the night with" (Metzger, *Textual Commentary*, p.278).

New Testament Usage

The difficulty rests on the interpretation of Acts 1:4: "And, being assembled together with them." Simple as it looks, rendering *sunalizō* "assembled together" in this verse creates certain problems. For example, it is difficult for one person to *assemble* (*sunalizomenos*, present middle participle masculine singular). The translators of the KJV realized this dilemma when they added the marginal note "eating together with them." This early marginal reading may prove to be a good interpretation of this text, since Luke does record that the Lord ate with His disciples after the Resurrection (Luke 24:42,43; Acts 10:41). The NIV reading "while he was eating with them" follows this understanding as well. A few manuscripts and quotations by early church fathers show *sunaulizō* as a variant in verse 4. The RSV seems to follow this reading: "while staying with them . . . " (see Hillyer, "Salt," *Colin Brown*, 3:449). Though Christ's resurrection body had no need of nourishment, this idea would only have been considered heretical to the Gnostics and those who denied a genuine, physical resurrection of the body (see Bruce, *New International Commentary on the New Testament, Acts*, pp.30,36).

Strong 4871, Bauer 783-84, Moulton-Milligan 601-2 (see "sunalizomai"), Liddell-Scott 1694, Colin Brown 3:443,449.

4722B. συναλλάσσω sunallassō verb

Reconcile someone.

Cross-Reference:

ἀλλάσσω allassō (234)

1. συνήλλασσεν sunēllassen 3sing indic imperf act

1 and he tried to reconcile them in peace, (NASB).... Acts 7:26

A compound verb of the preposition *sun* (4713), "together," and the verb *allassō* (234), "change, exchange," *sunallassō* fundamentally denotes a change in disposition by bringing together, hence "to reconcile someone." In the classical Greek period *sunallassō* occurs as early as in Aeschylus and Thucydides (Fifth Century B.C.) with the same meaning. In the Biblical literature this verb occurs only in Acts 7:26 where it describes the action attempted by Moses who tried to reconcile two Hebrew men at odds with one another.

Bauer 784, Moulton-Milligan 602, Liddell-Scott 1694.

4723. συναναβαίνω sunanabainō verb

To ascend with, to go up with.

Cross-Reference:

ὑπερβαίνω huperbainō (5070)

עָלָה 'ālâh (6148), Go up (Gn 50:7,9, Nm 13:31 [13:32], 2 Chr 18:2).

1. συναναβᾶσιν sunanabasin dat pl masc part aor act

2. συναναβᾶσαι sunanabasai nom pl fem part aor act

2 and many other women which came up with him ... Mark 15:41
1 of them which came up with him from Galilee ...... Acts 13:31

Classical Greek and Septuagint Usage

This word can be found in classical Greek since the Fifth Century B.C. and means "go up with or together" (*Liddell-Scott*). It often refers to people moving upward in both classical Greek and the Septuagint. Herodotus used it frequently of "going into" the mountainous region of central Asia (ibid.). It is used in the Septuagint frequently of how the Israelites "went up" to Canaan from Egypt (Genesis 50:7,9; Exodus 12:38).

New Testament Usage

The two New Testament occurrences of *sunanabainō* are in Mark 15:41 and Acts 13:31. In the first reference, the women present at the crucifixion of Jesus (Mary Magdalene, Mary the mother of James and Joses, and Salome) came up with (*sunanabasai*) Jesus to Jerusalem from Galilee. These faithful women "were last at the Cross as they stood afar and saw the dreadful end to all their hopes" (Robertson, *Word Pictures in the New Testament*, 1:397).

Paul in his sermon at Antioch of Syria (Acts 13) proclaimed that the risen Christ "was seen many days of them which came up with (*sunanabasin*) him from Galilee to Jerusalem" (13:31). The persons who were closest to Him during His ministry, who could not be easily deceived about the authenticity of His resurrection, saw Him in His resurrected form and were "witnesses unto the people" (13:31).

Strong 4872, Bauer 784, Moulton-Milligan 602, Liddell-Scott 1695.

4724. συνανάκειμαι sunanakeimai verb

Recline together (at table), eat with.

Cross-Reference:

κεῖμαι keimai (2719)

1. συνανακείμενοι sunanakeimenoi nom pl masc part pres mid

2. συνανακειμένων sunanakeimenōn gen pl masc part pres mid

3. συνανακειμένοις sunanakeimenois dat pl masc part pres mid

4. συνανακειμένους sunanakeimenous acc pl masc part pres mid

5. συνανέκειντο sunanekeinto 3pl indic imperf mid

5 came and sat down with him and his disciples........ Matt 9:10
4 and them which sat with him at meat,................. 14:9
5 publicans and sinners sat also together with Jesus ... Mark 2:15
3 and pleased Herod and them that sat with him,......... 6:22
4 oath's sake, and for their sakes which sat with him,..... 6:26
1 And they that sat at meat with him began to say .... Luke 7:49
2 in the presence of them that sit at meat with thee...... 14:10
2 And when one of them that sat at meat with him 14:15
2 Lazarus ... of them that sat at the table with him... John 12:2

Septuagint Usage

Sunanakeimai appears in the New Testament several times, but there are no references to the word in classical Greek, the papyri, or the Apostolic Fathers. The Septuagint offers one illustration of the word: "But the officials who were at table with (the king) . . . " (3 Maccabees 5:39). The late date of 3 Maccabees (First Century B.C.) presents a close parallel to New Testament language where the word occurs nine times (Mark 6:26; John 12:2, Received text only).

New Testament Usage

Sunanakeimai appears in John 12:2 as a textual variant to *anakeimai* (343). The reading which appears in the Received text of John does not occur in the majority of Greek manuscripts (Hodges and Farstad, *The Greek New Testament According to the Majority Text*, p.337). In parallel accounts of the supper at the house of Simon the leper two cognates appear: *anakeimai* (Matthew 26:7) and *katakeimai* (2591) (Mark 14:3). Aside from this variant *sunanakeimai* never appears in the Gospel of John. Either reading would carry the same meaning, and substitution between the three cognates is common in the Synoptics.

Two references to *sunanakeimai* in the Gospels relate to the story of Herod and John the Baptist. Herod did not want to behead John, but pressure from "them which sat with him at meat" compelled the evil act (Matthew 14:9; Mark 6:22,26—verse 26 is a Received text reading for *anakeimai*).

In the remaining Synoptic occurrences of *sunanakeimai* Jesus used the term in an illustration that taught a lesson with the meal, both in word and deed. Jesus had a varied audience at each session: Pharisees, publicans, sinners, women, and disciples (Matthew 9:10; Mark 2:15; Luke 7:49; 14:10,15). The lesson that Jesus taught was that all could come to Him for the necessities of life. To the Jew, *sunanakeimai* was only with peers; to Jesus, *sunanakeimai* was whosoever will. Jesus also taught a spiritual etiquette: humility, true honor, and genuine value.

STRONG 4873, BAUER 784, KITTEL 3:654-55, LIDDELL-SCOTT 1695.

4725. συναναμίγνυμι

sunanamignumi verb

Mix together, associate with, keep company with.

CROSS-REFERENCE:

μίγνυμι mignumi (3260)

בָּלַל bālal (1140), Mix, moisten, confuse; hithpolel: mix oneself among others (Hos 7:8—Codex Alexandrinus only).

1. συναναμίγνυσθαι sunanamignusthai inf pres mid

2. συναναμίγνυσθε sunanamignusthe 2pl indic/impr pres mid

1 wrote unto you ... not to company with fornicators: . . 1 Co 5:9
1 now I have written unto you not to keep company, ... 5:11
2 note that man, and have no company with him, ... 2 Th 3:14

Classical Greek and Septuagint Usage

This word, also spelled *sunanameignumi*, can be found in classical Greek meaning "mix up together," usually in reference to people (cf. *Liddell-Scott*). It is used twice in the Septuagint (Ezekiel 20:18; Hosea 7:8) in warnings given to the Israelites against intermingling with people or practices that would destroy the purity and devotion of God's people.

New Testament Usage

This word is used three times in the New Testament (always with a prohibition): 1 Corinthians 5:9,11 and 2 Thessalonians 3:14. The Corinthians were admonished not to mingle or keep company with immoral persons claiming to be believers. The Thessalonians were advised not to associate with a professing brother who did not obey the divine truth Paul wrote to them. Christians were thus to keep the church pure and undefiled. Association with professed unbelievers was appropriate, however (1 Corinthians 5:10), in order to bring sinners to Christ.

STRONG 4874, BAUER 784 (see "sunanameignumi"), MOULTON-MILLIGAN 602, KITTEL 7:852-55 (see "sunanameignumi"), LIDDELL-SCOTT 1695 (see "sunanameignumi").

4726. συναναπαύομαι

sunanapauomai verb

To refresh, rest together with.

CROSS-REFERENCE:

ἀναπαύω anapauō (372)

רָבַץ rāvats (7547), Lie down (Is 11:6).

1. συναναπαύσωμαι sunanapausōmai 1sing subj aor mid

1 by the will of God, and may with you be refreshed. Rom 15:32

The prefix *sun* (4713), "with," adds to the primary definition of *anapauō* (372), "rest, refresh," the idea of finding rest or repose "in the company of" or "with" others. Thus, in the single use of this word in the New Testament (Romans 15:32), the apostle Paul appealed to his Christian brothers at Rome to pray for him so he might someday meet with them and be refreshed in spirit by their company.

STRONG 4875, BAUER 784, MOULTON-MILLIGAN 602, LIDDELL-SCOTT 1695.

4727. συναντάω sunantaō verb

To meet with; happen.

COGNATE:
καταντάω katantaō (2628)
SYNONYMS:
ἀπαντάω apantaō (524)
συμβαίνω sumbainō (4670)
ὑπαντάω hupantaō (5059)

בּוֹא bô' (971), Come (Jb 30:26).

מָצָא mātsâ' (4834), Find (Prv 17:20).

נָגַע nāgha' (5236), Come (Jgs 20:41).

נָשַׂג nāsagh (5560), Hiphil: reach (Jb 41:26 [41:17]).

פָּגַע pāgha' (6534), Meet, find (Ex 5:20, Nm 35:19, Jos 2:16).

פָּגַשׁ pāghash (6539), Qal: meet (Gn 32:17, Ex 4:24, Is 34:14); niphal: meet (Ps 85:10 [84:10]); piel: meet (Jb 5:14).

קָבַץ qāvats (7192), Gather; niphal: be gathered (Is 34:15).

קָדַם qādham (7207), Piel: meet (Dt 23:4, Neh 13:2, Is 21:14).

קָרָא qārâ' (7410), Call; qal: meet, come (Ex 7:15, Jos 11:20, Prv 7:10); niphal: come to by chance, happen to meet (Dt 22:6, 2 Sm 18:9).

קָרָה qārâh (7424), Qal: happen (Eccl 2:14, 9:11): niphal: meet (Nm 23:16).

1. συνήντησεν sunēntēsen 3sing indic aor act
2. συναντήσας sunantēsas nom sing masc part aor act
3. συναντήσει sunantēsei 3sing indic fut act
4. συναντήσοντα sunantēsonta nom/acc pl neu part fut act

1 come down from the hill, much people met him..... Luke 9:37
3 there shall a man meet you, bearing a pitcher......... 22:10
2 And as Peter was coming in, Cornelius met him,... Acts 10:25
4 not knowing the things that shall befall me there:...... 20:22
2 priest of the most high God, who met Abraham..... Heb 7:1
1 loins of his father, when Melchisedec met him.......... 7:10

Classical Greek and Septuagint Usage

This verb can be found in classical Greek from the Eighth Century B.C. and means "meet with, encounter, happen to" (cf. *Liddell-Scott*). Occasionally it is used of something that would "befall" or "happen to" a person (ibid.), but usually it refers to two or more people "meeting face-to-face." This latter usage is most common in the Septuagint (e.g., Genesis 32:1,2; Ecclesiastes 2:14). There is at least one figurative use where "mercy and truth are *met* together" (Psalm 85:10 [LXX 84:10]).

New Testament Usage

Sunantaō is used in the New Testament six times (four by Luke and two by the writer of Hebrews). Coming down from the Mount of Transfiguration, Jesus was *met* (*sunēntēsen*) by a great crowd (Luke 9:37). In Luke 22:10 Jesus gave instructions to the disciples about preparing the Passover meal, "A man (shall) *meet* (*sunantēsei*) you, bearing a pitcher of water." According to Luke's account in Acts, Peter was *met* (*sunantēsas*) by Cornelius (10:25). In Hebrews 7:1 and 10 reference is made to the Old Testament incident when Melchizedek *met* Abraham returning from his defeat of the alliance of Canaanite kings.

The single figurative use of *sunantaō* is in Acts 20:22 where Paul announced that he was going to Jerusalem, compelled by the Spirit, not knowing what would *happen to* or *befall* him there (or what he would meet).

STRONG 4876, BAUER 784, MOULTON-MILLIGAN 602, LIDDELL-SCOTT 1696.

4728. συνάντησις sunantēsis noun

A meeting.

COGNATE:
καταντάω katantaō (2628)
SYNONYM:
ἀπάντησις apantēsis (525)

אֲגֻדָּה 'ăghuddāh (89), Troop (2 Sm 2:25).

קָרָא qārâ' (7410), Call; meet (Gn 24:17, 2 Kgs 1:6f., Is 7:3).

1. συνάντησιν sunantēsin acc sing fem

1 behold, the whole city came out to meet Jesus:...... Matt 8:34

This word, related to *sunantaō* (4727), "to meet," appears only once in the New Testament in Matthew 8:34 (*Textus Receptus*). After Jesus had healed the demon-possessed man of Gadara and allowed the demons to enter a herd of swine, the whole city came out to meet (literally, to a meeting with) Jesus, pleading with Him to depart from their country.

STRONG 4877, BAUER 784, MOULTON-MILLIGAN 602, LIDDELL-SCOTT 1696.

4729. συναντιλαμβάνομαι sunantilambanomai verb

Help, assist, take hold of together, help in obtaining.

COGNATE:
λαμβάνω lambanō (2956)
SYNONYMS:
ἀμύνομαι amunomai (290)
ἀντέχομαι antechomai (469)
ἀντιλαμβάνομαι antilambanomai (479)
βοηθέω boētheō (990)
ἐλεέω eleeō (1640)
παραγίνομαι paraginomai (3716)
συλλαμβάνω sullambanō (4666)

συμβάλλω sumballō (4671)
συμφέρω sumpherō (4702)
ὠφελέω ōpheleō (5456)

כּוּן kûn (3679), Niphal: be established (Ps 89:21 [88:21]).

נָשָׂא nāsâ' (5558), Bear (Nm 11:17).

1. **συναντιλαμβάνεται** **sunantilambanetai** 3sing indic pres mid

2. **συναντιλάβηται** **sunantilabētai** 3sing subj aor mid

2 to serve alone? bid her therefore that she **help** me. Luke 10:40
1 Likewise the Spirit also **helpeth** our infirmities:...... Rom 8:26

Classical Greek

This word can be found in classical Greek from the Third Century B.C. meaning "help in gaining, help in supporting" (cf. *Liddell-Scott*). Usually it is used of people who "render assistance" to others.

Septuagint Usage

Sunantilambanomai occurs four times in the Septuagint. Moses was encouraged by his father-in-law Jethro (Exodus 18:22) to let others judge in smaller matters and thus bear the burden (Hebrew, *nāsâ'*) with Moses. The same Hebrew word is used in Numbers 11:17 where God told Moses that 70 elders with the spirit of Moses upon them would "bear the burden" with him. (Cf. Psalm 89:21 [LXX 88:21].)

New Testament Usage

Various scholars provide picturesque definitions for this word which is used only two times in the New Testament. *Moulton-Milligan* identifies its meaning as "lend a hand along with." In Luke 10:40 Martha pleaded with Jesus, "Dost thou not care that my sister hath left me to serve alone? bid her therefore that she *help* (*sunantilambanomai*) me."

The use of *sunantilambanomai* is especially noteworthy in Romans 8:26. The indwelling Holy Spirit *helps* (*sunantilambanomai*) the believer's infirmities when it comes to prayer: "For we know not what we should pray for as we ought." The Spirit helps; He takes the believer's uncertainty in His hand along with the unarticulated prayer burden of the believer and makes intercession for him.

STRONG 4878, BAUER 784, MOULTON-MILLIGAN 602, KITTEL 1:375-76, LIDDELL-SCOTT 1696.

4730. συναπάγω sunapagō verb

To lead or carry away with another.

CROSS-REFERENCE:

ἄγω agō (70)

לָקַח lāqach (4089), Take (Ex 14:6).

1. **συναπαγόμενοι** **sunapagomenoi** nom pl masc part pres mid

2. **συναπήχθη** **sunapēchthē** 3sing indic aor pass

3. **συναπαχθέντες** **sunapachthentes** nom pl masc part aor pass

1 but **condescend** to men of low estate............... Rom 12:16
2 insomuch that Barnabas also **was carried away**........ Gal 2:13
3 **being led away** with the error of the wicked,......... 2 Pt 3:17

Classical Greek and Septuagint Usage

This word can be found in classical Greek from the Fourth Century B.C. meaning "lead away with or together" (cf. *Liddell-Scott*). In the papyri it can be found in reference to one who has been "arrested with" another (*Moulton-Milligan*). Its use in the Septuagint is limited. When the Israelites were finally allowed to leave Egypt after the 10th plague, Pharaoh again hardened his heart, prepared his chariot for pursuit, and *took* his army *with him* (Exodus 14:6).

New Testament Usage

Sunapagō is a compound of *sun* (4713), "with," and *apagō* (516), "to lead away" (compound also of *apo* [570], "from," and *agō* [70], "to lead"). The word is used figuratively and as a passive participle in the three New Testament references. The context in which the word is used, both in sacred and secular literature, sometimes makes "to be carried" a preferred translation over "to be led."

The occurrences of *sunapagō* in Galatians 2:13 and 2 Peter 3:17 convey a negative meaning. In defending his apostleship to the Galatians, Paul described how some Jews who advocated circumcision had influenced other apostles "insomuch that Barnabas also was *carried away* with their dissimulation" (Galatians 2:13). As Peter concluded his second epistle, he warned his readers, "Beware lest ye also, *being led away* with the error of the wicked, fall from your own steadfastness" (2 Peter 3:17). The Christian must always be alert against being misled or led astray, accepting the false or tainted rather than the true and pure.

The use of *sunapagō* in Romans 12:16 is particularly noteworthy. The form of the word can be translated as referring either to things or persons (*Bauer*). Note the marginal rendering in many versions. Paul told the Romans not to set their minds on exalted things but to "condescend" (KJV), "associate with" (Moffat), or "accommodate to" (Weymouth) the lowly things, ways, or people. The thrust of the word, however it is translated, is that the believer should be "led along with" the humble rather than the proud or the lofty.

STRONG 4879, BAUER 784, MOULTON-MILLIGAN 602-3, LIDDELL-SCOTT 1696.

4731. συναποθνῄσκω

sunapothnēskō verb

Die together with.

CROSS-REFERENCE:

θανατόω thanatoō (2266)

1. συναπεθάνομεν **sunapethanomen** 1pl indic aor act

2. συναποθανεῖν **sunapothanein** inf aor act

2 If I should die with thee, I will not deny thee ..... Mark 14:31
2 that ye are in our hearts to die and live with you.... 2 Co 7:3
1 For if we be dead with him, we shall also live .... 2 Tm 2:11

Classical Greek

This word is composed of several elements: *sun* (4713), "with"; *apo* (570), "off" or "out"; *thnēskō* (2325), "to die." It means "to die together with someone." Herodotus (Fifth Century B.C.) and Diodorus Siculus (First Century B.C.) both used the word to speak of the burning of widows in India with their deceased husbands (*Bauer*).

New Testament Usage

In two of the three New Testament references using the word the meaning is physical death. Peter vehemently declared that he would *die with* (*sunapothnēskō*) Jesus rather than deny Him (Mark 14:31). Paul declared in 2 Corinthians 7:3 that he had such great love for the Corinthians that he would *die with* (*sunapothnēskō*) them if necessary. The third usage of the word speaks of the believer's spiritual identification with Christ's death (2 Timothy 2:11).

STRONG 4880, BAUER 784-85, MOULTON-MILLIGAN 603, KITTEL 3:7-21; 7:766-97, LIDDELL-SCOTT 1697, COLIN BROWN 1:430-31,435.

4732. συναπόλλυμι sunapollumi verb

Destroy with, perish together with.

CROSS-REFERENCE:

ἀπόλλυμι apollumi (616)

אָסַף 'āsaph (636), Take away (Ps 26:9 [25:9]).

סָפָה sāphāh (5793), Qal: sweep away, bring disaster on something (Gn 18:23, Dt 29:19); niphal: be swept away, be destroyed (Gn 19:15, Nm 16:26).

קְטַל qᵉṭal (A7273), Kill; hithpeel: be killed (Dn 2:13—Aramaic).

1. συναπώλετο **sunapōleto** 3sing indic aor mid

1 Rahab perished not with them that believed not, ... Heb 11:31

The root of this word, *apollumi* (616), means "to perish" or "be destroyed." *Sunapollumi* means "to be destroyed with." The single occurrence of the word in the New Testament is in Hebrews 11:31 which says that the faith of Rahab the harlot preserved her from *perishing with* (*sunapollumi*) her unbelieving Jericho compatriots.

STRONG 4881, BAUER 785, MOULTON-MILLIGAN 603, LIDDELL-SCOTT 1697.

4733. συναποστέλλω

sunapostellō verb

Send with.

COGNATE:

ἀποστέλλω apostellō (643)

SYNONYM:

συμπέμπω sumpempō (4693)

שָׁלַח shālach (8365), Send (Ex 33:2,12).

1. συναπέστειλα **sunapesteila** 1sing indic aor act

1 I desired Titus, and with him I sent a brother...... 2 Co 12:18

Apostellō (643) means "to send" or "send out"; *sunapostellō* means "to send in company with someone." The single use of *sunapostellō* in the New Testament is 2 Corinthians 12:18. Paul, claiming that he had never taken any advantage of the Corinthians, told how he had *sent with* (*sunapostellō*) Titus another brother; he then asked the Corinthians, "Titus did not take any advantage of you (either), did he?" (NASB).

STRONG 4882, BAUER 785, MOULTON-MILLIGAN 603, LIDDELL-SCOTT 1697.

4734. συναρμολογέω

sunarmologeō verb

Fit closely, join together.

CROSS-REFERENCE:

λέγω legō (2978)

1. συναρμολογουμένη **sunarmologoumenē** nom sing fem part pres mid

2. συναρμολογούμενον **sunarmologoumenon** nom/acc sing neu part pres mid

1 In whom all the building fitly framed together .... Eph 2:21
2 From whom the whole body fitly joined together 4:16

This word has only been found in Christian literature (*Bauer*) in the passive voice meaning "to be fitted or framed together" (*Liddell-Scott*). It occurs in Ephesians 2:21 as an architectural metaphor of the Church (Robertson, *Word Pictures in the New Testament*, 4:529); in Christ, the chief cornerstone (literally, "head of the corner"), the entire structure is *joined together* (*sunarmologeō*). In Ephesians 4:16 the metaphor is that of a living organism; believers are members of the body (of which Christ is the head) *joined and knit together* (*sunarmologeō*).

STRONG 4883, BAUER 785, MOULTON-MILLIGAN 603, KITTEL 7:855-56, LIDDELL-SCOTT 1699.

4734B. συναρπάζω sunarpazō verb

Seize violently.

CROSS-REFERENCE:
ἁρπάζω harpazō (720)

SYNONYMS:
ἁρπάζω harpazō (720)
δράσσομαι drassomai (1399)
ἐπιλαμβάνομαι epilambanomai (1934)
ἔχω echō (2174)
καταλαμβάνω katalambanō (2608)
κρατέω krateō (2875)
λαμβάνω lambanō (2956)
παραφέρω parapherō (3772)
πιάζω piazō (3945)
συλλαμβάνω sullambanō (4666)

לָקַח lāqach (4089), Catch (Prv 6:25).

1. συνήρπασαν sunērpasan 3pl indic aor act
2. συναρπάσαντες sunarpasantes nom pl masc part aor act
3. συνηρπάκει sunērpakei 3sing indic plperf act
4. συναρπασθέντος sunarpasthentos gen sing neu part aor pass

3 For oftentimes it **had caught** him: .... Luke 8:29
1 the scribes, and came upon him, and **caught** him, ... Acts 6:12
2 and **having caught** Gaius and Aristarchus, ... 19:29
4 And when the ship **was caught**, ... 27:15

With the intensive prefix *sun* (4713), this word means "seize and keep a firm hold of" (*Moulton-Milligan*). Thus the KJV translation of "catch" in all four occurrences in the New Testament lacks the force portrayed in the original. An unclean spirit (Luke 8:29) *seized* (*sunarpazō*) the Gadarene man so violently that he broke the chains and fetters used to bind him. Stephen's opponents *seized* him (rather than caught him) and took him before the council (Acts 6:12). The rioting crowd in Ephesus *seized* Paul's companions and rushed them to the town theater (Acts 19:29). The ship carrying Paul to Rome was *seized* by a tempestuous wind and carried by the storm (Acts 27:15).

STRONG 4884, BAUER 785, MOULTON-MILLIGAN 603, LIDDELL-SCOTT 1699.

4735. συναυξάνω sunauxanō verb

To increase along with, grow together with.

CROSS-REFERENCE:
αὐξάνω auxanō (831)

1. συναυξάνεσθαι sunauxanesthai inf pres mid

1 Let both **grow together** until the harvest: .... Matt 13:30

This verb can be found in classical Greek from the Fourth Century B.C. and in the Septuagint meaning "increase along with or together." It can be found in reference to the "increasing" of size in both animate and inanimate things (cf. *Liddell-Scott*). The single New Testament usage of *sunauxanō* is in Matthew 13:30. In the Parable of the Wheat and the Tares the householder tells his servants to let the enemy's tares and the good wheat "grow together" or "side by side" (*sunauxanō*) until the harvest.

STRONG 4885, BAUER 785, MOULTON-MILLIGAN 603, LIDDELL-SCOTT 1700.

4736. σύνδεσμος sundesmos noun

Bond, fetter fastening; that which binds together.

CROSS-REFERENCE:
δεσμεύω desmeuō (1189)

בַּיִת bayith (1041), House (1 Kgs 6:10).
חַרְצֹב chartsōv (2890), Bond (Is 58:6).
מוֹטָה môṭāh (4269), Yoke (Is 58:9).
סָגַר sāghar (5646), Be shut (Jb 41:15 [41:6]).
קֶשֶׁר qesher (7490), Treason, conspiracy (2 Kgs 11:14, Jer 11:9).

1. σύνδεσμος sundesmos nom sing masc
2. συνδέσμῳ sundesmō dat sing masc
3. σύνδεσμον sundesmon acc sing masc
4. συνδέσμων sundesmōn gen pl masc

3 the gall of bitterness, and in the **bond** of iniquity..... Acts 8:23
2 to keep the unity of the Spirit in the **bond** of peace. Eph 4:3
4 from which all the body by joints and **bands** .... Col 2:19
1 put on charity, which is the **bond** of perfectness......... 3:14

Classical Greek and Septuagint Usage

This word is a compound of *sun* (4713), "with," and *desmos* (1193), "band" or "fetter." *Sundesmos* denotes the link or the fastening that binds two elements together (*Bauer*). One use of the term in secular literature identifies a grammatical conjunction (Aristotle, Fourth Century B.C.). It was used in a literal sense by Euripides (Fifth Century B.C.) to refer to the sinews of the body. It was used by Appianus (Second Century A.D.) to name the fastenings that hold a ship together. Others used it in connection with garments and the chains of the prisons.

The word was used figuratively by Plato (Fourth Century B.C.) when he called good men "the bond that keeps the state together" (*Liddell-Scott*). It is found in the phrase "the bond of peace" in Plutarch (First and Second Centuries A.D.). *Sundesmos* appears only eight times in the Septuagint translating six different Hebrew terms, the most frequent of which is *qesher*, "bind together." In 2 Kings 12:20 (LXX 4 Kings 12:20) the servants of Joash "*made a conspiracy* and slew Joash in the house of Millo."

New Testament Usage

Sundesmos is used in the New Testament as (1) a bond which holds things together in a positive sense and (2) a bond or fetter that hinders. The use in Colossians 2:19 is positive: Christ is the Head of the whole Body which in turn is supported and held together by spiritual ligaments and "bands" (*sundesmos*) connecting it with the Head.

Predating Plutarch's figurative use of the word in the phrase "bond of peace" is the description of Ephesians 4:3. Believers must endeavor "to keep the unity of the Spirit in the *bond* (*sundesmos*) of peace." Peace with other members of the Body is the bond that produces unity. Another figurative use of the word is found in Colossians 3:14. Love is the *bond* (*sundesmos*) that unites all the previously mentioned Christian virtues: compassion, kindness, humility, gentleness, patience, and forgiveness (verses 12-14).

The use of *sundesmos* in Acts 8:23 differs from the other three uses in the New Testament. Peter described the spiritual condition of Simon the sorcerer as a man who was "in the gall of bitterness, and in the bond (*sundesmos*) of iniquity (sin)." Some bonds prevent and hinder people from meeting God. Other bonds unite the body of Christ and are a joy (Richards, *Expository Dictionary of Bible Words*, "Bond").

Strong 4886, Bauer 785, Moulton-Milligan 604, Kittel 7:856-59, Liddell-Scott 1701, Colin Brown 3:591-92.

4737. συνδέω sundeō verb

Bind or tie together.

Cross-Reference:
δέω deō (1204)

דָּבַק dāvaq (1740), Cling, stick; hiphil: cause to stick (Ez 3:26).

פָּנָה pānâh (6680), Hiphil: turn (Jgs 15:4—Codex Alexandrinus only).

קָשַׁר qāshar (7489), Bind; niphal: be knit (1 Sm 18:1—Codex Alexandrinus only).

קָשַׁשׁ qāshash (7492), Gather (Zep 2:1).

שָׁבַץ shāvats (8129), Pual: be set (Ex 28:20).

מִשְׁבְּצוֹת mishbᵉtsôth (5051), Filigree setting (Ex 39:13 [36:20]).

תָּקַע tāqaʿ (8965), Thrust, strike hands; be a guarantor (Jb 17:3).

1. συνδεδεμένοι sundedemenoi
nom pl masc part perf mid

1 them that are in bonds, as **bound with them**; .... Heb 13:3

This word can be found in Homer (ca. Seventh Century B.C.), in papyri, and nine times in the Septuagint (*Moulton-Milligan*) with the varied meanings of the tying of two or more things, the binding of a wound, uniting together, and the forming of a union (*Liddell-Scott*). The prefix *sun* (4713), "with, together," intensifies the root *deō* (1204), "to bind." It appears only once in the New Testament: Hebrews 13:3. The writer urged the Jewish Christians to whom Hebrews was addressed to show brotherly love to strangers and those in prison, as though they were imprisoned and chained together with them (*sundeō*). According to Vincent, public intercession for prisoners has been a part of Christian church services since New Testament times (*Word Studies of the New Testament*, 4:561).

Strong 4887, Bauer 785, Moulton-Milligan 604, Liddell-Scott 1701.

4738. συνδοξάζω sundoxazō verb

Be glorified with, share glory with.

Cross-Reference:
δοξάζω doxazō (1386)

1. συνδοξασθῶμεν sundoxasthōmen
1pl subj aor pass

1 that we **may be also glorified together**. .... Rom 8:17

Classical Greek

In classical Greek literature, *sundoxazō* means "to join in approving" (Aristotle—Fourth Century B.C.), "to agree with" (Porphyry in Stobaeus—Third and Fifth Centuries A.D.), and "to join with others in praising something" (Ignatius to the Smyrnaeans—First Century A.D.) (see *Liddell-Scott*; *Bauer*).

New Testament Usage

The single use of the word in the New Testament (Romans 8:17), though developing from the secular use, is distinct. The children of God suffer with Christ so that they may also be glorified with Him (*sundaxazō*). In this one verse the writer used a compound of *sun* (4713) three times. As children of God, believers are joint heirs with Christ (*sunklēronomoi Christou*), provided they suffer with Christ (*sunpaschōmen*), so that they may be glorified with Him (*sundoxasthōmen*). The intensive use of *sun*, which describes the union of the believer as coheir with Christ and as glorified with Him through suffering, demonstrates emphatically the high privilege of a Christian.

Strong 4888, Bauer 785, Kittel 2:253-54; 7:766-97, Liddell-Scott 1703, Colin Brown 2:44.

4739. σύνδουλος sundoulos noun

A fellow slave, fellow servant.

Cross-Reference:
δουλόω douloō (1396)

כְּנָת kenāth (A3800), Colleague, associate (Ezr 4:7, 5:3, 6:6—Aramaic).

1. σύνδουλος sundoulos nom sing masc
2. συνδούλου sundoulou gen sing masc
3. σύνδουλον sundoulon acc sing masc
4. σύνδουλοι sundouloi nom pl masc
5. συνδούλων sundoulōn gen pl masc
6. συνδούλους sundoulous acc pl masc

5 went out, and found one of his **fellow servants,** .....Matt 18:28
1 And his **fellow servant** fell down at his feet, ... 18:29
4 So when his **fellow servants** saw what was done, ... 18:31
3 also have had compassion on thy **fellow servant,** 18:33
6 And shall begin to smite his **fellow servants,** 24:49
2 also learned of Epaphras our dear **fellow servant,** ..... Col 1:7
1 a faithful minister and **fellow servant** in the Lord: 4:7
4 until their **fellow servants** also and their brethren, ... Rev 6:11
1 See thou do it not: I am thy **fellow servant,** 19:10
1 See thou do it not: for I am thy **fellow servant,** 22:9

Classical Greek and Septuagint Usage

The root of this word, *doulos* (1395), is the most common word for "servant" or "slave." The prefix *sun* (4713), "with," adds the idea of being a slave together with others. Because *doulos* places stress on subjection and service that is not a matter of choice (cf. *Bauer*), *sundoulos* may be better understood as "fellow *slave*" rather than "fellow *servant*."

Sundoulos can be found in classical Greek from the Eighth Century B.C. as "fellow slave." Some early writers distinguish *sundoulos*, "slave of the same master," from *homodoulos*, "companion in slavery" (*Liddell-Scott*). The word appears eight times in the Septuagint, all in the Book of Ezra (LXX 2 Esdras) where it is translated "companions" (KJV) or "associates" (NIV).

New Testament Usage

The occurrence of the term in Matthew 24:49 illustrates the literal use of the word. As Jesus taught the disciples about the coming of the Son of Man, He referred to an evil servant who, believing his lord was delaying his coming, began to carouse and beat his "fellow servants" (*sundoulous*). A similar literal usage of the word is found in Matthew 18:28-31,33.

The figurative use of the word is seen in Colossians 1:7 and 4:7. Paul described Epaphras (1:7) and Tychicus (4:7) as *fellow servants* (*sundoulos*) because they were servants of Jesus Christ commissioned by Him to serve the Church.

The word is also used figuratively to emphasize that angels as well as humans are fellow servants of the same Lord. As John the Revelator is told by the angel what he should write about the Marriage Supper of the Lamb, the disciple is overwhelmed and falls at the feet of the angel to worship (Revelation 19:10). "Do not do it!" the angel says. "I am a *fellow servant* (*sundoulos*) with you and with your brothers who hold to the testimony of Jesus. Worship God!" (NIV). A similar scene is recorded in Revelation 22:9.

Strong 4889, Bauer 785, Moulton-Milligan 604, Kittel 2:261, Liddell-Scott 1703, Colin Brown 1:257; 3:596.

4740. συνδρομή sundromē noun

Running together, a tumultuous gathering together.

Cross-Reference:
δρόμος dromos (1402)

1. συνδρομή sundromē nom sing fem

1 and the people **ran together:** and they took Paul, ... Acts 21:30

Classical Greek and Septuagint Usage

Sundromē can be found in classical Greek from the Fourth Century B.C. in reference to a "tumultuous concourse" of people (cf. *Liddell-Scott*). It can also be found in the apocryphal books of the Septuagint with the same meaning (e.g., Judith 10:18). In other Greek writings *sundromē* means "tumultuously," and specifically it refers to a "determination" of blood, "concurrence" of symptoms, or even a "provisional concession" of an adversary's position (ibid.).

New Testament Usage

The word *sundromē* occurs once in the New Testament, in Acts 21:30. During Paul's last visit to Jerusalem, after he had been warned by Agabus and many believers about impending danger and difficulty, Asian Jews stirred up a great opposition against Paul. They ignited the fury of the crowd by charging Paul with bringing Greeks into the temple and defiling the Holy Place. The entire city was aroused and the people ran together (literally, "there was a running together" or rushing [*sundromē*] of the people), seized Paul, dragged him out of the temple, and tried to kill him.

STRONG 4890, BAUER 785, MOULTON-MILLIGAN 604, LIDDELL-SCOTT 1703.

4741. συνεγείρω sunegeirō verb

To rise or be raised up with another.

CROSS-REFERENCE:

ἐγείρω egeirō (1446)

עוּר 'āwar (5996), Be awake, rouse oneself; polel: arouse (Is 14:9).

עָזַב 'āzav (6013), Leave (Ex 23:5—only some Vaticanus texts).

1. συνήγειρεν sunēgeiren 3sing indic aor act
2. συνηγέρθητε sunēgerthēte 2pl indic aor pass

1 And hath raised us up together,...................... Eph 2:6
2 also ye are risen with him through the faith.......... Col 2:12
2 If ye then be risen with Christ,......................... 3:1

Septuagint Usage

This word is a late and rare verb, first found in the Septuagint (Exodus 23:5; Isaiah 14:9) and the intertestamental pseudepigraphic 4 Maccabees 2:14. The use of the Greek word in Isaiah 14:9 is typical of the meaning of the word prior to the New Testament usage. Isaiah's prophecy foretells a day when all the kings of the nations will be "raised up (together) from their thrones." In the First and Second Centuries A.D. *sunegeirō* was used by Plutarch with the meaning of "waking up together" (Robertson, *Word Pictures in the New Testament*, 4:492).

New Testament Usage

The use of the word in the New Testament is unique and does not carry a figurative meaning. In all three occurrences (Ephesians 2:6; Colossians 2:12; 3:1) the word refers to the believer's spiritual resurrection with Christ. The prefix *sun* (4713) is critical to the new purpose the word serves. The root *egeirō* (1446) means "to arise" and appears in classical literature as far back as Homer (Eighth Century B.C.). In the New Testament it is applied to the resurrection of Christ and human beings; it also has a metaphoric sense of the "lifting up" of a person in honor and position. But only in the three Pauline passages is the root joined with the prefix *sun* to describe the believer's participation in Christ's resurrection.

Ephesians 2:6 says that God has "raised us up together (*sunēgeiren*), and made us sit together in heavenly places in Christ Jesus." Colossians 2:12 uses the symbolism of water baptism in which the Colossians were "buried with him in baptism (and) . . . *risen with* him (*sunēgerthēte*) through the faith of the operation of God, who hath raised him from the dead." Growing out of that confession is the challenge given to every Christian at the beginning of the next chapter. "If ye then be *risen with* (*sunēgerthēte*) Christ, seek those things which are above, where Christ sitteth on the right hand of God" (Colossians 3:1). The word *sunegeirō* never carries such an eloquent meaning as when it describes the union of the believer with Christ in His resurrection.

STRONG 4891, BAUER 785-86, KITTEL 7:766,783, LIDDELL-SCOTT 1704, COLIN BROWN 1:643.

4742. συνέδριον sunedrion noun

The high council, the Sanhedrin.

SYNONYM:

συμβούλιον sumboulion (4675)

דִּין dîn (1835), Strife (Prv 22:10).

מַת math (5139), Men (Ps 26:4 [25:4]).

סוֹד ṣôdh (5660), Secret (Prv 11:13); counsel (Prv 15:22).

קָהָל qāhāl (7235), Assembly (Prv 26:26).

1. συνέδριον sunedrion nom/acc sing neu
2. συνεδρίου sunedriou gen sing neu
3. συνεδρίῳ sunedriō dat sing neu
4. συνέδρια sunedria nom/acc pl neu

3 say ... Raca, shall be in danger of the council:...... Matt 5:22
4 for they will deliver you up to the councils,........... 10:17
1 the chief priests, and elders, and all the council,....... 26:59
4 for they shall deliver you up to councils;.......... Mark 13:9
1 chief priests and all the council sought for witness..... 14:55
1 with the elders and scribes and the whole council,..... 15:1
1 came together, and led him into their council,..... Luke 22:66
1 gathered the ... priests and the Pharisees a council, John 11:47
2 commanded them to go aside out of the council,.... Acts 4:15
1 and called the council together,......................... 5:21
3 they set them before the council:...................... 5:27
3 Then stood there up one in the council, a Pharisee,..... 5:34
2 they departed from the presence of the council,......... 5:41
1 and caught him, and brought him to the council,......... 6:12
3 And all that sat in the council,........................ 6:15
1 commanded the chief priests and all their council...... 22:30
3 And Paul, earnestly beholding the council, said,....... 23:1
3 he cried out in the council, Men and brethren,........ 23:6
3 ye with the council signify to the chief captain......... 23:15
1 bring down Paul to morrow into the council,.......... 23:20
1 I brought him forth into their council:................ 23:28
2 while I stood before the council,...................... 24:20

Classical Greek and Septuagint Usage

Sunedrion is a compound formed from *sun* (4713), "together," and *hedra*, "a seat", and means "to sit together," that is, "to sit (with others) on a council." Initially the term referred to the place of meeting; later it described the assembly itself, the "council." In secular language *sunedrion* is used of a variety of official groups and councils including legislative bodies (Bertram, "sunedrion," *Kittel*, 7:861f.). The Septuagint records the term 12 times, but it carries no technical sense there.

Intertestamental Period

In the period prior to the birth of Christ *sunedrion* became a technical term for the "high court" of the Jews in Jerusalem. The Jews adopted the Greek into their own language (Hebrew/ Aramaic), calling the council the Sanhedrin (ibid.; 7:862-867).

Jews traced the origin of the council to the time of Moses (Numbers 11:16), when he, under the Lord's command, summoned 70 elders from the various tribes of Israel. These men were given some of God's Spirit that rested on Moses. From a historical standpoint the council can be traced to the time following the captivity in Babylon. During New Testament times the council consisted of 71 members of the priesthood and leading families in the land. Apparently the council itself determined who could belong. The highest official was the high priest. There were also some local councils throughout the Diaspora with 23 members, which were called *sunedrion*.

New Testament Usage

The Gospels reveal how the *sunedrion* tried to get rid of Jesus early in His ministry (John 11:47). Finally, with the help of Judas, they succeeded in having Him arrested, tried, and sentenced. However, since the Roman forces occupying Jerusalem did not allow the Jews to carry out the death penalty, Jesus had to be brought before the Roman governor, Pontius Pilate. Pilate, almost against his own will, sentenced Jesus to be crucified, the Roman death penalty.

The Sanhedrin continued to oppose the gospel even after Jesus rose from the dead. They persecuted the early disciples in Jerusalem (Acts 4:15f.; 6:12) as well as in other towns (Acts 9:1).

STRONG 4892, BAUER 786, MOULTON-MILLIGAN 604, KITTEL 7:860-71, LIDDELL-SCOTT 1704, COLIN BROWN 1:363.

4743. συνείδησις suneidēsis noun

Consciousness, conscience, scruples.

CROSS-REFERENCE:
εἶδον eidon (1481)

מַדָּע maddā' (4234I), Thoughts (Eccl 10:20).

1. **συνείδησις suneidēsis** nom sing fem
2. **συνειδήσεως suneidēseōs** gen sing fem
3. **συνειδήσει suneidēsei** dat sing fem
4. **συνείδησιν suneidēsin** acc sing fem
5. **συνειδήσεσιν suneidēsesin** dat pl fem

2 being convicted by their own **conscience**, ... John 8:9
3 I have lived in all good **conscience** before God ..... Acts 23:1
4 always a **conscience** void of offence toward God, ... 24:16
2 their **conscience** also bearing witness, ... Rom 2:15
2 I lie not, my **conscience** also bearing me witness 9:1
4 but also for **conscience** sake. 13:5
3 for some with **conscience** of the idol unto this hour . . 1 Co 8:7
1 and their **conscience** being weak is defiled. 8:7
1 shall not the **conscience** of him which is weak 8:10
4 wound their weak **conscience**, ye sin against Christ. 8:12
4 that eat, asking no question for **conscience** sake: 10:25
4 eat, asking no question for **conscience** sake. 10:27
4 his sake that showed it, and for **conscience** sake: 10:28
4 **Conscience**, I say, not thine own, but of the other: 10:29
2 is my liberty judged of another man's **conscience**? 10:29
2 rejoicing is this, the testimony of our **conscience**, ... 2 Co 1:12
4 commending ourselves to every man's **conscience** 4:2
5 I trust also are made manifest in your **consciences**. 5:11
2 and of a good **conscience**, and of faith unfeigned: ... 1 Tm 1:5
4 Holding faith, and a good **conscience**; 1:19
3 the mystery of the faith in a pure **conscience**. 3:9
4 having their **conscience** seared with a hot iron; 4:2
3 I serve from my forefathers with pure **conscience**, ... 2 Tm 1:3
1 but even their mind and **conscience** is defiled. .... Tit 1:15
4 the service perfect, as pertaining to the **conscience**; ... Heb 9:9
4 purge your **conscience** from dead works 9:14
4 should have had no more **conscience** of sins. 10:2
2 our hearts sprinkled from an evil **conscience**, ... 10:22
4 for we trust we have a good **conscience**, ... 13:18
4 if a man for **conscience** toward God endure grief, ... 1 Pt 2:19
4 Having a good **conscience**; 3:16
2 but the answer of a good **conscience** toward God, ... 3:21

Classical Greek

Formally a compound made up of *sun* (4713), "with, together," and *eidēsis*, "knowledge," *suneidēsis* (cf. the parent verb *sunoida* [4774]) means "knowledge, communication, information." Sometimes the term occurs in legal contexts of witnesses who share testimony. In a second, reflexive sense, *suneidēsis* signifies "consciousness" (in a neutral sense) and from that it means "inner consciousness," i.e., "conscience." "Conscience" particularly carries moral implications; it is a "knowledge" of right from wrong (*Liddell-Scott*; cf. Maurer, "suneidēsis," *Kittel*, 7:898-902).

Maurer concludes that *suneidēsis* as "conscience" generally has a negative nuance, because self-examination usually results in condemnation (ibid., 7:900). This is especially true among pre-Christian Greek authors, although Roman writers might speak of a "good" or "clear" conscience (Hahn, "Conscience," *Colin Brown*, 1:348f.).

Septuagint Usage

Suneidēsis occurs only once in the canonical writings of the Septuagint, in Ecclesiastes 10:20, and it appears twice in the apocryphal portions (Wisdom of Solomon 17:11; Ecclesiasticus 42:18, in Aleph). Likewise, the verb form occurs only twice in the canonical material (Leviticus 5:1; Job 27:6; cf. 1 Maccabees 4:21; 2 Maccabees 4:41).

Behind the single canonical instance of *suneidēsis* lies the Hebrew *maddā'*, "knowledge" (from *yāda'*, "to know"). "Inner thoughts" (cf. the NIV) adequately translates the Hebrew in Ecclesiastes 10:20. In the Wisdom of Solomon the negative classical meaning of "conscience" comes through: "Wickedness is . . . distressed by *conscience*" (17:11, RSV; cf. Sirach 42:18).

Although the Old Testament does not explicitly develop the idea of "conscience" with *suneidēsis*, it does know the concept in other terms. Here the "heart" rather than the mind (implicit in conscience) is the site of confrontation, judgment, confession, and penitence (see ibid., 1:349; cf. Romans 2:15).

New Testament Usage

Suneidēsis occurs 30 times in the Greek New Testament (not including 1 Corinthians 8:7 where the *Textus Receptus* reads it for *sunētheia* [4764], "being accustomed"). Paul used it more than any other writer (about 20 times); it is restricted to Romans, his Corinthian letters, and the Pastoral Epistles. Luke used it twice in Acts, where he also employed the verb form *sunoida*. The Book of Hebrews (five times) and 1 Peter (three times) contain the only other instances.

The simple idea of "consciousness, awareness" occurs only rarely. Peter wrote that it was commendable to endure suffering because of one's "consciousness" of God (1 Peter 2:19). Here the reflexive sense is absent and the more classical meaning comes through. Although *Bauer* suggests the same is true for Hebrews 10:2, to translate *suneidēsis* as "awareness" or "consciousness" overlooks the negative nuance and implied guilt in the overall condition of those who have lived under the old covenant sacrificial system. The need for "cleansing" is not simply ritualistic, it is a cleansing from sin's guilt (cf. the NIV's translation, "felt guilty"). Thus the major understanding of *suneidēsis* follows the latter interpretation. "Conscience" implies "moral consciousness." Many texts reading *suneidēsis* occur in a forensic (legal) context (e.g., Romans 2:15; 9:1). Often the conscience becomes the "court of appeal" (Hahn, "Conscience," *Colin Brown*, 1:350) where the believer makes moral decisions. The believer's conscience—controlled by the Spirit (Romans 9:1; cf. 2 Corinthians 1:12)—assumes a positive role in helping the Christian make the right decision. Thus Paul declared that his conscience was "clear" (2 Timothy 1:3; cf. Acts 24:16; 23:1).

One's conscience is not, however, to be exploited by others who would try to rob the freedom given by Christ. That is why Paul posed the rhetorical question: "Why should my freedom be judged by another's conscience?" (1 Corinthians 10:29 [NIV]; cf. verses 25-31). At the same time regard for another's weaker (not "stronger"!) conscience should govern one's actions. In other words, we should do what will be the most beneficial to others. We should not expect or force others to conform to our expectations against their conscience's direction, especially in the so-called gray areas of morality and ethics.

Since the conscience is a legitimate point of the appeal of the gospel (2 Corinthians 4:2; cf. 5:11), it is only natural to expect that the believer's life is to be marked with a conscience that has been "cleared" through the power of the gospel. A clear conscience signals faithfulness, especially among those in leadership (cf. 1 Timothy 1:5,19; 3:9; cf. 1 Peter 3:16). One trademark of those opponents of the Faith is a "seared conscience" (1 Timothy 4:2; Titus 1:15). They resist "sound teaching" and their behavior reflects their stubbornness (cf. Titus 1:16).

Hebrews presents the concept of the conscience purified by Christ's high priestly work (Hebrews 9:9,14; 10:2,22). The internal cleansing of the blood of Christ is ultimately more effective than the external ritual cleansing of the old covenant sacrifices (cf. 1 Peter 3:21, which uses baptismal imagery to make the same point). The high priestly sacrifice of Christ assures believers—as no former sacrifice or washing could do—that they have a clear conscience before God (Hebrews 13:18).

Strong 4893, Bauer 786-87, Moulton-Milligan 604-5, Kittel 7:898-919, Liddell-Scott 1704, Colin Brown 1:348-51,353.

4744. συνεῖδον suneidon verb

To perceive, understand, become aware of.

Cross-Reference:
εἶδον eidon (1481)

1. συνιδών sunidōn nom sing masc part aor act

2. συνιδόντες sunidontes nom pl masc part aor act

1 And when he had considered the thing, ... Acts 12:12
2 They were ware of it, and fled unto Lystra 14:6

Classical Greek and Septuagint Usage

This word is the second aorist form of *sunoraō*. It can be found in classical Greek from the Fourth Century B.C.; however, in the Septuagint and other Christian literature it is only used of mental seeing, i.e., to "perceive, become aware of, realize" (*Bauer*).

New Testament Usage

Suneidon occurs only a few times in the New Testament. For example, in Acts 12:12 Peter thought his deliverance from prison by the angel was just an imaginary or visionary experience (verse 9). But after he found himself alone on the street, he "came to himself" (verse 11). When the reality finally dawned on him (or he fully realized, *suneidōn*) that God had rescued him from his fate at the hand of Herod (verse 12), Peter headed for the house of Mary.

In Acts 14:6 Paul and his companions faced great persecution at Iconium. Gentiles, Jews, and city officials determined to stone the visiting apostles. Being aware of or realizing the situation (*sunidontes*), they fled to Lystra and Derbe.

Strong 4894, Bauer 787, Moulton-Milligan 605, Liddell-Scott 1704.

4745. σύνειμι suneimi verb

Be with someone, be joined with something.

Cognate:
εἰμί eimi (1498)

Synonym:
προσμένω prosmenō (4215)

רֵעַ rēaʿ (7739), Friend; husband (Jer 3:20).

1. **συνόντων** **sunontōn** gen pl masc part pres act
2. **συνῆσαν** **sunēsan** 3pl indic imperf act

2 his disciples were with him: and he asked them, ... Luke 9:18
1 being led by the hand of them that were with me, .. Acts 22:11

Classical Greek and Septuagint Usage

Suneimi is a compound of *sun* (4713), "with," and *eimi* (1498), "to be." This word has a variety of meanings in literature outside of Scripture. As used by various authors it means "to dream" (Aeschylus, Fifth Century B.C.), "to be acquainted with" (Sophocles, Fifth Century B.C.), "to be engaged in business" (Aristophanes, Fifth–Fourth Centuries B.C.), "to have intercourse with" (Euripides, Fifth Century B.C.), "to live with" (Herodotus, Fifth Century B.C.), "to attend a teacher (as a pupil)" (Xenophon, Fourth Century B.C.), and "to take part with" (Aeschylus, Fifth Century B.C.; cf. *Liddell-Scott*). It is found four times in the canonical Septuagint (e.g., Psalm 58:9 [LXX 57:9]; Proverbs 5:19; Jeremiah 3:20).

New Testament Usage

Suneimi occurs twice in the New Testament. After the feeding of the 5,000, Jesus was praying and the disciples were alone with Him (*suneimi*); Jesus used the occasion to ask the disciples, "Whom say the people that I am?" (Luke 9:18). In Acts 22:11 Paul reported how when blinded by his Damascus Road experience he was led into Damascus by those who were with him (*suneimi*).

Strong 4895, Bauer 787, Moulton-Milligan 605, Liddell-Scott 1705.

4746. σύνειμι suneimi verb

Come together, assemble.

1. **συνιόντος** **suniontos** gen sing masc part pres act

1 And when much people were gathered together, ... Luke 8:4

Classical Greek

This word differs from *suneimi* (4745) in that it is a compound of *sun* (4713), "with," and *eimi*, "to go" (not the same term as *eimi* [1498], "to be"). Hence the word means "to come together, to gather." In nonbiblical literature it is used in two different senses (cf. *Liddell-Scott*). In a hostile sense it means "to meet in battle" (*Iliad*) or "to engage in war" (Thucydides, Fifth Century B.C.). In a peaceable sense it means "to come together" or "meet to deliberate." In late papyri it is used as an accounting expression (cf. *Bauer*).

New Testament Usage

The single use of this word in the New Testament occurs in Luke 8:4. After a series of miracles by Jesus, a great crowd *came together* (*suneimi*), and He taught them by using the Parable of the Sower.

Strong 4896, Bauer 787, Moulton-Milligan 605, Liddell-Scott 1705.

4747. συνεισέρχομαι suneiserchomai verb

Enter together with, go in with.

Cross-Reference:
ἔρχομαι erchomai (2048)

1. **συνεισῆλθεν** **suneisēlthen** 3sing indic aor act

1 that Jesus went not with his disciples into the boat, .. John 6:22
1 and went in with Jesus into the palace 18:15

Classical Greek and Septuagint Usage

This compound verb can be found in classical Greek since the Fifth Century B.C. and in the Septuagint meaning "enter along with or together." It is usually used of people who "enter with" another (e.g., Exodus 21:3; Job 22:4), but it can also be used of things (cf. *Liddell-Scott*).

New Testament Usage

In the New Testament it occurs only in John 6:22 and 18:15. In the first instance (John 6:22), on the day after the feeding of the 5,000, the people who had seen the miracle wondered where Jesus was, for He had not gone with the disciples into the boat. In John 18:15, after Jesus was betrayed by Judas, Peter and the other disciple (possibly John) followed Jesus to the trial scene. Because the latter was known to the high priest, this disciple was able to "enter with" Jesus into the palace of the high priest.

STRONG 4897, BAUER 787, MOULTON-MILLIGAN 605, LIDDELL-SCOTT 1705, COLIN BROWN 1:321.

4748. συνέκδημος sunekdēmos noun

Fellow traveler, traveling companion.

CROSS-REFERENCE:

δῆμος dēmos (1211B)

1. συνέκδημος **sunekdēmos** nom sing masc

2. συνεκδήμους **sunekdēmous** acc pl masc

2 men of Macedonia, Paul's companions in travel,.... Acts 19:29
1 also chosen ... to travel with us with this grace,......2 Co 8:19

Classical Greek

This word is made up of three elements: *sun* (4713), "with" or "together," *ek* (1523), "from," and *dēmos* (1213), "people." The meaning of the word is "a fellow traveler" or "traveling companion." *Sunekdēmos* appears in Diodorus Siculus (First Century B.C.), Plutarch (First–Second Century A.D.), and Greek inscriptions from the First and Second Centuries A.D. (cf. *Bauer, Moulton-Milligan*).

New Testament Usage

The two occurrences of the word in the New Testament are Acts 19:29 and 2 Corinthians 8:19. In the first instance the Ephesian citizens seized Gaius and Aristarchus who were Paul's "companions in travel" (*sunekdēmous*) and rushed with them into the town theater. In 2 Corinthians 8:19 Paul wrote of an unnamed brother chosen to travel with (*sunekdēmos*, "fellow traveler") Paul's party.

STRONG 4898, BAUER 787, MOULTON-MILLIGAN 605, LIDDELL-SCOTT 1706.

4749. συνεκλεκτός suneklektos adj

Chosen together with, elect together with.

CROSS-REFERENCE:

ἐκλέγομαι eklegomai (1573)

1. συνεκλεκτή **suneklektē** nom sing fem

1 church ... elected together with you, saluteth you;.... 1 Pt 5:13

This compound term is formed by *sun* (4713), "with" or "together," and *eklegomai* (1573), "to select" or "to choose," and means "chosen along with or together."

New Testament Usage

The single use of *suneklektos* (1 Peter 5:13) has produced much controversy, mainly because of uncertain applications of associated words. In closing his first epistle Peter encouraged his readers saying, "The church that is at Babylon, elected together with you, saluteth you." "Church" is not in the Greek text, though the feminine definite article is. A.T. Robertson translates the beginning of the verse as "She that is in Babylon . . . " (*Word Pictures in the New Testament*, 6:135). The explanation by *Bauer* represents the majority scholarly interpretation: "No individual lady is meant, least of all Peter's wife, but rather a congregation w(ith) whom Peter is staying." Many scholars identify "Babylon" as a figurative reference to Rome, though it is possible that Peter was actually in Babylonia. Peter's farewell greeting links two Christian congregations with his use of the word *suneklektē*.

STRONG 4899, BAUER 787, MOULTON-MILLIGAN 605, LIDDELL-SCOTT 1706, COLIN BROWN 1:536-42.

4750. συνελαύνω sunelaunō verb

To drive together, compel; draw together, reconcile.

CROSS-REFERENCE:

ἐλαύνω elaunō (1630)

1. συνήλασεν **sunēlasen** 3sing indic aor act

1 and would have set them at one again, (NT)........ Acts 7:26

Classical Greek and Septuagint Usage

This verb appears as early as the Eighth Century B.C. meaning "drive together." It can be found of things "hammered together, welded" or just to describe the "force" it takes to "drive" or "compress" something together. In 2 Maccabees it is used to describe how some were "forced" to flee for their lives (4:26,42; 5:5).

New Testament Usage

It appears in Acts 7:26 in some manuscripts; others use the similar word *sunallassō* (4722B).

The word occurs in Stephen's sermon where he recounts Moses' attempt to bring together or to reconcile two men of Israel who were fighting. Both *sunelaunō*, "bring together," and *sunēllassō*, "change or exchange," carry the meaning of "to reconcile."

Strong 4900, Bauer 787, Liddell-Scott 1707.

4751. συνεπιμαρτυρέω
sunepimartureō verb

To bear witness together.

Cross-Reference:
μαρτυρέω martureō (3113)

1. συνεπιμαρτυροῦντος sunepimarturountos gen sing masc part pres act

1 God also **bearing them witness,** .... Heb 2:4

Classical Greek

Sunepimartureō is a compound verb made up by *sun* (4713), "with," *epi* (1894), "on, upon, in addition to," and *martureō* (3113), "to witness or testify." The verb means "to bear witness together or in addition to another." It can be found as far back as the Fourth Century B.C. meaning "join in attesting" and "add one's evidence" in a legal sense (*Liddell-Scott*). It is not found in the Septuagint.

New Testament Usage

Sunepimartureō is rare in the New Testament. The verb is used in Hebrews 2:4. God is said to be the One who bears witness, in addition to the Lord Jesus, to the Word, that is, the gospel. God bore witness through signs, wonders, and miracles. This confirms what Jesus said (Mark 16:12-18) would happen following the preaching of the gospel.

Strong 4901, Bauer 787, Moulton-Milligan 605, Kittel 4:508-10, Liddell-Scott 1710.

4751B. συνεπιτίθεμαι
sunepitithemai verb

Join in an attack.

Cross-Reference:
τίθημι tithēmi (4935)

נָכַר nākhar (5421), Piel: misjudge (Dt 32:27).

עָזַר ʿāzar (6038), To further (Zec 1:15).

שִׁית shîth (8308), Lay, appoint; hold responsible (Nm 12:11).

שָׁלַח shālach (8365), Send, stretch out; loot (Ob 13).

1. συνεπέθεντο sunepethento 3pl indic aor mid

1 And the Jews also **joined in the attack,** (NASB) .... Acts 24:9

This word is a compound verb of the prepositions *sun* (4713), "together," and *epi* (1894), "upon," and of the verb *tithēmi* (4935), "put, place, lay." It means "to join with others in an attack" (*Bauer*). The earliest occurrence of *sunepitithemai* comes from Thucydides in the Fifth Century B.C. In the New Testament this verb occurs only in Acts 24:9 and describes the efforts of the Jews who joined their lawyer Tertullus in bringing fabricated charges against the apostle Paul in the court of Felix.

Bauer 787, Moulton-Milligan 605, Liddell-Scott 1711.

4752. συνέπομαι sunepomai verb

To accompany, follow along with.

Synonyms:
προπέμπω propempō (4170)
συνέρχομαι sunerchomai (4755)

1. συνείπετο suneipeto 3sing indic imperf mid

1 there **accompanied him** into Asia Sopater of Berea; Acts 20:4

Classical Greek and Septuagint Usage

Sunepomai is a verb that can be found in classical Greek from the Fifth Century B.C. meaning "follow along with, accompany." It is used literally of "following" someone or something (cf. 2 Maccabees 15:2; 3 Maccabees 5:48). Figuratively it means "comply or be in accordance with" (cf. *Liddell-Scott*).

New Testament Usage

Sunepomai occurs only in Acts 20:4 where Luke listed all the travel companions of Paul when he left Greece. These travel companions were delegates from the various Gentile churches sent with their offerings to Jerusalem. Luke mentioned that though they accompanied Paul they went on ahead to meet him at Troas.

Strong 4902, Bauer 787, Moulton-Milligan 605, Liddell-Scott 1711.

4753. συνεργέω sunergeō verb

Work together with, assist, cooperate with.

Cross-Reference:
ἐργάζομαι ergazomai (2021)

1. συνεργεῖ sunergei 3sing indic pres act

2. συνεργοῦντος sunergountos gen sing masc part pres act

3. συνεργοῦντι sunergounti dat sing masc part pres act

4. συνεργοῦντες sunergountes nom pl masc part pres act

5. συνήργει sunērgei 3sing indic imperf act

2 Lord **working with** them, and confirming the word Mark 16:20
1 **work together** for good to them that love God, ... Rom 8:28
3 to every one that **helpeth with** us, and laboureth. . . . 1 Co 16:16
4 We then, as **workers together with** him, ... 2 Co 6:1
5 Seest thou how faith **wrought with** his works, ... Jas 2:22

Classical Greek and Septuagint Usage

This word can be found frequently in classical literature meaning "work together with" in the sense of positively contributing and being helpful (cf. *Liddell-Scott*). Philo (First Century A.D.) suggested that secondary powers cooperated together in creating man's physical vices. By contrast, no one can cooperate with God in creating and preserving the world (Bertram, "sunergeō," *Kittel*, 7:872f.). *Sunergeō* also occurs in 1 Esdras 7:2; 1 Maccabees 12:1; and Plutarch (First and Second Centuries A.D.) with the general meaning of "work together with." The usage is basically the same in secular and in New Testament writings.

New Testament Usage

The word occurs five times in the New Testament: three times in Paul's writings (Romans 8:28; 1 Corinthians 16:16; 2 Corinthians 6:1) and once each in Mark (16:20) and James (2:22). The "cooperation" or "working together" can be between God and man, man and man, or between forces or ideas. In Mark 16:20 *sunergeō* describes how, after the Ascension, the Lord worked with the disciples by confirming their message with accompanying signs. James 2:22 speaks of the intermingling of Abraham's faith with his works. The KJV terminology "faith wrought with his works" means that Abraham's faith was active along with (or in cooperation with) his works.

Sunergeō is a key word in one of the most cherished verses of the New Testament, Romans 8:28: "And we know that all things *work together* (*sunergei*) for good to them that love God, to them who are the called according to his purpose." A.T. Robertson notes that some manuscripts have *God* as the subject of *sunergei*. But whether or not the subject is included this is the idea being conveyed (*Word Pictures in the New Testament*, 4:377). God causes all things to work together for good; it does not happen magically simply because a believer claims to love God. Romans 8:29 explains what the "good" is.

In concluding his first letter to the Corinthians (16:16), Paul admonished the believers to submit themselves to every fellow worker (*sunergounti*), or as the KJV translates it, "to every one *that helpeth with* us." A final use of the word is in Paul's second letter to the Corinthians (6:1) where he described his party as working together (*sunergountes*, KJV: "workers together") with Christ.

Strong 4903, Bauer 787, Moulton-Milligan 605, Kittel 7:871-76, Liddell-Scott 1711, Colin Brown 3:1147-48,1152.

4754. συνεργός sunergos adj

Fellow worker.

Cognate:
ἐργάζομαι ergazomai (2021)

Synonym:
βοηθός boēthos (991)

1. συνεργός sunergos nom sing masc

2. συνεργῷ sunergō dat sing masc

3. συνεργόν sunergon acc sing masc

4. συνεργοί sunergoi nom pl masc

5. συνεργῶν sunergōn gen pl masc

6. συνεργούς sunergous acc pl masc

6 Greet Priscilla and Aquila my **helpers** in Christ . . . . Rom 16:3
3 Salute Urbane, our **helper** in Christ, ... 16:9
1 Timotheus my **workfellow**, and Lucius, and Jason, ... 16:21
4 For we are **labourers together with** God: . . . . 1 Co 3:9
4 but are **helpers** of your joy: for by faith ye stand. . . . 2 Co 1:24
1 he is my partner and **fellow helper** concerning you: 8:23
3 my brother, and **companion in labour**, ... Phlp 2:25
5 Clement also, and with other my **fellow labourers**, ... 4:3
4 are my **fellow workers** unto the kingdom of God, ... Col 4:11
3 Timothy, ... , God's **fellow-worker** (NASB) . . . . 1 Th 3:2
3 and our **fellow labourer** in the gospel of Christ, ... 3:2
2 Philemon our dearly beloved, and **fellow labourer**, . . Phlm 1:1
4 Aristarchus, Demas, Lucas, my **fellow labourers**. 1:24
4 that we might be **fellow helpers** to the truth. . . . . 3 Jn 1:8

Classical Greek

Sunergos is an adjective used mainly as a noun. It comes from *sun* (4713), "with," and *ergon* (2024), "act of work," and means "fellow worker" or "one who works with another" or "helper." *Sunergos* is found in Pindar of Cynoscephalae (518–446 B.C.) in his *Olympia* with the meaning "fellow worker" or "helper." Thucydides of Athens (460–396 B.C.) also used the term in his history of the Peloponnesian War. Plato stated that prudence must be on guard lest unreason become a "fellow-worker" in human actions and deeds. (See Bertram, "sunergos," *Kittel*, 7:871f.)

Philo used the word to oppose idolatry. He stated that the *sunergoi tēs apatēs*, "coworkers of deception," helped seduce men through idolatry. Philo used *sunergos*, as well as the verb form *sunergeō* (4753), to describe various helpers, i.e., sin and the "helpers" in creation (ibid., p.872).

The word is also used in Josephus, various papyri, and Polybius (Second Century B.C.) (cf. *Moulton-Milligan*).

Septuagint Usage

The word occurs twice in the Septuagint, both in the apocryphal book of 2 Maccabees. The night is said to be a *sunergos* with Maccabeus in his nightly raids on the enemy (2 Maccabees 8:7). The second reference is 2 Maccabees 14:5.

New Testament Usage

Other than in 3 John 8, all the New Testament occurrences are found in the Pauline writings. The New Testament uses the word only to describe the relationship between believers. For example, John wrote to Gaius and suggested that he continue to support the itinerant preachers of the gospel. In so doing, Gaius would be a *sunergos* with the itinerant preachers as well as in the truth they preached.

Paul used the term to describe such people as Priscilla and Aquila (Romans 16:3), Urbane (16:9), and Timothy (16:21). In 2 Corinthians 8:23 Paul called Titus his fellow worker. He appealed to the Corinthians to accept Titus and trust him with their gift to the Jerusalem saints. Paul also called Epaphroditus his fellow worker (Philippians 2:25). In each of these cases Paul used the term to make an association between those he was recommending to the various churches and himself. Paul used *sunergos* to give credibility to those mentioned. The use of the word does not suggest apostolic authority but apostolic recognition of the individuals in their ministries.

In 1 Corinthians 3:9 Paul used the term to describe the personalities associated with the factions in Corinth. Paul stated that Apollos, Cephas, and he were all "fellow workers" with God. These men were laborers in God's vineyard. Thus they were not to be admired to divide the Church, but to be seen as helpers of God used in different ways. They were not only helpers with one another but, more importantly, with God. The term suggests one who works alongside with or close by another. In this passage it was the apostles who worked closely with God.

STRONG 4904, BAUER 787-88, MOULTON-MILLIGAN 605, KITTEL 7:871-76, LIDDELL-SCOTT 1711-12, COLIN BROWN 3:1147-48.

4755. συνέρχομαι sunerchomai verb

To come together, assemble, sexual union, to travel with.

COGNATE:
ἔρχομαι erchomai (2048)

SYNONYMS:
προπέμπω propempō (4170)
συμπορεύομαι sumporeuomai (4699)
συνέπομαι sunepomai (4752)

אָסַף 'āsaph (636), Niphal: gather together (Ex 32:26).

בּוֹא bô' (971), Come (Ez 33:30).

הָלַךְ hālakh (2050), Walk (Jer 3:18).

חָבַק chāvaq (2354), Piel: embrace (Prv 5:20—Codex Vaticanus only).

יָעַד yā'adh (3366), Niphal: join forces (Jos 11:5).

פָּגַשׁ pāghash (6539), Meet; niphal: have something in common (Prv 29:13).

קָבַץ qāvats (7192), Assemble, gather; hithpael: gather together (Jos 9:2).

1. **συνῆλθεν sunēlthen** 3sing indic aor act
2. **συνῆλθαν sunēlthan** 3pl indic aor act
3. **συνῆλθον sunēlthon** 3pl indic aor act
4. **συνέλθῃ sunelthē** 3sing subj aor act
5. **συνελθόντα sunelthonta** acc sing masc part aor act
6. **συνελθόντες sunelthontes** nom pl masc part aor act
7. **συνελθόντων sunelthontōn** gen pl masc part aor act
8. **συνελθόντας sunelthontas** acc pl masc part aor act
9. **συνελθούσαις sunelthousais** dat pl fem part aor act
10. **συνελθεῖν sunelthein** inf aor act
11. **συνεληλύθεισαν sunelēlutheisan** 3pl indic plperf act
12. **συνεληλυθότας sunelēluthotas** acc pl masc part perf act
13. **συνεληλυθυῖαι sunelēluthuiai** nom pl fem part perf act
14. **συνέρχεται sunerchetai** 3sing indic pres mid
15. **συνέρχεσθε sunerchesthe** 2pl indic pres mid
16. **συνέρχονται sunerchontai** 3pl indic pres mid
17. **συνέρχησθε sunerchēsthe** 2pl subj pres mid
18. **συνερχόμενοι sunerchomenoi** nom pl masc part pres mid
19. **συνερχομένων sunerchomenōn** gen pl masc part pres mid
20. **συνήρχετο sunērcheto** 3sing indic imperf mid
21. **συνήρχοντο sunērchonto** 3pl indic imperf mid
22. **συνεληλυθότες sunelēluthotes** nom pl masc part perf act

10 before they **came together**, ... was found with child Matt 1:18
14 And the multitude **cometh together** again, ... Mark 3:20
3 and outwent them, and **came together** unto him. 6:33
16 and with him **were assembled** all the chief priests 14:53
21 and great multitudes **came together** to hear, ... Luke 5:15
13 which **came with** him from Galilee, followed after, ... 23:55
8 and the Jews also weeping which **came with** her, .. John 11:33
16 and in the temple, whither the Jews always **resort**; 18:20
6 When they therefore **were come together**, ... Acts 1:6
7 which **have companied with** us all the time 1:21

1 multitude **came together**, and were confounded, ... Acts 2:6
20 There **came** also a multitude out of the cities 5:16
1 Then Peter arose and **went with** them. 9:39
3 certain brethren from Joppa **accompanied** him. 10:23
12 and found many that **were come together**. 10:27
3 were astonished, as many as **came with** Peter, ... 10:45
10 And the Spirit bade me **go with** them, ... 11:12
5 and **went** not **with** them to the work. 15:38
9 and spake unto the women which **resorted** thither. 16:13
11 part knew not wherefore they **were come together**. 19:32
3 There **went with** us also certain of the disciples 21:16
10 the multitude must needs **come together**: 21:22
10 and all the Council **to assemble**, (NASB) 22:30
7 Therefore, when they **were come** hither, ... 25:17
7 when they **were come together**, he said unto them, ... 28:17
17 and **come together** again, that Satan tempt you not 1 Co 7:5
15 **come together** not for the better, but for the worse.... 11:17
19 when ye **come together** in the church, ... 11:18
19 When ye **come together** therefore into one place, ... 11:20
18 my brethren, when ye **come together** to eat, ... 11:33
17 that ye **come** not **together** unto condemnation. 11:34
4 the whole church be **come together** into one place, ... 14:23
17 How is it then, brethren? when ye **come together**, ... 14:26

Classical Greek

Sunerchomai is a compound verb from *sun* (4713), "with, together," and *erchomai* (2048), "to come"; thus, "to come together." The word is used in three ways. First, it means to come together in one place, such as a gathering or meeting. Plato, for example, used the term of a gathering together in one place. Diodorus Siculus likewise used the term for an assembling in one place. The various papyri also used the word in this sense. The Oxyrhynchus Papyri and the Tebtunis Papyri used this word for the gathering together of people in one place such as a house (cf. *Bauer*). Even Josephus used *sunerchomai* to mean "to gather together" (ibid.).

Second, it is used figuratively suggesting sexual union, a coming together of a man and woman. This meaning is attested to in Xenophon (Fourth Century B.C.) and Diodorus Siculus (First Century B.C.). This connotation is also found in the Psalms of Apollodorus (Second Century A.D.) and Philo.

Third, *sunerchomai* means to come or go with someone, i.e., travel. The word is used in this sense in the Epistle of Aristeas (Second Century B.C.) as well as various inscriptions and papyri. Josephus also used *sunerchomai* in this sense. All three usages are attested to in the New Testament.

Septuagint Usage

The Septuagint uses *sunerchomai* to mean "to gather together." Moses asked the question, "Who is on the Lord's side?" (Exodus 32:26). The sons of Levi "gathered together" at Moses' side. They stood with Moses in a concerted effort against those who played the harlot with the altar of Baal. The sons of Levi, at Moses' command, slew those who worshiped Aaron's golden calf. Another example can be found at Zechariah 8:21 which states that the inhabitants of many lands and cities shall "come together" in order to seek the Lord and pray.

New Testament Usage

The New Testament speaks of the crowds that gathered together around Jesus (Luke 5:15). Acts 1:6 says that the disciples gathered around Jesus just prior to His ascension. Paul seemed to use *sunerchomai* in a technical sense in 1 Corinthians 11 and 14. He used this term to describe the corporate church service/meeting. His usage in chapters 11 and 14 helps set apart these chapters (as well as 12 and 13) to refer to proper behavior in a corporate meeting. This should give further insight to the various regulations laid down in these important chapters.

There are two New Testament passages that use *sunerchomai* to refer to sexual union. Matthew 1:18 states that Mary was with child by the Holy Spirit before she "came together" (sexual union) with Joseph. This wording is significant because it attests to the virgin birth of the Lord Jesus.

Paul used the term in 1 Corinthians 7:5 to teach against withholding sexual intimacy in marriage. Apparently the Corinthians thought that celibacy was more "spiritual" than marriage. Many Corinthian couples attempted to be celibate within marriage. Paul wrote against this and gave specific guidelines regarding sexual compatibility within marriage (1 Corinthians 7:1-5).

In a third usage, John 11:33 speaks of the Jews who "came with" Mary to Lazarus' tomb. Acts 1:21 gives the apostolic requirement that the one chosen to replace Judas had to have "traveled" with Jesus since John's baptism. In addition, there are many verses in Acts that use *sunerchomai* to refer to the "travels" of the apostles (Acts 9:39; 10:23; 11:12; 15:38).

STRONG 4905, BAUER 788, MOULTON-MILLIGAN 605-6, KITTEL 2:684, LIDDELL-SCOTT 1712, COLIN BROWN 1:320,322.

4756. συνεσθίω sunesthiō verb

To eat together.

CROSS-REFERENCE:
ἐσθίω esthiō (2052)

אָכַל 'ākhal (404), Eat (Gn 43:32).

בָּרָה bārāh (1290), Eat (2 Sm 12:17).

1. συνεσθίει sunesthiei 3sing indic pres act
2. συνεσθίειν sunesthiein inf pres act

3. συνέφαγες sunephages 2sing indic aor act
4. συνεφάγομεν sunephagomen 1pl indic aor act
5. συνήσθιεν sunēsthien 3sing indic imperf act

1 This man receiveth sinners, and **eateth with** them... Luke 15:2
4 even to us, who did eat and drink with him........ Acts 10:41
3 in to men uncircumcised, and **didst eat with** them...... 11:3
2 or an extortioner; with such an one no not to **eat**.... 1 Co 5:11
5 he **did eat with** the Gentiles:........................ Gal 2:12

Classical Greek and Septuagint Usage

Sunesthiō is a compound verb made up of *sun* (4713), "with," and *esthiō* (2052), "to eat," and means "eat together." Its usage is consistent through classical Greek and the Septuagint. David said (Psalm 101:5 [LXX 100:5]) that he did not and would not eat with the slanderer, proud, or insatiable. David's words are in keeping with the Middle Eastern custom that equated table fellowship with companionship, friendship, or acceptance (cf. Genesis 43:32). David did not want to be associated with these sinners, thus he would not eat with them.

New Testament Usage

This connotation is also seen in the New Testament usage. The Pharisees were upset with Jesus because He received and "ate with" sinners, i.e., accepted them (Luke 15:2). Peter had to answer to the Jerusalem brethren concerning his eating with (acceptance of) the Gentiles (Acts 11:3). Paul rebuked the Corinthians for their lax stand with the immoral brother and thus commanded them not to "even" eat with an immoral brother (1 Corinthians 5:11). Paul also rebuked Peter for his hypocrisy concerning the Gentiles in Galatians 2:12. Each of these references show the implications of friendship or acceptance in the Eastern concept of table fellowship or "eating together."

Strong 4906, Bauer 788, Moulton-Milligan 606, Liddell-Scott 1712.

4757. σύνεσις sunesis noun

Understanding, knowledge, comprehension, insight, intelligence.

Cognate:
συνίημι suniēmi (4770)

Synonyms:
διάνοια dianoia (1265)
νοῦς nous (3426)

בִּין bîn (1032), Discern, understand; niphal: have understanding (Is 10:13); hiphil: have understanding (Ps 32:9 [31:9], Is 56:11).

בִּינָה bînāh (1035), Understanding, discernment (Dt 4:6, Jb 38:4, Is 29:14).

דַּעַת daʿath (1907), Knowledge (Jb 21:22, 33:3, Is 53:11).

חָכְמָה chokhmāh (2551), Skill, wisdom (Ex 31:6, Dt 34:9, Dn 1:20).

טַעַם ṭaʿam (3051), Discernment (Jb 12:20).

מַדָּע maddāʿ (4234I), Knowledge (2 Chr 1:10f.).

מַנְדַּע mandaʿ (4629B), Knowledge (Dn 2:21—Aramaic).

מַשְׂכִּיל maskîl (5030), Maskil (Pss 42, 45, 52-55: titles [41, 44, 51-54: titles]).

שָׂכַל sākhal (7959), Hiphil: give knowledge (Dn 1:17).

שֶׂכֶל sēkhel (7961I), Understanding (2 Chr 30:22, Ps 111:10 [110:10], Prv 13:15).

תְּבוּנָה tᵉvûnāh (8722), Understanding (1 Kgs 7:14, Prv 2:2f., Ob 7f.).

1. συνέσεως suneseōs gen sing fem
2. συνέσει sunesei dat sing fem
3. σύνεσιν sunesin acc sing fem

1 all the heart, and with all the **understanding**,...... Mark 12:33
2 were astonished at his **understanding** and answers.... Luke 2:47
3 bring to nothing the **understanding** of the prudent... 1 Co 1:19
3 understand my **knowledge** in the mystery of Christ... Eph 3:4
2 his will in all wisdom and spiritual **understanding**;.... Col 1:9
1 all riches of the full assurance of **understanding**,........ 2:2
3 and the Lord give thee **understanding** in all things... 2 Tm 2:7

Sunesis is the noun form of the verb *suniēmi* (4770). The verb's literal meaning is "to bring, flow," or "come together" as in the union of two rivers. It is used in the figurative sense of "to perceive, understand, comprehend." The noun likewise has a literal meaning of "union" or "joining together." However, it is most often used in the figurative sense of "understanding, knowledge," or "comprehension."

Classical Greek

The word group is abundant in classical Greek. *Sunesis* is used literally in Homer's Odyssey to describe the joining of two rivers. The term is used in the figurative sense of "understanding" in Thucydides' history of the Peloponnesian War, (Conzelmann, "suniēmi," *Kittel*, 7:888f.). Conzelmann further states that the word group, though used by the Sophists, did not "achieve the status of a philosophical term" (ibid.).

Septuagint Usage

Sunesis is found in the Septuagint. The word is used to translate Hebrew terms such as *sākhal*, *daʿath*, and *bîn* and describes practical judgment rather than theoretical understanding of the world. Isaiah used the term in 11:2 to describe the sevenfold Spirit of the coming Messiah. *Sunesis* is used with the Spirit of *sophia* (4531) and *gnōseōs*. The Messiah was to be filled with the Spirit of wisdom, knowledge, and understanding. *Sunesis* is used here to translate the Hebrew term *bîn*, "understanding." The noun is also found in

Proverbs to refer to the understanding that is needed to please the Lord (Proverbs 2:1-9). This understanding comes from the Lord (rather than a faculty native to man as in classical Greek) and is necessary to walk uprightly. One should pray to God for it (Psalm 119:34), and He can withdraw it (Isaiah 29:14).

New Testament Usage

Sunesis is used in Luke 2:47 to describe the understanding of Jesus at age 12 in the temple. The use of the word is significant because of Isaiah's prophecy (11:2) that the Messiah would have the Spirit of *sunesis*. That Spirit was already evident at age 12. The noun is also used in Mark 12:33 to describe the totality of one's being or existence that should be involved in one's love for God.

Paul used the term to define insight regarding the mysteries or ways of God. In Colossians his prayer was that these believers would be filled with spiritual understanding (1:9) and the full assurance of understanding (2:2) which is Christ himself. He told Timothy that God would give insight into what the Holy Spirit was saying through Paul (2 Timothy 2:7). Paul also wrote of the insight he had by the revelation of the Holy Spirit into the mysteries of God (Ephesians 3:1-4).

Paul used the term for insight in 1 Corinthians 1:19. However, here he stated that God will destroy man's insight because of his pride and folly. God will then grant such understanding to those who believe.

STRONG 4907, BAUER 788, MOULTON-MILLIGAN 606, KITTEL 7:888-96, LIDDELL-SCOTT 1712, COLIN BROWN 3:130.

4758. συνετός sunetos adj

Understanding, discerning, prudent, wise.

CROSS-REFERENCE:

συνίημι suniēmi (4770)

בִּין bîn (1032), Qal: prudent one (Jer 49:7 [29:7]); niphal: intelligent one, skilled person, discerning person (Eccl 9:11, Is 3:3, Hos 14:9 [14:10]); hiphil: be skillful, have understanding (1 Chr 15:22, Prv 17:24, Dn 1:4).

חָכָם chākhām (2550), Wise (Gn 41:33, Is 19:11, Jer 50:35 [27:35]).

יָדַע yādha' (3156), Experienced or respected person (Dt 1:13,15).

נְדִיבָה n^edhîvāh (5260), Noble thing (Is 32:8).

עָרוּם 'ārûm (6415), Prudent (Prv 12:23).

שָׂכַל sākhal (7959), Hiphil: wise person, expert (Prv 15:24, Jer 50:9 [27:9]); give attention to (Prv 16:20).

שֵׂכֶל sēkhel (7961I), Wisdom (Prv 12:8).

1. συνετῷ suneto dat sing masc

2. συνετῶν sunetōn gen pl masc

2 hast hid these things from the wise and **prudent**, ... Matt 11:25
2 hast hid these things from the wise and **prudent**, ... Luke 10:21
1 Sergius Paulus, a **prudent** man; .... Acts 13:7
2 bring to nothing the understanding of the **prudent**... 1 Co 1:19

Classical Greek

Sunetos is an adjective meaning "understanding, discerning, prudent, wise, having good sense." The word is found in Sophocles of Athens (496–406 B.C.) to describe Zeus and Apollos (cf. *Liddell-Scott*).

Septuagint Usage

Sunetos and its related forms (*suniēmi* [4770] and *sunesis* [4757]) are very common in the Septuagint, especially in Proverbs. The word group is used in a positive sense of man's faculty to know as given by God (Conzelmann, "suniemi," *Kittel*, 7:890).

New Testament Usage

Though used in a positive sense in the Greek literature and the Septuagint, the adjective is used in a demeaning sense in the New Testament. *Sunetos* describes the wise that were not enlightened by the Heavenly Father. These did not understand who Jesus really is (Matthew 11:25; Luke 10:21). Jesus said it was to the "babes" that God's revelation came.

This concept is further exemplified in Acts 13:7. Sergius Paulus was a *sunetos* man yet did not understand the gospel. He was following the magician Elymas. It was only after the blinding of Elymas and the instruction given through Paul and Barnabbas that Sergius Paulus believed. Yet he was "amazed" at their teaching (Acts 13:7ff.).

Paul used the term in a demeaning sense as well in 1 Corinthians 1:19. Paul quoted Isaiah 29:14 to prove that the word of the Cross would scandalize the "wisc" and yet save the "foolish" who believe.

STRONG 4908, BAUER 788, MOULTON-MILLIGAN 606, KITTEL 7:888-96, LIDDELL-SCOTT 1713.

4759. συνευδοκέω suneudokeō verb

To approve, be pleased with, consent, agree with, sympathize with.

COGNATE:

εὐδοκέω eudokeō (2085)

SYNONYMS:

ἐπινεύω epineuō (1947)

εὐδοκέω eudokeō (2085)
συγκατατίθημαι sunkatatithēmai (4635)
συμφωνέω sumphōneō (4707)

1. **συνευδοκεῖ** suneudokei 3sing indic pres act
2. **συνευδοκεῖτε** suneudokeite 2pl indic pres act
3. **συνευδοκοῦσιν** suneudokousin 3pl indic pres act
4. **συνευδοκῶν** suneudokōn nom sing masc part pres act

2 Truly ye bear witness that ye **allow** the deeds of... Luke 11:48
4 And Saul was **consenting** unto his death............Acts 8:1
4 standing by, and **consenting** unto his death,........... 22:20
3 but **have pleasure** in them that do them............ Rom 1:32
1 and she **be pleased** to dwell with him,.............. 1 Co 7:12
1 and if he **be pleased** to dwell with her,................ 7:13

Classical Greek

Suneudokeō is a compound verb from *sun* (4713), "with, together," and *eudokeō* (2085), "to think well, approve." The term means "to approve, agree, consent with another." The term was used by Polybius of the Second Century B.C. and is also found in Diodorus Siculus (First Century B.C.). The meanings used in classical Greek are the same as the Septuagint and New Testament.

Septuagint Usage

Suneudokeō occurs in 1 Maccabees 1:57. The text describes the reign of Antiochus over the Jews and his acts of desecration. He forbade any sacrifices in the temple, circumcision, and the reading or keeping of the Law. Any who were found to "agree" with the law of God were to be put to death by Antiochus' decree. *Suneudokeō* is also used in 2 Maccabees 11:24 to describe the willful, joyful agreement between Lysias and Quintus Memmius and Titus Manlius. (See also 2 Maccabees 11:35.)

New Testament Usage

In Luke 11:48 Jesus said that the Pharisees were just as guilty as their forefathers who killed the prophets of God. They were guilty because they consented or agreed with their father's actions. They were linked together with their fathers and thus also the sins of their fathers. This same concept is found in Acts 8:1 where Saul was in hearty agreement with those who were stoning Stephen. Saul was keeping watch over the belongings of those who stoned Stephen. This made Saul as guilty as those who actually cast the stones because he "heartily agreed" with them. Paul himself later gave evidence of his guilt before the Jews because of this consent over Stephen's death (Acts 22:20).

Paul used the term in Romans 1:32 to describe those having a depraved mind. These individuals not only did those things that they knew were against God's laws but also heartily supported others who did such sins. They were doubly guilty of doing the sin and encouraging others to sin with them.

The word also occurs in 1 Corinthians 7:12,13. Here Paul declared that if an unbelieving husband or wife agreed to live with the believing husband or wife, the believer should continue in such a marriage. The thought is that if the unbeliever is content with the different and new life of the believer, the believer should not attempt a separation or divorce.

Strong 4909, Bauer 788, Moulton-Milligan 606, Liddell-Scott 1713.

4760. συνευωχέομαι

suneuōcheomai verb

To entertain, to feast together.

Cross-Reference:
ἔχω echō (2174)

1. **συνευωχούμενοι** suneuōchoumenoi nom pl masc part pres mid

1 sporting themselves ... while they **feast with you**;.....2 Pt 2:13
1 when they **feast with you**, feeding themselves........Jude 1:12

Classical Greek

Suneuōcheomai is a compound verb stemming from *sun* (4713), "with," and *eucheō*, "to feast sumptuously," and means "to entertain" or "to feast together." *Suneuōcheomai* is found in Aristotle (Fourth Century B.C.) and Philo of Alexandria (First Century A.D.). It also occurs in Josephus. It does not appear in the Septuagint, however.

New Testament Usage

The word is rare in the New Testament. It occurs in 2 Peter 2:13 and Jude 12. In both references it refers to the false prophets who associated with the congregation. They were feasting with the other believers but were not part of them. Jude stated that they ate with the believers in their love-feasts, "agape" meals. (See 1 Corinthians 11:17-34.) Both Peter and Jude warned against the false prophets.

Strong 4910, Bauer 789, Moulton-Milligan 606, Liddell-Scott 1713.

4761. συνεφίστημι sunephistēmi verb

Rise up together, attack.

Cross-Reference:
ἵστημι histēmi (2449)

1. **συνεπέστη** sunepestē 3sing indic aor act

1 And the multitude **rose up together** against them:...Acts 16:22

Classical Greek

Sunephistēmi is a compound verb stemming from *sun* (4713), "with," and *ephistēmi* (2168), "stand by, be present," and means to "stand together" or "with one another" and also "to attack." The word is found in Thucydides (Fifth Century B.C.).

New Testament Usage

Sunephistēmi appears only in Acts 16:22 in the New Testament. The context shows that the word means more than to just "stand together"; it involves the idea of to "stand together against" someone or something. The term is used to describe the united, aggressive behavior against Paul and Silas in Philippi.

Strong 4911, Bauer 789, Liddell-Scott 1713.

4762. συνέχω sunechō verb

Hold fast, restrain, enclose; constrain, compel; press, pressure.

Cognate:

ἔχω echō (2174)

Synonyms:

ἀναγκάζω anankazō (313)
θλίβω thlibō (2323)
κελεύω keleuō (2724)
παραβιάζομαι parabiazomai (3711)
παραινέω paraineō (3728)
παρακαλέω parakaleō (3731)
παροξύνω paroxunō (3809)
προτρέπομαι protrepomai (4247)
στενοχωρέω stenochōreō (4580)
συνέχω sunechō (4762)
συνθλίβω sunthlibō (4768)
σωφρονίζω sōphronizō (4846)

אָחַז 'āchaz (270), Attach (1 Kgs 6:10).

אָטַר 'āṭar (335), Shut (Ps 69:15 [68:15]).

אָלַם 'ālam (487), Speechless (Ez 33:22).

בַּיִן bayin (1033), Between (Ez 43:8).

חָבַק chāvaq (2354), Embrace (Prv 5:20).

חָבַר chāvar (2357), Join, attach (Ex 26:3, 39:4 [36:11]).

חָזַק chāzaq (2480), Be strong; hiphil: restrain (Mi 7:18).

כָּלָא kālā' (3727), Keep back, restrain; niphal: be restrained (Gn 8:2).

לָכַד lākhadh (4058), Capture, take; niphal: be held (Jb 36:8); hithpael: clasp each other (Jb 41:17 [41:8]).

מָנַע mana' (4661), Withhold (Prv 11:26).

מַעְצוֹר ma'tsôr (4784), Hindrance (1 Sm 14:6—Codex Vaticanus only).

עָבַר 'āvar (5882), Go over, go through; be overcome (Jer 23:9).

עָצַר 'ātsar (6352), Qal: slave (2 Kgs 9:8); confine (Neh 6:10); niphal: be shut up (2 Chr 6:26).

צוּר tsûr (6961), Beseige (1 Sm 23:8).

צָרַר tsārar (7173), Shut up (2 Sm 20:3).

קָפַץ qāphats (7376), Withdraw (Ps 77:9 [76:9]).

1. **συνέχει sunechei** 3sing indic pres act
2. **συνέχουσιν sunechousin** 3pl indic pres act
3. **συνέχοντες sunechontes** nom pl masc part pres act
4. **συνέσχον suneschon** 3pl indic aor act
5. **συνέξουσιν sunexousin** 3pl indic fut act
6. **συνέχομαι sunechomai** 1sing indic pres mid
7. **συνεχόμενον sunechomenon** acc sing masc part pres mid
8. **συνεχομένους sunechomenous** acc pl masc part pres mid
9. **συνεχομένη sunechomenē** nom sing fem part pres mid
10. **συνείχετο suneicheto** 3sing indic imperf pass
11. **συνείχοντο suneichonto** 3pl indic imperf pass

8 that were **taken with** divers diseases and torments, . . Matt 4:24
9 Simon's wife's mother was **taken with** a ... fever; . . . Luke 4:38
11 for they **were taken with** great fear: 8:37
2 Master, the multitude **throng** thee and press thee, ... 8:45
6 and how **am I straitened** till it be accomplished! 12:50
5 thine enemies ... and **keep** thee **in** on every side, ... 19:43
3 men that **held** Jesus mocked him, and smote him. 22:63
4 cried out with a loud voice, and **stopped** their ears, Acts 7:57
10 Paul **was pressed** in the spirit, ... 18:5
7 that the father of Publius lay **sick of** a fever 28:8
1 For the love of Christ **constraineth** us; . . . . 2 Co 5:14
6 For I **am in a strait** betwixt two, ... Phlp 1:23

Classical Greek

Sunechō is derived from two words: *sun* (4713), meaning "with" or "together," and *echō* (2174), meaning "to have" or "to hold." Its basic sense is that of two things holding or pressing together, perhaps with something caught in the middle. It has a wide range of uses, such as holding two things together (coupling), holding someone prisoner (restraining), and being gripped with an inner pressure (constraint).

This wide range of meaning is observed in classical Greek, in the Septuagint, and in the papyri. Law was said to be the power that held the state together (Euripides *Supplices* 312), while God held the cosmos together (Xenophon *Cyropaedia* 8.7.22). Soldiers were held together to keep them from dispersing, and oarsmen stayed together to row in unison (Thucydides 7.14).

In the papyri *sunechō* is used of land that holds water (flooded), of sailors being held under arrest, of an individual in the grip of fever, of an individual compelled by force to repay a dowry, and of Attis as the one who holds all things together (*Moulton-Milligan*).

Septuagint Usage

In the Septuagint *sunechō* translates 17 different Hebrew words, only 3 of those more than once, but one (*'ātsar*), 13 times. In its most basic sense it refers to the literal holding together of things (e.g., the coupling of the curtains of the tabernacle, Exodus 26:3; 28:7; cf. 1 Kings 6:10 [LXX 3 Kings 6:10]). Such holding together came to signify imprisonment, inasmuch as a prisoner might have his hands bound together in fetters (Job 36:8) or be held fast by his captors. Figuratively, a person under the influence of alcohol is held fast by it (overcome, a prisoner, Jeremiah 23:9). Further, *sunechō* signifies restraint, the holding back of something: of rain ("shutting up the heavens," Genesis 8:2; Deuteronomy 11:17); of people (e.g., Doeg, 1 Samuel 21:7 [LXX 1 Kings 21:7]; or secluded women, withheld from the presence of men, 2 Samuel 20:3 [LXX 2 Kings 20:3]); of circumstances (the withdrawal of a plague, 2 Samuel 24:21,25 [LXX 2 Kings 24:21,25]); of speech (mute, Ezekiel 33:22). God alone is completely unrestrainable (1 Samuel 14:6 [LXX 1 Kings 14:6]). Finally, *sunechō* is translated "besiege" in the case of a city being pressed between hostile soldiers (1 Samuel 23:8 [LXX 1 Kings 23:8]).

New Testament Usage

A similar range of meaning is represented in *sunechō*'s 12 New Testament uses, 9 of them in Luke's writings. In the sense of restraining, the Lord Jesus was held prisoner by those who mocked and beat Him (Luke 22:63). Figuratively, the sick were in the grip of (captive to?) their illnesses (Matthew 4:24; Luke 4:38; Acts 28:8), and the Gadarenes were overcome by fear in the presence of Jesus (Luke 8:37).

The idea of "pressing" is seen literally in Acts 7:57: when the angry listeners wanted to cut off Stephen's words, they pressed their ears between their hands to cut off hearing. Elsewhere, the Lord Jesus warned Jerusalem of a day when it would be pressed (besieged) by armies on every side (Luke 19:43). He himself lived under the press (pressure) of the throngs that surrounded Him (Luke 8:45).

Such pressure can come from within as well as from without. Looking ahead to His death, the Lord referred to himself as pressed or gripped by that reality ("distressed," NASB) until it was finally accomplished (Luke 12:50), indicating the ever-present reality of His death that affected all He did. It is probably in a similar vein that Paul wrote that the love of Christ pressures ("compels," NIV, or "constrains," KJV) us to be faithful as ambassadors for Christ (2 Corinthians 5:14; cf. Acts 18:5). Because of that sense of duty to the Lord, Paul found himself pressed between two options (Philippians 1:23), his desire to go home to be with Christ and his obligation to stay and serve Christ.

STRONG 4912, BAUER 789, MOULTON-MILLIGAN 606-7, KITTEL 7:877-85, LIDDELL-SCOTT 1714.

4763. συνήδομαι sunēdomai verb

To rejoice, to delight together.

1. συνήδομαι sunēdomai 1sing indic pres mid

1 I delight in the law of God after the inward man: . . . Rom 7:22

Classical Greek

Sunēdomai is a compound verb that means to "rejoice or delight together." There is a broad range of meaning in classical Greek, from "malicious joy at misfortune" to genuinely "sympathize with" (cf. *Liddell-Scott*). It is not found in the Septuagint.

New Testament Usage

Sunēdomai is rare in the New Testament. Paul said he "joyfully agreed" or "delighted together with" the Law (Romans 7:22). The term is important because Paul argued that although he did not always keep the law of God, his inward/spiritual man joyfully agreed with the law of God. If he sinned, it was not because he enjoyed sin; instead, he sinned in spite of his delight in the law of the Lord.

STRONG 4913, BAUER 789, MOULTON-MILLIGAN 607, LIDDELL-SCOTT 1715.

4764. συνήθεια sunētheia noun

A mutual custom or habit, acquaintance, friendship, fellowship.

SYNONYM:

ἔθος ethos (1478)

1. συνήθεια sunētheia nom sing fem

2. συνήθειαν sunētheian acc sing fem

3. συνηθείᾳ sunētheia dat sing fem

1 But ye have a custom, that I should release ... one John 18:39
3 being accustomed to the idol (NASB) . . . . 1 Co 8:7
2 we have no such custom, neither the churches 11:16

Classical Greek

Sunētheia is a compound noun stemming from *sun* (4713), "with" or "together," and *ēthos* (2222), "custom" or "habit." The compound noun denotes a "shared custom" or "habit." The word can also denote friendship, intimacy, or intercourse. As well, it can be used of animals herding together. *Sunētheia* is used in Polybius (Second Century B.C.), Plutarch (First and Second Century A.D.), and Josephus (First Century A.D.) meaning "friendship" or "fellowship." This meaning is not found in the Septuagint or the New Testament. *Sunētheia* is used in the Homeric Hymns (Seventh Century B.C.), Plato (Fourth Century B.C.), and Philo (First Century A.D.) denoting "mutual habit" or "custom." This usage is also found in Josephus.

Septuagint Usage

In the Septuagint this word occurs only four times, all in 4 Maccabees. In the first two references the meaning is friendship or intimacy (2:12; 6:13). In the other two occurrences it denotes a habit or custom (13:22,27). Fourth Maccabees 13:22 reads, "As was the daily *custom*."

New Testament Usage

The word is rare in the New Testament. *Sunētheia* is found in John 18:39. Pilate addressed the Jews concerning their request to put Jesus to death. In spite of the fact Pilate found nothing worthy of death in Jesus, he feared the crowds. In an attempt to release Jesus, Pilate reminded the crowds of their mutual custom—that at Passover a criminal could be released by request of the Jews. However, instead of the Jews asking for Jesus' release, they demanded that Pilate free Barabbas, a thief and insurrectionist. (For a detailed history of this custom see Bruce, *The Gospel of John*, pp.355f.)

Paul used *sunētheia* in 1 Corinthians 11:16. Here he discussed the habit or custom of women wearing veils in church. In the passage Paul laid down various principles regarding proper attire and attitudes in worship concerning both hair length and head coverings. These principles were from a mutual custom or habit among the apostles as well as the Christian churches. Thus if the Corinthians should dispute such principles they were in essence disputing with the rest of Christendom. Paul used the term to strengthen his polemic. These principles were not just Paul's thinking or doing, but they had been adopted and maintained by all the churches.

STRONG 4914, BAUER 789, MOULTON-MILLIGAN 607, LIDDELL-SCOTT 1715.

4765. συνηλικιώτης sunēlikiōtēs noun

A person of equal age or stature; a peer.

1. συνηλικιώτας sunēlikiōtas acc pl masc

1 above many my equals in mine own nation,.......... Gal 1:14

Classical Greek

Sunēlikiōtēs is a noun that stems from *sun* (4713), "with," and *hēlikia* (2227), "maturity, age, stature." This compound denotes "a person of equal age or stature," thus "a peer." *Sunēlikiōtēs* can also be found without the *sun* prefix. It does not occur in the Septuagint.

New Testament Usage

The compound is found in Galatians 1:14. Paul stated that while a Pharisee, before conversion, he was far advanced beyond his *sunēlikiōtēs.* The terms *contemporaries* or *peers* make a good translation. Paul exceeded his peers in zeal for his Jewish roots and culture. This zeal led him to be one of the greatest persecutors of the Early Church, especially in comparison to his peers.

STRONG 4915, BAUER 789, MOULTON-MILLIGAN 607, LIDDELL-SCOTT 1715.

4766. συνθάπτω sunthaptō verb

To bury with someone, bury together.

CROSS-REFERENCE:

θάπτω thaptō (2267)

1. συνετάφημεν sunetaphēmen 1pl indic aor pass

2. συνταφέντες suntaphentes nom pl masc part aor pass

1 we are buried with him by baptism into death:...... Rom 6:4
2 Buried with him in baptism,......................... Col 2:12

Sunthaptō, a compound verb stemming from *sun* (4713), "with, together," and *thaptō* (2267), "to bury," means "to bury with someone" or "be buried together with another." The verb is found in two places in the New Testament. In both passages it is used figuratively. In Romans 6:4 and Colossians 2:12 Paul used the term for a believer's water baptism experience. Water baptism signifies the believer's death to self and sin, a burial with Christ, and a resurrection to the new life of the believer in Christ.

STRONG 4916, BAUER 789, MOULTON-MILLIGAN 607, KITTEL 7:766-97, LIDDELL-SCOTT 1716, COLIN BROWN 1:266.

4767. συνθλάω sunthlaō verb

To crush together, to break in pieces, shatter.

SYNONYMS:

θραύω thrauō (2329)
κατάγνυμι katagnumi (2579)
κατακλάω kataklaō (2592)
κλάω klaō (2779)
λύω luō (3061)
συνθρύπτω sunthruptō (4769)
συντρίβω suntribō (4789)

גָּדַע gādha' (1468), Piel: cut in two (Ps 107:16 [106:16]).

מָחַץ māchats (4410), Crush, shatter (Pss 68:21 [67:21], 110:5f. [109:5f.]).

נָתַץ nāthats (5606), Break (Ps 58:6 [57:6]).

נָקַר nāqar (5548), Piel: pierce (Jb 30:17—Codex Alexandrinus only).

פָּצַח pātsach (6723), Piel: break in pieces (Mi 3:3).

רָצַץ rātsats (7827), Qal: break (Is 42:3—Codex Alexandrinus only); piel: break in pieces (Ps 74:14 [73:14]—Codex Sinaiticus only); hiphil: crush (Jgs 9:53—Codex Alexandrinus only).

1. συνθλασθήσεται sunthlasthēsetai
3sing indic fut pass

1 whosoever shall fall on this stone shall be broken:.. Matt 21:44
1 shall fall upon that stone shall be broken;.......... Luke 20:18

Sunthlaō is a compound verb. The verb is made up of *sun* (4713), "with, together," and *thlaō*, "to break, destroy." The compound means "to crush together or break in pieces." It is used in the parallel passages of Matthew 21:44 and Luke 20:18. Taking His imagery from Isaiah 8:14f. and Daniel 2:34ff., Jesus talked about the judgment that was coming on the Jewish leaders and nation. The twofold description of judgment spoke of its certainty. Here *sunthlapō* is used to describe the crushing or breaking that would occur because the Jews rejected Jesus. Those, like pottery, who fall on the Rock (Messiah) will be broken in pieces; those on whom the Rock falls will be crushed.

Strong 4917, Bauer 790, Moulton-Milligan 607, Liddell-Scott 1717.

4768. συνθλίβω sunthlibō verb

To press or throng together, press upon.

Cognate:
θλίβω thlibō (2323)

Synonyms:
θλίβω thlibō (2323)
στενοχωρέω stenochōreō (4580)
συμπνίγω sumpnigō (4697)
συνέχω sunechō (4762)

רָצַץ rātsats (7827), Break (Eccl 12:6).

1. συνθλίβοντα sunthlibonta
acc sing masc part pres act

2. συνέθλιβον sunethlibon 3pl indic imperf act

2 and much people followed him, and thronged him... Mark 5:24
1 Thou seest the multitude thronging thee,.............. 5:31

Sunthlibō is made up of *sun* (4713), "together," and *thlibō* (2323), "to press upon" or "crowd." It means "to press together, to throng together" as in a massive crowd of people. *Sunthlibō* is found in Mark 5:24,31. Mark paints the picture well for the reader in describing the crowds of people who pressed upon Jesus. Yet with all the crowds pressing together around Him, He could tell He was touched in faith by the woman with the hemorrhage. The disciples were amazed at Jesus' question in verse 30. Because of the pressing crowds that surrounded them, they thought the question "Who touched me?" was one that could not be answered. But the woman had touched Jesus in a special way.

Strong 4918, Bauer 790, Liddell-Scott 1717.

4769. συνθρύπτω sunthruptō verb

To break in pieces.

Synonyms:
θραύω thrauō (2329)
κατάγνυμι katagnumi (2579)
κατακλάω kataklaō (2592)
κλάω klaō (2779)
λύω luō (3061)
συνθλάω sunthlaō (4767)
συντρίβω suntribō (4789)

1. συνθρύπτοντες sunthruptontes
nom pl masc part pres act

1 What mean ye to weep and to break mine heart?... Acts 21:13

Sunthruptō, from *sun* (4713), "with, together," and *thruptō*, "to break in small pieces," means "to break together in small pieces." Luke is the only New Testament writer to use *sunthruptō*. In Acts 21:13 the verb figuratively describes the emotions of the apostle Paul. His heart was being "broken in pieces" over the sentiments of the Christians in Caesarea. These Christians misunderstood the application of Agabus' prophecy and thus tried to prohibit Paul's journey to Jerusalem. Though Paul was moved by their love, he would not be deterred from going. He had already known that it was the Lord's will.

Strong 4919, Bauer 790, Moulton-Milligan 607, Liddell-Scott 1717.

4770. συνίημι suniēmi verb

Understand, comprehend, perceive.

Cognates:
ἀνίημι aniēmi (445)
ἀσύνετος asunetos (795)
ἀφίημι aphiēmi (856)
ἐγκάθετος enkathetos (1448)
καθίημι kathiēmi (2496)
παρίημι pariēmi (3797)
σύνεσις sunesis (4757)
συνετός sunetos (4758)

Synonyms:
αἰσθάνομαι aisthanomai (143)

γινώσκω ginōskō (1091)
ἐπιγινώσκω epiginōskō (1906)
ἐπίσταμαι epistamai (1971)
καταλαμβάνω katalambanō (2608)
νοέω noeō (3401)
οἶδα oida (3471)
ὁράω horaō (3571)
παρακολουθέω parakoloutheō (3738)
συνίημι suniēmi (4770)

בִּין bîn (1032), Qal: understand (Is 6:10); review, consider (Ezr 8:15, Ps 50:22 [49:22]); hiphil: discern, understand (1 Kgs 3:11, Neh 8:2f., Mi 4:12); hithpolel: consider, understand (Pss 107:43 [106:43], 119:95, [118:95], Is 1:3).

חוּשׁ chûsh (2456), Be disturbed (Jb 20:2).

יָדַע yādha' (3156), Know (Ex 36:1).

כּוּן kûn (3679), Make firm (Prv 21:29).

רָאָה rā'âh (7495), See; perceive (2 Sm 12:19).

שָׂכַל sākhal (7959), Qal: have success (1 Sm 18:30—Codex Alexandrinus only); hiphil: have success, understand(1 Sm 18:14f., Ps 106:7 [105:7]).

שָׁמַר shāmar (8490), Be careful (Jos 1:8—Codex Alexandrinus only).

1. **συνίετε suniete** 2pl indic/impr pres act
2. **συνίουσιν suniousin** 3pl indic pres act
3. **συνιῶσιν suniōsin** 3pl subj pres act
4. **συνίων suniōn** nom sing masc part pres act
5. **συνιέντος sunientos** gen sing masc part pres act
6. **συνιέντες sunientes** nom pl masc part pres act
7. **συνιέναι sunienai** inf pres act
8. **συνήκατε sunēkate** 2pl indic aor act
9. **συνῆκαν sunēkan** 3pl indic aor act
10. **συνῆτε sunēte** 2pl subj aor act
11. **συνῶσιν sunōsin** 3pl subj aor act
12. **συνήσουσιν sunēsousin** 3pl indic fut act
13. **συνιᾶσιν suniasin** 3pl indic pres act
14. **συνιείς sunieis** nom sing masc part pres act
15. **σύνετε sunete** 2pl impr aor act

2 hearing they hear not, neither **do they understand.** Matt 13:13
10 By hearing ye shall hear, and shall not **understand;**... 13:14
11 and **should understand** with their heart,.............. 13:15
5 word of the kingdom, and **understandeth** it not,...... 13:19
4 is he that heareth the word, and **understandeth** it;.... 13:23
8 **Have ye understood** all these things?................. 13:51
1 and said unto them, Hear, and **understand:**........... 15:10
9 Then **understood** they how that he bade them........ 16:12
9 Then the disciples **understood**...................... 17:13
3 and hearing they may hear, and not **understand;**... Mark 4:12
9 For they **considered** not the miracle of the loaves:..... 6:52
1 Hearken unto me every one ... and **understand:**........ 7:14
1 perceive ye not yet, neither **understand?**.............. 8:17
1 How is it that ye **do not understand?**................. 8:21
9 And they **understood** not the saying.............. Luke 2:50
3 and hearing they **might** not **understand**................ 8:10
9 And they **understood** none of these things:........... 18:34
7 that they **might understand** the scriptures,............ 24:45
7 he supposed his brethren **would have understood**.... Acts 7:25
9 but they **understood** not.............................. 7:25
10 Hearing ye shall hear, and shall not **understand;**...... 28:26
11 and **understand** with their heart,..................... 28:27
4 There is none that **understandeth,**................. Rom 3:11
12 and they that have not heard **shall understand.**.... Rom 15:21
2 and comparing themselves ... **are** not **wise**......... 2 Co 10:12
6 but **understanding** what the will of the Lord is...... Eph 5:17

Classical Greek

Suniēmi is a common verb in classical Greek literature meaning "to bring or set together." However, this nuance is never found in the New Testament. Figuratively, it means "to understand, to comprehend," or "to perceive" in the sense of gaining insight into something. In regard to this type of usage, the word signifies "perception, taking note of," and "grasping" in the sense of understanding (Goetzman, "Reason," *Colin Brown*, 3:130.)

Septuagint Usage

This verb appears over 120 times in the Septuagint with the majority in the Wisdom literature translating the Hebrew *bîn* ("to observe, to notice, to understand") and its derivatives. An important passage is Isaiah 43:10 where *suniēmi* means "to know" and "to believe." In Proverbs 2:5,9 "insight" comes when one is obedient to the Lord. The latest Old Testament literature connects the ability "to understand" with a gift imparted by God (Daniel 2:21).

New Testament Usage

In the New Testament the majority of *suniēmi*'s appearances occur in the Synoptics and Acts. Its primary meaning again is "to understand" or "to perceive," emphasizing not only the process of gaining information but also the process of obtaining comprehension. As in the later books of the Old Testament, this "understanding" is also tied to the action of God and the Holy Spirit in bestowing such insight. Quoting Isaiah 6:9 in reference to His use of parables, Jesus stated that physical hearing did not always bring mental comprehension (Matthew 13:13; Mark 4:12; Luke 8:10).

Suniēmi is used by Luke to describe Jesus' parents' inability to *understand* His actions at age 12 (Luke 2:50) and to describe Jesus' disciples' inability to *perceive* the prophecy of His death (Luke 18:34). It occurs in a positive way in Matthew 13:51 when the disciples acknowledged their *comprehension* of Jesus' parables; in Matthew 16:12 when the disciples "understood" what Jesus was telling them about the teaching of the Pharisees; and in Matthew 17:13 when they *perceived* that the prophecy about Elijah was describing John the Baptist.

Paul also used this verb but less frequently. In Romans 3:11 *suniēmi* is used to describe the original state of man as one in which he cannot *comprehend* God. It also occurs in Ephesians 5:17 where the Ephesians are encouraged to *understand* God's will.

Strong 4920, Bauer 790, Moulton-Milligan 607-8, Kittel 7:888-96, Liddell-Scott 1718, Colin Brown 3:130,132-33.

4771. συνίστημι sunistēmi verb

Recommend, demonstrate, endure, exist.

Cognate:
ἵστημι histēmi (2449)

Synonyms:
παράγω paragō (3717)
παρίστημι paristēmi (3798)

אָסַר 'āsar (646), Bind (Ps 118:27 [117:27]).

חָתַם chātham (2964), Seal; hiphil: be stopped (Lv 15:3).

יָקֹשׁ yāqosh (3483), Lay a snare (Ps 141:9 [140:9]).

כּוּן kûn (3679), Polel: found (Ps 107:36 [106:36]).

מִקְוָה miqwāh (4886), Reservoir (Ex 7:19).

עֲבַד ‛ăvadh (A5857), Do, make; wage (Dn 7:21—Aramaic).

עָמַד ‛āmadh (6198), Stand (1 Sm 17:26—Codex Alexandrinus only).

פָּקַד pāqadh (6734), Put in charge (Gn 40:4).

צָוָה tsāwâh (6943), Piel: commission, command (Nm 27:23, 32:28).

קָהַל qāhal (7234), Niphal: gather together (Ex 32:1).

שָׁלַח shālach (8365), Send; piel: stir up (Prv 6:14).

1. **συνίστημι sunistēmi** 1sing indic pres act
2. **συνίστησιν sunistēsin** 3sing indic pres act
3. **συνιστάνομεν sunistanomen** 1pl indic pres act
4. **συνιστῶν sunistōn** nom sing masc part pres act
5. **συνιστῶντες sunistōntes** nom pl masc part pres act
6. **συνιστανόντων sunistanontōn** gen pl masc part pres act
7. **συνιστάνειν sunistanein** inf pres act
8. **συνεστήσατε sunestēsate** 2pl indic aor act
9. **συνέστηκεν sunestēken** 3sing indic perf act
10. **συνεστῶτας sunestōtas** acc pl masc part perf act
11. **συνεστῶσα sunestōsa** nom sing fem part perf act
12. **συνίστασθαι sunistasthai** inf pres mid
13. **συνιστάνω sunistanō** 1sing indic pres act
14. **συνιστάνων sunistanōn** nom sing masc part pres act
15. **συνιστάντες sunistantes** nom pl masc part pres act
16. **συνιστάνοντες sunistanontes** nom pl masc part pres act

10 glory, and the two men that **stood with him**........ Luke 9:32
2 But if our unrighteousness **commend**.............. Rom 3:5
2 But God **commendeth** his love toward us,............. 5:8
1 I **commend** unto you Phebe our sister,............... 16:1
7 Do we begin again to **commend** ourselves?......... 2 Co 3:1
5 **commending** ourselves to every man's conscience...... 4:2
3 For we **commend** not ourselves again unto you,.... 2 Co 5:12
5 **approving** ourselves as the ministers of God,.......... 6:4
8 In all things ye **have approved** yourselves to be........ 7:11
6 or compare ourselves with some that **commend**....... 10:12
4 For not he that **commendeth** himself is approved,..... 10:18
2 but whom the Lord **commendeth**.................... 10:18
12 for I ought to **have been commended** of you:.......... 12:11
1 I **make** myself a transgressor....................... Gal 2:18
9 is before all things, and by him all things **consist**.... Col 1:17
11 earth **standing** out of the water and in the water:... 2 Pt 3:5

Classical Greek

Sunistēmi is a compound verb from *histēmi* (2449), "to put, place," or "set," and *sun* (4713), "with." The compound verb means "to put together, bring together, unite, collect." When used with people it can mean "introduce" or "recommend." When used with an object it usually means either to "stand by" or "to exist." The verb can be transitive or intransitive. Aristotle used the word in the sense of being composed or consisting of something (*Liddell-Scott*).

Philo used the word in the sense of "to hold together, cohere, or exist," the intransitive sense (*Bauer*). The word is found in 1 Clement 20:6 where the boundless seas are brought together in a gathering place. In the Oxyrhynchus Papyri IV of A.D. 16 there is the statement, "I am sure that I shall easily be introduced to the King" (*Moulton-Milligan*). Here *sunistēmi* refers to the recommending or bringing together of people.

Septuagint Usage

The Septuagint uses *sunistēmi* to describe the "pools of water" in Exodus 7:19. Literally, the Greek reads the "standing water." This water was contained or gathered together in pots or vessels as opposed to the water that ran freely in the Nile and canals.

In Numbers 16:3 *sunistēmi* refers to those who stood together with Korah against Moses and Aaron. They not only literally stood together in one place but were also figuratively standing together in their rebellion.

David talked to the armies of Israel who stood by him in the debate over Goliath. *Sunistēmi* is used in 1 Samuel 17:26 (LXX 1 Kings 17:26, Alexandrian text) to describe this literal act of standing by David.

In 1 Maccabees 12:43, Tryphon, seeing that Jonathan was greater in military strength than he could afford to deal with, "recommended" Jonathan to his friends and soldiers. The recommendation was to result in obedience. It is used frequently in the books of Maccabees.

New Testament Usage

The New Testament has *sunistēmi* in both the transitive and intransitive sense. *Sunistēmi* is seen in the transitive sense in Romans 16:1 where Paul recommended Phoebe to the Romans. Paul also used the word quite frequently in 2 Corinthians. He wrote to a church that doubted his apostolic authority and teaching. Thus Paul had much to say about recommendation and commendation. In 3:1 Paul asked if he needed some letter of recommendation as if the Corinthians did not know who Paul was or what he did. He made the point that the Corinthians themselves were his letter of recommendation. Paul also stated that his life and experiences recommended him (6:4ff.). His recommendation stood in contrast to the superapostles who were recommending themselves (10:12). They did this through their charismatic life-styles and miracles. Paul summarized the whole controversy of recommendation by stating that only God's recommendation really counts (10:18).

Sunistēmi is also used with the love of God in Romans 5:8. God proved or "set forth" His love by sending Christ to die, and that while we were yet sinners. Paul used *sunistēmi* in the sense of "to prove" in Galatians 2:18.

The New Testament also uses *sunistēmi* in the intransitive sense. In the Transfiguration (Luke 9:32) the two men who appeared with Jesus "stood with" Him. Paul stated that in Christ all things are held together or exist (Colossians 1:17). Peter likewise stated that the earth was formed, came to be, "out of water and with water" (2 Peter 3:5, NIV).

STRONG 4921, BAUER 790-91, MOULTON-MILLIGAN 608, KITTEL 7:896-98, LIDDELL-SCOTT 1718-19.

4772. συνοδεύω sunodeuō verb

Travel with, journey with.

CROSS-REFERENCE:
ὁδός hodos (3461)

הָלַךְ hālakh (2050), Go (Zec 8:21—only some Sinaiticus texts).

1. συνοδεύοντες sunodeuontes nom pl masc part pres act

1 **men which journeyed with him stood speechless,** ..... **Acts 9:7**

This is a compound verb from *sun* (4713), "with, together," and *hodeuō* (3456), "to journey" or "travel," and is found first in Koine Greek. Used with *tini* (see 4948), "someone," it refers to those who accompany one on his journey. In Acts 9:7, its only New Testament appearance, *sunodeuō* is used for those who were going with Paul to Damascus to persecute the Christians.

STRONG 4922, BAUER 791, MOULTON-MILLIGAN 610, LIDDELL-SCOTT 1720.

4773. συνοδία sunodia noun

Caravan, group of travelers.

CROSS-REFERENCE:
ὁδός hodos (3461)

יָחַשׂ yachas (3293), Hithpael: be enrolled by genealogy (Neh 7:5).

יַחַשׂ yachas (3294), Genealogical record (Neh 7:5,64).

1. συνοδίᾳ sunodia dat sing fem

1 **supposing him to have been in the company,** .... **Luke 2:44**

In the New Testament *sunodia* is found only in Luke 2:44 and refers to a "company of travelers" going in the same direction down a road. This was the "caravan" from which Jesus was missed by Mary and Joseph, who it seems were probably separated by custom. "The women usually went ahead and the men followed. Joseph may have thought Jesus was with Mary and Mary that he was with Joseph" (Robertson, *Word Pictures in the New Testament*, 2:33).

STRONG 4923, BAUER 791, MOULTON-MILLIGAN 610, LIDDELL-SCOTT 1720.

4774. σύνοιδα sunoida verb

Be aware of, be conscious of, share knowledge of.

CROSS-REFERENCE:
οἶδα oida (3471)

1. σύνοιδα sunoida 1sing indic perf act
2. συνειδυίας suneiduias gen sing fem part perf act
3. συνειδυίης suneiduiēs gen sing fem part perf act

2 **his wife also being privy to it,** .... **Acts 5:2**
1 **For I know nothing by myself;** .... **1 Co 4:4**

Classical Greek

In classical Greek *sunoida* is used in two primary ways. The first is "to share the knowledge of" or "to be privy to" as a witness would have in a trial. The other is in the reflexive form (with *emautō*, "myself") meaning "to be conscious of." (See Hahn, "Conscience," *Colin Brown*, 1:348.)

Sunoida is also related to the noun *suneidēsis* (4743), "consciousness, conscience." Although both the verb and the noun appear in the Septuagint translating *yādha'*, "know," and *māddā'*, "knowledge," there really are no Old

Testament words which convey the Greek concept of conscience. The focus of the Hebrews was not man's attitude and knowledge of himself, but his attitude and knowledge of God. Where these terms do appear in the Septuagint an assimilation of the Greek concept is observable (ibid., 1:349). These however are later passages of the Intertestamental Period (e.g., 1 Maccabees 4:21; Sirach 42:18).

New Testament Usage

In Acts 5:2 the context shows that the knowledge of Ananias' act of keeping back some money was shared with his wife Sapphira. They were both "privy to" (sharing the knowledge of) this information. The reflexive form of *sunoida* is found in 1 Corinthians 4:4 where Paul confessed his lack of personal knowledge concerning any matter that might show him guilty of an offense. The best translation would be, "I know nothing against myself."

This verb is also closely related to *suneidon* (4744), the aorist of *sunoraō*, meaning "to be aware" or "conscious." It is translated "considered" in Acts 12:12 (see also Acts 14:6).

Bauer 791, Moulton-Milligan 611, Kittel 7:898-919, Liddell-Scott 1720-21, Colin Brown 1:348,350-51,353.

4775. συνοικέω sunoikeō verb

Live with, dwell with.

Cross-Reference:
οἰκέω oikeō (3474)

בָּעַל bāʻal (1195), Married person, marry (Gn 20:3, Is 62:5).

יָבַם yāvam (3101), Piel: perform the duty of a brother-in-law (Dt 25:5).

1. συνοικοῦντες sunoikountes
nom pl masc part pres act

1 **dwell with them according to knowledge,** .... 1 Pt 3:7

Sunoikeō is a compound verb from the preposition *sun* (4713), "with, together," and *oikeō* (3474), "live, dwell," meaning to "live with" or "dwell with." Robertson calls it an old verb commonly used for domestic associations (*Word Pictures in the New Testament,* 6:110). The usual reference is to a husband and wife living under the same roof. *Sunoikeō* is found only in 1 Peter 3:7 where Peter instructed husbands and wives to live together in harmony.

Strong 4924, Bauer 791, Moulton-Milligan 611, Liddell-Scott 1721.

4776. συνοικοδομέω sunoikodomeō verb

Build together.

Cross-Reference:
οἰκοδομέω oikodomeō (3481)

1. συνοικοδομεῖσθε sunoikodomeisthe
2pl indic pres mid

1 In whom ye also **are builded together** .... Eph 2:22

Classical Greek

Formed from the preposition *sun* (4713), "with, together," and *oikodomeō* (3481), "to build," *sunoikodomeō* means to "build with" or "build together." It appears infrequently in classical Greek and always in a literal sense of constructing or building up some structure.

New Testament Usage

This compound verb appears only once in the New Testament in Ephesians 2:22. Here it is accompanied by five other terms related to *oikos* (3486), "house." Its figurative use here describes how Christ's body of believers has been brought into existence in unity. This tight-knit fellowship exists because of the work of Jesus.

Strong 4925, Bauer 791, Moulton-Milligan 611, Kittel 5:148, Liddell-Scott 1722, Colin Brown 2:249,251,253.

4777. συνομιλέω sunomileō verb

Talk with, converse.

Cognate:
ὁμιλέω homileō (3519)

Synonym:
συλλαλέω sullaleō (4665)

1. συνομιλῶν sunomilōn nom sing masc part pres act

1 And as he **talked with him,** he went in, ... Acts 10:27

Sunomileō is a rare compound verb from the common verb *homileō* (3519), "to be in company with" or "to consort with," and the preposition *sun* (4713), "with, together." It means "to talk with" someone. In Acts 10:27 it is a present active participle that describes concurrent action as Peter and Cornelius entered the house. They "talked together" as they went inside.

Strong 4926, Bauer 791, Moulton-Milligan 611, Liddell-Scott 1722.

4778. συνομορέω sunomoreō verb

Border on, be next to.

1. συνομοροῦσα sunomorousa
nom sing fem part pres act

1 whose house **joined hard** to the synagogue.......... Acts 18:7

This is a late verb found only once in the New Testament which refers to an object that shares a boundary with another object. It can be translated "to border on" or "to be joined to." In Acts 18:7 *sunomoreō* is used of the house of Titius Justus being "next door to" (NIV) the synagogue in Corinth.

STRONG 4927, BAUER 791, MOULTON-MILLIGAN 611, LIDDELL-SCOTT 1722.

4778B. συνοράω sunoraō

See word study at number 4744.

4779. συνοχή sunochē noun

Distress, anguish.

CROSS-REFERENCE:

ἔχω echō (2174)

מָצוֹר mātsôr (4857), Siege (Jer 52:5, Mi 5:1).

שׁוֹאָה shô'āh (8177), Desolation (Jb 30:3).

1. συνοχή sunochē nom sing fem

2. συνοχῆς sunochēs gen sing fem

1 upon the earth **distress** of nations, with perplexity; Luke 21:25
2 For out of much affliction and **anguish** of heart..... 2 Co 2:4

Classical Greek

This noun is used in two primary ways in classical Greek. First, it is used to mean "maintenance" or "control." Second, it is also used in various expressions from a narrow place in the road, to denote straights or narrows, to mean continuity or coherence, or to denote a conflict in battle (*Liddell-Scott*).

Septuagint Usage

It is used metaphorically in the Septuagint to symbolize the compressing of a person's inner emotions and can be translated "distress" or "anguish" in many cases. The context gives the best direction as to which would be the proper translation. Job 30:3, Micah 4:14, and Jeremiah 52:5 are examples where *sunochē* is used in the Septuagint.

New Testament Usage

In the New Testament it is used only in the metaphoric sense of "distress" or "anguish." In Luke 21:25 Jesus used *sunochē* to describe the great turmoil that will grip the nations at the end of the age. In its only other occurrence Paul wrote in 2 Corinthians 2:4 that his first epistle was born out of deep inner "distress" over the actions of those in the church. The noun describes situations of anxiety and stress created by "pressing" circumstances. The source of the pressure can be found either inside or outside the person or persons who are subject to these feelings.

STRONG 4928, BAUER 791, MOULTON-MILLIGAN 611, KITTEL 7:886-87, LIDDELL-SCOTT 1724.

4780. συνσρπάζω sunsrpazō

See word study at number 4734B.

4781. συντάσσω suntassō verb

Appoint, order, direct.

COGNATE:

τάσσω tassō (4872)

SYNONYMS:

διαμαρτύρομαι diamarturomai (1257)
διαστέλλω diastellō (1285)
διατάσσω diatassō (1293)
ἐντέλλομαι entellomai (1765)
ἐξορκίζω exorkizō (1828)
ἐπιτάσσω epitassō (1988)
κελεύω keleuō (2724)
λέγω legō (2978)
ὁρκίζω horkizō (3589)
παραγγέλλω parangellō (3715)
προστάσσω prostassō (4225)
τάσσω tassō (4872)

אָמַר 'āmar (569), Say (Jb 37:6).

דָּבַר dāvar (1744), Piel: speak, command (Ex 31:13, Jos 4:8, Jb 42:9).

דָּבָר dāvār (1745), Word (Ex 12:35).

חָבַר chāvar (2357), Hithpael: make an alliance (Dn 11:23).

טָרַף ṭāraph (3072), Tear in pieces; hiphil: feed (Prv 30:8 [24:31]).

יָעַד yā'adh (3366), Appoint; niphal: be assembled (1 Kgs 8:5—Codex Alexandrinus only).

יָצַר yātsar (3443), Form, shape; plan (Is 37:26).

פָּקַד pāqadh (6734), Seek, call to account; pual: be counted (Ex 38:21 [37:19]).

צָוָה tsāwâh (6943), Piel: command (Ex 16:16, Nm 31:21, Jer 32:13 [39:13]); pual: be commanded (Nm 3:16, 36:2).

1. συνέταξεν sunetaxen 3sing indic aor act

1 did just as Jesus **had directed** them, (NASB)....... Matt 21:6
1 And the disciples did as Jesus had **appointed** them;.... 26:19
1 for the potter's field, as the Lord **appointed** me........ 27:10

Suntassō is a compound of the preposition *sun* (4713), "with, together," and the verb *tassō* (4872), "to place in order, to arrange, to fix." It is best translated "to appoint" or "to direct."

Matthew is the only New Testament author who used this verb. In Matthew 26:19 the disciples did as they were "directed" by Jesus in regard to preparation for the Passover. *Suntassō* appears again in Matthew 27:10 in a quote from Jeremiah 32:6-9. The Old Testament passage says that Jeremiah bought a potter's field as "directed" by the Lord. It was a foreshadowing of the actions of the chief priests with Judas' money. (Some manuscripts have *suntassō* in Matthew 21:6 also.)

STRONG 4929, BAUER 791-92, MOULTON-MILLIGAN 613, LIDDELL-SCOTT 1725.

4782. συντέλεια sunteleia noun

Completion, consummation, end.

COGNATE:
τελέω teleō (4903)

SYNONYMS:
ἔκβασις ekbasis (1532)
πέρας peras (3872)
τέλος telos (4904)

אַחֲרִית 'achărîth (321), End (Dt 11:12).

אָסִיף 'āṣîph (628), Ingathering (Ex 23:16).

בֶּצַע betsa' (1240), Dishonest gain (1 Sm 8:3).

חָרַץ chārats (2888), Determine, cut; niphal: be decreed (Dn 9:27).

כֹּל kōl (3725), All (Am 8:8, 9:5, Hb 1:9,15).

כָּלָה kālâh (3735), Come to an end; piel: destroy (2 Kgs 13:17,19, Ezr 9:14).

כָּלָה kālāh (3737), End, destruction (Neh 9:31, Jer 5:10).

כָּלִיל kālîl (3752), Whole (Jgs 20:40—Codex Vaticanus only).

כּוּל kûl (3677), Hiphil: consume (Ez 21:28).

מִסְפָּר miṣpār (4709), Number (Jos 4:8).

סוּפָה ṣûphāh (5679), Whirlwind (Am 1:14, Na 1:3).

קֵץ qēts (7377), End (Dn 8:19).

קֶצֶב qetsev (7379I), Shape (1 Kgs 6:25).

תִּכְלָה tikhlāh (8831), Limit (Ps 119:96 [118:96]).

תַּכְלִית takhlîth (8832), Boundary (Jb 26:10).

תָּמַם tāmam (8882), Be finished (1 Kgs 6:22 [6:21]).

תְּקוּפָה t^eqûphāh (8958), The turn of the year (2 Chr 24:23).

1. **συντέλεια sunteleia** nom sing fem
2. **συντελείας sunteleias** gen sing fem
3. **συντελείᾳ sunteleia** dat sing fem

1 the harvest is the end of the world; .... Matt 13:39
3 so shall it be in the end of this world................ 13:40
3 So shall it be at the end of the world: 13:49
2 sign of thy coming, and of the end of the world? 24:3
2 with you alway, even unto the end of the world........ 28:20
3 now once in the end of the world hath he appeared . . Heb 9:26

Classical Greek

There are several related definitions for this word in classical Greek. Like Biblical Greek, *sunteleia* can mean "consummation" or "completion" in relation to time. A common meaning is "joint-contribution"; by extension the word denotes a "club, union, or contributor" (*Moulton-Milligan*). *Sunteleia* is also used metaphorically for instruction (*Liddell-Scott*).

Septuagint Usage

In the Septuagint *sunteleia* is also used in relation to time. It translates the Hebrew word *qēts* in an eschatological sense meaning "completion" (Schippers, "Goal," *Colin Brown*, 2:60) such as in Daniel 8:19 or 11:27. It can also mean the end of any period of time, such as one's life or a war.

Other Septuagintal meanings include the completion of crossing the Jordan (Joshua 4:8), "perfection" (Ezekiel 22:12), "conclusion" (Sirach 22:8), and "destruction" such as in Jeremiah 5:10,18; Nahum 1:8f.; and Zephaniah 1:18.

New Testament Usage

In the New Testament *sunteleia* appears only in eschatological settings, most of which are in Matthew. In the explanation of the Parable of the Wheat and the Tares the harvest is "the *end* of the world" (Matthew 13:39f.). In Matthew 24:3 the disciples asked Jesus what would be the sign of "the *end* of the world." In the Great Commission of Matthew 28:20 Jesus promised to be with the disciples He was sending out to "the *end* of the world." Most translations have "end of the age" in these verses. The confusion arises over the correct translation of the word *aiōn* (163), "age" or "world." In all five occurrences of the phrase "end of the world" in Matthew the Greek is the same: *sunteleia tou aiōnos*. Furthermore, in all five passages the second coming of Christ is indicated. This is the time of the great harvest (Matthew 13:39,40,49). Jesus assured His disciples that He would be with them until His physical return. In another sense, Hebrew 9:26 "stresses that the saving work accomplished in Christ is itself the event of the end time" (Delling, "telos," *Kittel*, 8:66).

STRONG 4930, BAUER 792, MOULTON-MILLIGAN 613, KITTEL 8:64-66, LIDDELL-SCOTT 1725-26, COLIN BROWN 2:59-62.

4783. συντελέω sunteleō verb

Bring to an end, complete, accomplish, fulfill.

COGNATE:
τελέω teleō (4903)
SYNONYMS:
ἀναπληρόω anaplēroō (376)
ἀνταναπληρόω antanaplēroō (463)
ἀποτελέω apoteleō (652)
διανύω dianuō (1268)
ἐκπληρόω ekplēroō (1590)
ἐκτελέω ekteleō (1602)
ἐξαρτίζω exartizō (1806)
ἐπιτελέω epiteleō (1989)
κατεργάζομαι katergazomai (2686)
πληρόω plēroō (3997)
τελειόω teleioō (4896)
τελέω teleō (4903)

אָסַף 'āṣaph (636), Gather (Lv 23:39).

בָּלָה bālâh (1126), Be worn out, become old; piel: spend (Jb 21:13).

בָּצַע bātsa' (1239), Cut off; qal: gain (Prv 1:19); piel: finish, fulfill (Is 10:12, Lam 2:17).

גָּמַר gāmar (1625), Come to an end (Ps 7:9).

גָּרַע gāra' (1686), Hinder (Jb 15:4).

חָתַם chātham (2964), Seal (Dn 9:24).

כֹּל kōl (3725), All, whole (Jb 14:14, Ez 11:15, Hos 13:2).

כָּלָה kālâh (3735), Qal: be finished, perish (2 Chr 29:34, Ez 5:12); be determined (1 Sm 20:7); piel: finish, destroy (Gn 6:16, 2 Sm 21:5, Ez 42:15); pual: be completed (Gn 2:1).

כָּלָה kālāh (3737), Destruction (Is 28:22).

כִּלָּיוֹן killāyôn (3750), Destruction (Is 10:22 [10:23]).

כָּלִיל kālîl (3752), Perfect (Ez 16:14).

כָּרַת kārath (3901), Cut; make (Jer 34:8,15 [41:8,15]).

מוּת mûth (4322), Die (Ez 6:12).

מָלֵא mālē' (4527), Qal: be completed (Dn 10:3); piel: fulfill (Gn 29:27).

נָקַף nāqaph (5545), Go around; complete a cycle (Jb 1:5).

עָשָׂה 'āsâh (6449), Qal: do, practice (Ex 36:2, Is 32:6, Mi 2:1); niphal: be done (Est 4:1, Is 46:10).

שָׁלַם shālam (8396), Qal: be finished (2 Chr 5:1 [4:22]); piel: finish? (1 Kgs 9:25 [3:1]).

תָּמַם tāmam (8882), Come to an end, be done (Dt 34:8, Jos 4:10f.).

1. **συντελῶν suntelōn** nom sing masc part pres act
2. **συνετέλεσεν sunetelesen** 3sing indic aor act
3. **συντελέσας suntelesas** nom sing masc part aor act
4. **συντελέσω suntelesō** 1sing indic fut act
5. **συντελεῖσθαι suntelcisthai** inf prcs mid
6. **συντελεσθεισῶν suntelestheisōn** gen pl fem part aor pass
7. **συνετελέσθη sunetelesthē** 3sing indic aor pass

2 when Jesus **had ended** these sayings, ... Matt 7:28
5 be the sign when all these things shall **be fulfilled**? Mark 13:4
6 when they **were ended**, he afterward hungered .... Luke 4:2
3 And when the devil **had ended** all the temptation, ... 4:13
5 And when the seven days were almost **ended**, ... Acts 21:27
1 For he **will finish** the work, ... Rom 9:28
4 the days come, ... when I **will make** a new covenant . .Heb 8:8

Classical Greek

In classical Greek writings *sunteleō* means "bring to an end, complete" (*Liddell-Scott*). In addition, it can be a technical term for "supply." In certain contexts it can also mean "pay, contribute, make good" (*Moulton-Milligan*) or "be brought about, pay to a common pot" (*Liddell-Scott*).

Septuagint Usage

In the Septuagint *sunteleō* does not mean "contribute" or "pay"; instead, it can mean "carry out, achieve, do" (Isaiah 32:6; Micah 2:1), and "complete" (Leviticus 16:20). In another sense of the word Scripture says that God executes His wrath *completely* (Lamentations 4:11; Ezekiel 5:13; Daniel 11:36). *Sunteleō* most frequently translates the Hebrew word *kālâh*, "to complete, destroy, be finished, be at an end."

New Testament Usage

In the New Testament *sunteleō* primarily means the completion of a period of time. Luke 2:21 (in some manuscripts) notes the end of the first 8 days of Jesus' life and thus the time for His dedication in the temple. Luke 4:2,13 records that after 40 days the temptation of Jesus by the devil *came to an end*. Acts 21:27 tells of the *end* of the 7-day period of purification by Paul and his associates before entering the temple.

In a related sense Matthew 7:28 states that when Jesus had "*ended* these sayings" (the Sermon on the Mount), the people were astonished. In Mark 13:4 the disciples asked when Jesus' prophecy about the destruction of the temple would *be fulfilled*. Finally, Romans 9:28 is a quotation of Isaiah 10:22 and states that the Lord will *finish* the work of establishing a remnant as He had promised.

STRONG 4931, BAUER 792, MOULTON-MILLIGAN 613-14, KITTEL 8:62-64, LIDDELL-SCOTT 1726, COLIN BROWN 2:59.

4784. συντέμνω suntemnō verb

Cut short, shorten.

CROSS-REFERENCE:
περιτέμνω peritemnō (3919)

חָרַץ chārats (2888), Decree (Is 10:22 [10:23]).

1. **συντέμνων suntemnōn** nom sing masc part pres act
2. **συντετμημένον suntetmēmenon** acc sing masc part perf mid

1 **finish** the work, and **cut it short** in righteousness: ....Rom 9:28
2 because a **short** work will the Lord make 9:28

Classical Greek

Suntemnō, a compound verb meaning "cut down" or "cut short," is used so often in reference to time that this connection is normally assumed. Vine suggests that it can be rendered "bring to an end" or "accomplish speedily" (*Expository Dictionary*, "Cut").

New Testament Usage

Suntemnō is used in the New Testament only in Romans 9:28 where Paul quoted Isaiah 10:22,23. The passage describes what will happen to Israel in the end times. A remnant of Israel will be saved, and the Lord will fulfill His Word. *Suntemnō* is used as a present active participle with *sunteleō* (4783), "complete, finish, close," another present active participle. Both participles describe how this sentence will be carried out. *Sunteleō* emphasizes the "completeness" of the action, while *suntemnō* suggests the "speed" by which it will be accomplished. The length of time will be "limited" or "shortened."

Strong 4932, Bauer 792, Moulton-Milligan 614, Liddell-Scott 1726.

4785. συντηρέω suntēreō verb

Protect, save, hold, keep.

Cross-Reference:
τηρέω tēreō (4931)

קַיָּם qayyām (A7290B) Sure (Dn 4:26 [4:23]—Aramaic).

שָׁמַר shāmar (8490), Keep (Ez 18:19).

1. συνετήρει sunetērei 3sing indic imperf act
2. συντηροῦνται suntērountai 3pl indic pres mid

2 new wine into new bottles, and both are preserved... Matt 9:17
1 and observed him; and when he heard him,.........Mark 6:20
1 But Mary kept all these things, and pondered them ..Luke 2:19
2 be put into new bottles; and both are preserved......... 5:38

Suntēreō is a compound of the preposition *sun* (4713), "with, together," and the verb *tereō*, "watch, keep, preserve." In the active voice it means "to protect" or "to defend," while in the passive it means "to be saved" or "to be preserved." It appears infrequently in classical Greek.

Septuagint Usage

In some manuscripts of the Septuagint *suntēreō* appears in Daniel 7:28. This is an interesting passage because it is used to mean "to hold" or "to keep" a matter in one's own mind. Daniel kept his divine vision to himself. It was certainly a way of "protecting" or "keeping safe" some very private and disturbing information. This same specialized meaning appears later in Luke 2:19. It appears also in the Septuagint in Ezekiel 18:19; Sirach 13:12; Tobit 1:11, etc.

New Testament Usage

In the New Testament *suntēreō* appears in Matthew 9:17, Mark 6:20, and Luke 2:19. The first passage refers to the "preservation" of new wineskins and new wine when the two are used together. In the Mark reference the verb is best translated "protect." Herod "protected" John the Baptist from Herodias' anger because he viewed John as a righteous and holy man. In Luke 2:19 Mary "kept" the words of the shepherds to herself. She was in awe of God's wondrous work and "protected" it from the scrutiny of the public.

Strong 4933, Bauer 792, Moulton-Milligan 614, Kittel 8:151, Liddell-Scott 1727.

4786. συντίθημι suntithēmi verb

Agree, covenant, decide.

Cross-Reference:
τίθημι tithēmi (4935)

קָשַׁר qāshar (7489), Conspire (1 Sm 22:13).

שָׁלַם shālam (8396), Be complete, be at peace; hiphil: make peace (1 Kgs 22:44 [16:28]—Codex Vaticanus only).

1. συνέθεντο sunethento 3pl indic aor mid
2. συνετέθειντο sunetetheinto 3pl indic plperf mid

1 were glad, and covenanted to give him money...... Luke 22:5
2 for the Jews had agreed already,................... John 9:22
1 The Jews have agreed to desire thee that...........Acts 23:20
1 And the Jews also assented,.......................... 24:9

The verb *tithēmi* (4935), "to put" or "to place," and the preposition *sun* (4713), "with, together," combine to form the verb *suntithēmi*. In both active and passive voices it means "put together." However, the middle voice is best translated "to agree with" or "to covenant with." In this way *suntithēmi* suggests the coming together of two parties to form a pact or agreement.

Although *suntithēmi* can be used in a positive manner, its appearances in Scripture are all negative, as certain groups of people came together to scheme against those who were godly. In Luke 22:5 the chief priests and teachers of the Law came to an "agreement" to pay Judas for betraying Jesus. In John 9:22 the Jewish leaders "decided" to excommunicate anyone who believed Jesus to be the Messiah. Finally, Acts 23:20 relates the "pact" among the Jews as they plotted to kill Paul.

Strong 4934, Bauer 792, Moulton-Milligan 614, Liddell-Scott 1727.

4787. συντόμως suntomōs adv

Briefly, concisely, promptly.

Cross-Reference:

περιτέμνω peritemnō (3919)

1. συντόμως suntomōs

1 wouldest hear us of thy clemency a few words...... Acts 24:4

This is an adverb related to the verb *suntemnō* (4784), "to cut short," and is best translated "promptly, readily, briefly, concisely." As an adverb it is often used in reference to the length of a discourse. In this case it describes someone who uses few words in getting to the point. Used only in Acts 24:4, *suntomōs* occurs in the speech of Tertullus as he promised to "briefly" state his remarks about Paul.

Strong 4935, Bauer 793, Moulton-Milligan 614, Liddell-Scott 1728.

4788. συντρέχω suntrechō verb

Run together, run with.

Cross-Reference:

τρέχω trechō (4983)

1. συντρεχόντων suntrechontōn gen pl masc part pres act

2. συνέδραμεν sunedramen 3sing indic aor act

3. συνέδραμον sunedramon 3pl indic aor act

3 and ran afoot thither out of all cities,.............. Mark 6:33
2 all the people ran together unto them in the porch ...Acts 3:11
1 run not with them to the same excess of riot,....... 1 Pt 4:4

Classical Greek and Septuagint Usage

The compound verb *suntrechō* means "to run with" or "to run together." When it is used figuratively it suggests close association, harmony, and even agreement between those involved in the interaction. In Psalm 50:18 (LXX 49:18) *suntrechō* is used in this figurative sense describing those who "join" with thieves.

New Testament Usage

Suntrechō appears three times in the New Testament. Both Mark 6:33 (those who "ran" ahead of Jesus) and Acts 3:11 (those who "ran" to see the healed beggar) are examples of the literal meaning. In 1 Peter 4:4 it is used metaphorically. Here the pagans are mentioned as not understanding why Christians do not "join" them in their actions of debauchery.

Strong 4936, Bauer 793, Moulton-Milligan 614-15, Liddell-Scott 1728.

4789. συντρίβω suntribō verb

Break, shatter, beat, bruise.

Synonyms:

θραύω thrauō (2329)
κατάγνυμι katagnumi (2579)
κατακλάω kataklaō (2592)
κλάω klaō (2779)
λύω luō (3061)
συνθλάω sunthlaō (4767)
συνθρύπτω sunthruptō (4769)

גָּדַע gādha' (1468), Qal: cut down (Is 10:33); niphal: be cut down (Is 14:12).

דָּכָא dākhâ' (1850), Niphal: lowly (Is 57:15).

הָרַס hāraṣ (2117), Break out (Ps 58:6 [57:6]).

חָתַת chāthath (2973), Qal: be shattered (Jer 48:20 [31:20]); niphal: go deeper (Prv 17:10).

טָרַף ṭāraph (3072), Tear (Dt 33:20).

כָּשַׁל kāshal (3911), Qal: fail (Neh 4:10); niphal: fall (Dn 11:34).

כָּתַת kāthath (3936), Grind (Dt 9:21—Codex Alexandrinus only).

נָכָה nākhâh (5409), Hiphil: strike down (Jos 7:5).

נָפַץ nāphats (5492), Piel: dash to pieces (Ps 2:9).

פָּצַע pātsa' (6728), Wound (1 Kgs 20:37 [21:37]).

צָלַע tsāla' (7027), Lame person (Mi 4:6f.).

קָרַם qāram (7449), Stoop (Is 46:1).

רָטַשׁ rāṭash (7660), Piel: slaughter (Is 13:18).

רָמַס rāmaṣ (7717), Trample (Dn 8:7).

רָצַץ rātsats (7827), Qal: break (Eccl 12:6); piel: crush (Ps 74:14 [73:14]).

שָׁבַר shāvar (8132), Qal: break (Lv 11:33, Ps 105:16 [104:16], Ez 30:18); niphal: be broken (Lv 6:28, Ps 34:20 [33:20]; piel: smash, demolish (Dt 12:3, 2 Chr 34:4, Jer 43:13 [50:13]).

שָׁטַף shāṭaph (8278), Sweep away, wash away; niphal: be swept away (Dn 11:22).

שָׁמַד shāmadh (8436), Niphal: be destroyed (Ez 32:12).

שָׁסַע shāṣa' (8538), Be split; piel: tear apart (Jgs 14:6).

תְּבַר t^evar (A8735), Be brittle (Dn 2:42—Aramaic).

1. συντρῖβον suntribon nom/acc sing neu part pres act

2. συντρίψασα suntripsasa nom sing fem part aor act

3. συντρίψει suntripsei 3sing indic fut act

4. συντρίβεται suntribetai 3sing indic pres mid

5. συντετριμμένον suntetrimmenon acc sing masc part perf mid

6. συντετριμμένους suntetrimmenous acc pl masc part perf mid

7. συντετρῖφθαι suntetriphthai inf perf mid

8. συντριβήσεται suntribēsetai 3sing indic fut pass

5 A bruised reed shall he not break,................ Matt 12:20
7 and the fetters broken in pieces:................... Mark 5:4
2 and she brake the box, and poured it on his head...... 14:3
6 he hath sent me to heal the brokenhearted,......... Luke 4:18
1 and bruising him hardly departeth from him............ 9:39
8 be fulfilled, A bone of him shall not be broken.....John 19:36
3 shall bruise Satan under your feet shortly.......... Rom 16:20
4 vessels of a potter shall they be broken to shivers:.... Rev 2:27

Classical Greek

This verb is used frequently in classical Greek. When used with things *suntribō* can be translated "break, crush, shatter," or "smash." When it is used with persons it means "beat, bruise," or "mistreat." *Suntribō* can mean "annihilate" in reference to enemies (*Bauer*).

Septuagint Usage

In the Septuagint it appears often in the passive voice describing a contrite heart. (See Psalm 51:17 [LXX 50:17]; Isaiah 57:15.) Vine suggests that it might possibly be "a figure of stones made smooth by being rubbed together in streams" (*Expository Dictionary*, "Break"). Exodus 32:19 refers to the "breaking" of the tables of the Law and Job 38:11 to the "crashing" of waves.

New Testament Usage

New Testament passages combine *suntribō* with both things and persons. Mark 14:3 describes the "smashing" of an alabaster flask. Matthew 12:20 refers to the "bruising" of a reed. John 19:36 mentions the "breaking" of bones. (See also Mark 5:4; Revelation 2:27.) In Luke 9:39 an evil spirit is described as "beating" a young boy before he is healed by Jesus. Paul wrote in Romans 16:20 about the "crushing" of Satan by the God of peace.

STRONG 4937, BAUER 793, MOULTON-MILLIGAN 615, KITTEL 7:919-25, LIDDELL-SCOTT 1728-29.

4790. σύντριμμα suntrimma noun

Destruction, calamity, ruin.

SYNONYMS:
ἀπώλεια apōleia (677)
καθαίρεσις kathairesis (2478)
ὄλεθρος olethros (3502)

עַצֶּבֶת ʿatstseveth (6329), Wound (Ps 147:3 [146:3]).

פֶּצַע petsaʿ (6729), Crush (Jb 9:17, Prv 20:30 23:29).

שֶׁבֶר shever (8133I), Broken thing, injury (Lv 21:19, Jer 10:19).

שִׁבָּרוֹן shibbārôn (8136), Destruction (Jer 17:18).

שֹׁד shōdh (8160), Destruction (Is 22:4, 59:7, 60:18).

1. σύντριμμα suntrimma nom/acc sing neu

1 **Destruction and misery are in their ways:........... Rom 3:16**

The primary meaning of the term *suntrimma* is "broken" or "shattered," for example, a fractured bone (Leviticus 21:19). It is similar to another verb, *suntribō* (4789), "to break into pieces." It is a compound verb composed of the preposition *sun* (4713), "together," and the noun *trimma* related to the verb *tribō*, "to rub." It is also used metaphorically to describe calamity or destruction. Thus Isaiah mourns over the destruction of Israel (22:4).

New Testament Usage

The only use of the term in the New Testament is metaphoric (Romans 3:16). Paul quoted from Isaiah 59:7 in his description of the sinful nature of man, " . . . *destruction* and misery are in their ways."

STRONG 4938, BAUER 793, MOULTON-MILLIGAN 615, KITTEL 7:919-25, LIDDELL-SCOTT 1729.

4791. σύντροφος suntrophos adj

Nourished with; brought up with.

CROSS-REFERENCE:
τρέφω trephō (4982)

1. σύντροφος suntrophos nom sing masc

1 **Manaen, which had been brought up with Herod.... Acts 13:1**

Classical Greek

Translated "brought up with, nourished with, comrade, foster brother," *suntrophos* can describe a companion of one's childhood and youth (*Liddell-Scott*).

New Testament Usage

Vine states that the word has been found in Hellenistic usage as a court term, identifying a close friend of a prince or king (*Expository Dictionary*, "Foster-Brother"). This appears to be its New Testament use, since it occurs only in Acts 13:1 where Manaen "had been brought up with" Herod the tetrarch. Robertson says this reference to Manaen "shows how the gospel was reaching some of the higher classes (home of Herod Antipas)" (*Word Pictures in the New Testament*, 3:177).

STRONG 4939, BAUER 793, MOULTON-MILLIGAN 615, LIDDELL-SCOTT 1729.

4792. συντυγχάνω suntunchanō verb

To meet with; to come to.

COGNATE:
τυγχάνω tunchanō (5018)

SYNONYM:
ἀπαντάω apantaō (524)

1. συντυχεῖν suntuchein inf aor act

1 **and could not come at him for the press........... Luke 8:19**

This is a verb describing the act of someone "joining" or "meeting" another person or people. It is a compound verb composed of the preposition *sun* (4713), "with, together," and *tunchanō* (5018), "to reach." *Liddell-Scott* identifies two uses of the term: (1) when used of persons it is translated "meet with, fall in with"; (2) when used of accidents and chances it is translated "happen to, befall." It occurs only once in the New Testament and is used in reference to persons. In Luke 8:19 the mother and brothers of Jesus came to Him and "were not able to get near him because of the crowd" (NIV).

STRONG 4940, BAUER 793, MOULTON-MILLIGAN 615, LIDDELL-SCOTT 1729.

4793. Συντύχη Suntuchē name

Syntyche.

1. Συντύχην Suntuchēn acc fem

1 I beseech Euodias, and beseech Syntyche,........... Phlp 4:2

A Christian woman in Philippi. Paul pleaded with her and Euodias to make peace with each other (Philippians 4:2).

4794. συνυποκρίνομαι sunupokrinomai verb

To dissemble with; act the hypocrite with.

CROSS-REFERENCE:
ὑποκρίνομαι hupokrinomai (5109)

1. συνυπεκρίθησαν sunupekrithēsan 3pl indic aor pass

1 And the other Jews dissembled likewise with him;.... Gal 2:13

Classical Greek

This is a rare term used only once in the New Testament and a few times in classical literature. It is a compound verb composed of the preposition *sun* (4713), "with," and the verb *hupokrinomai* (5109), "acting the hypocrite." In classical Greek it is used particularly to describe the role of the actors, thus meaning "play-acting" (Bruce, *New International Greek Testament Commentary, Galatians*, p.131).

New Testament Usage

It appears in Galatians 2:13 where Peter and other Christian Jews were eating with Christian Gentiles. When certain men of Jerusalem appeared, Peter arose and separated himself from the Gentiles. He pretended his motive was loyalty to the Mosaic law, but it was really fear of the visitors. This act influenced the other Christian Jews to depart also. Thus, the reading in Galatians 2:13, "And the other Jews *dissembled* likewise *with* him." (Cf. NIV, "The other Jews joined him in his hypocrisy.")

STRONG 4942, BAUER 793, MOULTON-MILLIGAN 615-16, KITTEL 8:559-70, LIDDELL-SCOTT 1730, COLIN BROWN 2:469.

4795. συνυπουργέω sunupourgeō verb

To work together; cooperate with.

CROSS-REFERENCE:
ἐργάζομαι ergazomai (2021)

1. συνυπουργούντων sunupourgountōn gen pl masc part pres act

1 Ye also helping together by prayer for us,.......... 2 Co 1:11

Sunupourgeō is an ordinary term identifying the act of working together, helping together, cooperating with. It is rarely found in other Greek literature and occurs only once in the New Testament. Paul used the term in 2 Corinthians 1:11 in soliciting prayers from the Corinthian believers, "Ye also *helping together* by prayer for us . . . . " That is, by prayer they were joining him in serving God.

STRONG 4943, BAUER 793, LIDDELL-SCOTT 1730.

4796. συνωδίνω sunōdinō verb

To be in travail together, suffer with.

1. συνωδίνει sunōdinei 3sing indic pres act

1 groaneth and travaileth in pain together until now... Rom 8:22

Classical Greek

A compound of *sun* and *ōdinō*, *sunōdinō* rarely occurs in classical Greek. When it does occur it means "be in travail together" or "share in the agony of woes" (*Liddell-Scott*). It does not appear in the Septuagint.

New Testament Usage

Sunōdinō is used only once in the New Testament, and that metaphorically. In Romans 8:22 Paul described creation suffering birth pangs for the new heavens and the new earth. As a father undergoes agony along with the mother in childbirth, even so all the elements of nature are sharing pains together until the rebirth of the world.

STRONG 4944, BAUER 793, LIDDELL-SCOTT 1730.

4797. συνωμοσία sunōmosia noun

A conspiracy; a swearing together.

Cross-Reference:
ὀμνύω omnuō (3523)

1. συνωμοσίαν sunōmosian acc sing fem

1 more than forty which had made this conspiracy.... Acts 23:13

This is the ordinary term for conspiracy. It is used throughout Greek literature (classical, papyri, etc.) to denote a conspiracy or confederacy. References usually identify soldiers or politicians entering into an oath together to put down a democracy or political union (*Liddell-Scott*). The meaning is apparent in its single occurrence in the New Testament (Acts 23:13). Over 40 Jews banded together to have Paul killed. Luke's use of the term aptly describes their "conspiracy."

Strong 4945, Bauer 793-94, Moulton-Milligan 616, Liddell-Scott 1730.

4798. Συράκουσαι Surakousai name

Syracuse.

1. Συρακούσας Surakousas acc pl fem

1 landing at Syracuse, we tarried there three days.... Acts 28:12

A city on the east coast of Sicily visited by Paul on his journey to Rome (Acts 28:12).

4798B. Συραφοινίκισσα Suraphoinikissa name-adj

Woman of Syrian Phoenicia.

1. Συροφοινίκισσα Surophoinikissa nom sing fem
2. Συραφοινίκισσα Suraphoinikissa nom sing fem
3. Συρα Φοινίκισσα Sura Phoinikissa

1 a Gentile, of the Syrophoenician race. (NASB)..... Mark 7:26

An unnamed Gentile woman from whose daughter Jesus expelled a demon in response to her great display of faith and humility (Mark 7:26).

4799. Συρία Suria name

Syria.

1. Συρίας Surias gen fem
2. Συρίαν Surian acc fem

2 And his fame went throughout all Syria:............Matt 4:24
1 first made when Cyrenius was governor of Syria..... Luke 2:2
2 of the Gentiles in Antioch and Syria and Cilicia:...Acts 15:23
2 And he went through Syria and Cilicia,............... 15:41
2 and sailed thence into Syria,......................... 18:18
2 as he was about to sail into Syria,.................... 20:3
2 we left it on the left hand, and sailed into Syria,...... 21:3
1 I came into the regions of Syria and Cilicia;......... Gal 1:21

Syria is the area north and northeast of the Holy Land. In New Testament times it was a Roman province which covered the area of the modern nations of Syria and Lebanon and also parts of Turkey and Iraq (Matthew 4:24; Luke 2:2; Acts 15:23,41; 18:18; 20:3; 21:3; Galatians 1:21).

4800. Σύρος Suros name

Syrian.

1. Σύρος Suros nom masc

1 none ... cleansed, saving Naaman the Syrian.........Luke 4:27

In Luke 4:27 "the Syrian" referred to Naaman whom Elisha the prophet healed of leprosy.

4801. Συροφοίνισσα Surophoinissa name-adj

Woman of Syrian Phoenicia.

1. Συροφοίνισσα Surophoinissa nom sing fem

1 woman was a Greek, a Syrophenician by nation;....Mark 7:26

A variant spelling of *Suraphoinikissa* (4798B).

4802. σύρτις surtis noun

Quicksands.

1. σύρτιν surtin acc sing fem

1 fearing lest they should fall into the quicksands,.... Acts 27:17

Classical Greek

This term is the proper name for two shallow coasts off the northern border of Africa, a dangerous coastal region. Syrtis Major, west of Cyrenaica (now called the Gulf of Sidra), and Syrtis Minor (now called the Gulf of Gabes) were dangerous due to their many sandbanks and shallows (Filson, "Syrtis," *Interpreter's Dictionary of the Bible*, 4:496). Often the wind would drive ships right into this peril. Metaphorically, the term is also used to mean "destruction" in classical Greek (*Liddell-Scott*).

New Testament Usage

The only New Testament use of the term is in Acts 27:17 where a shipwreck is described. It was the Syrtis Major upon which Paul's ship was in danger of being driven. However, the winds changed and drove them into the Sea of Adria, as this part of the Mediterranean is sometimes called.

Strong 4950, Bauer 794, Liddell-Scott 1733.

4803. σύρω surō verb

To draw, drag, haul.

COGNATE:

κατασύρω katasurō (2663)

SYNONYMS:

ἀντλέω antleō (498)
ἀποσπάω apospaō (639)
ἑλκύω helkuō (1657)
κατασύρω katasurō (2663)
σπάω spaō (4538)

1. σύρει surei 3sing indic pres act
2. σύρων surōn nom sing masc part pres act
3. σύροντες surontes nom pl masc part pres act
4. ἔσυρον esuron 3pl indic imperf act

3 **dragging** the net with fishes....................... John 21:8
2 **haling** men and women committed them to prison....Acts 8:3
4 and, having stoned Paul, **drew** him out of the city,..... 14:19
4 they **drew** Jason and certain brethren................. 17:6
1 his tail **drew** the third part of the stars of heaven,...Rev 12:4

Classical Greek

The term *surō* denotes an effort to draw or drag away someone or something. Its use in classical Greek includes persons "crawling" and waves or rivers "sweeping away" objects (*Liddell-Scott*). It is found in Josephus and other Greek literature (along with some compound forms) with the literal meaning. Metaphorically, *surō* is used to mean "to be dragged" or "drawn." It is also used in references to taxes "to be attached" to land (ibid.).

Septuagint Usage

The Septuagint uses are similar in meaning. In Deuteronomy 32:24 the term is used of divine judgment in the form of poisonous serpents "creeping" on the earth. In 2 Samuel 17:13 (LXX 2 Kings 17:13) if a city does not surrender it will be "pulled down" into the river.

New Testament Usage

The term occurs five times in the New Testament. In John 21:8 a fishing net was "dragged" to shore by the disciples. In Acts 8:3 Saul, the persecutor of the Church, was literally "dragging" men and women to prison for their faith. The reverse takes place in Acts 14:19 where Paul was stoned by the Jews of Lystra and "dragged" outside the city. In Acts 17:6 the Jews of Thessalonica could not find Paul, so they "dragged" Jason and his Christian friends to the judge. In Revelation 12:4 John's apocalyptic imagery describes the tail of the dragon as having "swept away" a third of the stars. According to Beasley-Murray this "may reflect in the original narrative an account of the war between Satan and the angels in which many angels were thrown down (cf. Daniel 8:10, which independently echoes the same tradition)" (*New Century Bible Commentary, Revelation*, p.199). He goes on to suggest, however, that this image may well be limited to portraying the dragon's terrible power (ibid.).

STRONG 4951, BAUER 794, MOULTON-MILLIGAN 616-17, LIDDELL-SCOTT 1733.

4804. συσπαράσσω susparassō verb

Cause one to shake or convulse violently, throw into a fit.

COGNATE:

σπαράσσω sparassō (4535)

SYNONYMS:

διαῤῥήσσω diarrhēssō (1278)
ῥήγνυμι rhēgnumi (4342)
σπαράσσω sparassō (4535)
σχίζω schizō (4829)

1. συνεσπάραξεν sunesparaxen 3sing indic aor act

1 the spirit **threw him into a convulsion**, (NASB)..... Mark 9:20
1 the devil threw him down, and **tare** him.............Luke 9:42

Susparassō is not found in any extant Greek texts prior to the New Testament, although its related term *sparassō* ("rend, tear apart, convulse") is found in both classical Greek and the Septuagint (2 Samuel 22:8; Jeremiah 4:19).

The term appears twice in the New Testament. In Luke 9:42 (and the parallel text Mark 9:20) it describes the force of a demon controlling a young boy. The demon was "tearing violently" or "pulling apart" the boy. Luke's medical background provided vivid details of the physical effects of demonic possession in this instance.

STRONG 4952, BAUER 794, LIDDELL-SCOTT 1733.

4805. σύσσημον sussēmon noun

A token; a signal.

CROSS-REFERENCE:

σημαίνω sēmainō (4446)

מַשְׂאֵת mas'ēth (5020), Smoke (Jgs 20:38).

נֵס nēs (5438), Banner (Is 5:26, 49:22, 62:10).

1. σύσσημον sussēmon nom/acc sing neu
2. σύνσημον sunsēmon nom/acc sing neu

1 And he that betrayed him had given them **a token**, Mark 14:44

Classical Greek and Septuagint Usage

This is a common word in the ancient Greek for a signal that has been made by an agreement of individuals. It is a compound term composed of the word for "sign," *sēmeion* (4447), and "with," *sun* (4713). According to Vine this was a "signal" agreed upon with others (*Expository Dictionary*,

"Token"). (Note that before the *sigma*, the *nu* in *sun* drops out. The Greek language did not tolerate dental [e.g., *nu*]—sibilant [e.g., *sigma*] combinations.) This form is used in classical literature as well as the Septuagint (Judges 20:38,40; Isaiah 5:26; 49:22; 62:10).

New Testament Usage

Sussēmon is used only once in the New Testament (Mark 14:44). The "signal" was the betrayal kiss used by Judas to identify Christ to the soldiers. Where the other Gospels use the simple term for "sign," only Mark uses this compound form with *sun*, emphasizing the plot made by Judas with the soldiers. Robertson concludes, "The signal was the kiss by Judas, a contemptible desecration of a friendly salutation" (Robertson, *Word Pictures in the New Testament,* 1:385).

STRONG 4953, BAUER 794, MOULTON-MILLIGAN 617, KITTEL 7:269, LIDDELL-SCOTT 1734.

4806. σύσσωμος sussōmos adj

Belonging to the same body.

CROSS-REFERENCE:
σῶμα sōma (4835)

1. σύσσωμα sussōma nom/acc pl neu

1 should be fellowheirs, and of the **same body**, ... Eph 3:6

A term unique to Christian literature, *sussōmos* is a compound form composed of the term for *sōma* (4835), "body," and the preposition *sun* (4713), "with." It is used only once in the New Testament, in Ephesians 3:6. Paul wrote of the union of Gentiles and Jews as belonging to "the same body," the Church. The word *body* is used metaphorically in reference to the universal Church, the body of Christ. Paul used the term to emphasize that Gentiles were of the same body, not attached nor distinguishable from the original members. Neither schism nor national variety nor previous condition nor any lines of separation exist in the Church, the body of Christ (Eadie, *John Eadie Greek Text Commentaries*, 2:220).

STRONG 4954, BAUER 794, KITTEL 7:1024-94, LIDDELL-SCOTT 1734.

4807. συστασιαστής sustasiastēs noun

Fellow rioter.

1. συστασιαστῶν sustasiastōn gen pl masc

1 them that **had made insurrection with** him, ... Mark 15:7

The term *sustasiastēs* denotes a companion in a riot or insurrection. It is a compound from the noun *stasiastēs* (4564B), referring to a revolutionist or rebel, and the prepositional prefix *sun* (4713), "with." It refers to one who stirs up an insurrection, the leader of the group. Usually the simple noun form alone is used; however, this rare compound form appears in the New Testament and in Josephus (*Antiquities* 14.2.1).

Occurring only once in the New Testament, it is used in the Gospel of Mark to describe the role of Barabbas at Jesus' trial. Barabbas was "bound with them that had made insurrection with him, who had committed murder in the insurrection" (Mark 15:7). Robertson describes him as "a desperate criminal, leader in the insurrection, sedition, or revolution against Rome, the very thing that the Jews up at Bethsaida Julias wanted Jesus to lead (John 6:15). Barabbas was the leader of these rioters and was bound with them" (Robertson, *Word Pictures in the New Testament,* 1:392).

STRONG 4955, BAUER 794, LIDDELL-SCOTT 1734.

4808. συστατικός sustatikos adj

Commendatory.

CROSS-REFERENCE:
ἵστημι histēmi (2449)

1. συστατικῶν sustatikōn gen pl fem

1 epistles of **commendation** to you, ... 2 Co 3:1
1 or letters of **commendation** from you? 3:1

Classical Greek

The term *sustatikos* is used frequently in the papyri and other Greek writings. It is used in two primary ways in the New Testament: to mean "putting together or drawing together," "a component"; and to mean "introductory, commendatory," "an introduction" either in person or by letter; "a deed of representation or power of attorney" (*Liddell-Scott*). It does not occur in the Septuagint.

New Testament Usage

Sustatikos is used only twice in the New Testament, both times by Paul in 2 Corinthians 3:1. Paul asked the Corinthians if he needed "letters of commendation" to confirm his character to them. Apparently letters or epistles of commendation were common according to numerous references in the New Testament (Acts 18:27; Romans 16:1; 1 Corinthians 16:10; Colossians 4:10, etc.).

STRONG 4956, BAUER 795, MOULTON-MILLIGAN 617, LIDDELL-SCOTT 1735.

4809. συσταυρόω sustauroō verb

To crucify along with.

Cross-Reference:

σταυρός stauros (4567)

1. συνεσταυρώθη sunestaurōthē 3sing indic aor pass

2. συσταυρωθέντος sustaurōthentos gen sing masc part aor pass

3. συσταυρωθέντες sustaurōthentes nom pl masc part aor pass

4. συνεσταύρωμαι sunestaurōmai 1sing indic perf mid

5. συνεσταυρωμένοι sunestaurōmenoi nom pl masc part perf mid

6. συνσταυρωθέντος sunstaurōthentos gen sing masc part aor pass

7. συνσταυρωθέντες sunstaurōthentes nom pl masc part aor pass

3 The thieves also, which **were crucified with him,**.... Matt 27:44
5 And they **that were crucified with him** reviled him. Mark 15:32
2 and of the other which **was crucified with him**...... John 19:32
1 that our old man **is crucified with him,**.............. Rom 6:6
4 I **am crucified with** Christ: nevertheless I live;........ Gal 2:20

The term *sustauroō* (cf. *stauroō* [4568], "crucify") does not mean simply "to crucify" but rather "to be crucified along with" or "among others" who are also being crucified.

This compound occurs five times in the New Testament, with both literal and figurative meanings. It is used in three of the Gospels to describe the literal crucifixion of Jesus with others, namely the two thieves (Matthew 27:44; Mark 15:32; John 19:32). Paul used the term figuratively to describe the spiritual death (crucifixion) of the carnal man through Christ's death on the cross (Romans 6:6; Galatians 2:20). For Paul baptism is a baptism into the death of Christ. It is the vehicle by which the individual mystically and spiritually participates in Christ's death. The concept of union is very prevalent in Romans 6:4-8 as seen in the use of several words with the prepositional prefix *sun*, "with." According to Stagg it is not that one dies *of* himself or *for* himself. Rather, the death that each believer dies with Jesus is like Jesus' death at Golgotha. It is a death of self and a yielding up of one's life and will to another (*New Testament Theology*, p.224).

Strong 4957, Bauer 795, Kittel 7:766-97, Liddell-Scott 1735 (see "sustauroomai"), Colin Brown 1:391,394,397-99,401.

4810. συστέλλω sustellō verb

To draw together; to wrap around.

Cross-Reference:

στέλλομαι stellomai (4575)

כָּנַע kānaʿ (3789), Niphal: be subdued (Jgs 8:28).

קָפַץ qāphats (7376), Be shut (Sir 4:31).

1. συνέστειλαν sunesteilan 3pl indic aor act

2. συνεσταλμένος sunestalmenos nom sing masc part perf mid

1 And the young men arose, **wound him up,**.......... Acts 5:6
2 But this I say, brethren, the time **is short:**.......... 1 Co 7:29

Classical Greek

The term *sustellō* is composed of the preposition *sun* (4713), "with" or "together," and the verb *stellomai* (4575), "bring" or "gather." In classical Greek it is a general term of restriction or constriction used variously to mean shortening a sail, reducing expenses, depriving of food and drink, humbling a person, or packing luggage (*Liddell-Scott*). It can also be used to mean "wrap up tightly, enshroud," or of cloaks that are "wrapped closely around oneself." In this way the term is also used as an expression of readiness for action (ibid.).

According to Vincent, the term has three specialized meanings: (1) to wrap garments about one's self, for example, tucking in the garments around the loins as preparation for a service; (2) to shroud a corpse for burial; and (3) medically, to bandage a limb or to describe the contraction of tumors or body organs (Vincent, *Word Studies in the New Testament*, 1:467).

New Testament Usage

Sustellō is found only twice in the New Testament. In Acts 5:6 it is used to describe the "enshrouding" of Ananias' corpse for burial. The term has been variously interpreted here to mean "enshroud, wrap up, pack up, remove" (*Bauer*). The second figurative occurrence is in 1 Corinthians 7:29 in the phrase "the time is short," signifying that time has been drawn together, contracted, into an abbreviated scale. Paul's reference to the imminent return of Christ for His church is graphically portrayed by the term.

Strong 4958, Bauer 795, Kittel 7:596-97, Liddell-Scott 1735.

4811. συστενάζω sustenazō verb

To groan together.

Cross-Reference:

στενάζω stenazō (4578)

1. συστενάζει sustenazei 3sing indic pres act

1 **groaneth** and travaileth in pain **together** until now... Rom 8:22

Classical Greek

Used only by Euripides (Fifth Century B.C.) in Greek writings prior to the New Testament, *sustenazō* means "groaning with" someone or some group. It is related to the term *stenazō* (4578), which refers to an unexpressed deep feeling of inner sorrow which is translated variously in the New Testament as "grieve, groan, sigh, murmur." This term is then prefixed with *sun* (4713) (with the standard loss of *n* before *s*), meaning "with," to signify a groaning "together." It means more than groaning "with" as alongside others, but a groaning "together" as in sharing the same inner sorrow (Schneider, "sustenazō," *Kittel*, 7:601).

New Testament Usage

Paul is the only New Testament writer to use the term. In Romans 8:22 he wrote, "The whole creation *groaneth* . . . until now." Schneider states, "It is a sighing in which all non-human creation is at one . . . . The reason for the sighing is that through the fall of Adam creation is subject to bondage (v. 20)" (ibid., 7:602).

STRONG 4959, BAUER 795, KITTEL 7:600-603, LIDDELL-SCOTT 1735.

4812. συστοιχέω sustoicheō verb

To answer to, to correspond to.

CROSS-REFERENCE:

στοιχεῖον stoicheion (4598)

1. συστοιχεῖ sustoichei 3sing indic pres act

1 **and answereth to Jerusalem which now is,** . . . . **Gal 4:25**

This is a common Greek word with a literal and figurative meaning. In classical literature it is used literally of soldiers standing in the same line or row (*Liddell-Scott*). More common is the related noun *sustoichia*, denoting a series of things or ideas. It is especially important to Pythagorean philosophy which speaks of series of coordinate pairs (ibid.). Paul used the term in Galatians 4:25 where he used Sarah and Hagar in a series of comparisons and contrasts to show the Galatians they were children of freedom and not slaves to the yoke of Judaism. In this series, which is in actuality and allegory, Paul carefully detailed each corresponding part of his allegory. In doing so he used *sustoicheō* to tell his readers that Hagar "corresponds" (or represents for the purpose of this story) to the earthly Jerusalem because, like Hagar who was bound to Sarah as her servant, Jerusalem (i.e., the Jews) is also in bondage to the Law.

STRONG 4960, BAUER 795, KITTEL 7:669, LIDDELL-SCOTT 1735, COLIN BROWN 2:451-52.

4813. συστρατιώτης sustratiōtēs noun

Fellow soldier.

CROSS-REFERENCE:

στρατεύομαι strateuomai (4605)

1. συστρατιώτῃ sustratiōtē dat sing masc

2. συστρατιώτην sustratiōtēn acc sing masc

2 **companion in labour, and fellow soldier,** . . . . **Phlp 2:25**

1 **beloved Apphia, and Archippus our fellow soldier,** . . **Phlm 1:2**

This is the ordinary term for fellow soldier, a comrade in battle. It consists of the noun *stratiōtēs* (4608), "soldier," and *sun* (4713), "with." It is used infrequently in classical writings, and always in a literal sense. However, it is used only figuratively in Christian literature in describing fellowship in Christian service.

The term is used twice in the New Testament, and both times by the apostle Paul (Philippians 2:25; Philemon 2). Figuratively used the term can refer to: (1) the fellowship in conflicts, victories, and disciplines of Christian life; (2) the honor of being associated with Paul and his sufferings (*Bauer*); and (3) according to Thayer, the common danger and endurance of hardships with others for the cause of Christ (*Greek-English Lexicon*).

STRONG 4961, BAUER 795, KITTEL 7:701-13, LIDDELL-SCOTT 1736.

4814. συστρέφω sustrephō verb

To gather; twist together.

COGNATES:

στρέφω strephō (4613)
συστροφή sustrophē (4815)

SYNONYMS:

ἀθροίζω athroizō (119B)
ἐπισυνάγω episunagō (1980)
συλλέγω sullegō (4667)
συνάγω sunagō (4714)
συναθροίζω sunathroizō (4718)
τρυγάω trugaō (5007)

הָלַךְ hālakh (2050), Go, walk; hithpael: move back and forth (Ez 1:13).

חוּל chûl (2435), Dance, go around; hithpolel: swirl (Jer 23:19).

כָּמַר kāmar (3770), Niphal: yearn (Gn 43:30).

לָקַט lāqaṭ (4092), Gather; hithpael: gather together (Jgs 11:3).

צָרַר tsārar (7173), Wrap up (Prv 30:4 [24:27]).

קָבַץ qāvats (7192), Gather (Jgs 12:4).

קָשַׁר qāshar (7489), Qal: be among, conspire (2 Sm 15:31, 1 Kgs 16:9, 2 Kgs 15:10); hithpael: conspire (2 Ks 9:14).

1. συστρέψαντος sustrepsantos gen sing masc part aor act

2. συστρεφομένων sustrephomenōn gen pl masc/neu part pres mid

2 while they were gathering together (NASB).........Matt 17:22
1 And when Paul had gathered a bundle of sticks,....Acts 28:3

Classical Greek and Septuagint Usage

Sustrephō is a compound form of *sun* (4713), "together," and *strephō* (4613), "to turn." It is used throughout the Greek documents (classical, papyri, Septuagint, et al.) meaning "to twist together" as a bundle of straw or sticks, or "to gather together" or "assemble" in reference to soldiers or other persons. The Septuagint records the judge Jephthah "gathering together" the men of Gilead in Judges 12:4. It is occasionally used in regard to twisting one's words, knotting hair, whirlwinds, etc. (*Liddell-Scott*).

New Testament Usage

Only two instances of *sustrephō* are found in the New Testament. In some texts of Matthew 17:22 it is used in place of *anastrephō* to describe Jesus and His followers as they "gathered together" in Galilee (cf. NIV), thus reflecting the word's use as a general term of constriction. After Paul's shipwreck on the island of Melita, he "gathered" a bundle of sticks to build a fire (Acts 28:3).

STRONG 4962, BAUER 795, MOULTON-MILLIGAN 617, LIDDELL-SCOTT 1736, COLIN BROWN 2:33.

4815. συστροφή sustrophē noun

A binding together, a coalition; an unruly gathering.

CROSS-REFERENCE:
συστρέφω sustrephō (4814)

סוֹד ṣôdh (5660), Secret council (Ps 64:2 [63:2]).

עֵדָה 'ēdhāh (5920), Assembly; swarm (Jgs 14:8—Codex Alexandrinus only).

צָרַר tsārar (7173), Bind up, be bound up (Hos 4:19, 13:12).

קֶשֶׁר qesher (7490), Conspiracy (2 Kgs 15:15).

1. συστροφῆς sustrophēs gen sing fem

2. συστροφήν sustrophēn acc sing fem

1 whereby we may give an account of this concourse. Acts 19:40
2 certain of the Jews banded together,.................. 23:12

Classical Greek

The word *sustrophē* is composed of two terms, *sun* (4713), "with," and *trophē* (5001), "to turn." It is used throughout classical Greek writings with both literal and metaphoric meanings. Literally, it refers to things that are twisted together, for example, yarn, chalkstones, nerves and sinews, twisted grain in wood, etc. The term is used likewise by classical writers in reference to a flock of birds, and even to the twisting together of a knot (*Liddell-Scott*). Metaphorically, it is used to denote communication between men in the form of a conspiracy or coalition, or a disorderly gathering such as a riot, as noted in the writings of Herodotus and Polybius (*Bauer*).

Septuagint Usage

The Septuagint uses the term with the same diversity as classical Greek. Judges 14:8 uses the term in reference to Samson's "*swarm* of bees" and the honey in the carcass. In this sense the "gathering" is of physical objects. In 2 Kings 15:15 *sustrophē* is used of the "conspiracy" of Shallum when he overthrew the evil king Zachariah. Similarly it is used in David's prayer to God against those who would bring an "insurrection" against him (Psalm 64:2), and in Amaziah's accusation of "conspiracy" against Jeroboam (Amos 7:10). In Hosea *sustrophē* is used twice. The first appearance is in 4:19 where it denotes the whirlwind (cf. the "spirit of whoredom" in 4:12), spoken of earlier, that will consume them (Wolff, *Hermeneia, Hosea*, p.92). In Hosea 13:12 Israel's sin is "bound up"; i.e., in keeping with the legal tone of the passage, their guilt remains as though laid away in a nonreversible legal record (ibid., p.228).

New Testament Usage

Only two instances of *sustrophē* are noted in the New Testament. Both are located in the Book of Acts, and both times a "conspiracy" is described. In Acts 19:40 the term is translated "concourse," in reference to the disorderly riot of Ephesians who were upset at Paul and his fellow workers for preaching against the goddess Diana (Artemis). In Acts 23:12 the term is translated "banded (twisted) together" in reference to a group of Jews who had conspired to have Paul killed.

STRONG 4963, BAUER 795, MOULTON-MILLIGAN 617, LIDDELL-SCOTT 1736.

4816. συσχηματίζω

suschēmatizō verb

To conform.

CROSS-REFERENCE:
σχῆμα schēma (4828)

1. συσχηματίζεσθε suschēmatizesthe 2pl impr pres mid
2. συσχηματιζόμενοι suschēmatizomenoi nom pl masc part pres mid
3. συσχηματίζεσθαι suschēmatizesthai inf pres mid

1 And be not **conformed** to this world:.............. Rom 12:2
2 not **fashioning yourselves** according ... former lusts... 1 Pt 1:14

Classical Greek

This term is related to the noun *schēma* (4828) which denotes outward appearance, form, or shape. The prepositional prefix *sun* (4713), "with," assumes the "form" was patterned after someone or something else. In classical literature *suschēmatizō* means to form or mold after something and is translated "conformed to" and "guided by" (*Bauer*).

New Testament Usage

The term is used twice in the New Testament. In Romans 12:2 Christians are commanded, "And be not *conformed* to this world," i.e., do not bring one's thinking and life into conformity with the world's pattern. In 1 Peter 1:14 a parallel directive is given: "As obedient children, not *fashioning* yourselves according to the former lusts in your ignorance."

STRONG 4964, BAUER 795, LIDDELL-SCOTT 1737, COLIN BROWN 1:708-9.

4817. Συχάϱ Suchar name

Sychar.

1. Συχάϱ Suchar fem

1 to a city of Samaria, which is called **Sychar**,........ John 4:5

This city in Samaria was the hometown of the woman with whom Jesus spoke at Jacob's well (John 4:5).

4818. Συχέμ Suchem name

Shechem.

1. Συχέμ Suchem fem

1 And were carried over into **Sychem**,................ Acts 7:16
1 of the sons of Emmor the father of **Sychem**............. 7:16

A city in Samaria briefly noted in the New Testament but occupying an important role in Old Testament history (cf. Acts 7:16).

4819. σφαγή sphagē noun

Slaughter.

COGNATE:
σφάζω sphazō (4821)
SYNONYM:
κοπή kopē (2843)

הָרַג hāragh (2103), Slay (Jer 15:3).
הֲרֵגָה hărēghāh (2105), Slaughter (Jer 12:3, Zec 11:4).
חֶרֶב cherev (2820), Sword (Jb 27:14).
טָבַח ṭāvach (2983), Slaughter (Jer 25:34 [32:34]).
טֶבַח ṭevach (2984), Slaughter (Prv 7:22, Is 53:7, Ez 21:15).
טִבְחָה ṭivchāh (2989), Slaughter (Ps 44:22 [43:22]).
כִּיד kîdh (3709), Destruction (Jb 21:20).
קֶטֶל qeṭel (7274), Slaughter (Ob 9 [10]).

1. σφαγῆς sphagēs gen sing fem
2. σφαγήν sphagēn acc sing fem

2 He was led as a sheep to the **slaughter**;............. Acts 8:32
1 we are accounted as sheep for the **slaughter**......... Rom 8:36
1 nourished your hearts, as in a day of **slaughter**........Jas 5:5

Classical Greek and Septuagint Usage

Sphagē is used in classical Greek for the "slaughter" of animals, particularly for sacrifices. The term is used literally to identify the throat, "the place between the collar-bones where sacrifices are usually slain" (Michel, "sphagē," *Kittel*, 7:935). It occurs 23 times in the Septuagint, mostly in reference to sacrifices. The Apocrypha uses the term in references to "massacres" resulting from wars, thus identifying people (ibid., 7:935f.).

New Testament Usage

There are three occurrences of *sphagē* in the New Testament. Two of these references are used in regard to "sheep being led to slaughter." In Acts 8:32 the Ethiopian eunuch was reading from Isaiah 53:7 which describes the sheep being led to the "slaughter" without resistance or complaint. Romans 8:36 quotes Psalm 44:22 as a song of triumph for the saints. The third occurrence is in James 5:5 where the rich are condemned for their luxurious living accomplished by withholding wages from the poor; such living is a "fattening" for the "day of *slaughter*," the impending Day of Judgment!

STRONG 4967, BAUER 795-96, KITTEL 7:935-38, LIDDELL-SCOTT 1737.

4820. σφάγιον sphagion noun

A slain animal; victim.

CROSS-REFERENCE:
σφάζω sphazō (4821)

זֶבַח zevach (2160), Sacrifice (Am 5:25).

טֶבַח ṭevach (2984), Slaughter (Ez 21:10).

נְדָבָה nᵉdhāvāh (5249), Freewill offering (Lv 22:23—Codex Vaticanus and some Alexandrinus texts only).

1. σφάγια sphagia nom/acc pl neu

1 have ye offered to me **slain beasts** and sacrifices ..... Acts 7:42

This is the common term in classical Greek literature and the Septuagint for a slaughtered animal being offered as a religious sacrifice (Herodotus, Philo, etc., *Liddell-Scott*). It is related to the verb *sphazō* (4821) which means "to slay." The emphasis of *sphagion* is upon the animal that is destined for slaughter, thus a victim. The term occurs only once in the New Testament (Acts 7:42). Stephen's message to the Sanhedrin included a quotation from Amos 5:25 where God asked Israel, "Have ye offered to me *slain beasts* and sacrifices . . . ?"

STRONG 4968, BAUER 796, LIDDELL-SCOTT 1737.

4821. σφάζω sphazō verb

To slay, slaughter.

COGNATES:
- κατασφάζω katasphazō (2664)
- πρόσφατος prosphatos (4230)
- προσφάτως prosphatōs (4231)
- σφαγή sphagē (4819)
- σφάγιον sphagion (4820)

SYNONYMS:
- ἀναιρέω anaireō (335)
- ἀποκτείνω apokteinō (609)
- ἀπόλλυμι apollumi (616)
- διαχειρίζομαι diacheirizomai (1309)
- θανατόω thanatoō (2266)
- θύω thuō (2357)
- κατασφάζω katasphazō (2664)
- νεκρόω nekroō (3362)
- φονεύω phoneuō (5244)

הָרַג hāragh (2103), Slaughter (Is 22:13).

זָבַח zāvach (2159), Make a sacrifice (Lv 17:5).

טָבַח ṭāvach (2983), Slay, slaughter (Gn 43:16, Dt 28:31); prepare food (Prv 9:2).

מַטְבֵּחַ maṭbēach (4430), Place for slaughtering (Is 14:21).

שָׁחַט shāchaṭ (8250), Qal: kill, slay (Lv 14:50, 1 Sm 14:32, Ez 40:41f.); niphal: be slaughtered (Nm 11:22—Codex Vaticanus and some Alexandrinus texts only).

שָׁסַף shāṣaph (8540), Piel: hew in pieces (1 Sm 15:33).

1. ἔσφαξεν esphaxen 3sing indic aor act

2. σφάξωσιν sphaxōsin 3pl subj aor act

3. ἐσφάγης esphagēs 2sing indic aor pass

4. ἐσφαγμένων esphagmenōn gen pl masc part perf mid

5. ἐσφαγμένην esphagmenēn acc sing fem part perf mid

6. ἐσφαγμένον esphagmenon nom/acc sing neu part perf mid

7. ἐσφαγμένου esphagmenou gen sing neu part perf mid

8. σφάξουσιν sphaxousin 3pl indic fut act

1 who was of that wicked one, and **slew** his brother.... 1 Jn 3:12
1 Not as Cain, ... And wherefore **slew** he him? 3:12
6 stood a Lamb as it **had been slain**, ... Rev 5:6
3 for thou **wast slain**, and hast redeemed us to God 5:9
6 the Lamb that **was slain** to receive power, ... 5:12
2 and that they **should kill** one another: 6:4
4 souls of them that **were slain** for the word of God, ... 6:9
5 saw one of his heads as it were **wounded** to death; 13:3
7 not written in the book of life of the Lamb **slain** 13:8
4 and of all that **were slain** upon the earth. 18:24

Classical Greek

This is the ordinary term meaning "to slay" or "to slaughter" an animal. In reference to men it means "to kill" or "to murder." The term denotes the "slaying" of the animal by the cutting the throat and draining the blood, the actual act of "slaughter." The majority of the uses refer to ritualistic animal sacrifices, but some instances refer to the slaughter of men as in war or murder. In classical Greek it was used by Homer especially for the slaughter of cattle. Herodotus and other authors occasionally referred to human victims as well as animals (*Liddell-Scott*). Josephus used the term specifically in describing the sacrificial system of the Old Testament. The papyri also use the term for sacrificial slayings of animals, with a few references to the slaying of men (*Moulton-Milligan*).

Septuagint Usage

Sphazō occurs about 85 times in the Septuagint. The majority of the references are in Leviticus where instructions for animal sacrifices are detailed, though they also occur elsewhere (Leviticus 1:5,11; 3:2,8,13; 4:15,24,29,33; 9:8, etc.; cf. 1 Samuel 1:25 [LXX 1 Kings 1:25]; 2 Kings 25:7 [LXX 4 Kings 25:7]; Psalm 37:14 [LXX 36:14]). It is used in regard to human beings on a few occasions, particularly with Abraham offering Isaac (Genesis 22:10) and Samuel slaying King Agag (1 Samuel 15:33 [LXX 1 Kings 15:33]) (Michel, "sphazō," *Kittel*, 7:929-30).

New Testament Usage

Sphazō occurs 10 times in the New Testament and is used exclusively by the apostle John. On eight occasions it means "slay" (1 John 3:12 [twice]; Revelation 5:6,9,12; 6:9; 13:8; 18:24). Jesus Christ is described as "the slaughtered Lamb," bearing the marks of the slaying in Revelation 5:6,9,12 and 13:8. It is used twice in 1 John 3:12 to denounce Cain's slaying of his brother. In Revelation 6:9 the martyrs were slain on account of the Word of God and their testimony; they were under the heavenly altar. The destruction of Babylon in Revelation 18:24 reveals the slaughter of the prophets, saints, and others.

On one occasion *sphazō* means "kill." In Revelation 6:4 the second horseman brings war and unrest which results in men slaying one another.

The participial form in Revelation 13:3 means "wound." The beast rising out of the sea has a mortal "wound" to its head but is then healed.

STRONG 4969, BAUER 796, KITTEL 7:925-35, LIDDELL-SCOTT 1737-38.

4822. σφοδρός sphodros adv

Violent, excessive.

SYNONYMS:
λίαν lian (3003)
σφοδρῶς sphodrōs (4823)

אַדִּיר 'addîr (116), Mighty (Ex 15:10).

עַז 'az (6006), Mighty (Neh 9:11).

1. σφόδρα sphodra

1 saw the star, ... rejoiced with **exceeding** great joy.... Matt 2:10
1 they fell on their face, and were **sore** afraid........... 17:6
1 And they were **exceeding** sorry....................... 17:23
1 they were **very** sorry, and came and told ... lord all.... 18:31
1 they were **exceedingly** amazed, saying,................ 19:25
1 And they were **exceeding** sorrowful,.................. 26:22
1 saw the earthquake, ... they feared **greatly**, saying,..... 27:54
1 the stone was rolled away: for it was **very** great.... Mark 16:4
1 he was very sorrowful: for he was **very** rich........ Luke 18:23
1 the disciples multiplied in Jerusalem **greatly**;.........Acts 6:7
1 hail; for the plague thereof was **exceeding** great..... Rev 16:21

Although the adjective *sphodros* ("vehement, violent, excessive") does not appear in the New Testament, *Liddell-Scott* shows widespread use of the word since Homer (Eighth Century B.C.). The term which does occur in the New Testament is *sphodra*, technically the neuter plural form of *sphodros*. As an adverb meaning "greatly" or "exceedingly," *sphodra* is used 11 times (mostly in the Gospels) to describe joy (Matthew 2:10), fear (Matthew 17:6; 27:54), sorrow (Matthew 17:23), amazement (Matthew 19:25), and riches (Luke 18:23). For other uses of this word see the *Concordance* and the related adverb *sphodrōs* (4823).

STRONG 4970, BAUER 796, LIDDELL-SCOTT 1741.

4823. σφοδρῶς sphodrōs adv

Exceedingly, greatly, violently.

SYNONYMS:
λίαν lian (3003)
σφοδρός sphodros (4822)

מְאֹד meʾōdh (4108), Great (Jos 3:16).

1. σφοδρῶς sphodrōs

1 And we being **exceedingly** tossed with a tempest,... Acts 27:18

This adverb was used in classical Greek as early as the time of Homer (Eighth Century B.C.) of something that occurred very violently (*Liddell-Scott*).

The word *sphodrōs* occurs only once in the New Testament. Luke employed this term to describe the nature of the Euroclydon or northeaster that violently battered the ship on which Paul and others were being taken to Rome (Acts 27:18). The ship was "being *exceedingly* tossed with a tempest."

STRONG 4971, BAUER 796, LIDDELL-SCOTT 1741.

4824. σφραγίζω sphragizō verb

Seal, seal up, set a seal upon, affirm, authenticate, certify, acknowledge.

COGNATES:
κατασφραγίζω katasphragizō (2665)
σφραγίς sphragis (4825)

חָתַם chātham (2964), Qal: seal (Dt 32:34, Est 8:10, Jer 32:11 [39:11]); niphal: be sealed (Est 8:8); piel: shut in (Jb 24:16).

חֲתַם chătham (A2965), Seal (Dn 6:17—Aramaic).

1. **σφραγίζωμεν sphragizōmen** 1pl subj pres act
2. **ἐσφράγισεν esphragisen** 3sing indic aor act
3. **σφραγίσῃς sphragisēs** 2sing subj aor act
4. **σφράγισον sphragison** 2sing impr aor act
5. **σφραγίσαντες sphragisantes** nom pl masc part aor act
6. **ἐσφραγίσθητε esphragisthēte** 2pl indic aor pass
7. **σφραγισάμενος sphragisamenos** nom sing masc part aor mid
8. **ἐσφραγισμένοι esphragismenoi** nom pl masc part perf mid
9. **ἐσφραγισμένων esphragismenōn** gen pl masc part perf mid
10. **σφραγίσεται sphragisetai** 3sing indic fut pass
11. **σφραγίσωμεν sphragisōmen** 1pl subj aor act

5 **sealing** the stone, and setting a watch.............Matt 27:66
2 hath **set to his seal** that God is true................John 3:33
2 Son of man ... for him hath God the Father **sealed**..... 6:27
7 and have **sealed** to them this fruit,................Rom 15:28
7 Who hath also **sealed** us, ... the Spirit in our hearts. 2 Co 1:22
10 no man **shall stop** me of this boasting................ 11:10
6 ye **were sealed** with that holy Spirit of promise,..... Eph 1:13
6 whereby ye **are sealed** unto the day of redemption..... 4:30
1 till we **have sealed** the servants of our God......... Rev 7:3
9 I heard the number of them which **were sealed**:........ 7:4
8 and there **were sealed** an hundred and forty and....... 7:4
8 Of the tribe of Juda **were sealed** twelve thousand....... 7:5
8 tribe of Reuben **were sealed** twelve thousand........... 7:5
8 Of the tribe of Gad **were sealed** twelve thousand....... 7:5
8 Of the tribe of Aser **were sealed** twelve thousand...... 7:6
8 tribe of Nephthalim **were sealed** twelve thousand....... 7:6

8 tribe of Manasses were sealed twelve thousand...... Rev 7:6
8 tribe of Simeon were sealed twelve thousand........... 7:7
8 Of the tribe of Levi were sealed twelve thousand....... 7:7
8 tribe of Issachar were sealed twelve thousand.......... 7:7
8 tribe of Zabulon were sealed twelve thousand.......... 7:8
8 Of the tribe of Joseph were sealed twelve thousand..... 7:8
8 tribe of Benjamin were sealed twelve thousand......... 7:8
4 Seal up those ... which the seven thunders uttered,... 10:4
2 and shut him up, and set a seal upon him,........... 20:3
3 Seal not the sayings of the prophecy of this book:.... 22:10

Classical Greek

Literally, *sphragizō* means "to close or enclose with a seal," and by extension, "to authenticate" or "to certify." In other circumstances an article may be "sealed" to show that it has been pledged. Metaphorically, one might be given the "seal of approval" (*Liddell-Scott*; cf. the noun *sphragis* [4825]). The act of sealing something not only ensures its not being tampered with, but the contents of the sealed object, especially a document, for example, remain unknown or "hidden" (*Moulton-Milligan*).

Septuagint Usage

The Septuagint translators employed *sphragizō* as a substitute for three Hebrew words; but one, *chātham*, clearly dominates. "Sealing" protects valuables (Deuteronomy 32:34; cf. 4 Kings 22:4, Septuagint only) or it "authenticates" a document (Esther 8:8,10). Jezebel sent a letter with Ahab's seal to ensure its authority (1 Kings 21:8 [LXX 3 Kings 20:8]).

Personal seals were a sign of endorsement of an agreement (Nehemiah 10:1; cf. 9:38ff.). Daniel was instructed to close up and "seal" the words of the scroll. This not only prevented the scroll from being opened, it implied that its contents would remain hidden (Daniel 12:4,9; cf. Theodotion's version, Daniel 8:26; 9:24). The sealing of a divine revelation was a typical feature of apocalyptic literature, which generally concerns divine secrets (cf. Revelation 10:4).

New Testament Usage

Most instances in the New Testament are figurative, but in Matthew 27:66 we have the only Gospel record that the tomb of Jesus was "sealed" at the command of Pilate. The intent was to protect the tomb from being opened and the body of Jesus stolen (cf. 27:64 and another literal use in Revelation 20:3 of Satan's confinement in the abyss).

John used it in two different ways: (1) The one accepting Jesus "authenticates" God's truthfulness (John 3:33); and (2) God placed His "seal of approval" upon the Son of Man (6:27).

Elsewhere, Paul used it five times. Once, in perhaps the imagery of commerce and trade, Paul described his intent to "make sure" of the reception of "fruit" by the poor in Jerusalem (Romans 15:28). The "seal of (God's) ownership" (NIV) is the "first installment" (*arrabōn* [722]) of the Spirit (2 Corinthians 1:22). Circumcision "sealed" Abraham's covenant relationship with God based upon faith (*sphragis*, Romans 4:11); now the "seal" of the Holy Spirit guarantees the inheritance (Ephesians 1:13; 4:30).

The Book of Revelation reads this word group more than any other New Testament book (verb, 18 times; noun, 13 times). The eschatological seal of God upon the foreheads of the faithful "protects" them and marks them as belonging to God (Revelation 7:3-8; cf. 2 Corinthians 1:22). The message of the thunders remains "sealed up," hence "hidden" (Revelation 10:4), but the book itself, unlike other apocalyptic literary, is "not sealed" (Revelation 22:10).

Strong 4972, Bauer 796, Moulton-Milligan 617-18, Kittel 7:939-53, Liddell-Scott 1742, Colin Brown 3:497,499.

4825. σφραγίς sphragis noun

A seal; signet.

Cross-Reference:
σφραγίζω sphragizō (4824)

חוֹתָם chôthām (2461), Seal, signet (Ex 28:21, S/S 8:6, Hg 2:23 [2:24]).

חָח chāch (2489), Brooch (Ex 35:22).

1. **σφραγίς sphragis** nom sing fem
2. **σφραγῖδα sphragida** acc sing fem
3. **σφραγίδων sphragidōn** gen pl fem
4. **σφραγῖσιν sphragisin** dat pl fem
5. **σφραγῖδας sphragidas** acc pl fem

2 a seal of the righteousness of the faith.............. Rom 4:11
1 for the seal of mine apostleship are ye in the Lord. 1 Co 9:2
2 this seal, The Lord knoweth them that are his...... 2 Tm 2:19
4 a book written within ... sealed with seven seals...... Rev 5:1
5 to open the book, and to loose the seals thereof?....... 5:2
5 open the book, and to loose the seven seals thereof..... 5:5
5 to take the book, and to open the seals thereof:........ 5:9
3 And I saw when the Lamb opened one of the seals,.... 6:1
2 And when he had opened the second seal,............. 6:3
2 And when he had opened the third seal,............... 6:5
2 And when he had opened the fourth seal,.............. 6:7
2 And when he had opened the fifth seal,................ 6:9
2 And I beheld when he had opened the sixth seal,....... 6:12
2 having the seal of the living God:...................... 7:2
2 And when he had opened the seventh seal,............. 8:1
2 which have not the seal of God in their foreheads....... 9:4

Classical Greek

A common term denoting a mark or "seal" upon something or someone, *sphargis* is used to denote an instrument that makes the seal; it can denote the impression or "seal." According to Thayer it can also denote a "seal" which secures a letter or book for secrecy or a confirmation of something or someone (*Greek-English Lexicon*). In the ancient world a seal served to identify a person's personal property, even a slave. Philo, Plato, papyri, etc., use the term to denote the "seal" upon a letter for secrecy and authority.

New Testament Usage

Sphragis is used 16 times in the New Testament. The apostle Paul used the term on three occasions, each time in a metaphoric sense. In 2 Timothy 2:19 Paul wrote, " . . . having this seal, The Lord knoweth them that are his," assuring Christians of His ownership and their security. Paul declared the Corinthian believers were the "seal" or "confirmation" of his apostleship. In Romans 4:11 Paul said, "Abraham received the sign of circumcision as something that simply confirms the righteousness through faith that was already present" (*Bauer*).

The other 13 occurrences of *sphragis* are located in the Book of Revelation. Fitzer divides these 13 references into two groups. The first group of "seal" references are directed to the book with seven seals, or "sealed book." Only Christ the Lamb has the authority to break open the seal (5:1,2,5,9). After one seal is broken, another one follows until all have been opened (6:1,3,5,7,9,12; 8:1). According to Fitzer this is similar to Roman law requiring six persons to place their individual seals upon a will, along with the testator; all six must break their seals before the will can be opened and made official ("sphargis," *Kittel*, 7:950f.). The second group of "seal" statements refers to the 144,000 from the 12 tribes of Israel (7:2-8). They are "sealed" which marks them as God's possession and protects them through the terrible judgments to come. This "sealing" is equivalent to the custom of marking one's property with a sign of ownership. As Fitzer states, "The sign became a seal, and the seal became a sign" (ibid., 7:951).

Strong 4973, Bauer 796, Moulton-Milligan 618, Kittel 7:939-53, Liddell-Scott 1742, Colin Brown 3:497,499.

4825B. σφυδρόν sphudron noun

Ankle, heel.

1. σφυδρά sphudra nom/acc pl neu

1 his feet and his ankles were strengthened. (NASB).. Acts 3:7

The earliest known occurrence of the noun *sphudron* is found in Acts 3:7 where it means "ankle." We see it in the famous story of the healing of the lame man at the temple gate called Beautiful. When Peter took him by the right hand and helped him up, this man's feet and ankles suddenly received strength from God (Acts 3:7) which enabled him to walk and leap as he praised God.

The only other instances where *sphudron* is used come from the Third and Fifth Century A.D. The variant reading in Acts 3:7, *sphuron* (4826), "ankle," is attested as early as in the writings of Homer (Eighth Century B.C.) with the meaning of "ankle," and in Euripedes (Fifth Century B.C.) with the meaning of "heel." In the New Testament, however, *sphuron* occurs only in relatively late manuscripts of Acts 3:7.

Strong 4974, Bauer 797, Moulton-Milligan 618, Liddell-Scott 1742.

4826. σφυρόν sphuron noun

Ankle.

תּוֹתָח tôthāch (8787), Club (Jb 41:29 [41:20]).

1. σφυρά sphura nom/acc pl neu

1 his feet and ankle bones received strength........... Acts 3:7

This is a variant spelling of *sphudron*. See the word study at number 4825B.

4827. σχεδόν schedon adv

Almost, nearly.

1. σχεδόν schedon

1 the next sabbath day came almost the whole city... Acts 13:44
1 but almost throughout all Asia,........................ 19:26
1 almost all things are by the law purged with blood;.. Heb 9:22

This common adverb was used from the time of Homer (Eighth Century B.C.) as an adverb of place ("near"), as an adverb of time (the time [is "near"]), or as an adverb of degree ("nearly" or "almost").

We find it twice in Acts. In 13:44 it describes "*almost* (*schedon*) all the city" assembling to hear Paul and Barnabas preach the Word of God. In 19:26 the silversmith Demetrius attempted to arouse those in his same trade against Paul by charging that Paul was leading astray *nearly* (*schedon*) the whole province of Asia.

Hebrews 9:22 utilizes *schedon* to remind us that the Law required "*nearly* everything" (NIV) to be purged or cleansed with blood because there is no forgiveness for sin without it.

Strong 4975, Bauer 797, Moulton-Milligan 618-19, Liddell-Scott 1744.

4828. σχῆμα schēma noun

Form, outward appearance.

Cognates:
ἀσχημονέω aschēmoneō (801)
εὐσχημόνως euschēmonōs (2137)
εὐσχημοσύνη euschēmosunē (2138)
εὐσχήμων euschēmōn (2139)
μετασχηματίζω metaschēmatizō (3215)
συσχηματίζω suschēmatizō (4816)

Synonyms:
εἶδος eidos (1482)
ἰδέα idea (2374)
μορφή morphē (3307)
μόρφωσις morphōsis (3309)
τύπος tupos (5020)

פֹּת pōth (6847), Head (Is 3:17).

1. σχῆμα schēma nom/acc sing neu
2. σχήματι schēmati dat sing neu

1 for the fashion of this world passeth away........... 1 Co 7:31
2 And being found in fashion as a man,.............. Phlp 2:8

Classical Greek and Septuagint Usage

Classical usage of *schēma* includes the meanings: "figure, shape"; "appearance" (as opposed to what is actually real); "disposition, character"; and other various related senses. Although *schēma* chiefly emphasizes the outward "form" of something, this should not be pressed, for the Greeks held that the outward reflected one's inward state. Naturally they were aware that the outward appearance of something could be deceptive. Therefore, *schēma* could also denote the "apparent" in contrast to the "actual" (Braumann, "Form," *Colin Brown*, 1:709; for an opposing view see Schneider, "schēma," *Kittel*, 7:954). *Schēma* and several other members of the same word group share similar meanings (e.g., *suschēmatizō* [4816], "to give the same form"; *metaschēmatizō* [3215], "to change form or appearance"). *Schēma* occurs only once in the Septuagint with a Hebrew counterpart (Isaiah 3:17).

New Testament Usage

Schēma occurs in the New Testament only two times, both of which are Pauline. Paul wrote in 1 Corinthians that the "*fashion* of this world passeth away" (7:31). This refers to the present form of existence that is rapidly passing away. Paul anticipated a transformation in the universe (Romans 8:19-22). The present form is subject to decay, but in the future it will be liberated.

The other occurrence of the term is in the Christological hymn of Philippians 2:5-11 where it is said that Christ was "found in appearance (*schēma*) as a man" (NIV). That is to say, in His outward appearance, His behavior and conduct in the eyes of men, He was "found as (*hōs*) a man". This complements the preceding verses, especially the terms *morphē* (3307), "form, manner, *nature*" (NIV), and *homoiōma* (3530), "likeness" (NIV), and it describes how men understood Jesus. He appeared as a man, and He was considered to be one. *Schēma* depicts the appearance (outward form) of Christ and *morphē*, the "essential and permanent" state (*Moulton-Milligan*).

An example of *schēma* in the sense of "outward manner, life-style" occurs in Romans 12:2 where the compound verb *suschēmatizō*, "to give the same form," appears. Believers are not to be "conformed" to the world's behavior and life-style; rather, they are to be transformed by the inner renewing of their minds and character.

Strong 4976, Bauer 797, Moulton-Milligan 619, Kittel 7:954-56, Liddell-Scott 1745, Colin Brown 1:708-9.

4829. σχίζω schizō verb

Break, chop, cleave, divide, open, rend, separate, split, tear.

Cognate:
σχίσμα schisma (4830)

Synonyms:
ἀποδιορίζω apodiorizō (587)
διακρίνω diakrinō (1246)
διαῤῥήσσω diarrhēssō (1278)
κρίνω krinō (2892)
μερίζω merizō (3177)
ῥήγνυμι rhēgnumi (4342)
σπαράσσω sparassō (4535)
συσπαράσσω susparassō (4804)
χωρίζω chōrizō (5398)

בָּקַע bāqa' (1260), Qal: split (Is 48:21); niphal: be divided (Ex 14:21); piel: split, chop up (Gn 22:3, 1 Sm 6:14).

קָרַע qāra' (7458), Tear (Is 36:22, 37:1).

1. σχίζει schizei 3sing indic pres act
2. σχίσωμεν schisōmen 1pl subj aor act
3. σχιζομένους schizomenous acc pl masc part pres mid
4. ἐσχίσθη eschisthē 3sing indic aor pass
5. ἐσχίσθησαν eschisthēsan 3pl indic aor pass
6. σχίσας schisas nom sing masc part aor act
7. σχίσει schisei 3sing indic fut act

4 **behold, the veil of the temple was rent in twain**.... Matt 27:51
5 **and the earth did quake, and the rocks rent;**.......... 27:51
3 **he saw the heavens opened, and the Spirit**.......... Mark 1:10
4 **And the veil of the temple was rent in twain**.......... 15:38
6 **"No one tears a piece from a new (NASB)**......... Luke 5:36
1 **if otherwise, then both the new maketh a rent,**.......... 5:36
7 **otherwise he will both tear the new, and (NASB)**....... 5:36
4 **and the veil of the temple was rent in the midst.**...... 23:45
2 **Let us not rend it, but cast lots for it,**............. John 19:24
4 **yet was not the net broken.**.......................... 21:11
4 **But the multitude of the city was divided:**.......... Acts 14:4
4 **a dissension ... and the multitude was divided.**......... 23:7

Classical Greek

This verb first appears in classical Greek in the Homeric Hymns (Seventh Century B.C.). Its general sense is "to break," and it can refer to a wide variety of splittings, breakings, etc. It is used of the branching of a river, the curdling of milk, and the splitting of wood (*Liddell-Scott*).

Septuagint Usage

The Septuagint uses *schizō* in Genesis 22:3 where Abraham was *splitting* wood to use for the sacrifice on Mount Moriah. It is also used to describe the *dividing* of the Red Sea (Exodus 14:21). We read of the people of Beth Shemesh *chopping* up the wood of the cart used to transport the ark of the covenant (1 Samuel 6:14 [LXX 1 Kings 6:14]). The "Preacher" warned people about the danger of being struck by pieces of logs while *splitting* them (Ecclesiastes 10:9). When King Hezekiah heard Sennacherib's threat to destroy Israel, Hezekiah *tore* his clothes, put on sackcloth, and went into the temple to seek God (Isaiah 37:1). The prophet Isaiah reminded the people of Israel about the way God *split* the rock in the wilderness in order to provide water for their ancestors (Isaiah 48:21).

New Testament Usage

The New Testament has the term for the rending of the veil in the temple in Jerusalem from top to bottom after the death of Jesus on the cross (Matthew 27:51; Mark 15:38). This was a sign that access to God had been made possible because of the redemptive work of Christ (Hebrews 6:19; 9:8; 10:19,20). Elsewhere the verb *schizō* describes heaven opening for the descent of the Holy Spirit in the form of a dove (Mark 1:10). Luke 5:36 states that patching an old garment with new cloth will result in the old material tearing. The soldiers decided to cast lots for Jesus' garments rather than *tearing* them (John 19:24). Peter's net did not *break* under the heavy load of 153 fish (John 21:11). *Schizō* is also used with a less literal sense. For example, the inhabitants of Iconium were *divided* over the preaching of Paul and Barnabas (Acts 14:4), and Acts 23:7 describes the *dissension* that broke out between the Pharisees and the Sadducees in the Sanhedrin over Paul's comments about the resurrection of the dead.

Strong 4977, Bauer 797, Moulton-Milligan 619, Kittel 7:959-63, Liddell-Scott 1746, Colin Brown 3:543-44.

4830. σχίσμα schisma noun

Split, division, tear; dissension, schism.

Cross-Reference:
σχίζω schizō (4829)

1. σχίσμα schisma nom/acc sing neu

2. σχίσματα schismata nom/acc pl neu

1 **and the rent is made worse.**........................ Matt 9:16
1 **and the rent is made worse.**........................ Mark 2:21
1 **So there was a division among the people**........... John 7:43
1 **And there was a division among them.**.................. 9:16
1 **There was a division therefore again**.................. 10:19
2 **and that there be no divisions among you;**.......... 1 Co 1:10
2 **I hear that there be divisions among you;**............. 11:18
1 **That there should be no schism in the body;**.......... 12:25

Classical Greek

The related verb *schizō* (4829), "to tear into pieces, split," functions in secular Greek in an almost exclusively literal sense, although it can be used of divided opinions. The noun *schisma*, "tear, split, division," in addition to a literal sense may also indicate a "division" between members of a group, i.e., a "faction." The noun is not found in the Septuagint.

New Testament Usage

Paul employed the term *schisma* in this way in 1 Corinthians 1:10; 11:18; and 12:25. The "factions" (or *schisms*) that had developed in Corinth were not because of false doctrine as in Galatia; consequently, Paul used the more forceful word *hairesis* (138), "dissension, division," in Galatians 5:20. Those who create divisions among the Body "shall not inherit the kingdom of God" (verse 21). Similarly, Paul wrote in 1 Corinthians 3:17 that if anyone destroyed the temple of God (i.e., the church in Corinth), God would destroy him.

Schisma carries another meaning in Matthew 9:16 and Mark 2:21. The issues in these contexts center around the irreconcilable differences existing between Christianity and Judaism. If one attempts to repair a torn garment with a new piece of cloth that has not been shrunk beforehand, the tear on the old garment will only worsen. The same can be said for attempting to merge Judaism and Christianity; eventually both would be destroyed.

Strong 4978, Bauer 797, Moulton-Milligan

619, Kittel 7:963-64, Liddell-Scott 1746, Colin Brown 3:543-44.

4831. σχοινίον schoinion noun

Cord, line, rope.

חֶבֶל chevel (2346), Rope, cord (2 Sm 17:13, Is 5:18): land (Ps 78:55 [77:55]).

נִקְפָּה niqpāh (5547), Rope (Is 3:24).

1. σχοινίων schoiniōn gen pl neu

2. σχοινία schoinia nom/acc pl neu

1 And when he had made a scourge of small **cords**,... John 2:15
2 Then the soldiers cut off the **ropes** of the boat,..... Acts 27:32

From the time of Herodotus (Fifth Century B.C.) this noun can be traced in classical Greek as referring to a rope made of rushes; a measuring line, hence a measure or portion (cf. Psalm 16:6 [LXX 15:6]); a girdle; and metaphorically, *cords* of care (which bind one) (*Liddell-Scott*). The term occurs twice in the New Testament. In John 2:15 Jesus is reported to have made a whip out of cords (*schoiniōn*), and in Acts 27:32 Luke reported that the soldiers "cut off the ropes (*schoinia*) of the boat."

Strong 4979, Bauer 797, Moulton-Milligan 619, Liddell-Scott 1746.

4832. σχολάζω scholazō verb

Be at leisure, loiter; be unoccupied, empty.

רָפָה rāphâh (7791), Become slack, sink; niphal: be lazy (Ex 5:8,17); hiphil: be still (Ps 46:10 [45:10]).

1. σχολάζητε scholazēte 2pl subj pres act

2. σχολάζοντα scholazonta acc sing masc part pres act

3. σχολάσητε scholasēte 2pl subj aor act

2 and when he is come, he findeth it **empty**, swept,.. Matt 12:44
1 that ye **may give yourselves** to fasting and prayer;.... 1 Co 7:5

Classical Greek

This verb is used of people who are at leisure, ceasing from labor, loitering, or resting. It also carries the idea of devoting one's spare time to the accomplishment of some activity. The word can be employed of things, especially of a place or a house being unoccupied.

Septuagint Usage

Scholazō appears three times in the Septuagint, translating the Hebrew word *rāphâh*, "to sink down, relax, be idle," on all three occasions. In Exodus 5:8,17 Pharaoh accused the Hebrews of being idle or lazy. Psalm 46:10 (LXX 45:10) exhorts the believer to "be *still*, and know that I am God."

New Testament Usage

In the New Testament the term occurs twice. It is used in Matthew 12:44 where Jesus described the return of a demon who was expelled from a life but later found it unoccupied: "And when he (the demon) comes he finds it empty (*scholazō*), swept, and put in order" (RSV). The Lord emphasized the absolute necessity of the life being occupied so that these evil beings could not reinhabit the person.

In 1 Corinthians 7:5 the apostle Paul also employed the word in his instructions to married couples: "Do not refuse one another except perhaps by agreement for a season, that you may devote yourselves to prayer" (RSV; literally, "in order that you may have *leisure* [or *time*] for prayer").

Strong 4980, Bauer 797-98, Moulton-Milligan 619-20, Liddell-Scott 1747.

4833. σχολή scholē noun

Freedom from labor, leisure time, school.

1. σχολῇ scholē dat sing fem

1 disputing daily in the **school** of one Tyrannus....... Acts 19:9

Classical Greek and Septuagint Usage

This interesting noun is used in the writings of Pindar (Fifth Century B.C.) to mean "leisure" (*Bauer*). In the classical world *scholē* could also mean "lecture, discussion" (*Liddell-Scott*). The meaning "school, lecture hall" appears to be attested as early as Aristotle (Fourth Century B.C.). In three occurrences in the Septuagint *scholē* means "leisure" (Genesis 33:14; Proverbs 28:19; Sirach 38:24).

New Testament Usage

Scholē appears only once in the New Testament. In Acts 19:9 Luke described how Paul left the synagogue at Ephesus and began discussions about Christianity in the "school" or, more properly, the "lecture hall" of Tyrannus. According to Louw and Nida it would be better to translate *scholē* with "lecture hall" "since one does not wish to give the impression of the typical classroom situation characteristic of present-day schools" (*Greek-English Lexicon*, 1:83).

Strong 4981, Bauer 798, Moulton-Milligan 620, Liddell-Scott 1747-48.

4834. σῴζω sōzō verb

Save, keep safe, preserve, rescue, make well.

COGNATES:
διασῴζω diasōzō (1289)
σωτήρ sōtēr (4842)
σωτηρία sōtēria (4843)
σωτήριος sōtērios (4844)

SYNONYMS:
διασῴζω diasōzō (1289)
ἐξαιρέω exaireō (1791)
λυτρόω lutroō (3056)
λύω luō (3061)
ῥύομαι rhuomai (4363)

בָּרַח bārach (1300), Flee (Jb 20:24).

חָיָה chāyâh (2513), Qal: live (Est 4:11, Prv 15:27, Ez 33:12); piel: keep alive (Ps 30:3 [29:3]); hiphil: save one's life (Gn 47:25).

חָסָה chāṣâh (2725), Find refuge (Is 14:32).

יָדַע yādha' (3156), Know (Ps 31:7 [30:7]).

יָשַׁע yāsha' (3588), Niphal: be saved (Ps 80:3,7,19 [79:3,7,19]); hiphil: save, deliver (Jgs 6:14f., Ps 106:8 [105:8], Is 43:11f.).

יֵשַׁע yēsha' (3589), Salvation (Hb 3:13).

יְשׁוּעָה y^eshû'āh (3568), Salvation (Ps 80:2 [79:2]).

מוֹשָׁעָה môshā'āh (4321), Salvation (Ps 68:20 [67:20]).

מָלַט mālaṭ (4561), Niphal: escape, be delivered (Gn 19:17, Ps 22:5 [21:5], Jer 48:19 [31:19]); piel; deliver, save (Ps 33:17 [32:17], Is 34:15); hiphil: rescue (Is 31:5).

מִפְלָט miphlāṭ (4817), Shelter (Ps 55:8 [54:8]).

נָצַל nātsal (5522), Niphal: be preserved, delivered oneself (Gn 32:30, Prv 6:3, Ez 14:18); piel: deliver (Ez 14:14); hiphil: bring a victory, deliver (1 Chr 11:14, Ps 69:14 [68:14], Jer 39:17 [46:17]).

עָזַר 'āzar (6038), Help (2 Chr 18:31, Ps 119:173 [118:173]).

פָּדָה pādhâh (6540), Qal: redeem (Jb 33:28); niphal: be redeemed (Is 1:27).

פָּלַט pālaṭ (6647), Piel: escape (Ps 56:7 [55:7]).

פָּלִיט pālîṭ (6654), One who escapes (Jer 44:28 [51:28]).

פָּלֵיט pālêṭ (6655), Survivor (Is 66:19).

פְּלֵיטָה p^elêṭāh (6656), One who escapes (Gn 32:9 [32:8], 2 Chr 20:24, Is 10:20).

רָאָה rā'âh (7495), See (Est 8:6).

שָׂגַב sāghav (7891), Pual: be safe (Prv 29:25).

שָׂרִיד sārîdh (8032), Survivor (Nm 24:19, Jos 10:33).

שׁוּב shûv (8178), Return (Is 10:22).

שֵׁיזִב shêziv (A8288), Haphel: deliver (Dn 3:28, 6:20—Aramaic).

שָׁלַם shālam (8396), Be complete, be at peace; pual: be rewarded (Prv 11:31).

1. **σῴζει sōzei** 3sing indic pres act
2. **σῴζετε sōzete** 2pl impr pres act
3. **σῴζειν sōzein** inf pres act
4. **σώσω sōsō** 1sing indic/subj fut/aor act
5. **ἔσωσεν esōsen** 3sing indic aor act
6. **σῶσον sōson** 2sing impr aor act
7. **σωσάτω sōsatō** 3sing impr aor act
8. **σώσας sōsas** nom sing masc part aor act
9. **σώσαντος sōsantos** gen sing masc part aor act
10. **σῶσαι sōsai** inf aor act
11. **σέσωκεν sesōken** 3sing indic perf act
12. **σώσεις sōseis** 2sing indic fut act
13. **σώσει sōsei** 3sing indic fut act
14. **σώσων sōsōn** nom sing masc part fut act
15. **σῴζεται sōzetai** 3sing indic pres mid
16. **σῴζεσθε sōzesthe** 2pl indic pres mid
17. **σῳζόμενοι sōzomenoi** nom pl masc part pres mid
18. **σῳζομένων sōzomenōn** gen pl masc part pres mid
19. **σῳζομένοις sōzomenois** dat pl masc part pres mid
20. **σῳζομένους sōzomenous** acc pl masc part pres mid
21. **σῴζεσθαι sōzesthai** inf pres mid
22. **ἐσώθη esōthē** 3sing indic aor pass
23. **ἐσώθημεν esōthēmen** 1pl indic aor pass
24. **σωθῆτε sōthēte** 2pl subj/impr aor pass
25. **σωθῶ sōthō** 1sing subj aor pass
26. **σωθῇ sōthē** 3sing subj aor pass
27. **σωθῶσιν sōthōsin** 3pl subj aor pass
28. **σωθῆναι sōthēnai** inf aor pass
29. **σέσωσται sesōstai** 3sing indic perf mid
30. **σεσῳσμένοι sesōsmenoi** nom pl masc part perf mid
31. **σωθήσομαι sōthēsomai** 1sing indic fut pass
32. **σωθήσῃ sōthēsē** 2sing indic fut pass
33. **σωθήσεται sōthēsetai** 3sing indic fut pass
34. **σωθησόμεθα sōthēsometha** 1pl indic fut pass
35. **ἐσῴζοντο esōzonto** 3pl indic imperf pass
36. **σέσωται sesōtai** 3sing indic perf mid

13 for he **shall save** his people from their sins......... Matt 1:21
6 saying, Lord, **save** us: we perish....................... 8:25
31 If I may but touch his garment, I **shall be whole**........ 9:21
11 thy faith **hath made** thee **whole**........................ 9:22
22 And the woman **was made whole** from that hour....... 9:22
33 but he that endureth to the end **shall be saved**........ 10:22
6 he cried, saying, Lord, **save** me....................... 14:30
10 For whosoever will **save** his life shall lose it:......... 16:25
10 the Son of man is come to **save** that which was lost... 18:11
28 amazed, saying, Who then can **be saved**?............. 19:25
33 shall endure unto the end, the same **shall be saved**.... 24:13
22 there should no flesh **be saved**:...................... 24:22
6 **save** thyself. If thou be the Son of God,............. 27:40
5 He **saved** others; himself he cannot save.............. 27:42
10 He saved others; himself he cannot **save**.............. 27:42
14 let us see whether Elias will come to **save** him........ 27:49
10 to **save** life, or to kill? But they held their peace... Mark 3:4
26 lay thy hands on her, that she **may be healed**;......... 5:23
31 If I may touch but his clothes, I **shall be whole**........ 5:28
11 Daughter, thy faith **hath made** thee **whole**;............ 5:34
35 and as many as touched him **were made whole**......... 6:56
10 For whosoever will **save** his life shall lose it;.......... 8:35
13 my sake and the gospel's, the same **shall save** it........ 8:35
28 saying among themselves, Who then can **be saved**?.... 10:26
11 Go thy way; thy faith **hath made** thee **whole**.......... 10:52
33 endure unto the end, the same **shall be saved**......... 13:13
22 no flesh **should be saved**: but for the elect's sake,..... 13:20
6 **Save** thyself, and come down from the cross.......... 15:30
5 He **saved** others; himself he cannot save.............. 15:31
10 He saved others; himself he cannot **save**.............. 15:31

33 He that believeth and is baptized **shall be saved**; .. Mark 16:16
10 or to do evil? **to save** life, or to destroy it? .... Luke 6:9
11 he said to the woman, Thy faith **hath saved** thee; 7:50
27 lest they should believe and **be saved**. 8:12
22 he that was possessed of the devils **was healed**. 8:36
11 thy faith **hath made** thee **whole**; go in peace. 8:48
33 believe only, and she **shall be made whole**. 8:50
10 For whosoever will **save** his life shall lose it: 9:24
13 will lose his life for my sake, the same **shall save** it. ... 9:24
10 not come to destroy men's lives, but **to save** them. 9:56
17 Lord, are there few that **be saved**? 13:23
11 Arise, go thy way: thy faith **hath made** thee **whole**. ... 17:19
10 Whosoever shall seek **to save** his life shall lose it; 17:33
28 they that heard it said, Who then can **be saved**? 18:26
11 Receive thy sight: thy faith **hath saved** thee. 18:42
10 For the Son of man is come to seek and **to save** 19:10
5 He **saved** others; let him save himself, ... 23:35
7 He saved others; **let** him **save** himself, ... 23:35
6 saying, If thou be the king of the Jews, **save** thyself. .. 23:37
6 saying, If thou be Christ, **save** thyself and us. 23:39
26 but that the world through him **might be saved**. .... John 3:17
24 but these things I say, that ye **might be saved**. 5:34
33 by me if any man enter in, he **shall be saved**, ... 10:9
33 Lord, if he sleep, he **shall do well**. 11:12
6 what shall I say? Father, **save** me from this hour: 12:27
4 came not to judge the world, but **to save** the world. ... 12:47
33 shall call on the name of the Lord **shall be saved**. ... Acts 2:21
24 **Save yourselves** from this untoward generation. 2:40
20 added to the church daily such as **should be saved**. 2:47
29 by what means he **is made whole**; 4:9
28 is none other name ... whereby we must **be saved**. 4:12
32 whereby thou and all thy house **shall be saved**. 11:14
28 and perceiving that he had faith **to be healed**, ... 14:9
28 Except ye be circumcised ... ye cannot **be saved**. 15:1
28 through the grace of the Lord ... we **shall be saved**, ... 15:11
25 and said, Sirs, what must I do **to be saved**? 16:30
32 and thou **shalt be saved**, and thy house. 16:31
21 all hope that we **should be saved** was then taken 27:20
28 Except these abide in the ship, ye cannot **be saved**. 27:31
34 we **shall be saved** from wrath through him. .... Rom 5:9
34 being reconciled, we **shall be saved** by his life. 5:10
23 For we **are saved** by hope: 8:24
33 be as the sand of the sea, a remnant **shall be saved**: 9:27
32 that God hath raised him ... thou **shalt be saved**. 10:9
33 call upon the name of the Lord **shall be saved**. 10:13
4 and **might save** some of them. 11:14
33 And so all Israel **shall be saved**: as it is written, ... 11:26
19 but unto us which **are saved** it is the power of God. 1 Co 1:18
10 foolishness of preaching **to save** them that believe. 1:21
33 but he himself **shall be saved**; yet so as by fire. 3:15
26 that the spirit **may be saved** in the day of the Lord 5:5
12 whether thou **shalt save** thy husband? 7:16
12 whether thou **shalt save** thy wife? 7:16
4 that I **might** by all means **save** some. 9:22
27 but the profit of many, that they **may be saved**. 10:33
16 By which also ye **are saved**, ... 15:2
19 in them that **are saved**, and in them that perish: .... 2 Co 2:15
30 by grace ye are **saved**; .... Eph 2:5
30 For by grace are ye **saved** through faith; 2:8
27 to speak to the Gentiles that they **might be saved**, .. 1 Th 2:16
28 received not the love ... that they **might be saved**... 2 Th 2:10
10 Christ Jesus came into the world **to save** sinners; ... 1 Tm 1:15
28 Who will have all men **to be saved**, ... 2:4
33 Notwithstanding **she shall be saved** in childbearing, ... 2:15
12 **shalt** both **save** thyself, and them that hear thee. 4:16
9 Who **hath saved** us, and called us .... 2 Tm 1:9
13 and **will preserve** me unto his heavenly kingdom: 4:18
5 but according to his mercy he **saved** us, ... Tit 3:5
3 unto him that was able **to save** him from death, ... Heb 5:7
3 Wherefore he is able also **to save** them 7:25
10 engrafted word, which is able **to save** your souls. .... Jas 1:21
10 and have not works? can faith **save** him? 2:14
10 is one lawgiver, who is able **to save** and to destroy: 4:12
13 And the prayer of faith **shall save** the sick, ... 5:15
13 the error of his way **shall save** a soul from death, ... 5:20
1 whereunto even baptism doth also now **save** us ..... 1 Pt 3:21
15 And if the righteous scarcely **be saved**, ... 4:18
8 **having saved** the people out of the land of Egypt, .. Jude 1:5
2 others **save** with fear, pulling them out of the fire; 1:23
18 them which are **saved** shall walk in the light of it: Rev 21:24

Classical Greek

Found in the writings of Homer (Eighth Century B.C.) on, *sōzō* is used in the sense of deliverance from danger, whether from enemies or the elements of weather. It also includes the idea of preservation from them. Greek religions attributed this work to their gods. Brown describes its usage by the adherents of the mystery cults who believed that " . . . deliverance comes through the initiates' sharing in the experience of the dying and rising god . . . " ("Redemption," *Colin Brown*, 3:205). The Gnostics, a heretical sect with beginnings in the First Century, held that it was "knowledge" of a supernatural sort that saved.

Septuagint Usage

Sōzō translates no less than 15 different Hebrew verbs in the Septuagint. *Sōzō*'s most important counterparts are the Hebrew terms *yāshaʿ* (verb), *yēshaʿ*, and *yeshûʿāh* (nouns). The root idea of these terms is "make wide, make adequate"; thus the verb *yāshaʿ* means "to give space to, to make room," and from that "to bring out (of tribulation)." The terms later denote "salvation, deliverance, releasing"; this involves the action itself ("to save") as well as the resulting condition. Therefore, the Old Testament concept of salvation includes "deliverance" from external and internal distress, captivity, and enemies, as well as the subsequent "peace, relief, liberty, rest, safety," and "prosperity." *Sōzō* very often denotes an idea very similar to the Hebrew concept of *shālom*, "peace, unity, completeness, happiness." In this regard it is important to note that in the Septuagint *shālom* is rendered by forms of the *sōzō* word group 68 times. In the Septuagint *sōzō* is often used experientially. It reflects the Hebrew concept of holistic salvation. One was both saved by God spiritually and saved from enemies or troubles physically. This holistic salvation is evidenced in historical books such as 1 and 2 Samuel, and in the Prophets (e.g., Isaiah and Ezekiel). The Apocrypha use the word (1 Maccabees 6:44) to describe someone who, desiring to save his people, runs into battle. Josephus used the word to signify deliverance from death or an enemy and the deliverance of the temple from demolition (ibid., 3:210).

New Testament Usage

In the New Testament *sōzō* means salvation from physical and/or spiritual death (Matthew

14:30; Romans 5:9), including deliverance from demon possession (Luke 8:36). In the passive voice it means "to be restored to health, to be cured" (Mark 5:34).

To be saved from spiritual death would imply escape from judgment and its cause, sin (Romans 5:10; Hebrews 7:25). God the Father and God the Son are the agents of this work (1 Corinthians 1:21; 2 Timothy 1:9; Titus 3:5). Human instruments or channels may be apostles (Romans 11:14; 1 Corinthians 9:22; 1 Timothy 4:16), the "saved" partner in a marriage (1 Corinthians 7:16), another believer (James 5:20), or oneself (Mark 8:35; 1 Timothy 4:16).

Salvation requires faith (Acts 16:30,31; 1 Corinthians 1:21; Ephesians 2:8) by corporate bodies, such as the remnant of Israel, and individuals (Romans 11:26; 1 Corinthians 3:15). It is by faith alone that one is saved, although genuine faith is never alone. It is always accompanied by works (James 2:14).

It is the sinner whom the Lord Jesus Christ came to save (1 Timothy 1:15). But while salvation is God's will for everyone, some refuse to accept His offer (1 Timothy 2:4). He is able to save men and women "to the uttermost" (Hebrews 7:25), meaning "completely, in every way." Baptism is imperative, in as much as it is a testimony of a clean conscience before God which is the result of salvation (1 Peter 3:21). A good illustration of the truth contained in the word *sōzō* is found in Acts 27:31: "Except these abide in the ship, ye cannot *be saved.*"

Two unique uses of *sōzō* are found. In John 11:12 it is translated, "He shall do well," referring to the recuperative powers of sleep. In 1 Timothy 2:15 it is used to describe the successful delivery of a baby, although any reference to "final eschatological redemption . . . cannot be ruled out" (Foerster, "sōzō," *Kittel*, 7:995).

Strong 4982, Bauer 798-99, Moulton-Milligan 620, Kittel 7:965-1003, Liddell-Scott 1748, Colin Brown 3:205-15.

4835. σῶμα sōma noun

Body, living body; dead body, corpse.

Cognates:

σύσσωμος sussōmos (4806)
σωματικός sōmatikos (4836)
σωματικῶς sōmatikōs (4837)

בָּשָׂר bāsār (1340), Body, flesh (Lv 15:2f., Jb 7:5, Dn 1:15).

גַּו gaw (1488), Back (Neh 9:26, Ez 23:35).

גֵּו gēw (1490), Back (Jb 20:25).

גְּוִיָּה g^ewîyāh (1505), Body, corpse (Gn 47:18, 1 Sm 31:10, Na 3:3).

גּוּפָה gûphāh (1512), Body (1 Chr 10:12).

גְּשֵׁם g^eshēm (A1702), Body (Dn 3:27f., 7:11—Aramaic).

חַיִל chayil (2524), Wealth (Gn 34:29).

טַף ṭaph (3054), Small children (Gn 47:12).

נְבֵלָה n^evēlāh (5215), Body, carcass (Dt 21:23, Jos 8:29, 1 Kgs 13:28).

נֶפֶשׁ nephesh (5497), Person (Gn 36:6).

עוֹר 'ôr (5997), Flesh (Jb 19:26).

פֶּגֶר pegher (6538), Carcass, corpse (Gn 15:11, 2 Kgs 19:35).

שְׁאֵר sh^e'ēr (8083), Body, oneself (Prv 5:11, 11:17).

1. σῶμα sōma nom/acc sing neu
2. σώματος sōmatos gen sing neu
3. σώματι sōmati dat sing neu
4. σώματα sōmata nom/acc pl neu
5. σωμάτων sōmatōn gen pl neu

1 not that thy whole **body** should be cast into hell..... Matt 5:29
1 not that thy whole **body** should be cast into hell........ 5:30
2 The light of the **body** is the eye:....................... 6:22
1 thy whole **body** shall be full of light.................... 6:22
1 thy whole **body** shall be full of darkness.............. 6:23
3 nor yet for your **body**, what ye shall put on............ 6:25
1 life more than meat, and the **body** than raiment?....... 6:25
1 And fear not them which kill the **body**,............... 10:28
1 able to destroy both soul and **body** in hell............ 10:28
1 And his disciples came, and took up the **body**,........ 14:12
2 in that she hath poured this ointment on my **body**,.... 26:12
1 and said, Take, eat; this is my **body**.................. 26:26
4 and many **bodies** of the saints which slept arose,....... 27:52
1 He went to Pilate, and begged the **body** of Jesus....... 27:58
1 Then Pilate commanded the **body** to be delivered...... 27:58
1 And when Joseph had taken the **body**,................ 27:59
3 felt in her **body** that she was healed of that plague. Mark 5:29
1 come aforehand to anoint my **body** to the burying...... 14:8
1 gave to them, and said, Take, eat: this is my **body**..... 14:22
1 boldly unto Pilate, and craved the **body** of Jesus...... 15:43
1 when he knew it ... he gave the **body** to Joseph........ 15:45
2 The light of the **body** is the eye:................. Luke 11:34
1 thy whole **body** also is full of light;.................. 11:34
1 thy **body** also is full of darkness..................... 11:34
1 If thy whole **body** therefore be full of light,.......... 11:36
1 Be not afraid of them that kill the **body**,............. 12:4
3 neither for the **body**, what ye shall put on............ 12:22
1 and the **body** is more than raiment.................... 12:23
1 And he said unto them, Wheresoever the **body** is,..... 17:37
1 This is my **body** which is given for you:.............. 22:19
1 went unto Pilate, and begged the **body** of Jesus........ 23:52
1 beheld the sepulchre, and how his **body** was laid....... 23:55
1 found not the **body** of the Lord Jesus.................. 24:3
1 And when they found not his **body**, they came,........ 24:23
2 But he spake of the temple of his **body**............ John 2:21
4 that the **bodies** should not remain upon the cross...... 19:31
1 besought Pilate that he might take away the **body**..... 19:38
1 He came therefore, and took the **body** of Jesus........ 19:38
1 Then took they the **body** of Jesus,.................... 19:40
1 where the **body** of Jesus had lain...................... 20:12
1 and turning him to the **body** said, Tabitha, arise..... Acts 9:40
4 to dishonour their own **bodies** between themselves:.. Rom 1:24
1 he considered not his own **body** now dead,............. 4:19
1 that the **body** of sin might be destroyed,............... 6:6
3 Let not sin therefore reign in your mortal **body**,........ 6:12

2 are become dead to the law by the **body** of Christ; .. Rom 7:4
2 who shall deliver me from the **body** of this death? 7:24
1 if Christ be in you, the **body** is dead because of sin; 8:10
4 shall also quicken your mortal **bodies** by his Spirit 8:11
2 through ... Spirit do mortify the deeds of the **body**, ... 8:13
2 the redemption of our **body**. 8:23
4 that ye present your **bodies** a living sacrifice, ... 12:1
3 For as we have many members in one **body**, ... 12:4
1 So we, being many, are one **body** in Christ, ... 12:5
3 I verily, as absent in **body**, but present in spirit, ... 1 Co 5:3
1 Now the **body** is not for fornication, ... 6:13
3 but for the Lord; and the Lord for the **body**. 6:13
4 that your **bodies** are the members of Christ? 6:15
1 that he which is joined to an harlot is one **body**? 6:16
2 Every sin that a man doeth is without the **body**; 6:18
1 fornication sinneth against his own **body**. 6:18
1 What? know ye not that your **body** is the temple 6:19
3 therefore glorify God in your **body**, ... 6:20
2 The wife hath not power of her own **body**, ... 7:4
2 the husband hath not power of his own **body**, ... 7:4
3 that she may be holy both in **body** and in spirit: 7:34
1 But I keep under my **body**, ... 9:27
2 is it not the communion of the **body** of Christ? 10:16
1 For we being many are one bread, and one **body**: 10:17
1 eat: this is my **body**, which is broken for you: 11:24
2 shall be guilty of the **body** and blood of the Lord. 11:27
1 not discerning the Lord's **body**. 11:29
1 For as the **body** is one, and hath many members, ... 12:12
2 and all the members of that one **body**, ... 12:12
1 being many, are one **body**: so also is Christ. 12:12
1 by one Spirit are we all baptized into one **body**, ... 12:13
1 For the **body** is not one member, but many. 12:14
2 Because I am not the hand, I am not of the **body**; 12:15
2 is it therefore not of the **body**? 12:15
2 Because I am not the eye, I am not of the **body**; 12:16
2 is it therefore not of the **body**? 12:16
1 whole **body** were an eye, where were the hearing? 12:17
3 the members every one of them in the **body**, ... 12:18
1 were all one member, where were the **body**? 12:19
1 now are they many members, yet but one **body**. 12:20
2 Nay, much more those members of the **body**, ... 12:22
2 And those members of the **body**, ... 12:23
1 but God hath tempered the **body** together, ... 12:24
3 That there should be no schism in the **body**; 12:25
1 are the **body** of Christ, and members in particular. 12:27
1 and though I give my **body** to be burned, ... 13:3
3 and with what **body** do they come? 15:35
1 sowest not that **body** that shall be, but bare grain, ... 15:37
1 But God giveth it a **body** as it hath pleased him, ... 15:38
1 and to every seed his own **body**. 15:38
4 are also celestial **bodies**, and bodies terrestrial: 15:40
4 are also celestial bodies, and **bodies** terrestrial: 15:40
1 It is sown a natural **body**; 15:44
1 is sown a natural body; it is raised a spiritual **body**. 15:44
1 There is a natural **body**, and there is a spiritual 15:44
1 is a natural body, and there is a spiritual **body**. 15:44
3 Always bearing about in the **body** the dying .... 2 Co 4:10
3 Jesus might be made manifest in our **body**. 4:10
3 knowing that, whilst we are at home in the **body**, ... 5:6
2 and willing rather to be absent from the **body**, ... 5:8
2 every one may receive the things done in his **body**, ... 5:10
2 but his **bodily** presence is weak, ... 10:10
3 whether in the **body**, I cannot tell; 12:2
2 or whether out of the **body**, I cannot tell: 12:2
3 whether in the **body**, or out of the body, ... 12:3
2 whether in the body, or out of the **body**, ... 12:3
3 for I bear in my **body** the marks of the Lord Jesus... Gal 6:17
1 Which is his **body**, the fulness of him .... Eph 1:23
3 reconcile both unto God in one **body** by the cross, ... 2:16
1 There is one **body**, and one Spirit, ... 4:4
2 for the edifying of the **body** of Christ: 4:12
1 From whom the whole **body** fitly joined together 4:16
2 maketh increase of the **body** unto the edifying 4:16
2 and he is the saviour of the **body**. 5:23
4 ought men to love their wives as their own **bodies**. 5:28
2 For we are members of his **body**, of his flesh, ... 5:30
3 so now also Christ shall be magnified in my **body**, ... Phlp 1:20
1 Who shall change our vile **body**, ... Phlp 3:21
3 it may be fashioned like unto his glorious **body**, ... 3:21
2 And he is the head of the **body**, the church: .... Col 1:18
3 In the **body** of his flesh through death, ... 1:22
2 afflictions of Christ in my flesh for his **body's** sake, ... 1:24
2 in putting off the **body** of the sins of the flesh 2:11
1 but the **body** is of Christ. 2:17
1 from which all the **body** by joints and bands 2:19
2 and humility, and neglecting of the **body**; 2:23
3 to the which also ye are called in one **body**; 3:15
1 spirit and soul and **body** be preserved blameless ..... 1 Th 5:23
1 but a **body** hast thou prepared me: .... Heb 10:5
2 the offering of the **body** of Jesus Christ once for all. ... 10:10
1 and our **bodies** washed with pure water. 10:22
3 as being yourselves also in the **body**. 13:3
4 For the **bodies** of those beasts, ... 13:11
2 not those things which are needful to the **body**; ...... Jas 2:16
1 For as the **body** without the spirit is dead, so faith 2:26
1 and able also to bridle the whole **body**. 3:2
1 and we turn about their whole **body**. 3:3
1 the tongue ... that it defileth the whole **body**, ... 3:6
3 Who his own self bare our sins in his own **body** ..... 1 Pt 2:24
2 Michael ... he disputed about the **body** of Moses, ... Jude 1:9
5 horses, and chariots, and **slaves**, and souls of men... Rev 18:13

Classical Greek

The original definition of *sōma* is uncertain. Its first known appearance describes a "dead body," a "corpse." Later it was used for the "trunk" of the human body. Thus it eventually means "body," the entire human body, and it denotes the "person" in a representative sense (Wibbing, "Body," *Colin Brown*, 1:232). In the dualism of certain Greek philosophers the body was regarded as the abode or the prison of the preexistent soul which needed to be delivered from the body.

Sōma acquired a somewhat figurative sense for describing the *kosmos* (2862), the physical universe. Certain philosophers believed that this *kosmos*/universe had its own divine *psuchē* (5425), "soul." Thus, just as the macrocosm of the universe had a soul, the microcosm of man involved his body and soul (Schweizer, "sōma," *Kittel*, 7:1029f.).

From a religious point of view such philosophical speculations were both negative and positive. Positively, dualism admits that man has a spiritual dimension. But negatively, such dualism—making the soul a prisoner in the body—stands in contradiction to the Biblical view of man.

Septuagint Usage

One might be justified in saying, therefore, that there is no true Hebrew equivalent to the Greek term *sōma* despite the fact that *sōma* consistently translated the Hebrew term *bāsār*, "flesh," in the Septuagint. In the Septuagint *sōma* principally stands for the "person." Just as man may be represented by his soul, likewise his body can speak of his whole being (Wibbing, "Body," *Colin Brown*, 1:233). The body is regarded as the total expression of the human makeup; it is not subordinate to the soul. Even heavenly beings have "bodies" (see e.g., Ezekiel 1:11,23; Daniel 10:6). Thus both earthly existence and heavenly existence are characterized by a body.

New Testament Usage

The New Testament appropriates its view of man from the Old Testament; however, here the term "body" takes on some added meanings as well. As in the Old Testament the body represents the total man. It is also considered to be an independent aspect of man: "Fear not them which kill the *body*, but are not able to kill the soul (*psuchē*)" (Matthew 10:28). When man is referred to in bipartite terms—as a mind and body—the soul is thought to be the center of the personality. The "inner man" equals the "heart" of man in the Old Testament.

Although a person may be identified by his body (John 19:40-42; Acts 9:37; 13:36), the body is not all of man, because man may exist apart from his body (2 Corinthians 12:2,3). The body is the visible, earthly form of man; consequently it would be in error to consider the body as the "shell," removed from the "inner man." For example, to engage in sexual immorality is to violate one's soul as well as one's body (see e.g., 1 Corinthians 6:13-20).

There are also indications in the New Testament that man is a tripartite being: spirit, soul, and body (1 Thessalonians 5:23). Some say that *sōma*, "body," and *pneuma* (4011), "spirit," can be separated; *pneuma* and *psuchē*, "soul," can only be distinguished between. It should be added, however, that clear distinction between the soul and spirit would be rather difficult.

In the Epistles we encounter "body" with ethical implications, often describing the nature of man. Paul ordinarily employed "flesh" (*sarx* [4418]) to express the sinful nature of man that opposes God (Romans 8:5-7; Galatians 5:17). He also used the phrase "*body* of . . . the flesh" (Colossians 2:11) in order to denote the sinful human nature in a more restricted sense. Parallel to this phrase are the "*body* of sin" (Romans 6:6) or the "*body* of . . . death" (Romans 7:24). "Body" in these cases does become the designation for the physical body in the sense that it is the seat of sin and the outlet for its expression.

However, Paul is not saying here that our bodies are sinful in and of themselves. Still, Scripture advises the "putting to death" of the body and its "members" (Colossians 3:5) as well as the "deeds of the body" (Romans 8:13); believers are to reckon themselves "dead . . . unto sin" (Romans 6:11). But this is not the "putting to death" of the normal impulses and desires of the body; it is not a charge for asceticism. Rather, it is a plea to "put to death" those impulses and lusts that are under the power of the sinful nature. The natural processes and desires of the body are not to be suppressed but channeled into godly expressions. But impulses and temptations such as gluttony, drunkenness, lewdness, and impurity are not to be satisfied (Ephesians 5:3ff.; Colossians 3:5; 1 Peter 4:3; cf. 1 Timothy 4:3).

Despite the inner transformation and renewal believers experience by the Spirit, the body will ultimately die. The life in our mortal bodies cannot be totally renewed by the Spirit until the resurrection (Romans 8:11). Our earthly bodies will perish, but as an integral dimension of our personality they will be resurrected in the form of a new spiritual body (1 Corinthians 15:35ff.). Our "lowly bodies" (NIV) will be like Christ's "glorious body" (KJV) (Philippians 3:21).

The resurrected body of Jesus Christ serves as the model for the resurrected body of the believer. His was a real body. Jesus ate while the disciples watched (Luke 24:43); they touched Him with their hands, and they felt His "flesh and bones" (Luke 24:39). He was no spirit without a body.

In addition the empty tomb of Jesus testifies to the relationship between the believer's earthly body and the body awaiting him in the resurrection. By "spiritual body" the New Testament means that it will be governed totally by the Holy Spirit, made alive and sustained by the eternal living power of the Spirit. That it is "heavenly" (1 Corinthians 15:40,48,51) indicates its glorious nature (Philippians 3:21). The body of the resurrected is of a new and different nature and quality. Consequently, this body is apparently not restricted by physical obstacles or the ordinary confines of space (John 20:19).

The Christology of the New Testament affirms that during His earthly life Christ had a human body (Colossians 2:9; cf. 1:19; Philippians 2:7; 1 Timothy 3:16). It is spoken of literally: during His ministry He "spake of the temple of his body" (John 2:21); Joseph asked for Jesus' body after He had died (Matthew 27:58); the women did not find "the *body* of the Lord Jesus" when they went to the tomb (Luke 24:3; cf. John 20:12). Figuratively, Jesus spoke of the bread of the Last Supper as His "body" (Matthew 26:26). The literal and figurative intersect on other occasions (1 Corinthians 10:16).

The image of "body" is used to depict the living quality of the Church. Unity as well as diversity in the Body are to be expected (Romans 12:4f.; 1 Corinthians 12:12f.). "By one Spirit are we all baptized into one *body*" (1 Corinthians 12:13). As the body of Christ, the Church is to mature and to strive for unity. Through the grace of the spiritual gifts God builds and edifies His church (Ephesians 4:4,12; cf. 1 Corinthians 12:27). Each believer belongs to the body of Christ (Romans 12:4,5; 1 Corinthians 12:27). Ephesians and Colossians also employ the image of the Church as the body of Christ. They, however, lay particular stress on the fact that Christ is the Head to whom all others are subordinate (Ephesians 1:22; 4:15; 5:23; Colossians 1:18; 2:19).

Strong 4983, Bauer 799-800, Moulton-Milligan 620-21, Kittel 7:1024-94, Liddell-Scott 1749, Colin Brown 1:232-37,241-42; 2:523-25,537.

4836. σωματικός sōmatikos adj

Bodily, pertaining to the body.

Cross-Reference:
σῶμα sōma (4835)

1. σωματικῇ sōmatikē nom sing fem
2. σωματικῷ sōmatikō dat sing neu

2 And the Holy Ghost descended in a **bodily** shape....Luke 3:22
1 For **bodily** exercise profiteth little:................. 1 Tm 4:8

Classical Greek

Aristotle's use of this adjective in the Fourth Century B.C. is the oldest known example of this word in classical Greek. He used it to mean something corporeal, bodily, or consisting of a body.

New Testament Usage

Luke utilized the term when he recorded the story of Jesus' baptism. The Holy Spirit descended on the Lord in the bodily form of a dove (Luke 3:22). Lastly, Paul employed the word when he told Timothy that "*bodily* exercise" profits a little (1 Timothy 4:8). Paul exhorted Timothy to train himself in godliness which has value not only in this life but also in the life to come. "*Bodily* exercise" does not refer to asceticism but to the physical training which was so prized among the Greeks and a standard part of the education of Greek youths.

Strong 4984, Bauer 800, Moulton-Milligan 621, Kittel 7:1024-94, Liddell-Scott 1749.

4837. σωματικῶς sōmatikōs adv

Bodily, in bodily form.

Cross-Reference:
σῶμα sōma (4835)

1. σωματικῶς sōmatikōs

1 dwelleth all the fulness of the Godhead **bodily**........Col 2:9

Classical Greek

The earliest extant occurrence of *sōmatikōs* is found in Philo who referred to the "bodily" exit of the high priest from the Holy of Holies (*Quis Rerum Diuinarum Heres* 84). Plutarch (Second Century A.D.) also used the word with the meaning "bodily" (*Moralia* 424e; cf. *Bauer*). It is not used in the Septuagint.

New Testament Usage

The apostle Paul employed *sōmatikōs* in his classic statement about Jesus being the fullness of deity manifested in bodily form (Colossians 2:9). It is believed that he was countering Gnostic heresy which propagated the existence of many so-called intermediaries between God and man.

Strong 4985, Bauer 800, Moulton-Milligan 621, Liddell-Scott 1749.

4838. Σώπατρος Sōpatros name

Sopater.

1. Σώπατρος Sōpatros nom masc

1 there accompanied him into Asia **Sopater** of Berea; Acts 20:4

Sopater the son of Pyrrhus was a Christian from Beroea in central Greece. He and others from the churches planted by Paul accompanied the apostle on his final journey to Jerusalem (Acts 20:4).

4839. σωρεύω sōreuō verb

Heap, pile up.

Synonym:
ἐπισωρεύω episōreuō (1986)

חָתָה chāthar (2972), Heap (Prv 25:22).

1. σωρεύσεις sōreuseis 2sing indic fut act
2. σεσωρευμένα sesōreumena nom/acc pl neu part perf mid

1 so doing thou shalt **heap** coals of fire on his head...Rom 12:20
2 and lead captive silly women **laden** with sins,....... 2 Tm 3:6

Classical Greek

In classical Greek *sōreuō* means "to heap" or "pile up." Examples of this verb can be seen as far back in classical Greek as the writings of Aristotle in the Fourth Century B.C. and of Polybius in the Second Century B.C. Eusebius, the first major church historian after Luke, compiled his monumental work around A.D. 300. He made considerable use of the word.

Septuagint Usage

The Septuagint uses *sōreuō* in Proverbs 25:22 where the Lord instructed righteous people not to retaliate against their enemies. Instead, they were to feed them and give them water to drink. By so doing the righteous would be "heaping" (*sōreuō*) coals on their enemies; that is, they would be overwhelming with love the wrongs committed by these enemies.

New Testament Usage

In the New Testament *sōreuō* occurs only twice, once at Romans 12:20 and again at 2 Timothy 3:6. Both occurrences have the connotation of heaping or piling up. In Romans 12:20 Paul quoted the Septuagint, Proverbs 25:22. Two interpretations of "heaping burning coals" exist. One sees in the burning coals a reference to future punishment which the "enemy" will receive. The other understands the coals to indicate "shame and contrition" (Cranfield, *International Critical Commentary*, *Romans*, 2:648f.). According to Cranfield the latter interpretation "is to be preferred . . . for it is congruous with the context in Romans" (ibid.). Thus by ministering to his enemy the believer will cause him to feel shame and hopefully to repent. The origin of the expression "heap burning coals" may be an Egyptian repentance ritual in which a man carried a dish of burning coals on his head (ibid., 2:650).

In 2 Timothy 3:6 Paul gave exhortation concerning those who were opposing the truth of the gospel: "They are the kind who worm their way into homes and gain control over weak-willed women, who are *loaded down* (*sōreuō*) with sins" (NIV). Here, the sense of *sōreuō* is "overwhelmed" (*Moulton-Milligan*). Fee notes that their "less-than-satisfying social position in Greco-Roman society and their religious hunger . . . made women easy prey" for these religious charlatans (*Good News Commentary, 1 and 2 Timothy and Titus*, p.221). He interprets *sōreuō* "burdened with a sinful past" (ibid., p.222).

STRONG 4987, BAUER 800, MOULTON-MILLIGAN 621, KITTEL 7:1094-96, LIDDELL-SCOTT 1750.

4840. Σωσθένης Sōsthenēs name

Sosthenes.

1. Σωσθένης **Sōsthenēs** nom masc
2. Σωσθένην **Sōsthenēn** acc fem

2 Then all the Greeks took **Sosthenes**, ... Acts 18:17
1 Paul, ... and **Sosthenes** our brother, ... 1 Co 1:1

The name appears twice in the New Testament. It is very possible that both references are to the same man. The first Sosthenes was a ruler of the synagogue in Corinth at the time of Paul's visit. He was beaten by "the Jews" in an attempt to influence the proconsul Gallio against Paul (Acts 18:17). The second was a Christian who joined Paul in addressing the church at Corinth (1 Corinthians 1:1).

4841. Σωσίπατρος Sōsipatros name

Sosipater.

1. Σωσίπατρος **Sōsipatros** nom masc

1 and Jason, and **Sosipater**, my kinsmen, salute you. Rom 16:21

He joined Paul and others in sending greetings to the church in Rome (Romans 16:21). His name may be a variant of *Sopater* (4838).

4842. σωτήρ sōtēr noun

Savior, redeemer, deliverer, preserver.

CROSS-REFERENCE:
σῴζω sōzō (4834)

יְשׁוּעָה yeshûʿāh (3568), Salvation (Dt 32:15, Ps 62:2 [61:2], Is 12:2).

יָשַׁע yāshaʿ (3588), Hiphil: deliverer (Jgs 3:9, Neh 9:27); deliver (1 Sm 10:19).

יֵשַׁע yēshaʿ (3589), Salvation (Pss 24:5 [23:5], 65:5 [64:5], Hb 3:18).

1. σωτήρ **sōtēr** nom sing masc
2. σωτῆρος **sōtēros** gen sing masc
3. σωτῆρι **sōtēri** dat sing masc
4. σωτῆρα **sōtēra** acc sing masc

3 And my spirit hath rejoiced in God my **Saviour**..... Luke 1:47
1 is born this day in the city of David a **Saviour**, ... 2:11
1 this is indeed the Christ, the **Saviour** of the world... John 4:42
4 God exalted ... to be a Prince and a **Saviour**, ... Acts 5:31
4 hath God ... raised unto Israel a **Saviour**, Jesus: 13:23
1 and he is the **saviour** of the body.................... Eph 5:23
4 we look for the **Saviour**, the Lord Jesus Christ: ..... Phlp 3:20
2 by the commandment of God our **Saviour**, ... 1 Tm 1:1
2 acceptable in the sight of God our **Saviour**; 2:3
1 the living God, who is the **Saviour** of all men, ... 4:10
2 by the appearing of our **Saviour** Jesus Christ, ... 2 Tm 1:10
2 the commandment of God our **Saviour**; .... Tit 1:3
2 the Father and the Lord Jesus Christ our **Saviour**....... 1:4
2 the doctrine of God our **Saviour** in all things........... 2:10
2 of the great God and our **Saviour** Jesus Christ; 2:13
2 love of God our **Saviour** toward man appeared, ... 3:4
2 abundantly through Jesus Christ our **Saviour**; 3:6
2 righteousness of God and our **Saviour** Jesus Christ: .. 2 Pt 1:1

2 kingdom of our Lord and **Saviour** Jesus Christ....... 2 Pt 1:11
2 knowledge of the Lord and **Saviour** Jesus Christ,....... 2:20
2 us the apostles of the Lord and **Saviour**:............... 3:2
2 in the knowledge of our Lord and **Saviour** Jesus........ 3:18
4 Father sent the Son to be the **Saviour** of the world. 1 Jn 4:14
3 To the only wise God our **Saviour**,................. Jude 1:25

Classical Greek

The noun *sōtēr*, "savior," carries the same broad meaning in classical Greek as the related verb *sōzō* (4834) and the noun *sōtēria* (4843). The term ordinarily occurs in connection with men or gods and only rarely in connection with objects (Foerster, "sōzō," *Kittel*, 7:1004). Of the gods Zeus was especially honored as *sōtēr*. At times a physician or a philosopher was called a *sōtēr*, but normally the title was reserved for politicians and rulers. Philip of Macedon was honored as *sōtēr*, and the Grecian kings of the Orient often adopted the title *theos sōtēr*, "divine savior," for themselves (ibid., 7:1009). Later this custom was taken over by the Roman emperors. Caesar was called *sōtēr tēs oikoumenēs*, "savior of the inhabited world," and Hadrian was termed *sōtēr tou kosmou*, "the savior of the world" (ibid., 7:1010). Such "saviors" might be highly esteemed and popular. The famous Roman orator and senator Cicero says: "*Sōtēr* . . . how much this word contains! So much that it cannot be expressed by just one Latin word" (*In Verrem* 2.2.63.154).

Septuagint Usage

Sōtēr appears about 35 times in the Septuagint for the Hebrew term *y^eshû'āh* (in various forms). This Hebrew term for "savior, salvation" forms part of many personal names in the Bible; for example, Hosea (Greek, *Osee*) and Joshua (Greek, *Iēsous* [2400]; i.e., "Jesus").

The word "saviors" appears in the Old Testament under a variety of situations. Judges are often called saviors (Judges 3:9,15; cf. Nehemiah 9:27) because they were sent from God as His instruments to bring relief and salvation to His people. As channels of God's saving intervention kings were often called saviors. For example, this is the case with Jeroboam, the son of Joash (2 Kings 13:5; cf. 14:27), who delivered the people from the hands of the Syrians. Any "deliverer" sent by God in response to the prayers of the people was a *sōtēr* (Isaiah 19:20). During the final reestablishment of the kingdom of Israel, saviors would appear among the people and, like the ancient judges, would defend them, conquering their oppressors (Obadiah 21).

But first and foremost the Lord God is Saviour; only He can claim this title in the absolute sense. He revealed himself as the Saviour of His people when He delivered them from their bondage in Egypt and led them into the Promised Land (Isaiah 63:7-9). During times of natural disaster and catastrophe the people of Israel trusted in the Lord, the Saviour of Israel (Jeremiah 14:1-8). Reflecting upon his life of victorious struggle, David worshiped the God of Israel as his personal Saviour (2 Samuel 22:3). God demonstrated His great wisdom and His power as Saviour when He freed the captives in Babylon who were in captivity for 70 years (Isaiah 43:3,11). Ultimately, in the last days the Lord will reappear as the Saviour of His people (Isaiah 49:22-26); He will gather Israel from all the nations of the earth to their homeland. He will grant them unbelievable prosperity, abundant life, and happiness (Isaiah chapter 60).

New Testament Usage

Sōtēr occurs 24 times in the Greek New Testament. On 8 occasions it is applied to God and 16 times to Christ.

At the dawn of the arrival of God's kingdom, Mary glorified God as Saviour because of the great blessings He had bestowed upon her, Israel, and all of humanity (Luke 1:47f.). Paul's pastoral letters emphasize that God is the Saviour of all men. We should recognize the context of Paul's comments. He was here struggling with a heresy that became more fully expressed in later gnosticism; i.e., that salvation does not include everyone willing to call upon the name of the Lord, but only a select few. Consequently, every time Paul used *sōtēr* in these epistles it has the ring of universal invitation (e.g., 1 Timothy 1:1f.; 2:3,4; 4:10; Titus 1:3f.; 2:10,11; 3:4). On each occasion *sōtēr* carries a religiomoral implication. In contrast to the deluded teaching and the misguided understanding of the false teachers, Paul held up knowledge of the living God, "who is the Saviour of all men," and the salvation He offers (1 Timothy 4:9,10; cf. verses 1-8). Jude closed his epistle with praise "to the only wise God our Saviour" (verse 25).

Jesus Christ is the Saviour sent from God. He is the Saviour proclaimed by thc prophets. Accordingly, the angel of the Lord announced to Mary that the baby she carried was the promised Saviour. The shepherds outside Bethlehem were told of the birth of the Saviour (Luke 2:11). Jesus himself bore witness to His calling as Saviour (Luke 19:10). His apostles declared Him to be Saviour (1 Timothy 1:15; cf. Acts 4:12).

Jesus as Saviour delivers from the guilt of sin as well as from sin's power (He is the Redeemer). Each person, having been justified through the blood of Christ (cf. Romans 5:1), is delivered from the guilt of sin. Being made holy in Christ, believers are freed from sin's power. The first is an act, the second a process that culminates at Jesus' return when believers will be transformed into His likeness and their bodies will be redeemed by the Saviour (Philippians 3:20,21).

Strong 4990, Bauer 800-801, Moulton-Milligan 621-22, Kittel 7:1003-21, Liddell-Scott 1751, Colin Brown 3:216-23.

4843. σωτηρία sōtēria noun

Salvation, deliverance, preservation.

Cross-Reference:

σώζω sōzō (4834)

יְשׁוּעָה yeshûʿāh (3568), Salvation, deliverance (Ex 14:13, Jb 13:16, Is 26:18).

יָשַׁע yāshaʿ (3588), Hiphil: deliverer (2 Kgs 13:5).

יֵשַׁע yēshaʿ (3589), Salvation (2 Sm 22:3, Ps 18:46 [17:46], Hb 3:13).

פְּלֵיטָה pelēṭāh (6656), Deliverance, remnant (2 Chr 12:7, Ezr 9:8, Jer 25:35 [32:35]).

שָׁלֵו shālēw (8355), Quietness (Jb 20:20).

שָׁלוֹם shālôm (8361), Peace, safety (Gn 26:31, 28:21).

שֶׁלֶם shelem (8399), Offering (Nm 6:14—only some Vaticanus texts).

תְּשׁוּעָה teshûʿāh (9009), Deliverance, victory (1 Sm 11:9, 2 Kgs 13:17, Ps 146:3 [145:3]).

תּוּשִׁיָּה tûshîyāh (8786), Sound wisdom (Prv 2:7).

1. **σωτηρία sōtēria** nom sing fem
2. **σωτηρίας sōtērias** gen sing fem
3. **σωτηρίαν sōtērian** acc sing fem

2 And hath raised up an horn **of salvation** for us ...... Luke 1:69
3 That we **should be saved** from our enemies, ... 1:71
2 To give knowledge **of salvation** unto his people 1:77
1 This day is **salvation** come to this house, ... 19:9
1 for **salvation** is of the Jews. .... John 4:22
1 Neither is there **salvation** in any other: .... Acts 4:12
3 how that God by his hand would **deliver** them: 7:25
2 to you is the word of this **salvation** sent. 13:26
3 that thou shouldest be for **salvation** 13:47
2 which show unto us the way **of salvation**. 16:17
2 to take some meat: for this is for your **health**: 27:34
3 for it is the power of God unto **salvation** .... Rom 1:16
3 prayer ... for Israel is, that they **might be saved**. 10:1
3 with the mouth confession is made unto **salvation**. 10:10
1 but rather through their fall **salvation** is come 11:11
1 for now is our **salvation** nearer than when we 13:11
2 it is for your consolation and **salvation**, ... 2 Co 1:6
2 it is for your consolation and **salvation**. 1:6
2 and in the day **of salvation** have I succoured thee: 6:2
2 behold, now is the day **of salvation**. 6:2
3 For godly sorrow worketh repentance to **salvation** 7:10
2 the word of truth, the gospel of your **salvation**: ...... Eph 1:13
3 For I know that this shall turn to my **salvation** ...... Phlp 1:19
2 but to you **of salvation**, and that of God. .... Phlp 1:28
3 work out your own **salvation** with fear 2:12
2 and for an helmet, the hope **of salvation**. .... 1 Th 5:8
2 but to obtain **salvation** by our Lord Jesus Christ, ... 5:9
3 to **salvation** through sanctification of the Spirit ...... 2 Th 2:13
2 that they may also obtain the **salvation** ... in Christ 2 Tm 2:10
3 which are able to make thee wise unto **salvation** 3:15
3 minister for them who shall be heirs of **salvation**? .... Heb 1:14
2 escape, if we neglect so great **salvation**; 2:3
2 to make the captain of their **salvation** perfect 2:10
2 he became the author of eternal **salvation** 5:9
2 and things that accompany **salvation**, ... 6:9
3 appear the second time without sin unto **salvation**. 9:28
3 prepared an ark to the **saving** of his house; 11:7
3 by the power of God through faith unto **salvation** .... 1 Pt 1:5
3 even the **salvation** of your souls. 1:9
2 Of which **salvation** the prophets have inquired 1:10
3 you may grow in respect to **salvation**, (NASB) 2:2
3 that the longsuffering of our Lord is **salvation**; .... 2 Pt 3:15
2 to write unto you of the common **salvation**, ... Jude 1:3
1 with a loud voice, saying, **Salvation** to our God ...... Rev 7:10
1 voice saying in heaven, Now is come **salvation**, ... 12:10
1 **Salvation**, and glory, and honour, and power, ... 19:1

The principal conveyers of the concept of salvation in the New Testament are members of the *sōzō* (4834) word group, the noun *sōtēria*, the adjective *sōtērios* (4844), the noun *sōtēr* (4842), as well as the compound *diasōzō* (1289). The stem of these words, *sao* or *sō*, means "whole, fresh, healthy," and the verb means "to keep (whole, healthy), to save (from danger, illness, death)."

Classical Greek

Words derived from this root have a broad understanding in classical Greek. They may depict being "rescued" from serious danger such as war, shipwreck, etc. They may involve "being assisted" out of a difficult legal situation, or "being helped" by a physician in a time of illness. They also might describe a "safe return" from a perilous journey. Inherent in the words are the ideas of "protection, mercy," and "security." They also imply a healthy, prosperous condition, an inner well-being and personal self-esteem. The terms frequently occur in a religious and moral context (see Foerster, "sōzō," *Kittel*, 7:966-969).

Septuagint Usage

In the Septuagint *sōtēria* occurs over 100 times, predominantly translating forms of the root *yshʿ*, "deliver, protect, preserve." On three occasions it translates *shālôm*, "peace, health" (Genesis 26:31; 28:21; 44:17). *Sōtēria* preserves many of the same senses as in classical usage. In Exodus 14:13 Moses cries out, "Stand firm and you will see the *deliverance* the Lord will bring you today" (NIV). Isaiah 45:17 declares that "Israel shall be saved . . . with an everlasting *salvation*."

Old Testament Background

The concept of salvation in the Old Testament is quite broad. It concerns every aspect of human existence. "To be saved/delivered" means deliverance from anything that threatens to destroy. It also stands for the resultant safety and security. Positively, salvation connotes everything promoting happiness, wealth, progress, and well-being. God's acts of deliverance on behalf of His people Israel become the model of His messianic eschatological salvation through Christ (cf. 1 Corinthians 10:11).

Salvation has a national, corporate dimension; the Lord delivered His people from their bondage in Egypt, destroyed their enemies, and led them into the land of promise (Exodus 14:13,30; 15:1-19). Through judges God saved Israel from its threatening neighbors and gave them peace and prosperity in the land (Judges 2:16-18; 3:9,31; 6:11f.; 10:1,12; 13:5). Saul's mission was to deliver God's people from the power of the Philistines (1 Samuel 9:16). His son Jonathan brought salvation to the people through his bravery that resulted from his trust in God (1 Samuel 14:6,23). By defeating Israel's enemies David brought salvation to Israel (1 Samuel 23:5). In response to Hezekiah's prayer for God's intervention during the siege of the Assyrians, God promised deliverance. That same night the Lord extended His saving hand through His angel and delivered the people, giving them victory (Isaiah 37:36,38). Following the 70 years of bondage in Babylon, Israel was delivered by Cyrus, the Lord's instrument. Cyrus conquered the neo-Babylonian Empire. Judah was delivered from captivity, returned to its own land, and restored as a nation (Isaiah 45:1-7). Its enemies were vanquished (Isaiah 45:16).

Salvation, however, is individual as well as corporate. God rescues the individual from his/her personal enemies (Psalm 18:3), persecutors (Psalm 7:1f.), slanderous speech (Job 5:15f.), and the clutches of the powerful (Job 5:15). He saves in times of sickness (Job 33:19-25). But first and foremost salvation means "divine help" in spiritual/moral distress: God forgives sins, and He delivers from sin's power (Psalms 40:12-17; 51:8-14).

Salvation is not only salvation *from* something (negative); it is also positive. We are saved *for* happiness, prosperity, and blessing by God in every way (Psalms 21:1-7; 85:10-13). Salvation puts joy in one's heart (Psalm 51:12); it gives one a sense of security. It evokes praise to God who allows His people to share in the fullness of His divine life (Psalm 116:13; Isaiah 12:2-6; 61:10). Those delivered by God experience His miraculous power and keeping grace (Psalm 118:14). They have a long life under the care and blessing of God (Psalm 91:14-16).

Salvation also has eschatological implications. After being scattered throughout the earth and among all peoples, Israel will once again see the Lord's salvation. There will be national, social, but most importantly religious and spiritual restoration (Isaiah 62:10-12; Jeremiah 30:7-11; 31:8-14; Ezekiel 36:23-38; 37:1f.; Amos 9:11f.). Salvation will be universal, that is, available to all; all peoples will see God's salvation (Isaiah 25:6-9; 52:10).

The arrival of eschatological salvation will be accompanied by "new heavens and a new earth" (Isaiah 65:17; 66:22). Those who are His will be raised to eternal life in the resurrection (Psalm 16:8-11; Isaiah 26:19; Daniel 12:1-3). The relationship between an end-time salvation and the original purpose of creation prior to the Fall is specific. Through His salvation God will restore creation; He will heal it from all the corruption and destruction that came as a result of the Fall. He will return His people to the unity, completeness, and freedom from disease and sickness formerly found in paradise (Isaiah 11:4-9; Ezekiel 47).

Salvation originates with God in heaven. False gods and idols stand powerless before Him (Isaiah 45:20; 46:6,7; Jeremiah 11:12), as do astrologers and practitioners of the occult (Isaiah 47:13f.). Human power is also inadequate to effect salvation. Only the name of God—that is, His personal revelation—brings salvation (Psalm 54:1-3). Salvation is a gift of God (Isaiah 46:13), an expression of His grace and His authority as judge and king (Isaiah 33:22). A proper response is the only mandate for experiencing God's grace and salvation (Job 22:20-30). Repentance from selfish ways and a turning to peace and trust accomplishes salvation (Isaiah 30:15). God saves those who take refuge in Him (Psalm 37:40), who trust in Him (Psalm 86:2), and who sincerely turn to Him (Isaiah 45:22). To forsake the Lord is to forfeit salvation and to become subject to judgment and damnation (Deuteronomy 32:15-22; Isaiah 17:10f.).

The richest and fullest expression of salvation in the Old Testament occurs in Isaiah's words of comfort (Isaiah 40–66). Here we encounter the various shades of meaning intrinsic to *sōtēria*: national, universal, corporate, and individual, in the present and future. The central figure throughout this section of Isaiah is the Suffering Servant of the Lord who at the same time is the exalted Messiah (as He is depicted in Isaiah 52:13 to 53:12). The true meaning of salvation in its most forceful and distinct presentation in the Old Testament can be found here. Here, too, is found in sublime form the ultimate salvation declared by the New Testament.

New Testament Usage

The New Testament writings contain the verb *sōzō* about 110 times while the compound *diasōzō* occurs 8. The noun *sōtēria* is used 45 times. The noun *sōtēria* has a wide range of meanings in the New Testament. The meaning "personal salvation"—that is, the deliverance of the individual from bondage to sin, his regeneration, redemption, and assurance of eternal life—cannot be forced into every occurrence of *sōtēria*. In the majority of appearances "personal salvation" is in view. Thus, Paul wrote that repentance leads to "salvation," he has in mind the believer's salvation (2 Corinthians 7:10). Second Thessalonians 2:13 acknowledges that God has chosen the believers for "salvation" through the work of the Spirit. Here, Paul referred to all of the blessings that God desires to bestow on the Christian. In 2 Timothy 3:15 Paul stated that the Scriptures show the way to "salvation."

When it refers to the salvation of the believer, *sōtēria* can indicate either the "state of having been saved" or "the process of being saved" (Louw and Nida, *Greek-English Lexicon*, 1:241f.). Louw and Nida, however, acknowledge the difficulty of discerning the difference in each occurrence.

Sōtēria has other meanings in the New Testament. It can mean "deliverance, rescue," as in Acts 7:25 where Stephen says that Moses thought God would use him for the deliverance of Israel. In Zechariah's song (Luke 1:69-71) the emphasis is on deliverance and freedom from the oppression of enemies. Regeneration of individuals is not in view until verse 77 in which it is clear that God will work His deliverance via the salvation of the people "through the forgiveness of their sins" (NIV).

Sōtēria can also denote the final deliverance at the second coming of Christ. In Romans 13:11 Paul warned the believers to "wake up" for "our *salvation* is nearer now than when we first believed" (NIV). According to Barrett, "Paul is not thinking of salvation in a pietistic way as something that happens to *us* in *our* experience, but as a universal eschatological event" (*Harper's New Testament Commentaries*, 6:253). Peter noted that "salvation" will "be revealed in the last time" (1 Peter 1:5, NIV). He referred to the final deliverance of the Christian from all suffering.

Sōtēria further denotes "what is beneficial." In Philippians 1:19 Paul notes that his imprisonment will "turn out for (his) *deliverance*" (NIV). He believed that through the prayers of the Philippians the circumstances would be beneficial to him. In Acts 27:34 Paul exhorted the crew of the ship to eat, "for this is for your *health*." Here *sōtēria* means "what is beneficial." One could hardly argue that personal salvation could result from the consumption of food. With the wide range of meaning for *sōtēria* one must carefully study the context in which it appears to discern its exact sense.

The understanding of salvation in the New Testament is more restricted than in the Old Testament. The dominating concept is the religious one, although a somewhat physical understanding occurs in a number of places. For example, Jesus saved the disciples from the stormy seas (Matthew 8:25); He saved/rescued the sinking Peter (Matthew 14:30). Paul and his fellow travelers were saved from death when they experienced shipwreck (Acts 27:20,31). Noah and his family were saved by the ark which delivered them from the floodwaters (Hebrews 11:7; 1 Peter 3:20).

However, in the New Testament salvation is essentially a religious and ethical concept. The underlying premise of salvation is that the chief enemy of mankind is sin. Sin, therefore, is the source of all peril and hardship, of distress and death. Sin is separation from God. Thus from a negative point of view Christians are saved *from*: the wrath of God (Romans 5:9; 1 Thessalonians 1:10), the guilt of sin (Matthew 1:21; Luke 1:77; Ephesians 1:7; Colossians 1:14; 1 Peter 1:18,19), condemnation (John 3:17), the power of darkness (Colossians 1:13), the bondage of sin and its power (Luke 7:50; Romans 7:24,25; Galatians 5:16), temptations (2 Peter 2:9), the Evil One and everything evil (Matthew 6:13).

But first and foremost salvation is positive. It reestablishes fellowship with God (Luke 1:68,69,74,75), and by it men are justified (Romans 5:1). Salvation makes them the adopted children of God (Galatians 4:5; Ephesians 1:5). Through salvation they are granted communion with the glorified Christ by the Spirit (Romans 8:9,10; Ephesians 1:13,14). To them belongs a citizenship in heaven—the kingdom of God (Colossians 1:13). Salvation means men are restored to the image of God, i.e., reborn (Titus 3:5). Through salvation their spirits, souls, and bodies are sanctified so they may walk in newness of life in fellowship with God and according to the will of God (1 Thessalonians 5:23,24; Titus 2:11-14). Finally, salvation entitles men to the glorious resurrection and to participation in the eschatological community of God in the age to come (2 Timothy 4:18; cf. Ephesians 2:6,7; 2 Peter 3:13; Revelation chapters 21 and 22).

The New Testament's view of salvation is built on the assumption that it is messianic and eschatological. The first advent of Christ initiated the arrival of eschatological salvation. The consummation of salvation, however, will occur in the future. "We are saved by hope" (Romans 8:24,25; cf. 13:11; Hebrews 9:28; 1 Peter 1:5,9; 4:18; 2 Peter 3:15).

Salvation is entirely an act of God (Ephesians 2:8-10). Man lacks any power to save himself; neither the "revelations" of gnosticism (cf. 1 Corinthians 1:17 to 2:16; Colossians 2:8,23), the "ecstatic experiences" of the mystery religions (Colossians 2:18), nor the keeping of the Law by the likes of the Pharisees (Romans 3:20,28; Galatians 2:16; Ephesians 2:8,9) are able to save mankind. Salvation is of God (Luke 3:6; Acts 28:28). The plan of salvation, the means of salvation, and the results of salvation are under God's charge, the ruler of all things, and His Son Jesus Christ (Revelation 7:10).

God's salvation in Christ is preached and offered to men through the gospel (Romans 1:16; 1 Corinthians 15:2; Ephesians 1:13; 2 Timothy 3:15). The preaching of the gospel brings salvation (Acts 11:14; 1 Timothy 4:16). The goal of every preacher is to win men to Christ (1 Corinthians 9:22). Every believer has the potential to be an instrument for God in the salvation of mankind (James 5:20; Jude 22,23).

Salvation must be received by faith (Acts 16:31; Romans 3:22; Galatians 3:26) which is expressed in humility (Acts 2:21; Romans 10:13) and in obedience to Christ (Hebrews 5:9). Faith is a gift from God (Ephesians 2:8; Philippians 2:13); nevertheless, it can be rejected by the stubborn (Hebrews 4:2; 10:39).

The various aspects of salvation can be seen in a threefold manner: Salvation is a present reality; believers *are* saved (Luke 7:50; Ephesians 2:8; 2 Timothy 1:9). They are currently delivered from the condemnation and penalty of sin and have been given fellowship with God in Christ (Galatians 2:20; Colossians 3:3) and a sharing in His life (1 John 5:12). Secondly, they are justified (Romans 5:1; 8:30). However, salvation is also something continually taking place; Christians are continually "being saved" (Philippians 2:12,13). They are being made holy in the image of Christ (Ephesians 4:20-24; Colossians 3:12f.). The final phase (future) of salvation will come at the return of Christ (Philippians 3:20,21; Hebrews 9:28; 1 Peter 1:5,9) when believers will be glorified (Romans 8:23).

Strong 4991, Bauer 801, Moulton-Milligan 622, Kittel 7:965-1003, Liddell-Scott 1751, Colin Brown 3:205-7,209-16,218-19.

4844. σωτήριος sōtērios adj

Delivering, saving, salvation.

Cross-Reference:

σῴζω sōzō (4834)

שֶׁלֶם shelem (8399), Offering (Am 5:22).

1. **σωτήριος** **sōtērios** nom sing fem
2. **σωτήριον** **sōtērion** nom/acc sing neu
3. **σωτηρίου** **sōtēriou** gen sing neu

2 For mine eyes have seen thy salvation,............. Luke 2:30
2 And all flesh shall see the salvation of God............ 3:6
2 that the salvation of God is sent unto the Gentiles, Acts 28:28
3 And take the helmet of salvation,.................. Eph 6:17
1 For the grace of God that bringeth salvation......... Tit 2:11

Classical Greek

In classical Greek the adjective *sōtērios* indicates the act of saving, delivering, or preserving (*Liddell-Scott*). *Sōtērios* had a wide usage as a substantive (acting as a noun) and is at times synonymous with *sōtēria* (4843), "deliverance." As a substantive it could refer to a thank-offering for salvation or a physician's fee (ibid.).

Septuagint Usage

The Septuagint contains *sōtērios* with reference to someone seeing the salvation of God (Psalm 50:23 [LXX 49:23]). David asked God to restore to him the joy of salvation that he enjoyed before his sin with Bathsheba (Psalm 51:12 [LXX 50:12]). Isaiah prophesied that John the Baptist would prepare the way for the revelation of Christ as the Messiah, and this Old Testament prophet promised that all flesh would see the salvation of the Lord (Isaiah 40:5). On many occasions *sōtērios* is used as a substantive to refer to the "peace offering" (Leviticus 3:1-16). In these instances (57 occurrences) *sōtērios* translates *shelem*, "peace offering" or "fellowship offering." The translators of the Septuagint understand it as a "salvation offering."

New Testament Usage

In the New Testament *sōtērios* is always used of spiritual salvation. The just and devout Simeon rejoiced that God allowed him to live long enough to see the Messiah whom he designated as the salvation provided by God (Luke 2:30). Luke quoted Isaiah 40:3-5 when he referred to the ministry of John the Baptist as the preparer of the way of the Lord. This was done so all mankind could see the salvation of God (Luke 3:6).

At the outset of his 2-year Roman imprisonment, Paul preached to certain Jews about Jesus being the salvation of God and that he (Paul) was presenting this offer of salvation to Gentiles (Acts 28:28). While Paul was in this imprisonment he instructed his readers to take the helmet of salvation (Ephesians 6:17), using the term here in a metaphoric sense. He assured Titus that God's grace that brings salvation has appeared to all people (Titus 2:11).

STRONG 4992, BAUER 801-2, MOULTON-MILLIGAN 622, KITTEL 7:1021-24, LIDDELL-SCOTT 1751, COLIN BROWN 3:216-17,221.

4845. σωφρονέω sōphroneō verb

Be of sound mind, sensible, serious.

COGNATE:

σωφρονίζω sōphronizō (4846)

SYNONYM:

νήφω nēphō (3387)

1. σωφρονοῦμεν sōphronoumen 1pl indic pres act

2. σωφρονοῦντα sōphronounta acc sing masc part pres act

3. σωφρονεῖν sōphronein inf pres act

4. σωφρονήσατε sōphronēsate 2pl impr aor act

2 sitting, and clothed, and **in his right mind:** .... Mark 5:15
2 clothed, and in his **right mind:** .... Luke 8:35
3 but to think **soberly,** according as God hath dealt .. Rom 12:3
1 or whether we **be sober,** it is for your cause......... 2 Co 5:13
3 Young men likewise exhort to **be sober minded**........ Tit 2:6
4 **be ye** therefore **sober,** and watch unto prayer........ 1 Pt 4:7

Classical Greek

This verb means "to be sound-minded" (cf. the noun *sōphrosunē* [4849], "soundness of mind"). In a more ethical sense it means "to be moderate, to show self-control." The main idea of the word is "restraint" of one's passions and desires. *Sōphroneō* does not occur in the Septuagint.

New Testament Usage

Sōphroneō occurs six times in the New Testament. Jesus restored the Gerasene demoniac to his "right mind" (cf. NIV; see Mark 5:15; Luke 8:35). We know from Mark's description of the man in 5:3ff. that he was formerly completely out of control and under the bondage of the legion of demons (cf. Aquila's Greek translation of Isaiah 38:16 which uses *sōphronizō* [4846] with a similar understanding).

Paul, in a like manner, advised his Roman readers to "be sober" in estimating their own righteousness. Here, "sober" is not referring to the opposite of drunkenness; rather they were not to think more highly of themselves than they should (Romans 12:3). Mental soundness is again the issue in 2 Corinthians 5:13, but in Titus 2:6 the ethical sense comes to the fore. Young men are encouraged to maintain self-control. This explicitly expects the general attitude of the young men to be godly (cf. verse 5; 1 Timothy 3:2; cf. Titus 1:8; 2:2). But implied is the advice to be morally and ethically moderate (cf. verse 12).

STRONG 4993, BAUER 802, MOULTON-MILLIGAN 622, KITTEL 7:1097-1104, LIDDELL-SCOTT 1751, COLIN BROWN 1:501-2.

4846. σωφρονίζω sōphronizō verb

Admonish, chasten, train.

COGNATES:

σωφρονέω sōphroneō (4845)
σωφρονισμός sōphronismos (4847)
σωφρόνως sōphronōs (4848)
σωφροσύνη sōphrosunē (4849)
σώφρων sōphrōn (4850)
φρονέω phroneō (5262)

SYNONYMS:

ἀναγκάζω anankazō (313)
κελεύω keleuō (2724)
παραβιάζομαι parabiazomai (3711)
παραινέω paraineō (3728)
παρακαλέω parakaleō (3731)
παραμυθέομαι paramutheomai (3749)
παροξύνω paroxunō (3809)
παροτρύνω parotrunō (3813)
προτρέπομαι protrepomai (4247)
συμβουλεύω sumbouleuō (4674)
συνέχω sunechō (4762)

1. σωφρονίζωσιν sōphronizōsin 3pl subj pres act

2. σωφρονίζουσιν sōphronizousin 3pl indic pres act

1 That they **may teach** the young women to be sober,... Tit 2:4

Classical Greek

From the time of Euripides, in the Fifth Century B.C., this verb was commonly used in classical Greek of bringing someone to his senses or simply encouraging or advising someone (*Bauer*). Its general sense is " 'to make someone a *sōphrōn*,' i.e., 'to bring him to reason' " (Luck, "sōphrōn," *Kittel*, 7:1104). It does not appear in the Septuagint.

New Testament Usage

The only New Testament occurrence of this word is in Paul's letter to Titus where the writer instructed the older women to train the younger women to live honorable Christian lives (Titus 2:4). The passage exhorts them to pass on the character of *sōphronismos* (4847), "good judgment, prudence, moderation," or *sōphrosunē* (4849), "mental soundness, self-control," in order to produce someone who is *sōphrōn* (4850), "prudent, chaste, modest."

STRONG 4994, BAUER 802, MOULTON-MILLIGAN 622, KITTEL 7:1104, LIDDELL-SCOTT 1751.

4847. σωφρονισμός sōphronismos noun

Moderation, prudence, self-control.

CROSS-REFERENCE:
σωφρονίζω sōphronizō (4846)

1. σωφρονισμοῦ sōphronismou gen sing masc

1 but of power, and of love, and of a sound mind..... 2 Tm 1:7

Classical Greek

Around the time of the coming of Christ this noun was used in secular Greek in the sense of good judgment, improvement, moderation, self-control, etc. It also could mean the teaching of morality, the giving of advice, the admonishing of others to manifest moderation, self-control, and general soundness of mind (*Bauer*). Thus, it could have a "definite, active sense in secular literature" (Luck, "sōphrōn," *Kittel*, 7:1104). It does not appear in the Septuagint.

New Testament Usage

The New Testament contains *sōphronismos* in Paul's admonition to his son in the Lord, Timothy (2 Timothy 1:7). Negatively, the apostle reminded his spiritual son that God had not given him a spirit of fear, i.e., cowardice or timidity. This statement follows the writer's encouragement for Timothy to stir up the gift of God that he had received through the laying on of Paul's hands. Apparently Timothy had a problem with timidity.

Positively, Paul explained to Timothy what he had received. (1) He had been given a spirit of power or ability to accomplish by the Holy Spirit that which God had called him to do. (2) He was granted God's love that is to be the motivational force behind all that believers do for God (1 Corinthians 13). (3) God endued him with a sound mind or a spirit of self-control or self-discipline (*sōphronismos*). His mind was to be disciplined in the sense of not being shaken by the intimidation he would have to face as he served God. This kind of self-discipline comes from continuous reliance on the grace that God gives to individuals who trust Him implicitly.

STRONG 4995, BAUER 802, MOULTON-MILLIGAN 622, KITTEL 7:1104, LIDDELL-SCOTT 1751.

4848. σωφρόνως sōphronōs adv

Soberly, temperately, with moderation, showing self-control.

CROSS-REFERENCE:
σωφρονίζω sōphronizō (4846)

1. σωφρόνως sōphronōs

1 we should live soberly, righteously, and godly,........ Tit 2:12

This word occurs only once in the Septuagint (Wisdom of Solomon 9:11) and once in the New Testament (Titus 2:12). The apocryphal reference indicates the "prudent" manner in which wisdom will lead, while *sōphronōs* in Titus describes the life of "self-control" taught by the grace of God. It is one of three adverbs used by Paul to indicate what manner of life Christians are to lead in this present age. It should be characterized by *sōphronōs*, "self-control"; *dikaiōs* (1339B), "uprightness"; and *eusebōs* (2134), "godliness." This entire word group conveys the idea of "sane, sensible, in one's right mind." It pictures a person who is well-balanced, who has all aspects of his life under control and in proper relationship.

STRONG 4996, BAUER 802, LIDDELL-SCOTT 1752, COLIN BROWN 1:501-2.

4849. σωφροσύνη sōphrosunē noun

Mental soundness, moderation, good sense, self-control.

CROSS-REFERENCE:
σωφρονίζω sōphronizō (4846)

1. σωφροσύνης sōphrosunēs gen sing fem

1 but speak forth the words of truth and soberness. . . .Acts 26:25
1 modest apparel, with shamefacedness and sobriety; . . 1 Tm 2:9
1 in faith and charity and holiness with sobriety. 2:15

Classical Greek

Sōphrosunē is a contraction of *saophrosunē* found in Homer (Eighth Century B.C.). Its etymological meaning is "of sound mind," a combination of *saos* ("sound, whole, healthy") and *phrenes* ("mind"). In classical Greek it could denote the "rational," what is "intellectually sound," or "discretion," i.e., moderation and self-control (Luck, "sōphrōn," *Kittel,* 7:1097).

Philosophers wrangled over the exact definition of *sōphrosunē* (Plato discussed it at length in his *Charmides*). In general, it refers "to a basic attitude which alone makes possible certain concrete modes of conduct" (Luck, ibid., 7:1098). Its main manifestation is restraint, an effort to control one's emotions using reason. Thus, *sōphrosunē* is an attitude arising from within oneself and manifests itself in an outward life of moderation and self-control. An antonym in classical Greek is the word *hubris* (5036B), "lack of self-restraint," which reveals itself in greed, pride, gluttony, overstepping of bounds, etc. *Sōphrosunē* was expected of people in the Greek world.

Following Plato the Stoics classified *sōphrosunē* as one of the four cardinal virtues of life. In popular philosophy these virtues could be subdivided into long lists of virtue and vices (ibid., 7:1100). *Sōphrosunē,* when applied to women, meant self-control and restraint in sexual desires, and hence, "chastity."

Septuagint Usage

In the Septuagint *sōphrosunē* does not appear in the canonical books. According to Luck its main Hebrew equivalent is *mûsār,* "discipline, correction." (*Mûsār* is generally translated *paideia* [3672] in the Septuagint.) An analysis of *mûsār,* however, shows a profound difference in emphasis from *sōphrosunē.* According to Gilchrist *mûsār* denotes "correction which results in education." The theological basis for *mûsār* is "grounded in the covenant relationship which Yahweh establishes with His people." It is "education that is theocentric," and "*mûsār* primarily points to a God-centered way of life, and only secondarily to ethical behavior" (*Theological Wordbook of the Old Testament,* "yāsar"). Thus, *mûsār* is restraint and discipline that originates from without, while Greek understanding of *sōphrosunē* arises from within. The translators of the Septuagint thus avoided the use of *sōphrosunē* (and its cognates, none of which appear in canonical books). *Sōphrosunē* only appears "in texts extant in Greek alone or giving clear evidence of Hellenistic influence" (Luck, "sōphrōn," *Kittel,* 7:1100). In Philo *sōphrosunē* has its normal Hellenistic usage.

In the noncanonical books of the Septuagint *sōphrosunē* appears nine times. In Esther 3:13 (Septuagint only) it is (according to Artaxerxes) a quality of Haman. He has "sound judgment" (RSV). In Wisdom of Solomon 8:7 it appears with Plato's other cardinal virtues as a product of the teaching of personified Wisdom. The writer has combined Greek and Jewish concepts. *Sōphrosunē* is the result of having wisdom; wisdom is attained through instruction (*paideia,* 6:17).

Sōphrosunē appears six times in the highly Stoic 4 Maccabees. The Greek understanding of the word predominates. Emotions hinder *sōphrosunē* (1:3). The writer refers to the four cardinal virtues in 1:6,18. He calls these virtues "kinds of wisdom" (1:18, RSV). Reason (*logismos* [3027]) rules over the emotions through "the restraining power of *self-control*" (1:30, RSV). He defines *sōphrosunē* as "mastery over desires" (1:31). The writer shows his Jewish adherence to the Law when he attributes the attainment of the virtues to study of the Law (5:16-24). Via *sōphrosunē* the Jew can "master all pleasures and desires" (verse 23, RSV). Thus, *sōphrosunē* becomes a virtue which results from instruction in the Law.

New Testament Usage

In the New Testament the word group "plays a comparatively minor role." It is "chiefly used to characterize Christian life in the world" (Luck, "sōphrōn," *Kittel,* 7:1102f.). Paul employed this noun when he stood before Agrippa as well as before Festus who interrupted the speaker's defense by accusing him of being out of his mind. He acknowledged the apostle's abundant learning and even claimed Paul was insane precisely because of his constant study of the Scriptures. Festus' implication was that Paul was confused because of the nature of what he studied. The apostle countered this impugning of the Old Testament by claiming that what he studied consisted of words of truth and words of soberness (*sōphrosunē*); that is, words that produced mental soundness, rationality, and self-control (Acts 26:25).

This crucial term also occurs in Paul's first epistle to his spiritual son Timothy. After giving instructions concerning public worship Paul instructed women to dress orderly, *kosmiō* (see 2860), a term which comes from the same Greek noun *kosmos* (2862) which means "world." The idea is that the outward apparel should be arranged in an orderly fashion so it reflects the orderly arrangement of the redeemed soul. If this is done the clothing will manifest two things: (1) modesty, a quality which does not unnecessarily expose the human body so as to draw undue attention to itself; and (2) sobriety (*sōphrosunē*), which has to do with a soundness of mind that reflects scriptural discretion and chastity (1 Timothy 2:9).

Strong 4997, Bauer 802, Moulton-Milligan 622, Kittel 7:1097-1104, Liddell-Scott 1751, Colin Brown 1:494,501-2.

4850. σώφρων sōphrōn adj

Chaste, discreet, prudent, sober-minded, self-controlled.

Cognate:
σωφρονίζω sōphronizō (4846)

Synonym:
νηφάλεος nēphaleos (3386)

1. σώφρονας sōphronas acc pl masc/fem

2. σώφρονα sōphrona acc sing masc

2 **vigilant**, sober, of good behaviour, ... 1 Tm 3:2
2 a lover of good men, **sober**, just, holy, temperate; .... Tit 1:8
1 That the aged men be sober, grave, **temperate**, ... 2:2
1 To be **discreet**, chaste, keepers at home, good, ... 2:5

Classical Greek

Examples of this Greek adjective can be found in classical Greek all the way back to the time of Homer (Eighth Century B.C.). Later, Aristotle (Fourth Century B.C.) contrasted the temperate (*sōphrōn*) man with the self-indulgent man and concluded that the temperate man desired *what* he should *as* he should and *when* he should (*Nichomachean Ethics* 1119b15). Hence, the term can mean "chaste, discreet, moderate, sober, temperate." It can even take on the meaning of being "sane." The same kind of usage continued until the time of Josephus and Philo in the First Century A.D.

Septuagint Usage

In the Septuagint *sōphrōn* is only found in 4 Maccabees, but its use aptly demonstrates its secular Greek meaning. The writer sees *sōphrōn* as a quality of the mind (*nous* [3426]) which enables one to "restrain his emotions and desires" (1:35). Thus, Joseph is *sōphrōn* because by mental effort he overcame and restrained his sexual desires when tempted by Potiphar's wife (2:2). *Sōphrōn* is a quality of reason and gives the persecuted strength to suffer (3:19ff.). God gave the individual his emotions, but He also gave the mind to rule the emotions. Finally, He provided the Law to teach the mind (2:21-23). Thus, for this writer the Law was the source of "temperance" (5:16-24, *sōphrosunē* [4849]). Moses and Jacob are also used to illustrate the behavior of the temperate man. They restrained their anger by reason (2:18-20).

New Testament Usage

In the New Testament this word is confined to the Pastoral Epistles. Paul included it in his list of qualifications for a bishop in 1 Timothy 3. Among other qualities this individual is to be sober or sensible (1 Timothy 3:2). When Paul enumerated a similar list to Titus, in order to assist him in the appointment of elders, he also employed *sōphrōn* to describe these individuals as sober or sensible people (Titus 1:8). They must be able to restrain themselves and behave rationally.

Lastly, in Titus 2:2,5 the apostle utilized this adjective in conjunction with his description of the ideal assembly. First, he specified that aged men are to be sober or sensible. Secondly, he instructed Titus to teach the older women in the congregation to meet certain qualifications. They, in turn, were to train the younger women to do certain things, among them to be discreet or sensible.

Strong 4998, Bauer 802, Kittel 7:1097-1104, Liddell-Scott 1751-52, Colin Brown 1:501-2.

τ

4850B. ταβερνῶν tabernōn noun

Tavern, shop.

1. ταβερνῶν tabernōn gen pl fem

1 **and The three taverns: whom when Paul saw,**...... **Acts 28:15**

This word is part of a proper noun, "Three Taverns." (See 4979.)

4851. Ταβιθά Tabitha name

Tabitha.

1. Ταβιθά Tabitha fem

1 **was at Joppa a certain disciple named Tabitha,**...... **Acts 9:36**
1 **and turning him to the body said, Tabitha, arise**......... **9:40**

A Christian woman raised from the dead after Peter prayed (Acts 9:36,40). Her Aramaic name is also given in its Greek form *Dorcas.* The etymology of both words can be traced to the meaning "gazelle."

4852. τάγμα tagma noun

Something ordered, arranged; class, corps, division, group.

CROSS-REFERENCE:
τάσσω tassō (4872)

דֶּגֶל deghel (1764), Standard (Nm 2:2f.,10, 10:14,18).
חַיָּה chayyāh (2518), Troop (2 Sm 23:13).
רַגְלִי raghlî (7561), Foot soldier (1 Sm 4:10, 15:4).

1. τάγματι tagmati dat sing neu

1 **every man in his own order: Christ the firstfruits;**.. **1 Co 15:23**

Classical Greek

This Greek noun often has a military connotation. It is related to the verb *tassō* (4872) which means "to order," sometimes of a battle. Hence, it can refer in classical Greek to a corps, division, or some specific group of soldiers. To illustrate, the writings of Polybius (Second Century B.C.) contain the term in the sense of military personnel being arranged in some orderly fashion (3.85.3). This type of usage can be traced as far back as the time of Xenophon in the Fourth Century B.C. The word can also be used of any order or arrangement.

Septuagint Usage

The Septuagint contains *tagma* in 2 Samuel 23:13 (LXX 2 Kings 23:13) where it refers to the army of the Philistines encamped in the Valley of Rephaim. David's three mighty men broke through their ranks in order to obtain water from the well by the gate of Bethlehem. David, however, poured it out before the Lord. Some commentators remark that to him it represented the blood of his loyal followers, and he remembered the prohibition in the Law against drinking blood (Leviticus 17:10-14).

New Testament Usage

The New Testament has the word with a different application. The term can stand for any group arranged in an orderly manner. Paul employed it this way in the classic resurrection chapter (1 Corinthians 15). After including an enumeration of testimonies to the resurrection of Christ (verses 1-11), he suggested some consequences of denying the reality of the Lord's resurrection (verses 12-19).

Then he countered with a beautiful list of the consequences of accepting the reality of Jesus' resurrection. Among other important matters Paul specified the *order* or arrangement of the first resurrection (verse 23) by using this Greek noun. He spoke of Christ as the firstfruit or the beginning of this resurrection which started nearly two millennia ago. Then he added that the bulk of the harvest will consist of those people who are in Christ, i.e., those who belong to Him. They will be resurrected at His glorious coming to this earth.

STRONG 5001, BAUER 802-3, MOULTON-MILLIGAN 624, KITTEL 8:31-32, LIDDELL-SCOTT 1752.

4853. τακτός taktos adj

Set, appointed.

Cross-Reference:
τάσσω tassō (4872)

שַׁאֲנָן sha'ănān (8077), At ease (Jb 12:5).

1. τακτῇ taktē dat sing fem

1 upon a set day Herod, arrayed in royal apparel, ... Acts 12:21

Taktos, derived from *tassō* (4872), means of a "set or appointed time or place." It can describe a *fixed* quantity of any sort or refer to a *prescribed* way. *Taktos* occurs once in the Septuagint and once in the New Testament. Job 12:5 uses it in the sense of a *set* time. In Acts 12:21 *taktos* is used of Herod Agrippa I's action on the set or appointed day. He was arrayed in silver robes which reflected the sun's rays.

Strong 5002, Bauer 803, Moulton-Milligan 624, Liddell-Scott 1753.

4854. ταλαιπωρέω talaipōreō verb

Endure distress, be in misery.

Cognates:
ταλαιπωρία talaipōria (4855)
ταλαίπωρος talaipōros (4856)
πωρόω pōroō (4313)

Synonym:
βασανίζω basanizō (922)

עָוָה 'āwâh (5971), Niphal: be bowed down (Ps 38:6 [37:6]).

שָׁדַד shādhadh (8161), Qal: destroyer (Is 33:1, Jer 12:12); niphal: be ruined (Mi 2:4); pual: be destroyed, be ruined (Jer 4:20, Jl 1:10, Zec 11:2f.); polel: destroy (Hos 10:2).

1. ταλαιπωρήσατε talaipōrēsate 2pl impr aor act

1 Be afflicted, and mourn, and weep: .... Jas 4:9

Classical Greek

Talaipōreō means "to endure distress and/ or sorrow" and hence to be miserable and wretched. An extended meaning is to express by complaining or lamenting. It may also mean "to afflict or torment," and in the passive voice, "to be afflicted or tormented" (*Bauer*).

In classical literature this verb is used to describe those who undergo distress and/or hardship, often to the point of becoming emotionally or physically worn out. It is also used to mean to "do hard work."

Septuagint Usage

The Septuagint uses this verb frequently in the prophetic literature for the Hebrew verb *shādad* with the meaning "to despoil, to deal violently." It is also used for *'āwâh*, "to do wrong and to pervert the right." Isaiah 33:1 uses this verb for those who destroy (KJV: spoil) but are not destroyed. Jeremiah 4:13 emphasizes the result: "We are *spoiled*" (ruined). The same usage is true of verse 20. Perhaps the best translation of the verb in Jeremiah 10:20 is, "My tent is *wrecked*" (destroyed; KJV: spoiled). Its usage stresses the serious negative effect of an action or event. In Psalm 17:9 (LXX 16:9) this verb is used in the sense "to oppress" (mistreat).

New Testament Usage

In the New Testament *talaipōreō* is used only in James 4:9 where it means "to be wretched" (KJV: afflicted). It is followed by verbs which mean "to mourn" and "to cry." In the context of this passage, James calls for true repentance and humility before God.

Strong 5003, Bauer 803, Liddell-Scott 1753, Colin Brown 3:858-59.

4855. ταλαιπωρία talaipōria noun

Distress, misery.

Cross-Reference:
ταλαιπωρέω talaipōreō (4854)

מַהֲמֹרוֹת mahămōrôth (4254), Deep pit (Ps 140:10 [139:10]).

מַחְשָׁךְ machshākh (4423), Darkness (Ps 88:18 [87:18]).

מְשׁוֹאָה mᵉshô'āh (5060), Waste (Jb 30:3).

נוּשׁ nûsh (5316), Be sick (Ps 69:20 [68:20]).

שָׁאוֹן shā'ôn (8065), Mire (Ps 40:2 [39:2]).

שֶׁבֶר shever (8133I), Destruction (Is 60:18).

שֹׁד shōdh (8160), Destruction, oppression (Jer 6:7, Ez 45:9, Hb 2:17).

שָׁדַד shādhadh (8161), Destroyer (Jer 6:26, 51:56 [28:56]).

שׁוֹאָה shô'āh (8177), Disaster (Zec 1:15—only some Sinaiticus texts).

1. ταλαιπωρία talaipōria nom sing fem
2. ταλαιπωρίαις talaipōriais dat pl fem

1 Destruction and misery are in their ways: .... Rom 3:16
2 ye rich men, weep and howl for your miseries .... Jas 5:1

Talaipōria, the noun form of *talaipōreō* (4854), means "distress, misery, trouble, wretchedness." It is common in the Septuagint, being found, for example, in Hosea 9:6 meaning "destruction" and in Micah 2:4 meaning "lamentation" (bitter wailing). Its usage in the Septuagint has less emphasis on the extent and nature of the destruction than the Hebrew text (Harrison, "Torment," *Colin Brown*, 3:859). In the New

Testament it is used in Romans 3:16 as a quotation from Isaiah 59:7, with the meaning of "misery," and in James 5:1 in the plural, "miseries" or "sufferings."

STRONG 5004, BAUER 803, MOULTON-MILLIGAN 624, LIDDELL-SCOTT 1753, COLIN BROWN 3:858-59.

4856. ταλαίπωρος talaipōros adj

Wretched, devastated.

CROSS-REFERENCE:

ταλαιπωρέω talaipōreō (4854)

שָׁדַד shādhadh (8161), Be destroyed (Ps 137:8 [136:8]).

1. ταλαίπωρος talaipōros nom sing masc

1 O wretched man that I am! .... Rom 7:24
1 and knowest not that thou art wretched, ... Rev 3:17

In classical Greek *talaipōros* simply means "wretched, miserable." It can be used to describe things, persons, or life in general. The Hebrew counterpart of *talaipōros* is *shādhadh* which means "to devastate, overpower." In Isaiah 33:1 the Septuagint uses this word to mean "not spoiled" (better: "not devastated"). The Apocrypha frequently uses it to describe the persecutions suffered by Jesus during the Maccabean period (e.g., 2 Maccabees 4:47). In the New Testament *talaipōros* occurs in Romans 7:24, "O *wretched* man that I am!" In Revelation 3:17 the term is used to describe the wretched condition of the Laodicean believers.

STRONG 5005, BAUER 803, MOULTON-MILLIGAN 624, LIDDELL-SCOTT 1753, COLIN BROWN 3:858-59.

4857. ταλαντιαῖος talantiaios adj

Of a talent's weight.

1. ταλαντιαία talantiaia nom sing fem

1 every stone about the weight of a talent: .... Rev 16:21

Talantiaios is used in Hellenistic literature and by Josephus as a measure of weight. In the New Testament it is used in the apocalyptic imagery of Revelation 16:21 to refer to huge hailstones, a *talantiaios* each. The reference is probably to the Roman system of weights. In weight, a talent in the English system would be about 75 pounds.

STRONG 5006, BAUER 803, MOULTON-MILLIGAN 624, LIDDELL-SCOTT 1753.

4858. τάλαντον talanton noun

Talent.

אֵיפָה 'êphāh (380), Ephah (Zec 5:7—Codex Alexandrinus only).

כַּכַּר kakkar (A3723), Talent (Ezr 7:22—Aramaic).

כִּכָּר kikkār (3724), Talent (Ex 38:24 [39:1], 2 Chr 9:9, Est 3:9).

1. τάλαντον talanton nom/acc sing neu

2. ταλάντων talantōn gen pl neu

3. τάλαντα talanta nom/acc pl neu

2 which owed him ten thousand talents. .... Matt 18:24
3 And unto one he gave five talents, to another two, ... 25:15
3 Then he that had received the five talents 25:16
3 and made them other five talents. 25:16
3 And so he that had received five talents came 25:20
3 and brought other five talents, saying, Lord, ... 25:20
3 saying, Lord, thou deliveredst unto me five talents: 25:20
3 I have gained beside them five talents more. 25:20
3 also that had received two talents came and said, ... 25:22
3 Lord, thou deliveredst unto me two talents: 25:22
3 I have gained two other talents beside them. 25:22
1 which had received the one talent came and said, ... 25:24
1 afraid, and went and hid thy talent in the earth: 25:25
1 Take therefore the talent from him, ... 25:28
3 and give it unto him which hath ten talents. 25:28

Talanton was a Greek unit of weight and the translated term for Hebrew *kikkar*, a term used for a large measure of weight in Canaan, Israel, and Mesopotamia. It varied in weight from 56 to 80 pounds (*Bauer*). In Scripture passages its weight was about 75 pounds.

The talent was also a Greek unit of money. Its value depended on the specific time and the prevailing monetary system. The value differed depending whether it was in copper, silver, or gold (ibid.). A silver talent was worth approximately 6,000 denarii; a gold talent was probably worth at least 30 times as much. A denarius was worth a day's pay for one who worked by the day. These differing values give insight to Jesus' use of this term in Matthew 18:24 and 25:14-28.

STRONG 5007, BAUER 803, MOULTON-MILLIGAN 624, LIDDELL-SCOTT 1753-54.

4859. ταλιθά talitha noun

Girl, maiden.

1. ταλιθα talitha fem

1 Talitha cumi; which is, being interpreted, Damsel, ... Mark 5:41

Talitha is a Greek transliteration of an Aramaic word meaning "little girl," as found in Mark 5:41. Jesus used this emphatic form when He raised the daughter of Jairus from the dead. The term expresses an affectionate concern. Luke 8:42 notes that she was about 12 years old.

STRONG 5008, BAUER 803, COLIN BROWN 1:581.

4860. ταμεῖον tameion noun

Inner room, a hidden or secret room.

אָסָם ’āsām (632), Barn (Dt 28:8, Prv 3:10).

חֶדֶר chedher (2410), Chamber, bedroom (Gn 43:30, 2 Kgs 6:12, S/S 1:4).

מָזוּ māzû (4330), Granary (Ps 144:13 [143:13]).

תָּוֶךְ tāwekh (8761), Middle (Ez 28:16).

1. **ταμεῖον tameion** nom/acc sing neu
2. **ταμείοις tameiois** dat pl neu

2 behold, he is in the **secret chambers**; believe it not. Matt 24:26
2 and that which ye have spoken in the ear in **closets** Luke 12:3
1 ravens: ... which neither have **storehouse** nor barn;.... 12:24

Classical Greek

Tameion is a contracted form of *tamieion* (4860B) which was used, for example, by Thucydides to mean "a treasury." *Tameion* is found in inscriptions as early as the First Century B.C., but it became common in the First Century A.D. (*Bauer*).

Septuagint Usage

Tameion is generally used of inner rooms, e.g., a hidden, innermost, or secret room. The Septuagint uses this term in Genesis 43:30 when Joseph was overcome by his emotions upon seeing his younger brother Benjamin. As a result he retired to an "inner room" (KJV: chamber) to shed tears in private, away from his servants and officials. Song of Songs 1:4 speaks of the king bringing the woman into his "chambers" (inner rooms).

New Testament Usage

Jesus used this term in Matthew 6:6 to exhort His hearers to pray privately in an "inner room" (KJV: closet) rather than seeking to demonstrate their piety in public. The same meaning of the term occurs in its use in Matthew 24:26 (KJV: secret chambers) as well as in Luke 12:3. In Luke 12:24 the term is used with *apothēkē* (591) in the sense of "storeroom."

STRONG 5009, BAUER 803, MOULTON-MILLIGAN 624-25, LIDDELL-SCOTT 1754.

4860B. ταμιεῖον tamieion noun

A hidden or secret room.

1. **ταμιεῖον tamieion** nom/acc sing neu
2. **ταμιείοις tamieiois** dat pl neu

1 when thou prayest, enter into thy **closet**,............ Matt 6:6

This is a variant spelling of *tameion*. Scc thc word study at number 4860.

4860C. τανῦν tanun adv

Now, at present.

CROSS-REFERENCE:
νῦν nun (3431)

1. **τανῦν tanun**

1 And **now**, brethren, I commend you to God,....... Acts 20:32
1 And **now** I exhort you to be of good cheer:........... 27:22

Usually written as two words (*ta* and *nun*), this adverb literally means "the things that now are." See word study at *nun* (3431).

4861. τάξις taxis noun

Order, nature, orderly manner.

CROSS-REFERENCE:
τάσσω tassō (4872)

דִּבְרָה divrāh (1750), Order (Ps 110:4 [109:4]).

זְבֻל zᵉvul (2166), Habitation (Hb 3:11).

מוּצָק mûtsāq (4299), Casting (1 Kgs 7:37).

מַחֲנֶה machăneh (4402), Camp (Nm 1:52).

מְסִלָּה mᵉsillāh (4697), Course (Jgs 5:20—Codex Alexandrinus only).

מָקוֹם māqôm (4887), Place (Jb 38:12).

פֹּעַל pō‘al (6714), Work (Jb 24:5).

קֵץ qēts (7377), End (Jb 16:3, 28:3).

תּוֹרָה tôrāh (8784), Teaching (Prv 31:26 [31:24]).

1. **τάξει taxei** dat sing fem
2. **τάξιν taxin** acc sing fem

1 office before God in the **order** of his course,........ Luke 1:8
2 Let all things be done decently and in **order**....... 1 Co 14:40
2 joying and beholding your **order**,.................... Col 2:5
2 a priest for ever after the **order** of Melchisedec...... Heb 5:6
2 an high priest after the **order** of Melchisedec............ 5:10
2 high priest for ever after the **order** of Melchisedec....... 6:20
2 priest should rise after the **order** of Melchisedec,........ 7:11
2 and not be called after the **order** of Aaron?............ 7:11
2 a priest for ever after the **order** of Melchisedec......... 7:17
2 a priest for ever after the **order** of Melchisedec:........ 7:21

Classical Greek

Taxis has several meanings in its wider usage, especially in Hellenistic literature. Its meaning of "position, post," and "administration" is not found in Biblical usage. Thus, *taxis* can refer to the order of an army or a battle array. It can denote the body of soldiers itself. It also refers to any "order" or "arrangement" and at times is used of an ordinance, law, or prescription (*Liddell-Scott*).

Septuagint Usage

In the Septuagint *taxis* appears several times. It denotes the "camp" to which each man must go (Numbers 1:52). The ten stands for the temple were all in one *taxis*, "arrangement" (1 Kings 7:37 [LXX 3 Kings 7:37]). In 2 Maccabees 8:22 it refers to the *division* of an army.

New Testament Usage

Taxis is used in Luke 1:8 to state that Zechariah was serving "in the *order* of his course" (division of priests). Paul instructed the church at Corinth to do everything "decently and *in order*" (1 Corinthians 14:40). Perhaps "orderly manner" is a better translation of the Greek in this instance. In Colossians 2:5 Paul used the term *taxis* to compliment the Colossians for the *orderly* manner in which they conducted themselves.

The writer of Hebrews used this word to express a comparison of Christ to Melchizedek when he wrote: "Thou art a priest for ever after the *order* of Melchizedek" (5:6). He used this term again with the same meaning in 5:10; 6:20; 7:11,17,21. The writer of Hebrews stressed that Jesus Christ, as the perfect high priest, was in the nature (order, pattern) of Melchizedek's priesthood (Genesis 14:18-20).

STRONG 5010, BAUER 803-4, MOULTON-MILLIGAN 625, LIDDELL-SCOTT 1756.

4862. ταπεινός tapeinos adj

Humble, lowly, undistinguished, poor, downcast, subservient.

COGNATES:

ταπεινοφροσύνη tapeinophrosunē (4863)
ταπεινόφρων tapeinophrōn (4863B)
ταπεινόω tapeinoō (4864)
ταπείνωσις tapeinōsis (4865)

אֶבְיוֹן 'evyôn (33), Needy (Am 8:6).

דַּךְ dakh (1847), Oppressed (Ps 10:18 [9:39]).

דַּכָּא dakkā' (1851), Crushed (Ps 34:18 [33:18]).

דַּל dal (1859), Poor, lowly (Is 25:4, Zep 3:12).

עָמֹק 'āmōq (6233), Deeper (Lv 13:3f.,25).

עָנָו 'ānāw (6262), Meek, humble (Am 2:7, Zep 2:3).

עָנִי 'ānî (6270), Afflicted, poor (Ps 18:27 [17:27]).

עַרְעָר 'ar'ār (6436), Destitute (Ps 102:17 [101:17]).

צָנוּעַ tsānûa' (7067), Humble (Prv 11:2).

רוּשׁ rûsh (7609), Poor person (1 Sm 18:23).

שָׁפֵל shāphēl (8584), Qal: be humbled (Is 2:11); hiphil: humble (Ps 113:6 [112:6]).

שֵׁפֶל shēphel (8586), Humble place (Eccl 10:6).

שָׁפָל shāphāl (8587), Lower, lowly (Lv 13:20, Jb 5:11, Ez 17:24).

שְׁפֵלָה sh^ephēlāh (8590), Lowland (Jos 11:16).

תַּחְתִּי tachtî (8812), Lower (Jgs 1:15).

1. **ταπεινοῖς tapeinois** dat pl masc/neu
2. **ταπεινός tapeinos** nom sing masc
3. **ταπεινούς tapeinous** acc pl masc

2 and learn of me; for I am meek and lowly in heart: Matt 11:29
3 and exalted them of low degree.................... Luke 1:52
1 but condescend to men of low estate.............. Rom 12:16
3 God, that comforteth those that are cast down,...... 2 Co 7:6
2 who in presence am base among you,................. 10:1
2 Let the brother of low degree rejoice................ Jas 1:9
1 but giveth grace unto the humble...................... 4:6
1 and giveth grace to the humble.................... 1 Pt 5:5

Classical Greek

Tapeinos in classical usage refers to a "low" region or place, or of something's "low" (physical) position. When describing persons, *tapeinos* means "humble, lowly," and it includes the ideas of "despised, rejected, poor" (*Liddell-Scott*). It is not without significance that classical writers invested *tapeinos* (and its cognates) with almost exclusively negative connotations. The *tapeinos* individual was "grovelling, slavish and mean-spirited" according to Greek standards (cf. Trench, *Synonyms of the New Testament*, p.139).

Septuagint Usage

Tapeinos occurs about 65 times in the Septuagint where it translates as many as 15 Hebrew terms. Physically *tapeinos* refers to sores "beneath" the skin, i.e., more than "skin deep." These infections rendered the victim ceremonially unclean (Leviticus 13:3ff.). Elsewhere it may refer to "lower" springs which were given by Caleb to Achsah (Judges 1:15; cf. Joshua 11:16).

The Psalmist knows God is "defending the fatherless and the *oppressed*" (Psalm 10:18 [LXX 9:39], NIV). God "saves" (*sōzō* [4834]) the "humble" (Psalm 18:27 [LXX 17:27], NIV), but He destroys the proud. Thus *tapeinos* in the Septuagint begins to take on very positive connotations in contrast to the traditional usage in classical Greek. This becomes critical for the New Testament understanding and usage of the term. The "lowly" are treasured by God (cf. Psalm 102:17 [LXX 101:17]; Isaiah 11:4; 66:2).

New Testament Usage

Tapeinos occurs eight times in the New Testament. It appears twice in the Gospels. In Matthew 11:29 the word describes Jesus as being "lowly in heart." In language reminiscent of the Old Testament theme that God favors the "humble," Luke recorded Mary's song: "(God) has brought down rulers from their thrones but has lifted up the *humble*" (Luke 1:52, NIV; cf. 2 Corinthians 7:6).

Paul used it almost neutrally in Romans 12:16, but even here the idea is that the gospel demands a shift of perspective. Paul may have alluded to Jesus' own words about humility (Matthew 11:29) in 2 Corinthians 10:1 ("meekness [*praotētos* (see 4099)] and gentleness [*epieikeia* (1917)] of Christ"); however, he applied *tapeinos*, "timid" (NIV), to himself in contrast to *tharreō*, "bold."

The Biblical reversal of roles—the lowly are exalted, the proud brought down—comes through sharply in James. Those who are "lowly" can "boast," knowing that their Father loves them (James 1:9). God even gives grace to those despised by the world, while He opposes the proud (James 4:6; cf. Proverbs 3:34; 1 Peter 5:5). Being "humble" is tantamount to "submitting yourselves one to another" (Ephesians 5:21; cf. 1 Peter 5:5).

STRONG 5011, BAUER 804, MOULTON-MILLIGAN 625, KITTEL 8:1-26, LIDDELL-SCOTT 1756-57, COLIN BROWN 2:259-64.

4863. ταπεινοφροσύνη

tapeinophrosunē noun

Humility, modesty.

CROSS-REFERENCES:

ταπεινός tapeinos (4862)
φρονέω phroneō (5262)

1. **ταπεινοφροσύνης** **tapeinophrosunēs** gen sing fem
2. **ταπεινοφροσύνῃ** **tapeinophrosunē** dat sing fem
3. **ταπεινοφροσύνην** **tapeinophrosunēn** acc sing fem

1 Serving the Lord with all **humility** of mind,........ Acts 20:19
1 With all **lowliness** and meekness,.................... Eph 4:2
2 in **lowliness** of mind let each esteem other better.... Phlp 2:3
2 in a voluntary **humility** and worshipping of angels,.... Col 2:18
2 and **humility**, and neglecting of the body;............. 2:23
3 bowels of mercies, kindness, **humbleness of mind**,....... 3:12
3 clothed with **humility**: for God resisteth the proud,.. 1 Pt 5:5

This noun, normally translated as "humbleness, lowliness," does not occur in classical Greek, being found only in the early centuries after the birth of Christ. When it does appear it denotes something "poor, weak," something "groveling" and "submissive." Outside of Biblical writings it always has a negative connotation. It does not appear in the Septuagint.

New Testament Usage

The term is found seven times in the New Testament, and there only in Acts and the Epistles. True "humbleness" (*tapeinophrosunē*) is encouraged for the believer (Acts 20:19; Ephesians 4:2; Philippians 2:3; Colossians 3:12; 1 Peter 5:5). This "humility," however, has nothing to do with "groveling" or "weakness." It describes a humility that naturally evolves out of a heart of love for the exalted Lord. It is the attitude of the Christian servant, first exemplified by Jesus. In fact, it is only in an attitude of humility, a contrite heart, that the spiritual life can prosper. Humility should characterize relationships among the children of God (Philippians 2:3). Paul likewise is a model of humility (Acts 20:19). Nevertheless, believers are cautioned against having a false humility (Colossians 2:18,23).

STRONG 5012, BAUER 804, KITTEL 8:1-26, LIDDELL-SCOTT 1757, COLIN BROWN 2:259-64.

4863B. ταπεινόφρων

tapeinophrōn adj

Humbleminded; lowly.

CROSS-REFERENCES:

ταπεινός tapeinos (4862)
φρονέω phroneō (5262)

1. **ταπεινόφρονες** **tapeinophrones** nom pl masc/fem

1 kindhearted, and **humble** in spirit. (NASB).......... 1 Pt 3:8

Tapeinophrōn does not occur in Greek literature prior to the New Testament. It appears in certain manuscripts of the Septuagint at Proverbs 29:23, "A man of *lowly spirit* gains honor" (NIV).

New Testament Usage

Occurring only once in the New Testament (in some texts of 1 Peter 3:8), *tapeinophrōn* is related to *tapeinoō* (4864), used in Luke 3:5 to denote the leveling of a mountain. Some texts of 1 Peter 3:8 contain the related term *philophrōn* (5228), "courteous." According to Peter the believer should seek the place of lowliness and absolute dependence upon God. Like water he should always seek the lowest place. This affects his desire to retaliate (1 Peter 3:9), for such an attitude must be restrained. Rather, he must be willing to "suffer for righteousness' sake" (1 Peter 3:13,14). Such a disposition is both proper and divinely rewarded (1 Peter 3:8-12).

BAUER 804, KITTEL 8:1-26, LIDDELL-SCOTT 1757, COLIN BROWN 2:259-64.

4864. ταπεινόω tapeinoō verb

Make low, humble, abase.

CROSS-REFERENCE:

ταπεινός tapeinos (4862)

אָנָה 'ānāh (589), Mourn (Is 3:26 [3:25]).

אֲנִיָּה 'ănîyāh (606), Lamentation (Lm 2:5).

בָּלָה bālâh (1126), Be worn out, be rotten; piel: waste (1 Chr 17:9).

דַּךְ dakh (1847), Oppressed (Ps 74:21 [73:21]).

דָּכָא dākhā' (1850), Piel: crush (Pss 72:4 [71:4], 94:5 [93:5], Lm 3:34); hithpael: be crushed (Jb 34:25).

דָּכָה dākhâh (1852), Qal: be crushed (Ps 10:10 [9:31]);

niphal: be crushed (Ps 38:8 [37:8]); something contrite (Ps 51:17 [50:17]); piel: crush, break (Pss 44:19 [43:19], 51:8 [50:8]).

דָּלַל dālal (1870), Be brought low (Pss 116:6 [114:6], 142:6 [141:6]).

זָלַל zālal (2236), Despise (Lm 1:8).

יָגָה yāghâh (3122), Piel: grieve (Lm 3:33); hiphil: cause grief (Lm 1:5, 3:32).

כָּנַע kāna' (3789), Niphal: be subdued, be subjected (1 Sm 7:13, Ps 106:42 [105:42]); hiphil: subdue, humble (1 Chr 17:10, 2 Chr 28:19).

כָּרַע kāra' (3895), Bow down (Jb 31:10).

מוּךְ mûkh (4270), Become poor (Lv 25:39).

מָכַךְ mākhakh (4493), Qal: sink down (Ps 106:43 [105:43]); niphal: sag (Eccl (10:18).

נָפַל nāphal (5489), Fall (Est 6:13).

עָנָה 'ānâh (6257), Qal: testify (Ru 1:21, Hos 7:10); be afflicted (Ps 116:10 [115:1]); niphal: be afflicted (Ps 119:107 [118:107]); afflicted person (Is 58:10); piel: violate, rape (Gn 34:2, 2 Sm 13:12); humble (Is 58:5); pual: humble oneself, be afflicted (Lv 23:29, Ps 119:71 [118:71]); hiphil: afflict (1 Kgs 8:35, Ps 55:19 [54:19]); hithpael: humble oneself, be afflicted (Ezr 8:21, Ps 107:17 [106:17], Dn 10:12).

עֲנָוָה 'ănāwāh (6265), Humility (Prv 18:12).

עָנִי 'ānî (6270), Afflicted (Is 51:21).

עָצַב 'ātsav (6321), Pain (1 Chr 4:10).

רוּשׁ rûsh (7609), Be poor; hithpolel: pretend to be poor (Prv 13:7).

שׁוּחַ shûach (8190), Be bowed down (Ps 44:25 [43:25]).

שָׁחַח shāchach (8249), Qal: bow down, be brought low (Ps 35:14 [34:14], Is 2:11,17); niphal: be brought down (Is 5:15); be soft in sound (Eccl 12:4); hiphil: bring down (Is 26:5).

שָׁחַת shāchath (8271), Hiphil: destroy (1 Sm 26:9).

שָׁפֵל shāphēl (8584), Qal: be brought low, be made low (Is 10:33, 29:4, 40:4); hiphil: bring down (2 Sm 22:28, Ps 75:7 [74:7], Ez 17:24).

שְׁפֵל shephēl (A8585), Haphel: subdue (Dn 7:24—Aramaic).

תַּאֲנִיָּה ta'ănîyāh (8713), Mourning (Lm 2:5).

1. ταπεινῶν tapeinōn nom sing masc part pres act
2. ἐταπείνωσεν etapeinōsen 3sing indic aor act
3. ταπεινώσῃ tapeinōsē 3sing subj aor act
4. ταπεινώσει tapeinōsei 3sing indic fut act
5. ταπεινοῦσθαι tapeinousthai inf pres mid
6. ταπεινώθητε tapeinōthēte 2pl impr aor pass
7. ταπεινωθήσεται tapeinōthēsetai 3sing indic fut pass

3 Whosoever therefore **shall humble** himself .... Matt 18:4
7 And whosoever shall exalt himself **shall be abased**; 23:12
4 and he that **shall humble** himself shall be exalted. 23:12
7 and every mountain and hill **shall be brought low**; ... Luke 3:5
7 For whosoever exalteth himself **shall be abased**; 14:11
1 and he that **humbleth** himself shall be exalted. 14:11
7 for every one that exalteth himself **shall be abased**; 18:14
1 and he that **humbleth** himself shall be exalted. 18:14
1 in **abasing** myself that ye might be exalted, ... 2 Co 11:7
3 my God **will humble** me among you, ... 12:21
2 found in fashion as a man, he **humbled** himself, ... Phlp 2:8
5 I know both how **to be abased**, and ... to abound: 4:12
6 **Humble yourselves** in the sight of the Lord, ... Jas 4:10
6 **Humble yourselves** therefore under the mighty .... 1 Pt 5:6

Classical Greek

Tapeinoō appears in Greek literature from the Fifth Century B.C. It means "to make small" or "to weaken." When used of persons it can mean "to humiliate, to be dispirited, to exploit" (Grundmann, "tapeinos," *Kittel,* 8:4,5).

Septuagint Usage

Tapeinoō is used approximately 165 times in the Septuagint as a translation for several Hebrew words. The emphasis is not so much on a state but on an action. Its use in 1 Samuel 2:7 (LXX 1 Kings 2:7), Psalm 75:7 (LXX 74:7), and Ezekiel 21:26 speaks of God's action in exalting the humble and laying low the mighty. God graciously receives those who humble themselves through the Spirit's work (Psalm 51:17 [LXX 50:17]).

New Testament Usage

Tapeinoō is found 14 times in the New Testament. Luke 3:5 uses the verb figuratively in quoting Isaiah 40:4 (LXX): "Every mountain and hill shall be *brought low*" (i.e., leveled).

In Matthew 23:12 Jesus stated, "Whosoever shall exalt himself shall be *abased* (humbled); and he that shall *humble* himself shall be exalted." Luke 14:11 uses this verb twice in making the same point. In the closing words of the Parable of the Pharisee and the Tax Collector (Luke 18:14), Jesus used *tapeinoō* to emphasize this same truth.

Seemingly Paul was criticized for not taking support from the church at Corinth in his missionary endeavor. Paul replied, "Have I committed an offense in *abasing* (humbling) myself that ye might be exalted?" (2 Corinthians 11:7).

In answer to attacks by his opponents, Paul indirectly stressed that he was Christ's apostle and as Christ was humble (see Matthew 11:29) so he also dealt humbly with them; he did not flaunt his apostolic authority. His concern was the spiritual welfare and growth of the church (2 Corinthians 12:21).

In thanking the church at Philippi for its gifts toward his missionary endeavors, Paul stated that he had learned to be content when he was *abased* (i.e., to be humbled by having little) or when he had much (Philippians 4:12). In so doing he followed Christ's example, who even *humbled* himself even to the point of death on the cross (Philippians 2:8).

James (4:10) and Peter (1 Peter 5:6) exhorted believers to humble themselves before God. Both reflect Proverbs 3:34 (Septuagint only).

STRONG 5013, BAUER 804-5, MOULTON-MILLIGAN 625, KITTEL 8:1-26, LIDDELL-SCOTT 1757, COLIN BROWN 2:259-64.

4865. ταπείνωσις tapeinōsis noun

Humiliation, humble state.

CROSS-REFERENCE:
ταπεινός tapeinos (4862)

דַּכָּא dakkā' (1851), Dust (Ps 90:3 [89:3]).

עָנִי 'ānî (6270), Humble (Prv 16:19).

עֳנִי 'ŏnî (6271), Affliction (Gn 31:42, Ps 25:18 [24:18], Lm 1:3).

עֹצֶר 'ōtser (6354), Oppression (Is 53:8).

שֵׁפֶל shēphel (8586), Low (Ps 136:23 [135:23]).

תַּעֲנִית ta'ănîth (8922), Self-abasement (Ezr 9:5).

1. **ταπεινώσεως tapeinōseōs** gen sing fem
2. **ταπεινώσει tapeinōsei** dat sing fem
3. **ταπείνωσιν tapeinōsin** acc sing fem

3 hath regarded the **low estate** of his handmaiden: .... Luke 1:48
2 In his **humiliation** his judgment was taken away: ..... Acts 8:33
1 Who shall change our **vile** body, ... Phlp 3:21
2 But the rich, in that he is **made low**: .... Jas 1:10

Classical Greek

In classical Greek *tapeinōsis* denoted the act of reducing or lessening. Thus, it could refer to the reducing of a swelling in the body, the humiliation of a man, or a lowering motion in a dance (*Liddell-Scott*).

Septuagint Usage

In the Septuagint *tapeinōsis* appears several times. Genesis 16:11 reports that the angel of the Lord acknowledged that God had heard Hagar's *misery* (NIV). It refers to suffering in Genesis 41:52. The Psalmist cried out to God to look upon his *affliction* (Psalm 25:18 [LXX 24:18]). Sirach exhorted his reader: "In the changes of *humiliation* be patient" (2:4).

New Testament Usage

In her beautiful words of praise in the Magnificat, Mary said that God had looked at the *low estate* of His handmaiden (Luke 1:48). She, a young unknown maiden of the insignificant town of Nazareth in Galilee, would become the virgin mother of the promised Saviour (Isaiah 7:14). The stress of the noun is on her humble status.

The Ethiopian official was reading from Isaiah 53:7,8 (Septuagint) which speaks about Christ's humiliation as the obedient, suffering Servant. Verse 8 (cf. Acts 8:33) uses the Greek noun *tapeinōsei* which means "humiliation." Isaiah used a graphic illustration of an innocent lamb to stress the true nature and significance of Christ's humiliation.

In warning his readers against false teachers, the apostle Paul reminded the Philippians that to be citizens of heaven is far more significant than to be citizens of the prestigious Roman colony of Philippi (Philippians 3:20,21). He reminded them that at Christ's coming He would transform our *vile* bodies (Greek: *to sōma tēs tapeinōseōs*; the body of our humble state) to be like the body of His glory (following the Greek).

STRONG 5014, BAUER 805, MOULTON-MILLIGAN 625, KITTEL 8:1-26, LIDDELL-SCOTT 1757, COLIN BROWN 2:259-64.

4866. ταράσσω tarassō verb

Stir up, be troubled, trouble.

COGNATES:
διαταράσσω diatarassō (1292)
ἐκταράσσω ektarassō (1600)
ταραχή tarachē (4867)
τάραχος tarachos (4868)

SYNONYMS:
ἀνασείω anaseiō (381)
σαλεύω saleuō (4388)
σείω seiō (4434)

בָּהַל bāhal (963), Niphal: be terrified, be dismayed (Gn 45:3, Ps 6:2f., 83:17 [82:17]); piel: terrify (Pss 2:5, 83:15 [82:15]).

בְּהַל b^ehal (A964), Pael: trouble (Dn 7:15—Aramaic).

בּוּךְ bûkh (978), Niphal: be perplexed (Est 3:15).

בָּלַע bāla' (1142), Swallow; piel: confuse (Is 3:12).

בָּעַת bā'ath (1227), Niphal: be terrified (Est 7:6).

בָּקַק bāqaq (1265), Niphal: loose heart (Is 19:3).

גָּעַשׁ gā'ash (1649), Shake (2 Sm 22:8).

דָּלַח dālach (1865), Trouble (Ez 32:2,13).

הוּם hûm (2016), Hiphil: be distraught (Ps 55:2 [54:2]).

הָמָה hāmāh (2064), Uproar, noise (Ps 46:6 [45:6], Is 17:12).

הָמוֹן hāmôn (2066), Tumult (Ps 65:7 [64:7]).

זָעַף zā'aph (2280), Be dejected (Gn 40:6).

חָגַג chāghagh (2379), Stagger (Ps 107:27 [106:27]).

חִיל chîl (2523), Qal: be in anguish (Ps 55:4 [54:4]); hithpalpal: be in distress (Est 4:4).

חָלַל chālal (2591), Be wounded (Ps 109:22 [108:22]).

חָמַר chāmar (2666), Qal: foam (Ps 46:3 [45:3]); poalal: be troubled (Lm 1:20, 2:11).

חֹמֶר chōmer (2672), Surging (Hb 3:15).

חָרַד chāradh (2829), Tremble (Jb 37:1).

חָרֵד chārēdh (2830), Trembling (Gn 42:28).

כָּמַר kāmar (3770), Niphal: yearn (1 Kgs 3:26).

כָּרַע kāraʻ (3895), Kneel; hiphil: bring low (Jgs 11:35).

לָהַט lāhaṯ (3993), Something on fire (Ps 57:4 [56:4]).

לָפַת lāphath (4085), Niphal: turn (Ru 3:8).

מָהַהּ māhahh (4244), Hithpalpel: hesitate, delay (Gn 19:16, Ps 119:60 [118:60]).

מָהַר māhar (4257), Piel: hurry (Gn 43:30).

מוּג mûgh (4265), Niphal: go here and there (1 Sm 14:16); melt (Is 14:31).

מוּר mûr (4306), Hiphil: change (Ps 46:2 [45:2]).

נָדַד nādhadh (5252), Hithpolel: flee (Ps 64:8 [63:8]).

נָפַל nāphal (5489), Fall; hiphil: cause to fall (Dn 11:12).

סָחַר s̱āchar (5692), Travel, be merchant; pilpel: throb (Ps 38:10 [37:10]).

סַר s̱ar (5821), Sullen (1 Kgs 21:5 [20:5]).

עָוָה ʻāwâh (5971), Piel: make crooked (Lm 3:9).

עָוַת ʻāwath (6003), Piel: pervert (Jb 8:3).

עָרַץ ʻārats (6442), Hiphil: dread (Is 8:12).

עָשֵׁשׁ ʻāshēsh (6485), Waste away (Pss 6:7, 31:9f. [30:9f.]).

פָּעַם pāʻam (6717), Niphal: be troubled (Gn 41:8, Ps 77:4 [76:4]); hithpael: be troubled (Dn 2:1).

צָהַל tsāhal (6934), Cry out (Is 24:14).

צָמַת tsāmath (7059), Pilpel: destroy (Ps 88:16 [87:16]—Codex Vaticanus only).

קָלַל qālal (7327), Be insignificant, be swift; pilpel: sharpen (Eccl 10:10); hithpalpel: move back and forth (Jer 4:24).

רָגַז rāghaz (7553), Tremble, be convulsed (Dt 2:25, Ps 77:16 [76:16], Am 8:8).

רָגַע rāghaʻ (7567), Stir up (Is 51:15).

רָעַשׁ rāʻash (7782), Quake (Ps 46:3 [45:3]).

רָפַשׂ rāphas (7806), Muddy (Ez 34:18).

שָׁחָה shāchâh (8246), Bow down; hiphil: weigh down (Prv 12:25).

שָׁחַח shāchach (8249), Hithpolel: be cast down (Ps 42:6 [41:6]).

שָׁלַל shālal (8394), Plunder; hithpolel: be plundered (Ps 76:5 [75:5]).

שָׁמֵם shāmēm (8460), Hithpolel: be appalled (Ps 143:4 [142:4]).

1. **ταράσσων tarassōn** nom sing masc part pres act
2. **ταράσσοντες tarassontes** nom pl masc part pres act
3. **ἐτάραξεν etaraxen** 3sing indic aor act
4. **ἐτάραξαν etaraxan** 3pl indic aor act
5. **ἐτάρασσεν etarassen** 3sing indic imperf act
6. **ταρασσέσθω tarassesthō** 3sing impr pres mid
7. **ἐταράχθη etarachthē** 3sing indic aor pass
8. **ἐταράχθησαν etarachthēsan** 3pl indic aor pass
9. **ταραχθῇ tarachthē** 3sing subj aor pass
10. **ταραχθῆτε tarachthēte** 2pl subj aor pass
11. **τετάρακται tetaraktai** 3sing indic perf mid
12. **τεταραγμένοι tetaragmenoi** nom pl masc part perf mid

7 Herod ... **he was troubled,** and all Jerusalem .... Matt 2:3
8 saw him walking on the sea, they **were troubled,** 14:26
8 For they all saw him, and **were troubled.** .... Mark 6:50
7 And when Zacharias saw him, he **was troubled,** .... Luke 1:12
12 And he said unto them, Why **are** ye **troubled?** 24:38
5 into the pool, and **troubled** the water: .... John 5:4
9 when the water **is troubled,** to put me into 5:7
3 he groaned in the spirit, and was **troubled,** 11:33
11 Now is my soul **troubled;** and what shall I say? 12:27
7 he **was troubled** in spirit, and testified, and said, ... 13:21
6 Let not your heart **be troubled:** ye believe in God, ... 14:1
6 Let not your heart **be troubled,** 14:27
4 that certain ... **have troubled** you with words, ... Acts 15:24
4 they **troubled** the people and the rulers of the city, ... 17:8
2 agitating and **stirring up** the crowds. (NASB) 17:13
2 but there be some that **trouble** you, ... Gal 1:7
1 but he that **troubleth** you shall bear his judgment, ... 5:10
10 be not afraid of their terror, neither **be troubled;** ... 1 Pt 3:14

Classical Greek

In classical Greek *tarassō* has a wide variety of usage, expressing various levels of physical or emotional agitation. It can refer to the troubling of the sea, plowing the ground, or the wagging of a tongue (*Liddell-Scott*). It can also mean "to cause confusion, to throw into disorder, to agitate," or "to disturb."

Septuagint Usage

In the Septuagint the verb is used for what happens when water is stirred up (Isaiah 24:14 [Septuagint only]; Ezekiel 32:2). It also describes human agitation. The baker and cupbearer were *troubled* by their dreams (Genesis 40:6). The Psalmist declares that no bones are *shaken* (Psalm 6:2). *Tarassō* can also signify fear. Psalm 2:5 notes that the Lord *terrifies* the kings of the earth.

New Testament Usage

Tarassō is used of the reaction of Zechariah to the angel Gabriel who appeared to him in the temple (Luke 1:12). Luke also employed *tarassō* of the disciples' reaction when the resurrected Jesus appeared to them on the first Easter evening (Luke 24:38). They thought He was a ghost (Luke 24:37).

John 5:7 uses *tarassō* in speaking of the belief that an angel at times stirred up the water of the pool of Bethesda. In the passive *tarassō* can mean "being troubled, agitated," or "frightened," and also "terrified." John 11:33 notes that when

Jesus saw Martha and the Jews weeping loudly at Lazarus' tomb, He groaned inwardly and was deeply *troubled*. John used the same word to describe Jesus' emotional state in the temple on Tuesday before His passion. Jesus said, "Now my soul is deeply *troubled*" (in turmoil), knowing all that lay ahead of Him in His role as the obedient, suffering Servant (John 12:27).

After eating the Passover with His disciples, Jesus told them, "Let not your heart be *troubled*" (John 14:1,27). In these two instances the verb refers to the inward anxiety and emotional shock they would experience that night and in the coming days. But, as Jesus told them in this chapter, their anxiety would be overcome by their faith in God through the work of the Holy Spirit. The phrase Jesus used reflects Psalms 55:4 (LXX 54:4) and 143:4 (LXX 142:4).

Tarassō describes the action of people who stirred up others and caused a riot. When the unbelieving Jews learned that many Jews and God-fearers in Thessalonica came to believe in Christ through Paul's preaching, they formed a street mob and *stirred up* the crowd (Acts 17:8). Then when the Jews at Thessalonica heard about the success of Paul's work at Beroea, they went there and again stirred up the people (Acts 17:13; some texts contain the word *saleuō* [4388] instead).

In Galatians 1:7 Paul in graphic language referred to the action of the Judaizers who were deeply *troubling* and thereby confusing believers, stressing that to be saved all had to live as Jews. However, the false teachers who were doing so would be punished (5:10).

Strong 5015, Bauer 805, Moulton-Milligan 625, Liddell-Scott 1757-58, Colin Brown 3:709-10.

4867. ταραχή tarachē noun

Disturbance, tumult, stirring up (of something or of people).

Cross-Reference:

ταράσσω tarassō (4866)

בַּלָּהָה ballāhāh (1130), Terror (Jb 24:17—Codex Alexandrinus and some Sinaiticus texts only).

בְּעָתָה be'āthāh (1228), Terror (Jer 14:19).

זַעֲוָה za'ăwāh (2272), Terror (Ez 23:46).

חִיל chîl (2523), Writhe (Ez 30:16).

חַלְחָלָה chalchālāh (2580), Anguish (Ez 30:4,9).

חִפָּזוֹן chippāzôn (2754), Haste (Is 52:12).

חָרַר chārar (2893), Burn; pilpel: kindle (Prv 26:21).

כָּרַע kāra' (3895), Kneel; hiphil: bring low (Jgs 11:35).

מָדוֹן mādhôn (4209II) Strife (Prv 6:14).

מְהוּמָה mehûmāh (4245), Tumult (Is 22:5).

עַוָּתָה 'awwāthāh (6004), Wrong (Lm 3:59).

רֹכֶס rōkhes (7696), Plot (Ps 31:20 [30:20]).

רָעַע rā'a' (7778), Be broken up (Is 24:19).

1. **ταραχήν** **tarachēn** acc sing fem
2. **ταραχαί** **tarachai** nom pl fem

2 and there shall be famines and troubles:..........Mark 13:8
1 troubling of the water stepped in was made whole...John 5:4

Classical Greek

In nonbiblical literature *tarachē* is used for a state of perplexity, a disturbance, riot, disorder of a physiological or psychological nature, and political disturbances. It is used by Claudius of a *disturbance* by the Jews (*Moulton-Milligan*).

Septuagint Usage

This term appears about 30 times in the Septuagint to reflect perplexity, tumult, and the like. For example, in Judges 11:35, Jephthah said of his daughter, "You are my *trouble*." Jephthah had promised the Lord that he would sacrifice the first thing he saw upon returning from the victory over the enemy. It was his daughter he saw first. Some scholars believe that Jephthah did not actually sacrifice his daughter; they believe she was merely forced into perpetual virginity. In Job 24:17, Job said that the Lord is the One who is familiar with the *terrors* of thick darkness. Psalm 31:20 (LXX 30:20) states that the Lord hides the righteous from the *conspiracies* (KJV: "pride") of men. Ezekiel 23:46 states that Aholah and Aholibah, two adulteresses, were to be judged by being given over to *terror* and plunder. Ezekiel 30:4 prophesied that *anguish* would be in Ethiopia.

New Testament Usage

Tarachē has the same general meaning in the New Testament as the classical usage, i.e., a "disturbance" of the normal order. It is used in John 5:4 of the water in the pool of Bethesda being stirred up. The stirring of the water was due to the action of an angel coming down from heaven. Several variants to the text of Mark 13:8 add *tarachē* with the meaning of "rebellion, riot, tumult."

Strong 5016, Bauer 805, Moulton-Milligan 625, Liddell-Scott 1758, Colin Brown 3:709.

4868. τάραχος tarachos noun

Confusion, consternation, commotion.

Cross-Reference:
ταράσσω tarassō (4866)

בַּלָּהָה ballāhāh (1130), Terror (Jb 24:17).

מְהוּמָה mehûmāh (4245), Panic (1 Sm 5:9).

עָכַר 'ākhar (6138), One who causes trouble (Jgs 11:35).

1. τάραχος tarachos nom sing masc

1 **there was no small stir among the soldiers,.........Acts 12:18**
1 **same time there arose no small stir about that way..... 19:23**

Tarachos is a noun related to the verb *tarassō* (4866). Its meaning in Koine Greek is essentially the same as in the classical Greek and the Septuagint: "disturbance, agitation," etc. Acts 12:18 underlines the *consternation* and acute distress of the soldiers when Peter was not found in prison. They knew, as verse 19 states, that this would result in their execution. Acts 19:22ff. speaks about the results of Paul's missionary activity and its effect on the business of the silversmiths who made silver shrines of the great goddess Artemis (Diana). They instigated a serious *commotion* hoping to arouse public opinion against Paul.

Strong 5017, Bauer 805, Moulton-Milligan 626, Liddell-Scott 1758.

4869. Ταρσεύς Tarseus name-adj

From Tarsus.

1. Ταρσεύς Tarseus nom sing masc
2. Ταρσέα Tarsea acc sing masc

2 **one called Saul, of Tarsus: for, behold, he prayeth,.. Acts 9:11**
1 **Paul said, I am a man which am a Jew of Tarsus,..... 21:39**

The word is used at Acts 9:11 and 21:39 to describe Paul, who was born in Tarsus.

4870. Ταρσός Tarsos name

Tarsus.

1. Ταρσῷ Tarsō dat fem
2. Ταρσόν Tarson acc fem

2 **and sent him forth to Tarsus...................... Acts 9:30**
2 **departed Barnabas to Tarsus, for to seek Saul:........ 11:25**
1 **I am verily a man which am a Jew, born in Tarsus,.... 22:3**

Tarsus was a large city, the capital of the Roman province of Cilicia. It was famous as a city of learning.

The apostle Paul was born at Tarsus. However, at Acts 22:3 he describes himself as brought up in Jerusalem. Soon after his conversion he lived for a while in Tarsus. It is therefore not clear how much influence his native city had upon him, either in childhood or as an adult.

4871. ταρταρόω tartaroō verb

Hold captive in Tartarus, send to Tartarus.

1. ταρταρώσας tartarōsas nom sing masc part aor act

1 **but cast them down to hell,.........................2 Pt 2:4**

Classical Greek

Tartaroō is a word of Christian origin based on the term *Tartarus* (Turner, *Christian Words*, p.210). In Greek mythology Tartarus was the place of punishment for the wicked. Homer described it as "a black hole, a bottomless pit" with iron gates and bronze walls; it was as far below Hades as heaven was above the earth (Iliad 8:13). Thus, Greeks believed Tartarus lay under the earth.

According to mythology, Tartarus was the place in which the Titans, the children of the gods Ouranos and Gaia (Sky and Earth), were confined after they rebelled against the Olympian gods (Zeus, Poseidon, etc.) (Hesiod *Theogony* 715-722). There they supposedly are kept, bound with chains and hidden in "misty gloom." Tartarus was also the place in which the wicked dead were confined and was the opposite of the Elysian Fields. In earlier mythology those in Tartarus were punished solely for having offended the gods, not necessarily for ethical moral reasons (Rose, *Handbook of Greek Mythology*, p.80). Later, however, people were cast into Tartarus for moral misdeeds—treason, abuse of power, offenses against close blood relations, as well as offenses against the gods (ibid., p.90). Plato described Tartarus as a place under the earth which was both the origin and goal of all subterranean rivers (Phaed. 112a). Here all sinners were kept, those who committed moral or ethical crimes (Gorgias 523b).

Septuagint Usage

The verb *tartaroō* does not appear in the Septuagint. The noun *tartaros* appears a few times. In Job 40:15 (LXX) and 41:23 it is not a deep place under the earth but the "deep," i.e., the sea. In Job 41:23 it is synonymous with *abussos* (12), "the deep." In some manuscripts *tartaros* appears at Proverbs 24:51 (LXX 30:16). In this passage it is synonymous with *hadēs* (85), "hell."

The concept of Tartarus as a place of imprisonment appears in noncanonical Jewish literature. Pseudo-philo 60:3 refers to Tartarus as the place where evil spirits walk. The book of

First Enoch (Greek text) states that Tartarus is ruled by the archangel Uriel (20:2).

New Testament Usage

This verb is used only in 2 Peter 2:4 in the New Testament. Peter wrote: "God spared not the angels that sinned, but cast them down to hell (*tartarōsas*), and delivered them into chains of darkness, to be reserved unto judgment." This passage was written to Jews of the Diaspora who would have been very familiar with the term *Tartarus*. They would have understood Peter to say that these fallen angels received the gravest punishment imaginable. This is not to say that the New Testament teaches the existence of the literal "Tartarus" described in Greek mythology. Rather, the writer used a concept that was meaningful to those who received his epistle.

Adam Clarke states that God cast the apostate angels out of His presence into that *zophos tou skotous*, blackness of darkness (2 Peter 2:17; Jude 13) where they will be forever banished from the light of His countenance (*Clarke's Commentaries*, 6:885).

Strong 5020, Bauer 805, Moulton-Milligan 626, Liddell-Scott 1759.

4872. τάσσω tassō verb

Place, fix, determine, appoint, direct.

Cognates:

ἀνατάσσω anatassō (390)
ἀντιτάσσομαι antitassomai (495)
ἀποτάσσω apotassō (651)
διαταγή diatagē (1290)
διάταγμα diatagma (1291)
διατάσσω diatassō (1293)
ἐπιδιατάσσομαι epidiatassomai (1913)
ἐπιταγή epitagē (1987)
ἐπιτάσσω epitassō (1988)
προστάσσω prostassō (4225)
προτάσσω protassō (4243)
συντάσσω suntassō (4781)
τάγμα tagma (4852)
τακτός taktos (4853)
τάξις taxis (4861)
ὑποταγή hupotagē (5130)
ὑποτάσσω hupotassō (5131)

Synonyms:

διαμαρτύρομαι diamarturomai (1257)
διαστέλλω diastellō (1285)
διατάσσω diatassō (1293)
ἐντέλλομαι entellomai (1765)
ἐξορκίζω exorkizō (1828)
ἐπιτάσσω epitassō (1988)
καθίστημι kathistēmi (2497)
κελεύω keleuō (2724)
λέγω legō (2978)
ὁρίζω horizō (3587)
ὁρκίζω horkizō (3589)
παραγγέλλω parangellō (3715)
προστάσσω prostassō (4225)
προχειρίζομαι procheirizomai (4258)
συντάσσω suntassō (4781)
τίθημι tithēmi (4935)
χειροτονέω cheirotoneō (5336)

אָחַז 'āchaz (270), Fasten (Est 1:6—only some Sinaiticus texts).

דָּגַל dāghal (1763), Niphal: host [military? celestial?] (S/S 6:4,10 [6:3,9]).

הָלַךְ hālakh (2050), Go, walk; hiphil: bring (Hos 2:14).

יָעַד yā'adh (3366), Qal: appoint (2 Sm 20:5); niphal: meet (Ex 29:43).

מוֹעֵד mô'ēdh (4287), Appointment (1 Sm 20:35).

נָשָׂא nāsâ' (5558), Lift up (Jb 30:22).

נָתַן nāthan (5598), Give, put; appoint, assign (1 Chr 16:4,7).

עָמַד 'āmadh (6198), Stand, arise; hiphil: appoint (2 Chr 31:2).

פָּאַר pā'ar (6526), Glorify; hithpael: have an honor (Ex 8:9).

צָוָה tsāwâh (6943), Piel: appoint (2 Sm 7:11, 1 Chr 17:10); set (Is 38:1).

שִׂים sîm (7947), Station, put (2 Kgs 10:24, Ez 14:4,7); make (Zec 7:12,14).

שׁוּב shûv (8178), Return; hiphil: recall (Lm 3:21).

שִׁית shîth (8308), Appoint, make (Jb 14:13, Jer 2:15, Hos 2:3).

1. **ἔταξαν etaxan** 3pl indic aor act
2. **τασσόμενος tassomenos** nom sing masc part pres mid
3. **ἐτάξατο etaxato** 3sing indic aor mid
4. **ταξάμενοι taxamenoi** nom pl masc part aor mid
5. **τέτακται tetaktai** 3sing indic perf mid
6. **τεταγμένοι tetagmenoi** nom pl masc part perf mid
7. **τεταγμέναι tetagmenai** nom pl fem part perf mid
8. **τεταχέναι tetachenai** inf perf act

3 into a mountain where Jesus had **appointed** them... Matt 28:16
2 For I also am a man set under authority,........... Luke 7:8
6 as many as were **ordained** to eternal life believed... Acts 13:48
1 they **determined** that Paul and Barnabas,.............. 15:2
5 of all things which are **appointed** for thee to do........ 22:10
4 And when they **had appointed** him a day,............. 28:23
7 the powers that be are **ordained** of God...........Rom 13:1
1 that they **have addicted** themselves to the ministry.. 1 Co 16:15

Classical Greek

Tassō is a common verb in classical Greek for arranging troops or ships in proper position for battle. This verb can also mean "to impose a punishment" or "assess a tax" (*Liddell-Scott*). It came to have a variety of meanings such as, "to appoint or order someone to a task, to put into proper order," and "to command." Priests were appointed as supervisors and judges. The senses are "appointed" to serve.

Septuagint Usage
The Septuagint uses it to translate a wide range of Hebrew verbs. Mainly, *tassō* renders the Hebrew word *sîm* (or *sôm*). Depending on the context, the verb *tassō* may be translated "to appoint, draw up, ordain, prohibit, set," and in the middle voice, "to command, fix, make disposition, to set one's heart" and similar meanings. All these imply that God or humans are the agents of the action.

New Testament Usage
Tassō is used in the New Testament in a variety of meanings: "to appoint, order, arrange, determine, establish, set in place," depending on the immediate context. A glance at a concordance indicates that Luke used *tassō* more than any other writer of the New Testament, especially in the Book of Acts. He drew on a variety of meanings of this verb to present his message. For example, in Luke 7:8 the centurion at Capernaum said: "I am a man *set* (*tassomenos*) under authority."

In Acts 13:48 Luke noted the success of Paul's work in Galatian Antioch: "As many as were ordained (*tetagmenoi*, appointed) to eternal life believed." Because of the turmoil caused by the Judaizers, "they determined (*etaxsen*) that Paul and Barnabas . . . should go up to Jerusalem" (Acts 15:2).

Acts 18:2 reflects another meaning of the verb: "Claudius had commanded (*diatetachenai*, ordered) all Jews to depart from Rome." Paul told the mob in the temple what Christ had told him on the Damascus Road, "There it shall be told thee of all things which are appointed for thee to do" (*tetaktai soi poiēsai*, ordered, Acts 22:10).

Luke recorded in Acts 28:23 that Paul met with the Jewish leaders in Rome. They appointed (*taxamenoi*, set) a day on which to meet with him.

In Romans 13:1 Paul exhorted his readers to "be subject" (*hupotassesthō*, submit) to the government *ordained* by God. In his closing verses to the church in Corinth, Paul reminded them that the house of Stephanas had "addicted" (*etaxan*, committed, devoted) themselves to the service of the saints (1 Corinthians 16:15).

STRONG 5021, BAUER 806, MOULTON-MILLIGAN 626, KITTEL 8:27-31, LIDDELL-SCOTT 1759-60, COLIN BROWN 1:476.

4873. ταῦρος tauros noun
Bull, ox.

אַבִּיר 'abbîr (48), Bull, large bull (Ps 50:13 [49:13], Is 34:7); stallion (Jer 50:11 [27:11]).

אֶלֶף 'eleph (511), Oxen (Is 30:24).

מְרִיא m^erî' (4968), Fatling (Is 11:6).

פַּר par (6749), Bull (Gn 32:15, Is 1:11).

שׁוֹר shôr (8228), Ox, bull (Ex 21:28f.,32,35f., Dt 33:17).

1. ταῦροι tauroi nom pl masc
2. ταύρων taurōn gen pl masc
3. ταύρους taurous acc pl masc

1 my oxen and my fatlings are killed, ... Matt 22:4
3 brought oxen and garlands unto the gates, ... Acts 14:13
2 For if the blood of bulls and of goats, ... Heb 9:13
2 blood of bulls and of goats should take away sins. 10:4

Classical Greek and Septuagint Usage
Tauros may denote a "bull" or an "ox." It may also be used as a generic term for "cattle." The Septuagint makes frequent use of this term in its various designations.

New Testament Usage
In the Parable of the Marriage Feast the king sent out his servants to tell those invited, "My oxen (*tauroi*) and my fatlings are killed" (Matthew 22:4). After Paul and Barnabas had healed the cripple at Lystra, the priest of Jupiter and Mercury brought oxen (*taurous*) and garlands for sacrifice (Acts 14:13). References to bulls (*taurōn*) for sacrifice occur in Hebrews 9:13 and 10:4.

STRONG 5022, BAUER 806, MOULTON-MILLIGAN 626, LIDDELL-SCOTT 1761, COLIN BROWN 1:116.

4874. ταὐτά tauta dem-pron
In like manner, even so, like things.

1. ταὐτά tauta nom/acc pl neu

Tauta is equal to *ta auta* in variant readings of older editions of the Greek New Testament text; for example, Luke 6:23 ("in like manner"), 6:26 ("so"); 17:30 ("even thus"); 1 Thessalonians 2:14 ("like things"). Modern critical texts (*Nestle-Aland 26th* and *UBS 3rd*) no longer include *tauta* as a variant reading. (See the word study at *houtos* [3642].)

STRONG 5023, BAUER 806, LIDDELL-SCOTT 1761.

4875. ταφή taphē noun
Burial, tomb.

CROSS-REFERENCE:
θάπτω thaptō (2267)

חֲנֻטִים chănuṯîm (2693), Embalming (Gn 50:3).

קְבוּרָה q^evûrāh (7185), Burial (Jer 22:19).

קָבַר qāvar (7196), Bury (Dt 21:23).

קֶבֶר qever (7197), Grave (Is 53:9, Na 1:14).

1. ταφήν taphēn acc sing fem

1 bought ... the potter's field, to **bury** strangers in.... Matt 27:7

In the Septuagint *taphē* translates two Hebrew words: *qever* and *q^evûrāh*. Depending on the context it usually denotes "tomb" but at times can also be translated as "burial." As seen in classical Greek, it can also refer to a "mummy" or "mummy-wrappings" (*Liddell-Scott*). In Isaiah 53:9 *taphē* refers to "grave." In Matthew 27:7 *taphē* denotes a place "to bury strangers in." The passage is discussing the potter's field. It may also be translated "for the burial" (*eis taphēn*) of strangers or as a burial place (grave).

STRONG 5027, BAUER 806, MOULTON-MILLIGAN 626, LIDDELL-SCOTT 1761, COLIN BROWN 1:263-64.

4876. τάφος taphos noun

Sepulcher, tomb.

COGNATE:
θάπτω thaptō (2267)

SYNONYMS:
μνῆμα mnēma (3282)
μνημεῖον mnēmeion (3283)

קְבוּרָה q^evûrāh (7185), Burial place, tomb (Gn 47:30, 1 Sm 10:2, 2 Kgs 21:26).

קָבַר qāvar (7196), Bury (Eccl 8:10).

קֶבֶר qever (7197), Burial site, grave (Gn 23:4, 1 Kgs 13:30f., Ps 88:5 [87:5]).

1. τάφος taphos nom sing masc
2. τάφου taphou gen sing masc
3. τάφον taphon acc sing masc
4. τάφοις taphois dat pl masc
5. τάφους taphous acc pl masc

4 for ye are like unto whited **sepulchres**,............ Matt 23:27
5 because ye build the **tombs** of the prophets,........... 23:29
2 sitting over against the **sepulchre**........................ 27:61
3 that the **sepulchre** be made sure until the third day,.... 27:64
3 So they went, and made the **sepulchre** sure,........... 27:66
3 and the other Mary to see the **sepulchre**............... 28:1
1 Their throat is an open **sepulchre**;................... Rom 3:13

Classical Greek and Septuagint Usage

This term is a derivative of *thaptō* (2267) and is one of three words used both in the Septuagint and in the New Testament for "tomb" (cf. *mnēma* [3282], *mnēmeion* [3283]). (In the Septuagint no real significance should be seen in the variations of words.) *Taphos* is almost always translated "funeral rites" in Homer. Later Greek literature translates *taphos* as "tomb" (Hemer, "Bury," *Colin Brown*, 1:263-266).

New Testament Usage

According to Vincent the references in Matthew 23:27,29 and Romans 3:13 refer to *graves* covered with plastered surfaces. Cemeteries were usually placed outside cities. However, dead bodies found in a field would be buried on the spot where they were found. A person coming to Passover might inadvertently pass by such a grave and thus become ceremonially unclean. (See Numbers 19:16.) Thus all sepulchers were whitewashed one month previous to the Passover. This would make graves very obvious and give a person the opportunity to avoid defilement (*Word Studies in the New Testament*, 1:125f.; see also Hemer, "Bury," *Colin Brown*, 1:265).

This custom was occurring during the time Jesus spoke to the Pharisees, thus providing Him the obvious comparison of the outward appearance of cleanliness and the death (the evil of inner motives) that was covered up. This would be the inference in the Romans 3:13 usage as well. The Matthew 23:29 usage of the word *tomb* further delineates Jesus' alluding to the Pharisees' practice of embellishing the tomb of prophets their forebears had rejected and killed (ibid.).

The context of the usage of *taphos* in Matthew 27 and 28 would indicate a different type of sepulcher (i.e., those hewn out of rock and owned by the rich, as with Joseph of Arimathea cited in Matthew 27:57-61).

STRONG 5028, BAUER 806, MOULTON-MILLIGAN 626, LIDDELL-SCOTT 1761, COLIN BROWN 1:263-65.

4877. τάχα tacha adv

Perhaps, possibly.

CROSS-REFERENCE:
τάχος tachos (4882)

1. τάχα tacha

1 yet **peradventure** for a good man some would....... Rom 5:7
1 For **perhaps** he therefore departed for a season,.... Phlm 1:15

Tacha has the meaning of a low probability of something happening or being done. Depending on the context it may be translated "maybe, perhaps, possibly." In classical Greek *tacha* has a wide semantic range, but the New Testament does not utilize this range of definitions. To emphasize the idea of improbability, Romans 5:7 (KJV) has *tacha* translated as "*peradventure* for a good man some would even dare to die." Philemon 15 uses *tacha* in the sense of "perhaps."

STRONG 5029, BAUER 806, MOULTON-MILLIGAN 626, LIDDELL-SCOTT 1762.

4878. ταχέως tacheōs adv

Quickly, shortly, hastily, soon.

COGNATE:
 τάχος tachos (4882)

SYNONYMS:
 ἐξαυτῆς exautēs (1808)
 εὐθέως eutheōs (2091)
 εὐθύς euthus (2098)
 παραχρῆμα parachrēma (3777)

מָהַר māhar (4257), Piel: make haste, do hastily (Jgs 9:48, Prv 25:8).

מְהֵרָה m^ehērāh (4259), Quickly, speedily (2 Sm 17:18, 2 Kgs 1:11, Jl 3:4).

רָגַע rāgha' (7567), Be still; hiphil: do something in an instant (Jer 50:44 [27:44]).

1. ταχέως tacheōs

1 Go out **quickly** into the streets and lanes of the city, Luke 14:21
1 Take thy bill, and sit down **quickly**, and write fifty..... 16:6
1 that she rose up **hastily** and went out,............. John 11:31
1 But I will come to you **shortly**, if the Lord will,..... 1 Co 4:19
1 I marvel that ye are so **soon** removed from him...... Gal 1:6
1 to send Timotheus **shortly** unto you,................ Phlp 2:19
1 But I trust ... that I also myself shall come **shortly**...... 2:24
1 That ye be not **soon** shaken in mind,............... 2 Th 2:2
1 Lay hands **suddenly** on no man,.................... 1 Tm 5:22
1 Do thy diligence to come **shortly** unto me:......... 2 Tm 4:9

Classical Greek and Septuagint Usage

Tacheōs is an adverb related to *tachus* (4884) meaning "swift." In the Septuagint *tacheōs* has similar meanings. Judges 9:48 says that Abimelech ordered his men to do quickly as he has done. Proverbs 25:8 warns the reader not to bring anything *hastily* into court. In 2 Maccabees 6:23 Eleazer quickly replies to his tormentors.

New Testament Usage

From the time of Homer into the era of New Testament, it is most frequently translated "quickly, shortly, hastily." In Luke 14:21 and 16:6 *tacheōs* is translated "quickly." Luke 16:6 carries with it the picture of a financial transaction that is supposed to be carried out in secret. It is to be done *quickly* and carried through and completed with haste (Vincent, *Word Studies in the New Testament*, 1:393).

According to Thayer, Paul's use of *tacheōs* in 1 Timothy 5:22 carries with it an "added suggestion of inconsiderateness" (*Greek-English Lexicon*). This is one of the examples where the usage of *tacheōs* takes on special import. First Timothy 5:22 might be better rendered "hastily" and is probably a reference to the procedure of formal restoration for those who had been expelled from the Church for gross sins (Vincent, *Word Studies in the New Testament*, 4:229). Subsequently, this passage focuses on the idea of avoiding rash action (Earle, *Word Meanings*, 5:211).

Another special usage should be noted in Galatians 1:6 where *tacheōs* is translated "soon": "I marvel that ye are so *soon* removed from him that called you." Paul did not speak here about a subsequent event that had occurred, i.e., either their conversion, his latest visit, or coming under the influence of a false teacher. Paul referred to the rapidity of their move toward apostasy.

STRONG 5030, BAUER 806-7, MOULTON-MILLIGAN 627, LIDDELL-SCOTT 1762.

4879. ταχινός tachinos adj

Shortly, soon, swift.

COGNATE:
 τάχος tachos (4882)

SYNONYMS:
 ὀξύς oxus (3554)
 ταχύς tachus (4884)

מָהַר māhar (4257), Niphal: impetuous (Hb 1:6); piel: hasten (Is 59:7).

1. ταχινὴ tachinē nom sing fem

2. ταχινήν tachinēn acc sing fem

1 that **shortly** I must put off this my tabernacle,....... 2 Pt 1:14
2 and bring upon themselves **swift** destruction............ 2:1

Related to *tachos* (4882), this adjective appears from the time of Theocritus (Third Century B.C.) onward. The term carries the implication of events "soon to come or just impending" (Thayer, *Greek-English Lexicon*). Suddenness or imminent action is conveyed by this word. It is found in the Septuagint in Proverbs 1:16; Ecclesiastes 11:22; 18:26; Isaiah 59:7; Habbakuk 1:6; and Wisdom of Solomon 13:2. In the New Testament it is used only in 2 Peter in connection with the writer's anticipation of his imminent death (1:14) and with the sudden or swift destruction of false prophets (2:1).

STRONG 5031, BAUER 807, MOULTON-MILLIGAN 627, LIDDELL-SCOTT 1762.

4880. τάχιον tachion adv

More swiftly, more quickly.

CROSS-REFERENCE:
 τάχος tachos (4882)

1. τάχιον tachion comp

1 said Jesus unto him, That thou doest, do **quickly**... John 13:27
1 disciple ran ahead **faster** than Peter, (NASB).......... 20:4
1 things write I ... hoping to come unto thee **shortly**:..1 Tm 3:14
1 that I may be restored to you the **sooner**.......... Heb 13:19
1 with whom, if he come **shortly**, I will see you.......... 13:23

This word is the comparative form of *tacheōs* (4878), and it is used either in a comparative way to mean "more quickly, earlier," or "sooner" (John 20:4; Hebrews 13:19) or simply to mean "quickly, soon," and "without delay" (John 13:17; 1 Timothy 3:14; Hebrews 13:23). *Tachion* appears five times in the New Testament. In John 13:27 Jesus told Judas to carry out his intention "quickly." In 20:4 the anonymous disciple (probably John), literally translated, "ran on in front faster than Peter" to reach the tomb first on resurrection day.

The word may be translated as "shortly" or "soon" in 1 Timothy 3:14. In Hebrews 13:19 the writer urged his readers to pray earnestly for his release from imprisonment so he could return "sooner" to be with them. The same comparative is used in verse 23 of the same chapter, but it has the meaning of the positive form—"soon."

STRONG 5032, BAUER 807, MOULTON-MILLIGAN 627, LIDDELL-SCOTT 1762.

4881. τάχιστα tachista adv

With all speed.

CROSS-REFERENCE:

τάχος tachos (4882)

1. τάχιστα tachista sup

1 and Timotheus for to come to him with **all speed**,.. Acts 17:15

Tachista is an adverb related to the adjective *tacheōs* (4878). From the time of Homer on the term meant "very quickly" or "as quickly as possible." *Tachista* is used only once in the New Testament, in Acts 17:15. Robertson points out that this term is really a very good Greek (Attic) idiom. In this passage the term appears as *hōs tachista* and conveys the idea of "as quickly as possible" (*Word Pictures in the New Testament*, 3:276).

STRONG 5033, BAUER 807, MOULTON-MILLIGAN 627, LIDDELL-SCOTT 1762-63.

4882. τάχος tachos noun

Speed; quickness, shortness.

COGNATES:

τάχα tacha (4877)
ταχέως tacheōs (4878)
ταχινός tachinos (4879)
τάχιον tachion (4880)
τάχιστα tachista (4881)
ταχύ tachu (4883)
ταχύς tachus (4884)

יְעָף yeʿāph (3397), Flight (Dn 9:21).

מָהַר māhar (4257), Piel: do quickly (2 Chr 18:8).

מְהֵרָה meherāh (4259), Swiftly (Ps 147:15 [147:4]).

1. τάχει tachei dat sing neu

1 I tell you that he will avenge them **speedily**........ Luke 18:8
1 Arise up **quickly**. And his chains fell off........... Acts 12:7
1 and get thee **quickly** out of Jerusalem:................ 22:18
1 and that he himself would depart **shortly** thither....... 25:4
1 shall bruise Satan under your feet **shortly**.......... Rom 16:20
1 things which must **shortly** come to pass;............. Rev 1:1
1 or else I will come unto thee **quickly**,.................. 2:5
1 to show ... the things which must **shortly** be done...... 22:6

Classical Greek and Septuagint Usage

In classical Greek, from Homer on, this word means "quickness" or "speed." However, it is often used with a preposition to function as an adverbial phrase and is frequently found from the period of Aeschylus and Pindar on. The Septuagint uses *tachos* over 40 times in the historical, wisdom, and prophetic literature of the Old Testament.

New Testament Usage

Tachos is used seven times in the New Testament. It appears in Luke 18:8 in conjunction with *en* and is translated "speedily"; in Acts 12:7 and 22:18 as "quickly"; and in Acts 25:4, Romans 16:20, Revelation 1:1, and 22:6 as "shortly." It is also a variant in 1 Timothy 3:14.

Plummer suggests the phrase *en tachei*, in all of its usages in the New Testament, can be translated as "quickly, without delay." In the New Testament He seems to wait too long to act for those who are suffering, yet He really acts "speedily." The action is swift and decisive, but in His own time (*The International Critical Commentary, St. Luke*, pp.414,415). The term *tachos* thus is placed in the text for emphasis on the sure action of God.

The two usages in Revelation 1:1 and 22:6 find the same clause being used, i.e., "things which must shortly come to pass" (1:1) and "things which must shortly be done" (22:6). In these contexts it is the revelatory initiative of God that is shown through the angel. The subsequent speaker in each case is Jesus himself. Again we see God acting swiftly, i.e., with clarity and assuredness.

STRONG 5034, BAUER 807, MOULTON-MILLIGAN 627, LIDDELL-SCOTT 1762.

4883. ταχύ tachu adv

Quickly, swiftly, without delay, soon.

CROSS-REFERENCE:

τάχος tachos (4882)

1. ταχύ tachu

1 Agree with thine adversary **quickly**,................ Matt 5:25
1 And go **quickly**, ... tell his disciples that he is risen.... 28:7

1 And they departed **quickly** from the sepulchre ..... Matt 28:8
1 in my name, that can **lightly** speak evil of me....... Mark 9:39
1 went out **quickly**, and fled from the sepulchre; 16:8
1 **Quickly** bring out the best robe (NASB) .... Luke 15:22
1 she arose **quickly**, and came unto him............ John 11:29
1 Repent; or else I will come unto thee **quickly**,....... Rev 2:16
1 I come **quickly**: hold that fast which thou hast,......... 3:11
1 and, behold, the third woe cometh **quickly**............. 11:14
1 Behold, I come **quickly**: blessed is he that............. 22:7
1 behold, I come **quickly**; and my reward is with me,.... 22:12
1 He which testifieth ... Surely I come **quickly**........... 22:20

Classical Greek and Septuagint Usage

The adverb *tachu* (formally a neuter singular of the adjective *tachus* [4884]; see Blass and DeBrunner, *Greek Grammar of the New Testament*, p.55f.; cf. *Bauer*) means "quickly" or "soon." The difference between the two ideas—immediacy (soon), suddenness (quickly)—is not always easy to determine (*Bauer*). *Tachu* does not appear in the Septuagint, but its related adjective *tachus* does.

New Testament Usage

Tachu is the form most common to the New Testament where it appears 13 times. *Tachus* occurs once, in James 1:19, with essentially the same meaning. The sense of "immediately" (in a short time) should probably be understood in Mark 9:39. The notion of "quickly" (with speed) comes through elsewhere in the Gospels (e.g., Matthew 5:25; 28:7; Luke 15:22 [some texts]; John 11:29). Nevertheless, a clear-cut distinction is not always possible.

Revelation uses *tachu* in unique reference to the coming of the Lord or His power in judgment (Revelation 2:16; 11:14) or reward (3:11; cf. 22:7,12,20). The refrain of Jesus, "Behold (or "indeed"), I come quickly soon (*tachu*)" (Revelation 22:7,12,20) refers to the immediacy of Jesus' return rather than to His style of coming. Nevertheless, the suddenness of His return cannot be ruled out since we read elsewhere that He will come "as a thief in the night" (1 Thessalonians 5:2).

Strong 5035, Bauer 807 (see "tachus"), Moulton-Milligan 627, Liddell-Scott 1762 (see "tachus").

4884. ταχύς tachus adj

Swift, speedy.

Cognate:
 τάχος tachos (4882)

Synonyms:
 ὀξύς oxus (3554)
 ταχινός tachinos (4879)

אוּץ 'ûts (211), Be hasty (Prv 29:20).

מָהִיר māhîr (4248), Skilled (Ezr 7:6).

מָהַר māhar (4257), Piel: do something quickly, a swift person (Ex 32:8, Ps 79:8 [78:8], Mal 3:5).

מְהֵרָה m^ehērāh (4259), Quickly, soon (2 Sm 17:16, Ps 37:2 [36:2], Is 58:8).

קָרוֹב qārôv (7427), At hand (Is 13:22 [14:1]).

רָגַע rāgha' (7567), Be at rest; hiphil: be momentary (Prv 12:19).

1. ταχύς tachus nom sing masc

1 let every man be **swift** to hear, slow to speak,........ Jas 1:19

Classical Greek and Septuagint Usage

This adjective can be found in classical Greek from the Eighth Century B.C. meaning "swift, fleet, quick, hasty" (*Liddell-Scott*). In reference to persons, animals, and things it is used of motion as well as of thought and purpose (ibid.). *Tachus* usually translates the Hebrew word *māhar*, "to hurry, be quick," in the Septuagint. It is used of the shortened period of time between Israel's faithfulness to God and her "turning away" to idols (cf. Exodus 32:8; Deuteronomy 9:12,16; Judges 2:17). In Judges 9:54 it is used of Abimelech's hurried urging of his armor-bearer to kill him before he died from a woman's hand. Elsewhere the Psalmist asked the Lord to answer him "speedily" or "without delay" (Psalm 69:17 [LXX 68:17]) and to show him mercy "speedily" (Psalm 79:8 [78:8]; cf. Isaiah 58:8).

New Testament Usage

Ropes suggests that the phrase "swift to hear," used in James 1:19 (i.e., *tachus eis to akousai*), relates primarily to the hearing of or the ready obedience to the Word (referring to 1:18). It is not just an imperative concerning normal social interaction or communication. It is, in fact, the trait of a good pupil, "quick to learn, slow to forget" (Ropes, *International Critical Commentary*, *James*, pp.168f.). The imperative given in this text is really a conventional Jewish exhortation. The same form or pattern (not exactly the same directive) can be seen in Ecclesiastes 7:9, Matthew 5:22, and Ephesians 4:26 (Sidebottom, *Century Bible*, *James*, p.33). Greek moralists also use such short, concise moralisms in their writings. Robertson suggests that the picture presented is one of listening to the word of truth, and the directive is aimed against "violent and disputatious speech." This is emphasized in James 3:1-12 (*Word Pictures in the New Testament*, 6:21).

The directive to be "swift to hear" is a reference to what has preceded the statement. It implies that the hearers are well aware or have knowledge of the word of truth. Consequently, they should be "swift to hear" (*tachus eis to akousai*) the word of truth that has such great power for good and for life (Alford, *The Greek Testament*, 4:285).

Strong 5036, Bauer 807, Liddell-Scott 1762.

4885. τέ te conj

Also, and, both, even, then, whether.

1. τέ te

This word is a common enclitic particle that appears in all types of Greek literature. It is used most frequently as a conjunction meaning "and, both." It joins words, phrases, clauses, or sentences (cf. *Liddell-Scott*).

New Testament Usage

Te appears about 200 times in the New Testament, most often in the Book of Acts (about 150 times, probably reflecting the writer's style) followed by its usage in Romans and Hebrews (about 20 times in each). It appears in a number of combinations. It can stand alone or be followed by another *te* or by *kai* (2504) or be joined with another particle. When it stands alone it can join equal parts of the same sentence or connect complete sentences.

When *te* is used with *kai* it is more emphatic and may be translated "as well." Kindred thoughts are connected by usages of *te* and *kai* (see Luke 12:45). They also may be united by some inner bond, either logical or real. According to Thayer *te* and *kai* express the closest connection between ideas and thoughts (*Greek-English Lexicon*).

Te and *de* (1156) may be joined together. *Te*, like *kai*, brings together in a sentence what has been said beforehand with an additional thought (see Acts 19:3). *Te* may also be used with another *te* to present parallel ideas or connecting sentences. This correlative *te* is found in classical poetry and only once in the New Testament. It may be translated "as . . . so" or "not only . . . but also" (Acts 26:16; see Turner, *A Grammar of New Testament Greek*, 4:329).

Te may be used with *gar* (1056) where *te* serves as the connective and *gar* provides the qualifying amplification. (Romans 1:26 serves as an example of this usage.) This is the combination most used in the Septuagint.

The usages of *te* seem to vary as evidenced by the considerable freedom in placing the word. *Te* is most properly used to connect parallel words or ideas.

Strong 5037, Bauer 807, Moulton-Milligan 627, Liddell-Scott 1763-64.

4886. τεῖχος teichos noun

Wall.

Cognates:

μεσότοιχον mesotoichon (3190)
τοῖχος toichos (4956)

Synonym:

φραγμός phragmos (5254)

חוֹמָה chômāh (2440), Wall (Lv 25:30f., Neh 2:8, Ez 26:9f.).

מְצוּרָה m^e^tsûrāh (4859), Fortress (2 Chr 11:11—Codex Alexandrinus only).

קִיר qîr (7306), Wall (Ez 33:30).

קִיר qîr (7307), Kir (Is 15:1).

שׁוּר shûr (8229), Wall (2 Sm 22:30, Ps 18:29 [17:29]).

שׁוּר shûr (A8232), Wall (Ezr 4:12f.,16—Aramaic).

תֵּל tēl (8839), Ruins (Jer 30:18 [37:18]—Codex Alexandrinus only).

1. τεῖχος teichos nom/acc sing neu
2. τείχους teichous gen sing neu
3. τείχη teichē nom/acc pl neu

2 and let him down by the wall in a basket. . . . . Acts 9:25
2 in a basket was I let down by the wall, ... 2 Co 11:33
3 By faith the walls of Jericho fell down, ... Heb 11:30
1 had a wall great and high, and had twelve gates, ... Rev 21:12
1 And the wall of the city had twelve foundations, ... 21:14
1 city, and the gates thereof, and the wall thereof. 21:15
1 wall thereof, an hundred and forty and four cubits, ... 21:17
2 And the building of the wall of it was of jasper: 21:18
2 And the foundations of the wall of the city 21:19

This noun is common in classical Greek from the Eighth Century B.C. and in the Septuagint. It generally means a "wall" but is most frequently used of a city wall, fortification, or embankment, in contrast to that of a house, temple, or ship (cf. *Liddell-Scott*).

New Testament Usage

Teichos appears nine times in the New Testament. It is used in Acts 9:25, 2 Corinthians 11:33, and Hebrews 11:30 to describe city walls. It is also used to refer to the wall of the heavenly city in Revelation 21:12,14,15,17-19.

The multiple usage of the term in Revelation frequently describes a wall that is high. The measuring of this high wall by the angel in 21:17 draws attention to its height and thus indicates eternal protection for the inhabitants. The angels depicted in 21:12 as stationed at the gates are present more to show honor to the city than to guard the entrance. The wall displayed in Revelation 21 is built of jasper and adorned with

12 different jewels (Hillyer, "Wall," *Colin Brown*, 3:948).

STRONG 5038, BAUER 808, MOULTON-MILLIGAN 627, LIDDELL-SCOTT 1767, COLIN BROWN 3:948.

4887. τεκμήριον tekmērion noun

Positive proofs.

1. τεκμηρίοις tekmēriois dat pl neu

1 after his passion by many infallible proofs,.......... Acts 1:3

The word is used in the New Testament only in Acts 1:3. It is a derivative of *tekmar* which means a "goal, mark, sign." The Authorized Version translates the passage "infallible proofs," though a proof does not require the word "infallible" which Vine sees as somewhat superfluous (*Expository Dictionary*, "Proof"). It seems the Scripture is emphasizing the truth of the Resurrection.

Tekmērion is also related to *tekmariō* which means "to show or prove by sure signs." The word indicates something that is surely and plainly known, an indisputable evidence or proof.

STRONG 5039, BAUER 808, MOULTON-MILLIGAN 628, LIDDELL-SCOTT 1768, COLIN BROWN 3:571.

4888. τεκνίον teknion noun

Little child.

CROSS-REFERENCE:
τέκνον teknon (4891)

1. τεκνία teknia nom/acc pl neu

1 Little children, yet a little while I am with you..... John 13:33
1 My little children, of whom I travail in birth......... Gal 4:19
1 My little children, these things write I unto you,..... 1 Jn 2:1
1 I write unto you, little children,........................ 2:12
1 And now, little children, abide in him;................. 2:28
1 Little children, let no man deceive you:................ 3:7
1 My little children, let us not love in word,............. 3:18
1 Ye are of God, little children,......................... 4:4
1 Little children, keep yourselves from idols. Amen....... 5:21

The word *teknion* is used nine times in the New Testament, seven of those occurrences in 1 John. It is a late and somewhat rare usage, and the term is actually a nursery term meaning "little child." It does not occur in the Septuagint or early Christian literature outside the New Testament.

Its usage in the New Testament occurs in the vocative plural. It is used as a special endearing term by both Jesus and the apostles as they address their spiritual children (Oepke, "pais," *Kittel*, 5:637).

STRONG 5040, BAUER 808, MOULTON-MILLIGAN 628, KITTEL 5:636-54, LIDDELL-SCOTT 1768, COLIN BROWN 1:285-86.

4889. τεκνογονέω teknogoneō verb

To bear children, be a child bearer.

CROSS-REFERENCES:
γίνομαι ginomai (1090)
τέκνον teknon (4891)

1. τεκνογονεῖν teknogonein inf pres act

1 that the younger women marry, bear children,...... 1 Tm 5:14

This term is a compound verb which comes from *teknon* (4891), "child," and the base of *ginomai* (1090), "be born." (Greenlee suggests that the verb derives from *tiktō* [4936], "bring forth," and *ginō* [*ginomai*], "become, be born" [see *Greek Morpheme Lexicon*].) It occurs once in the New Testament, in 1 Timothy 5:14, and is not seen in the Septuagint or classical Greek. A similar derivative, *teknogonia* (4890), is seen in 1 Timothy 2:15 and is translated "childbearing."

It is in keeping with Paul's affirmation that childbearing is a unique function of womanhood which should not be viewed as demeaning. Childbearing carries a glory and dignity all its own (Robertson, *Word Pictures in the New Testament*, 4:570f.).

STRONG 5041, BAUER 808, MOULTON-MILLIGAN 628, LIDDELL-SCOTT 1768.

4890. τεκνογονία teknogonia noun

Bearing children, childbearing.

CROSS-REFERENCES:
γίνομαι ginomai (1090)
τέκνον teknon (4891)

1. τεκνογονίας teknogonias gen sing fem

1 Notwithstanding she shall be saved in childbearing, 1 Tm 2:15

The noun *teknogonia* is a compound from *teknon* (4891) and *ginomai* (1090). It occurs once in the New Testament, in 1 Timothy 2:15, and it denotes bearing children or implies duties of motherhood. The context of its usage lends itself to somewhat cloudy interpretation. A common explanation of its usage is that it is a reference to all Christian mothers who will be saved by fulfilling their proper destiny as women. However, the best explanation may be to note references to Eve in 2:13 and her being saved "by the relation in which the woman stood to the Messiah" (see

Genesis 3:15; Vincent, *Word Studies in the New Testament*, 4:226).

Strong 5042, Bauer 808, Moulton-Milligan 628, Liddell-Scott 1768.

4891. τέκνον teknon noun

Child, descendant, posterity.

Cognates:

τεκνίον teknion (4888)
τεκνογονέω teknogoneō (4889)
τεκνογονία teknogonia (4890)
τεκνοτροφέω teknotropheō (4892)
τίκτω tiktō (4936)
φιλότεκνος philoteknos (5225)

Synonyms:

βρέφος brephos (1018)
μικρός mikros (3262)
νήπιος nēpios (3378)
παιδάριον paidarion (3671)
παῖς pais (3679)

אַחֲרִית 'achărîth (321), Posterity, children (Ps 109:13 [108:13], Jer 31:17 [38:17]).

בַּיִת bayith (1041), Household (1 Kgs 17:15).

בֵּן bēn (1158), Son, children (Gn 27:25, Prv 17:6, Jl 1:3).

בַּר bar (1275), Son (Prv 31:2 [24:70]).

בַּר bar (A1280), Children (Dn 6:24—Aramaic).

דּוֹר dôr (1810), Generations (Jos 22:27—Codex Alexandrinus only).

טַף ṭaph (3054), Children, little ones (Dt 2:34, 3:19, Ezr 8:21).

יֶלֶד yeledh (3315), Children (Gn 33:7, Neh 12:43, Is 2:6).

עוֹלֵל 'ôlēl (5985II) Infant (Is 13:16).

צֶאֱצָאִים tse'ětsā'îm (6889), Offspring, descendants (Jb 5:25, 21:8, Is 44:3).

1. **τέκνον teknon** nom/acc sing neu
2. **τέκνου teknou** gen sing neu
3. **τέκνῳ teknō** dat sing neu
4. **τέκνα tekna** nom/acc pl neu
5. **τέκνων teknōn** gen pl neu
6. **τέκνοις teknois** dat pl neu

4 Rachel weeping for her **children**, ... Matt 2:18
4 of these stones to raise up **children** unto Abraham. ... 3:9
6 know how to give good gifts unto your **children**, ... 7:11
1 **Son**, be of good cheer; thy sins be forgiven thee. ... 9:2
1 deliver up the brother ... and the father the **child**: ... 10:21
4 and the **children** shall rise up against their parents, ... 10:21
5 But wisdom is justified of her **children**. ... 11:19
5 It is not meet to take the **children's** bread, ... 15:26
4 and his wife, and **children**, and all that he had, ... 18:25
4 or wife, or **children**, or lands, for my name's sake, ... 19:29
4 But what think ye? A certain man had two **sons**; ... 21:28
1 and he came to the first, and said, **Son**, ... 21:28
4 Moses said, If a man die, having no **children**, ... 22:24
4 often would I have gathered thy **children** together, ... 23:37
4 His blood be on us, and on our **children**. ... 27:25
1 **Son**, thy sins be forgiven thee. ... Mark 2:5
4 Let the **children** first be filled: ... 7:27
5 for it is not meet to take the **children's** bread, ... 7:27
4 answereth again, and saith unto them, **Children**, ... Mark 10:24
4 or father, or mother, or wife, or **children**, ... 10:29
4 and **children**, and lands, with persecutions; ... 10:30
4 leave his wife behind him, and leave no **children**, ... 12:19
1 betray the brother ... and the father the **son**; ... 13:12
4 and **children** shall rise up against their parents, ... 13:12
1 And they had no **child**, ... Elisabeth was barren, ... Luke 1:7
4 to turn the hearts of the fathers to the **children**, ... 1:17
1 and his mother said unto him, **Son**, ... 2:48
4 of these stones to raise up **children** unto Abraham. ... 3:8
5 But wisdom is justified of all her **children**. ... 7:35
6 know how to give good gifts unto your **children**: ... 11:13
4 often would I have gathered thy **children** together, ... 13:34
4 and wife, and **children**, and brethren, and sisters, ... 14:26
1 And he said unto him, **Son**, thou art ever with me, ... 15:31
1 **Son**, remember that thou in thy lifetime receivedst ... 16:25
4 wife, or **children**, for the kingdom of God's sake, ... 18:29
4 thy **children** within thee; and they shall not leave ... 19:44
4 the seven also: and they left no **children**, and died. ... 20:31
4 but weep for yourselves, and for your **children**. ... 23:28
4 to them gave he power to become the **sons** of God, John 1:12
4 If ye were Abraham's **children**, ... 8:39
4 the **children** of God that were scattered abroad. ... 11:52
6 For the promise is unto you, and to your **children**, ... Acts 2:39
2 to his seed after him, when as yet he had no **child**. ... 7:5
6 God hath fulfilled the same unto us their **children**, ... 13:33
6 brought us on our way, with wives and **children**, ... 21:5
4 that they ought not to circumcise their **children**, ... 21:21
4 beareth witness ... that we are the **children** of God: Rom 8:16
4 And if **children**, then heirs; heirs of God, ... 8:17
5 into the glorious liberty of the **children** of God. ... 8:21
4 Neither, ... seed of Abraham, are they all **children**: ... 9:7
4 That is, They which are the **children** of the flesh, ... 9:8
4 of the flesh, these are not the **children** of God: ... 9:8
4 **children** of the promise are counted for the seed. ... 9:8
4 but as my beloved **sons** I warn you. ... 1 Co 4:14
1 I sent unto you Timotheus, who is my beloved **son**, ... 4:17
4 else were your **children** unclean; ... 7:14
6 I speak as unto my **children**, be ye also enlarged. ... 2 Co 6:13
4 the **children** ought not to lay up for the parents, ... 12:14
6 but the parents for the **children**. ... 12:14
5 this Agar ... and is in bondage with her **children**. ... Gal 4:25
4 more **children** than she which hath an husband. ... 4:27
4 we, ... as Isaac was, are the **children** of promise. ... 4:28
4 not **children** of the bondwoman, but of the free. ... 4:31
4 and were by nature the **children** of wrath, ... Eph 2:3
4 Be ye therefore followers of God, as dear **children**; ... 5:1
4 light in the Lord: walk as **children** of light: ... 5:8
4 **Children**, obey your parents in the Lord: ... 6:1
4 ye fathers, provoke not your **children** to wrath: ... 6:4
4 and harmless, the **sons** of God, without rebuke, ... Phlp 2:15
1 the proof of him, that, as **a son** with the father, ... 2:22
4 **Children**, obey your parents in all things: ... Col 3:20
4 Fathers, provoke not your **children** to anger, ... 3:21
4 even as a nurse cherisheth her **children**: ... 1 Th 2:7
4 how we exhorted ... as a father doth his **children**, ... 2:11
3 Unto Timothy, my own **son** in the faith: ... 1 Tm 1:2
1 This charge I commit unto thee, **son** Timothy, ... 1:18
4 having his **children** in subjection with all gravity; ... 3:4
5 ruling their **children** and their own houses well. ... 3:12
4 But if any widow have **children** or nephews, ... 5:4
3 To Timothy, my dearly beloved **son**: Grace, ... 2 Tm 1:2
1 Thou therefore, my **son**, be strong in the grace ... 2:1
3 To Titus, mine own **son** after the common faith: ... Tit 1:4
4 faithful **children** not accused of riot or unruly. ... 1:6
2 I beseech thee for my **son** Onesimus, ... Phlm 1:10
4 As obedient **children**, ... 1 Pt 1:14
4 whose **daughters** ye are, as long as ye do well, ... 3:6
4 exercised with covetous practices; cursed **children**: ... 2 Pt 2:14
4 that we should be called the **sons** of God: ... 1 Jn 3:1
4 Beloved, now are we the **sons** of God, ... 3:2
4 In this the **children** of God are manifest, ... 3:10
4 of God are manifest, and the **children** of the devil: ... 3:10
4 By this we know that we love the **children** of God, ... 5:2
6 The elder unto the elect lady and her **children**, ... 2 Jn 1:1
5 that I found of thy **children** walking in truth, ... 1:4
4 The **children** of thy elect sister greet thee. Amen. ... 1:13

4 than to hear that my children walk in truth..........3 Jn 1:4
4 And I will kill her children with death;..............Rev 2:23
1 for to devour her child as soon as it was born......... 12:4
1 child was caught up unto God, and to his throne....... 12:5

Classical Greek

Teknon (often plural *tekna*) denotes a "child" and connotes particularly the child-parent relationship. From the earliest days, in the days of the city-state's glory, children, especially sons, were highly prized. Malformed children or handicapped offspring were often abandoned, particularly in Sparta. As the emphasis upon individualism flourished in Greek society the desire for children diminished. At the same time a more sentimental attitude toward children developed.

Septuagint Usage

Teknon translates no less than 11 Hebrew terms in the Septuagint including *yeledh* and *ṯaph*, "infant," as well as *bar* and *bēn*, "son." *Teknon* could also refer to descendants of later generations. Metaphorically *teknon* was an intimate form of address used often of the relationship between a student and a teacher.

Old Testament Background

Children are shown as important in the Old Testament. They perpetuate the family, the tribe, and the nation (Deuteronomy 25:6; Ruth 4:11). Consequently, Israelites regarded childbearing as a duty (Genesis 1:28)—the more the better. It was a great blessing to see one's descendants of various generations (Genesis 50:23; Proverbs 17:6). Childbearing acquires religious connotations because God "blessed" people with children (cf. the creation account, Genesis 1:28). Children or offspring were also integral to God's covenant with Abraham (Genesis 12:2,7; 13:16; 22:17). At the giving of the covenant (Genesis 17:5) Abraham's original name, Abram, was changed to Abraham which means the "father of many."

Children are a gift from God (Psalm 127:3), a reward, an expression of His delight, and a blessing of the covenant (Psalms 113:9; 128:3,4; cf. Ecclesiastes 6:3). Barrenness, the inability to have children, therefore, was regarded as a sign of God's disfavor (Job 18:19,21) and punishment (Leviticus 20:20; Isaiah 47:9; Jeremiah 15:7). Therefore, the desire for children was strong (Genesis 30:1).

If a married woman continued to be childless she might allow her maid to lie with her husband in hopes of having a child (Genesis 16:1,2; 30:1,3,9). The child of the maid was considered the child of the wife. Moreover, if a brother died without having children it was the duty of another brother to marry the widow and give her children on behalf of his brother. The firstborn of this union was regarded as the son of the deceased (Deuteronomy 25:5; cf. Matthew 22:24f.). If the nearest brother could not fulfill this obligation the next closest relative was to take his place (Ruth 4:4,5). This practice is known as "levirate" marriage.

In ancient times children were named immediately after their birth (Genesis 19:37,38). Later the male children were named on the day of their circumcision, i.e., the eighth day (Luke 1:59; 2:21). Either the mother (Genesis 19:37,38) or the father (Genesis 4:26; Luke 1:62,63) named the child. The name might echo the events surrounding the birth of the child (Exodus 2:10; 1 Samuel 1:20), or it might indicate some kind of physical trait or a psychological tendency of an infant (Genesis 25:25,26). The name might also reflect events or conditions at the time of the infant's birth (1 Samuel 4:21; Isaiah 7:3; 8:3; cf. Exodus 2:10). Children were named after relatives (cf. Luke 1:59), and names often captured the desires, hopes, and wishes of the parents for the child (Genesis 4:25; 29:32-35; 30:24). Under certain circumstances the Lord determined the name of the child, either before birth (1 Kings 13:2; Matthew 1:21; Luke 1:13) or after (Isaiah 8:3; Hosea 1:6-9).

Children were dedicated to God before they were born on some occasions (1 Samuel 1:11; Judges 13:7). The firstborn belonged to God (Exodus 13:2) and thus had to be redeemed (Exodus 34:19,20; Numbers 3:44f.).

Both the father and mother shared in the rearing and educating of the child (Proverbs 1:8; 6:20; cf. 2 Timothy 1:5; 3:15). As long as the child was an infant the mother cared for it, and daughters were under her supervision until they were married. The rearing and educating of boys was the father's responsibility from the time the child was five. Those families who could afford it left the education of the child in the hands of special tutors (2 Kings 10:1; 1 Chronicles 27:32; cf. Galatians 4:1f.). Most education took place in the home; schools appeared on the scene relatively late (cf. Oepke, "pais," *Kittel*, 5:647f.).

The Talmud indicates that schools for children began around the year 1000 B.C. (ibid.). By the time of Jesus they were fairly common. Children sat on the floor at the feet of the teacher (cf. Acts 22:3). Lessons mainly focused upon reading and writing. The skill of writing developed rather early in Israel's history (Isaiah 8:1; 10:19). The young boy also learned a trade, usually his father's (cf. Mark 6:3). The ordinances, commandments, teachings, and rituals of the Law became part of the psychological makeup of children at a very early age (Deuteronomy 4:8,9; 6:7; 32:46). For example, Timothy knew the Holy Scriptures from his early childhood (2 Timothy 3:15).

Children were totally under the authority and control of their parents. Respect and obedience were mandates (Exodus 20:12; Leviticus 19:3). Disobedience against one's parents resulted in severe punishment (Deuteronomy 21:18-21; 27:16). On the other hand, the Law protected children against abuse and mistreatment by their parents (Numbers 30:4,5; Deuteronomy 21:15-17).

New Testament Usage

Teknon occurs in the New Testament about 100 times. As in the Old Testament, children are discussed frequently. Jesus' love for children is unmistakable; He gave His time, concern, and blessing freely to them (Mark 10:13f.). He defended them (Mark 7:27) and healed them (9:27). The kingdom of heaven belongs to them, Jesus said (Matthew 19:13f.). As a teacher Jesus frequently used children to illustrate a point (Matthew 18:1f.; 11:16f.).

From the basis of the fourth commandment the New Testament stresses the responsibility of children to obey their parents (Ephesians 6:1-3; Colossians 3:20). Jesus is their model in this regard (Luke 2:51; cf. John 19:26,27). One earmark of paganism's decline, which will be repeated in the falling away of the last days, is disobedience to parents (Romans 1:30; 2 Timothy 3:2).

The New Testament likewise emphasizes the responsibilities of parents toward their children (2 Corinthians 12:14; Ephesians 6:4). Parents, especially church leaders (1 Timothy 3:4,5), are entrusted with the responsibility to educate their children. A proper relationship with children is a model for the pastor's relationship with his congregation (1 Thessalonians 2:7,11).

Much of Christian teaching employs the example of children to make its point. Jesus presented a child's dependency upon others and its humility and vulnerability as an example of qualities for entering the kingdom of God (Matthew 18:1f.). However, a child's immaturity, helplessness, and lack of understanding represent obstacles to Christian development and maturity (1 Corinthians 3:1f.; 14:20; Ephesians 4:13f.; Hebrews 5:11f.). The immaturity of childhood contrasts the maturity of adulthood in a representation of our present limitations in contrast to our future perfection (1 Corinthians 13:11,12).

Teknon in the New Testament frequently draws upon its Hebrew heritage for meaning (cf. Braumann, "Child," *Colin Brown*, 1:286). In a religious sense it depicts the believer's relationship to God the Father (John 1:12; 1 John 3:1) and with Christ (Mark 10:24; John 13:33; 21:5). Paul called those he had led to faith his "children" (Galatians 4:19; 1 Timothy 1:2; Philemon 10). John understood the term in the same way (1 John 2:1,28; 4:4; 5:21). Figuratively, *teknon* is concerned with the children of God (John 1:12); the children of light (Ephesians 5:8); obedient children (1 Peter 1:14); the children of promise (Romans 9:8; Galatians 4:28). In another sense the term may be used figuratively of the devil's children (1 John 3:10) or the children of wrath (Ephesians 2:3).

The diminutive form *teknion* (4888), "little child," is used only figuratively in the New Testament where it appears many times in John's first epistle. Jesus used it only once (John 13:33), as did Paul (Galatians 4:19).

Strong 5043, Bauer 808, Moulton-Milligan 628, Kittel 5:636-54, Liddell-Scott 1768, Colin Brown 1:284-87.

4892. τεκνοτροφέω

teknotropheō verb

To rear young, to bring up children.

Cross-References:

τέκνον teknon (4891)
τρέφω trephō (4982)

1. ἐτεκνοτρόφησεν eteknotrophēsen
3sing indic aor act

1 **if she have brought up children,** .... **1 Tm 5:10**

This is a compound verb from *teknon* (4891), "child," and *tropheō*, "to serve as a wet nurse." It is not used in the Septuagint and is very rare in classical Greek. It is used once in the New Testament, in 1 Timothy 5:10, when referring to the widow eligible to be put on the roll. Here the term does not denote childbirth so much as the virtuous bringing up of children. These could be the widow's own children or those entrusted to her charge (Nicholl, *The Expositor's New Testament*, 4:131).

The meaning of *teknotropheō* includes an expressed virtue that goes beyond one's own home. This would be especially true of church widows who later had charge of orphans under the church's care (Luck, *International Critical Commentary, 1 Timothy*, p.60).

STRONG 5044, BAUER 808-9, MOULTON-MILLIGAN 628, LIDDELL-SCOTT 1768.

4893. τέκτων tektōn noun

Craftsman, carpenter.

COGNATES:

ἀρχιτέκτων architektōn (748)
τεχνίτης technitēs (4927)
τέχνη technē (4926)

חָרַשׁ chārash (2896), Metalworker, carpenter (1 Kgs 7:14, Is 44:13); devise (Prv 14:22).

חָרָשׁ chārāsh (2900), Carpenter, craftsman (2 Sm 5:11, 1 Chr 4:14, Hos 8:6).

עָשָׂה 'āsâh (6449), Do, make; worker (Sir 38:27).

1. **τέκτων tektōn** nom sing masc
2. **τέκτονος tektonos** gen sing masc

2 Is not this the carpenter's son?....................Matt 13:55
1 Is not this the carpenter, the son of Mary,..........Mark 6:3

Classical Greek and Septuagint Usage

This noun is used to denote any craftsman. In classical Greek *tektōn* meant a craftsman in wood, stone, or metal. In the Septuagint the word translates *chārāsh* which refers to craftsmen in general. The Jews, unlike the Greeks and Romans, held a high regard for manual labor and a deep respect for those who worked skillfully.

New Testament Usage

This term appears only in the identification of Jesus by the people of Nazareth (Matthew 13:55; Mark 6:3). Though "carpenter" is the most common usage, it could also mean that Jesus and Joseph were both carpenters and masons (Packer, "Carpenter," *Colin Brown*, 1:279).

Tektōn is a descriptive term which gives us one of the few glimpses into a central part of Jesus' life from childhood to manhood (Vincent, *Word Studies in the New Testament*, 1:192).

STRONG 5045, BAUER 809, MOULTON-MILLIGAN 628-29, LIDDELL-SCOTT 1769, COLIN BROWN 1:279.

4894. τέλειος teleios adj

Complete, perfect, whole; full-grown, mature, adult.

CROSS-REFERENCE:

τέλος telos (4904)

שָׁלוֹם shālôm (8361), Whole (Jer 13:19).

שֶׁלֶם shelem (8399), Peace offering (Jgs 20:26).

שָׁלֵם shālēm (8400), Wholly (1 Kgs 8:61, 15:3, 1 Chr 28:9).

תַּכְלִית takhlîth (8832), Something complete (Ps 139:22 [138:22]).

תָּם tām (8865), Perfect one (S/S 5:2, 6:9 [6:8]).

תָּמִים tāmîm (8879), Unblemished, blameless (Ex 12:5, Dt 18:13, 2 Sm 22:26).

תֻּמִּים tummîm (8880), Thummin (Ezr 2:63).

1. **τέλειον teleion** nom/acc sing masc/neu
2. **τέλειος teleios** nom sing masc
3. **τέλειοι teleioi** nom pl masc
4. **τελείων teleiōn** gen pl masc
5. **τελείοις teleiois** dat pl masc
6. **τελεία teleia** nom sing fem
7. **τελειοτέρας teleioteras** comp gen sing fem

3 Be ye therefore perfect, even as your Father ... is... Matt 5:48
2 even as your Father which is in heaven is perfect........ 5:48
2 If thou wilt be perfect, go and sell that thou hast,..... 19:21
1 that good, and acceptable, and perfect, will of God. Rom 12:2
5 we speak wisdom among them that are perfect:..... 1 Co 2:6
1 But when that which is perfect is come,............... 13:10
3 but in understanding be men.......................... 14:20
1 unto a perfect man,................................. Eph 4:13
3 Let us therefore, as many as be perfect,.............Phlp 3:15
1 we may present every man perfect in Christ Jesus:....Col 1:28
3 that ye may stand perfect and complete................ 4:12
4 strong meat belongeth to them that are of full age,...Heb 5:14
7 by a greater and more perfect tabernacle,............... 9:11
1 But let patience have her perfect work,.............. Jas 1:4
3 ye may be perfect and entire, wanting nothing.......... 1:4
1 good gift and every perfect gift is from above,.......... 1:17
1 But whoso looketh into the perfect law of liberty,....... 1:25
2 offend not in word, the same is a perfect man,.......... 3:2
6 but perfect love casteth out fear:................... 1 Jn 4:18

Classical Greek

Teleios (also in the form *teleos*) is a highly complex and versatile adjective in classical Greek. Essentially the ideas behind the term include: "mature, perfect, full-grown, ripe, complete," and these can refer to quality, quantity, development, skill, extent, and so on. Thus the notion of "whole, complete" is characteristic of *teleios* in whatever it modifies, from "full-grown" animals to a "perfect" (of quality) sacrifice, i.e., one that is "without blemish" (see *Liddell-Scott*; cf. Delling, "teleios," *Kittel*, 8:67-78 for a fuller discussion).

Teleios was a significant term in Greek philosophical and ethical discussions. In simplified terms "perfection" is variously expressed as "attainment of purpose," an "acquisition of wisdom or insight," and the "ability to make the correct ethical or moral choices" (however arbitrary these might be). "Perfection" thus became particularly defined or judged by human standards. The Hellenistic Jew Philo attempted to merge the more Hebraic understanding—that *teleios* particularly relates to God—with the Greek, humanistic concept (Delling, ibid., 8:70-72).

Septuagint Usage

Teleios appears 16 times in the Septuagint, with a Hebrew parallel, and twice in apocryphal texts (Wisdom 9:6; Sirach 44:17). Two Hebrew terms (or their cognates) usually stand behind it: *shelem* and *tāmîm*. The basic idea is "whole, complete, unblemished" (of sacrifices, e.g., Exodus 12:5; cf. Judges 20:26). A religious nuance appears in Ezra 2:63 where *hoi teleios* (substantive use, "the perfect ones/things") apparently refers to Urim and Thummim, the tangible means of discerning God's will that was part of the high priest's breastplate (cf. Exodus 28:30; Leviticus 8:8; Numbers 27:21).

A frequent union of *teleios* with "heart," *kardia* (2559), in speaking of an attitude before God, suggests the relational dimension of *teleios* intrinsic in Hebrew thought (e.g., 1 Kings 8:61; 11:4; 15:3 [LXX 3 Kings 8:61; 11:4; 15:3]). It is virtually synonymous with "righteous" (*diakios* [1335B]) on at least one occasion. Noah is a "righteous" (*diakios*) and "blameless" (NIV, *teleios*) man (Genesis 6:9; cf. Sirach 44:17 which uses the same terminology in its description of Noah).

New Testament Usage

Teleios occurs 19 times in the Greek New Testament, being found in various books. Of the Gospels only Matthew used it (5:48; 19:21), and he did so drawing clearly upon the Old Testament understanding that *teleios* is a comparative adjective that presents God as the absolute model of perfection. Only through Jesus Christ can we as imperfect beings have a relationship with a perfect God.

Jesus' command, "Be ye therefore perfect, even as your Father which is in heaven is perfect" (Matthew 5:48), can be correctly interpreted only in light of this. Jesus was not commanding moral and ethical "perfection" in the Greek sense of "flawless behavior." Rather, He was inviting men and women to share a relationship with the living God through belief in Him. Obviously this "perfection" approximates "righteousness," another key concept in Matthew. Furthermore, it does demand radical behavior, but it is behavior based upon love for God rather than a belief in one's ability to achieve "perfection" (cf. Matthew 19:21).

The idea of "wholeness, completeness" is always inherent in *teleios*. Whether it is one's mature spiritual character (1 Corinthians 2:6; cf. 14:20; Ephesians 4:13; Philippians 3:15; Hebrews 5:14; James 1:4) or God's "perfect" (i.e., "complete, ultimate") will (Romans 12:2), "totality" is in view.

Mature Christian behavior is the goal of teaching and exhortation (Colossians 1:28f.; 4:12). Moreover, it is consistently a relational quality rather than a positional state achieved by being sinless or faultless. Just as sin is a broken relationship with God and not simply specific acts, so too, *teleios* is relational. With love as the premise of Christian life-style rather than an ethic, John wrote: "*Perfect* love drives out fear" (1 John 4:18, NIV).

The "more perfect" (NIV, *teleiotepas*) tabernacle of Hebrews 9:11 can be misleading unless it is kept in mind that it was in the thematic interest of the writer of Hebrews to show that Christ "fulfills, completes, consummates" the Old Testament covenant.

Strong 5046, Bauer 809, Moulton-Milligan 629, Kittel 8:67-78, Liddell-Scott 1769-70, Colin Brown 2:59-65.

4895. τελειότης teleiotēs noun

Perfection, perfectness.

Cognate:
τέλος telos (4904)

Synonym:
κατάρτισις katartisis (2646)

תֻּמָּה tummāh (8870), Integrity (Prv 11:3—Codex Alexandrinus only).

תָּמִים tāmîm (8879), Integrity (Jgs 9:16,19).

1. τελειότητος teleiotētos gen sing fem
2. τελειότητα teleiotēta acc sing fem

1 put on charity, which is the bond of perfectness.......Col 3:14
2 let us go on unto perfection;.........................Heb 6:1

Classical Greek and Septuagint Usage

A word denoting a state of being, *teleiotēs* connotes an end or actual accomplishment of an end in view. Septuagintal usages denote "wholeness" or "completeness." (See Judges 9:16,19; Proverbs 11:3; Wisdom of Solomon 6:15; 12:17; Jeremiah 2:2.)

New Testament Usage

Teleiotēs appears twice in the New Testament. The Colossians 3:14 usage of the word may be translated "perfectedness" and emphasizes the oneness of the community which unites itself into a whole. In the Hebrews 6:1 usage it means "completion" and denotes the "highest stage" of Christian teaching. In the strictest sense, only God has true *teleiotēs* (Delling, "teleiotēs," *Kittel*, 8:78f.).

Strong 5047, Bauer 809, Moulton-Milligan 629, Kittel 8:86-87, Liddell-Scott 1770, Colin Brown 2:59,61.

4896. τελειόω teleioō verb

Make perfect, complete, finish, accomplish; bring to completion, perfect.

Cognate:

τέλος telos (4904)

Synonyms:

ἀναπληρόω anaplēroō (376)
ἀνταναπληρόω antanaplēroō (463)
ἀποτελέω apoteleō (652)
διανύω dianuō (1268)
ἐκπληρόω ekplēroō (1590)
ἐκτελέω ekteleō (1602)
ἐξαρτίζω exartizō (1806)
ἐπιτελέω epiteleō (1989)
ἐργάζομαι ergazomai (2021)
καταρτίζω katartizō (2645)
κατεργάζομαι katergazomai (2686)
κατεστρώννυμι katestrōnnumi (2689)
πληρόω plēroō (3997)
πράσσω prassō (4097)
συντελέω sunteleō (4783)
τελέω teleō (4903)

כָּלַל kālal (3754), Make perfect (Ez 27:11).

מָלֵא mālē' (4527), Piel: ordain (Ex 29:9, Nm 3:3); be fulfilled (Lv 8:33).

עָשָׂה 'āsâh (6449), Do, make; niphal: be accomplished (Neh 6:16).

תָּמַם tāmam (8882), Qal: be all gone (1 Kgs 14:10—Codex Alexandrinus only); hithpael: show oneself blameless (2 Sm 22:26).

1. **ἐτελείωσα eteleiōsa** 1sing indic aor act
2. **ἐτελείωσεν eteleiōsen** 3sing indic aor act
3. **τελειώσω teleiōsō** 1sing subj aor act
4. **τελειωσάντων teleiōsantōn** gen pl masc part aor act
5. **τελειῶσαι teleiōsai** inf aor act
6. **τετελείωκεν teteleiōken** 3sing indic perf act
7. **τελειοῦμαι teleioumai** 1sing indic pres mid
8. **τελειοῦται teleioutai** 3sing indic pres mid
9. **ἐτελειώθη eteleiōthē** 3sing indic aor pass
10. **τελειωθῇ teleiōthē** 3sing subj aor pass
11. **τελειωθῶσιν teleiōthōsin** 3pl subj aor pass
12. **τελειωθείς teleiōtheis** nom sing masc part aor pass
13. **τετελείωμαι teteleiōmai** 1sing indic perf mid
14. **τετελείωται teteleiōtai** 3sing indic perf mid
15. **τετελειωμένον teteleiōmenon** acc sing masc part perf mid
16. **τετελειωμένοι teteleiōmenoi** nom pl masc part perf mid
17. **τετελειωμένων teteleiōmenōn** gen pl masc part perf mid
18. **τετελειωμένη teteleiōmenē** nom sing fem part perf mid
19. **τελειώσας teleiōsas** nom sing masc part aor act

4 And when they **had fulfilled** the days, ... Luke 2:43
7 and the third day I **shall be perfected**. 13:32
3 to do the will of him ... and to **finish** his work. .... John 4:34
3 works which the Father hath given me to **finish**, ... 5:36
1 I **have finished** the work which thou gavest me 17:4
16 that they may be **made perfect** in one; 17:23
10 that the scripture **might be fulfilled**, saith, I thirst. 19:28
5 so that I **might finish** my course with joy, ... Acts 20:24
8 for my strength **is made perfect** in weakness. ...... 2 Co 12:9
13 already attained, either **were** already **perfect**: .... Phlp 3:12
5 to **make** the captain of their salvation **perfect** .... Heb 2:10
12 And being **made perfect**, he became the author 5:9
2 For the law made nothing **perfect**, ... 7:19
15 maketh the Son, who **is consecrated** for evermore. 7:28
5 could not make him that did the service **perfect**, ... 9:9
5 make the comers thereunto **perfect**. 10:1
6 he **hath perfected** for ever them that are sanctified. ... 10:14
11 that they without us **should** not **be made perfect**. 11:40
17 and to the spirits of just men **made perfect**, ... 12:23
9 and by works **was** faith **made perfect**? .... Jas 2:22
14 in him verily is the love of God **perfected**: .... 1 Jn 2:5
18 God dwelleth in us, and his love is **perfected** in us. 4:12
14 Herein is our love **made perfect**, ... 4:17
14 He that feareth is not **made perfect** in love. 4:18

Classical Greek

In classical usage the verb *teleioō* is used most often in its generic sense of "finish, complete," or "bring to completion." It is found in common use from Herodotus onward. In some texts the idea of completion means to be successful in a task such as a battle or war. In other texts the word is used biologically with the meaning to allow fruit to ripen to maturity.

During the Hellenistic period this verb was used in legal papyri to indicate a legal document had been executed, i.e., completed. In the mystery religions one who had completed the initiatory rites was complete or perfect. Philo also used it to indicate moral completeness or perfection.

Septuagint Usage

Some Septuagintal usage connotes perfection as in Ezekiel 27:11 where his lament for Tyre mentions that the Gentiles brought the beauty of Tyre to completeness or perfection. Elsewhere this verb is used in Exodus and Leviticus in the expression "to complete/fill the hands" and means to be pure enough/perfect so that one might become or act as a priest (cf. Exodus 29:9,29, etc.). This may be the background for the concept "kingdom of priests" used in the New Testament to refer to the perfection of Christians.

New Testament Usage

This verb is used 24 times in the New Testament; 18 of the 24 occurrences are in Hebrews and the Johannine literature. There are generic references as in Acts 20:24 where Paul mentioned finishing his course. The same expression occurs in 2 Timothy 4:6, but the verb for "finish" is *teleō* (4903), a synonym in this case. Luke 2:43 refers to the fulfilling of Scripture, and James 2:22 refers to faith as being completed by works.

Most of the New Testament references are to the completion of the work of salvation either by Jesus or in the Christian. In John 4:34 Jesus said His "meat" was to accomplish the will of God. In Hebrews 5:9 Jesus is referred to as having been made complete and thus able to be the cause of eternal salvation to the obedient ones. In Hebrews 9:9 the idea of completion as perfection is seen. The old covenant gifts and sacrifices were not able to eliminate the faults in the conscience of the worshiper, but the new covenant could perfect the one approaching God. In Hebrews the process of salvation through Christ is seen in sacrificial terms in the negative sense. In Hebrews 7:19; 9:9; and 10:1 the Law's sacrifices cannot perfect the worshiper, but Christ's single offering completes/perfects for all time. Thus, completion/perfection is not accomplished by the Christian but is accomplished for him by Christ. "Perfect" is therefore an appropriate description of the Christian only when one understands that Christ is the cause of perfection (cf. Hebrews 10:14).

First John has four occurrences of the verb—all connected with the love of God and love by the Christian. If we obey God's Word this is a demonstration that God's love is completed in us (2:5). As John wrote in 4:12, if we love one another it is a demonstration that God's love is completed in us. Another sign that God's love is completed in us is our lack of fear of judgment; since God's love is perfected in us, we can live confidently. Note again that the perfection of love is accomplished by God and not by our own effort. That love is most demonstrably seen in our obedience to God's Word and in our love for one another.

Strong 5048, Bauer 809-10, Moulton-Milligan 629, Kittel 8:79-84, Liddell-Scott 1770, Colin Brown 2:59-66.

4896B. τελείως teleiōs adv

To the end, perfectly, fully.

Cross-Reference:

τέλος telos (4904)

1. τελείως teleiōs

1 be sober, and hope to the end for the grace......... 1 Pt 1:13

This term is an adverb related to *teleios*, carrying with it the implication of not wavering. It appears only once in the New Testament, in 1 Peter 1:13. Though it is translated "hope *to the end*," a better translation might be "fix your hope *completely*," with the idea of unreservedly, or "hope with a *perfect* hope" (Bigg, *International Critical Commentary, 1 Peter*, p.112).

The injunction to be sober in this context is in keeping with Peter's directive to be steadfast in a sea of wild and disorderly movement. It is with this disciplined mindset that a person who has hope because of Christ's resurrection should now persevere in assurance of the hope of Christ's return. The context and the verse itself carry definite eschatological overtones.

Strong 5049, Bauer 810, Moulton-Milligan 629, Liddell-Scott 1770.

4897. τελείωσις teleiōsis noun

Fulfillment, perfection.

Cross-Reference:

τέλος telos (4904)

מִלֻּאִים millu'îm (4533), Ordination, consecration (Ex 29:26f., Lv 8:31).

1. τελείωσις teleiōsis nom sing fem

1 for there shall be a performance of those things..... Luke 1:45
1 If ... perfection were by the Levitical priesthood,..... Heb 7:11

Classical Greek and Septuagint Usage

In classical Greek the word *teleiōsis* carries the idea of actualization or execution of a resolve or an oath. This is the way Aristotle and Philo used the term. Thayer notes other usages in classical Greek that have the connotation of conclusion or the processes of maturation (*Greek-English Lexicon*). In the Septuagint the word is used in other ways including execution of a plan or completion of a plan (e.g., Exodus 29:22; cf. Delling, "teleiōsis," *Kittel*, 8:84).

New Testament Usage

The usage of the word in Luke 1:45 suggests that Mary was blessed because the things she hoped for would certainly come to pass; through an angel God said they would. The emphasis here is on the substance of her faith that was so crucial to the fulfillment of the promise given to her (Nicholl, *Expositor's New Testament*, 1:446).

Hebrews is the book where the greatest frequency of *teleios* and its derivatives occur. Hebrews 7:11 is perhaps a technical use of the term common in the Septuagint (Delling, "teleiōsis," *Kittel*, 8:85). The context indicates that priests of the Levitical line could not reach the state of a "perfection" by means of the Law. The inference is that an institution (i.e., priesthood) can only bring perfection when it carries out the purpose for which it was developed and reaps a result that is in accordance with its foundational ideas. If there is a failure in the priestly service the whole system falls apart. It is therefore inappropriate to give a law without providing at the same time the possibility that the law can be fulfilled. Thus, in Christ, as the Melchizedek-Priest, the ideal of a priesthood is presented, and there is the establishment of a perfect fellowship between God and the worshiper (Vincent, *Word Studies in the New Testament*, 4:459f.).

STRONG 5050, BAUER 810, MOULTON-MILLIGAN 629, KITTEL 8:84-86, LIDDELL-SCOTT 1770, COLIN BROWN 2:59,61,63-64.

4898. τελείως teleiōs

See word study at number 4896B.

4899. τελειωτής teleiōtēs noun

Finisher, accomplisher.

CROSS-REFERENCE:
τέλος telos (4904)

1. **τελειωτήν teleiōtēn** acc sing masc

1 **Jesus the author and finisher of our faith;** .... **Heb 12:2**

This is one of a great number of words formed from the basic root word *telos* (4904), "goal, end," or "purpose," and means "finisher, accomplisher" (*Liddell-Scott*). It is used once in the New Testament, in Hebrews 12:2. The writer described Christ in this text as both "the author and *finisher* (or consummator) of our faith." It is thus similar to another expression from both the Old and New Testaments where Jesus is described as the alpha (beginning) and the omega (end; cf. Isaiah 44:6; 48:12; Revelation 2:8,11; 22:13).

STRONG 5051, BAUER 810, KITTEL 8:86-87, LIDDELL-SCOTT 1770, COLIN BROWN 2:59,61.

4900. τελεσφορέω telesphoreō verb

Bring fruit to completion or maturity.

CROSS-REFERENCES:
τελέω teleō (4903)
φέρω pherō (5179)

1. **τελεσφοροῦσιν telesphorousin** 3pl indic pres act

1 **among thorns ... and bring no fruit to perfection.** .... **Luke 8:14**

This word is a combination of *telos* (4904), "goal, end," and *pherō* (5179), "to bear, carry." This word was often used in early Greek literature of fruits maturing and of pregnant women and animals bringing their young to maturity (cf. *Liddell-Scott*).

Telesphoreō is used only once in the New Testament, in Luke 8:14. Here Luke recorded the Parable of the Sower and described the seed which fell among thorns; it was choked out and was not brought to maturity.

STRONG 5052, BAUER 810, MOULTON-MILLIGAN 629, LIDDELL-SCOTT 1770-71.

4901. τελευτάω teleutaō verb

Bring to pass, finish, die.

COGNATES:
τελευτή teleutē (4902)
τελέω teleō (4903)

SYNONYMS:
ἀποθνήσκω apothnēskō (594)
θνήσκω thnēskō (2325)

גָּוַע gāwaʿ (1510), Perish (Gn 6:17, Jb 34:15).

מוּת mûth (4322), Qal: die (Ex 2:23, 2 Chr 24:15, Am 7:11): hophal: be put to death (Ex 19:12, 35:2, Lv 24:16).

נָפַל nāphal (5489), Fall (Ez 6:12—Codex Alexandrinus only).

1. **τελευτᾷ teleuta** 3sing indic pres act
2. **τελευτάτω teleutatō** 3sing impr pres act
3. **τελευτῶν teleutōn** nom sing masc part pres act
4. **τελευτᾶν teleutan** inf pres act
5. **ἐτελεύτησεν eteleutēsen** 3sing indic aor act
6. **τελευτήσαντος teleutēsantos** gen sing masc part aor act
7. **τετελευτηκότος teteleutēkotos** gen sing masc/neu part perf act

6 But when Herod **was dead**, ... dream to Joseph ...... **Matt 2:19**
5 My daughter is even now **dead**: **9:18**
2 curseth father or mother, **let him die** the death. **15:4**
5 married a wife, **deceased**, and, having no issue, ... **22:25**
2 curseth father or mother, **let him die** the death: ..... **Mark 7:10**
1 Where their worm **dieth** not, ... **9:44**
1 Where their worm **dieth** not, ... **9:46**
1 Where their worm **dieth** not, ... **9:48**
4 who was dear unto him, was sick, and ready **to die**. **Luke 7:2**
7 Martha, the sister of the **deceased**, (NASB) .... **John 11:39**
5 patriarch David, that he is both **dead** and buried, ... **Acts 2:29**
5 So Jacob went down into Egypt, and **died**, ... **7:15**
3 By faith Joseph, when he **died**, made mention ...... **Heb 11:22**

Classical Greek and Septuagint Usage
This verb is related to the term *telos* (4904), "end," and can be found in classical Greek from the Eighth Century B.C. meaning "bring to pass, accomplish, fulfill, finish" (cf. *Liddell-Scott*). It was used in a wide variety of ways, especially in reference to "fulfilling" an oath or "finishing" life (i.e., "dying"; ibid.). In the Septuagint it almost always translates the Hebrew term *mûth*, meaning "die" or "end one's life," especially in reference to physical death.

New Testament Usage
The word *teleutaō* occurs 11 times in the New Testament. It appears four times in Matthew; two times in Mark; once each in Luke, some texts of John, and Hebrews; and twice in Acts. Of these occurrences, three are quotations from the Old Testament (Matthew 15:4; Mark 7:10; 9:48). Of greatest note are the occurrences in Matthew 9:18 and John 11:39. Both of these usages refer to persons who are raised from the dead by Jesus. The word usage here carries with it the certainty of the death of the persons in question, i.e., Lazarus and Jairus' daughter.

The word is also used to describe the death of Herod in Matthew 2:19. It refers to the deaths of David, Jacob, and Joseph in Acts 2:29; 7:15; and Hebrews 11:22. It is also used in the story of brothers who died, recorded in Matthew 22:25. The usage in Mark 9:48 is somewhat different in that it refers to the powerful impact of self-destructive thought on a person's conscience. Some texts duplicate Mark 9:48 in 9:44 and 46.

Strong 5053, Bauer 810, Moulton-Milligan 629-30, Liddell-Scott 1771, Colin Brown 1:429-30; 2:59.

4902. τελευτή teleutē noun

Death, end.

Cross-Reference:

τελευτάω teleutaō (4901)

אַחֲרִית 'achărîth (321), End; future (Prv 24:14).

מוּת mûth (4322), Die; death (Jos 1:1, Jgs 1:1, 2 Chr 24:17).

מָוֶת māweth (4323), Death (Gn 27:2, 1 Chr 22:5, 2 Chr 26:21).

1. τελευτῆς teleutēs gen sing fem

1 And was there until the death of Herod:............Matt 2:15

The ordinary Greek word for death is *thanatos* (2265). *Teleutē* is more of a figure of speech for death, taken from the root *teleō* (4903), "to end," and literally meaning "the end." *Teleutē* is common in classical Greek and is used in the Septuagint to translate *mûth*, the Hebrew word for death.

The only occurrence of this word in the New Testament is in Matthew 2:15. Here Matthew's record says Jesus stayed in Egypt until the end (death) of Herod.

Strong 5054, Bauer 810, Moulton-Milligan 630, Liddell-Scott 1771, Colin Brown 2:59.

4903. τελέω teleō verb

To complete, finish, perform.

Cognates:

ἀποτελέω apoteleō (652)
διατελέω diateleō (1294)
ἐκτελέω ekteleō (1602)
ἐπιτελέω epiteleō (1989)
λυσιτελέω lusiteleō (3053)
ὁλοτελής holotelēs (3514)
πολυτελής polutelēs (4045)
συντέλεια sunteleia (4782)
συντελέω sunteleō (4783)
τελεσφορέω telesphoreō (4900)
τελευτάω teleutaō (4901)
τέλος telos (4904)
τελώνιον telōnion (4906)

Synonyms:

ἀναπληρόω anaplēroō (376)
ἀνταναπληρόω antanaplēroō (463)
ἀποτελέω apoteleō (652)
διανύω dianuō (1268)
ἐκπληρόω ekplēroō (1590)
ἐκτελέω ekteleō (1602)
ἐξαρτίζω exartizō (1806)
ἐπιτελέω epiteleō (1989)
ἐργάζομαι ergazomai (2021)
καταρτίζω katartizō (2645)
κατεστρώννυμι katestrōnnumi (2689)
πληρόω plēroō (3997)
πράσσω prassō (4097)
συντελέω sunteleō (4783)
τελειόω teleioō (4896)

גְּמַר g[e]mar (A1626), Something perfect? something complete? (Ezr 7:12—[Codex Vaticanus only]—Aramaic).

כָּלָה kālâh (3735), Qal: be fulfilled (Ezr 1:1—only some Vaticanus texts); piel: finish, settle (Ru 2:21, 3:18, Ezr 10:17).

סוּף ṣûph (5673), Be fulfilled (Dn 4:33 [4:30]—Aramaic).

עָשָׂה 'āsâh (6449), Accomplish (Is 55:11).

צָמַד tsāmadh (7044), Niphal: join oneself to someone (Nm 25:5, Ps 106:28 [105:28]).

קָדֵשׁ qādhēsh (7228), Temple prostitute (Hos 4:14).

שֵׁיצִיא shêtsê' (A8300), Shaphel: be completed (Ezr 6:15—Aramaic).

שָׁלַם shālam (8396), Be completed (Neh 6:15).

שְׁלֵם shᵉlēm (A8397), Be finished (Ezr 5:16—Aramaic).

1. **τελεῖ telei** 3sing indic pres act
2. **τελεῖτε teleite** 2pl indic pres act
3. **τελοῦσα telousa** nom sing fem part pres act
4. **ἐτέλεσεν etelesen** 3sing indic aor act
5. **ἐτέλεσαν etelesan** 3pl indic aor act
6. **τελέσητε telesēte** 2pl subj aor act
7. **τελέσωσιν telesōsin** 3pl subj aor act
8. **τετέλεκα teteleka** 1sing indic perf act
9. **ἐτελέσθη etelesthē** 3sing indic aor pass
10. **τελεσθῇ telesthē** 3sing subj aor pass
11. **τελεσθῶσιν telesthōsin** 3pl subj aor pass
12. **τελεσθῆναι telesthēnai** inf aor pass
13. **τετέλεσται tetelestai** 3sing indic perf mid
14. **τελεσθήσεται telesthēsetai** 3sing indic fut pass
15. **τελεῖται teleitai** 3sing indic pres mid
16. **τελεσθήσονται telesthēsontai** 3pl indic fut pass

4 when Jesus **had finished** these words, (NASB) ...... Matt 7:28
6 Ye **shall not have** gone over the cities of Israel, ... 10:23
4 when Jesus **had made an end** of commanding 11:1
4 when Jesus had **finished** these parables, ... 13:53
1 and said, Doth not your master **pay** tribute? 17:24
4 that when Jesus had **finished** these sayings, ... 19:1
4 when Jesus **had finished** all these sayings, ... 26:1
5 **had performed** all things according to the law ...... Luke 2:39
10 and how am I straitened till it **be accomplished!** 12:50
14 concerning the Son of man **shall be accomplished.** 18:31
12 that this that is written must yet **be accomplished** 22:37
13 knowing that all things were now **accomplished,** ... John 19:28
13 he said, It **is finished:** ... and gave up the ghost. 19:30
5 when they **had fulfilled** all that was written of him, Acts 13:29
3 if it **fulfil** the law, judge thee, who by the letter .... Rom 2:27
2 For for this cause **pay** ye tribute also: 13:6
15 for my power **is perfected** in weakness." (NASB) 2 Co 12:9
6 and ye **shall not fulfil** the lust of the flesh. ....Gal 5:16
8 I **have finished** my course, I have kept the faith: ... 2 Tm 4:7
2 If ye **fulfil** the royal law according to the scripture, .. Jas 2:8
10 the mystery of God should **be finished,** .... Rev 10:7
7 And when they **shall have finished** their testimony, ... 11:7
9 for in them **is filled up** the wrath of God. 15:1
11 seven plagues of the seven angels **were fulfilled.** 15:8
10 until the words of God **shall be fulfilled.** 17:17
10 till the thousand years **should be fulfilled:** 20:3
10 not again until the thousand years **were finished.** 20:5
10 And when the thousand years **are expired,** 20:7

Classical Greek

This is a very common verb in both classical and Biblical Greek meaning "to complete, perform, fulfill." In classical Greek it was frequently used from Homer (Eighth Century B.C.) on and often carried the sense of completing one's will (cf. *Liddell-Scott*). Plato thus described the universe as being completed according to a plan. It is likewise used to "carry out" a promise and to "carry out" the instructions given to soldiers. Plato likewise used the word to refer to the carrying out of God's will (see Delling, "teleō," *Kittel*, 8:57).

A similar use in classical Greek is to "complete" or "perform" obligations, especially taxes or tribute. The concept of perform is used to signify the execution of a dangerous feat. *Teleō* also refers to the carrying out of religious duties and the performing of prayers. It is often translated "to pay debts." A final use of the word in classical Greek is "to complete" in the sense of bringing to an end. Aristotle used the word to denote the bringing to an end the years of a person's life (*Liddell-Scott*). Josephus used *teleō* meaning to "fulfill" a promise and also to pay a tribute to masters (*Bauer*).

Septuagint Usage

Teleō appears in the Septuagint and often in the Apocrypha with the sense of "to complete" or "to fulfill." The meaning "to render" or "to pay," which appears in the classical Greek, is not found in the Septuagint. The use of this word for fulfilling a religious obligation is likewise rare, and when it does occur it applies mostly to keeping vows to heathen gods (cf. Delling, "teleō," *Kittel*, 8:58f.). Examples of the latter include Numbers 25:3 and Psalm 106:28 (LXX 105:28).

New Testament Usage

In the New Testament *teleō* has three primary meanings according to Thayer (*Greek-English Lexicon*). The first is "to bring to a close, finish," which parallels its most common use in classical Greek. It is thus used for completing the Word (Matthew 11:1; 19:1; 26:1) and completing the parable (Matthew 13:53). Vine points out that the word is used to signify not merely termination but carrying out a thing to its full conclusion (*Expository Dictionary*, "Finish"). This sense is used especially in Revelation where the word is translated eight times as "finish" (see Revelation 15:1,8). Paul likewise wrote about "finishing" the course (2 Timothy 4:7), and John referred to Scripture being "fulfilled" (John 19:28).

The second meaning of *teleō* in the New Testament is "to perform, execute, complete." It is especially used of completing a task or finishing an order. Paul used it several times to refer to performing a command (Romans 2:27). A variation of this use is in Galatians 5:16 where Paul used it to denote the satisfaction (completion) of fleshly desires.

The final use of *teleō* in the New Testament is the sense of "paying (completing) an obligation." While this use is common in the classical writers it appears only twice in the New Testament and is not the usual word for "pay back." It is used in Matthew 17:24 where the question was asked if Jesus paid the tribute tax. It appears again in Romans 13:6 where the readers are told they are to "*pay* tribute" (taxes).

Strong 5055, Bauer 810-11, Moulton-Milligan 630, Kittel 8:57-61, Liddell-Scott 1771-72, Colin Brown 2:59-65; 3:752-56.

4904. τέλος telos noun

End, termination, conclusion, aim, result, goal, outcome; taxes, obligations.

Cognates:

τέλειος teleios (4894)
τελειότης teleiotēs (4895)
τελειόω teleioō (4896)
τελείως teleiōs (4896B)
τελείωσις teleiōsis (4897)
τελειωτής teleiōtēs (4899)
τελέω teleō (4903)

Synonyms:

ἔκβασις ekbasis (1532)
κῆνσος kēnsos (2750)
λοιπός loipos (3036)
πέρας peras (3872)
συντέλεια sunteleia (4782)
φόρος phoros (5247)

מֶכֶס mekhes (4508), Tribute (Nm 31:28,37-41).

מִכְסָה mikhsāh (4509), Amount (Lv 27:23).

מַס mas (4671), Tribute (Est 10:1).

סוֹף sôph (5677), End, conclusion (Eccl 3:11, 12:13).

סוֹף sôph (A5678), End (Dn 7:26—Aramaic).

קֵץ qēts (7377), End (2 Sm 15:7).

קָצֶה qātseh (7381), End (2 Sm 24:8, 2 Kgs 8:3, 18:10).

1. τέλος telos nom/acc sing neu
2. τέλους telous gen sing neu
3. τέλη telē nom/acc pl neu

1 but he that endureth to the **end** shall be saved..... Matt 10:22
3 of whom do the kings of the earth take **custom**........ 17:25
1 things must come to pass, but the **end** is not yet....... 24:6
1 But he that shall endure unto the **end**, ... be saved..... 24:13
1 unto all nations; and then shall the **end** come.......... 24:14
1 went in, and sat with the servants, to see the **end**...... 26:58
1 Satan ... he cannot stand, but hath **an end**.......... Mark 3:26
1 such ... needs be; but the **end** shall not be yet......... 13:7
1 but he that shall endure unto the **end**, ... be saved..... 13:13
1 and of his kingdom there shall be **no end**........... Luke 1:33
1 lest by her **continual** coming she weary me. (NT)...... 18:5
1 first come to pass; but the **end** is not by and by....... 21:9
1 for the things concerning me have **an end**.............. 22:37
1 he loved them unto the **end**...................... John 13:1
1 for the **end** of those things is death................ Rom 6:21
1 and the **end** everlasting life........................... 6:22
1 is the **end** of the law for righteousness to every one.... 10:4
1 **custom** to whom custom;............................ 13:7
1 custom to whom **custom**;............................ 13:7
2 Who shall also confirm you unto the **end**,........... 1 Co 1:8
3 upon whom the **ends** of the world are come........... 10:11
1 Then cometh the **end**,................................ 15:24
2 and I trust ye shall acknowledge even to the **end**;... 2 Co 1:13
1 look to the **end** of that which is abolished:............ 3:13
1 whose **end** shall be according to their works........... 11:15
1 Whose **end** is destruction, whose God is their belly, Phlp 3:19
1 for the wrath is come upon them to the **uttermost**... 1 Th 2:16
1 Now the **end** of the commandment is charity....... 1 Tm 1:5
2 and the rejoicing of the hope firm unto the **end**...... Heb 3:6
2 beginning of our confidence stedfast unto the **end**;...... 3:14
1 is nigh unto cursing; whose **end** is to be burned......... 6:8
2 to the full assurance of hope unto the **end**:.......... Heb 6:11
1 having neither beginning of days, nor **end** of life;....... 7:3
1 and have seen the **end** of the Lord;................. Jas 5:11
1 Receiving the **end** of your faith,.................... 1 Pt 1:9
1 **Finally**, be ye all of one mind,......................... 3:8
1 But the **end** of all things is at hand:.................. 4:7
1 what shall the **end** be of them that obey not............ 4:17
1 Alpha and Omega, the beginning and the **ending**,.... Rev 1:8
2 overcometh, and keepeth my works unto the **end**,....... 2:26
1 Alpha and Omega, the beginning and the **end**......... 21:6
1 Alpha and Omega, the beginning and the **end**,........ 22:13

Classical Greek

From the stem *tel-*, "to turn round," *telos* "originally meant the turning point, hinge, the culminating point at which one stage ends and another begins; later goal" (Schippers, "Goal," *Colin Brown*, 2:59). Delling reduces the major meanings of *telos* to five: (1) "achievement"; (2) "completion"; (3) "obligation" (such as taxes); (4) "offering" (religious); (5) "detachment, group" ("telos," *Kittel*, 8:49-51). These, of course, are oversimplified; the term is extremely diverse in meaning in classical Greek (see *Liddell-Scott*). Essentially *telos* indicates "fulfillment, execution of an act, consummation" or a state, such as "complete, perfect, total." In philosophy *telos* was particularly linked to "goal," such as the goal of an ethical life (Schippers, "Goal," *Colin Brown*, 2:60).

Septuagint Usage

The complexity of *telos* is further accented by its occurrences in the Septuagint which uses it in place of 7 Hebrew terms as well as 12 cognate forms within those 7. Curiously *eis to telos*, literally "for ever," appears in the title of over 50 psalms.

Elsewhere *telos* refers to a "tribute" (offering) to the Lord (Numbers 31:28,37,38ff.). And in the temporal sense *telos* is "for ever" (1 Chronicles 28:9; cf. Job 20:7) or the end of a series of events (2 Chronicles 31:1; cf. Daniel 11:13). "Completeness" is implied in Job 14:20 (NIV, "once for all").

New Testament Usage

Telos appears about 40 times in the Greek New Testament. The Synoptic Gospels use *telos* in reference to "The End," the eschatological close of this age. Jesus himself used the term in this way (e.g., Matthew 10:22; 24:6; Mark 13:7,13; Luke 21:9). He was perhaps picking up on the language of the Jewish apocalypticism of His day, although not necessarily (see Delling, "telos," *Kittel*, 8:53).

The sense of "end" as a point in time appears also. The kingdom of Messiah has no "end" (Luke 1:33). *Telos* as the "outcome" of something is the idea in Luke 18:5, and in Luke 22:37 it denotes the "fulfillment" of prophecy about Jesus. (Note: *Telos* occurs in the Gospel of Luke but not in Acts.)

John's single use recalls the "full extent" (NIV) of Jesus' love in going to the cross. Jesus' love, ultimate and total, expressed itself in His desire to do the will of the Father (John 13:1; cf. 3:16f.).

At times Paul used *telos* as the "result" or "outcome" of understanding (cf. above, Luke 18:5; Philippians 3:19; 1 Thessalonians 2:16). Death is the result of sin, but the end of righteousness through faith is eternal life (Romans 6:21,22; cf. 2 Corinthians 11:15).

Romans 13:7 approximates the classical usage of "obligation" or, in this case, probably a "tax" (NIV). In other contexts some eschatological connection with the end seems intended, for example, 1 Corinthians 1:8; nevertheless, Paul's tendency not to use the terminology in a technical manner elsewhere (unless it functions this way in 1 Corinthians 15:24) indicates he was merely thinking of the end point.

The author of Hebrews refers to "until the end" (*mechri telous*) twice (3:6,14) and "up to the end" (*achri telous*) once (6:11). Reading technical status here does not appear justified either. It simply means until the "finish" or perhaps "outcome" (as it does in 6:8 and 7:3). The author was not thinking in terms of "The End" as an apocalyptic, cataclysmic close of this age; he was merely reflecting upon the end of the present situation (cf. Schippers, "Goal," *Colin Brown*, 2:64).

"Conclusion," too, is the sense in James 5:11. Like Hebrews, though, at the conclusion of the Lord's work those enduring in suffering will be vindicated. The Lord's own example of perseverance is presented here as incentive for enduring suffering.

Revelation 21:6 and 22:13 declare God and Christ *hē archē kai to telos*, "the beginning and the end." This suggests the power and authority invested in Jesus (cf. the Old Testament passages Isaiah 41:4; 44:6).

STRONG 5056, BAUER 811-12, MOULTON-MILLIGAN 630-31, KITTEL 8:49-57, LIDDELL-SCOTT 1772-74, COLIN BROWN 2:59-66; 3:752,754,756,759.

4905. τελώνης telōnēs noun

Tax collector, revenue officer.

CROSS-REFERENCE:
τελώνιον telōnion (4906)

1. τελώνης telōnēs nom sing masc
2. τελώνην telōnēn acc sing masc
3. τελῶναι telōnai nom pl masc
4. τελωνῶν telōnōn gen pl masc

3 do not even the **publicans** the same? .... Matt 5:46
3 more than others? do not even the **publicans** so? 5:47
3 many **publicans** and sinners came and sat down 9:10
4 Why eateth your Master with **publicans** and 9:11
1 Thomas, and Matthew the **publican**; 10:3
4 a friend **of publicans** and sinners. 11:19
1 let him be ... as a heathen man and **a publican**. 18:17
3 **publicans** and the harlots go into the kingdom 21:31
3 but the **publicans** and the harlots believed him: 21:32
3 **publicans** and sinners sat also together with Jesus ... Mark 2:15
4 Pharisees saw him eat with **publicans** and sinners, ... 2:16
4 he eateth and drinketh with **publicans** and sinners? 2:16
3 Then came also **publicans** to be baptized, ... Luke 3:12
2 he went forth, and saw **a publican**, named Levi, ... 5:27
4 and there was a great company **of publicans** 5:29
4 do ye eat and drink with **publicans** and sinners? 5:30
3 all the people that heard him, and the **publicans**, ... 7:29
4 a winebibber, a friend **of publicans** and sinners! 7:34
3 Then drew near unto him all the **publicans** 15:1
1 the one a Pharisee, and the other **a publican**. 18:10
1 unjust, adulterers, or even as this **publican**. 18:11
1 And the **publican**, standing afar off, ... 18:13

Classical Greek

The term *telōnēs*, "tax collector," had a negative sound in Jewish ears (as is seen so clearly in the Gospels). Greeks also had their own sayings about them: "All are *telōnēs*, all are thieves" (Xenophon; cf. Hillyer, "Tax," *Colin Brown*, 3:755). The association of thieves with tax collectors evolved from the system of taxation in the ancient world. Since the time of the Greek city-state, individuals were hired to collect taxes and customs. These tax collectors guaranteed the city-state a certain amount of revenue; anything above the guaranteed revenue for the state went into the pockets of the tax collectors. Thus their income was determined by their ability to exact money. The imposition of taxes and the right to collect them was auctioned off each year to the highest bidder. This naturally increased the tax pressure upon the common people.

Romans employed the same taxation system as did the Greek city-states. Eventually, however, many provinces were so financially depleted that the emperor had to revise the system of taxation. The change began during the reign of Emperor Augustus, but it was not completed until the Second Century A.D. (ibid.). The collection of taxes passed through many channels. Rich citizens bought tax-collecting rights from the state. They then engaged agents or magistrates who in turn appointed local civil servants to collect the taxes from the people. In Judea, a Roman province under the jurisdiction of a Roman-appointed ruler, the tax was paid to the emperor (Mark 12:14). But Herod Antipas, the tetrarch of Galilee who had the authority to collect taxes in Galilee and Peraea, used a system of renting the collection of taxes to independent collectors.

Josephus distinguishes between two types of tax collectors: those responsible for personal taxes and those who collected customs (ibid., 3:756). Custom stations were set up along the extensive Roman roads, next to bridges, and in port cities. The subordinates, the local civil servants who came in direct contact with the public, were despised and hated by the common people. This public disdain, which was the attitude toward that position everywhere, was even greater among the Jewish population. Tax collectors were considered "unclean" because of their daily contact with Gentiles and because they violated the Sabbath commandment. (The payment of taxes was also extremely distasteful to the Jew because it reminded him that he was ruled by a foreign power.) Tax collectors were regarded as traitors and liars; they were excluded from synagogue fellowship, and they were considered as among the worst sinners, being compared to prostitutes, thieves, adulterers, Gentiles, and the ungodly (Matthew 9:10; 21:31; Luke 18:11; cf. Matthew 18:17).

New Testament Usage

It is noteworthy that even before Jesus appeared on the scene John the Baptist showed a different attitude toward the tax collectors. John did not require either the soldier or tax collector to leave their position; rather, he demanded that they carry out their duties in an honorable and just way (Luke 3:12-14). Jesus, too, refused to participate in the general condemnation of tax collectors despite the fact that He did use the current jargon of the day when He referred to those excluded from the fellowship of believers: "Let him be unto thee as a heathen man and a publican" (Matthew 18:17). This suggests that Jesus did not have any illusions about the actual moral condition of this segment of society. He knew they needed conversion (Luke 5:32; 15:7) and salvation (Luke 19:9,10). This was precisely the reason He came into contact with them. It is the "sick" who need a physician. Zaccheus the chief tax collector in Jericho is a perfect example of this.

That Jesus would have fellowship with "publicans and sinners" caused a public uproar (Matthew 9:10; Luke 15:1,2). The fact that Jesus' circle of disciples included both a Zealot (who bitterly opposed taxation) and a tax collector (see the list of apostles in Matthew 10:3: "Matthew the publican" and in Luke 6:15, "Simon . . . the Zealot" [NIV]) must have caused tremendous consternation.

The customhouse in Capernaum where Levi (Matthew) was employed was along an important trade route for both land and sea (at the Sea of Galilee) (ibid., 3:757). Those working this tax station must have mastered several languages, accounting, and probably shorthand of some sort, perhaps that developed by Marcus Tullius Tiro which was widely known. The writer of the First Gospel would have been very capable of taking notes. Matthew may have recorded Jesus' sermons.

Matthew probably knew Peter and John, as well as other fishermen at the Sea of Galilee, since it is quite likely he would have collected duty on their fish catches. Two inscriptions from an Asian province mention "those having their occupation in collecting duties on fish" (ibid.).

Strong 5057, Bauer 812, Moulton-Milligan 631, Kittel 8:88-105, Liddell-Scott 1774, Colin Brown 3:755,757.

4906. τελώνιον telōnion noun

Tollhouse, tax office.

Cognates:

ἀρχιτελώνης architelōnēs (749)
τελέω teleō (4903)
τελώνης telōnēs (4905)

1. τελώνιον telōnion nom/acc sing neu

1 Matthew, sitting at the receipt of custom:........... Matt 9:9
1 he saw Levi ... sitting at the receipt of custom,......Mark 2:14
1 named Levi, sitting at the receipt of custom:.........Luke 5:27

This word is derived from *telos* (4904), a "custom" or "toll," and refers to the place of collection where the tax collector sat to collect taxes. *Telōnion* is used three times in the New Testament: in Matthew 9:9, Mark 2:14, and Luke 5:27. In all three appearances the use is identical, referring to Jesus' commanding Matthew (Levi) to follow Him.

Although *telōnion* is found in some early classical Greek literature, it does not appear in the Septuagint.

Strong 5058, Bauer 812, Moulton-Milligan 631, Liddell-Scott 1774, Colin Brown 3:755-57,759.

4907. τέρας teras noun

Portent, omen, wonder.

מוֹפֵת môphēth (4295), Wonder, marvel (Dt 7:19, Ps 105:5 [104:5]); sign (Ez 12:6,11).

פָּלָא pālâ' (6623), Hiphil: be wonderful (Is 28:29).

פֶּלֶא pele' (6624), Wonder (Ex 15:11).

שַׁמָּה shammāh (8439), Desolations (Ps 46:8 [45:8]).

תְּמַהּ t^emahh (A8868), Wonder (Dn 4:2 [3:32]—Aramaic).

1. τέρατα terata nom/acc pl neu
2. τεράτων teratōn gen pl neu
3. τέρασιν terasin dat pl neu
4. τέρασι terasi dat pl neu

1 and shall show great signs and **wonders**;........... Matt 24:24
1 For false Christs ... shall show signs and **wonders**, Mark 13:22
1 Except ye see signs and **wonders**, ye ... not believe...John 4:48
1 And I will show **wonders** in heaven above,.......... Acts 2:19
3 approved ... by miracles and **wonders** and signs,........ 2:22
1 **wonders** and signs were done by the apostles........... 2:43
1 and that signs and **wonders** may be done............... 4:30
1 signs and **wonders** wrought among the people;.......... 5:12
1 did great **wonders** and miracles among the people....... 6:8
1 after that he had showed **wonders** and signs............ 7:36
1 signs and **wonders** to be done by their hands.......... 14:3
1 declaring what miracles and **wonders** God had......... 15:12
2 Through mighty signs and **wonders**,................Rom 15:19
3 in signs, and **wonders**, and mighty deeds........... 2 Co 12:12
3 with all power and signs and lying **wonders**,.........2 Th 2:9
3 witness, both with signs and **wonders**,............... Heb 2:4

Classical Greek

Teras, "wonder, sign, omen," refers in classical literature especially to cosmic wonders or signs, although there might be "signs" of an impending event in the less supernatural sense. The definition of "monster" or "monstrosity" occurs in some cases (e.g., the Gorgon's head, *Liddell-Scott*). In a religious context the term might denote divine "omens" or "portents," often requiring interpretation (Hofius, "Miracle," *Colin Brown*, 2:633; cf. Rengstorf, "teras," *Kittel*, 8:113-117).

Septuagint Usage

Teras ordinarily replaces the Hebrew word *môphēth* in the Septuagint (34 times), although *pele'/pālâ'* (twice), *shammāh* (once), and *t^emah* (once) also appear. In Hebrew *môphēth* means "sign, portent, miracle," and it frequently stands in relation to *'ôth*, "sign" (cf. the Greek word *sēmeion* [4447]). The "wonders" (*terata*) Moses performed before the eyes of Pharaoh (Exodus 4:21) did not necessarily promote faith; in fact, they may even have had a hardening effect upon him (cf. Exodus 7:3).

In and of themselves "wonders" are no guarantee of God's being behind the activity (Deuteronomy 13:1ff.). The term can refer to God's miraculous power and intervention on behalf of Israel, especially of the "miracles" worked through Moses in Egypt (e.g., Deuteronomy 29:3; cf. 1 Chronicles 16:12). Or it may depict divine punishment (e.g., Deuteronomy 28:45ff., of the curses that will come upon covenant violators). "Signs" can confirm significant events (e.g., Josiah's advent as king, 1 Kings 13:3 [LXX 3 Kings 13:3]; Hezekiah's recovery, 2 Chronicles 32:31). Cosmic portents will declare the arrival of that great eschatological Day of the Lord (Joel 2:30; cf. Acts 2:19).

New Testament Usage

Teras appears 16 times in the New Testament. The Synoptic Gospels, excluding Luke, recall Jesus' warning that false prophets would come claiming divine authority and working miracles and yet deceiving everyone they can (Matthew 24:24; parallel Mark 13:22). John's Gospel seemingly downplays the importance of seeing the miraculous for faith. Jesus said, "Unless you see signs and *wonders* you will not believe" (John 4:48, RSV; cf. John 20:29).

The term *teras* does not play any role in Luke's Gospel whatsoever; however, it plays a major role in Acts, occurring more there (nine times) than in any other New Testament book. Invariably it occurs in the construction *semeia kai terata*, "signs and wonders." These may refer to the cosmic portents announcing the arrival of the Day of the Lord (e.g., Acts 2:19; cf. Joel 2:30). But mainly signs and wonders confirm the apostolic testimony (Acts 2:43; 4:30; 5:12; 6:8; 14:3; 15:12) just as they attest to Jesus' own authority from God (Acts 2:22; cf. Hebrews 2:4).

Paul took a similar view of the affirming power of "wonders" (Romans 15:19). They are accomplished through the power of the Spirit, a thought Luke agreed with, for it was clearly by the Spirit's power that the apostles ministered in the name of Jesus (cf. 2 Corinthians 12:12, marks of the apostle). Paul apparently referred to the same idea expressed in the Gospels that counterfeit miracles of the deceiver will accompany the close of this age (2 Thessalonians 2:9; cf. Matthew 24:24; Mark 13:22). (Cf. *pseudoprophētēs* [5413], "false prophet," a term closely associated with this phenomenon; e.g., Revelation 19:20.)

STRONG 5059, BAUER 812, MOULTON-MILLIGAN 631, KITTEL 8:113-26, LIDDELL-SCOTT 1776, COLIN BROWN 2:633-34.

4908. Τέρτιος Tertios name

Tertius.

1. Τέρτιος Tertios nom masc

1 I **Tertius**, who wrote this epistle, salute you........Rom 16:22

In Romans 16:22 Tertius greets the Christians of Rome and identifies himself as the writer of the letter, that is, Paul's secretary. He alone of all Paul's secretaries does so, and this leads scholars to surmise that he was a Roman Christian.

4909. Τέρτυλλος Tertullos name

Tertullus.

1. Τέρτυλλος Tertullos nom masc
2. Τερτύλλου Tertullou gen masc

2 and with a certain orator named **Tertullus**,.........Acts 24:1
1 **Tertullus** began to accuse him, saying,................ 24:2

A lawyer who acted as counsel for the prosecution in Paul's trial before Felix (Acts 24:1). There Luke recorded a summary of his eloquent speech.

4910. τεσσαράκοντα tessarakonta num

Forty.

1. τεσσεράκοντα tesserakonta card
2. τεσσαράκοντα tessarakonta card

2 when he had fasted **forty** days and forty nights,..... Matt 4:2
2 when he had fasted forty days and **forty** nights,......... 4:2
2 And he was there in the wilderness **forty** days,..... Mark 1:13
2 Being **forty** days tempted of the devil.............. Luke 4:2
2 **Forty** and six years was this temple in building,..... John 2:20
2 being seen of them **forty** days,......................Acts 1:3
2 For the man was above **forty** years old,................ 4:22
2 And when **forty** years were expired,.................... 7:30
2 in the Red sea, and in the wilderness **forty** years........ 7:36
2 by the space of **forty** years in the wilderness?........... 7:42
2 by the space of **forty** years.......................... 13:21
2 more than **forty** which had made this conspiracy....... 23:13
2 lie in wait for him of them more than **forty** men,...... 23:21
2 five times received I **forty** stripes save one......... 2 Co 11:24
2 proved me, and saw my works **forty** years........... Heb 3:9
2 But with whom was he grieved **forty** years?............ 3:17
2 one hundred and **forty**-four thousand (NASB)....... Rev 7:4
2 shall they tread under foot **forty** and two months...... 11:2
2 given unto him to continue **forty** and two months...... 13:5
2 and with him an hundred **forty** and four thousand,..... 14:1
2 but the hundred and **forty** and four thousand,......... 14:3
2 wall thereof, an hundred and **forty** and four cubits,.... 21:17

Classical Greek and Septuagint Usage

The word *tessarakonta* is a variant spelling of *tesserakonta* and is the ordinary word used in the Bible for 40. This particular spelling occurs often in the Septuagint and early papyri, but seldom in the first three centuries A.D. outside of the Biblical references. It does appear in early Christian literature in the writings of 1 Clement, Barnabas, and the Shepherd of Hermas (cf. *Bauer*). There is one papyrus document which contains both spellings, dating from A.D. 125. The *Textus Receptus* uses the spelling *tessarakonta.* It is a compound word based upon the root *tessares* (4911B), the normal word for "four."

The number 40 is commonly used in Greek literature to represent a specific number of days and years, and for men and things. Frequently it is used as a round number rather than an exact count. Forty years, for example, was often considered a generation and therefore represents a long time period. The number 40 also denotes maturity. Some important positions, such as lawgivers, required that a man be 40 years old.

New Testament Usage

Tessarakonta is used 21 times in the New Testament, usually for 40 days or years but on one occasion used to refer to a 40-year-old man. Vine suggests that the number is used at times in the New Testament to suggest probation, separation, or judgment (*Expository Dictionary*, "Forty"; cf. Matthew 4:2; Acts 1:3; Hebrews 3:9,17). Perhaps the background of this use is that suggested by *Liddell-Scott* which points out that the word was also used as the name of a formal group, the *tessarakonta* (the "Forty"), who were a body of justices that went around the Attic demes (units of local government in ancient Greece) to hear all cases up to 10 drachmas and all assault cases.

Strong 5062, Bauer 813, Moulton-Milligan 631 (see "tesserakonta"), Kittel 8:135-39 (see "tesserakonta"), Liddell-Scott 1779 (see "tesserakonta"), Colin Brown 2:689,696.

4911. τεσσαρακονταετής tessarakontaetēs adj

Forty years old.

1. τεσσαρακονταετής tessarakontaetēs nom sing masc
2. τεσσαρακονταετῆ tessarakontaetē acc sing masc
3. τεσσερακονταετής tesserakontaetēs nom sing masc

1 And when he was full **forty years old**,............. Acts 7:23
3 And about the time of **forty years**.................... 13:18

This ordinary word for "40 years of age" is a compound of *tessarakonta* (4910), "forty," and *etos* (2073), "years." It is used in the New Testament in two places, Acts 7:23 and 13:18, the latter of which, according to Balz ("tessarakontaetēs," *Kittel*, 8:138), represents a "typological rather than a chronological period." Typologically the number 40 is significant in the history of salvation, going back to the Israelites' wilderness period under the wrath of God.

Strong 5063, Bauer 813, Kittel 8:135-39.

4911B. τέσσαρες tessares num

Four.

1. **τέσσαρες tessares** card nom masc/fem
2. **τέσσαρσιν tessarsin** card dat masc/fem
3. **τέσσαρας tessaras** card acc masc/fem
4. **τεσσάρων tessarōn** card gen masc/neu
5. **τέσσαρα tessara** card nom/acc neu
6. **τέσσερα tessera** card pl neu

4 shall gather together his elect from the **four** winds, Matt 24:31
4 one sick of the palsy, which was borne of **four**...... Mark 2:3
4 gather together his elect from the **four** winds,......... 13:27
3 he had lain in the grave **four** days already......... John 11:17
5 took his garments, and made **four** parts,.............. 19:23
2 a great sheet knit at the **four** corners,..............Acts 10:11
2 let down from heaven by **four** corners;................ 11:5
2 and delivered him to **four** quaternions of soldiers...... 12:4
1 And the same man had **four** daughters, virgins,........ 21:9
1 We have **four** men which have a vow on them;........ 21:23
3 they cast **four** anchors out of the stern,............... 27:29
1 about the throne were **four** and twenty seats:........ Rev 4:4
3 upon the seats I saw **four** and twenty elders sitting,..... 4:4
5 were **four** beasts full of eyes before and behind......... 4:6
5 And the **four** beasts had each of them six wings........ 4:8
1 The **four** and twenty elders fall down before him....... 4:10
4 in the midst of the throne and of the **four** beasts,....... 5:6
5 **four** beasts and four and twenty elders fell down....... 5:8
1 creatures and the twenty-four elders (NASB)........... 5:8
5 And the **four** beasts said, Amen...................... 5:14
4 one of the **four** beasts saying, Come and see............ 6:1
4 I heard a voice in the midst of the **four** beasts say,..... 6:6
3 And after these things I saw **four** angels.............. 7:1
3 angels standing on the **four** corners of the earth,........ 7:1
3 holding the **four** winds of the earth,................... 7:1
2 and he cried with a loud voice to the **four** angels,....... 7:2
1 one hundred and forty-**four** thousand (NASB).......... 7:4
4 throne, and about the elders and the **four** beasts,....... 7:11
4 **four** horns of the golden altar which is before God,..... 9:13
3 Loose the **four** angels which are bound................. 9:14
1 the **four** angels were loosed, which were prepared....... 9:15
1 the **four** and twenty elders, which sat before God...... 11:16
1 and with him an hundred forty and **four** thousand,..... 14:1
4 and before the **four** beasts, and the elders:............ 14:3
1 but the hundred and forty and **four** thousand,......... 14:3
4 one of the **four** beasts gave unto the seven angels...... 15:7
1 And the **four** and twenty elders and the four beasts.... 19:4
5 And the four and twenty elders and the **four** beasts.... 19:4
2 nations which are in the **four** quarters of the earth,.... 20:8
4 wall thereof, an hundred and forty and **four** cubits,.... 21:17

Classical Greek

This is the ordinary Greek word for "four." Because of the basic four sides or directions from man (front, back, left, right), as well as the four compass directions of the earth, the number *four* in classical Greek carried not only a literal numerical sense but also a figurative sense of completeness or wholeness. The word appears as early as Thucydides and Homer (Eighth Century B.C.; cf. *Liddell-Scott*). It is often used as a number to summarize types or listings, such as: the four kinds of quality or Aristotelian senses, the four simple bodies of Empedocles, the four cardinal principles of Epicurus, the four constitutions of Plato, or the four divisions of work of Plato (see Balz, "tessares," *Kittel*, 8:127-135).

Septuagint Usage

Tessares is used in the Septuagint to express its common usage of completion or totality. Thus it expresses the four quarters of heaven and the four borders of Israel (Ezekiel 7:2). The number is of particular significance to Ezekiel who, in addition to the four corners of the earth, described the four creatures having four faces and four wings, and the four wheels (Ezekiel 1). The number *four* also is significant to the prophecy of Daniel (the four kingdoms of 2:31f.; four beasts of 7:3f., with one having four wings and four heads; and the four horns of 8:8f.) and of Zechariah (the four angels, four craftsmen and horns, and four chariots of chapters 1 and 6).

New Testament Usage

In the New Testament *tessares* appears only in the Gospels, Acts of the Apostles, and Revelation, occurring very often in the latter. The usage in the Gospels and Acts are to the general numerical use, as in four anchors (Acts 27:29), fourth watch (Mark 6:48), fourth day (John 11:17), and four parts into which Jesus' garments were divided (John 19:23).

In Revelation the use of *tessares*, which appears 29 times, parallels that found in the apocalyptic passages of the Old Testament prophets, particularly Ezekiel, having a symbolic meaning of wholeness or completeness. The 4 living creatures appear in 11 verses in 7 different chapters of Revelation (chapters 4–7, 14, 15, 19). The concept of the four horses also reappears in Revelation 6:1-8. Revelation also presents four destroying angels (9:14) and the four corners of the earth (20:8).

Strong 5064, Bauer 813, Moulton-Milligan 631, Kittel 8:127-35, Liddell-Scott 1778, Colin Brown 2:688,703.

4912. τεσσαρεσκαιδέκατος tessareskaidekatos num

Fourteenth.

1. **τεσσαρεσκαιδεκάτη tessareskaidekatē** ord nom sing fem
2. **τεσσαρεσκαιδεκάτην tessareskaidekatēn** ord acc sing fem

1 But when the fourteenth night was come,.......... Acts 27:27
2 This day is the fourteenth day that ye have tarried..... 27:33

This word, the ordinal number *14*, consists of *tessares* (4911B), "four," and *deka* (1171), "ten." *Tessareskaidekatos* appears in the New Testament twice, in Acts 27:27 ("the *fourteenth* night") and in Acts 27:33 ("the *fourteenth* day"). The same two root words (*tessares* and *deka*) also appear in reverse order (*dekatessares* [1175]) with the same meaning in five places in the New Testament.

STRONG 5065, BAUER 813, MOULTON-MILLIGAN 631, LIDDELL-SCOTT 1778.

4913. τέσσαρες tessares

See word study at number 4911B.

4913B. τεσσερακονταετής tesserakontaetēs

Forty years old.

This is an alternate spelling of *tessarakontaetēs*. See the word study at number 4911.

4914. τεταρταῖος tetartaios adj

Fourth day.

רְבִיעִי r^evî'î (7536), Fourth (2 Sm 3:4—Codex Alexandrinus only).

1. τεταρταῖος tetartaios nom sing masc

1 he stinketh: for he hath been dead four days....... John 11:39

This term can be found in classical Greek from the Fifth Century B.C. meaning "on the fourth day." *Tetartaios* appears in the Septuagint only once (2 Samuel 3:4 [LXX 2 Kings 3:4]) in reference to the fourth son of David. The only use of this word in the New Testament is in John 11:39 in reference to the fourth day of death. The more common word for *fourth* is *tetartos* (4915).

STRONG 5066, BAUER 813, MOULTON-MILLIGAN 631, KITTEL 8:127-35, LIDDELL-SCOTT 1779.

4915. τέταρτος tetartos num

Fourth.

1. τέταρτον tetarton ord nom/acc sing masc/neu
2. τετάρτου tetartou ord gen sing masc/neu
3. τέταρτος tetartos ord nom sing masc
4. τετάρτης tetartēs ord gen sing fem
5. τετάρτῃ tetartē ord dat sing fem
6. τετάρτην tetartēn ord acc sing fem

5 And in the fourth watch of the night Jesus went... Matt 14:25
6 fourth watch of the night he cometh unto them,.... Mark 6:48
4 Four days ago I was fasting until this hour;........ Acts 10:30
1 and the fourth beast was like a flying eagle.......... Rev 4:7
6 And when he had opened the fourth seal,.............. 6:7
2 And when he had opened the fourth seal,.............. 6:7
1 power was given unto them over the fourth part........ 6:8
3 And the fourth angel sounded,........................ 8:12
3 the fourth angel poured out his vial upon the sun;..... 16:8
3 the third, a chalcedony; the fourth, an emerald;....... 21:19

This is the normal word used for the ordinal "fourth." *Tetartos* occurs 10 times in 9 verses of the New Testament. In two places it refers to the fourth watch of the day, the period from 3–6 a.m. (Matthew 14:25; Mark 6:48). A variation in use appears in Acts 10:30 where the text makes reference to a fast being literally "from the fourth day" meaning that it began 4 days before.

Tetartos appears seven times in the Book of Revelation where it identifies the fourth angel (8:12; 16:8), the fourth creature (4:7; 6:7), the fourth seal (6:7), the fourth stone (21:19), and the fourth part of the earth (6:8).

STRONG 5067, BAUER 813, MOULTON-MILLIGAN 632, KITTEL 8:127-35, LIDDELL-SCOTT 1779.

4916. τετράγωνος tetragōnos adj

Square, four-sided.

רָבַע rāva' (7541), Qal: be square (Ex 27:1, 30:2, Ez 43:16); pual: be square (1 Kgs 7:31, Ez 45:2).

רְבִיעִי r^evî'î (7536), Fourth; foursquare (Ez 28:20).

1. τετράγωνος tetragōnos nom sing fem

1 And the city lieth foursquare,......................Rev 21:16

This term is a combination of the words *tetra*, "four," and *gōnia* (1131), "corner, angle." It can be found in classical Greek from the Fifth Century B.C. literally meaning "with four angles" but usually is used for "square" (cf. *Liddell-Scott*). It also occurs 13 times in the Septuagint, primarily in Exodus and Ezekiel. The only appearance of *tetrogōnos* in the New Testament is in Revelation 21:16. Here the New Jerusalem is described as being "foursquare."

STRONG 5068, BAUER 813, MOULTON-MILLIGAN 632, LIDDELL-SCOTT 1780.

4917. τετράδιον tetradion noun

Four soldiers, squad.

1. τετραδίοις tetradiois dat pl neu

1 and delivered him to four **quaternions** of soldiers ... Acts 12:4

This is the normal word for a quaternion, a "guard" of soldiers for one prisoner normally consisting of four men (*Liddell-Scott*). Two soldiers were to keep guard over the prisoner while another two were to stand watch outside. *Tetradion* occurs only once in the New Testament. Acts 12:4 tells how Peter was arrested and kept by four squads, one to be on duty during each watch of the day. An interesting background passage is John 19:23 where the outer garments of Jesus were divided into four parts, one for each member of the *tetradion*.

STRONG 5069, BAUER 813, MOULTON-MILLIGAN 632, LIDDELL-SCOTT 1780, COLIN BROWN 2:689.

4918. τετρακισχίλιοι tetrakischilioi num

Four thousand.

1. τετρακισχιλίων tetrakischiliōn card gen masc/fem/neu
2. τετρακισχίλιοι tetrakischilioi card nom masc
3. τετρακισχιλίους tetrakischilious card acc masc

2 And they that did eat were **four thousand** men, ... Matt 15:38
1 Neither the seven loaves of the **four thousand**, ... 16:10
2 And they that had eaten were about **four thousand**: Mark 8:9
3 And when the seven among **four thousand**, ... 8:20
3 and leddest out into the wilderness **four thousand** ... Acts 21:38

This is the ordinary Greek word for 4,000, comprised of the root words *tetra*, "four," and *chilioi* (5343), "thousand." It appears five times in the Septuagint; however, it is not used to translate any Hebrew terms. *Tetrakischilioi* appears five times in three books of the New Testament (Matthew 15:38; 16:10; Mark 8:9,20; Acts 21:38). In each of the five occurrences this word is used to refer to 4,000 men.

STRONG 5070, BAUER 813, MOULTON-MILLIGAN 632, LIDDELL-SCOTT 1780, COLIN BROWN 2:699.

4919. τετρακόσιοι tetrakosioi num

Four hundred.

1. τετρακοσίων tetrakosiōn card gen masc/fem/neu
2. τετρακοσίοις tetrakosiois card dat masc/neu
3. τετρακόσια tetrakosia card nom/acc neu

1 to whom a number of men, about **four hundred**, ... Acts 5:36
3 and entreat them evil **four hundred** years. 7:6
2 about the space of **four hundred** and fifty years, ... 13:20
3 which was **four hundred** and thirty years after, ... Gal 3:17

This is the common Greek word for 400. The word *tetrakosioi* appears 4 times in the New Testament, 3 times referring to 400 years (Acts 7:16; 13:20; Galatians 3:17) and 1 time describing 400 men (Acts 5:36). *Tetrakosioi* is found often in the Septuagint and the Apocrypha with the same usage.

STRONG 5071, BAUER 813, MOULTON-MILLIGAN 632, LIDDELL-SCOTT 1781, COLIN BROWN 2:689.

4920. τετράμηνος tetramēnos adj

Four months.

1. τετράμηνον tetramēnon nom/acc sing neu
2. τετράμηνος tetramēnos nom sing masc

1 Say not ye, There are yet **four months**, ... John 4:35

This is the typical Greek word to describe a period of time which lasts 4 months. *Tetramēnos* is a combination of the two root words *tetra*, "four," and *men*, "month." It is found twice in the Septuagint with both appearances in the same book (Judges 19:2; 20:47). The word is used only once in the New Testament, in John 4:35, where Jesus quoted the disciples as saying "yet *four months*" before harvest, just prior to His announcement that the fields were white unto harvest.

STRONG 5072, BAUER 813, MOULTON-MILLIGAN 632, LIDDELL-SCOTT 1781.

4921. τετραπλοῦς tetraplous adj

Fourfold, quadruple.

1. τετραπλοῦν tetraploun nom/acc sing neu

1 by false accusation, I restore him **fourfold**. .... Luke 19:8

This is the common Greek word for "fourfold." It appears only once in the New Testament, in Luke 19:8. Following his encounter with Christ, Zaccheus pledged that if he had defrauded anyone he would restore to him "fourfold" of that which he had taken. The implication is that Zaccheus had been dishonest and had extorted funds from others. Zaccheus' fourfold restitution was in keeping with the Mosaic law (cf. Exodus 22:1; 1 Samuel 12:3).

BAUER 813, MOULTON-MILLIGAN 632, LIDDELL-SCOTT 1781.

4922. τετράπους tetrapous adj

Four-footed, beast.

בְּהֵמָה b[e]hēmāh (966), Animal, beast (Gn 34:23, Lv 18:23, Jb 18:3).

חַיָּה chayyāh (2516), Beast (Jb 40:20 [40:15], Is 40:16).

1. τετράποδα tetrapoda nom/acc pl neu
2. τετραπόδων tetrapodōn gen pl neu

1 Wherein were all manner of **fourfooted beasts** ...... Acts 10:12
1 and saw **fourfooted beasts** of the earth, ... 11:6
2 and to birds, and **fourfooted beasts**, ... Rom 1:23

This is the common Greek word for "four-footed." It is a combination of two root words: *tetra*, "four," and *pous* (4087), "foot." *Tetrapous* literally means "four-footed." In later uses the word connoted "beast" (i.e., a four-footed animal or quadruped). It appears about 25 times in the Septuagint where it translates the Hebrew word *b^ehēmāh* which is a general word for "animal" and is usually translated "beast." It is also used three times in the New Testament, each referring to a four-footed animal (beast). In Acts 10:12 and 11:6 *terapous* is used of the "fourfooted beasts" in Peter's vision that were no longer to be considered unclean. Paul used this term in reference to the images reprobate men made and worshiped (Romans 1:23).

Strong 5074, Bauer 814, Moulton-Milligan 632, Liddell-Scott 1782.

4923. τετραρχέω tetrarcheō verb

To be a tetrarch.

Cross-Reference:
ἀρχή archē (741)

1. τετραρχοῦντος tetrarchountos
gen sing masc part pres act
2. τετρααρχοῦντος tetraarchountos
gen sing masc part pres act

1 and Herod **being tetrarch** of Galilee, ... Luke 3:1
1 and his brother Philip **tetrarch** of Ituraea and 3:1
1 and Lysanias the **tetrarch** of Abilene, ... 3:1

This word refers to someone who has been made a tetrarch, a governor or ruler over a tetrarchy. A tetrarchy was one division of a region that had been divided into four sections, each governed by a tetrarch. Later the term *tetrarch* came to be used for any "petty, dependent prince" whose rank and authority were below the level of a king. *Tetrarcheō* appears three times in Luke 3:1, in reference to Herod, Philip, and Lysanias, all of whom were tetrarchs. The word is not found in the Septuagint, nor does it appear in Greek literature before the Christian times.

Strong 5075, Bauer 814, Liddell-Scott 1782.

4924. τετράρχης tetrarchēs noun

Tetrarch.

Cross-Reference:
ἀρχή archē (741)

1. τετράρχης tetrarchēs nom sing masc
2. τετράρχου tetrarchou gen sing masc
3. τετραάρχης tetraarchēs nom sing masc
4. τετραάρχου tetraarchou gen sing masc

1 Herod the **tetrarch** heard of the fame of Jesus, ... Matt 14:1
1 But Herod the **tetrarch**, being reproved by him for .. Luke 3:19
1 Now Herod the **tetrarch** heard of all that was done 9:7
2 had been brought up with Herod the **tetrarch**, ... Acts 13:1

Classical Greek

Literally *tetrarchēs* (normally *tetrarchos* in classical Greek) is a compound from *tetra*, "four," and *archos*, "ruler"; thus, it means a "ruler of one-fourth" of a given district, region, empire, etc.; in other words, a "tetrarch." The precision originally implied by the term eventually broke down, and *tetrarch* came to describe any ruler over one or more districts. The status of the tetrarch also declined (cf. *Bauer*). *Tetrarchēs* does not occur in the Septuagint.

New Testament Usage

Four instances of *tetrarchēs* are recorded in the New Testament. Each instance is a reference to Herod Antipas, the tetrarch of Galilee and Peraea (ca. 4 B.C.–A.D. 39). Recounting the imprisonment of John the Baptist by Herod, Luke described him as "Herod the tetrarch" (Luke 3:19; cf. Matthew 14:1; Mark 6:14,17; Luke 9:7). And, in a descriptive comment, Luke noted that Manaen, a member of the church in Antioch, "had been brought up with Herod the tetrarch" (Acts 13:1, NIV). (Cf. Josephus who also called Herod "the tetrarch" [Antiquities 18.4.5; 18.5.1; 18.6.3].)

Strong 5076, Bauer 814, Liddell-Scott 1782.

4925. τεφρόω tephroō verb

To reduce or burn to ashes.

1. τεφρώσας tephrōsas nom sing masc part aor act

1 And turning ... Sodom and Gomorrha **into ashes** .... 2 Pt 2:6

This word is derived from the root *tephra* which refers to "ashes," such as those of the funeral pyre after the bodies are burnt. It is not found in the Septuagint, although the noun form *tephra* is used six times in the Apocrypha. The verb *tephroō* appears only once in the New Testament, in 2 Peter 2:6. Here God is described as dealing with Sodom and Gomorrah by "turning" them "into ashes."

Strong 5077, Bauer 814, Moulton-Milligan 632, Liddell-Scott 1784.

4926. τέχνη technē noun

Art, craft, skill.

Cognate:
τέκτων tektōn (4893)

Synonym:
ἐργασία ergasia (2022)

חָכְמָה chokhmāh (2551), Wisdom (1 Kgs 7:14, Dn 1:17).

מַעֲשֶׂה ma'ăseh (4801), Mixture (Ex 30:25).

עֲבֹדָה 'ăvōdhāh (5865), Service (1 Chr 28:21).

1. **τέχνης technēs** gen sing fem
2. **τέχνην technēn** acc sing fem
3. **τέχνῃ technē** dat sing fem

1 or silver, or stone, graven **by art** and man's device. Acts 17:29
2 for by their **occupation** they were tentmakers.......... 18:3
1 and no craftsman, of whatsoever **craft** he be,....... Rev 18:22

This is the only term used in the New Testament for "craft, trade," or "occupation." It is derived from *tektōn*, a "craftsman in wood, stone, or metal." *Technē* appears four times in the Septuagint and six times in the Apocrypha. It occurs three times in the New Testament. In Revelation 18:22 the word is used to describe a craft. In Acts 17:29 it describes those who work in stone. In Acts 18:3 the word refers to a trade or occupation.

Strong 5078, Bauer 814, Moulton-Milligan 633, Liddell-Scott 1785, Colin Brown 1:279.

4927. τεχνίτης technitēs noun

Craftsman, architect, designer, artisan.

Cross-Reference:
τέκτων tektōn (4893)

אָמָּן 'ommān (554), Artificer (S/S 7:1).

חָצַב chātsav (2778), Stonecutter (1 Chr 22:15).

חָרָשׁ chārāsh (2900), Craftsman (1 Chr 29:5, Jer 10:9, 24:1).

1. **τεχνίτης technitēs** nom sing masc
2. **τεχνῖται technitai** nom pl masc
3. **τεχνίταις technitais** dat pl masc

3 brought no small gain unto the **craftsmen**;..........Acts 19:24
2 Demetrius, and the **craftsmen** which are with him,..... 19:38
1 whose **builder** and maker is God..................Heb 11:10
1 and no **craftsman**, of whatsoever craft he be,....... Rev 18:22

Classical Greek

Throughout classical Greek *technitēs* was a term used to describe a variety of skilled craftsmen such as engravers, wood-carvers, stonemasons, and potters (cf. *Liddell-Scott*). In general, *technitēs* referred to any number of skilled individuals—artists, musicians, designers, etc. A second- or third-century document (*Dio Cassius* 63.29) supposedly records the words of Nero just prior to his suicide (a fatal stab wound into the throat): "*Hoios technitēs parapollumai*"; that is, "O what a great *artist* I am wasting (destroying)" (cf. Latin = "*qualis artifex pereo*"; ibid.). Although a rare figurative use translates the word as "trickster" (one *skilled* in trickery), the most common meaning is a "craftsman."

Septuagint Usage

The Septuagint translates three Hebrew terms as *technitēs*: *chātsav* (a hewer of stones—2 Kings 12:12 [LXX 4 Kings 12:12]), *'ommān* (a master workman, an artist—Song of Solomon 7:1,2), *chārāsh* (an engraver, a woodworker—Jeremiah 10:9, 24:1). The common classical meaning is evident in each Septuagintal occurrence.

New Testament Usage

In the New Testament four passages contain the word *technitēs*. Acts 19:24,38 describes a guild of skilled craftsmen who were associated with the temple of Artemis in the city of Ephesus. One *technitēs* named Demetrius (verse 24f.) stirred up a riot in this heathen town because the rise of Christianity was creating a decline in the sale of handcrafted religious artifacts. In Hebrews 11:10 God is called the "*builder* and maker" of the heavenly city for which Abraham looked. Lastly, Revelation 18:22 uses the word *technitēs* as a general term to describe the various musicians, artists, and other craftsmen who perished in the "great city Babylon" (verse 21) when the wrath of God destroyed it in 1 hour.

Strong 5079, Bauer 814, Moulton-Milligan 633, Liddell-Scott 1785, Colin Brown 1:279.

4928. τήκω tēkō verb

To make liquid, to melt.

בָּקַע bāqa' (1260), Break open, split; hithpael: be split (Mi 1:4).

דְּאָבוֹן d^e'āvôn (1719), Despair (Dt 28:65).

זָרַב zārav (2302), Pual: be dried up (Jb 6:17).

כָּלָה kālâh (3735), Qal: fail (Jb 11:20); piel: cause to fail (Jb 31:16—Codex Alexandrinus only).

מוּג mûgh (4265), Niphal: melt away (Ex 15:15); totter (Ps 75:3 [74:3]); hithpael: melt away (Ps 107:26 [106:26]).

מָזֶה māzeh (4328), Wasting (Dt 32:24).

מָסָה māsâh (4678), Hiphil: melt (Ps 147:18 [147:7]).

מָסַס māsas (4701), Niphal: melt (Ex 16:21, 2 Sm 17:10, Ps 68:2 [67:2]).

מָקַק māqaq (4905), Niphal: waste away, rot (Lv 26:39, Ez 33:10, Zec 14:12); hiphil: be made to rot (Zec 14:12).

נָזַל nāzal (5320), Flow down (Is 64:1).

נָתַךְ nāthakh (5597), Niphal: be poured out (Na 1:6).

שָׁחַח shāchach (8249), Crouch, stoop; collapse (Hb 3:6).

תָּמַם tāmam (8882), Be finished, be complete; hiphil: make something be completely done (Ez 24:10).

תֶּמֶס temes (8886), Melting (Ps 58:8 [57:8]).

1. τήκεται tēketai 3sing indic pres mid

1 and the elements shall melt with fervent heat? .... 2 Pt 3:12

Classical Greek and Septuagint Usage

This term has several nuances in Greek literature. With the active voice it could be used transitively meaning "melt down" (of metals) or "bring down" (of rain). Used metaphorically it means "dissolve" or "pine away" (of the spirit). In the passive voice it could be translated "melt" or "thaw" (of snow) or "fall away" (of putrefying flesh). It appears frequently in the Septuagint, a common example of which can be found at Isaiah 34:4: "And all the host of heaven shall be *dissolved*" ("rot away," RSV).

New Testament Usage

Tēkō occurs once in the New Testament (2 Peter 3:12), where it means "melt," of the "elements (which) will *melt* with fire" (RSV). *Luō* (3061) may also be translated "melt" or "dissolve" (cf. 2 Peter 3:10ff.).

Strong 5080, Bauer 814, Moulton-Milligan 633, Liddell-Scott 1786-87.

4929. τηλαυγῶς tēlaugōs adv

Clearly.

1. τηλαυγῶς tēlaugōs

1 and he was restored, and saw every man clearly..... Mark 8:25

This term appears in classical Greek from the Fifth Century B.C. literally meaning "far-shining," but it is generally used as "clear, plain" (*Bauer*). *Tēlaugōs* also appears several times in the Septuagint where it is translated "clear spot." It is used only once in the New Testament, in Mark 8:25, where Jesus healed the blind man at Bethsaida, and he "began to see everything *clearly*" (NASB).

Strong 5086, Bauer 814, Moulton-Milligan 633, Liddell-Scott 1787.

4930. τηλικοῦτος tēlikoutos dem-pron

So old, so young, so great, so important.

1. τηλικοῦτος tēlikoutos nom sing masc
2. τηλικούτου tēlikoutou gen sing masc
3. τηλικαύτης tēlikautēs gen sing fem
4. τηλικαῦτα tēlikauta nom pl neu
5. τηλικούτων tēlikoutōn gen pl masc

2 Who delivered us from so great a death, ... 2 Co 1:10
3 escape, if we neglect so great salvation; .... Heb 2:3
4 also the ships, which though they be so great, ... Jas 3:4
1 so mighty an earthquake, and so great. .... Rev 16:18

Tēlikoutos is a demonstrative pronoun used by the ancient Greeks to describe the age, size, or magnitude of a person or thing. In the New Testament the word is used only of things, physical or otherwise. Hebrews 2:3 speaks of neglecting "*so great* salvation," and Paul wrote that Christians have been delivered from "*so great* a death" (2 Corinthians 1:10).

Speaking of physical objects James 3:4 uses *tēlikoutos* to say, "the ships . . . though they be *so great* . . . . " Revelation 16:18, "*so mighty* an earthquake," is an unusual use of the term because a synonymous phrase, *houtōs megas*, "so great," is added for emphasis.

Strong 5082, Bauer 814, Moulton-Milligan 633, Liddell-Scott 1787-88.

4931. τηρέω tēreō verb

Watch carefully, guard; keep, hold in reserve, preserve; observe, obey, pay attention to.

Cognates:
- διατηρέω diatēreō (1295)
- παρατηρέω paratēreō (3767)
- συντηρέω suntēreō (4785)
- τήρησις tērēsis (4932)

Synonyms:
- ἀντέχομαι antechomai (469)
- ἀσφαλίζω asphalizō (799)
- κατέχω katechō (2692)
- κρατέω krateō (2875)
- παρατηρέω paratēreō (3767)
- φυλάσσω phulassō (5278)

נָטַר nātar (5386), Caretaker (S/S 8:11); tend (S/S 8:12).

נָצַר nātsar (5526), Guard, keep (Prv 2:11, 3:1, 4:6).

צָפַן tsāphan (7121), Store up (S/S 7:13).

קוּם qûm (7251), Stand, arise; hiphil: carry out (1 Sm 15:11).

שְׁכַח shᵉkhach (A8320), Haphel: find (Dn 6:11—Aramaic).

שָׁמַע shāmaʿ (8471), Hear; heed (Prv 15:32 [16:3]).

שָׁמַר shāmar (8490), Keep, watch (Ezr 8:29, Prv 7:5, Eccl 11:4).

1. τηρῶ tērō 1sing indic pres act
2. τηρεῖ tērei 3sing indic pres act
3. τηροῦμεν tēroumen 1pl indic pres act
4. τηρῇ tērē 3sing subj pres act
5. τηρῶμεν tērōmen 1pl subj pres act
6. τήρει tērei 2sing impr pres act
7. τηρεῖτε tēreite 2pl impr pres act
8. τηρῶν tērōn nom sing masc part pres act
9. τηροῦντες tērountes nom pl masc part pres act
10. τηρούντων tērountōn gen pl masc part pres act
11. τηρεῖν tērein inf pres act
12. ἐτήρησα etērēsa 1sing indic aor act
13. ἐτήρησας etērēsas 2sing indic aor act
14. ἐτήρησαν etērēsan 3pl indic aor act
15. τηρήσῃς tērēsēs 2sing subj aor act
16. τηρήσῃ tērēsē 3sing subj aor act
17. τηρήσητε tērēsēte 2pl subj aor act
18. τήρησον tērēson 2sing impr aor act
19. τηρήσατε tērēsate 2pl impr aor act
20. τηρήσαντας tērēsantas acc pl masc part aor act
21. τηρῆσαι tērēsai inf aor act
22. τετήρηκα tetērēka 1sing indic perf act
23. τετήρηκας tetērēkas 2sing indic perf act
24. τετήρηκεν tetērēken 3sing indic perf act
25. τετηρήκασιν tetērēkasin 3pl indic perf act
26. τηρήσω tērēsō 1sing indic fut act
27. τηρήσει tērēsei 3sing indic fut act
28. τηρήσουσιν tērēsousin 3pl indic fut act
29. ἐτήρουν etēroun 1/3sing/pl indic imperf act
30. τηρούμενοι tēroumenoi nom pl masc part pres mid
31. τηρεῖσθαι tēreisthai inf pres mid
32. τηρηθείη tērētheiē 3sing opt aor pass
33. τηρηθῆναι tērēthēnai inf aor pass
34. τετήρηται tetērētai 3sing indic perf mid
35. τετηρημένοις tetērēmenois dat pl masc part perf mid
36. τετηρημένους tetērēmenous acc pl masc part perf mid
37. τετηρημένην tetērēmenēn acc sing fem part perf mid
38. ἐτηρεῖτο etēreito 3sing indic imperf pass
39. τετήρηκαν tetērēkan 3pl indic perf act
40. τηρήσετε tērēsete 2pl indic fut act
41. τηρουμένους tēroumenous acc pl masc part pres mid
42. τηρήσωμεν tērēsōmen 1pl subj aor act

18 thou wilt enter into life, **keep** the commandments. Matt 19:17
11 All therefore whatsoever they bid you **observe**, ... 23:3
7 they bid you observe, that **observe** and do; 23:3
29 And sitting down they **watched** him there; 27:36
9 and they that were with him, **watching** Jesus, ... 27:54
9 And for fear of him the **keepers** did shake, ... 28:4
11 Teaching them **to observe** all things whatsoever 28:20
17 that ye **may keep** your own tradition. .... Mark 7:9
23 but thou **hast kept** the good wine until now. .... John 2:10
16 If a man **keep** my saying, he shall never see death. 8:51
16 thou sayest, If a man **keep** my saying, ... 8:52
1 but I know him, and **keep** his saying. .... John 8:55
2 because he **keepeth** not the sabbath day. 9:16
24 against the day of my burying **hath** she **kept** this. 12:7
19 If ye love me, **keep** my commandments. 14:15
8 hath my commandments, and **keepeth** them, ... 14:21
27 If a man love me, he **will keep** my words: 14:23
2 He that loveth me not **keepeth** not my sayings: 14:24
17 If ye **keep** my commandments, ye shall abide 15:10
22 even as I **have kept** my Father's commandments, ... 15:10
14 if they **have kept** my saying, ... 15:20
28 they **will keep** yours also. 15:20
25 gavest them me; and they **have kept** thy word. 17:6
18 Holy Father, **keep** through thine own name 17:11
29 I **kept** them in thy name: 17:12
15 but that thou **shouldest keep** them from the evil. 17:15
38 Peter therefore **was kept** in prison: .... Acts 12:5
29 and the keepers before the door **kept** the prison. 12:6
11 and to command them **to keep** the law of Moses. 15:5
11 saying, Ye must be circumcised, and **keep** the law: 15:24
11 charging the jailor **to keep** them safely: 16:23
11 and concluded that they **observe** no such thing, ... 21:25
31 And he commanded a centurion **to keep** Paul, ... 24:23
31 that Paul **should be kept** at Caesarea, ... 25:4
33 **to be reserved** unto the hearing of Augustus, ... 25:21
31 him **to be kept** till I might send him to Caesar. 25:21
11 decreed in his heart that he **will keep** his virgin, ... 1 Co 7:37
12 I **have kept** myself from being burdensome .... 2 Co 11:9
26 and so **will I keep** myself. 11:9
11 **to keep** the unity of the Spirit in the bond of peace. Eph 4:3
32 spirit and soul and body **be preserved** blameless .... 1 Th 5:23
6 **keep** thyself pure. .... 1 Tm 5:22
21 That thou **keep** this commandment without spot, ... 6:14
22 I have finished my course, I **have kept** the faith: ... 2 Tm 4:7
11 and **to keep** himself unspotted from the world. ...... Jas 1:27
27 For whosoever **shall keep** the whole law, ... 2:10
37 that fadeth not away, **reserved** in heaven for you, ... 1 Pt 1:4
36 **to be reserved** unto judgment; .... 2 Pt 2:4
11 and **to reserve** the unjust unto the day of judgment 2:9
34 to whom the mist of darkness **is reserved** for ever. 2:17
30 **reserved** unto fire against the day of judgment 3:7
5 that we know him, if we **keep** his commandments. .. 1 Jn 2:3
8 and **keepeth** not his commandments, is a liar, ... 2:4
4 But whoso **keepeth** his word, ... 2:5
3 we receive ... because we **keep** his commandments, ... 3:22
8 that **keepeth** his commandments dwelleth in him, ... 3:24
5 when we love God, and **keep** his commandments. 5:2
5 the love of God, that we **keep** his commandments: 5:3
2 but he that is begotten of God **keepeth** himself, ... 5:18
35 and **preserved** in Jesus Christ, and called: .... Jude 1:1
20 And the angels which **kept** not their first estate, ... 1:6
24 **hath reserved** in everlasting chains under darkness 1:6
34 **is reserved** the blackness of darkness for ever. 1:13
19 **Keep** yourselves in the love of God, ... 1:21
9 and **keep** those things which are written therein: .... Rev 1:3
8 overcometh, and **keepeth** my works unto the end, ... 2:26
6 hast received and heard, and **hold fast**, and repent. 3:3
13 **hast kept** my word, and hast not denied my name. 3:8
13 Because thou **hast kept** the word of my patience, ... 3:10
26 I also **will keep** thee from the hour of temptation, ... 3:10
10 which **keep** the commandments of God, ... 12:17
9 here are they that **keep** the commandments of God, .. 14:12
8 he that watcheth, and **keepeth** his garments, ... 16:15
8 **keepeth** the sayings of the prophecy of this book. 22:7
10 and of them which **keep** the sayings of this book: 22:9

Classical Greek

Essentially *tēreō* means "to watch over, to keep, to guard." Implied in this is a sense of protection, care, and maintenance. A second major definition emphasizes the "watching" aspect of *tēreō*. Thus, it can mean "to observe carefully, to keep" (as in "not lose," *Bauer*), or "to watch" (for something). Furthermore, it can mean "to keep" in the sense of "to observe" (such as "to keep" a holiday). The broad sense of *tēreō* is reflected in both Biblical and nonbiblical sources alike (*Liddell-Scott*).

Septuagint Usage

Although seven Hebrew words are replaced by *tēreō*, the most important (and common) equivalents are *nātsar*, "to keep, preserve, comply with," and *shāmar*, "to guard, protect, keep watch," etc. Most of the 38 instances are found in so-called Wisdom literature (e.g., Proverbs, Sirach), and only 2 occur in the canonical historical books (Ezra 8:29 [LXX 2 Esdras 8:29], of *guarding* silver; 1 Samuel 15:11 [LXX 1 Kings 15:11], of Saul's failure to *carry out* God's instructions).

The writer of Proverbs views discretion and understanding (i.e., aspects of "Wisdom") as capable of *protecting* one from wickedness (Proverbs 2:11; cf. 4:6; 7:5; cf. Wisdom of Solomon 10:5). Moreover, *keeping* the commandments adds years to one's life (Proverbs 3:1,21; cf. Sirach 6:26). The heart must be *guarded*, for it is the wellspring of life. It is *kept* through the observance of God's instructions (Proverbs 4:20-23; 8:32f.). As a man *observes* the commandments, *watches* what he says, exhibits *care* in his ways, he *guards* (*phulassō* [5278]) his soul (cf. Proverbs 13:3; 16:17; 19:16). God also *keeps* His covenant with His people (Daniel 9:4).

New Testament Usage

Tēreō is particularly important in the New Testament and is used of *keeping* (i.e., obeying) the commandments (Matthew 19:17; 1 Timothy 6:14; James 2:10; cf. Revelation 12:17; 14:12). It especially refers to *keeping* Jesus' commands or His word—synonymous ideas (John 8:51,52; 14:15,21,23,24; 1 John 2:3-5; 5:3). Jesus himself modeled such obedience by *keeping* the word of the Father (John 8:55; 15:10; 17:6).

Acts uses *tēreō* almost exclusively of imprisonment. The same holds true in 2 Peter (2:4,9,17) and in Jude (6,13). Jude 1 and 21, however, speak of believers *being kept* by Jesus Christ (cf. John 17:11,12,15) and *keeping* themselves in God while they await their Lord.

Strong 5083, Bauer 814-15, Moulton-Milligan 633, Kittel 8:140-46, Liddell-Scott 1789, Colin Brown 2:132-33,135,137.

4932. τήρησις tērēsis noun

Custody, prison, guarding; obeying, keeping.

Cross-Reference:
τηρέω tēreō (4931)

1. **τήρησις tērēsis** nom sing fem
2. **τηρήσει tērēsei** dat sing fem
3. **τήρησιν tērēsin** acc sing fem

3 **and put them in hold unto the next day:** .... Acts 4:3
2 **and put them in the common prison.** 5:18
1 **but the keeping of the commandments of God.** ...... 1 Co 7:19

Classical Greek

In classical Greek literature *tērēsis* is used primarily with the idea of a "vigilance" or "watch." Later it came to be used of medical or scientific "observations." Classical usage also includes "preservation" of one's health (*Liddell-Scott*).

Septuagint Usage

By the time of the Septuagint the term had acquired three quite different meanings. Each of these is found in the Septuagint's apocryphal books, but *tērēsis* is never used to translate any Old Testament Hebrew term. One use was for a military "watch" of a city (1 Maccabees 5:18). Another was for "guarding" a person against a robbery (2 Maccabees 3:40). And the third was for the "observance" of commandments (Wisdom of Solomon 6:18; Sirach 32:23 [LXX 35:23]).

New Testament Usage

In the New Testament *tērēsis* is used twice of a "prison." Acts 4:3 states that Peter and John were put "in hold" (i.e., "jail"), and Acts 5:18 mentions that all the apostles were thrown into the "common prison." In addition, the Septuagintal usage, "observance" of commandments, is found in 1 Corinthians 7:19. Here Paul contrasted the demands of the Christian way with the practice of circumcision: "Circumcision is nothing, and uncircumcision is nothing, but the keeping (*tērēsis*) of the commandments of God (matters)." The word "keeping" seems to be the pivotal meaning between the two main uses. This is consistent with *tēreō* (4931), "keep, hold," which has the same root.

Strong 5084, Bauer 815, Moulton-Milligan 633-34, Kittel 8:146, Liddell-Scott 1789, Colin Brown 2:132-33.

4933. Τιβεριάς Tiberias name

Tiberias.

1. **Τιβεριάδος Tiberiados** gen fem

1 **the sea of Galilee, which is the sea of Tiberias.** ..... John 6:1
1 **Howbeit there came other boats from Tiberias** 6:23
1 **again to the disciples at the sea of Tiberias;** 21:1

A city on the west coast of the Sea of Galilee. It was built by Herod Antipas (ca. A.D. 20–25) as the capital of his tetrarchy and was named for the Emperor Tiberius. Although it was a major city by the time of Jesus' public ministry, there is no record that He visited it. It is only mentioned in the New Testament at John 6:23. The Sea of Galilee came to be known as the Sea of Tiberias and is twice so named in John (6:1; 21:1).

4934. Τιβέριος Tiberios name

Tiberius.

1. Τιβερίου Tiberiou gen masc

1 Now in the fifteenth year of the reign of Tiberius... Luke 3:1

Tiberius was the emperor of Rome from A.D. 14—37, succeeding his adoptive father Augustus. Tiberius is mentioned by name in the New Testament only at Luke 3:1, but the references to "Caesar" during Jesus' adult lifetime and the first few years of the church would have had him in mind.

4935. τίθημι tithēmi verb

To put, set, place, lay down.

COGNATES:

ἀθέμιτος athemitos (111)
ἄθεσμος athesmos (113)
ἀναθεματίζω anathematizō (330)
ἀνατίθημι anatithēmi (392)
ἀντιδιατίθημι antidiatithēmi (472)
ἀντίθεσις antithesis (474)
ἀποθήκη apothēkē (591)
ἀποτίθημι apotithēmi (653)
διαθήκη diathēkē (1236)
διατίθημι diatithēmi (1297)
ἔκθετος ekthetos (1557)
ἐκτίθημι ektithēmi (1606)
ἐπιτίθημι epitithēmi (1991)
εὔθετος euthetos (2090)
θεμελιόω themelioō (2288)
θήκη thēkē (2313)
καταθεματίζω katathematizō (2586C)
κατατίθημι katatithēmi (2667)
μετατίθημι metatithēmi (3216)
νομοθεσία nomothesia (3411)
νομοθετέω nomotheteō (3412)
νομοθέτης nomothetēs (3413)
ὁροθεσία horothesia (3597)
παραθήκη parathēkē (3727)
παρακαταθήκη parakatathēkē (3733)
παρατίθημι paratithēmi (3769)
περίθεσις perithesis (3888)
περιτίθημι peritithēmi (3920)
προθεσμία prothesmia (4146)
προσανατίθημι prosanatithēmi (4181)
προστίθημι prostithēmi (4227)
προτίθημι protithēmi (4246)
συγκατάθεσις sunkatathesis (4634)
συγκατατίθημι sunkatatithēmi (4635)
συνεπιτίθεμαι sunepitithemai (4751B)
συντίθημι suntithēmi (4786)
υἱοθεσία huiothesia (5047)
ὑποτίθημι hupotithēmi (5132)

SYNONYMS:

ἀποτίθημι apotithēmi (653)
βάλλω ballō (900)
ἵστημι histēmi (2449)
καθίστημι kathistēmi (2497)
κατατίθημι katatithēmi (2667)
ὁρίζω horizō (3587)
προχειρίζομαι procheirizomai (4258)
ῥίπτω rhiptō (4352)
τάσσω tassō (4872)
ὑποτίθημι hupotithēmi (5132)
χειροτονέω cheirotoneō (5336)

אָסַף 'āṣaph (636), Put together (Gn 42:17).

בּוֹא bô' (971), Go, come; hiphil: bring (Ex 34:26).

יָצַג yātsagh (3431), Hiphil: put (Jgs 6:37).

יָצַק yātsaq (3441), Hiphil: spread out (Jos 7:23).

יָשַׁב yāshav (3553), Sit, dwell; hiphil: set (1 Kgs 2:24).

כּוּן kûn (3679), Be stable, be firm; hiphil: take (Jb 29:7).

כָּרַת kārath (3901), Cut; make (Ex 34:10, Jb 41:4 [40:23]).

מוּר mûr (4306), Hiphil: change (Hos 4:7).

נָגַע nāgha' (5236), Touch, reach; hiphil: bring down (Ez 13:14).

נוּחַ nûach (5299), Rest, settle; hiphil: deposit (Dt 14:28); put, set (1 Kgs 8:9, Ez 37:1); hophal: be set (Zec 5:11).

נָחָה nāchâh (5328), Hiphil: station, put (1 Kgs 10:26, 2 Kg 18:11).

נָחֵת nāchēth (5365), Go down; piel: bend (Ps 18:34 [17:34]).

נְחֵת nechēth (A5366), Come down; haphel: deposit (Ezr 5:15—Aramaic).

נָפַל nāphal (5489), Fall; hiphil: destroy (Est 9:24).

נָשָׂא nāsâ' (5558), Lift up (Ez 18:12,15).

נָתַן nāthan (5598), Give, put; write (Jb 19:23).

סָבַב ṣāvav (5621), Turn; hiphil: change (2 Kgs 24:17—Codex Alexandrinus only).

סְבַל ṣeval (A5629), Be laid (Ezr 6:3—Aramaic).

עָלָה 'ālâh (6148), Go up; hiphil: set up (Ez 14:4).

עָשָׂה 'āsâh (6449), Do, make; grant, set (Jb 10:12, 14:5, Prv 22:28).

פָּקַד pāqadh (6734), Seek, call to account; hiphil: store (Is 10:28).

צָוָה tsāwâh (6943), Piel: command (Ps 78:5 [77:5]—only some Sinaiticus texts).

קוּם qûm (7251), Qal: rise up (1 Sm 22:13); hiphil: set up (Is 29:3).

רוּם rûm (7597), Be high; hiphil: raise (Is 14:13).

רְמָה remâh (A7701), Set in place (Dn 7:9—Aramaic).

שִׂים sîm (7947), Place, put (Ex 40:24, 2 Sm 8:6, Is 5:20).

שָׁוָה shāwâh (8187), Be like; piel: set, bestow (2 Sm 22:34, Ps 89:19 [88:19]).

שִׁית shîth (8308), Establish, make (Ex 23:31, 2 Sm 22:12, Is 26:1).

שָׁמַר shāmar (8490), Keep, guard (1 Sm 9:24, Ps 39:1 [38:1]).

שָׁתַת shāthath (8701), Set, make (Ps 73:9,28 [72:9,28]).

תָּקַע tāqaʿ (8965), Fasten (1 Chr 10:10).

1. **τίθημι tithēmi** 1sing indic pres act
2. **τίθησιν tithēsin** 3sing indic pres act
3. **τιθέασιν titheasin** 3pl indic pres act
4. **τιθέτω tithetō** 3sing impr pres act
5. **τιθείς titheis** nom sing masc part pres act
6. **τιθέντες tithentes** nom pl masc part pres act
7. **τιθέναι tithenai** inf pres act
8. **ἔθηκα ethēka** 1sing indic aor act
9. **ἔθηκας ethēkas** 2sing indic aor act
10. **ἔθηκεν ethēken** 3sing indic aor act
11. **ἔθηκαν ethēkan** 3pl indic aor act
12. **θῶ thō** 1sing subj aor act
13. **θῇ thē** 3sing subj aor act
14. **θείς theis** nom sing masc part aor act
15. **θέντος thentos** gen sing masc part aor act
16. **θέντες thentes** nom pl masc part aor act
17. **θεῖναι theinai** inf aor act
18. **τέθεικα tetheika** 1sing indic perf act
19. **τεθείκατε tetheikate** 2pl indic perf act
20. **τεθεικώς tetheikōs** nom sing masc part perf act
21. **θήσω thēsō** 1sing indic fut act
22. **θήσεις thēseis** 2sing indic fut act
23. **θήσει thēsei** 3sing indic fut act
24. **ἐτίθει etithei** 3sing indic imperf act
25. **ἐτίθουν etithoun** 3pl indic imperf act
26. **τίθεται tithetai** 3sing indic pres mid
27. **ἐτέθην etethēn** 1sing indic aor pass
28. **ἔθου ethou** 2sing indic aor mid
29. **ἐτέθη etethē** 3sing indic aor pass
30. **ἔθετο etheto** 3sing indic aor mid
31. **ἔθεσθε ethesthe** 2pl indic aor mid
32. **ἐτέθησαν etethēsan** 3pl indic aor pass
33. **ἔθεντο ethento** 3pl indic aor mid
34. **τεθῇ tethē** 3sing subj aor pass
35. **τεθῶσιν tethōsin** 3pl subj aor pass
36. **θέσθε thesthe** 2pl impr aor mid
37. **θέμενος themenos** nom sing masc part aor mid
38. **τεθῆναι tethēnai** inf aor pass
39. **θῶμεν thōmen** 1pl subj aor act
40. **θέτε thete** 2pl impr aor act
41. **ἐτίθεσαν etithesan** 3pl indic imperf act
42. **τέθειται tetheitai** 3sing indic perf mid
43. **τεθειμένος tetheimenos** nom sing masc part perf mid

3 light a candle, and **put** it under a bushel, ... Matt 5:15
21 I **will put** my spirit upon him, ... 12:18
30 and **put** him in prison for Herodias' sake, ... 14:3
12 till I **make** thine enemies thy footstool? 22:44
23 and **appoint** him his portion with the hypocrites: 24:51
10 And **laid** it in his own new tomb, ... 27:60
34 Is a candle brought **to be put** under a bushel, ... Mark 4:21
34 brought **to be put** on the lampstand? (NASB) 4:21
39 by what parable shall we present it? (NASB) (NT) 4:30
11 took up his corpse, and **laid** it in a tomb. 6:29
25 they **laid** the sick in the streets, ... 6:56
5 **put** his hands upon them, and blessed them. 10:16
12 till I **make** thine enemies thy footstool. 12:36
6 and **bowing** their knees worshipped him. 15:19
26 the mother of Joses beheld where he **was laid**. 15:47
11 is not here: behold the place where they **laid** him. 16:6
33 they that heard them **laid** them **up** in their hearts, .. Luke 1:66
17 means to bring him in, and **to lay** him before him. 5:18
10 and **laid** the foundation on a rock: 6:48
2 covereth it with a vessel, or **putteth** it under a bed; 8:16
2 but he **puts** it on a lampstand, (NASB) 8:16
36 Let these sayings **sink down** into your ears: 9:44
2 **putteth** it in a secret place, neither under a bushel, ... 11:33
23 **will appoint** him his portion with the unbelievers. 12:46
15 Lest haply, after he **hath laid** the foundation, ... 14:29
9 thou takest up that thou **layedst** not **down**, ... 19:21
8 Thou knewest ... taking up that I **laid** not **down**, ... 19:22
12 Till I **make** thine enemies thy footstool. 20:43
36 **Settle** it therefore in your hearts, ... 21:14
14 he ... withdrawn ... and **kneeled down**, and prayed, ... 22:41
10 and **laid** it in a sepulchre that was hewn in stone, ... 23:53
29 beheld the sepulchre, and how his body **was laid**. 23:55
2 at the beginning **doth set forth** good wine; .... John 2:10
2 the good shepherd **giveth** his life for the sheep. 10:11
1 and I **lay down** my life for the sheep. 10:15
1 my Father love me, because I **lay down** my life, ... 10:17
1 but I **lay** it **down** of myself. 10:18
17 I have power **to lay** it **down**, ... 10:18
19 And said, Where **have** ye **laid** him? 11:34
2 riseth from supper, and **laid aside** his garments; 13:4
21 I **will lay down** my life for thy sake. 13:37
22 **Wilt** thou **lay down** thy life for my sake? 13:38
13 that a man **lay down** his life for his friends. 15:13
8 but I have chosen you, and **ordained** you, ... 15:16
10 And Pilate wrote a title, and **put** it on the cross. 19:19
29 a new sepulchre, wherein was never man yet **laid**. 19:41
11 There **laid** they Jesus therefore 19:42
11 and we know not where they **have laid** him. 20:2
11 and I know not where they **have laid** him. 20:13
9 tell me where thou **hast laid** him, ... 20:15
30 which the Father hath **put** in his own power. .... Acts 1:7
12 Until I **make** thy foes thy footstool. 2:35
25 whom they **laid** daily at the gate of the temple 3:2
33 and **put** them in hold unto the next day: 4:3
25 And **laid** them down at the apostles' feet: 4:35
10 the money, and **laid** it at the apostles' feet. 4:37
10 a certain part, and **laid** it, at the apostles' feet. 5:2
28 why **hast** thou **conceived** this thing in thine heart? 5:4
7 and **laid** them on beds and couches, ... 5:15
33 and **put** them in the common prison. 5:18
31 whom ye **put** in prison are standing in the temple, ... 5:25
32 and **laid** in the sepulchre that Abraham bought 7:16
14 And he kneeled **down**, and cried with a loud voice, ... 7:60
11 they **laid** her in an upper chamber. 9:37
14 But Peter put them all forth, and kneeled **down**, ... 9:40
30 he had apprehended him, **he put** him in prison, ... 12:4
11 and **laid** him in a sepulchre. 13:29
18 I **have set** thee to be a light of the Gentiles, ... 13:47
30 Paul **purposed** in the spirit, ... 19:21
30 which the Holy Ghost **hath made** you overseers, ... 20:28
14 he kneeled **down**, and prayed with them all. 20:36
16 and we kneeled **down** on the shore, and prayed. 21:5
33 the more part advised to depart thence also, (NT) 27:12
18 I **have made** thee a father of many nations, ... Rom 4:17
1 I **lay** in Sion a stumblingstone and rock of offence: 9:33
7 that no man **put** a stumblingblock or an occasion 14:13
18 as a wise masterbuilder, I **have laid** the foundation, 1 Co 3:10

17 other foundation can no man **lay** than that is laid, 1 Co 3:11
21 I **may make** the gospel of Christ without charge,....... 9:18
30 But now hath God **set** the members every one....... 12:18
30 God **hath set** some in the church, first apostles,....... 12:28
13 reign, till he **hath put** all enemies under his feet...... 15:25
4 let every one of you **lay** by him in store,............ 16:2
24 And not as Moses, which **put** a veil over his face,..2 Co 3:13
37 **hath committed** unto us the word of reconciliation..... 5:19
30 For God **hath** not **appointed** us to wrath,.......... 1 Th 5:9
37 counted me faithful, **putting** me into the ministry;..1 Tm 1:12
27 Whereunto I **am ordained** a preacher,................. 2:7
27 Whereunto I **am appointed** a preacher,............ 2 Tm 1:11
10 his Son, whom he **hath appointed** heir of all things, Heb 1:2
12 until I **make** thine enemies thy footstool?............ 1:13
35 expecting till his enemies **be made** his footstool....... 10:13
1 Behold, I **lay** in Sion a chief corner stone,......... 1 Pt 2:6
32 whereunto also they **were appointed**.................. 2:8
20 Sodom and ... **making** them an ensample..........2 Pt 2:6
10 because he **laid down** his life for us:............... 1 Jn 3:16
7 we ought to **lay down** our lives for the brethren........ 3:16
10 He **laid** His right hand upon me, saying, (NASB)... Rev 1:17
10 and he **set** his right foot upon the sea,............... 10:2
38 not suffer their dead bodies **to be put** in graves....... 11:9

Classical Greek

This word carries both a local sense, "to set" or "to put down," as well as a derived sense, "to make, fix," or "establish." It occurs first among classical writers in Homer (Eighth Century B.C.) and is very common in subsequent writers. The word is found in a variety of usages: to place down a garment, to put down a foundation, to put someone in prison, and to place something before one's eyes. In a slightly different sense it is used to pay (lay down) the tax, to make (lay down) offerings, and to lay down shields (negotiate).

Classical writers also used *tithēmi* in an applied or derived sense. Thus, Homer speaks of building (putting down) a house or establishing (making) a friendship. An even more interesting use by Homer is the phrase "to place a child under one's girdle," i.e., to conceive (see Friedrich, "tithēmi," *Kittel,* 8:152f.). Similar applied uses would include to establish (make) a law, to take (make) a wife, and to value someone or something.

Septuagint Usage

The verb *tithēmi* is used approximately 560 times in the Septuagint where it again is generally translated as "set down, place, put on." Hence, a sword is put on (Exodus 32:27), fruits are brought (placed) to the temple (Exodus 34:26), and Achan's booty is set before the Lord (Joshua 7:23). In an applied sense, overseers are appointed (2 Kings 11:18 [LXX 4 Kings 11:18]), and people reach an agreement (Exodus 34:10). Friedrich points out that in more than a quarter of all uses of this verb in the Septuagint, God is the subject (ibid., 8:154). God placed the stars (Genesis 1:17), set boundaries for waters (Job 38:10), made Abraham the father of nations (Genesis 17:5), appointed Jeremiah as prophet (Jeremiah 1:5), established David's throne forever (Psalm 89:27 [LXX 88:27]), and sets aside man's sin (Psalm 90:8 [89:8]).

New Testament Usage

In the New Testament *tithēmi* carries four primary interpretations according to *Liddell-Scott.* The first two are local—something is set or placed, or is put down or laid down. The second two are applied meanings, "to make something" or "to establish something." The most common of approximately 100 uses in the New Testament is to "set, put," or "place." In this sense the New Testament often quotes Old Testament verses which use *tithēmi* in the Septuagint, such as 1 Peter 2:6, one of several verses to quote "I *lay* in Zion a choice stone" (NASB) from Isaiah 28:16. Another common usage in the New Testament of this first meaning is to lay the dead to rest. Twelve passages use the word this way. Similar meanings are found in putting one in prison (Acts 12:4), receiving (placing) in one's ears (Luke 9:44), and laying up (remembering) in one's heart.

The second broad meaning of *tithēmi* is "to lay down" or "put down." This sense is found in expressions such as to lay down one's life (John 10:17), to lay aside money (1 Corinthians 16:2), and to set forth (John 2:10).

The third meaning of *tithēmi* is "to make" or "appoint." Vine describes the use of this word for appointment to any kind of service (*Expository Dictionary,* "Appoint"). Christ used it of His followers (John 15:16). Paul used it of his service in the ministry (1 Timothy 1:12) and also of the appointment of overseers or elders in the church at Ephesus (Acts 20:28). It is likewise used for appointment to punishment as in the cases of the unfaithful servant (Matthew 24:51) and unbelieving Israel (1 Peter 2:8).

The final use of *tithēmi* is the meaning of "fix, establish," or "set." The New Testament use of this meaning is infrequent. One illustration is the use in Acts 27:12 to settle (resolve) something in the heart.

Strong 5087, Bauer 815-16, Moulton-Milligan 634, Kittel 8:152-58, Liddell-Scott 1790-91, Colin Brown 1:477.

4936. τίκτω tiktō verb

To bring forth, bear children, generate.

Cognates:

πρωτότοκος prōtotokos (4274)
τέκνον teknon (4891)

Synonyms:
ἀποκυέω apokueō (610)
γεννάω gennaō (1074)

הָרָה hārâh (2106), Conceive (Hos 2:5).

יָלַד yāladh (3314), Qal: give birth, bear (Gn 4:1f., 1 Chr 7:14, Is 7:14); niphal: be born (Lv 22:27, 1 Chr 2:9, Ps 78:6 [77:6]); pual: be born (Gn 24:15, 2 Sm 21:20, Jer 20:15); hiphil: beget, bring forth (Jb 38:28, Is 59:4); hophal: be born (Ez 16:4f.).

יִלּוֹד yillôdh (3318), Born (Ex 1:22, 2 Sm 12:14).

לֵדָה lēdhāh (3985), Childbirth, labor (Is 37:3, Jer 13:21).

מָלַט mālaṯ (4561), Escape; hiphil: give birth (Is 66:7).

1. **τίκτει tiktei** 3sing indic pres act
2. **τίκτῃ tiktē** 3sing subj pres act
3. **τίκτουσα tiktousa** nom sing fem part pres act
4. **ἔτεκεν eteken** 3sing indic aor act
5. **τέκῃ tekē** 3sing subj aor act
6. **τεκεῖν tekein** inf aor act
7. **ἐτέχθη etechthē** 3sing indic aor pass
8. **τεχθείς techtheis** nom sing masc part aor pass
9. **τέξῃ texē** 2sing indic fut mid
10. **τέξεται texetai** 3sing indic fut mid

10 And she **shall bring forth** a son, ... Matt 1:21
10 and **shall bring forth** a son, ... his name Emmanuel, ... 1:23
4 And knew her not till **she had brought forth** 1:25
8 Saying, Where is he that **is born** King of the Jews? 2:2
9 conceive in thy womb, and **bring forth** a son, ... Luke 1:31
6 full time came that she should **be delivered**; 1:57
6 were accomplished that she **should be delivered**. 2:6
4 And she **brought forth** her firstborn son, ... 2:7
7 **is born** this day in the city of David a Saviour, ... 2:11
2 A woman when she **is in travail** hath sorrow, ... John 16:21
3 Rejoice, thou barren that **bearest** not; .... Gal 4:27
3 and **bringeth forth** herbs meet for them .... Heb 6:7
4 **was delivered** of a child when she was past age, ... 11:11
1 when lust hath conceived, it **bringeth forth** sin: ...... Jas 1:15
6 travailing in birth, and pained **to be delivered**. ..... Rev 12:2
6 the woman which was ready **to be delivered**, ... 12:4
5 for to devour her child as soon as it **was born**. 12:4
4 And she **brought forth** a man child, ... 12:5
4 the woman which **brought forth** the man child. 12:13

Classical Greek

From the time of Homer (Eighth Century B.C.) on, *tiktō* was used with a variety of meanings. Sometimes it was used of "breeding" animals, other times of "begetting" (by the father) or "bearing" (by the mother) children. Furthermore, it referred to the earth "producing" fruit. Finally, it meant "to generate" or "to produce" (metaphorically) something (*Liddell-Scott*).

Septuagint Usage

Most of the time the Septuagint translators followed the secular Greek usage of *tiktō* except that, when referring to children, it is normally used only of the mother. As a participle, "the one who bears," *tiktō* is practically equivalent to "mother" in the Septuagint (*Moulton-Milligan*). *Gennaō* (1074) is largely used for the act of fathering a child. The Septuagint uses *tiktō* some 215 times, almost always to translate *yāladh*, "to bear." (See Bauer, "Birth," *Colin Brown*, 1:186). Once it is used for *hārâh*, "conceive" (Hosea 2:5), and once for *mālaṯ*, "give birth" (Isaiah 66:7). Elsewhere in the Septuagint the variant form *ektiktō* refers to producing fruit from the earth (Isaiah 55:10). On several occasions the word is used metaphorically, to express how something is brought forth. Numbers 11:12 and Isaiah 66:8 both speak of a nation being "brought forth" while Psalm 7:14 says, "He hath conceived mischief, and *brought forth* (*tiktō*) falsehood."

New Testament Usage

The New Testament follows closely the Septuagintal usage of the word. Here *tiktō* is used only of the woman's role in childbearing. For instance, Matthew and Luke use *gennaō* to speak of the conception of Jesus (Matthew 1:20; Luke 1:35) but *tiktō* to speak of the actual birth process (Matthew 1:21; Luke 2:7). Hence the New Testament use of *yāladh* continues to be dependent on the subject. When the subject is female it means "to bear" as in childbirth; with a male subject it means "to bring forth." If the king is the subject the definition is enhanced to mean "to bring forth as a coregent"—a common practice in Old Testament times. Thus the claim that Christ is not preexistent according to Psalm 2 is unfounded.

Only two New Testament passages use *tiktō* to describe anything but human birth. Hebrews 6:7 speaks of the land which drinks in the rain and "*produces* a crop" (NIV). Finally, James 1:15 uses the word metaphorically when it says, "After desire has conceived, it gives *birth* (*tiktō*) to sin" (NIV). Interestingly, *tiktō* is never used of spiritual birth.

Strong 5088, Bauer 816-17, Moulton-Milligan 634, Liddell-Scott 1792, Colin Brown 1:176,186-87.

4937. τίλλω tillō verb

To pull, pluck off.

מָרַט māraṯ (4965), Qal: pull out (Ezr 9:3); pual: be smooth-skinned (Is 18:7).

מְרַט mᵉraṯ (A4966), Be plucked (Dn 7:4—Aramaic).

1. **τίλλοντες tillontes** nom pl masc part pres act
2. **τίλλειν tillein** inf pres act
3. **ἔτιλλον etillon** 3pl indic imperf act

2 his disciples ... and began **to pluck** the ears of corn, Matt 12:1

1 his disciples began, ... to **pluck** the ears of corn..... Mark 2:23
3 his disciples **plucked** the ears of corn, and did eat,.. Luke 6:1

This is a verb commonly used to describe the action of picking or plucking something such as grass or heads of grain. For example, Jesus' disciples were criticized because they "began *to pick* some heads of grain" (Matthew 12:1, NIV; Mark 2:23; Luke 6:1) and eat them on the Sabbath Day which, according to the Pharisees, constituted work.

Strong 5089, Bauer 817, Moulton-Milligan 634, Liddell-Scott 1792.

4938. Τιμαῖος Timaios name

Timeus.

1. Τιμαίου Timaiou gen masc

1 blind Bartimaeus, the son **of Timaeus**,............. Mark 10:46

A blind beggar whom Jesus healed at Jericho is identified only as Bartimeus, that is, "son of Timeus" (Mark 10:46).

4939. τιμάω timaō verb

Set a price on, value; honor, regard, respect.

Cognates:

ἀτιμάζω atimazō (812)
ἀτιμία atimia (813)
ἄτιμος atimos (814)
ἀτιμόω atimoō (815)
βαρύτιμος barutimos (921)
ἔντιμος entimos (1768)
ἐπιτιμάω epitimaō (1992)
ἰσότιμος isotimos (2445)
πολύτιμος polutimos (4046)
τιμή timē (4940)
τίμιος timios (4941)
τιμιότης timiotēs (4942)
τιμωρέω timōreō (4945)
φιλοτιμέομαι philotimeomai (5226)

Synonym:

δοξάζω doxazō (1386)

הָדַר hādhar (1991), Honor (Lv 19:32).

יָקַר yāqar (3478), Be precious (Ps 139:17 [138:17]).

כָּבֵד kāvēdh (3632), Be heavy; piel: honor (Nm 22:17, Prv 3:9, Dn 11:38); pual: be honored (Prv 27:18).

נָשָׂא nāsâ' (5558), Lift up, carry; piel: help (Est 9:3).

עָרַךְ 'ārakh (6424), Set in order, arrange; hiphil: value (Lv 27:8,14).

עֵרֶךְ 'ērekh (6425), Value (Lv 27:12).

שָׁקַל shāqal (8620), Spend (Is 55:2).

1. **τιμῶσιν timōsin** 3pl indic/subj pres act
2. **τιμῶ timō** 1sing indic pres act
3. **τιμᾷ tima** 3sing indic pres act
4. **τίμα tima** 2sing impr pres act
5. **τιμᾶτε timate** 2pl impr pres act
6. **τιμῶν timōn** nom sing masc part pres act
7. **ἐτίμησαν etimēsan** 3pl indic aor act
8. **τιμήσῃ timēsē** 3sing subj aor act
9. **τιμήσατε timēsate** 2pl impr aor act
10. **τιμήσει timēsei** 3sing indic fut act
11. **ἐτιμήσαντο etimēsanto** 3pl indic aor mid
12. **τετιμημένου tetimēmenou** gen sing masc part perf mid
13. **τιμῶσι timōsi** 3pl indic/subj pres act

4 **Honour** thy father and mother:.................. Matt 15:4
8 And **honour** not his father or his mother,............ 15:6
3 and **honoureth** me with their lips;.................. 15:8
4 **Honour** thy father and thy mother:.................. 19:19
12 the price of him that was **valued**,.................... 27:9
11 whom they of the children of Israel **did value**;........ 27:9
3 This people **honoureth** me with their lips,......... Mark 7:6
4 Moses said, **Honour** thy father and thy mother;........ 7:10
4 Defraud not, **Honour** thy father and mother.......... 10:19
4 **Honour** thy father and thy mother................ Luke 18:20
1 That all men **should honour** the Son,.............. John 5:23
1 honour the Son, even as they **honour** the Father....... 5:23
6 He that **honoureth** not the Son ... not the Father...... 5:23
3 **honoureth** not the Father which hath sent him......... 5:23
2 but I **honour** my Father, and ye do dishonour me...... 8:49
10 if any man serve me, him **will** my Father **honour**...... 12:26
7 Who also **honoured** us with many honours;........ Acts 28:10
4 **Honour** thy father and mother;.................... Eph 6:2
4 **Honour** widows that are widows indeed...........1 Tm 5:3
9 **Honour** all men. Love the brotherhood. Fear God. 1 Pt 2:17
5 Love the brotherhood. Fear God. **Honour** the king..... 2:17

Classical Greek

Timaō, "to honor, revere, respect," refers to honor or respect bestowed upon someone or something. In classical Greek it can be used of men showing "respect, honor, reverence" to the gods or of gods conferring "honor and respect" upon man. From this latter sense comes the meaning "to reward, to give honors to" (*Liddell-Scott*). It can also mean "to esteem, to value, to prize" when used of things. Its active forms frequently function as legal terms meaning "to estimate the amount of punishment, to award the penalty," plus various other shades of meaning derived from this (ibid.). The idea of "setting a value, a price" in the nonlegal sense is also attested (*Moulton-Milligan*).

Septuagint Usage

Timaō occurs in the Septuagint approximately 50 times, but only 21 of these are canonical. Most often *kāvēdh,* "to honor/be honored," and *'ārakh* (in the hiphil), "to value, to estimate," are the Hebrew words behind *timaō;* but four other terms are also replaced by it. In the Ten Commandments *timaō* is used in the command, "*Honor* your father and your mother" (Exodus 20:12, NIV; Deuteronomy 5:16). This command continued to play an important role in Israel's ethics (e.g., Tobit 4:3; Sirach 3:3,5).

Leviticus 19:32 commands Israelites to "show respect" (NIV) for the elderly (cf. Esther 9:3 of respect shown to the Jews). And in another usage *timaō* refers to the practice of setting a value when dedicating persons to the Lord (Leviticus 27:8,12). In Numbers 22:17,37 and 24:11 it refers to a reward.

God is also the object of mankind's "honor" or "respect" (Proverbs 3:9; cf. 7:2 in the Septuagint; Wisdom of Solomon 14:15-20). This is also true of His wisdom (Proverbs 4:8; cf. 6:8 in the Septuagint; Wisdom of Solomon 6:21) and His temple (2 Maccabees 3:2; cf. 3 Maccabees 3:16). Proverbs makes it vividly clear that honoring God is not merely a vertical relationship (Proverbs 14:31; cf. James 1:27).

New Testament Usage

On six occasions the New Testament writers endorsed the Old Testament command (Exodus 20:12; Deuteronomy 5:16) to "honor" mother and father (Matthew 15:4; 19:19; Mark 7:10; 10:19; Luke 18:20; Ephesians 6:2). Moreover, that this command mainly comes from Jesus himself reflects how seriously the Biblical writers—and God—took this command.

God is likewise to be the object of men's honor and respect. The kind of reverence God expects is not lip service but heartfelt devotion (Matthew 15:4-9; parallel Mark 7:6). In addition, men honor God by their relationship with others. We particularly evidence our "honor" of God in our attitude and response to His Son (John 5:23).

A more secular understanding of *timaō* occurs in Acts where the islanders on Malta honored Paul and his party in a tangible way (28:10). Paul was concerned in 1 Timothy (5:3) that genuine widows received "honor" (perhaps monetary; cf. the noun *timē* [4940], especially in the Pastoral Epistles). For civil reasons Peter encouraged his readers to show respect to the king (1 Peter 2:17). He was not suggesting that the kind of honor due to God alone be given to the emperor; rather, without compromising faith, he advised Christians to live peaceably in the world.

STRONG 5091, BAUER 817, MOULTON-MILLIGAN 634-35, KITTEL 8:169-80, LIDDELL-SCOTT 1793, COLIN BROWN 2:48-50.

4940. τιμή timē noun

Price, value; honor, recognition, respect.

CROSS-REFERENCE:

τιμάω timaō (4939)

הָדָר hādhār (1994), Majesty (Jb 40:10 [40:5]).

הוֹד hôdh (2003), Majesty (Jb 37:22).

יָקַר yāqar (3478), Be costly (Ps 49:8 [48:8]).

יָקָר yāqār (3479), Honorable (Ps 45:9 [44:9]).

יְקָר y^eqār (3480), Honor, favor (Est 1:20, Dn 1:9); pomp (Ps 49:12 [48:12]).

יְקָר y^eqār (A3481), Strength, glory (Dn 2:37, 7:14—Aramaic).

כָּבוֹד kāvôdh (3638), Glory, honor (Ex 28:2, 2 Chr 32:33, Is 14:18).

כֶּסֶף keseph (3826B), Silver, money (Gn 44:2, Jb 31:39).

מְחִיר m^echîr (4379), Price (Is 55:1).

מֶכֶר mekher (4514), Price (Nm 20:19).

עֹז 'ōz (6010), Strength (Pss 29:1 [28:1], 96:7 [95:7]).

עֵרֶךְ 'ērekh (6425), Value, valuation (Lv 5:15, 27:2f.,16f.).

שְׂאֵת $s^{e'}$ēth (7874), High position (Ps 62:4 [61:4]).

1. τιμή timē nom sing fem
2. τιμῆς timēs gen sing fem
3. τιμῇ timē dat sing fem
4. τιμήν timēn acc sing fem
5. τιμαῖς timais dat pl fem
6. τιμάς timas acc pl fem

1 because it is the **price** of blood.................... Matt 27:6
4 the **price** of him that was valued,..................... 27:9
4 that a prophet hath no **honour** in his own country... John 4:44
6 and brought the **prices** of the things that were sold,..Acts 4:34
2 And kept back part of the **price**,...................... 5:2
2 and to keep back part of the **price** of the land?......... 5:3
2 bought for a **sum** of money of the sons of Emmor...... 7:16
6 and they counted the **price** of them,................. 19:19
5 Who also honoured us with many **honours**;............ 28:10
4 seek for glory and **honour** and immortality,......... Rom 2:7
1 But glory, **honour**, and peace,......................... 2:10
4 of the same lump to make one vessel unto **honour**,..... 9:21
3 in **honour** preferring one another;.................... 12:10
4 **honour** to whom honour............................. 13:7
4 honour to whom **honour**............................. 13:7
2 For ye are bought **with a price**:.....................1 Co 6:20
2 bought **with a price**; be not ye the servants of men...... 7:23
4 upon these we bestow more abundant **honour**;......... 12:23
4 more abundant **honour** to that part which lacked:...... 12:24
3 not in any **honour** to the satisfying of the flesh....... Col 2:23
3 to possess his vessel in sanctification and **honour**;... 1 Th 4:4
1 God, be **honour** and glory for ever and ever........ 1 Tm 1:17
2 be counted worthy of double **honour**,................. 5:17
2 count their own masters worthy of all **honour**,.......... 6:1
1 to whom be **honour** and power everlasting. Amen....... 6:16
4 and some to **honour**, and some to dishonour........ 2 Tm 2:20
4 he shall be a vessel unto **honour**, sanctified,............ 2:21
3 thou crownedst him with glory and **honour**,..........Heb 2:7
3 we see Jesus, ... crowned with glory and **honour**;........ 2:9
4 hath more **honour** than the house...................... 3:3
4 And no man taketh this **honour** unto himself,.......... 5:4
4 might be found unto praise and **honour** and glory... 1 Pt 1:7
1 Unto you therefore which believe he **is precious**:........ 2:7
4 giving **honour** unto the wife,.......................... 3:7
4 received from God the Father **honour** and glory,.... 2 Pt 1:17
4 And when those beasts give glory and **honour**....... Rev 4:9
4 worthy, ... to receive glory and **honour** and power:...... 4:11
4 and strength, and **honour**, and glory, and blessing....... 5:12
1 heard I saying, Blessing, and **honour**, and glory,....... 5:13
1 and thanksgiving, and **honour**, and power,.............. 7:12
1 and **honour**, and power, unto the Lord our God:...... 19:1

4 do bring their glory and **honour** into it............ Rev 21:24
4 bring the glory and **honour** of the nations into it....... 21:26

Classical Greek

Throughout the classical period the noun *timē* reflected three general meanings. First, there was the idea of "worth" being ascribed to an individual. (The etymological roots of the English word *worship*, i.e., "worth-ship," maintain this sense.) This ascribed worth or "honor" was given to Roman senators, kings, and those considered superior (socially or materially). In addition, heathen gods were honored or "esteemed" through hymns of praise and worship. In return, they supposedly "honored" men with wealth, gifts, and a variety of material rewards. This latter aspect of material wealth conveys the second meaning of *timē* which relates to the concept of "worth, value, price." It also parallels a third, almost synonymous meaning which has to do with "commendations, awards, rewards." Some, in fact, believe that the original sense of *timē* was "compensation" (Schneider, "timē," *Kittel*, 8:169).

Concerning the early Greek concepts of *timē* Schneider reports, "Gradually *timē* detaches itself from real possessions and becomes an abstract concept of honour. That the original elements in the meaning of the word were never wholly lost can be seen in the fact that in the Koine *timē* can mean both 'honour' and 'price' " (ibid., p.171). Plato, Aristotle, and later Stoic philosophers refined the concept of honor and applied it more strictly to inward morality. Aristotle, for example, concluded that the "high-minded man must be virtuous, for there is no honour without virtue" (idem). The fullest development of honor as an inward virtue was set forth by the Stoics who believed that a wise person is one who is free from passion, unmoved by grief, pain, or pleasure, and who is submissive to the natural laws. They viewed *timē*, "inward honor," as the sense of one's own worth and therefore of primary importance.

Septuagint Usage

As in classical Greek literature, the Septuagint use of *timē* shows a variety of meanings. This can be seen in that 11 different Hebrew terms are translated by this Greek word. Among the range of possible meanings are examples in Ezekiel 22:25 where *timē* refers to "treasure" or valuable things, and in Job 31:39 where it is translated as "payment" in the New International Version. (See also Exodus 34:20, where *timē* refers to the ransom paid for the firstborn, and Numbers 20:19 where it denotes the price offered to the Edomites by Israel as they neared their borders en route to the Promised Land [see Septuagint research section above for other examples].)

The more significant use of *timē* in the Septuagint can be seen in passages where it refers to honor in the sense of affording due regard or esteem. Of course, God is honored and given glory (Psalms 29:1 [LXX 28:1]; 96:7 [95:7]), but the Scriptures teach that God has also crowned man with "glory and *honor*" (Psalm 8:4-9). In other words, man has "value, honor," or "worth" because the Creator has "crowned" (Hebrew *ʿāṭar*, "to surround or encircle"; Greek *stephanoō* [4588], "to crown, honor, reward") him with value, honor, and worth. A man's or woman's self-worth, therefore, exists not as a result of achievement, power, wealth, class, appearance, etc., but because God has attributed or imputed worth. The sacrifice of the only begotten Son reflects the price the Father was willing to pay in order to redeem fallen man.

The Old Testament records that honor (i.e., reverence, respect, esteem) must be given to various individuals not only because of their God-given worth but because of their social position in the culture. Kings, for example, are to be honored (Job 34:19; Proverbs 24:21; 25:6), as are the elderly (Leviticus 19:32) and one's parents (Exodus 20:12). Others who receive honor include wealthy individuals (Genesis 31:1) and people of influence (Job 29:20).

New Testament Usage

As in classical Greek, the word *timē* conveys several meanings in the New Testament. First and foremost, God is to be honored and given glory (see 1 Timothy 6:16; Revelation 4:11). Christ too is crowned with "glory and *honor*" (Hebrews 2:7,9). Next, the New Testament teaches that *all* people—regardless of position, sex, race, social status, etc.—are to be honored (1 Peter 2:17). Again this is true because God has crowned man with "glory and *honor*" (Psalm 8:4-9) and because the image of God remains as an element of man's basic nature even though this image is warped and perverted due to sin.

Beyond the basic honor given to all, the New Testament requires that special honor be given to certain individuals such as rulers (Romans 13:7), wives (1 Peter 3:7), slave owners (1 Timothy 6:1), church elders (1 Timothy 5:17), widows (1 Timothy 5:3), and "responsible leaders of the congregation in general (Philippians 2:29)" (Aalen, "Glory, Honour," *Colin Brown*, 2:50f.).

In a unique contrast to the above standards (and to standards of the world) 1 Corinthians 12 teaches that the "parts of the body (of Christ) that seem to be weaker are indispensable, and the parts that we think are less honorable we (should) treat with special honor" (verses 22,23, NIV). Each of the above examples employs an aspect of the word *timē* which relates to "worth, honor, respect," or "esteem."

As noted earlier, however, the Koine Greek (including that of the New Testament) did not altogether lose the aspect of *timē*'s meaning which relates to "price." First Corinthians 6:20 and 7:23, for example, state that the believer has been bought with a *timē*, "price," i.e., the blood of Jesus. Contrary to a popular but erroneous doctrine, this "price" was not paid to the devil but served as a "propitiation" to God for the sin of man (see *hilasmos* [2410]). The idea of "price" is seen also in Acts 4:34 and 5:2,3 where Ananias and Sapphira claimed to be presenting the "price" that a certain possession brought when sold. Similarly, Acts 19 records that, having been seized by conviction, Jews and Greeks living in Ephesus burned scrolls that were used in the practice of sorcery. The "value" (*timas*) came to 50,000 drachmas—a drachma being the equivalent of a day's wage. (See the *Concordance* above for other such uses of the word.)

STRONG 5092, BAUER 817-18, MOULTON-MILLIGAN 635, KITTEL 8:169-80, LIDDELL-SCOTT 1793-94, COLIN BROWN 2:48-50,52.

4941. τίμιος timios adj

Precious, costly, esteemed, respected.

COGNATE:
τιμάω timaō (4939)

SYNONYM:
ἔντιμος entimos (1768)

חֵפֶץ chēphets (2761), Something desirable (Prv 3:15, 8:11).

יַקִּיר yaqqîr (A3468), Honorable (Ezr 4:10—Aramaic).

יָקָר yāqār (3479), Costly, precious (1 Kgs 7:9f., 2 Chr 9:9f., Lm 4:2).

יְקָר yeqār (3480), Something precious (Jb 28:10—Codex Alexandrinus only).

רָחוֹק rāchôq (7632), Far (Prv 31:10).

1. **τιμίῳ timiō** dat sing masc/neu
2. **τίμιος timios** nom sing masc
3. **τιμίου timiou** gen sing masc
4. **τίμιον timion** acc sing masc
5. **τιμίους timious** acc pl masc
6. **τιμίαν timian** acc sing fem
7. **τιμιώτερον timiōteron** comp sing neu
8. **τίμια timia** nom/acc pl neu
9. **τιμιωτάτῳ timiōtatō** sup dat sing masc
10. **τιμιωτάτου timiōtatou** sup gen sing neu

2 had in **reputation** among all the people, ... Acts 5:34
6 neither count I my life **dear** unto myself, ... 20:24
5 gold, silver, **precious** stones, wood, hay, stubble; ... 1 Co 3:12
2 Marriage is **honourable** in all, ... Heb 13:4
4 the husbandman waiteth for the **precious** fruit .... Jas 5:7
7 much **more precious** than of gold that perisheth, ... 1 Pt 1:7
1 But with the **precious** blood of Christ, ... 1:19
8 exceeding great and **precious** promises: .... 2 Pt 1:4
1 decked with gold and **precious** stones and pearls, .. Rev 17:4
3 and **precious** stones, and of pearls, and fine linen, ... 18:12
10 and all manner vessels of **most precious** wood, ... 18:12
1 decked with gold, and **precious** stones, and pearls! 18:16
9 and her light was like unto a stone **most precious**, ... 21:11
1 were garnished with all manner of **precious** stones. ... 21:19

Classical Greek

The adjective *timios* has two basic uses. When used to describe a thing it normally refers to the object's value or cost. When used to describe a person it indicates one who is held in honor. Both usages can be traced back to the earliest classical writers. For example, Homer (Eighth Century B.C.) uses *timios* in its metaphoric sense in the *Odyssey* (10:38), while Hesiod (ca. 700 B.C.) has the more literal rendering in one of his passages. In later Greek literature, including Josephus, both the literal and the metaphoric uses of *timios* occur (compare *Antiquities* 17.9.1 and 1.18.6).

Septuagint Usage

In the Septuagint *timios* appears only in its literal sense, of things. It is usually used to translate *yāqār*, "costly, precious" (Lamentations 4:2). Most commonly it refers to "pure gold" (*lithon timion*, literally "a costly stone," see Psalm 19:10 [LXX 18:10]).

New Testament Usage

The New Testament normally uses *timios* in its literal sense. For instance, 1 Corinthians 3:12 speaks of "costly stones" (*lithous timious*; NIV) (see also James 5:7; Revelation 17:4). Particularly interesting among those passages using *timios* literally are Acts 20:24, 1 Peter 1:19, and 2 Peter 1:4. In the first, Paul said his life was not precious (literally "of no account I make my life precious to myself") compared to the preaching of the gospel. In the second, Peter contrasted the truly "precious blood of Christ" with things we normally consider valuable: gold and silver (verse 18). In the third, Peter described God's promises as "precious," especially compared to the corruption of the world.

There are only two instances in the New Testament of *timios* used in its metaphoric sense. The first (Acts 5:34) describes a person (Gamaliel), as is usually the case. The second (Hebrews 13:4) departs from the usual metaphoric usage. Instead of a person, *timios* here refers to *marriage* as "honorable."

Like other Greek adjectives, *timios* admits of degrees of comparison. Thus, 1 Peter 1:7 gives us the comparative degree of *timios*: " . . . your faith, being much more *precious* (*polu timiōteron*) than of gold." We find a rare instance of a superlative degree in Revelation: " . . . a stone most *precious* (*timiōtatō*)" (21:11).

Strong 5093, Bauer 818, Moulton-Milligan 635, Liddell-Scott 1794.

4942. τιμιότης timiotēs noun

Preciousness, costliness.

Cross-Reference:
τιμάω timaō (4939)

1. τιμιότητος timiotētos gen sing fem

1 were made rich ... by reason of her **costliness!** ...... Rev 18:19

Timiotēs—from *timē* (4940), "price, value," or "precious thing"—is found but once in the New Testament. Although it is an abstract term it is used in Revelation 18:19 to refer to an abundance of costly material goods: "All who had ships on the sea became *rich* through her wealth" (NIV).

Strong 5094, Bauer 818, Moulton-Milligan 635, Liddell-Scott 1794.

4943. Τιμόθεος Timotheos name

Timothy.

1. Τιμόθεος Timotheos nom masc
2. Τιμοθέου Timotheou gen masc
3. Τιμοθέῳ Timotheō dat masc
4. Τιμόθεον Timotheon acc masc
5. Τιμόθεε Timothee voc masc

1 a certain disciple was there, named **Timotheus,** ..... Acts 16:1
1 but Silas and **Timotheus** abode there still. 17:14
4 and **Timotheus** for to come to him with all speed, ... 17:15
1 Silas and **Timotheus** were come from Macedonia, ... 18:5
4 that ministered unto him, **Timotheus** and Erastus; 19:22
1 Secundus; and Gaius of Derbe, and **Timotheus;** 20:4
1 **Timotheus** my workfellow, and Lucius, and Jason, .. Rom 16:21
4 For this cause have I sent unto you **Timotheus,** ..... 1 Co 4:17
1 if **Timotheus** come, see that he may be with you 16:10
1 Paul, an apostle ... and **Timothy** our brother, ... 2 Co 1:1
2 even by me and Silvanus and **Timotheus,** 1:19
1 Paul and **Timotheus,** the servants of Jesus Christ, ... Phlp 1:1
4 But I trust in the Lord Jesus to send **Timotheus** 2:19
1 Paul, an apostle ... and **Timotheus** our brother, ... Col 1:1
1 Paul, and Silvanus, and **Timotheus,** .... 1 Th 1:1
4 sent **Timotheus,** our brother, and minister of God, ... 3:2
2 But now when **Timotheus** came from you unto us, ... 3:6
1 Paul, and Silvanus, and **Timotheus,** .... 2 Th 1:1
3 Unto **Timothy,** my own son in the faith: .... 1 Tm 1:2
5 This charge I commit unto thee, son **Timothy,** 1:18
5 O **Timothy,** keep that which is committed 6:20
3 To **Timothy,** my dearly beloved son: Grace, ... 2 Tm 1:2
1 prisoner of Jesus Christ, and **Timothy** our brother, .. Phlm 1:1
4 Know ye that our brother **Timothy** is set at liberty; Heb 13:23

On his second missionary visit to Lystra in Asia Minor, Paul met a young man named Timothy (Acts 16:1-3). He was a Christian whose mother Eunice and grandmother Lois were also Christians (1 Timothy 1:5). As they were Jewish, he was considered a Jew, although his father was Greek. Paul felt personally involved in his conversion and addressed him as his "son in the faith" (1 Timothy 1:2; cf. 1 Corinthians 4:17).

Timothy was well respected by the local believers (Acts 16:2) and singled out by words of prophecy (1 Timothy 1:18). It may well have been at this time that the elders laid hands on him (1 Timothy 4:14). Paul had him circumcised to forestall Jewish charges of neglecting the Law (Acts 16:3), and he became a constant companion of Paul (e.g., Acts 20:4) and an increasingly trusted coworker. He was at times left to complete a task for Paul (Acts 17:14) or sent on a specific mission (Acts 19:22; 1 Timothy 1:3, in Ephesus). His name appears with Paul's at the head of six of the apostle's letters (2 Corinthians 1:1; Philippians 1:1; Colossians 1:1; 1 Thessalonians 1:1; 2 Thessalonians 1:1; Philemon 1). Philippians 2:19-23 bears witness to the love and esteem Paul held for Timothy late in his life.

Nevertheless, the relationship remained one of mentor and assistant. In the Pastoral Epistles Timothy is shown as timid (2 Timothy 1:7) and liable to be discounted (1 Corinthians 16:10f.) because of his youth (1 Timothy 4:12). He was frequently ill (1 Timothy 5:23). Most of the other references to him are general exhortations to keep the true faith, guard his holiness, and stay full of zeal, together with specific instructions to guide him in leading the church and performing his ministry.

There is only one reference to Timothy outside of Acts and the Pauline letters. It is usually assumed that he is the Timothy whose release is reported in Hebrews 13:23.

4944. Τίμων Timōn name

Timon.

1. Τίμωνα Timōna acc masc

1 Philip, and Prochorus, and Nicanor, and **Timon,** ..... Acts 6:5

One of the seven chosen by the Early Church to supervise the daily distribution to the needy (Acts 6:5).

4945. τιμωρέω timōreō verb

To avenge, to punish; to have someone punished.

Cognates:
τιμάω timaō (4939)
τιμωρία timōria (4946)

Synonym:
κολάζω kolazō (2822)

שָׁכֹל shākhōl (8323), Be bereaved; piel: bereave, leave childless (Ez 5:17, 14:15).

1. **τιμωρῶν timōrōn** nom sing masc part pres act
2. **τιμωρηθῶσιν timōrēthōsin** 3pl subj aor pass

2 bound unto Jerusalem, for **to be punished**. . . . . Acts 22:5
1 And I **punished** them oft in every synagogue, ... 26:11

To the early Greeks this word could mean "to help," to redress an injury, or to avenge or punish a wrong. The verb is used twice in the New Testament, both times by Paul. The first instance is in Acts 22:5 where Paul recounted how he went to Damascus to take Christians to Jerusalem "as prisoners *to be punished*" (NASB). Later, in Acts 26:11, Paul used *timōreō* in the active voice when he said, "I *punished* them often in all the synagogues" (NASB).

Strong 5097, Bauer 818, Moulton-Milligan 636, Liddell-Scott 1794-95.

4946. τιμωρία timōria noun

Punishment, retribution.

Cognate:
τιμωρέω timōreō (4945)

Synonyms:
ἐκδίκησις ekdikēsis (1544)
ἐπιτιμία epitimia (1993)
κόλασις kolasis (2824)

מַהֲלֻמוֹת mahălumôth (4253), Beating (Prv 19:29).

פִּיד pîdh (6608), Ruin (Prv 24:22).

תַּמְרוּרִים tamrûrîm (8894), Guidepost (Jer 31:21 [38:21]).

1. **τιμωρίας timōrias** gen sing fem

1 Of how much sorer **punishment**, suppose ye, ... Heb 10:29

Timōria is related to *timōreō* (4945), "to punish, to avenge." It could mean "help," or "vengeance" or "punishment." The word is used only once in the New Testament, in Hebrews 10:29: "How much severer *punishment* do you think he will deserve who has trampled under foot the Son of God" (NASB). The writer to the Hebrews warns us here not to fall back into sin (10:26). *Moulton-Milligan* argues that the main thought of the word is "punishment," not "discipline." The word indicates giving an offender what he deserves.

Strong 5098, Bauer 818, Moulton-Milligan 636, Liddell-Scott 1795.

4947. τίνω tinō verb

Pay a penalty, suffer punishment, pay a price.

Cross-Reference:
ἀποτίνω apotinō (655)

1. **τίσουσιν tisousin** 3pl indic fut act

1 Who **shall be punished** with everlasting destruction . . . 2 Th 1:9

From the time of Homer on, *tinō* meant "to pay" or "to recompense." Classical writers used it several times in connection with *dikē* (1343), "a judicial hearing, a sentence," to mean "pay a penalty" or "suffer punishment." This is the way it is used in 2 Thessalonians 1:9, its only occurrence in the New Testament: "They will be *punished* with everlasting destruction" (NIV).

Strong 5099, Bauer 818, Moulton-Milligan 636, Liddell-Scott 1795.

4948. τις tis indef-pron

Someone, anyone, a certain one, something, anything, some, certain, in a manner, a kind of.

1. **τινός tinos** gen sing masc/fem/neu
2. **τινί tini** dat sing masc/fem/neu
3. **τις tis** nom sing masc/fem
4. **τινῶν tinōn** gen pl masc/fem
5. **τινά tina** nom/acc sing/pl masc/neu
6. **τῳ tō** dat sing masc
7. **τινές tines** nom pl masc
8. **τισίν tisin** dat pl masc
9. **τινάς tinas** acc pl masc
10. **τι ti** nom/acc sing neu

5 so that **no man** might pass by that way. . . . . Matt 8:28
7 **certain** of the scribes said within themselves, ... 9:3
3 neither shall **any man** hear his voice in the streets. 12:19
3 Then **one** said unto him, ... 12:47
7 **some** standing here, which shall not taste of death, . . . 16:28
3 neither durst **any man** from that day forth ask him . . . 22:46
7 the Pharisees, and **certain** of the scribes, ... Mark 7:1
2 nor tell it to **any** in the town. 8:26
10 if thou canst do **any thing**, have compassion on us, ... 9:22
3 and he would not that **any man** should know it. 9:30
3 and saith unto them, If **any man** desire to be first, ... 9:35
7 **certain** of them that stood there said unto them, ... 11:5
10 he came, if haply he might find **any thing** thereon: . . . 11:13
3 And would not suffer that **any man** should carry 11:16
7 **some** of them that stood by, when they heard it, ... 15:35
3 if **any man** be in Christ, he is a new creature: . . . . . . 2 Co 5:17

Tis (with grave accent) is an indefinite pronoun which is capable of a variety of meanings. It is commonly found in all Greek literature from the classical period to the Koine period, including the Septuagint and the New Testament.

Dana and Mantey (*A Manual Grammar of the Greek New Testament*, pp.134f.) identify five categories of uses of *tis*. These various constructions can be found in Greek literature from Homer on.

(1) The Pronominal Use. When used as a pronoun *tis* may stand alone. It can refer to a person ("someone," Matthew 12:47) or persons ("some," Luke 13:1) who are part of a larger number of people. It may also be used with a noun in the genitive case (a "partitive genitive") to indicate someone who is part of a specific group (see Luke 7:36, "one of the Pharisees," and Matthew 9:3, "certain of the scribes"). Sometimes it refers to a specific person (Luke 9:49) or persons (Romans 3:8), and other times it refers to "anyone" in general (Mark 11:25). In its neuter form (*ti*) it means "anything" or "something" (see Matthew 5:23), and its uses are parallel to those described above for *tis*.

As a pronoun *tis* may also be linked with the conjunction *ean* (1430), "if" (Mark 11:3), to indicate a hypothetical condition. If it is paired with one of the negative adverbs *ou* (3620), *oute* (3641), or *oude* (3624), or with *mē* (3231), *tis* takes the meaning of "nobody" or "no one" (see Matthew 11:27; 24:4; John 10:28; Acts 28:21).

(2) The Adjectival Use. *Tis* may also be used as an adjective to modify a noun. The noun described may be either proper (*tina Simona*, "a certain Simon" [Mark 15:21]) or common (*hiereus tis*, "a certain priest" [Luke 1:5]). Like other Greek adjectives *tis* may appear before or after the noun it modifies. For example: *tis aner*, "a certain man" (Acts 14:8), or *aner tis*, "a certain man" (Luke 8:27). Normally, when it functions as an adjective *tis* appears after the noun.

Besides modifying nouns, *tis* may be joined to an expression to make it less definite. In such cases the word is commonly translated "a kind of" or "some kind of" (see James 1:18).

In addition, *tis* may be joined, like an adverb, with an adjective of quality or quantity. In the New Testament, when *tis* is used to modify such an adjective, it sometimes functions as a superlative (i.e., the greatest degree possible). Thus, in Hebrews 10:27 *phobera de tis ekdochē kriseōs* is translated "but a certain terrifying expectation of judgment" (NASB). Another example of *tis* used to emphasize quantity or quality is Hebrews 2:7,9: "a little lower than the angels."

(3) The Emphatic Use. Sometimes *tis* may be used with the verb *einai* (see 1498), "to be," to indicate the importance or distinctness of its antecedent. Note Paul's use of the word: *apo de tōn dokountōn einai ti*, "but of those who seemed to be somewhat (important)" (Galatians 2:6; see also Acts 5:36).

(4) The Numerical Use. Coupled with a number *tis* gives the idea of approximation. Hence, Luke 7:19 indicates that John called "(some) two of his disciples" (*duo tinas tōn mathētōn autou*). Used without a number *tis* can indicate "several" people or things (Luke 8:2). Similarly, *tis* may be used with words such as *chronos* (5385), "time," and *hēmerai* (see 2232), "days," to indicate an approximate passage of time (Acts 9:19; 18:23).

(5) The Alternative Use. Sometimes *tines . . . tines* ("some . . . some") or *tis . . . heteros* ("some . . . others") are used in alternative expressions, as in "*some* indeed preach Christ even of envy and strife; and *some* also of good will" (*tines men kai dia phthonon kai epin, tines de kai di eudokian ton Christon kērussousin*, Philippians 1:15) and, "For while *one* saith, I am of Paul; and another, I am of Apollos" (*otan gar legē tis, egō men eimi Paulou, heteros de egō Apollō*, 1 Corinthians 3:4). (For further information see *Bauer*.)

STRONG 5100, BAUER 819-20, MOULTON-MILLIGAN 636-37, LIDDELL-SCOTT 1796-97.

4949. τίς tis intr-pron

Who, what, why, wherefore, how very.

1. τίνα tina nom/acc sing/pl masc/fem/neu
2. τίνι tini dat sing masc/fem/neu
3. τίς tis nom sing masc/fem
4. τίνος tinos gen sing masc/neu
5. τίνων tinōn gen pl masc/neu
6. τίνες tines nom pl masc
7. τίσιν tisin dat pl masc
8. τίνας tinas acc pl fem
9. τί ti nom/acc sing neu

2 Whereunto shall we liken the kingdom of God? .....Mark 4:30
4 Whose is this image and superscription? 12:16
4 whose wife shall she be of them? for the seven had 12:23

As an interrogative pronoun *tis* (with acute accent) occurs in several forms: *tis, ti, tinos, tini,* and *tina*. There are several distinct uses of *tis* which can be found in Greek literature from the time of Homer on (see Dana and Mantey, *A Manual Grammar of the Greek New Testament*, pp.132f.).

(1) The Interrogative Use. *Tis* is the usual pronoun used to introduce common questions (such as Matthew 3:7). There are three types of questions introduced by *tis*: direct, indirect, and rhetorical. Direct questions, such as "*Who* hit you?" (Matthew 26:68, NIV), are most common. More rarely *tis* is used for *hostis* (3610) in indirect questions where the question is put in reported form: "And they went out to see *what* (*ti*) it was that was done" (Mark 5:14). *Tis* is used especially in rhetorical questions where the answer is implied (see 1 Corinthians 9:7).

While the masculine/feminine form, *tis* ("who, which"), is used with questions concerning people, the neuter form, *ti* ("what, why, which"), always introduces questions dealing with things. Compare Matthew 3:7 and 18:12.

Sometimes *tis* and *ti* are used as synonyms for *poios* (4029), "what sort of person, who," and *poion*, "what sort of thing, what," respectively (for example, see Mark 1:27; James 4:12).

(2) The Adverbial Use. When *tis* is used as an adverb, it is translated "why." See, for example, Matthew 6:28.

(3) The Exclamatory Use. Occasionally, when *ti* is used as an adverb, it introduces an exclamation rather than a question. In the Septuagint *ti* is sometimes used to translate the Hebrew *māh* in exclamations (Song of Solomon 4:10). For New Testament examples see Luke 12:49; 22:46.

(4) The Relative Use. *Tis* may also introduce a relative clause, such as Mark 14:36, "Not *what* (*ti*) I will, but *what* (*ti*) thou wilt."

(5) The Alternative Use. Where the classical writers used *poteros* (4079), "which of two (persons)," and *poteron*, "which of two (things)," the New Testament writers employ *tis* (Matthew 9:5) and *ti* (1 Corinthians 4:21).

Strong 5101, Bauer 818-19, Moulton-Milligan 636, Liddell-Scott 1797-98.

4949B. Τίτιος Titios name

Titius.

1. Τιτίου Titiou gen masc

1 **a certain man named Titius Justus, (NASB)** .... **Acts 18:7**

Titius, surnamed Justus, was "one that worshipped God," that is, a Gentile who accepted the Jewish faith but stopped short of a full commitment. His house became the center for Paul's mission in Corinth after the synagogue was closed to him (Acts 18:7).

4950. τίτλος titlos noun

Title, inscription, epitaph.

1. τίτλον titlon acc sing masc

1 **And Pilate wrote a title, and put it on the cross.... John 19:19**
1 **This title then read many of the Jews: 19:20**

This is the technical term used by the Romans (the Latin is *titulus*) denoting the inscription which listed the crime for which a criminal was being punished. This inscription would normally be hung around the neck of the accused for all to see. Or, in the case of crucifixion, it would be affixed to the cross, as was the case with Jesus. John (19:19,20) is the only Gospel to use the term. Mark and Luke each use a synonym, *epigraphē* (1908), "superscription," while Matthew uses the phrase *tēn aitian gegrammenēn*, "the written charge."

Strong 5102, Bauer 820, Moulton-Milligan 637, Liddell-Scott 1799, Colin Brown 1:392.

4951. Τίτος Titos name

Titus.

1. Τίτος Titos nom masc
2. Τίτου Titou gen masc
3. Τίτῳ Titō dat masc
4. Τίτον Titon acc masc

4 **because I found not Titus my brother: .... 2 Co 2:13**
2 **God, ... comforted us by the coming of Titus; 7:6**
2 **exceedingly the more joyed we for the joy of Titus, ... 7:13**
2 **even so our boasting, which I made before Titus, ... 7:14**
4 **Insomuch that we desired Titus, ... 8:6**
2 **same earnest care into the heart of Titus for you. 8:16**
2 **Whether any do inquire of Titus, ... 8:23**
4 **I desired Titus, and with him I sent a brother. 12:18**
1 **Did Titus make a gain of you? 12:18**
4 **with Barnabas, and took Titus with me also. .... Gal 2:1**
1 **neither Titus, who was with me, being a Greek, ... 2:3**
1 **Crescens to Galatia, Titus unto Dalmatia. .... 2 Tm 4:10**
3 **To Titus, mine own son after the common faith: ...... Tit 1:4**

Titus was a valued friend and coworker of Paul. He is mentioned repeatedly in 2 Corinthians (chapters 2, 7, 8, and 12). He was the named recipient of the letter to Titus. Elsewhere he is only mentioned in Galatians 2:1,3 and 2 Timothy 4:10.

From these limited references we learn that he was Greek. He and Barnabas joined Paul on a comparatively early visit by the apostle to Jerusalem (Galatians 2:1-10). Paul refused to submit to the demands of Judaizing Christians that Titus should be circumcised. The issue became a test case of the freedom of the gospel in contrast to the half-Jewish Timothy (Acts 16:3).

Titus was a valued representative of Paul in his relationship with the church at Corinth. He was sent there on several missions at a time of great tension between the apostle and the church he founded. Paul was very eager for news of his success in Corinth (2 Corinthians 2:13) and was delighted with the news he received (7:6f.,13-16). He praised the enthusiasm Titus showed in this task (8:16f.) and his care not to exploit the believers (12:18).

The letter to Titus is addressed to him as Paul's missionary in Crete (Titus 1:5) and encourages and instructs Titus in that task.

4952. τοιγαροῦν toigaroun partic

Well then, so then, therefore, for that very reason, accordingly.

1. τοιγαροῦν toigaroun

1 He **therefore** that despiseth, despiseth not man,..... 1 Th 4:8
1 **Wherefore** seeing we also are compassed about..... Heb 12:1

Toigaroun is a combination of the particles *toi*, "so," *gar* (1056), "for," and *oun* (3631), "then," to give *toi* a greater emphasis than it would have alone. This is one of over a dozen Greek words or phrases which can be translated the same way. However, *toigaroun* is used especially as a formal introduction to some conclusion. Hence, it normally appears at the beginning of a sentence (in an inference or exhortation). For example, 1 Thessalonians 4:8: "*Therefore*, he who rejects this instruction . . . " (NIV); Hebrews 12:1: "*Therefore*, since we are surrounded by such a great cloud of witnesses . . . " (NIV).

STRONG 5105, BAUER 821, MOULTON-MILLIGAN 637, LIDDELL-SCOTT 1801.

4953. τοίνυν toinun partic

Therefore, then, accordingly, well then, therefore now.

1. τοίνυν toinun

1 Render **therefore** unto Caesar the things which be..Luke 20:25
1 I **therefore** so run, not as uncertainly;............. 1 Co 9:26
1 go forth **therefore** unto him without the camp,......Heb 13:13
1 Ye see **then** how that by works a man is justified,.... Jas 2:24

Toinun appears four times in the New Testament acting as a coordinating conjunction. It introduces a conclusion or inference drawn from material which the writer has just presented. In classical usage *toinun* was postpositive (i.e., it did not appear first in a clause). Later writers used it first in a sentence (for instance, the translators of Isaiah in the Septuagint [3:10; 5:13; 27:4]). New Testament writers employ it as either the first (Luke 20:25; Hebrews 13:13) or second (1 Corinthians 9:26; James 2:24) word in a clause.

As an inferential conjunction *toinun* was weaker than *oun* (3631) or *toigaroun* (4952), but it still signaled a conclusion drawn from previous arguments. Thus, after determining the figure on a coin, Jesus commanded, "*Therefore* (consequently, accordingly), render unto Caesar . . . " (Luke 20:25). Paul likewise concluded that self-discipline is necessary for good Christian service, after referring to the need for strict training in competitive sports. Hebrews 13:13 notes that since Jesus suffered outside the city, "therefore" believers should join Him there (used figuratively of being rejected by the world). (See James 2:14-23 for a similar use of the term.)

STRONG 5106, BAUER 821, MOULTON-MILLIGAN 637, LIDDELL-SCOTT 1801.

4954. τοιόσδε toiosde dem-pron

Such as this, such as follows, of this kind.

1. τοιᾶσδε toiasde gen sing fem

1 came **such** a voice to him from the excellent glory,.. 2 Pt 1:17

Toiosde is an emphatic form of *toios*, "such." It is used only once in the New Testament, in its genitive singular feminine form, *toiasde*. From the ancient Greek writers on, it was used to refer to the quality of some person or object, generally in a superlative sense, "so great" or "so bad" (*Liddell-Scott*). Second Peter 1:17 retains this idea: "For he received from God the Father honor and glory, when there came *such* (*toiasde*) a voice to him from the excellent glory . . . . "

STRONG 5107, BAUER 821, MOULTON-MILLIGAN 637, LIDDELL-SCOTT 1802.

4955. τοιοῦτος toioutos dem-pron

Such like, such a person, such a thing.

1. **τοιούτων toioutōn** gen pl masc/fem/neu
2. **τοιοῦτον toiouton** nom/acc sing masc/neu
3. **τοιούτοις toioutois** dat pl masc/neu
4. **τοιοῦτος toioutos** nom sing masc

5. τοιούτου toioutou gen sing masc
6. τοιούτῳ toioutō dat sing masc
7. τοιοῦτοι toioutoi nom pl masc
8. τοιούτους toioutous acc pl masc
9. τοιαύτη toiautē nom sing fem
10. τοιαύτην toiautēn acc sing fem
11. τοιαῦται toiautai nom pl fem
12. τοιαύταις toiautais dat pl fem
13. τοιαύτας toiautas acc pl fem
14. τοιαῦτα toiauta acc pl neu
15. τοιοῦτο toiouto nom/acc sing neu

10 God, which had given **such** power unto men....... Matt 9:8
2 And whoso shall receive one **such** little child......... 18:5
1 for of **such** is the kingdom of heaven................ 19:14
12 And with many **such** parables spake he the word.. Mark 4:33
11 even **such** mighty works are wrought by his hands?.... 6:2
14 and many other **such** like **things** ye do............... 7:8
14 and many **such** like **things** do ye..................... 7:13
1 Whosoever shall receive one of **such** children.......... 9:37
1 for of **such** is the kingdom of God.................. 10:14
9 **such as** was not from the beginning of the creation... 13:19
14 but who is this, of whom I hear **such things?**...... Luke 9:9
14 were sinners ... because they suffered **such things?**.... 13:2
1 children ... for of **such** is the kingdom of God........ 18:16
8 for the Father seeketh **such** to worship him........ John 4:23
13 that **such** should be stoned: but what sayest thou?..... 8:5
14 How can a man that is a sinner do **such** miracles?..... 9:16
10 Who, having received **such** a charge,.............Acts 16:24
14 together with the workmen of **like occupation**,........ 19:25
2 and concluded that they observe no **such thing**,....... 21:25
2 Away with **such** a fellow from the earth:............. 22:22
8 and altogether **such** as I am, except these bonds...... 26:29
14 which commit **such things** are worthy of death,.....Rom 1:32
14 against them which commit **such things**................ 2:2
14 that judgest them which do **such things**,............... 2:3
7 they that are **such** serve not our Lord Jesus Christ,... 16:18
9 and **such** fornication as is not so much as named...1 Co 5:1
2 To deliver **such an one** unto Satan.................... 5:5
6 or an extortioner; with **such an one** no not to eat...... 5:11
3 or a sister is not under bondage in **such** cases:........ 7:15
7 Nevertheless **such** shall have trouble in the flesh:...... 7:28
10 we have no **such** custom, neither the churches........ 11:16
7 As is the earthy, **such** are they also that are earthy:.. 15:48
7 the heavenly, **such** are they also that are heavenly.... 15:48
3 That ye submit yourselves unto **such**,................ 16:16
8 therefore acknowledge ye them that are **such**......... 16:18
6 Sufficient to **such** a man is this punishment,....... 2 Co 2:6
4 lest perhaps **such a one** should be swallowed up....... 2:7
10 **such** trust have we through Christ to God-ward:....... 3:4
10 Seeing then that we have **such** hope,.................. 3:12
4 Let **such an one** think this, that, such as we are...... 10:11
7 **such** will we be also in deed when we are present..... 10:11
7 For **such** are false apostles, deceitful workers,........ 11:13
2 **such an one** caught up to the third heaven........... 12:2
2 And I knew **such** a man,.......................... 12:3
5 Of **such an one** will I glory:........................ 12:5
14 which do **such things** shall not inherit the kingdom.. Gal 5:21
1 against **such** there is no law........................ 5:23
2 restore **such an one** in the spirit of meekness;......... 6:1
1 not having spot, or wrinkle, or any **such thing**;......Eph 5:27
8 Receive him ... and hold **such** in reputation:....... Phlp 2:29
3 Now them that are **such** we command and exhort.. 2 Th 3:12
1 from **such** withdraw thyself...................... 1 Tm 6:5
4 Knowing that he that is **such** is subverted,.......... Tit 3:11
4 being **such** an one as Paul the aged,............. Phlm 1:9
4 For **such** an high priest became us, who is holy,.... Heb 7:26
2 this is the sum: We have **such** an high priest,.......... 8:1
14 For they that say **such things** declare plainly......... 11:14
10 him that endured **such** contradiction of sinners....... 12:3
12 for with **such** sacrifices God is well pleased........... 13:16
9 rejoice in your boastings: all **such** rejoicing is evil....Jas 4:16
8 We therefore ought to receive **such**,............... 3 Jn 1:8

Classical Greek

Toioutos, found in ancient Greek writings from Homer on, is a stronger form of *toios*. Normally it is used as an adjective ("such as, like this") or as a correlative adjective with *hoios* (3497), "of such a kind," or *hopoios* (3560), "of such a manner." But often it is used as a substantive in place of a noun ("such a person, such a thing").

Septuagint Usage

In the Septuagint we find all three uses of *toioutos* (cf. Genesis 41:19; Joshua 10:14; Job 16:2). In addition, the Septuagint writers sometimes use *toioutos* as a pleonasm, a redundant word or phrase, to match the emphatic redundancy of the Hebrew Old Testament. For instance, note Exodus 9:18,24: "hail, *such as* hath not been in Egypt." The correlative and pleonastic uses of *toioutos* can also be found in Josephus (see *Antiquities* 7.15.1; 12.6.3).

New Testament Usage

In the New Testament *toioutos* occurs over 60 times, normally as an adjective and usually in the attributive position where it describes the noun it modifies. For example, see 2 Corinthians 12:3, *ton toiouton anthrōpon*, "such a man." Sometimes *toioutos* occurs in the predicate position, where it makes an assertion about the noun it modifies, as in Mark 6:2, *kai dunameis toiautai*, "such miracles as these" (NASB). In the first case the adjective is merely an incidental description of the noun; in the second, it is the main point.

As a substantive *toioutos* may refer to a person or a thing. The New Testament writers used it both ways (see Acts 19:25; 22:22). When used of a person *toioutos* may indicate either a specific individual with certain characteristics or any person with those characteristics.

Finally, as in the Septuagint, the New Testament occasionally uses *toioutos* pleonastically for added emphasis (see Mark 13:19).

STRONG 5108, BAUER 821, MOULTON-MILLIGAN 637, LIDDELL-SCOTT 1802.

4956. τοῖχος toichos noun

Wall.

CROSS-REFERENCE:
τεῖχος teichos (4886)

גָּדֵר gādhēr (1474), Wall (Is 5:5).
חוֹמָה chômāh (2440), Fortified wall (Is 25:12).
חַיִץ chayits (2534), Wall (Ez 13:10).
כְּתַל kᵉthal (3925), Wall (Ezr 5:8, Dn 5:5—Aramaic).

כֹּתֶל kōthel (3926), Wall (S/S 2:9).

קִיר qîr (7306), Wall (Lv 14:37, 1 Kgs 6:15, Ez 41:5f.).

קִיר חֲרֶשֶׂת qîr chăreseth (7309), Kir (2 Kgs 3:25 [Kir Hareseth]).

1. **τοῖχε** **toiche** voc sing masc

1 God shall smite thee, thou whited **wall:**............ Acts 23:3

Classical Greek and Septuagint Usage

The classical Greek writers commonly used *toichos* for the wall of a house as opposed to the wall of a city (*teichos* [4886]). The Septuagint retains this distinction, normally using *toichos* to translate *qîr*, which usually refers to the wall of a house or of the temple (for example, Leviticus 14:37; 1 Kings 6:15 [LXX 3 Kings 6:15]), and *teichos* to translate *chômāh*, the wall of a city (see Jeremiah 1:15).

New Testament Usage

In the New Testament *toichos* is found once, in Acts 23:3. Here Paul used the term figuratively when he called Ananias, the high priest, a "whitewashed wall" (NIV). Hillyer ("Wall," *Colin Brown*, 3:948f.) suggests that the idea here is that Ananias' devotion to upholding the Law is neither firm nor true but is like a precarious old wall which has been whitewashed to hide its decay. On the outside it looks fine, but in reality it is rotten (see Ezekiel 13:10-16).

Strong 5109, Bauer 821, Moulton-Milligan 637, Liddell-Scott 1802, Colin Brown 3:948-49.

4957. τόκος tokos noun

Interest.

לֵדָה lēdhāh (3985), Birth (Hos 9:11).

נְשִׁי n^eshî (5569), Debt (2 Kgs 4:7).

נֶשֶׁךְ neshekh (5575), Interest (Dt 23:20 [23:19], Prv 28:8, Ez 18:8).

תֹּךְ tōkh (8826), Oppression (Ps 72:14 [71:14]).

1. **τόκῳ** **tokō** dat sing masc

1 I should have received mine own with **usury**....... Matt 25:27
1 I might have required mine own with **usury?**....... Luke 19:23

Classical Greek

The ancient Greeks originally used *tokos* (from *tiktō* [4936], "to bear children") to refer to the birth process or to children themselves. Metaphorically it came to refer to lending money at interest (or increasing money by "producing" it) (*Liddell-Scott*).

Septuagint Usage

The Septuagint translators used *tokos* to translate *neshek*, "usury," i.e., "money lent at interest." See, for example, Deuteronomy 23:19 where God forbade the Israelites to lend money at interest to their countrymen.

New Testament Usage

The New Testament follows the Septuagintal usage. *Tokos* is found twice, in Matthew 25:27 and in Luke 19:23, both times to indicate lending money at interest.

Strong 5110, Bauer 821, Moulton-Milligan 637-38, Liddell-Scott 1803.

4958. τολμάω tolmaō verb

To be brave, to dare, to presume.

Cognates:
- ἀποτολμάω apotolmaō (656)
- τολμηρός tolmēros (4959)
- τολμηροτέρως tolmēroterōs (4959B)
- τολμητής tolmētēs (4960)

Synonyms:
- εὐθυμέω euthumeō (2093)
- εὐψυχέω eupsucheō (2155)
- θαῤῥέω tharrheō (2269)
- θαρσέω tharseō (2270)

לָקַח lāqach (4089), Take; carry away (Jb 15:12).

1. **τολμᾷ** **tolma** 3sing indic/subj pres act
2. **τολμῶ** **tolmō** 1sing indic pres act
3. **τολμῶμεν** **tolmōmen** 1pl indic pres act
4. **τολμᾶν** **tolman** inf pres act
5. **ἐτόλμησεν** **etolmēsen** 3sing indic aor act
6. **τολμήσας** **tolmēsas** nom sing masc part aor act
7. **τολμῆσαι** **tolmēsai** inf aor act
8. **τολμήσω** **tolmēsō** 1sing indic fut act
9. **ἐτόλμα** **etolma** 3sing indic imperf act
10. **ἐτόλμων** **etolmōn** 3pl indic imperf act

5 neither **durst** any man from that day forth ask him Matt 22:46
9 And no man after that **durst** ask him any question. Mark 12:34
6 Joseph ... and went in **boldly** unto Pilate,............ 15:43
10 And after that they **durst** not ask him any question Luke 20:40
9 none of the disciples **durst** ask him, Who art thou? John 21:12
9 And of the rest **durst** no man join himself to them: Acts 5:13
9 Then Moses trembled, and **durst** not behold........... 7:32
1 for a good man some would even **dare** to die...... Rom 5:7
8 For I **will** not **dare** to speak of any of those things... 15:18
1 **Dare** any of you, having a matter against another,.. 1 Co 6:1
7 wherewith I think **to be bold** against some,........ 2 Co 10:2
3 For we **dare** not make ourselves of the number,...... 10:12
1 Howbeit whereinsoever any **is bold**,................ 11:21
2 I speak foolishly, I **am bold** also.................... 11:21
4 much more **bold** to speak the word without fear.... Phlp 1:14
5 **durst** not bring against him a railing accusation,.... Jude 1:9

Classical Greek

In classical usage *tolmaō* has several usages. It can mean "to endure, to bear with," or it can mean "to dare" in either a positive or negative sense. Positively it can mean "to have courage" or "to be courageous" (Fitzer, "tolmaō," *Kittel*, 8:182).

The emphasis here is on boldness. Negatively *tolmaō* can mean "to presume, be rash."

Septuagint Usage

In the Septuagint *tolmaō* appears seven times, usually in a very negative sense. Thus, when Esther related the schemes of Haman to King Xerxes, Xerxes replied, "Where is the man who has *dared* to do such a thing?" (7:5, NIV). The emphasis is upon presumption; i.e., an individual has misdirected courage based on assumptions he had made about a certain situation. *Tolmaō* can have a less negative sense, as in 3 Maccabees 3:21 where Ptolemy writes that he is making a legal change in citizenship; he "ventured" to make the change.

New Testament Usage

The New Testament writers, especially Paul, used *tolmaō* approximately 15 times. In Mark 15:43 we read that Joseph of Arimathea "went in boldly" to Pilate to ask for Jesus' body. Some commentators doubt that this was an act of great courage. Joseph's position in the Sanhedrin would have enabled him to approach the Roman governor without fear of reprisal. However, he may have had reason to fear the Sanhedrin itself if it were discovered that he was a disciple of Jesus. Elsewhere, Acts 7:32 tells us that Moses did not dare (in the negative sense) to look at the burning bush.

Paul's writings also represent both uses of *tolmaō*. In 2 Corinthians 11:21 Paul rebuked those who dare to boast of their sufferings for Christ. Earlier he chastised those who would "dare" to take a fellow Christian before an unbelieving judge (1 Corinthians 6:1). But in 2 Corinthians 10:2 Paul declared that he would "*be bold* against" his adversaries because he knew his position was right.

STRONG 5111, BAUER 821-22, MOULTON-MILLIGAN 638, KITTEL 8:181-86, LIDDELL-SCOTT 1803, COLIN BROWN 1:364-65.

4959. τολμηρός tolmēros adj

Bold, daring, rash.

CROSS-REFERENCE:
τολμάω tolmaō (4958)

1. τολμηρότερον tolmēroteron comp nom/acc sing neu

1 written the more boldly unto you in some sort, ... Rom 15:15

Classical Greek

Tolmēros is an adjective derived from *tolmaō* (4958), "to have courage." Like *tolmaō*, the ancient Greek writers used *tolmerōs* with both good and bad connotations. In its good sense it describes a person who is "bold" or "confident." In its bad sense it refers to an "audacious" or "rash" person. The distinction depends on the writer's understanding of the person's motives for his actions.

Septuagint Usage

In the Septuagint *tolmēros* appears twice. Sirach cautions his readers to not "travel on the road with a *foolhardy* fellow . . . for he will act as he pleases" (8:15, RSV). In 19:2,3 he describes the *tolmēros* man as one who "consorts with harlots . . . . Decay and worms will be snatched away."

New Testament Usage

In the New Testament *tolmēros* is used only once, in its adjectival form (comparative degree), *tolmēroteron*. Paul spoke of having written "more boldly" to the Romans (15:15). The context here indicates that Paul was using the term in its good sense. His boldness came from his conviction that his doctrine was correct and that he was commissioned by God to be a minister to the Gentiles.

BAUER 822, KITTEL 8:181-86, LIDDELL-SCOTT 1803, COLIN BROWN 1:364-65.

4959B. τολμηροτέρως tolmēroterōs adv

Rather boldly.

CROSS-REFERENCE:
τολμάω tolmaō (4958)

1. τολμηροτέρως tolmēroterōs comp

This word is an adverbial form of the adjective *tolmēros*. It appears as a variant to the *Textus Receptus* at Romans 15:15. See the word study at number 4959.

4960. τολμητής tolmētēs noun

One who is bold, one who is audacious.

CROSS-REFERENCE:
τολμάω tolmaō (4958)

1. τολμηταί tolmētai nom pl masc

1 Presumptuous are they, selfwilled, ... 2 Pt 2:10

Classical Greek

Tolmētēs is a noun derived from *tolmaō* (4958). It is found in classical writings from the time of Thucydides (Fifth Century B.C.) on. It is sometimes used in a positive sense of one who is bold and sometimes in a negative sense of one who is audacious or presumptuous.

The word does not occur in the Septuagint, but Josephus used the term to refer to those bold but untrained Jewish patriots who fought bravely against the Romans (*Wars of the Jews* 3.10.1).

New Testament Usage

In the New Testament only Peter used *tolmētēs*. In 2 Peter 2:10 he referred to false teachers in the church as "bold" or "daring" in the negative sense: they had no respect for divine authority.

Strong 5113, Bauer 822, Moulton-Milligan 638, Kittel 8:181-86, Liddell-Scott 1803, Colin Brown 1:364-65.

4961. τομώτερος tomōteros adj

Sharper.

1. τομώτερος tomōteros comp nom sing masc

1 and sharper than any twoedged sword, ... Heb 4:12

Classical Greek

Tomōteros is the comparative form of *tomos*, "sharp," from *temnō*, "to cut" (*Liddell-Scott*). *Tomos* occurs first among classical writers in the Fifth Century B.C. in the works of Sophocles. *Tomōteros* is found first in extant papyri dating from the Third Century B.C. In its earliest extant appearances the word is used literally of objects such as swords.

The word can be used metaphorically also. For instance, pseudo-Phocylides (First Century A.D.) says, "Surely, a word is sharper to a man than an iron weapon" (124). The word does not appear in the Septuagint.

New Testament Usage

In the New Testament *tomōteros* is found only in Hebrews 4:12 where the Word of God is described as "*sharper* than any two-edged sword." The Word of God can thus penetrate and cut through any "shield" man may erect to hide from the truth.

Strong 5114, Bauer 822 (see "tomos"), Moulton-Milligan 638 (see "tomos"), Liddell-Scott 1804 (see "tomos").

4962. τόξον toxon noun

A bow.

אַשְׁפָּה 'ashpāh (855), Quiver (Jb 39:23).

חֵץ chēts (2777), Arrow (2 Kgs 13:18, Pss 58:7 [57:7], 64:3 [63:3]).

קֶשֶׁת qesheth (7493), Rainbow (Gn 9:13f.,16); bow (Gn 27:3, Ps 46:9 [45:9], Jer 50:14 [27:14]).

1. τόξον toxon nom/acc sing neu

1 a white horse: and he that sat on him had a bow; .... Rev 6:2

Classical Greek and Septuagint Usage

In classical Greek *toxon* normally means "a bow," i.e., the weapon. In the Septuagint, however, in place of the normal Greek term *iris* (2438), "halo, rainbow," *toxon* is also used to refer to a "rainbow" (Genesis 9:13ff.). This departure is consistent with the Hebrew term *qesheth* which is used both of a warrior's bow (Genesis 27:3) and of a rainbow (Genesis 9:13ff.). The rainbow in Genesis 9:13 was a sign of God's covenant with Noah never to destroy the world by flood again.

New Testament Usage

The New Testament reflects the classical use of the term. *Toxon* is used only once, in Revelation 6:2, where it refers to a weapon. In the two New Testament passages which mention a rainbow (Revelation 4:3; 10:1) John used *iris* each time.

Strong 5115, Bauer 822, Moulton-Milligan 638, Liddell-Scott 1805.

4963. τοπάζιον topazion noun

Topaz.

פַּז paz (6580), Pure gold (Ps 119:127 [118:127]).

פִּטְדָה pitdhāh (6600), Topaz (Ex 28:17, Jb 28:19, Ez 28:13).

1. τοπάζιον topazion nom/acc sing neu

1 the ninth, a topaz; the tenth, a chrysoprasus; .... Rev 21:20

Septuagint Usage

In the Septuagint *topazion* denotes one of the stones in the breastplate of the high priest in Exodus 28:17. Job 28:19 notes the high value of the topaz of Ethiopia. Ezekiel 28:13 mentions a "covering" similar to that of the high priest. Here the covering is for the king of Tyre (verse 12) who some believe represents Satan here.

New Testament Usage

This word occurs only once in the New Testament. In the description of the New Jerusalem in Revelation 21 the ninth foundation stone of the new city is *topazion* (verse 20). It is a bright yellow stone that is somewhat transparent. It is possible that the chrysolith stone is intended here (also a yellow gem), but this is not certain (*Bauer*).

Strong 5116, Bauer 822, Moulton-Milligan 638, Liddell-Scott 1805, Colin Brown 3:396-97.

4964. τόπος topos noun

Place, location; area, region; room; station, office; possibility, opportunity.

אֲתַר 'ăthar (A902), Place, site (Ezr 5:15, 6:7—Aramaic).

בַּיִת bayith (1041), House (1 Sm 10:25, 1 Kgs 8:42, Ps 119:54 [118:54]).

יָד yādh (3135), Hand; memorial (Is 56:5).

כֵּן kēn (3774), Place (Dn 11:21).

כַּר kar (3862), Pasture (Is 30:23).

מָכוֹן mākhôn (4487), Area, place (Is 4:5, Dn 8:11).

מָעוֹן mā'ôn (4737), Habitation (Pss 68:5 [67:5], 71:3 [70:3]).

מָקוֹם māqôm (4887), Place (Gn 28:11, 2 Chr 6:21, Ez 3:12).

נָוֶה nāweh (5295), Habitation (Ps 79:7 [78:7]).

נָוָה nāwāh (5297), Pasture (Ps 23:2 [22:2]).

נַחֲלָה nachălāh (5338), Inheritance (Jos 24:28).

סָךְ şākh (5710), Multitude (Ps 42:4 [41:4]).

סֹךְ şōkh (5711), Tent (Ps 76:2 [75:2]).

1. **τόπος topos** nom sing masc
2. **τόπου topou** gen sing masc
3. **τόπῳ topō** dat sing masc
4. **τόπον topon** acc sing masc
5. **τόπων topōn** gen pl masc
6. **τόποις topois** dat pl masc
7. **τόπους topous** acc pl masc

5 he walketh through dry **places**, seeking rest, ... Matt 12:43
4 departed thence by ship into a desert **place** apart: 14:13
1 This is a desert **place**, and the time is now past; 14:15
2 when the men of that **place** had knowledge of him, ... 14:35
7 pestilences, and earthquakes, in divers **places**. 24:7
3 spoken of by Daniel ... stand in the holy **place**, ... 24:15
4 Put up again thy sword into his **place**: 26:52
4 when they were come unto **a place** called Golgotha, ... 27:33
1 Golgotha, that is to say, a **place** of a skull, ... 27:33
4 Come, see the **place** where the Lord lay. 28:6
4 departed into a solitary **place**, and there prayed. .... Mark 1:35
6 but was without in desert **places**: 1:45
1 And any **place** that does not receive you (NASB) 6:11
4 Come ye yourselves apart into a desert **place**, ... 6:31
4 they departed into a desert **place** by ship privately. 6:32
1 This is a desert **place**, ... 6:35
7 and there shall be earthquakes in divers **places**, ... 13:8
4 And they bring him unto the **place** Golgotha, ... 15:22
1 which is, being interpreted, The **place** of a skull. 15:22
1 is not here: behold the **place** where they laid him. 16:6
1 because there was no **room** for them in the inn. ..... Luke 2:7
4 he found the **place** where it was written, ... 4:17
4 And the fame of him went out into every **place** 4:37
4 he departed and went into a desert **place**: 4:42
2 He ... stood on a level **place**; (NASB) 6:17
4 and went aside privately into a desert **place** 9:10
3 and get victuals: for we are here in a desert **place**. 9:12
4 sent them two and two ... into every city and **place**, ... 10:1
4 And likewise a Levite, when he was at the **place**, ... 10:32
3 that, as he was praying in a certain **place**, ... 11:1
5 he walketh through dry **places**, seeking rest; 11:24
4 come and say to thee, Give this man **place**; 14:9
4 and thou begin with shame to take the lowest **room**. ... 14:9
4 go and sit down in the lowest **room**; 14:10
1 as thou hast commanded, and yet there is **room**. 14:22
4 lest they also come into this **place** of torment. 16:28
4 And when Jesus came to the **place**, he looked up, .. Luke 19:5
7 And great earthquakes shall be in divers **places**, ... 21:11
2 And when he was at the **place**, he said unto them, ... 22:40
4 And when they were come to the **place**, ... Calvary, ... 23:33
1 Jerusalem is the **place** ... men ought to worship. ..... John 4:20
3 a multitude being in that **place**. 5:13
3 Now there was much grass in the **place**. 6:10
2 nigh unto the **place** where they did eat bread, ... 6:23
4 into the **place** where John at first baptized; 10:40
3 he abode two days still in the same **place** 11:6
3 but was in that **place** where Martha met him. 11:30
4 and take away both our **place** and nation. 11:48
4 I go to prepare **a place** for you. 14:2
4 And if I go and prepare **a place** for you, ... 14:3
4 Judas also, which betrayed him, knew the **place**: 18:2
4 in **a place** that is called the Pavement, ... 19:13
4 into a **place** called the place of a skull, ... 19:17
1 for the **place** where Jesus was crucified was nigh to 19:20
3 **place** where he was crucified there was a garden; 19:41
4 but wrapped together in a **place** by itself. 20:7
4 to occupy this ministry (NASB) (NT) .... Acts 1:25
4 that he might go to his own **place**. 1:25
1 the **place** was shaken where they were assembled 4:31
2 speak blasphemous words against this holy **place**, ... 6:13
4 that this Jesus of Nazareth shall destroy this **place**, ... 6:14
3 shall they come forth, and serve me in this **place**. 7:7
1 for the **place** where thou standest is holy ground. 7:33
1 or what is the **place** of my rest? 7:49
4 And he departed, and went into another **place**. 12:17
6 because of the Jews which were in those **quarters**: 16:3
2 against the people, and the law, and this **place**: 21:28
4 and hath polluted this holy **place**. 21:28
4 **licence** to answer for himself concerning the crime 25:16
7 meaning to sail by the **coasts** of Asia; 27:2
4 came unto **a place** which is called The fair havens; 27:8
7 fearing lest we should have fallen upon rocks, (NT) 27:29
4 And falling into **a place** where two seas met, ... 27:41
4 In the same **quarters** were possessions of the chief 28:7
3 that in the **place** where it was said unto them, ... Rom 9:26
4 but rather give **place** unto wrath: 12:19
4 But now having no more **place** in these parts, ... 15:23
3 with all that in every **place** call upon the name ...... 1 Co 1:2
4 he that occupieth the **room** of the unlearned 14:16
3 the savour of his knowledge by us in every **place**. ... 2 Co 2:14
4 Neither give **place** to the devil. .... Eph 4:27
3 in every **place** your faith to God-ward is spread ..... 1 Th 1:8
3 I will therefore that men pray every **where**, ... 1 Tm 2:8
1 should no **place** have been sought for the second. .... Heb 8:7
4 to go out into a **place** which he should after receive ... 11:8
4 for he found no **place** of repentance, ... 12:17
3 as unto a light that shineth in a dark **place**, ... 2 Pt 1:19
2 and will remove thy candlestick out of his **place**, ... Rev 2:5
5 and island were moved out of their **places**. 6:14
4 where she hath **a place** prepared of God, ... 12:6
1 neither was their **place** found any more in heaven. 12:8
4 she might fly into the wilderness, into her **place**, ... 12:14
4 a **place** called in the Hebrew tongue Armageddon. 16:16
4 all shipmasters and seafaring men (RSV) (NT) 18:17
1 fled away; and there was found no **place** for them. 20:11

Classical Greek

Essentially *topos* denotes a "place, region," or "location." It may denote a geographical "region" or a specific "site." It can also mean a "place," such as a "passage" in a book, or a "space," such as that between words on a page (*Liddell-Scott*). Metaphorically *topos* indicates an "occasion" or "room (for)" or "opportunity" (ibid.). The "condition" of someone or something may also be described as *topos* (*Moulton-Milligan*). In a unique sense *topos* refers to a "sanctuary" (Köster, "topos," *Kittel*, 8:189f.).

Furthermore, *topos* was part of philosophical, cosmological, and scientific terminology (ibid., pp.191f.).

Septuagint Usage

Topos occurs extensively in the Septuagint, and although it replaces as many as 17 Hebrew words or constructions, one (occurring about 400 times) predominates: *māqôm*, "place, location," or an open "space." The Septuagint reads *topos* over 100 times without a Hebrew counterpart. Generally the same meanings found in classical Greek follow in the Septuagint, for example: a region of land (Exodus 3:8; Ruth 1:7) and other locations (Deuteronomy 1:33; 2 Samuel 6:8 [LXX 2 Kings 6:8]).

Köster notes *topos* is "not used technically for the promised land" (ibid., p.195); it is, however, employed for holy sites, both Jewish and non-Jewish alike (Genesis 12:6; 28:11-19; Judges 2:4,5). *Topos* achieves special significance as the place where God dwells (e.g., Deuteronomy 12:5,11; cf. 16:16; 17:8). Thus, as Köster notes, the establishment of the "Place" as God's habitation is directly linked to the destruction of the "places" of the pagans, i.e., their idolatrous shrines with which Israel had flirted (ibid., p.197; cf. the "high places" or "places on the high mountains" [NIV], Deuteronomy 12:2; these idolatrous shrines must be destroyed before God would establish His place with Israel).

The Place as the site of God's presence continued to play a role in the history of Israel, especially following the return from exile. Religious activities centered around various places in and around the temple (e.g., 2 Maccabees 2:18; 8:17; 4 Maccabees 4:12; cf. Leviticus 6:9,19,20 [LXX 6:16,26,27]; see Köster, ibid., pp.195-202).

New Testament Usage

The vast majority of New Testament occurrences of *topos* are found in the Gospels and Acts (a total of about 75), but the term does occur in the writings of Paul (9 times), Hebrews (3 times), 2 Peter (1 time), and Revelation (7 times).

Frequently *topos* denotes a geographical region (Matthew 14:15; Mark 6:32; John 6:10) or a specific site (e.g., Matthew 27:33; Luke 10:1; John 11:6) or location (Mark 16:6). Luke referred to the "place" (location) where something was written (Luke 4:17), a unique usage. Elsewhere he wrote of a "place" of seating at a banquet (Luke 14:9).

John 4:20 and 11:48 make the most obvious connection between *topos* and the temple, although Matthew and Luke (in Acts) also refer to that aspect ("holy place," Matthew 24:15; cf. Acts 6:13; 7:7; 21:28). John may present the idea of *topos* as the site of God's presence in chapter 14 (verses 2,3; cf. Revelation 12:8). *Topos* as an "opportunity" is to be understood in Ephesians 4:27 (NASB): "Do not give the devil an *opportunity* (*topos*)" (cf. Romans 12:19).

The temple is called the "holy place" (Matthew 24:15; Acts 6:13), but Jesus declared that the true worshiper is no longer connected to any single place (John 4:20ff.). In John 14:2,3 *topos* is used of the place which Jesus is preparing for believers, but it can also be used of the dwelling place of the ungodly: the rich man called it a "place of torment" (Luke 16:28).

The New Testament shows that *topos* continued to be flexible in definition. At the same time it is obvious that the more technical understanding of *topos* as the temple or the site of God's presence was not unknown.

Strong 5117, Bauer 822, Moulton-Milligan 638-39, Kittel 8:187-208, Liddell-Scott 1806.

4965. τοσοῦτος tosoutos dem-pron

So much, so many, so great, such.

1. **τοσοῦτον tosouton** acc sing masc/neu
2. **τοσοῦτος tosoutos** nom sing masc
3. **τοσοῦτοι tosoutoi** nom pl masc
4. **τοσούτων tosoutōn** gen pl masc
5. **τοσούτους tosoutous** acc pl masc
6. **τοσαύτην tosautēn** acc sing fem
7. **τοσούτου tosoutou** gen sing neu
8. **τοσούτῳ tosoutō** dat sing neu
9. **τοσαῦτα tosauta** nom/acc pl neu
10. **τοσοῦτο tosouto** nom/acc sing neu

6 not found **so great** faith, no, not in Israel. .... Matt 8:10
3 Whence should we have **so much** bread 15:33
1 **so much** bread ... as to fill **so great** a multitude? 15:33
6 I have not found **so great** faith, no, not in Israel. ....Luke 7:9
9 Lo, these **many** years do I serve thee, ... 15:29
5 but what are they among **so many**? ....John 6:9
9 though he had done **so many** miracles before them, ... 12:37
1 Have I been **so long** time with you, ... 14:9
4 and for all there were **so many**, ... 21:11
7 Tell me whether ye sold the land for **so much**? ...... Acts 5:8
7 And she said, Yea, for **so much**. 5:8
9 it may be, **so many** kinds of voices in the world, ... 1 Co 14:10
9 Have ye suffered **so many** things in vain? .... Gal 3:4
8 Being made **so much** better than the angels, ... Heb 1:4
1 To day, after **so long** a time; as it is said, ... 4:7
1 By **so much** was Jesus made a surety 7:22
8 **so much** the more, as ye see the day approaching. 10:25
1 compassed about with **so great** a cloud of witnesses, ... 12:1

1 so much torment and sorrow give her: .... Rev 18:7
2 For in one hour so great riches is come to nought...... 18:17
1 and the length is as large as the breadth: 21:16

Classical Greek

Tosoutos, which can be translated "so much, so large, so far," etc., is an adjective of quality or quantity in use from Homer (Eighth Century B.C.) onward, perhaps being a combined form of *tosos*, "so great, so many, so much," and *houtos* (3642), "this." It generally meant "so great, so much."

Septuagint Usage

Tosoutos occurs only 4 times in the canonical Septuagint but more than 20 times in the apocryphal books. It functions in much the same way as in classical Greek. It can be an adjective of degree: "For if thou didst punish with *such great* care and indulgence . . . " (Wisdom of Solomon 12:20, RSV). Here it describes the quality of God's care. It can also function as an adjective of quantity: "How can we, few as we are, fight against *so great* and strong a multitude?" (1 Maccabees 3:17, RSV). In 4 Maccabees 15:5 the correlative use with *hosos* (3607) appears: "For to the degree that (*hosos*) mothers are weaker and the more children they bear, the more (*tosoutos*) they are devoted to their children" (RSV margin).

New Testament Usage

In the New Testament *tosoutos* is used in a variety of places with meanings found in the classical and Old Testament usage. It gives specific applications to the substance quantified. Thus, in Matthew 15:33 the word is used twice, emphasizing the impossibility of the situation: "Whence should we have *so much* bread in the wilderness, as to fill *so great* a multitude?" It is used to emphasize number in John 12:37: "But though he had done *so many* miracles before them, yet they believed not on him." John 14:9 emphasizes length of time: "Have I been *so long* time with you, and yet hast thou not known me, Philip?" In Matthew 8:10 it emphasizes the character of faith exercised by the Roman centurion: "I have not found *so great* faith, no, not in Israel." The only time *tosoutos* is used with the article is in Revelation 18:17: "For in one hour *so great* riches is come to nought."

Tosoutos can also be used unemphatically without a noun to indicate a quantity, as in Acts 5:8 where Peter asked Sapphira if she and her husband had sold their land "for *so much*," and she answered with *tosoutos*, "for *so much*." It has an emphatic meaning in Hebrews 1:4 where Jesus is declared to have been made "*so much* better than the angels." It occurs adverbially in Hebrews 10:25, " . . . and *so much* the more, as ye see the day approaching." In both of these Hebrews occurrences (and 7:20-22) the correlative use with *hosos* occurs. In 1:4 the writer draws a comparison between the qualities of the names of angels and the Son of God along with their relative greatness: "In proportion as (*hosos*) the name he (Jesus) has inherited is superior to that of the angels, by so much (tosoutos) he has become better than the angels." In 10:25 the comparison is between the quantity and level of intimate fellowship as Christ's return approaches: "In proportion as (*hosos*) you see the day approaching, encourage (one another) by so much more (or all that much more) (*tosoutos*)."

STRONG 5118, BAUER 823, MOULTON-MILLIGAN 639, LIDDELL-SCOTT 1807-8.

4966. τότε tote adv

Then.

אֱדַיִן 'ědhayin (A115), Then (Ezr 5:4f., Dn 2:15, 6:14—Aramaic).

אָז 'āz (226), Then (Lv 26:41, 1 Chr 11:16, Is 35:5f.).

אַחַר 'achar (313), Afterward (Lv 22:7).

אַךְ 'akh (395), Only (Dt 28:29).

כֵּן kēn (3772), Thus, so; the rest (Neh 2:16).

רַק raq (7828), Only (Dt 28:13).

1. τότε tote

1 Then Herod, ... he had privily called the wise men, . . Matt 2:7
1 Then Herod, when he saw that he was mocked 2:16
1 Then was fulfilled that which was spoken 2:17
1 Then went out to him Jerusalem, and all Judaea, ... 3:5
1 Then cometh Jesus from Galilee to Jordan 3:13
1 to fulfil all righteousness. Then he suffered him......... 3:15
1 Then was Jesus led up of the Spirit 4:1
1 Then the devil taketh him up into the holy city, ... 4:5
1 Then saith Jesus unto him, Get thee hence, Satan: 4:10
1 Then the devil leaveth him, and, behold, ... 4:11
1 From that time Jesus began to preach, and to say, ... 4:17
1 and then come and offer thy gift...................... 5:24
1 and then shalt thou see clearly to cast out the mote 7:5
1 then will I profess unto them, I never knew you: 7:23
1 Then he arose, and rebuked the winds and the sea; 8:26
1 then saith he to the sick of the palsy, ... 9:6
1 Then came to him the disciples of John, saying, ... 9:14
1 bridegroom ... from them, and then shall they fast....... 9:15
1 Then touched he their eyes, saying, ... 9:29
1 Then saith he unto his disciples, ... 9:37
1 Then began he to upbraid the cities wherein 11:20
1 Then saith he to the man, Stretch forth thine hand..... 12:13
1 Then was brought unto him one possessed 12:22
1 and then he will spoil his house...................... 12:29
1 Then certain of the scribes and of the Pharisees 12:38
1 Then he saith, I will return into my house 12:44
1 Then goeth he, ... taketh with himself seven other 12:45
1 brought forth fruit, then appeared the tares also....... 13:26
1 Then Jesus sent the multitude away, ... 13:36
1 Then shall the righteous shine forth as the sun 13:43
1 Then came to Jesus scribes and Pharisees, ... 15:1

1 **Then** came his disciples, and said unto him, ... Matt 15:12
1 **Then** Jesus answered and said unto her, ... 15:28
1 **Then** understood they how that he bade them 16:12
1 **Then** charged he his disciples 16:20
1 From **that time forth** began Jesus to show 16:21
1 **Then** said Jesus unto his disciples, ... 16:24
1 and **then** he shall reward every man 16:27
1 **Then** the disciples understood 17:13
1 **Then** came the disciples to Jesus apart, and said, ... 17:19
1 **Then** came Peter to him, and said, Lord, ... 18:21
1 **Then** his lord, after that he had called him, ... 18:32
1 **Then** were there brought unto him little children, ... 19:13
1 **Then** answered Peter and said unto him, ... 19:27
1 **Then** came to him ... mother of Zebedee's children 20:20
1 **then** sent Jesus two disciples, ... 21:1
1 **Then** saith he to his servants, ... 22:8
1 **Then** said the king to the servants, ... 22:13
1 **Then** went the Pharisees, and took counsel 22:15
1 **Then** saith he unto them, ... 22:21
1 **Then** spake Jesus to the multitude, ... 23:1
1 **Then** shall they deliver you up to be afflicted, ... 24:9
1 And **then** shall many be offended, ... 24:10
1 unto all nations; and **then** shall the end come 24:14
1 **Then** let them which be in Judaea flee 24:16
1 For **then** shall be great tribulation, ... 24:21
1 **Then** if any man shall say unto you, Lo, ... 24:23
1 And **then** shall appear the sign of the Son of man 24:30
1 and **then** shall all the tribes of the earth mourn, ... 24:30
1 **Then** shall two be in the field; 24:40
1 **Then** shall the kingdom of heaven be likened 25:1
1 **Then** all those virgins arose, ... 25:7
1 **then** shall he sit upon the throne of his glory: 25:31
1 **Then** shall the King say unto them on his right 25:34
1 **Then** shall the righteous answer him, saying, ... 25:37
1 **Then** shall he say also unto them on the left hand, ... 25:41
1 **Then** shall they also answer him, saying, ... 25:44
1 **Then** shall he answer them, saying, ... 25:45
1 **Then** assembled together the chief priests, ... 26:3
1 **Then** one of the twelve, called Judas Iscariot, ... 26:14
1 And from **that time** he sought opportunity 26:16
1 **Then** saith Jesus unto them, ... 26:31
1 **Then** cometh Jesus with them 26:36
1 **Then** saith he unto them, My soul is ... sorrowful, ... 26:38
1 **Then** cometh he to his disciples, and saith 26:45
1 **Then** came they, and laid hands on Jesus, ... 26:50
1 **Then** said Jesus unto him, ... 26:52
1 **Then** all the disciples forsook him, and fled 26:56
1 **Then** the high priest rent his clothes, saying, ... 26:65
1 **Then** did they spit in his face, and buffeted him; 26:67
1 **Then** began he to curse and to swear, saying, ... 26:74
1 **Then** Judas, which had betrayed him, ... 27:3
1 **Then** was fulfilled that which was spoken 27:9
1 **Then** said Pilate unto him, Hearest thou not 27:13
1 they had **then** a notable prisoner, called Barabbas 27:16
1 **Then** released he Barabbas unto them: 27:26
1 **Then** the soldiers of the governor took Jesus 27:27
1 **Then** were there two thieves crucified with him, ... 27:38
1 **Then** Pilate commanded the body to be delivered 27:58
1 **Then** said Jesus unto them, Be not afraid: 28:10
1 and **then** shall they fast in those days .... Mark 2:20
1 and **then** he will spoil his house 3:27
1 **then** let them that be in Judaea flee 13:14
1 And **then** if any man shall say to you, ... 13:21
1 And **then** shall they see the Son of man coming 13:26
1 And **then** shall he send his angels, ... 13:27
1 and **then** shall they fast in those days .... Luke 5:35
1 and **then** shalt thou see clearly to pull out the mote 6:42
1 **Then** goeth he, and taketh to him seven other 11:26
1 **Then** shall ye begin to say, ... 13:26
1 and thou begin with shame to take (NT) 14:9
1 Friend, go up higher: **then** shalt thou have worship 14:10
1 **Then** the master of the house being angry said 14:21
1 since **that time** the kingdom of God is preached, ... 16:16
1 **Then** said he unto them, Nation shall rise against 21:10
1 **then** know that the desolation thereof is nigh 21:20
1 **Then** let them which are in Judaea flee 21:21
1 And **then** shall they see the Son of man coming 21:27
1 **Then** shall they begin to say to the mountains, ... Luke 23:30
1 **Then** opened he their understanding, ... 24:45
1 men have well drunk, **then** that which is worse: ..... John 2:10
1 **then** went he also up unto the feast, not openly, ... 7:10
1 **then** shall ye know that I am he, ... 8:28
1 **Then** came the Feast of Dedication (NIV) 10:22
1 he abode two days still in the same place (NT) 11:6
1 **Then** said Jesus unto them plainly, ... 11:14
1 when Jesus was glorified, **then** remembered they 12:16
1 And after the sop Satan entered into him. (NT) 13:27
1 **Then** Pilate therefore took Jesus, ... 19:1
1 **Then** delivered he him therefore unto them 19:16
1 **Then** went in also that other disciple, ... 20:8
1 **Then** returned they unto Jerusalem .... Acts 1:12
1 **Then** Peter, filled with the Holy Ghost, said 4:8
1 **Then** went the captain with the officers, ... 5:26
1 **Then** they suborned men, which said, ... 6:11
1 **Then** came he out of the land of the Chaldaeans, ... 7:4
1 **Then** laid they their hands on them, ... 8:17
1 **Then** answered Peter, ... 10:46
1 **Then** prayed they him to tarry certain days 10:48
1 And when **they** had fasted and prayed, ... 13:3
1 **Then** the deputy, when he saw what was done, ... 13:12
1 **Then** pleased it the apostles and elders, ... 15:22
1 And **then** immediately the brethren sent away Paul 17:14
1 **Then** Paul answered, What are you doing, (NASB) 21:13
1 **Then** Paul took the men, ... 21:26
1 **Then** the chief captain came near, and took him, ... 21:33
1 **Then** said Paul unto him, God shall smite thee, ... 23:3
1 **Then** Festus, when he had conferred 25:12
1 **Then** Paul stretched forth the hand, ... 26:1
1 But **after** long abstinence Paul stood forth 27:21
1 **Then** the soldiers cut off the ropes of the boat, ... 27:32
1 **then** they knew that the island was called Melita 28:1
1 What fruit had ye **then** in those things .... Rom 6:21
1 and **then** shall every man have praise of God .... 1 Co 4:5
1 **then** that which is in part shall be done away 13:10
1 see through a glass, darkly; but **then** face to face: 13:12
1 but **then** shall I know even as also I am known 13:12
1 **then** shall the Son also himself be subject unto him 15:28
1 **then** shall be brought to pass the saying 15:54
1 **that** there be no gatherings when I come 16:2
1 for when I am weak, **then** am I strong .... 2 Co 12:10
1 Howbeit **then**, when ye knew not God, ... Gal 4:8
1 But as **then** he that was born after the flesh 4:29
1 and **then** shall he have rejoicing in himself alone, ... 6:4
1 **then** shall ye also appear with him in glory .... Col 3:4
1 **then** sudden destruction cometh upon them, ... 1 Th 5:3
1 And **then** shall that Wicked be revealed, ... 2 Th 2:8
1 **Then** said I, Lo, I come .... Heb 10:7
1 **Then** said he, Lo, I come to do thy will, O God 10:9
1 Whose voice **then** shook the earth: 12:26
1 Whereby the world that **then** was, ... perished: ...... 2 Pt 3:6

New Testament Usage

In the New Testament the word is used in two primary fashions: First, *tote* has a simple meaning of "then, at that time," usually with a past meaning (*Bauer*). Matthew 4:17 says, "*From that time* (*apo tote*) Jesus began to preach." In 2 Peter 3:6 *ho tote kosmos* is translated "the world *that then was*." It stands in contrast to *arti* (732), "right now," in 1 Corinthians 13:12 where it has a future connotation: "For now we see through a glass, darkly, but *then* face to face: now I know in part; but *then* shall I know even as also I am known." *Tote* is also used not specifically related to chronological time but to a period characterized by a state: "When I am weak, *then* am I strong" (2 Corinthians 12:10).

Secondly, *tote* is used as a simple consecutive conjunction that indicates the general period in which events occurred without reference to a specific time or sequence (cf. *Bauer*). For example, Matthew 2:7 states: "*Then* Herod, when he had privily called the wise men, inquired of them diligently what time the star appeared." The order of the clauses can be reversed, as in 1 Thessalonians 5:3: "For when they shall say, Peace and safety; *then* sudden destruction cometh upon them, as travail upon a woman with child; and they shall not escape." *Tote* is used with other temporal particles, but it retains its more general meaning in these cases (see *Bauer*).

STRONG 5119, BAUER 823-24, MOULTON-MILLIGAN 639, LIDDELL-SCOTT 1808.

4967. τοὐναντίον tounantion noun

Contrariwise, instead.

1. τοὐναντίον tounantion nom/acc sing neu

1 that **contrariwise** ye ought rather to forgive him, ... 2 Co 2:7
1 But **contrariwise**, when they saw that the gospel ...... Gal 2:7
1 Not rendering evil ... but **contrariwise** blessing; ...... 1 Pt 3:9

Tounantiou is a rare word, being a contraction of *to* (see 3450), "the," and *enantios* (1711), "opposite, contrary." It acts as an adversative adverb which draws a contrast between what has just been written and what is about to be written.

Tounantion occurs only three times in the New Testament. In 2 Corinthians 2:7 Paul told the Corinthians they should not punish a repentant erring member but instead forgive him. In Galatians 2:7 Paul said that church leaders in Jerusalem, upon seeing his ministry, did not add anything to his message, but "contrariwise" they recognized his call to preach to the Gentiles. Peter said persecuted Christians should "not render evil for evil, or railing for railing: but *contrariwise* blessing" (1 Peter 3:9).

STRONG 5121, BAUER 824, LIDDELL-SCOTT 554-55.

4968. τοὔνομα tounoma noun

Named, by name.

1. τοὔνομα tounoma nom/acc sing neu

1 came a rich man of Arimathaea, **named** Joseph, ... Matt 27:57

This word, which simply means "named," is a contraction of the neuter singular article *to* (see 3450), "the," and the word *onoma* (3549), "name." It occurs only in Matthew 27:57: "When the even was come, there came a rich man of Arimathea, *named* Joseph, who also himself was Jesus' disciple."

STRONG 5122, BAUER 824.

4969. τουτέστιν toutestin verb

Meaning, that is, (to say).

1. τουτέστιν toutestin

1 Aceldama, **that is** to say, The field of blood. .... Acts 1:19
1 should come after him, **that is**, on Christ Jesus. 19:4
1 For I know that in me **that is**, in my flesh, ... Rom 7:18
1 **That is**, They which are the children of the flesh, ... 9:8
1 therefore receive him, **that is**, mine own bowels: .... Phlm 1:12
1 him that had the power of death, **that is**, the devil; .. Heb 2:14
1 to take tithes ... **that is**, of their brethren, ... 7:5
1 **that is** to say, not of this building; 9:11
1 **that is** to say, his flesh; 10:20
1 But now they desire a better country, **that is**, ... 11:16
1 **that is**, the fruit of our lips giving thanks 13:15
1 few, **that is**, eight souls were saved by water. .... 1 Pt 3:20

This explanatory word, which is used 17 times in the New Testament, is a compound term composed of the demonstrative pronoun *touto* (see 3642), "this," and the singular verb of being, *eimi* (1498), "I am." Hence, its literal meaning is "this is." It serves as a copula (a connecting word) uniting an explanatory construction to the main point of discussion and could be translated "is a representation of, is the equivalent of, this means," or "that is to say." The Latin equivalent is *id est*, used in English: "i.e." Twice it introduces translations of Aramaic statements. One example can be seen at Matthew 27:46: "And about the ninth hour Jesus cried with a loud voice, saying, Eli, Eli, lama sabach'thani? *that is to say*, My God, my God, why hast thou forsaken me?" (Compare Acts 1:19.) Other verses using this term include Mark 7:2; Acts 19:4; Romans 7:18, and 9:8, to name a few.

STRONG 5123, BAUER 824, MOULTON-MILLIGAN 639 (see "toutesti"), LIDDELL-SCOTT 1808 (see "toutesti").

4970. τράγος tragos noun

He-goat, male goat.

עַתּוּד 'attûdh (6500), Ram, male goat (Gn 31:10, Ps 50:13 [49:13], Ez 39:18).

צָפִיר tsāphîr (7117), He-goat (Dn 8:5,8).

תַּיִשׁ tayish (8825), He-goat, male goat (Gn 30:35, 32:14, Prv 30:31 [24:66).

1. τράγων tragōn gen pl masc

1 Neither by the blood **of goats** and calves, ... Heb 9:12
1 For if the blood of bulls and **of goats**, ... 9:13
1 he took the blood of calves and **of goats**, ... 9:19
1 blood of bulls and **of goats** should take away sins...... 10:4

This is the normal Greek word for a male goat as opposed to *aix*, "a female goat." It is common in all Greek dialects. In the New Testament it occurs only in Hebrews (9:12,13,19; 10:4) where it refers to a sacrificial animal whose blood was shed for the covering of sins under the Law but whose blood is not sufficient to take away sins.

STRONG 5131, BAUER 824, MOULTON-MILLIGAN 639, LIDDELL-SCOTT 1809.

4971. τράπεζα trapeza noun

Table, bank.

CROSS-REFERENCE:
τραπεζίτης trapezitēs (4972)

לֶחֶם lechem (4035), Food, meal (1 Sm 20:24,27).

שְׁאֵר sheʾēr (8083), Meat (Ps 78:20 [77:20]).

שֻׁלְחָן shulchān (8374), Table (Ex 26:35, 2 Sm 9:10f., Ez 40:41ff.).

1. τράπεζα trapeza nom sing fem
2. τραπέζης trapezēs gen sing fem
3. τράπεζαν trapezan acc sing fem
4. τραπέζαις trapezais dat pl fem
5. τραπέζας trapezas acc pl fem

2 dogs eat of the crumbs ... from their masters' **table**. Matt 15:27
5 and overthrew the **tables** of the moneychangers, ... 21:12
2 dogs under the **table** eat of the children's crumbs.... Mark 7:28
5 and overthrew the **tables** of the moneychangers, ... 11:15
2 the crumbs which fell from the rich man's **table**:... Luke 16:21
3 then gavest not thou my money into the **bank**, ... 19:23
2 of him that betrayeth me is with me on the **table**...... 22:21
2 ye may eat and drink at my **table** in my kingdom, ... 22:30
5 the changers' money, and overthrew the **tables**; ..... John 2:15
4 leave the word of God, and serve **tables**............. Acts 6:2
3 he set meat before them, and rejoiced, (NT) 16:34
1 And David saith, Let their **table** be made a snare, .. Rom 11:9
2 ye cannot be partakers of the Lord's **table**, ... 1 Co 10:21
2 of the Lord's table, and of the **table** of devils.......... 10:21
1 the candlestick, and the **table**, and the showbread; ... Heb 9:2

Classical Greek

Related to the word for square, in classical writings *trapeza* referred to a four-legged or square table. It came to be used in a transferred sense for the table of a money changer, hence a "bank," as well as a dining table. It also was used of cultic tables or altars where one entered into the presence of the gods through the cultic meal (see Klappert, "Lord's Supper," *Colin Brown*, 2:520).

Septuagint Usage

The Septuagint uses the word to mean a simple table: "He made also ten *tables*" (2 Chronicles 4:8). It also can refer to the table of showbread (Exodus 39:36 [LXX 39:18]). Figuratively *trapeza* can refer to the food upon a table: "You prepare a *table* before me" (Psalm 23:5, NIV [LXX 22:5]).

New Testament Usage

New Testament writers use *trapeza* of the physical table (Matthew 15:27; Mark 7:28) and of the food on the table (Acts 6:2; 16:34). The table of showbread is mentioned in Hebrews 9:2. The table is a place of fellowship (Matthew 9:10-13; Mark 2:15-17; Luke 22:21; Revelation 3:20). It is this sense of intimate fellowship which forms the basis for Paul's argument in 1 Corinthians 10:21 that one cannot have intimate fellowship with God and at the same time have intimate fellowship with demons. The point is that while one may freely eat meat offered to idols, one must not combine idolatry with the worship of God at the Lord's table (cf. 1 Corinthians 11).

On two occasions *trapeza* refers to the table of the money changers erected in the Court of the Gentiles in the Jerusalem temple (Matthew 21:12; Mark 11:15). These money changers converted various types of coinage into Tyrian shekels to enable the worshipers to pay the temple tax commanded in Exodus 30:13-16. A slight surcharge of 1/24th of a shekel was charged (Lane, *New International Commentary on the New Testament*, 2:405).

In Luke 19:23 *trapeza* refers to the "bank" made up of money changers (Matthew uses *trapezitais* [see 4972], "bankers" [25:27]). There were no banks, as we understand them, in the ancient world, but it was possible to make loans and investments and so gain interest on money. Finley notes that in the ancient world there was "endless money lending" but not for productive purposes such as agriculture, trade, or manufacture; rather, loans were made for prestige reasons. On one occasion the Roman orator Cicero borrowed a huge sum of money to build a large house for entertainment purposes (*Ancient Economy*, pp.53-57,141). Thus, the ancient bank was primarily a money-changing establishment with pawnbroking facilities. It was not a modern bank, that is, a "credit institution, designed to encourage productive investment" (Austin and Vidal-Nacquet, *Economic and Social History of Ancient Greece*, p.149). A very common method of storing cash was to bury it in the ground in a strong box (Finley, *Ancient Economy*, p.141; Matthew 25:18).

STRONG 5132, BAUER 824, MOULTON-MILLIGAN

639-40, Kittel 8:209-15, Liddell-Scott 1810, Colin Brown 2:520,522.

4972. τραπεζίτης trapezitēs noun

Money changer, banker.

Cross-Reference:
τράπεζα trapeza (4971)

1. τραπεζίταις trapezitais dat pl masc

1 therefore to have put my money to the **exchangers,** Matt 25:27

Even in classical Greek this word referred to a banker, a money exchanger, someone who sat at a square table (*trapēza* [4971]) and changed currencies for travelers and merchants. In the New Testament it occurs only in Matthew 25:27. In the Parable of the Talents it denotes a banker with whom money is invested at interest. See *trapeza* for further information on ancient banking.

Strong 5133, Bauer 824, Moulton-Milligan 640, Liddell-Scott 1810.

4973. τραῦμα trauma noun

An open wound.

Synonyms:
μώλωψ mōlōps (3330)
πληγή plēgē (3987)

חֳלִי chōlî (2582), Sickness (Jer 10:19).

חָלָל chālāl (2592), Wounded, slain (Ps 69:26 [68:26], Ez 32:29).

נֶתֶק netheq (5608), Infection (Lv 13:31).

פֶּצַע petsa' (6729), Wound (Ex 21:25, Prv 27:6, Is 1:6).

1. τραύματα traumata nom/acc pl neu

1 And went to him, and bound up his **wounds,** ...... Luke 10:34

This is a common classical word used to denote a physical injury or a blow or defeat in war. *Trauma* is used only once in the New Testament (Luke 10:34). Jesus said that the Samaritan bound up the "wounds" of the man who had fallen prey to robbers. The use of oil and wine as medicine on such wounds was common in New Testament times.

Strong 5134, Bauer 824, Moulton-Milligan 640, Liddell-Scott 1811.

4974. τραυματίζω traumatizō verb

To wound.

חִיל chîl (2523), Writhe; be severely wounded (1 Sm 31:3).

חָלַל chālal (2591), Piel: profane (Ez 28:16); polal: be wounded (Is 53:5).

חָלָל chālāl (2592), Slain (Jer 9:1 [8:23], Ez 30:4, 35:8).

פָּצַע pātsa' (6728), Wound (S/S 5:7).

1. τραυματίσαντες traumatisantes
nom pl masc part aor act

2. τετραυματισμένους tetraumatismenous
acc pl masc part perf mid

1 again he sent a third: and they **wounded** him also, Luke 20:12
2 they fled out of that house naked and **wounded.**.... Acts 19:16

Though the word is found in classical Greek from Aeschylus (Fifth Century B.C.), it occurs only in Luke's writings in the New Testament. It refers to the injuries inflicted upon a servant (Luke 20:12) and upon the sons of Sceva (Acts 19:16). In the latter case the wounds were given when they attempted an exorcism in the name of Jesus.

Strong 5135, Bauer 824, Moulton-Milligan 640, Liddell-Scott 1811.

4975. τραχηλίζω trachēlizō verb

Stretch out so as to expose, lay open, lay bare.

1. τετραχηλισμένα tetrachēlismena
nom/acc pl neu part perf mid

1 but all things are naked and **opened** unto the eyes ... Heb 4:13

This word, which appears only in Hebrews 4:13 in the New Testament, and then in its passive form, has an unclear meaning. In classical Greek the term meant to twist the neck of an opponent either in a combatant or a sporting sense, as in wrestling. Here the word has no necessary hostile meaning but merely emphasizes the passivity and helplessness of the subject in being exposed (a further classical sense was "to be overpowered" [*Liddell-Scott*]). The writer of Hebrews declared that nothing is hidden from God. Everything is laid open before Him. The metaphoric use of *trachēlizō* may originate with the bending back of a victim's neck in a sacrifice (*Moulton-Milligan*).

Strong 5136, Bauer 824-25, Moulton-Milligan 640, Liddell-Scott 1811.

4976. τράχηλος trachēlos noun

Neck, throat.

גַּרְגְּרוֹת garg^erôth (1664), Neck (Prv 1:9, 3:3,22).

גָּרוֹן gārôn (1671), Neck (Is 3:16, Ez 16:11).

עֹרֶף 'ōreph (6439), Neck (Dt 10:16, 2 Chr 36:13, Neh 9:16f.).

צַוָּאר tsawwā'r (6939), Neck (Gn 45:14, Jgs 8:21, Jer 28:10ff. [35:10ff.]).

צַוְּרֹנִים tsawwerōnîm (6968), Necklace (S/S 4:9).

1. τράχηλον trachēlon acc sing masc

1 that a millstone were hanged about his **neck**,.......Matt 18:6
1 that a millstone were hanged about his **neck**,....... Mark 9:42
1 and ran, and fell on his **neck**, and kissed him...... Luke 15:20
1 that a millstone were hanged about his **neck**,.......... 17:2
1 to put a yoke upon the **neck** of the disciples,.......Acts 15:10
1 And they all wept sore, and fell on Paul's **neck**,....... 20:37
1 Who have for my life laid down their own **necks**:.. Rom 16:4

Classical Greek

Trachēlos was used by classical writers to describe the necks of humans and animals. It came to be used of the narrow part of the abdomen, the neck of a vessel or gourd, or of the middle portion of a ship's mast (*Liddell-Scott*).

Septuagint Usage

The Septuagintal usage of the word includes Jacob's neck, disguised by his mother in order to deceive his father (Genesis 27:16), and the necks of camels (Judges 8:21). *Trachēlos* is often used figuratively: of burdens (Genesis 27:40), of falling on one's neck in greeting (Genesis 33:4), of stubbornness (Deuteronomy 10:16; Isaiah 48:4), of a point of mortal danger (Isaiah 30:28), of personal struggle (Nehemiah 3:5), of victory (Joshua 10:24), and of the place where one wears truth (Proverbs 3:3).

New Testament Usage

New Testament usage mirrors the Septuagint. Jesus said that a millstone around the neck and drowning was less to be feared than offending one who comes to Him (Matthew 18:6). Paul spoke highly of those who risked their necks for his sake (Romans 16:4). The Oriental custom of falling on one's neck for greeting or comfort in sorrow was demonstrated by the prodigal's father (Luke 15:20) and by Paul's companions in Ephesus (Acts 20:37). Acts 15:10 speaks of the Law as a yoke around men's necks which they are not able to bear.

Strong 5137, Bauer 825, Moulton-Milligan 640, Liddell-Scott 1811-12.

4977. τραχύς trachus adj

Rough, jagged.

אֵיתָן 'êthān (393), Running (Dt 21:4).

רֶכֶס rekhes (7695), Rugged terrain (Is 40:4).

1. τραχεῖς tracheis acc pl masc

2. τραχεῖαι tracheiai nom pl fem

2 and the **rough** ways shall be made smooth;......... Luke 3:5
1 fearing lest we should have fallen upon **rocks**,...... Acts 27:29

This word was used in ancient literature to denote severe or crude circumstances, such as warfare or natural forces, rough and rocky places, and figuratively of the actions of crude persons (*Liddell-Scott*). In the New Testament *trachus* is used in Luke 3:5 of the rough ways that will be made smooth by the forerunner of Christ (cf. Isaiah 40:4). It is also used in Acts 27:29 of the jagged rocks upon which the sailors feared their vessel would be broken.

Strong 5138, Bauer 825, Moulton-Milligan 640, Liddell-Scott 1812.

4978. Τραχωνῖτις

Trachōnitis name-adj

Trachonitis.

1. Τραχωνίτιδος Trachōnitidos gen fem

1 of Ituraea and of the region of **Trachonitis**,......... Luke 3:1

Trachonitis was a forbidding area of volcanic rock south of Damascus. With Ituraea, it formed the tetrarchy of Herod Philip (Luke 3:1).

4979. Τρεῖς Τάβερναι

Treis Tabernai name

Three taverns.

1. Τριῶν Ταβερνῶν Triōn Tabernōn gen fem

1 and **The three taverns**: whom when Paul saw,...... Acts 28:15

A town about 30 miles south of Rome. Here, and at the nearby Forum of Appius, Paul met the Roman Christians who came out to meet him on his journey to Rome (Acts 28:15).

4980. τρεῖς treis num

Three.

1. τρεῖς treis card nom masc/fem

2. τριῶν triōn card gen masc/fem

3. τρισίν trisin card dat masc/fem

4. τρία tria card nom/acc neu

1 **three** days and **three** nights in the whale's belly;... Matt 12:40
1 **three** days and **three** nights in the whale's belly;....... 12:40
1 so shall the Son of man be **three** days................ 12:40
1 the Son of man be **three** days and **three** nights........ 12:40
4 leaven, ... and hid in **three** measures of meal,......... 13:33
1 because they continue with me now **three** days,........ 15:32
1 if thou wilt, let us make here **three** tabernacles;....... 17:4
2 that in the mouth of two or **three** witnesses........... 18:16
1 two or **three** are gathered together in my name,....... 18:20
2 destroy the temple ... and to build it in **three** days..... 26:61
3 destroyest the temple, and buildest it in **three** days,.... 27:40
1 After **three** days I will rise again..................... 27:63

1 because they have now been with me three days, ... Mark 8:2
1 and be killed, and after three days rise again........... 8:31
1 and let us make three tabernacles; one for thee,........ 9:5
1 He will rise three days later." (NASB)................. 9:31
1 and three days later He will rise again." (NASB)...... 10:34
2 and within three days I will build another............. 14:58
3 destroyest the temple, and buildest it in three days,.... 15:29
1 And Mary abode with her about three months,......Luke 1:56
1 that after three days they found him in the temple,..... 2:46
4 heaven was shut up three years and six months,........ 4:25
1 and let us make three tabernacles; one for thee,........ 9:33
2 Which now of these three, thinkest thou,.............. 10:36
1 and say unto him, Friend, lend me three loaves;....... 11:5
1 three against two, and two against three.............. 12:52
3 three against two, and two against three.............. 12:52
4 three years I come seeking fruit on this fig tree,....... 13:7
4 a woman took and hid in three measures of meal,..... 13:21
1 containing two or three firkins apiece............... John 2:6
3 and in three days I will raise it up..................... 2:19
3 and wilt thou rear it up in three days?................. 2:20
2 large fish, a hundred and fifty-three: (NASB)......... 21:11
2 And it was about the space of three hours after,.....Acts 5:7
1 nourished up in his father's house three months:........ 7:20
1 And he was three days without sight,.................. 9:9
1 Spirit said unto him, Behold, three men seek thee...... 10:19
1 And, behold, immediately there were three men....... 11:11
4 and three sabbath days reasoned with them........... 17:2
1 and spake boldly for the space of three months,....... 19:8
1 And there abode three months........................ 20:3
1 after three days he ascended from Caesarea........... 25:1
1 received us, and lodged us three days courteously...... 28:7
1 And after three months we departed in a ship......... 28:11
1 landing at Syracuse, we tarried there three days........ 28:12
2 and The three taverns: whom when Paul saw,......... 28:15
1 And it came to pass, that after three days............ 28:17
4 And now abideth faith, hope, charity, these three;..1 Co 13:13
1 let it be by two, or at the most by three,.............. 14:27
1 Let the prophets speak two or three,.................. 14:29
2 In the mouth of two or three witnesses............2 Co 13:1
4 Then after three years I went up to Jerusalem....... Gal 1:18
2 an accusation, but before two or three witnesses.....1 Tm 5:19
3 died without mercy under two or three witnesses:...Heb 10:28
1 and it rained not on the earth by the space of three.. Jas 5:17
1 For there are three that bear record in heaven,......1 Jn 5:7
1 Father, ... Word, ... Ghost: and these three are one..... 5:7
1 And there are three that bear witness in earth,......... 5:8
1 and these three agree in one.......................... 5:8
1 and three measures of barley for a penny;........... Rev 6:6
2 other voices of the trumpet of the three angels,......... 8:13
2 By these three was the third part of men killed,........ 9:18
1 shall see their dead bodies three days and an half,..... 11:9
1 And after three days and an half the Spirit of life..... 11:11
4 I saw three unclean spirits like frogs come out of...... 16:13
4 And the great city was divided into three parts,....... 16:19
1 On the east three gates; on the north three gates;..... 21:13
1 On the east three gates; on the north three gates;..... 21:13
1 on the north three gates; on the south three gates;..... 21:13
1 south three gates; and on the west three gates......... 21:13

The word *treis,* "three," is used frequently in both the Old and New Testaments. Its most sacred connotation is its relationship to the triunity of the Godhead, although this is not specifically spelled out in Scripture. Nowhere is the number treated with superstitious reverence as may have been true in the Greek and Roman worlds (cf. Delling, "treis," *Kittel,* 8:216f.).

Classical Greek

In classical Greek *treis* had several usages. First, it denotes the number three, used in a purely literal sense. It could also be used in a figurative way to mean "completion": "I am thrice, i.e., *utterly* undone" (*Liddell-Scott*). *Treis* plays "no inconsiderable role in the divine world and especially the cultus of antiquity" (Delling, "treis," *Kittel,* 8:216). Various cultic acts are done in threes to make them effective; divine triads (groups of three gods) are common.

Septuagint Usage

In the Septuagint *treis* is also used to denote the quantity "three." David had three mighty men (2 Samuel 23:8-12); Job had three comforters. *Treis* also symbolizes perfection or completeness. Three strands make a strong cord (Ecclesiastes 4:12). Water was poured over Elijah's sacrifice three times (1 Kings 18:30-34). In addition, the number three played a role in worship. Worshipers went to Jerusalem three times per year (Exodus 23:14); Solomon offered special offerings three times per year (1 Kings 9:25 [LXX 3 Kings 9:25]); and Daniel prayed three times daily (Daniel 6:10,13). The use of three and groupings of three is a "general stylistic device in poetry" (Delling, ibid., p.219; Isaiah 6:11).

New Testament Usage

In the New Testament these same usages appear. In a literal sense, Peter asked to erect "*three* tabernacles" on the Mount of Transfiguration (Matthew 17:4; Mark 9:5; Luke 9:33). It is the number of days between the crucifixion and resurrection of the Lord Jesus (Matthew 12:40; Mark 8:31). Jesus had three companions with whom He seemed more intimate than with the rest of the Twelve (Matthew 26:37; Mark 9:2). Paul described "three" virtues: faith, hope, and love (1 Corinthians 13:13).

Three can also signify "a few," especially when combined with "two." "Two or three witnesses" refers to "a few" witnesses as opposed to only one. When Jesus stated that He would be among His people even when only two or three were gathered together (Matthew 18:20), He meant "the smallest group who meet" (Delling, ibid., p.220). Repetition of an event three times emphasizes it. Peter received the vision three times (Acts 10); Jesus prayed in Gethsemane three times; Paul three times asked to have his thorn removed (2 Corinthians 12:7-10).

Strong 5140, Bauer 825, Moulton-Milligan 640-41, Kittel 8:216-25, Liddell-Scott 1812, Colin Brown 2:686-87.

4981. τρέμω tremō verb

To tremble, quiver.

חָרֵד chārēdh (2830), Trembling (Is 66:2,5).

נוּד nûdh (5290), Wanderer (Gn 4:12,14).

רָעַד rā'adh (7746), Hiphil: tremble (Dn 10:11).

רָעַשׁ rā'ash (7782), Quake (Jer 4:24).

1. τρέμουσιν tremousin 3pl indic pres act
2. τρέμων tremōn nom sing masc part pres act
3. τρέμουσα tremousa nom sing fem part pres act

3 But the woman fearing and **trembling**, ... Mark 5:33
3 she came **trembling**, and falling down before him, ... Luke 8:47
2 And he **trembling** and astonished said, Lord, ... Acts 9:6
1 they are not **afraid** to speak evil of dignities......... 2 Pt 2:10

In its earliest extant appearances *tremō* meant "to shake or quiver" or "to shiver with the chills" (associated with malaria) (*Liddell-Scott*). It came to be used of shaking in fear, as of the woman with the issue of blood when she approached Jesus (Mark 5:33; Luke 8:47). Saul trembled on the Damascus Road when he asked, "Lord, what wilt thou have me to do?" (Acts 9:6). *Tremō* is the proper (but absent) emotion of those who blaspheme dignitaries (2 Peter 2:10).

Strong 5141, Bauer 825, Moulton-Milligan 641, Liddell-Scott 1813.

4982. τρέφω trephō verb

Feed, nurture, bring up.

Cognates:
ἀνατρέφω anatrephō (395)
ἀποτρέπω apotrepō (659)
διατροφή diatrophē (1299)
ἐκτρέφω ektrephō (1611)
ἐντρέφω entrephō (1773)
σύντροφος suntrophos (4791)
τεκνοτροφέω teknotropheō (4892)

Synonyms:
ἀνατρέφω anatrephō (395)
βόσκω boskō (999)
ἐκτρέφω ektrephō (1611)
χορτάζω chortazō (5361)
ψωμίζω psōmizō (5430)

אָכַל 'ākhal (404), Eat; hiphil: give someone food (Prv 25:21).

גָּדַל gādhal (1461), Become great, grow up; piel: let grow (Nm 6:5).

חָיָה chāyâh (2513), Live; piel: keep alive (Is 7:21); hiphil: keep alive (Gn 6:19f. [6:20f.]).

חִיל chîl (2523), Writhe; polel: beget (Dt 32:18).

כּוּל kûl (3677), Hold, seize; pilpel: supply with food (1 Kgs 18:13).

מַרְבֵּק marbēq (4932), Fattened calf (Jer 46:21 [26:21]).

רָעָה rā'âh (7749), Shepherd (Gn 48:15).

1. τρέφει trephei 3sing indic pres act
2. τρέφωσιν trephōsin 3pl subj pres act
3. ἐθρέψαμεν ethrepsamen 1pl indic aor act
4. ἐθρέψατε ethrepsate 2pl indic aor act
5. τρέφεται trephetai 3sing indic pres mid
6. τρέφεσθαι trephesthai inf pres mid
7. τεθραμμένος tethrammenos nom sing masc part perf mid
8. ἔθρεψαν ethrepsan 3pl indic aor act
9. τρέφηται trephētai 3sing subj pres mid

1 yet your heavenly Father **feedeth** them. .... Matt 6:26
3 when saw we thee an hungered, and **fed** thee? 25:37
7 came to Nazareth, where he had been **brought up**: ...Luke 4:16
1 storehouse nor barn; and God **feedeth** them: 12:24
8 and the breasts that never **nursed**. (NASB) 23:29
6 their country **was nourished** by the king's country... Acts 12:20
4 ye **have nourished** your hearts, ... Jas 5:5
2 a place prepared ... that they **should feed** her there ..Rev 12:6
5 **is nourished** for a time, and times, and half a time, ... 12:14

Classical Greek

Trephō has many usages throughout the classical and Koine Greek periods related to the basic idea of enlarging. In the classical Greek period the term was used of inanimate as well as animate objects. When used of inanimate objects like liquids it could mean "to thicken" or "congeal" or even "curdle" when used of milk. When used of the earth or the sea the term could mean "breed, produce," or "teem with." When used of animate objects the term could mean, in an active or middle voice, "cause to grow, increase, bring up," or "rear." In the passive voice the term could mean simply "to be." Another usage carries the sense of "supporting" or "maintaining," hence "to feed" or "nourish."

Septuagint Usage

In the Septuagint *trephō* is used of feeding animals (Genesis 6:19) and people (1 Kings 18:13 [LXX 3 Kings 18:13]), of taking care of one's hair (Numbers 6:5), and of generally caring for one's needs (Genesis 48:15, "shepherd," NASB; Hebrew *rā'âh*).

New Testament Usage

These same senses are found in the New Testament. God feeds the birds (Matthew 6:26; Luke 12:24) and likewise cares for the physical needs of His children. Herod dominated Tyre and Sidon because he was their source of food (Acts 12:20). As Israel of old was cared for by God, the persecuted woman has her needs met in the wilderness during the Tribulation (Revelation 12:6,14). The ungodly who exploit the helpless in order to live luxuriously are fattening themselves up for slaughter (James 5:5).

One final usage deserves special comment. Jesus praised His "sheep" (Matthew 25:37) for vicariously feeding Him when He was hungry by feeding His needy brethren. This passage does not teach either salvation by works or salvation by surprise.

Strong 5142, Bauer 825, Moulton-Milligan 641, Liddell-Scott 1814.

4983. τρέχω trechō verb

Run, strive to advance, exert effort, make progress.

Cognates:

εἰστρέχω eistrechō (1516)
ἐπισυντρέχω episuntrechō (1982)
κατατρέχω katatrechō (2670)
περιτρέχω peritrechō (3923)
προστρέχω prostrechō (4228)
προτρέχω protrechō (4248)
συντρέχω suntrechō (4788)
ὑποτρέχω hupotrechō (5133)

Synonym:

ἐκπηδάω ekpēdaō (1587B)

דּוּץ dûts (1805), Dance (Jb 41:22 [41:13]).

רוּץ rûts (7608), Qal: run (Gn 24:28f., 2 Sm 18:22ff., Jer 12:5); hiphil: carry quickly (2 Chr 35:13).

1. **τρέχω trechō** 1sing indic/subj pres act
2. **τρέχει trechei** 3sing indic pres act
3. **τρέχουσιν trechousin** 3pl indic pres act
4. **τρέχῃ trechē** 3sing subj pres act
5. **τρέχωμεν trechōmen** 1pl subj pres act
6. **τρέχετε trechete** 2pl impr pres act
7. **τρέχοντος trechontos** gen sing masc part pres act
8. **τρέχοντες trechontes** nom pl masc part pres act
9. **τρεχόντων trechontōn** gen pl masc part pres act
10. **ἔδραμον edramon** 1/3sing/pl indic aor act
11. **ἔδραμεν edramen** 3sing indic aor act
12. **δραμών dramōn** nom sing masc part aor act
13. **ἐτρέχετε etrechete** 2pl indic imperf act
14. **ἔτρεχον etrechon** 3pl indic imperf act

12 straightway one of them **ran**, and took a sponge,..Matt 27:48
10 and **did run** to bring his disciples word.............. 28:8
11 he saw Jesus afar off, **he ran** and worshipped him, Mark 5:6
12 And one **ran** and filled a sponge full of vinegar,...... 15:36
12 his father saw him, and had compassion, and **ran**, Luke 15:20
11 Then arose Peter, and **ran** unto the sepulchre;....... 24:12
2 Then she **runneth**, and cometh to Simon Peter,... John 20:2
14 So they **ran** both together:......................... 20:4
7 is not of him that willeth, nor of him that **runneth**, Rom 9:16
8 Know ye not that they which **run** in a race run all, 1 Co 9:24
3 Know ye not that they which run in a race **run** all,.... 9:24
6 So **run**, that ye may obtain.......................... 9:24
1 I therefore so **run**, not as uncertainly;................. 9:26
1 lest by any means I **should run**, ... in vain..........Gal 2:2
10 by any means I should run, or **had run**, in vain........ 2:2
13 Ye **did run** well; who did hinder you................. 5:7
10 I **have** not **run** in vain, neither laboured in vain.....Phlp 2:16
4 that the word of the Lord **may have free course**,....2 Th 3:1
5 and let us **run** with patience the race............ Heb 12:1
9 sound of chariots of many horses **running** to battle. Rev 9:9

Classical Greek

Among the Greeks *trechō* described the act of "running" or "hurrying away." Particularly it was used in connection with the running events in the athletic games. Further examples show that *trechō* could also refer to intellectual "striving" and/or spiritual "achievement" (Ebel, "Walk," *Colin Brown*, 3:946).

Septuagint Usage

Trechō occurs about 60 times in the Septuagint, normally for the Hebrew *rûts*, "to run" in the literal sense. A few times *trechō* does function figuratively, for example, in Psalm 119:32 (LXX 118:32) of "running" in the path of God's commands. In the apocryphal 4 Maccabees it concerns "running on the road of immortality" (14:5).

New Testament Usage

The literal understanding of *trechō* is evident in the Gospels: of a possessed man who ran and fell at Jesus' feet (Mark 5:6); of the soldiers at the cross who ran to offer Jesus vinegar (Matthew 27:48); of the women who ran from the empty tomb of Jesus as they hurried to give the angel's message that Jesus had risen (Matthew 28:8); and of Peter and John who ran to the tomb (John 20:4). In the Parable of the Prodigal Son Luke used it of the father who ran to meet his lost son (15:20).

Paul, emphasizing that salvation is not the consequence of human effort but a free gift of God, wrote, "So then it is not of him that willeth, nor of him that *runneth*, but of God that showeth mercy" (Romans 9:16). Paul also used *trechō* in connection with the ongoing Christian life which he compared to the athletic running event. Just as an athlete runs to win the prize, so too, the Christian must exert every effort to finish the race and win the prize (1 Corinthians 9:24-26; cf. Hebrews 12:1). Paul described his preaching and ministry in terms of "running" (Galatians 2:2; Philippians 2:16). He asserted that he had not "*run* in vain." Paul also prayed in 2 Thessalonians (3:1) that the word of the Lord might have "free course" and that it might thereby increase (cf. Acts 6:7).

Strong 5143, Bauer 825-26, Moulton-Milligan 641, Kittel 8:226-33, Liddell-Scott 1814-15, Colin Brown 3:945-47.

4983B. τρῆμα trēma noun

Opening, hole, point, aperture.

1. **τρήματος trēmatos** gen sing neu

1 camel to go through the eye of a needle, (NASB)..Matt 19:24
1 camel to go through the eye of a needle, (NASB)..Luke 18:25

Trēma could be used in classical literature to refer to a hole or opening of any sort. In the New Testament it appears only as a variant at Matthew 19:24 and Luke 18:25. See *trumalia* (5009) for a discussion on the meaning of this word.

BAUER 826, MOULTON-MILLIGAN 641, LIDDELL-SCOTT 1815.

4984. τριάκοντα triakonta num

Thirty.

1. τριάκοντα triakonta card

1 **brought forth fruit, ... some thirtyfold.** .... **Matt 13:8**
1 **some an hundredfold, some sixty, some thirty.** **13:23**
1 **they covenanted with him for thirty pieces of silver.** **26:15**
1 **and brought again the thirty pieces of silver** **27:3**
1 **And they took the thirty pieces of silver,** **27:9**
1 **some thirty, and some sixty, and some an hundred. Mark 4:8**
1 **some thirtyfold, some sixty, and some an hundred.** **4:20**
1 **Jesus himself began to be about thirty years of age, Luke 3:23**
1 **which had been thirty-eight years (NASB)** .... **John 5:5**
1 **rowed about five and twenty or thirty furlongs,** **6:19**
1 **which was four hundred and thirty years after,** .... **Gal 3:17**

Triakonta is used 10 times in the New Testament, 4 times referring to the yield of good seed in the Parable of the Sower (Matthew 13:8,23; Mark 4:8,20). It is also used in Luke 3:23 to tell that Jesus was "about thirty years of age" at the time of His baptism by John in the Jordan. The number of silver coins Judas accepted for Jesus was 30, the price of a slave (Matthew 27:3,9; cf. Zechariah 11:12,13). John used *triakonta* to give the approximate distance the disciples had rowed when they saw Jesus: "five and twenty or *thirty* furlongs" (6:19).

STRONG 5144, BAUER 826, MOULTON-MILLIGAN 641, LIDDELL-SCOTT 1815.

4985. τριακονταοκτώ triakontaoktō num

Thirty-eight.

1. τριακονταοκτώ triakontaoktō card

1 **which had an infirmity thirty and eight years.** .... **John 5:5**

Triakontaoktō appears only once in the New Testament, at John 5:5. It describes the length of a time a certain man had been crippled: 38 years. John included the length of his infirmity to emphasize "the intractability of the complaint" (Morris, *New International Commentary*, 4:302) and to point to the greatness of Jesus' healing power. The waters could not heal him, but Jesus could, and that with only a word.

4986. τριακόσιοι triakosioi num

Three hundred.

1. τριακοσίων triakosiōn card gen masc/fem/neu

1 **might have been sold for more than three hundred Mark 14:5**
1 **sold for three hundred pence,** .... **John 12:5**

This word is used in Mark 14:5 and John 12:5. Judas calculated the value of the spikenard ointment which Mary the sister of Lazarus used to anoint the feet of Jesus at 300 pence. See the word study on *dēnarion* (1214), "denarius."

STRONG 5145, BAUER 826, LIDDELL-SCOTT 1816.

4987. τρίβολος tribolos noun

Thistle.

SYNONYM:
ἄκανθα akantha (171)

דַּרְדַּר dardar (1923), Thistle (Gn 3:18 [3:19], Hos 10:8).

חָרִיץ chārîts (2862), Iron pick (2 Sm 12:31—Codex Vaticanus only).

צֵן tsēn (7060), Thorn (Prv 22:5).

1. τριβόλων tribolōn gen pl masc
2. τριβόλους tribolous acc pl masc

1 **Do men gather grapes of thorns, or figs of thistles? Matt 7:16**
2 **that which beareth thorns and briers is rejected,** ..... **Heb 6:8**

First denoting a three-spiked weapon, *tribolos* came to be used for a variety of spiked or thorny plants (Motyer, "Fruit," *Colin Brown*, 1:726). It is used in the New Testament of the thistle which is abundant everywhere in Palestine (*Bauer*). Matthew 7:16 uses the word figuratively as a contrast to figs. Hebrews 6:8 is a reminder of Genesis 3:18 where the Septuagint uses *tribolos* for thorns that are part of the curse of God on the earth as a result of man's sin.

STRONG 5146, BAUER 826, MOULTON-MILLIGAN 641, LIDDELL-SCOTT 1817, COLIN BROWN 1:726.

4988. τρίβος tribos noun

A path or beaten track.

SYNONYMS:
ἄμφοδον amphodon (294)
ὁδός hodos (3461)
ῥύμη rhumē (4362)

אֹרַח 'ōrach (758), Path (Jb 22:15, Ps 25:4 [24:4], Mi 4:2).

דֶּרֶךְ derekh (1932), Way (Prv 2:20, 30:19 [24:54], Is 3:12).

מְסִלָּה m^esillāh (4697), Highway (2 Sm 20:12f., Is 40:3).

מַעְגָּל ma'gāl (4724), Path, wayside (Pss 17:5 [16:5], 23:3 [22:3], 140:5 [139:5]).

נָתִיב nāthîv (5593), Path (Jb 18:10, 28:7, Ps 78:50 [77:50]).

נְתִיבָה nethîvāh (5594), Path (Jb 30:13, Ps 142:3 [141:3], Lam 3:9).

שְׁבִיל shevîl (8111), Path (Ps 77:19 [76:19]).

1. τρίβους tribous acc pl fem

1 Prepare ye the way ... make his **paths** straight....... Matt 3:3
1 Prepare ye the way ... make his **paths** straight.......Mark 1:3
1 Prepare ye the way ... make his **paths** straight....... Luke 3:4

Tribos was used in secular literature for a path, usually one worn and well beaten. Among other usages the Septuagint uses *tribos* to refer to the upright person's path that departs from evil (Proverbs 2:20). Its usage in the New Testament is a citation of Isaiah 40:3 given by John the Baptist. John's ministry was to prepare the way of the Lord and to "make his *paths* straight" (Matthew 3:3; Mark 1:3; Luke 3:4).

Strong 5147, Bauer 826, Moulton-Milligan 641, Liddell-Scott 1817.

4989. τριετία trietia noun

A period of 3 years.

1. τριετίαν trietian acc sing fem

1 that by the space of **three years** I ceased not....... Acts 20:31

The only use of this word in the New Testament is in Acts 20:31. Paul reminded the elders at Ephesus that he had faithfully preached to them and warned them of coming spiritual dangers "by the space of three years."

Strong 5148, Bauer 826, Moulton-Milligan 641-42, Liddell-Scott 1818.

4990. τρίζω trizō verb

Grind with the teeth, gnash.

1. τρίζει trizei 3sing indic pres act

1 and he foameth, and **gnasheth** with his teeth,....... Mark 9:18

Trizō is used for a variety of sounds produced by animals, ranging from shrill cries to hissing noises (*Liddell-Scott*). It can also be used for the sound of creaking when a wheel rubs an axle, hence the usage of grinding or gnashing of the teeth. This is the usage in the New Testament where a father reported to Jesus that his demon-possessed son gnashed his teeth when under the control of the dumb spirit (Mark 9:8).

Strong 5149, Bauer 826, Moulton-Milligan 642, Liddell-Scott 1818-19.

4991. τρίμηνος trimēnos adj

Three months.

1. τρίμηνον trimēnon nom/acc sing neu

1 was hid **three months** of his parents,............... Heb 11:23

Trimēnos is used a few times in secular Greek and the Septuagint but just once in the New Testament. Second Kings 24:8 (LXX 4 Kings 24:8) and 2 Chronicles 36:2 record the reigns of Jehoiachin and Jehoahaz respectively as each being 3 months.

The only New Testament reference containing this word is Hebrews 11:23. This verse notes that by faith his parents hid Moses for 3 months, not being afraid of the edict of Pharaoh.

Strong 5150, Bauer 826, Moulton-Milligan 642, Liddell-Scott 1820.

4991B. τρίς tris adv

Three, three times.

1. τρίς tris

1 before the cock crow, thou shalt deny me **thrice**.... Matt 26:34
1 Before the cock crow, thou shalt deny me **thrice**....... 26:75
1 before the cock crow ... thou shalt deny me **thrice**. Mark 14:30
1 the cock crow twice, thou shalt deny me **thrice**......... 14:72
1 thou shalt **thrice** deny that thou knowest me....... Luke 22:34
1 Before the cock crow, thou shalt deny me **thrice**....... 22:61
1 cock shall not crow, till thou hast denied me **thrice**. John 13:38
1 This was done **thrice**:............................. Acts 10:16
1 And this was done **three times**:....................... 11:10
1 **Thrice** was I beaten with rods, once was I stoned,..2 Co 11:25
1 once was I stoned, **thrice** I suffered shipwreck,........ 11:25
1 For this thing I besought the Lord **thrice**,............. 12:8

Tris occurs 12 times in the New Testament, meaning "three times." Matthew 26:34,75; Mark 14:30,72; Luke 22:34,61; and John 13:38 all record Jesus' prophecy that Peter would deny Him three times and Peter's subsequent remembrance of the foretelling. In 2 Corinthians 11:25 Paul wrote about some of his hardships. He was beaten three times with rods and was shipwrecked three times. Paul prayed three times for the "thorn in his flesh" to be removed (2 Corinthians 12:8). Acts 10:16 records a vision that Peter saw three times. Peter told about this same experience in Acts 11:10. (For more information concerning the significance of the number *3*, see *tritos* [4995].)

Strong 5151, Bauer 826, Moulton-Milligan 642, Kittel 8:216-25, Liddell-Scott 1822, Colin Brown 2:686,703.

4992. τρίστεγος tristegos noun

The third story.

1. τριστέγου tristegou gen sing neu

1 and fell down from the **third loft**,.................. Acts 20:9

This word occurs only once in the New Testament. While the word can mean "three stories high," the New Testament meaning is "the third story" of a building, or "third window" up from the ground.

In Acts 20:9 Eutychus, having fallen asleep because of Paul's long sermon, fell "from the third loft." He was taken up dead. But Paul fell upon him (undoubtedly in prayer) much as Elisha did on the Shunnamite's dead son (2 Kings 4:34), and Eutychus was restored to life.

Strong 5122, Bauer 826 (see "tristegon"), Moulton-Milligan 642, Liddell-Scott 1823.

4993. τρισχίλιοι trischilioi num

Three thousand.

1. τρισχίλιαι trischiliai card nom fem

1 were added unto them about **three thousand** souls.... Acts 2:41

This is a combination of two Greek terms: *tris* (4991B) and *chilioi* (5343). The first one is an adverb generally meaning "three times." The second word is a noun often used in combination with various prefixes and suffixes.

Both words occur in classical Greek as early as Homer's writings (Eighth Century B.C.) and can also be found in the Septuagint and the papyri. They are combined in Acts 2:41 to designate the number of believers who were added to the infant New Testament Church on the Day of Pentecost.

Strong 5153, Bauer 826, Liddell-Scott 1823, Colin Brown 2:699.

4994. τρίς tris

See word study at number 4991B.

4995. τρίτος tritos num

Third.

1. τρίτον triton ord nom/acc sing masc/neu
2. τρίτου tritou ord gen sing masc/neu
3. τρίτος tritos ord nom sing masc
4. τρίτη tritē ord nom sing fem
5. τρίτης tritēs ord gen sing fem
6. τρίτῃ tritē ord dat sing fem
7. τρίτην tritēn ord acc sing fem

6 and be killed, and be raised again the **third** day.... Matt 16:21
6 and the **third** day he shall be raised again............ 17:23
7 And he went out about the **third** hour,.............. 20:3
6 crucify him: and the **third** day he shall rise again... Matt 20:19
3 Likewise the second also, and the **third**,.............. 22:26
2 and prayed the **third time**, saying the same words...... 26:44
5 that the sepulchre be made sure until the **third** day,... 27:64
6 after that he is killed, he shall rise the **third** day.... Mark 9:31
6 and the **third** day he shall rise again.................. 10:34
3 neither left he any seed: and the **third** likewise........ 12:21
1 he cometh the **third time**, and saith unto them,........ 14:41
4 And it was the **third** hour, and they crucified him...... 15:25
6 and be slain, and be raised the **third** day........... Luke 9:22
6 or come in the **third** watch, and find them so,......... 12:38
6 and the **third** day I shall be perfected................ 13:32
6 put him to death: ... **third** day he shall rise again...... 18:33
1 again he sent **a third**: and they wounded him also,..... 20:12
3 **third** took her; and in like manner the seven also:..... 20:31
1 And he said unto them the **third time**, Why,.......... 23:22
6 and be crucified, and the **third** day rise again.......... 24:7
7 to day is the **third** day since these ... were done....... 24:21
6 and to rise from the dead the **third** day:.............. 24:46
6 And the **third** day there was a marriage in Cana.... John 2:1
1 is now **the third time** that Jesus showed himself........ 21:14
1 He saith unto him the **third time**,..................... 21:17
1 he said unto him the **third time**, Lovest thou me?...... 21:17
4 seeing it is but the **third** hour of the day........... Acts 2:15
6 Him God raised up the **third** day,.................... 10:40
5 at **the third** hour of the night;........................ 23:23
6 And the **third** day we cast out with our own hands.... 27:19
1 secondarily prophets, **thirdly** teachers,............. 1 Co 12:28
6 and that he rose again the **third** day.................. 15:4
2 such an one caught up to the **third** heaven......... 2 Co 12:2
1 Behold, the **third time** I am ready to come to you;..... 12:14
1 This is the **third time** I am coming to you............ 13:1
1 and the **third** beast had a face as a man,............ Rev 4:7
7 And when he had opened the **third** seal,............... 6:5
2 I heard the **third** beast say, Come and see............ 6:5
1 **a third** of the earth was burned up, (NASB)........... 8:7
1 and the **third** part of trees was burnt up,............... 8:7
1 and the **third** part of the sea became blood;............ 8:8
1 **third** part of the creatures which were in the sea,....... 8:9
1 and the **third** part of the ships were destroyed.......... 8:9
3 And the **third** angel sounded,.......................... 8:10
1 and it fell upon the **third** part of the rivers,............ 8:10
1 the **third** part of the waters became wormwood;........ 8:11
1 and the **third** part of the sun was smitten,.............. 8:12
1 and the **third** part of the moon,........................ 8:12
1 and the **third** part of the stars;........................ 8:12
1 stars; so as the **third** part of them was darkened,....... 8:12
1 and the day shone not for a **third** part of it,............ 8:12
1 were prepared ... for to slay the **third** part of men...... 9:15
1 By these three was the **third** part of men killed,........ 9:18
4 and, behold, the **third** woe cometh quickly............. 11:14
1 his tail drew the **third** part of the stars of heaven,..... 12:4
3 And the **third** angel followed them, saying............ 14:9
3 the **third** angel poured out his vial upon the rivers..... 16:4
3 the **third**, a chalcedony; the fourth, an emerald;....... 21:19

Classical Greek

According to Delling ("treis," *Kittel*, 8:216), the cardinal number *three* and the ordinal number *third* play a significant role in the cultus of antiquity. The use of *three* makes what is being referred to definitive, giving it "full validity and power" (ibid.). *Three* is used to indicate completeness, the totality of the universe, or to designate the beginning, middle, and end of something.

Septuagint Usage

Both in the Old and New Testaments *tritos* is used as an adjective, substantive, or adverb to indicate the third in a series of three or more. It also represents the fraction one-third. Thus, in the Septuagint *tritos* occurs as an adjective in Genesis 1:13, "on the third day." It appears as a substantive in Numbers 15:6,7: "prepare a grain offering . . . mixed with a third of a hin of oil" (NIV). It appears in Exodus 5:14 as an adverb: "Wherefore have ye not fulfilled your task in making brick both yesterday (*tritēn hēmeran*) and today, as heretofore?"

New Testament Usage

There are several significant "thirds" in the New Testament. Most significant are the 15 references to the resurrection of the Lord Jesus on the third day, 13 of these in the Synoptic Gospels. Such usage seems always to be calculated from the present perspective of the speaker, so the third day means the "day after tomorrow" (cf. *Liddell-Scott*; Numbers 7:24; Luke 13:32, "today, and tomorrow, and the third day"). The use of the idiom "three days and three nights" does not contradict this (cf. Esther 4:16; 5:1).

Another significant "third" is the "third hour." Daytime was reckoned from sunrise, so the third hour of the day (Matthew 20:3; Mark 15:25; Acts 2:15) was approximately 9 a.m., depending upon the season. However, because of the lack of precise timekeeping instruments among the general populace, the term also referred to the quarter of a day that began with the third hour, approximately 9 a.m. till 12 noon. Thus John's reckoning of the trial of Christ ("about the sixth hour," John 19:14) and Mark's chronicling of the Crucifixion ("it was the third hour," Mark 15:25) do not contradict, but both point to the same period of the morning sun (cf. Morris, *The Gospel According to John, New International Commentary on the New Testament*, p.801). The third hour of the night was reckoned from sundown, and timed roughly with such devices as water clocks (Acts 23:23). The third watch of the night (Luke 12:38) probably fell between midnight and 3 a.m. (cf. Carcopino, *Daily Life in Ancient Rome*, pp.143-150; Ramsay, "About the Sixth Hour," pp.216-223).

The third witness or third attempt seems significant as indicating a sincere or complete effort (Matthew 26:44; Mark 14:41; Luke 20:12; 23:22; John 21:14,17; 2 Corinthians 12:8). The third heaven is the abode of God (2 Corinthians 12:2), above the localized atmosphere and stellar space.

The Book of Revelation has the most references to "thirds." It portends both the breadth and restraint of God's progressive judgments upon a third of the earth (8:7-12; 9:15,18). It also denotes the number of "stars" which the red dragon swept to earth with its tail (a third, 12:4).

STRONG 5154, BAUER 826-27, MOULTON-MILLIGAN 642, KITTEL 8:216-25, LIDDELL-SCOTT 1824, COLIN BROWN 2:687-88.

4996. τρίχινος trichinos adj

Hairy, made of hair.

שֵׂעָר sēʻār (7998), Hair (Zec 13:4).

1. τρίχινος trichinos nom sing masc

1 and the sun became black as sackcloth of hair,.......Rev 6:12

This term can signify something hairy or something made from hair. It occurs in Revelation 6:12, the sixth seal judgment of the tribulation period, which refers to the sun turning black as sackcloth made of hair.

STRONG 5155, BAUER 827, MOULTON-MILLIGAN 642, LIDDELL-SCOTT 1825.

4997. τρόμος tromos noun

Quaking, quivering, trembling.

אֵימָה 'êmāh (372), Terror (Ex 15:16).

מוֹרָא môrā' (4307), Fear (Gn 9:2).

מְחִתָּה m^echittāh (4425), Terror (Is 54:14).

עִיר ʻîr (6112), Anguish (Jer 15:8).

פַּחַד pachadh (6586), Trembling, fear (Dt 2:25, Is 19:16).

רֶטֶט reṯeṯ (7658), Panic (Jer 49:24 [30:24]).

רַעַד raʻadh (7747), Trembling (Ex 15:15).

רְעָדָה r^eʻādhāh (7748), Trembling (Jb 4:14, Ps 2:11, Is 33:14).

1. τρόμος tromos nom sing masc
2. τρόμου tromou gen sing masc
3. τρόμῳ tromō dat sing masc

1 for they trembled and were amazed:.............. Mark 16:8
3 in weakness, and in fear, and in much trembling.....1 Co 2:3
2 how with fear and trembling ye received him........2 Co 7:15
2 that are your masters ... with fear and trembling,.... Eph 6:5
2 your own salvation with fear and trembling..........Phlp 2:12

This term is often combined with the word for "fear" (*phobos* [5238]) in the Septuagint and in the New Testament. Hence, it generally relates to a trembling caused by fear.

It is used in Mark 16:8 of the women who fled from the sepulcher of Jesus after an angel appeared to them. Paul employed it to describe his sense of personal inadequacy when preaching the gospel in Corinth (1 Corinthians 2:3), of the way the Corinthians received Titus (2 Corinthians 7:15), of servants obeying their masters (Ephesians 6:5), and of Christians working out their own salvation, i.e., with fear and *trembling* (Philippians 2:12).

STRONG 5156, BAUER 827, MOULTON-MILLIGAN 642, LIDDELL-SCOTT 1826, COLIN BROWN 1:622.

4998. τροπή tropē noun

Turning, variation, change.

CROSS-REFERENCE:
τρόπος tropos (4999)

אֵיד 'êdh (344), Disaster (Jer 49:32 [30:10]).

חֲלוּשָׁה chălûshāh (2577), Defeat (Ex 32:18).

מַכָּה makkāh (4485), Wound (1 Kgs 22:35).

פֶּרֶץ perets (6806), Abandonment (Sir 45:23).

1. τροπῆς tropēs gen sing fem

1 is no variableness, neither shadow of turning......... Jas 1:17

Classical Greek

While the word *tropē* is found only one time in the New Testament (James 1:17), its classical Greek usage is quite significant. As early as 300 B.C. the term was used to describe the two solstices of the solar year (*Moulton-Milligan*). (These usually occur on June 22 and December 22—the days having the longest and shortest amount of sunlight.) A less technical use of the word *tropē* was also quite common and simply meant "to turn" or "to change." For example, it described a "change" in the weather or food "turning" bad (see *Liddell-Scott*). In a third-century A.D. writing *tropē* refers to the turning of waterwheels used in irrigation (*Moulton-Milligan*).

Septuagint Usage

In the Septuagint *tropē* describes various kinds of "turnings" or "changings." In Sirach 45:23 the writer describes how Phinehas stood fast for the Lord while the people *turned* away. It is used several times to denote the flight of an army, i.e., its retreat from battle (Exodus 32:18; 1 Maccabees 4:35; 5:61; 2 Maccabees 12:27,37). Further, it refers to the changes of seasons or the sun (Job 38:33; Deuteronomy 33:14).

New Testament Usage

With this varied range of meanings in view, Bible commentators have interpreted James 1:17 in a number of ways. Some see a very technical use of the term, such as Adam Clarke (see *Clarke's Commentaries*, 6:806-808). After a complex analysis of solstices and resultant parallax phenomena, Clarke (and others) supports a rendering of verse 17 which reads " . . . from the Father of lights, with whom is no parallax, nor *tropical shadow*." This interpretation is based on the occurrence of several other technical terms in the verse which were also used in the science of astronomy. (See word studies at *phōs* [5292B], "light, that which gives light"; *parallagē* [3744], "change, variation"; and *aposkiasma* [638], "shadow, a shadow cast by variation" [cf. *Bauer*].)

Bauer insists that the KJV translation "shadow of turning" cannot be supported lexically. This view adopts a more general understanding of the word *tropē*, as seen in the NIV translation, for example, which reads " . . . the Father of heavenly lights, who does not change like *shifting* shadows." An even more general use of the word is seen in this translation quoted in *Bauer* (see "aposkiasma") which says that the Father of lights is one "who is without change and knows neither *turning* nor darkness." Regardless of how the Greek is rendered, the truth arrived at is identical: that unlike everything else in life, God our Father is unchangeable! All that is good and perfect comes from Him.

STRONG 5157, BAUER 827, MOULTON-MILLIGAN 642, LIDDELL-SCOTT 1826.

4999. τρόπος tropos noun

Character, conduct, fashion, manner, way, guise.

COGNATES:
ἐπιτρέπω epitrepō (1994)
πολυτρόπως polutropōs (4047)
τροπή tropē (4998)
τροποφορέω tropophoreō (5000)

SYNONYM:
ἀναστροφή anastrophē (389)

דָּבָר dāvār (1745), Thing, matter (Nm 18:7, Dn 1:14).

טַעַם ṭa'am (3051), Judgment (1 Sm 25:33).

1. τρόπος tropos nom sing masc
2. τρόπῳ tropō dat sing masc
3. τρόπον tropon acc sing masc

3 as a hen gathereth her chickens under her wings,...Matt 23:37
3 as a hen doth gather her brood under her wings,...Luke 13:34
3 shall so come in like manner as ye have seen him... Acts 1:11
3 Wilt thou kill me, as thou diddest the Egyptian......... 7:28
3 we shall be saved, even as they. (NT)................. 15:11
3 that it shall be even as it was told me. (NT).......... 27:25
3 Much every way: chiefly, because that unto them.... Rom 3:2
2 What then? notwithstanding, every way,............ Php 1:18
3 Let no man deceive you by any means:............. 2 Th 2:3
2 the Lord ... give you peace always by all means......... 3:16
3 Now as Jannes and Jambres withstood Moses,...... 2 Tm 3:8
1 Let your conversation be without covetousness;..... Heb 13:5
3 Sodom ... and the cities about them in like manner, Jude 1:7

Classical Greek
This common noun occurs in Greek writings in numerous locations and with varied usage. It is applied to one person coming in the guise of another person, a person's character, the manner or way something occurs, etc. However, it is found in a figurative sense far more than in a literal sense. Metaphorically, in the papyri it often relates to a certain manner or way of life or to the actual character of an individual (*Moulton-Milligan*).

Septuagint Usage
In the Septuagint *tropos* has several usages. In Numbers 18:7 it means "custom" or "method"; the sons of Aaron were to minister according to the custom of the altar. In 1 Samuel 25:33 (LXX 1 Kings 25:33) it refers to the good judgment or conduct Abigail showed when she prevented David from slaughtering Nabal's household. It can also mean "appearance." The predominant usage of *tropos*, however, is in conjunction with the relative pronoun *hon* (see 3601B). In this usage *hon tropon* translates several Hebrew words and phrases which describe comparison, especially phrases containing *ka'asher*, "as, just as." In these cases *hon tropon* is equivalent to *hōs* (5445A), "as, like." Thus, in Exodus 2:14 Moses is asked: "Are you thinking of killing me *as* you killed the Egyptian?" (NIV). *Hon tropon* means "in the same way." Joshua 10:1 describes how Joshua destroyed Ai *just as* he destroyed Jericho.

New Testament Usage
In the New Testament these same senses also appear. *Tropos* refers to "conduct" as when the writer of Hebrews exhorted his readers to keep their *lives* free from the love of money (13:5). *Tropos* can also mean variation, kind, or possibility, for instance, when Paul rejoiced that in every *way* Christ was preached (cf. 2 Thessalonians 3:16). As in the Septuagint the main use of *tropos* is in conjunction with *hon* as a comparative adverb or conjunction. Jesus said, "*Even as* a hen gathereth her chickens under her wings . . . " (Matthew 23:37). Acts 1:11 says that Jesus will return *just as* (in the same *way* as) He left. Paul noted that in the last days evil men will resist the truth "*as* Jannes and Jambres withstood Moses" (2 Timothy 3:8).

STRONG 5158, BAUER 827, MOULTON-MILLIGAN 642, LIDDELL-SCOTT 1827.

5000. τροποφορέω tropophoreō verb

Bear, endure, put up with (another person).

CROSS-REFERENCES:
τρόπος tropos (4999)
φορέω phoreō (5246)

נָשָׂא nāsâ' (5558), Carry (Dt 1:31—only some Vaticanus texts).

1. ἐτροποφόρησεν etropophorēsen 3sing indic aor act

1 suffered he their manners in the wilderness......... Acts 13:18

This verb is a combination of *tropos* (4999), "fashion, manner, mode, way," and *pherō* (5179), "to bear" or "carry," and carries the idea of putting up with someone else's character or manners. Cicero used it this way when he said to Atticus, "*Bear with* my nonsense (or whim)" (*Letters to Atticus* 13.29.1). One text of the Septuagint uses it in Deuteronomy 1:31 of God's enduring the people of Israel as a parent would endure a child. From the context it appears that *trophophoreō* (5003B) is the better reading.

In his sermon in Pisidian Antioch Paul utilized the term to describe how God endured the manners of the Israelites for 40 years in the wilderness (Acts 13:18).

STRONG 5159, BAUER 827, MOULTON-MILLIGAN 643, LIDDELL-SCOTT 1827.

5001. τροφή trophē noun

Food, nourishment, victuals, means of support.

אֹכֶל 'ōkhel (406), Food (Pss 104:27 [103:27], 145:15 [144:15]).
דָּגָן dāghān (1765), Grain (65:9 [64:9]).
טֶרֶף ṭereph (3074), Food (Ps 111:5 [110:5]).
לֶחֶם lechem (4035), Food (Pss 136:25 [135:25], 147:9 [146:9], Prv 30:25 [24:60]).
מָזוֹן māzôn (4332), Provisions (2 Chr 11:23).
תַּעֲנוּג ta'ănûgh (8921), Abundance of food (Sir 41:1).

1. τροφή trophē nom sing fem
2. τροφῆς trophēs gen sing fem
3. τροφήν trophēn acc sing fem
4. τροφάς trophas acc pl fem

1 and his meat was locusts and wild honey........... Matt 3:4
2 Is not the life more than meat,........................ 6:25
2 for the workman is worthy of his meat............... 10:10
3 wise servant, ... to give them meat in due season?..... 24:45
2 The life is more than meat,....................... Luke 12:23
4 were gone away unto the city to buy meat.......... John 4:8
2 eat ... meat with gladness and singleness of heart,....Acts 2:46
3 when he had received meat, he was strengthened........ 9:19
2 filling our hearts with food and gladness............. 14:17
2 Paul besought them all to take meat, saying,.......... 27:33
2 Wherefore I pray you to take some meat:............ 27:34
2 and they also took some meat....................... 27:36
2 And when they had eaten enough, (NT).............. 27:38
2 such as have need of milk, and not of strong meat... Heb 5:12

1 strong meat belongeth to them that are of full age,.. Heb 5:14
2 or sister be naked, and destitute of daily food,....... Jas 2:15

Classical Greek

This noun is a cognate of the verb *trephō* (4982), "to feed, nourish, rear." The New Testament, as well as the papyri and other Greek sources, contains the noun with the literal meaning of "food." Symbolically, the word is used in common Greek writings in a variety of ways: of one's livelihood, of nursing and rearing children, of tending animals, etc. *Trophē* can also denote the place where animals are fed (*Liddell-Scott*).

Septuagint Usage

In the Septuagint *trophē* is a common word. In Genesis 49:20 it is used to refer to food which Jacob prophesied would be rich for Asher's descendants. In Job 36:31 (LXX 36:32) Elihu stated that God is the provider of food for the people of the earth. In Psalm 104:27 (LXX 103:27) the Psalmist noted that God provides food for all the animals as well.

New Testament Usage

The King James' translators normally translated *trophē* with the word *meat*, but this refers to grain; *flesh* is the King James' term for "meat." It is used literally of the food John the Baptist ate (Matthew 3:4), in Jesus' command about not worrying over how to acquire necessary food (Matthew 6:25; Luke 12:23), and in His instructions to the 12 disciples not to take food for their preaching mission (Matthew 10:10). Thus, *trophē* is a word for "food," any kind of food or nourishment for the body.

The New Testament utilizes the term metaphorically to refer to the solid food of the Scriptures that only mature believers are capable of digesting (Hebrews 5:14). Conversely, new converts or people who remain babes in Christ are not capable of digesting solid food (Hebrews 5:12). Therefore, they must mature by depending on God's grace to help them progress beyond the elementary truths of the Bible, or what Scripture designates as the "milk" of the Word.

STRONG 5160, BAUER 827, MOULTON-MILLIGAN 643, LIDDELL-SCOTT 1827-28.

5002. Τρόφιμος Trophimos name

Trophimus.

1. Τρόφιμος Trophimos nom masc
2. Τρόφιμον Trophimon acc masc

1 and of Asia, Tychicus and **Trophimus**............. Acts 20:4
2 with him in the city **Trophimus** an Ephesian,....... Acts 21:29
2 but **Trophimus** have I left at Miletum sick......... 2 Tm 4:20

Trophimus was a Christian from Ephesus who was one of those who joined Paul on his last journey to Jerusalem (Acts 20:4). As a Greek convert he was uncircumcised and was the subject of the capital charge against Paul: "He has brought Greeks into the temple area and defiled this holy place" (Acts 21:28f., NIV).

Second Timothy 4:20 records that Paul "left (Trophimus) at Miletus sick." This statement conflicts with Acts which records his presence in Jerusalem. Assuming that the statement is true, and that it refers to the same Trophimus, it must refer to a later period in Paul's life after his trial in Rome.

5003. τροφός trophos noun

Feeder, nurse, rearer.

יָנַק yānaq (3352), Suck; hiphil: nurse (Gn 35:8, 2 Kgs 11:2, 2 Chr 22:11).

1. τροφός trophos nom sing fem

1 even as a **nurse** cherisheth her children:.............1 Th 2:7

This noun can be traced back in classical Greek to the writings of Homer (Eighth Century B.C.). The Septuagint uses it of Rebecca's nurse (Genesis 35:8), of Joash's nurse (2 Kings 11:2 [LXX 4 Kings 11:2]), and of queens becoming nursing mothers (Isaiah 49:23).

In the New Testament the apostle Paul selected this term to speak of the gentle care he and his associates manifested toward the Thessalonians (1 Thessalonians 2:7). Paul said he cared for them in the same way concerned parents would express care for their children.

STRONG 5162, BAUER 827-28, MOULTON-MILLIGAN 643, LIDDELL-SCOTT 1828, COLIN BROWN 1:282.

5003B. τροφοφορέω trophophoreō verb

Nourish, sustain.

1. ἐτροφοφορησεν etrophophorēsen 3sing indic aor act

1 **suffered** he their manners in the wilderness........ Acts 13:18

Septuagint Usage

Trophophoreō, "to nourish," is an extremely rare word in ancient Greek. It appears only as a variant in the Septuagint reading of Deuteronomy 1:31 and at 2 Maccabees 7:27. For Patristic Greek,

Lampe supplies only one reference (*Patristic Greek Lexicon*). Because it is generally a variant reading for *tropophoreō* (5000), some scholars have doubted whether *trophophoreō* actually existed as a word prior to the New Testament times (Metzger, *Textual Commentary on the Greek New Testament*, p.405). However, the context of Deuteronomy seems to favor *trophophoreō*: "The Lord your God will *nourish* you" is better than "The Lord your God will *endure* or *bear with* (*tropophoreō*) you." *Tropophoreō* has a negative connotation which is out of place in the context. At 2 Maccabees 7:27 the mother of the seven martyred sons exhorted her youngest son to stand firm and reminded him that she nourished or took care of him as a child.

New Testament Usage

Trophophoreō appears only once in the New Testament as a variant reading in Acts 13:18. Paul alluded to Deuteronomy 1:31 when he described the conduct of God toward the Israelites in the desert: He *nourished* them. The textual evidence is almost evenly balanced, but scholars generally accept *tropophoreō* as the better reading.

Bauer 828, Moulton-Milligan 643, Liddell-Scott 1828.

5004. τροχιά trochia noun

Course, path, rut, track.

מַעְגָּל maʿgāl (4724), Way, path (Prv 2:15, 4:11, 5:6).

1. τροχιάς trochias acc pl fem

1 And make straight paths for your feet,............. Heb 12:13

Although this noun was used as early as Philo (First Century A.D.) of the literal track or rut made by a wheel, it was also used in a metaphoric way. It occurs, for example, in Proverbs 4:26 which speaks of straight *paths* for the feet.

The same idea comes into the New Testament where the writer of Hebrews urged his readers to make straight *paths* for their feet (Hebrews 12:13). It is located in the context of God's discipline of His children and is symbolic of a moral life.

Strong 5163, Bauer 828, Liddell-Scott 1828.

5005. τροχός trochos noun

Circular course for running, wheel.

אוֹפַן 'ôphan (210), Wheel (1 Kgs 7:33, Prv 20:26, Ez 10:10).

גַּלְגַּל galgal (1574), Whirlwind (Ps 77:18 [76:18], Is 5:28); wheels (Ez 10:2).

מוֹרַג môragh (4308), Threshing sledge (2 Sm 24:22, Is 41:15).

1. τροχόν trochon acc sing masc

1 and setteth on fire the course of nature;............ Jas 3:6

From the time of Homer (Eighth Century B.C.) classical Greek contains a plethora of references to this common term that can denote a circular track for running, a wheel of a machine, or a waterwheel.

James employed it in a figurative way when he delineated the problems the tongue can cause (James 3:6). According to James an uncontrolled tongue is like a raging blaze that sets on fire the "whole direction" of a person in a way that would be like the continuous burning of Gehenna. Hence, it actually is inflamed by hell itself. The phrase *ton trochon tēs geneseōs*, "the course of nature," probably refers to the "whole world" (see Ropes, *International Critical Commentary, James*, p.235).

Strong 5164, Bauer 828, Moulton-Milligan 643, Liddell-Scott 1829, Colin Brown 1:182.

5006. τρυβλίον trublion noun

Bowl, cup.

טֶנֶא ṭene' (3046), Food container (Sir 34:14).

כַּף kaph (3834), Palm; bowl (1 Kgs 7:50).

קְעָרָה qeʿārāh (7370), Dish, plate (Ex 25:29, Nm 4:7, 7:84).

1. τρυβλίῳ trubliō dat sing neu

2. τρύβλιον trublion nom/acc sing neu

1 He that dippeth his hand with me in the dish,..... Matt 26:23

2 one of the twelve, that dippeth with me in the dish. Mark 14:20

This noun normally was used for a bowl, though sometimes the Greeks even used it of a measuring cup for medical prescriptions.

The Gospels contain this word when referring to the bowl used at the Last Supper (Matthew 26:23; Mark 14:20). Christ designated His betrayer as the one who dipped the sop in the dish used at this historic meal. According to Lane, "To dip one's hand into the bowl together with someone is to share one's meal with him. The expression thus heightens the baseness of the betrayal" (*New International Commentaries*, 2:500).

Strong 5165, Bauer 828, Moulton-Milligan 643, Liddell-Scott 1829.

5007. τρυγάω trugaō verb

Gather ripe fruit, harvest.

SYNONYMS:

ἀθροίζω athroizō (119B)
ἐπισυνάγω episunagō (1980)
συλλέγω sullegō (4667)
συνάγω sunagō (4714)
συναθροίζω sunathroizō (4718)
συστρέφω sustrephō (4814)

אָרָה 'ārâh (741), Pick (Ps 80:12 [79:12]).

בָּצַר bātsar (1245), Gather, gatherer (Dt 24:21, Jgs 9:27, Jer 6:9).

דָּרַךְ dārakh (1931), Tread (Jer 25:30 [32:30]).

חֹל chōl (2555), Use (Dt 28:30).

חָמַס chāmaṣ (2659), Shake off (Jb 15:33).

קָצִיר qātsîr (7392), Harvest (Hos 6:11 [6:12]).

קָצַר qātsar (7403), Reap (1 Sm 8:12, Hos 10:13).

1. τρυγῶσιν trugōsin 3pl indic pres act
2. ἐτρύγησεν etrugēsen 3sing indic aor act
3. τρύγησον trugēson 2sing impr aor act

1 nor of a bramble bush **gather** they grapes........... Luke 6:44
3 and **gather** the clusters of the vine of the earth;.....Rev 14:18
2 and **gathered** the vine of the earth,.................. 14:19

Classical Greek and Septuagint Usage

From Homer on to New Testament times, this verb commonly expressed the harvesting of ripe fruit, especially grapes (*Bauer*). It even included the aspect of gathering the harvest. *Trugaō* appears several times in the Septuagint with the same meaning. Deuteronomy 28:30 notes that if the Israelites were unfaithful to the Covenant they would plant a vineyard, but would "surely not *harvest* it."

New Testament Usage

The Gospel of Luke utilizes the term in a metaphoric sense to speak of the fruit of a person's heart (Luke 6:44). The apostle John included the word twice in the same figurative sense when he alluded to the harvesting of the earth during the Battle of Armageddon (Revelation 14:18,19).

STRONG 5166, BAUER 828, MOULTON-MILLIGAN 643-44, LIDDELL-SCOTT 1829.

5008. τρυγών trugōn noun

Turtledove.

תּוֹר tôr (8782), Turtledove (Lv 12:8, Nm 6:10, Jer 8:7).

1. τρυγόνων trugonōn gen pl fem

1 A pair of **turtledoves**, or two young pigeons......... Luke 2:24

This noun is related to the verb *truzō* which means "to coo, murmur, sigh" (*Bauer*). It is found in the Septuagint in Leviticus 12:8 which permitted the poor to offer two turtledoves, one for a whole burnt offering and one for a sin offering.

When Mary's time for purification arrived, Mary and Joseph presented Jesus to God along with a pair of turtledoves or pigeons (Luke 2:24). This offering of two turtledoves shows they could not afford a lamb for a burnt offering. According to Louw and Nida (*Greek-English Lexicon*, 1:45), the Greek of the New Testament does not make a clear distinction between doves (which have pointed tails) and pigeons (which have squared-off tails).

STRONG 5167, BAUER 828, MOULTON-MILLIGAN 644, KITTEL 6:63-72, LIDDELL-SCOTT 1830.

5009. τρυμαλιά trumalia noun

Hole, eye of a needle.

חָגוּ chāghû (2380), Cleft (Jer 49:16 [29:16]).

מִנְהָרָה minhārāh (4636), Den (Jgs 6:2).

נָקִיק nāqîq (5540), Crevice, cleft (Jer 13:4, 16:16).

סָעִיף ṣā'îph (5780), Cleft (Jgs 15:8).

1. τρυμαλιᾶς trumalias gen sing fem

1 for a camel to go through the **eye** of a needle,..... Mark 10:25
1 is easier for a camel to go through a needle's **eye**, Luke 18:25

Classical Greek and Septuagint Usage

Trumalia appears very rarely in classical Greek but seems to be a word that denotes holes in general. The Septuagint uses this noun of the hole in the rock of Etam (Judges 15:11), of the hole in the rock at the Euphrates (Jeremiah 13:4), and of the Israelites' hiding in caves (Jeremiah 16:16).

New Testament Usage

The Greek New Testament, however, uses the word in a metaphoric sense of the impossibility of a camel going through the *eye* of a needle (Mark 10:25; Luke 18:25). Some Bible students believe there actually was a gate by this title, but these smaller gates were not constructed until the Fourth Century A.D. The picture is that of the largest animal passing through the smallest opening. The important fact is that Jesus used the expression to explain the difficulty involved in the salvation of a rich person.

STRONG 5168, BAUER 828, MOULTON-MILLIGAN 644, LIDDELL-SCOTT 1830.

5010. τρύπημα trupēma noun

Hole, eye of a needle, porthole.

1. τρυπήματος trupēmatos gen sing neu

1 easier for a camel to go through the eye of a needle,Matt 19:24

The noun *trupēma* was employed by Greeks in a number of ways. It could refer to a hole in a ship or to nearly any kind of hole. It is related to the verb *trupaō*, "to bore."

The New Testament uses *trupēma* only to refer to the eye of a needle (Matthew 19:24). It is found in the context of Jesus' appeal to the rich young ruler who obviously was possessed by his possessions. Jesus told His disciples that it is easier for a camel to pass through a needle's eye than for a rich person to enter the kingdom of God. (See *trumalia* [5009].)

STRONG 5169, BAUER 828.

5011. Τρύφαινα Truphaina name

Tryphaena.

1. Τρύφαιναν Truphainan acc fem

1 Salute Tryphena and Tryphosa, ... Rom 16:12

A Christian woman whom Paul greets at Romans 16:12.

5012. τρυφάω truphaō verb

Live in luxury, live sumptuously, revel, carouse.

COGNATE:

τρυφή truphē (5013)

SYNONYMS:

σπαταλάω spatalaō (4537)
στρηνιάω strēniaō (4614)

עָדַן ʿādhan (5939), Hithpael: revel (Neh 9:25).

עָנֹג ʿānōgh (6253), Hithpael: be delighted (Is 66:11).

1. ἐτρυφήσατε etruphēsate 2pl indic aor act

1 Ye have lived in pleasure on the earth, ... Jas 5:5

Classical Greek

Classical Greek commonly employs the word *truphaō* when speaking about well-fed, contented animals. It can carry the connotation of being insolent or putting on an air of superiority. It is also used figuratively of reveling in doing good (*Bauer*).

Septuagint Usage

The Septuagint uses it of the Israelites growing fat from enjoying the bounties of Canaan after they occupied it (Nehemiah 9:25). It also speaks of this same kind of experience during the Millennium when the Israelites will enjoy the abundance of the land God will give them (Isaiah 66:11). (See also Sirach 14:4.)

New Testament Usage

The New Testament contains the term *truphaō* in James' warning to the rich men who were living luxuriously at the expense of the poor (James 5:5). He wrote that the self-indulgence of these wealthy people would be cut short because their wealth would be corrupted, their expensive clothing would be eaten by moths, and their gold and silver would rust (James 5:1-3). He added that they would be judged by God for hoarding material goods and cheating their employees (James 5:4,6).

STRONG 5171, BAUER 828, MOULTON-MILLIGAN 644, LIDDELL-SCOTT 1831.

5013. τρυφή truphē noun

Self-indulgence, luxury, reveling, enjoyment, delight, softness, delicateness.

CROSS-REFERENCE:

τρυφάω truphaō (5012)

מַעֲדַנִּים maʿadhannîm (4729), Dainties (Gn 49:20).

עֵדֶן ʿēdhen (5941), Delight, delicacies (Ps 36:8 [35:8], Jer 51:34 [28:34]).

עֵדֶן ʿēdhen (5942), Eden (Gn 3:23f. [3:24f.], Ez 31:9).

תַּעֲנוּג taʿănûgh (8921), Luxury, delights (Prv 19:10, S/S 7:6).

תִּפְאֶרֶת tiph'ereth (8930), Beauty (Prv 4:9).

1. τρυφῇ truphē dat sing fem
2. τρυφήν truphēn acc sing fem

1 are gorgeously apparelled, and live delicately, ... Luke 7:25
2 they that count it pleasure to riot in the day time.... 2 Pt 2:13

Classical Greek

This noun is used throughout Greek writings in a variety of ways. It normally speaks of a dainty, delicate, indulgent, luxurious, soft, splendid lifestyle. It even can refer to males who are effeminate. It is also used of a fastidious person who is overly difficult to please, especially relative to edible delicacies. It can denote a conceited, insolent, and scornful individual who wallows in luxury and detests other people.

Septuagint Usage

In the Septuagint *truphē* is used to describe Eden, the luxurious garden (Genesis 2:15; 3:23). Proverbs 4:5 describes how wisdom will present the one who attains it with a "crown of *luxury*." In Ezekiel 28:13 the prophet referred to the Garden of Eden in a metaphoric sense. The verse describes the blessings of the Lord that the king of Tyre forfeited because of his violence and sin.

New Testament Usage

Luke employed this term describing the scene where Jesus informed the crowd that John the Baptist was not a dainty, effeminate individual who would resemble a reed shaken by the wind. Neither was he a man adorned in splendid garments. Nor did he live in the lap of luxury like a king in a royal palace (Luke 7:24,25). Instead, John was a prophet, but not just an ordinary prophet. He was the one selected by God to be the forerunner of Christ (Luke 7:26,27). Hence, up to that time no human ever was given a higher honor than John the Baptist. However, even the least in the kingdom of God has greater privileges than John (Luke 7:28), because John preceded the events of Calvary, and believers enjoy the benefits of the redemptive work of Christ.

In another usage the apostle Peter warned his readers about false teachers who introduce destructive heresies, exploit innocent people, blaspheme God, and live in the lap of luxury (2 Peter 2:13). Peter carefully added that these individuals will face the wrath of God.

STRONG 5172, BAUER 828, MOULTON-MILLIGAN 644, LIDDELL-SCOTT 1830.

5014. Τρυφῶσα Truphōsa name

Tryphosa.

1. Τρυφῶσαν Truphōsan acc fem

1 **Salute Tryphena and Tryphosa,** .... Rom 16:12

A Christian woman whom Paul greets at Romans 16:12.

5015. Τρῳάς Trōas name

Troas.

1. Τρῳάδος Trōados gen fem

2. Τρῳάδι Trōadi dat fem

3. Τρῳάδα Trōada acc fem

3 **And they passing by Mysia came down to Troas.**... Acts 16:8
1 **Therefore loosing from Troas,** 16:11
2 **These going before tarried for us at Troas.** 20:5
3 **and came unto them to Troas in five days;** 20:6
3 **when I came to Troas to preach Christ's gospel,** ..... 2 Co 2:12
2 **The cloak that I left at Troas with Carpus,** .... 2 Tm 4:13

A city and area in northwest Asia Minor which Paul visited several times. It was 10 miles south of ancient Troy and was the gateway from Asia to Europe.

Paul visited the city at least three times. At Troas, on his second missionary journey, he had his vision of the man of Macedonia, in response to which he first journeyed to Europe (Acts 16:8,11). On his third journey he gave up an "open door" to preach the gospel there in his anxiety to hear news from Titus of the church in Corinth (2 Corinthians 2:12f.). Lastly, on his return from that journey to Jerusalem, he spent a week in Troas. On this visit he raised a young believer named Eutychus from death after a fatal fall (Acts 20:5-12).

5016. Τρωγύλλιον Trōgullion name

Trogyllium.

1. Τρωγυλλίῳ Trōgulliō dat neu

1 **and tarried at Trogyllium;** .... Acts 20:15

A headland near Ephesus on the coast of Asia Minor, facing the island of Samos. According to some manuscripts of Acts 20:15 Paul and his party anchored there overnight en route to Jerusalem. Others give Samos as the place of anchorage.

5017. τρώγω trōgō verb

Chew, crunch, gnaw, nibble, eat.

SYNONYMS:

γεύω geuō (1083)
ἐσθίω esthiō (2052)
καταπίνω katapinō (2636)
κατεσθίω katesthiō (2688)

1. τρώγων trōgōn nom sing masc part pres act

2. τρώγοντες trōgontes nom pl masc part pres act

2 **they were eating and drinking,** .... Matt 24:38
1 **Whoso eateth my flesh, and drinketh my blood,** ..... John 6:54
1 **He that eateth my flesh, and drinketh my blood,** 6:56
1 **so he that eateth me, even he shall live by me.** 6:57
1 **he that eateth of this bread shall live for ever.** 6:58
1 **He that eateth bread with me** 13:18

Classical Greek

From the time of Homer (Eighth Century B.C.) to New Testament times this verb can be traced in Greek writings as referring to the audible chewing and munching of food by animals. It normally speaks of a slow process that consumes much of an animal's time. It even speaks of the gnawing of bones and other hard substances. It can simply mean "to eat," however. At times it is used of people chewing raw fruit and vegetables, as opposed to eating cooked foods (*Liddell-Scott*). *Trōgō* is not found in the Septuagint.

New Testament Usage

Matthew 24:38 employs this word as a present participle (*trōgontes*, "eating") when Jesus said that the mind-set of most people surrounding the time of His second advent would be similar to what it was like the days of Noah. The tenses of the verbs express duration in eating, drinking, marrying, and being given in marriage, all done without any consciousness whatever of the imminency of the Lord's return. Hence, He cautioned people to keep watching for His imminent return.

The term is utilized four times as a present participle (*ho trōgōn*, "the one eating") in the metaphoric sense of enjoying a continuous relationship with Christ (John 6:54-58). Jesus figuratively called himself the manna that God supplied the Israelites in the wilderness, and He encouraged His listeners to partake of that same manna. Otherwise, they would not be able to share the eternal life He alone is able to provide.

John used *trōgō* as the present tense form "to eat." In late Hellenistic usage there was a trend to use *trōgō* instead of *esthiō* (2052) (Goppelt, "trōgō," *Kittel*, 8:236). While John used the aorist stem *phag-*, he did not use *esthiō*. This is particularly evident at 13:18 where he used *trōgō* even though the Septuagint uses *esthiō*. Thus, *trōgō* means any kind of eating, not necessarily a "noisy feeding" (like "munch" or "crunch"). An analysis of John's Gospel reveals that the source of Christian life is the abiding power of the Holy Spirit, not a material act of eating.

Christ referred to Psalm 41:9 (LXX 40:10) during His last meal with His disciples before the Cross (John 13:18). Jesus acknowledged His impending betrayal by Judas. The betrayal would be made by a friend, "one who eats with me."

STRONG 5176, BAUER 829, MOULTON-MILLIGAN 644, KITTEL 8:236-37, LIDDELL-SCOTT 1832.

5018. τυγχάνω tunchanō verb

Happen to be, meet, meet by chance, find oneself, find a thing, hit a mark, obtain something.

COGNATES:

ἐντυγχάνω entunchanō (1777)
ἐπιτυγχάνω epitunchanō (1997)
παρατυγχάνω paratunchanō (3770)
συντυγχάνω suntunchanō (4792)

מָצָא mātsâ' (4834), Find, reach; hit by accident (Dt 19:5).

1. **τυγχάνοντα tunchanonta** acc sing masc part pres act
2. **τυγχάνοντες tunchanontes** nom pl masc part pres act
3. **τύχωσιν tuchōsin** 3pl subj aor act
4. **τύχοι tuchoi** 3sing opt aor act
5. **τυχών tuchōn** nom sing masc part aor act
6. **τυχοῦσαν tuchousan** acc sing fem part aor act
7. **τυχούσας tuchousas** acc pl fem part aor act
8. **τυχόν tuchon** nom/acc sing neu part aor act
9. **τυχεῖν tuchein** inf aor act
10. **τέτευχεν teteuchen** 3sing indic perf act
11. **τέτυχεν tetuchen** 3sing indic perf act

1 and departed, leaving him half dead. (NT)........Luke 10:30
9 shall be accounted worthy to obtain that world,....... 20:35
7 And God wrought special miracles by ... Paul:.... Acts 19:11
2 Seeing that by thee we enjoy great quietness,......... 24:2
5 Having therefore obtained help of God,.............. 26:22
9 go unto his friends to refresh himself. (NT).......... 27:3
6 the barbarous people showed us no little kindness:... 28:2
4 it may be, so many kinds of voices in the world,.. 1 Co 14:10
4 it may chance of wheat, or of some other grain:...... 15:37
8 And it may be that I will abide,..................... 16:6
3 that they may also obtain the salvation ... in Christ 2 Tm 2:10
10 now hath he obtained a more excellent ministry,.... Heb 8:6
3 that they might obtain a better resurrection:.......... 11:35

Classical Greek

This verb is used in Greek writings in numerous ways. It can mean to hit with an arrow, to light upon someone or something, to fall in with someone, to gain one's purpose, to be in a place, to succeed, to suffer violence, to become master of, to experience something, to turn out a certain way, to obtain something, etc. (*Liddell-Scott*). It occurs in both a positive and negative sense, and it can be used of people, of things, or of circumstances.

Septuagint Usage

In the Septuagint *tunchanō* is used in Deuteronomy 19:5 to refer to the head of an ax which happened to come loose, striking a fellow worker. Proverbs 30:23 (LXX 24:58) tells of a despised woman who *marries* a good man (in the sense "obtains"). In many other references, especially in the apocryphal books, *tunchanō* is almost the same as *eimi* (1498), the simple verb of being (Bauernfeind, "tunchanō," *Kittel*, 8:240).

New Testament Usage

Luke 10:30 employs the term in the story of the Good Samaritan: the Lord said that by *chance* a priest came down the same road (Luke 10:30). Jesus also spoke of the ones counted worthy of *obtaining* or taking part in the resurrection of believers (Luke 20:35).

Luke recorded Tertullus' comment about *obtaining* or enjoying peace under Felix's rule (Acts 24:2). Luke also recorded Paul's statement before King Agrippa that the apostle had *obtained* the help of God from the time of his conversion (Acts 26:22). In addition, Luke recorded Paul's use of the word when telling how his friends helped *provide* for his needs (Acts 27:3).

In 1 Corinthians 15:37 Paul used *tunchanō* to indicate an example. He noted that the farmer does not sow a full-grown object; rather, he plants a seed "perhaps" (or "for example") of wheat or something else. Paul used this verb in the subjunctive mood (*may obtain*) when he wrote of the eternal glory that God's children will experience when Jesus returns (2 Timothy 2:10).

The writer of Hebrews employed the word as a perfect tense verb to describe the more excellent ministry Jesus *has obtained* because He is the mediator of a better covenant (Hebrews 8:6). In addition, the writer used the word when speaking of the tortured saints *receiving* a better resurrection (Hebrews 11:35). Thus, in the New Testament *tunchanō* is used to denote acquisition of any sort of occurrence, including a chance occurrence.

Strong 5177, Bauer 829, Moulton-Milligan 644-45, Kittel 8:238-42, Liddell-Scott 1832.

5019. τυμπανίζω tumpanizō verb

To torture, torment.

תָּוָה tāwâh (8757), Piel: scribble (1 Sm 21:14 [21:13]).

1. ἐτυμπανίσθησαν etumpanisthēsan 3pl indic aor pass

1 others were tortured, not accepting deliverance; ..... Heb 11:35

Classical Greek and Septuagint Usage

In its earliest known occurrences *tumpanizō* refers to beating a drum or "drumming" upon an object. This is the meaning in its only appearance in the Septuagint. David, when he feigned insanity before the king of Gath, "beat" upon the doors of the gate (1 Samuel 21:13 [LXX 1 Kings 21:13]).

By extension *tumpanizō* could also refer to beating people, and hence, "to torture" or "torment." Thayer describes an ancient implement of torture called the *tumpanon*, a wheel-shaped instrument upon which an individual would be stretched and then beaten with clubs or whips (*Greek-English Lexicon*). According to 2 Maccabees 6:19,28 Eleazer was tortured upon the *tumpanon*.

New Testament Usage

In the classic listing of the people of faith we read of some faithful believers who were perhaps beaten to death on this kind of device (Hebrews 11:35). According to Louw and Nida, the use of *tumpanizō* may imply "some special form of torture," but "it is probably employed in a more generic sense" (*Greek-English Lexicon*, 1:491). If torture upon the *tumpanon* was in view when the writer wrote chapter 11 he may have been referring to Eleazer, who refused to be released.

Strong 5178, Bauer 829, Moulton-Milligan 645, Liddell-Scott 1834.

5019B. τυπικῶς tupikōs adv

By way of example, typologically.

Cross-Reference:
τύπος tupos (5020)

1. τυπικῶς tupikōs

1 happened to them as an example (NASB) (NT).... 1 Co 10:11

The adverb *tupikōs* is related to the adjective *tupikos*, "impressionable, conforming to type," and means "by way of example" (*Liddell-Scott*). It is rare in classical Greek and is not found in the Septuagint. Its only occurrence in the New Testament is as a variant in 1 Corinthians 10:11 (cf. *Nestle-Aland 26th*; *Textus Receptus* has *tupoi* [see 5020], "types"). There Paul declared that the incidents experienced by the Jews in the Old Testament were "types" ("*typologically* happening") or lessons of history, "written down as warnings for us, on whom the fulfillment of the ages has come" (NIV).

Bauer 829, Moulton-Milligan 645, Kittel 8:246-59, Liddell-Scott 1835, Colin Brown 3:903.

5020. τύπος tupos noun

Mark, image, statue, form, figure, pattern, model, example.

Cognates:
ἀντίτυπος antitupos (496)
ἐντυπόω entupoō (1779)
τυπικῶς tupikōs (5019B)
τύπτω tuptō (5021)
ὑποτύπωσις hupotupōsis (5134)

Synonyms:
εἰκών eikōn (1494)
ἰδέα idea (2374)
μορφή morphē (3307)
μόρφωσις morphōsis (3309)
σχῆμα schēma (4828)
ὑπόδειγμα hupodeigma (5100)
χάραγμα charagma (5316)

צֶלֶם tselem (7021), Image (Am 5:26).

תַּבְנִית tavnîth (8732), Pattern (Ex 25:40 [25:39]).

1. τύπος tupos nom sing masc
2. τύπον tupon acc sing masc
3. τύποι tupoi nom pl masc
4. τύπους tupous acc pl masc

2 Except I shall see in his hands the **print** of ... nails, John 20:25
2 and put my finger into the **print** of the nails, ... 20:25
4 **figures** which ye made to worship them: .... Acts 7:43
2 make it according to the **fashion** that he had seen....... 7:44
2 And he wrote a letter after this **manner**: 23:25
1 who is the **figure** of him that was to come........... Rom 5:14
2 that **form** of doctrine which was delivered you.......... 6:17
3 Now these things were our **examples**, ... 1 Co 10:6
3 these things happened unto them for **ensamples**: 10:11
2 them which walk so as ye have **us for an ensample**... Phlp 3:17
4 So that ye were **ensamples** to all that believe .... 1 Th 1:7
2 make ourselves **an ensample** unto you to follow us... 2 Th 3:9
1 but be thou **an example** of the believers, ... 1 Tm 4:12
2 showing thyself **a pattern** of good works: .... Tit 2:7
2 all things according to the **pattern** showed to thee .... Heb 8:5
3 but being **ensamples** to the flock.................... 1 Pt 5:3

Classical Greek

Tupos exhibits a strange dual meaning: on the one hand it denotes an "original, model, pattern"; on the other hand, it indicates a "copy." Thus it can describe a model as well as a copy. Scholars are unsure about the origin of the term. It may be a derivative of *tuptō* (5021), "to beat." If that is the case, a *tupos* then is the "mark" of a beating, i.e., a "wound." The term functions in this way in John's Gospel in reference to the *scars* of the nails in the hands of Jesus that He presented to His disciples following His resurrection (John 20:25). Others think that *tupos* originally meant "form" or "impression" (Müller, "Type," *Colin Brown*, 3:903-904).

Tupos had both literal and figurative senses in classical Greek. In a concrete sense it could denote the "imprint" of something upon something else. Figuratively it represented the "example" of conduct or the "pattern" for establishing doctrine.

Septuagint Usage

Only four instances of *tupos* occur in the Septuagint. One is a translation of the Hebrew word *tavnîth* (Exodus 25:40, of the tabernacle as a "model" of the divine tabernacle; cf. Hebrews 8:5). The other (two of the four are in apocryphal writings which lack a Hebrew original) translates *tselem* (Amos 5:25, of idolatries). (Cf. the other two instances in 3 Maccabees 3:30 and 4 Maccabees 6:19.)

New Testament Usage

Sixteen occurrences of *tupos* are attested in the New Testament. Several times it clearly means "example." Paul encouraged the believers in Philippi to follow the example they had from Paul and his coworkers if they wished to live the Christian life (Philippians 3:17; cf. 2 Thessalonians 3:9). The recent converts in Thessalonica, because of their eagerness and piety, were already "examples" for other churches (1 Thessalonians 1:7). Paul encouraged his younger coworkers Timothy and Titus to conduct themselves properly so they might be examples to their congregations in both word and life-style (1 Timothy 4:12; Titus 2:7).

Tupos, however, also functions in a metaphoric way. Adam is a *tupos* of Christ; Adam is the head of the race and represents it. When he fell he allowed sin to enter the world, and consequently men were subject to condemnation. Christ, however, as the last Adam (cf. 1 Corinthians 15:45-49), came on the scene as the new representative of the human race; He reestablished what the first Adam forfeited.

Paul wrote in 1 Corinthians (10:6-11) that the things that happened to Israel during the old covenant serve as *tupoi* to believers in these days. Israel's "missing of God's will" is a grave warning to the church of the New Testament.

STRONG 5179, BAUER 829-30, MOULTON-MILLIGAN 645, KITTEL 8:246-59, LIDDELL-SCOTT 1835, COLIN BROWN 3:903-7.

5021. τύπτω tuptō verb

Beat, smite, strike (someone else or oneself), sting, wound.

COGNATE:
τύπος tupos (5020)

SYNONYMS:
κολαφίζω kolaphizō (2826)
μαστιγόω mastigoō (3118)
μαστίζω mastizō (3119)
παίω paiō (3680)
πατάσσω patassō (3822)
πλήσσω plēssō (4001)
ῥαπίζω rhapizō (4331)
φραγελλόω phragelloō (5253)

חָלַק chālaq (2606), Divide, allot; hiphil: make smooth (Is 41:7).

כָּרַת kārath (3901), Cut; hiphil: kill (1 Kgs 18:4).

נָגַף nāghaph (5238), Smite (Ex 8:2).

נָכָה nākhâh (5409), Hiphil: strike, kill (Dt 25:11, 2 Kgs 6:22, Ez 7:9).

1. **τύπτοντι tuptonti** dat sing masc part pres act
2. **τύπτοντες tuptontes** nom pl masc part pres act
3. **τύπτειν tuptein** inf pres act
4. **ἔτυπτεν etupten** 3sing indic imperf act
5. **ἔτυπτον etupton** 3pl indic imperf act
6. **τύπτεσθαι tuptesthai** inf pres mid

3 And shall begin **to smite** his fellowservants, ... Matt 24:49
5 and took the reed, and **smote** him on the head........ 27:30
5 And they **smote** him on the head with a reed, ... Mark 15:19
1 And unto him that **smiteth** thee on the one cheek ... Luke 6:29
3 shall begin **to beat** the menservants and maidens, ... 12:45
4 but **smote** upon his breast, saying, God be merciful 18:13
5 they **struck** him on the face, and asked him, ... 22:64

2 all the people ... smote their breasts, and returned. Luke 23:48
5 and beat him before the judgment seat............ Acts 18:17
2 saw the chief captain ... they left beating of Paul....... 21:32
3 them that stood by him to smite him on the mouth..... 23:2
3 God shall smite thee, thou whited wall:............... 23:3
6 commandest me to be smitten contrary to the law?..... 23:3
2 wound their weak conscience, ye sin against Christ... 1 Co 8:12

Classical Greek

This verb can be found in classical Greek writings as far back as Homer (Eighth Century B.C.). It is used commonly of striking someone on the face, on the cheek, or on the mouth. Although it normally signifies a violent blow, it also is used as a sign of sincere sorrow or even of wounding someone's conscience (*Liddell-Scott*).

Septuagint Usage

We see it in the Septuagint of God's warning to smite Egypt with a plague of frogs (Exodus 8:2), of the angel of the Lord smiting the people of Israel (2 Samuel 24:17 [LXX 2 Kings 24:17]), and of God striking Israel because of their adoption of heathen ways (Ezekiel 7:9).

New Testament Usage

In the New Testament *tuptō* is used of the evil servant who began to smite his fellow servants (Matthew 24:49; Luke 12:45). It also was used of Jesus when the Roman soldiers began to spit on Him, mock Him, and strike Him (Matthew 27:30). Matthew put the word in the form of an imperfect verb to indicate repeated blows. Mark did the same thing (Mark 15:19). Jesus instructed His disciples to offer the other cheek when struck on one (Luke 6:29). The publican beat on his breast to show his personal sorrow over sin (Luke 18:13). The viewers were constantly beating their breasts after Jesus' death on the cross (Luke 23:48).

Acts 18:17 uses the word in the imperfect tense to show that Sosthenes, the ruler of the synagogue, received many blows. Acts 21:32 describes the beating of Paul by the rioters. The high priest Ananias ordered the striking of Paul on the mouth (Acts 23:2,3).

In 1 Corinthians 8:12 Paul cautioned the believers against *wounding* their brothers' consciences by eating meat sacrificed to idols. To sin against the believer is to sin against Christ.

STRONG 5180, BAUER 830, MOULTON-MILLIGAN 646, KITTEL 8:260-69, LIDDELL-SCOTT 1835-36, COLIN BROWN 3:903.

5022. Τύραννος Turannos name

Tyrannus.

1. Τυράννου Turannou gen masc

1 disputing daily in the school of one Tyrannus....... Acts 19:9

Paul lectured daily for 2 years in the lecture hall of Tyrannus after the synagogue in Ephesus became closed to him (Acts 19:9). It is unknown whether Tyrannus was the owner of the hall, the philosopher who usually lectured there, or the donor of money to build the public hall.

5023. τυρβάζω turbazō verb

Confuse, disturb, trouble.

SYNONYMS:

θορυβέω thorubeō (2327)
σκύλλω skullō (4515)

1. τυρβάζῃ turbazē 2sing indic pres mid

1 thou art careful and troubled about many things:... Luke 10:41

In the New Testament *turbazō* is used with respect to Martha's state of confusion and her personal anxiety when attempting to serve Jesus (Luke 10:41). (Some ancient manuscripts have the form *thorubazō* [2326B].) In this passage anxiety (*merimna* [3178]) refers to Martha's mental distraction; *turbazē*, to her external agitation (Plummer, *International Critical Commentary*, 28:291).

STRONG 5182, BAUER 830, LIDDELL-SCOTT 1837.

5024. Τύριος Turios name

Tyrian; of or from Tyre.

1. Τυρίοις Turiois dat pl masc

1 highly displeased with them of Tyre and Sidon:..... Acts 12:20

The people of Tyre and Sidon at one point quarreled with King Herod Agrippa I. He accepted their worship of him as divine, and Luke ascribed his death to this blasphemy (Acts 12:20-23).

5025. Τύρος Turos name

Tyre.

1. Τύρου Turou gen fem
2. Τύρῳ Turō dat fem
3. Τύρον Turon acc fem

2 done in you, had been done in Tyre and Sidon,.... Matt 11:21
2 It shall be more tolerable for Tyre and Sidon.......... 11:22
1 and departed into the coasts of Tyre and Sidon....... 15:21
3 beyond Jordan; and they about Tyre and Sidon,.... Mark 3:8
1 and went into the borders of Tyre and Sidon,........... 7:24
1 departing from the coasts of Tyre and Sidon,........... 7:31
1 and from the sea coast of Tyre and Sidon,.......... Luke 6:17
2 for if the mighty works had been done in Tyre........ 10:13
2 But it shall be more tolerable for Tyre and Sidon...... 10:14

3 and sailed into Syria, and landed at Tyre:.......... Acts 21:3
1 And when we had finished our course from Tyre,...... 21:7

Tyre was an ancient city-state on the southern coast of Phoenicia. It is recorded with Sidon as the scene of ministry among the Gentiles by Jesus (Matthew 15:21; Mark 7:24,31), and people from there came to hear Him (Mark 3:8; Luke 6:17). Jesus contrasted the inhabitants' openness to the word and works of God with the lack of response in Israel (Matthew 11:21f.; Luke 10:13f.). Paul passed through it on his journey to Jerusalem and spent time with a group of Christians there (Acts 21:3,4,7).

5026. τυφλός tuphlos adj

Blind.

Cross-Reference:
τυφλόω tuphloō (5027)

עִוֵּר 'iwwēr (5999), Blind (Dt 15:21, 2 Sm 5:6, Is 42:18f.).

עַוֶּרֶת 'awwereth (6001), Blind animal (Lv 22:22—only Codex Vaticanus and some Alexandrinus texts).

1. **τυφλός tuphlos** nom sing masc
2. **τυφλοῦ tuphlou** gen sing masc
3. **τυφλῷ tuphlō** dat sing masc
4. **τυφλόν tuphlon** acc sing masc
5. **τυφλέ tuphle** voc sing masc
6. **τυφλοί tuphloi** nom pl masc
7. **τυφλῶν tuphlōn** gen pl masc
8. **τυφλοῖς tuphlois** dat pl masc
9. **τυφλούς tuphlous** acc pl masc

6 two **blind** men followed him, crying, and saying,..... Matt 9:27
6 the **blind** men came to him:.......................... 9:28
6 The **blind** receive their sight, and the lame walk,...... 11:5
1 **blind**, and dumb: and he healed him,.................. 12:22
4 that the **blind** and dumb both spake and saw.......... 12:22
6 Let them alone: they be **blind** leaders of the blind..... 15:14
7 Let them alone: they be blind leaders **of the blind**...... 15:14
1 And if the **blind** lead the blind, both shall fall......... 15:14
4 And if the blind lead the **blind**, both shall fall......... 15:14
9 lame, **blind**, dumb, maimed, and many others,......... 15:30
9 the lame to walk, and the **blind** to see:................ 15:31
6 behold, two **blind** men sitting by the way side,......... 20:30
6 the **blind** and the lame came to him in the temple;.... 21:14
6 Woe unto you, ye **blind** guides, which say,............ 23:16
6 Ye fools and **blind**: for whether is greater,............ 23:17
6 Ye fools and **blind**: for whether is greater, the gift,.... 23:19
6 Ye **blind** guides, which strain at a gnat,............... 23:24
5 Thou **blind** Pharisee, cleanse first ... within the cup.... 23:26
4 and they bring **a blind** man unto him,.............. Mark 8:22
2 And he took the **blind** man by the hand,............... 8:23
1 **blind** Bartimaeus, the son of Timaeus,................ 10:46
4 And they call the **blind** man, saying unto him,......... 10:49
1 The **blind** man said unto him, Lord,.................. 10:51
8 and recovering of sight **to the blind**,................ Luke 4:18
1 Can the **blind** lead the blind?......................... 6:39
4 Can the blind lead the **blind**?......................... 6:39
8 and unto many that were **blind** he gave sight........... 7:21
6 how that the **blind** see, the lame walk,................ 7:22
9 call the poor, the maimed, the lame, the **blind**:........ 14:13
9 poor, and the maimed, and the halt, and the **blind**..... 14:21
1 a certain **blind** man sat by the way side begging:... Luke 18:35
7 impotent folk, of **blind**, halt, withered,.............. John 5:3
4 he saw a man which was **blind** from his birth........... 9:1
1 this man, or his parents, that he was born **blind**?....... 9:2
2 anointed the eyes of the **blind** man with the clay,....... 9:6
1 they which before had seen him that he was **blind**,...... 9:8
4 to the Pharisees him that aforetime was **blind**........... 9:13
3 They say unto the **blind** man again,.................... 9:17
1 that he had been **blind**, and received his sight,.......... 9:18
1 Is this your son, who ye say was born **blind**?........... 9:19
1 that this is our son, and that he was born **blind**:........ 9:20
1 Then again called they the man that was **blind**,......... 9:24
1 I know, that, whereas I was **blind**, now I see............ 9:25
2 opened the eyes of one that was born **blind**............. 9:32
6 and that they which see might be made **blind**........... 9:39
6 and said unto him, Are we **blind** also?................. 9:40
6 If ye were **blind**, ye should have no sin:................ 9:41
7 Can a devil open the eyes **of the blind**?............... 10:21
2 this man, which opened the eyes of the **blind**,......... 11:37
1 thou shalt be **blind**, not seeing the sun for a season. Acts 13:11
7 confident that thou thyself art a guide **of the blind**,.. Rom 2:19
1 But he that lacketh these things is **blind**,............ 2 Pt 1:9
1 and miserable, and poor, and **blind**, and naked:...... Rev 3:17

Classical Greek

The adjective *tuphlos*, "blind," denotes the inability to see in both a literal and figurative sense. One can be "blind" intellectually (or spiritually) as well as physically. Further definitions are also attested. Thus one can speak of "blind" waterways and ports, that is, muddied waters (*Liddell-Scott*). Matters which are mysterious and unintelligible are also considered *tuphlos*.

Septuagint Usage

Tuphlos translates the Hebrew term *'iwwēr* in the Septuagint. There, blindness was considered to be divine judgment against sinners (Deuteronomy 28:28f.); however, the practice of blinding violators of a law—common among Greeks and Israel's neighbors—was foreign to Mosaic law (cf. 1 Samuel 11:2; 2 Kings 25:7; Jeremiah 39:7). Individuals who were blind enjoyed special protection under the law of Israel (Leviticus 19:14; Deuteronomy 27:18).

God both gives sight to the blind and blinds the seeing (Exodus 4:11). A unique feature of Old Testament messianic prophecies is that the blind will receive their sight (Isaiah 29:18; 35:5; 42:7).

On many occasions "blindness" refers to spiritual or intellectual blindness. The Law forbids bribery; it asserts that receiving bribes makes a judge "blind" (to the truth; Exodus 23:8; Deuteronomy 16:19). Spiritual blindness—the inability to see or understand the truth—can be God's judgment against those who choose to harden themselves against His Word (Isaiah 6:10; 29:9f.).

New Testament Usage

The legalism which pervaded later Judaism perverted the Biblical attitude toward the blind;

this was especially true of the religious leaders. A clear example of this is seen in the harsh words of the Pharisees to the man born blind whom Jesus had just healed: "Thou wast altogether born in sins, and dost thou teach us?" (John 9:34). In order to make their theological system consistent they had to view blindness as a punishment, either for the sins of one's parents or for one's own sins. Upon meeting a blind person they coldly recited the formula, "Blessed be the truthful judge!" (Graber, "Blind," *Colin Brown*, 1:219). Although many Jewish synagogues were not so harsh, we can see how far this judgmental attitude had spread by looking at Qumran. That community excluded the blind from their fellowship (ibid.).

Jesus confronted and challenged these merciless attitudes head-on. Concerning the man who had been born blind, Jesus said that neither the sins of the man nor of his parents were responsible for his blindness. Moreover, He did not simply say it was the result of misfortune in this world. Rather, Jesus taught that this blindness had a function in God's divine plan: "that the works of God should be made manifest in him" (John 9:3). By healing the blind man Jesus revealed himself as the Light of the World (verse 5).

Jesus healed many blind people. In the programmatic (pertaining to a program or plan) sermon in the Nazareth synagogue (Luke 4), Jesus viewed restoring the sight of the blind as part of His messianic ministry (Luke 4:18; cf. Isaiah 61:1). Giving sight to the blind was also among the messianic signs given to John the Baptist (Matthew 11:5; cf. Isaiah 29:18; 35:5).

The New Testament, like the Old, understands blindness as spiritual blindness on occasion. Jesus employed this imagery in His saying about the "blind leaders of the blind" (Luke 6:39; cf. John 9:39-41; Romans 2:19). This kind of blindness results from Satan's having blinded the unbeliever (2 Corinthians 4:4); at the same time it can be God's judgment on mankind's refusal to believe the truth (John 9:39-41).

STRONG 5185, BAUER 830-31, MOULTON-MILLIGAN 646, KITTEL 8:270-94, LIDDELL-SCOTT 1838, COLIN BROWN 1:218,220.

5027. τυφλόω tuphloō verb

Make blind, deprive of sight.

COGNATES:

τυφλός tuphlos (5026)
τύφω tuphō (5029)

עִוֵּר ʿiwwēr (5999), Blind (Is 42:19).

1. **ἐτύφλωσεν etuphlōsen** 3sing indic aor act
2. **τετύφλωκεν tetuphlōken** 3sing indic perf act

2 He **hath blinded** their eyes, ... John 12:40
1 **hath blinded** the minds of them which believe not, .. 2 Co 4:4
1 because that darkness hath **blinded** his eyes. .... 1 Jn 2:11

Classical Greek

In classical Greek *tuphloō* can be used in a literal or figurative way. Literally, it can refer to the blinding of an individual. Figuratively, it can mean "to baffle, to render ineffectual," or "to stop up" (cf. *Liddell-Scott*; Schrage, "tuphlos," *Kittel*, 8:271).

Septuagint Usage

Although this term literally refers to making a person physically blind, its use in the Septuagint also relates to spiritual blindness (Isaiah 42:19) that results from allowing the mind to be dulled with respect to spiritual realities.

New Testament Usage

The Gospel of John uses the term in the same fashion when Jesus upbraided the spiritually blind of His day (John 12:40). The apostle Paul spoke of the "god of this world" blinding the minds of unbelievers (2 Corinthians 4:4), and the apostle John ascribed this kind of darkness to the person motivated by hate (1 John 2:11).

STRONG 5186, BAUER 831, MOULTON-MILLIGAN 646, KITTEL 8:270-94, LIDDELL-SCOTT 1838.

5028. τυφόω tuphoō verb

To be puffed up (with pride), to become blinded or foolish.

CROSS-REFERENCE:

τύφω tuphō (5029)

1. **τυφωθείς tuphōtheis** nom sing masc part aor pass
2. **τετύφωται tetuphōtai** 3sing indic perf mid
3. **τετυφωμένοι tetuphōmenoi** nom pl masc part perf mid

1 Not a novice, lest **being lifted up with pride** he fall .. 1 Tm 3:6
2 He **is proud**, knowing nothing, ... 6:4
3 Traitors, heady, **highminded**, lovers of pleasures ..... 2 Tm 3:4

Classical Greek

This word occurs in both classical and post-Christian Greek writings, although not in the Septuagint. In these extra-Biblical contexts the meaning includes both literal as well as figurative usages. Literally *tuphoō* means "to delude," but most frequently in the perfect passive it means "to be crazy" or "demented" (*Liddell-Scott*). Figuratively the term takes on the sense of "to be puffed up, conceited" or "to be blinded, become foolish" (*Bauer*).

New Testament Usage

In the New Testament *tuphoō* only occurs figuratively, and that in the Pastoral Epistles (1 Timothy 3:6; 6:4; 2 Timothy 3:4). The meaning is "to be puffed up with conceit." The use of *tuphoō* in 1 Timothy is a pointed condemnation of the potential of arrogance in the ministry. In 3:6 Paul warned that maturity is a prerequisite to humility in the ministry; a "novice" is vulnerable to "being lifted up with pride" and falling prey to Satan's schemes. First Timothy 6:4 warns against those who teach contrary to Paul's instructions, identifying such teachers as "*proud*, knowing nothing."

Not only is this foolish arrogance something for ministers to avoid, it is a common characteristic of men in the last days. Paul's description of what men will be like in the "perilous times" (2 Timothy 3:1-7) includes *tuphoō*. The King James renders this as "high-minded" in verse 4.

The Pastoral Epistles issue a timely warning to those in ministry in the end times. Foolish pride is a common characteristic of men, but it must be earnestly avoided by those in the ministry.

Strong 5187, Bauer 831, Moulton-Milligan 646, Liddell-Scott 1838.

5029. τύφω tuphō verb

Smolder, smoke, burn slowly.

Cognates:

τυφλόω tuphloō (5027)
τυφόω tuphoō (5028)

1. τυφόμενον tuphomenon
nom/acc sing neu part pres mid

1 **and smoking flax shall he not quench,** .... **Matt 12:20**

Classical Greek

In classical Greek *tuphō* generally means "to smoke, to make smoke." It can also have the sense "to burn slowly" or "to smolder." Figuratively, it can refer to the "fire of love" (*Liddell-Scott*). It is not found in the Septuagint.

New Testament Usage

Matthew utilized the word when he wrote that Jesus would not quench smoldering flax (Matthew 12:20). This statement, which Jesus quoted from one of the Servant Songs of Isaiah (42:1-4) detailing the work of the Messiah (the Septuagint uses *kapnizō*, "to smoke," at verse 3), emphasizes the compassion with which Jesus ministered.

Strong 5188, Bauer 831, Liddell-Scott 1838.

5030. τυφωνικός tuphōnikos adj

Like a hurricane, tempestuous, stormy.

1. τυφωνικός tuphōnikos nom sing masc

1 **against it a tempestuous wind, called Euroclydon.** ... **Acts 27:14**

The only New Testament occurrence of *tuphōnikos* is in Acts 27:14, a reference to the great storm which resulted in Paul's shipwreck. The word comes from *tuphōn* which means "typhoon." It is not found before the Christian Era, nor in the Septuagint.

Strong 5189, Bauer 831, Moulton-Milligan 646, Liddell-Scott 1838.

5031. Τυχικός Tuchikos name

Tychicus.

1. Τυχικός Tuchikos nom masc
2. Τυχικοῦ Tuchikou gen masc
3. Τυχικόν Tuchikon acc masc

1 **and of Asia, Tychicus and Trophimus.** .... **Acts 20:4**
1 **Tychicus, a beloved brother and faithful minister** ..... **Eph 6:21**
1 **All my state shall Tychicus declare unto you,** .... **Col 4:7**
3 **And Tychicus have I sent to Ephesus.** .... **2 Tm 4:12**
3 **When I shall send Artemas unto thee, or Tychicus,** ... **Tit 3:12**

Tychicus was a Christian from the province of Asia who joined Paul on his last journey to Jerusalem (Acts 20:4). Paul spoke warmly of him in Colossians 4:7f. In verse 8 (and at Ephesians 6:21f.; 2 Timothy 4:12; and Titus 3:12) he is shown as one to whom Paul entrusted tasks on several occasions.

υ

5032. ὑακίνθινος huakinthinos adj

Hyacinth-colored, dark blue or purple.

תַּחַשׁ tachash (8807), Ram? sea cow? animal yielding fine leather (Ex 25:5, 35:7, Nm 4:10ff.).

תְּכֵלֶת t^ekhēleth (8833), Blue material, blue cloth (Ex 26:4, 39:22 [36:30], Nm 4:11f.).

1. ὑακινθίνους huakinthinous acc pl masc

1 breastplates of fire, and of jacinth, and brimstone:... Rev 9:17

Huakinthinos occurs in classical and Christian writings and refers to the deep blue color (occasionally deep red) of the hyacinth gemstone. (In many cases it is nearly impossible to know for certain which specific stone is being referred to.) The only New Testament use of this word is found in Revelation 9:17. Here it describes the deep blue color of the breastplates worn by the army or horsemen loosed by the sixth angel.

The hyacinth gem is possibly the same as zircon. *Moulton-Milligan* understands Revelation 9:17 to refer to "a dusky blue colour as of sulphurous smoke," thus painting a more graphic mental image of the scene in Revelation.

Strong 5191, Bauer 831, Moulton-Milligan 647, Liddell-Scott 1840.

5033. ὑάκινθος huakinthos noun

A blue-colored precious stone.

תַּחַשׁ tachash (8807), Ram? sea cow? animal yielding fine leather (Ez 16:10).

תְּכֵלֶת t^ekhēleth (8833), Blue material, embroidered material (Ex 26:1, 2 Chr 3:14, Ez 27:7).

1. ὑάκινθος huakinthos nom sing masc

1 the eleventh, a jacinth; the twelfth, an amethyst..... Rev 21:20

The word is used in classical Greek in reference to the hyacinth flower and occurs as a proper name in post-Christian writings (*Moulton-Milligan*). In New Testament and Christian writings it refers to a stone of a blue color.

The only use of this word is found in Revelation 21:20 and is translated "jacinth" in the King James Version. Named after the hyacinth flower with the same deep blue color, this stone is most likely today's sapphire.

Strong 5192, Bauer 831, Moulton-Milligan 647, Liddell-Scott 1840, Colin Brown 3:396-97.

5034. ὑάλινος hualinos adj

Of glass, transparent like glass.

1. ὑαλίνη hualinē nom sing fem

2. ὑαλίνην hualinēn acc sing fem

1 And before the throne there was a sea of glass...... Rev 4:6
2 I saw as it were a sea of glass mingled with fire:...... 15:2
2 stand on the sea of glass, having the harps of God..... 15:2

The term *hualinos* refers to a sea which is composed either of glass or transparent as glass. Both verses using this word occur in Revelation. The King James Version renders the translation in 4:6 and 15:12 as the sea actually being a sea of glass. The context does not clearly indicate if an alternative translation, "a sea transparent as glass," is preferred.

The fact that the sea is further likened to crystal in 4:6 and is mingled with fire in 15:2 suggests that the sea is a "glassy sea," and these words add to the description of the word picture.

Strong 5193, Bauer 831, Moulton-Milligan 647, Liddell-Scott 1840.

5035. ὕαλος hualos noun

Glass, crystal.

זְכוֹכִית z^ekhôkhîth (2220), Crystal (Jb 28:17).

1. ὕαλος hualos nom sing masc

2. ὑάλῳ hualō dat sing masc

2 and the city was pure gold, like unto clear **glass**.....Rev 21:18
1 was pure gold, as it were transparent **glass**........... 21:21

Found in classical literature, as well as in the Septuagint and Christian writings, *hualos* refers to glass, crystal, or a hard transparent stone. This word is used twice in the New Testament, in Revelation 21:18 and 21. Both references refer to the crystal or glasslike appearance of certain features of the New Jerusalem.

Strong 5194, Bauer 831, Moulton-Milligan 647, Liddell-Scott 1840.

5036. ὑβρίζω hubrizō verb

Treat disgracefully, be insolent to, mistreat, abuse, insult.

Cognates:
- ἐνυβρίζω enubrizō (1780)
- ὕβρις hubris (5036B)
- ὑβριστής hubristēs (5037)

Synonyms:
- βλασφημέω blasphēmeō (980)
- κακολογέω kakologeō (2522)
- καταλαλέω katalaleō (2605)
- λοιδορέω loidoreō (3032)
- ὀνειδίζω oneidizō (3542)

גֵּאֶה gē'eh (1373), Proud (Jer 48:29 [31:29]).

גַּאֲוָה ga'ăwāh (1375), Loftiness (Is 13:3).

עָלַז 'ālaz (6159), Exult (Is 23:12).

קָלַל qālal (7327), Be small, be trifling; hiphil: treat with contempt (2 Sm 19:44 [19:43]).

1. **ὑβρίζεις hubrizeis** 2sing indic pres act
2. **ὕβρισαν hubrisan** 3pl indic aor act
3. **ὑβρίσαι hubrisai** inf aor act
4. **ὑβρισθέντες hubristhentes** nom pl masc part aor pass
5. **ὑβρισθήσεται hubristhēsetai** 3sing indic fut pass

2 and entreated them **spitefully**, and slew them....... Matt 22:6
1 Master, thus saying thou **reproachest** us also........Luke 11:45
5 mocked, and **spitefully entreated**, and spitted on:....... 18:32
3 to use them **despitefully**, and to stone them,........Acts 14:5
4 were **shamefully entreated**, as ye know, at Philippi,.. 1 Th 2:2

Classical Greek

Hubrizō means "to run riot," especially "in the use of superior strength or power, or in sensual indulgence" (*Liddell-Scott*; cf. the noun *hubris* [5036B], "wanton violence," and *hubristēs* [5037], "a violent person"). Thus, it can mean "to mistreat, to insult," or passively, "to be arrogant, rude." The word has the connotation of severity and harshness. In the papyri it occurs at times in connection with a husband's mistreatment of his wife; the example illustrates the intensity behind *hubrizō* (*Moulton-Milligan*; cf. Trench's comments on *hubris*; he suggests the motive for *hubris* is the "pleasure" of the inflicting party [*Synonyms of the New Testament*, pp.97f.]).

Septuagint Usage

The verb *hubrizō* occurs infrequently in the Septuagint (cf. the noun). There are two apocryphal occurrences (2 Maccabees 14:42; 3 Maccabees 6:9). The texts themselves reveal the various aspects of *hubrizō* as outlined above.

It refers to "contemptible treatment" (2 Samuel 19:43 [LXX 2 Kings 19:43]) or to a country's "wanton reveling" (Isaiah 23:12; cf. 23:7). The idea of arrogance and pride comes through clearly in Jeremiah 48:29 (LXX 31:29). Second Maccabees 14:42 is a good illustration of the violence implied in *hubrizō*. There it is almost synonymous with "torture."

New Testament Usage

Only five instances of *hubrizō* are recorded in the New Testament (cf. *hubris*, three; and *hubristēs*, two). Luke (11:45) wrote of the legal experts who complained that Jesus "insulted" them with His denouncement of the Pharisees. Here we have a more mild usage (cf. 2 Samuel 19:43).

The physical aspect of mistreatment is illustrated by other texts. Later in Luke's Gospel Jesus foretold He would be "treated with contempt" by the Gentiles (Luke 18:32). The idea here may more closely follow the one in 2 Maccabees, which includes the notion of physical mistreatment. A similar understanding should be read in Matthew's account of the Parable of the Wedding Banquet. In that passage the king's servants are "mistreated" (Matthew 22:6; cf. Acts 14:5; 1 Thessalonians 2:2).

Strong 5195, Bauer 831-32, Moulton-Milligan 647, Kittel 8:295-307, Liddell-Scott 1841, Colin Brown 3:27-29.

5036B. ὕβρις hubris noun

Insult, insolence, mistreatment; damage, loss, hurt, disaster.

Synonyms:
- ἀτιμία atimia (813)
- ὀνειδισμός oneidismos (3543)
- ὄνειδος oneidos (3544)

גֵּאָה gē'āh (1372), Arrogance (Prv 8:13).

גֵּאֶה gē'eh (1373), Proud (Prv 16:19—Codex Alexandrinus only).

גַּאֲוָה ga'ăwāh (1375), Pride (Prv 14:3, Is 25:11, Zep 3:11).

גָּאוֹן gā'ôn (1377), Pride (Lv 26:19, Ez 30:6, Zec 9:6).

גֵּאוּת gē'ûth (1378), Pride (Is 28:1,3).

גֵּוָה gēwāh (1498), Pride (Jer 13:17).

זָדוֹן zādhôn (2171), Pride, arrogance (Prv 11:2, 13:10, Jer 50:32 [27:32]).

לָצוֹן lātsôn (4087), Scoffing (Prv 1:22).

עַלִּיז 'allîz (6171), Exultant (Is 23:7).

רוּם rûm (7599), Pride (Is 2:17).

1. **ὕβρεως** **hubreōs** gen sing fem
2. **ὕβριν** **hubrin** acc sing fem
3. **ὕβρεσιν** **hubresin** dat pl fem

1 I perceive that this voyage will be with hurt........Acts 27:10
2 and to have gained this harm and loss................. 27:21
3 in reproaches, in necessities, in persecutions,........2 Co 12:10

Classical Greek

In classical usage *hubris* has a wide variety of meanings. According to Bertram it originally meant "an act which invades the sphere of another to his hurt, a 'trespass,' a 'transgression' of the true norm in violation of divine and human right" ("hubris," *Kittel*, 8:295). Involved in *hubris* are arrogance, insult, violence, and contempt. In fact, the term describes any act or attitude associated with a lack of self-control and with attempts to seize what the gods have not allotted. *Sōphrosunē* (4849), "restraint, self-control," is the antonym of *hubris. Hubris* is not necessarily an act "directed against the gods" (Güting, "Pride," *Colin Brown*, 3:27); rather, it is "the overbearing attitude of man toward both the gods and his fellow men," hence, "egotism" (Ehrenberg, *From Solon to Socrates*, p.184). It can, however, be the "classical expression . . . of the Greek sense of sin from the religious standpoint," especially in certain tragedians (Bertram, "hubris," *Kittel*, 8:297).

Septuagint Usage

In the Septuagint *hubris* appears approximately 50 times. Its main Hebrew equivalents are words derived from the root *g'h*, "to be high, lofty, arrogant." *Hubris* only translates this word group in the negative sense. Proverbs 29:23 states, "A man's *pride* brings him low" (NIV). A wide variety of meanings also appears in the Septuagint including "presumptuousness" (Proverbs 11:2) or "rebellion" (LXX Job 15:26). According to Bertram, it "can denote disposition, attitude, and conduct, sinful turning from or provocation of God, secularism, as well as vainglorious arrogance, encroachment, and tyranny against one's fellows" (ibid., p.301).

New Testament Usage

In the New Testament the usage of *hubris* is very restricted. Its meanings, "hardship, insult," are attested in popular usage (see *Moulton-Milligan*). Three citations appear in the New Testament. Of these, two separate meanings can be discerned. First, the ideas of shame, insult, or mistreatment are found in 2 Corinthians 12:10 (translated "reproaches" in the King James Version). However, more than verbal abuse is implied. Because of God's promise (2 Corinthians 12:9), Paul actually anticipated hardships.

Second, disaster or damage are the concepts in Acts 27:10,21. In the account of Paul's shipwreck on his way to Rome, two references are made to the destruction of the vessel. One was a prophecy (Acts 27:10); the other was the fulfillment (Acts 27:21). According to Louw and Nida, *hubris* means "harm, damage, injury," and "the condition resulting from violence or mistreatment" (*Greek-English Lexicon*, 1:230).

Strong 5196, Bauer 832, Moulton-Milligan 647, Kittel 8:295-307, Liddell-Scott 1841, Colin Brown 3:27,29-30,32.

5037. ὑβριστής hubristēs noun

A relentless, insolent, cruel, and violent man.

Cross-Reference:
ὑβρίζω hubrizō (5036)

גֵּא gē' (1370), Pridefulness (Is 16:6).

גֵּאֶה gē'eh (1373), Proud (Jb 40:11 [40:6], Prv 15:25, Is 2:12).

זָדוֹן zādhôn (2171), Proud ones (Sir 32:18).

לִיץ lîts (4054), Injurious or scornful person (Sir 8:11).

רוּם rûm (7599), Something haughty (Prv 6:17).

שָׁלוֹם shālôm (8361), Welfare, peace (Gn 43:27, 1 Sm 25:6, Dn 10:19).

שָׁלַם shālam (8396), Be complete, be whole; pual: be rewarded (Prv 13:13).

1. **ὑβριστήν** **hubristēn** acc sing masc
2. **ὑβριστάς** **hubristas** acc pl masc

2 Backbiters, haters of God, despiteful, proud,........ Rom 1:30
1 a blasphemer, and a persecutor, and injurious:...... 1 Tm 1:13

This word is found in Greek literature from classical to Christian writings, and it occurs in the New Testament in Romans 1:30 and 1 Timothy 1:13. The King James Version translates the word "despiteful" in Romans and "injurious" in 1 Timothy.

The usage in Romans refers to self-centered and violent cruelty, having no regard for others. This provides a description of man's fallen, depraved nature. In Timothy the word refers to Paul's former cruelty to Christians.

Strong 5197, Bauer 832, Moulton-Milligan 647, Kittel 8:295-307, Liddell-Scott 1841, Colin Brown 3:27-29,31.

5038. ὕβρις hubris

See word study at number 5036B.

5039. ὑγιαίνω hugiainō verb

Be in good health, be sound, wholesome, correct.

Cross-Reference:

ὑγιής hugiēs (5040)

שָׁלוֹם shālôm (8361), Completeness, welfare, peace (Gn 29:6, 37:14, 1 Sm 25:6).

שָׁלֵם shālam (8396), Complete, finish; pual: be rewarded (Prv 13:13).

1. **ὑγιαίνωσιν hugiainōsin** 3pl subj pres act
2. **ὑγιαίνοντα hugiainonta** acc sing masc part pres act
3. **ὑγιαίνοντες hugiainontes** nom pl masc part pres act
4. **ὑγιαινόντων hugiainontōn** gen pl masc part pres act
5. **ὑγιαίνουσιν hugiainousin** dat pl masc part pres act
6. **ὑγιαίνοντας hugiainontas** acc pl masc part pres act
7. **ὑγιαινούσης hugiainousēs** gen sing fem part pres act
8. **ὑγιαινούσῃ hugiainousē** dat sing fem part pres act
9. **ὑγιαίνειν hugiainein** inf pres act

3 They that are **whole** need not a physician; .... Luke 5:31
2 found the servant **whole** that had been sick............ 7:10
2 because he hath received him **safe and sound**........... 15:27
8 any other thing that is contrary to **sound** doctrine; .. 1 Tm 1:10
5 and consent not to **wholesome** words,.................. 6:3
4 Hold fast the form of **sound** words,............... 2 Tm 1:13
7 when they will not endure **sound** doctrine;.............. 4:3
8 may be able by **sound** doctrine both to exhort and.... Tit 1:9
1 that they may **be sound** in the faith;.................... 1:13
8 the things which become **sound** doctrine:.............. 2:1
6 temperate, **sound** in faith, in charity, in patience........ 2:2
9 that thou mayest prosper and **be in health**,.......... 3 Jn 1:2

Classical Greek

Hugiainō means "to be physically or mentally healthy or sound." The idea of "soundness" extended into other realms as well. For example, in a figurative sense "soundness" could refer to being "sound" in political or religious matters (*Liddell-Scott*). *Hugiainō* frequently occurs in the opening and closing of personal letters. As a closure it virtually means "good-bye" (*Moulton-Milligan*).

Septuagint Usage

The numerous occurrences of *hugiainō* in the Septuagint provide an interesting picture. First, of the 12 canonical appearances, all except 1 are replacements for the Hebrew word *shālôm* (often "Peace!" or "Well-being!" as a greeting). But, counting all the readings of Codex Sinaiticus and including a noncanonical reading in Job (24:23), there are 41 instances of *hugiainō* (e.g., Tobit 5:15,16,20; 7:1). Second, virtually all of the instances of *hugiainō* occur in a form of greeting or salutation in the canonical material (e.g., Jacob's inquiry of Laban's health [Genesis 29:6]; cf. 37:14; 43:27f.; cf. Jethro's wishing Moses "well" [Exodus 4:18]; 1 Samuel 25:6 [LXX 1 Kings 25:6]). The idea includes not only a wish for good physical health, it also includes a wish for general well-being (as conveyed by the Hebrew *shālôm*; e.g., Proverbs 13:13; Daniel 10:19).

New Testament Usage

The understanding of *hugiainō* in the New Testament is a curious mixture of literal and figurative. When Jesus insisted that "those who are well (*hoi hugianontes*) have no need of a physician" (RSV), Luke was obviously using it in the literal sense within the metaphor but in the figurative sense overall (Luke 5:31). Its use is literal in Lukc 7:10 and 15:27 (of the prodigal who returns "safe and *sound*"). In 3 John (verse 2) *hugiainō* occurs in the greeting of the letter (a typical prayer-wish for the recipient's good health).

When we reach the Pastoral Epistles, however, *hugiainō* acquires a figurative sense which reflects the dire circumstances confronting the Pauline churches. Here Paul cautioned against those who falsely teach things contrary to "sound doctrine." This sound doctrine—the gospel of Jesus Christ—was under attack by the "sick" teachings of the false teachers (cf. 2 Timothy 2:17 which describes the doctrine of false teachers that spreads "like gangrene"; see also 1 Timothy 1:10; 6:3; 2 Timothy 1:13; 4:3; Titus 1:9,13; 2:1,2). Thus in the Pastoral Epistles *hugiainō* especially refers to the "soundness" of the gospel in contrast to the false doctrines taught by others. (On this word as well as other terminology see Malherbe, "Medical Imagery in the Pastoral Epistles," pp.19-35.)

Strong 5198, Bauer 832, Moulton-Milligan 647-48, Kittel 8:308-13, Liddell-Scott 1841-42, Colin Brown 2:169-71.

5040. ὑγιής hugiēs adj

Healthy, sound, whole; well, cured.

Cross-Reference:

ὑγιαίνω hugiainō (5039)

חַי chay (2508), Life; flesh (Lv 13:15f.).

1. **ὑγιής hugiēs** nom sing masc/fem
2. **ὑγιῆ hugiē** acc sing masc
3. **ὑγιεῖς hugieis** acc pl masc

1 and it was restored **whole**, like as the other........ Matt 12:13
3 the maimed to be **whole**, the lame to walk,............ 15:31
1 and his hand was restored **whole** as the other....... Mark 3:5
1 go in peace, and be **whole** of thy plague................ 5:34
1 and his hand was restored **whole** as the other....... Luke 6:10
1 was made **whole** of whatsoever disease he had.......John 5:4
1 he saith unto him, Wilt thou be made **whole**?........... 5:6
1 And immediately the man was made **whole**,............ 5:9
2 He that made me **whole**, the same said unto me,....... 5:11
1 and said unto him, Behold, thou art made **whole**:....... 5:14
2 that it was Jesus, which had made him **whole**........... 5:15
2 made a man every whit **whole** on the sabbath day?..... 7:23
1 by him doth this man stand here before you **whole**...Acts 4:10
2 **Sound** speech, that cannot be condemned;............Tit 2:8

Classical Greek

The word *hugiēs* is an adjective describing someone or something as healthy or sound. The term occurs from the days of Homer onward. People can be healthy and ideas can be healthy, in the sense of being true. Thus, *hugiēs* is used of that which is healthy, whole, unbroken. It can be used of *virtuous* behavior and *wise* words (*Liddell-Scott*).

Septuagint Usage

The Septuagint contains six citations of *hugiēs*. Four are in Leviticus where the context is the laws concerning leprosy (13:10,15 [twice],16). "All the people returned to the camp to Joshua at Makkedah in peace" (*hugieis*, "in health, whole," Joshua 10:21). Isaiah instructed those attending King Hezekiah, "Let them take a lump of figs, and lay it for a plaster upon the boil, and he shall recover" (*kai hugiēs esē*, "be cured," Isaiah 38:21).

New Testament Usage

In the New Testament *hugiēs* appears 14 times. The King James Version translates it as "whole" 13 times, signifying wholeness, literally and physically. The one exception is found in Titus 2:8 where it is translated "sound." Jesus healed many different people and therefore made them literally "healthy." Some examples are: Matthew 12:13; Mark 3:5; Luke 6:10; John 5:4,6,9,11,14,15. In the Book of Acts, Peter and John by the power of the Holy Spirit made the lame man at the Beautiful Gate "whole" (Acts 4:10).

Figuratively, Paul used *hugiēs* of the type of speech which should exemplify the minister, that is, "sound speech, that cannot be condemned" (Titus 2:8). Nothing spiritually "unhealthy" should proceed from his lips.

Strong 5199, Bauer 832, Moulton-Milligan 648, Kittel 8:308-13, Liddell-Scott 1842, Colin Brown 2:169-71.

5041. ὑγρός hugros adj

Moist, pliant, green.

לַח lach (4026), New, not dried (Jgs 16:7f.).

רָטֹב rāṭōv (7656), Green (Jb 8:16).

1. **ὑγρῷ hugrō** dat sing neu

1 For if they do these things in a **green** tree,........ Luke 23:31

Found only in Luke 23:31, aside from extra-Biblical usage, this word in context means moist, sappy, and green. More general meanings of the word outside Scripture include wet, moist, or dampened.

Verse 31 is a proverbial saying whose meaning is disputed (partially by variations in translation; compare KJV and NIV). The "green wood" could refer to Jesus or to the present "mild" wickedness of the Jews (other interpretations exist; see Morris, *Tyndale New Testament Commentaries, Luke*, p.355). The best interpretation may be to equate the coming period of trouble prophesied by Jesus with the "dry" wood, that is, a future period when wickedness would be much greater. The "green wood" then refers to the time of Jesus' crucifixion; that is, a period when the wickedness of the Jews had not yet reached its full measure.

Strong 5200, Bauer 832, Moulton-Milligan 648, Liddell-Scott 1843.

5042. ὑδρία hudria noun

Water jar.

Cross-Reference:
ὕδωρ hudōr (5045)

כַּד kadh (3656), Jar (Gn 24:14-18, Jgs 7:19f., 1 Kgs 17:12).

1. **ὑδρίαν hudrian** acc sing fem
2. **ὑδρίαι hudriai** nom pl fem
3. **ὑδρίας hudrias** acc pl fem

2 And there were set there six **waterpots** of stone,.... John 2:6
3 Fill the **waterpots** with water........................... 2:7
1 The woman then left her **waterpot**,..................... 4:28

Hudria, which literally means "water jar," is cognate with the verb *huō*, "rain," and the noun *hudōr* (5045), "water." Broader extra-Biblical use of the word refers to jars or pots used for a variety of purposes from storing coins to baking bread (*Moulton-Milligan*). In the New Testament *hudria* occurs only in John's Gospel, in 2:6,7 and 4:28. These references are to large water pots or jars that were generally used as receptacles for a family's water supply.

Strong 5201, Bauer 832, Moulton-Milligan 648, Liddell-Scott 1844.

5043. ὑδροποτέω hudropoteō verb

To drink water.

Cross-References:

πίνω pinō (3956)
ὕδωρ hudōr (5045)

1. ὑδροπότει hudropotei 2sing impr pres act

1 **Drink no longer water, but use a little wine........ 1 Tm 5:23**

Classical Greek

The word *hudropoteō* comes from two root words: *hudōr* (5045), "water," and *pinō*, "to drink" (*Liddell-Scott*). Their combination and resulting meaning brings an exclusive element to the word. Thus *hudropoteō* refers to drinking exclusively water (see *Bauer*). Herodotus, for example, used the word of the Persians who drank water and not wine (1.71).

Septuagint Usage

Septuagint use of the word in Daniel 1:12 gives perhaps the most elaborate understanding of the term. Here, Daniel and the chosen youth of Israel refused to drink King Nebuchadnezzar's wine. The "Hebrew children" preferred to drink only water.

New Testament Usage

In 1 Timothy 5:23 Paul admonished Timothy that he should no longer drink only water, but also some wine for medicinal purposes. Understanding the implied exclusiveness of *hudropoteō*, we realize Paul was not telling Timothy to give up water altogether ("drink no longer water"), but to cease insisting on drinking nothing but water, and to do so for the sake of his health.

Strong 5202, Bauer 832, Moulton-Milligan 648, Liddell-Scott 1845.

5044. ὑδρωπικός hudrōpikos adj

Dropsy, suffering from dropsy.

Cross-Reference:

ὕδωρ hudōr (5045)

1. ὑδρωπικός hudrōpikos nom sing masc

1 **a certain man before him which had the dropsy.... Luke 14:2**

The word *hudrōpikos* occurs in writings two to five centuries before Christ and means "dropsy" or "suffering from dropsy." *Hudrōpikos* is understood to be a medical term, most likely describing a condition of edema, "an abnormal accumulation of serous fluids in connective tissues or cavities of the body accompanied by swelling, distension, or defective circulation . . . usually symptomatic of more serious problems" (Fitzmyer, *The Anchor Bible*, 28a:1041). The only New Testament occurrence of this word is in Luke 14:2. It is appropriate that Luke the physician is the Gospel writer to make the only recorded note of Christ's healing this disease.

Strong 5203, Bauer 832, Moulton-Milligan 648, Liddell-Scott 1845.

5045. ὕδωρ hudōr noun

Water.

Cognates:

ἄνυδρος anudros (501)
ὑδρία hudria (5042)
ὑδροποτέω hudropoteō (5043)
ὑδρωπικός hudrōpikos (5044)

מַיִ may (4448), Water (Gn 1:6f., 1 Kgs 18:35, Is 30:20).

מִקְוָה miqwāh (4886), Water supply (Sir 48:17).

נָזַל nāzal (5320), Flow (Ex 15:8).

1. ὕδωρ hudōr nom/acc sing neu
2. ὕδατος hudatos gen sing neu
3. ὕδατι hudati dat sing neu
4. ὕδατα hudata nom/acc pl neu
5. ὑδάτων hudatōn gen pl neu
6. ὕδασιν hudasin dat pl neu

3 I indeed baptize you with water unto repentance:....Matt 3:11
2 Jesus, ... went up straightway out of the water:......... 3:16
6 into the sea, and perished in the waters............... 8:32
4 if it be thou, bid me come unto thee on the water..... 14:28
4 he walked on the water, to go to Jesus............... 14:29
1 he falleth into the fire, and oft into the water.......... 17:15
1 but that rather a tumult was made, he took water,..... 27:24
3 I indeed have baptized you with water:............Mark 1:8
2 And straightway coming up out of the water,........... 1:10
4 it hath cast him into the fire, and into the waters,...... 9:22
2 shall give you a cup of water to drink in my name,..... 9:41
2 shall meet you a man bearing a pitcher of water:...... 14:13
3 I indeed baptize you with water;................... Luke 3:16
1 thou gavest me no water for my feet:................. 7:44
2 and rebuked the wind and the raging of the water:...... 8:24
3 for he commandeth even the winds and water,.......... 8:25
2 that he may dip the tip of his finger in water,......... 16:24
2 a man meet you, bearing a pitcher of water;........... 22:10
3 John answered them, saying, I baptize with water:...John 1:26
3 therefore am I come baptizing with water............... 1:31
3 but he that sent me to baptize with water,.............. 1:33
2 Fill the waterpots with water.......................... 2:7
1 When the ruler of the feast had tasted the water........ 2:9
1 but the servants which drew the water knew;........... 2:9
2 Except a man be born of water and of the Spirit,....... 3:5
4 baptizing ... because there was much water there:....... 3:23
1 There cometh a woman of Samaria to draw water:...... 4:7
1 and he would have given thee living water............. 4:10
1 from whence then hast thou that living water?.......... 4:11
2 Whosoever drinketh of this water shall thirst........... 4:13
2 of the water that I shall give him shall never thirst;..... 4:14
1 but the water that I shall give him shall be in him...... 4:14
2 a well of water springing up into everlasting life......... 4:14
1 give me this water, that I thirst not,.................. 4:15

1 Cana of Galilee, where he made the water wine..... John 4:46
2 waiting for the moving of the water.................... 5:3
1 into the pool, and troubled the water:.................. 5:4
2 troubling of the water stepped in was made whole...... 5:4
1 when the water is troubled, to put me into............. 5:7
2 out of his belly shall flow rivers of living water......... 7:38
1 After that he poureth water into a basin,.............. 13:5
1 and forthwith came there out blood and water......... 19:34
3 For John truly baptized with water;................. Acts 1:5
1 came unto a certain water: and the eunuch said,........ 8:36
1 here is water; what doth hinder me to be baptized?..... 8:36
1 they went down both into the water, both Philip........ 8:38
2 And when they were come up out of the water,........ 8:39
1 Can any man forbid water,............................ 10:47
3 John indeed baptized with water;..................... 11:16
2 cleanse it with the washing of water by the word,.... Eph 5:26
2 blood of calves and of goats, with water,............ Heb 9:19
3 and our bodies washed with pure water................ 10:22
1 so can no fountain both yield salt water and fresh.... Jas 3:12
2 few, that is, eight souls were saved by water......... 1 Pt 3:20
2 earth standing out of the water and in the water:.... 2 Pt 3:5
2 earth standing out of the water and in the water:....... 3:5
3 world that then was, being overflowed with water,...... 3:6
2 This is he that came by water and blood,........... 1 Jn 5:6
3 not by water only, but by water and blood.............. 5:6
3 not by water only, but by water and blood.............. 5:6
1 the Spirit, and the water, and the blood:............... 5:8
5 and his voice as the sound of many waters........... Rev 1:15
5 shall lead them unto living fountains of waters:......... 7:17
5 the rivers, and upon the fountains of waters;............ 8:10
5 a third of the waters became wormwood; (NASB)...... 8:11
5 and many men died of the waters,...................... 8:11
5 and have power over waters to turn them to blood,.... 11:6
1 out of his mouth water as a flood after the woman,.... 12:15
5 a voice from heaven, as the voice of many waters,..... 14:2
5 and earth, and the sea, and the fountains of waters..... 14:7
5 his vial upon the rivers and fountains of waters;....... 16:4
5 And I heard the angel of the waters say,.............. 16:5
1 Euphrates; and the water thereof was dried up,........ 16:12
5 of the great whore that sitteth upon many waters:..... 17:1
4 waters which thou sawest, where the whore sitteth,.... 17:15
5 a great multitude, and as the voice of many waters,.... 19:6
2 athirst of the fountain of the water of life freely....... 21:6
2 And he showed me a pure river of water of life,....... 22:1
1 let him take the water of life freely.................. 22:17

Classical Greek

Generally *hudōr* denotes "water" of any kind (e.g., "rainwater, the water of a river," etc.), although in reference to sea water *hudōr* is usually qualified. It can also stand for a "liquid" of any kind. Many places had *hudōr* in their name, especially if the site was associated with hot or mineral waters (*Liddell-Scott*).

Old Testament Background

From the very outset of Israel's history water played an important part in the life of the people. Water, being a mainstay of existence, was easily adopted to describe in figurative terms need, dependency, and existence. Thus in the patriarchal narratives we read of the digging of wells (Genesis 21:25,30; 26:15,18) whose supply proved mandatory in the arid regions of the Middle East. During the wilderness journeyings Israel received water in a miraculous way (Exodus 17:5f.). This became a fundamental example of God's faithfulness throughout the history of Israel (e.g., Deuteronomy 8:15f.; Psalm 78:14f.). Its recollection evoked praise and thanksgiving (Psalms 42:7,8; 74:15).

After Israel entered the Promised Land the people began to depend upon regular rainfall. In contrast to Egypt, whose primary source of water was irrigation of the Nile, Canaan was a land that "drinketh water of the rain of heaven" (Deuteronomy 11:10,11). The requirement of regular rainfall was met when Israel obeyed the commands of the Lord (Deuteronomy 11:13-15). If the people worshiped other gods, the Lord withheld rain from the land (verses 16,17; cf. Deuteronomy 28:12; 1 Kings 17:1; Isaiah 3:1; Jeremiah 5:23,24; Ezekiel 4:16,17; Amos 4:7,8). Water is often mentioned in conjunction with bread as one of the essentials for the maintenance of life (Genesis 21:14; Proverbs 25:21; Ezekiel 4:17).

Prophecies concerning the end time speak of the abundant rains that will drench the land and make the desert into a garden rich in water. Here the literal and figurative meanings overlap. The Messianic Age will usher in material and spiritual blessing (Isaiah 32:15 combines the outpouring of the Spirit from on high with the fact that the desert will become fertile soil; see also Isaiah 12:3; 30:22-25; 35:1,6,7; 41:17-20; 44:3,4; 49:10; 58:11; Jeremiah 31:9,12; Ezekiel 36:25-27; 47:1-12; Joel 3:18; Zechariah 14:8; cf. Numbers 24:5-7).

Water also played an important role in the cultic practices of Israel. Exodus 29:4 notes that the sons of Aaron were to wash before entering the tabernacle. Water was used in leprosy cleansings (Leviticus 14:2-9). Leviticus 8:6,7 refers to a "water of cleansing" used to set apart the Levites. Water was even used as a drink offering (1 Samuel 7:6; 2 Samuel 23:14-17).

Water's power and violent capabilities often form images in the Old Testament. It may symbolize God's power, His judgment or wrath, or as a broad symbol it may represent disaster and distress (Genesis 49:4; Isaiah 59:19; Psalm 69:2,3; Isaiah 30:20, etc.).

New Testament Usage

Thus, the background for the New Testament understanding and usage of *hudōr* more closely follows the Old Testament usage (over 450 times in the Septuagint) than that of secular Greek. In the New Testament there are about 80 instances of *hudōr*; of these, more than half occur in the writings of John (24 in his Gospel, 18 in Revelation). Both the literal and figurative understandings are attested in the New Testament.

Many instances of *hudōr*, both literal and figurative, occur in religious contexts in the New Testament. John the Baptist baptized "in water"; similarly, early and later Christian baptism took place in water (e.g., John 1:26; Acts 8:36-38; 1 Peter 3:20,21). Jesus' first miracle recorded in John's Gospel involved changing water into wine (John 2:7f.). The person giving a cup of cold water to a follower of Jesus will not lose his reward (Mark 9:41).

As Jesus conversed with the Samaritan woman He told her of the "living water" that He came to give. This was unlike mere "water" of the kind she drew from Jacob's well (John 4:10f.). The water Jesus gives is a fountain springing up in the one who believes. On the last, great day of the Feast of Tabernacles Jesus stood up and cried out that any who were thirsty should come to Him and drink. From the one believing in Him (some interpret this as meaning that from Jesus himself) would flow streams of living water (John 7:37,38).

On the first 7 days of the Feast of Tabernacles, water was poured into a bowl beside the altar. This water symbolized the water which God had provided the Israelites in the past (particularly the water from the rock in the desert). It also represented a prayer for rain for the next year (Morris, *The New International Commentary*, 4:420). John notes that Jesus made His proclamation on the last (eighth) day of the feast, on which (see Morris, p.422) no water was poured. Thus Jesus' exhortation is that much more significant. At a time when the people were concerned for their health, Jesus turned their attention to the emptiness of their souls and offered the Holy Spirit, the "living water." The imagery comes from the rock in the desert out of which flowed life-giving water. The believer, filled with the Spirit, not only finds complete satisfaction for his own soul, but becomes a source of life for all those around him.

The turning of water into a bitter and poisonous drink is among the most severe of the judgments of the last days (Revelation 8:10,11). But those who remain faithful until the end will drink of the waters of the fountain of life—freely! (Revelation 21:6; 22:17). The river of life's clear waters flow from "the throne of God and of the Lamb" (Revelation 22:1f.).

STRONG 5204, BAUER 832-33, MOULTON-MILLIGAN 648, KITTEL 8:314-33, LIDDELL-SCOTT 1845, COLIN BROWN 3:988-90.

5046. ὑετός huetos noun

Rain, a rain shower.

גֶּשֶׁם geshem (1700), Rain (Gn 8:2, 1 Kgs 18:44f., Ez 13:11).

מָטָר māṭār (4443), Rain (Ex 9:33f., 2 Chr 6:26f., Is 5:6).

מַי may (4448), Water (Jb 36:27).

שׁוֹאָה shô'āh (8177), Storm (Ez 38:9).

1. ὑετός huetos nom sing masc
2. ὑετόν hueton acc sing masc
3. ὑετούς huetous acc pl masc

3 in that he did good, and gave us **rain** from heaven, **Acts 14:17**
2 because of the present **rain**, and ... the cold.......... **28:2**
2 which drinketh in the **rain** that cometh oft upon it,.. **Heb 6:7**
2 until he receive the early and latter **rain**............. **Jas 5:7**
2 And he prayed again, and the heaven gave **rain**,........ **5:18**
1 that it **rain** not in the days of their prophecy:....... **Rev 11:6**

This word occurs throughout the history of the Greek language and means "rain," especially in the sense of a shower. According to Morris, *huetos* denotes a "heavy shower" as compared to *ombros* (3518), a "continuous rain," and *psekas*, a "drizzle" ("Weather," *Colin Brown*, 3:1003f.).

The ancient Greeks believed rain to be a gift from Zeus. Paul contradicted this pagan belief by giving God glory for all aspects of creation, including rain, in Acts 14:17. Hebrews 6:7 makes similar reference to *huetos*, as does James 5:7,18. Acts 28:2 refers simply to the rain at the time of Paul's shipwreck. In Revelation 11:6 the two witnesses are granted authority by God to control the rain.

STRONG 5205, BAUER 833, MOULTON-MILLIGAN 648, LIDDELL-SCOTT 1846, COLIN BROWN 3:1000,1003-4.

5047. υἱοθεσία huiothesia noun

Adoption.

CROSS-REFERENCE:
υἱός huios (5048)

1. υἱοθεσία huiothesia nom sing fem
2. υἱοθεσίας huiothesias gen sing fem
3. υἱοθεσίαν huiothesian acc sing fem

2 but ye have received the Spirit of **adoption**,......... **Rom 8:15**
3 waiting for the **adoption**, to wit,...................... **8:23**
1 Israelites; to whom pertaineth the **adoption**,............ **9:4**
3 that we might receive the **adoption** of sons.......... **Gal 4:5**
3 the **adoption** of children by Jesus Christ to himself,.. **Eph 1:5**

Classical Greek

Huiothesia, "adoption, the taking of a child as one's own," occurs only rarely before the Christian period. W. von Martitz indicates it was known in the Second Century B.C. ("kuios," *Kittel*, 8:397f.), as does *Moulton-Milligan*. Almost certainly there was a precedent for the concept in the Old Testament, despite the fact that the term does not occur in the Septuagint. Israel as God's sons is a prevalent theme (e.g., Exodus 4:22; Isaiah 1:2; Hosea 1:10; 11:1; cf. *Bauer*).

Huiothesia was a legal technical term in antiquity. It was not present in the language of religion where "descent" was the most common view of relationship between human and divine (but cf. the adoption terminology in Diodorus Siculus 4.39.2 cited by von Martitz, ibid., p.398).

New Testament Usage

Only five instances of *huiothesia* occur in the New Testament, and all are attributed to Paul (Romans 8:15,23; 9:4; Galatians 4:5; Ephesians 1:5). Ridderbos is correct—despite the absence of the term in the Septuagint—in saying that the Old Testament, rather than secular Greek or the Greek of the mystery cults, must be the basis for understanding "adoption" in the New Testament (*Paul: An Outline of His Theology*, pp.197-204).

First and foremost, adoption concerns the believer's relationship to God. The legal nuances are secondary, for adoption primarily concerns redemption (cf. Romans 8:23) that comes through Christ. This redemption, in turn, makes believers God's children (Galatians 4:4ff.; see the word studies on *huios* [5048] and *teknon* [4891]). Furthermore, adoption is defined in terms of receiving the Spirit (Romans 8:15; Galatians 4:6) which effects sonship. In contrast, Christ is the eternal Son and did not need to be adopted. Because the believer is by nature a child of wrath, he needs adoption into sonship. This adoption is given on the basis of undeserved grace.

Adoption involves both the redemption of Israel (Romans 9:4)—probably on the basis of the Old Testament precedent (2 Samuel 7:14; Hosea 1:10; cf. in Paul's understanding Romans 8:14; 9:26; 2 Corinthians 6:18)—and the new people of God, His church (Ephesians 1:5).

Paul's description of the believers' relationship to God in terms of adoption is further elaborated in the broader concept that Christians are now God's children. They become God's children through the new birth (James 1:18; 1 Peter 1:3), not through adoption which signifies a special relationship with the Father yet to be received (cf. Romans 8:23). A product of this new relationship is the imparting of all the rights and privileges as sons. From this, as Abraham's offspring, the believer is also an "heir" to the promises made to Abraham, specifically eternal life (cf. Romans 8:17; Galatians 3:26,29; 4:7; so Ridderbos, ibid., p.203).

Sonship/adoption thus relates to the present and also to the future consummation of adoption and the inheritance of eternal life (Ridderbos, ibid.; cf. Schweizer, "huios," *Kittel*, 8:399). Now, God's children may cry, "Abba, Father," and the power of the Spirit overcomes the enslaving power of the Law, ensuring their status as God's sons and daughters (cf. Galatians 3:23 to 4:11).

Strong 5206, Bauer 833, Moulton-Milligan 648-49, Kittel 8:397-99, Liddell-Scott 1846, Colin Brown 1:286-87,289.

5048. υἱός huios noun

Son, offspring, descendant.

Cross-Reference:

υἱοθεσία huiothesia (5047)

אִישׁ ʼîsh (382), Man (Jos 9:7).

בַּיִת bayith (1041), House (Ex 16:31, Jos 18:5, Jer 2:26).

בֵּן bēn (1158), Son (Gn 46:8-19, 1 Chr 4:9, Jer 43:2f. [50:2f.]).

בַּר bar (1275), Son (Prv 31:2 [24:70]).

בַּר bar (A1280), Son, young (Ezr 5:2, 6:9,14—Aramaic); Son (Dn 7:13—Aramaic).

זֶרַע zeraʻ (2320), Seed; descendant (Neh 9:2).

יֶלֶד yeledh (3315), Child, son (Ru 1:5, 2 Kgs 4:1).

יָלִיד yālîdh (3320), Descendant (1 Chr 20:4).

1. **υἱός huios** nom sing masc
2. **υἱοῦ huiou** gen sing masc
3. **υἱῷ huiō** dat sing masc
4. **υἱόν huion** acc sing masc
5. **υἱέ huie** voc sing masc
6. **υἱοί huioi** nom pl masc
7. **υἱῶν huiōn** gen pl masc
8. **υἱοῖς huiois** dat pl masc
9. **υἱούς huious** acc pl masc

2 the **son** of David, the son of Abraham. . . . . Matt 1:1
2 the son of David, the **son** of Abraham. 1:1
1 saying, Joseph, thou **son** of David, ... 1:20
4 And she shall bring forth **a son**, ... 1:21
4 and shall bring forth **a son**, ... his name Emmanuel, ... 1:23
4 her firstborn **son**: 1:25
4 saying, Out of Egypt have I called my **son**. 2:15
1 my beloved **Son**, in whom I am well pleased. 3:17
1 the tempter ... said, If thou be the **Son** of God, ... 4:3
1 And saith unto him, If thou be the **Son** of God, ... 4:6
6 for they shall be called the **children** of God. 5:9
6 That ye may be the **children** of your Father 5:45

1 if his **son** ask bread, will he give him a stone? ...... Matt 7:9
6 But the **children** of the kingdom 8:12
1 but the **Son** of man hath not where to lay his head..... 8:20
5 What have we to do with thee, ... thou **Son** of God? 8:29
1 that ye may know that the **Son** of man hath power 9:6
6 Can the **children** of the bridechamber mourn, ... 9:15
5 and saying, Thou **son** of David, have mercy on us....... 9:27
1 not ... cities of Israel, till the **Son** of man be come..... 10:23
4 and he that loveth **son** or daughter more than me 10:37
1 The **Son** of man came eating and drinking, ... 11:19
4 and no man knoweth the **Son**, but the Father; 11:27
1 neither knoweth any man the Father, save the **Son**, ... 11:27
1 and he to whomsoever the **Son** will reveal him.......... 11:27
1 the **Son** of man is Lord even of the sabbath day....... 12:8
1 Is not this the **son** of David? 12:23
6 by whom do your **children** cast them out? 12:27
2 whosoever speaketh a word against the **Son** of man, ... 12:32
1 so shall the **Son** of man be three days 12:40
1 He that soweth the good seed is the **Son** of man; 13:37
6 the good seed are the **children** of the kingdom; 13:38
6 but the tares are the **children** of the wicked one; 13:38
1 The **Son** of man shall send forth his angels, ... 13:41
1 Is not this the carpenter's **son?** 13:55
1 Of a truth thou art the **Son** of God................... 14:33
5 Have mercy on me, O Lord, thou **son** of David; 15:22
4 Whom do men say that I the **Son** of man am? 16:13
1 Thou art the Christ, the **Son** of the living God......... 16:16
1 For the **Son** of man shall come in the glory 16:27
4 till they see the **Son** of man coming in his kingdom.... 16:28
1 This is my beloved **Son**, ... 17:5
1 until the **Son** of man be risen again from the dead..... 17:9
1 Likewise shall also the **Son** of man suffer of them..... 17:12
4 Lord, have mercy on my **son**: for he is a lunatic, ... 17:15
1 The **Son** of man shall be betrayed 17:22
7 of their own **children**, or of strangers? 17:25
6 Jesus saith unto him, Then are the **children** free....... 17:26
1 the **Son** of man is come to save that which was lost.... 18:11
1 in the regeneration when the **Son** of man shall sit 19:28
1 and the **Son** of man shall be betrayed 20:18
7 the mother of Zebedee's **children** with her sons, ... 20:20
7 the mother of Zebedee's children with her **sons**, ... 20:20
6 Grant that these my two **sons** may sit, ... 20:21
1 the **Son** of man came not to be ministered unto, ... 20:28
1 Have mercy on us, O Lord, thou **son** of David......... 20:30
1 Have mercy on us, O Lord, thou **son** of David......... 20:31
4 and a colt the **foal** of an ass.......................... 21:5
3 cried, saying, Hosanna to the **son** of David: 21:9
3 and saying, Hosanna to the **son** of David; 21:15
4 But last of all he sent unto them his **son**, saying, ... 21:37
4 saying, They will reverence my **son**.................... 21:37
4 But when the husbandmen saw the **son**, ... 21:38
3 a certain king, which made a marriage for his **son**, ... 22:2
1 What think ye of Christ? whose **son** is he? 22:42
1 If David then call him Lord, how is he his **son?** 22:45
4 twofold more the **child** of hell than yourselves......... 23:15
6 the **children** of them which killed the prophets......... 23:31
2 unto the blood of Zacharias **son** of Barachias, ... 23:35
2 so shall also the coming of the **Son** of man be......... 24:27
2 shall appear the sign of the **Son** of man in heaven: 24:30
4 see the **Son** of man coming in the clouds of heaven 24:30
1 the angels of heaven, nor the **Son**, (NASB) 24:36
2 so shall also the coming of the **Son** of man be......... 24:37
2 so shall also the coming of the **Son** of man be......... 24:39
1 an hour as ye think not the **Son** of man cometh....... 24:44
1 day nor the hour wherein the **Son** of man cometh...... 25:13
1 When the **Son** of man shall come in his glory, ... 25:31
1 and the **Son** of man is betrayed to be crucified........ 26:2
1 The **Son** of man goeth as it is written of him: 26:24
1 woe ... by whom the **Son** of man is betrayed! 26:24
9 took with him Peter and the two **sons** of Zebedee, ... 26:37
1 **Son** of man is betrayed into the hands of sinners...... 26:45
1 tell us whether thou be the Christ, the **Son** of God.... 26:63
4 the **Son** of man sitting on the right hand of power, ... 26:64
7 whom they of the **children** of Israel did value; 27:9
1 If thou be the **Son** of God, come down 27:40
1 for he said, I am the **Son** of God.................... 27:43
1 Truly this was the **Son** of God........................ 27:54
7 and the mother of Zebedee's **children**............. Matt 27:56
2 the Father, and of the **Son**, and of the Holy Ghost: ... 28:19
2 the gospel of Jesus Christ, the **Son** of God; .... Mark 1:1
1 Thou art my beloved **Son**, ... I am well pleased......... 1:11
1 that ye may know that the **Son** of man hath power 2:10
6 Can the **children** of the bridechamber fast, ... 2:19
1 the **Son** of man is Lord also of the sabbath............ 2:28
1 and cried, saying, Thou art the **Son** of God............ 3:11
6 Boanerges, which is, The **sons** of thunder: 3:17
8 All sins shall be forgiven unto the **sons** of men, ... 3:28
5 Jesus, thou **Son** of the most high God? 5:7
1 Is not this the carpenter, the **son** of Mary, ... 6:3
4 that the **Son** of man must suffer many things, ... 8:31
1 of him also shall the **Son** of man be ashamed, ... 8:38
1 saying, This is my beloved **Son**: hear him.............. 9:7
1 till the **Son** of man were risen from the dead.......... 9:9
4 and how it is written of the **Son** of man, ... 9:12
4 Master, I have brought unto thee my **son**, ... 9:17
1 The **Son** of man is delivered into the hands of men, ... 9:31
1 and the **Son** of man shall be delivered 10:33
6 And James and John, the **sons** of Zebedee, ... 10:35
1 the **Son** of man came not to be ministered unto, ... 10:45
1 blind Bartimaeus, the **son** of Timaeus, ... 10:46
1 Jesus, thou **son** of David, have mercy on me.......... 10:47
5 Thou **son** of David, have mercy on me................ 10:48
4 Having yet therefore one **son**, his wellbeloved, ... 12:6
4 he sent him also ... They will reverence my **son**........ 12:6
1 How say the scribes that Christ is the **son** of David? ... 12:35
1 and whence is he then his **son?** 12:37
4 And then shall they see the **Son** of man coming 13:26
1 no man, ... neither the **Son**, but the Father............ 13:32
1 **Son** of man indeed goeth, as it is written of him: 14:21
1 but woe to that man by whom the **Son** of man........ 14:21
1 **Son** of man is betrayed into the hands of sinners...... 14:41
1 Art thou the Christ, the **Son** of the Blessed? 14:61
4 the **Son** of man sitting on the right hand of power, ... 14:62
1 he said, Truly this man was the **Son** of God........... 15:39
4 and thy wife Elisabeth shall bear thee **a son**, ... Luke 1:13
7 And many of the **children** of Israel shall he turn 1:16
4 conceive in thy womb, and bring forth **a son**, ... 1:31
1 and shall be called the **Son** of the Highest: 1:32
1 be born of thee shall be called the **Son** of God......... 1:35
4 she hath also conceived **a son** in her old age: 1:36
4 should be delivered; and she brought forth **a son**........ 1:57
4 And she brought forth her firstborn **son**, ... 2:7
4 word of God came unto John the **son** of Zacharias 3:2
1 which said, Thou art my beloved **Son**; 3:22
1 being as was supposed the **son** of Joseph, ... 3:23
1 If thou be the **Son** of God, command this stone that 4:3
1 If thou be the **Son** of God, cast thyself down 4:9
1 And they said, Is not this Joseph's **son?** 4:22
1 and saying, Thou art Christ the **Son** of God............ 4:41
9 so was also James, and John, the **sons** of Zebedee, ... 5:10
1 that ye may know that the **Son** of man hath power 5:24
9 Can ye make the **children** of the bridechamber fast, ... 5:34
1 That the **Son** of man is Lord also of the sabbath........ 6:5
2 out your name as evil, for the **Son** of man's sake....... 6:22
6 and ye shall be the **children** of the Highest: 6:35
1 the only **son** of his mother, and she was a widow: 7:12
1 The **Son** of man is come eating and drinking; 7:34
5 thou **Son** of God most high? ... torment me not......... 8:28
4 Saying, The **Son** of man must suffer many things, ... 9:22
1 of him shall the **Son** of man be ashamed, ... 9:26
1 saying, This is my beloved **Son**: hear him.............. 9:35
4 look upon my **son**: for he is mine only child........... 9:38
4 Jesus answering said, ... Bring thy **son** hither........... 9:41
1 the **Son** of man shall be delivered into the hands 9:44
1 the **Son** of man is not come to destroy men's lives, ... 9:56
1 but the **Son** of man hath not where to lay his head..... 9:58
1 if the **son** of peace be there, your peace shall rest 10:6
1 no man knoweth who the **Son** is, but the Father; 10:22
1 but the Father; and who the Father is, but the **Son**, ... 10:22
1 the Son, and he to whom the **Son** will reveal him...... 10:22
1 If a **son** shall ask bread of any ... that is a father, ... 11:11
6 by whom do your **sons** cast them out? 11:19
1 so shall also the **Son** of man be to this generation..... 11:30
1 him shall the **Son** of man also confess 12:8

4 And whosoever shall speak a word against the **Son** Luke 12:10
1 ready also: for the **Son** of man cometh at an hour..... 12:40
3 The father shall be divided against the **son**,........... 12:53
1 against the son, and the **son** against the father;........ 12:53
1 of you shall have a **son** or an ox (NASB)............. 14:5
9 And he said, A certain man had two **sons**:............ 15:11
1 the younger **son** gathered all together,................ 15:13
1 And am no more worthy to be called thy **son**:......... 15:19
1 And the **son** said unto him, Father, I have sinned..... 15:21
1 and am no more worthy to be called thy **son**.......... 15:21
1 For this my **son** was dead, and is alive again;......... 15:24
1 Now his elder **son** was in the field:.................. 15:25
1 But as soon as this thy **son** was come,................ 15:30
6 **children** of this world are in their generation wiser..... 16:8
9 in their generation wiser than the **children** of light..... 16:8
2 desire to see one of the days of the **Son** of man,...... 17:22
1 so shall also the **Son** of man be in his day............ 17:24
2 so shall it be also in the days of the **Son** of man....... 17:26
1 Even thus shall it be in the day when the **Son**......... 17:30
1 Nevertheless when the **Son** of man cometh,.......... 18:8
3 concerning the **Son** of man shall be accomplished...... 18:31
5 Jesus, thou **son** of David, have mercy on me........... 18:38
5 but he cried so much the more, Thou **son** of David,... 18:39
1 forsomuch as he also is **a son** of Abraham............. 19:9
1 For the **Son** of man is come to seek and to save...... 19:10
4 What shall I do? I will send my beloved **son**:.......... 20:13
6 The **children** of this world marry, and are given....... 20:34
6 and are the **children** of God,......................... 20:36
6 being the **children** of the resurrection.................. 20:36
4 How say they that Christ is David's **son**?.............. 20:41
1 therefore calleth him Lord, how is he then his **son**?.... 20:44
4 And then shall they see the **Son** of man coming....... 21:27
2 worthy to escape ... to stand before the **Son** of man.... 21:36
1 truly the **Son** of man goeth, as it was determined:..... 22:22
4 Judas, betrayest thou the **Son** of man with a kiss?..... 22:48
1 Hereafter shall the **Son** of man sit on the right........ 22:69
1 Then said they all, Art thou then the **Son** of God?.... 22:70
4 Saying, The **Son** of man must be delivered............ 24:7
1 hath seen God at any time; the only begotten **Son**,..John 1:18
1 I saw, and bare record that this is the **Son** of God...... 1:34
1 Thou art Simon the **son** of Jona:...................... 1:42
4 Jesus of Nazareth, the **son** of Joseph.................. 1:45
1 thou art the **Son** of God; ... the King of Israel.......... 1:49
4 ascending and descending upon the **Son** of man......... 1:51
1 even the **Son** of man which is in heaven............... 3:13
4 even so must the **Son** of man be lifted up:............ 3:14
4 that he gave his only begotten **Son**,.................... 3:16
4 For God sent not his **Son** ... to condemn the world;.... 3:17
2 in the name of the only begotten **Son** of God........... 3:18
4 The Father loveth the **Son**,........................... 3:35
4 He that believeth on the **Son** hath everlasting life:...... 3:36
3 and he that believeth not the **Son** shall not see life;..... 3:36
3 parcel of ground that Jacob gave to his **son** Joseph...... 4:5
6 and drank thereof himself, and his **children**,............ 4:12
1 whose **son** was sick at Capernaum...................... 4:46
4 that he would come down, and heal his **son**:............ 4:47
1 Jesus saith unto him, Go thy way; thy **son** liveth........ 4:50
1 in the which Jesus said unto him, Thy **son** liveth:....... 4:53
1 The **Son** can do nothing of himself,.................... 5:19
1 these also doeth the **Son** likewise...................... 5:19
4 For the Father loveth the **Son**,....................... 5:20
1 even so the **Son** quickeneth whom he will............. 5:21
3 but hath committed all judgment unto the **Son**:......... 5:22
4 That all men should honour the **Son**,.................. 5:23
4 He that honoureth not the **Son** ... not the Father....... 5:23
2 the dead shall hear the voice of the **Son** of God:....... 5:25
3 so hath he given to the **Son** to have life in himself;..... 5:26
1 execute judgment ... because he is the **Son** of man...... 5:27
1 meat ... which the **Son** of man shall give unto you:..... 6:27
4 that every one which seeth the **Son**,.................. 6:40
1 And they said, Is not this Jesus, the **son** of Joseph,..... 6:42
2 Except ye eat the flesh of the **Son** of man,............. 6:53
4 the **Son** of man ascend up where he was before?....... 6:62
1 that thou art that Christ, the **Son** of the living God..... 6:69
4 When ye have lifted up the **Son** of man,............... 8:28
1 servant abideth not ... but the **Son** abideth ever......... 8:35
1 If the **Son** therefore shall make you free,.............. 8:36
1 Is this your **son**, who ye say was born blind?....... John 9:19
1 We know that this is our **son**, ... he was born blind:.... 9:20
4 Dost thou believe on the **Son** of God?................. 9:35
1 because I said, I am the **Son** of God?................ 10:36
1 that the **Son** of God might be glorified thereby........ 11:4
1 I believe that thou art the Christ, the **Son** of God,.... 11:27
1 that the **Son** of man should be glorified............... 12:23
4 The **Son** of man must be lifted up? who is this Son.... 12:34
1 Son ... must be lifted up? who is this **Son** of man?.... 12:34
6 that ye may be the **children** of light.................. 12:36
1 Now is the **Son** of man glorified,..................... 13:31
3 that the Father may be glorified in the **Son**............ 14:13
4 Father, the hour is come; glorify thy **Son**,............. 17:1
1 that thy **Son** also may glorify thee:................... 17:1
1 and none of them is lost, but the **son** of perdition;..... 17:12
4 to die, because he made himself the **Son** of God....... 19:7
1 he saith unto his mother, Woman, behold thy **son**!..... 19:26
1 believe that Jesus is the Christ, the **Son** of God;....... 20:31
6 and your **sons** and your daughters shall prophesy,....Acts 2:17
6 Ye are the **children** of the prophets,.................. 3:25
1 which is, being interpreted, The **son** of consolation,..... 4:36
7 and all the senate of the **children** of Israel,............ 5:21
7 bought for a sum of money of the **sons** of Emmor...... 7:16
4 and nourished him for her own **son**.................... 7:21
9 to visit his brethren the **children** of Israel............... 7:23
9 in the land of Madian, where he begat two **sons**........ 7:29
8 which said unto the **children** of Israel,................. 7:37
4 the **Son** of man standing on the right hand of God...... 7:56
4 I believe that Jesus Christ is the **Son** of God........... 8:37
7 the Gentiles, and kings, and the **children** of Israel:...... 9:15
1 preached Christ ... that he is the **Son** of God........... 9:20
8 word which God sent unto the **children** of Israel,...... 10:36
5 thou **child** of the devil,.............................. 13:10
4 and God gave unto them Saul the **son** of Cis,......... 13:21
6 **children** of the stock of Abraham,.................... 13:26
1 Thou art my **Son**, this day have I begotten thee....... 13:33
1 the **son** of a certain woman, which was a Jewess,...... 16:1
6 And there were seven **sons** of one Sceva, a Jew,........ 19:14
1 I am a Pharisee, the **son** of a Pharisee:.............. 23:6
1 Paul's sister's **son** heard of their lying in wait,......... 23:16
2 Concerning his **Son** Jesus Christ our Lord,..........Rom 1:3
2 And declared to be the **Son** of God with power,........ 1:4
2 I serve with my spirit in the gospel of his **Son**,......... 1:9
2 we were reconciled to God by the death of his **Son**,.... 5:10
4 sending his own **Son** in the likeness of sinful flesh,..... 8:3
6 led by the Spirit of God, they are the **sons** of God...... 8:14
7 waiteth for the manifestation of the **sons** of God........ 8:19
2 to be conformed to the image of his **Son**,............. 8:29
2 He that spared not his own **Son**, but delivered him..... 8:32
1 this time will I come, and Sarah shall have **a son**........ 9:9
6 shall they be called the **children** of the living God....... 9:26
7 **children** of Israel be as the sand of the sea,............ 9:27
2 the fellowship of his **Son** Jesus Christ our Lord......1 Co 1:9
1 then shall the **Son** also himself be subject unto him.... 15:28
1 For the **Son** of God, Jesus Christ,..................2 Co 1:19
9 so that the **children** of Israel could not................ 3:7
9 that the **children** of Israel could not stedfastly........... 3:13
9 and ye shall be my **sons** and daughters,................ 6:18
4 To reveal his **Son** in me,.......................... Gal 1:16
2 live by the faith of the **Son** of God, who loved me,..... 2:20
6 are of faith, the same are the **children** of Abraham...... 3:7
6 are all the **children** of God by faith in Christ Jesus...... 3:26
4 God sent forth his **Son**, made of a woman,............. 4:4
6 because ye are **sons**, God hath sent forth the Spirit..... 4:6
2 God hath sent forth the Spirit of his **Son**............... 4:6
1 Wherefore thou art no more a servant, but a **son**;...... 4:7
1 and if a **son**, then an heir of God through Christ........ 4:7
9 For it is written, that Abraham had two **sons**,.......... 4:22
4 Cast out the bondwoman and her **son**:................. 4:30
1 for the **son** of the bondwoman shall not be heir........ 4:30
2 shall not be heir with the **son** of the freewoman........ 4:30
8 that now worketh in the **children** of disobedience:....Eph 2:2
8 was not made known unto the **sons** of men,............ 3:5
2 and of the knowledge of the **Son** of God,.............. 4:13
9 wrath of God upon the **children** of disobedience........ 5:6
2 translated us into the kingdom of his dear **Son**:...... Col 1:13
9 wrath ... cometh on the **children** of disobedience:....... 3:6

4 And to wait for his **Son** from heaven, ... 1 Th 1:10
6 Ye are all the **children** of light, ... 5:5
6 and the **children** of the day: 5:5
1 that man of sin be revealed, the **son** of perdition; ... 2 Th 2:3
3 Hath in these last days spoken unto us by his **Son**, .. Heb 1:2
1 Thou art my **Son**, this day have I begotten thee? 1:5
4 be to him a Father, and he shall be to me a **Son**? 1:5
4 But unto the **Son** he saith, Thy throne, O God, ... 1:8
1 or the **son** of man, that thou visitest him? 2:6
9 in bringing many **sons** unto glory, ... 2:10
1 But Christ as a **son** over his own house; 3:6
4 a great high priest, ... Jesus the **Son** of God, ... 4:14
1 Thou art my **Son**, to day have I begotten thee. 5:5
1 Though he were a **Son**, yet learned he obedience 5:8
4 they crucify to themselves the **Son** of God afresh, ... 6:6
3 but made like unto the **Son** of God; 7:3
7 And verily they that are of the **sons** of Levi, ... 7:5
4 maketh the **Son**, who is consecrated for evermore. 7:28
4 who hath trodden under foot the **Son** of God, ... 10:29
7 By faith Jacob, ... blessed both the **sons** of Joseph; 11:21
7 of the departing of the **children** of Israel; 11:22
1 refused to be called the **son** of Pharaoh's daughter; 11:24
8 which speaketh unto you as **unto children**, ... 12:5
5 My **son**, despise not thou the chastening 12:5
4 and scourgeth every **son** whom he receiveth. 12:6
8 God dealeth with you as **with sons**; 12:7
1 for what **son** is he whom the father chasteneth not? 12:7
6 then are ye bastards, and not **sons**. 12:8
4 when he had offered Isaac his **son** upon the altar? .... Jas 2:21
1 saluteth you; and so doth Marcus my **son**. .... 1 Pt 5:13
1 from the excellent glory, This is my beloved **Son**, ... 2 Pt 1:17
2 is with the Father, and with his **Son** Jesus Christ. .... 1 Jn 1:3
2 and the blood of Jesus Christ his **Son** cleanseth us 1:7
4 is antichrist, that denieth the Father and the **Son**. 2:22
4 denieth the **Son**, the same hath not the Father: 2:23
3 also shall continue in the **Son**, and in the Father. 2:24
1 For this purpose the **Son** of God was manifested, ... 3:8
2 should believe on the name of his **Son** Jesus Christ, ... 3:23
4 because that God sent his only begotten **Son** 4:9
4 and sent his **Son** to be the propitiation for our sins. 4:10
4 Father sent the **Son** to be the Saviour of the world. 4:14
1 shall confess that Jesus is the **Son** of God, ... 4:15
1 but he that believeth that Jesus is the **Son** of God? 5:5
2 witness of God which he hath testified of his **Son**. 5:9
4 He that believeth on the **Son** of God 5:10
2 believeth not the record that God gave of his **Son**. 5:10
3 given to us eternal life, and this life is in his **Son**. 5:11
4 He that hath the **Son** hath life; 5:12
4 and he that hath not the **Son** of God hath not life. 5:12
2 you that believe on the name of the **Son** of God; 5:13
2 ye may believe on the name of the **Son** of God. 5:13
1 And we know that the **Son** of God is come, ... 5:20
3 even in his **Son** Jesus Christ. This is the true God, ... 5:20
2 from the Lord Jesus Christ, the **Son** of the Father, .. 2 Jn 1:3
4 he hath both the Father and the **Son**. 1:9
3 And in the midst ... one like unto the **Son** of man, .. Rev 1:13
7 cast a stumblingblock before the **children** of Israel, ... 2:14
1 These things saith the **Son** of God, ... 2:18
7 of all the tribes of the **children** of Israel. 7:4
4 And she brought forth a man **child**, ... 12:5
3 upon the cloud one sat like unto the **Son** of man, ... 14:14
1 and I will be his God, and he shall be my **son**. 21:7
7 names of the twelve tribes of the **children** of Israel: 21:12

Classical Greek

Huios means "son" in the broadest sense in classical Greek. Thus it means not only "son" as in the male offspring of human parents but also "offspring" as in the offspring of animals or even plants. Neither is it restricted to meaning the offspring of the first generation, for it can be used of "grandchildren" or of "descendants" in general.

The relationship between a teacher and a student may also be conveyed in terms of the father-son relationship. In addition it can describe nationality (e.g., son of Achaia; cf. Braumann, "Child," *Colin Brown*, 1:287). Finally *huios* functions in a religious capacity, such as in the expressions "the sons of darkness" or "the sons of light" (ibid.).

Septuagint Usage

The understanding of *huios* in classical Greek closely parallels the understanding of *bēn*, "son," in Hebrew, an equivalency that occurs in the Septuagint no less than 4,800 times. Besides the simple denotation of "male child" the words *son* or *sons* carry quite a number of nuances in Scripture. Thus, *huios* can stand for a "grandson" (Genesis 29:5; 2 Samuel 19:24 [LXX 2 Kings 19:24]) or for "descendants" in general (Numbers 2:14), or it can denote a people (for example the "*children* of the east," 1 Kings 4:30 [LXX 3 Kings 4:30]). Furthermore, the high priest Eli called his disciple Samuel his "son" (1 Samuel 3:6 [LXX 1 Kings 3:6]). Figuratively an arrow is the "son" of a bow (Job 41:28, see NASB, margin note; cf. the expression "the arrows of his quiver," Psalm 127:4,5 [LXX 126:4,5], a figure of speech for children).

The metaphoric use of *son* was even more common in Israel than among the Greeks. The Hellenistic Jews of the New Testament period commonly used the terminology in this way. The documents from the Qumran community provide us with a valuable example of how extensive such usage was. The members of that group distinguish between "sons of light" and "sons of darkness," or "sons of righteousness" and "sons of unrighteousness," and the "sons of Belial" and the "sons of the good pleasure of God." They saw the world in dualistic terms, and the line of separation is between the "sons of heaven and grace" and the "sons of the world, the sons of transgressions and destruction" (ibid., 1:288).

Being able to have many children was considered a blessing in Israel (Genesis 1:28); it was a tremendous privilege to see one's descendants (Genesis 50:23; Proverbs 17:6). Corresponding to this view, the birth of a child was a time of great joy and celebration (cf. Genesis 30:23). This was even more the case if the child were a boy (Psalm 127:4,5, see RSV). Unlike daughters who would leave the family when they married, male offspring insured ongoing protection and provision under the patriarchal family system.

Within a family the eldest son held the privileged position among his siblings. Upon the father's death he assumed the duties and responsibilities of the head of the family. He received a double portion of the inheritance (see also *teknon* [4891]).

Son acquires a unique significance when it concerns a relationship with God. The title "Son of God" is given a wide and diverse range of meaning in the Biblical account (ibid.). Essentially it describes a personal being who somehow, either spiritually or morally, stands in a unique relation to God. The angels are depicted as "sons of God" because they are considered to be particularly near God and because they are spirit beings (Job 1:6; 2:1; 38:7; Psalm 89:6).

The first man, Adam, who was a direct creation of the Creator, was the son of God in a very unique way (cf. Luke 3:38). On a grander scale, Israel, as God's chosen people, was called the "son of God" or the "sons of God." The Lord called Israel "my *son* . . . my firstborn," an allusion to His having chosen them (Exodus 4:22). Israelites were the sons of God because they were a people created for His glory and called by His name (Isaiah 43:6; cf. Deuteronomy 32:6; Isaiah 64:8; Malachi 2:10). As the chosen sons of God they were uniquely the object of His love and care (Jeremiah 31:20; Hosea 11:1). Along with the privileges of sonship came a special demand for obedience and service. As a "son" Israel was also the "servant" of the Lord (Isaiah 1:2; 44:1; 45:4; Malachi 1:6). The people of Israel recognized that the status of son belonged first and foremost to them (Romans 9:4). They were initially participants in that relationship, and they are the "first" to whom salvation is offered (Romans 1:16).

The king of the people represented the entire nation. He, likewise, was the one responsible for establishing God's kingdom on earth; i.e., he was God's representative. This relationship is depicted in terms of "the chosen one" whose Father is God: "I will be his father, and he shall be my *son*" (2 Samuel 7:14). The king—as God's son—came under God's special care and protection (Psalm 89:27f.). He was uniquely charged to obey God and to execute His will on earth. Nonetheless, despite this unique relationship, the kings of Israel were never regarded as divine themselves; the same could not be said for the practices of some of its neighbors. The king was God's son only because he was the instrument chosen for carrying out the will (i.e., the kingdom) of God. The king of Israel was God's son only as he functioned in the theocratic (i.e., "God-ruled") government in Israel.

The coming Messiah was seen as God's Son to an even larger degree. The starting point for the view that Messiah was the Son of God is found in Nathan's prophecy in 2 Samuel (7:13f.). This messianic prophecy declares: "I will be his father, and he shall be my *son*." The hope for a future, eschatological king emerged most prominently after the kingdom in Israel had fallen. In Psalms 2:7 and 89:28,29, both of which are eschatological psalms, Messiah is called the Son of God. Of all the Old Testament messianic passages Psalm 89 draws the most complete picture of the Messiah as God's Son. Isaiah 9:6 connects the deity of the Messiah with the fact that He is God's Son.

All the privileges of sonship granted to Israel, as well as to kings as God's sons, are bestowed upon Messiah in a unique way. He is the only begotten of God and His chosen one in a sense unlike any before Him. He is God's absolute representative on earth; He, in God's stead, makes known the promises of salvation. Israel's role as God's servant is realized in His person, and He fulfills this role in perfect obedience.

New Testament Usage

These Old Testament prophecies are resumed in the New Testament. Here, however, the title "Son of God" is exclusively applied to God's only Son, Jesus Christ. Jesus' unique status as God's Son is declared by angels upon His entrance into the history of mankind: "The Holy Ghost shall come upon thee (Mary), and the power of the Highest shall overshadow thee: therefore also that holy thing which shall be born of thee shall be called the *Son* of God" (Luke 1:35).

Jesus' own testimony about himself defines further His unique status as God's Son. As He offers praise to the Father He says: "All things are delivered unto me of my Father: and no man knoweth the *Son*, but the Father; neither knoweth any man the Father, save the *Son*, and he to whomsoever the *Son* will reveal him" (Matthew 11:27). In His eschatological discourse in Mark chapter 13 Jesus comments about the time of His return: "But of that day and that hour knoweth no man, no, not the angels which are in heaven, neither the *Son*, but the Father" (verse 32). He shows us in this statement that He sees himself above both heavenly and earthly beings.

Another significant witness to Jesus' sonship is contained in Jesus' own summons to missions: "Go ye therefore, and teach all nations, baptizing them in the name of the Father, and of the *Son*, and of the Holy Ghost" (Matthew 28:19). Here Jesus unites himself with the Father and the Spirit and gives us a glimpse of the divine Trinity.

Jesus' self-testimony of His status as Son climaxes in John's Gospel. He acknowledges that He is the only begotten Son of God whom the Father in His love sent to save the world (John 3:16-18). No one else can claim the position of Son as Jesus does. He alone is the object of the Father's love (John 3:35; 5:20; 17:24-26). He is aware of His preexistent nature: "Before Abraham was, I am" (John 8:58). "Glorify thou me with thine own self with the glory which I had with thee before the world was" (John 17:5; cf. 3:13; 6:62).

Jesus further witnessed to His unique status as Son through His works. His miracles far surpass mere human ability; they point to the Father who has given Him the authority to do them (John 5:19-30). The Father has entrusted the Son with two important tasks: to make alive and to judge (cf. 5:21,22). Both take place on two different planes; the one is eternal, and the other is spiritual (verses 24-29). Jesus realizes that not even His most ardent followers can achieve the kind of relationship He has with His Father. Therefore, we see He exclusively refers to "my Father" and "your Father" but never "our Father." He did teach His disciples to pray the Lord's Prayer, but He never included himself in this prayer: "After this manner therefore pray ye: Our Father . . . " (Matthew 6:9).

God's testimony to His Son resounds throughout the New Testament writings in various ways. First, God attests to His Son in the voice which was heard at Jesus' baptism and on the Mount of Transfiguration: "This is my beloved *Son*, in whom I am well pleased" (Matthew 3:17; 17:5). In these instances God is giving express testimony to His Son.

Second, the writings of John purport to be written so the readers "might believe (keep believing) that Jesus is the Christ, the *Son* of God; and that believing (they) might have (keep having) life through his name" (John 20:31) and that they might have fellowship with "the Father, and with his *Son* Jesus Christ" (1 John 1:3). He greeted the readers of his second letter with: "Grace be with you, mercy, and peace, from God the Father, and from the Lord Jesus Christ, the *Son* of the Father, in truth and love" (2 John 3).

The apostolic witnesses consistently confirm that Jesus is the Son of God in the ultimate sense of that relationship. Even on the way to the suffering awaiting Jesus in Jerusalem, Peter, as spokesman for the disciples, confessed: "Thou art the Christ, the *Son* of the living God" (Matthew 16:16). This confession was confirmed further by the disciple's experience on the Mount of Transfiguration: "For he received from God the Father honor and glory, when there came such a voice to him from the excellent glory, This is my beloved *Son*, in whom I am well pleased" (2 Peter 1:17).

Following Paul's dramatic conversion in which God revealed "his *Son*" to him (Galatians 1:16), Paul made this a fundamental element of his preaching: "And straightway he preached Christ in the synagogues, that he is the *Son* of God" (Acts 9:20). The essence of his gospel message was Jesus, who was "declared to be the *Son* of God with power, according to the Spirit of holiness, by the resurrection from the dead" (Romans 1:4).

The testimony of the Church to Jesus' status as God's Son appears in various New Testament passages, such as Romans 1:3,4, a confession, and Philippians 2:6-9, possibly an early hymn.

Huios is also used in the New Testament to denote the relationship of the "son" to his father (Mark 10:46) or to his mother (Luke 1:13) or even to ancestors (Matthew 1:20; 23:31; Luke 19:9). Paul, in particular, also called attention to the "sons of God" (e.g., Romans 8:14f.) where those who become Christians receive "sonship" by adoption (Galatians 4:5). A believer's "sonship" to God is both a present reality and the goal of hope for future fulfillment in eternity (Romans 8:23; cf. James 1:18; 1 Peter 1:23; ibid., 1:288f.).

STRONG 5207, BAUER 833-35, MOULTON-MILLIGAN 649, KITTEL 8:334-97, LIDDELL-SCOTT 1846-47, COLIN BROWN 1:286-90.

5049. ὕλη hulē noun

Wood, fuel, material for burning; stand of trees.

יָוֵן yāwēn (3223), Mire (Ps 69:2 [68:2]—only Codex Sinaiticus and some Vaticanus texts).

סְכָּה ṣukkāh (5712), Covert (Jb 38:40).
שָׁמִיר shāmîr (8455), Thorns (Is 10:17).

1. **ὕλην hulēn** acc sing fem

1 how great a matter a little fire kindleth! .... Jas 3:5

Classical Greek

There is considerable variety in the meaning of *hulē* in Greek literature. In classical Greek *hulē* indicates wood that is cut down for some purpose: firewood or wood for building. *Hulē* also means "a stand of trees," as in a forest. This kind of forest is not in the mountains or on cultivated plains; thus, it is a wild woodland (*Bauer*; *Moulton-Milligan*). In uncommon usage *hulē* refers not to wood in its rough form but to wood that has been fashioned into furniture. Further, *hulē* can denote any material and in philosophy was the word for "matter."

Hulē was also a raw material used in the construction of idols; it was generically understood as the "stuff" of which man was made. (Later, Mani [the founder of the Manichaeans] named the dark lord of the material realm "Hyle.") Such matter could be seen as sinful or in opposition to God (*Bauer*).

The most unique occurrence of *hulē* appears in a second-century B.C. papyrus in which some interpret the term to mean "mud" or "slime" (see *Moulton-Milligan*).

Septuagint Usage

Hulē occurs in the Septuagint as well as in early Christian writings and secular usage contemporary with New Testament literature. In the Septuagint *hulē* was used to translate at least two Hebrew terms: *ṣukkāh*, "thicket," (Job 38:40, NIV), and *shāmîr*, "thorns" (Isaiah 10:17).

New Testament Usage

In its only New Testament occurrence James referred to *hulē* in the context of wood used as firewood. Thus, James 3:5 teaches that just as a large mass of firewood (*hulēn*) can become an inferno from a small flame, so also a few small words can cause extensive damaging consequence. To paraphrase James' reference to the great matter of fuel, "Wrong words are like kindling wood producing a blaze of evil."

STRONG 5208, BAUER 836, MOULTON-MILLIGAN 649, LIDDELL-SCOTT 1847-48.

5050. ὑμεῖς humeis prs-pron

You, yourselves.

1. **ὑμεῖς humeis** nom 2pl
2. **ὑμῶν humōn** gen 2pl
3. **ὑμῖν humin** dat 2pl
4. **ὑμᾶς humas** acc 2pl

2 otherwise ye have no reward of your Father .... Matt 6:1
4 your Father knoweth ... before ye ask him. 6:8
3 Unto you it is given to know the mystery .... Mark 4:11
1 for it is not ye that speak, but the Holy Ghost. 13:11
2 he be of you that forsaketh not all that he hath, ... Luke 14:33
2 But we were gentle among you, ... 1 Th 2:7
3 Grace unto you, and peace, from God our Father ... 2 Th 1:2

Humeis serves as the plural form of the second person singular pronoun "you" (*su*). Verb forms in Greek indicate by their endings the person and number of their antecedent. Consequently, when a pronoun such as *humeis* is added to the verb as an expressed subject, it is generally translated "yourselves" or "you yourselves" for emphasis. The pronoun occurs as the subject of the verb in Matthew 14:16 where the King James Version reads, "They need not depart; give *ye* them to eat." The presence of *humeis* in the text renders the stronger translation "you *yourselves* give them to eat" or "*you* give them (something) to eat." See also Matthew 7:12; Luke 17:10; and numerous other passages throughout the New Testament for this common pronoun.

STRONG 5210, BAUER 836, LIDDELL-SCOTT 1848.

5051. Ὑμέναιος Humenaios name

Hymeneus.

1. **Ὑμέναιος Humenaios** nom masc

1 Of whom is Hymenaeus and Alexander; .... 1 Tm 1:20
1 a canker: of whom is Hymenaeus and Philetus; ..... 2 Tm 2:17

A member of the church who had "shipwrecked (his) faith" and whom Paul "handed over to Satan to be taught not to blaspheme" (1 Timothy 1:19f., NIV). The punishment involved at least a removal from fellowship (cf. 1 Corinthians 5:5) and had a redemptive purpose. Hymeneus' errors were apparently doctrinal. He taught that the resurrection of the dead had already taken place (2 Timothy 2:17f.).

5052. ὑμέτερος humeteros adj

Yours, belonging or pertaining to you.

1. **ὑμετέρῳ humeterō** dat 2sing masc/neu
2. **ὑμέτερον humeteron** nom/acc 2sing masc/neu
3. **ὑμέτερος humeteros** nom 2sing masc
4. **ὑμετέρα humetera** nom 2sing fem
5. **ὑμετέρας humeteras** gen 2sing fem

6. ὑμετέρᾳ humetera dat 2sing fem
7. ὑμετέραν humeteran acc 2sing fem

4 ye poor: for **yours** is the kingdom of God. . . . . Luke 6:20
2 who shall give you that which is **your** own? 16:12
3 but **your** time is alway ready. . . . . John 7:6
1 It is also written in **your** law, ... 8:17
2 they will keep **yours** also. 15:20
5 to take some meat: for this is for **your** health: . . . . . Acts 27:34
1 through **your** mercy they also may obtain mercy. . . . Rom 11:31
7 I protest, brethren, by the boasting in **you**, (NASB) 1 Co 15:31
2 supplied what was lacking on **your** part. (NASB) 16:17
5 and to prove the sincerity of **your** love. . . . . 2 Co 8:8
6 you circumcised, that they may glory in **your** flesh. . . . Gal 6:13

This is the possessive form of the second person plural pronoun *humeis* (5050). Found only 10 times in the New Testament, *humeteros* occurs in the Gospels and in Pauline literature. Possession in the second person plural is most often indicated by the genitive plural of the pronoun *humeis*, "of you"; translators shift it to the possessive adjective *your* for a more idiomatic expression in English.

The possessive is never found in the New Testament in reference to material ownership. The meaning is more of attribute or heritage. In Luke 6:20 Christ referred to the kingdom of God being "yours"; John 7:6 mentions "*your* time"; 8:17, "*your* law"; 15:20, "*your* sayings." See also Acts 27:34; Romans 11:31; 1 Corinthians 15:31; (some texts of) 16:17; 2 Corinthians 8:8; Galatians 6:13.

STRONG 5212, BAUER 836, MOULTON-MILLIGAN 649, LIDDELL-SCOTT 1849.

5053. ὑμνέω humneō verb

To sing a hymn of praise.

COGNATE:
ὕμνος humnos (5054)

SYNONYMS:
ᾄδω adō (102)
ψάλλω psallō (5402)

הָלַל hālal (2054), Piel: sing praises, praise (2 Chr 29:30, Ps 22:22 [21:22]).

זָמַר zāmar (2252), Piel: sing praises, sing (1 Chr 16:9, Is 12:5).

יָדָה yādhâh (3142), Hiphil: give thanks, praise (Is 12:4, 25:1).

יָדַע yādha' (3156), Know; hiphil: lead (2 Chr 23:13).

רָנַן rānan (7728), Cry aloud, cry out (Prv 1:20, 8:3).

שִׁיר shîr (8301), Shout for joy, sing (Ps 65:13 [64:13], Is 42:10).

1. ὑμνήσαντες humnēsantes nom pl masc part aor act
2. ὑμνήσω humnēsō 1sing indic fut act
3. ὕμνουν humnoun 3pl indic imperf act

1 And when they **had sung an hymn**, they went out . . Matt 26:30
1 And when they **had sung an hymn**, they went out . . Mark 14:26
3 Paul and Silas prayed, and **sang praises** unto God: Acts 16:25
2 in the midst of the church will I **sing praise** . . . . Heb 2:12

Classical Greek

In classical Greek *humneō* first refers to singing a song or hymn. By extension it means to extol, praise, or affirm solemnly the nature of another. The general use of *humneō* in classical Greek is to sing a hymn of praise to the gods (Delling, "humnos," *Kittel*, 8:490).

Septuagint Usage

Humneō is found in the Septuagint with abundant occurrences in the third chapter of Daniel (36 times). The basic meaning is similar to that of its classical Greek use "sing the praise of" or "magnifying through songs or hymns of praise."

New Testament Usage

Humneō in the vocabulary of the New Testament refers both to the singing of hymns of praise as well as praise to God which is not necessarily to be sung. *Humneō* appears four times in the New Testament.

In Matthew 26:30 Christ and His disciples sang a hymn at the close of the Last Supper before departing to the Mount of Olives. Mark 14:26 is the synoptic parallel to Matthew 26 and also uses *humneō* to indicate that the Last Supper was closed with a time of worship through singing a hymn.

Both Gospel uses of *humneō* probably refer to the musical recitation of the second half of the Hallel (Psalms 113–118), a customary part of the Passover ritual. This was obviously a significant time of praise at the close of their meal together. Luke did not highlight the closing of the Lord's Supper but focused on the transition from the supper to the garden at the Mount of Olives. Thus, Luke did not mention the singing of the hymn.

Acts 16:25 gives an account of the hymns of praise sung by Paul and Silas in the Philippian jail. In the Gospels a hymn of praise was sung as commemoration of one of the most meaningful times the disciples spent with Christ; it was on the verge of the darkest hour they would face. In Acts, Christ's followers were not discouraged by the bleakness of their prison situation; instead, they sang with joy.

Hebrews 2:12 is the final New Testament use of *humneō*. Here the hymn may not necessarily be a song to be sung by Christ as much as an expression of exaltation and praise. It is a quotation from Psalm 22:22, "In the midst of the congregation will I praise thee."

Strong 5214, Bauer 836, Moulton-Milligan 649, Kittel 8:489-503, Liddell-Scott 1849, Colin Brown 3:668-70.

5054. ὕμνος humnos noun

Hymn, song of praise.

Cross-Reference:

ὑμνέω humneō (5053)

הָלַל hālal (2054), Piel: praise (2 Chr 7:6).

נְגִינָה n^eghînāh (5234), Stringed instrument (Pss 54:title [53:title], 61:title [60:title], 76:title [75:title]).

שִׁיר shîr (8302), Song (Is 42:10).

תְּהִלָּה t^ehillāh (8747), Praise song, praise (Pss 40:3 [39:3], 65:1 [64:1], 119:171 [118:171]).

תְּפִלָּה t^ephillāh (8940), Prayer (Ps 72:20 [71:20]).

1. ὕμνοις humnois dat pl masc

1 in psalms and hymns and spiritual songs, ... Eph 5:19
1 in psalms and hymns and spiritual songs, ... Col 3:16

This is one of the three terms used by Paul in Ephesians 5:19 for Christian "songs" (cf. *psalmos* [5403], "psalm"; *ōdē* [5437], "song"). Their usage in classical Greek suggests some slight differences in meaning; however, this should not be pressed. They might have represented different forms or aspects of a song, such as those found in the Early Church. Despite the influence of local customs or ethnic traditions, undoubtedly the most influential force behind the content of Christian songs would have been the Old Testament and the songs of the synagogue.

Classical Greek

In classical Greek *humnos* predominantly refers to a hymn or ode that praises the gods (*Liddell-Scott*). The *humnos* could either be a song of joy or a mourning song. It could also be sung to heroes or men.

Septuagint Usage

Evidence in support of the contention that one should not draw too much distinction between the various terms is found in the Septuagint. There these three terms are all freely used to translate the same Hebrew terms. These Hebrew words are, in large measure, associated with Old Testament psalms.

New Testament Usage

The use of the verb *humneō* in the New Testament also suggests a relationship between New Testament songs and Old Testament psalms. When the Gospels of Matthew (26:30) and Mark (14:26) report that Jesus and His disciples, having "sung a hymn . . . went out into the mount of Olives," they are almost certainly referring to a psalm of the Old Testament. In this particular case they probably sang the Hallel, a song commonly sung at Passover, which was taken from Psalms 113–118. Thus *humnos* may refer to Biblical psalms, although not necessarily so.

Strong 5215, Bauer 836, Moulton-Milligan 649, Kittel 8:489-503, Liddell-Scott 1849, Colin Brown 2:874; 3:668-70,672,674-75.

5055. ὑπάγω hupagō verb

Go, go away, depart.

Cognate:

ἄγω agō (70)

Synonyms:

ἀναλύω analuō (358)
ἀναχωρέω anachōreō (400)
ἀπαλλάσσω apallassō (521)
ἀπέρχομαι aperchomai (562)
ἀποβαίνω apobainō (571)
ἀπολύω apoluō (624)
ἀποχωρέω apochōreō (666)
ἀφίστημι aphistēmi (861)
διαχωρίζω diachōrizō (1310)
ἐγκαταλείπω enkataleipō (1452)
ἐξέρχομαι exerchomai (1814)
ἐξιέναι exienai (1821)
μεταίρω metairō (3202)
παράγω paragō (3717)
πορεύομαι poreuomai (4057)
χωρέω chōreō (5397)

הָלַךְ hālakh (2050), Go, walk; hiphil: cause to go back (Ex 14:21).

1. ὑπάγω hupagō 1sing indic pres act
2. ὑπάγεις hupageis 2sing indic pres act
3. ὑπάγει hupagei 3sing indic pres act
4. ὑπάγῃ hupagē 3sing subj pres act
5. ὑπάγητε hupagēte 2pl subj pres act
6. ὕπαγε hupage 2sing impr pres act
7. ὑπάγετε hupagete 2pl impr pres act
8. ὑπάγοντες hupagontes nom pl masc part pres act
9. ὑπάγοντας hupagontas acc pl masc part pres act
10. ὑπάγειν hupagein inf pres act
11. ὑπῆγον hupēgon 3pl indic imperf act

6 Then saith Jesus unto him, Get thee hence, Satan: .. Matt 4:10
6 Leave there thy gift ... and go thy way; 5:24
6 compel thee to go a mile, go with him twain. 5:41
6 See thou tell no man; but go thy way, ... 8:4
6 And Jesus said unto the centurion, Go thy way; 8:13
7 And he said unto them, Go. 8:32
6 Arise, take up thy bed, and go unto thine house. 9:6
3 for joy thereof goeth and selleth all that he hath, ... 13:44
6 said unto Peter, Get thee behind me, Satan: 16:23
6 go and tell him his fault between thee and him 18:15
6 go and sell that thou hast, and give to the poor, ... 19:21
7 And said unto them; Go ye also into the vineyard, ... 20:4
7 He saith unto them, Go ye also into the vineyard; 20:7
6 Take that thine is, and go thy way: 20:14
6 and said, Son, go work to day in my vineyard. 21:28
7 Go into the city to such a man, and say unto him, ... 26:18

3 The Son of man goeth as it is written of him: .... Matt 26:24
7 go your way, make it as sure as ye can. ... 27:65
7 go tell my brethren that they go into Galilee, ... 28:10
6 but go thy way, show thyself to the priest, ... Mark 1:44
6 take up thy bed, and go thy way into thine house. ... 2:11
6 Go home to thy friends, and tell them how great ... 5:19
6 go in peace, and be whole of thy plague. ... 5:34
8 for there were many coming and going, ... 6:31
9 people saw them departing, and many knew him, ... 6:33
7 How many loaves have ye? go and see. ... 6:38
6 And he said unto her, For this saying go thy way; ... 7:29
6 rebuked Peter, saying, Get thee behind me, Satan: ... 8:33
6 go thy way, sell whatsoever thou hast, ... 10:21
6 Go thy way; thy faith hath made thee whole. ... 10:52
7 Go your way into the village over against you: ... 11:2
7 and saith unto them, Go ye into the city, ... 14:13
3 Son of man indeed goeth, as it is written of him: ... 14:21
7 But go your way, tell his disciples and Peter that ... 16:7
6 Get thee behind me, Satan: for it is written, ... Luke 4:8
10 But as he went the people thronged him. ... 8:42
7 Go your ways: behold, I send you forth as lambs ... 10:3
2 thou goest with thine adversary to the magistrate, ... 12:58
10 that, as they went, they were cleansed. ... 17:14
7 Saying, Go ye into the village over against you; ... 19:30
3 not tell whence it cometh, and whither it goeth: ... John 3:8
6 Go, call thy husband, and come hither. ... 4:16
11 the ship was at the land whither they went. ... 6:21
10 said Jesus unto the twelve, Will ye also go away? ... 6:67
6 Depart hence, and go into Judaea, ... 7:3
1 and then I go unto him that sent me. ... 7:33
1 for I know whence I came, and whither I go; ... 8:14
1 ye cannot tell whence I come, and whither I go. ... 8:14
1 Then said Jesus again unto them, I go my way, ... 8:21
1 whither I go, ye cannot come. ... 8:21
1 because he saith, Whither I go, ye cannot come. ... 8:22
6 And said unto him, Go, ... 9:7
6 and said unto me, Go to the pool of Siloam, ... 9:11
2 sought to stone thee; and goest thou thither again? ... 11:8
3 saying, She goeth unto the grave to weep there. ... 11:31
10 Jesus saith unto them, Loose him, and let him go. ... 11:44
11 by reason of him many of the Jews went away, ... 12:11
3 walketh in darkness knoweth not whither he goeth. ... 12:35
3 and that he was come from God, and went to God; .. 13:3
1 Whither I go, ye cannot come; ... 13:33
2 Simon Peter said unto him, ... whither goest thou? ... 13:36
1 Whither I go, thou canst not follow me now; ... 13:36
1 And whither I go ye know, and the way ye know. ... 14:4
2 Lord, we know not whither thou goest; ... 14:5
1 I go away, and come again unto you. ... 14:28
5 that ye should go and bring forth fruit, ... 15:16
1 But now I go my way to him that sent me; ... 16:5
2 and none of you asketh me, Whither goest thou? ... 16:5
1 Of righteousness, because I go to my Father, ... 16:10
1 ye shall see me, because I go to the Father. ... 16:16
1 and, Because I go to the Father? ... 16:17
10 if therefore ye seek me, let these go their way: ... 18:8
1 Simon Peter saith unto them, I go a fishing. ... 21:3
7 And one of you say unto them, Depart in peace, ... Jas 2:16
3 in darkness, and knoweth not whither he goeth, ... 1 Jn 2:11
6 Go and take the little book which is open ... Rev 10:8
3 that leadeth into captivity shall go into captivity: ... 13:10
4 which follow the Lamb whithersoever he goeth. ... 14:4
7 Go your ways, and pour out the vials of the wrath ... 16:1
10 out of the bottomless pit, and go into perdition: ... 17:8
3 and is of the seven, and goeth into perdition. ... 17:11

Classical Greek

Hupagō is a common verb in secular Greek literature. In its earliest use *hupagō* had a variety of meanings. In Homer (Eighth Century B.C.) and elsewhere *hupagō* ranged in meaning from "to lead under" (as horses or oxen might be led "under" a yoke) to others such as "to go on a journey." A common early use is the idea of subjection: "to lead" someone before a court, "to go" devote oneself to service (to a god or master), "to go" put oneself at another's disposal (Delling, "hupagō," *Kittel*, 8:504).

Septuagint Usage

Septuagint and pre-New Testament usage of *hupagō* reflects the sense of "to go" as well as the descriptive use found in Exodus 14:21: "Yahweh caused the sea *to go* back" (ibid.). *Hupagō* also expresses a wish for good fortune, "to go" in peace.

New Testament Usage

The meaning of *hupagō* generally narrowed over time to the common New Testament meaning of "go, go away, withdraw from one's presence." Post-New Testament use is generally consistent with New Testament occurrences.

In the New Testament *hupagō* generally occurs without a direct object; the "where" of going is usually understood from the context. About 70 of approximately 80 New Testament occurrences are found in the Gospels; John used the word with the greatest frequency.

The synoptic Evangelists testify to the authority of Christ. He had power to command as evidenced by the imperative use of *hupagō*: i.e., over physical illness (Matthew 8:13); in directing His followers on a mission (Luke 10:3); in directing the disciples with details for His triumphal entry (Mark 11:2); and over the power of Satan. Matthew 8:32 shows the ultimate spiritual dominance of Christ over the power of Satan when He commands demons with just a single word—*hupagō*, "Go."

John used *hupagō* in his Gospel about 30 times. Nearly 20 of these occurrences refer to the going or going away of Christ. *Hupagō* plays a key role in John's theology in showing that Christ was *going to* the Father. This first occurs in 7:33 and 8:14, but it is not fully communicated nor understood by the disciples until the last discourse of Christ in chapters 13 through 18. Christ's going to the Father is a vital part of John's message; it is from the Father that Christ was sent, and through Him access to the Father is now available.

Strong 5217, Bauer 836-37, Moulton-Milligan 649-50, Kittel 8:504-6, Liddell-Scott 1850.

5056. ὑπακοή hupakoē noun

Responsive obedience, obedient answer.

Cross-Reference:

ὑπακούω hupakouō (5057)

עֲנָוָה ʽănāwāh (6265), Gentleness (2 Sm 22:36).

1. **ὑπακοή hupakoē** nom sing fem
2. **ὑπακοῆς hupakoēs** gen sing fem
3. **ὑπακοῇ hupakoē** dat sing fem
4. **ὑπακοήν hupakoēn** acc sing fem

4 for **obedience** to the faith among all nations, ... Rom 1:5
2 so by the **obedience** of one shall many be 5:19
4 that to whom ye yield yourselves servants to **obey**, ... 6:16
2 or of **obedience** unto righteousness? 6:16
4 to make the Gentiles **obedient**, by word and deed, ... 15:18
1 For your **obedience** is come abroad unto all men. 16:19
4 known to all nations for the **obedience** of faith: 16:26
4 whilst he remembereth the **obedience** of you all, ...2 Co 7:15
4 captivity every thought to the **obedience** of Christ; 10:5
1 when your **obedience** is fulfilled. 10:6
3 Having confidence in thy **obedience** I wrote ....Phlm 1:21
4 Though he were a Son, yet learned he **obedience** .....Heb 5:8
4 unto **obedience** and sprinkling of the blood ....1 Pt 1:2
2 As **obedient** children, ... 1:14
3 ye have purified your souls in **obeying** the truth 1:22

Classical Greek

This word is a combination of *hupo* (5097), a preposition meaning "by" or "below," and *akoē* (187), "that which is heard" (from the verb *akouō* [189], "to hear"). This noun refers to the appropriate submissive obedience to an authority beyond oneself, whether human or divine.

Evidence (or lack of it) indicates that *hupakoē* is a term of primarily Biblical usage, although its meaning deals with a common concept of authority. There is a very limited use of the word in extra-Biblical literature. When it does occur, it conforms to the Biblical usage of the term and is consistent with the New Testament meanings. Early Christian writers (Clement and others) are the most common users of the word, although even their use is rare.

Septuagint Usage

Hupakoē is not found in secular Greek literature before the writings of Christianity. The only Septuagint usage of *hupakoē* is in 2 Samuel 22:36 (LXX 2 Kings 22:36). Here it refers to the answers to prayer which God gives.

New Testament Usage

The New Testament uses the word *hupakoē* 15 times, 11 of which are found in Pauline literature, 7 in Romans. In the Book of Romans *hupakoē* carries the following meanings: obedience that grows in response to the believer's faith (1:5; 16:26); the perfect obedience of Christ to God (5:19); and obedient submission to either the ways of righteousness or the way of sin (6:16; 16:19). Such obedience, in contrast to the outward conformity of Old Testament legalism, is thorough obedience—both internal and external. It is obedience "by word and deed" (15:18).

Paul expanded the application of *hupakoē* to include the believer's obedience to Christ (2 Corinthians 10:6) as well as to those appointed to positions of authority (for example, Titus who was appointed by Paul, 2 Corinthians 7:15). Such obedience is often at the cost of great consequence or personal suffering, as demonstrated by Christ (Hebrews 5:8).

Peter's use of *hupakoē* relies on family parallels, as the obedience of children (1 Peter 1:14) and the obedience that compels believers to exhibit brotherly love (1:22). Thus *hupakoē* is used with other words; however, when used by itself it "signifies the believing state of Christians as this consists in obedience" (Kittel, "akouō," *Kittel*, 1:224). "Only through *hupakoē* and conduct which fulfills the commandments of God does faith come to completion (James 2:22)" (Michel, "Faith," *Colin Brown*, 1:604).

STRONG 5218, BAUER 837, MOULTON-MILLIGAN 650, KITTEL 1:224-25, LIDDELL-SCOTT 1851, COLIN BROWN 1:604; 2:179.

5057. ὑπακούω hupakouō verb

Listen to, obey, respond, answer, follow, be subject to.

COGNATES:
ἀκούω akouō (189)
ὑπακοή hupakoē (5056)
ὑπήκοος hupēkoos (5093)

SYNONYMS:
ἀκούω akouō (189)
διακούω diakouō (1245)
εἰσακούω eisakouō (1508)
ἐνωτίζομαι enōtizomai (1785)
ἐπακούω epakouō (1858)
ἐπακροάομαι epakroaomai (1859)
πειθαρχέω peitharcheō (3842)
πειθώ peithō (3843B)
πείθω peithō (3844)

אָזַן ʼāzan (237), Hiphil: listen (2 Chr 24:19).

מִשְׁמַעַת mishmaʽath (5109), Subjects (Is 11:14).

נָשַׁק nāshaq (5583), Kiss; do homage (Gn 41:40).

עָנָה ʽānâh (6257), Qal: answer (2 Sm 22:42, Jb 9:3, Is 65:12); hiphil: respond (Prv 29:19).

קָשַׁב qāshav (7477), Hiphil: make attentive (Prv 2:2).

שָׁלַם shālam (8396), Be complete, be whole; hiphil: make peace (Dt 20:12).

שָׁמַע shāmaʽ (8471), Qal: listen (Lv 26:14, Dt 17:12, Jer 13:10); niphal: obey (Ps 18:44 [17:44]).

1. **ὑπακούετε hupakouete** 2pl indic/impr pres act
2. **ὑπακούουσιν hupakouousin** dat pl masc indic/part pres act

3. **ὑπακούει hupakouei** 3sing indic pres act
4. **ὑπακούειν hupakouein** inf pres act
5. **ὑπήκουσεν hupēkousen** 3sing indic aor act
6. **ὑπηκούσατε hupēkousate** 2pl indic aor act
7. **ὑπήκουσαν hupēkousan** 3pl indic aor act
8. **ὑπακοῦσαι hupakousai** inf aor act
9. **ὑπήκουον hupēkouon** 3pl indic imperf act

2 that even the winds and the sea **obey** him!.......... Matt 8:27
2 even the unclean spirits, and they **do obey** him...... Mark 1:27
2 that even the wind and the sea **obey** him?.............. 4:41
2 even the winds and water, and they **obey** him....... Luke 8:25
5 be thou planted in the sea; and it **should obey** you..... 17:6
9 and a great company of the priests **were obedient**.... Acts 6:7
8 a damsel came to **hearken**, named Rhoda............. 12:13
4 that ye **should obey** it in the lusts thereof.......... Rom 6:12
1 his servants ye are to whom ye **obey**;................. 6:16
6 but ye **have obeyed** from the heart..................... 6:17
7 But they have not all **obeyed** the gospel............... 10:16
1 Children, **obey** your parents in the Lord:............ Eph 6:1
1 Servants, **be obedient** to ... your masters................ 6:5
6 Wherefore, my beloved, as ye have always **obeyed**,.. Phlp 2:12
1 Children, **obey** your parents in all things:............ Col 3:20
1 Servants, **obey** in all things your masters.............. 3:22
2 that **obey** not the gospel of our Lord Jesus Christ:...2 Th 1:8
3 And if any man **obey** not our word by this epistle,...... 3:14
2 of eternal salvation unto all them **that obey** him;..... Heb 5:9
5 **obeyed**; and he went out,.............................. 11:8
5 Even as Sara **obeyed** Abraham, calling him lord:.....1 Pt 3:6

Classical Greek

Hupakouō, from the preposition *hupo* (5097) and the verb *akouō* (189), "I hear," means "to listen, give ear to" (*Liddell-Scott*). The idea of "response" or "answer" is implied; thus, it can refer to someone "answering" a door or to legal parties who appear in court (in response to a summons). *Hupakouō* also connotes "obedience" that comes from "hearing." Thus one "regards" instruction or warning, or one "submits" or "complies with" a rule or law (ibid.; cf. *Moulton-Milligan*).

Septuagint Usage

Ordinarily *hupakouō* translates either *shāmaʿ* (qal, "to hear"; often simply *akouō* in the Septuagint) or *ʿānâh* (qal, "to answer") in the Septuagint. However, six other Hebrew words are rendered by it. Abraham listened to Sarah's advice to sleep with her maidservant Hagar (Genesis 16:2). And because Abraham "obeyed" in the matter of sacrificing Isaac, the Lord God promised to bless him (Genesis 22:18).

The negative construction frequently occurs in the Septuagint. In contrast to the consequences of obedience, if Israel failed to listen and to obey (often the subjunctive *mē hupakousēte*), God is justified in punishing them (e.g., Leviticus 26:14,18,21,27; cf. Proverbs 15:23; 21:13). Regularly it is the voice of God or others that is obeyed or disobeyed (e.g., Deuteronomy 21:18,20; 26:14; Joshua 22:2; Judges 2:20).

New Testament Usage

Twenty-one instances of *hupakouō* occur in the New Testament, 11 of which are attributed to Paul. The Gospel writers tell of evil spirits or strong winds which obey Jesus' command (Mark 1:27; 4:41, with parallels; cf. Luke 8:25; 17:6, of disciples' commands being obeyed). Luke utilized *hupakouō* in a religious connection in Acts 6:7 when he wrote of priests who "were *obedient* to the faith." But in Acts 12:13 he more closely followed the secular understanding of "to answer" (of Rhoda's answering the door).

Paul used *hupakouō* in terms of being obedient (as a slave) to either sin or righteousness (Romans 6:12,16,17; cf. Ephesians 6:5; Colossians 3:20). He also (indirectly) spoke of being obedient to the gospel (cf. 2 Thessalonians 1:8; 3:14).

The Book of Hebrews tells of Christ's obedience (*hupakoē* [5056]) as a son (Hebrews 5:8) which enables those who "obey" (*hupakouō*) Him to participate in the salvation He secures (Hebrews 5:9; cf. Ephesians 6:1; Colossians 3:20, of children's obedience to parents).

STRONG 5219, BAUER 837, MOULTON-MILLIGAN 650, KITTEL 1:223-24, LIDDELL-SCOTT 1851, COLIN BROWN 2:179.

5058. ὕπανδρος hupandros adj

Subject to a man, married.

CROSS-REFERENCE:
ἀνήρ anēr (433)

1. **ὕπανδρος hupandros** nom sing fem

1 For the woman which **hath an husband** is bound..... Rom 7:2

This word is a compound of *hupo* (5097), "under, subject to," and *anēr* (433), "man, husband." It appears once in the New Testament, Romans 7:2. In this verse it identifies the status of "the *married* woman (who) is bound by law to her husband while he is living" (NASB).

STRONG 5220, BAUER 837, MOULTON-MILLIGAN 650, LIDDELL-SCOTT 1852.

5059. ὑπαντάω hupantaō verb

To meet, come against, oppose.

COGNATE:
καταντάω katantaō (2628)

SYNONYMS:
ἀπαντάω apantaō (524)
συμβαίνω sumbainō (4670)
συναντάω sunantaō (4727)

קָדַם qādham (7207), Meet (Sir 15:2).

קָרָא qārâ' (7410), Call; come to (Sir 12:17).

קָרֵב qārēv (7414), Meet (Sir 9:3).

קָרָה qārâh (7424), Happen (Dn 10:14).

1. ὑπήντησεν hupēntēsen 3sing indic aor act
2. ὑπήντησαν hupēntēsan 3pl indic aor act
3. ὑπαντῆσαι hupantēsai inf aor act

2 there met him two possessed with devils,........... Matt 8:28
1 behold, Jesus met them and greeted them. (NASB).... 28:9
1 a man ... with an unclean spirit met Him. (NASB)..Mark 5:2
1 there met him out of the city a certain man,........Luke 8:27
3 with ten thousand men to encounter (NASB).......... 14:31
2 his slaves met him, saying that his son (NASB)..... John 4:51
1 heard that Jesus was coming, went and met him:...... 11:20
1 but was in that place where Martha met him.......... 11:30
1 For this cause the people also met him,............... 12:18
3 having a spirit of divination met us, (NASB).......Acts 16:16

Classical Greek

This verb is actually a combination of two prepositions: *hupo* (5097), "by, below, through," and a derivative of *anti* (470), "in place of, because of, opposite." *Hupantaō* means "to go to meet" someone or something with a sense of purpose or directness. Such meeting may include an element of hostility or opposition.

In each of the extra-Biblical uses *hupantaō* apparently means "to meet" or "to present oneself" (*Moulton-Milligan*). The confrontational aspect of *hupantaō* is more commonly found in the New Testament usage. The word occurs in the Septuagint in Tobit 7:1; Sirach 9:3; Daniel 10:14.

New Testament Usage

Hupantaō occurs five times in the New Testament, all of these in the Gospels. In Matthew 8:28, some texts of Mark 5:2, and Luke 8:27 the continuity of the synoptic accounts is demonstrated by the use of *hupantaō* by all three writers in describing the way in which Jesus was approached at Gerasa by those possessed by demons.

In some texts of Matthew 28:9 Jesus "met" Mary Magdalene and Mary as they fled from the tomb. This occasion, as any time Christ met His followers, brought them great joy and a response of heartfelt worship.

Luke's use of *hupantaō* (*apantaō* [524] in the *Textus Receptus*) describes the hostile meeting of rival kings (Luke 14:31) as well as those who met Christ from their position of need (10 lepers, 17:12). John's use of *hupantaō* is consistent; in references where people are "going to meet" with Christ, there is great excitement and anticipation over what He had done or would do (4:51 [some texts]; 11:20; 12:18).

The Book of Acts reminds us that the followers of Christ are also met with confrontations by foreign spirits. Paul and Silas were "met" (*apantaō, Textus Receptus*) (confrontational) by the possessed young woman in 16:16. Similar to Christ's experience, the demon spirit cried out that the apostles were true messengers of God. The apostles demonstrated the same victorious power of Christ over the demon spirit as described in the Gospels.

Strong 5221, Bauer 837, Moulton-Milligan 650, Kittel 3:625-26, Liddell-Scott 1852, Colin Brown 1:324-25.

5060. ὑπάντησις hupantēsis noun

A meeting, a going to meet.

Cross-Reference:
κατaντάω katantaō (2628)

קָרָא qārâ' (7410), Meet (Jgs 11:34).

1. ὑπάντησιν hupantēsin acc sing fem

1 city came out to meet Jesus; (NASB)...............Matt 8:34
1 and went out to meet the bridegroom. (NASB)........ 25:1
1 and went forth to meet him, and cried, Hosanna:.. John 12:13

Hupantēsis is an abstract noun related to *hupantaō* (5059), "to meet." It means "a meeting," especially a purposeful one; "a going out *to meet*" or "*for a meeting with* someone."

It appears three times in the New Testament: in Matthew 8:34 of the Gadarenes who were going out to meet Jesus (*sunantēsis* [4728], *Textus Receptus*); in Matthew 25:1 of the 10 virgins who were going out to meet the bridegroom (*apantēsis* [525], *Textus Receptus*); and in John 12:13 of the crowds who were going out to meet Jesus at the Triumphal Entry. In all three cases it is preceded by the verb form "came" or "went out" and the preposition *eis* (1506B), "into, for." It is followed by the identification of the persons being met.

Strong 5222, Bauer 837, Moulton-Milligan 650, Kittel 3:625-26, Liddell-Scott 1852, Colin Brown 1:324-25.

5061. ὕπαρξις huparxis noun

Existence, substance, property.

Cognate:
ἀρχή archē (741)

Synonym:
οὐσία ousia (3639)

הוֹן hôn (2019), Wealth (Prv 13:11, 18:11, 19:14).

יֵשׁ yēsh (3552), There is, existence; wealth (Prv 8:21).

מִקְנֶה miqneh (4898), Flock, cattle (Ps 78:48 [77:48], Jer 9:10).

רְכוּשׁ rᵉkhûsh (7688), Possessions, property (2 Chr 35:7, Ezr 10:8).

1. **ὕπαρξιν huparxin** acc sing fem
2. **ὑπάρξεις huparxeis** acc pl fem

2 And sold their possessions and **goods**,.............. Acts 2:45
1 in heaven a better and an enduring **substance**....... Heb 10:34

Huparxis is an abstract noun pressed into a concrete usage in its New Testament occurrence. It is derived from the verb *huparchō* (5062) and shares the same range of meanings as that verb. It is used either of being ("existence, reality, substance") or of property ("possessions"; *Bauer*).

In the New Testament it is used only with the latter meaning, "possessions," similar in meaning to *ta huparchonta*, the neuter plural participle of *huparchō* (cf. Acts 2:45). In Hebrews 10:34 it appears in parallel with and slightly contrasted to *ta huparchonta*: ". . . and accepted joyfully the seizure of your *property* (*tōn huparchontōn*), knowing that you have . . . a better *possession* (*huparxin*)" (NASB).

Strong 5223, Bauer 837, Moulton-Milligan 650, Liddell-Scott 1853, Colin Brown 2:845-47.

5062. ὑπάρχω huparchō verb

Be, exist; have, possess.

Cross-Reference:
ἀρχή archē (741)

הָיָה hāyâh (2030), Is, be (Dt 20:14, Ps 109:12 [108:12], Ob 16).

יֵשׁ yēsh (3552), There is, have (Est 3:8, Mal 1:14).

לִין lîn (4053), Lodge (Jer 4:14).

מְכוֹנָה mᵉkhônāh (4488), Estate (Sir 41:1).

1. **ὑπάρχουσιν huparchousin** dat pl neu indic/part pres act
2. **ὑπάρχει huparchei** 3sing indic pres act
3. **ὑπάρχωσιν huparchōsin** 3pl subj pres act
4. **ὑπάρχοντα huparchonta** nom/acc sing/pl masc/neu part pres act
5. **ὑπάρχοντος huparchontos** gen sing masc/neu part pres act
6. **ὑπάρχων huparchōn** nom sing masc part pres act
7. **ὑπάρχοντες huparchontes** nom pl masc part pres act
8. **ὑπάρχοντας huparchontas** acc pl masc part pres act
9. **ὑπαρχούσης huparchousēs** gen sing fem part pres act
10. **ὑπαρχόντων huparchontōn** gen pl neu part pres act
11. **ὑπάρχειν huparchein** inf pres act
12. **ὑπῆρχεν hupērchen** 3sing indic imperf act
13. **ὑπῆρχον hupērchon** 3pl indic imperf act

4 go and sell **that thou hast**, and give to the poor,.. Matt 19:21
1 That he shall make him ruler over all his **goods**....... 24:47
4 and delivered unto them his **goods**.................. 25:14
7 are gorgeously apparelled, and **live** delicately,...... Luke 7:25
10 which ministered unto him of their **substance**.......... 8:3
12 Jairus, and he **was** a ruler of the synagogue:........... 8:41
6 **is** least among you all, the same shall be great......... 9:48
7 If ye then, **being** evil, know how to give good gifts... 11:13
4 armed keepeth his palace, his **goods** are in peace:.... 11:21
10 the abundance of the things which he **possesseth**...... 12:15
4 Sell **that ye have**, and give alms;..................... 12:33
1 that he will make him ruler over all **that he hath**..... 12:44
1 he be of you that forsaketh not all **that he hath**,...... 14:33
4 accused unto him that he had wasted his **goods**....... 16:1
7 And the Pharisees also, who **were** covetous,.......... 16:14
6 And in hell he lift up his eyes, **being** in torments,.... 16:23
10 Lord, the half of my **goods** I give to the poor;....... 19:8
6 there was a man named Joseph, a counsellor; (NT)... 23:50
6 Therefore **being** a prophet,........................ Acts 2:30
6 a certain man lame from his mother's (NT)........... 3:2
2 Then Peter said, Silver and gold **have** I none;......... 3:6
10 the things which he **possessed** was his own;............ 4:32
12 Neither **was** there any among them that lacked:....... 4:34
13 **were** possessors of lands or houses sold them,......... 4:34
5 **Having** land, sold it, and brought the money,.......... 4:37
12 after it was sold, **was** it not in thine own power?...... 5:4
6 But he, **being** full of the Holy Ghost,................ 7:55
13 only **they were** baptized in the name of the Lord...... 8:16
12 Wherein **were** all manner of fourfooted beasts........ 10:12
6 **being** a cripple from his mother's womb,............ 14:8
12 for they knew all that his father **was** a Greek.......... 16:3
7 men, **being** Jews, do exceedingly trouble our city,..... 16:20
8 beaten us openly uncondemned, **being** Romans,....... 16:37
6 seeing that he **is** Lord of heaven and earth,.......... 17:24
4 though he **be** not far from every one of us:.......... 17:27
7 Forasmuch then as we **are** the offspring of God,...... 17:29
11 ye ought **to be** quiet, and to do nothing rashly........ 19:36
5 there **being** no cause whereby we may give........... 19:40
1 and they **are** all zealous of the law:.................. 21:20
6 and **was** zealous toward God, as ye all are this day... 22:3
5 the haven **was** not commodious to winter in,......... 27:12
9 But after long abstinence Paul stood forth (NT)...... 27:21
2 to take some meat: for this **is** for your health:....... 27:34
12 In the same quarters **were** possessions of the chief.... 28:7
11 because there **was** no cause of death in me........... 28:18
6 when he **was** about an hundred years old,......... Rom 4:19
11 I suppose therefore that this **is** good.............. 1 Co 7:26
6 forasmuch as he **is** the image and glory of God:...... 11:7
11 I hear that **there be** divisions among you;........... 11:18
11 those members ... which seem **to be** more feeble,..... 12:22
4 And though I bestow all my **goods** to feed the poor,.. 13:3
6 but **being** more forward, of his own accord he went 2 Co 8:17
6 nevertheless, **being** crafty, I caught you with guile..... 12:16
6 **being** more exceedingly zealous of the traditions.... Gal 1:14
6 unto Peter before them all, If thou, **being** a Jew,...... 2:14
6 Who, **being** in the form of God,................. Phlp 2:6
2 For our conversation **is** in heaven;.................... 3:20
10 and took joyfully the spoiling of your **goods**,...... Heb 10:34
3 or sister **be** naked, and destitute of daily food,...... Jas 2:15
4 For if these things **be** in you, and abound,......... 2 Pt 1:8
7 they themselves **are** the servants of corruption:........ 2:19
11 **to be** in all holy conversation and godliness,........... 3:11

Classical Greek

Huparchō occurs as early as Homer (Eighth Century B.C.) with the meaning "begin, initiate." In classical Greek it developed other specialized shades of meaning, e.g., "an *existing* property, *current* price, *proper* nature, *subsistence* of a quality (in philosophy)" (*Liddell-Scott*). The Koine papyri exhibit the following meanings; "be, exist; have, possess," or, as a participle, "possessions" (*Moulton-Milligan*).

Septuagint Usage

The word occurs over 150 times in the Septuagint. It has the same variety of meanings as in the classical literature. Frequently *huparchō* appears as a plural participle with the sense "possessions." Thus, Genesis 12:5 notes that Abram took all his possessions from Haran. As a finite verb *huparchō* can mean "possess": "Whom *have* I in heaven" (Psalm 73:25 [LXX 72:25]). It can also be used to denote existence. In Genesis 42:13 the sons of Jacob state that Joseph "is not," i.e., he no longer exists; he is dead.

New Testament Usage

Among the New Testament usages, a significant group (especially in the Gospels) involves the neuter plural participle *ta huparchonta* which means "possessions" (Matthew 19:21; 24:47; 25:14; Luke 8:3; 11:21; 12:15,33,44; 14:33; 16:1; 19:8; Acts 4:32; 1 Corinthians 13:3; Hebrews 10:34). These passages commonly involve a related possessive form (yours, his, etc.). Three passages form the bridge between the idea of "being" and this idea of "being possessed." They use the verb form with a related dative form ("to" or "for" someone). These verses are Acts 3:6 (literally "there is no silver and gold to me," i.e., "I have no silver and gold" [KJV]); 4:37 (literally "a field being to him" i.e., "having land" [KJV]); and 2 Peter 1:8 (literally "these things belonging to you," i.e., "these things be in you" [KJV]).

The most common New Testament usages, however, are in the meaning range "be, exist, exist as, live." There are about 40 such occurrences. It appears nine times in the sense "be, exist, live" with a preposition following, e.g., "in fine clothes" (Luke 7:25, NIV); "in torments" (Luke 16:23); "in heaven" (Philippians 3:20); "in holy conduct" (2 Peter 3:11, NASB). As a verb of being, it is followed regularly by a noun (e.g., synagogue ruler, prophet, a Greek, a Jew, God's offspring) or by an adjective or participle (e.g., lesser, evil, money-loving, blind, zealous, 100-year-old). It occurs 17 times in each of these two constructions.

A notable occurrence of the word involving a preposition is Philippians 2:6: "who, being in the form of God . . . . " In this verse the verb *huparchō* is appropriate to the idea of Christ's original existence in that form. However, the full proof of that concept comes from the total context, not from the verb form alone.

Strong 5225, Bauer 838, Moulton-Milligan 650-51, Liddell-Scott 1853-54.

5063. ὑπείκω hupeikō verb

Yield (to), submit (to).

1. ὑπείκετε hupeikete 2pl impr pres act

1 submit yourselves: for they watch for your souls,... Heb 13:17

This word is a compound of *eikō* (1493), "give way, withdraw, yield," and *hupo* (5097), "under." The preposition in this case emphasizes the basic meaning of the simple verb form. Thus *hupeikō* means "yield" or "submit" to someone or some authority. It is used in the New Testament only in Hebrews 13:17 where it is parallel in meaning to *peithō* (3844): "Obey them that have the rule over you, and *submit* yourselves."

Strong 5226, Bauer 838, Moulton-Milligan 651, Liddell-Scott 1854-55.

5064. ὑπεναντίος hupenantios adj

Opposite to, against, hostile to.

אָיַב 'āyav (342), Enemy (Lv 26:16, 2 Chr 20:29, Jb 33:10).

צַר tsar (7141), Enemy (Dt 32:27, Is 26:11, Na 1:2).

קוּם qûm (7251), Rise up (Ex 15:7); enemy (Ex 32:25).

שָׂנֵא sānē' (7983), One who hates, enemy (Gn 24:60, Ex 1:10, 2 Chr 1:11).

1. ὑπεναντίους hupenantious acc pl masc
2. ὑπεναντίον hupenantion nom/acc sing neu

2 that was against us, which was contrary to us,........Col 2:14
1 which shall devour the adversaries..................Heb 10:27

Classical Greek and Septuagint Usage

Hupenantios is a double compound of *antios*, "over against, opposite," an adjectival counterpart of the preposition *anti* (470). (For the first level compound see *enantios* [1711].) The additional compounding with *hupo* (5097) seems to strengthen the idea of opposition. In classical Greek *hupenantios* can refer to an "enemy" or a meeting of armies. It means "opposite" or "contrary" and used as a substantive can mean "incongruities" (*Liddell-Scott*). *Hupenantios* occurs over three dozen times in the Septuagint, always in reference to "the adversaries" or "(the) enemy" (cf. Genesis 22:17).

New Testament Usage

It appears in the New Testament twice, once purely as an adjective (Colossians 2:14, "the handwriting of ordinances . . . , which was *contrary to* us") and once functioning as a plural noun (Hebrews 10:27, "fiery indignation, which shall devour the *adversaries*").

STRONG 5227, BAUER 838, MOULTON-MILLIGAN 651, LIDDELL-SCOTT 1856.

5065. ὑπέρ huper prep

Over, above, more than; for, for the sake of.

1. ὑπέρ huper

1 and pray **for** them which despitefully use you,....... Matt 5:44
1 The disciple is not **above** his master,.................. 10:24
1 nor the servant **above** his lord....................... 10:24
1 He that loveth father or mother **more than** me........ 10:37
1 and he that loveth son or daughter **more than** me...... 10:37
1 For he that is not against us is **on** our part......... Mark 9:40
1 blood ... which is poured out **for** many. (NASB)....... 14:24
1 and pray **for** them which despitefully use you........ Luke 6:28
1 The disciple is not **above** his master:.................. 6:40
1 for he that is not against us is **for** us.................. 9:50
1 in their generation wiser **than** the children of light..... 16:8
1 This is my body which is given **for** you:............... 22:19
1 new testament in my blood, which is shed **for** you..... 22:20
1 This is He **on behalf of** whom I said, (NASB)....... John 1:30
1 my flesh, which I will give **for** the life of the world...... 6:51
1 the good shepherd giveth his life **for** the sheep......... 10:11
1 and I lay down my life **for** the sheep................. 10:15
1 sickness is not unto death, but **for** the glory of God,... 11:4
1 that one man should die **for** the people,............... 11:50
1 prophesied that Jesus should die **for** that nation;....... 11:51
1 And not **for** that nation only,........................ 11:52
1 I will lay down my life **for** thy **sake**................. 13:37
1 Wilt thou lay down thy life **for** my **sake?**............. 13:38
1 that a man lay down his life **for** his friends........... 15:13
1 And **for** their sakes I sanctify myself,................. 17:19
1 expedient that one man should die **for** the people...... 18:14
1 were counted worthy to suffer shame **for** his name... Acts 5:41
1 and said, Pray ye to the Lord **for** me,................... 8:24
1 great things he must suffer **for** my name's **sake**.......... 9:16
1 without ceasing of the church unto God **for** him....... 12:5
1 Men that have hazarded their lives **for** the name....... 15:26
1 to die at Jerusalem **for** the name of the Lord Jesus..... 21:13
1 offering should be offered **for** every one of them....... 21:26
1 Thou art permitted to speak **for** thyself............... 26:1
1 **above** the brightness of the sun,...................... 26:13
1 to the faith among all nations, **for** his name:........ Rom 1:5
1 I thank my God through Jesus Christ **for** you all,....... 1:8
1 in due time Christ died **for** the ungodly................. 5:6
1 For scarcely **for** a righteous man will one die:.......... 5:7
1 **for** a good man some would even dare to die........... 5:7
1 while we were yet sinners, Christ died **for** us........... 5:8
1 but the Spirit itself maketh intercession **for** us.......... 8:26
1 because he maketh intercession **for** the saints........... 8:27
1 If God be **for** us, who can be against us?.............. 8:31
1 not his own Son, but delivered him up **for** us all,....... 8:32
1 who also maketh intercession **for** us.................... 8:34
1 myself were accursed from Christ **for** my brethren,...... 9:3
1 Esaias also crieth **concerning** Israel,.................... 9:27
1 my heart's desire and prayer to God **for** Israel is,...... 10:1
1 Destroy not him ... **for** whom Christ died............. 14:15
1 a minister of the circumcision **for** the truth of God,.... 15:8
1 that the Gentiles might glorify God **for** his mercy;..... 15:9
1 together with me in your prayers to God **for** me;...... 15:30
1 Who have **for** my life laid down their own necks:...... 16:4
1 Is Christ divided? was Paul crucified **for** you?....... 1 Co 1:13
1 not to think of men **above** that which is written,..... 1 Co 4:6
1 of you be puffed up **for** one against another............ 4:6
1 For even Christ our passover is sacrificed **for** us:........ 5:7
1 suffer you to be tempted **above** that ye are able;....... 10:13
1 evil spoken of **for** that for which I give thanks?....... 10:30
1 eat: this is my body, which is broken **for** you:......... 11:24
1 should have the same care one **for** another............ 12:25
1 Christ died **for** our sins according to the scriptures;.... 15:3
1 shall they do which are baptized **for** the dead,......... 15:29
1 why are they then baptized **for** the dead?............. 15:29
1 it is **for** your consolation and salvation,............. 2 Co 1:6
1 it is **for** your consolation and salvation................ 1:6
1 And our hope **of** you is stedfast,....................... 1:7
1 have you ignorant **of** our trouble which came to us..... 1:8
1 we were pressed out of measure, **above** strength,........ 1:8
1 Ye also helping together by prayer **for** us,.............. 1:11
1 thanks may be given by many **on** our **behalf**........... 1:11
1 but give you occasion to glory **on** our **behalf**,........... 5:12
1 that if one died **for** all, then were all dead:............. 5:14
1 And that he died **for** all,............................. 5:15
1 but unto him which died **for** them, and rose again....... 5:15
1 Now then we are ambassadors **for** Christ,.............. 5:20
1 we pray you **in** Christ's **stead**,........................ 5:20
1 For he hath made him to be sin **for** us,................ 5:21
1 great is my glorying **of** you:.......................... 7:4
1 your mourning, your fervent mind **toward** me;.......... 7:7
1 our care **for** you in the sight of God might appear...... 7:12
1 For if I have boasted any thing to him **of** you,.......... 7:14
1 yea, and **beyond** their power they were willing.......... 8:3
1 same earnest care into the heart of Titus **for** you........ 8:16
1 Whether any do inquire **of** Titus,...................... 8:23
1 and of our boasting **on** your **behalf**.................... 8:24
1 for which I boast **of** you to them of Macedonia,........ 9:2
1 lest our boasting **of** you should be in vain............. 9:3
1 And by their prayer **for** you,......................... 9:14
1 I was not a whit behind the **very** chiefest apostles...... 11:5
1 ministers of Christ? I speak as a fool I am **more**;...... 11:23
1 **Of** such an one will I glory:......................... 12:5
1 **of** myself I will not glory, but in mine infirmities....... 12:5
1 think of me **above** that which he seeth me to be,...... 12:6
1 **For** this thing I besought the Lord thrice,............ 12:8
1 in persecutions, in distresses **for** Christ's sake:......... 12:10
1 in nothing am I behind the **very** chiefest apostles,...... 12:11
1 is it wherein ye were inferior **to** other churches,....... 12:13
1 And I will very gladly spend and be spent **for** you;.... 12:15
1 we do all things, dearly beloved, **for** your edifying..... 12:19
1 can do nothing against the truth, but **for** the truth...... 13:8
1 Who gave himself **for** our sins,..................... Gal 1:4
1 And profited in the Jews' religion **above** many.......... 1:14
1 who loved me, and gave himself **for** me............... 2:20
1 being made a curse **for** us: for it is written,............ 3:13
1 Cease not to give thanks **for** you,................... Eph 1:16
1 to be the head **over** all things to the church,............ 1:22
1 the prisoner of Jesus Christ **for** you Gentiles,........... 3:1
1 I desire that ye faint not at my tribulations **for** you,..... 3:13
1 to do **exceeding** abundantly above all that we ask....... 3:20
1 **abundantly** above all that we ask or think,.............. 3:20
1 and hath given himself **for** us an offering............... 5:2
1 Giving thanks always **for** all things unto God........... 5:20
1 also loved the church, and gave himself **for** it;.......... 5:25
1 And **for** me, that utterance may be given unto me,...... 6:19
1 **For** which I am an ambassador in bonds:............... 6:20
1 Always in every prayer of mine **for** you all......... Phlp 1:4
1 Even as it is meet for me to think this **of** you all,...... 1:7
1 For unto you it is given in the **behalf of** Christ,......... 1:29
1 but also to suffer **for** his **sake**;......................... 1:29
1 and given him a name which is **above** every name:...... 2:9
1 both to will and to do **of** his good pleasure............ 2:13
1 your care **of** me hath flourished again;................. 4:10
1 who is **for** you a faithful minister of Christ;.......... Col 1:7
1 since ... we heard it, do not cease to pray **for** you,...... 1:9
1 Who now rejoice in my sufferings **for** you,............. 1:24
1 afflictions of Christ in my flesh **for** his body's sake,..... 1:24
1 great a struggle I have **on** your **behalf**, (NASB)......... 2:1
1 always labouring fervently **for** you in prayers,........... 4:12
1 bear him record, that he hath a great zeal **for** you,...... 4:13
1 and encourage you **as to** your faith, (NASB)........ 1 Th 3:2

1 praying exceedingly that we might see (NT)......... 1 Th 3:10
1 Who died for us, that, whether we wake or sleep,....... 5:10
1 And to esteem them very highly in love............... 5:13
1 in the churches of God for your patience and faith.. 2 Th 1:4
1 worthy of the kingdom ... for which ye also suffer:...... 1:5
1 by the coming of our Lord Jesus Christ,................ 2:1
1 and giving of thanks, be made for all men;......... 1 Tm 2:1
1 For kings, and for all that are in authority;............ 2:2
1 Who gave himself a ransom for all,.................... 2:6
1 Who gave himself for us,........................... Tit 2:14
1 that in thy stead he might have ministered unto me Phlm 1:13
1 but above a servant, a brother beloved,................ 1:16
1 knowing that thou wilt also do more than I say......... 1:21
1 should taste death for every man.................... Heb 2:9
1 and sharper than any twoedged sword,................. 4:12
1 is ordained for men in things pertaining to God,........ 5:1
1 that he may offer both gifts and sacrifices for sins:...... 5:1
1 for the people, so also for himself, to offer for sins...... 5:3
1 Whither the forerunner is for us entered,............... 6:20
1 seeing he ever liveth to make intercession for them...... 7:25
1 first for his own sins, and then for the people's:........ 7:27
1 which he offered for himself, and for ... the people:..... 9:7
1 now to appear in the presence of God for us:.......... 9:24
1 after he had offered one sacrifice for sins for ever,..... 10:12
1 submit yourselves: for they watch for your souls,...... 13:17
1 Confess your faults ... and pray one for another,..... Jas 5:16
1 Christ also suffered for us, leaving us an example,... 1 Pt 2:21
1 hath once suffered for sins, the just for the unjust,...... 3:18
1 Forasmuch then as Christ hath suffered for us.......... 4:1
1 because he laid down his life for us:............... 1 Jn 3:16
1 we ought to lay down our lives for the brethren......... 3:16
1 Because that for his name's sake they went forth,... 3 Jn 1:7

Huper, a common preposition, appears approximately 160 times in the New Testament, about 135 times with the genitive case meaning "for," etc.; 20 times with the accusative case meaning "above, beyond," etc.; and once as a separate adverb meaning "more" (2 Corinthians 11:23). In compounds with verbs, nouns, or adverbs it adds the ideas of: (1) "over" or "beyond," spatially; (2) "for" someone or something; or (3) "beyond (normal) limits." (Compare the English *hyper-* and *super-* forms which are derived from this Greek word and its cognate Latin form, respectively.)

Classical Greek

From an original meaning of "over" or "above" *huper* developed a variety of other literal and figurative meanings. The figurative meanings are concerned with relative position, e.g., "more than, beyond." It conveys the idea of a person being "above" or "over" another, either literally or figuratively. This person may be acting to protect or represent another, thus such meanings as "for (the sake of), in behalf of," and even "instead of" developed.

Moulton-Milligan cites examples of the same variety of usages in the papyri as well as the more general meaning of "concerning" or "about." In such cases *huper* is roughly equivalent to *peri* (3875). *Moulton-Milligan* also calls attention to the decreasing use of *huper* with the accusative case in later Greek.

Septuagint Usage

In the Septuagint *huper* is used about 450 times, slightly over half of them with the accusative (objective) case. This frequent use with the accusative is in contrast with the New Testament where the genitive case is predominant. According to *Bauer* none of the Septuagint uses are in a local (literal) sense; all are figurative.

New Testament Usage

In the New Testament *huper*, used with the genitive or accusative cases, is not used literally of position. The most common usage is with the sense of "for" someone or something (genitive). Some of these involve the more specific idea of "in their behalf" or "for their sake." Specific usage of this type involves the following constructions: (1) after verbs of speaking, praying, etc. (e.g., Acts 26:1, "thou art permitted to speak *for* [i.e., in behalf of] thyself"); (2) with verbs of being (e.g., Mark 9:40, Luke 9:50, "he that is not against us is *for* us"); (3) following verbs of personal concern, effort, sacrifice, dying, etc. (Luke 22:20, "my blood . . . shed *for* you"; Romans 8:32, "delivered him up *for* us all"). Related to this last construction is a usage with the genitive case of the thing affected, e.g., "the life of the world" (= to bring life to), John 6:51; "the glory of God," John 11:4; "sins" (= to atone for), Galatians 1:4. *Huper* is also used to refer to actions as done for Christ (2 Corinthians 5:20; 12:10) or "his name" (Acts 5:41, etc.).

Huper is also used in instances where someone goes beyond just acting in behalf of someone to actually being God's representative or substitute, i.e., being "in place of" or "instead of" the other (e.g., Romans 9:3; 1 Corinthians 15:29; 2 Corinthians 5:14,15; Galatians 3:13; Philemon 13). This meaning is more precisely expressed by *anti* (470) which is more commonly used for this idea.

At the other extreme, *huper* is used in some passages in the weaker sense of "concerning, with reference to" (compare *peri* [3875]): e.g., Romans 9:27; 2 Corinthians 1:7,8; 5:12; 7:4,14; 8:23,24; 9:2,3; 12:5 (twice),8; Philippians 1:7; 2 Thessalonians 1:4; 2:1.

In the 20 New Testament occurrences with the accusative case *huper* is used only figuratively in the sense of excelling or surpassing: "over, above, beyond, more than." Examples include 1 Corinthians 4:6, "*beyond* what is written" (NIV); Philemon 16, "*more than* a slave" (RSV); Philemon 21, "even *more than* I ask" (NIV). A special form of this usage is its appearance after comparative adjectives (e.g., Luke 16:8; Hebrews 4:12) or a verb expressing a comparison (2 Corinthians 12:13).

Strong 5228, Bauer 838-39, Moulton-Milligan 651-52, Kittel 8:507-16, Liddell-Scott 1857-58, Colin Brown 3:1171-74,1176,1180,1193,1196-97, 1199,1203,1207-8.

5067 and 5066

5066. ὑπεραίρω huperairō verb

Raise up over, exalt.

Cross-Reference:

αἴρω airō (142)

נָשָׂא nāsâ' (5558), Lift up, carry; niphal: be exalted (2 Chr 32:23).

עָבַר 'āvar (5882), Go over (Ps 38:4 [37:4]).

1. ὑπεραίρωμαι **huperairōmai** 1sing subj pres mid

2. ὑπεραιρόμενος **huperairomenos** nom sing masc part pres mid

1 **And lest I should be exalted above measure** .... 2 Co 12:7
1 **lest I should be exalted above measure**................. 12:7
2 **and exalteth himself above all that is called God,**.... 2 Th 2:4

Classical Greek

This word is a compound of *huper* (5065), "over, above," and *airō* (142), "I lift up." The literal idea of lifting or raising something over or beyond some reference point gave rise to figurative uses, both positive and negative. Literally *huperairō* can mean "to raise up, jump over, pass beyond," or "overflow." Figuratively it can mean "to excel, surpass, exceed" (*Liddell-Scott*).

Septuagint Usage

In the Septuagint *huperairō* appears six times, all in a figurative sense. In 2 Chronicles 32:23 the Lord is *exalted* before all. The Psalmist declares that his sins had *risen over* his head (Psalm 38:4 [LXX 37:4]). The good woman *surpasses* all other women (Proverbs 31:29).

New Testament Usage

In the New Testament it appears always in the middle form, *huperairomai*, and always in a negative, figurative sense. It occurs in 2 Corinthians 12:7 (twice) as "lest I *should be exalted above measure*" and in 2 Thessalonians 2:4 of the one "who . . . *exalteth himself* above all that is called God."

Strong 5229, Bauer 839, Moulton-Milligan 652, Liddell-Scott 1858.

5067. ὑπέρακμος huperakmos adj

Past one's prime, excessive passions.

1. ὑπέρακμος **huperakmos** nom sing masc/fem

1 **pass the flower of her age, and need so require,**...... 1 Co 7:36

This word is derived from the preposition *huper* (5065) ("above, beyond" [either in terms of time or intensity]) and the noun *akmē* ("peak" [of development], "climax"). It does not occur in pre-Christian Greek literature, including the Septuagint. Literally this adjective means "beyond the peak" (temporally), such as a woman who has exceeded the age of marriageability, or "beyond the limit" (in terms of intensity), such as passions that are at their height of being able to control them (cf. *Bauer*). Both of these definitions are linguistically justified, and moreover, either definition fits within the context of 1 Corinthians 7:36, the only occurrence of the term in the New Testament.

There are two potential understandings of *huperakmos* in that passage. It may refer to a woman who has exceeded the age of marriageability and whose father or guardian is concerned that she marry. It may also refer to a man whose sexual desire is on the verge of being out of control with the woman to whom he is engaged.

The choice in 1 Corinthians 7:36, however, is beset with difficulties. Resolution of the issue demands answering several questions which are related to the overall dilemma:

(1) How should *parthenos* (3795), which normally means "virgin," be translated in verses 36 and 37? For example, cf. verse 36: the *LB*, which totally avoids the issue by not translating it; Phillips, "woman he loves"; RSV, "betrothed"; KJV, "virgin"; NASB, "virgin *daughter*"; *GNB*, "the girl" (of an engaged couple); NIV, "virgin he is engaged to." The most widely accepted view is that presented by NASB.

(2) Who is the subject ("anyone," NIV) of verse 36 who behaves improperly ("unseemly," KJV—see *aschēmoneō* [801]) toward his *parthenos*? Is it a father/guardian, or is it a fiance?

(3) Is the meaning of *gamizō* (1053B) "to marry" or "to give in marriage"? The latter seems correct. (Except in verse 38, where *ekgamizō* [1534] appears, *gameō* [1053], "marry," occurs.)

(4) What is the definition of *huperakmos*? Does it refer to the woman who is at her "peak" in terms of her age for marrying (this takes the "anyone" to be the father/guardian)? Or does it refer to the man who is "oversexed" (so Barrett, *Harper New Testament Commentaries*, 7a:182),

who Paul then advises to marry? Again, many prefer the translation as a reference to the father. (See Hamar, *Complete Biblical Library, 1 Corinthians*, pp. 349 ff.)

A further thought on the definition of *huperakmos* was made by Ford who wrote that *huperakmos* is linked with the Mishnaic Hebrew *bôgereṯ* meaning "wrinkled." According to Ford, the word refers to the age at which levirate marriage is "incumbent on her" ("The Rabbinic Background of St. Paul's use of *huperakmos*" pp.89ff.; cf. Brown, "Marriage," *Colin Brown*, 2:588).

STRONG 5230, BAUER 839, MOULTON-MILLIGAN 652, LIDDELL-SCOTT 1859, COLIN BROWN 2:587-88.

5068. ὑπεράνω huperanō prep

Far above, above.

CROSS-REFERENCE:
ἄνω anō (504)

1. ὑπεράνω huperanō

1 Far above all principality, and power, and might, ... Eph 1:21
1 same also that ascended up far above all heavens, ... 4:10
1 And over it the cherubims of glory shadowing . . . . Heb 9:5

Huperanō is an adverb which is a compounded form of the adverb *anō* (504), "above," and the preposition *huper* (5065), "over, above." The result is a potentially emphatic adverb, or adverbial preposition, meaning "high above" or "far above." Sometimes, however, it means simply "above"; this meaning was common in the Septuagint.

Huperanō occurs three times in the New Testament and is used exclusively as a preposition. In Ephesians 1:21 and 4:10 it refers, respectively, to Christ's exalted position and to His ascent. In Hebrews 9:5 it describes the position of the "cherubim of glory" *over* the ark of the covenant.

STRONG 5231, BAUER 840, MOULTON-MILLIGAN 652, LIDDELL-SCOTT 1859.

5069. ὑπεραυξάνω huperauxanō verb

Grow exceedingly, increase beyond.

CROSS-REFERENCE:
αὐξάνω auxanō (831)

1. ὑπεραυξάνει huperauxanei 3sing indic pres act

1 because that your faith groweth exceedingly, ... 2 Th 1:3

Huperauxanō is a compound of *huper* (5065), "over, above," and *auxanō*, "grow, increase." The resultant meaning is to "grow or increase beyond normal expectations or limits." It appears once in the New Testament, in 2 Thessalonians 1:3, describing the growth of the faith of the Thessalonian believers.

STRONG 5232, BAUER 840, MOULTON-MILLIGAN 652, KITTEL 8:517-19, LIDDELL-SCOTT 1860, COLIN BROWN 2:128.

5070. ὑπερβαίνω huperbainō verb

Go over/beyond, transgress.

COGNATES:
ἀναβαίνω anabainō (303)
ἀποβαίνω apobainō (571)
βάσις basis (932)
βεβαιόω bebaioō (943)
βέβηλος bebēlos (945)
βῆμα bēma (961)
διαβαίνω diabainō (1218)
ἐκβαίνω ekbainō (1530B)
ἔκβασις ekbasis (1532)
ἐμβαίνω embainō (1671)
ἐπιβαίνω epibainō (1895)
καταβαίνω katabainō (2568)
κατάβασις katabasis (2571)
μεταβαίνω metabainō (3197)
παραβαίνω parabainō (3707)
προβαίνω probainō (4119)
προσαναβαίνω prosanabainō (4178)
συγκαταβαίνω sunkatabainō (4633)
συμβαίνω sumbainō (4670)
συναναβαίνω sunanabainō (4723)

SYNONYMS:
ἁμαρτάνω hamartanō (262)
παραβαίνω parabainō (3707)
παραπίπτω parapiptō (3756)

דָּלַג dālagh (1860), Piel: leap (2 Sm 22:30, Ps 18:29 [17:29]).

יָסַף yāsaph (3362), Add, do again; hiphil: go farther (Jb 38:11).

סוּג sûgh (5657), Deviate, move away; hiphil: remove (Jb 24:2).

עָבַר 'āvar (5882), Go past, go by (2 Sm 18:23, Jb 9:11, Jer 5:22).

1. ὑπερβαίνειν huperbainein inf pres act

1 go beyond and defraud his brother in any matter: . . . 1 Th 4:6

This word is a compound of *huper* (5065), "over, above, beyond," and *bainō*, "I go." It thus involves the idea of going over or beyond something, either literally or figuratively.

Classical Greek

It appears throughout the classical period from Homer (Eighth Century B.C.) on. It is used in either a literal/physical sense ("step over, go beyond"), or in nonphysical ("exceed, transcend, surpass") or figurative/ethical senses ("overstep, transgress") (*Liddell-Scott*). It can also mean "overlook, bypass," or "presume." It is commonly used with a direct object of the thing "gone beyond" but is used intransitively meaning "transgress, sin."

In the ethical sense, "transgress, trespass," it is similar in meaning to *parabainō* (3707). Insofar as they differ, *parabainō* may suggest straying outside the bounds, while *huperbainō* suggests going beyond the limits.

Septuagint Usage

Huperbainō is used over a dozen times in the Septuagint, generally in the literal or physical senses. Examples are David's leaping over a wall (2 Samuel 22:30 [LXX 2 Kings 22:30]; Psalm 18:29 [LXX 17:29]), of the divinely set bounds that the sea must obey (Job 38:11; Jeremiah 5:22, twice), of man's life (Job 14:5) which does not go beyond the days determined for it, or of Ahimaaz' outrunning the Cushite (2 Samuel 18:23 [LXX 2 Kings 18:23]). It is used once in a nonphysical, ethical sense of God's *passing over* "the transgression of the remnant" (Micah 7:18). The Koine usages are essentially the same.

New Testament Usage

The word occurs only once in the New Testament, in 1 Thessalonians 4:6. In this verse it may be taken either absolutely, "transgress," or with the understood direct object of the person wronged (compare the NASB translation ["that no man *transgress* and defraud his brother in the matter,"] with the NIV ["and that in this matter no one should *wrong his brother* or take advantage of him"]). In either case, the flow of thought in the passage contrasts this action with the "sanctification" (*hagiasmos* [38]), i.e., the abstaining from sexual immorality, which is presented in verse 3 as God's will.

STRONG 5233, BAUER 840, MOULTON-MILLIGAN 652, KITTEL 5:743-44, LIDDELL-SCOTT 1860, COLIN BROWN 3:583-84.

5071. ὑπερβαλλόντως huperballontōs adv

Above measure, immeasurably.

CROSS-REFERENCE:
βάλλω ballō (900)

1. ὑπερβαλλόντως huperballontōs

1 **in stripes above measure,** .... **2 Co 11:23**

Huperballontōs is an adverb derived from the participle *huperballōn* and is related to the verb *huperballō*, "to surpass, excel, exceed." It thus means "surpassing measure, exceedingly, immeasurably"; or, comparatively, "to a greater extent." It appears in the Septuagint in Job 15:11, "You (Job) have spoken greatly *to excess*" (author's translation), a paraphrase differing substantially from the Hebrew text.

In the New Testament *huperballontōs* appears once, in 2 Corinthians 11:23. Here it is translated *above measure* (or "more frequently") with reference to the "stripes" (beatings) Paul endured.

STRONG 5234, BAUER 840, MOULTON-MILLIGAN 652, KITTEL 8:520-22, LIDDELL-SCOTT 1860.

5072. ὑπερβάλλω huperballō verb

Surpass, excel, exceed.

CROSS-REFERENCE:
βάλλω ballō (900)

1. ὑπερβάλλοντα huperballonta
acc sing masc part pres act

2. ὑπερβαλλούσης huperballousēs
gen sing fem part pres act

3. ὑπερβάλλουσαν huperballousan
acc sing fem part pres act

4. ὑπερβάλλον huperballon
nom/acc sing neu part pres act

2 **by reason of the glory that excelleth** .... **2 Co 3:10**
3 **for the exceeding grace of God in you** **9:14**
4 **And what is the exceeding greatness of his power** .... **Eph 1:19**
1 **the exceeding riches of his grace in his kindness** **2:7**
3 **know the love of Christ, which passeth knowledge,** **3:19**

Classical Greek

Huperballō is a compound of the preposition *huper* (5065), "above, beyond," and the verb *ballō* (900), "cast, place, put." The idea resulting from the compounding is that of doing or going beyond that which is usual or expected, i.e., "outdoing, surpassing, excelling." In classical Greek usage it appears with both positive ("outshoot, outstrip, outdo") and occasionally negative meanings ("overshoot" or "exceed" in the sense of "be excessive") (*Liddell-Scott*).

Septuagint Usage

In the Septuagint it appears half a dozen times in the apocryphal books and possibly once in Job 15:11. In the Job passage it appears as a variant of *huperballontōs* (5071) in a reference to *exceedingly* "great (i.e., boastful) speech." The Septuagint here is a free paraphrase differing greatly from the Hebrew text. In Ecclesiasticus 5:7 it is used of "postponement" or "delay" of turning to the Lord, and in 25:11 it is used to describe the fear of the Lord as "*surpassing* all things." In 2 Maccabees 4:24 it is used of Menelaus' "outbidding" Jason for the office of high priest. In the other apocryphal references participle forms are used to describe various things as "surpassing, exceedingly great," or "extreme"; for example, wickedness (2 Maccabees 4:13), tortures (2 Maccabees 7:42), and fear (3 Maccabees 2:23).

These various meanings, "exceed, surpass, postpone(ment), outbid," are all supported by contemporary papyri (*Moulton-Milligan*).

New Testament Usage

Huperballō appears five times in the New Testament, in 2 Corinthians and Ephesians. In all five passages the participle is used to describe the overwhelming greatness of some attribute or work of God. In 2 Corinthians 3:10 Paul wrote of "the glory that *excelleth*" that of Moses' face and ministrations, and in 9:14 of the "*exceeding* grace of God." In Ephesians he used the term in still more complex constructions to further emphasize the awesomeness of the things described: "the *exceeding* greatness of his power" (1:19); "the *exceeding* riches of his grace" (2:7); and "the love of Christ, *which passeth* knowledge" (3:19).

STRONG 5235, BAUER 840, MOULTON-MILLIGAN 652, KITTEL 8:520-22, LIDDELL-SCOTT 1860.

5073. ὑπερβολή huperbolē noun

Superiority, excellence.

CROSS-REFERENCE:
βάλλω ballō (900)

1. **ὑπερβολή huperbolē** nom sing fem
2. **ὑπερβολῇ huperbolē** dat sing fem
3. **ὑπερβολήν huperbolēn** acc sing fem

3 that sin by the commandment ... exceeding sinful.... Rom 7:13
3 and yet show I unto you a more excellent way..... 1 Co 12:31
3 we were pressed out of measure, above strength,.... 2 Co 1:8
1 that the excellency of the power may be of God,....... 4:7
3 a far more exceeding and eternal weight of glory;....... 4:17
3 a far more exceeding and eternal weight of glory;....... 4:17
2 through the abundance of the revelations,............. 12:7
3 beyond measure I persecuted the church of God,..... Gal 1:13

Huperbolē is an abstract noun related to *huperballō* (5072), "exceed, excel." It thus suggests a surpassing quality or character: "excellence, superiority, extraordinariness, preeminence," or, negatively, "excess."

Classical Greek and Septuagint Usage

The classical writers used it in the literal senses of "overshooting" mountain passes and of "crossing over" mountains or rivers. *Huperbolē* possesses all the figurative meanings given in the preceding paragraph. In addition, the term refers to deliberate excessive speech, i.e., *hyperbole.* From one meaning of the verb *huperballō,* "delay," the noun referred to a "delay, putting off, postponement."

Huperbolē occurs in 4 Maccabees 3:18 and means "*extreme* bodily agonies." The papyri use it in prepositional phrases in such senses as "exceedingly, excessively (vexed)" and in negative statements of "not *exaggerating*" and "no further *delays*" (*Moulton-Milligan*).

New Testament Usage

In the New Testament Paul used it eight times in four books; Romans, 1 and 2 Corinthians, and Galatians. In five passages it occurs adverbially (in a phrase with the prepositional form *kath',* see *kata* [2567]) to mean "beyond all measure" or "exceedingly." It refers to *exceeding* sinfulness (Romans 7:13); to Paul's *excessive* persecution of the church (Galatians 1:13); to the "*more excellent* way" of love (1 Corinthians 12:31); to Paul's *excessive* burdening in Asia (2 Corinthians 1:8); and to the "*far more exceeding* . . . weight of glory" (2 Corinthians 4:17). Elsewhere in 2 Corinthians it describes "the *excellency* of the power . . . of God" (4:7) and "the *abundance* of the revelations" given to Paul (12:7).

STRONG 5236, BAUER 840, MOULTON-MILLIGAN 652-53, KITTEL 8:520-22, LIDDELL-SCOTT 1860.

5074. ὑπερεῖδον hupereidon verb

Overlook, disregard.

CROSS-REFERENCE:
εἶδον eidon (1481)

עָזַב ʿāzav (6013), Forsake (Jos 1:5).

עָלַם ʿālam (6180), Niphal: be hidden (Na 3:11); hiphil: hide (Ps 10:1 [9:22]); hithpael: hide oneself (Is 58:7).

רָאָה rā'âh (7495), See (Dt 22:4—only some Alexandrinus texts).

1. **ὑπεριδών huperidōn** nom sing masc part aor act

1 And the times of this ignorance God winked at;.... Acts 17:30

This word is a compound of *huper* (5065), "over," and *eidon* (1481), the aorist (simple past tense) of the irregular verb *horaō* (3571), "see, look." Hence, it means "to look over" or "to look down upon" (e.g., "to look down upon" the sea). From this basic meaning is derived the sense of "to overlook" or "take no notice of." By extension, then, it means "to despise" or "to disdain."

The participle form of this compound (*huperidōn*) appears once in the New Testament, in Acts 17:30, with the meaning "to overlook": "The times of this ignorance God *winked at* (i.e., He overlooked)."

STRONG 5237, BAUER 841 (see "huperoraō"), MOULTON-MILLIGAN 653, LIDDELL-SCOTT 1867 (see "huperoraō").

5075. ὑπερέκεινα huperekeina prep

Beyond.

CROSS-REFERENCE:
ἐκεῖ ekei (1550)

1. ὑπερέκεινα huperekeina

1 To preach the gospel in the regions **beyond** you,... 2 Co 10:16

Huperekeina is an adverb compounded of *huper* (5065) and a form of *ekeinos* (1552), "that." The resulting compound means "beyond, on the far side of," etc. *Huperekeina* is used in the New Testament only in 2 Corinthians 10:16. It appears there with the definite article in a phrase used as a noun substitute, "to preach the gospel in *the regions beyond* you."

STRONG 5238, BAUER 840, MOULTON-MILLIGAN 653, LIDDELL-SCOTT 1862.

5076. ὑπερεκπερισσοῦ huperekperissou adv

Superabundantly, exceeding abundantly, beyond all measure.

CROSS-REFERENCE:
περισσεύω perisseuō (3915)

1. ὑπερεκπερισσοῦ huperekperissou

1 **exceedingly abundantly** beyond all (NASB).......... Eph 3:20
1 praying **most earnestly** that we may see (NASB).....1 Th 3:10
1 esteem them **very highly** in love (NASB)............... 5:13

This compound adverb is formed by *huper* (5065), "over"; *ek* (1523), "out of"; and *perissos* (3916), "above measure," and means "exceedingly above and beyond all measure." This heightened form of comparative almost defies any single, simple English translation. All three occurrences in the New Testament are in Paul's letters. In Ephesians 3:20 Paul prayed for the Ephesians to God who is "able to do *exceeding abundantly* above all that we ask or think." This same sense of infinite capacity and ability is seen in Paul's praying "exceedingly" for the Thessalonians (1 Thessalonians 3:10) and in his admonition to the Thessalonians that they "esteem them (those who labor for God among them) *very highly* in love for their work's sake" (1 Thessalonians 5:13). The *Textus Receptus* reads *perissos* in all three verses.

BAUER 840, MOULTON-MILLIGAN 653, KITTEL 6:61-62, LIDDELL-SCOTT 1862.

5076B. ὑπερεκπερισσῶς huperekperissōs adv

Exceedingly, beyond measure.

CROSS-REFERENCE:
περισσεύω perisseuō (3915)

1. ὑπερεκπερισσῶς huperekperissōs

This is an alternate spelling of *huperekperissou*. See the word study at number 5076.

5077. ὑπερεκτείνω huperekteinō verb

Overextend, overstretch.

CROSS-REFERENCE:
ἐκτείνω ekteinō (1601)

1. ὑπερεκτείνομεν huperekteinomen
1pl indic pres act

1 For we **stretch** not ourselves **beyond** our measure,.. 2 Co 10:14

Huperekteinō is a compound of *huper* (5065), "over, beyond," and *ekteinō* (1601), "stretch out." *Ekteinō* is itself a compound of *ek* (1523), "out," and *teinō*, "stretch, extend." The resulting meaning is that of stretching out beyond a normal or suitable extent.

In 2 Corinthians 10:14 Paul denied the suitability of describing his relations to the Corinthians; "We are not *going too far* in our boasting, as . . . if we had not come to you" (NIV).

STRONG 5239, BAUER 840, KITTEL 2:465, LIDDELL-SCOTT 1862.

5078. ὑπερεκχύννω huperekchunnō verb

Pour out over; (passive), overflow.

פּוּץ pûts (6571), Overflow (Prv 5:16).

שׁוּק shûq (8224), Hiphil: overflow (Jl 3:13).

1. ὑπερεκχυνόμενον huperekchunomenon
nom/acc sing neu part pres mid

2. ὑπερεκχυννόμενον huperekchunnomenon
nom/acc sing neu part pres mid

1 and running over, shall men give into your bosom... Luke 6:38

Huperekchunnō is a rare word occurring perhaps first in Diodorus Siculus (First Century B.C.). It is equivalent in meaning to *huperekcheō*, which occurs in the Septuagint at Proverbs 5:15 and Joel 2:24. (This word also appears in manuscript Alexandrinus of the Septuagint at Joel 2:24.) *Huperekchunnō* appears once in the New Testament, in the passive, in Luke 6:38: " . . . and *running over*, shall men give into your bosom."

STRONG 5240, BAUER 840, MOULTON-MILLIGAN 653, LIDDELL-SCOTT 1862.

5079. ὑπερεντυγχάνω

huperentunchanō verb

Intercede for.

CROSS-REFERENCE:

ἐντυγχάνω entunchanō (1777)

1. ὑπερεντυγχάνει huperentunchanei
3sing indic pres act

1 but the Spirit itself **maketh intercession for** us....... Rom 8:26

In this compound *huper* (5065) adds the idea of interceding "for" someone. The *entunchanō* (1777) part of this term is itself a compound which has among its meanings the idea of interceding with someone. Thus *huperentunchanō* means to "intercede" or "plead" with someone "for" someone. It occurs in the New Testament in Romans 8:26: "The Spirit Himself *intercedes for* us" (NASB). *Huperentunchanō* places "specific emphasis upon the fact that what is being done is for the sake of someone else" (Louw and Nida, *Greek-English Lexicon*, 1:428). The Christian is reminded that the Holy Spirit is interceding on his behalf when he does not know how to pray himself.

STRONG 5241, BAUER 840, MOULTON-MILLIGAN 653, LIDDELL-SCOTT 1863, COLIN BROWN 2:874,882.

5080. ὑπερέχω huperechō verb

Be superior, surpass, excel.

CROSS-REFERENCE:

ἔχω echō (2174)

אַדִּיר 'addîr (116), Lordly (Jgs 5:25).

אָמֵץ 'āmēts (563), Be stronger (Gn 25:23).

אָרַךְ 'ārēkh (773), Hiphil: be long (1 Kgs 8:8).

גָּדוֹל gādhôl (1448), Greater (Gn 39:9).

עָדַף 'ādhaph (5951), What is left over (Ex 26:13).

1. ὑπερέχοντι huperechonti
dat sing masc part pres act

2. ὑπερέχοντας huperechontas
acc pl masc part pres act

3. ὑπερέχουσα huperechousa
nom sing fem part pres act

4. ὑπερεχούσαις huperechousais
dat pl fem part pres act

5. ὑπερέχον huperechon
nom/acc sing neu part pres act

4 Let every soul be subject unto the **higher** powers... Rom 13:1
2 let each esteem other **better than** themselves........ Phlp 2:3
5 loss for the **excellency** of the knowledge of Christ....... 3:8
3 the peace of God, **which passeth** all understanding,...... 4:7
1 whether it be to the king, as **supreme**;............. 1 Pt 2:13

Classical Greek

Huperechō is a compound of the verb *echō* (2174), "have, hold" (or even "be [something]") and *huper* (5065), here in the sense of "over" or "beyond." In classical Greek it is used both literally, of "holding" something "over" someone to protect him, and figuratively, of "being" or "rising above" something. It can also mean "prevail over."

Septuagint Usage

Huperechō appears about a dozen times in the Septuagint, translating a half dozen different Hebrew words or phrases. They have in common some idea of superiority or excelling. This superiority or excelling has to do with physical strife (Genesis 25:23), authority (Genesis 39:9; 41:40), excess of length or amount (Exodus 26:13; Leviticus 25:27; 1 Kings 8:8 [LXX 3 Kings 8:8]; 2 Chronicles 5:9), and size or appearance (of a bowl, Judges 5:25). Other Septuagint usages are in Daniel 5:12; Wisdom of Solomon 6:5; and Sirach 33:7 (LXX 36:7) and 43:30.

The word was used for similar kinds of superiority or excelling in the Hellenistic papyri and inscriptions (*Moulton-Milligan*).

New Testament Usage

In the New Testament *huperechō* is used five times, four by Paul and one by Peter. Twice it refers to governmental authority: "whether it be to the king, as *supreme*" (1 Peter 2:13) and "be subject unto the *higher* powers" (Romans 13:1). Once it is used of the proper attitude toward others: "Let each esteem other *better* than themselves" (Philippians 2:3). The other two usages, also in Philippians, speak of some aspect of our relation to God. In 3:8 Paul considered all else valueless because of "the *excellency* of the knowledge of Christ Jesus my Lord." In 4:7 he desired for them "the peace of God, *which passeth* ('surpasses,' NASB; 'transcends,' NIV) all understanding."

STRONG 5242, BAUER 840-41, MOULTON-MILLIGAN 653, KITTEL 8:523-24, LIDDELL-SCOTT 1863.

5081. ὑπερηφανία huperēphania noun

Pride, arrogance, haughtiness.

CROSS-REFERENCE:
ὑπερήφανος huperēphanos (5082)

בֶּצַע betsa' (1240), Dishonest gain (Ex 18:21).

גַּאֲוָה ga'ăwāh (1375), Something proud, pride (Pss 31:23 [30:23], 36:11 [35:11], 73:6 [72:6]).

גָּאוֹן gā'ôn (1377), Pride, arrogance (Ps 59:12 [58:12], Ez 7:20, 16:49).

גֵּאוּת gē'ûth (1378), Arrogance (Ps 17:10 [16:10]).

זָדוֹן zādhôn (2171), Something presumptuous, pride (Dt 17:12, Ob 3).

רוּם rûm (7597), Do defiantly (Nm 15:30).

שָׁאוֹן shā'ôn (8064), Uproar (Ps 74:23 [73:23]).

1. ὑπερηφανία huperēphania nom sing fem

1 lasciviousness, an evil eye, blasphemy, **pride**, ... Mark 7:22

Classical Greek

An abstract noun, *huperēphania* refers to the quality shown by a person who is *huperēphanos* (5082), "arrogant." It generally means "pride" or "arrogance." According to Barclay, "It does not so much mean the man who is conspicuous and someone to whom others look up; instead it refers to the man who stands on his own little self-created pedestal and looks down" (*New Testament Words*, p.134).

Septuagint Usage

Huperēphania appears over 50 times in the Septuagint. It translates five different Hebrew words, especially *ga'ăwāh*, "be high, arrogant," or is used with no Hebrew text counterpart. It is nearly synonymous with *hubris* (5036B).

New Testament Usage

On the other hand, *huperēphania* is found only once in the New Testament. It appears in Mark 7:22 near the end of the list of internal things that defile a person: *blasphēmia* (981), *huperēphania*, *aphrosunē* (869) ("slander, *arrogance* and folly," NIV).

STRONG 5243, BAUER 841, MOULTON-MILLIGAN 653, KITTEL 8:525-29, LIDDELL-SCOTT 1864, COLIN BROWN 3:28-30.

5082. ὑπερήφανος huperēphanos adj

Arrogant, haughty, proud.

COGNATES:
ὑπερηφανία huperēphania (5081)
φαίνω phainō (5154)

SYNONYM:
ἀλαζονεία alazoneia (210)

גֵּאֶה gē'eh (1373), Proud (Jb 40:12 [40:7], Pss 94:2 [93:2], 140:5 [139:5]).

גַּאֲיוֹן ga'ăyôn (1379), Proud (Ps 123:4 [122:4]).

גָּבֹהַּ gāvōahh (1393), Haughty (Ps 101:5 [100:5]).

זֵד zēdh (2170), Arrogant (Ps 119:21,69,122 [118:21,69,122]).

לִיץ lîts (4054), Scorn, scorner (Prv 3:34, Is 29:20).

עָרִיץ 'ārîts (6422), Ruthless person (Is 13:11).

רַהַב rahav (7581), Rahab (Ps 89:10 [88:10]).

רוּם rûm (7599), Something uplifted, something haughty (Jb 38:15, Ps 18:27 [17:27]); proud person (Is 2:12).

1. ὑπερήφανοι huperēphanoi nom pl masc
2. ὑπερηφάνοις huperēphanois dat pl masc
3. ὑπερηφάνους huperēphanous acc pl masc

3 strength with his arm; he hath scattered the **proud** .. Luke 1:51
3 Backbiters, haters of God, despiteful, **proud**, ... Rom 1:30
1 covetous, boasters, **proud**, blasphemers, ... 2 Tm 3:2
2 Wherefore he saith, God resisteth the **proud**, ... Jas 4:6
2 clothed with humility: for God resisteth the **proud**, .. 1 Pt 5:5

Classical Greek

This adjective—from *huper* (5065), "above," and *phainō* (5154), "I appear"—means "arrogant, proud." It almost always carries an unfavorable sense in classical writings (cf. *Liddell-Scott*). The ideas of "insolence" and "brutality" may be implied. Trench—discussing *huperēphanos* in the notorious company of *hubristēs* (5037), "insolent, violent man," and *alazōn* (211) "boaster, braggart"—suggests such cruelty may often be the consequence of the "arrogant one" being denied the "honor" he or she felt was deserved (*Synonyms of the New Testament*, p.96). He further notes that *huperēphanos* is particularly an inner condition not always expressed externally (ibid.).

Septuagint Usage

Huperēphanos, as well as its cognates, appears primarily in the Psalms and the Wisdom writings of the Septuagint, but not exclusively (e.g., Isaiah 2:12; 13:11). The Septuagint, like all other Biblical writings, uses *huperēphanos* unfavorably. It is used to translate seven Hebrew words, and no single one predominates. It is associated with ungodly "pride" (Job 38:15 [Hebrew *rûm*, "be high, rise up" (such as a raised hand, a gesture of defiance)]). The proud are destined to be humiliated by God (Psalm 18:27 [LXX 17:27]; cf. 89:10 [88:10]; 101:5 [100:5]; 119:78 [118:78]; Isaiah 13:11). For the author of Sirach there is no cure for their "sickness" (Sirach 3:28). It even infects those who come in contact with the "arrogant" (Sirach 13:1). In 4 Maccabees 4:15 it is applied to Antiochus IV Epiphanes.

New Testament Usage

Only five instances of *huperēphanos* occur in the New Testament. Two of these are allusions to Proverbs 3:34 which says that God opposes the *arrogant* but gives grace to the lowly (cf. James 4:6; 1 Peter 5:5). According to Barclay the basic sin of the *huperēphanos* "is that he has forgotten that he is a creature and that God is the Creator; for the *huperēphanos* has erected an altar to himself within his own heart, and worships there" (*New Testament Words*, p.138).

Paul's two usages are in reference to the "proud" or "arrogant" who have repeatedly and willfully rejected God's revelation (Romans 1:30; cf. the conjunction with *hubris* [5036B] also in Isaiah 2:12) both in his present day (including the past) and in the future (2 Timothy 3:2).

Luke's single usage certainly captures the Old Testament belief that arrogance is a condition of the heart's "inmost thoughts" (cf. Deuteronomy 8:14, "proud heart" [NIV], literally "high heart"; Ezekiel 31:10). Here, in Mary's song (Luke 1:51), the strength of the Lord is manifest in His overthrow of the "proud" and His lifting up of the humble (cf. above on Proverbs 3:34).

Strong 5244, Bauer 841, Moulton-Milligan 653, Kittel 8:525-29, Liddell-Scott 1864, Colin Brown 3:27-32.

5082B. ὑπερλίαν huperlian adv

Very much, exceedingly.

1. ὑπερλίαν huperlian

1 inferior to the most eminent apostles. (NASB) ..... 2 Co 11:5
1 inferior to the most eminent apostles, (NASB) 12:11

Huperlian appears as a variant in 2 Corinthians 11:5 and 12:11. The *Textus Receptus* reads *huper lian*. The confusion arises because ancient scribes did not place any spaces between words in their manuscripts. The only other occurrence of *huperlian* in Greek literature is in a 12th-century A.D. work.

Huperlian means "exceedingly, chief" and is used as an adjective in its two New Testament appearances. Paul referred to the "*very chiefest* apostles" ("super-apostles," NIV) who had come to Corinth. There may have been a note of sarcasm in Paul's tone when he referred to these men. Although some scholars believe Paul referred to the original apostles (Peter, John, etc.), it is clear from the text that this is inaccurate. Paul said that these men preach a different Jesus, a different spirit, and a different gospel (11:4); and he called them "false apostles . . . masquerading as apostles of Christ" (11:13, NIV). These were false teachers who boasted of their spiritual status, whom Paul felt the need to challenge. He also was a Jew (11:22); he also had suffered (1:23-33); he also had received visions (12:1-10). The Corinthians were being seduced by these "super-apostles," and Paul resisted them.

Bauer 841, Moulton-Milligan 653, Liddell-Scott 1866.

5083. ὑπερνικάω hupernikaō verb

Be completely victorious, overcome completely.

Cross-Reference:
νικάω nikaō (3390)

1. ὑπερνικῶμεν hupernikōmen 1pl indic pres act

1 more than conquerors through him that loved us..... Rom 8:37

Hupernikaō is an emphatic compound of *nikaō* (3390), "conquer, be victor(ious)." *Huper* (5065) adds the idea of "going" even "beyond the usual force of" an idea; i.e., "to be completely victorious, to overcome completely."

Classical Greek

Hupernikaō, though very rare, goes back at least to the medical writer Hippocrates (Fifth Century B.C.). *Liddell-Scott* cites only four references for its use: Hippocrates, the New Testament usage, and two post-New Testament writers. It suggests "prevail completely over" as the meaning in Hippocrates and in a passage in Galen, a medical writer of the Second Century A.D.

New Testament Usage

There is only one occurrence of *hupernikaō* in the New Testament. Paul used it in Romans 8:37 to describe the believer's confidence of overwhelming victory through Christ: "In all these things we *are more than conquerors* through him that loved us" ("we overwhelmingly conquer," NASB).

Strong 5245, Bauer 841, Moulton-Milligan 653, Kittel 4:942-45, Liddell-Scott 1866.

5084. ὑπέρογκος huperonkos adj

Excessive, bombastic.

גָּדוֹל gādhôl (1448), Great (Ex 18:22).

פָּלָא pālā' (6623), Niphal: be too difficult, seem hard (Dt 30:11, 2 Sm 13:2).

פֶּלֶא pele' (6624), Something astounding (Lam 1:9).

קָשֶׁה qāsheh (7482), Difficult (Ex 18:26).

1. ὑπέρογκα huperonka nom/acc pl neu

1 when they speak **great swelling** words of vanity, ... 2 Pt 2:18
1 and their mouth speaketh great **swelling** words, ... Jude 1:16

This word is a compound of *huper* (5065) and the adjective *onkos,* "bulky, swollen." *Onkos* is related to the verb *onkoō,* "to enlarge, 'bulk' up, swell or puff up." *Huperonkos* thus means "oversized, overgrown, overblown, immoderate" and was used to describe the size of attitudes, of speech ("verbose"), and in various other ways.

Huperonkos appears twice in the New Testament, in the parallel descriptions in 2 Peter and Jude that refers to the manner of speech of the false teachers: "They speak *great swelling words* of vanity" (2 Peter 2:18), and, "Their mouth speaketh *great swelling words*" (Jude 16). In these passages the NASB uses "arrogant words" and "arrogantly"; the NIV, "boastful words" and "they boast."

STRONG 5246, BAUER 841, MOULTON-MILLIGAN 653, LIDDELL-SCOTT 1866.

5085. ὑπεροχή huperochē noun

Projection, preeminence, superiority, excellency.

CROSS-REFERENCE:
ἔχω echō (2174)

קוֹמָה qômāh (7253), Height (Jer 52:22).

1. ὑπεροχῇ huperochē dat sing fem
2. ὑπεροχὴν huperochēn acc sing fem

2 came not with **excellency** of speech or of wisdom, ... 1 Co 2:1
1 For kings, and for all that are in **authority**; .... 1 Tm 2:2

Classical writers used *huperochē* to describe the peak of a mountain, the top of a beam, an excess of money, a rank that exceeds another, and the like (*Liddell-Scott*). In the New Testament *huperochē* occurs twice. In 1 Corinthians 2:1 Paul used the word with reference to his speech: "I . . . came not with *excellency* of speech." The second occurrence of *huperochē* occurs in 1 Timothy 2:2 where Paul exhorted Timothy that prayer be made "for all that are in *authority*."

STRONG 5247, BAUER 841, MOULTON-MILLIGAN 653-54, KITTEL 8:523-24, LIDDELL-SCOTT 1867.

5086. ὑπερπερισσεύω huperperisseuō verb

Be present in abundance, greatly increase, cause to overflow; overflow, run over.

CROSS-REFERENCE:
περισσεύω perisseuō (3915)

1. ὑπερεπερίσσευσεν hupereperisseusen 3sing indic aor act
2. ὑπερπερισσεύομαι huperperisseuomai 1sing indic pres mid

1 grace did **much more abound**: .... Rom 5:20
2 I am **exceeding joyful** in all our tribulation. .... 2 Co 7:4

Classical Greek

This regular verb is related to the adverb *huperperissōs* (5087), meaning "beyond all measure" (Mark 7:37). It is a compound verb composed of the preposition *huper* (5065), "over," and the verb *perisseuō* (3915), "abound." A word with similar meaning is *huperpleonazō* (5088), "to be present in great abundance," although it is rare in classical Greek. *Huperperisseuō* does not appear in the Septuagint.

New Testament Usage

Since little or no attestation from pre-New Testament Greek has been discovered as yet, the apostle Paul may have coined this word himself under the inspiration of the Holy Spirit to express the overwhelming sense of surplus he felt of both joy and grace. *Huperperisseuō* occurs twice in the New Testament.

The verb has both transitive and intransitive uses in the New Testament. The transitive is translated "to cause overflow" or "overflow" if in the passive voice (*Bauer*). This usage can be found in 2 Corinthians 7:4: "I overflow with joy" (author's translation).

The intransitive usage is rendered "be present in abundance" (*Bauer*). Romans 5:20 states, "Grace did *much more abound* (than sin and guilt)." Grace did not just abound; it overflowed and far surpassed the power of sin. It was greater by far than sin.

STRONG 5248, BAUER 841, KITTEL 6:58-61, LIDDELL-SCOTT 1867.

5087. ὑπερπερισσῶς huperperissōs adv

Beyond measure, exceedingly.

CROSS-REFERENCE:
περισσεύω perisseuō (3915)

1. ὑπερπερισσῶς huperperissōs

1 And were **beyond measure** astonished, saying, ... Mark 7:37

Huperperissōs is an adverb related to the verb *huperperisseuō* (5086). These words are rare in classical Greek literature and do not occur in the Septuagint or papyri. *Huperperissōs* consists of *huper* (5065), "over" or "above," and *perissōs*, denoting "abundantly." When placed together the word is a strengthened form of *perissōs* and means "exceedingly abundant." The verb appears in Romans 5:20 and 2 Corinthians 7:4, but the adverb *huperperissōs* occurs only in Mark 7:37. Here the word expresses the extremely astounding effects that Jesus' miracle had upon those who witnessed His great power.

STRONG 5249, BAUER 842, LIDDELL-SCOTT 1867, COLIN BROWN 1:728-29.

5088. ὑπερπλεονάζω

huperpleonazō verb

Abound exceedingly, overflow.

CROSS-REFERENCE:

πλεονάζω pleonazō (3981)

1. ὑπερεπλεόνασεν huperepleonasen 3sing indic aor act

1 And the grace of our Lord was **exceeding abundant** 1 Tm 1:14

This verb rarely occurs in the classical Greek literature or papyri. It is not found in the Septuagint. *Huperpleonozō* is a strengthened form of *pleonazō* (3981), "abound." *Huperpleonazō* occurs once in the New Testament, in 1 Timothy 1:14. In this verse the apostle said that the Lord's grace superabounded toward him. Ordinary words could not express how great that grace was and is. Thus the apostle added a preposition to an already strong verb to lay greater emphasis on the exceedingly abundant grace of the Lord Jesus Christ.

STRONG 5250, BAUER 842, MOULTON-MILLIGAN 654, KITTEL 6:263-66, LIDDELL-SCOTT 1868, COLIN BROWN 2:130-31.

5089. ὑπερυψόω huperupsoō verb

To exalt highly, exalt to the highest place.

CROSS-REFERENCE:

ὑψόω hupsoō (5150)

עָלָה 'ālâh (6148), Go up; niphal: be exalted (Ps 97:9 [96:9]).

עָרִיץ 'ārîts (6422), Violent (Ps 37:35 [36:35]).

1. ὑπερύψωσεν huperupsōsen 3sing indic aor act

1 Wherefore God also hath **highly exalted** him, ... Phlp 2:9

This verb is formed by the preposition *huper* (5065), "over" or "above," and the verb *upsoō*, "to lift up high." The preposition strengthens the verb *upsoō*, thus forming an intensified word. The strengthened form rarely occurs in the classical writings and papyri. In the Septuagint the verb appears in Psalms 37:35 (LXX 36:35); 97:9 (96:9); and in Daniel 4:34. In Psalm 37:35 (LXX 36:35) the Psalmist noted that he saw the wicked highly exalting himself. In Daniel 4:34 Nebuchadnezzar highly exalted God. Psalm 97:9 (LXX 96:9) applies the word to God. The apostle Paul did the same in the only New Testament occurrence of the word (Philippians 2:9). Here Paul wrote that God "highly exalted" Christ because He "humbled himself, and became obedient unto death, even the death of the cross" (verse 8).

STRONG 5251, BAUER 842, KITTEL 8:606-13, LIDDELL-SCOTT 1869.

5090. ὑπερφρονέω

huperphroneō verb

To think highly, to be overly proud, to be high-minded, to have high thoughts.

CROSS-REFERENCE:

φρονέω phroneō (5262)

1. ὑπερφρονεῖν huperphronein inf pres act

1 not to **think of himself more highly** than he ought.. Rom 12:3

Classical Greek and Septuagint Usage

Classical writers used *huperphroneō* to express how a person thought of himself in the sense of being proud and how a person thought of others in looking down upon them. Thus the meaning was "to despise, to overlook, to think slightly of or with contempt." The verb also contains the idea of surpassing in knowledge or excelling in wisdom (*Liddell-Scott*). In three occurrences in the Septuagint (4 Maccabees 13:1; 14:11; 16:2) *huperphroneō* means "to treat with contempt, to despise." The writer noted that those who were martyred treated their sufferings with contempt; they despised them.

New Testament Usage

Huperphroneō is found only in Romans 12:3 in the New Testament. The apostle used the word in its negative sense, i.e., *not* to think more highly of one's self than one ought to think. The warning is balanced by describing the way a Christian ought to think of himself—with a sober mind (i.e., with restraint) (Greek *sōphroneō* [4845], "to be of sound mind").

Strong 5252, Bauer 842, Moulton-Milligan 654, Liddell-Scott 1870.

5091. ὑπερῷον huperōon noun

Upper room, upper story, roof chamber.

עִלִּי ʿillî (A6164), Upstairs room (Dn 6:10—Aramaic).

עֲלִיָּה ʿălîyāh (6168), Roof chamber, upper room (Jgs 3:23, 2 Kgs 4:10f., Jer 22:13f.).

עֶלְיוֹן ʿelyôn (6169), Upper, highest (Jer 20:2, Ez 41:7).

1. ὑπερῴῳ huperōō dat sing neu
2. ὑπερῷον huperōon nom/acc sing neu

2 they went up into an **upper room,** .... Acts 1:13
1 they laid her in an **upper chamber** 9:37
2 they brought him into the **upper chamber:** 9:39
1 And there were many lights in the **upper chamber,** 20:8

Classical Greek and Septuagint Usage

This is a commonly used word in both literary and nonliterary (e.g., papyri) sources. The term denotes upper chambers such as those belonging to women (see *Liddell-Scott*; *Moulton-Milligan*). (In Greek homes the women's quarters were upstairs and the men's, downstairs.) The Septuagint contains *huperōon* about 25 times. Judges 3:20,23-25 refer to the upper chamber of Eglon. In 1 Kings 17:19 (LXX 3 Kings 17:19) Elijah carried the dead boy into the upper room.

New Testament Usage

The New Testament uses *huperōon* four times, all in Acts (1:13; 9:37,39; 20:8). The first of these references denotes the upper chamber where the apostles stayed while waiting for the descent of the Holy Spirit at Pentecost. The second and third occurrences (9:37,39) refer to the room in which Dorcas was raised from the dead. The last reference is to the room where Christians met to hear Paul preach at Troas. This *huperōon* was high enough to cause Eutychus' death when he fell from the chamber.

Strong 5253, Bauer 842, Moulton-Milligan 654, Liddell-Scott 1871.

5092. ὑπέχω hupechō verb

Suffer, hold under, undergo.

Cross-Reference:
ἔχω echō (2174)

נָשָׂא nāsâʾ (5558), Bear (Ps 89:50 [88:50]).

סָבַל sāval (5628), Bear (Lam 5:7).

1. ὑπέχουσαι hupechousai nom pl fem part pres act

1 an example, **suffering** the vengeance of eternal fire...Jude 1:7

Classical Greek, including the papyri, used this verb in a variety of ways. Men are *held under* other men and laws; animals and things *submit* to others; a cup is *held under* another vessel until something is poured into it; wax is *held under* a pressed seal to authenticate a document; a man *stands under* a shower for a bath, etc. (see *Liddell-Scott*). This word occurs twice in the canonical Septuagint and once in the New Testament. In Psalm 89:50 (LXX 88:50) *hupechō* means "reproach." Lamentations 5:7 states that sons are "held under" their fathers' lawlessness, i.e., the sons suffer for what their fathers had done. The translators of the King James Version rendered *hupechō* as "suffering" in Jude 7. In a few words, Jude painted a graphic scene of God holding Sodom and Gomorrah under the punishment of eternal fire as an example to the world.

Strong 5254, Bauer 842, Moulton-Milligan 654, Liddell-Scott 1871.

5093. ὑπήκοος hupēkoos adj

Obedient, subject.

Cross-Reference:
ὑπακοή hupakoē (5056)

עָבַד ʿāvadh (5856), Serve (Dt 20:11).

שָׁמַע shāmaʿ (8471), Listen (Prv 21:28).

1. ὑπήκοος hupēkoos nom sing masc
2. ὑπήκοοι hupēkooi nom pl masc

2 To whom our fathers would not **obey,** .... Acts 7:39
2 whether ye be **obedient** in all things.................2 Co 2:9
1 and became **obedient** unto death, ... Phlp 2:8

Classical Greek and Septuagint Usage

This adjective is related to *akoē* (187), "hearing." The idea is that one hears to the point of obeying. Thus *hupēkoos* may be used to describe a hearer, scholar, or subject (see *Liddell-Scott*). The Septuagint uses this word five times (Deuteronomy 20:11; Joshua 17:13; Proverbs 4:3; 13:1; 21:28). It is clear from the first two references that *hupēkoos* means "obedient" or "subject."

New Testament Usage

In the New Testament *hupēkoos* occurs three times (Acts 7:39; 2 Corinthians 2:9; Philippians 2:8). The first two references are to man's obedience to God's laws. The last refers to the complete obedience of Jesus to the Father's will.

The obedience and subjection of Jesus to the Father is man's supreme example.

Strong 5255, Bauer 842, Moulton-Milligan 654, Kittel 1:224-25, Liddell-Scott 1871-72, Colin Brown 2:179.

5094. ὑπηρετέω hupēreteō verb

Serve, minister.

Cognate:

ὑπηρέτης hupēretēs (5095)

Synonyms:

διακονέω diakoneō (1241)
δουλεύω douleuō (1392)
θεραπεύω therapeuō (2300)
λατρεύω latreuō (2973)
λειτουργέω leitourgeō (2982)

1. **ὑπηρετεῖν hupēretein** inf pres act
2. **ὑπηρέτησαν hupēretēsan** 3pl indic aor act
3. **ὑπηρετήσας hupēretēsas** nom sing masc part aor act

3 For David, after he **had served** his own generation . . Acts 13:36
2 these hands have **ministered** unto my necessities, ... 20:34
1 his acquaintance **to minister** or come unto him. 24:23

Classical Greek

This is a verb form of the noun *hupēreteia* which means "to do service." It can be used to describe the grueling work of a rower on a ship. The classical Greek usage also means to do service as a minister, to submit to a ruling, to support, to render military service, and to help until a task is completed (*Liddell-Scott*). Papyri and other nonliterary sources use *hupēreteō* to mean "serve" and "minister" in secular activity (*Moulton-Milligan*).

Septuagint Usage

This verb does not occur in the canonical Septuagint, but it does occur in the apocryphal Septuagint in Wisdom 16:21,24,25; 19:6; Ecclesiasticus 39:4. In Wisdom 16:21-25 the author, in an extended passage discussing God's treatment of the Israelites, describes how both the manna and the whole creation served God. Ecclesiasticus 39:4 notes that the man who studies the Law will serve great men.

New Testament Usage

Three instances of *hupēreteō* occur in the New Testament, all in the Book of Acts (13:36; 20:34; 24:23). In the first of these, Paul spoke of David who "*served* his own generation." David's service was the faithful execution of God's call to minister in God's kingdom and to His people.

The second instance of the verb relates to Paul's emphasis on service for others. He said that while he was with the Ephesian church at its founding, he worked with his own hands to supply the needs of himself and his evangelistic team. He did this so that no one could undermine the gospel by accusing him of ministering for money. He also supported himself to set an example of the blessedness of giving over that of receiving. In other words, Paul showed what it means to serve or minister.

The last use of this word in Acts relates to Felix's command concerning Paul as a prisoner. Though Paul was confined, he was to have liberty, and his friends were allowed to "minister" to his needs. According to Rengstorf the help Paul's friends gave him included "not merely seeing and supplying his needs but also meeting his wishes" ("hupēretēs," *Kittel*, 8:540). In this instance Paul was the recipient of help. The aid his friends gave him doubtless enabled Paul to minister to others through the messengers to the churches.

Strong 5256, Bauer 842, Moulton-Milligan 654-55, Kittel 8:530-44, Liddell-Scott 1872, Colin Brown 3:544,547.

5095. ὑπηρέτης hupēretēs noun

Minister, officer, servant, attendant.

Cognate:

ὑπηρετέω hupēreteō (5094)

Synonyms:

διάκονος diakonos (1243)
θεράπων therapōn (2301)
λειτουργός leitourgos (2985)

כִּילַי kîlay (3716), Scoundrel (Is 32:5).

עֶבֶד ʿevedh (5860), Servant (Prv 14:35).

1. **ὑπηρέτῃ hupēretē** dat sing masc
2. **ὑπηρέτην hupēretēn** acc sing masc
3. **ὑπηρέται hupēretai** nom pl masc
4. **ὑπηρετῶν hupēretōn** gen pl masc
5. **ὑπηρέταις hupēretais** dat pl masc
6. **ὑπηρέτας hupēretas** acc pl masc

1 and the judge deliver thee to the **officer**, ... Matt 5:25
4 went in, and sat with the **servants**, to see the end. 26:58
4 and he sat with the **servants**, and warmed himself . . Mark 14:54
3 and the **servants** did strike him with the palms 14:65
3 were eyewitnesses, and **ministers** of the word; . . . . Luke 1:2
1 and he gave it again to the **minister**, and sat down. 4:20
6 and the Pharisees and the chief priests sent **officers** John 7:32
3 Then came the **officers** to the chief priests 7:45
3 **officers** answered, Never man spake like this man. 7:46
6 having received a band of men and **officers** 18:3
3 and the captain and **officers** of the Jews took Jesus, ... 18:12
3 And the servants and **officers** stood there, ... 18:18
4 one of the **officers** which stood by struck Jesus 18:22
3 then would my **servants** fight, ... 18:36
3 the chief priests therefore and **officers** saw him, ... 19:6
3 But when the **officers** came, and found them not . . . . Acts 5:22
5 Then went the captain with the **officers**, ... 5:26
2 and they had also John to their **minister**. 13:5

2 to make thee a minister and a witness .... Acts 26:16
6 as of the ministers of Christ, ... 1 Co 4:1

Classical Greek

This word is related to the verb *hupēreteō* (5094), "serve." The noun occurs frequently in classical Greek with the meanings of a rower, an underling, a servant, an attendant. The meaning is that of a subordinate with authority but under another's authority. Thus the thought of an officer often occurs (*Liddell-Scott*). According to Rengstorf the earliest appearances of *hupēretēs* have the meaning "servant." Hermes, for example, is a *hupēretēs* of the gods; he carries out the will of Zeus ("hupēretēs," *Kittel*, 8:530). The traditional derivation of this word, "under-rower," is very dubious. The references to rowing are relatively rare, and even in these occurrences it is not the rowing "which makes him a *hupēretēs*, but only the fact that he rows according to directions" (ibid., p.533). With *hupēretēs* the "reference is always to a service of any kind which in structure and goal is controlled by the will of him to whom it is rendered" (ibid., p.532). The *hupēretēs*, though a servant, had considerable authority and was still free; he could dissolve his obligations, unlike the *doulos* (1395) who was a slave, unable to free himself. The *hupēretēs* retained his own sense of dignity and worth (ibid., p.533). In the papyri the word has the meaning of doing service in behalf of another (see *Moulton-Milligan*).

Septuagint Usage

Two instances of *hupēretēs* are recorded in the canonical Septuagint. The first is found in Proverbs 14:35 where the word is translated "servant." The wise servant finds favor from the king, and the servant's behavior causes no embarrassment for his king. The second instance (Isaiah 32:5 of the Septuagint) refers to servants who have authority to say "be silent." Thus the classical Greek meaning is carried over into the Septuagint.

New Testament Usage

Hupēretēs occurs about 20 times in the New Testament. Twelve times the noun means "officers." But the word is used in the Christian sense of a minister. In Luke 1:2 the word is coupled with "eyewitnesses" indicating that they were eyewitnesses, recipients, and servants of the Word. Jesus spoke of His disciples as *hupēretēs* in John 18:36 where the word is translated "servants." This is probably the best translation for the context since the term *officers* would surely convey a military connotation. In Acts 13:5 the word is rendered "minister" or "attendant" because John Mark was a novice and a subordinate to Barnabas and Saul.

This word appears in Acts 26:16 connected with Paul's testimony of his conversion. Jesus said that He was going to make Paul a "minister" (hupēretēs) of the things he had seen. This term expresses Paul's lowly and subordinate position. He was a man under the authority of Jesus Christ the Lord! In all humility Paul applied this word to himself as well as to Apollos and Peter (1 Corinthians 3:22 to 4:1). By *hupēretēs* the apostle indicated the minister is but a servant and Christ is the Master.

Strong 5257, Bauer 842, Moulton-Milligan 655, Kittel 8:530-44, Liddell-Scott 1872, Colin Brown 3:544,546.

5096. ὕπνος hupnos noun

Sleep, slumber.

Cognates:
ἐξυπνίζω exupnizō (1836)
ἔξυπνος exupnos (1837)

חֵזוּ chēzû (A2468), Vision (Dn 7:2—Aramaic).

חָזוֹן chāzôn (2469), Vision (Dn 9:21).

חֲלוֹם chălôm (2573), Dream (Gn 31:10f., Nm 12:6, 1 Kgs 3:5).

חָלַם chālam (2593), Dream (Is 29:8).

יָשֵׁן yāshēn (3585), Smoldering (Hos 7:6).

שֵׁנָא shēnā' (8517), Sleep (Ps 127:2 [126:2]).

שֵׁנָה shēnāh (8524), Sleep (Gn 28:16, Prv 6:4, Jer 31:26 [38:26]).

שְׁנָת sh^enāth (8535), Sleep (Ps 132:4 [131:4]).

1. ὕπνου hupnou gen sing masc

2. ὕπνῳ hupnō dat sing masc

1 Then Joseph being raised from sleep .... Matt 1:24
2 they that were with him were heavy with sleep: ..... Luke 9:32
1 thought ... he had spoken of taking of rest in sleep. John 11:13
2 named Eutychus, being fallen into a deep sleep: .... Acts 20:9
1 Paul was long preaching, he sunk down with sleep, ... 20:9
1 that now it is high time to awake out of sleep: ..... Rom 13:11

This is the ordinary word for sleep. It occurs in both literary and nonliterary Greek writings. The Septuagint contains *hupnos* about 50 times. In the New Testament it is used six times. Five of these occurrences indicate natural sleep; one signifies a figurative meaning. *Hupnos* should be distinguished from *koimaomai* (2810) which often means the sleep of death (John 11:11; 1 Corinthians 11:30; 15:6). At times, sleep is the locus of divine revelation. *Hupnos* is never used figuratively to mean "death," neither does it mean "dream." Natural sleep is the denotation in Matthew 1:24; Luke 9:32; John 11:13; and Acts

20:9, twice. But in Romans 13:11 the apostle Paul used *hupnos* figuratively to mean worldliness. He told the Romans "to wake up from (their) *slumber*" (NIV), to become aware of the times, cast off the "deeds of darkness," and behave decently. "Sleep" indicates the state of stupor, unconsciousness, and unawareness that accompanies indulging the flesh.

STRONG 5258, BAUER 843, MOULTON-MILLIGAN 655, KITTEL 8:545-56, LIDDELL-SCOTT 1873, COLIN BROWN 1:441-43.

5097. ὑπό hupo prep

Under, by, by means of, about, subject to.

1. ὑφ' huph'

2. ὑπ' hup'

3. ὑπό hupo

3 fulfilled ... spoken **of** the Lord by the prophet, ... Matt 1:22
3 fulfilled ... was spoken **of** the Lord by the prophet, ... 2:15
3 when he saw that he was mocked **of** the wise men, ... 2:16
3 fulfilled ... was spoken **by** Jeremy the prophet, ... 2:17
3 For this is he that was spoken of **by** the prophet 3:3
2 And were baptized **of** him in Jordan, ... 3:6
2 cometh Jesus ... unto John, to be baptized **of** him. 3:13
3 I have need to be baptized **of** thee, ... 3:14
3 was Jesus led up **of** the Spirit into the wilderness 4:1
3 into the wilderness to be tempted **of** the devil. 4:1
3 cast out, and to be trodden under foot **of** men. 5:13
3 light a candle, and put it **under** a bushel, ... 5:15
3 hypocrites do ... that they may have glory **of** men. 6:2
3 that thou shouldest come **under** my roof: 8:8
3 For I am a man **under** authority, ... 8:9
2 a man under authority, having soldiers **under** me: 8:9
3 insomuch that the ship was covered **with** the waves: 8:24
3 ye shall be hated **of** all men for my name's sake: 10:22
3 A reed shaken **with** the wind? 11:7
3 All things are delivered unto me **of** my Father: 11:27
3 And she, being **before** instructed of her mother, ... 14:8
3 tossed **with** waves: for the wind was contrary. 14:24
2 Likewise shall also the Son of man suffer **of** them. 17:12
3 which were made eunuchs **of** men: 19:12
3 for whom it is prepared **of** my Father. 20:23
3 not read that which was spoken unto you **by** God, ... 22:31
3 and to be called **of** men, Rabbi, Rabbi. 23:7
3 as a hen gathereth her chickens **under** her wings, ... 23:37
3 ye shall be hated **of** all nations for my name's sake. ... 24:9
3 when he was accused **of** the chief priests and elders, ... 27:12
3 be fulfilled which was spoken **by** the prophet, ... 27:35
2 and were all baptized **of** him in the river of Jordan, Mark 1:5
3 and was baptized **of** John in Jordan. 1:9
3 in the wilderness forty days, tempted **of** Satan; 1:13
3 one sick of the palsy, which was borne **of** four. 2:3
3 Is a candle brought to be put **under** a bushel, ... 4:21
3 brought to be put under a bushel, or **under** a bed? 4:21
3 fowls of the air may lodge **under** the shadow of it. 4:32
2 and the chains had been plucked asunder **by** him, ... 5:4
3 And had suffered many things **of** many physicians, ... 5:26
3 and be rejected **by** the elders (NASB) 8:31
3 ye shall be hated **of** all men for my name's sake: 13:13
3 of desolation, spoken of **by** Daniel the prophet, ... 13:14
2 was alive, and had been seen **of** her, believed not. 16:11
3 Gabriel was sent **from** God unto a city of Galilee, ... Luke 1:26
3 things which were told them **by** the shepherds. 2:18
3 called JESUS, which was so named **of** the angel 2:21
3 And it was revealed unto him **by** the Holy Ghost, ... 2:26
2 multitude that came forth to be baptized **of** him, ... 3:7
2 the tetrarch, being reproved **by** him for Herodias 3:19
3 Being forty days tempted **of** the devil. .... Luke 4:2
3 taught in their synagogues, being glorified **of** all. 4:15
2 and to be healed **by** him of their infirmities. 5:15
3 And they that were vexed **with** unclean spirits: 6:18
3 worthy that thou shouldest enter **under** my roof: 7:6
3 For I also am a man set **under** authority, ... 7:8
2 under authority, having **under** me soldiers, ... 7:8
3 to see? A reed shaken **with** the wind? 7:24
2 the Pharisees and ... being not baptized **of** him. 7:30
3 and are choked **with** cares and riches and pleasures 8:14
3 and was driven **of** the devil into the wilderness. 8:29
2 had spent all ... neither could be healed **of** any, ... 8:43
2 the tetrarch heard of all that was done **by** him: 9:7
3 he was perplexed, because that it was said **of** some, ... 9:7
3 **of** some, that Elias had appeared; and of others, ... 9:8
3 All things are delivered to me **of** my Father: 10:22
3 putteth it in a secret place, neither **under** a bushel, ... 11:33
2 all the glorious things that were done **by** him. 13:17
3 as a hen doth gather her brood **under** her wings, ... 13:34
3 When thou art bidden **of** any man to a wedding, ... 14:8
2 more honourable ... than thou be bidden **of** him; 14:8
3 was carried **by** the angels into Abraham's bosom: 16:22
3 And when he was demanded **of** the Pharisees, ... 17:20
2 that lighteneth out of the one part **under** heaven, ... 17:24
2 shineth unto the other part **under** heaven; 17:24
3 And ye shall be betrayed both **by** parents, ... 21:16
3 ye shall be hated **of** all men for my name's sake. 21:17
3 ye shall see Jerusalem compassed **with** armies, ... 21:20
3 Jerusalem shall be trodden down **of** the Gentiles, ... 21:24
2 he hoped to have seen some miracle done **by** him. 23:8
3 when thou wast **under** the fig tree, I saw thee. ...... John 1:48
3 being convicted **by** their own conscience, ... 8:9
3 and know my sheep, and am known **of** mine. 10:14
3 and he that loveth me shall be loved **of** my Father, ... 14:21
3 devout men, out of every nation **under** heaven. ...... Acts 2:5
2 it was not possible that he should be holden **of** it. 2:24
1 the stone which was set at nought **of** you builders, ... 4:11
3 none other name **under** heaven given among men, ... 4:12
3 who **by** the apostles was surnamed Barnabas, ... 4:36
3 and them which were vexed **with** unclean spirits: 5:16
3 into the temple early in the morning, (NT) 5:21
3 attention to what was said **by** Philip, (NASB) 8:6
3 men who had been sent **by** Cornelius (NASB) 10:17
3 of good report **among** all the nation of the Jews, ... 10:22
3 was warned from God **by** an holy angel 10:22
3 to hear all things that are commanded thee **of** God. ... 10:33
3 and healing all that were oppressed **of** the devil; 10:38
3 but unto witnesses chosen before **of** God, ... 10:41
3 it is he which was ordained **of** God to be the Judge ... 10:42
3 but prayer was made without ceasing **of** the church 12:5
3 So they, being sent forth **by** the Holy Ghost, ... 13:4
3 against those things which were spoken **by** Paul, ... 13:45
3 And being brought on their way **by** the church, ... 15:3
3 they were received **of** the church, ... 15:4
3 and departed, being recommended **by** the brethren 15:40
3 Which was well reported of **by** the brethren 16:2
3 that were ordained **of** the apostles and elders 16:4
3 and were forbidden **of** the Holy Ghost to preach 16:6
3 she attended unto the things ... spoken **of** Paul. 16:14
3 the word of God was preached **of** Paul at Berea, ... 17:13
3 what this new doctrine, **whereof** thou speakest, is? 17:19
3 Neither is worshipped **with** men's hands, ... 17:25
3 And when the Jews laid wait for him, (NT) 20:3
3 that he was borne **of** the soldiers for the violence 21:35
3 being led by the hand **of** them that were with me, ... 22:11
3 having a good report **of** all the Jews 22:12
3 why he had been accused **by** the Jews, (NASB) 22:30
2 Paul should have been pulled in pieces **of** them, ... 23:10
3 This man was taken **of** the Jews, ... 23:27
2 and should have been killed **of** them: 23:27
3 how that the Jews laid wait for the man, (NT) 23:30
1 I am called in question **by** you this day. 24:21
3 that money should have been given him **of** Paul, ... 24:26
3 There is a certain man left in bonds **by** Felix: 25:14
3 all the things whereof I am accused **of** the Jews: 26:2
3 hope of the promise made **of** God unto our fathers: ... 26:6
3 For which hope's sake, ... I am accused **of** the Jews. ... 26:7

3 than those things which were spoken **by** Paul....... Acts 27:11
3 was broken **with** the violence of the waves............. 27:41
1 both Jews and Gentiles, that they are all **under** sin; Rom 3:9
3 the poison of asps is **under** their lips:.................. 3:13
3 being witnessed **by** the law and the prophets;........... 3:21
3 for ye are not **under** the law, but under grace........... 6:14
3 for ye are not under the law, but **under** grace........... 6:14
3 shall we sin, because we are not **under** the law,......... 6:15
3 not under the law, but **under** grace? God forbid......... 6:15
3 but I am carnal, sold **under** sin........................ 7:14
3 Be not overcome **of** evil,............................. 12:21
3 there is no authority except **from** God, (NASB)....... 13:1
3 the powers that be are ordained **of** God............... 13:1
3 because of the grace that is given to me **of** God,...... 15:15
1 and to be brought on my way thitherward **by** you,..... 15:24
3 shall bruise Satan **under** your feet shortly.............. 16:20
3 **by** them which are of the house of Chloe,.......... 1 Co 1:11
3 know the things that are freely given to us **of** God...... 2:12
2 yet he himself is judged **of** no man..................... 2:15
1 I should be judged **of** you, or of man's judgment:....... 4:3
3 I should be judged of you, or **of** man's judgment:....... 4:3
3 but I will not be brought under the power **of** any....... 6:12
3 hath obtained mercy **of** the Lord to be faithful.......... 7:25
2 if any man love God, the same is known **of** him........ 8:3
3 to them that are **under** the law, as under the law,........ 9:20
3 to them that are under the law, as **under** the law,........ 9:20
3 though not being myself **under** the Law, (NASB)....... 9:20
3 that I might gain them that are **under** the law;.......... 9:20
3 how that all our fathers were **under** the cloud,......... 10:1
3 also tempted, and were destroyed **of** serpents.......... 10:9
3 murmured, and were destroyed **of** the destroyer........ 10:10
3 is my liberty judged **of** another man's conscience?..... 10:29
3 when we are judged, we are chastened **of** the Lord,.... 11:32
3 he is convinced **of** all, he is judged of all:............ 14:24
3 he is convinced of all, he is judged **of** all:............ 14:24
3 reign, till he hath put all enemies **under** his feet....... 15:25
3 For he hath put all things **under** his feet............... 15:27
3 wherewith we ourselves are comforted **of** God....... 2 Co 1:4
1 **of** you to be brought on my way toward Judaea......... 1:16
3 this punishment, which was inflicted **of** many............ 2:6
3 no advantage be taken of us **by** Satan; (NASB)......... 2:11
3 written in our hearts, known and read **of** all men:...... 3:2
1 to be the epistle of Christ ministered **by** us,............ 3:3
3 that mortality might be swallowed up **of** life............ 5:4
3 but who was also chosen **of** the churches to travel...... 8:19
1 which is administered **by** us to the glory............... 8:19
1 in this abundance which is administered **by** us:......... 8:20
3 **Of** the Jews ... received I forty stripes save one......... 11:24
1 for I ought to have been commended **of** you:.......... 12:11
2 gospel which was preached **of** me is not after man.... Gal 1:11
3 are of the works of the law are **under** the curse:........ 3:10
3 confirmed before **of** God in Christ, the law,............ 3:17
3 But the scripture hath concluded all **under** sin,.......... 3:22
3 But before faith came, we were kept **under** the law,..... 3:23
3 we are no longer **under** a schoolmaster................. 3:25
3 But is **under** tutors and governors until the time........ 4:2
3 were in bondage **under** the elements of the world:...... 4:3
3 his Son, made of a woman, made **under** the law,........ 4:4
3 To redeem them that were **under** the law,.............. 4:5
3 ye have known God, or rather are known **of** God,...... 4:9
3 Tell me, ye that desire to be **under** the law,........... 4:21
3 take heed that ye be not consumed one **of** another...... 5:15
3 if ye be led of the Spirit, ye are not **under** the law...... 5:18
3 And hath put all things **under** his feet,.............. Eph 1:22
3 **by** that which is called the Circumcision................ 2:11
2 those things which are done **of** them in secret........... 5:12
3 that are reproved are made manifest **by** the light:....... 5:13
3 And in nothing terrified **by** your adversaries:........ Phlp 1:28
3 for which also I am apprehended **of** Christ Jesus........ 3:12
3 preached to every creature which is **under** heaven;.... Col 1:23
3 vainly puffed up **by** his fleshly mind,.................. 2:18
3 Knowing, brethren beloved, your election **of** God.... 1 Th 1:4
3 allowed **of** God to be put in trust with the gospel,...... 2:4
3 have suffered like things **of** your own countrymen,...... 2:14
3 have suffered ... even as they have **of** the Jews:......... 2:14
3 brethren beloved **of** the Lord,...................... 2 Th 2:13
3 Let as many servants as are **under** the yoke........ 1 Tm 6:1
2 who are taken captive **by** him at his will........... 2 Tm 2:26
3 was confirmed unto us **by** them that heard him;..... Heb 2:3
3 For every house is builded **by** some man;.............. 3:4
3 but he that is called **of** God, as was Aaron............. 5:4
3 Called **of** God an high priest........................... 5:10
3 the less is blessed **of** the better......................... 7:7
3 Moses had spoken every precept (NT)................. 9:19
3 was hid three months **of** his parents,.................. 11:23
3 him that endured such contradiction **of** sinners......... 12:3
2 nor faint when thou art rebuked **of** him:.............. 12:5
3 he is drawn away **of** his own lust, and enticed........ Jas 1:14
3 Stand thou there, or sit here **under** my footstool:....... 2:3
3 and are convinced **of** the law as transgressors........... 2:9
3 also the ships, ... and are driven **of** fierce winds,........ 3:4
3 yet are they turned about **with** a very small helm,...... 3:4
3 and it is set on fire **of** hell............................. 3:6
3 So that you may not fall **under** judgment. (NASB)...... 5:12
3 as unto a living stone, disallowed indeed **of** men,.... 1 Pt 2:4
3 Humble yourselves therefore **under** the mighty.......... 5:6
3 came such a voice to him **from** the excellent glory,.. 2 Pt 1:17
3 spake as they were moved **by** the Holy Ghost............ 1:21
3 vexed **with** the filthy conversation of the wicked:....... 2:7
3 clouds that are carried **with** a tempest;................. 2:17
3 which were spoken before **by** the holy prophets,......... 3:2
3 Demetrius hath good report **of** all men,............. 3 Jn 1:12
2 hath good report of all men, and **of** the truth itself:..... 1:12
3 hath reserved in everlasting chains **under** darkness... Jude 1:6
3 clouds ... without water, carried about **of** winds;........ 1:12
3 the words which were spoken before **of** the apostles..... 1:17
3 and with death, and **with** the beasts of the earth...... Rev 6:8
3 when she is shaken **of** a mighty wind................... 6:13
3 **By** these three was the third part of men killed,........ 9:18

This preposition is usually rendered "under" or "below," but other translations in the Authorized Version also occur, such as, "of" (Matthew 1:22), "by" (Matthew 2:17), "with" (Matthew 8:24), "in" (Acts 5:21), "among" (Acts 10:22), etc. It is used variously with the genitive, dative, accusative, as an adverb, and as a prefix attached to a verb. *Hupo* is often prefixed to other words to intensify them or alter their meaning. *Hupo* appears many times in both literary and nonliterary sources as well as in the Septuagint and the New Testament. The meanings are similar throughout, however.

In canonical texts *hupo* is used with two cases of the Greek: with the genitive case it signifies agent; with the accusative, "under," it is used of place, time, or subjection to authority. In the New Testament *hupo* occurs as a preposition about 220 times. A perusal of the lexicons reveals that *hupo* is prefixed to at least 40 Biblical words.

In the New Testament *hupo* is employed with the genitive case to indicate the agent from which a fact, event, or action originates. Thus the translation is "of" or "by." Two illustrations of this are found in Matthew 4:1: "Then was Jesus led up *of* the Spirit into the wilderness to be tempted *of* the devil." The cause of an action is seen in Luke 7:24: "A reed shaken *with* the wind?" Another example showing agency occurs in Luke 7:30: " . . . being not baptized *of* him." *Hupo* is used in a figurative sense as in Luke

8:14: "And that which fell among thorns are they, which, when they have heard, go forth, and are choked *with* cares and riches and pleasures of this life."

With the accusative case *hupo* is used both literally and figuratively. The literal sense occurs in Matthew 5:15, "put it *under* a bushel"; Matthew 8:8, "thou shouldest come *under* my roof"; and Luke 13:34, "as a hen doth gather her brood *under* her wings." The figurative use of *hupo* with the accusative case appears many times. Four times we see *hupo* in this sense in Romans 6:14,15: "For ye are not *under* the law, but *under* grace. What then? shall we sin, because we are not *under* the law, but *under* grace? God forbid." Galatians 3 illustrates three figurative senses: verse 10, "*under* the curse"; verse 22, "*under* sin"; verse 23, "*under* the law." Thus, *hupo* can indicate subordination. The figurative sense occurs once in respect to time: Acts 5:21, "early *in* the morning."

STRONG 5259, BAUER 843, MOULTON-MILLIGAN 655-56, LIDDELL-SCOTT 1873-75, COLIN BROWN 3:1197-98,1208.

5098. ὑποβάλλω hupoballō verb

Suborn, instigate, suggest, prompt.

CROSS-REFERENCE:
βάλλω ballō (900)

1. ὑπέβαλον hupebalon 3pl indic aor act

1 Then they **suborned** men, which said, ... Acts 6:11

This verb is made up of *hupo* (5097), an intensifying preposition, and *ballō* (900), "to throw." Thus the word signifies "to throw forcefully." *Hupoballō* is used numerous times in literary and nonliterary (e.g., papyri) Greek documents. The translations are varied: "throw, lay under, put down, subject, submit." Sometimes *hupoballō* means "suggest" and "whisper" as a prompter (*Liddell-Scott*). In the New Testament *hupoballō* occurs but once. In Acts 6:11 the word is rendered "suborn," i.e., to procure in a secret or unlawful way. The members of the Synagogue of the Freedmen obtained (secretly) some men to slander Stephen.

STRONG 5260, BAUER 843, MOULTON-MILLIGAN 656, LIDDELL-SCOTT 1875.

5099. ὑπογραμμός hupogrammos noun

Example, pattern, copy, model, outline.

COGNATE:
γράφω graphō (1119)

SYNONYMS:
δεῖγμα deigma (1159)
ὑπόδειγμα hupodeigma (5100)

1. ὑπογραμμόν hupogrammon acc sing masc

1 Christ also suffered for us, leaving us **an example**, ... 1 Pt 2:21

Classical Greek

This is one of four Greek words translated "example." Both literary and nonliterary sources contain the word which is translated "pattern, model, outline." Some of the occurrences denote "copy-heads" for children containing all the letters of the alphabet (see *Liddell-Scott*). The most common use of the noun refers to the faint outline of letters which pupils traced over when learning to write. (Occasionally pupils would practice copying a line of text recorded at the top of the page [Bruce, "Image," *Colin Brown*, 2:291].)

Septuagint Usage

This noun appears in the Septuagint in 2 Maccabees 2:28 (the verb *hupographō* is found in Esther 8:13). In this reference the meaning is "a copy of a letter."

New Testament Usage

In the New Testament *hupogrammos* occurs only in 1 Peter 2:21. Peter wrote, "Christ also suffered for us, leaving us an *example*, that ye should follow his steps." Christ is the example, pattern, and model for living in times of suffering.

STRONG 5261, BAUER 843, KITTEL 1:772-73, LIDDELL-SCOTT 1877, COLIN BROWN 2:291.

5100. ὑπόδειγμα hupodeigma noun

Example, sign, model, pattern, copy, imitation.

COGNATE:
δείκνυμι deiknumi (1161)

SYNONYMS:
δεῖγμα deigma (1159)
ὑπογραμμός hupogrammos (5099)

1. ὑποδείγματι hupodeigmati dat sing neu
2. ὑπόδειγμα hupodeigma nom/acc sing neu
3. ὑποδείγματα hupodeigmata nom/acc pl neu

2 For I have given you **an example**, ... John 13:15
1 any man fall after the same **example** of unbelief. ..... Heb 4:11
1 unto the **example** and shadow of heavenly things, ... 8:5
3 that the **patterns** of things in the heavens 9:23
2 **an example** of suffering affliction, and of patience. .... Jas 5:10
2 Sodom and ... making them **an ensample** .... 2 Pt 2:6

Classical Greek

In classical Greek *hupodeigma* (from *hupo* [5097], "by," and *deiknumi* [1161], "to show, demonstrate") is used in three primary ways: (1) as a "sign, indication" of something (a picture of how something should be done); (2) as a "pattern" for something (a model after which something is built); and (3) as an "example" or "specimen" of something (a sample of a certain number of specimens) (*Liddell-Scott*; cf. *Moulton-Milligan*).

Septuagint Usage

Only five instances of *hupodeigma* occur in the Septuagint, none of which are canonical, although all are instructive. The author of 2 Maccabees wrote of the elderly expert in the Law, Eleazar, who left the young men a "noble example" (RSV) of how to die (6:28,31). The "example" of other Jewish martyrs was apparently so great, Antiochus allegedly proclaimed them to be "examples" to his soldiers (4 Maccabees 17:23; cf. Sirach 44:16, of Enoch's example of repentance). In a noncanonical use in Ezekiel it refers to the "model" of the priests' rooms adjacent to the temple, which Ezekiel "saw" in his vision (Ezekiel 42:15, Septuagint only).

New Testament Usage

Three of the six instances of *hupodeigma* in the New Testament appear in the Book of Hebrews. Twice the usage there echoes the New Testament perspective that the Old Testament sanctuary, along with the sacrificial system as a whole, was only "a *copy* and shadow" of the heavenly (Hebrews 8:5, NIV; cf. 9:23).

Elsewhere *hupodeigma* concerns an example of behavior, either good (James 5:10; cf. John 13:15, of Jesus) or bad (Hebrews 4:11). God's destruction of Sodom and Gomorrah was an example of what will happen to the ungodly (2 Peter 2:6).

STRONG 5262, BAUER 844, MOULTON-MILLIGAN 656, LIDDELL-SCOTT 1878, COLIN BROWN 2:290,293.

5101. ὑποδείκνυμι

hupodeiknumi verb

Show plainly, point out, give direction, warn, set forth, inform.

COGNATE:

δείκνυμι deiknumi (1161)

SYNONYMS:

δείκνυμι deiknumi (1161)
ἐνδείκνυμι endeiknumi (1715)
ἐπιδείκνυμι epideiknumi (1910)

בִּין bîn (1032), Discern, understand; hiphil: make understand (Dn 10:14).

חֲוָה chăwâh (A2426), Pael: show an interpretation (Dn 5:7—Aramaic).

יְדַע yᵉdhaʿ (A3157), Know; haphel: explain, make known (Dn 2:17, 5:16—Aramaic).

יָרָה yārâh (3498), Throw, shoot; hiphil: teach (2 Chr 15:3).

נָגַד nāghadh (5222), Hiphil: tell, make known (2 Chr 20:2, Est 2:10, Dn 11:2).

סָפַר sāphar (5807), Count; piel: recount (Est 5:11).

רָאָה rā'âh (7495), See; choose (Est 2:9—Sixtine Edition only).

שָׂכַל sākhal (7959), Hiphil: give insight (Dn 9:22).

1. ὑπέδειξα **hupedeixa** 1sing indic aor act
2. ὑπέδειξεν **hupedeixen** 3sing indic aor act
3. ὑποδείξω **hupodeixō** 1sing indic fut act

2 who ... warned you to flee from the wrath to come? Matt 3:7
2 who hath warned you to flee from the wrath........ Luke 3:7
3 I will show you to whom he is like:.................... 6:47
3 But I will forewarn you whom ye shall fear:........... 12:5
3 I will show him how great things he must suffer..... Acts 9:16
1 I have showed you all things,......................... 20:35

Classical Greek

This verb is composed of the preposition *hupo* (5097), "under," and *deiknumi* (1161), "show, make known, explain, prove." Classical Greek writings reveal numerous examples of the use of this word: to show by tracing out, to set a pattern or example, to teach, to indicate, to give a glimpse of, to indicate one's will, intimate, lay out information, report, bring to the notice of, produce evidence, etc. (see *Liddell-Scott* and *Moulton-Milligan*).

Septuagint Usage

Hupodeiknumi occurs 14 times in the canonical Septuagint. In Esther the verb indicates Queen Esther had kept her nationality secret (2:10,20); she did not *reveal* it. The queen's uncle, Mordecai, *made known* that he resisted the king's command because he was a Jew.

New Testament Usage

In Matthew 3:7 (cf. Luke 3:7) this verb is translated "warn." Note the intensified meaning as the result of *hupo* prefixed to *deiknumi*, "to show." The other four occurrences mean "plainly setting forth" or "pointing out strongly." In the first of the four references (Luke 6:47) Jesus pressed upon His hearers the utter necessity of practicing His teachings. In Luke 12:5 Jesus stressed what to fear and what not to fear. Acts 9:16 reports that Jesus told Ananias that Saul would no longer bring havoc on the Church, but He would plainly show Saul what he himself must suffer. Lastly, in Acts 20:35 Paul reminded the Ephesians that he had plainly and emphatically set forth how they ought to help each other. Paul's use of this emphatic verb pointed out how important he felt it was to help others.

STRONG 5263, BAUER 844, MOULTON-MILLIGAN 656, LIDDELL-SCOTT 1878.

5102. ὑποδέομαι hupodeomai verb

Shod, bind on, bind under, put on.

CROSS-REFERENCE:

δέω deō (1204)

נָעַל nā'al (5457), Qal: put sandals on someone (Ez 16:10); hiphil: provide sandals (2 Chr 28:15).

1. ὑπόδησαι hupodēsai 2sing impr aor mid
2. ὑποδησάμενοι hupodēsamenoi nom pl masc part aor mid
3. ὑποδεδεμένους hupodedemenous acc pl masc part perf mid

3 **be shod with** sandals; and not put on two coats..... Mark 6:9
1 Gird thyself, and **bind on** thy sandals..............Acts 12:8
2 **shod with** the preparation of the gospel of peace;.... Eph 6:15

Classical Greek and Septuagint Usage

In classical Greek this verb means to underbind, e.g., to fasten a binding on one's sandals or put on one's shoes (see *Liddell-Scott*). The verb appears twice in the Septuagint (2 Chronicles 28:15; Ezekiel 16:10). Second Chronicles 28:15 records how the Israelites clothed their prisoners, gave them food and drink, and *put sandals on their feet.* In Ezekiel 16:10 God recounts how He treated the Israelites; He bathed them (verse 9), clothed them, and placed sandals on their feet.

New Testament Usage

In the New Testament the word occurs three times. In Mark 6:9 it is translated "shod." Jesus sent out the Twelve and told them, among other things, to be *shod* with sandals. The angel told Peter to *bind on* his sandals (Acts 12:8). The last use of *hupodeomai* occurs in Ephesians 6:15. Here Paul says to have our feet *shod* with the preparation of the gospel. The preparation of the gospel of peace "is not the readiness for conflict given by the Gospel but the readiness for active propagation of the Gospel, which is the most effective means of combatting satanic powers" (Oepke, "hupodeō," *Kittel,* 5:312).

STRONG 5265, BAUER 844 (see "hupodeō"), MOULTON-MILLIGAN 657 (see "hupodeō"), KITTEL 5:310-12 (see "hupodeō"), LIDDELL-SCOTT 1879 (see "hupodeō").

5103. ὑποδέχομαι hupodechomai verb

Receive as a guest, welcome, entertain.

COGNATE:

δέχομαι dechomai (1203)

SYNONYMS:

ἀναδέχομαι anadechomai (322)
ἀπέχω apechō (563)
ἀποδέχομαι apodechomai (583)
ἀπολαμβάνω apolambanō (612)
δέχομαι dechomai (1203)
εἰσδέχομαι eisdechomai (1509)
ἐπιδέχομαι epidechomai (1911)
κομίζω komizō (2837)
λαμβάνω lambanō (2956)
μεταλαμβάνω metalambanō (3205)
παραδέχομαι paradechomai (3720)
παραλαμβάνω paralambanō (3741)
προσδέχομαι prosdechomai (4185)
προσλαμβάνω proslambanō (4213)
ὑπολαμβάνω hupolambanō (5112)

1. ὑπεδέξατο hupedexato 3sing indic aor mid
2. ὑποδεξαμένη hupodexamenē nom sing fem part aor mid
3. ὑποδέδεκται hupodedektai 3sing indic perf mid

1 and a certain woman named Martha **received** him.. Luke 10:38
1 and came down, and **received** him joyfully............ 19:6
3 Whom Jason **hath received**:........................Acts 17:7
2 justified ... when she **had received** the messengers,.... Jas 2:25

This verb is used to mean entertain at a meal, *harbor* a runaway slave, *take up* a burden, undertake, promise, etc. (see *Liddell-Scott*). It occurs four times in the New Testament. Each occurrence of *hupodechomai* has a positive connotation. In Luke 10:38 Martha *received* Jesus into her house; she invited Him into her home and entertained Him. Zaccheus *received* (welcomed) Christ into his house. Thus, Jesus became a guest in the tax collector's home (Luke 19:6,7).

Acts 17:7 indicates Jason welcomed Paul into his house. James wrote that Rahab received (invited to her home) the spies Joshua sent to Jericho (James 2:25). These references indicate *hupodechomai* is used of a warm and hospitable welcome.

STRONG 5264, BAUER 844, MOULTON-MILLIGAN 656-57, LIDDELL-SCOTT 1879.

5104. ὑπόδημα hupodēma noun

Shoes, sandals.

CROSS-REFERENCE:

δέω deō (1204)

מִנְעָל min'āl (4663), Lock (Dt 33:25).

נַעַל na'al (5458), Shoe, sandal (Ex 3:5, Ps 60:8 [59:8], Am 8:6).

1. ὑποδήματος hupodēmatos gen sing neu
2. ὑπόδημα hupodēma nom/acc sing neu
3. ὑποδημάτων hupodēmatōn gen pl neu
4. ὑποδήματα hupodēmata nom/acc pl neu

4 whose **shoes** I am not worthy to bear: .... Matt 3:11
4 neither two coats, neither **shoes**, nor yet staves: 10:10
3 the latchet of whose **shoes** I am not worthy .... Mark 1:7
3 latchet of whose **shoes** I am not worthy to unloose: Luke 3:16
4 Carry neither purse, nor scrip, nor **shoes**: 10:4
4 and put a ring on his hand, and **shoes** on his feet: 15:22
3 I sent you without purse, and scrip, and **shoes**, ... 22:35
1 whose **shoe's** latchet I am not worthy to unloose..... John 1:27
2 Put off thy **shoes** from thy feet: .... Acts 7:33
2 whose **shoes** of his feet I am not worthy to loose...... 13:25

Classical Greek

This is the primary word for shoes. It is related to the verb *hupodeomai* (5102), "to bind under." In the nonbiblical writings this word is used for sandals, shoes, and half-boots (see *Liddell-Scott*). These were generally leather soles fastened to the foot by means of straps.

New Testament Usage

This noun occurs 10 times in the New Testament. It is consistently rendered "shoes" in the King James Version. It seems evident from culture and the use of the word in such references as Mark 1:7, Luke 3:16, and John 1:27 that the word means "sandals."

STRONG 5266, BAUER 844, MOULTON-MILLIGAN 657, KITTEL 5:310-12, LIDDELL-SCOTT 1879.

5105. ὑπόδικος hupodikos adj

Guilty, brought to trial, answerable, liable to punishment.

CROSS-REFERENCE:
δικαιόω dikaioō (1338)

1. ὑπόδικος hupodikos nom sing masc

1 and all the world may become **guilty** before God.... Rom 3:19

In classical Greek the word *hupodikos* means "brought to trial, liable to be tried," and "liable to action" (see *Liddell-Scott*). This word is translated "guilty" in the King James Version. *Hupodikos* occurs once in the New Testament (Romans 3:19). Here the word signifies that the world is under the judgment of God because of the Law before which no one can stand blameless.

STRONG 5267, BAUER 844, MOULTON-MILLIGAN 657, KITTEL 8:557-58, LIDDELL-SCOTT 1880.

5106. ὑποζύγιος hupozugios noun

Ass, donkey, beast of burden.

CROSS-REFERENCE:
ζυγός zugos (2201)

אָתוֹן 'āthôn (888), Donkey (Jgs 5:10—Codex Alexandrinus only).

חֲמוֹר chămôr (2645), Donkey (Ex 20:17, Dt 5:14, 2 Chr 28:15).

1. ὑποζύγιον hupozugion nom/acc sing neu
2. ὑποζυγίου hupozugiou gen sing neu

2 and a colt the foal **of an ass**. .... Matt 21:5
1 the dumb **ass** speaking with man's voice .... 2 Pt 2:16

Literally this noun signifies "under the yoke" (*hupo* [5097], "under," and *zugos* [2201], "yoke"). This word should not be confused with the usual word for an ass, *onos* (3551); the diminutive form, *onarion* (3541), denoting a young ass; nor with *pōlos* (4311), referring to "a colt" (see Vine's *Expository Dictionary*, "Ass"). In its earliest usage *hupozugios* denoted any animal used as a beast of burden. Later, in Biblical Greek, it came to denote only the donkey (*Liddell-Scott*), perhaps because in the East the ass was the main beast of burden (Thayer, *Greek-English Lexicon*). Only two occurrences of *hupozugios* are found in the New Testament (Matthew 21:5; 2 Peter 2:16). The first reference seems to indicate the parent of the colt on which Jesus sat (Matthew 21:2). Peter refers to the ass (*hupozugios*) speaking to Balaam.

STRONG 5268, BAUER 844 (see "hupozugion"), MOULTON-MILLIGAN 657 (see "hupozugion"), LIDDELL-SCOTT 1881 (see "hupozugion").

5107. ὑποζώννυμι hupozōnnumi verb

To undergird, strengthen, brace.

CROSS-REFERENCE:
ζῷον zōon (2209)

1. ὑποζωννύντες hupozōnnuntes
nom pl masc part pres act

1 they used helps, **undergirding** the ship; .... Acts 27:17

This is the verb for "undergird," and is a compound form of *hupo* (5097), "under," and *zōnnumi* (2207), "gird." The verb occurs without *hupo* in John 21:18. Classical writings use *hupozōnnumi* to denote the undergirding of ships. Whatever is used to gird is called a girdle (*hupozōnē*). *Hupozōnnumi* occurs once in the New Testament. Acts 27:17 describes the storm that threatened to break apart the ship on which Paul was sailing. The crew attempted to strengthen the ship by undergirding it with cables or ropes that went around the outside of the hull to protect the ship from the pounding waves of the hurricane. Generally *hupozōmata* (undergirdings for ships) were used only on warships. However, the large grain ships (on one of which Paul was riding) may have needed these heavy cables for reinforcement and stability. (For an excellent discussion on these grain ships, see Hirschfeld, "The Ship of Saint Paul: Historical Background.")

Strong 5269, Bauer 844, Moulton-Milligan 657, Liddell-Scott 1881.

5108. ὑποκάτω hupokatō prep

Under, underneath, below.

Cross-Reference:

κατώτερος katōteros (2707)

1. ὑποκάτω hupokatō

1 until I put your enemies **under** your feet." (NIV) .. Matt 22:44
1 shake off the dust **under** your feet for a testimony .. Mark 6:11
1 dogs **under** the table eat of the children's crumbs........ 7:28
1 I put your enemies **under** your feet." (NASB) 12:36
1 covereth it with a vessel, or putteth it **under** a bed; Luke 8:16
1 I saw thee **under** the fig tree, believest thou? .... John 1:50
1 hast put all things in subjection **under** his feet........Heb 2:8
1 in heaven, nor in earth, neither **under** the earth,..... Rev 5:3
1 and on the earth, and **under** the earth,................ 5:13
1 I saw **under** the altar the souls of them 6:9
1 clothed with the sun, and the moon **under** her feet,.... 12:1

This is an adverb used as a preposition. The word is composed of *hupo* (5097), "under," and *katō* (2706), "under, down, beneath, lower, bottom." *Hupokatō* appears in the New Testament nine times. In these references literal things are under objects, such as dust under the feet, dogs under a table, a lamp under a bed, Nathanael under a fig tree, etc. *Hupokatō* is also used figuratively, as in the following: " . . . all things in subjection under his feet" (Hebrews 2:8); and "I saw under the altar the souls of them that were slain for the word of God" (Revelation 6:9). The use of *hupokatō* in John 1:50 is interesting because in 1:48 the word for "under" is *hupo* but in 1:50 it is *hupokatō*. The use of *hupokatō* strengthens the meaning of *hupo* in 1:48.

Strong 5270, Bauer 844, Moulton-Milligan 657, Liddell-Scott 1883.

5109. ὑποκρίνομαι hupokrinomai verb

Feign, pretend, play a part on stage, be a hypocrite.

Cognates:

ἀνυπόκριτος anupokritos (502)
κρίνω krinō (2892)
συνυποκρίνομαι sunupokrinomai (4794)
ὑπόκρισις hupokrisis (5110)
ὑποκριτής hupokritēs (5111)

לָהָה lāhâh (3992), Behave insanely; hithpalpel: act like a hypocrite (Sir 35:15).

עָנָה ʿānâh (6257), Answer (Jb 40:2 [39:32]).

1. ὑποκρινομένους hupokrinomenous acc pl masc part pres mid

1 which **should feign** themselves just men,........... Luke 20:20

Classical Greek

Hupokrinomai appears in classical literature as early as Homer (Eighth Century B.C.). Its early uses included "to explain, interpret." As well, it could mean "to answer" (Wilckens, "hupokrinomai," *Kittel,* 8:559). In Attic Greek *hupokrinomai* also means "to play a part" on the stage (here it is connected with the *hupokritēs,* the actor introduced into Athenian tragedy by Thespis in 536 B.C.). Occasionally it could mean "to deliver a speech, to represent dramatically," or "to exaggerate" (*Liddell-Scott*).

Septuagint Usage

In the Septuagint *hupokrinomai* assumes a negative sense absent in classical literature. In Sirach 1:29 the RSV translates this word as "hypocrite": "Be not a *hypocrite*" in men's sight. In 2 Maccabees 5:25 it describes a man who *pretended* to be favorable toward the Jews (cf. 2 Maccabees 6:21). In 4 Maccabees 6:15 certain followers of the king exhorted Eleazer to "pretend" to eat pork. In its only canonical appearance, *hupokrinomai* means "to answer" (Job 40:2 [LXX 39:32]).

New Testament Usage

Hupokrinomai occurs once in the New Testament (Luke 20:20). The enemies of the Lord Jesus sent spies who pretended to be righteous men in an effort to entrap Jesus. These enemies pretended or feigned to be what they were not, but Jesus saw through their duplicity. Thus *hupokrinomai* expresses the action of the noun for hypocrisy. "As Luke sees it, this role is a hubris which typifies the Pharisee, Luke 16:15; 18:9" (Wilckens, "hupokrinomai," *Kittel,* 8:568).

Strong 5271, Bauer 845, Moulton-Milligan 657, Kittel 8:559-70, Liddell-Scott 1885-86, Colin Brown 2:468 (see "hupokrinō").

5110. ὑπόκρισις hupokrisis noun

Hypocrisy, pretense, insincerity.

Cross-Reference:

ὑποκρίνομαι hupokrinomai (5109)

1. ὑπόκρισις hupokrisis nom sing fem
2. ὑποκρίσεως hupokriseōs gen sing fem

3. **ὑποκρίσει hupokrisei** dat sing fem
4. **ὑπόκρισιν hupokrisin** acc sing fem
5. **ὑποκρίσεις hupokriseis** acc pl fem

2 but within ye are full of **hypocrisy** and iniquity..... Matt 23:28
4 But he, knowing their **hypocrisy**, said unto them,.. Mark 12:15
1 leaven of the Pharisees, which is **hypocrisy**......... Luke 12:1
3 also was carried away with their **dissimulation**........ Gal 2:13
3 Speaking lies in **hypocrisy**;........................ 1 Tm 4:2
4 swear not, ... lest ye fall into condemnation. (NT).... Jas 5:12
5 and **hypocrisies**, and envies, and all evil speakings,...1 Pt 2:1

Classical Greek

This term, generally translated as "hypocrisy," is a compound term from the preposition *hupo* (5097), "by," and the verb *krinō* (2892), "to judge." In classical Greek it can denote a "reply" (cf. the verb *hupokrinomai* [5109], "pretend, make believe"). *Hupokrisis* can refer to "playing a part on the stage," or to the *delivery* of an orator which included "mime and gesture" (Wilckens, "hupokrinomai," *Kittel*, 8:559-561). Later in classical Greek, under the influence of its role in the world of drama, *hupokrisis* assumed the meaning "pretense," the unreality and deception associated with acting, although the word is not "intrinsically a deceiving" (ibid., 8:563). *Hupokrisis* only assumes a wholly negative sense in Jewish Greek, perhaps as a response by Jews to the pagan Greek stage.

Septuagint Usage

Only one instance of *hupokrisis* occurs in the Septuagint, and it is noncanonical (cf. the verb, only one of nine instances is canonical). Eleazar, about to be executed for refusing to eat unclean food, refused to carry out a "pretense" of eating it because of the effect such capitulation would have upon himself and others (2 Maccabees 6:18-31).

New Testament Usage

Hupokrisis is used in the New Testament only of religious "hypocrisy." It refers to the Pharisees and teachers of the Law (e.g., Mark 12:15). Jesus saw their inner man as full of hypocrisy (Matthew 23:28). Any "righteousness" they had was merely superficial and external pomp which served to disguise their true nature.

Paul and Peter equated hypocrisy with lying (1 Timothy 4:2; 1 Peter 2:1), following Hellenistic Jewish usage (see Wilckens, "hupokrinomai," *Kittel*, 8:566-569). Jesus strongly cautioned against the presence of hypocrisy in one's prayer life (Matthew 6:5). In addition, man can be carried away by the hypocrisy of others, for even an upright man like Barnabas was guilty of this (Galatians 2:13). Care must be taken to avoid hypocrisy (Luke 12:1).

Hypocrites try to conceal their true identity and their secret sins by wearing a "mask." Externally their conduct may seem very pious and upright, but it is all an act. The hypocrite is never the person he or she pretends to be.

Strong 5272, Bauer 845, Moulton-Milligan 657, Kittel 8:559-70, Liddell-Scott 1886, Colin Brown 2:468-69.

5111. ὑποκριτής hupokritēs noun

Hypocrite, pretender.

Cross-Reference:

ὑποκρίνομαι hupokrinomai (5109)

חָנֵף chānēph (2715), Godless, hypocrite (Jb 34:30, 36:13).

1. **ὑποκριτά hupokrita** voc sing masc
2. **ὑποκριταί hupokritai** nom pl masc
3. **ὑποκριτῶν hupokritōn** gen pl masc

2 **hypocrites** do in the synagogues and in the streets,.. Matt 6:2
2 thou shalt not be as the **hypocrites** are:................ 6:5
2 Moreover when ye fast, be not, as the **hypocrites**,....... 6:16
1 Thou **hypocrite**, first cast out the beam................. 7:5
2 Ye **hypocrites**, well did Esaias prophesy of you,........ 15:7
2 O ye **hypocrites**, ye can discern the face of the sky;.... 16:3
2 Why tempt ye me, ye **hypocrites**?..................... 22:18
2 woe unto you, scribes and Pharisees, **hypocrites**!....... 23:13
2 Woe unto you, scribes and Pharisees, **hypocrites**!...... 23:14
2 Woe unto you, scribes and Pharisees, **hypocrites**!...... 23:15
2 Woe unto you, scribes and Pharisees, **hypocrites**!...... 23:23
2 Woe unto you, scribes and Pharisees, **hypocrites**!...... 23:25
2 Woe unto you, scribes and Pharisees, **hypocrites**!...... 23:27
2 Woe unto you, scribes and Pharisees, **hypocrites**!...... 23:29
3 and appoint him his portion with the **hypocrites**:....... 24:51
3 Well hath Esaias prophesied of you **hypocrites**,..... Mark 7:6
1 Thou **hypocrite**, cast out first the beam out of thine Luke 6:42
2 Woe unto you, scribes and Pharisees, **hypocrites**!...... 11:44
2 Ye **hypocrites**, ye can discern the face of the sky...... 12:56
1 answered him, and said, Thou **hypocrite**,.............. 13:15

Classical Greek

In classical Greek this noun (a compound form related to *krinō* [2892], "judge") denotes the individual who "answers" or "replies" on stage. At the same time, it can depict the "interpreter" or "expounder" who explained the drama to the audience. In 536 B.C. Thespis introduced an individual who replied to the chorus (a group of male dancers and singers) in the festival of Dionysius held every spring in Athens. This individual wore a mask (as did the chorus) and was called the *hupokritēs*, the one who "answers" or "interprets." The *hupokritēs* came to be the actor in Greek theater. *Hupokritēs* alone never had an unfavorable ethical meaning in classical Greek (Wilckens, "hupokrinomai," *Kittel*, 8:563).

Septuagint Usage

Negative meanings of *hupokritēs* developed in the Septuagint and in Hellenistic Jewish usage, where it occurs most regularly in later writings. Found only in Job 34:30 and 36:13, *hupokritēs* (Hebrew *chānēph*, "estranged from God, godless") contains clearly negative ethical implications. According to Wilckens, in Jewish thinking "the *hupokritēs* is the ungodly man, the ungodly man is the *hupokritēs*" (ibid., 8:564). The negative sense attached to this word perhaps derived from Jewish dislike of the pagan Greek theater and *hupokritēs*' association with lying and deception (ibid., 8:566).

New Testament Usage

Every New Testament instance of *hupokritēs* occurs in the Synoptic Gospels and every one occurs in a saying of Jesus. Moreover, every instance but two (parallel texts) is in the plural form (cf. Matthew 7:5; Luke 6:42).

Hupokritēs is often found in Matthew as a descriptive epithet for the experts in the Law and for the Pharisees (e.g., Matthew 15:7; 22:18; 23:13-15, etc.). His portrait of the "hypocrites" (Matthew 6:2,5,16) shows what spiritual "actors" and "pretenders" these fakes were.

Mark's single usage (7:6; cf. Matthew 15:7) concerns the tradition created by the Pharisees and scribes. They perverted the Law's intent, and their external religiosity was an attempt to conceal their inner corruption. Jesus applied the words of Isaiah 29:13 to them showing that God does not tolerate such pretense.

Luke's usage carries an intimation of the hardness and lack of compassion characteristic of the hypocrite (Luke 12:56; 13:15). Jesus' attitude is similarly reflected in His pronouncement of "Woe!" upon the hypocritical Pharisees and legal experts; they not only perverted the Law but also prevented others from knowing God (Matthew 23; cf. Luke 11).

STRONG 5273, BAUER 845, MOULTON-MILLIGAN 657, KITTEL 8:559-70, LIDDELL-SCOTT 1886, COLIN BROWN 2:468-70.

5112. ὑπολαμβάνω

hupolambanō verb

Receive, answer, suppose, take up, bear up, support.

COGNATE:

λαμβάνω lambanō (2956)

SYNONYMS:

ἀναδέχομαι anadechomai (322)
ἀποδέχομαι apodechomai (583)
ἀπολαμβάνω apolambanō (612)
δέχομαι dechomai (1203)
δοκέω dokeō (1374)
εἰσδέχομαι eisdechomai (1509)
ἐνθυμέομαι enthumeomai (1744)
ἐπιδέχομαι epidechomai (1911)
ἡγέομαι hēgeomai (2216)
κρίνω krinō (2892)
λαμβάνω lambanō (2956)
λογίζομαι logizomai (3023)
μεταλαμβάνω metalambanō (3205)
νοέω noeō (3401)
νομίζω nomizō (3406)
οἴομαι oiomai (3496)
παραδέχομαι paradechomai (3720)
παραλαμβάνω paralambanō (3741)
προσδέχομαι prosdechomai (4185)
προσλαμβάνω proslambanō (4213)
ὑποδέχομαι hupodechomai (5103)
φρονέω phroneō (5262)

אָחַז 'āchaz (270), Seize (Ps 48:6 [47:6]—Codex Alexandrinus only).

בּוֹא bô' (971), Go (2 Chr 25:8).

דָּלָה dālâh (1861), Piel: lift out (Ps 30:1 [29:1]).

דָּמָה dāmâh (1880), Be like, cease; piel: think about (Ps 48:9 [47:9]).

חָשַׁב chāshav (2913), Think out (Ps 73:16 [72:16]).

יָתַר yāthar (3613), Niphal: be left (2 Kgs 20:17—Codex Alexandrinus only).

עָנָה 'ānâh (6257), Answer, reply (Jb 4:1, 6:1, 8:1).

עֲנָה 'ănâh (A6258), Respond (Dn 3:9,28—Aramaic).

1. **ὑπολαμβάνω hupolambanō** 1sing indic pres act
2. **ὑπολαμβάνετε hupolambanete** 2pl indic pres act
3. **ὑπέλαβεν hupelaben** 3sing indic aor act
4. **ὑπολαβών hupolabōn** nom sing masc part aor act
5. **ὑπολαμβάνειν hupolambanein** inf pres act

1 I suppose that he, to whom he forgave most.........Luke 7:43
4 And Jesus answering said, A certain man............ 10:30
3 and a cloud received him out of their sight.......... Acts 1:9
2 For these are not drunken, as ye suppose,.............. 2:15
5 Therefore we ought to support such (NASB)........ 3 Jn 1:8

Classical Greek

Classical Greek usage of this frequently used verb varies greatly. The verb is used literally to mean "bear up, support, seize." Figuratively, the word means "interpret, understand, assume" (*Liddell-Scott*). Papyri use this verb both in the figurative sense and the literal sense. "Suppose" and "assume" are common meanings, as well as "take up" and "carry away" (*Moulton-Milligan*).

Septuagint Usage

Hupolambanō occurs about 50 times in the Septuagint. The Book of Job contains 27 occurrences of this verb. In Job 2:4 this word means "take up" or "answer." The Lord *took up* the devil's challenge concerning Job. The turn of debate between Job and his friends opens with the words "*answered* and said" (Job 4:1; 6:1; 8:1; 9:1; 11:1; 12:1; 15:1, etc.). In English it may seem redundant to follow "answered" with "said," but this is simply a Hebrew idiom for "reply."

New Testament Usage

In the New Testament *hupolambanō* is recorded four times. In Luke 7:43 the rendering is "suppose," indicating Simon thought about Jesus' question and answered having weighed the two possible responses. Here the words "answered" and "suppose" are similar in meaning; however, the result of Simon's reasoning is translated "suppose" (or "assume") while the word "answered" verbalizes the conclusion. Luke 10:30 describes Jesus answering a lawyer's question. The King James Version rendering is, "And Jesus answering (*hupolambanō*) said . . . " (*eipen* [see 1500]). Jesus "took up" or received the lawyer's question and answered. In Acts 1:9 this verb is used of the cloud which "received" (*hupolambanō*) Jesus. *Hupo* (5097) perhaps intensifies the meaning of *lambanō* (2956), "receive."

In Acts 2:15 Luke used this verb in a figurative sense rendered "suppose." Some who observed the phenomena on the Day of Pentecost attributed speaking in tongues to drunkenness. But Peter said it was not as they supposed or imagined. They had reached the wrong conclusion. In some texts of 3 John 8 *hupolambanō* has the idea of "support" (other texts contain the related word *apolambanō*, "receive"). John commended Gaius for taking care of traveling ministers who came to his home.

Strong 5274, Bauer 845, Moulton-Milligan 658, Kittel 4:15, Liddell-Scott 1886-87, Colin Brown 3:747,749.

5112B. ὑπόλειμμα hupoleimma noun

A remnant.

Cross-Reference:

λείπω leipō (2981)

שָׂרִיד sārîdh (8032), What is left (Jb 20:21).

שָׁאַר shā'ar (8080), Niphal: what is kept (1 Sm 9:24).

שְׁאֵר sh^{e}'ēr (8083), Flesh (Mal 2:15).

שְׁאֵרִית sh^{e}'erîth (8086), Remnant (2 Kgs 21:4, Mi 4:7, 5:7f.).

1. ὑπόλειμμα hupoleimma nom/acc sing neu

1 REMNANT THAT WILL BE SAVED: (NASB)..... Rom 9:27

Found in classical Greek literature as early as the Fifth Century B.C., this noun occurs only one time in the New Testament. Romans 9:27 quotes Isaiah 10:22f. and reads, "Though the number of the children of Israel be as the sand of the sea, a *remnant* shall be saved." (The *Textus Receptus* contains the word *kataleimma* [2610], "remnant," in this verse.) For a discussion of the term *remnant* see the word study at *leimma* (2979).

Bauer 845, Moulton-Milligan 658, Kittel 4:194-214, Liddell-Scott 1887, Colin Brown 3:247-48,251.

5113. ὑπολείπω hupoleipō verb

Leave, leave remaining, be left.

Cross-Reference:

λείπω leipō (2981)

אָצַל 'ātsal (702), Reserve (Gn 27:36—Sixtine Edition only).

גָּרַם gāram (1677), Leave (Zep 3:3).

יָצַר yātsar (3443), Set, place; hophal: be left behind (Ex 10:24—Codex Vaticanus only).

יָתַר yāthar (3613), Niphal: the rest, be left (Gn 30:36, 1 Kgs 18:22, Ez 14:22); hiphil: leave, have left (Ex 10:15, 2 Sm 17:12); spare (Ez 12:16).

יֶתֶר yether (3615), Remnant (Jos 12:4).

עָדַף 'ādhaph (5951), What is left over (Ex 26:12).

עָזַב 'āzav (6013), Leave (Gn 50:8, Mal 4:1).

עָמַד 'āmadh (6198), Stand (Jos 10:8).

שִׂים sîm (7947), Set, put; preserve (Gn 45:7).

שָׁאַר shā'ar (8080), Niphal: be left, remain (Gn 47:18, 1 Sm 11:11, Zec 9:7); hiphil: leave, spare (1 Sm 25:22, 2 Kgs 13:7, Jer 50:20 [27:20]).

1. ὑπελείφθην hupeleiphthēn 1sing indic aor pass

1 and I am left alone, and they seek my life.......... Rom 11:3

This verb occurs often in classical Greek and the Septuagint. Found as early as Homer (Eighth Century B.C.), *hupoleipō* occurs only once in the New Testament. In Romans 11:3 the apostle Paul quoted 1 Kings 19:10 where Elijah told God in his prayer that he was "left" (*hupoleipō*) as the only prophet of the Lord. But God was faithful to preserve a remnant. Paul noted this principle in Romans 11.

Strong 5275, Bauer 845, Moulton-Milligan 658, Liddell-Scott 1887, Colin Brown 3:247-48.

5114. ὑπολήνιον hupolēnion noun

Winevat, trough, pit.

יֶקֶב yeqev (3449), Winepress, wine vat (Is 16:10, Hg 2:16 [2:17], Zec 14:10).

1. ὑπολήνιον hupolēnion nom/acc sing neu

1 and digged a place for the winefat, ... Mark 12:1

The word *hupolēnion* denotes a container or pit located underneath a winepress that received and held the wine after the grapes were pressed (*Bauer*). The two elements of this compound term are *hupo* (5097), meaning "under, below, an inferior position," and *lēnos*, "trough, winevat."

The word is found in classical Greek, the Septuagint, and other early literature. It is used only once in the New Testament, at Mark 12:1. There it is rendered "winevat" in the KJV while the RSV more accurately translates it "a *pit* for the wine press."

Strong 5276, Bauer 845, Moulton-Milligan 658, Kittel 4:254-57, Liddell-Scott 1887.

5115. ὑπολιμπάνω hupolimpanō verb

Leave behind.

Synonyms:
ἀνίημι aniēmi (445)
ἀπολείπω apoleipō (614)
ἀποτάσσω apotassō (651)
ἀφίημι aphiēmi (856)
ἐγκαταλείπω enkataleipō (1452)
καταλείπω kataleipō (2611)

1. ὑπολιμπάνων hupolimpanōn
nom sing masc part pres act

1 Christ also suffered for us, leaving us an example, ... 1 Pt 2:21

This word is the Ionic Greek form of *hupoleipō* which has the same meaning (*Bauer*). Included in the sense of the word is the idea of "bequeathing" or "leaving" something for a specific purpose.

Although used throughout early literature and papyri, it only occurs once in the New Testament. At 1 Peter 2:21 the specific sense noted above can be seen: "Because Christ also suffered for us, *leaving* us an example, that ye should follow his steps . . . . "

Strong 5277, Bauer 845, Moulton-Milligan 658, Liddell-Scott 1887.

5116. ὑπομένω hupomenō verb

Abide, wait, endure, undergo, be patient, suffer, stay behind.

Cognates:
μένω menō (3176)
ὑπομονή hupomonē (5119)

Synonyms:
ἀνέχομαι anechomai (428)
ἀπολείπω apoleipō (614)
αὐλίζομαι aulizomai (829)
διαμένω diamenō (1259)
διατελέω diateleō (1294)
διατρίβω diatribō (1298)
ἐμμένω emmenō (1682)
ἐπιμένω epimenō (1946)
καθίζω kathizō (2495)
καρτερέω kartereō (2565)
καταμένω katamenō (2620)
μένω menō (3176)
παραμένω paramenō (3748)
περιλείπομαι perileipomai (3898)
στέγω stegō (4573)
ὑποφέρω hupopherō (5135)
φέρω pherō (5179)

חָכָה chākhâh (2542), Piel: wait (Jb 32:4, Is 64:4, Hb 2:3).

טָמַן ṭāman (3045), Be held in reserve (Jb 20:26).

יָחַל yāchal (3282), Piel: hope, wait (Jb 6:11, 14:14); hiphil: wait, have hope (2 Kgs 6:33, Jb 32:16, Lam 3:21).

יָשַׁב yāshav (3553), Stay (Nm 22:19).

כּוּל kûl (3677), Pilpel: endure (Mal 3:2).

מָהַהּ māhahh (4244), Hithpalpel: tarry (Ex 12:39—Codex Alexandrinus only).

קָוָה qāwâh (7245), Qal: wait, hope (Ps 37:9 [36:9], Is 40:31, Lam 3:25); piel: look for, wait for (Jb 17:13, Ps 37:9 [36:9], Jer 14:19).

קוּם qûm (7251), Stand, arise; endure (Jb 8:15).

1. ὑπομένετε hupomenete 2pl indic/impr pres act
2. ὑπομένω hupomenō 1sing indic pres act
3. ὑπομένει hupomenei 3sing indic pres act
4. ὑπομένομεν hupomenomen 1pl indic pres act
5. ὑπομένοντες hupomenontes
nom pl masc part pres act
6. ὑπομένοντας hupomenontas
acc pl masc part pres act
7. ὑπέμεινεν hupemeinen 3sing indic aor act
8. ὑπεμείνατε hupemeinate 2pl indic aor act
9. ὑπομείνας hupomeinas nom sing masc part aor act
10. ὑπομεμενηκότα hupomemenēkota
acc sing masc part perf act
11. ὑπομενεῖτε hupomeneite 2pl indic fut act
12. ὑπέμενον hupemenon 1/3sing/pl indic imperf act
13. ὑπέμειναν hupemeinan 3pl indic aor act
14. ὑπομείναντας hupomeinantas
acc pl masc part aor act

9 but he that endureth to the end shall be saved.... Matt 10:22
9 But he that shall endure unto the end, ... be saved.... 24:13
9 but he that shall endure unto the end, ... be saved.Mark 13:13
7 the child Jesus tarried behind in Jerusalem; .... Luke 2:43
13 but Silas and Timotheus abode there still. ....Acts 17:14
5 Rejoicing in hope; patient in tribulation; ....Rom 12:12
3 hopeth all things, endureth all things. ....1 Co 13:7
2 Therefore I endure all things for the elect's sakes, 2 Tm 2:10
4 If we suffer, we shall also reign with him: 2:12
8 ye endured a great fight of afflictions; .... Heb 10:32
7 endured the cross, despising the shame, ... 12:2
10 him that endured such contradiction of sinners 12:3

1 If ye **endure** chastening, ... Heb 12:7
3 Blessed is the man that **endureth** temptation: .... Jas 1:12
6 Behold, we count them happy **which endure**. 5:11
11 buffeted for your faults, ye shall **take it patiently**? .. 1 Pt 2:20
11 ye **take it patiently**, this is acceptable with God. 2:20

Classical Greek

Classical literature has a great number of renderings for this verb: "stay behind, to be left behind, to abide, to be patient under, submit, stand one's ground," etc. (*Liddell-Scott*).

In nonliterary writings *hupomenō* includes the idea of "suffering." To endure may likely involve suffering. Thus we read of one "who suffered (*hupomenō*) many ills for the sake of his only daughter" (*Moulton-Milligan*).

Septuagint Usage

The Septuagint uses *hupomenō* about 85 times. This verb appears three times in Psalm 25 (verses 3,5,21) (LXX Psalm 24). "Waiting on" the Lord here typifies Old Testament faith or trust in God. The writer began with a known fact that those who "wait" (*hupomenō*) on the Lord will not be ashamed. He moved in his prayer to the fact that he had spent the whole day "waiting" upon the Lord (verse 5). Finally, the Septuagint says that those who "wait" with him are the harmless and upright. They joined him because he waited (*hupomenō*) upon the Lord. Waiting here is also an equivalent of Old Testament faith.

New Testament Usage

The verb *hupomenō* is recorded 17 times in the New Testament. Only twice does the word occur in a literal sense. Once it is used when Jesus as a young boy remained behind at Jerusalem (Luke 2:43) and again when Silas and Timothy stayed behind at Beroea while Paul went on to Athens (Acts 17:14). Other references mean "endure, bear patiently," or "suffer." Jesus taught that the Christian must "endure" to the end for salvation (Matthew 10:22; 24:13; Mark 13:13). Christians are also encouraged to "endure" in difficult times and circumstances (1 Corinthians 13:7; Hebrews 10:32; 12:7, etc.). Not only that, they are to endure "patiently" (Romans 12:12; 1 Peter 2:20).

In 2 Timothy 2:12 *hupomenō* is rendered as "suffer." The very thought of continued endurance may entail suffering. While enduring and suffering the Christian is admonished to be patient. Thus we notice the close relationship between endure, be patient, and suffer, all of which are translated from *hupomenō*.

Strong 5278, Bauer 845-46, Moulton-Milligan 658, Kittel 4:581-88, Liddell-Scott 1888-89, Colin Brown 2:772-76.

5117. ὑπομιμνῄσκω

hupomimnēskō verb

Remember, bring to remembrance, put in mind, remind of, mention, suggest.

Cognate:
μιμνῄσκω mimnēskō (3267)

Synonyms:
ἀναμιμνῄσκω anamimnēskō (362)
μιμνῄσκω mimnēskō (3267)
μνημονεύω mnēmoneuō (3285)

זָכַר zākhar (2226), Remember; hiphil: recorder (1 Kgs 4:3—Codex Vaticanus only).

1. **ὑπομίμνῃσκε hupomimnēske** 2sing impr pres act
2. **ὑπομιμνῄσκειν hupomimnēskein** inf pres act
3. **ὑπομνῆσαι hupomnēsai** inf aor act
4. **ὑπομνήσω hupomnēsō** 1sing indic fut act
5. **ὑπομνήσει hupomnēsei** 3sing indic fut act
6. **ὑπεμνήσθη hupemnēsthē** 3sing indic aor pass

6 And Peter **remembered** the word of the Lord, ... Luke 22:61
5 and bring all things to your **remembrance**, ... John 14:26
1 Of these things **put** them **in remembrance**, ... 2 Tm 2:14
1 **Put** them **in mind** to be subject to principalities .... Tit 3:1
2 to **put** you always **in remembrance** of these things, ... 2 Pt 1:12
4 I **will remember** his deeds which he doeth, ... 3 Jn 1:10
3 I will therefore **put** you **in remembrance**, ... Jude 1:5

Classical Greek

Classical authors used the word *hupomimnēskō* to mean "to remind of, put in mind, mention, suggest, provoke, remember," and "observe" (*Liddell-Scott*). A characteristic of words related to its stem, *mimnēskō* (3267), is that both the simple nouns and verbs, as well as the compounds, are used rather interchangeably. Thus *anamimnēskō* is often substituted with *hupomimnēskō* and vice versa (see Bartels, "Remember," *Colin Brown*, 3:230).

Septuagint Usage

The Septuagint uses *hupomimnēskō* four times. In 1 Kings 4:3 (LXX 3 Kings 4:3) it has the variant *anamimnēskō*, a reading found in the Codex Alexandrinus. It is also found in Wisdom of Solomon 12:1; 18:22; 4 Maccabees 18:14. In Wisdom of Solomon 12:1 God is the One who *reminds* people of the things "wherein they sin" (RSV).

New Testament Usage

In each of its seven New Testament occurrences, the word *hupomimnēskō* is related either to rightful or wrongful behavior. In Luke 22:61 Peter "remembered" what the Lord had said about his act of denial. Jesus said that the Holy Spirit would "bring to remembrance" all things He had spoken to them (John 14:26). Paul admonished Timothy to remind the church, i.e., "put them in remembrance," about the important aspects of the gospel instead of being sidetracked into futile disputes (2 Timothy 2:14). Likewise, Paul encouraged Titus "to remind" his hearers of proper Christian conduct (Titus 3:1). Peter admonished his readers by saying, "Wherefore I will not be negligent to put you always in remembrance of these things" (2 Peter 1:12). Peter emphasized that if they did the things he "reminded" them of they would have an abundant entrance into the everlasting kingdom (verses 10,11).

In 3 John 10 the apostle John said, "If I come, I will *remember* his (Diotrephes') deeds"; that is, John would bring up before the church the matter or raise the question concerning the malicious words and sinful behavior of the man. In Jude 5 the writer reminded his readers of the judgment of God which fell on His chosen people, who on account of their unbelief died in the wilderness instead of inheriting the blessings promised to them.

STRONG 5279, BAUER 846, MOULTON-MILLIGAN 658-59, LIDDELL-SCOTT 1889, COLIN BROWN 3:240-43.

5118. ὑπόμνησις hupomnēsis noun

Recollection, remembrance, reminder.

COGNATE:
μιμνῄσκω mimnēskō (3267)

SYNONYMS:
ἀνάμνησις anamnēsis (363)
μνεία mneia (3281)
μνήμη mnēmē (3284)

תְּהִלָּה tehillāh (8747), Praise (Ps 71:6 [70:6]—Codex Sinaiticus only).

1. **ὑπομνήσει hupomnēsei** dat sing fem
2. **ὑπόμνησιν hupomnēsin** acc sing fem

2 When I call to remembrance the unfeigned faith.... 2 Tm 1:5
1 to stir you up by putting you in remembrance;....... 2 Pt 1:13
1 I stir up your pure minds by way of remembrance:...... 3:1

Classical Greek

Hupomnēsis appears as early as the late Fifth Century B.C. In classical Greek it denotes the act of reminding. Thus, it can mean "a reminding, a suggestion," or "a mention." It appears in constructions with *echō* (2174) to indicate action, "to remind, suggest." In medical terminology *hupomnēsis* can refer to a *revival* of normal functions in the body or a *relapse* into sickness (*Liddell-Scott*).

Septuagint Usage

In the Septuagint *hupomnēsis* appears three times. In Psalm 71:6 (LXX 70:6, certain manuscripts only) the Psalmist declared, "In you is my remembrance continually." Wisdom of Solomon 16:11 says that the Israelites were bitten by serpents as a reminder of the words of God. In 2 Maccabees 6:17 the compiler interjects comments which will "serve as a *reminder*" of the faithfulness of God.

New Testament Usage

In the New Testament it occurs three times (2 Timothy 1:5; 2 Peter 1:13; 3:1). The KJV renders it "remembrance" at all three locations. At 2 Peter 1:13 the RSV translates it "to arouse you by way of reminder."

This noun seems to encompass both the act of remembering and its effect on the person, not merely the idea of a memory. A full participation in the act of remembering past teaching (including the Word of God) is suggested. This active remembering will make the truth of the Lord's teaching more alive in His children and strengthen them in difficult times (Bartels, "Remember," *Colin Brown*, 3:241). Bartels also calls it "a positive force which affects one's behavior . . . " (ibid.).

Peter stated he wished to remind his readers of the "words which were spoken before by the holy prophets, and of the commandment of us the apostles of the Lord and Saviour: knowing . . . that there shall come in the last days scoffers . . . " (2 Peter 3:1-3). This seems to indicate that Peter was exhorting the reader to relive past experiences or times of learning. In other words he was asking them to contemplate more deeply the teachings and the Word of God in order to develop stronger faith and greater strength to endure the hardships of life.

STRONG 5280, BAUER 846, MOULTON-MILLIGAN 659, KITTEL 1:348-49, LIDDELL-SCOTT 1890, COLIN BROWN 3:230,241-43,247.

5119. ὑπομονή hupomonē noun

Patience, endurance, steadfastness, perseverance.

CROSS-REFERENCE:
ὑπομένω hupomenō (5116)

מִקְוֶה miqweh (4884), Hope (1 Chr 29:15, Ezr 10:2, Jer 14:8).

קָוָה qāwâh (7245), Piel: wait (Ps 39:7 [38:7]).

תִּקְוָה tiqwāh (8951), Hope (Jb 14:19, Pss 62:5 [61:5], 71:5 [70:5]).

1. **ὑπομονή hupomonē** nom sing fem
2. **ὑπομονῆς hupomonēs** gen sing fem
3. **ὑπομονῇ hupomonē** dat sing fem
4. **ὑπομονήν hupomonēn** acc sing fem

3 keep it, and bring forth fruit with **patience**.......... Luke 8:15
3 In your **patience** possess ye your souls................. 21:19
4 To them who by **patient** continuance in well doing .. Rom 2:7
4 knowing that tribulation worketh **patience**;.............. 5:3
1 And **patience**, experience; and experience, hope:........ 5:4
2 then do we with **patience** wait for it.................... 8:25
2 we through **patience** and comfort of the scriptures..... 15:4
2 Now the God of **patience** and consolation grant you... 15:5
3 is effectual in the **enduring** of the same sufferings... 2 Co 1:6
3 as the ministers of God, in much **patience**,............. 6:4
3 signs ... were wrought among you in all **patience**,...... 12:12
4 unto all patience and **longsuffering** with joyfulness;... Col 1:11
2 and **patience** of hope in our Lord Jesus Christ,...... 1 Th 1:3
2 in the churches of God for your **patience** and faith .. 2 Th 1:4
4 and into the **patient waiting** for Christ................. 3:5
4 godliness, faith, love, **patience**, meekness............ 1 Tm 6:11
3 purpose, faith, **longsuffering**, charity, patience,...... 2 Tm 3:10
3 temperate, sound in faith, in charity, in **patience**...... Tit 2:2
2 For ye have need of **patience**,..................... Heb 10:36
2 run **with patience** the race that is set before us,........ 12:1
4 that the trying of your faith worketh **patience**......... Jas 1:3
1 But let **patience** have her perfect work,................. 1:4
4 Ye have heard of the **patience** of Job,.................. 5:11
4 to temperance **patience**; and to patience godliness;... 2 Pt 1:6
3 to temperance patience; and to **patience** godliness;...... 1:6
3 and in the kingdom and **patience** of Jesus Christ,..... Rev 1:9
4 know thy works, and thy labour, and thy **patience**,...... 2:2
4 And hast borne, and hast **patience**,.................... 2:3
4 and faith, and thy **patience**, and thy works;............. 2:19
2 Because thou hast kept the word of my **patience**,....... 3:10
1 Here is the **patience** and the faith of the saints......... 13:10
1 Here is the **patience** of the saints:.................... 14:12

Classical Greek

In classical Greek *hupomonē* means "a remaining behind" or "under" (based on the words *hupo* [5097], "under," and *menō* [3176], "remain"). From this the idea of "remaining steadfast" or "enduring" developed. The noun was known from the time of Plato. Among the philosophers *hupomonē* was a virtue associated with *andreia*, "manliness" (courage, bravery), and *kartareia*, "perseverance" (Hauck, "menō," *Kittel*, 4:582,583). *Liddell-Scott* says that negatively it denotes "stubbornness."

Septuagint Usage

Nine canonical instances of *hupomonē* occur in the Septuagint, along with 16 noncanonical (Sirach and 4 Maccabees only). The Hebrew term which is translated by *hupomonē* is some form of *qāwâh* ("to wait" [eagerly, expectantly]). The idea behind *hupomonē* might be best expressed as "patient hope." It expresses confidence and "hope" (cf. the NIV's translation in 1 Chronicles 29:15; Ezra 10:2 [LXX 2 Esdras 10:2]; Job 14:19; Psalms 9:18; 39:7 [LXX 38:7]), in spite of circumstances of distress. *Hupomonē* is possible because of God's mercy and faithfulness, even when His people are unfaithful (Ezra 10:2; cf. Sirach 17:24). He himself is the believers' source of "hope" (NIV, Psalms 62:5 [LXX 61:5]; 71:5 [70:5]); He alone is their reason for enduring.

We see the appearance of *hupomonē* as a term for "endurance," particularly in the face of adversity and suffering (Sirach 41:2; especially in 4 Maccabees 1:11; 7:9, cf. verse 8; 9:8; etc.). Nonetheless, "endurance" remained a religious virtue (cf. 4 Maccabees 17:4,12,17f.).

New Testament Usage

The New Testament use of *hupomonē*, "patience, perseverance, endurance," is quite interesting. Surprisingly the Gospels record *hupomonē* only twice—both in Luke (8:15; 21:19)—and they never use it of Jesus (cf. 2 Thessalonians 3:5). Of the Synoptic accounts of the interpretation of the Parable of the Sower (Matthew 13:18-23; Mark 4:13-20; Luke 8:11-15), only Luke (8:15) qualified the "bearing fruit" of the good seed as being "with patience" (*en hupomonē*). There is probably a hint of persecution here, for his second usage explicitly concerns "endurance" in the face of persecutions (21:19).

The majority of the occurrences of *hupomonē* are attributed to the apostle Paul. "Perseverance" is not passively waiting out difficult circumstances; rather, it is active, often being depicted in terms of work on behalf of the gospel or of suffering on behalf of it (Romans 2:7; 5:3; 2 Corinthians 1:6; 6:4; 2 Thessalonians 1:4; cf. James 1:3; Revelation 1:9; 2:2). It is closely connected with hope, just as it was in the Old Testament (Romans 8:25; 15:4; 2 Corinthians 1:6,7); furthermore, it comes from God (Romans 15:5; Colossians 1:11). "Endurance" (patience) joins the noble company of godliness, faith, and love as one of the many virtues of Christian living (1 Timothy 6:11; cf. 2 Timothy 3:10; Titus 2:2; Revelation 2:19). In addition, *hupomonē* generates further confidence in God (cf. James 1:3,4; 2 Peter 1:6).

As in the Old Testament, *hupomonē* is closely connected with confidence in God, and it is particularly grounded in the future (Hebrews 12:1). It is also equated with Christian faithfulness and obedience in the face of adversity (Revelation 14:12; cf. 13:10). Believers show God and others the quality of their Christian character and benefit themselves spiritually when they "endure patiently" the sufferings that come upon them because of the gospel.

Strong 5281, Bauer 846, Moulton-Milligan 659, Kittel 4:581-88, Liddell-Scott 1890, Colin Brown 2:772-76.

5120. ὑπονοέω huponoeō verb

Think privately, suppose, surmise.

COGNATE:
νοέω noeō (3401)
SYNONYMS:
δοκέω dokeō (1374)
οἴομαι oiomai (3496)

1. ὑπονοεῖτε huponoeite 2pl indic pres act
2. ὑπενόουν hupenooun 1/3sing/pl indic imperf act

1 Whom **think** ye that I am? I am not he............ Acts 13:25
2 none accusation of such things as I **supposed**:.......... 25:18
2 **deemed** that they drew near to some country;......... 27:27

This verb is formed from *hupo* (5097), "under," and *noeō*, "to exercise the mind." The word is scattered throughout early classical literature, the papyri, and Septuagint. *Bauer* suggests "to suspect" as a proper rendering, and when used with the accusative case it adds the idea "to suspect or suppose *something*."

Huponoeō occurs three times in the New Testament, all in Acts: 13:25, "Whom *think* ye that I am?"; 25:18, "they brought none accusation of such things as I *supposed*"; 27:27, "the shipmen *deemed* that they drew near to some country." Louw and Nida define *huponoeō* in this way: "to have an opinion based on scant evidence, often with the implication of regarding a false opinion as true" (*Greek-English Lexicon*, 1:370).

STRONG 5282, BAUER 846, MOULTON-MILLIGAN 659, KITTEL 4:1017-19, LIDDELL-SCOTT 1890.

5121. ὑπόνοια huponoia noun

Suspicion.

CROSS-REFERENCE:
νοέω noeō (3401)

דִּמְיֹן dimyōn (1886), Similarity; conclusion (Sir 3:24).
רַעְיוֹן ra'yôn (A7764), Thoughts (Dn 4:19 [4:16], 5:6—Aramaic).

1. ὑπόνοιαι huponoiai nom pl fem

1 cometh envy, strife, railings, evil **surmisings**,........ 1 Tm 6:4

Huponoia is a noun related to the verb *huponoeō* (5120). It denotes a "surmising" or "conjecture" (cf. *Bauer*).

Found throughout classical literature, papyri, and the Septuagint (Sirach 3:24: "wrong opinion" [RSV]), it only appears once in the New Testament. First Timothy 6:4 translates it "(evil) *surmisings*." The RSV contains "(base) *suspicions*." The negative connotation should not be rigidly applied to this word; rather, it is a contextual matter. The meaning of *huponoia* is "an opinion based on scant evidence" (Louw and Nida, *Greek-English Lexicon*, 1:370). To express "*evil* suspicions" Paul needed to qualify *huponoia* with the adjective *ponēros* (4050), "evil."

STRONG 5283, BAUER 846, MOULTON-MILLIGAN 659, KITTEL 4:1017-19, LIDDELL-SCOTT 1890.

5121B. ὑποπιάζω hupopiazō verb

To treat roughly, to blacken the eye.

CROSS-REFERENCE:
πιάζω piazō (3945)

1. ὑποπιάζῃ hupopiazē 3sing subj pres act

This is a variant spelling of *hupōpiazō*. See the word study at number 5137.

5122. ὑποπλέω hupopleō verb

Sail to leeward of.

CROSS-REFERENCE:
πλέω pleō (3986)

1. ὑπεπλεύσαμεν hupepleusamen 1pl indic aor act

1 launched from thence, we **sailed under** Cyprus,..... Acts 27:4
1 we **sailed under** Crete, over against Salmone;.......... 27:7

A term of maritime use, *hupopleō* is composed of *hupo* (5097), "under," and *pleō* (3986), "to pass in a vessel." More specifically it means "to sail under the lee of" an island so that the landmass serves as a protection from difficult or contrary winds (*Bauer*). (*Lee* generally denotes a "protecting shelter," and specifically, the side of a ship that is protected from the wind.)

This idea is clearly borne out in both of its New Testament occurrences. The first is Acts 27:4, "We sailed *under* Cyprus, because the winds were contrary," and the second is Acts 27:7 where a similar thought is conveyed.

STRONG 5284, BAUER 846, MOULTON-MILLIGAN 659, LIDDELL-SCOTT 1892.

5123. ὑποπνέω hupopneō verb

Breathe softly, blow gently.

CROSS-REFERENCE:
πνέω pneō (4014)

1. ὑποπνεύσαντος hupopneusantos gen sing masc part aor act

1 And when the south wind **blew softly**,............ Acts 27:13

A unique term of rare use, *hupopneō* appears to be a compound form of *hupo* (5097) (in this case does not take one of its many prepositional forms; rather, it has a generally diminutive application), and *pneō* (4014), "to breathe," and the resulting compound means "to breathe softly." Applying the term to the wind the verb means to "blow gently, blow softly." Its single appearance in classical Greek is in Aristotle's *Problemata* at 8.6 where it is translated "blow underneath." New Testament translators differ little in their renderings of its only appearance; in Acts 27:13 it refers to a light wind. The KJV states: "And when the south wind *blew softly* . . . they sailed close by Crete." RSV simply changes it to "when the wind *blew gently*."

STRONG 5285, BAUER 846, LIDDELL-SCOTT 1892.

5124. ὑποπόδιον hupopodion noun

Footstool.

הֲדֹם hădhōm (1986), Footstool (Ps 99:5 [98:5], Is 66:1, Lam 2:1).

1. ὑποπόδιον hupopodion nom/acc sing neu

1 Nor by the earth; for it is his **footstool:** .... Matt 5:35
1 till I make thine enemies thy **footstool?** 22:44
1 till I make thine enemies thy **footstool.** .... Mark 12:36
1 Till I make thine enemies thy **footstool.** .... Luke 20:43
1 Until I make thy foes thy **footstool.** .... Acts 2:35
1 Heaven is my throne, and earth is my **footstool:** 7:49
1 until I make thine enemies thy **footstool?** .... Heb 1:13
1 expecting till his enemies be made his **footstool.** 10:13
1 Stand thou there, or sit here under my **footstool:** ..... Jas 2:3

Classical Greek

This word first appeared during the Fourth Century B.C. It is a compound of *hupo* (5097), "under," and *pous* (4087), "foot," and denotes a "footstool."

Septuagint Usage

Hupopodion occurs four times in the Septuagint. Isaiah 66:1 says that the earth serves as a *footstool* for God himself (cf. Matthew 5:35). In Psalm 99:5 (LXX 98:5) the temple seems to be likened to His footstool; and in Lamentations 2:1 the city of Zion is considered His footstool. It is also used in the sense of making someone subject (i.e., a footstool) to another (Psalm 110:1 [LXX 109:1]; cf. Matthew 22:44; Mark 12:36). It served as a loanword in rabbinic writings.

New Testament Usage

In the New Testament also, *hupopodion* denotes a "footstool" (James 2:3). However, depending on the context, *hupopodion* has three different connotations: (1) the earth serves as God's footstool (Matthew 5:35; Acts 7:49); (2) the enemies of God's people will become their footstool (Matthew 22:44; Mark 12:36; Luke 20:43; Acts 2:35; Hebrews 1:13; 10:13). Here *hupopodion* serves as a poignant metaphor that speaks of complete or total conquest of one's enemies. Finally, it is a small piece of furniture which literally serves as a resting place for someone's feet (James 2:3).

STRONG 5286, BAUER 846-47, MOULTON-MILLIGAN 659, LIDDELL-SCOTT 1892.

5125. ὑπόστασις hupostasis noun

Underlying essence, nature, reality; confidence, conviction, assurance, steadfastness.

CROSS-REFERENCE:
ἵστημι histēmi (2449)

חֶלֶד cheledh (2566), Lifetime, span of one's life (Pss 39:5 [38:5], 89:47 [88:47]).

יְקוּם y^e^qûm (3462), Living things (Dt 11:6).

כִּנְעָה kin'āh (3790), Bundle (Jer 10:17).

מָעֳמָד mo'ŏmādh (4772), Foothold (Ps 69:2 [68:2]).

מַצָּב matstsāv (4835), Garrison (1 Sm 14:4—Codex Vaticanus only).

מַצֵּבָה matstsēvāh (4838), Pillar (Ez 26:11).

מַשָּׂא massā' (5014), Burden (Dt 1:12).

נָצַב nātsav (5507), Stand; hiphil: be a set rate (1 Sm 13:21—Codex Vaticanus only); hophal: be decreed (Na 2:7).

סוֹד sôdh (5660), Council (Jer 23:22).

רָקַם rāqam (7844), Weave; pual: be woven together (Ps 139:15 [138:15]).

תּוֹחֶלֶת tôcheleth (8760), Hope (Ps 39:7 [38:7]).

תְּכוּנָה t^e^khûnāh (8828), Design (Ez 43:11).

תִּקְוָה tiqwāh (8951), Hope (Ru 1:12, Ez 19:5).

1. ὑπόστασις hupostasis nom sing fem
2. ὑποστάσεως hupostaseōs gen sing fem
3. ὑποστάσει hupostasei dat sing fem

3 should be ashamed in this same **confident** boasting... 2 Co 9:4
3 as it were foolishly, in this **confidence** of boasting...... 11:17
2 and the express image of his **person,** .... Heb 1:3
2 if we hold the beginning of our **confidence** stedfast 3:14
1 Now faith is the **substance** of things hoped for, ... 11:1

Hupostasis is related to the verb *huphistēmi* ("to place under"). However, they are virtually unrelated in definition except for some features *hupostasis* holds in common with the middle voice form of the verb (Köster, "hupostasis," *Kittel*, 8:572; cf. *Liddell-Scott*).

Classical Greek

In classical writings *hupostasis* has a variety of definitions. It denotes an act ("of standing under, supporting"), a thing ("sediment," something that settles to the "bottom"), a "foundation" or "groundwork," as well as the more philosophical meanings of "substance, nature, substantial existence" (*Liddell-Scott*; cf. Harder, "Form," *Colin Brown*, 1:710f.).

Köster notes that originally it belonged "almost exclusively to the specialized vocabulary of science and medicine" ("hupostasis," *Kittel*, 8:572). From the papyri we see the nontechnical sense of "property" (i.e., "land") or "title-deed" (cf. *Moulton-Milligan*).

Harder also informs us that as a human attitude "*hypostasis* means putting oneself between, . . . enduring (Poly[bius] 4.50.10)." It is further related to hope, conviction, and perseverance ("Form," *Colin Brown*, 1:710).

A fourth—composite—usage of *hupostasis* transpires in the realm of philosophy. Here "systems" such as Stoicism and Neoplatonism utilize the terminology to denote "reality," that which exists. They also use it to describe the relationship between reality and something. Early on *hupostasis* referred to "being (including matter) which has attained reality" (Köster, "hupostasis," *Kittel*, 8:572). Later, as reality and appearance became opposed to one another in philosophy, *hupostasis* became an "actuality" totally divorced from matter. In general usage *hupostasis* came to denote the "reality behind the appearances," particularly denoting the plan or purpose governing a phenomenon (ibid., 8:575-578; Harder, "Form," *Colin Brown*, 1:711).

Septuagint Usage

The extreme complexity of *hupostasis* is further mirrored in the Septuagint, where in the 18 instances with a Hebrew original there are 12 different Hebrew expressions behind it. There is only one apocryphal occurrence (Wisdom of Solomon 16:21).

Generally it can refer to the "burdens" of existence; even here, however, the more philosophical sense creeps in (Deuteronomy 1:12). It can refer to "things that live" (Hebrew *yeqûm*, Deuteronomy 11:6; cf. Judges 6:4). In Ruth 1:12 it suggests "enduring (existence)" or perhaps "length of life" (cf. Psalms 39:5 [LXX 38:5]; 89:47 [88:47]). "Hope" or "confidence" (*tôcheleth*, Psalm 39:7 [LXX 38:7]; *tiqwāh*, Ezekiel 19:5) placed in God is also rendered by *hupostasis*. This more philosophical understanding may be implying that God is the "basis of existence," therefore, it is only fitting that the creation place its confidence in Him. The kind of hope pictured here is not wishful hope, but enduring trust.

New Testament Usage

Hupostasis occurs five times in the New Testament, twice in 2 Corinthians and three times in the Book of Hebrews. The sense in 2 Corinthians is probably not "confidence" (cf. NIV; 2 Corinthians 9:4; 11:17) as much as it is the "condition" of boasting (cf. *Bauer*; Harder, "Form," *Colin Brown*, 1:712).

The Son of God, the writer of Hebrews tells us, is the "exact representation" (*charaktēr tēs hupostaseōs*) of God (Hebrews 1:3). That is, in terms of the reality behind the appearance of the person of Jesus Christ, stands God (cf. "he . . . bears the very stamp of his [God's] nature" [RSV]). We therefore know God's true nature, essence, and being—embodied in Jesus—by knowing Jesus (cf. John 10:30; 14:8-10).

Even in Hebrews 3:14 the sense of "being" is still preferable to "confident" (cf. Köster, "hupostasis," *Kittel*, 8:578; *Bauer*). Some manuscripts (e.g., A 629 2495 and a few others) support (indirectly) the interpretation "being" by adding the possessive pronoun "his" (*autou*). This forces the word to refer to "Christ's nature," just as was seen in 1:3. The idea then would be that the believers are to hold fast to the Christlike nature they possessed since the day of their salvation.

According to Harder's useful breakdown, three options for translating *hupostasis* are available in Hebrews 11:1: (1) "confidence, expectation"; (2) "guarantee, pledge"; and (3) "realization, actualization" ("Form," *Colin Brown*, 1:713). Each of these options has some merit. Granted that numbers 1 and 2 have the least lexical support, there remains an element of truth in each definition. Perhaps it is most helpful to see each of these as contributing to a larger idea, namely, that faith is not only the "essence" (number 3) of what we hope for, it is also essentially an expression of "conviction" (number 1). Moreover, it has inherent in it an element of endurance precisely because God is the source of hope (see articles on *hupomonē* [5119], *elpis* [1667], *pistis* [3963]).

Strong 5287, Bauer 847, Moulton-Milligan 659-60, Kittel 8:572-89, Liddell-Scott 1895, Colin Brown 1:710-14.

5126. ὑποστέλλω hupostellō verb

Draw back, withdraw, shrink from, avoid, turn back, keep back, keep silent about, conceal.

גּוּר gûr (1513), Be afraid (Dt 1:17).

כָּלָא kālâʼ (3727), Withhold (Hg 1:10).
עָפַל ʻāphal (6306), Swell; pual: be puffed (Hb 2:4).

1. **ὑπέστελλεν hupestellen** 3sing indic imperf act
2. **ὑπεστειλάμην hupesteilamēn** 1sing indic aor mid
3. **ὑποστείληται huposteilētai** 3sing subj aor mid

2 I **kept back** nothing that was profitable unto you,... Acts 20:20
2 For I have not **shunned** to declare unto you 20:27
1 he **withdrew** and separated himself,.................. Gal 2:12
3 but if any man **draw back**,....................... Heb 10:38

Hupostellō appears in secular Greek writings since the Fifth Century B.C. and generally means "to draw aside, to draw back," "always for a specific purpose" (Rengstorf, "stellō," *Kittel*, 7:597). It could mean "to hide" or "to keep to oneself." Further uses include "to abstain" from something or "place restrictions on oneself" (*Liddell-Scott*).

Septuagint Usage

Hupostellō appears five different times in the canonical books of the Septuagint. It occurs in Exodus 23:21 which says, "For he will not *pardon* your transgressions." Deuteronomy 1:17 reads, "Ye shall not *be afraid of* (draw back from) the face of man." Habakkuk 2:4 is quoted by the writer to the Hebrews (10:38). Haggai 1:10 reads, "The earth *is stayed* from her fruit." It is also found in Job 13:8; Wisdom 6:7; 3 Maccabees 5:20.

New Testament Usage

Four citations of this verb may be found in the New Testament. It has two uses. In the active voice it means "draw back, withdraw" (Galatians 2:12). When used in the middle voice it also can mean "draw back"; however, in Hebrews 10:38 the context suggests to *draw back* in fear. Elsewhere, *hupostellō* should be translated "shrink from" or "avoid" (Acts 20:27) and "keep silent about" (Acts 20:20). *Hupostellō* is the exact opposite action which faith calls for. It denotes a shrinking back instead of pressing forward.

STRONG 5288, BAUER 847, MOULTON-MILLIGAN 660, KITTEL 7:597-98, LIDDELL-SCOTT 1895-96.

5127. ὑποστολή hupostolē noun

Drawing back, timidity.

CROSS REFERENCE:
στέλλομαι stellomai (4575)

1. **ὑποστολῆς hupostolēs** gen sing fem

1 we are not of them who **draw back** unto perdition;..Heb 10:39

Hupostolē has been variously defined as "a drawing or shrinking back, shrinkage, shrinking." It is related to the Greek verb *hupostellō* (5126) which means "to draw back" or, reflexively, "to cower, shrink."

Although found occasionally in classical literature, in the New Testament this noun occurs only at Hebrews 10:39. Usage of the word in that context suggests a negative implication: "But we are not of them who *draw back* unto perdition . . . . " The phrase "unto perdition" suggests to some that this is a reference to apostasy, or a complete withdrawal from God resulting in permanent separation from Him. The context seems to support this interpretation. (Notice verse 38: "but if any man *draw back*, my [God's] soul shall have no pleasure in him.")

STRONG 5289, BAUER 847, MOULTON-MILLIGAN 660, KITTEL 7:599, LIDDELL-SCOTT 1896.

5128. ὑποστρέφω hupostrephō verb

To turn back, to return.

COGNATE:
στρέφω strephō (4613)

SYNONYMS:
ἀνακάμπτω anakamptō (342)
ἀποστρέφω apostrephō (648)
ἐπανέρχομαι epanerchomai (1865)
ἐπιστρέφω epistrephō (1978)
στρέφω strephō (4613)

אֲזַל ʼăzal (A235), Go (Dn 6:18—Aramaic).
דָּחַף dāchaph (1821), Hurry (Est 6:12).
פָּנָה pānâh (6680), Turn (Jos 7:12—only some Vaticanus texts).
שׁוּב shûv (8178), Qal: return (Gn 43:10, Jos 2:23); hiphil: turn away (Prv 24:18—only some Sinaiticus texts).

1. **ὑπόστρεφε hupostrephe** 2sing impr pres act
2. **ὑποστρέφων hupostrephōn** nom sing masc part pres act
3. **ὑποστρέφοντι hupostrephonti** dat sing masc part pres act
4. **ὑποστρέφειν hupostrephein** inf pres act
5. **ὑπέστρεψα hupestrepsa** 1sing indic aor act
6. **ὑπέστρεψεν hupestrepsen** 3sing indic aor act
7. **ὑπέστρεψαν hupestrepsan** 3pl indic aor act
8. **ὑποστρέψας hupostrepsas** nom sing masc part aor act
9. **ὑποστρέψαντι hupostrepsanti** dat sing masc part aor act
10. **ὑποστρέψαντες hupostrepsantes** nom pl masc part aor act
11. **ὑποστρέψασαι hupostrepsasai** nom pl fem part aor act
12. **ὑποστρέψαι hupostrepsai** inf aor act
13. **ὑποστρέψω hupostrepsō** 1sing indic fut act
14. **ὑπέστρεφον hupestrephon** 3pl indic imperf act

8 when he **returned**, he found them asleep again,... Mark 14:40
6 and **returned** to her own house.................. Luke 1:56

7 The shepherds **returned**, glorifying and (NIV)...... Luke 2:20
7 **returned** into Galilee, to their own city Nazareth....... 2:39
4 they had fulfilled the days, as they **returned**,.......... 2:43
7 they **turned back again** to Jerusalem, seeking him...... 2:45
6 And Jesus being full of the Holy Ghost **returned**...... 4:1
6 And Jesus **returned** in the power of the Spirit......... 4:14
10 And they that were sent, **returning** to the house,...... 7:10
6 he went up into the ship, and **returned back again**...... 8:37
1 **Return** to thine own house, and show how great....... 8:39
12 it came to pass, that, when Jesus **was returned**,........ 8:40
10 And the apostles, when they **were returned**,........... 9:10
7 And the seventy **returned** again with joy, saying,..... 10:17
13 **I will return** unto my house whence I came out....... 11:24
6 **turned back**, and with a loud voice glorified God,..... 17:15
10 are not found that **returned** to give glory to God,..... 17:18
12 to receive for himself a kingdom, and **to return**....... 19:12
14 all the people ... smote their breasts, and **returned**.... 23:48
11 they **returned**, and prepared spices and ointments;.... 23:56
11 And **returned** from the sepulchre,.................. 24:9
7 rose up the same hour, and **returned** to Jerusalem,... 24:33
7 they worshipped him, and **returned** to Jerusalem...... 24:52
7 Then **returned** they unto Jerusalem................ Acts 1:12
7 **returned** to Jerusalem, and preached the gospel........ 8:25
2 Was **returning**, and sitting in his chariot............... 8:28
7 And Barnabas and Saul **returned** from Jerusalem,..... 12:25
6 John departing from them **returned** to Jerusalem...... 13:13
4 now no more **to return** to corruption,................ 13:34
7 they **returned** again to Lystra, and to Iconium,....... 14:21
4 he purposed **to return** through Macedonia............ 20:3
7 we took ship; and they **returned** home again.......... 21:6
9 when I **was come again** to Jerusalem,................. 22:17
7 left the horsemen ... and **returned** to the castle:...... 23:32
5 into Arabia, and **returned** again unto Damascus..... Gal 1:17
3 **returning** from the slaughter of the kings,.......... Heb 7:1
12 **to turn** away from the holy commandment (NASB) 2 Pt 2:21

Classical Greek

The semantic range of this verb is narrow, meaning simply "to return." It could also be used in the sense of "returning" from sorrow to joy, or of "turning away" in order to elude an attack (*Liddell-Scott*).

Septuagint Usage

Hupostrephō appears 24 times in the Septuagint, 4 of which are in the Apocrypha. Although it translates three Hebrew terms and one Aramaic term, its meaning varies little from the idea of "returning." The most common Hebrew equivalent is *shûv* ("to turn back"), occurring 16 times. Examples of *hupostrephō* in historical narrative (such as "and Moses *returned* unto the Lord" [Exodus 32:31]) abound. A variation of this describes the raven released by Noah, who flew "to and fro" (literally "going and returning") searching for dry land (Genesis 8:7). It also describes the Lord's anger being "turned away" from an enemy of Israel because of the rejoicing it provoked (Proverbs 24:18). In Joshua 7:12 Israel "turned" (Hebrew *pānāh*) their backs before the men of Ai because of Achan's sin. A final example has King Darius "returning" (Aramaic *'ăzal*) to his palace to fast during Daniel's ordeal in the lions' den (Daniel 6:18 [LXX 6:19]). Common variants for *hupostrephō* are *epistrephō* (1978) and *anastrephō* (388).

New Testament Usage

The New Testament follows the same pattern as the Septuagint in that historical narratives use *hupostrephō* to describe movement. Thirty-two of the thirty-five occurrences are found in Luke–Acts. An exception is found in Acts 13:34 where Paul, speaking of Christ's resurrection, said that His body is "no more to *return* to corruption." Peter used *hupostrephō* (the *Textus Receptus* has *epistrephō* in this verse) to describe the act of apostasy. Such individuals "turn from" the holy commandment they once embraced and are in a far worse state than if they had never known the way of righteousness (2 Peter 2:21).

Strong 5290, Bauer 847, Moulton-Milligan 660, Liddell-Scott 1896.

5129. ὑποστρώννυμι

hupostrōnnumi verb

To spread out.

Cross-Reference:

στρώννυμι strōnnumi (4617)

יָצַע yātsa' (3440), Hiphil: spread out (Is 58:5); hophal: lay (Est 4:3—only some Sinaiticus texts).

פָּלַשׁ pālash (6672), Hithpael: wallow (Ez 27:30—Codex Alexandrinus only).

צָעָה tsā'âh (7084), Make oneself subservient (Sir 4:27).

1. ὑπεστρώννυον hupestrōnnuon 3pl indic imperf act

1 as he went, they **spread** their clothes in the way.... Luke 19:36

This verb's only New Testament occurrence (Luke 19:36) is used to describe the multitude's reaction as Jesus triumphantly entered Jerusalem on a colt. The people honored their Messiah by "spreading out" their garments on the road before Jesus as He traveled from Bethany to the Holy City, about 2 miles distant (cf. John 11:18). They were not haphazardly thrown on the road but were spread out as one would prepare a bed (cf. Isaiah 58:5).

Strong 5291, Bauer 847 (see "hupostrōnnuō"), Moulton-Milligan 660 (see "hupostrōnnuō"), Liddell-Scott 1896.

5130. ὑποταγή hupotagē noun

Subjection, obedience.

Cross-Reference:

τάσσω tassō (4872)

1. ὑποταγῇ hupotagē dat sing fem

1 they glorify God for your professed **subjection**...... 2 Co 9:13
1 To whom we gave place by **subjection**, no,........... Gal 2:5

1 Let the woman learn in silence with all **subjection**... 1 Tm 2:11
1 having his children in **subjection** with all gravity; 3:4

Hupotagē occurs four times in the New Testament, all of which are found in the Pauline corpus. It is used to denote the willful submission of one to another in the sense of renouncing the initiative, i.e., giving up the leadership (Delling, "hupotassō," *Kittel*, 8:46). God received glory through the "submission" of the Corinthians to the gospel, as evidenced by their testimony and generosity (2 Corinthians 9:13). Conversely, Paul refused to "submit" to the false brothers in Jerusalem who sought to impose Jewish requirements on his Gentile converts (Galatians 2:5).

Paul instructed Timothy that a woman should "learn in silence with all *subjection*" (1 Timothy 2:11). He explains her "subjection" in the following verse: she is neither to teach, nor to have authority (see *authenteō* [825]) over the man. Whether this is to be understood in the context of church or family is unclear.

The would-be deacon must have his children "in subjection with all gravity" (1 Timothy 3:4); that is, they must respectfully obey him. Failure in his parental duties would render him unfit for a leadership role in the church.

STRONG 5292, BAUER 847, MOULTON-MILLIGAN 660, KITTEL 8:46-47, LIDDELL-SCOTT 1897, COLIN BROWN 1:347.

5131. ὑποτάσσω hupotassō verb

To subject to, put in submission to, to be or make subject; to submit oneself.

COGNATE:
τάσσω tassō (4872)

SYNONYM:
ὑπακούω hupakouō (5057)

דָּבַר dāvar (1744), Speak; hiphil: subdue (Ps 18:47 [17:47]).

דּוּמִיָּה dûmîyāh (1800), Silence (Ps 62:1 [61:1]).

דָּמַם dāmam (1887), Be still, wait for (Pss 37:7 [36:7], 62:5 [61:5]).

כָּבַשׁ kāvash (3653), Subjugate; niphal: be subdued (1 Chr 22:18).

פְּלַח p^elach (A6643), Serve (Dn 7:27—Aramaic).

רָדַד rādhadh (7574), Subdue (Ps 144:2 [143:2]).

שִׂים sîm (7947), Set, put; consider (Hg 2:18 [2:19]).

שִׁית shîth (8308), Put (Ps 8:6).

1. **ὑπέταξας hupetaxas** 2sing indic aor act
2. **ὑπέταξεν hupetaxen** 3sing indic aor act
3. **ὑποτάξαντος hupotaxantos** gen sing masc part aor act
4. **ὑποτάξαντι hupotaxanti** dat sing masc part aor act
5. **ὑποτάξαντα hupotaxanta** acc sing masc part aor act
6. **ὑποτάξαι hupotaxai** inf aor act
7. **ὑποτάσσεται hupotassetai** 3sing indic pres mid
8. **ὑποτάσσησθε hupotassēsthe** 2pl subj pres mid
9. **ὑποτασσέσθω hupotassesthō** 3sing impr pres mid
10. **ὑποτάσσεσθε hupotassesthe** 2pl impr pres mid
11. **ὑποτασσόμενος hupotassomenos** nom sing masc part pres mid
12. **ὑποτασσόμενοι hupotassomenoi** nom pl masc part pres mid
13. **ὑποτασσόμεναι hupotassomenai** nom pl fem part pres mid
14. **ὑποτασσομένας hupotassomenas** acc pl fem part pres mid
15. **ὑποτάσσεσθαι hupotassesthai** inf pres mid
16. **ὑπετάγη hupetagē** 3sing indic aor pass
17. **ὑπετάγησαν hupetagēsan** 3pl indic aor pass
18. **ὑποταγῇ hupotagē** 3sing subj aor pass
19. **ὑποτάγητε hupotagēte** 2pl impr aor pass
20. **ὑποταγέντων hupotagentōn** gen pl masc part aor pass
21. **ὑποτέτακται hupotetaktai** 3sing indic perf mid
22. **ὑποτεταγμένα hupotetagmena** nom/acc pl neu part perf mid
23. **ὑποταγήσεται hupotagēsetai** 3sing indic fut pass
24. **ὑποταγησόμεθα hupotagēsometha** 1pl indic fut pass
25. **ὑποτασσέσθωσαν hupotassesthōsan** 3pl impr pres mid

11 and came to Nazareth, and was **subject** unto them: Luke 2:51
7 the devils **are subject** unto us through thy name....... 10:17
7 rejoice not, that the spirits **are subject** unto you;...... 10:20
7 for it is not **subject** to the law of God,............ Rom 8:7
16 For the creature **was made subject** to vanity,........... 8:20
5 but by reason of him who **hath subjected** the same..... 8:20
17 **have not submitted** themselves unto.................. 10:3
9 Let every soul **be subject** unto the higher powers...... 13:1
15 Wherefore ye must needs **be subject**,................ 13:5
7 spirits of the prophets **are subject** to the prophets. 1 Co 14:32
15 but they are commanded **to be under obedience**,...... 14:34
2 For he **hath put** all things **under** his feet............. 15:27
21 But when he saith all things **are put under** him,....... 15:27
3 which **did put** all things **under** him.................. 15:27
18 And when all things **shall be subdued** unto him,...... 15:28
23 then shall the Son also himself **be subject** unto him... 15:28
4 be subject unto him **that put** all things **under** him,.... 15:28
8 That ye **submit** yourselves unto such,................ 16:16
2 And **hath put** all things under his feet,............ Eph 1:22
12 **Submitting yourselves** one to another................ 5:21
10 Wives, **submit yourselves** unto your own husbands,..... 5:22
7 Therefore as the church **is subject** unto Christ,......... 5:24
6 he is able even **to subdue** all things unto himself.... Phlp 3:21
10 Wives, **submit** yourselves unto your own husbands,.. Col 3:18
14 good, **obedient** to their own husbands,............. Tit 2:5
15 Exhort servants **to be obedient** unto ... masters,........ 2:9
15 be subject to principalities ... to obey **magistrates**,..... 3:1
2 For unto the angels hath he not **put in subjection**... Heb 2:5
1 **hast put** all things **in subjection** under his feet.......... 2:8
6 For in that he **put** all **in subjection under** him,......... 2:8
22 But now we see not yet all things **put under** him....... 2:8

24 rather **be in subjection** unto the Father of spirits,.. Heb 12:9
19 **Submit yourselves** therefore to God................ Jas 4:7
19 **Submit** yourselves to every ordinance of man...... 1 Pt 2:13
12 Servants, **be subject** to your masters with all fear;...... 2:18
13 ye wives, **be in subjection** to your own husbands;...... 3:1
13 **being in subjection** unto their own husbands:.......... 3:5
20 and powers **being made subject** unto him.............. 3:22
19 ye younger, **submit yourselves** unto the elder.......... 5:5
12 Yea, all of you **be subject** one to another,............ 5:5

Classical Greek

Hupotassō is an important word with a wide semantic range. In addition to the definitions given above, its meanings include: "to subject to or unto, to be or make subject, to be under obedience, to subordinate, to put under, subdue, submit oneself," and "be in subjection." In classical Greek it frequently occurs in the middle voice and often indicates involuntary submission or obedience. Throughout Hellenistic literature *hupotassō* (and its cognates) is found in lists expressing rules on ethical standards and appropriate levels of subordination. For example, lists of duties appear in Aristotle, Seneca, and Plutarch (Fourth Century B.C., First Century A.D., and Second Century A.D., respectively) (Martin, "Virtue," *Colin Brown*, 3:930).

In addition, the middle voice is also used to indicate involuntary submission, i.e., to "submit oneself" out of fear. It may describe voluntary submission or obedience, but this sense occurs less often. Submission to spiritual laws and to God is also indicated by the middle form.

In references to literary matters the word means "to attach or append" one document to another (*Bauer*). The verb is found frequently throughout the papyri with that very meaning: e.g., "I append the claims of both of us" (*Moulton-Milligan*).

Septuagint Usage

The Septuagint contains several Hebrew equivalents to *hupotassō* with the same range of meanings found in classical usage (see Septuagint section above). In addition, the concept of overcoming is included, e.g., Moses overcame Pharaoh (Wisdom of Solomon 18:22). This is in contrast to the idea of submission to governmental authority.

Regarding the lists of ethical standards noted above, New Testament examples of such lists appear to be more closely linked to Old Testament Jewish tradition than to classical sources (for instance, the Testament of Judah 21:2 ["God set the monarchy under the priesthood"] and Philo *De Opificio Mundi* 84 ["God set all creatures . . . under man"]; cf. Delling, "hupotassō," *Kittel*, 8:40). In addition, the Testament of Judah 20:1 and the Testament of Levi 19:1 teach an ethical dualism found in Psalm 1; Proverbs 4:18,19; Jeremiah 21:8; Galatians 5:16-23, and in postapostolic Christian literature.

New Testament Usage

The New Testament frequently displays the same meanings found in the classical and Septuagintal literature. Again the connotation involves both involuntary and voluntary submission. The main themes discussed within the contexts containing the word *hupotassō* are the subjection of powers unto Christ, the submission of men unto Christ, and the subjection of men to one another and to authorities, either out of fear or respect. Among the examples that could be cited are the following: God subjects "all things unto Christ" (Ephesians 1:22); and all things, including death, are subjected to Christ (Philippians 3:21). In a slightly different use, 1 Peter 5:5 tells believers to be "subject one to another, and be clothed with humility."

In the middle voice the term has various applications. Perhaps the one of highest import is found in 1 Corinthians 15:28. Here Paul expressed the relative positions of God the Father, Christ, Christians, and "all things." He states that when all things are subdued under Christ, He will be subject to God, as will *all* things. Christ's power as well as His right and manner of acting in that power are subject to the will of the Father.

The middle voice of *hupotassō* is also used to indicate submission to God and submission among men. Regarding one's own family, Jesus submitted to His parents (Luke 2:51). With respect to relationships among equals, Christians are asked to submit to one another "in the fear of God" (Ephesians 5:21). This same idea occurs at 1 Peter 2:13 (including the context of 2:17, "Honor all men"): "*Submit yourselves* to every ordinance of man for the Lord's sake." Although this clearly includes man's duty toward authority, it also encompasses the greater rule of *voluntary* submission.

Four passages containing *hupotassō* deal specifically with the marriage relationship. Ephesians 5:22-24 discusses the submission of wives to their own husbands, but the passage provides a powerful balance: "Submit to one another out of reverence for Christ" (verse 21, NIV). The commands given here to husbands call for a response on their part that will make it easy for wives to submit; that is, husbands are to love their wives as "Christ loved the church and gave himself for it" (verse 25). Furthermore, they are to love their wives "as their own bodies" (verse 28), even as they would love themselves (verse 33).

Markus Barth points out that the concepts of "submission and headship" described in this passage are "qualified, interpreted, and limited by Christ alone" and do not involve "an unlimited headship that can be arbitrarily defined and (that) has to be obeyed" (*Anchor Bible*, 24a:618f.). Verse 24 defines the parameters of this submission: "as the church submits to Christ" (NIV). The relationship of the wife to her husband defined by Ephesians 5, then, is intended to be that of a partnership; the wife is joined with one who loves and cherishes her unselfishly and unreservedly—just as Christ loves and cherishes the Church.

Colossians 3:18 is a parallel passage that also commands wives to submit to their own husbands "as is fitting in the Lord" (i.e., as is pleasing or proper in the sight of God). As in Ephesians 5, the imperative is followed immediately by a command to husbands that they love their wives. Again, submission is set within the general context of mutual obedience to the Lord. Like the Ephesians passage, this text "is an appeal to free and responsible agents that can only be heeded voluntarily" (O'Brien, *Word Biblical Commentary*, 4:222).

First Peter 3:1-5 also reflects this theme. As in the two previous passages, the writer is addressing the submission of wives to their *own* husbands (as an act of obedience which is pleasing to God, verses 3-5). Verse 2 suggests that another factor is sometimes present: an unbelieving husband. The passage states that God may be able to use the submissive attitude of the wife to bring her husband to Christ. Once again there is advice for husbands (verse 7); they are reminded to honor and care for their wives "as heirs together of the grace of life." (Titus 2:5 provides a similar usage of *hupotassō*.)

Submission to authority is another extremely important issue. Although they are equal in Christ, believers are to give deference to elders and those in positions of high standing (1 Peter 5:5; cf. 1 Corinthians 16:16).

Hupotassō often occurs in passages which deal with the ethical standards by which the Christian community was to live. Specifically, these rules addressed the issue of conforming to the existing society from a Christian perspective. They were imperatives addressed to masters, slaves, wives, husbands, children, and to Christians in general.

Paul had a special message for slaves who comprised up to one-third of the Roman Empire's population. Though Paul did not condone slavery, classifying "menstealers" (slave traders) with evildoers of the worst sort (1 Timothy 1:10), he did not advocate revolt on their part. They were told to "submit" (*hupotassomenoi*) to their masters (1 Peter 2:18; cf. Titus 2:9). Paul presented a high motivation for doing so: "that the name of God . . . be not blasphemed" (1 Timothy 6:1) and "that they may adorn the doctrine of God our Saviour in all things" (Titus 2:10).

Paul also made a powerful statement concerning slaves in Colossians 3. After telling slaves in verse 22 to obey their masters "in all things," in verse 23 he tells them, "Whatsoever ye do, do it heartily, as to the Lord, and not unto men"—as though they were working for Christ, not a master. In doing so God would give them a well-deserved reward (verse 24). That slaves could be asked to do this makes an emphatic statement to believers who serve in far more favorable circumstances.

Romans 13:1-7 defines the role of believers with respect to governmental authority. This epistle was written to Christians living in Rome, the capital of the Roman Empire. At that time the empire was under the rule of an absolute dictator. For the most part Rome's dictators (for example, Nero) were corrupt, sinful men. Nevertheless, Paul told believers to be "subject unto the higher powers" (verse 1). However, when the dictates of the state conflicted with the clear teachings of Scripture, another Biblical principal took precedent: "We ought to obey God rather than man" (Acts 5:29). For this very reason, Christians throughout history have fled homelands and have even forfeited their lives rather than submit themselves to the sinful demands of a godless government.

The abrogation of unjust laws or actions against commands that are contrary to Scripture should first be approached through legitimate protest and not disobedience. Initially the individual or group should work through the legislative and legal systems to correct the injustices.

There are some who feel that Christians may ultimately be justified in taking sterner measures. For example, Francis Schaeffer, in his provocative work *Christian Manifesto* (especially pp.89-93) maintains that when a state acts outside of the authority delegated by God as defined in Romans 13:1-4, its actions are no longer ordained by God. He sets forth appropriate levels of response, based on *Lex Rex* by Samuel Rutherford: (1) defense by protest or legal action, (2) flight, (3) use of force as a last resort if necessary to defend oneself or the Church body. Thus when the state acts to oppress any class of people rather than to "do good," Christians have a duty to stand against evil and injustice. Several Biblical and historical examples are cited to support his view, e.g., Moses overcame Pharaoh; Daniel defied King Darius; and, in an example from Church history, Christians opposed Roman law demanding the worship of Caesar, an action that Rome regarded as civil disobedience; they died for their beliefs.

In today's complicated society, many issues demand that people take a stand. Obviously, even Bible principles are subject to varied interpretations, but at least these principles provide guidance and are to be preferred over the ideas of men who do not approach issues from a Christian viewpoint.

STRONG 5293, BAUER 847-48, MOULTON-MILLIGAN 660, KITTEL 8:39-46, LIDDELL-SCOTT 1897.

5132. ὑποτίθημι hupotithēmi verb

To lay down, to risk, to make known.

COGNATE:
τίθημι tithēmi (4935)

SYNONYMS:
ἀποτίθημι apotithēmi (653)
βάλλω ballō (900)
ἵστημι histēmi (2449)
κατατίθημι katatithēmi (2667)
ῥίπτω rhiptō (4352)
τίθημι tithēmi (4935)

בּוֹא bôʼ (971), Go, come; hiphil: put (Sir 51:26).

נָטָה nāṭâh (5371), Bow (Gn 49:15).

נָתַן nāthan (5598), Put (Ex 27:5).

פָּגַע pāghaʻ (6534), Meet, reach, encounter; hiphil: urge (Jer 36:25 [43:25]).

שִׂים sîm (7947), Put (Gn 47:29, Ex 17:12).

1. **ὑπέθηκαν hupethēkan** 3pl indic aor act
2. **ὑποτιθέμενος hupotithemenos** nom sing masc part pres mid

1 Who have for my life **laid down** their own necks:...Rom 16:4
2 **put** the brethren **in remembrance** of these things,....1 Tm 4:6

Classical Greek

This verb carries a variety of meanings in classical Greek. It can mean "to place under" one's feet, or "to lay down" as a foundation or a beginning. One would "put down" a deposit or a pledge. *Hupotithēmi* can be used to indicate the act of "assuming" or of "risking" something. It also means "to counsel" or "to suggest" a course of action (*Liddell-Scott*).

Septuagint Usage

Hupotithēmi appears 13 times in the Septuagint, 5 of which are in the Apocrypha. The remaining eight references translate four Hebrew terms, with *sûm* ("to put or place") accounting for four. A stone was "placed" as a pillow for Jacob (Genesis 28:18), and as a seat for a weary Moses (Exodus 17:12). In making a pledge Joseph "placed" his hand under the thigh of Jacob (Genesis 47:29). This concept of "placing underneath" is also found in Genesis 49:15 and Exodus 27:5, as well as Sirach 6:25 and 51:26.

The meaning "to counsel" is found in both the Septuagint and the Apocrypha. King Jehoiakim was "strongly urged" (Hebrew *pāgaʻ*) not to burn Jeremiah's prophecy recorded by Baruch (Jeremiah 36:25 [LXX 43:25]), and Ptolemy "suggested" that the Jews be forced to participate in pagan sacrifices (2 Maccabees 6:8).

New Testament Usage

The New Testament records only two occurrences of *hupotithēmi*: Romans 16:4 and 1 Timothy 4:6. The former expresses Paul's gratitude for Priscilla and Aquila, who "*laid down* (i.e., risked) their own necks" on Paul's behalf. This reflects a classical meaning not found in the Septuagint, i.e., the idea of "giving counsel." Paul informed Timothy that by "putting" the brethren "in remembrance" of certain truths already mentioned, he would be a good minister of Jesus Christ. It is interesting to note that neither of the New Testament references reflect the general meaning "to set" or "place" found throughout the Septuagint.

STRONG 5294, BAUER 848, MOULTON-MILLIGAN 660-61, LIDDELL-SCOTT 1898-99.

5133. ὑποτρέχω hupotrechō verb

To run in under.

CROSS-REFERENCE:
τρέχω trechō (4983)

1. **ὑποδραμόντες hupodramontes** nom pl masc part aor act

1 And **running under** a certain island................Acts 27:16

The verb *hupotrechō* describes the action of moving to safety under the would-be blows of an assailant. In a nautical sense the term describes the maneuvering of a ship to shelter it from the wind. This is how it is used in Acts 27:16, its only New Testament appearance. Setting sail contrary to Paul's advice to remain in Fair Havens, the voyage to Rome was jeopardized by a violent wind known to the sailors as Euroclydon (i.e., "northeaster"). The crew managed to "run in under" to the shelter of the southwest side of the island of Clauda. This respite was short-lived, however, as they eventually were shipwrecked on the island of Malta.

Strong 5295, Bauer 848, Moulton-Milligan 661, Liddell-Scott 1899.

5134. ὑποτύπωσις hupotupōsis noun

Pattern, example, form, standard.

Cross-Reference:
τύπος tupos (5020)

1. ὑποτύπωσιν hupotupōsin acc sing fem

1 a pattern to them which should hereafter believe .... 1 Tm 1:16
1 Hold fast the form of sound words, (NT) .... 2 Tm 1:13

Classical Greek

Classical writers used this noun to indicate a "sketch" or an "outline" for something, especially something written. It could also stand as a model or a "pattern" for something (*Liddell-Scott*). The term does not occur in the Septuagint in either canonical or apocryphal material of any version.

New Testament Usage

Hupotupōsis occurs only in 1 Timothy 1:16 and 2 Timothy 1:13 in the New Testament. Paul considered his own salvation as an "example" of God's unlimited patience toward sinners (1 Timothy 1:16). His role as "model" for Timothy is a repeated theme in the Pastoral Epistles (e.g., 2 Timothy 1:8,13; 2:3; 3:10). *Moulton-Milligan* is wrong in rejecting "example" at 1 Timothy 1:16 in favor of "outline." However, it is likely that the idea of "sketch" or "outline" is appropriate in 2 Timothy 1:13 (cf. the NIV, "pattern"). There Paul encouraged Timothy to keep the "essence" of the gospel message intact. Coupled with this desire is the urging of Timothy to "pass on what he received" from Paul (cf. 2 Timothy 3:14; Titus 1:9; 2:1).

Strong 5296, Bauer 848, Moulton-Milligan 661, Kittel 8:246-59, Liddell-Scott 1900, Colin Brown 3:903-5.

5135. ὑποφέρω hupopherō verb

To bear, to endure, to submit to.

Cognate:
φέρω pherō (5179)

Synonyms:
ἀνέχομαι anechomai (428)
καρτερέω karthereō (2565)
στέγω stegō (4573)
ὑπομένω hupomenō (5116)
φέρω pherō (5179)

יָכֹל yākhōl (3310), Be able (Jb 4:2, 31:23).

כּוּל kûl (3677), Hiphil: bear (Am 7:10).

כּוּן kûn (3679), Be firm, be stable; hiphil: prepare (Jb 15:35).

מָצָא mātsâ' (4834), Get (Prv 6:33).

נָשָׂא nāsâ' (5558), Bear (Ps 55:12 [54:12], Prv 18:14, Mi 7:9).

קָבַל qāval (7186), Piel: accept (Jb 2:10).

1. ὑποφέρει hupopherei 3sing indic pres act
2. ὑπήνεγκα hupēnenka 1sing indic aor act
3. ὑπενεγκεῖν hupenenkein inf aor act

3 a way to escape, that ye may be able to bear it..... 1 Co 10:13
2 at Lystra; what persecutions I endured:............. 2 Tm 3:11
1 if a man for conscience toward God endure grief,.... 1 Pt 2:19

Classical Greek

The general meaning of *hupopherō* in the classical period was "to carry away" in the sense of escaping a dangerous situation. Passively, it meant "to be carried away" as though by a stream. One author used *hupopherō* to mean "to add" or "suggest." It was also used metaphorically to mean "to endure" a hardship or "to sink down" in decay.

Septuagint Usage

This sense of "enduring" a hardship dominates the use of *hupopherō* in the Septuagint, with one notable exception: the Book of Job. There, three unexpected Hebrew terms are translated by *hupopherō*. Job rebuked his wife by asking whether one should not expect to *endure* (*qāval*) both good and evil from the Lord (Job 2:10). Proverbs 6:33 reflects a related concept (*mātsâ'*, "to acquire"). The Hebrew *yākhōl* ("to be able, to have power") is behind *hupopherō* in Job 4:2, where Eliphaz expressed his "inability" to withhold from rebuking Job. It is also found in Job 31:23 in a more traditional sense. Job "could not endure" (literally, "has no ability") in light of God's loftiness. Finally, Eliphaz spoke of the deceit "prepared" (*kûn*) in the bellies of hypocrites (Job 15:35). The meanings of *hupopherō* derived solely from Job are somewhat questionable since the Septuagint version of this Old Testament book is regarded as a loose paraphrase. Therefore, the sense conveyed by the Greek term may not be equivalent to the meaning of the word contained in the Old Testament Hebrew text.

Five of the remaining seven Septuagint references reflect the metaphoric sense of "enduring" difficulties, as do the nine apocryphal passages. The godly man can "bear" *(nāsâ')* the reproach of the Lord's enemies (Psalms 55:12 [LXX 54:12]; 69:7 [68:7]), as well as the Lord's anger for sin (Micah 7:9). No one can "bear" a wounded spirit (Proverbs 18:14), nor could Israel "endure" *(kûl)* the words of the prophet (Amos 7:10). The remaining two passages do not have Hebrew equivalents (1 Kings 8:64 [LXX 3 Kings 8:64]; Proverbs 14:17).

New Testament Usage

In all three New Testament references *hupopherō* denotes "enduring" hardships. Paul encouraged the Corinthian believers to expect the Lord's enabling to endure the inevitable times of temptation (1 Corinthians 10:13). He himself had experienced the Lord's deliverance, as he "endured" the afflictions and persecutions encountered on his missionary journeys (2 Timothy 3:11). And lastly, Peter commends the Christian who is willing to "endure" grief from sufferings generated by righteous living (1 Peter 2:19). Jesus said that such individuals are blessed, for theirs is the kingdom of God (Matthew 5:10).

STRONG 5297, BAUER 848, MOULTON-MILLIGAN 661, LIDDELL-SCOTT 1901.

5136. ὑποχωρέω hupochōreō verb

Withdraw, retreat.

CROSS-REFERENCE:

χωρέω chōreō (5397)

1. ὑποχωρῶν hupochōrōn nom sing masc part pres act

2. ὑπεχώρησεν hupechōrēsen 3sing indic aor act

1 And he withdrew himself into the wilderness,....... Luke 5:16
2 and went aside privately into a desert place............. 9:10

Although *hupochōreō* is found only in Luke, the clear testimony of the Gospel writers is that Jesus would often withdraw for various reasons (see *anachōreō* [400]). He withdrew in order to avoid the murderous plots of His enemies (Matthew 12:15; Mark 3:7), as well as the overzealous intentions of His followers (John 6:15). The execution of John the Baptist caused Jesus to withdraw, perhaps to receive strengthening from the Father for His mission (Matthew 14:13). The construction in Luke 5:16 (*ēn hupochōrōn*) indicates that Jesus customarily withdrew to pray. The imperfect form (*ēn*) of the verb *eimi* (1498), "to be," is iterative, indicating a practice or custom. Jesus would also withdraw from the crowds in order to rest (Luke 9:10; cf. Mark 6:31).

STRONG 5298, BAUER 848, MOULTON-MILLIGAN 661, LIDDELL-SCOTT 1903.

5137. ὑπωπιάζω hupōpiazō verb

To treat roughly, to blacken the eye.

1. ὑπωπιάζω hupōpiazō 1sing indic pres act

2. ὑπωπιάζῃ hupōpiazē 3sing subj pres act

2 lest by her continual coming she weary me......... Luke 18:5
1 But I keep under my body,......................... 1 Co 9:27

The verb *hupōpiazō* is not found in the Septuagint and occurs only twice in the New Testament. It is a boxing term whose meaning is "to strike under the eye" or "to give a black eye" (*Liddell-Scott*). The unjust judge in the parable feared such consequences should he fail to take up the widow's case (Luke 18:5). This is to be understood figuratively. The widow's continual pleading would show the judge either as incapable of fulfilling his function or as guided by personal considerations. In either case, his prestige is assaulted and he is effectively disgraced. His "face has been blackened" (Derrett, "Law in the New Testament: the Unjust Judge," pp.189f.).

Paul used *hupōpiazō* to describe the manner in which he disciplined his body for service (1 Corinthians 9:27). Just as an athlete must train and master his body to compete, so the Christian must "keep under" or discipline his body in order to bring it into subjection. Paul was not guided by physical comforts; if he were, the hardships he suffered for the gospel's sake would have compelled him to quit. Rather, Paul disciplined his body to accept these sufferings so that he might receive the prize: an incorruptible crown from the Lord's own hand (cf. 2 Timothy 4:7,8). Conversely, Paul also had a high regard for the body as the temple of the Holy Spirit, and he commanded believers to treat it as such (1 Corinthians 6:19).

STRONG 5299, BAUER 848, MOULTON-MILLIGAN 661, KITTEL 8:590-91, LIDDELL-SCOTT 1904, COLIN BROWN 1:162-63.

5137B. ὗς hus noun

Sow, a female pig.

חֲזִיר chăzîr (2478), Pig, swine (Lv 11:7, Dt 14:8, Prv 11:22).

1. ὗς hus nom sing fem

1 **sow that was washed to her wallowing in the mire...** 2 Pt 2:22

This word occurs in a proverb quoted in 2 Peter 2:22, although the proverb's source is uncertain. Peter likened a backsliding Christian to a dog returning to its vomit (quoting Proverbs 26:11) and a sow returning to the mire. Such an analogy is poignant, for dogs and sows were "species of animals . . . traditionally coupled together as unclean and beneath contempt" (Kelly, *Harper's New Testament Commentaries, Peter and Jude*, p.350). Jesus coupled them together in a negative context in Matthew 7:6, although *choiros* (5355) is used for "swine."

Strong 5300, Bauer 848, Moulton-Milligan 661, Liddell-Scott 1904.

5138. ὕσσωπος hussōpos noun

Hyssop.

אֵזוֹב 'ēzôv (230), Hyssop (Lv 14:4,6, 1 Kgs 4:33, Ps 51:7 [50:7]).

1. **ὑσσώπου hussōpou** gen sing masc
2. **ὑσσώπῳ hussōpō** dat sing masc

2 and put it upon **hyssop**, and put it to his mouth.... John 19:29
1 with water, and scarlet wool, and **hyssop**,............Heb 9:19

Hussōpos is a noun denoting a class of plants thought to include thyme and marjoram. Among the Jews they were used in sacrifices of purification and cleansing (Leviticus 14:4; Numbers 19:6,18). At Passover bunches of the plants were used to apply the blood of the lamb to the doorposts and lintels of the homes where the Passover meal was eaten (Exodus 12:22).

In English translations of the Bible it is transliterated as "hyssop." In Hebrews 9:19 *hussōpos* is used in reference to the sprinkling of sacrificial blood on the Day of Atonement. And John 19:29 describes the scene when our crucified Lord thirsted. He was given a sponge full of sour, vinegary wine held by the hyssop.

Strong 5301, Bauer 849, Moulton-Milligan 661, Liddell-Scott 1905.

5139. ὑστερέω hustereō verb

To come too late, to lack, to fail, to be inferior.

Cognate:
ὕστερος husteros (5143)

Synonym:
λείπω leipō (2981)

גָּרַע gāra' (1686), Diminish, shave; niphal: be kept from doing something (Nm 9:7).

חָדַל chādhal (2403), Neglect (Nm 9:13).

חָדֵל chādhēl (2404), Fleeting (Ps 39:4 [38:4]).

חָסֵר chāṣēr (2741), Lack (Eccl 9:8, 10:3).

חָסֵר chāṣēr (2742), Lacking (Eccl 6:2).

מָהַהּ māhahh (4244), Hithpael: tarry (Hb 2:3).

מָנַע māna' (4661), Withhold (Ps 84:11 [83:11]).

1. **ὑστερῶ husterō** 1sing indic pres act
2. **ὑστερεῖ husterei** 3sing indic pres act
3. **ὑστερῶν husterōn** nom sing masc part pres act
4. **ὑστεροῦντι husterounti** dat sing masc part pres act
5. **ὑστέρησα husterēsa** 1sing indic aor act
6. **ὑστερήσατε husterēsate** 2pl indic aor act
7. **ὑστερήσαντος husterēsantos** gen sing masc part aor act
8. **ὑστερηκέναι husterēkenai** inf perf act
9. **ὑστερούμεθα husteroumetha** 1pl indic pres mid
10. **ὑστεροῦνται husterountai** 3pl indic pres mid
11. **ὑστερούμενοι husteroumenoi** nom pl masc part pres mid
12. **ὑστερεῖσθαι hustereisthai** inf pres mid
13. **ὑστερηθείς husterētheis** nom sing masc part aor pass
14. **ὑστερουμένῳ husteroumenō** dat sing neu part pres mid

1 these ... I kept from my youth up: what **lack** I yet? Matt 19:20
2 One thing thou **lackest**: ... sell whatsoever........Mark 10:21
12 and he began **to be in want**..................... Luke 15:14
6 **lacked ye** any thing? And they said, Nothing......... 22:35
7 And when they **wanted** wine,..................... John 2:3
10 sinned, and **come short** of the glory of God;....... Rom 3:23
12 So that ye **come behind** in no gift;............... 1 Co 1:7
9 neither, if we eat not, are we **the worse**.............. 8:8
4 more abundant honour to that part **which lacked**:..... 12:24
8 I **was** not a whit **behind** the very chiefest apostles. 2 Co 11:5
13 And when I was present with you, and **wanted**,....... 11:9
5 in nothing **am I behind** the very chiefest apostles,..... 12:11
12 both to abound and **to suffer need**................ Phlp 4:12
8 any of you should seem **to come short of it**......... Heb 4:1
11 **being destitute**, afflicted, tormented;................ 11:37
3 Looking diligently lest any man **fail** of the grace...... 12:15

Classical Greek

The primary sense of *hustereō* in the classical period was temporal, denoting one who "came too late." One author wrote of an individual who "came one day after the appointed day," while another lamented "they came too late for the battle by five days" (Lane, "Want," *Colin Brown*, 3:952). It came to be used metaphorically to mean "failing" in a task or "being inferior." *Hustereō* also indicated the "lack" of some personal quality or possession.

Septuagint Usage

This last meaning occurs in 14 of the 21 Septuagint passages (8 of 14 canonical references, and 6 of 7 apocryphal entries). King David's reflections on the transient nature (Hebrew *chādhēl*) of life are expressed as a "lack" in Psalm 39:4 (LXX 38:4). The Psalmist desired to know his lack so he might appear approved before God (ibid., 3:953). King Belshazzar was weighed in the balances and found "wanting" (Hebrew *chāsēr*, Daniel 5:27), while the man "lacking" strength will be sustained by God (Sirach 11:12). The Israelites "lacked" nothing in the wilderness (Nehemiah 9:21 [LXX 2 Esdras 19:21]), nor will the man whose shepherd is the Lord (Psalm 23:1 [LXX 22:1]).

The concept of "failing" is also present in the Septuagint. One should not "fail" those who weep (Sirach 7:34). The man who "failed" to keep the Passover was to be cut off from the people (Numbers 9:13). This was in contrast to the individual who was "kept back" (Hebrew *gāra'*) from doing so due to defilement (Numbers 9:7). The concept of time is found in Habakkuk 2:3, where the Lord assured the prophet of the reliability of His promises, even though now they "tarry" (Hebrew *māhahh*).

New Testament Usage

Eight of the sixteen New Testament references reflect the concept of "lacking," or "being in need." Although the rich young man had kept the commandments since his youth, he still sensed some "lack" that would deny him eternal life (Matthew 19:20). Jesus revealed to him that he lacked proper priorities, for he loved his riches more than he loved God (Mark 10:21). Physical needs are amply represented. The Prodigal Son was "in want" when his resources were spent and the famine hit (Luke 15:14). The apostles did not "lack" anything when Jesus sent them out to evangelize (Luke 22:35), and Paul's "needs" were met by fellow Christians from Macedonia (2 Corinthians 11:9).

Paul used *hustereō* in the context of being "inferior." In the analogy of the body as representing the Church, Paul spoke of those members which "lack" the spectacular gifts—they are worthy of "more abundant honor" (1 Corinthians 12:24). He also defended his apostleship as being in no way "behind the very chiefest apostles" (2 Corinthians 11:5; 12:11).

The last concept expressed by *hustereō* is that of "failing." Because of sin, all have "come short" of the glory of God (Romans 3:23). Israel's unbelief in the wilderness provides a warning for others not to "come short" of entering God's rest (Hebrews 4:1), a plea restated as "failing" of the grace of God (Hebrews 12:15).

Strong 5302, Bauer 849, Moulton-Milligan 661-62, Kittel 8:592-601, Liddell-Scott 1905-6, Colin Brown 3:952-54.

5140. ὑστέρημα husterēma noun

Need, want, poverty, absence; shortcoming.

Cross-Reference:

ὕστερος husteros (5143)

חֶסְרוֹן chesrôn (2747), What is lacking (Eccl 1:15).

מַחְסוֹר machsôr (4408), Lack, want (Jgs 18:10, 19:19, Ps 34:9 [33:9]).

1. **ὑστερήματος husterēmatos** gen sing neu
2. **ὑστέρημα husterēma** nom/acc sing neu
3. **ὑστερήματα husterēmata** nom/acc pl neu

1 her **penury** hath cast in all the living that she had. Luke 21:4
2 for that **which was lacking** on your part .... 1 Co 16:17
2 your abundance may be a supply for their **want**, ... 2 Co 8:14
2 abundance also may be a supply for your **want**: 8:14
3 not only supplieth the **want** of the saints, ... 9:12
2 for that which **was lacking** to me 11:9
2 to supply your **lack** of service toward me. .... Phlp 2:30
3 **which is behind** of the afflictions of Christ .... Col 1:24
3 might perfect that which is **lacking** in your faith? .... 1 Th 3:10

Septuagint Usage

The noun *husterēma* appears for the first time in the Septuagint. The Hebrew behind it (*chesrôn* or *machsôr*) denotes a "deficit, what is missing, lacking" (e.g., Judges 18:10, of a land which lacked nothing; 19:19,20; cf. the Aramaic *chăshach*, "what is needed," Ezra 6:9 [LXX 2 Esdras 6:9]). Those fearing the Lord "lack nothing" according to the Psalmist (34:9 [LXX 33:9]). (Cf. the cognate *husterēsis* [5141].)

New Testament Usage

Of its nine instances in the New Testament, eight are attributed to Paul and one to Luke (Luke 21:4). The poor widow gave her offering in spite of her "deficiency" (Luke 21:4, note the association of *husterēma* with the means of existence; cf. Septuagint usage above and 2 Corinthians 8:14; 9:12; 11:9).

Paul understood it in a spiritual sense (1 Thessalonians 3:10). He, through his prayers, hoped to come and visit the Thessalonians and supply what was deficient in their faith. He may have hoped to impart to them some spiritual gift as he did the believers in Rome (Romans 1:11) and Corinth (see 1 Corinthians 1:7, the use of the verb *hustereō* [5139]).

By far the most perplexing use of *husterēma* in the New Testament, theologically speaking, is found in Colossians 1:24: "Who (I, Paul) now rejoice in my sufferings for you, and fill up *that which is behind* of the afflictions of Christ in my flesh for his body's sake, which is the church." Paul was not speaking of a deficiency in the atoning work of Christ. Neither was he concluding that somehow Christ's sufferings (*thlipseōn tou Christou*) were incomplete. Lane notes that *thlipsis* nowhere in the New Testament refers to the sufferings of Jesus during His ministry ("Want," *Colin Brown*, 3:956.)

Lane also notes that the phrase makes sense within the framework of early Christian apocalyptic, which saw the end-time sufferings and afflictions as preceding the end of the age and the coming of Messiah. God had determined the duration and extent of these "messianic woes" (cf. Mark 13:5-27; Ethiopian Enoch 47:1-4; 2 Baruch 30:2). As these were complete, the new age would break through. Thus Paul could see his sufferings as helping the Church move toward this goal (ibid., 3:956).

However, other interpretations exist. Carson also rejects the view that the Atonement is incomplete but opts for a mystical explanation: "We may take these sufferings as being those which Christ suffers in Paul because of the mystical union of the apostle with his Saviour" (*Tyndale New Testament Commentaries*, 12:51). Abbott, on the other hand, argues that "the notion that Christ suffers affliction in His people is nowhere found in the N.T. . . . It is true that he sympathizes with the afflictions of His people; but sympathy is not affliction" (*International Critical Commentary, Ephesians and Colossians*, pp.231f.). Rather, Paul called *his own* sufferings the "afflictions of Christ." "Christ's afflictions are regarded as the type of all those that are endured by His followers on behalf of the church" (ibid.). Finally, Bruce concurs that there may be the notion of an apocalyptic/Rabbinic concept of "the messianic birth pangs," but he decides that "Paul and his fellow preachers . . . in the fulfillment of (their) ministry . . . are exposed to sufferings for Christ's sake, and these sufferings are their share in the afflictions of Christ" (*New International Commentary on the New Testament, Colossians, Philemon, and Ephesians*, p.83).

STRONG 5303, BAUER 849, KITTEL 8:592-601, LIDDELL-SCOTT 1905-6, COLIN BROWN 3:952-53,955.

5141. ὑστέρησις husterēsis noun

Need, lack, want, poverty.

CROSS-REFERENCE:
ὕστερος husteros (5143)

1. ὑστερήσεως husterēseōs gen sing fem
2. ὑστέρησιν husterēsin acc sing fem

1 but she of her **want** did cast in all that she had, . . . Mark 12:44
2 Not that I speak in respect of **want**: . . . . Phlp 4:11

This is a noun related to the verb *hustereō* (5139) which means "to be in need, to lack," or "to go without." So *husterēsis* signifies a state of need. In Mark 12:44 this term refers to the poverty of the widow who gave her last mite. In Philippians 4:11 Paul used it in a disclaimer. He did not want the Philippians to think that his praise for their giving was a backhanded way of asking them to give again. He denied that he had any real need, any lack of material necessities. He steadfastly maintained that he relied on inner spiritual resources, not material externals.

STRONG 5304, BAUER 849, KITTEL 8:592-601, LIDDELL-SCOTT 1905, COLIN BROWN 3:952-53,955.

5142. ὕστερον husteron adv

Afterward, in the second place, at last, finally.

CROSS-REFERENCE:
ὕστερος husteros (5143)

אַחַר 'achar (313), After (Jer 29:2 [36:2], 31:19 [38:19]).
אַחֲרִית 'achărîth (321), End (Prv 5:4).

1. ὕστερον husteron comp

1 he had fasted ... he was **afterward** an hungered. . . . . . Matt 4:2
1 but **afterward** he repented, and went. 21:29
1 repented not **afterward**, that ye might believe him. 21:32
1 But **last** of all he sent unto them his son, saying, ... 21:37
1 And **last** of all the woman died also. 22:27
1 **Afterward** came also the other virgins, ... 25:11
1 At the **last** came two false witnesses, ... 26:60
1 **Afterward** he appeared unto the eleven . . . . Mark 16:14
1 when they were ended, he **afterward** hungered. . . . . . . Luke 4:2
1 **Last** of all the woman died also. 20:32
1 but thou shalt follow me **afterwards**. . . . . John 13:36
1 **afterward** it yieldeth the peaceable fruit . . . . Heb 12:11

A neuter form of the adjective *husteros* (5143), *husteron* is used adverbially. These adverbial meanings fall into two categories. Sometimes the meaning is purely chronological and the word describes one event which comes after another (see Matthew 4:2; 21:29,32; 25:11; Mark 16:14; Luke 4:2; John 13:36; Hebrews 12:11). In other instances it refers to the last item or event in a series and carries the meaning "finally" (see Matthew 21:37; 22:27; Luke 20:32).

STRONG 5305, BAUER 849 (see "husteros"), MOULTON-MILLIGAN 662, KITTEL 8:592-601, LIDDELL-SCOTT 1906, COLIN BROWN 3:952-53.

5143. ὕστερος husteros adj

Second, last, or later.

COGNATES:
ὑστερέω hustereō (5139)
ὑστέρημα husterēma (5140)

ὑστέρησις husterēsis (5141)
ὕστερον husteron (5142)

אַחֲרוֹן 'achărôn (315), Last (1 Chr 29:29).

1. ὑστέροις husterois comp dat pl masc
2. ὕστερος husteros comp nom sing masc

2 They said, "The latter." (NASB) .... Matt 21:31
1 in the latter times some shall depart from the faith, 1 Tm 4:1

Husteros is an adjective that means "second, last." In most of its uses in the New Testament, the neuter form *husteron* (5142) is used. The neuter form of the adjective is generally in the accusative case and functions adverbially, meaning "afterward, in the second place," or "at last, finally."

In its strict adjectival usage, *husteros* is used in two ways and has two meanings. First of all, it is a comparative adjective, meaning "the second" or "the latter." We find this usage in Matthew 21:30. This context displays both the adjectival and the adverbial use of *husteros.* In verse 29 the word translated "afterward" is *husteron.* In verse 30 the word translated "the second" is, in some of the manuscripts, *husteros.* (For a fuller discussion of the manuscript variations see Metzger, *A Textual Commentary on the Greek New Testament*, pp.55,56.)

The second adjectival usage of *husteros* is a superlative use. In this usage it means "the last." We discover this meaning employed in the eschatological teaching of the apostle Paul in 1 Timothy 4:1. Here Paul was warning Timothy about the great religious apostasy of the final days when many people would follow after the teaching of evil spirits and would be influenced by demons. He described this as taking place in *husterois kairois*, meaning "the last seasons" or "latter times." This phrase refers not to a second period of time in comparison to a former time period but to a later, future time period in the whole series of ages that comprise human history.

Strong 5306, Bauer 849, Moulton-Milligan 662, Kittel 8:592-601, Liddell-Scott 1906, Colin Brown 3:952-53.

5144. ὗς hus

See word study at number 5137B.

5144B. ὑφαίνω huphainō verb

Weave.

Cross-Reference:
φαίνω phainō (5154)

אָרַג 'āragh (730), Weave (Jgs 16:13, Is 59:5): weaver (2 Sm 21:19).

עָלָה 'ālâh (6148), Go up; hiphil: work something into a fabric (2 Chr 3:14).

1. ὑφαίνει huphainei 3sing indic pres act

1 they neither toil nor spin; (NASB) (NT) .... Luke 12:27

As early as the Eighth Century B.C., *huphainō* meant the process of "weaving," for example, tunics, carpets, and linen items for the temple (cf. *Moulton-Milligan*). There is also evidence that the word had a figurative use. *Liddell-Scott* references a work of Homer describing plans that were "craftily imagined." Its only New Testament occurrence is at Luke 12:27, a literal use which states that the lilies of the field "toil not" and "they *weave* not." Some manuscripts contain the word *nēthō* (3376), "to spin." Weaving is "the process of interlacing previously spun lengthwise threads with previously spun crosswise threads to form cloth" (Lee, *International Standard Bible Encyclopedia*, "Weaving"). It is seen as early as 6000 B.C. Looms (devices used to weave cloth) were known in the Biblical period, both horizontal and vertical looms being attested (ibid.).

Bauer 849, Moulton-Milligan 662, Liddell-Scott 1906-7.

5145. ὑφαντός huphantos adj

Woven.

Cross-Reference:
φαίνω phainō (5154)

אָרַג 'āragh (730), Weave (Ex 39:22,27 [36:30,35]).

חָשַׁב chāshav (2913), Weaver, skilled craftsman (Ex 35:35, 39:8 [36:15]); weave (Ex 39:3 [36:10]).

רָקַם rāqam (7844), Embroiderer (Ex 36:37 [37:5]).

1. ὑφαντός huphantos nom sing masc

1 without seam, woven from the top throughout...... John 19:23

Huphantos, "woven," is an adjective related to the verb *huphainō* (5144B), "to weave" (see Luke 12:27). In his Passion narrative the apostle John used *huphantos* to describe the seamless garment of Jesus over which the soldiers gambled. It was a single piece of weaving (John 19:23, "without seam, *woven* from the top throughout").

Strong 5307, Bauer 849, Moulton-Milligan 662, Liddell-Scott 1907.

5146. ὑψηλός hupsēlos adj

High, a high thing.

Cross-Reference:
ὑψόω hupsoō (5150)

בָּמָה bāmāh (1154), High place (1 Kgs 3:2f., 2 Kgs 14:4, Ez 6:3).

גֵּאֶה gē'eh (1373), Proud (Is 2:12).

גֵּאוּת gē'ûth (1378), An excellent thing (Is 12:5).

גָּבַהּ gāvahh (1391), Qal: be high (Jb 35:5 [35:4]); hiphil: go upward, a high place above the earth (Ps 113:5 [112:5]).

גָּבֹהַּ gāvōahh (1393), High (Gn 7:19, Jer 2:20); proud (1 Sm 2:3).

גֹּבַהּ gōvahh (1394), Height (Jb 11:8, 22:12).

גַּבְהוּת gavhûth (1395), Arrogance (Is 2:11).

גֹּדֶל gōdhel (1465), Pride (Is 9:9).

חָזָק chāzāq (2481), Strong, mighty (Ex 6:1, Dn 9:15).

מִדָּה middāh (4201), Stature (Is 45:14).

מוֹרֶה môreh (4310B), Moreh (Gn 12:6, Dt 11:30).

מָרוֹם mārôm (4953), High place, heights (Ps 93:4 [93:3], Prv 9:3, Is 26:5).

מֹרִיָּה mōrîyāh (4974), Moriah (Gn 22:2).

נָטָה nāṭâh (5371), Something outstretched (Dt 4:34, 2 Chr 6:32, Is 3:16).

נָשָׂא nāsâ' (5558), Lift up, carry; niphal: Lofty One (Is 57:15).

עֹז 'ōz (6010), Strong (Jgs 9:51—Codex Alexandrinus only).

עֶלְיוֹן 'elyôn (6169), Heap (1 Kgs 9:8); highest, upper (Ps 89:27 [88:27], Ez 9:2).

רוּם rûm (7597), Do something boldly, be high (Nm 33:3, Ps 138:6 [137:6]).

רוּם rûm (7599), Height (Prv 25:3).

רָמָה rāmāh (7703), Ramah (Hos 5:8).

1. **ὑψηλοῦ hupsēlou** gen sing masc
2. **ὑψηλοῖς hupsēlois** dat pl masc
3. **ὑψηλόν hupsēlon** nom/acc sing neu
4. **ὑψηλά hupsēla** nom/acc pl neu
5. **ὑψηλότερος hupsēloteros** comp nom sing masc

3 devil taketh ... into an exceeding **high** mountain,.... Matt 4:8
3 and bringeth them up into an **high** mountain apart,.... 17:1
3 up into an **high** mountain apart by themselves:..... Mark 9:2
3 the devil, taking him up into an **high** mountain,..... Luke 4:5
3 for that which is **highly esteemed** among men.......... 16:15
1 and with an **high** arm brought he them out of it.... Acts 13:17
4 Do not be conceited, but fear. (NASB) (NT)...... Rom 11:20
4 Mind not **high things**,.............................. 12:16
2 sat down on the right hand of the Majesty on **high**;.. Heb 1:3
5 and made **higher** than the heavens;.................. 7:26
3 away in the spirit to a great and **high** mountain,.... Rev 21:10
3 had a wall great and **high**, and had twelve gates,...... 21:12

Generally *hupsēlos* is used as an adjective. In its literal meaning, "high," it modifies things like mountains and walls (see Matthew 4:8; 17:1; Mark 9:2; Luke 4:5; Revelation 21:10,12). As is the case with most other Greek adjectives, it can also be used as a noun on occasion.

In Hebrews 1:3 it appears in the phrase "on high." In this instance it refers to "heaven," for it speaks of the location of our Lord Jesus Christ after His resurrection and ascension. He is now located at the right hand of God in heaven. In Luke 16:15 *hupsēlos* is again used as a noun. Here it has a figurative, metaphoric usage. It is modified by the prepositional phrase "among men" and is translated "highly esteemed." Literally, the Greek reads "the among men high thing." In this context Jesus was confronting the Pharisees and condemning them for their greed. They had made the love of money into one of their greatest values, and Jesus was telling them that this is a reversal of God's value system. Their pursuit of material gain was an abomination to God.

In Romans 12:16 there is a similar usage of the term. Christians are told not to set their minds upon *ta hupsēla*, "the high things." Here the neuter plural form of the adjective functions as a noun. It has reference to mankind's inverted value system. Cranfield understands this expression as a reference to haughtiness (*International Critical Commentary, Romans*, 2:644; cf. NIV: "Do not be proud").

Once *hupsēlos* appears in its comparative form, *hupsēloteros*. In Hebrews 7:26 the Lord Jesus Christ is described in His exalted high priesthood as One who "has become higher than the heavens." He has been elevated beyond the highest imaginable part of the creation; He has ascended from the humiliation of His incarnation to the right hand of God.

Sometimes *hupsēlos* is used figuratively as an adjective. A case in point is found in Acts 13:17. The phrase "an high arm" is a figure of speech for the display of God's power through Moses in the miraculous deliverance of the Children of Israel at the Red Sea (see Exodus 14).

Strong 5308, Bauer 849-50, Moulton-Milligan 662, Liddell-Scott 1909, Colin Brown 2:198-200; 3:1009-10.

5147. ὑψηλοφρονέω
hupsēlophroneō verb

To be proud, arrogant.

Cross-Reference:
φρονέω phroneō (5262)

1. **ὑψηλοφρόνει hupsēlophronei** 2sing impr pres act
2. **ὑψηλοφρονεῖν hupsēlophronein** inf pres act

1 standest by faith. Be not **highminded**, but fear:..... Rom 11:20
2 rich in this world, that they be not **highminded**,..... 1 Tm 6:17

In the two places where this term is used in the New Testament it has a negative meaning. In Romans 11:20 the Gentiles of the present age are commanded not to be proud because God is blessing them instead of blessing the unbelieving Jews. The blessing of God on the Gentiles is by divine mercy, not by merit. The day will come when God's mercy will again fall upon the Jews, and "all Israel" will be saved.

In 1 Timothy 6:17 Paul counseled Timothy to command those who were wealthy not to be proud of their material wealth which was temporary, but to rest in God who lives forever. In both references the "high things" people set their minds upon are not the highest, that is, God himself, but something they have put in God's place.

STRONG 5309, BAUER 850, LIDDELL-SCOTT 1909.

5148. ὕψιστος hupsistos adj

The highest, the Most High.

CROSS-REFERENCE:
ὑψόω hupsoō (5150)

אֵל 'ēl (418), The Most High (Sir 12:6).

מָרוֹם mārôm (4953), Heights, Someone high (Jb 25:2, Ps 148:1, Mi 6:6).

עִלָּי 'illāy (A6162), The Most High (Dn 3:26, 4:2 [3:32], 7:25—Aramaic).

עֶלְיוֹן 'elyôn (6169), The Most High (Gn 14:18ff., Ps 18:13 [17:13], Lam 3:35).

עֶלְיוֹן 'elyôn (A6170), The Most High (Dn 7:18,22—Aramaic).

רוּם rûm (7599), High place (Is 57:15).

1. **ὕψιστος hupsistos** sup nom sing masc
2. **ὑψίστου hupsistou** sup gen sing masc
3. **ὑψίστοις hupsistois** sup dat pl neu

3 in the name of the Lord; Hosanna in the **highest**... Matt 21:9
2 Jesus, thou Son of the **most high** God?............Mark 5:7
3 in the name of the Lord: Hosanna in the **highest**....... 11:10
2 and shall be called the Son of the **Highest**:......... Luke 1:32
2 the power of the **Highest** shall overshadow thee:........ 1:35
2 child, shalt be called the prophet of the **Highest**:........ 1:76
3 Glory to God in the **highest**, and on earth peace,....... 2:14
2 and ye shall be the children of the **Highest**:............ 6:35
2 thou Son of God **most high**? ... torment me not......... 8:28
3 peace in heaven, and glory in the **highest**.............. 19:38
1 Howbeit the **most High** dwelleth not in temples......Acts 7:48
2 These men are the servants of the **most high** God,..... 16:17
2 king of Salem, priest of the **most high** God,......... Heb 7:1

Classical Greek and Septuagint Usage

This term is used in classical Greek literature to denote the highest of all heights with reference to places (e.g., mountains or heaven), to gods (e.g., Zeus), or to things (e.g., crowns, profits, fears; *Liddell-Scott*). In the Septuagint *hupsistos* is used to make topographical distinctions (e.g., Psalm 148:1) or as an appellation for God (e.g., Psalm 21:7 [LXX 20:7]). It primarily translates *'elyôn*, "most high, upper." When used with a divine figure, *'elyôn* is always used of God (Bertram, "hupsistos," *Kittel*, 8:616). Melchizedek was Priest of God *Most High* (Genesis 14:18-22). The "voice of the Most High thunders" (Psalm 18:13 [LXX 17:13]).

New Testament Usage

This superlative of the adverb *hupsi*, "high," is used in the New Testament as a noun. It appears in two usages: (1) as a reference to heaven, the abode of God; (2) the name of God. As a reference to heaven it is found in the mouths of the crowd praising Jesus on Palm Sunday: "Hosanna in the *highest*" (Matthew 21:9; Mark 11:10). (This could also mean "to the highest degree" rather than heaven.) See also the account of the Triumphal Entry in Luke 19:38. We also hear this worship expressed by the angelic hosts at the birth of Jesus (Luke 2:14).

All of the other appearances of this word in the New Testament are in the second category. It is used when Jesus is identified as the Son of God (Mark 5:7; Luke 1:32; 8:28). Thus, in Mark 5:7 the demon-possessed man asks, "What do you want with me, Jesus, son of the Most High God?" (NIV). Elsewhere it speaks of the power, the prophet, the children, the servants, and the priest of God *Most High* (Luke 1:35,76; 6:35; Acts 16:17; Hebrews 7:1). Stephen used it when insisting that God *Most High* does not live in a temple built by men (Acts 7:48).

STRONG 5310, BAUER 850, MOULTON-MILLIGAN 662, KITTEL 8:614-20, LIDDELL-SCOTT 1910, COLIN BROWN 2:198-200.

5149. ὕψος hupsos noun

Height.

CROSS-REFERENCE:
ὑψόω hupsoō (5150)

בָּמָה bāmāh (1154), High place (2 Sm 1:25, 22:34, Am 4:13).

גָּאוֹן gā'ôn (1377), Majesty (Jb 40:10 [40:5]).

גָּבֹהַּ gāvōahh (1393), High (Ez 41:22).

גֹּבַהּ gōvahh (1394), Height (2 Sm 22:34, Ez 31:14); pride (2 Chr 32:26).

גֹּדֶל gōdhel (1465), Greatness, majesty (Ez 31:2,7).

מַעַל ma'al (4762), High, above (1 Chr 14:2, 29:3); greater (2 Chr 17:12).

מָרוֹם mārôm (4953), High place, place on high (Jgs 5:18, Ps 68:18 [67:18], Is 37:23).

קוֹמָה qômāh (7253), Height (Ex 27:1, 2 Chr 4:2, Jer 52:21).

רוּם rûm (7597), Be high; hiphil: raise (1 Chr 15:16).

רוּם rûm (7599), Pride, haughtiness (Is 2:11, 10:12).

רוּם rûm (A7600), Height (Ezr 6:3, Dn 3:1—Aramaic).

רוֹם rôm (7601), Place on high (Hb 3:10).

תּוֹעָפוֹת tô'āphôth (8776), Peak (Ps 95:4 [94:4]).

1. ὕψος hupsos nom/acc sing neu
2. ὕψους hupsous gen sing neu
3. ὕψει hupsei dat sing neu

2 the dayspring from on high hath visited us,......... Luke 1:78
2 until ye be endued with power from on high........... 24:49
1 the breadth, and length, and depth, and height;...... Eph 3:18
1 Wherefore he saith, When he ascended up on high,..... 4:8
3 brother of low degree rejoice in that he is exalted:... Jas 1:9
1 length and the breadth and the height ... are equal. Rev 21:16

Classical Greek

This neuter noun, which is used both literally and figuratively from the classical Greek period onward, is related to the adverb *hupsi*, "high, aloft." Literally, *hupsos* refers to a measurable height, for example, a height that is too great to leap over. Figuratively, the term may refer to the concept of royalty, dignity, sublimity, grandeur, or ignorance (*Liddell-Scott*).

Septuagint Usage

In the Septuagint the term could be used to denote the height of an object like a mountain (2 Kings 19:23 [LXX 4 Kings 19:23]), the temple (Ezra 6:3), or a tree (Ezekiel 31:14). The term may indicate the realm of heaven, of God, or of that which relates to God (Psalms 68:18 [LXX 67:18]; 102:19 [101:19]; 144:7 [143:7]; Isaiah 40:26). *Hupsos* may also denote man's pride (Isaiah 2:17).

New Testament Usage

Hupsos is used in four different ways in the New Testament. First, like *hupsistos* (5148), it can refer to heaven as the place where God dwells, or perhaps even to God himself. In Luke 1:78, the prophecy of Zechariah, it depicts the Messiah as "the dayspring from on high." This is either a reference to the Messiah's heavenly origin or His coming from God. There is no difference. If He comes from heaven, He comes from God. Jesus made the same application in His promise of the Holy Spirit where He commanded His disciples to wait in Jerusalem "until ye be endued with power from on high" (Luke 24:49). The Holy Spirit came both from heaven and from God at Pentecost. Likewise, in Ephesians 4:8 Christ's giving of gifts to the Church is associated with His ascension "on high," a reference to His ascension to the right hand of God the Father.

Secondly, *hupsos* is used in Revelation 21:16 to refer literally to the measurement of the dimensions of the New Jerusalem; the New Jerusalem was as *high* as it was long. A third use of a figurative kind appears in Ephesians 3:18 where Paul prayed that believers will know the greatness of the dimensions of God's love in Christ Jesus: "how *high* the love of Christ is."

Finally, in James 1:9 *hupsos* indicates the exaltation of the humble believer who has placed faith in Jesus Christ. The humblest believers can rejoice because they are "on high," that is, seated in heaven at the right hand of God the Father in Jesus.

STRONG 5311, BAUER 850, MOULTON-MILLIGAN 662, KITTEL 8:602-6, LIDDELL-SCOTT 1910, COLIN BROWN 2:198-200.

5150. ὑψόω hupsoō verb

To exalt, to raise high.

COGNATES:
ὑπερυψόω huperupsoō (5089)
ὑψηλός hupsēlos (5146)
ὑψηλοφρονέω hupsēlophroneō (5147)
ὕψιστος hupsistos (5148)
ὕψος hupsos (5149)
ὕψωμα hupsōma (5151)

SYNONYMS:
αἴρω airō (142)
ἐπαίρω epairō (1854)

אָרֵךְ 'ārēkh (773), Become long (Ez 31:5—Codex Alexandrinus only).

גָּאוֹן gā'ôn (1377), Pride (Is 4:2).

גָּבַהּ gāvahh (1391), Qal: be taller (1 Sm 10:23); be proud, be lifted up (Prv 18:12, Ez 28:2); hiphil: make high, exalt (2 Chr 33:14, Ez 17:24).

גֹּבַהּ gōvahh (1394), Height (Ez 31:10).

גָּבַר gāvar (1428), Rise, flood (Gn 7:20,24).

גָּדוֹל gādhôl (1448), Great (Is 12:6).

גָּדַל gādhal (1461), Qal: become rich, grow (Gn 24:35, Dn 8:10); piel: exalt (Jos 3:7); rear (Is 51:18); hiphil: be excellent, magnify oneself (Is 28:29, Dn 8:4,25); hithpael: boast of oneself, magnify oneself (Is 10:15, Dn 11:36f.).

מָרָא mārā' (4916), Hiphil: lift oneself on high (Jb 39:18).

מָרוֹם mārôm (4953), Place on high (Jer 17:12).

נָטָה nāṭāh (5371), Be stretched out (Is 14:26—only some Sinaiticus texts).

נָשָׂא nāsā' (5558), Qal: release (2 Kgs 25:27); rise up, lift up (Ps 88:15 [87:15], Is 52:8); piel: lift up oneself, rise up (Pss 7:6, 94:2 [93:2], Is 33:10); piel: advance, carry (Est 3:1, Is 63:9); hithpael: exalt oneself (Ez 29:15).

עָלַז 'ālaz (6159), Exult (Ps 108:7 [107:7]).

פָּאַר pā'ar (6526), Piel: beautify (Ps 149:4).

פָּרָה pārâh (6759), Bear fruit; hiphil: make fruitful (Gn 41:52—Codex Alexandrinus only).

רָבָה rāvâh (7528), Become numerous, become great; hiphil: do something exceedingly (Ezr 10:1).

רוּם rûm (7597), Qal: be exalted, rise (Nm 24:7, Ps 18:46 [17:46], Is 30:18); polel: exalt (2 Sm 22:49, Ps 37:34 [36:34]); bring up (Is 1:2); hiphil: raise, exalt oneself (Gn 39:15, Ps 89:42 [88:42], Is 13:2).

רוּם rûm (7599), Haughtiness (Jer 48:29 [31:29]).

רֹמֹם rāmōm (7715), Qal: be exalted (Ps 118:16 [117:16]); be extolled (Ps 66:17 [65:17]).

רָנַן rānan (7728), Piel: sing joyfully (Ps 145:7 [144:7]—only some Alexandrinus texts).

שָׂגַב sāghav (7891), Niphal: be exalted, be safe (Ps 148:13, Prv 18:10, Is 2:11).

שָׂגָה sāghâh (7892), Grow (Jb 8:11).

1. **ὑψῶν hupsōn** nom sing masc part pres act
2. **ὕψωσεν hupsōsen** 3sing indic aor act
3. **ὑψώσῃ hupsōsē** 3sing subj aor act
4. **ὑψώσητε hupsōsēte** 2pl subj aor act
5. **ὑψώσει hupsōsei** 3sing indic fut act
6. **ὑψωθῶ hupsōthō** 1sing subj aor pass
7. **ὑψωθῆτε hupsōthēte** 2pl subj aor pass
8. **ὑψωθείς hupsōtheis** nom sing masc part aor pass
9. **ὑψωθεῖσα hupsōtheisa** nom sing fem part aor pass
10. **ὑψωθῆναι hupsōthēnai** inf aor pass
11. **ὑψωθήσεται hupsōthēsetai** 3sing indic fut pass
12. **ὑψωθήσῃ hupsōthēsē** 2sing indic fut pass
13. **ὑψώθης hupsōthēs** 2sing indic aor pass

9 Capernaum, which **art exalted** unto heaven,....... Matt 11:23
5 And whosoever **shall exalt** himself shall be abased;... 23:12
11 and he that shall humble himself **shall be exalted**...... 23:12
2 and **exalted** them of low degree.................. Luke 1:52
9 thou, Capernaum, which **art exalted** to heaven,........ 10:15
1 For whosoever **exalteth** himself shall be abased;...... 14:11
11 and he that humbleth himself **shall be exalted**......... 14:11
1 for every one that **exalteth** himself shall be abased;... 18:14
11 and he that humbleth himself **shall be exalted**......... 18:14
2 as Moses **lifted up** the serpent in the wilderness,... John 3:14
10 even so must the Son of man **be lifted up**:............ 3:14
4 When ye **have lifted up** the Son of man,.............. 8:28
6 And I, if I **be lifted up** from the earth,.............. 12:32
10 The Son of man must **be lifted up**? who is this Son... 12:34
8 Therefore **being** by the right hand of God **exalted**,..Acts 2:33
2 Him hath God **exalted** with his right hand............ 5:31
2 **exalted** the people when they dwelt as strangers...... 13:17
7 in abasing myself that ye **might be exalted**,........2 Co 11:7
5 Humble yourselves ... and he **shall lift** you **up**....... Jas 4:10
3 that he **may exalt** you in due time:............... 1 Pt 5:6

Classical Greek and Septuagint Usage

The term *hupsoō* is used in the classical Greek as well as in the Septuagint with the meaning of "to exalt" or "raise high." In the classical Greek period it was rare and generally meant "to lift up." In the Hellenistic period (330–30 B.C.) it could refer to a mystical "elevation" in mystery cult experiences (Bertram, "hupsos," *Kittel*, 8:606). In the Septuagint *hupsoō* is used to refer to the exaltations of the righteous, the exaltation of God, and self-exaltation (Müller, "Height," *Colin Brown*, 2:201-202).

New Testament Usage

This term has two basic meanings in the New Testament. One is literal, the other figurative. The figurative usage appears more frequently.

In the Gospel of John *hupsoō* occurs in a somewhat cryptic, prophetic reference to the Crucifixion. It is first employed when Jesus spoke about Moses lifting up the brazen serpent in the wilderness; He likened this to His own lifting up and its consequent effect of delivering men to eternal life (John 3:14). The use of the term there is something of a paradox. In His being physically lifted up He was also humiliated because the lifting took place in His execution as a criminal. But that very same humiliation produces eternal life for those who will look to Him and live—as the Israelites who looked to the brazen serpent lived to escape the fiery serpents who were slaying them in the wilderness.

When He confronted His opponents in John 8:28, Jesus informed them they would know the truth about His relationship to the Father after He had been "lifted up," that is, crucified. In John 12:32 He announced that His crucifixion would attract all men to Him. In the following verse John noted that Jesus thus indicated the means of this death, and in verse 34 the people responded by repeating His words and questioning Him about the meaning of His term "Son of man."

The figurative uses of the word appear for the most part in statements condemning human pride (Matthew 11:23; Luke 10:15); sayings contrasting human pride with God's exaltation of the humble individual (Matthew 23:12; Luke 14:11; 18:14); or in declarations concerning God's exaltation of men, including Jesus (Luke 1:52; Acts 2:33; 5:31; 13:17; James 4:10; 1 Peter 5:6). Many of these references involve the paradox that God's way of doing things inverts the value system of human culture, just as the humiliation of the cross led to the exaltation of Jesus Christ. Paul's use of the word when reporting his own self-abasement as a means of exalting the Corinthians was also rooted in his preaching of the value system derived from the cross of Jesus Christ (2 Corinthians 11:7).

STRONG 5312, BAUER 850-51, MOULTON-MILLIGAN 662, KITTEL 8:606-13, LIDDELL-SCOTT 1910, COLIN BROWN 2:200-204.

5151. ὕψωμα hupsōma noun

Height, stronghold, obstacle, exaltation, something elevated.

CROSS-REFERENCE:
ὑψόω hupsoō (5150)

1. ὕψωμα hupsōma nom/acc sing neu

1 Nor **height,** nor depth, nor any other creature,...... Rom 8:39
1 and every **high thing** that exalteth itself............2 Co 10:5

Classical Greek

Hupsōma is relatively rare in classical Greek. J. Blunck provides information concerning its classical background: *Hupsōma* "is first attested in late G(ree)k. after the translation of the LXX, meaning height, exaltation, what is exalted. It was always used in figurative senses, e.g . . . . for the closest approach of a star to the zenith" ("Height," *Colin Brown*, 2:198). Its antonym would be *bathos* (893), "deep" or "depth."

Septuagint Usage

Hupsōma appears in the Septuagint in Job 24:24; Judith 10:8; 13:4; and 15:9. Job explained how the proud are humbled, "They are exalted for a little while, but are gone and brought low" (Job 24:24). In Judith 10:8 the elders prayed for the *exaltation* of Jerusalem (cf. 13:4; 15:9).

New Testament Usage

In the New Testament Romans 8:39 says that "height" cannot separate believers from the love of God. Nor are they subject to "every *high thing* that exalteth itself against the knowledge of God" (2 Corinthians 10:5). These two references, which are the only locations the term may be found in the New Testament, show how space or position have no influence over the believer, unless he allows it. Second Corinthians 10:5 could be an apt description of pride. The Revised Standard Version translates it "every proud obstacle."

STRONG 5313, BAUER 851, MOULTON-MILLIGAN 662, KITTEL 8:613-14, LIDDELL-SCOTT 1910, COLIN BROWN 2:198,200.

5152. φάγος phagos noun
A glutton.

1. **φάγος phagos** nom sing masc

1 Behold a man gluttonous, and a winebibber, ... Matt 11:19
1 Behold a gluttonous man, and a winebibber, ... Luke 7:34

This noun is related to the verb *phagō*, "to eat." It refers to someone who can be characterized by eating, one who lives to eat. Thus it means "glutton" in Matthew 11:19 and Luke 7:34. It is linked with "winebibber" in a false, libelous charge hurled at Jesus by His enemies who could not fathom His concern for lost sinners.

STRONG 5314, BAUER 851, MOULTON-MILLIGAN 663, LIDDELL-SCOTT 1911.

5153. φαιλόνης phailonēs noun
Outer garment, cloak.

1. **φαιλόνην phailonēn** acc sing masc

1 The cloak that I left at Troas with Carpus, ... 2 Tm 4:13

In 2 Timothy 4:13 *phailonēs* (also spelled *phelonēs* or *phenolēs* in some manuscripts) refers to a winter garment, i.e., the cloak which Paul asked Timothy to fetch from Troas where it had been left with Carpus. Although some have tried to interpret this as a reference to a valise or a leather covering for a scroll, it seems best to understand it as a Latin loanword meaning "cloak" (see *Bauer*).

BAUER 851, MOULTON-MILLIGAN 665-66 (see "phelonēs"), LIDDELL-SCOTT 1912.

5154. φαίνω phainō verb
To shine, to appear, to be seen, to seem.

COGNATES:
- ἀναφαίνω anaphainō (396)
- ἀφανίζω aphanizō (846)
- διαφανής diaphanēs (1301)
- ἐμφανίζω emphanizō (1702)
- ἐπιφαίνω epiphainō (1998)
- πρόφασις prophasis (4250)
- συκοφαντέω sukophanteō (4662)
- ὑπερήφανος huperēphanos (5082)
- ὑφαίνω huphainō (5144B)
- ὑφαντός huphantos (5145)
- φανερός phaneros (5156)
- φανερόω phaneroō (5157)
- φανερῶς phanerōs (5157B)
- φανέρωσις phanerōsis (5158)
- φανός phanos (5160)
- φαντάζω phantazō (5162)
- φαντασία phantasia (5163)
- φάντασμα phantasma (5164)
- φωτίζω phōtizō (5297)

SYNONYMS:
- ἀναφαίνω anaphainō (396)
- αὐγάζω augazō (820)
- ἐμφανίζω emphanizō (1702)
- ἐπιφαίνω epiphainō (1998)
- ἐπιφαύσκω epiphauskō (2001)
- λάμπω lampō (2962)
- ὀπτάνομαι optanomai (3563)
- ὁράω horaō (3571)
- φωτίζω phōtizō (5297)

אוֹר 'ôr (213), Be light, be bright; hiphil: give light, light up (Gn 1:15, Ps 97:4 [96:4]).

בָּחַן bāchan (1010), Test; niphal: be tested (Gn 42:15).

גָּלָה gālâh (1580), Give away, uncover; niphal: reveal oneself (Gn 35:7—Sixtine Edition only).

הָיָה hāyâh (2030), Be (Prv 26:5).

זָהַר zāhar (2178), Hiphil: shine (Dn 12:3).

זָרַח zārach (2311), Rise (Is 60:2).

מָאוֹר mā'ôr (4115), Shining lights (Ez 32:8).

נְפַל nᵉphal (A5490), Fall; provide (Ezr 7:20—Aramaic).

קָרָה qārâh (7424), Happen, come; niphal: come to meet (Nm 23:3f.).

רָאָה rā'âh (7495), See; niphal: be seen, be observed (Is 47:3, Dn 1:13).

1. **φάνῃ phanē** 3sing subj aor pass
2. **φαίνει phainei** 3sing indic pres act
3. **φαίνῃ phainē** 3sing subj pres act
4. **φαίνωσιν phainōsin** 3pl subj pres act
5. **φαίνων phainōn** nom sing masc part pres act

6. **φαίνοντι phainonti** dat sing masc part pres act
7. **φαίνεσθε phainesthe** 2pl indic/impr pres mid
8. **φαίνεται phainetai** 3sing indic pres mid
9. **φαίνονται phainontai** 3pl indic pres mid
10. **φαινομένου phainomenou** gen sing masc part pres mid
11. **φαινομένη phainomenē** nom sing fem part pres mid
12. **φαινομένων phainomenōn** gen pl neu part pres mid
13. **ἐφάνη ephanē** 3sing indic aor pass
14. **ἐφάνησαν ephanēsan** 3pl indic aor pass
15. **φανῇς phanēs** 2sing subj aor pass
16. **φανῶμεν phanōmen** 1pl subj aor pass
17. **φανῶσιν phanōsin** 3pl subj aor pass
18. **φανήσεται phanēsetai** 3sing indic fut pass
19. **φανεῖται phaneitai** 3sing indic fut mid

13 angel of the Lord **appeared** unto him in a dream, .. Matt 1:20
10 inquired ... diligently what time the star **appeared**...... 2:7
8 angel of the Lord **appeareth** to Joseph in a dream, ... 2:13
8 angel of the Lord **appeareth** in a dream to Joseph 2:19
17 they love to pray ... that **they may be seen** of men...... 6:5
17 that **they may appear** unto men to fast................ 6:16
15 That **thou appear** not unto men to fast, ... 6:18
13 saying, It was never so **seen** in Israel................. 9:33
13 brought forth fruit, then **appeared** the tares also...... 13:26
9 which indeed **appear** beautiful outward, ... 23:27
7 so ye also outwardly **appear** righteous unto men, ... 23:28
8 and **shineth** even unto the west; 24:27
18 **shall appear** the sign of the Son of man in heaven: ... 24:30
8 Ye have heard the blasphemy: what **think** ye? .... Mark 14:64
13 **he appeared** first to Mary Magdalene, ... 16:9
13 of some, that Elias **had appeared**; and of others, ... Luke 9:8
14 And their words **seemed** to them as idle tales, ... 24:11
2 And the light **shineth** in darkness; .... John 1:5
5 He was a burning and a **shining** light: 5:35
1 But sin, that it **might appear** sin, ... Rom 7:13
16 not that we **should appear** approved, ... 2 Co 13:7
7 among whom ye **shine** as lights in the world; ...... Phlp 2:15
12 were not made of things which **do appear**.......... Heb 11:3
11 It is even a vapour, that **appeareth** for a little time, Jas 4:14
19 where shall the ungodly and the sinner **appear**? .... 1 Pt 4:18
6 as unto a light **that shineth** in a dark place, ... 2 Pt 1:19
2 darkness is past, and the true light now **shineth**..... 1 Jn 2:8
2 countenance was as the sun **shineth** in his strength. Rev 1:16
3 and the day **shone** not for a third part of it, ... 8:12
1 light of a candle **shall shine** no more at all in thee; ... 18:23
4 need of the sun, neither of the moon, **to shine** in it: .. 21:23

Classical Greek

This term appears from Homer (Eighth Century B.C.) on in the active voice meaning "to bring to light" or "to cause to appear." When used in the passive voice it means "to come to light" or "to appear." Thus *phainō* can mean "reflect" or "reveal." Other figurative meanings are "set forth, expound, denounce, ordain," and "proclaim" (*Liddell-Scott*).

Septuagint Usage

In the Septuagint *phainō* appears over 60 times, translating a variety of Hebrew words (see Septuagint section above). It can mean "to shine," as when God gave the sun "to shine" on the earth (Genesis 1:15). Proverbs 21:2 notes that every man appears righteous to himself. In Genesis 35:7 it means "reveal": "God revealed himself."

New Testament Usage

The verb *phainō* has several meanings in the New Testament. In the active voice it means "to shine." In some instances this shining is literal: of the sun (Revelation 1:16); of the moon (Revelation 21:23); of a candle or lamp (Revelation 18:23). In other cases it is figurative: of the incarnation of the Word of God (John 1:5); of the witness of John the Baptist (John 5:35); of the power of Scripture as God's revelation to men (2 Peter 1:19); of the gospel of Jesus Christ and its effect in the world (1 John 2:8). Occasionally a passive form of the verb means "to shine": literally of the sun (Revelation 8:12); of lightning (Matthew 24:37); of a candle or lamp (Revelation 18:23); or figuratively of the testimony of Christians among sinners (Philippians 2:15).

Passive and middle forms of the verb are most common in New Testament usage. Our English word *phenomenon* is a transliteration of one of its passive forms. It refers to "something which is visible, something which appears." Most other New Testament uses revolve around this idea of appearing.

In some places it refers literally to the appearance of people or things: an angel (Matthew 1:20); a star (Matthew 2:7); a dream or someone or something in a dream (Matthew 2:13,19). It is also used of Elijah (Luke 9:8); of sin (Romans 7:13); of vapor (James 4:14); of tares (Matthew 13:26); of a sign (Matthew 24:30); of a miracle (Matthew 9:23); and of the resurrected Jesus (Mark 16:9). These things are thought of as either being displayed (passive voice) or of showing themselves (middle voice).

In some uses the verb means "to seem or to appear externally." It is used this way of hypocrites (Matthew 6:5,16; 23:27,28).

On a few occasions it refers to the opinion or judgment of men, what they think about a situation. In Mark 14:64 this verb is used by the high priest during the trial of Jesus when the high priest asked, "What *think* ye?" A similar use occurs in Luke 24:11 where the women's reports of the Resurrection are said to have "*seemed* to them (the apostles) as idle tales."

Finally, in Hebrews 11:3 the verb occurs in the phrase "not made of things which do appear." In other words, God did not use existing materials to create the universe; He created it *ex nihilo*, i.e., "out of nothing."

Strong 5316, Bauer 851-52, Moulton-Milligan 663, Kittel 9:1-2, Liddell-Scott 1912-13, Colin Brown 2:487-88,496; 3:320.

5155. Φάλεκ Phalek name

Peleg.

1. **Φάλεκ Phalek** masc
2. **Φάλεγ Phaleg** masc

1 which was the son of **Phalec**, ... Luke 3:35

A figure in the genealogy of Jesus (Luke 3:35).

5156. φανερός phaneros adj

Visible, clear, plain, known.

Cross-Reference:

φαίνω phainō (5154)

גָּלָה gālâh (1580), Reveal, go away; niphal: something revealed (Dt 29:29).

1. **φανερόν phaneron** nom/acc sing masc/neu
2. **φανεροί phaneroi** nom pl masc
3. **φανερούς phanerous** acc pl masc
4. **φανερά phanera** nom/acc sing/pl fem/neu
5. **φανερῷ phanerō** dat sing neu

5 thy Father ... himself shall reward thee **openly**. ...... Matt 6:4
5 thy Father ... shall reward thee **openly**. 6:6
5 thy Father, ... shall reward thee **openly**. 6:18
1 that they should not make him **known**: 12:16
1 charged ... that they should not make him **known**. .. Mark 3:12
1 kept secret, but that it should come abroad. (NT) 4:22
1 for his name was **spread abroad**: and he said, ... 6:14
1 nothing is secret, that shall not be made **manifest**; .. Luke 8:17
1 that shall not be known and come **abroad**. 8:17
1 miracle hath been done by them **is manifest** to all ... Acts 4:16
1 Joseph's kindred was made **known** unto Pharaoh. 7:13
1 which may be known of God is **manifest** in them; ... Rom 1:19
5 For he is not a Jew, which is one **outwardly**; 2:28
5 circumcision, which is **outward** in the flesh: 2:28
1 Every man's work shall be made **manifest**: .... 1 Co 3:13
2 they which are approved may be made **manifest** 11:19
4 thus are the secrets of his heart made **manifest**; 14:25
4 Now the works of the flesh are **manifest**, ... Gal 5:19
3 my bonds in Christ are **manifest** in all the palace, ... Phlp 1:13
4 that thy profiting **may appear** to all. .... 1 Tm 4:15
4 In this the children of God are **manifest**, ... 1 Jn 3:10

Classical Greek

This adjective is related to the verb *phainō* (5154), "to bring to light, to appear," and it basically means "visible, manifest, that which can be seen" (especially in contrast to that which is "secret or hidden"; see Thayer's *Greek-English Lexicon*). In addition to this, it can also mean "shining" (in appearance) or "conspicuous." Thus a person or object described as *phaneros* is "revealed to the public, plainly known" (cf. *Liddell-Scott*).

Septuagint Usage

Phaneros's usage in the Septuagint essentially follows the classical pattern. Nineteen total occurrences are counted, but only nine of these are canonical. A peculiar use in Genesis 42:16 refers to the imprisonment of Joseph's brothers until their words were *made clear*, i.e., proven to be true (cf. 2 Maccabees 1:33). The contrast between something "secret" and something "revealed" is most plain in Deuteronomy 29:29 (the secret things belong to God, but the *revealed things* belong to the people as contained in the Law; cf. 2 Maccabees 12:41). As a replacement for *yādha'* ("to know") *phaneros einai* suggests making something "known," often on a figuratively universal scale (Isaiah 64:2; 1 Maccabees 15:9). The divine "manifestation" (cf. *epiphaneia* [1999]) of God and two of His angels is "visible" to everyone but the Jews according to 3 Maccabees 6:18.

New Testament Usage

Phaneros is used 21 times in the New Testament. Nine occur in the Synoptic Gospels, and only two of these are parallel (Mark 3:12; Matthew 12:16). Two instances in Mark refer to Jesus' becoming "known" publicly (3:12; 6:14; cf. 1 Timothy 4:15). Mark's third usage (4:22) resembles Luke's saying in 8:17 about the "disclosure" of secret things ("What is hidden shall be *manifest*"; cf. 1 Corinthians 3:13; 14:25).

Phaneros as a manifestation of something divine is implied in Acts 4:16, but the usage should not be pressed into a technical understanding (that is, a divine revelation), as Luke's only other use in Acts makes clear (Acts 7:13; cf. Romans 1:19).

The notion that outward "appearance" does not guarantee reality comes through in Romans 2:28, for a man is not a Jew simply by the external sign of circumcision. Conversely, the acts of the sinful nature are "plain" to all (Galatians 5:19; cf. 1 John 3:10).

Strong 5318, Bauer 852, Moulton-Milligan 663, Kittel 9:2-3, Liddell-Scott 1915, Colin Brown 3:317,320.

5157. φανερόω phaneroō verb

To manifest, show, reveal, disclose.

Cognate:

φαίνω phainō (5154)

Synonyms:

ἀναδείκνυμι anadeiknumi (320)
ἀποδείκνυμι apodeiknumi (579)
ἀποκαλύπτω apokaluptō (596)

γνωρίζω gnōrizō (1101)
δείκνυμι deiknumi (1161)
δηλόω dēloō (1207)
ἐμφανίζω emphanizō (1702)
ἐπιδείκνυμι epideiknumi (1910)
ἐπιφαίνω epiphainō (1998)
μηνύω mēnuō (3245)

גָּלָה gālâh (1580), Piel: reveal (Jer 33:6 [40:6]).

1. **φανεροῦντι** phanerounti dat sing masc part pres act
2. **ἐφανέρωσα** ephanerōsa 1sing indic aor act
3. **ἐφανέρωσεν** ephanerōsen 3sing indic aor act
4. **φανερώσω** phanerōsō 1sing subj aor act
5. **φανέρωσον** phanerōson 2sing impr aor act
6. **φανερώσει** phanerōsei 3sing indic fut act
7. **φανεροῦται** phaneroutai 3sing indic pres mid
8. **φανερούμενοι** phaneroumenoi nom pl masc part pres mid
9. **φανερούμενον** phaneroumenon nom/acc sing neu part pres mid
10. **ἐφανερώθη** ephanerōthē 3sing indic aor pass
11. **ἐφανερώθησαν** ephanerōthēsan 3pl indic aor pass
12. **φανερωθῇ** phanerōthē 3sing subj aor pass
13. **φανερωθῶσιν** phanerōthōsin 3pl subj aor pass
14. **φανερωθέντος** phanerōthentos gen sing masc part aor pass
15. **φανερωθέντες** phanerōthentes nom pl masc part aor pass
16. **φανερωθεῖσαν** phanerōtheisan acc sing fem part aor pass
17. **φανερωθῆναι** phanerōthēnai inf aor pass
18. **πεφανέρωται** pephanerōtai 3sing indic perf mid
19. **πεφανερώμεθα** pephanerōmetha 1pl indic perf mid
20. **πεφανερῶσθαι** pephanerōsthai inf perf mid
21. **φανερωθήσεσθε** phanerōthēsesthe 2pl indic fut pass
22. **φανερώσαντες** phanerōsantes nom pl masc part aor act

12 nothing hid, which **shall not be manifested**;........ Mark 4:22
10 After that he **appeared** in another form unto two..... 16:12
10 Afterward he **appeared** unto the eleven............ 16:14
12 but that he **should be made manifest** to Israel,......John 1:31
3 and **manifested** forth his glory;...................... 2:11
12 that his deeds **may be made manifest**,................. 3:21
5 If thou do these things, **show** thyself to the world...... 7:4
12 the works of God **should be made manifest** in him...... 9:3
2 I **have manifested** thy name unto the men............ 17:6
3 After these things Jesus **showed** himself again........ 21:1
3 and on this wise **showed** he himself.................. 21:1
10 is now the third time that Jesus **showed** himself....... 21:14
3 for God **hath showed** it unto them................. Rom 1:19
18 righteousness of God without the law **is manifested**,.... 3:21
14 But now **is made manifest**,......................... 16:26
6 and **will make manifest** the counsels of the hearts:.. 1 Co 4:5
1 and **maketh manifest** the savour of his knowledge.. 2 Co 2:14
8 Forasmuch as ye **are manifestly declared**.............. 3:3
12 that the life also of Jesus **might be made manifest**...... 4:10
12 that the life also of Jesus **might be made manifest**...... 4:11
17 must all **appear** before the judgment seat of Christ;.... 5:10
19 but we **are made manifest** unto God;.................. 5:11
20 I trust also **are made manifest** in your consciences...... 5:11
17 our care for you in the sight of God **might appear**..2 Co 7:12
15 but we **have been** thoroughly **made manifest**.......... 11:6
7 But all things that are reproved **are made manifest**.. Eph 5:13
9 for whatsoever **doth make manifest** is light............ 5:13
10 but now **is made manifest** to his saints:............. Col 1:26
12 When Christ, who is our life, **shall appear**,............ 3:4
21 then shall ye also **appear** with him in glory........... 3:4
4 That I **may make** it **manifest**, as I ought to speak....... 4:4
10 God **was manifest** in the flesh,................... 1 Tm 3:16
16 But is now **made manifest** by the appearing........2 Tm 1:10
3 But hath in due times **manifested** his word.......... Tit 1:3
20 into the holiest of all was not yet **made manifest**,... Heb 9:8
18 now once in the end of the world hath he **appeared**.... 9:26
14 but **was manifest** in these last times for you,........1 Pt 1:20
14 And when the chief Shepherd **shall appear**,............ 5:4
10 For the life **was manifested**, and we have seen it,... 1 Jn 1:2
10 was with the Father, and **was manifested** unto us;...... 1:2
13 that they **might be made manifest** ... not all of us....... 2:19
12 when he **shall appear**, we may have confidence,........ 2:28
10 and it doth not yet **appear** what we shall be:.......... 3:2
12 when he **shall appear**, we shall be like him;........... 3:2
10 know that he **was manifested** to take away our sins;.... 3:5
10 For this purpose the Son of God **was manifested**,...... 3:8
10 In this **was manifested** the love of God toward us,..... 4:9
12 that the shame of thy nakedness **do not appear**;.....Rev 3:18
11 worship ... for thy judgments **are made manifest**....... 15:4

Classical Greek and Septuagint Usage

This term is almost nonexistent in classical Greek and the Septuagint. Only a few occurrences of the term have been found in the classical literature and only one occurrence in the Septuagint (Jeremiah 33:6 [LXX 40:6]). It generally means "to make known" or "reveal."

New Testament Usage

Most of the appearances of *phaneroō* are found in the writings of Paul and John. It means "to reveal" (active voice) or "to be revealed" (passive voice). In the King James Version there are several places where it is translated by the word "appear." In all of these instances the passive form of the verb is being translated.

In most references *phaneroō* refers to divine revelation, God's disclosure of himself, His character, His works, and His saving grace and deeds in Jesus Christ. Sometimes it depicts a disclosure made by one person to another or to others. The people, things, or ideas that are revealed have previously been hidden or unknown. Thus Paul, for instance, used *phaneroō* synonymously with *apokaluptō* (596).

In Mark 4:22 the verb is used to indicate that none of the hidden meanings of Jesus' parables will remain unrevealed. Mark also used the verb to describe Jesus' self-revelation in His resurrected body (Mark 16:12,14).

Paul declared that God's power and godhead are revealed in the creation (Romans 1:19). Other objects of divine revelation announced in Paul's use of *phaneroō* are: righteousness (Romans 3:31); the mystery of the gospel (Romans 16:26; Colossians 1:26); the plans of men's hearts (1

Corinthians 4:5); Christ's work in the lives of Corinthian believers (2 Corinthians 3:3); Jesus' life (2 Corinthians 4:10); the hidden facts and realities in the lives of Christians (2 Corinthians 5:10); the deeds of all men (Ephesians 5:13); the glorified Christ and glorified believers (Colossians 3:4); God in the flesh, i.e., the incarnation of Jesus Christ (1 Timothy 3:16); and God's purpose (2 Timothy 1:10). For the most part Paul's references are either to God's revelation in Christ and the proclamation of that message or to divine revelation, i.e., the Second Coming and judgment.

The writings of the apostle John show similar usage. The things revealed are: God's glory (John 2:11); His deeds (John 3:21); God himself (John 7:4); His works (John 9:3); the Father's name (John 17:6); Jesus himself (John 21:1,14); Jesus, the eternal life (1 John 1:2); Jesus and believers at the Second Coming (1 John 3:2); the incarnation and atoning work of Jesus (1 John 3:5,8; 4:9).

Similar revelations are mentioned in Hebrews: the way into the holy sanctuary of heaven (Hebrews 9:8) and the atoning sacrifice of Jesus (Hebrews 9:26). Likewise, Peter referred to divine revelation in the Incarnation (1 Peter 1:20) and the Second Coming (1 Peter 5:4).

Strong 5319, Bauer 852-53, Moulton-Milligan 663, Kittel 9:3-6, Liddell-Scott 1915, Colin Brown 3:317,320-23.

5157B. φανερῶς phanerōs adv

Publicly, clearly.

Cross-Reference:
φαίνω phainō (5154)

1. φανερῶς phanerōs

1 **Jesus could no more openly enter into the city,..... Mark 1:45**
1 **then went he also up unto the feast, not openly,.... John 7:10**
1 **a vision evidently about the ninth hour of the day.. Acts 10:3**

An adverb related to the verb *phaneroō* (5157), "to make known, to reveal, to show," *phanerōs* has two basic meanings in the New Testament. In Mark 1:45 and John 7:10 it refers to Jesus' restrictions regarding travel in Palestine. In the Markan reference He was denied public ministry in the city because of the crowds. In John 7:10 it was His enemies who hindered Jesus from going "openly" to the Feast of Tabernacles. In Acts 10:3, however, this same word refers to the clarity with which Peter saw the angel who appeared to him in the vision that sent him to the house of Cornelius the centurion.

Strong 5320, Bauer 853, Moulton-Milligan 663, Liddell-Scott 1915, Colin Brown 3:317,320.

5158. φανέρωσις phanerōsis noun

Disclosure, manifestation.

Cross-Reference:
φαίνω phainō (5154)

1. φανέρωσις phanerōsis nom sing fem
2. φανερώσει phanerōsei dat sing fem

1 **But the manifestation of the Spirit is given.........1 Co 12:7**
2 **but by manifestation of the truth................... 2 Co 4:2**

A noun related to the verb *phaneroō* (5157), "to make known, to reveal, to show," *phanerōsis* means the act of "disclosure" or "manifestation." In 2 Corinthians 4 Paul explained the nature of his ministry and the reasons he spoke so boldly and frankly to the believers at Corinth. In verse 2 Paul wrote that he did not use deceit or craftiness in his ministry, but he lived and preached "by manifestation of the truth." He did not hide anything but, rather, uncovered the truth in public. In 1 Corinthians 12:7 he referred to the charismatic gifts of the Holy Spirit as "the manifestation of the Spirit." He taught that the gifts exercised by Christians make the Holy Spirit evident.

Strong 5321, Bauer 853, Moulton-Milligan 663, Kittel 9:6, Liddell-Scott 1915, Colin Brown 3:317.

5159. φανερῶς phanerōs

See word study at number 5157B.

5160. φανός phanos noun

Lantern, torch.

Cross-Reference:
φαίνω phainō (5154)

1. φανῶν phanōn gen pl masc

1 **cometh thither with lanterns and torches...........John 18:3**

In John 18:3, the only occurrence of *phanos* in the New Testament, the soldiers who accompanied Judas in the arrest and betrayal of Jesus are described as carrying "lanterns and torches," *phanōn* and *lampadōn* (see 2958). *Phanos* refers to an object which bears light. Originally it meant "torch" but came to be used of lanterns or lamps with wicks in oil. Another type of light-giving device was the *lampas* (2958). The lanterns carried by this crowd may have been

Roman lanterns made of "a metal frame with a surrounding cylinder of translucent material, such as horn or bladder" (Hasel, "Lantern," *International Standard Bible Encyclopedia*, 3:72).

Strong 5322, Bauer 853, Moulton-Milligan 663, Liddell-Scott 1915.

5161. Φανουήλ Phanouēl name

Phanuel.

1. Φανουήλ Phanouēl masc

1 Anna, a prophetess, the daughter of Phanuel,....... Luke 2:36

The father of the prophetess Anna who gave thanks for the infant Jesus when He was presented in the temple (Luke 2:36).

5162. φαντάζω phantazō verb

To make or become visible, appear.

Cross-Reference:
φαίνω phainō (5154)

1. φανταζόμενον phantazomenon nom/acc sing neu part pres mid

1 And so terrible was the sight, that Moses said,..... Heb 12:21

Generally this verb is used to describe the appearance of unusual sights in the natural world. In Hebrews 12:21 the neuter form of the present passive participle is used to describe the terrifying phenomena that accompanied the giving of the Law at Mount Sinai. In this verse (its only New Testament use) it means "the sight which appeared."

Strong 5324, Bauer 853, Moulton-Milligan 664, Kittel 9:6, Liddell-Scott 1915, Colin Brown 3:317,324.

5163. φαντασία phantasia noun

Appearance, pomp, parade.

Cross-Reference:
φαίνω phainō (5154)

חָזִיז chăzîz (2477), Storm cloud (Zec 10:1).

1. φαντασίας phantasias gen sing fem

1 Agrippa was come, and Bernice, with great pomp,.. Acts 25:23

The arrival of Agrippa and Bernice is described by *phantasia* in Acts 25:23, its only New Testament appearance. This noun refers to that which appears. It connotes great activity. A big impression was made on the crowds because there were many things to watch at the same time. In this usage the word came to refer to the outward ceremony and pageantry used to impress people with the importance of government dignitaries.

Strong 5325, Bauer 853, Moulton-Milligan 664, Liddell-Scott 1915-16.

5164. φάντασμα phantasma noun

Apparition, ghost.

Cross-Reference:
φαίνω phainō (5154)

חִזָּיוֹן chizzāyôn (2476), Vision (Jb 20:8—Codex Alexandrinus only).

1. φάντασμα phantasma nom/acc sing neu

1 saying, It is a spirit; and they cried out for fear.... Matt 14:26
1 they supposed it had been a spirit, and cried out:...Mark 6:49

A *phantasma* refers to something which becomes visible. It generally is used of a ghost, a dream, or an apparition. In the Gospels it refers to what the disciples saw as they rowed against the wind on the Sea of Galilee at night. Suddenly they saw Jesus walking toward them. They thought He was a *phantasma*, a "ghost" (Matthew 14:26; Mark 6:49).

Strong 5326, Bauer 853, Moulton-Milligan 664, Kittel 9:6, Liddell-Scott 1916, Colin Brown 2:552; 3:317,324.

5165. φάραγξ pharanx noun

Valley, ravine.

אָפִיק 'āphîq (665), Channel, ravine (Is 8:7, Ez 32:6, 34:13).

גַּי gay (1547II) Valley (Jos 15:8).

גֵּיא gê' (1548I), Valley (Is 22:5).

גַּיְא gay[e]' (1548III Valley (Dt 4:46, Neh 2:15).

גֵּיא(־)(הַ)מֶּלַח gê'(-)(ha)melach (1550), Valley of Salt (Ps 60:title ([59:title]).

מַדְרֵגָה madhrēghāh (4238), Cliff (Ez 38:20).

מַעְבָּרָה ma'bārāh (4723), Pass (Is 10:29).

נַחַל nachal (5337), Valley (Dt 2:24); brook, stream (Jos 15:4, Is 35:6).

עֵמֶק 'ēmeq (6231), Valley (Gn 14:3, Jos 10:12, Is 28:21).

1. φάραγξ pharanx nom sing fem

1 Every valley shall be filled,........................ Luke 3:5

When John the Baptist came preaching as the forerunner of Jesus the Messiah, he talked about preparing a highway for the coming of the Messiah. In building a road the high places must be leveled and the low places (valleys) filled. In Luke 3:5 the Greek word for "valley" is *pharanx.*

This is the only place where the term is used in the New Testament.

STRONG 5327, BAUER 853, MOULTON-MILLIGAN 664, LIDDELL-SCOTT 1916.

5166. Φαραώ Pharaō name

Pharaoh.

1. Φαραώ Pharaō masc

1 wisdom in the sight of **Pharaoh** king of Egypt; ...... Acts 7:10
1 Joseph's kindred was made known unto **Pharaoh**........ 7:13
1 **Pharaoh's** daughter took him up,.................... 7:21
1 For the scripture saith unto **Pharaoh**,............... Rom 9:17
1 refused to be called the son of **Pharaoh's** daughter; Heb 11:24

The word *pharaoh* was a title for the monarch of ancient Egypt. It became used as a proper name (Acts 7:10,13,21; Romans 9:17; Hebrews 11:24).

5167. Φαρές Phares name

Pharez.

1. Φαρές Phares masc

1 And Judas begat **Phares** and Zara of Thamar;...... Matt 1:3
1 and **Phares** begat Esrom; and Esrom begat Aram;...... 1:3
1 which was the son of **Phares**,...................... Luke 3:33

The son of the patriarch Judah and twin brother of Zerah. The story of his birth is told in Genesis 38. He is listed in both versions of the genealogy of Jesus (Matthew 1:3; Luke 3:33).

5168. Φαρισαῖος Pharisaios name

Pharisee.

1. Φαρισαῖος Pharisaios nom sing masc
2. Φαρισαίου Pharisaiou gen sing masc
3. Φαρισαῖε Pharisaie voc sing masc
4. Φαρισαῖοι Pharisaioi nom pl masc
5. Φαρισαίων Pharisaiōn gen pl masc
6. Φαρισαίοις Pharisaiois dat pl masc
7. Φαρισαίους Pharisaious acc pl masc

5 many of the **Pharisees** and Sadducees come......... Matt 3:7
5 the righteousness of the scribes and **Pharisees**,.......... 5:20
4 And when the **Pharisees** saw it,....................... 9:11
4 Why do we and the **Pharisees** fast oft,................. 9:14
4 But the **Pharisees** said, He casteth out devils........... 9:34
4 But when the **Pharisees** saw it, they said unto him,.... 12:2
4 Then the **Pharisees** went out, and held a council....... 12:14
4 But when the **Pharisees** heard it, they said,............ 12:24
5 certain of ... scribes and of the **Pharisees** answered,.... 12:38
4 Then came to Jesus scribes and **Pharisees**,............ 15:1
4 Knowest thou that the **Pharisees** were offended,....... 15:12
4 The **Pharisees** also with the Sadducees came,.......... 16:1
5 the leaven of the **Pharisees** and of the Sadducees...... 16:6
5 the leaven of the **Pharisees** and of the Sadducees?..... 16:11
5 the doctrine of the **Pharisees** and of the Sadducees..... 16:12
4 The **Pharisees** also came unto him, tempting him,...... 19:3
4 chief priests and **Pharisees** had heard his parables, Matt 21:45
4 Then went the **Pharisees**, and took counsel........... 22:15
4 But when the **Pharisees** had heard that he........... 22:34
5 While the **Pharisees** were gathered together,........... 22:41
4 The scribes and the **Pharisees** sit in Moses' seat:...... 23:2
4 But woe unto you, scribes and **Pharisees**,............. 23:13
4 Woe unto you, scribes and **Pharisees**, hypocrites!...... 23:14
4 Woe unto you, scribes and **Pharisees**, hypocrites!...... 23:15
4 Woe unto you, scribes and **Pharisees**, hypocrites!...... 23:23
4 Woe unto you, scribes and **Pharisees**, hypocrites!...... 23:25
3 Thou blind **Pharisee**, cleanse first ... within the cup.... 23:26
4 Woe unto you, scribes and **Pharisees**, hypocrites!...... 23:27
4 Woe unto you, scribes and **Pharisees**, hypocrites!...... 23:29
4 priests and **Pharisees** came together unto Pilate,....... 27:62
4 And when the scribes and **Pharisees** saw him eat... Mark 2:16
5 disciples of John and of the **Pharisees** used to fast:..... 2:18
5 Why do the disciples of John and ... **Pharisees** fast,..... 2:18
4 And the **Pharisees** said unto him, Behold,.............. 2:24
4 And the **Pharisees** went forth,......................... 3:6
4 Then came together unto him the **Pharisees**,............ 7:1
4 For the **Pharisees**, and all the Jews,.................... 7:3
4 Then the **Pharisees** and scribes asked him,............. 7:5
4 the **Pharisees** came forth, and began to question........ 8:11
5 Take heed, beware of the leaven of the **Pharisees**,...... 8:15
4 And the **Pharisees** came to him, and asked him,........ 10:2
5 And they send unto him certain of the **Pharisees**...... 12:13
4 were **Pharisees** and doctors of the law sitting by,.... Luke 5:17
4 And the scribes and the **Pharisees** began to reason,..... 5:21
4 But their scribes and **Pharisees** murmured.............. 5:30
5 and likewise the disciples of the **Pharisees**;............. 5:33
5 And certain of the **Pharisees** said unto them,........... 6:2
4 And the scribes and **Pharisees** watched him,............ 6:7
4 But the **Pharisees** and lawyers rejected the counsel...... 7:30
5 **Pharisees** desired him that he would eat with him....... 7:36
2 And he went into the **Pharisee's** house,................ 7:36
2 that Jesus sat at meat in the **Pharisee's** house,........... 7:37
1 Now when the **Pharisee** which had bidden him saw..... 7:39
1 a certain **Pharisee** besought him to dine with him:..... 11:37
1 And when the **Pharisee** saw it, he marvelled.......... 11:38
4 Now do ye **Pharisees** make clean the outside.......... 11:39
6 But woe unto you, **Pharisees**!......................... 11:42
6 Woe unto you, **Pharisees**!........................... 11:43
4 Woe unto you, scribes and **Pharisees**, hypocrites!...... 11:44
4 the scribes and the **Pharisees** began to urge him....... 11:53
5 Beware ye of the leaven of the **Pharisees**,............. 12:1
4 The same day there came certain of the **Pharisees**,..... 13:31
5 went into the house of one of the chief **Pharisees**...... 14:1
7 spake unto the lawyers and **Pharisees**, saying,......... 14:3
4 And the **Pharisees** and scribes murmured, saying,...... 15:2
4 And the **Pharisees** also, who were covetous,............ 16:14
5 And when he was demanded of the **Pharisees**,.......... 17:20
1 the one a **Pharisee**, and the other a publican........... 18:10
1 The **Pharisee** stood and prayed thus with himself,....... 18:11
5 of the **Pharisees** from among the multitude said....... 19:39
5 And they which were sent were of the **Pharisees**..... John 1:24
5 There was a man of the **Pharisees**,..................... 3:1
4 **Pharisees** had heard that Jesus ... baptized more........ 4:1
4 The **Pharisees** heard that the people murmured......... 7:32
4 and the **Pharisees** and the chief priests sent officers..... 7:32
7 came the officers to the chief priests and **Pharisees**;..... 7:45
4 Then answered them the **Pharisees**,.................... 7:47
5 Have any of the rulers or of the **Pharisees** believed..... 7:48
4 scribes and **Pharisees** brought unto him a woman....... 8:3
4 The **Pharisees** therefore said unto him,................. 8:13
7 brought to the **Pharisees** him that ... was blind.......... 9:13
4 Then again the **Pharisees** also asked him............... 9:15
5 Therefore said some of the **Pharisees**,................... 9:16
5 **Pharisees** which were with him heard these words,...... 9:40
7 But some of them went their ways to the **Pharisees**,... 11:46
4 Then gathered the chief priests and the **Pharisees**...... 11:47
4 Now both the chief priests and the **Pharisees**.......... 11:57
4 The **Pharisees** therefore said among themselves,........ 12:19
7 because of the **Pharisees** they did not confess him,..... 12:42
5 and officers from the chief priests and **Pharisees**,...... 18:3
1 Then stood there up one in the council, a **Pharisee**,..Acts 5:34
5 of the sect of the **Pharisees** which believed, saying,.... 15:5
5 one part were Sadducees, and the other **Pharisees**,..... 23:6

1 Men and brethren, I am a **Pharisee**, ... Acts 23:6
2 I am a **Pharisee**, the son of a **Pharisee**: 23:6
5 between the **Pharisees** and the Sadducees: 23:7
4 no resurrection, ... but the **Pharisees** confess both...... 23:8
5 the scribes that were of the **Pharisees'** part arose, ... 23:9
1 most straitest sect of our religion I lived a **Pharisee**.... 26:5
1 as touching the law, a **Pharisee**; .... Phlp 3:5

The word *Pharisaios* refers to a member of the Pharisees, a strict, legalistic, religious party that arose after Jewish exiles returned from Babylon. They were very popular and highly respected among the masses during the time of Christ. Because of their popularity, the Sadducees usually had to submit to their decisions or else evoke the wrath of the people (Josephus *Antiquities* 18.1.4).

The word *Pharisaios* is most likely derived from the Hebrew word *pārash*, "to separate" or "to separate oneself." A Pharisee, then, was a "separated one" or a "separatist" (*Bauer*). It could refer to their separating themselves from a particular group of the Hasidim, from the Gentiles and their heathen practices, or from the elements forcing the hellenization of the Jewish people. All are true, but the most probable explanation is that the designation arose because they separated themselves from the great mass of godless Jews who were not living by their conception of the Law. The Pharisees looked upon themselves as the ones who were keeping alive the true worship of the Lord.

The Pharisees are traced back to the Hasidim, a religious group during the Second Century B.C., and were firmly established by 100 B.C. (Meyer, "Pharisaios," *Kittel*, 9:16). The Hasidim strongly resisted the hellenization being forced on the Jews by Antiochus Epiphanes. In particular they were opposed to the priestly party that had submitted to Hellenistic influence (the predecessors of the Sadducees). The Hasidim, as well as the Pharisees, were more concerned with maintaining religious purity than with political matters.

The word *Pharisaios* is found in Josephus and the New Testament, occurring 90 times in the Gospels, 9 times in Acts, and once in the Epistles (Philippians 3:5). It is not found in classical Greek or the Septuagint. The date the word came into usage cannot be determined precisely. Josephus mentions that the Pharisees were active during the time of Jonathan and Hyrcanus I, about 150–135 B.C. (*Antiquities* 13.5.9; 13.10.5).

The Pharisees were known for their strict observance of the letter of the Law, for their austere life, and for their obsession with oral tradition. The oral tradition was designed to be a hedge around the Torah to prevent possible infringements. They held that the oral law was equally as inspired and authoritative as the written Torah. They believed it was given to Moses at Sinai; eventually the oral law was written down and is known as the Mishnah. The Sadducees accepted only the written law as binding. The Pharisees also believed in the resurrection of the dead, immortality of the soul, future judgment, and the existence of supernatural beings (angels, demons, Satan). All of these were rejected by the Sadducees. Paul capitalized on these differences to his advantage when on trial (Acts 23:6-10). Furthermore, the Pharisees depended on the intervention of God rather than turning to force in order to liberate the Jews from oppression (contrary to the Zealots). They also awaited the coming of the Messiah (contrary to the Sadducees). Although there were differences among the Jewish religious parties, they united in their opposition against Jesus (Matthew 16:1; Mark 3:6).

The Pharisees were the chief opponents of Jesus. A major area of conflict between Jesus and the Pharisees was regarding the oral tradition (Matthew 15:1-20; Mark 7:8-13; Luke 11:38-42). Jesus condemned their following the tradition of men, for it was causing them to overlook the spirit of the Law and to ignore the need of inward holiness. He accused them of being like whitewashed sepulchers, "which indeed appear beautiful outward, but are within full of dead men's bones, and of all uncleanness" (Matthew 23:27). He denounced this outward piety by quoting Isaiah 29:13, "This people honoreth me with their lips, but their heart is far from me" (Mark 7:6).

The Pharisees likewise condemned Jesus for mingling with sinners (Matthew 9:11; Mark 2:16), for not washing before eating (Mark 7:1-5; Luke 11:37,38), and for allowing His disciples to violate the Sabbath (Mark 2:23,24). It was their self-appointed task to scrutinize any religious teacher to see whether his teachings were in line with their legalistic perception of the Law.

Not all Pharisees were bad. Some, perhaps like Nicodemus, were dissatisfied with an external religion and were attracted to Jesus. They often invited Him to dinner (Luke 7:36; 11:37; 14:1), but at least one did so without the courtesy of a kiss, an anointing, or foot washing (Luke 7:44-46). This suggests that he could not fully accept Jesus. Some even warned Jesus that Herod

Antipas was seeking to kill Him (Luke 13:31). A number of Pharisees became members of the early Christian community (Acts 15:5).

Strong 5330, Bauer 853-54, Kittel 9:11-48, Colin Brown 2:810-14.

5169. φαρμακεία pharmakeia noun

Sorcery, witchcraft, magic.

Cognates:

φαρμακεύς pharmakeus (5170)
φάρμακον pharmakon (5170B)
φάρμακος pharmakos (5171)

Synonym:

μαγεία mageia (3067)

כֶּשֶׁף kesheph (3914), Sorcery (Is 47:9,12).

לְהָטִים l^ehāṭîm (3995), Secret arts (Ex 7:11).

לָט lāṭ (4044), Secret arts (Ex 7:22, 8:18).

1. φαρμακεία pharmakeia nom sing fem
2. φαρμακείᾳ pharmakeia dat sing fem
3. φαρμακειῶν pharmakeiōn gen pl fem

1 Idolatry, witchcraft, hatred, variance, emulations,..... Gal 5:20
3 nor of their sorceries, nor of their fornication,....... Rev 9:21
2 for by thy sorceries were all nations deceived.......... 18:23

The family of words from which we get our English word *pharmacy* is derived from the Greek word *pharmakeuō* which means "to mix potions or poison." The term also refers to the practice of magic. Thus *pharmakeia* (also spelled *pharmakia*) refers to the practice of the arts associated with magic, which in the time of the New Testament involved the use of potions or drugs. In Galatians 5:20 this practice is identified as a work of the flesh. In Revelation 9:21 it is listed among the sins which humanity refuses to repent of—even after the plague of the sixth trumpet. In Revelation 18:23 it refers to the magical arts practiced by the great whore Babylon in her seduction of all the nations of the earth.

Strong 5331, Bauer 854, Moulton-Milligan 664, Liddell-Scott 1917, Colin Brown 2:552,558.

5170. φαρμακεύς pharmakeus noun

Sorcerer, magician, poison mixer.

Cognate:

φαρμακεία pharmakeia (5169)

Synonyms:

μάγος magos (3069)
φάρμακος pharmakos (5171)

1. φαρμακεῦσιν pharmakeusin dat pl masc

1 and sorcerers, and idolaters, and all liars,.......... Rev 21:8

This term, related to *pharmakeuō*, identifies those who practiced mixing potions, poisons, or drugs, i.e., magicians or sorcerers. In Revelation 21:8 they are numbered with sinners who are cast into the lake of fiery brimstone to experience eternal death, the second death. (See *pharmakeia* [5169].)

Strong 5332, Bauer 854, Liddell-Scott 1917, Colin Brown 2:552,558.

5170B. φάρμακον pharmakon noun

Witchcraft, sorcery, magic potion, drug.

כֶּשֶׁף kesheph (3914), Witchcraft, sorcery (2 Kgs 9:22, Na 3:4).

1. φαρμάκων pharmakōn gen pl neu

1 their sorceries nor of their immorality (NASB).......Rev 9:21

Classical Greek

Pharmakon is a noun which occurs in Greek literature from the time of Homer (Eighth Century B.C.). In classical Greek it is used of a healing remedy or medicine, of a toxic drug or poison, and of a sedative or stimulative drug. Used figuratively it refers to an enchanted potion or to any means of attaining something. This latter meaning denotes a concoction made of various drugs and exotic ingredients that was used in the magical arts. In Herodotus 3.85 Oebares said to Darius, "No other man will be king but you; trust (my) *pharmaka* for that." This refers to magical formulas or charms such as those used in witchcraft.

Pharmakon is often used for drugs, medicine, and poison in the papyri and in the writings of Josephus. Philo used it in the general sense of a remedy: "God holds out . . . the most all-healing *remedy*" (*On the Migration of Abraham* 124). It takes occult connotations in *The Shepherd of Hermas*: "Be not like the sorcerers, for sorcerers carry their charms (*pharmaka*) in boxes, but you carry your *charms* and poison in your hearts" (*Vision* 3.9.7).

Septuagint Usage

In the Septuagint *pharmakon* means witchcraft, magical charms, poison, or medicine. There is a reference to Jezebel's witchcraft in 2 Kings 9:22 (LXX 4 Kings 9:22; see also Micah 5:12; Nahum 3:4). Some manuscripts of Tobit 6:4 use *pharmakon* to refer to a magical charm to keep away evil spirits. The charm consisted of the smoke from burning a fish heart and liver.

New Testament Usage

In the New Testament *pharmakon* occurs only in Revelation 9:21 in some manuscripts. Men did not repent of their *sorceries*, despite the trumpet judgments. It could be rendered "magic" (*GNB*), "magic arts" (NIV), or "witchcraft" (*Jerusalem Bible*). The reference is clearly to that which is an offense against God, i.e., the practice of magic or witchcraft. It most likely involved the use of drugs (magic potions) and the casting of spells. The *Textus Receptus* has the related term *pharmakeia* (5169) at Revelation 9:21.

Bauer 854, Moulton-Milligan 664, Liddell-Scott 1917, Colin Brown 2:552,558.

5171. φάρμακος pharmakos noun

Sorcerer, magician, poisoner.

Cognate:
- φαρμακεία pharmakeia (5169)

Synonyms:
- μάγος magos (3069)
- φαρμακεύς pharmakeus (5170)

חָבַר chāvar (2357), Charmer (Ps 58:5 [57:5]).

חַרְטֹם chartōm (A2852), Enchanter (Dn 2:27—Aramaic).

כָּשַׁף kāshaph (3913), Piel: sorcerer (Ex 7:11, Dn 2:2, Mal 3:5).

כַּשָּׁף kashshāph (3915), Sorcerer (Jer 27:9 [34:9]).

1. **φάρμακοι pharmakoi** nom pl masc
2. **φαρμάκοις pharmakois** dat pl masc

2 and sorcerers and idolaters and all liars, (NASB) . . . Rev 21:8
1 For without are dogs, and sorcerers, ... 22:15

Classical Greek and Septuagint Usage

The word *pharmakos* refers to one involved in the occult arts or witchcraft. In the Septuagint *pharmakos* is used of the Egyptian magicians (Exodus 7:11) who used enchantments to duplicate some of the miracles God performed through Moses. It is also used in God's injunction, "Thou shalt not suffer a witch to live" (Exodus 22:18; see Deuteronomy 18:10). Accented on the last syllable, *pharmakos* means "scapegoat."

New Testament Usage

The word occurs only once in the New Testament (Revelation 22:15). It refers to one who practices magical arts, such as mixing potions from herbs and exotic ingredients and muttering magical formulas or charms. The potions and enchantments did not have magical powers in themselves but were used to evoke the services of evil spirits. However, some potions were mixed as a poison. There is no essential difference between sorcery and witchcraft.

Strong 5333, Bauer 854, Moulton-Milligan 664, Liddell-Scott 1917, Colin Brown 2:552,554-55,558.

5172. φάσις phasis noun

Information, news, report, announcement.

1. **φάσις phasis** nom sing fem

1 tidings came unto the chief captain of the band, ... Acts 21:31

Related to the verb *phēmi* (5183), *phasis* is a noun meaning "information." It only occurs once in the New Testament (Acts 21:31) where it is translated "tidings." The word was originally used of a report that contained information against someone who had committed fraud. It then came to be used of information, a report, or an announcement in general (*Bauer*). *Phasis* is very common in the papyri meaning "news." One papyrus fragment reads, "Good *news* will come from me in the boats which are on their way" (*Moulton-Milligan*). In Acts 21:31 *phasis* could refer to "rumor" (see *Liddell-Scott*), but it seems best to interpret it as "news" or "report."

Strong 5334, Bauer 854, Moulton-Milligan 664-65, Liddell-Scott 1918.

5173. φάσκω phaskō verb

Say, allege, affirm, profess.

אָמַר 'āmar (569), Say (Gn 26:20).

1. **φάσκοντες phaskontes** nom pl masc part pres act
2. **φάσκοντας phaskontas** acc pl masc part pres act
3. **ἔφασκεν ephasken** 3sing indic imperf act

1 saying that these things were so. . . . . Acts 24:9
3 which was dead, whom Paul affirmed to be alive. 25:19
1 Professing themselves to be wise, ... became fools, . . . Rom 1:22
2 thou hast tried them which say they are apostles, ... Rev 2:2

Phaskō is related to the verb *phēmi* (5183). It usually denotes a strong affirmation that something is true. Sometimes the context reveals that the assertion is false or lacks objective, convincing proof. In Revelation 2:2 the Ephesian church was commended for trying those who *claimed* to be apostles and were not. In Romans 1:22 Paul condemned those who *profcsscd* themselves to be wise but were fools. In Acts 24:9 Luke wrote that the Jews *alleged* the facts to be just as Tertullus reported. However, it was only a verbal assertion. They offered no objective proof of their claims. When Festus reported Paul's case to King Agrippa (Acts 25:19), he mentioned that Paul *affirmed* that Jesus was still alive. Festus' use of the word may reveal (1) that he was not convinced of what Paul was affirming or (2) that Paul was forcibly presenting his case.

STRONG 5335, BAUER 854, MOULTON-MILLIGAN 665, LIDDELL-SCOTT 1918.

5174. φάτνη phatnē noun

Manger, stall, feeding trough.

אֵבוּס 'ēvûs (16), Manger (Prv 14:4, Is 1:3).

אֻרְוָה 'urwāh (747), Stall (2 Chr 32:28).

בְּלִיל b^elîl (1137), Fodder (Jb 6:5).

רֶפֶת repheth (7808), Stall (Hb 3:17).

1. φάτνης **phatnēs** gen sing fem
2. φάτνῃ **phatnē** dat sing fem

2 and wrapped him ... and laid him in a manger; ...... Luke 2:7
2 wrapped in swaddling clothes, lying in a manger........ 2:12
2 Mary, and Joseph, and the babe lying in a manger...... 2:16
1 on the sabbath loose his ox or his ass from the stall,... 13:15

Classical Greek

Phatnē appears as early as Homer (Eighth Century B.C.) and refers to a manger or feeding trough (Hengel, "phatnē," *Kittel*, 9:49). The meaning of *phatnē* broadened to include the organs of digestion, a cavity in a tooth, or a star cluster (ibid., p.50).

Septuagint Usage

The Septuagint also uses the word to mean "manger" and in a transferred sense to indicate the room or area enclosed around the manger (Proverbs 14:4). Such mangers were often made of stones laid like blocks, then plastered over with a substance to make them waterproof. These feeding troughs could also be carved from a single block of stone or simply made of dried mud. The animals ate from them. Hezekiah had many such stalls. Actually, several references may be found (2 Chronicles 32:28; Job 6:5; 39:9; Isaiah 1:3; Joel 1:17; Habakkuk 3:17).

One of the most pungent analogies in the Old Testament is in Isaiah: "The ox knoweth his owner, and the ass his master's crib: but Israel doth not know, my people doth not consider" (Isaiah 1:3). For a person or people to forget where they regularly receive nourishment tells of their inconsideration and lack of gratitude.

New Testament Usage

The term appears three times in the birth narratives of the Lord Jesus Christ (Luke 2:7,12,16). It is possible that the idea refers only to the room where Jesus was born or to a feeding place out-of-doors.

The Luke account typically stressed God's interest in the humble things of life. Jesus was laid in a manger upon birth. The angels gave this as a sign to the shepherds that they had found the newborn king of Israel. They would not have been allowed to visit Him in a palace. But they could come where possibly some of their own children had been laid.

In a later reference Jesus told a story about an ox that fell into a ditch; He did so in response to questions about His healings on the Sabbath Day (Luke 13:15).

STRONG 5336, BAUER 854, MOULTON-MILLIGAN 665, KITTEL 9:49-55, LIDDELL-SCOTT 1919.

5175. φαῦλος phaulos adj

Worthless, evil, vile.

SYNONYMS:
ἄτοπος atopos (818)
κακός kakos (2527)
πονηρός ponēros (4050)

אֱוִיל 'ĕwîl (188), Foolish person (Prv 29:9).

לָעַע lā'a' (4082), Be rash (Jb 6:3).

סָלַף sālaph (5751), Overthrow (Prv 13:6—Codex Alexandrinus only).

עַוְלָה 'awlāh (5983), Iniquity (Prv 22:8).

1. φαῦλον **phaulon** nom/acc sing neu
2. φαῦλα **phaula** nom/acc pl neu

2 For every one that doeth evil hateth the light,...... John 3:20
2 and they that have done evil,.......................... 5:29
1 not done anything good or bad, (NASB)............Rom 9:11
1 he has done, whether good or bad. (NASB).........2 Co 5:10
1 having no evil thing to say of you....................Tit 2:8
1 there is confusion and every evil work............... Jas 3:16

Classical Greek

From the classical perspective *phaulos* is not first and foremost a condition or act of wickedness or cruelty. Rather, it means to be "worthless, unable," such as a good-for-nothing person. More precisely it means to be "inconsistent, wavering," like the refuse blown around by the wind on the threshing floor. *Phaulos* suggests "indifference" or simply "worthlessness." Among the Greek philosophers, the Stoics divided men into two groups: those who were *spoudaios* (4558), "eager, energetic, purposeful," and those who were *phaulos*, "lazy, worthless, useless" (see Trench, *Synonyms of the New Testament*, p.296).

Septuagint Usage

Occurring only in the so-called Wisdom literature of the Septuagint, *phaulos* shows its versatility in that out of eight canonical occurrences there are three texts where the Hebrew is doubtful (Job

6:25; 9:23; Proverbs 16:21), and one which lacks the Hebrew altogether (Proverbs 5:2). Of the remaining four texts there are four different Hebrew originals. We see a shade of the classical sense of "worthless" (cf. NIV's "impetuous") in reference to words (Job 6:3; cf. 6:25; Sirach 20:16). The nuance of "wickedness," however, is usually present (Proverbs 22:8, in parallel with *kakos* [2527]; cf. 3 Maccabees 3:22).

New Testament Usage

The New Testament's use of *phaulos* is not totally removed from the original classical idea of "worthless," but there is more at stake in the New Testament. Here *phaulos* describes the spiritual barrenness and uselessness in terms of sin. Indeed, it denotes a serious sin, being associated with envy and selfish ambition (James 3:16).

Elsewhere the term is related to something evil. Thus in John 3:20 we read "every one who doeth *evil*" as a translation for *pas ho phaula prassōn.* Later, Jesus declared that a "resurrection of judgment" awaits "those practicing *evil*" (John 5:29, author's translation). Before the judgment seat of Christ the *phaulos* stands in contrast to the "good" (*agathos* [18]) (2 Corinthians 5:10; some texts contain *kakos* instead of *phaulos*). The New Testament understands *phaulos* in terms of "being incapable" or "being worthless." In addition, it denotes "sin" in the broadest terms. It especially suggests that the offender does not take God seriously; consequently, this is evidenced by "laziness" and "wickedness."

STRONG 5337, BAUER 854, MOULTON-MILLIGAN 665, LIDDELL-SCOTT 1919-20, COLIN BROWN 1:561,564.

5176. φέγγος phengos noun

Light, brilliance, radiance.

אוֹר 'ôr (214), Light (Jb 41:18 [41:9]).

לֶהָבָה lehāvāh (3988), Flame (Hos 7:6).

נֹגַהּ nōghahh (5227), Brightness, flashing (2 Sm 22:13, Ez 1:4, Hb 3:4).

נְהָרָה neharāh (5284), Light (Jb 3:4).

1. φέγγος phengos nom/acc sing neu

1 and the moon shall not give her **light**, ... Matt 24:29
1 and the moon shall not give her **light**, ... Mark 13:24
1 that they which come in may see the **light**. .... Luke 11:33

Classical Greek

The word *phengos*, like *phōs* (5292B), refers to various kinds of light. Often their meanings overlap. In classical Greek both words could refer to daylight, moonlight, or the light of torches. Some grammarians distinguish between the two saying that *phengos* was the light of the moon and *phōs* was the light of the sun. This distinction was observed most of the time, but not always (Trench, *Synonyms of the New Testament,* p.153). Figuratively, *phengos* refers to the radiance of a person (delight, joy, glory) (*Liddell-Scott*).

Septuagint Usage

In the Septuagint *phengos* is often used of the light of the heavenly bodies. The absence of this light was a sign of divine judgment (Joel 2:10; 3:15; Amos 5:20).

New Testament Usage

Phengos occurs three times in the New Testament. Twice it refers to the light of the moon (Matthew 24:29 and Mark 13:24, both quoting Isaiah 13:10). Once it refers to the light of a lamp (Luke 11:33) (Hahn, "Light," *Colin Brown,* 2:484).

STRONG 5338, BAUER 854, COLIN BROWN 2:484.

5177. φείδομαι pheidomai verb

Spare, refrain from, abstain.

חוּס chûs (2441), Show pity, have pity (Dt 25:12, Ps 72:13 [71:13], Jon 4:10f.).

חָמַל chāmal (2654), Have pity, have compassion (Ex 2:6, 2 Chr 36:17, Lam 2:2).

חֶמְלָה chemlāh (2655), Mercy (Gn 19:16, Is 63:9).

חָשַׂךְ chāsakh (2910), Deep, restrain (Gn 26:6, Jb 7:17).

מַחֲסֶה machăseh (4406I), Refuge (Jer 17:17, Jl 3:16).

1. φείδομαι pheidomai 1sing indic pres mid
2. φειδόμενος pheidomenos nom sing masc part pres mid
3. φειδόμενοι pheidomenoi nom pl masc part pres mid
4. ἐφείσατο epheisato 3sing indic aor mid
5. φείσηται pheisētai 3sing subj aor mid
6. φείσομαι pheisomai 1sing indic fut mid
7. φείσεται pheisetai 3sing indic fut mid

3 grievous wolves enter in ... not **sparing** the flock.... Acts 20:29
4 He that **spared** not his own Son, but delivered him .. Rom 8:32
4 For if God **spared** not the natural branches, ... 11:21
5 take heed lest he also **spare** not thee. 11:21
1 shall have trouble in the flesh: but I **spare** you...... 1 Co 7:28
2 that to **spare** you I came not as yet unto Corinth.... 2 Co 1:23
1 for I will say the truth: but now I **forbear**, ... 12:6
6 to all other, that, if I come again, I **will** not **spare**: 13:2
4 For if God **spared** not the angels that sinned, ... 2 Pt 2:4
4 And **spared** not the old world, but saved Noah 2:5

Classical Greek

Pheidomai is a common verb with the basic meaning "to spare." The word has various meanings in classical Greek. It often refers to sparing persons or things from their certain doom, as in war. With the negative ("not spare") it would mean "to destroy" or "judge." It also refers to using things sparingly. A negative would yield the meaning "to use or give freely." At times it can mean to draw back or refrain from doing something, such as a dangerous expedition. Lastly, it sometimes refers to having consideration for someone or something (*Liddell-Scott*).

Several meanings are found in the papyri. For example, it can mean "to use freely" or "to have consideration for" (*Moulton-Milligan*). The idea of sparing one from certain doom is found in *The Epistle of Barnabas* (5.13), "*Spare* my soul from the sword."

Septuagint Usage

The Septuagint retains most of the classical meanings. Jeremiah 13:14 speaks of God's destroying the enemy and not sparing them. Isaiah 54:2 refers to not sparing one's cords and stakes, i.e., to use them freely. The idea of refraining oneself is common. "He that refraineth his lips is wise" (Proverbs 10:19); and "He that spareth his rod hateth his son" (Proverbs 13:24).

New Testament Usage

The New Testament retains the meaning of sparing someone or something from certain doom or certain trouble. In 2 Corinthians 1:23 Paul spared the Corinthians by not coming to them and scolding them personally. This would be equivalent to showing mercy on them. It is usually used with the negative meaning "to judge" or "condemn." God spared not His own Son (Romans 8:32), the natural branches (Romans 11:21), or the angels that sinned (2 Peter 2:4). The New Testament also retains the meaning of refraining from or avoiding doing something. In 2 Corinthians 12:6 Paul refrained from saying more about being caught up into the third heaven.

STRONG 5339, BAUER 854, MOULTON-MILLIGAN 665, LIDDELL-SCOTT 1920-21.

5178. φειδομένως pheidomenōs adv

Sparingly.

1. φειδομένως pheidomenōs

1 which soweth **sparingly** shall reap also sparingly; .... 2 Co 9:6
1 which soweth sparingly shall reap also **sparingly**; 9:6

Pheidomenōs is a very rare adverb related to the verb *pheidomai* (5177) "to spare." Plutarch wrote, "But now use *sparingly* those things which you have" (*Alexander* 25.7). It only occurs in the New Testament at 2 Corinthians 9:6 where it is used twice. Following the Greek word order, the verse reads, "He who sows sparingly, sparingly also he will reap." This construction places emphasis on the miserly use of one's resources and the meagerness of the consequent return. This reflects the divine principle that the more one gives, the fuller his life becomes.

STRONG 5340, BAUER 854, MOULTON-MILLIGAN 665, LIDDELL-SCOTT 1921.

5179. φέρω pherō verb

Carry, bear, endure, produce, bring, lead.

COGNATES:

ἀναφέρω anapherō (397)
ἀποφέρω apopherō (661)
διαφέρω diapherō (1302)
διάφορος diaphoros (1307)
εἰσφέρω eispherō (1517)
ἐκφέρω ekpherō (1613)
ἐπιφέρω epipherō (2002)
εὐφορέω euphoreō (2145)
καρποφορέω karpophoreō (2563)
καρποφόρος karpophoros (2564)
καταφέρω katapherō (2671)
παραφέρω parapherō (3772)
παρεισφέρω pareispherō (3785)
περιφέρω peripherō (3924)
ποταμοφόρητος potamophorētos (4075)
προσφέρω prospherō (4232)
προσφορά prosphora (4234)
προφέρω propherō (4251)
συμφέρω sumpherō (4702)
τελεσφορέω telesphoreō (4900)
τροποφορέω tropophoreō (5000)
ὑποφέρω hupopherō (5135)
φορέω phoreō (5246)
φόρος phoros (5247)
φωσφόρος phōsphoros (5294)

SYNONYMS:

ἄγω agō (70)
αἴρω airō (142)
ἀνέχομαι anechomai (428)
βαστάζω bastazō (934)
ἐπιφέρω epipherō (2002)
καρτερέω kartereō (2565)
κινέω kineō (2767)
κομίζω komizō (2837)
μεταβαίνω metabainō (3197)
προσάγω prosagō (4175)
προσφέρω prospherō (4232)
στέγω stegō (4573)
ὑπομένω hupomenō (5116)
ὑποφέρω hupopherō (5135)

אָתָה 'āthâh (885), Come; hiphil: bring (Is 21:14).

אָתָה 'ăthâh (A886), Come; haphel: bring (Dn 5:3,23, 6:17—Aramaic).

בּוֹא bô' (971), Qal: come (Ex 35:22, 2 Kgs 10:6, 2 Chr 9:13); hiphil: bring (Gn 4:3f., 1 Sm 15:15, Jer 49:5 [30:5]); hophal: be brought (Gn 33:11).

הָב hav (1957), Bring (Ru 3:15); ascribe (Ps 29:1f. [28:1f.]).

יָבַל yāval (3095), Hiphil: bring (Pss 68:29 [67:29], 76:11 [75:11], Zep 3:10).

יָעֵף yā'ēph (3395), Be tired; hophal: do swiftly (Dn 9:21).

יָצָא yātsâ' (3428), Come out, go out; hiphil: import (2 Chr 1:17).

יָרַד yāradh (3495), Go down; hiphil: bring (Gn 43:22).

כּוּל kûl (3677), Pilpel: contain (2 Chr 2:6).

כּוּן kûn (3679), Be firm, be stable; hiphil: prepare (Jb 15:35—only some Sinaiticus texts).

לָקַח lāqach (4089), Get (Gn 27:13).

נָגַשׁ nāghash (5242), Come near, approach; hiphil: bring (2 Sm 17:28).

נָדַב nādhav (5246), Be willing (Ex 35:29).

נָדַף nādhaph (5264), Drive, blow away; niphal: chase (Lv 26:36).

נוּף nûph (5311), Hiphil: present as a wave offering (Ex 35:22 [35:23]).

נְפַק n^{e}phaq (A5494), Go out, go forth; haphel: bring (Dn 5:2—Aramaic).

נָשָׂא nāsâ' (5558), Support, carry (Gn 36:7, Nm 11:14, Is 30:6).

נָתַן nāthan (5598), Give (Gn 43:24—Codex Alexandrinus only).

סְעָרָה s^{ee}ārāh (5788), Whirlwind (Is 29:6).

עָבַר 'āvar (5882), Go over, go through; blow away (Is 29:5, Jer 13:24).

עָלָה 'ālâh (6148), Go up; hiphil: pay, offer a sacrifice (2 Kgs 17:4, 2 Chr 35:16, Ezr 4:2).

עָשָׂה 'āsâh (6449), Do, make; bear (Hos 9:16).

פָּנָה pānâh (6680), Turn (Jos 15:2).

שׁוּב shûv (8178), Return; hiphil: do what was done before (2 Chr 27:5).

שָׁטַף shātaph (8278), Pass through (Is 28:15,18).

שָׁלַח shālach (8365), Send (1 Kgs 9:14).

1. **φέρετε pherete** 2pl indic/impr pres act
2. **φέρει pherei** 3sing indic pres act
3. **φέρουσιν pherousin** 3pl indic pres act
4. **φέρῃ pherē** 3sing subj pres act
5. **φέρητε pherēte** 2pl subj pres act
6. **φέρε phere** 2sing impr pres act
7. **φέρων pherōn** nom sing masc part pres act
8. **φέροντες pherontes** nom pl masc part pres act
9. **φέρουσαν pherousan** acc sing fem part pres act
10. **φέρουσαι pherousai** nom pl fem part pres act
11. **φέρον pheron** nom/acc sing neu part pres act
12. **φέρειν pherein** inf pres act
13. **ἤνεγκα ēnenka** 1sing indic aor act
14. **ἤνεγκεν ēnenken** 3sing indic aor act
15. **ἤνεγκαν ēnenkan** 3pl indic aor act
16. **ἐνέγκατε enenkate** 2pl impr aor act
17. **ἐνέγκας enenkas** nom sing masc part aor act
18. **ἐνέγκαντες enenkantes** nom pl masc part aor act
19. **οἴσει oisei** 3sing indic fut act
20. **οἴσουσιν oisousin** 3pl indic fut act
21. **ἔφερεν epheren** 3sing indic imperf act
22. **ἔφερον epheron** 3pl indic imperf act
23. **φερώμεθα pherōmetha** 1pl subj pres mid
24. **φερόμενοι pheromenoi** nom pl masc part pres mid
25. **φερομένης pheromenēs** gen sing fem part pres mid
26. **φερομένην pheromenēn** acc sing fem part pres mid
27. **φέρεσθαι pheresthai** inf pres mid
28. **ἠνέχθη ēnechthē** 3sing indic aor pass
29. **ἐνεχθείσης enechtheisēs** gen sing fem part aor pass
30. **ἐνεχθεῖσαν enechtheisan** acc sing fem part aor pass
31. **ἐνεχθῆναι enechthēnai** inf aor pass
32. **ἐφερόμεθα epherometha** 1pl indic imperf pass
33. **ἐφέροντο epheronto** 3pl indic imperf pass
34. **ἐνέγκαι enenkai** inf aor act
35. **ἐνεγκεῖν enenkein** inf aor act

35 A good tree cannot **bear** bad fruit, (NIV) .... Matt 7:18
35 and a bad tree cannot **bear** good fruit. (NIV) 7:18
28 And his head **was brought** in a charger, ... 14:11
14 and **she brought** it to her mother. 14:11
1 He said, **Bring** them hither to me. 14:18
1 Jesus answered ... **bring** him hither to me. 17:17
22 they **brought** unto him all that were diseased, ... Mark 1:32
8 they come unto him, **bringing** one sick of the palsy, ... 2:3
21 and **brought forth**, some thirty, and some sixty, ... 4:8
31 and commanded his head **to be brought**: 6:27
14 And **brought** his head in a charger, ... 6:28
3 And **they bring** unto him one that was deaf, ... 7:32
3 and **they bring** a blind man unto him, ... 8:22
13 Master, I **have brought** unto thee my son, ... 9:17
1 how long shall I suffer you? **bring** him unto me. 9:19
15 And **they brought** him unto him: 9:20
1 colt tied ... untie it and **bring** it (NASB) 11:2
3 And they **brought** the colt to Jesus (NASB) 11:7
1 **bring** me a penny, that I may see it. 12:15
15 And they **brought** it. And he saith unto them, ... 12:16
3 And they **bring** him unto the place Golgotha, ... 15:22
8 And, behold, men **brought** in a bed a man .... Luke 5:18
18 And **bring** hither the fatted calf, and kill it; 15:23
12 the cross, that he **might bear** it after Jesus. 23:26
10 **bringing** the spices which they had prepared, ... 24:1
1 and **bear** unto the governor of the feast. .... John 2:8
15 unto the governor of the feast. And they **bare** it. 2:8
14 Hath any man **brought** him ought to eat? 4:33
2 but if it die, it **bringeth forth** much fruit. 12:24
11 Every branch ... **beareth** not fruit he taketh away: 15:2
11 and every branch that **beareth** fruit, he purgeth it, ... 15:2
4 he purgeth it, that it **may bring forth** more fruit. 15:2
12 As the branch cannot **bear** fruit of itself, ... 15:4
2 the same **bringeth forth** much fruit: 15:5
5 is my Father glorified, that ye **bear** much fruit; 15:8
5 that ye should go and **bring forth** fruit, ... 15:16
1 What accusation **bring** ye against this man? 18:29
7 and **brought** a mixture of myrrh and aloes, ... 19:39
6 Then saith he to Thomas, **Reach** hither thy finger, ... 20:27
6 **reach** hither thy hand, and thrust it into my side: 20:27
16 **Bring** of the fish which ye have now caught. 21:10
19 and **carry** thee whither thou wouldest not. 21:18
25 a sound from heaven as of a **rushing** mighty wind, . . Acts 2:2

22 and **brought** the prices of the things that were sold, Acts 4:34
14 Having land, sold it, and **brought** the money,.......... 4:37
17 and **brought** a certain part,.......................... 5:2
8 round about unto Jerusalem, **bringing** sick folks,....... 5:16
9 came unto the iron gate that **leadeth** unto the city;... 12:10
17 **brought** oxen and garlands unto the gates,........... 14:13
8 **laid** many and grievous complaints against Paul,...... 25:7
22 they began **bringing** charges against him (NASB)..... 25:18
32 could not bear up into the wind, we let her **drive**..... 27:15
33 struck sail, and so **were driven**...................... 27:17
14 **endured** with much longsuffering the vessels........Rom 9:22
6 The cloak ... when thou comest, **bring** with thee,.. 2 Tm 4:13
7 and **upholding** all things by the word of his power, Heb 1:3
23 let us **go on** unto perfection;........................ 6:1
27 must also of necessity **be** the death of the testator...... 9:16
22 they **could** not **endure** that which was commanded,... 12:20
8 unto him without the camp, **bearing** his reproach..... 13:13
26 the grace that is to **be brought** unto you.......... 1 Pt 1:13
29 when **there came** such a voice to him............. 2 Pt 1:17
30 And this voice which **came** from heaven we heard,..... 1:18
28 prophecy **came** not in old time by the will of man:.... 1:21
24 but holy men of God spake as they **were moved**....... 1:21
3 **bring** not railing accusation against them............ 2:11
2 come any unto you, and **bring** not this doctrine,....2 Jn 1:10
3 and the kings of the earth do **bring** their glory.... Rev 21:24
20 And they **shall bring** the glory and honour........... 21:26

Pherō, a common verb, derives from the root *pher-*, meaning "to bear." Together with its many compounds, *pherō* is capable of denoting multiple processes in the literal, as well as in the figurative, sense of the verb. Grammatically, *pherō* has only one principal part which supplies the base for the present and imperfect tenses; otherwise it is dependent upon other roots, as seen in the future tense *oisō* and the aorist *ēnenka*.

Classical Greek

The classical Greek literature reflects many of the meanings of *pherō* which are also found later in the New Testament. Already in Homer (Eighth Century B.C.), the verb means "to bring" or "lead" men, animals, or things; "to bring forth," hence "to express" a word; "to bring" gifts; and "to bear" burdens or fruit. The figurative sense of "bearing" or "enduring" afflictions, both physical and spiritual, occurs early as well.

Septuagint Usage

In the Septuagint *pherō* predominantly translates the Hebrew *bô'* ("bring gifts") and *nāsâ'* ("bear"). While the former is used with all kinds of objects, it also carries a special cultic sense. It means to bring gifts as offerings to the temple or priest. At times it may even become synonymous with the action of sacrificing itself (e.g., Jeremiah 6:20; Amos 4:4; Malachi 1:13; see Weiss, "pherō," *Kittel*, 9:56). When *pherō* is the translation for the latter Hebrew term it means "to bear" a burden, "to bring" a gift, or "to bear" fruit (e.g., Joel 2:22). The figurative sense can be seen, for example, in Numbers 11:14,17 where Moses complained to God that he was no longer able to bear the burdens of Israel (cf. Deuteronomy 1:9,12). In Isaiah 53:4 the servant of the Lord bears our sins (*hamartias* [see 264], rather than griefs or sorrows).

New Testament Usage

The New Testament usage of *pherō* is no less diverse and reflects meanings which are already found in secular literature and in the Septuagint. Some of the figurative meanings of *pherō* are worth pointing out. Bearing good or bad fruit (Mark 4:8) means more than distinguishing the quality of fruit trees; it also represents the criterion of the authentic follower of Jesus. "To bear fruit" is also the Father's will for the disciples (John 15:2,4,16). Jesus' own fruitfulness in His death and resurrection is expressed in the metaphor of the grain of wheat that falls into the ground and dies in order to "bring much fruit" (John 12:24).

In terms of carrying burdens *pherō* is used only in Luke 23:26, namely, of Simon of Cyrene who was coerced to carry the cross of Jesus. In Hebrew 13:13 Christians are called upon to go to Jesus outside the camp, "bearing" (the burden of) the shame He bore. For Paul, God's power is displayed in that He "bears" patiently with those who are objects of His wrath, thus demonstrating His long-suffering and mercy to those He calls (Romans 9:22-24).

Pherō is also used in Acts 2:2 to describe what happened at Pentecost when a "rushing" mighty wind from heaven filled the house. The work of the Spirit is also in mind when the prophets (of the Old Testament) are described as those who spoke as they were "moved along" or "impelled" by the Holy Spirit (2 Peter 1:21).

Finally, in Hebrew 1:3 *pherō* serves to describe the function of the Son of God with reference to the created order: He "bears up," i.e., "rules," the universe by His powerful Word (Weiss, "pherō," *Kittel*, 9:56).

STRONG 5342, BAUER 854-55, MOULTON-MILLIGAN 666, KITTEL 9:56-60, LIDDELL-SCOTT 1922.

5180. φεύγω pheugō verb

Flee, escape, shun.

COGNATES:

ἀποφεύγω apopheugō (662)
διαφεύγω diapheugō (1303)
ἐκφεύγω ekpheugō (1614)
καταφεύγω katapheugō (2672)
φυγή phugē (5273)

SYNONYMS:

ἀποφεύγω apopheugō (662)
διαφεύγω diapheugō (1303)

ἐκκλίνω ekklinō (1565)
ἐκτρέπω ektrepō (1610)
ἐκφεύγω ekpheugō (1614)
καταφεύγω katapheugō (2672)
περιΐστημι periistēmi (3889)
στέλλομαι stellomai (4575)

בָּרַח bārach (1300), Flee (Nm 24:11, 1 Sm 22:17, Is 48:20).

בָּרִחַ bāriach (1301), Something fleeing, fugitive (Is 27:1, 43:14).

מְנוּסָה m^enûsāh (4643), Fleeing (Lv 26:36).

נָדַד nādhadh (5252), Flee, fugitive (Ps 31:11 [30:11], Is 21:14).

נָדַח nādhach (5258), Niphal: wanderer (Is 16:3); hophal: something hunted (Is 13:14).

נוּס nûs (5308), Qal: flee (Dt 19:4, 2 Kgs 9:27, Jer 51:6 [28:6]); hiphil: flee (Jgs 7:21—Codex Vaticanus only).

נָסַס nāsas (5449), Qal: waste away (Is 10:18); hithpolel: be displayed (Ps 60:4 [59:4]).

נָפַל nāphal (5489), Fall; desert (Jer 37:13 [44:13], 38:19 [45:19]).

עָרַק ʿāraq (6443), Gnaw (Jb 30:3).

שָׂרִיד sārîdh (8032), Survivor (Ob 14).

1. **φεύγει pheugei** 3sing indic pres act
2. **φεῦγε pheuge** 2sing impr pres act
3. **φεύγετε pheugete** 2pl impr pres act
4. **φευγέτωσαν pheugetōsan** 3pl impr pres act
5. **ἔφυγεν ephugen** 3sing indic aor act
6. **ἔφυγον ephugon** 3pl indic aor act
7. **φύγητε phugēte** 2pl subj aor act
8. **φυγεῖν phugein** inf aor act
9. **φεύξεται pheuxetai** 3sing indic fut mid
10. **φεύξονται pheuxontai** 3pl indic fut mid

2 young child and his mother, and **flee** into Egypt, ... Matt 2:13
8 who ... warned you to **flee** from the wrath to come? ... 3:7
6 And they that kept them **fled**, ... 8:33
3 persecute you in this city, **flee** ye into another: 10:23
7 how can ye **escape** the damnation of hell? 23:33
4 which be in Judaea **flee** into the mountains: 24:16
6 Then all the disciples forsook him, and **fled**. 26:56
6 And they that fed the swine **fled**, ... Mark 5:14
4 let them that be in Judaea **flee** to the mountains: 13:14
6 And they all forsook him, and **fled**. 14:50
5 he left the linen cloth, and **fled** from them naked. 14:52
6 went out quickly, and **fled** from the sepulchre; 16:8
8 warned you to **flee** from the wrath to come? .... Luke 3:7
6 they that fed them saw what was done, they **fled**, ... 8:34
4 them which are in Judaea **flee** to the mountains; 21:21
10 will they not follow, but **will flee** from him: .... John 10:5
1 and leaveth the sheep, and **fleeth**: 10:12
1 The hireling **fleeth**, because he is an hireling, ... 10:13
5 Then **fled** Moses at this saying, ... Acts 7:29
8 as the shipmen were about to **flee** out of the ship, ... 27:30
3 **Flee** fornication. .... 1 Co 6:18
3 Wherefore, my dearly beloved, **flee** from idolatry. 10:14
2 But thou, O man of God, **flee** these things; .... 1 Tm 6:11
2 **Flee** also youthful lusts: but follow righteousness, .. 2 Tm 2:22
6 **escaped** the edge of the sword, ... Heb 11:34
6 **escaped** not who refused him that spake on earth, ... 12:25
9 Resist the devil, and he **will flee** from you. .... Jas 4:7
9 shall desire to die, and death **shall flee** from them... Rev 9:6
5 And the woman **fled** into the wilderness, ... 12:6
5 And every island **fled** away, ... Rev 16:20
5 whose face the earth and the heaven **fled** away; 20:11

Classical Greek

Pheugō is a common verb which occurs from the time of Homer (Eighth Century B.C.). In classical Greek it means (1) to flee from or to a certain place; (2) to escape out of a predicament; (3) to shun or avoid things such as evil or a dangerous campaign; (4) to be exiled from a country; (5) to live in exile; (6) to slip from one's hand; or (7) to be prosecuted at law (*Liddell-Scott*). The early church fathers often used *pheugō* in moral contexts, such as shunning evil doctrine and ungodliness.

Septuagint Usage

In the Septuagint *pheugō* retains the basic meaning of fleeing from or to a certain place, or from a person or army. For example, a person who accidentally killed another could flee to a city of refuge (Deuteronomy 4:42). It also means to escape as in the statement, "To escape from thy hand is impossible" (Wisdom of Solomon 16:15, RSV). Finally, it means to shun or avoid evil as in "flee from sin as from a snake" (*Sirach* 21:2, RSV).

New Testament Usage

In the New Testament *pheugō* keeps the basic meaning of fleeing from impending or anticipated danger or difficulty (Matthew 2:13; 10:23; 24:16; John 10:5). It may also mean to escape out of a predicament, such as to escape the edge of the sword (Hebrews 11:34). Four times it is used figuratively to denote shunning evil, e.g., flee fornication (1 Corinthians 6:18); flee idolatry (1 Corinthians 10:14); flee evil doctrine (1 Timothy 6:11); flee youthful lusts (2 Timothy 2:22). Twice it takes on the connotation of vanishing or becoming invisible to the sight, as when every island disappeared (Revelation 16:20; also 20:11).

STRONG 5343, BAUER 855-56, MOULTON-MILLIGAN 666, LIDDELL-SCOTT 1924-25, COLIN BROWN 1:558-59.

5181. Φῆλιξ Phēlix name

Felix.

1. **Φῆλιξ Phēlix** nom masc
2. **Φήλικος Phēlikos** gen masc
3. **Φήλικι Phēliki** dat masc
4. **Φήλικα Phēlika** acc masc

4 and bring him safe unto **Felix** the governor. .... Acts 23:24
3 most excellent governor **Felix** sendeth greeting. 23:26

1 most noble Felix, with all thankfulness............ Acts 24:3
1 And when Felix heard these things,.................. 24:22
1 when Felix came with his wife Drusilla,.............. 24:24
1 Felix trembled, and answered, Go thy way............ 24:25
1 Porcius Festus came into Felix' room:................ 24:27
1 and Felix, willing to show the Jews a pleasure,........ 24:27
2 There is a certain man left in bonds by Felix:......... 25:14

Antonius Felix was the procurator of Judea from ca. A.D. 52–60, the period which covers the arrest of Paul in Jerusalem. He heard Paul's initial defense in Caesarea and kept him under arrest for 2 years, hoping thereby to appease the Jews and to give every opportunity for the offering of a bribe. His time in office was marked by great cruelty and corruption and did much to provoke the disastrous revolt of 66–70. He was recalled to Rome in disgrace and was succeeded by Festus, probably in A.D. 60. (Cf. Acts 23:24 through 25:14.)

5182. φήμη phēmē noun

Report, news, fame.

COGNATE:
φημί phēmi (5183)

SYNONYMS:
ἀκοή akoē (187)
ἦχος ēchos (2256)

שְׁמוּעָה shemûʻāh (8444), News (Prv 15:30 [16:2]).

1. φήμη phēmē nom sing fem

1 And the **fame** hereof went abroad into all that land. Matt 9:26
1 and there went out a **fame** of him through all....... Luke 4:14

Classical Greek

Phēmē is a noun which is derived from *phēmi* (5183), "to say, to make known." It originally referred to a divine oracle; for example, in Homer's *Odyssey* it refers to omens from Zeus (*Liddell-Scott*). It then took on the meaning of a report, news, message, or even rumor.

Septuagint Usage

In the Septuagint *phēmē* appears four times. In 2 Maccabees 4:39 it refers to the news or *report* of certain sacrileges being committed in Judea. In 3 Maccabees 3:2 it means a *rumor*, that is, false knowledge spread around the land. This same sense occurs in 4 Maccabees 4:22. A false story (*phēmē*) spread throughout Judea that Antiochus Epiphanes had died. Proverbs 15:30 notes that "*good news* gives health to the bones" (NIV).

New Testament Usage

The word occurs twice in the New Testament, both times being translated "fame." After the Lord raised Jairus' daughter from the dead, "the fame hereof went abroad into all that land" (Matthew 9:26). Here it refers to the news about Jesus' being able to raise the dead. The second occurrence is when Jesus returned to Galilee from the temptation and a "fame" of Him spread throughout the land (Luke 4:14). In both passages the NIV translates it "news" and the RSV translates it "report." In 1611, when the KJV came into existence, the word *fame* meant "report" or "news."

STRONG 5345, BAUER 856, MOULTON-MILLIGAN 666, LIDDELL-SCOTT 1925.

5183. φημί phēmi verb

Say, mean, assert.

COGNATES:
βλασφημέω blasphēmeō (980)
διαφημίζω diaphēmizō (1304)
δυσφημέω dusphēmeō (1418B)
δυσφημία dusphēmia (1419)
εὐφημία euphēmia (2143)
εὔφημος euphēmos (2144)
προφητεύω prophēteuō (4253)
σύμφημι sumphēmi (4703)
φήμη phēmē (5182)

SYNONYMS:
ἀπαγγέλλω apangellō (514)
διαλέγομαι dialegomai (1250)
διηγέομαι diēgeomai (1328)
ἐκδιηγέομαι ekdiēgeomai (1542)
ἐξηγέομαι exēgeomai (1817)
ἐρεύγομαι ereugomai (2027)
λαλέω laleō (2953)
λέγω legō (2978)
ὁμιλέω homileō (3519)
φθέγγομαι phthengomai (5187)
φωνέω phōneō (5291)

אָמַר 'āmar (569), Say (Gn 24:47, Ex 2:6, Prv 30:20 [24:55]).

נָאַם nā'am (5176), Say, declare (2 Kgs 9:26, Ps 36:1 [35:1], Jer 31:32f. [38:32f.]).

נְאֻם neʼum (5177), Oracle (Nm 24:3f.,15).

1. φημί phēmi 1sing indic pres act
2. φησίν phēsin 3sing indic pres act
3. φασίν phasin 3pl indic pres act
4. ἔφη ephē 3sing indic imperf/aor act
5. ἐφημίσθη ephēmisthē 3sing indic aor pass

4 Jesus **said** unto him, It is written again,............Matt 4:7
4 The centurion answered and **said**, Lord,................ 8:8
4 He **said** unto them, An enemy hath done this.......... 13:28
4 But he **said**, Nay; lest while ye gather up the tares,.... 13:29
2 being before instructed of her mother, **said**,........... 14:8
4 Jesus **saith** unto him, Then are the children free....... 17:26
4 "Which ones?" And Jesus **said**, (NASB).............. 19:18
4 Jesus **said** unto him, If thou wilt be perfect,........... 19:21
4 And he **said** unto them, Neither tell I you............ 21:27
4 And He **said** to him, (NASB)........................ 22:37
4 His lord **said** unto him, Well done, thou good......... 25:21
4 His lord **said** unto him, Well done, good............. 25:23
4 Jesus **said** unto him, Verily I say unto thee,........... 26:34
4 This fellow **said**, I am able to destroy the temple...... 26:61

4 And Jesus **said** unto him, Thou sayest............ Matt 27:11
4 the governor **said**, Why, what evil hath he done?...... 27:23
4 Pilate **said** unto them, Ye have a watch:............. 27:65
4 And He **said** to them, (NASB).................... Mark 9:12
4 John **said** to Him, "Teacher, (NASB).................. 9:38
4 And he **said** to Him, "Teacher, (NASB)............. 10:20
4 Jesus **said**, "Truly I say to you, (NASB)............. 10:29
4 Jesus **said** to them, "Is this not the reason (NASB).... 12:24
4 But Peter **said** unto him, Although all shall be........ 14:29
2 I have somewhat to say unto thee. And he **saith**,.... Luke 7:40
4 he turned to the woman, and **said** unto Simon,......... 7:44
4 But when he came to his senses, he **said**, (NASB)..... 15:17
4 And after a little while another saw him, and **said**,.... 22:58
4 one of them too!" But Peter **said** (NASB)............ 22:58
4 And he **said** unto them, Ye say that I am............. 22:70
4 And he answered him and **said**, Thou sayest it......... 23:3
4 answered, and rebuking him **said**, (NASB)............ 23:40
4 He **said**, I am the voice of one crying............. John 1:23
4 he **said**, Lord, I believe. And he worshipped him........ 9:38
2 Pilate ... went out to them, and **said**, (NASB)......... 18:29
4 Then Peter **said** unto them, Repent,................ Acts 2:38
4 And he **said**, Men, brethren, and fathers, hearken;...... 7:2
2 came unto a certain water: and the eunuch **said**,........ 8:36
4 And he **said** unto them,............................ 10:28
4 And Cornelius **said**,................................ 10:30
2 And **said**, Cornelius, thy prayer is heard,............. 10:31
4 and **said**, Sirs, what must I do to be saved?........... 16:30
4 But Paul **said** unto them,........................... 16:37
4 Paul stood in the midst of Mars' hill, and **said**,........ 17:22
2 he **said**, Ye men of Ephesus, what man is there........ 19:35
4 Who **said**, Canst thou speak Greek?.................. 21:37
2 they kept the more silence: and he **saith**,.............. 22:2
4 Tell me, art thou a Roman? He **said**, Yea............. 22:27
4 And Paul **said**, But I was free born.................. 22:28
4 Then **said** Paul, I wist not, brethren,.................. 23:5
4 called one of the centurions unto him, and **said**,....... 23:17
2 and brought him to the chief captain, and **said**,........ 23:18
4 I will hear thee, **said** he,........................... 23:35
2 therefore, **said** he, which among you are able,......... 25:5
4 Then Agrippa **said** unto Festus,...................... 25:22
2 To morrow, **said** he, thou shalt hear him............. 25:22
2 And Festus **said**, King Agrippa, and all men.......... 25:24
4 Then Agrippa **said** unto Paul,........................ 26:1
4 Festus **said** with a loud voice, Paul,.................. 26:24
2 But he **said**, I am not mad, most noble Festus;........ 26:25
4 Then Agrippa **said** unto Paul,........................ 26:28
4 Then **said** Agrippa unto Festus,...................... 26:32
3 and as some **affirm** that we say, Let us do evil,..... Rom 3:8
2 for two, **saith** he, shall be one flesh................ 1 Co 6:16
1 But this I **say**, brethren, the time is short:............ 7:29
1 I speak as to wise men; judge ye what I **say**.......... 10:15
1 What **say** I then? that the idol is any thing,........... 10:19
1 Now this I **say**, brethren, that flesh and blood......... 15:50
2 For his letters, **say** they, are weighty and powerful; 2 Co 10:10
2 for, See, **saith** he, that thou make all things......... Heb 8:5

Classical Greek

Phēmi is a common verb related to *phaō*, "to bring to light" (Thayer, *Greek-English Lexicon*). In classical Greek it means "say, affirm," or "assert." When it involves a belief or opinion it means "think" or "suppose."

In the papyri it often means "to affirm" or "to profess." For example, in one papyrus someone affirmed that he had bought a certain piece of land by a contract (*Moulton-Milligan*). It is frequent in the subscriptions of letters where one person signed for another who professed to be illiterate (ibid.).

Josephus also used it for asserting that something is true: "Some *say* that Homer did not leave his poems in writing" (*Against Apion* 1.2). In early Christian literature it could mean "say, reply," or "answer." Clement used it to introduce a quotation from Scripture: "The Holy Word says . . . " (1 *Clement* 13:3). This could have the notion of "affirms."

Septuagint Usage

In the Septuagint *phēmi* has several meanings. It introduces a simple statement: "And she said . . . " (Genesis 24:47). It can mean "utter" in the sense of a solemn pronouncement, as when Balaam uttered his prophecy (Numbers 24:3,15). It can also be used to introduce a declaration of the Lord (1 Samuel 2:30 [LXX 1 Kings 2:30]; Jeremiah 31:31 [LXX 38:31]). Thus *phēmi* is used of various types of speaking.

New Testament Usage

In the New Testament *phēmi* seems to be a generic verb of speaking with the general meaning "to say." It can be translated as "answer" or "reply" (Matthew 13:29; Luke 7:40), "ask" (Matthew 27:23), "remark" (Acts 26:32), "declare" (Matthew 13:28), or "say" (Acts 16:37). The classical sense of asserting or affirming is seen when Peter asserted that he would never leave the Lord (Mark 14:29). Paul sometimes used *phēmi* to introduce an explanation. For example, Paul's statement, "But this I *say*," conveys the idea "this is what I mean" (1 Corinthians 7:29). Also, his question, "What say I then?" has the meaning, "What do I mean by this?" (1 Corinthians 10:19). *Phēmi* is also used with an unnamed or implied subject to introduce a discourse, a scriptural quotation, or a parenthetic insertion, "It is said." The subject could be God (Hebrews 8:5), Scriptures (1 Corinthians 6:16), or something indefinite (2 Corinthians 10:10).

STRONG 5346, BAUER 856, MOULTON-MILLIGAN 666, LIDDELL-SCOTT 1926.

5184. Φῆστος Phēstos name

Festus.

1. **Φῆστος Phēstos** nom masc
2. **Φήστου Phēstou** gen masc
3. **Φήστῳ Phēstō** dat masc
4. **Φῆστον Phēston** acc masc
5. **Φῆστε Phēste** voc masc

4 But after two years Porcius **Festus** came........... Acts 24:27
1 Now when **Festus** was come into the province,......... 25:1
1 But **Festus** answered, that Paul should be kept........ 25:4
1 But **Festus**, willing to do the Jews a pleasure,......... 25:9
1 **Festus**, when he had conferred with the council,....... 25:12
4 Agrippa ... came unto Caesarea to salute **Festus**........ 25:13

1 **Festus** declared Paul's cause unto the king, ... Acts 25:14
4 Then Agrippa said unto **Festus**, ... 25:22
2 at **Festus'** commandment Paul was brought forth. 25:23
1 And **Festus** said, King Agrippa, and all men 25:24
1 **Festus** said with a loud voice, Paul, ... 26:24
5 But he said, I am not mad, most noble **Festus**; 26:25
3 Then said Agrippa unto **Festus**, ... 26:32

Porcius Festus succeeded the corrupt and cruel Felix as procurator of Judea, probably in A.D. 60. His term in office was beneficial but too short to halt the slide toward revolt which finally occurred in A.D. 66.

On arrival, Festus was immediately faced with the problem of Paul who had been left under arrest by Felix. His understanding of Jewish law and religion at the time was slight. To win favor with the Jewish establishment, Festus proposed to hear Paul's case in Jerusalem rather than the civil capital of Caesarea. Paul was well aware both of the dangers this involved and of the long-term value for Christianity if a successful defense could be presented before Emperor Nero. He therefore exercised his right as a Roman citizen to appeal to Caesar. In those circumstances, Festus had no choice but to send Paul to Rome, and he did so. (See Acts 25, 26.)

5185. φθάνω phthanō verb

Arrive, precede, attain.

Cognate:

προφθάνω prophthanō (4257)

Synonyms:

διέρχομαι dierchomai (1324)
ἐγγίζω engizō (1443)
ἐπέρχομαι eperchomai (1889)
ἔρχομαι erchomai (2048)
ἐφικνέομαι ephikneomai (2167)
ἥκω hēkō (2223)
καταντάω katantaō (2628)
παραβάλλω paraballō (3708)
παραγίνομαι paraginomai (3716)
παρέρχομαι parerchomai (3790)
παρίστημι paristēmi (3798)
προσέρχομαι proserchomai (4193)
προσάγω prosagō (4175)
προσεγγίζω prosengizō (4189)
προσέρχομαι proserchomai (4193)
προσπορεύομαι prosporeuomai (4223)
συνίστημι sunistēmi (4771)

אָמֵץ 'āmēts (563), Be strong; hithpael: manage (1 Kgs 12:18).

דָּבַק dāvaq (1740), Cling, stick; hiphil: overtake (Jgs 20:42).

יָגָה yāghâh (3122), Hiphil: remove (2 Sm 20:13).

נָגַע nāgha' (5236), Qal: be near, come (Jgs 20:34, Ezr 3:1, Neh 7:73 [8:1]); hiphil: meet, happen (2 Chr 28:9, Eccl 8:14).

1. ἔφθασεν ephthasen 3sing indic aor act
2. ἐφθάσαμεν ephthasamen 1pl indic aor act
3. φθάσωμεν phthasōmen 1pl subj aor act
4. ἔφθακεν ephthaken 3sing indic perf act

1 then the kingdom of God **is come** unto you. .... Matt 12:28
1 no doubt the kingdom of God **is come** upon you... Luke 11:20
1 **hath not attained** to the law of righteousness. .... Rom 9:31
2 for we **are come** as far as to you also .... 2 Co 10:14
2 Nevertheless, whereto we **have already attained**, ... Phlp 3:16
1 for the wrath **is come** upon them to the uttermost... 1 Th 2:16
3 shall not **prevent** them which are asleep. 4:15

Classical Greek

The verb *phthanō* occurs in Greek literature from the time of Homer (Eighth Century B.C.). In classical Greek it is used with the connotation of priority (doing something or coming before someone or something else), for example, overtaking someone else in a footrace. It was also used to convey the notion of having done something previously or of anticipating something, such as a coming storm (*Liddell-Scott*). The papyri, for example, include this statement: "I have already written to you." It was also used of simply coming or arriving with or without prepositions (*Moulton-Milligan*). Josephus also used it in the original sense of priority when he wrote that Ahimaaz *arrived before* Chushi with the news of Joab's victory (*Antiquities* 7.10.4).

Septuagint Usage

In the Septuagint *phthanō* is used with the basic idea of priority. "One must rise before the sun to give thee thanks" (Wisdom of Solomon 16:28). But it is also used with the sense of simply arriving or coming (the idea of priority being lost). For example, the priests and Levites came on the seventh of the month (Nehemiah 7:73 [LXX 8:1]), and the time came (Daniel 7:22). Another use is with prepositions following, for example, "come against" (Judges 20:34) and "come unto" (Daniel 7:13).

New Testament Usage

The original sense of priority occurs only once in the New Testament: "We which are alive and remain unto the coming of the Lord shall not *prevent* them which are asleep" (1 Thessalonians 4:15). The KJV's "prevent" means "to precede." On other occasions it is used with a preposition without the idea of priority. With the preposition *epi* (1894) it means "to come upon" (Matthew 12:28; 1 Thessalonians 2:16), with *eis* (1506B) it means "to attain" (Romans 9:31; Philippians 3:16), and with *achri* (884) it means "to come as far as" (2 Corinthians 10:14).

Strong 5348, Bauer 856, Moulton-Milligan 666-67, Kittel 9:88-92, Liddell-Scott 1926-27.

5186. φθαρτός phthartos adj

Perishable, corruptible.

מָשְׁחָת moshchāth (5076), Defect (Lv 22:25—Codex Alexandrinus and some Vaticanus texts only).

1. **φθαρτόν phtharton** nom/acc sing masc/neu
2. **φθαρτοῦ phthartou** gen sing masc
3. **φθαρτῆς phthartēs** gen sing fem
4. **φθαρτοῖς phthartois** dat pl neu

2 into an image made like to **corruptible** man, ... Rom 1:23
1 Now they do it to obtain a **corruptible** crown; .... 1 Co 9:25
1 For this **corruptible** must put on incorruption, ... 15:53
1 this **corruptible** shall have put on incorruption, ... 15:54
4 that ye were not redeemed with **corruptible things**, ... 1 Pt 1:18
3 Being born again, not of **corruptible** seed, ... 1:23

Classical Greek

Phthartos is an adjective related to *phtheirō* (5188), "destroy, ruin." It refers to that which is perishable or subject to decay or destruction (*Bauer*). It is opposed to that which is *aidios* (126), "eternal," or *aphthartos* (855), "imperishable." *Phthartos* may refer to persons or things.

Septuagint Usage

In the Septuagint *phthartos* appears five times. Leviticus 22:25 forbids the offering of animals which are "corrupted" or deformed. Wisdom of Solomon 9:15 declares that a "*perishable* body weighs down the soul" (RSV). In 14:8 *phthartos* describes an idol made with hands. Second Maccabees 7:16 describes Antiochus as *phthartos*, "mortal."

New Testament Usage

When the word refers to persons it denotes "being subject to the processes that lead to death" (Romans 1:23). In 1 Corinthians 15:53,54 Paul used *phthartos* in parallel with *thnētos* (2326), "mortal": "For this corruptible (*phthartos*) must put on incorruption, and this mortal (*thnētos*) must put on immortality." Paul employed this literary parallelism to emphasize and climax his absolute certainty of a future Christian resurrection.

Phthartos may also refer to things, such as crowns (1 Corinthians 9:25), silver and gold (1 Peter 1:18), or seed (1 Peter 1:23). The idea in 1 Peter 1:18 is not that gold is subject to rust and decay but that it is one of the temporal things of this world. This, then, is contrasted with the permanency of the spiritual, such as Christ's sacrifice for sin. The reference to that which is passing may also lie behind its use in 1 Corinthians 9:25.

Strong 5349, Bauer 857, Kittel 9:93-106, Liddell-Scott 1927, Colin Brown 2:468.

5187. φθέγγομαι phthengomai verb

Utter, speak.

Synonyms:

ἀναγγέλλω anangellō (310)
ἀνατίθημι anatithēmi (392)
ἀπαγγέλλω apangellō (514)
ἀποδείκνυμι apodeiknumi (579)
ἀποκρίνω apokrinō (605B)
διαλέγομαι dialegomai (1250)
ἐρεύγομαι ereugomai (2027)
καταγγέλλω katangellō (2576)
κηρύσσω kērussō (2756)
λαλέω laleō (2953)
λέγω legō (2978)
ὁμιλέω homileō (3519)
φημί phēmi (5183)
φωνέω phōneō (5291)

דָּבַר dāvar (1744), Piel: speak (Jb 13:7).

נָבַע nāvaʻ (5218), Touch, reach; hiphil: utter, pour out (Pss 78:2 [77:2], 94:4 [93:4]).

עָנָה ʻānāh (6257), Shout, answer (Jer 51:14 [28:14], Hb 2:11).

שִׂיחַ sîach (7943), Talk about (Jgs 5:10—Codex Alexandrinus only).

שָׁאַג shā'agh (8057), Roar (Am 1:2).

תָּפַף tāphaph (8943), Polel: beat (Na 2:7).

1. **φθεγγόμενοι phthengomenoi** nom pl masc part pres mid
2. **φθέγγεσθαι phthengesthai** inf pres mid
3. **φθεγξάμενον phthenxamenon** nom/acc sing neu part aor mid

2 called them, and commanded them not to **speak** ..... Acts 4:18
3 the dumb ass **speaking** with man's voice .... 2 Pt 2:16
1 when they **speak** great swelling words of vanity, ... 2:18

Classical Greek

Phthengomai means "to produce a sound," the opposite of remaining silent. It can also mean "to say something loudly and clearly." In classical Greek it is used of any sound or voice, whether made by something living or not. It can refer to an utterance or cry of a person; the whinny of a horse; the creaking of a door; the sound of a musical instrument; or even the sound of thunder (see *Liddell-Scott*).

Septuagint Usage

In the Septuagint *phthengomai* appears several times. It can mean simply "to speak." Job asked, "Will you *speak* deceitfully" (13:7). In Psalm 119:172 (LXX 118:172) the Psalmist cries, "My tongue shall *speak* of thy word." It has the sense of "beating" in conjunction with sorrow and moaning in Nahum 2:7.

New Testament Usage

It occurs three times in the New Testament. The general sense of the word is in Acts 4:18 where the Jewish leaders commanded Peter and John not to speak at all or teach in the name of Jesus. They wanted them to remain perfectly silent about Christ—to stop "proclaiming" Him as the Messiah. The basic idea is also seen in 2 Peter 2:18 where it refers to the boastful and hollow words of false prophets. They produced much sound, but signified nothing. *Phthengomai* focuses on the sound itself rather than the specific content of any utterance (Louw and Nida, *Greek-English Lexicon*, 1:398).

STRONG 5350, BAUER 857, MOULTON-MILLIGAN 667, LIDDELL-SCOTT 1927.

5188. φθείρω phtheirō verb

To destroy, corrupt, defile, ruin, spoil.

COGNATES:

ἀδιαφθορία adiaphthoria (89)
ἀφθαρσία aphtharsia (854)
διαφθείρω diaphtheirō (1305)
διαφθορά diaphthora (1306)
καταφθείρω kataphtheirō (2673)
φθορά phthora (5193)

SYNONYMS:

ἀνατρέπω anatrepō (394)
ἀπόλλυμι apollumi (616)
ἀφανίζω aphanizō (846)
διαφθείρω diaphtheirō (1305)
καθαιρέω kathaireō (2479)
καταλύω kataluō (2617)
καταργέω katargeō (2643)
καταστρέφω katastrephō (2660)
καταφθείρω kataphtheirō (2673)
κενόω kenoō (2729)
λύω luō (3061)
ὀλοθρεύω olothreuō (3508)
πορθέω portheō (4058)

בָּקַק bāqaq (1265), Lay waste; niphal: be plundered (Is 24:3).

חָבַל chāval (2341), Pledge; piel: destroy (Is 54:16).

חֲבַל chăval (A2342), Destroy; hithpaal: be destroyed (Dn 2:44, 7:14—Aramaic).

נָבֵל nāval (5209), Wither (Is 24:4).

נוּס nûs̱ (5308), Abate (Dt 34:7).

שָׁחַת shāchath (8271), Niphal: be corrupt (Gn 6:11); piel: be deeply corrupted (Hos 9:9); hiphil: cut off (Lv 19:27); waste, destroy (1 Chr 20:1, Dn 8:24).

1. φθείρει phtheirei 3sing indic pres act
2. φθείρουσιν phtheirousin 3pl indic pres act
3. ἐφθείραμεν ephtheiramen 1pl indic aor act
4. φθερεῖ phtherei 3sing indic fut act
5. ἔφθειρεν ephtheiren 3sing indic imperf act
6. φθείρονται phtheirontai 3pl indic pres mid
7. φθειρόμενον phtheiromenon acc sing masc part pres mid
8. φθαρῇ phtharē 3sing subj aor pass
9. φθαρήσονται phtharēsontai 3pl indic fut pass

1 If any man **defile** the temple of God, ... 1 Co 3:17
4 defile the temple of God, him **shall** God **destroy**; 3:17
2 evil communications **corrupt** good manners............ 15:33
3 wronged no man, we **have corrupted** no man,....... 2 Co 7:2
8 so your minds **should be corrupted**.................... 11:3
7 which is **corrupt** according to the deceitful lusts;..... Eph 4:22
9 and like beasts they too **will perish**. (NIV).......... 2 Pt 2:12
6 in those things they **corrupt themselves**.............. Jude 1:10
5 which **did corrupt** the earth with her fornication,.... Rev 19:2

The primary meaning of this verb is "to destroy," particularly by means of corrupting. It may convey a literal sense or, as is generally true in the seven New Testament texts where it is used, a figurative one. The context usually clarifies the significance of *phtheirō*. When used in the sphere of religion and morality, it refers to ruining or corrupting a person's inner life, either by false instruction or by immoral conduct. This spoiling of another's character is often accomplished by means of misleading tactics.

Classical Greek

In classical Greek as early as Homer (Eighth Century B.C.) the primary meaning is "to destroy." Epicurus, for one, used it in the literal sense of "passing away, cease to be" (*Liddell-Scott*); but it often had a figurative meaning. For example, *phtheirō* was sometimes used of "seducing a female," of "women pining away," or of "wandering off" (ibid.). Even the simple meaning of "to kill" is common in literature with reference to battles (Harder, "phtheirō," *Kittel*, 9:93). "A literal sense is seen . . . where provision is made against the nurse's 'spoiling' her milk" (*Moulton-Milligan*).

Septuagint Usage

In the Septuagint *phtheirō* sometimes means "to be morally corrupted" (as in Genesis 6:11 and Hosea 9:9) or to destroy (Exodus 10:15). It is equivalent to the Hebrew *shāchath*, which means "to become corrupt" in the niphal stem and "to wipe out, ruin, corrupt" in the piel stem (Harder, "phtheirō," *Kittel*, 9:96).

New Testament Usage

New Testament usage also is varied. First Corinthians 3:17 uses *phtheirō* in two different senses, warning that if anyone "corrupts" the church, God will "destroy" him. Unworthy associates will "corrupt" or "lead astray" the upright (1 Corinthians 15:33; 2 Corinthians 7:2; 11:3), just as Eve was led astray. Our personal evil desires or lack of knowledge also "corrupt" or "destroy" us (Ephesians 4:22; Jude 10). And the great prostitute of Revelation 19:2 "ruins" the earth by her adulteries. Destruction is the destiny of false teachers (2 Peter 2:12).

STRONG 5351, BAUER 857, MOULTON-MILLIGAN 667, KITTEL 9:93-106, LIDDELL-SCOTT 1928, COLIN BROWN 1:467-69.

5189. φθινοπωρινός phthinopōrinos adj

Autumnal (late autumn).

1. φθινοπωρινά phthinopōrina nom/acc pl neu

1 trees whose fruit withereth, without fruit, ... Jude 1:12

This adjective means "belonging to late autumn" (*Bauer*) and is used only once in the New Testament. Related to *phthinō*, "to wane or waste away," and *opōra* (3566), "autumn," *phthinopōrinos* is applied (Jude 12) to certain godless men who, like leafless and fruitless trees at the close of autumn, have failed to achieve their purpose in existence (ibid.).

STRONG 5352, BAUER 857, MOULTON-MILLIGAN 667, LIDDELL-SCOTT 1928.

5190. φθόγγος phthongos noun

Sound, (musical) tone.

קַו qāw (7241), Line? sound? (Ps 19:4 [18:4]).

1. φθόγγος phthongos nom sing masc
2. φθόγγοις phthongois dat pl masc

1 Yes verily, their sound went into all the earth, ... Rom 10:18
2 except they give a distinction in the sounds, ... 1 Co 14:7

This word denotes a clear and distinct sound, whether of a musical instrument (1 Corinthians 14:7) or of the human voice. Romans 10:18, in quoting Psalm 19:4, compares the gospel message to a voice "like that of the starry sky proclaiming God's glory to all the earth" (Vincent, *Word Studies in the New Testament*, 3:117).

STRONG 5353, BAUER 857, MOULTON-MILLIGAN 667, LIDDELL-SCOTT 1929.

5191. φθονέω phthoneō verb

To envy, be jealous of, resent.

COGNATE:
φθόνος phthonos (5192)

SYNONYM:
ζηλόω zēloō (2189)

1. φθονοῦντες phthonountes
nom pl masc part pres act

1 provoking one another, envying one another. .... Gal 5:26

In its single New Testament occurrence *phthoneō* means "to be envious" or "jealous" of someone (Galatians 5:26). Elsewhere the word sometimes means "to have ill will or malice" or "to hold a grudge against someone" (*Liddell-Scott*). It is closely related to the noun *phthonos* (5192), "envy," which Trench (*Synonymns of the New Testament*, pp.82-86) believes always has an evil signification. Used with *tini* (see 4948), "someone," it can mean to simply "dislike" or "be resentful" without a grudge or jealousy being involved (*Bauer*).

STRONG 5354, BAUER 857, MOULTON-MILLIGAN 667, LIDDELL-SCOTT 1929-30, COLIN BROWN 1:557-58.

5192. φθόνος phthonos noun

Envy, jealousy.

CROSS-REFERENCE:
φθονέω phthoneō (5191)

1. φθόνος phthonos nom sing masc
2. φθόνου phthonou gen sing masc
3. φθόνῳ phthonō dat sing masc
4. φθόνον phthonon acc sing masc
5. φθόνοι phthonoi nom pl masc
6. φθόνους phthonous acc pl masc

4 For he knew that for envy they had delivered him. Matt 27:18
4 that the chief priests had delivered him for envy... Mark 15:10
2 full of envy, murder, debate, deceit, malignity; .... Rom 1:29
5 Envyings, murders, drunkenness, revellings, ... Gal 5:21
4 Some ... preach Christ even of envy and strife; ...... Phlp 1:15
1 whereof cometh envy, strife, railings, ... 1 Tm 6:4
3 living in malice and envy, hateful, and hating .... Tit 3:3
4 The spirit that dwelleth in us lusteth to envy? .... Jas 4:5
6 and hypocrisies, and envies, and all evil speakings, ... 1 Pt 2:1

Classical Greek

Classical evidence shows that the word *phthonos* denotes "ill will" or a "desire to harm others," especially stemming from "envy" or "jealousy" of others' good fortune. From this it refers to an act of "refusal" based on feelings of envy or jealousy (*Liddell-Scott*).

Septuagint Usage

The use of *phthonos* (as well as *phthoneō* [5191] and *phthoneros*) in the Septuagint is restricted to the apocryphal writings. One interesting text illustrating the use of *phthonos* is found in the Wisdom of Solomon: "But through the devil's envy (*phthonos*) death entered the world" (2:24, RSV). Here we see the devil's desire to be like

God; and his jealousy of men who were created in God's image caused the entrance of death and corruption into the world. "Envious slander" caused Daniel to be cast to the lions (3 Maccabees 6:7). Thus *phthonos* describes that which is particularly evil, deceitful, and covetous (cf. Sirach 14:10; Tobit 4:7,16).

New Testament Usage

The Gospels of Mark and Matthew observe that "envy" prompted the chief priests to deliver Jesus to Pilate (Mark 15:10; Matthew 27:18; cf. 3 Maccabees 6:7). Thus we note "envy" is not passive but active, being accomplished in treacherous acts.

Unlike *zēlos* (2188), "jealousy," which may have a positive meaning, *phthonos* almost always carries a negative sense (see Trench's discussion on the differences in *Synonyms of the New Testament*, pp.82-86; but see below on James 4:5). Paul regularly couples it with other heinous sins in his "vice-lists" (e.g., Romans 1:29; Galatians 5:21; cf. 1 Timothy 6:4; Titus 3:3, of former life-styles; see also 1 Peter 2:1).

James 4:5 presents an interpreting challenge. It reads: "Or do you think Scripture says without reason that the spirit he caused to live in us tends toward envy . . . ?" (NIV). First, we do not know to which Scripture passage James is referring (on this problem see Davids, *New International Greek Testament Commentary, James*, p.162ff.).

Second, the subject of this verse may be: (1) God; (2) the Holy Spirit; or (3) the human spirit (number 3 is the NIV's choice, but cf. the RSV which takes God as the subject). Because *phthonos* generally has such unfavorable overtones, and because the idea of the human spirit which envies (against) God is in keeping with later Jewish anthropology which saw man as having a good and a bad "impulse" (*yetser*), some interpret "the spirit" (*to pneuma*) as the human spirit. This is viewed as resisting God and choosing instead the ways of the world (cf. James 4:4).

Others see James as using *phthonos* positively as a synonym for *zēlos* (cf. 1 Maccabees 8:16; 1 Clement 3:2; 4:7) and choose to read God as the subject. Thus it is God who "yearns jealously" (RSV) over the spirit He has put in us (on this concept see Genesis 6:3 [LXX 6:4]; 7:15; Psalm 104:29,30 [LXX 103:29,30]). Of course this approach is entirely in keeping with the Old Testament truth that the Lord God is a jealous God (Exodus 20:5; 34:14; Deuteronomy 4:24). Therefore, as we tend to "become friends with the world," God, because of His "jealous grace," is wanting to rescue us (cf. 4:7ff.).

Strong 5355, Bauer 857, Moulton-Milligan 667-68, Liddell-Scott 1930, Colin Brown 1:557-58.

5193. φθορά phthora noun

Destruction, ruin, deterioration, corruption, loss.

Cognate:
φθείρω phtheirō (5188)

Synonym:
διαφθορά diaphthora (1306)

בָּקַק bāqaq (1265), Lay waste; niphal: be plundered (Is 24:3).

חֲבָל chăvāl (A2343), Harm (Dn 3:25—Aramaic).

חֶבֶל chevel (2347), Destruction (Mi 2:10).

מַשְׁחִית mashchîth (5072), Deathly pale color (Dn 10:8).

נָבַל nāval (5209), Wear out (Ex 18:18).

שַׁחַת shachath (8273), Pit (Ps 103:4 [102:4]).

1. **φθορά phthora** nom sing fem
2. **φθορᾶς phthoras** gen sing fem
3. **φθορᾷ phthora** dat sing fem
4. **φθοράν phthoran** acc sing fem

2 shall be delivered from the bondage of **corruption** ... Rom 8:21
3 is sown in **corruption**; it is raised in incorruption: .. 1 Co 15:42
1 neither doth **corruption** inherit incorruption. 15:50
4 shall of the flesh reap **corruption**; .... Gal 6:8
4 Which all are to **perish** with the using; .... Col 2:22
2 having escaped the **corruption** that is in the world ... 2 Pt 1:4
4 brute beasts, made to be taken and **destroyed**, ... 2:12
3 and shall utterly perish in their own **corruption**; 2:12
2 they themselves are the servants **of corruption**: 2:19

Classical Greek

A cognate of the verb *phtheirō* (5188), "to destroy," *phthora* signifies a destruction or corruption that reduces something to an inferior condition. It has a literal usage in connection with physical objects; however, at other times it is used figuratively, as when applied to moral and ethical issues. In the physical sense this corruption is decomposition, deterioration, decay, and death. Its figurative use points to the ruin or disintegration of one's character, a display of depravity.

Classical usage exhibits these shades of meaning. Hippocrates wrote of the world coming into existence and "passing away," and it is used in philosophy with this meaning of "ceasing to be" (*Liddell-Scott*). One writer reported the case of a man whose body "decomposed" while he was still living (*Bauer*). *Phthora* sometimes means a destruction by "abortion" or "miscarriage";

closely related, a *phthorion* was a means of producing an abortion (*Bauer*). In classical (and later Greek) literature it also means the seduction or rape of a maiden (ibid.).

Septuagint Usage

The Septuagint applies this word to cases of ruining one's health (Exodus 18:18), moral depravity, and religious unfaithfulness (Micah 2:10). "God is the one who can redeem life from destruction (*phthora*, Psalm 103:4)" (Merkel, "Destroy," *Colin Brown*, 1:468).

New Testament Usage

In the New Testament *phthora*'s primary thrust of "destruction" and "ruin" is often associated with a process of deterioration and decay. The term is mainly applied to the physical world which is in bondage to decay (Romans 8:21) and with its contents is certain to perish (Colossians 2:22). Wild beasts in it are destined to be killed (2 Peter 2:12); and human bodies decompose after death (1 Corinthians 15:42). *Phthora* is therefore the "corruptibility" which must pass away as our bodies "put on incorruption" (1 Corinthians 15:50). The word often is to be understood in an eschatological sense (Harder, "phtheirō," *Kittel*, 9:104).

However, this destruction is also a spiritual danger, a moral disintegration resulting from living unrighteously (Galatians 6:8; 2 Peter 2:19). *Phthora*, as a final consequence of depravity, is the opposite of eternal life and is connected with final judgment (2 Peter 2:12).

STRONG 5356, BAUER 858, MOULTON-MILLIGAN 668, KITTEL 9:93-106, LIDDELL-SCOTT 1930, COLIN BROWN 1:467-70.

5194. φιάλη phialē noun

Bowl, basin.

כּוֹס kôs̱ (3683), Cup (Prv 23:31).

מִזְרָק mizrāq (4353), Bowl (Nm 7:13,19, 1 Kgs 7:40, Zec 14:20).

עֲרוּגָה ʿărûghāh (6410), Flower bed (S/S 6:2 [6:1]).

קְשָׂוָה qaswāh (7472), Bowl (1 Chr 28:17).

1. φιάλην phialēn acc sing fem

2. φιάλας phialas acc pl fem

2 harps, and golden **vials** full of odours, ... Rev 5:8
2 seven golden **vials** full of the wrath of God, ... 15:7
2 and pour out the **vials** of the wrath of God 16:1
1 first went, and poured out his **vial** upon the earth; 16:2
1 the second angel poured out his **vial** upon the sea; 16:3
1 the third angel poured out his **vial** upon the rivers 16:4
1 the fourth angel poured out his **vial** upon the sun; 16:8
1 poured out his **vial** upon the seat of the beast; 16:10
1 And the sixth angel poured out his **vial** .... Rev 16:12
1 the seventh angel poured out his **vial** into the air; 16:17
2 one of the seven angels which had the seven **vials**, ... 17:1
2 had the seven **vials** full of the seven last plagues, ... 21:9

A *phialē* is a broad, flat, and shallow bowl rather than a small bottle as might be suggested by the rendering "vial" (KJV). Its features make it an appropriate vessel for boiling liquids or for pouring out libations in worship. Vine (*Expository Dictionary*, "Bowl") finds the word "suggestive of rapidity in the emptying of the contents." The Septuagint employs this word for basins used in the tabernacle or temple worship (e.g., Numbers 7:13). The New Testament uses *phialē* only in the Book of Revelation.

STRONG 5357, BAUER 858, MOULTON-MILLIGAN 668, LIDDELL-SCOTT 1930.

5195. φιλάγαθος philagathos adj

Loving goodness.

CROSS-REFERENCES:
ἀγαθός agathos (18)
φιλέω phileō (5205)

1. φιλάγαθον philagathon acc sing masc

1 But a lover of hospitality, a **lover of good** men, ... Tit 1:8

A compound form of *phileō* (5205), "to love," and *agathos* (18), "good," this adjective depicts the person who loves what is good. The word occurs only in Titus 1:8 as a qualification of a bishop; but its opposite, *aphilagathos* (858), "no lover of good," is found in 2 Timothy 3:3.

STRONG 5358, BAUER 858, MOULTON-MILLIGAN 668, KITTEL 1:18, LIDDELL-SCOTT 1931, COLIN BROWN 2:549.

5196. Φιλαδέλφεια Philadelpheia name

Philadelphia.

1. Φιλαδελφείᾳ Philadelpheia dat fem

2. Φιλαδέλφειαν Philadelpheian acc fem

2 and unto **Philadelphia**, and unto Laodicea. .... Rev 1:11
1 to the angel of the church in **Philadelphia** write; 3:7

A city in the west of Asia Minor, 60 miles inland from Smyrna. Its modern name is Alasehir. The church was addressed in one of the seven letters of Revelation (1:11; 3:7-13).

5197. φιλαδελφία philadelphia noun

Brotherly love, love toward brothers.

Cross-References:
ἀδελφός adelphos (79)
φιλέω phileō (5205)

1. **φιλαδελφία philadelphia** nom sing fem
2. **φιλαδελφίας philadelphias** gen sing fem
3. **φιλαδελφίᾳ philadelphia** dat sing fem
4. **φιλαδελφίαν philadelphian** acc sing fem

3 affectioned one to another with **brotherly love**; ..... Rom 12:10
2 But as touching **brotherly love** .... 1 Th 4:9
1 Let **brotherly love** continue. .... Heb 13:1
4 unto unfeigned **love of the brethren**, ... 1 Pt 1:22
4 And to godliness **brotherly kindness**; .... 2 Pt 1:7
3 and to **brotherly kindness** charity. 1:7

Philadelphia is love for brother, sister, or other near kinsmen. The noun is a compound of *adelphos* (79), "brother" or "near kinsman," and a root of *philia* (5210), "love, friendship, devotion, affection."

Classical Greek and Septuagint Usage

In its earliest appearances *philadelphia* denotes the love for blood brothers, sisters, and other family members (*Bauer*). This use predominates in classical sources and also in the Septuagint where *philadelphia* occurs three times, but only in the Apocrypha (4 Maccabees 13:23,26; 14:1). *Moulton-Milligan* indicates that secular documents of New Testament times share this meaning of "the love of those who are brothers by common descent . . . and . . . of kindness to sisters."

New Testament Usage

In the New Testament the definition extends to those who are brothers and sisters in the Christian faith, those who have entered the family of God. This spiritual "brotherly love" is commanded (Romans 12:10; Hebrews 13:1) and must be genuine rather than counterfeit (1 Peter 1:22). *Philadelphia* is a virtue that Christians must cultivate (2 Peter 1:7). In either its literal or figurative sense, then, *philadelphia* emphasizes a loving relationship among people closely connected, whether by kinship or by faith.

Strong 5360, Bauer 858, Moulton-Milligan 668, Kittel 1:144-46, Liddell-Scott 1931, Colin Brown 1:254,257; 2:547,549-50.

5198. φιλάδελφος philadelphos adj

Loving one's brother or sister.

Cross-References:
ἀδελφός adelphos (79)
φιλέω phileō (5205)

1. **φιλάδελφοι philadelphoi** nom pl masc

1 **love as brethren**, be pitiful, be courteous: .... 1 Pt 3:8

This word's meaning of "loving one's brother or sister," has been found on ancient gravestones (*Bauer*). It is a compound of *phileō* (5205), "to love," and *adelphos* (79), "brother, near kinsman." In 1 Peter 3:8 (its only usage in the New Testament) *philadelphos* conveys the idea of "loving as brethren."

Strong 5361, Bauer 858, Moulton-Milligan 668, Kittel 1:144-46, Liddell-Scott 1931, Colin Brown 1:254,257; 2:549.

5199. φίλανδρος philandros adj

Loving a husband.

Cross-References:
ἀνήρ anēr (433)
φιλέω phileō (5205)

1. **φιλάνδρους philandrous** acc pl fem

1 **to love their husbands**, to love their children, ... Tit 2:4

The New Testament uses this word only once, referring to the virtue of a young wife in loving her husband (Titus 2:4). Although this meaning of the adjective differs from its earlier classical sense of "loving men or masculine habits; lewd," it does correspond to its tender use in epitaphs (Vincent, *Word Studies in the New Testament*, 4:341).

Strong 5362, Bauer 858, Moulton-Milligan 668, Liddell-Scott 1931-32, Colin Brown 2:549.

5200. φιλανθρωπία philanthrōpia noun

Kindness, loving-kindness, kindheartedness.

Cross-References:
ἄνθρωπος anthrōpos (442)
φιλέω phileō (5205)

1. **φιλανθρωπία philanthrōpia** nom sing fem
2. **φιλανθρωπίαν philanthrōpian** acc sing fem

2 the barbarous people showed us no little **kindness**: ..Acts 28:2
1 love of God our Saviour **toward man** appeared, ... Tit 3:4

Classical Greek

Philanthrōpia, composed of the words *phileō* (5205), "to love," and *anthrōpos* (442), "man, mankind," has the meaning of loving-kindness extended to others. The word normally applies to specific expressions of humane feeling and kindness rather than to a generalized love for mankind as in our English word *philanthropy*.

Its earliest usage in classical Greek (Fifth Century B.C.) signifies "a friendly relation." The gods showed *philanthrōpia* to people, and kings to their subjects; such examples display a similar "benevolent condescension" (Luck, "philanthrōpia," *Kittel*, 9:107).

Secular usage in the New Testament world indicates *philanthrōpia* was in common use. It is recorded on inscriptions and papyrus fragments. These indicate a variety of meanings: benevolence, hospitality, humane feeling, kindness, and even courtesy (*Moulton-Milligan*).

Septuagint Usage

Although the Septuagint includes *philanthrōpia* five times, each is in the Apocrypha rather than the canonical text. They all maintain the classical sense and some speak of kindness toward the nations. (Cf. Esther 8:13; 2 Maccabees 6:22; 14:9; 3 Maccabees 3:15,18.)

New Testament Usage

In Acts 28:2 *philanthrōpia* fits this normal Greek usage: the residents of Malta showed *kindness* to Paul and his fellow victims of shipwreck. However, *philanthrōpia* is elevated to a higher significance in Titus 3:4, "The kindness and love (*philanthrōpia*) of God our Saviour toward man appeared." Here, the whole redemptive ministry of Christ is viewed as the supreme revelation of the highest *philanthrōpia*.

STRONG 5363, BAUER 858, MOULTON-MILLIGAN 668-69, KITTEL 9:107-12, LIDDELL-SCOTT 1932, COLIN BROWN 2:547,549,551.

5201. φιλανθρώπως philanthrōpōs adv

Humanely, kindly, benevolently.

CROSS-REFERENCES:

ἄνθρωπος anthrōpos (442)
φιλέω phileō (5205)

1. φιλανθρώπως philanthrōpōs

1 **And Julius courteously entreated Paul,............Acts 27:3**

This adverb is a compound form of *phileō* (5205), "to love," and *anthrōpos* (442), "man, mankind." It depicts actions taken "in a man-loving way," i.e., humanely, benevolently, philanthropically. The New Testament uses *philanthrōpōs* only in Acts 27:3 where the KJV translates it "courteously." Julius the centurion allowed Paul to "go to his friends and receive care" (NASB). It was a benevolent act to allow this. Vincent (*Word Studies in the New Testament*, 1:590f.) finds "humanely" preferable to "courteously," which suggests good manners rather than genuine kindness.

STRONG 5364, BAUER 858, MOULTON-MILLIGAN 669, KITTEL 9:107-12, LIDDELL-SCOTT 1932 (see "philanthrōpos"), COLIN BROWN 2:550.

5202. φιλαργυρία philarguria noun

Love of money, avarice.

COGNATES:

ἀργύριον argurion (688)
φιλάργυρος philarguros (5203)
φιλέω phileō (5205)

SYNONYM:

πλεονεξία pleonexia (3984)

1. φιλαργυρία philarguria nom sing fem

1 **For the love of money is the root of all evil:........1 Tm 6:10**

Like many New Testament words this noun combines two others: *phileō* (5205), "to love" or "have affection for," and *arguros* (690), "silver" (money). *Philarguria* is an unwarranted attachment to money which expresses itself in greed and miserliness. In contemporary Greek literature *philarguria* is often listed with other vices (see 4 Maccabees 1:26; 2:15 in which it appears in lists of vices conquered by reason). The New Testament uses it only in 1 Timothy 6:10, "The *love of money* is the root of all evil."

STRONG 5365, BAUER 859, MOULTON-MILLIGAN 669, LIDDELL-SCOTT 1932, COLIN BROWN 1:138; 2:550.

5203. φιλάργυρος philarguros adj

Avaricious, fond of money.

CROSS-REFERENCE:

φιλαργυρία philarguria (5202)

1. φιλάργυροι philarguroi nom pl masc

1 **And the Pharisees also, who were covetous,....... Luke 16:14**
1 **lovers of their own selves, covetous, boasters,.......2 Tm 3:2**

This adjective (*-os* ending as opposed to *philarguria* with *-ia*, a noun ending) describes those obsessed with concern for money and thus embodies the content of the words from which it comes: *phileō* (5205), "to love" or "have affection for," and *arguros* (690), "silver" (money). *Philarguros* is a cognate of *philarguria* (5202) and means "covetous" or "avaricious" in Luke 16:14 and 2 Timothy 3:2.

STRONG 5366, BAUER 859, MOULTON-MILLIGAN 669, LIDDELL-SCOTT 1932, COLIN BROWN 2:550.

5204. φίλαυτος philautos adj

Self-centered, selfish.

CROSS-REFERENCE:

φιλέω phileō (5205)

1. **φίλαυτοι philautoi** nom pl masc

1 For men shall be **lovers of their own selves,** .... 2 Tm 3:2

Philautos is a compound of the Greek words *phileō* (5205), "to love" or "to have affection for," and *autos* (840), "self." In classical Greek the term is used in a positive sense of "loving oneself" but more frequently in a bad sense of "selfishness" (*Liddell-Scott*). Philo of Alexandria linked *philautos* with *atheos* (112), "without God, godless" (*Bauer*). *Philautos*, "selfishness," is the first of 18 vices listed in 2 Timothy 3:2-5 as characteristics of people in the "last days."

Strong 5367, Bauer 859, Moulton-Milligan 669, Liddell-Scott 1932, Colin Brown 2:550.

5205. φιλέω phileō verb

Love, have affection for, delight in, like, kiss.

Cognates:

ἀφιλάγαθος aphilagathos (858)
ἀφιλάργυρος aphilarguros (859)
καταφιλέω kataphileō (2674)
προσφιλής prosphilēs (4233)
φιλάγαθος philagathos (5195)
φιλαδελφία philadelphia (5197)
φιλάδελφος philadelphos (5198)
φίλανδρος philandros (5199)
φιλανθρωπία philanthrōpia (5200)
φιλανθρώπως philanthrōpōs (5201)
φιλαργυρία philarguria (5202)
φιλάργυρος philarguros (5203)
φίλαυτος philautos (5204)
φιλήδονος philēdonos (5206)
φίλημα philēma (5207)
φιλία philia (5210)
φιλόθεος philotheos (5214)
φιλονεικία philoneikia (5216)
φιλόνεικος philoneikos (5217)
φιλοξενία philoxenia (5218)
φιλόξενος philoxenos (5219)
φιλοπρωτεύω philoprōteuō (5220)
φίλος philos (5220B)
φιλοσοφία philosophia (5221)
φιλόσοφος philosophos (5222)
φιλόστοργος philostorgos (5223)
φίλος philos (5224)
φιλότεκνος philoteknos (5225)
φιλοτιμέομαι philotimeomai (5226)
φιλοφρόνως philophronōs (5227)
φιλόφρων philophrōn (5228)

Synonyms:

ἀγαπάω agapaō (25)
καταφιλέω kataphileō (2674)

אָהֵב 'āhēv (154), Qal: love (Gn 27:4, Prv 29:3, Hos 3:1); piel: love (Jer 22:22).

נָשַׁק nāshaq (5583), Qal: kiss (Gn 27:26f., Job 31:27, S/S 1:2); piel: kiss (Gn 29:13).

רֵעַ rēa' (7739), Friend (Lam 1:2).

1. **φιλῶ philō** 1sing indic/subj pres act
2. **φιλεῖς phileis** 2sing indic pres act
3. **φιλεῖ philei** 3sing indic pres act
4. **φιλοῦσιν philousin** 3pl indic pres act
5. **φιλῶν philōn** nom sing masc part pres act
6. **φιλούντων philountōn** gen pl masc part pres act
7. **φιλοῦντας philountas** acc pl masc part pres act
8. **φιλήσω philēsō** 1sing subj aor act
9. **φιλῆσαι philēsai** inf aor act
10. **πεφιλήκατε pephilēkate** 2pl indic perf act
11. **ἐφίλει ephilei** 3sing indic imperf act

4 for they **love** to pray standing in the synagogues .... Matt 6:5
5 He that **loveth** father or mother more than me 10:37
5 and he that **loveth** son or daughter more than me 10:37
4 And **love** the uppermost rooms at feasts, ... 23:6
8 Whomsoever I **shall kiss,** that same is he: 26:48
8 saying, Whomsoever I **shall kiss,** that same is he; Mark 14:44
6 and **love** greetings in the markets, ... Luke 20:46
9 Judas, ... drew near unto Jesus to **kiss** him. 22:47
3 For the Father **loveth** the Son, ... John 5:20
2 Lord, behold, he whom thou **lovest** is sick. 11:3
11 Then said the Jews, Behold how he **loved** him! 11:36
5 He that **loveth** his life shall lose it; 12:25
11 the world would **love** his own: 15:19
3 For the Father himself **loveth** you, ... 16:27
10 Father ... loveth you, because ye **have loved** me, ... 16:27
11 and to the other disciple, whom Jesus **loved,** 20:2
1 Yea, Lord; thou knowest that I **love** thee. 21:15
1 Yea, Lord; thou knowest that I **love** thee. 21:16
2 Simon, son of Jonas, **lovest** thou me? 21:17
2 he said unto him the third time, **Lovest** thou me? 21:17
1 knowest all things; thou knowest that I **love** thee. 21:17
3 If any man **love** not the Lord Jesus Christ, ... 1 Co 16:22
7 Greet them **that love** us in the faith. .... Tit 3:15
1 As many as I **love,** I rebuke and chasten: .... Rev 3:19
5 idolaters, and whosoever **loveth** and maketh a lie. 22:15

Classical Greek

Phileō, "love, have affection for," is quite common in Greek antiquity, exhibiting a wide semantic range. The *phil-* stem became the basis for a rich variety of compounds (e.g., *philadelpheia* [5197], *philanthrōpia* [5200]). The kind of emotions encompassed by *phileō* include the innate love of a parent for a child or that of a husband for his wife. It can also indicate the kind of love friends have for one another. Under other circumstances it can describe sensual love between a man and a woman (*Liddell-Scott*). It was also used of "greeting" (with a kiss) or "kissing." Stählin notes that while *phileō* often denotes an attraction to those who belong (e.g., love for a family member), it shifts at times to include those things or people which are chosen (e.g., friends) and may even denote sensual love between the sexes ("phileō," *Kittel*, 9:115f.). Other general meanings include "to like doing (something), to value," or "to be accustomed to" (*Liddell-Scott*).

Stählin further observes that in classical Greek the distinction between *phileō* and *agapaō* (25) is at times vague or negligible. *Phileō* occurs more frequently in secular Greek than *agapaō*, a circumstance reversed in the Septuagint as well as in the New Testament. These are important reminders before observing the Biblical text. A common oversimplification in seeking to distinguish between *phileō* and *agapaō* is discussed by Stählin who contends that when a distinction could be made, it was one of intensity; *phileō* more closely approximating "I like" and *agapaō*, "I love" ("phileō," *Kittel*, 9:115f.). Such generalizations do not reflect the diversity with which *phileō* is used in classical or New Testament Greek.

Septuagint Usage

Compared to *agapaō*, *phileō* occurs only infrequently in the Septuagint but continues its broad usage. Genesis contains the most instances of *phileō* (11 times). It first appears in Isaac's request that Esau prepare him the kind of food "he likes" (Genesis 27:4,9,14; Hebrew *'āhēv*). Then, in the same context, it refers to Isaac's request that Esau (so he thinks) come and "kiss" him (Genesis 27:26,27; Hebrew *nāshaq*; cf. Genesis 50:1; Proverbs 7:13; Tobit 5:16). Later it is used when Jacob "kissed" Rachel (Genesis 29:11; cf. Tobit 5:16) as well as when Laban greeted Jacob with a kiss (Genesis 29:13). The love between a man and a woman is to be understood in Tobit 6:17 (cf. Song of Songs 1:2; 8:1).

In a religious connection Wisdom "loves" (*agapaō*) those that "love" (*phileō*) her (Proverbs 8:17). The "lovers" (*agapōntōn*) and "friends" (*philountes*) have rejected Jerusalem in her distress (Lamentations 1:2). These lovers and friends are figures for the faithless allies of Israel. Only YHWH was to be the protector of Israel, the One who fought her battles. Thus, the prophets regarded it as the most serious form of apostasy and is often pictured as adultery (cf. Hosea 2:1-13 where Israel put herself under the rule and protection of political alliances).

New Testament Usage

The use of *phileō* in the New Testament does not depart from the classical pattern except for being less frequent. It describes the affection between members of the same family. This kind of affection may stand in the way of one becoming a disciple (cf. John 12:25; 15:19 with Matthew 10:37). It also depicts the affection that members of God's household share with one another (Titus 3:15).

Judas signaled the religious leaders by *kissing* Jesus (Matthew 26:48; Mark 14:44; cf. Luke 22:47). This gesture of greeting and friendship must have pained Jesus deeply. The betrayal took place at a time that would otherwise be a time of joyous response and affection.

The notion of "liking, enjoying" comes through most plainly in Jesus' condemnation of religiosity's "love" of public attention (Matthew 6:5; Luke 20:46). This kind of satisfaction, which is grounded in human fallible judgment, is exactly the opposite of God's desire for mankind (cf. Matthew 23:6; Revelation 22:15).

In a religious context *phileō* can speak of God's love for man (Revelation 3:19) or man's love for God (1 Corinthians 16:22; cf. John 16:27). John used it of the Father's great love for the Son (John 5:20) and of the Father's love for humanity (John 16:27). Lazarus was loved by Jesus (John 11:3,36).

As seen above, *phileō* is used at times to convey qualities of love typically associated only with *agapaō*. Consequently, some scholars see no significance in the alternating use of these words when John reported the conversation Jesus had with Peter by the Sea of Galilee (John 21:15-17). The first two times Jesus asked Peter if he loved Him the word *agapaō* is used; Peter's response is conveyed with the word *phileō*. The third time Jesus asked this question John used a form of the word *phileō*, but again John recorded Peter's response with *phileō*. Other scholars see a significance in this; that Peter, who had formerly asserted his love for Jesus so strongly was now unsure of himself. He could not bring himself to use the stronger word. They infer Jesus had a reason for changing to the ideas or emotions portrayed in the word *phileō*.

STRONG 5368, BAUER 859, MOULTON-MILLIGAN 669-70, KITTEL 9:114-46, LIDDELL-SCOTT 1933, COLIN BROWN 2:538-39,542-43,547-51.

5206. φιλήδονος philēdonos adj

Pleasure-seeking, given to pleasure.

CROSS-REFERENCES:

ἡδονή hēdonē (2220)
φιλέω phileō (5205)

1. φιλήδονοι philēdonoi nom pl masc

1 lovers of pleasures more than lovers of God;........2 Tm 3:4

A compound of *phileō* (5205), "to love" or "to have affection for," and *hēdonē* (2220), "pleasure, lust, strong desire," *philēdonos* is found from the Second Century B.C. (Polybius) and means "fond of pleasure" (*Liddell-Scott*). Used as an adjective in 2 Timothy 3:4, *philēdonos* describes one whose search for pleasure is so all-consuming as to displace one's *philotheos* (5214), "love for God."

STRONG 5369, BAUER 859, MOULTON-MILLIGAN 670, KITTEL 2:909-26, LIDDELL-SCOTT 1934, COLIN BROWN 1:458,460; 2:550.

5207. φίλημα philēma noun

Kiss.

CROSS-REFERENCE:

φιλέω phileō (5205)

נְשִׁיקָה nᵉshîqāh (5573), Kiss (Prv 27:6, S/S 1:2).

1. φιλήματι philēmati dat sing neu

2. φίλημα philēma nom/acc sing neu

2 Thou gavest me no **kiss**: but this woman since...... Luke 7:45
1 Judas, betrayest thou the Son of man with a **kiss**?..... 22:48
1 Salute one another with an holy **kiss**.............. Rom 16:16
1 Greet ye one another with an holy **kiss**........... 1 Co 16:20
1 Greet one another with an holy **kiss**............... 2 Co 13:12
1 Greet all the brethren with an holy **kiss**............ 1 Th 5:26
1 Greet ye one another with a **kiss** of charity.......... 1 Pt 5:14

This noun denoting a "kiss" belongs to the family of words with the root *phil-*, "love" or "affection," the relationship being that a kiss is a token or symbol of love. In the ancient world the kiss was used in friendly greetings as well as in affectionate farewells. For Jewish rabbis the kiss was a common courtesy greeting, as when Judas kissed Jesus (Luke 22:48). For Christ and the church the kiss was a token of brotherhood (Luke 7:45) and an expression of holy love and equality (1 Thessalonians 5:26; 1 Peter 5:14).

STRONG 5370, BAUER 859, MOULTON-MILLIGAN 670, KITTEL 9:114-46, LIDDELL-SCOTT 1934, COLIN BROWN 2:538,547-49.

5208. Φιλήμων Philēmōn name

Philemon.

1. Φιλήμονι Philēmoni dat masc

2. Φιλήμονα Philēmona acc masc

1 unto **Philemon** our dearly beloved,................. Phlm 1:1

Philemon is known only from the letter of Paul which is addressed to him (Philemon 1) and by what we may infer from it. Names and circumstances in common link the letter closely to Paul's letter to the Colossians (Epaphras in Colossians 1:7 and Philemon 23; Onesimus in Colossians 4:9 and Philemon 10; Archippus in Colossians 4:17 and Philemon 1; Paul was in prison when he wrote Colossians 4:3,18 and Philemon 10,23).

Philemon was apparently a leading Christian of Colossae. A slave of his, Onesimus (the name simply means "profitable") had run away and perhaps stolen from him (cf. verses 18f.). Paul makes a play on this meaning in the epistle. Paul had led Onesimus to faith in Christ (verse 10) and sent him back with an appeal to Philemon (verses 17-21) to welcome and forgive him. This was no light appeal since the penalty for a runaway slave could be death.

5209. Φίλητος Philētos name

Philetus.

1. Φίλητος Philētos nom masc

1 a canker: of whom is Hymenaeus and **Philetus**;..... 2 Tm 2:17

Philetus was condemned in 2 Timothy 2:17f. as a misled and misleading thinker, who was teaching with Hymeneus that "the resurrection is past already." This overspiritualized understanding of the resurrection of the dead was probably an early form of gnosticism.

5210. φιλία philia noun

Friendship, fondness, devotion.

CROSS-REFERENCE:

φιλέω phileō (5205)

אַהַב 'ahav (156), Something loving (Prv 5:19).

אַהֲבָה 'ahăvāh (157), Love (Prv 5:19, 17:9, 27:5).

דּוֹד dôdh (1782), Love (Prv 7:18).

רֵעַ rēaʿ (7739), Friend (Prv 19:7).

1. φιλία philia nom sing fem

1 the **friendship** of the world is enmity with God?...... Jas 4:4

The word *philia* is an abstract noun related to *philos* (5220B), "friend," and *phileō* (5205), "to love." Its single New Testament usage (James 4:4) follows the classical Greek meaning of "friendship" and "devotion" and warns against that type of relationship with "the world." This diametrically opposed pair, friendship and enmity, reflects a radical ethical dualism that is often seen in the writings of John (cf. 1 John 2:15-17). Such a dualism is similar to that seen in the writings of the Qumran community and the apocalyptic communities (cf. Ethiopian Enoch 108:8 which speaks of hating the world; Jubilees 30:14-22 which talks of being a friend or enemy of God).

There is no middle ground; one who courts the values, mores, and institutions of this world is not simply a poor Christian; he is an enemy of God (Davids, *New International Greek Testament Commentary, James,* p.161).

Strong 5373, Bauer 859, Moulton-Milligan 670, Kittel 9:146-71, Liddell-Scott 1934, Colin Brown 2:538,547-48.

5211. Φιλιππήσιος

Philippēsios name-adj

Of or from Philippi.

1. Φιλιππήσιοι Philippēsioi nom pl masc

2. Φιλιππησίους Philippēsious acc pl masc

1 Now ye **Philippians** know also, ... Phlp 4:15

The word is used in Philippians 4:15 to refer to the inhabitants of the city of Philippi in northern Greece.

5212. Φίλιπποι Philippoi name

Philippi.

1. Φιλίππων Philippōn gen masc

2. Φιλίπποις Philippois dat masc

3. Φιλίππους Philippous acc masc

3 And from thence to **Philippi,** .... Acts 16:12
1 And we sailed away from **Philippi** 20:6
2 all the saints in Christ Jesus which are at **Philippi,** .. Phlp 1:1
2 were shamefully entreated, as ye know, at **Philippi,** .. 1 Th 2:2

A city in northern Greece which had an important location on the Via Egnatia, the main west-east route of the eastern Roman Empire. Luke, in Acts 16:12, refers to Philippi as a Roman colony and as *prōtē* (see 4270B), "most important, most prominent," of the area. A colony was a city in which legionary veterans were given land grants and Roman citizenship on retirement from the military. It was thus a center for Roman influence and a place of importance and pride in the Empire. The implication of *prōtē* is less certain. Philippi belonged to the first of the four districts of the province of Macedonia. Amphipolis was the capital of that district. Luke's reference therefore must be taken to mean either "a leading city, the leading city" (but not capital) or (reading *prōtēs* for *prōtē*) "a city of the first district." Philippi is now uninhabited, but its port city Neapolis, at which Paul landed, was 10 miles away and is the modern Kavalla.

This was the city in which Paul and his companions began their missionary preaching in Europe. It seems that in this largely Roman city there was no synagogue (10 Jewish men were needed to form a synagogue), a factor which must have made their task harder. They looked for "a place of prayer" outside the city and found only women gathered there (Acts 16:13, NIV). Acts 16 records the eventful progress of the mission. Luke may well have settled in Philippi, for the narrative reverts from "we" to "they" in chapter 16 and only returns to "we" in 20:5, the point when Paul again passed through Philippi.

From small beginnings there grew a flourishing church. Paul's special esteem and love for this first church he planted in Europe are reflected in Philippians (e.g., 1:3-8), and they were constant in their support for him with gifts of money and personal help (cf. 2 Corinthians 11:9; Philippians 2:25; 4:10-19). Paul visited the city on several later occasions.

5213. Φίλιππος Philippos name

Philip.

1. Φίλιππος Philippos nom masc

2. Φιλίππου Philippou gen masc

3. Φιλίππῳ Philippō dat masc

4. Φίλιππον Philippon acc masc

5. Φίλιππε Philippe voc masc

1 **Philip,** and Bartholomew; Thomas, and Matthew ... Matt 10:3
2 for Herodias' sake, his brother **Philip's** wife. 14:3
2 Jesus came into the coasts of Caesarea **Philippi,** 16:13
4 And Andrew, and **Philip,** and Bartholomew, ... Mark 3:18
2 his brother **Philip's** wife: for he had married her. 6:17
2 into the towns of Caesarea **Philippi:** 8:27
2 and his brother **Philip** tetrarch of Ituraea and .... Luke 3:1
2 for Herodias his brother **Philip's** wife, ... 3:19
4 James and John, **Philip** and Bartholomew, ... 6:14
4 and findeth **Philip,** and saith unto him, Follow me... John 1:43
1 Now **Philip** was of Bethsaida, ... 1:44
1 **Philip** findeth Nathanael, and saith unto him, ... 1:45
1 **Philip** saith unto him, Come and see. 1:46
4 Before that **Philip** called thee, ... I saw thee. 1:48
4 he saith unto **Philip,** Whence shall we buy bread, ... 6:5
1 **Philip** answered him, ... 6:7
3 The same came therefore to **Philip,** 12:21
1 **Philip** cometh and telleth Andrew: 12:22
1 and again Andrew and **Philip** tell Jesus. 12:22
1 **Philip** saith unto him, Lord, show us the Father, ... 14:8
5 and yet hast thou not known me, **Philip?** 14:9
1 and Andrew, **Philip,** and Thomas, Bartholomew, ... Acts 1:13
4 **Philip,** and Prochorus, and Nicanor, and Timon, ... 6:5
1 Then **Philip** went down to the city of Samaria, ... 8:5
2 gave heed unto those things which **Philip** spake, ... 8:6
3 But when they believed **Philip** preaching 8:12
3 when he was baptized, he continued with **Philip,** 8:13
4 And the angel of the Lord spake unto **Philip,** 8:26
3 Then the Spirit said unto **Philip,** Go near, ... 8:29
1 And **Philip** ran thither to him, ... 8:30
4 And he desired **Philip** that he would come up 8:31
3 And the eunuch answered **Philip,** and said, ... 8:34
1 Then **Philip** opened his mouth, ... 8:35
1 **Philip** said, If thou believest with all thine heart, ... 8:37
1 both **Philip** and the eunuch; and he baptized him. 8:38

4 the Spirit of the Lord caught away **Philip**, ... Acts 8:39
1 But **Philip** was found at Azotus: 8:40
2 we entered into the house of **Philip** the evangelist, ... 21:8

Philip is the name of four men in the New Testament, of whom two were of the royal house of Herod and two were leaders of the Early Church.

Philip the tetrarch (son of Herod the Great and Cleopatra of Jerusalem) was ruler of Ituraea and Trachonitis throughout Jesus' lifetime. He is mentioned at Luke 3:1. His half-brother Philip (the son of Herod the Great and Mariamne, daughter of Simon the high priest) was the first husband of Herodias (Matthew 14:3; Mark 6:17).

Philip the apostle is named in every list of the Twelve after Peter, Andrew, James, and John (Matthew 10:3; Mark 3:18; Luke 6:14; Acts 1:13). He is not mentioned elsewhere in the New Testament except in John where he plays quite an important part. Like Andrew, he was one of the first disciples to be called by Jesus (1:43); he immediately responded by bringing another, Nathanael (1:45f.). Again like Andrew, he was from the fishing town of Bethsaida on the north shore of the Sea of Galilee (1:44). His name was Greek.

Philip the apostle is revealed as possessing a mixture of spiritual insight and dullness. He spoke to Nathanael of Jesus as Messiah and answered his doubting sarcasm with a simple "come and see" (1:45f.). He was approached by some Greeks who wanted to see Jesus and, joined by Andrew, led them to Him. This happening seems to have been for Jesus a signal that "the hour is come, that the Son of man should be glorified" (12:20-23). On the other hand, when Jesus and the disciples faced a need to feed a very large crowd, he answered Jesus' question about what to do in terms solely of the everyday world, in contrast to Andrew (6:4-7). And, finally, at the Last Supper Philip's request, "Lord, show us the Father," drew from Jesus the sharp answer, "He that hath seen me hath seen the Father" (14:8f.).

Although there are several traditions which link him later with the province of Asia, nothing definite is known of his later life.

Philip "the evangelist . . . one of the seven," is so described by Luke (Acts 21:8) from his two major ministries. He was one of those chosen to supervise the daily distribution to the needy (Acts 6:5) but is known chiefly as an evangelist. In Acts 8 we read of two evangelistic enterprises he undertook which moved the gospel past new frontiers. They occurred soon after the martyrdom of Stephen when the members of the church were persecuted and scattered. First, his preaching of the gospel, confirmed by signs and miracles, led to a large number of conversions in Samaria (verses 5-13). Even a well-known local wonder-worker, Simon, was converted. As the Holy Spirit did not at first come openly upon the new Samaritan believers, Peter and John came down and prayed for them (verses 14-25), thus affirming the reception of the gospel by a people whom Jews ordinarily despised (but with whom Jesus had contact [cf. John 4]).

From there, in response to directions from an angel, Philip went to the desert road from Jerusalem to Gaza. In this unpromising location he met an important Ethiopian official whom he led to a declaration of faith and then baptized (Acts 8:26-38). After this "the Spirit of the Lord caught away Philip" to Azotus, and he started to evangelize the coastal region between Azotus and Caesarea where he eventually settled (Acts 8:39f.). In Acts 21:8f. Luke records that Paul and his party stayed for a period at his house. By this time, he was the father of four unmarried daughters who had a ministry of prophecy.

5214. φιλόθεος philotheos adj

Pious, God-loving (person).

Cross-References:
θεός theos (2292B)
φιλέω phileō (5205)

1. φιλόθεοι philotheoi nom pl masc

1 lovers of pleasures more than **lovers of God**; .... 2 Tm 3:4

The compound adjective *philotheos* combines *theos* (2292B), "God," and *phileō* (5205), "to love." The "God-loving person" is pious and allows nothing else to infringe upon his devotion. The New Testament uses *philotheos* only once and that in a play on words (2 Timothy 3:4) contrasting *philēdonos* (5206) and *philotheos* ("pleasure-loving" rather than "God-loving"). This contrast demonstrates the virtuous nature of *philotheos*.

Strong 5377, Bauer 860, Moulton-Milligan 670, Liddell-Scott 1936, Colin Brown 2:550.

5215. Φιλόλογος Philologos name

Philologus.

1. Φιλόλογον Philologon acc masc

1 Salute **Philologus**, and Julia, Nereus, and his sister, Rom 16:15

A Christian whom Paul greets at Romans 16:15.

5216. φιλονεικία philoneikia noun

Contention, strife, dispute.

COGNATE:

φιλέω phileō (5205)

SYNONYMS:

ἀντιλογία antilogia (482)
ἐριθεία eritheia (2036)
ἔρις eris (2038)
μάχη machē (3135)
στάσις stasis (4565)

1. φιλονεικία philoneikia nom sing fem

1 And there was also a **strife** among them, ... Luke 22:24

Classical Greek

Philoneikia appears as early as the Fifth Century B.C. and is used by such writers as Plato, primarily in a bad sense of "contentiousness, love of rivalry" (*Liddell-Scott*). The term is also used, however, in a good sense of "competition, ambition," or "the desire to emulate the excellence of another," especially in the games (ibid.).

Papyrus documents in New Testament times employ *philoneikia* with the primary meaning of "dispute" or "strife." This reflects the word's derivation from *phileō* (5205), "to love," and *nikē* (3391), "victory" (*Moulton-Milligan*). *Philoneikia* is the product of a zeal to contend, i.e., a contentious spirit.

New Testament Usage

Its only New Testament use fits this pattern (Luke 22:24). Here the word is used in a negative sense of the strife that arose among the disciples (a strife linked by the use of *kai* [2504] to the previous verses) and the contention over who would betray Jesus (Luke 22:21-23). As noted by Marshall, the appearance of *dokeō* (1374) in the reply of Jesus indicates that the disciples were concerned about how they would appear to others (*New International Greek Testament Commentary, Luke*, p.811).

STRONG 5379, BAUER 860, MOULTON-MILLIGAN 670-71, LIDDELL-SCOTT 1937, COLIN BROWN 2:550.

5217. φιλόνεικος philoneikos adj

Contentious, quarrelsome.

CROSS-REFERENCE:

φιλέω phileō (5205)

1. φιλόνεικος philoneikos nom sing masc

1 But if any man seem to be **contentious**, ... 1 Co 11:16

The adjective *philoneikos* is a compound from the words *phileō* (5205), "to love," and *nikos* (3396), "victory." It's meaning is to be quarrelsome (1 Corinthians 11:16, its only occurrence in the New Testament), contentious, or stubborn (as in the Septuagint of Ezekiel 3:7).

STRONG 5380, BAUER 860, LIDDELL-SCOTT 1937-38, COLIN BROWN 2:550.

5218. φιλοξενία philoxenia noun

Hospitality.

CROSS-REFERENCES:

ξένος xenos (3443)
φιλέω phileō (5205)

1. φιλοξενίας philoxenias gen sing fem

2. φιλοξενίαν philoxenian acc sing fem

2 given to **hospitality**. .... Rom 12:13
1 Be not forgetful to **entertain strangers**: .... Heb 13:2

A rare term in classical Greek, *philoxenia*, "hospitality," is referred to as a Christian responsibility in Romans 12:13 and Hebrews 13:2. Christians are to be hospitable to others—known or unknown—who are in need. The related word *xenia* (3440) denotes a "guest room" in Philemon 22.

BAUER 860, MOULTON-MILLIGAN 671, KITTEL 5:1-36, LIDDELL-SCOTT 1938, COLIN BROWN 1:686,690; 2:547,550.

5219. φιλόξενος philoxenos adj

Hospitable.

CROSS-REFERENCES:

ξένος xenos (3443)
φιλέω phileō (5205)

1. φιλόξενον philoxenon acc sing masc

2. φιλόξενοι philoxenoi nom pl masc

1 given to **hospitality**, apt to teach; .... 1 Tm 3:2
1 But a lover of **hospitality**, a lover of good men, ... Tit 1:8
2 Use **hospitality** one to another without grudging. ..... 1 Pt 4:9

The compound adjective *philoxenos* describes persons as "hospitable" in 1 Timothy 3:2; Titus 1:8; and 1 Peter 4:9. A compound of the root *phil-*, "love," and *xenos* (3443), "hospitality shown to a guest" (*Liddell-Scott*), *philoxenos* suggests both a fondness for and a natural desire to serve the needs of others ("given to hospitality," 1 Timothy 3:2).

STRONG 5382, BAUER 860, MOULTON-MILLIGAN 671, KITTEL 5:1-36, LIDDELL-SCOTT 1938, COLIN BROWN 1:686,690; 2:550.

5220. φιλοπρωτεύω

philoprōteuō verb

To love to be first, desire to be preeminent.

Cross-Reference:

φιλέω phileō (5205)

1. φιλοπρωτεύων philoprōteuōn
nom sing masc part pres act

1 who **loveth to have the preeminence among them,**.... 3 Jn 1:9

The verb *philoprōteuō* indicates an aspiration to achieve not merely prominence but preeminence. Although the New Testament uses it only once (3 John 9), secular literature of that time used it for "loving the chief place" and "desiring to be first" (*Moulton-Milligan*). In 3 John 9 the writer addressed the problem of Diotrephes. As noted by Brown, the verb appears in the present participle form here, "The-liking-to-be-first Diotrephes." This construction that implies what follows is the direct result of his ambition to be first (*Anchor Bible*, 30:717).

Strong 5383, Bauer 860-61, Moulton-Milligan 671, Liddell-Scott 1939, Colin Brown 2:550.

5220B. φίλος philos adj

Friend, loved one.

Cross-Reference:

φιλέω phileō (5205)

אָהֵב 'āhēv (154), Qal: friend, loved one (Est 5:10, Ps 38:11 [37:11], Jer 20:4); piel: lover (Jer 30:14 [37:14]).

אַלּוּף 'allûph (443), Close friend, intimate friend (Prv 16:28, 17:9).

יָדַע yādha' (3156), Know; pual: intimate friend (Job 19:14).

מֵרֵעַ mērēa' (4991), Neighbor (Prv 12:26).

רֵעַ rēa' (7739), Friend, neighbor (Job 2:11, Prv 6:3, Mi 7:5).

שָׁלוֹם shālôm (8361), Peace, prosperity; friend (Jer 20:10).

1. **φίλος philos** nom sing masc
2. **φίλον philon** acc sing masc
3. **φίλε phile** voc sing masc
4. **φίλοι philoi** nom pl masc
5. **φίλων philōn** gen pl masc
6. **φίλοις philois** dat pl masc
7. **φίλους philous** acc pl masc
8. **φίλας philas** acc pl fem

1 a **friend** of publicans and sinners.................. Matt 11:19
7 the centurion sent **friends** to him, saying unto him,.. Luke 7:6
1 a winebibber, a **friend** of publicans and sinners!......... 7:34
2 Which of you shall have a **friend**,..................... 11:5
3 and say unto him, **Friend**, lend me three loaves;....... 11:5
1 For a **friend** of mine in his journey is come to me,..... 11:6
2 because he is his **friend**, yet because ... importunity.... 11:8
6 And I say unto you my **friends**,.................. Luke 12:4
3 he may say unto thee, **Friend**, go up higher:........... 14:10
7 call not thy **friends**, nor thy brethren,................. 14:12
7 he calleth together his **friends** and neighbours,......... 15:6
8 she calleth her **friends** and her neighbours together,.... 15:9
5 that I might make merry with my **friends**:............ 15:29
7 Make to yourselves **friends** of the mammon.......... 16:9
5 parents, and brethren, and kinsfolks, and **friends**;...... 21:16
4 Pilate and Herod were made **friends** together:......... 23:12
1 but the **friend** of the bridegroom,.................. John 3:29
1 Our **friend** Lazarus sleepeth;......................... 11:11
5 that a man lay down his life for his **friends**........... 15:13
4 Ye are my **friends**, if ye do whatsoever I command.... 15:14
7 but I have called you **friends**;........................ 15:15
1 If thou let this ... go, thou art not Caesar's **friend**:..... 19:12
7 had called together his kinsmen and near **friends**....Acts 10:24
4 certain of the chief of Asia, which were his **friends**,.... 19:31
7 and gave him liberty to go unto his **friends**........... 27:3
1 and he was called the **Friend** of God................Jas 2:23
1 a **friend** of the world is the enemy of God............. 4:4
4 Peace be to thee. Our **friends** salute thee...........3 Jn 1:14
7 Our friends salute thee. Greet the **friends** by name...... 1:14

Classical Greek

Although primarily an adjective with the meaning of "beloved, friendly," or "dear," *philos* came to be used as a noun meaning "friend." Neither Greek nor Hebrew tradition requires a distinction between a relative and a friend; a *philos* may also be a relative.

Philos bears this sense in classical Greek as early as the writings of Homer (Eighth Century B.C.). The word denotes a friendly relationship, a helping and caring attitude between persons whether related by blood or not. It can further denote several aspects of close relations. *Philos* can mean "lover" in an erotic sense; it can also refer to "followers" of a politician or "clients" of a wealthy man. Thus it can express both equal and unequal relationships (Stählin, "philos," *Kittel*, 9:147). Many Greek and Roman authors wrote on the subject of friendship, particularly Cicero. Aristotle, for instance, gives four qualities of friendship: friends are a single soul; they share all things; they are equal; and friendship begins in the home (*Nicomachean Ethics* 1168b. 6-8). Greeks believed that a man could have only a few *real* friends and that a pair of friends was the true ideal.

The supreme duty of a friend was to sacrifice himself for his friend, and examples of sacrifice are highly extolled in Greek literature (Stählin, "philos," *Kittel*, 9:151-152). Cicero gave several qualities of a friend. First, friendship could only exist between good men, men who lived pure lives, free from greed, lust, and violence. Friends had complete agreement on all subjects and good will toward one another. Friendship was based on love. Friends would not ask one another to do what was wrong and only did good to one another. Permanence and stability in friendship were the product of mutual loyalty. The golden rule for a friend was to put himself on the same level as his friend (*De Amicitia* 5,6,8,12,13,18,19).

Other Greek literature uses *philos* in its normal meaning of "friend." *Moulton-Milligan* reports its frequent use in letters of commendation and even in legal documents.

Septuagint Usage

The Septuagint employs *philos* approximately 180 times. In about 40 texts *philos* renders the Hebrew *rēaʿ* "friend" or "fellow," but in the majority of cases it does not translate a specific Hebrew word. In the Septuagint *philos* conveys several shades of meaning: a close friend (Deuteronomy 13:6); a closest friend (1 Chronicles 27:33); a friend of the house (Proverbs 27:10); a political supporter of someone in authority (Esther 6:13); and even a best man (1 Maccabees 9:39). *Philos* often appears either in combination with or parallel to other terms (Stählin, "philos," *Kittel*, 9:154).

The Jewish world also knew and understood the concept of deep friendship. The classic example is that of David and Jonathan. Scripture notes that Jonathan loved David as he loved himself (1 Samuel 20:17). David, in his lament for Saul and Jonathan declared, "Your (Jonathan's) love for me was wonderful, more wonderful than that of women" (2 Samuel 1:26, NIV). Curiously, *philos* is not used to describe this relationship (nor *rēaʿ*). According to Stählin, there was no technical term for this kind of friendship in Hebrew; substitute phrases were needed (ibid., 9:156).

New Testament Usage

The New Testament employs *philos* about 30 times, often to indicate "a friend to whom one is under a basic obligation" (Günther, "Love," *Colin Brown*, 2:549). Although friends and relatives are sometimes differentiated (Luke 21:16; Acts 10:24), this need not be the case (John 15:13-15). Scripture notes several interesting examples of friendship: John the Baptist is best man to Jesus (John 3:29); Jesus is a "friend" to sinners (Matthew 11:19; Luke 7:34); Abraham is "the *friend* of God" (James 2:23); and believers cannot be friends both of the world and God (James 4:4).

In Luke 14:12 Jesus exhorted his hearers not to invite their friends, etc., to a meal, but rather to invite those unable to repay. In the ancient world a man invited individuals to his home in order to obligate them to himself. In this way when he desired a favor, he could demand a response, for ancient social custom obligated a man to return favors. Thus, many invited only those who could repay them or who could in the future provide them with favors. To invite the poor, etc., was unthinkable, since they could not repay. Jesus exhorted his disciples to create a new custom, not based on selfish reciprocity but on selfless giving without seeking return favors.

In the New Testament the supreme example of a friend was Jesus. His example of love crosses all cultural boundaries. To the Jews he represented one who loved His disciples as He loved himself; to the Greeks and Romans He was the one who laid down His life for His friends. In John 15:15 Jesus declared that His followers were His friends not merely His servants (*doulos* [1395]). The believer is more than a *servant* of God, i.e., one who ignorantly obeys orders under fear of punishment; rather, he is a friend—one who knows the Lord's will and follows Him out of love and desire.

STRONG 5384, BAUER 861, MOULTON-MILLIGAN 671, KITTEL 9:146-71, LIDDELL-SCOTT 1939, COLIN BROWN 2:547-51.

5221. φιλοσοφία philosophia noun

Philosophy, love of wisdom or knowledge.

CROSS-REFERENCES:

σοφία sophia (4531)
φιλέω phileō (5205)

1. φιλοσοφίας philosophias gen sing fem

1 **Beware lest any man spoil you through philosophy... Col 2:8**

A compound built on the *phil-* ("love") root and *sophia* (4531), "wisdom," *philosophia* denotes either the love and search for wisdom or the knowledge resulting from that pursuit.

Classical Greek

The use of the word *philosophia* in classical Greek dates back to the Fifth Century B.C. with the Ionians to whom Aristotle credits the start of philosophy. They sought an underlying unity, or being, beneath the diversity of things. The later Sophists turned their methodical reflections towards acquiring ethical knowledge. Plato located the nature of *philosophia* in combining the search for truth with educational and political action (Michel, "philosophia," *Kittel*, 10:172ff.).

For Aristotle, "doing philosophy" was a methodical search to understand the world. He applied *philosophia* both to comprehensive knowledge and also to individual disciplines, sometimes interchanging *philosophia* and *epistemē*, "knowledge." He used *protē philosophia*, "first philosophy," to denote basic principles and fundamental reality, including the "unmoved Mover." In contrast, investigating reality that is open to the senses constituted *deutera* ("second") *philosophia* (ibid., 10:174f.).

In the Hellenistic period the term *philosophia* was also applied to the teachings of the Epicureans and Stoics, increasingly being identified with ethics. Later Platonists and Oriental mystery cults associated *philosophia* with devotion to the gods and salvation by knowledge (ibid., 10:178f.).

Septuagint Usage

The Septuagint employs *philosophia* in the apocryphal book of 4 Maccabees (1:1; 5:11,22; 7:9,21) but not in any canonical text. These usages present Jewish religion as a "philosophy" with virtues that lead to glory for the true God. The stress is ethical and parallels the Stoic claim that reason must rule over impulses and passions in human actions (ibid., 10:180).

Clearly, even though the word *philosophia* and the idea it represents were essentially Greek, both had come into Jewish thought. Philo attempted to show a relationship between Greek *philosophia* and Biblical *sophia*, "wisdom," by making the former a handmaiden to the latter. He went on to say that Biblical wisdom corrects philosophy, but philosophical exegesis can clarify Biblical teaching. Philo applied the word to both the Mosaic law and Jewish religion (ibid., 10:181).

Josephus' use of *philosophia* is limited. He employed the term to denote the pre-Socratics, pagan sages, and priests. On occasions, Jewish religious instruction is referred to as *philosophia*. He also spoke of the three Jewish sects (Pharisees, Sadducees, and Essenes) as "philosophies" within Judaism (O'Brien, *Word Biblical Commentary*, 44:109).

New Testament Usage

Colossians 2:8 is the only New Testament instance of *philosophia*, although the related word *philosophos* (5222), "philosopher," designates the Epicureans and Stoics at Athens (Acts 17:18). Elsewhere the New Testament uses the terms *sophia*, "wisdom" (1 Corinthians 1:17ff.), and *gnosis* (1102), "knowledge" (1 Timothy 6:20), in alluding to the contemporary philosophy. But in Colossians 2:8 "philosophy" refers neither to Greek philosophy in general nor to any single school. Rather, *philosophia* here is a specific religious heresy, one attempting to combine Christian teachings with other teachings from non-Christian sources. Scripture does not condemn philosophy in itself, but it does condemn this particular philosophy "which depends on human tradition and the basic principles of this world rather than on Christ" (NIV).

The context shows that this Colossian heresy advocated separation, promised unique insight into the nature of the cosmos, and claimed a long tradition. It is likely that Scripture calls this *philosophia* because that is how its advocates designated it.

Strong 5385, Bauer 861, Moulton-Milligan 671, Kittel 9:172-88, Liddell-Scott 1940, Colin Brown 2:550; 3:1034-36.

5222. φιλόσοφος philosophos noun

Philosopher, lover of wisdom.

Cross-References:

σοφία sophia (4531)
φιλέω phileō (5205)

אַשָּׁף 'ashshāph (853), Enchanter (Dn 1:20).

1. φιλοσόφων philosophōn gen pl masc

1 Then certain philosophers of the Epicureans,....... Acts 17:18

Classical Greek

Philosophos is a compound of *philos* (5220B), "love," and *sophos* (4533), that which refers to wisdom and practical knowledge. In classical Greek *philosophos* denotes men of learning. The philosopher was not necessarily an authority in possession of absolute truth or wisdom. But his was an inquiring mind, motivated by a strong desire to know and be a lover of wisdom. As Paul wrote, "The Greeks seek after wisdom" (1 Corinthians 1:22). A philosopher searched for wisdom his whole life without attaining it fully (Weigelt, "Wisdom," *Colin Brown*, 3:1034).

New Testament Usage

The term occurs only once in the New Testament. When Paul preached in Athens, philosophers, both Epicureans and Stoics, ridiculed him as a "babbler" (Acts 17:18). Paul countered that "the world by (earthly) wisdom knew not God" (1 Corinthians 1:21). Without revelation, philosophy is a vain search. But the wisdom of God provided "Christ Jesus, who of God is made unto us wisdom, and righteousness, and sanctification, and redemption" (verse 30). Christ takes us beyond the questions raised by philosophy.

Strong 5386, Bauer 861, Moulton-Milligan 671, Kittel 9:172-88, Liddell-Scott 1940, Colin Brown 2:550; 3:1034-36.

5223. φιλόστοργος philostorgos adj

Tenderly loving, loving dearly, affectionate.

Cross-Reference:

φιλέω phileō (5205)

1. φιλόστοργοι philostorgoi nom pl masc

1 Be **kindly affectioned** one to another with .... Rom 12:10

This word appears only once in the New Testament. It is a compound adjective meaning "devoted to (i.e., a lover of) family affection (*storgē*)." Though the word *storgē* never appears alone in the New Testament, Paul used its negation, *astorgos* (788), in Romans 1:31. It is translated "without natural affection," describing the depths of human depravity in sin. In the light of all that God has done, the proper response of believers is to be devoted to one another, having tender affection, *philadelphia* (5197)—the kind of love that binds true brothers together (Romans 12:10). Nothing less will produce true spiritual health and Christian ethics in the family of God.

Strong 5387, Bauer 861, Moulton-Milligan 671-72, Liddell-Scott 1940, Colin Brown 2:538-39,542,550.

5224. φίλος philos

See word study at number 5220B.

5225. φιλότεκνος philoteknos adj

Loving one's children.

Cross-References:

τέκνον teknon (4891)
φιλέω phileō (5205)

1. φιλοτέκνους philoteknous acc pl fem

1 to love their husbands, **to love their children**,......... Tit 2:4

This is an adjectival form that functions as a noun and denotes a "lover of children." In the one instance of *philoteknos* in the New Testament the reference is to a young mother's relation to her children (Titus 2:4). These instructions are given so that those outside the community of faith will not disparage the gospel as a result of the behavior of believers. Paul's exhortation (for the young women to love their husbands and their children) matches a pair of qualities frequently found in secular writings that praise good wives (Fee, *Good News Commentary, 1 and 2 Timothy and Titus*, p.141).

Strong 5388, Bauer 861, Moulton-Milligan 672, Liddell-Scott 1940, Colin Brown 2:550.

5226. φιλοτιμέομαι philotimeomai verb

Have as one's ambition, aim, aspire; to love, honor.

Cross-References:

τιμάω timaō (4939)
φιλέω phileō (5205)

1. φιλοτιμούμεθα philotimoumetha 1pl indic pres mid

2. φιλοτιμούμενον philotimoumenon acc sing masc part pres mid

3. φιλοτιμεῖσθαι philotimeisthai inf pres mid

2 Yea, so **have I strived** to preach the gospel,........ Rom 15:20
1 Wherefore we **labour**, that, whether present or...... 2 Co 5:9
3 And that ye **study** to be quiet,..................... 1 Th 4:11

This verb is a compound of *philos* (5220B), "friend," and *timē* (4940), "honor." It expresses, in Pauline literature at least, the strong inclination of his affection for the highest and most honorable values for which he was willing to spend and be spent (2 Corinthians 12:15). In the context of Paul's one ambition to be "accepted of (Christ)," the word is translated "labor" to express the strength of his aspiration (2 Corinthians 5:9). In Romans 15:20 this word is translated "strived" in a description of the missionary zeal of spreading the gospel. And in his exhortation to the Thessalonians, Paul used the same word to insist that they "study" (or be zealous) to live an acceptable life (1 Thessalonians 4:11). In each case the prize, the esteem of Christ, is of eternal value.

Strong 5389, Bauer 861, Moulton-Milligan 672, Liddell-Scott 1941, Colin Brown 2:550.

5227. φιλοφρόνως philophronōs adv

Kindly disposed, with friendliness, hospitably.

Cross-References:

φιλέω phileō (5205)
φρονέω phroneō (5262)

1. φιλοφρόνως philophronōs

1 received us, and lodged us three days **courteously**... Acts 28:7

Literally the word *philophronōs* is an adverb meaning "in a friendly state of mind." It is composed of the word for friend (*philos* [5220B]) and the adverbial use of *phroneō* (5262), "to set one's mind." It can refer to a person's disposition or may suggest a deliberate ethical choice to act in a kindly manner. Both occurrences in the apocryphal sections of the Septuagint use *philophronōs* in the context of a high public official "courteously receiving" someone (cf. 2

Maccabees 3:9; 4 Maccabees 8:5). In the New Testament it was by deliberate ethical choice that Publius received Paul and his many shipwrecked companions "and lodged (them) three days *courteously*" (Acts 28:7).

STRONG 5390, BAUER 861, MOULTON-MILLIGAN 672, LIDDELL-SCOTT 1942, COLIN BROWN 2:550.

5228. φιλόφρων philophrōn adj

Friendly, kind, kindly-disposed.

CROSS-REFERENCES:
φιλέω phileō (5205)
φρονέω phroneō (5262)

1. φιλόφρονες philophrones nom pl masc

1 love as brethren, be pitiful, **be courteous:**............1 Pt 3:8

In the New Testament the adjective *philophrōn* is found only in 1 Peter 3:8 and then only in the *Textus Receptus*. But the word is well attested in other literature. As with the adverb *philophronōs* (5227), it means "of a friendly state of mind." The root *phron* of the latter part of the adjective indicates that the love or friendliness of the first part could be volitional and intentional. It is a "mindedness." The idea of mindedness occurs twice in the same verse: "Be ye all of one mind" (*homophrones* [see 3538], of one deliberate attitude) and "be courteous" (*philophrones*, "have a friendly mind-set") (1 Peter 3:8). Those manuscripts which do not have *philophrones* do have another similar word of the same ethical import: *tapeinophrones* (see 4863B), "of a humble mind-set."

STRONG 5391, BAUER 861, LIDDELL-SCOTT 1942, COLIN BROWN 2:550.

5229. φιμόω phimoō verb

Muzzle, tie shut, silence.

חָסַם chāsam (2733), Muzzle (Dt 25:4).

1. φιμοῦν phimoun inf pres act
2. ἐφίμωσεν ephimōsen 3sing indic aor act
3. φιμώσεις phimōseis 2sing indic fut act
4. ἐφιμώθη ephimōthē 3sing indic aor pass
5. φιμώθητι phimōthēti 2sing impr aor pass
6. πεφίμωσο pephimōso 2sing impr perf mid

4 how camest thou in ... And he **was speechless**...... Matt 22:12
2 heard that he had **put** the Sadducees **to silence**,........ 22:34
5 And Jesus rebuked him, saying, **Hold thy peace**,.... Mark 1:25
6 and said unto the sea, Peace, **be still**.................. 4:39
5 And Jesus rebuked him, saying, **Hold thy peace**,.....Luke 4:35
3 Thou shalt not **muzzle** the mouth of the ox......... 1 Co 9:9
3 shalt not **muzzle** the ox that treadeth out the corn... 1 Tm 5:18
1 ye may **put to silence** the ignorance of foolish men:.. 1 Pt 2:15

Classical Greek

This verb is related to the noun *phimos*, "muzzle." Aristophanes, the Athenian dramatist (Fifth Century B.C.), used the word in his satiric comedies with the meaning "to make fast" (cf. *Liddell-Scott*).

Septuagint Usage

Phimoō appears in the Septuagint, translating into Greek the commandment of God, "Thou shalt not *muzzle* the ox when he treadeth out the corn" (Deuteronomy 25:4; see also 4 Maccabees 1:35; Susanna 61). The muzzle is a strap or metal piece fastened over the mouth to keep an animal from eating the grain that was being threshed. The muzzle was forbidden because it was cruel and inhumane to walk an ox over the grain all day and never allow him to satisfy his own hunger.

New Testament Usage

In the New Testament Paul twice quoted Deuteronomy 25:4 and applied it to one who spends his days ministering in spiritual things. As it was cruel to muzzle the ox, it is equally cruel to muzzle the minister to prevent his participation in the benefits of the more earthly labors (1 Corinthians 9:9; 1 Timothy 5:18).

The concept of "muzzling" was so graphic that Jesus and the Gospel writers made use of it. Figuratively, Jesus muzzled or "put the Sadducees to silence" (Matthew 22:34). They could say no more. Jesus had "shut them up." Again, Jesus *muzzled* and commanded unclean spirits to *hold their peace* (or be silent) and come out of a demon-possessed man (Mark 1:25; Luke 4:35). Jesus also muzzled the storm at sea: "Peace, *be still*" (Mark 4:39). The winds and the waves were immediately silenced and stayed calm (perfect passive tense of *phimoō*).

STRONG 5392, BAUER 861-62, MOULTON-MILLIGAN 672, LIDDELL-SCOTT 1943.

5230. Φλέγων Phlegōn name

Phlegon.

1. Φλέγοντα Phlegonta acc masc

1 Salute Asyncritus, **Phlegon**, Hermas, Patrobas,..... Rom 16:14

A Christian whom Paul greets at Romans 16:14.

5231. φλογίζω phlogizō verb

Set on fire, burn, burn up.

Cross-Reference:
φλόξ phlox (5232)

לָהַט lāhaṯ (3993), Qal: flaming (Sir 3:30); piel: burn up (Ps 97:3 [96:3]).

לָקַח lāqach (4089), Take, seize; hithpael: do something continually (Ex 9:24).

1. φλογίζουσα phlogizousa nom sing fem part pres act
2. φλογιζομένη phlogizomenē nom sing fem part pres mid

1 and setteth on fire the course of nature;..............Jas 3:6
2 and it is set on fire of hell............................ 3:6

Classical Greek and Septuagint Usage

This verb is related to the noun *phlox* (5232), "a flame," and the verb *phlegō* which means "set on fire, burn." Instances of the noun go back to Homer (Eighth Century B.C.), and the verb *phlogizō* has been found in Sophocles (Fifth Century B.C.) with a range of meaning from "singe" to "be burnt up, consumed" (cf. *Liddell-Scott*).

In Exodus 9:24 *phlogizō* is used of the "fire mingled" with the plague of hail wrought on the unrelenting Pharaoh of Egypt. This type of burning is often associated with the power and judgment of God (cf. Psalm 97:3 [LXX 96:3]; Revelation 8:7; 16:21).

New Testament Usage

Figuratively, James used the verb twice in one verse: "And the tongue is a fire, a world of iniquity: so is the tongue among our members, that it defileth the whole body, and *setteth on fire* the course of nature; and it is *set on fire* of hell" (James 3:6). In this very difficult verse, James describes the devastating effects wrought by the tongue. Kindled by the devil, the evil influence of the tongue spreads like a fire from its source out to the entire circumference of our lives.

Strong 5394, Bauer 862, Moulton-Milligan 672, Liddell-Scott 1945.

5232. φλόξ phlox noun

Flame, flaming fire.

Cognate:
φλογίζω phlogizō (5231)

Synonyms:
ἀνθρακιά anthrakia (437)
πῦρ pur (4300)

אֵשׁ 'ēsh (813), Fire (Ex 3:2).

זִיקוֹת zîqôth (2214), Firebrand (Is 50:11).

לַבָּה labbāh (3958), Flame (Ex 3:2—Codex Alexandrinus only).

לַהַב lahav (3987), Flame (Jgs 13:20, Job 41:21 [41:12], Jl 2:5).

לֶהָבָה lehāvāh (3988), Flame (Nm 21:28, Ps 106:18 [105:18], Is 43:2).

קִיטֹר qîṯōr (7290I), Smoke (Gn 19:28).

שְׁבִיב sh^e^vîv (A8109), Something flaming (Dn 7:9—Aramaic).

שַׁלְהֶבֶתְיָה shalhevethyāh (8354), Mighty flame (S/S 8:6).

1. φλόξ phlox nom sing fem
2. φλογός phlogos gen sing fem
3. φλογί phlogi dat sing fem
4. φλόγα phloga acc sing fem

3 cool my tongue; for I am tormented in this flame...Luke 16:24
3 an angel of the Lord in a flame of fire in a bush.....Acts 7:30
2 In flaming fire taking vengeance on them...........2 Th 1:8
4 and his ministers a flame of fire.....................Heb 1:7
1 and his eyes were as a flame of fire;................Rev 1:14
4 who hath his eyes like unto a flame of fire,............ 2:18
1 His eyes were as a flame of fire,...................... 19:12

Classical Greek and Septuagint Usage

This noun is related to the verb *phegō*, "set on fire, burn," and can be found in classical Greek from the Eighth Century B.C. meaning "flame" of fire, or lightning; "heat" of the sun; or the "flash" of heavenly bodies, precious stones, or a sword (cf. *Liddell-Scott*). It can sometimes be found with *puros* (the more common word for "fire"), as in Exodus 3:2 which refers to the "flame of fire" that Moses saw come out of the bush (cf. Isaiah 66:15).

New Testament Usage

As in the Old Testament and Septuagint, the divine manifestation of God was sometimes accompanied by fire in the New Testament, often in association with divine judgment (2 Thessalonians 1:7,8; Hebrews 12:29). *Phlox* is also used anthropomorphically to positively describe the "eyes" of the glorified Christ (Revelation 1:14; 2:18; 19:12) or negatively, the evil influence of man's "tongue" (James 3:6). (For the latter reference see also word study on *phlogizō* [5231].)

Strong 5395, Bauer 862, Moulton-Milligan 673, Liddell-Scott 1945.

5233. φλυαρέω phluareō verb

Talk nonsense, charge falsely, gossip.

1. φλυαρῶν phluarōn nom sing masc part pres act

1 prating against us with malicious words:............3 Jn 1:10

This verb is used only once in the New Testament, at 3 John 10. John warned against

Diotrephes who was "prating" (trumping up false charges) against John and other traveling representatives of the Church. *Phluareō* implies that the attacks were pure nonsense and unfounded gossip. The word is found in similar contexts from Herodotus (ca. Fifth Century B.C.) to Philo and the papyri. *Moulton-Milligan* illustrates the more general meaning "talk nonsense": one person expressed the desire "that I may not by much writing *prove myself an idle babbler.*"

STRONG 5396, BAUER 862, MOULTON-MILLIGAN 673, LIDDELL-SCOTT 1945-46.

5234. φλύαρος phluaros adj

Gossipy, foolish, nonsensical.

1. φλύαροι phluaroi nom pl fem

1 and not only idle, but tattlers also and busybodies, . . 1 Tm 5:13

The adjective *phluaros,* which can mean a person "given to gossip" or the "gossip" itself (when used substantively), occurs once in the New Testament. Paul used the word in its plural form, *phluaroi,* to describe the indiscreet conversation and conduct of young widows who seek position in the social and religious ministry of the church but then lose their Christian motivation. The result is they degenerate to gossipy busybodies in the community (1 Timothy 5:13).

STRONG 5397, BAUER 862, LIDDELL-SCOTT 1946.

5235. φοβερός phoberos adj

Fearful, terrible, frightful.

CROSS-REFERENCE:

φοβέω phobeō (5236)

אָיֹם 'āyōm (371), Dreadful (Hb 1:7).

דְּחַל d^echal (A1819), Something awesome or dreadful (Dn 2:31, 7:7—Aramaic).

יָרֵא yārē' (3486), Fear; niphal: be awesome, be feared (Dt 10:17, 1 Chr 16:25, Ps 99:3 [98:3]).

מוֹרָא môrā' (4307), One to be feared (Ps 76:11 [75:11]).

1. φοβερά phobera nom sing fem

2. φοβερόν phoberon nom/acc sing neu

1 But a certain fearful looking for of judgment . . . . Heb 10:27
2 It is a fearful thing ... the hands of the living God. 10:31
2 And so terrible was the sight, that Moses said, ... 12:21

Phoberos seems to be used at least in part as an intensive form of *phobos* (5238). *Phobos* focuses on the object or person causing fear. *Phoberos* is often used when it would be appropriate to call attention to the intensity of the fear or terror itself (cf. *Liddell-Scott*). *Phoberos* occurs three times in the New Testament. In Hebrews 10:27,31 Christ is exalted and man is confronted with the fearful judgment of God. Hebrews 12:21 describes Mount Sinai when God presented the Ten Commandments to Moses: the sight of it was "terrifying" (NIV). However, the King James Version uses the strong word "terror" to translate the less dramatic term *phobos* (Romans 13:3; 2 Corinthians 5:11; 1 Peter 3:14) where the reference is to the respect for human authority or a more general reference to the supreme authority of Christ.

STRONG 5398, BAUER 862, MOULTON-MILLIGAN 673, LIDDELL-SCOTT 1946, COLIN BROWN 1:621-23.

5236. φοβέω phobeō verb

Fear, be afraid, become terrified; worship, reverence, respect.

COGNATES:

ἀφόβως aphobōs (863)
ἐκφοβέω ekphobeō (1615)
ἔκφοβος ekphobos (1616)
ἔμφοβος emphobos (1703)
φοβερός phoberos (5235)
φόβητρον phobētron (5237)
φόβος phobos (5238)

SYNONYM:

εὐλαβέομαι eulabeomai (2106)

גּוּר gûr (1513), Be afraid (Nm 22:3).

דָּאַג dā'agh (1720), Be anxious (Jer 17:8).

חִיל chîl (2523), Tremble (1 Chr 16:30, Ps 77:16 [76:16]).

חָרַד chāradh (2829), Tremble (Ez 26:16,18).

חָתַת chāthath (2973), Niphal: be dismayed, be terrified (Jos 1:9, Jer 1:17, 10:2).

יָגֹר yāghōr (3133), Be afraid (Jer 39:17 [46:17]).

יָרֵא yārē' (3486), Be afraid (Dt 20:1, 2 Kgs 17:35-39, Is 41:10).

יָרֵא yārē' (3487), Afraid (Gn 22:12, Ps 60:4 [59:4], Mal 3:16).

יִרְאָה yir'āh (3488), Fearing (Is 63:17).

נוּעַ nûa' (5309), Tremble (Ex 20:18).

עָרַץ 'ārats (6442), Hiphil: be in awe (Is 29:23).

פָּחַד pāchadh (6585), Qal: be in dread, be afraid (Dt 28:66f., Is 12:2, Jer 33:9 [40:9]); piel: fear (Is 51:13).

פְּלַח p^elach (A6643), Serve (Dn 3:17—Aramaic).

רָגַז rāghaz (7553), Tremble (Ex 15:14—Codex Alexandrinus only).

רָעַשׁ rā'ash (7782), Shake (Ez 27:28).

שִׂים sîm (A7948), Set up (Dn 3:12—Aramaic).

1. **φοβοῦμαι phoboumai** 1sing indic pres mid
2. **φοβῇ phobē** 2sing indic pres mid
3. **φοβούμεθα phoboumetha** 1pl indic pres mid
4. **φοβῆται phobētai** 3sing subj pres mid
5. **φοβοῦ phobou** 2sing impr pres mid
6. **φοβεῖσθε phobeisthe** 2pl impr pres mid
7. **φοβούμενος phoboumenos** nom sing masc part pres mid
8. **φοβούμενοι phoboumenoi** nom pl masc part pres mid
9. **φοβουμένοις phoboumenois** dat pl masc part pres mid
10. **φοβούμεναι phoboumenai** nom pl fem part pres mid
11. **φοβεῖσθαι phobeisthai** inf pres mid
12. **ἐφοβήθη ephobēthē** 3sing indic aor pass
13. **ἐφοβήθησαν ephobēthēsan** 3pl indic aor pass
14. **φοβηθῇς phobēthēs** 2sing subj aor pass
15. **φοβηθῇ phobēthē** 3sing subj aor pass
16. **φοβηθῶμεν phobēthōmen** 1pl subj aor pass
17. **φοβηθῆτε phobēthēte** 2pl subj aor pass
18. **φοβήθητε phobēthēte** 2pl impr aor pass
19. **φοβηθείς phobētheis** nom sing masc part aor pass
20. **φοβηθέντες phobēthentes** nom pl masc part aor pass
21. **φοβηθεῖσα phobētheisa** nom sing fem part aor pass
22. **φοβηθήσομαι phobēthēsomai** 1sing indic fut pass
23. **ἐφοβούμην ephoboumēn** 1sing indic imperf mid
24. **ἐφοβεῖτο ephobeito** 3sing indic imperf mid
25. **ἐφοβοῦντο ephobounto** 3pl indic imperf mid

14 **fear** not to take unto thee Mary thy wife: .... Matt 1:20
12 Archelaus did reign ... **he was afraid** to go thither: 2:22
13 they were filled with awe, (NASB) 9:8
17 **Fear** them not therefore: 10:26
17 And **fear** not them which kill the body, ... 10:28
18 **fear** him which is able to destroy ... soul and body ... 10:28
17 **Fear** ye not therefore, ye are of more value 10:31
12 put him to death, **he feared** the multitude, ... 14:5
6 Be of good cheer; it is I; **be not afraid**. 14:27
12 when he saw the wind boisterous, **he was afraid**; 14:30
13 they fell on their face, and **were** sore **afraid**. 17:6
6 touched them, and said, Arise, and **be not afraid**. 17:7
3 But if we shall say, Of men; **we fear** the people; 21:26
13 to lay hands on him, **they feared** the multitude, ... 21:46
19 And I **was afraid**, and went and hid thy talent 25:25
13 saw the earthquake, ... they **feared** greatly, saying, ... 27:54
6 **Fear** not ye: for I know that ye seek Jesus, ... 28:5
6 Then said Jesus unto them, **Be not afraid**: 28:10
13 **they feared** exceedingly, and said one to another, .. Mark 4:41
13 and in his right mind: and they **were afraid**. 5:15
21 But the woman **fearing** and trembling, ... 5:33
5 Be not **afraid**, only believe. 5:36
24 For Herod **feared** John, knowing that he was a just 6:20
6 Be of good cheer: it is I; be not **afraid**. 6:50
25 they understood not ... and **were afraid** to ask him. 9:32
25 amazed; and as they followed, they **were afraid**. 10:32
25 how they might destroy him: for they **feared him**, ... 11:18
25 they **feared** the people: 11:32
13 sought to lay hold on him, but **feared** the people: 12:12
25 neither said they any thing ... for they **were afraid**. 16:8
5 But the angel said unto him, **Fear** not, Zacharias: .. Luke 1:13
5 And the angel said unto her, **Fear** not, Mary: 1:30
9 his mercy is on them that **fear** him from generation 1:50
13 angel of the Lord ... and they **were** sore afraid. 2:9
6 And the angel said unto them, **Fear** not: for, ... Luke 2:10
5 **Fear** not; from henceforth thou shalt catch men. 5:10
20 they **being afraid** wondered, saying one to another, ... 8:25
13 and in his right mind: and they **were afraid**. 8:35
5 he answered him, saying, **Fear** not: believe only, ... 8:50
13 and they **feared** as they entered into the cloud. 9:34
25 and they **feared** to ask him of that saying. 9:45
17 **Be not afraid** of them that kill the body, ... 12:4
17 But I will forewarn you whom ye **shall fear**: 12:5
18 **Fear** him, which after he hath killed hath power 12:5
18 to cast into hell; yea, I say unto you, **Fear** him. 12:5
6 **Fear** not therefore: ye are of more value than 12:7
5 **Fear** not, little flock; for it is your Father's good 12:32
7 There was in a city a judge, which **feared** not God, ... 18:2
1 Though I **fear** not God, nor regard man; 18:4
23 I **feared** thee, because thou art an austere man: 19:21
13 to lay hands on him; and they **feared** the people: 20:19
25 how they might kill him; ... they **feared** the people. ... 22:2
2 rebuked him, saying, **Dost** not thou **fear** God, ... 23:40
13 Jesus walking on the sea, ... and they **were afraid**... John 6:19
6 But he saith unto them, It is I; be not **afraid**. 6:20
25 because they **feared** the Jews: 9:22
5 **Fear** not, daughter of Sion: 12:15
12 Pilate ... heard that saying, he **was** the more **afraid**; ... 19:8
25 without violence: for they **feared** the people, ... Acts 5:26
25 but they were all **afraid** of him, ... 9:26
7 and one that **feared** God with all his house, ... 10:2
7 centurion, a just man, and one that **feareth** God, ... 10:22
7 But in every nation he that **feareth** him, ... 10:35
8 Men of Israel, and ye **that fear** God, give audience. ... 13:16
8 and whosoever among you **feareth** God, ... 13:26
13 **feared**, when they heard that they were Romans. 16:38
5 **Be not afraid**, but speak, and hold not thy peace: 18:9
12 and the chief captain also **was afraid**, ... 22:29
19 commander was **afraid** Paul (NASB) 23:10
8 **fearing** lest they should fall into the quicksands, ... 27:17
5 Saying, **Fear** not, Paul; 27:24
8 **fearing** lest we should have fallen upon rocks, ... 27:29
5 standest by faith. Be not highminded, but **fear**: .... Rom 11:20
11 Wilt thou then not **be afraid** of the power? 13:3
5 if you do evil ... **be afraid**; 13:4
1 But I **fear**, lest by any means, ... 2 Co 11:3
1 For I **fear**, lest, when I come, ... 12:20
7 **fearing** them which were of the circumcision. .... Gal 2:12
1 I **am afraid** of you, ... labour in vain. 4:11
4 and the wife see that she **reverence** her husband. .... Eph 5:33
8 but in singleness of heart, **fearing** God: .... Col 3:22
16 **Let** us therefore **fear**, lest, a promise being left us ... Heb 4:1
13 they were not **afraid** of the king's commandment. 11:23
19 forsook Egypt, not **fearing** the wrath of the king: 11:27
22 and I **will** not **fear** what man shall do unto me. 13:6
6 Honour all men. Love the brotherhood. **Fear** God. 1 Pt 2:17
10 do well, and are not **afraid** with any amazement. 3:6
17 **be not afraid** of their terror, neither be troubled; 3:14
7 He that **feareth** is not made perfect in love. .... 1 Jn 4:18
5 **Fear** not; I am the first and the last: .... Rev 1:17
5 **Fear** none of those things which thou shalt suffer: 2:10
9 and to the saints, and them **that fear** thy name, ... 11:18
18 with a loud voice, **Fear** God, and give glory to him; .. 14:7
15 **shall** not **fear** thee, O Lord, and glorify thy name? 15:4
8 and ye that **fear** him, both small and great. 19:5

Classical Greek

This word can be found in classical Greek from the Eighth Century B.C. meaning "to cause to run" (actively) or "to be put to flight" (passively) (*Liddell-Scott*). By the Fifth Century B.C. it can also be found meaning "to terrify, frighten, startle," or "to be afraid" (ibid.). Thus generally it denotes "flight because of terror"; more narrowly it describes "fear, anxiety," or "apprehension" of someone or something. According to Balz it came to have religious connotations, and its related noun *phobos* (5238), in fact, was "from primitive times a real and powerful deity" ("phobos," *Kittel*, 9:191).

A variety of emotions are conjured by *phobeō* and its cognates. It suggests first of all a response to some (superior) force or power (ibid., 9:193). The range of emotions covers "terror, respect," and "reverence." A sense of utter dread is not always present; rather, the term can simply suggest "regard" for something.

Septuagint Usage

The versatility of *phobeō* is somewhat continued by the Septuagint whose translators equate *phobeō* with as many as 16 different Hebrew expressions. These data, however, are a bit misleading since *phobeō* predominantly translates *yārē'*, "to fear" (in different forms).

In general, *phobeō* denotes religious "fear," either directed toward the one true God (e.g., Genesis 22:12; Exodus 1:17,21; 9:30; Proverbs 14:2) or His word (Exodus 9:20). It can also be used of "fearing" other gods (Judges 6:10; cf. 2 Kings 17:37,38 [LXX 4 Kings 17:37,38]). Most especially "those fearing the Lord" are those regarded as His people (Psalms 22:23 [LXX 21:23]; 33:18 [32:18]; 34:9 [33:9] [note the parallel here with *hoi hagioi*, "the holy ones"]; Psalms 103:17 [102:17]; 112:1 [111:1]; 115:11 [113:19]; cf. especially Sirach; Psalm 145:19 [144:19]; Micah 6:8).

Phobeō stands for the kind of fear experienced in the presence of deity or higher authority (e.g., Daniel 10:12; cf. 1 Samuel 3:15 [LXX 1 Kings 3:15]) as well as "fear" of one's enemies (1 Samuel 7:7 [LXX 1 Kings 7:7]; Psalm 3:6). It also suggests "regard" or "paying attention to" (and obey) a command (Daniel 3:12). Certainly the idea of "obedience" is implicit in the religious use of *phobeō* (cf. Zephaniah 3:7).

New Testament Usage

In the New Testament *phobeō* occurs only in the passive form *phobeomai*. Without an object it denotes the condition of fear (Matthew 14:5; 17:6; 21:26; etc.). With an object the verb depicts something or someone as the source of fear (e.g., Matthew 10:26; Mark 6:20; 11:18). *Phobeomai* particularly denotes the response on the part of those witnessing Jesus' miracles (Mark 4:41; Luke 8:35; John 6:19). These miracles evoked the response of fear, awe, and reverence (cf. also Luke 1:13,30; 2:9,10). This idea is repeated in a limited fashion in Acts where "fear" (only the noun functions this way) is generated among the people because of events in the Church (e.g., Acts 5:5,11; 19:17; cf. 2:43; Revelation 11:11).

"Those fearing God" is a designation given to Gentiles who were sympathetic to Judaism but who had not become proselytes (Acts 10:2,22, coupled with *dikaios* [1335B], "righteous"; 13:16). These "God-fearers" were generally receptive to the gospel.

"Fearing God"—not anxious, desperate terror (cf. Luke 8:50; Hebrews 13:6; Romans 8:15) but heartfelt awe and reverence—is essential to the Christian faith. Reward awaits those who "fear (His) name" (Revelation 11:18; cf. Romans 11:20). In one sense "fear" is expressed not only in an attitude toward God (Revelation 19:5) but also in life-style before others.

Strong 5399, Bauer 862-63, Moulton-Milligan 673 (see "phobeomai"), Kittel 9:189-219, Liddell-Scott 1946, Colin Brown 2:596.

5237. φόβητρον phobētron noun

A fearful sight, a terror.

Cross-Reference:

φοβέω phobeō (5236)

חָגָּא chāggā' (2375), Terror (Is 19:17).

1. φόβητρα phobētra nom/acc pl neu

1 and fearful sights and great signs shall there be.... Luke 21:11

Classical Greek and Septuagint Usage

This word can be found in classical Greek from the Fifth Century B.C. (usually in the plural) meaning "terrors" (cf. *Liddell-Scott*). It is related to the verb *phobizō*, "scare, terrify." It can be found in the Septuagint at Isaiah 19:17. There it occurs in Isaiah's prophecy of the "terror" that Judah would become to Egypt.

New Testament Usage

The one time that the word *phobētron* occurs in the New Testament is in Jesus' prophecies about the destruction of Jerusalem and the end times (Luke 21:11). In the midst of wars, earthquakes, famine, and pestilence there will be "fearful events" (*phobētra*, NIV) and great signs from heaven. According to Louw and Nida, *phobētron* refers to the "object, event, or condition which causes fear" (*Greek-English Lexicon*, 1:317). In comparison, *phobos* (5238) is seen as a state of distress or the occasion or source of fear, and *phoberos* (5235) refers to something or someone who causes the fear (ibid., 1:316).

Strong 5400, Bauer 863, Liddell-Scott 1946.

5238. φόβος phobos noun

Fear, terror, alarm; reverence, respect.

CROSS-REFERENCE:

φοβέω phobeō (5236)

אֵימָה 'êmāh (372), Dread, terror (Gn 15:12, Jos 2:9, Job 9:34).

אֵימְתָן 'êmethān (A374), Terrifying (Dn 7:7—Aramaic).

חָרֵד chāradh (2829), Tremble (Is 19:16).

חֲרָדָה chărādhāh (2832), Fear, terror (Is 21:4, Jer 30:5 [37:5], Dn 10:7).

חַת chath (2952), Dread (Gn 9:2).

חִתָּה chittāh (2955), Terror (Gn 35:5).

חִתִּית chittîth (2959), Terror (Ez 32:23f.,26,30,32).

יִרְאָה yir'āh (3488), Fear (Ex 20:20, Prv 8:13, Is 7:25).

מוֹרָא môrā' (4307), Fear (Is 8:12).

פַּחַד pachadh (6586), Fear, dread (Gn 31:42, Ps 64:1 [63:1], Jer 49:5, 30:5]).

רַעְמָה ra'māh (7771), Mane (Job 39:19).

1. **φόβος phobos** nom sing masc
2. **φόβου phobou** gen sing masc
3. **φόβῳ phobō** dat sing masc
4. **φόβον phobon** acc sing masc
5. **φόβοι phoboi** nom pl masc

2 saying, It is a spirit; and they cried out for **fear**.... Matt 14:26
2 And for **fear** of him the keepers did shake,........... 28:4
2 quickly from the sepulchre with **fear** and great joy;.... 28:8
4 they feared exceedingly, and said (NT).............Mark 4:41
1 saw him, he was troubled, and **fear** fell upon him....Luke 1:12
1 And **fear** came on all that dwelt round about them:..... 1:65
4 angel of the Lord ... and they were sore **afraid**.......... 2:9
2 glorified God, and were filled **with fear**, saying,......... 5:26
1 there came a **fear** on all: and they glorified God,....... 7:16
3 for they were taken **with** great **fear**:.................... 8:37
2 Men's hearts failing them for **fear**,.................... 21:26
4 no man spake openly of him for **fear** of the Jews.... John 7:13
4 but secretly for **fear** of the Jews,..................... 19:38
4 the disciples were assembled for **fear** of the Jews,...... 20:19
1 And **fear** came upon every soul:....................Acts 2:43
1 **fear** came on all them that heard these things........... 5:5
1 And great **fear** came upon all the church,.............. 5:11
3 were edified; and walking in the **fear** of the Lord,...... 9:31
1 and **fear** fell on them all,........................... 19:17
1 There is no **fear** of God before their eyes........... Rom 3:18
4 not received the spirit of bondage again to **fear**;........ 8:15
1 For rulers are not **a terror** to good works,............. 13:3
4 **fear** to whom fear;.................................. 13:7
4 fear to whom **fear**;.................................. 13:7
3 And I was with you in weakness, and in **fear**,....... 1 Co 2:3
4 Knowing therefore the **terror** of the Lord,.......... 2 Co 5:11
3 perfecting holiness in the **fear** of God................. 7:1
5 without were fightings, within were **fears**................ 7:5
4 yea, what indignation, yea, what **fear**,.................. 7:11
2 how with **fear** and trembling ye received him........... 7:15
3 Submitting yourselves ... in the **fear** of God..........Eph 5:21
2 that are your masters ... with **fear** and trembling,....... 6:5
2 work out your own salvation with **fear**..............Phlp 2:12
4 rebuke before all, that others also may **fear**......... 1 Tm 5:20
3 through **fear** of death were ... subject to bondage.....Heb 2:15
3 pass the time of your sojourning here in **fear**:....... 1 Pt 1:17
3 Servants, be subject to your masters with all **fear**;....... 2:18
3 behold your chaste conversation coupled with **fear**....... 3:2
4 be not afraid of their **terror**, neither be troubled;....... 3:14
2 the hope that is in you with meekness and **fear**:........ 3:15
1 There is no **fear** in love;.......................... 1 Jn 4:18
4 love casteth out **fear**: because fear hath torment......... 4:18
1 love casteth out fear: because **fear** hath torment......... 4:18
3 others save with **fear**, pulling them out of the fire;.. Jude 1:23
1 and great **fear** fell upon them which saw them...... Rev 11:11
4 Standing afar off for the **fear** of her torment,.......... 18:10
4 shall stand afar off for the **fear** of her torment,........ 18:15

Classical Greek

As early as Homer (Eighth Century B.C.) the Greeks used *phobos* in the sense of "fright" or "panic." The word is related to *phobeō* (5236), "to flee" or "run away" (*Liddell-Scott*). Throughout the classical period the word was used not only for "terror" and "headlong flight" but "fear" or "apprehension," whatever the cause. Fear of death was a common example. Sometimes the word was used in the positive sense of "respect, awe," or "reverence," especially toward authorities to whom one is responsible or to deity. As early as Homer the god *Phobos* was ranked high in the mythological system, depicted as a typical war-god (ibid.).

In ordinary speech, fear that oppressed and caused anxiety was to be avoided if possible. But unavoidable fear had its uses in exhortation and could even be the basis of respect and reverence. For some, to repudiate fear was to promote anarchy. The rationalistic philosophers before Socrates sharply rejected emotional fear as disturbing to calmness and peace of mind. Even "fear of God (or the gods)" was said to be invented to scare men. The Stoics defined fear as an irrational emotion and repudiated it as harmful. The Epicureans sharply rejected fear along with the pains of the body and upsets of the soul. (See Balz, "phobos," *Kittel*, 9:191-197.)

Septuagint Usage

In the Septuagint *phobos* is the usual word that translates the Hebrew root *yir'āh*, "to fear" or "to be afraid." The noun form in Hebrew can designate the cause of the fear or its object. *Phobos* is used instead of *deos* (1183B) because the reference is to a "more abiding fear" or a "watchfulness." *Phobos* and the corresponding verb are frequently used in the Old Testament with men or God as the object.

But there is a difference between classical and Septuagint Greek. The glory and majesty of God is *terrible*—strikes with terror. But the terror is for the enemies of God. He is a mighty deliverer to His people but terrible to the enemies (Deuteronomy 11:25) that would destroy them.

God's sovereign power and holiness demand *reverence* and worship. Those who love God are *watchful* and *fearful* lest they displease God. They also respect, esteem, and obey those whom God has placed over them (Joshua 4:14). Already in the Old Testament this fear of God was very positive; it distinguished between the people of God and the unbelievers. "In the fear of the Lord is strong confidence: and his children shall have a place of refuge" (Proverbs 14:26).

New Testament Usage

In the New Testament *phobos* takes for granted and enlarges on the classical concepts as purified and enriched by divine revelation and by inspiration. There is still the sudden alarm, the deliberate fear and caution, the dread of impending doom. There is the slavish fear (Romans 8:15) called "bondage." Each was a fact to be reckoned with. But the glory of the gospel is that a new relationship with God overwhelms these negative aspects of fear, delivers believers from bondage, and gives them the spirit of adoption (son-placing) so that they confidently call God "Father."

This is what God does for those who *fear* Him and keep His commandments. It is a relationship of love and trust. "Fear" (*phobos*) is no longer a fear of judgment for the believer. In addition, reverence toward God is always to be coupled with love of Him; this love, then, will cast out all "fear" (1 John 4:18). This type of a relationship with the Lord will break the bondage fear brings (cf. Romans 8:15; 2 Timothy 1:7; Hebrews 2:15). The fear that remains is a function of love—fear lest a believer hurt the heart of the Saviour and Lord or that he fails to love his neighbor as himself. In addition, fear is the caution that makes believers respect and obey legitimate authority. Furthermore, it is the proper concern for one's own health and safety and that of others.

The Bible is full of assurance to those who "fear God, and keep his commandments" (Ecclesiastes 12:13). Again and again a reader comes across the words "fear not." Those who "fear God" can trust Him and "not be afraid" (Psalm 56:11). Knowing his own weakness and dependence upon God, and knowing that God will judge every man according to his own works, the Christian is commanded to "pass the time of (his) sojourning here in *fear*" (1 Peter 1:17). In doing so the believer will be kept from the self-confidence which so often leads to falling. In light of this Paul wrote to Christians saying "work out your own salvation with *fear* and trembling" (Philippians 2:12).

Strong 5401, Bauer 863-64, Moulton-Milligan 673, Kittel 9:189-219, Liddell-Scott 1947, Colin Brown 1:621-24.

5239. Φοίβη Phoibē name

Phoebe.

1. Φοίβην Phoibēn acc fem
2. Φοίβης Phoibēs gen fem

1 **I commend unto you Phebe our sister,** .... **Rom 16:1**

Phoebe was a leading member of the church at Cenchreae, a port on the isthmus east of Corinth. She is described as a *diakonos* (1243); this may mean "minister" in a general sense or, specifically, "deacon." Paul praised her ministry and urged the Roman church to welcome and help her (Romans 16:1f.).

5240. Φοινίκη Phoinikē name

Phoenicia.

1. Φοινίκης Phoinikēs gen fem
2. Φοινίκην Phoinikēn acc fem

1 **travelled as far as Phenice, and Cyprus,** .... **Acts 11:19**
2 **they passed through Phenice and Samaria,** **15:3**
2 **And finding a ship sailing over unto Phenicia,** **21:2**

In New Testament times Phoenicia was a geographical term which referred to the coastal area of Syria, roughly corresponding to the modern state of Lebanon. The Phoenicians were among the most famous traders of the era before Christ. Tyre and Sidon were their chief cities.

The Gentile woman whose daughter Jesus healed was from Syrian Phoenicia (Mark 7:26), and inhabitants of the area had other contacts with Jesus. The gospel was preached there, though at first only to resident Jews (Acts 11:19). Paul stayed twice with the members of the church in Phoenicia. On the first occasion he was traveling with Barnabas on their way to the Council of Jerusalem (Acts 15:3). On the second he was on his last journey to Jerusalem and stayed at Tyre and Ptolemais (Acts 21:3-7).

5241. φοῖνιξ phoinix noun

Date palm, palm, Phoenix.

תָּמָר tāmār (8887), Palm tree (Lv 23:40, Jgs 3:13, Jl 1:12).

תֹּמֶר tōmer (8890), Palm tree (Jgs 4:5).

תִּמֹרָה timōrāh (8891), Palm tree, palm tree decoration (1 Kgs 6:29, 2 Chr 3:5, Ez 40:22, 26).

1. **φοίνικες phoinikes** nom pl masc
2. **φοινίκων phoinikōn** gen pl masc
3. **φοίνικας phoinikas** acc pl masc

2 Took branches of **palm trees**, ... John 12:13
1 with white robes, and **palms** in their hands; .... Rev 7:9

The primary meaning of *phoinix* is the "palm tree," more particularly the date palm. This was a common tree in ancient Palestine, especially in Jericho, the "city of palms" (Judges 3:13; Josephus *Antiquities* 14.4.1; 15.4.2). Modern Israel now proudly cultivates choice dates in an oasis by the Dead Sea. Palms or palm branches were a common symbol on coins of the period. In the Christian tradition, palms became a symbol of victory, reminiscent of Jesus' triumphal entry into Jerusalem (John 12:13). Furthermore, the multitudes around the throne wear white robes and hold palms in their hands (Revelation 7:9).

Outside the Scriptures *phoinix* is also used in reference to the mythological bird of Egypt and as the name of an ancient port city on the south coast of Crete (Acts 27:12).

Strong 5404, Bauer 864, Moulton-Milligan 673-74, Liddell-Scott 1948.

5242. Φοῖνιξ Phoinix name

Phoenix.

1. **Φοίνικα Phoinika** acc masc

1 if by any means they might attain to **Phenice**, ... Acts 27:12

Phoenix was a sheltered harbor on the south coast of Crete. The crew of the ship carrying Paul to Rome hoped to winter there, but they were prevented from doing so by the sudden onset of a fierce northeasterly storm. This carried the ship far off course to its eventual shipwreck on Malta (Acts 27:12).

5243. φονεύς phoneus noun

Murderer, slayer.

Cognate:
φόνος phonos (5245)

Synonym:
ἀνθρωποκτόνος anthrōpoktonos (441)

1. **φονεύς phoneus** nom sing masc
2. **φονέα phonea** acc sing masc
3. **φονεῖς phoneis** nom/acc pl masc
4. **φονεῦσιν phoneusin** dat pl masc

3 and destroyed those **murderers**, ... Matt 22:7
2 and desired **a murderer** to be granted unto you; ..... Acts 3:14
3 ye have been now the betrayers and **murderers**: 7:52
1 No doubt this man is **a murderer**, ... 28:4
1 But let none of you suffer as **a murderer**, ... 1 Pt 4:15
4 abominable, and **murderers**, and whoremongers, ... Rev 21:8
3 and sorcerers, and whoremongers, and **murderers**, ... 22:15

Phoneus, "murderer," occurs seven times in the New Testament, though other words for "killing" are fairly common. It is apparently distinct from the killing of animal or plant life or even the unavoidable or judicial taking of human life. A murderer is one who deliberately takes the life of another human being for personal and evil reasons. Usually it was used to describe the Jewish leaders (Matthew 22:7; Acts 7:52; 28:4; 1 Peter 4:15), but it can also be found in general lists of vices (Revelation 21:8; 22:15).

Strong 5406, Bauer 864, Moulton-Milligan 674, Liddell-Scott 1949.

5244. φονεύω phoneuō verb

Murder.

Cognate:
φόνος phonos (5245)

Synonyms:
ἀναιρέω anaireō (335)
ἀποκτείνω apokteinō (609)
ἀπόλλυμι apollumi (616)
διαχειρίζομαι diacheirizomai (1309)
θανατόω thanatoō (2266)
θύω thuō (2357)
νεκρόω nekroō (3362)
σφάζω sphazō (4821)

הָרַג hāragh (2103), Qal: kill (Neh 4:11, 6:10, Prv 1:32); niphal: be slain (Lam 2:20).

חָרַם chāram (2868), Hiphil: destroy (Jos 10:35).

נָכָה nākhâh (5409), Hiphil: smite, strike (Jos 10:28,35); kill (2 Chr 25:3).

רָצַח rātsach (7815), Qal: manslayer (Nm 35:12); murder (1 Kgs 21:19 [20:19], Jer 7:9); niphal: be murdered (Jgs 20:4); piel: murder (Pss 62:3 [61:3], 94:6 [93:6], Hos 6:9 [6:10]).

1. **φονεύετε phoneuete** 2pl indic pres act
2. **ἐφονεύσατε ephoneusate** 2pl indic aor act
3. **φονεύσῃς phoneusēs** 2sing subj aor act
4. **φονεύσῃ phoneusē** 3sing subj aor act
5. **φονευσάντων phoneusantōn** gen pl masc part aor act
6. **φονεύσεις phoneuseis** 2sing indic fut act
7. **φονεύεις phoneueis** 2sing indic pres act

6 **Thou shalt not kill**; and whosoever **shall kill** .... Matt 5:21
4 whosoever **shall kill** ... in danger of the judgment: 5:21
6 **Thou shalt do no murder**, ... 19:18
5 the children of **them which killed** the prophets. 23:31
2 whom **ye slew** between the temple and the altar. 23:35
3 Do not commit adultery, **Do not kill**, ... Mark 10:19
3 Do not commit adultery, **Do not kill**, ... Luke 18:20
6 **Thou shalt not kill**, ... Rom 13:9
3 Do not commit adultery, said also, **Do not kill**. .... Jas 2:11
6 Now if thou commit no adultery, yet if **thou kill**, ... 2:11

1 ye **kill**, and desire to have, and cannot obtain:....... Jas 4:2
2 Ye have condemned and **killed** the just;................ 5:6

Phoneuō is a verb meaning "to commit murder." The Septuagint uses this word commonly to translate the Hebrew *rātsach* which is used in the commandment, "Thou shalt commit no *murder*" (Exodus 20:13 [LXX 20:15]; Deuteronomy 5:17, free translation). Though there are 10 Hebrew words (Old Testament) and 6 Greek (New Testament) words translated "kill" in the King James Version, *phoneuō* and its Hebrew counterpart clearly imply the taking of human life for intentional and personal evil reasons. Such conduct is specifically forbidden by God and is certain to be judged with severity (Matthew 5:21; 19:18; 23:31,35; Mark 10:19; Luke 18:20; Romans 13:9; James 2:11; 5:6).

Strong 5407, Bauer 864, Moulton-Milligan 674, Liddell-Scott 1949.

5245. φόνος phonos noun

Murder, killing.

Cognates:

φονεύς phoneus (5243)
φονεύω phoneuō (5244)

דָּם dām (1879), Blood, bloodshed (Ex 22:2, Dt 22:8, Prv 28:17).

חֶרֶב cherev (2820), Sword (Ex 5:3, Lv 26:7).

פֶּגֶר pegher (6538), Corpse (Ez 43:7,9).

פֶּה peh (6552), Mouth; edge (Ex 17:13, Nm 21:24, Dt 20:13).

רֶצַח rātsach (7815), Murder (Hos 4:2).

1. **φόνου phonou** gen sing masc
2. **φόνῳ phonō** dat sing masc
3. **φόνον phonon** acc sing masc
4. **φόνοι phonoi** nom pl masc
5. **φόνων phonōn** gen pl masc

4 For out of the heart proceed ... **murders**,.......... Matt 15:19
4 evil thoughts, adulteries, fornications, **murders**,......Mark 7:21
3 who had committed **murder** in the insurrection......... 15:7
3 Who ... for **murder**, was cast into prison........... Luke 23:19
3 that for sedition and **murder** was cast into prison,...... 23:25
1 yet breathing out threatenings and **slaughter**.........Acts 9:1
1 full of envy, **murder**, debate, deceit, malignity;...... Rom 1:29
4 Envyings, **murders**, drunkenness, revellings,.......... Gal 5:21
2 were tempted, were **slain** with the sword:...........Heb 11:37
5 Neither repented they of their **murders**,............. Rev 9:21

Classical Greek

Phonos signifies "murder, slaughter," in classical Greek. Generally this concerned the literal "killing" of someone or something. Trench, however, notes the figurative use of the cognate term, *phoneus* (5243), "murderer," in reference to a "murderer of godliness" (i.e., a wicked man who destroys the piety of others [*Synonyms of the New Testament*, p.314]). He further suggests that such usage was "not infrequent."

Septuagint Usage

Five Hebrew words are translated by *phonos* in the Septuagint. The 21 canonical instances are fairly distributed among the various forms. Several times it is linked to a word meaning "sword" (*cherev*; cf. Exodus 5:3; Leviticus 26:7; Deuteronomy 28:22). On two occasions it equals a term usually denoting a "corpse" (Ezekiel 43:7,9). Thus we see the absence of any direct equivalent to *phonos* in the Old Testament. Perhaps this is because "murder" is such a verbal idea (cf. *phoneuō* [5244], Hebrew *rātsach*; *apokteinō* [609]). With respect to "murder" as a concept, it is certainly denounced early in the Scriptures (Genesis 4:8ff.).

Respect for human life is a basic tenet in the Old Testament. Premeditated and willful murder is considered a great sin and does not go unnoticed by God (cf. Genesis 4:10). In Genesis 9:5,6 the blood of the murderer is claimed by God who may execute His judgment through men (Genesis 9:6). The murderer loses his own right to live. The premise for such a high regard for human life is that man was made in the "image of God" (Genesis 1:27).

In the Law given at Sinai the fifth commandment says, "Thou shalt not kill" (Exodus 20:13). Anyone who intentionally murdered was guilty of trespassing this commandment and would be punished by death (Exodus 21:12; Leviticus 24:17-21; Numbers 35:16,17). The Law distinguished between intentional and unintentional murder (Numbers 35:22f.), and in order to protect one who committed an unintentional murder from the "avenger of blood," cities of refuge were established (Numbers 35:1-10).

New Testament Usage

Phonos occurs only 10 times in the New Testament (cf. *phoneuō* [5244], 12 times; *phoneus*, 7 times). Murder continues to be a violation of God's covenant relationship, only now we can commit the crime in our hearts and be equally guilty in God's eyes (cf. Matthew 5:21,22 with Exodus 20:13,14).

Murder is one of the many by-products of the sinful nature which are inherited from the Fall (cf. Genesis 4:8ff.; Matthew 15:19; Mark 7:21; Romans 1:29). Being the victim of murder has often been the fate of the faithful (Hebrews 11:37; cf. Acts 9:1; James 5:6) and will continue to be. Satan is the ultimate originator of all murderous intent. Jesus called him a "murderer from the beginning" (John 8:44). Murder will be especially rampant among the unrepentant in the end times (Revelation 9:21).

Strong 5408, Bauer 864, Moulton-Milligan 674, Liddell-Scott 1949-50.

5246. φορέω phoreō verb

Bear, carry regularly, wear.

Cognates:

πληροφορέω plērophoreō (3995)
πληροφορία plērophoria (3996)
φέρω pherō (5179)

יָסַף yāsaph (3362), Hiphil: add (Prv 16:23).

עָטָה 'ātâh (6057), Wear (Sir 11:5).

1. **φορεῖ phorei** 3sing indic pres act
2. **φορῶν phorōn** nom sing masc part pres act
3. **φοροῦντα phorounta** acc sing masc part pres act
4. **φοροῦντες phorountes** nom pl masc part pres act
5. **ἐφορέσαμεν ephoresamen** 1pl indic aor act
6. **φορέσομεν phoresomen** 1pl indic fut act
7. **φορέσωμεν phoresōmen** 1pl subj aor act

4 they that **wear** soft clothing are in kings' houses.... Matt 11:8
2 **wearing** the crown of thorns, and the purple robe. John 19:5
1 for he **beareth** not the sword in vain: .... Rom 13:4
5 And as we **have borne** the image of the earthy,.... 1 Co 15:49
6 we **shall** also **bear** the image of the heavenly........... 15:49
3 have respect to him that **weareth** the gay clothing,.... Jas 2:3

Classical Greek

This verb is a form of *pherō* (5179) which means to "bear, carry," or "bring." It replaces *pherō* especially in reference to a lasting, continuing, repeated, or customary action (Weiss, "phoreō," *Kittel*, 9:83). Weiss lists many examples of its use: of a steady wind or raging waves that "carry something forward," of swirling dust, of the chariot that usually carries the hero to battle, of the cupbearer who keeps the cup full, and many more. The most common reference is to wearing (or carrying) clothes, weapons, the scepter, or what belongs to a person—even the parts of the body (ibid., 9:83f.). Classical usage also included bearing a name.

Septuagint Usage

The Septuagint seldom used the word. Two significant instances are in Proverbs. Figuratively it is used of "*carrying* learning on the lips" (Proverbs 16:23) and of one who "*bears* destruction in his mouth" (Proverbs 16:27, Septuagint).

New Testament Usage

The verb is used six times in the New Testament meaning "to bear for a longer time or continually." Jesus said, "They that *wear* soft clothing are in kings' houses" (Matthew 11:8). John said, "Then came Jesus forth, *wearing* the crown of thorns" (John 19:5). The thorns were not a momentary cruelty; Jesus *wore* them. Paul warned believers to respect civil authority, for the officer "*beareth* not the sword in vain" (Romans 13:4). James condemns favoritism toward "him that *weareth* the gay clothing" (James 2:3). And Paul referred to one's identity as a characteristic likeness: "As we have *borne* the image of the earthy, we *shall* also *bear* the image of the heavenly" (1 Corinthians 15:49).

Strong 5409, Bauer 864-65, Moulton-Milligan 674, Kittel 9:83-84, Liddell-Scott 1951.

5247. φόρος phoros noun

Tax, tribute, payment.

Cognate:

φέρω pherō (5179)

Synonyms:

κῆνσος kēnsos (2750)
τέλος telos (4904)

מִדָּה middāh (4202), Tax (Neh 5:4).

מִדָּה middāh (A4203), Tribute, revenue (Ezr 4:20, 6:8—Aramaic).

מַס maṣ (4671), Forced labor (Jgs 1:28, 1 Kgs 4:6, 2 Chr 8:8).

1. **φόρον phoron** acc sing masc
2. **φόρους phorous** acc pl masc

1 Is it lawful for us to give **tribute** unto Caesar,...... Luke 20:22
2 and forbidding to give **tribute** to Caesar,.............. 23:2
2 For for this cause pay ye **tribute** also: .... Rom 13:6
1 **tribute** to whom tribute is due; 13:7
1 tribute to whom **tribute** is due; 13:7

This term is related to *pherō* (5179), "bear" or "carry," and means literally "that which is brought in by way of payment" (*Liddell-Scott*). Its meaning includes the broad sense of "payment" which is owed for whatever cause. The papyri have examples of bills for the "payment" of rent on property (*Moulton-Milligan*). For the Jews in the time of Jesus *phoros* denoted the "tax" or "tribute" exacted by the Roman emperor from all subject peoples, including the Jews. This tax was to support the hated Roman government and army of occupation. Since the only alternative for the subject nation was destruction or anarchy, Jesus implied that the tax was owed and should be paid (Luke 20:22-25), as every Roman coin bore witness. Paul said that government is ordained of God and should be respected, obeyed, and financed for one's own safety and "for conscience sake." Even a corrupt government is better than anarchy (Romans 13:1-7).

STRONG 5411, BAUER 865, MOULTON-MILLIGAN 674, KITTEL 9:78-83, LIDDELL-SCOTT 1951, COLIN BROWN 3:752,754.

5248. φορτίζω phortizō verb

Load, burden, lade.

COGNATES:
φορτίον phortion (5249)
φόρτος phortos (5250)

SYNONYM:
βαρέω bareō (911)

שָׁחַד shāchadh (8244), Give a gift (Ez 16:33).

1. φορτίζετε phortizete 2pl indic pres act
2. πεφορτισμένοι pephortismenoi nom pl masc part perf mid

2 all ye that labour and are **heavy laden,**............Matt 11:28
1 for ye **lade** men with burdens grievous to be borne, Luke 11:46

Classical Greek

Phortizō is related to *phortos* (5250), the "cargo of a ship," and *phortis*, a "freighter." The verb was used as early as Homer (Eighth Century B.C.) to indicate "loading a ship" or "shipping." It can also be found generally meaning "to carry away a load" or "be burdened with a load" (cf. *Liddell-Scott*). *Moulton-Milligan* mentions papyri that use the participial form for "beasts loaded with dry hay" and "ships loaded with produce."

Septuagint Usage

One use is noted in the Septuagint (Ezekiel 16:33). Backslidden Israel is likened to an unfaithful wife that scorns the taking of fees for her prostitution but rather loads her lovers with gifts to gain more attention. The verb seems to have an intensive effect—to indicate the horror of Israel's sin.

New Testament Usage

Phortizō is used only twice in the New Testament. Jesus rebuked the lawyers who loaded people with detailed interpretations of the Law. He said, "Ye *lade* men with burdens grievous to be borne, and ye yourselves touch not the burdens with one of your fingers" (Luke 11:46). In contrast to the method of the lawyers, Jesus offered rest to the loaded or burdened. He said, "Come unto me, all ye that labor and are *heavy laden*, and I will give you rest" (Matthew 11:28). It is not the rest of no responsibility; it is joining Christ in wearing His yoke. The well-fitted yoke is not an instrument of torture. Its purpose is to make life's tasks bearable and to make the burden lighter with Christ himself as a partner in the yoke (verses 29,30).

STRONG 5412, BAUER 865, MOULTON-MILLIGAN 674, KITTEL 9:86-87, LIDDELL-SCOTT 1951-52, COLIN BROWN 1:260.

5249. φορτίον phortion noun

Load, burden, cargo; obligation, duty.

COGNATE:
φορτίζω phortizō (5248)

SYNONYM:
βάρος baros (916)

מַשָּׂא massā' (5014), Burden (2 Sm 19:35, Job 7:20, Is 46:1).

שׂוֹךְ sôkh (7913), Branch (Jgs 9:49—Codex Alexandrinus only).

שׂוֹכָה sôkhāh (7914), Branch (Jgs 9:48—Codex Alexandrinus only).

1. φορτίον phortion nom/acc sing neu
2. φορτίοις phortiois dat pl neu
3. φορτία phortia nom/acc pl neu
4. φορτίου phortiou gen sing neu

1 For my yoke is easy, and my **burden** is light....... Matt 11:30
3 they bind heavy **burdens** and grievous to be borne,.... 23:4
3 for ye lade men with **burdens** grievous to be borne, Luke 11:46
2 touch not the **burdens** with one of your fingers......... 11:46
1 For every man shall bear his own **burden**........... Gal 6:5

Phortion is the diminutive form of *phortos* (5250). Its literal meaning is "load" or "cargo" but by extension becomes "burden, obligation," or "duty." The diminutive form of the noun is more common than the original (*Liddell-Scott*).

Classical Greek

In the classical and Koine Greek, including Josephus and the papyri, the word is common for "ship's lading, wagon load, lading, freight." It is used of sacks of grain on a beast of burden and even of a child in its mother's womb (cf. ibid.). It has the general sense of "goods." From Demosthenes through the papyri it also means "burdening" with cares, duties, tasks, sickness, age, etc. (*Moulton-Milligan*).

Septuagint Usage

The Septuagint uses *phortion* for the Hebrew word *massā'* both in the literal sense of "bearing a load" and for "burdens" in general. Job became a "burden" to himself (Job 7:20), and an aged friend of David did not want to be a "burden" to the king (2 Samuel 19:35 [LXX 2 Kings 19:35]).

In rabbinic texts the Hebrew *massā'* means "bearing, trade, business," or "occupation." In some instances it means "obligation" or "duty" (Weiss, "phortion," *Kittel*, 9:85).

New Testament Usage

In the New Testament *phortion* has the literal meaning of a ship's "cargo" (Acts 27:10, some texts). But more often it refers to the "load" or "burden" of life's "responsibilities, cares, obligations, duties." Jesus indignantly criticized the Pharisaic rabbis for laying on the people "*heavy burdens* . . . grievous to be borne" (Matthew 23:4). As Weiss says, "The over-heavy burden is not the Law itself nor is it the fact of interpretation by the rabbis. What Jesus is criticizing is the one side of the contradiction between the rabbis' own conduct and the duties they impose on men, and on the other the perverted direction in which their exposition of the Law leads" (ibid.). If the "heavy laden" will but come to Jesus, there is release from the unreasonable "burden" of legalism. Jesus' well-fitted yoke eases the strain of the responsibility, and sharing the yoke with Jesus makes the *burden* lighter (Matthew 11:28-30).

If one is overtaken with a failure, he should be able to claim the help and support of the Christian community to restore him so together the heavy load can be carried again (Galatians 6:1,2). But there is a "burden" of responsibility (*phortion*) that the individual must carry (Galatians 6:5). His help is in the Lord and the yoke of true discipleship (Matthew 11:28-30).

Strong 5413, Bauer 865, Moulton-Milligan 674-75, Kittel 9:84-86, Liddell-Scott 1952, Colin Brown 1:260-61.

5250. φόρτος phortos noun

Cargo, load, freight, burden.

Cross-Reference:
φορτίζω phortizō (5248)

1. φόρτου phortou gen sing masc

1 and much damage, not only of the **lading** and ship, Acts 27:10

Phortos occurs only once in the New Testament (in the *Textus Receptus* version of Acts 27:10). It is translated "lading" and refers to the cargo of the ship that was threatened in a storm. This is the literal meaning of *phortos* from the time of Homer (Eighth Century B.C.) to at least New Testament times.

The diminutive form, *phortion* (5249), however, came into much more common use both in the sense of "cargo, load, burden" and in the more figurative meanings of "obligation, duty, responsibility."

Strong 5414, Bauer 865, Liddell-Scott 1952.

5251. Φουρτουνᾶτος Phourtounatos name

Fortunatus.

1. Φουρτουνάτου Phourtounatou gen masc
2. Φορτουνάτου Phortounatou gen masc

1 coming of Stephanas and **Fortunatus** and Achaicus: 1 Co 16:17

An otherwise unknown Christian of Corinth who, with Stephanas and Achaicus, brought Paul encouraging news of the church (1 Corinthians 16:17).

5252. φραγέλλιον phragellion noun

Whip, lash, scourge.

Cross-Reference:
φραγελλόω phragelloō (5253)

1. φραγέλλιον phragellion nom/acc sing neu

1 And when he had made a **scourge** of small cords, . . . John 2:15

Phragellion is a loanword from the Latin *flagellum.* According to Vine, the Roman "lash" or "scourge was made of leathern thongs, weighted with sharp pieces of bone or lead, which tore the flesh of both the back and the breast" (*Expository Dictionary,* "Scourge"). Slaves or others without Roman citizenship, when condemned to crucifixion, were generally prepared by the scourging until the flesh hung down in bloody shreds. Many died from the beating itself (Schneider, "mastigoō," *Kittel,* 4:516-519). It occurs once in the New Testament of the whip Jesus used to clear the temple (John 2:15).

Strong 5416, Bauer 865, Moulton-Milligan 675, Liddell-Scott 1952, Colin Brown 1:162.

5253. φραγελλόω phragelloō verb

Scourge, flog.

Cognate:
φραγέλλιον phragellion (5252)

Synonyms:
κολαφίζω kolaphizō (2826)
μαστιγόω mastigoō (3118)
μαστίζω mastizō (3119)
παίω paiō (3680)
πατάσσω patassō (3822)
πλήσσω plēssō (4001)
ῥαπίζω rhapizō (4331)
τύπτω tuptō (5021)

1. φραγελλώσας phragellōsas nom sing masc part aor act

1 and when he **had scourged** Jesus, he delivered him Matt 27:26
1 and delivered Jesus, when he **had scourged** him, . . . Mark 15:15

Classical Greek

The word *phragelloō* is borrowed from the Latin *flagellare*, to "flog" or "scourge." Among the several Greek words for beat, whip, flog, or scourge, *phragelloō* more specifically indicates the Roman type of punishment usually inflicted on slaves and provincials after a sentence of death had been pronounced (*Bauer*). According to Vine, the scourging of Roman citizens was prohibited by the Porcian law of 197 B.C. (*Expository Dictionary*, "Scourge"). The word does not occur in the Septuagint.

Vine describes the method of scourging as follows: "The person was stripped and tied in a bending position to a pillar, or stretched on a frame. The scourge was made of leathern thongs, weighted with sharp pieces of bone or lead, which tore the flesh of both the back and the breast" (ibid.). Schneider says further: "The number of strokes was not prescribed. It continued until the flesh hung down in bloody shreds" (Schneider, "mastigoō," *Kittel*, 4:517).

New Testament Usage

Phragelloō occurs only twice in the New Testament. Both references are to the scourging that Pilate ordered immediately prior to the crucifixion of Jesus (Matthew 27:26; Mark 15:15). In foretelling His own scourging Jesus used the word *mastigoō* (3118) (Matthew 20:19; Mark 10:34; Luke 18:33), as did John in describing the event (John 19:1). Apparently this word covered either the Roman or Jewish type of scourging and did not indicate who would do the deed. Luke used the same word in referring to the intent of the chief captain to examine Paul by scourging, until he learned of Paul's Roman citizenship (Acts 22:25). Jewish scourging had more humanitarian restraint according to the Mishnah. According to Vine, it "was by the use of three thongs of leather. The offender received thirteen stripes on the bare breast and thirteen on each shoulder, 'the forty stripes save one,' as administered to Paul five times (2 Corinthians 11:24)" (*Expository Dictionary*, "Scourge").

STRONG 5417, BAUER 865, MOULTON-MILLIGAN 675, LIDDELL-SCOTT 1952, COLIN BROWN 1:162.

5254. φραγμός phragmos noun

Fence, wall, hedge, partition.

COGNATE:
φράσσω phrassō (5256)

SYNONYM:
χάραξ charax (5318)

גָּדֵר gādhēr (1474), Wall, fence (Nm 22:24, Ps 62:3 [61:3], Eccl 10:8).

גְּדֵרָה gᵉdhērāh (1477), Wall (Ps 89:40 [88:40], Na 3:17).

מְשׂוּכָּה mᵉsûkkāh (5023), Hedge (Is 5:5).

מֹשְׁכוֹת mōshᵉkhôth (5087), Cords (Job 38:31).

פֶּרֶץ perets (6806), Breach, gap (Gn 38:29, 1 Kgs 11:27, Is 58:12).

1. **φραγμοῦ phragmou** gen sing masc
2. **φραγμόν phragmon** acc sing masc
3. **φραγμούς phragmous** acc pl masc

2 planted a vineyard, and **hedged** it round about, ... Matt 21:33
2 man planted a vineyard, and set an **hedge** about it, Mark 12:1
3 Go out into the highways and **hedges**, ... Luke 14:23
1 and hath broken down the middle wall of **partition** ... Eph 2:14

Phragmos is literally the "fence" around a vineyard. It can also take the form of a wall or a living hedge. The word is used in the Septuagint in the Parable of the Vineyard (Isaiah 5:2). It occurs twice in the Gospels in Jesus' Parable of the Vineyard (Matthew 21:33; Mark 12:1) and once of the host of a great supper who sent his servants into "the highways and *hedges*" (of the vineyards) to bring the workers in (Luke 14:23).

The only other reference is figurative, of the Law that separates Jews and Gentiles, leading to enmity. Christ has broken down this "middle wall of *partition*" (Ephesians 2:14) and has united all believers in himself.

STRONG 5418, BAUER 865, MOULTON-MILLIGAN 675, LIDDELL-SCOTT 1952, COLIN BROWN 3:950-51.

5255. φράζω phrazō verb

Declare, explain, interpret.

SYNONYMS:
διερμηνεύω diermēneuō (1323)
διηγέομαι diēgeomai (1328)
ἐκδιηγέομαι ekdiēgeomai (1542)
ἐξηγέομαι exēgeomai (1817)
ἑρμηνεύω hermēneuō (2043)
ὁρίζω horizō (3587)

בִּין bîn (1032), Understand, perceive; hiphil: show (Job 6:24).

חֲוָה chăwâh (A2426), Pael: show (Dn 2:4—Aramaic).

יָרָה yārâh (3498), Throw, shoot; hiphil: teach (Job 12:8).

1. **φράσον phrason** 2sing impr aor act

1 **Declare** unto us the parable of the tares of the field. Matt 13:36
1 **Declare** unto us this parable. 15:15

Classical Greek and Septuagint Usage

Phrazō is found from Homer (Eighth Century B.C.) to the papyri and inscriptions as well as in the Septuagint and Josephus meaning "make known, declare, explain," or "interpret." Job, in pleading his case, said, "*Cause me to understand* wherein I have erred" (Job 6:24). *Moulton-Milligan* cites a papyrus instance in which *phrazō* was used of the requirement that orchard owners "register" themselves, that is, to "make clear" their names and the village where they live.

New Testament Usage

The two New Testament instances of the word occur in contexts where the disciples asked Jesus to make the meaning of parables clear to them. Both times they said, "*Declare* unto us the parable" (Matthew 13:36; 15:15).

Strong 5419, Bauer 865, Moulton-Milligan 675, Liddell-Scott 1952-53.

5256. φράσσω phrassō verb

To shut, to stop, close, fence in, secure, fortify.

Cross-Reference:

φραγμός phragmos (5254)

אָטַם 'āṯam (334), Shut (Prv 21:13).

סוּג ṣûgh (5657), Move away, be disloyal; be encircled (S/S 7:2).

סָכַךְ ṣākhakh (5718), Cover, set apart; hiphil: shut up (Job 38:8).

סָתַם ṣātham (5845), Seal up (Dn 8:26).

רָפַשׂ rāphas (7806), Make muddy; niphal: be muddied (Prv 25:26).

שׂוּךְ sûkh (7912), Hedge up (Hos 2:6).

1. **ἔφραξαν ephraxan** 3pl indic aor act
2. **φραγῇ phragē** 3sing subj aor pass
3. **φραγήσεται phragēsetai** 3sing indic fut pass

2 that every mouth may be stopped,.................. Rom 3:19
3 boasting of mine will not be stopped (NASB)...... 2 Co 11:10
1 obtained promises, stopped the mouths of lions,.... Heb 11:33

Classical Greek

Phrassō is cognate with *phragmos* (5254), "fence, hedge, wall," and literally means "to fence in" or "to put a hedge around." This sense was predominant in the classical literature (*Liddell-Scott*). A secondary sense was "to block up" a road, river, etc. Also, a metaphoric use, "to shut," is attested (ibid.).

Septuagint Usage

In its eight appearances in the Septuagint *phrassō* is used in much the same way—the six Hebrew words which are translated expressing various shades of the concept "to fence in, to shut" (see Hillyer, "Wall," *Colin Brown*, 3:950). Thus, the sea is spoken of as being fenced in (Job 38:8), and God can "hedge up" an individual (Hosea 2:6). Ears can be "shut" (Proverbs 21:13); a valley can be closed (Zechariah 14:5); visions can be "shut . . . up" (Daniel 8:26); and wells can be stopped (Proverbs 25:26).

In its history, then, *phrassō* is used in the general sense "to erect a barrier" of some sort; this is in harmony with the basic meaning "to fence in." The Septuagint reflects a growing use of the previously rare sense "to shut, to stop," both literally (of a well) and figuratively (of ears). This use predominates in the New Testament also. A later use (A.D. 190) found in the papyri attests the same sense—"to block up" a road and, hence, to shut off all traffic (*Moulton-Milligan*).

New Testament Usage

In its two occurrences in the New Testament *phrassō* is used in connection with the mouth. In Hebrews 11:33 the mouths of lions are shut, and in Romans 3:19 the mouths of men are shut—left defenseless when faced with their own sinfulness. (Paul answered his own question in verse 9, "Are we [Jews] better than they?" by demonstrating that the whole Old Testament testifies to their iniquities [verses 10 through 18]. Thus both Gentiles and Jews have no defense and are left speechless before God.) Certain manuscripts attest a use of *phrassō* in 2 Corinthians 11:10. In this occurrence Paul said that no one would stop his boasting.

Strong 5420, Bauer 865, Moulton-Milligan 675, Liddell-Scott 1953, Colin Brown 3:950-51.

5257. φρέαρ phrear noun

Well, pit, shaft.

בְּאֵר b^e'ēr (908), Well, pit (Gn 26:18-23, Ps 55:23 [54:23, Prv 5:15).

בְּאֵר b^e'ēr (909), Beer (Nm 21:16).

בְּאֵר אֵילִים b^e'ēr 'êlîm (911), Beer-Elim (Is 15:8).

בְּאֵר לַחַי רֹאִי b^e'ēr lachay rō'î (915), Beer Lahai Roi (Gn 16:14, 24:62, 25:11).

בְּאֵר שֶׁבַע b^e'ēr sheva' (916), Beer Sheba (Gn 21:14, 31, Am 5:5).

בּוֹר bôr (988), Well, cistern (1 Sm 19:22, 2 Sm 3:26, Jer 41:7 [48:7]).

גֵּב gēv (1386), Cistern (Jer 14:3).

1. **φρέαρ phrear** nom/acc sing neu
2. **φρέατος phreatos** gen sing neu

1 of you shall have an ass or an ox fallen into a pit, Luke 14:5
1 nothing to draw with, and the well is deep:......... John 4:11
1 which gave us the well, and drank thereof himself,...... 4:12
2 and to him was given the key of the bottomless pit...Rev 9:1
1 And he opened the bottomless pit;..................... 9:2
2 and there arose a smoke out of the pit,................ 9:2
2 were darkened by reason of the smoke of the pit........ 9:2

Classical Greek and Septuagint Usage
The word *phrear* denotes a "cistern, pit," or "well." Essentially it describes a hole dug in the ground for various purposes, notably water collection and storage. It is contrasted with *pēgē* (3938), which was a natural spring or fountain, as well as with *krēnē*, also a spring (*Liddell-Scott*). In the Septuagint it predominantly translates *b*[e]*'ēr*, "a well" (as in *Beer*sheba).

New Testament Usage
In Luke 14:5 the word *phrear* is the hole into which an ox may fall. In Revelation 9:1,2 it is the shaft of the abyss out of which issue smoke and the locusts. In John 4:11,12 Jacob's well is called a *phrear*. This well is 138 feet deep with a water level 75–80 feet below ground and was surrounded by a short wooden or stone wall upon which one might sit. In John 4:6 this well is also called a *pēgē*. Apparently due to its depth it not only collected surface water but had subterranean sources as well (Pellett, "Jacob's Well," *Interpreter's Dictionary of the Bible*, 2:787).

STRONG 5421, BAUER 865, MOULTON-MILLIGAN 675, LIDDELL-SCOTT 1954, COLIN BROWN 3:986.

5258. φρεναπατάω phrenapataō verb

To deceive.

COGNATES:
ἀπατάω apataō (534)
φραγέλλιον phragellion (5252)

SYNONYMS:
ἀπατάω apataō (534)
ἐξαπατάω exapataō (1802)
παραλογίζομαι paralogizomai (3745)
πλανάω planaō (3966)

1. φρεναπατᾷ phrenapata 3sing indic pres act

1 **when he is nothing, he deceiveth himself**............ **Gal 6:3**

This compound verb is derived from *phrēn* (5260), "mind, thought," and *apataō* (534), "to deceive," and essentially means "to deceive in the mind" or simply "to deceive." It is a coinage of Christian Greek and appears nowhere previously (Turner, *Christian Words*, p.447). In Galatians 6:3 it is coupled with *heauton* (see 1431), "himself." The one who thinks he is "something, when he is nothing, he *deceiveth himself*." In this way Paul cautioned believers against the dangers of pride and self-exaltation and exhorted them to self-examination instead.

STRONG 5422, BAUER 865, MOULTON-MILLIGAN 675, LIDDELL-SCOTT 1954.

5259. φρεναπάτης phrenapatēs noun

A deceiver.

COGNATES:
ἀπατάω apataō (534)
φρονέω phroneō (5262)

SYNONYM:
πλάνος planos (3969)

1. φρεναπάται phrenapatai nom pl masc

1 **are many unruly and vain talkers and deceivers,**...... **Tit 1:10**

This noun is a combination of *phrēn* (5260), "mind, thought," and *apataō* (534), "to deceive." The suffix *-ēs* indicates the agent of the action, and thus *phrenapatēs* is one who deceives the mind, "a deceiver." It is a rare word, but it is used earlier than the New Testament to denote a proud man (perhaps one who is self-deceived) (Turner, *Christian Words*, pp.447f.). In Titus 1:10 *phrenapatēs* is coupled with *anupotaktoi* (see 503), the "unruly" or "rebellious," and *mataiologoi* (see 3123), "vain talkers," and refers to certain church members who were teaching false doctrine closely related to that found in Ephesus and Colossae. This errant teaching was composed of Jewish myths, human commandments, and "endless genealogies" (Colossians 2:21,22; 1 Timothy 1:4; and Titus 1:14).

STRONG 5423, BAUER 865, MOULTON-MILLIGAN 675, LIDDELL-SCOTT 1954.

5260. φρήν phrēn noun

Thinking, understanding.

CROSS-REFERENCE:
φρονέω phroneō (5262)

לֵב lēv (3949), Heart; sense, understanding (Prv 6:32, 9:4, 15:21).

1. φρεσίν phresin dat pl fem

1 **Brethren, be not children in understanding:**........ **1 Co 14:20**
1 **but in understanding be men**......................... **14:20**

Classical Greek
Early on *phrēn* denoted the midriff region (diaphram) of the body. It especially suggested the "heart" in a more figurative sense and picked up on its role as the seat of emotions. This also included the idea of the "mind" as the site of mental activity. The broad range of function along these lines includes "will, intelligence, rationality," etc. (*Liddell-Scott*).

Septuagint Usage
As is typical of its use in classical writings, *phrēn* occurs mainly in the plural in the Septuagint (but cf. 3 Maccabees 4:16; 5:47, an irrational mind).

Lēv, the normal Hebrew equivalent to "heart" (including all its dimensions, see *kardia* [2559]), is the main word behind *phrēn* (7 out of 10 instances). Eight of these occur in Proverbs where it refers to (rational) "understanding" or the ability to judge (which is conspicuously absent in the sin of adultery, Proverbs 6:32; 7:7). This lack of "understanding/judgment" contrasts with Wisdom's understanding (Proverbs 9:4; 15:21; cf. 18:2), and it implies an attitude of laziness (Proverbs 12:11; 24:30 [LXX 24:45]) in both practical and spiritual matters.

New Testament Usage

The two New Testament instances of *phrēn* (both plural) occur in Paul's first letter to Corinth, both in 14:20. Paul advised his readers to stop "thinking" like children and instead be mature (*teleios* [4894]) in their "understanding."

Quite likely Paul was simply advising the Corinthians to use some common sense in their estimate and exercise of tongues (14:18f.). Tongues in the congregation are only of value if they are made intelligible through an interpreter (cf. 14:5). Paul implied that common sense should have led them to this conclusion. The need to make tongues intelligible concerns both believers in the assembly who are edified by an interpretation and the nonbelievers who, apart from an interpretation, would only be confused by tongues.

Strong 5424, Bauer 865-66, Moulton-Milligan 675, Kittel 9:220-35, Liddell-Scott 1954.

5261. φρίσσω phrissō verb

Shake, shudder.

סָמַר sāmar (5763), Piel: bristle (Job 4:15).

שָׂעַר sā'ar (7994), Shudder in horror (Jer 2:12).

1. φρίσσουσιν phrissousin 3pl indic pres act

1 the devils also believe, and tremble.................. Jas 2:19

This onomatopoeic verb is found as early as Homer (Eighth Century B.C.) and is cognate with *phrix*, "a ruffling, a ripple." *Phrissō* means "to shudder, to shake, to bristle"—physical movement with various causes. The sense "to shudder with fear" is vividly attested in the *Iliad* which speaks of the Trojans who trembled in fear before the Greeks as "bleating goats before a lion" (11.383; cf. *Liddell-Scott*). Also, in Job, Eliphaz says, "Fear and trembling seized me and made all my bones shake. A spirit glided past my face, and the hair on my body *stood on end* (*phrissō*)" (4:14,15, NIV). Shuddering with extreme fear is the response of demons who know God exists and will judge them (James 2:19). Although their knowledge instills terror within them, they will not do God's will; thus their belief, like faith without works, is useless.

Strong 5425, Bauer 866, Moulton-Milligan 676, Liddell-Scott 1955.

5262. φρονέω phroneō verb

Think, decide, judge, set one's mind on, seek for, observe.

Cognates:

ἄφρων aphrōn (871)
εὐφραίνω euphrainō (2146)
καταφρονέω kataphroneō (2675)
καταφρονητής kataphronētēs (2676)
παραφρονέω paraphroneō (3773)
παραφρονία paraphronia (3774)
περιφρονέω periphroneō (3925)
σωφρονίζω sōphronizō (4846)
ταπεινοφροσύνη tapeinophrosunē (4863)
ταπεινόφρων tapeinophrōn (4863B)
ὑπερφρονέω huperphroneō (5090)
ὑψηλοφρονέω hupsēlophroneō (5147)
φιλοφρόνως philophronōs (5227)
φιλόφρων philophrōn (5228)
φρεναπατάω phrenapataō (5258)
φρεναπάτης phrenapatēs (5259)
φρήν phrēn (5260)
φρόνησις phronēsis (5264)
φροντίζω phrontizō (5267)

Synonyms:

ἀναλογίζω analogizō (355)
βουλεύομαι bouleuomai (1003)
διαλογίζομαι dialogizomai (1254)
δοκέω dokeō (1374)
ἐνθυμέομαι enthumeomai (1744)
ἐπιβλέπω epiblepō (1899)
ἔχω echō (2174)
ἡγέομαι hēgeomai (2216)
κατανοέω katanoeō (2627)
κρίνω krinō (2892)
λογίζομαι logizomai (3023)
νοέω noeō (3401)
νομίζω nomizō (3406)
οἴομαι oiomai (3496)
συμβάλλω sumballō (4671)
συμβουλεύω sumbouleuō (4674)
ὑπολαμβάνω hupolambanō (5112)

בִּין bîn (1032), Understand (Is 44:18).

חָכַם chākham (2549), Be wise (Dt 32:29, Zec 9:2).

שָׂכַל sākhal (7959), Hiphil: be wise (Ps 94:8 [93:8]).

1. **φρονεῖτε phroneite** 2pl indic/impr pres act
2. **φρονεῖς phroneis** 2sing indic pres act
3. **φρονεῖ phronei** 3sing indic pres act
4. **φρονοῦσιν phronousin** 3pl indic prcs act
5. **φρονῶμεν phronōmen** 1pl subj pres act
6. **φρονῆτε phronēte** 2pl subj pres act

7. φρονῶν phronōn nom sing masc part pres act
8. φρονοῦντες phronountes nom pl masc part pres act
9. φρονεῖν phronein inf pres act
10. φρονήσετε phronēsete 2pl indic fut act
11. ἐφρόνουν ephronoun 1sing indic imperf act
12. ἐφρονεῖτε ephroneite 2pl indic imperf act
13. φρονείσθω phroneisthō 3sing impr pres mid
14. φρόνει phronei 2sing impr pres act

2 for thou **savourest** not the things that be of God, Matt 16:23
2 for thou **savourest** not the things that be of God,.. Mark 8:33
2 But we desire to hear of thee what thou **thinkest**: Acts 28:22
4 are after the flesh do **mind** the things of the flesh; Rom 8:5
14 Do not be conceited, but fear. (NASB) (NT)......... 11:20
9 not to think ... more highly than he ought **to think**;... 12:3
9 but **to think** soberly, according as God hath dealt..... 12:3
8 Be of the same **mind** one toward another............. 12:16
8 **Mind** not high things,.............................. 12:16
7 He that **regardeth** the day,......................... 14:6
3 **regardeth** it unto the Lord;........................ 14:6
7 and he that **regardeth** not the day,................... 14:6
3 to the Lord he doth not **regard** it.................... 14:6
9 God of patience ... grant you **to be likeminded**........ 15:5
9 not **to think** of men above that which is written,... 1 Co 4:6
11 I **understood** as a child, I thought as a child:......... 13:11
1 Be perfect, be of good comfort, be of one **mind**,.. 2 Co 13:11
10 that ye will **be** none otherwise **minded**:............. Gal 5:10
9 Even as it is meet for me **to think** this of you all,.. Phlp 1:7
6 Fulfil ye my joy, that ye be **likeminded**,............... 2:2
8 being of one accord, of one **mind**.................... 2:2
13 Let this **mind be** in you, which was also in Christ...... 2:5
5 therefore, as many as be perfect, **be** thus **minded**:...... 3:15
1 and if in any thing ye **be** otherwise **minded**,........... 3:15
9 let us **mind** the same thing.......................... 3:16
8 glory is in their shame, who **mind** earthly things....... 3:19
9 that they be of the same **mind** in the Lord........... 4:2
9 your **care** of me hath flourished again;................ 4:10
12 ye were also **careful**, but ye lacked opportunity........ 4:10
1 Set your **affection** on things above,................. Col 3:2

Classical Greek

This highly adaptable term, from the stem *phren-*, occurs extensively in classical writings. Its definitions span a broad range: "to have understanding, to have a certain frame of mind, to comprehend, to intend," etc. (*Liddell-Scott*).

Septuagint Usage

Phroneō occurs 15 times in the Septuagint, but only 4 of these have a Hebrew counterpart. It is associated with "having wisdom" (Hebrew *chākham*, e.g., Deuteronomy 32:29; Zechariah 9:2) or "having understanding, regard for" (Hebrew *bîn*; Isaiah 44:18, of spiritual discernment; cf. Deuteronomy 32:29). Usage in the apocryphal writings is even less precise (cf. Wisdom of Solomon 1:1; 1 Maccabees 10:20; 2 Maccabees 9:12).

New Testament Usage

Phroneō appears nearly 30 times in the New Testament. Apart from two (parallel) instances in Matthew and Mark (16:23 and 8:33 respectively) and one in Acts (28:22), *phroneō* is exclusively a member of the Pauline vocabulary. Paul used it most in the letters to Rome (10 times) and Philippi (11 times).

In Romans 8:5 *phroneō* refers to an "attitude" or "disposition" of the mind. It is either fixed upon the sinful nature (*sarx* [4418]) or on the Spirit. This perception is reflected elsewhere in Paul's writings (cf. Philippians 3:19; Colossians 3:2).

Paul desired that God would grant the Romans unity (literally "the same understanding") in order that He would be glorified (Romans 15:5f.). The outcome would be peace (cf. 2 Corinthians 13:11; Philippians 2:2) and an attitude like Christ's (Philippians 2:5). This is a sign of true maturity (Philippians 3:15).

In another usage Paul warned against being haughty or arrogant in understanding. This attitude (*hupsēlophronei* [see 5147]) promotes a false sense of security in the individual (Romans 11:20) and disunity among the congregation (cf. Romans 12:3,16 and 1 Timothy 6:17, *hupsēlophronein*, which some manuscripts read as *hupsēla phronein*).

Strong 5426, Bauer 866, Moulton-Milligan 676, Kittel 9:220-35, Liddell-Scott 1955-56, Colin Brown 2:259,616-19.

5263. φρόνημα phronēma noun

Mind, thought, aspiration, mind-set, aim.

Cross-Reference:
φρόνησις phronēsis (5264)

1. φρόνημα phronēma nom/acc sing neu

1 For to be carnally **minded** is death;.................Rom 8:6
1 but to be spiritually **minded** is life and peace............ 8:6
1 Because the carnal **mind** is enmity against God:........ 8:7
1 knoweth what is the **mind** of the Spirit,................ 8:27

Classical Greek

Occurring as early as Homer (Eighth Century B.C.), *phronēma* denotes the "mind, will," or "spirit." It could also be used with the sense "highmindedness"—in a positive way as "courage" or a negative way, "arrogance, conceit" (cf. *Liddell-Scott*). It is derived from *phrēn* (5260) which originally denoted the diaphragm and was seen as the seat of intellectual and spiritual activity (perhaps as controller of the breath, and hence, the human spirit) (Bertram, "phrēn," *Kittel*, 9:220). *Phrēn* and its cognates soon lost the physical sense, and in Homer the intellectual sense of "mind, thought" predominates (*ibid.*). Thus *phronēma* to Plato (Fourth Century B.C.) was an intellectual or spiritual attitude (*Laws*

9.865d) or the disposition of a person (*Republic* 9.573b; cf. *Liddell-Scott*). Josephus used *phronēma* to refer to the attitude or disposition (*Antiquities* 12.6.3).

Septuagint Usage

In the Septuagint *phronēma* only appears twice—both times in the apocryphal literature. In 2 Maccabees 7:21 it is "courageous thought" and in 13:9, "intentions" or "ideas."

New Testament Usage

Phronēma occurs four times in the New Testament, all in Romans 8. In verse 27 the *phronēma* of the Spirit refers to the whole sphere of the Spirit's personality—thoughts, will, desires, and reasonings. In verses 6 and 7 *phronēma* is "the content of *phroneō*, the general bent of thought and motive" (Sanday and Headlam, *International Critical Commentary, Romans*, p.195). In verse 5 it includes the "affections and will, as well as the reason" (ibid.). So Paul had more than mere rational and mental activity in mind. Present in the verb *phroneō* is the sense "to strive after." This is seen, for example, in Colossians 3:1,2 where Paul wrote "seek these things which are above" and "set your *affection* (*phroneō*) on things above." Both injunctions are related.

In verse 27 (and elsewhere) the whole sphere of human personality and activity is in view in the use of *phronēma*. The mind of the flesh represents the individual whose goals and energies (his very being) are devoted to satisfying the flesh. The mind of the Spirit represents the individual controlled by the Holy Spirit and yielded to His desires and goals. The mind (strivings, thoughts, etc.) of the flesh is death, for it is at variance with God and will not submit to Him. On the other hand, the mind of the Spirit is life and peace, for its goals are the will of God and His pleasure. To Paul, only these two "minds" exist. There is no in-between "lukewarm" mind. Either a person is living for the flesh or the Spirit.

Strong 5427, Bauer 866, Moulton-Milligan 676, Kittel 9:220-35, Liddell-Scott 1956, Colin Brown 2:616-17.

5264. φρόνησις phronēsis noun

Thought, understanding, way of thinking, frame of mind, intention, judgment.

Cognates:

φρονέω phroneō (5262)
φρόνημα phronēma (5263)
φρόνιμος phronimos (5265)
φρονίμως phronimōs (5266)

בִּינָה bînāh (1035), Understanding (Prv 1:2, 8:14, 30:2 [24:25]).

דַּעַת daʿath (1907), Knowledge (Prv 24:5).

חָכְמָה chokhmāh (2551), Wisdom (1 Kgs 3:28, 4:30, 10:4).

לֵב lēv (3949), Heart; understanding (Prv 9;16).

עָרְמָה ʿormāh (6430), Craftiness (Job 5:13).

רוּחַ rûach (7593), Spirit, wind; courage (Jos 5:1).

שָׂכַל sākhal (7959), Hiphil: give knowledge (Dn 1:17).

שֶׂכֶל sekhel (7961II) Understanding (Job 17:4—Codex Vaticanus and some Sinaiticus texts only).

תְּבוּנָה tevûnāh (8722), Understanding (Prv 10:23, Is 44:19, Jer 10:12).

1. φρονήσει phronēsei dat sing fem

1 and the disobedient to the wisdom of the just;...... Luke 1:17
1 abounded toward us in all wisdom and prudence;.... Eph 1:8

Classical Greek

Phronēsis is related to *phrēn* (5260) (see *phronēma* [5263] for further information) and first appears in the latter half of the Fifth Century B.C. In classical literature *phronēsis* can refer to "purposes" or "intentions, sense, judgment," and even "arrogance" or "pride" (*Liddell-Scott*). Pertinent to Biblical studies is its use with the sense "practical wisdom." Aristotle carefully delineated between *phronēsis* and *sophia* (4531), "wisdom." To him *sophia* was a combination of intelligence and scientific knowledge, whereas *phronēsis* was practical wisdom concerned with what is best for oneself. Thus men could have *sophia* without having *phronēsis*. (He refers to Thales and Anaxagoras, early Greek philosophers who studied the origin and nature of the universe but not ethics and morality. These men perhaps were knowledgeable on scientific matters but not necessarily adept at governing their own behavior; *Nicomachean Ethics* 6.7; cf. *Bauer*). Later, Philo of Alexandria said *sophia* was for the worship of God but *phronēsis* for regulation of human life (*On Rewards and Punishments* 14.81; cf. ibid.). "*Phronēsis* can help man in the battle between good and evil" (Bertram, "phronēsis," *Kittel*, 9:221).

Septuagint Usage

This carefully defined distinction is not maintained in the Septuagint. In over 60 occurrences *phronēsis* can mean both practical wisdom and scientific knowledge (notably in 1 Kings 10 [LXX 3 Kings 10; five appearances] in which the Queen of Sheba marveled at Solomon's *phronēsis* when he answered many questions). *Phronēsis* predominantly translates *chokhmāh*, "wisdom," in 1 Kings and *tᵉvûnāh,* "understanding," in Proverbs and Isaiah. *Sophia* is also translated (predominantly) by *chokhmāh.* Thus, these words cannot be clearly distinguished; rather, "*phronēsis, sophia,* and *aisthēsis* constitute a unity as practical wisdom with a religious slant" (Bertram, "phrēn," *Kittel,* 9:226). In one place *phronēsis* denotes a peasant's knowledge about his occupation (Goetzmann, "Mind," *Colin Brown,* 2:616).

New Testament Usage

Phronēsis occurs twice in the New Testament. In Luke 1:17 it essentially refers to "thoughts." John the Baptist came to turn the disobedient so they might have the thoughts of the righteous. In Ephesians 1:8 Paul coupled *phronēsis* with *sophia* to describe the fullness with which God has given His grace to believers. It may be possible in the combining of these two words to see an element of the Aristotelian distinction. But more than likely it reflects the Septuagintal sense in which they together emphasize the totality of doctrine, knowledge, ethics, and especially practical wisdom.

Strong 5428, Bauer 866, Moulton-Milligan 676, Kittel 9:220-35, Liddell-Scott 1956, Colin Brown 2:616-17,620.

5265. φρόνιμος phronimos adj

Prudent, sensible, shrewd, arrogant, wise, thoughtful.

Cross-Reference:

φρόνησις phronēsis (5264)

בִּין bîn (1032), Niphal: one who is discerning, one who has understanding (Gn 41:33, Prv 14:6); hiphil: one who has understanding (Prv 17:10).

חָכָם chākhām (2550), Wise (1 Kgs 5:7, 3:7).

חָכְמָה chokhmāh (2551), Wisdom (1 Kgs 4:30).

מְזִמָּה mᵉzimmāh (4343), Evil device (Prv 14:17).

עָרוּם ʿārûm (6415), Crafty (Gn 3:1 [3:2]).

תְּבוּנָה tᵉvûnāh (8722), Understanding (Prv 17:27, 20:5).

1. **φρόνιμοι phronimoi** nom pl masc/fem
2. **φρονίμοις phronimois** dat pl masc/fem
3. **φρόνιμος phronimos** nom sing masc
4. **φρονίμῳ phronimō** dat sing masc
5. **φρονιμώτεροι phronimōteroi** comp nom pl masc

4 I will liken him unto a wise man,.................. Matt 7:24
1 be ye therefore wise as serpents,...................... 10:16
3 Who then is a faithful and wise servant,............... 24:45
1 And five of them were wise, and five were foolish..... 25:2
1 the wise took oil in their vessels with their lamps...... 25:4
2 And the foolish said unto the wise,................... 25:8
1 But the wise answered, saying, Not so;................ 25:9
3 Who then is that faithful and wise steward,........ Luke 12:42
5 in their generation wiser than the children of light. Luke 16:8
1 lest ye should be wise in your own conceits;....... Rom 11:25
1 Be not wise in your own conceits..................... 12:16
1 We are fools ... but ye are wise in Christ;...........1 Co 4:10
2 I speak as to wise men; judge ye what I say............ 10:15
1 suffer fools gladly, seeing ye yourselves are wise....2 Co 11:19

Classical Greek

Phronimos appears in extant Greek literature as early as the time of the tragedian Sophocles. It is related to *phrēn* (5260), "mind, spirit." As an adjective it describes one who "uses his head" and consequently is "sensible, prudent," or regarded as "in his right mind" (cf. *Liddell-Scott*).

Septuagint Usage

In the Septuagint this word occurs over 40 times (mostly in the Wisdom literature) and is used to translate four Hebrew words. *Bîn,* "discerning," occurs in the majority of appearances and *chākhām,* "wise," is also found several times. In one occurrence *ʿārûm,* "crafty," is translated by *phronimos*—Genesis 3:1 where the serpent is described. Thus *phronimos* can also have the negative connotation: "crafty" or "shrewd."

New Testament Usage

In the New Testament *phronimos* appears several times, almost always with the positive sense "prudent." In Romans 11:25 and 12:16, however, it means "arrogant" in a warning against an incorrect self-evaluation (perhaps this sense derived from the cognate noun *phronēsis* [5264] which could mean "arrogance"). In Matthew 7:24-27 and 25:1-11 *phronimos* is used several times as an antonym to *mōros* (3336), "foolish, fool" (also in 1 Corinthians 4:10). The Matthew parables teach that the *phronimos* man or woman is one who *does* Jesus' words and shows forethought by being prepared for times of crisis. The King James Version translation of Matthew 6:34, "Take therefore no thought for the morrow," translates the verb *merimnaō* (3179) meaning "worry." This does not prohibit forethought and rational judgment with respect to future events. Instead, it warns against yielding to the nonconstructive, disabling worry that often accompanies speculation about the uncertainties of the future. A man who uses forethought is *phronimos,* and Jesus commends him.

In Matthew 24:45 (paralleled by Luke 12:42) *phronimos* is coupled with *pistos* (3964) to describe the ideal Christian servant as a "faithful" steward. He is characterized as one who does his job in contrast to the "evil" man who neglects his duties and takes advantage of those in his care. "Hence the idea behind *phronimos* in the Gospels may be summarized thus: the believer's wisdom lies in his obedience" (Goetzmann, "Mind," *Colin Brown*, 2:620).

The unjust steward was commended by his master because he "used his head" in a desperate situation (Luke 16:8). The disciples were admonished to be as "*wise* as serpents" (Matthew 10:16). Here the language parallels Genesis 3:1, but Jesus qualified this use of *phronimos* with the charge to be as "harmless as doves"; thus the meaning of *phronimos* does not inherently contain moral or ethical connotations. The believer is expected to think, to use his God-given reasoning capabilities as he lives out his Christian life, but always with proper motives and purity.

STRONG 5429, BAUER 866, MOULTON-MILLIGAN 676, KITTEL 9:220-35, LIDDELL-SCOTT 1956, COLIN BROWN 2:616-20; 3:1025-26.

5266. φρονίμως phronimōs adv

Shrewdly.

CROSS-REFERENCE:
φρόνησις phronēsis (5264)

1. φρονίμως phronimōs

1 the unjust steward, because he had done wisely:....Luke 16:8

Phronimōs is the adverbial form of *phronimos* (5265), "prudent, sensible." It appears as early as the comedy writer Aristophanes where it means "sensibly" (cf. *Liddell-Scott*). Its only occurrence in the New Testament is in the difficult Parable of the Unjust Steward (Luke 16:8). Its best rendering here is "shrewdly." On the strategy of the steward Bertram writes, "Cleverly resolute action is imposed by the hopelessness of the situation and the resultant urgency. In acting as he does, even the worldly man can be a model for the children of light" ("phrēn," *Kittel*, 9:234). It possibly derives this somewhat negative connotation from its associated adjective *phronimos* which in Genesis 3:1 has the meaning "shrewd" or "crafty."

STRONG 5430, BAUER 866, MOULTON-MILLIGAN 676, LIDDELL-SCOTT 1956, COLIN BROWN 2:617,619.

5267. φροντίζω phrontizō verb

To consider carefully, to put one's mind to it.

CROSS-REFERENCE:
φρονέω phroneō (5262)

דָּאַג dā'agh (1720), Become anxious (1 Sm 9:5—Codex Vaticanus only).

חָשַׁב chāshav (2913), Think of (Ps 40:17 [39:17]).

יָרֵא yārē' (3486), Be afraid (Prv 31:21).

פָּחַד pāchadh (6585), Be afraid (Job 23:15 [23:14]).

1. φροντίζωσιν phrontizōsin 3pl subj pres act

1 might be careful to maintain good works.............Tit 3:8

This verb, related to *phrēn* (5260), "mind, spirit" (see *phronēma* [5263]), has the force "to put one's mind to it, to consider carefully" a course of action. It emphasizes the use of one's rational faculties to assess a situation. This sense is also present in the cognate verb *phroneō* (5262) (e.g., Colossians 3:2; Romans 8:5). The papyri attest *phrontizō* several times with such translations as "to take care; to make careful, dedicated effort." This same sense is found in Titus 3:8 where Paul exhorted Titus to make sure the believers "put their minds to" and "consider carefully" how they might do good works. Thus, the Christian life involves the use of the mind in cooperation with the prompting of the Holy Spirit in doing good works.

STRONG 5431, BAUER 866-67, MOULTON-MILLIGAN 676, LIDDELL-SCOTT 1956-57.

5268. φρουρέω phroureō verb

Guard, keep watch over, confine, protect, keep.

SYNONYMS:
ἀσφαλίζω asphalizō (799)
παρατηρέω paratēreō (3767)
τηρέω tēreō (4931)
φυλάσσω phulassō (5278)

1. φρουρήσει phrourēsei 3sing indic fut act
2. ἐφρούρει ephrourei 3sing indic imperf act
3. φρουρουμένους phrouroumenous acc pl masc part pres mid
4. ἐφρουρούμεθα ephrouroumetha 1pl indic imperf pass

2 kept the city of the Damascenes with a garrison,... 2 Co 11:32
4 But before faith came, we were kept under the law,.. Gal 3:23
1 shall keep your hearts and minds through Christ.....Phlp 4:7
3 Who are kept by the power of God through faith....1 Pt 1:5

Classical Greek

"To watch over, to guard, to keep watch over" are among the various nuances of this verb. Further shades of meaning include "to be on guard against" or "to protcct" (*Liddcll-Scott*).

Septuagint Usage

Only four instances of *phroureō* are found in the Septuagint, and all of these are apocryphal. It can literally mean "guarding" a city (1 Esdras 4:56; Judith 3:6; 1 Maccabees 11:3). It may also be used figuratively of "being captured" and "restrained" (by fear; Wisdom of Solomon 17:16).

New Testament Usage
Of the four uses in the New Testament (three of which are Pauline) there is a literal usage in 2 Corinthians 11:32. Paul recalled that while he was in Damascus the governor sought to arrest him and therefore ordered the city guarded against his flight. In a figurative use, similar to that found in the Septuagint (Wisdom of Solomon 17:16), Paul wrote of being imprisoned by the Law (Galatians 3:23).

On the other side, Paul saw God's peace as "guarding, keeping watch over" "hearts and minds (of believers) through Christ Jesus" (Philippians 4:7). Similarly—and remarkably—by faith God guards the Christian. During times of distress and suffering (a particular concern in this letter) God himself shields by His power (1 Peter 1:5). Moreover, He enables the believer to overcome these trials despite circumstances.

STRONG 5432, BAUER 867, MOULTON-MILLIGAN 677, LIDDELL-SCOTT 1957-58, COLIN BROWN 2:134-35.

5269. φρυάσσω phruassō verb

To be arrogant, to be haughty, to rage.

רָגַשׁ rāghash (7570), Rage (Ps 2:1).

1. ἐφρύαξαν ephruaxan 3pl indic aor act

1 Why did the heathen rage, ... **Acts 4:25**

Classical Greek
This onomatopoeic verb was used originally of the "vehement neighing" of horses (*Moulton-Milligan*). It still had this sense after the First Century A.D. (e.g., Plutarch *Lycias* 22; cf. *Liddell-Scott*).

New Testament Usage
In Acts 4:25 the praying apostles quoted from Psalm 2:1. Here *phruassō* has the sense "to be arrogant, haughty," perhaps reminiscent of the neighing of a high-spirited horse. The disciples identified with the Psalmist in their present situation in which the "kings of the earth" were opposing their witness (Psalm 2:2). They also appear to see these verses from Psalm 2 as prophetically fulfilled in the crucifixion of Christ.

STRONG 5433, BAUER 867, MOULTON-MILLIGAN 677, LIDDELL-SCOTT 1958.

5270. φρύγανον phruganon noun

Brushwood.

חָרוּל chārûl (2839), Undergrowth (Job 30:7).

קֶצֶף qetseph (7398), Stick (Hos 10:7).

קַשׁ qash (7475), Chaff, stubble (Is 41:2, 47:14, Jer 13:24).

1. φρυγάνων phruganōn gen pl neu

1 And when Paul had gathered a bundle of sticks,.... **Acts 28:3**

This word appears as early as the Fifth Century B.C. in classical Greek. Herodotus has the meaning "brushwood, wood for fire" as does Xenophon (e.g., *Anabasis* 4.3.11; cf. *Liddell-Scott*). The papyri also attest such a use in the Third Century B.C. (*Moulton-Milligan*). In its single New Testament occurrence it refers to the pile of combustible material collected by Paul on the island of Malta (Acts 28:3).

STRONG 5434, BAUER 867, MOULTON-MILLIGAN 677, LIDDELL-SCOTT 1958.

5271. Φρυγία Phrugia name

Phrygia.

1. Φρυγίας Phrugias gen fem

2. Φρυγίαν Phrugian acc fem

2 Phrygia, and Pamphylia, in Egypt, ... **Acts 2:10**
2 Now when they had gone throughout Phrygia **16:6**
2 all the country of Galatia and Phrygia in order, ... **18:23**

A large area of west central Asia Minor whose limits varied considerably at different periods of history. In New Testament times it was divided between the two Roman provinces of Asia and Galatia. Phyrgians were among the crowd on the Day of Pentecost (Acts 2:10).

Phrygia was very mixed racially and culturally and had a strong Jewish presence. It had long been open to new religions of many sorts and was thus fertile ground for Christianity also to take root. However, there was likely to be some doctrinal confusion, and Paul's letters to the Galatians and Colossians address distortions that arose. Paul visited Phrygia on all three of his missionary journeys, though the name only occurs at Acts 16:6 and 18:23. But the cities of Iconium, Lystra, and Antioch in Pisidia are within Phrygia.

5272. Φύγελλος Phugellos name

Phygellus.

1. Φύγελλος Phugellos nom masc

2. Φύγελος Phugelos nom masc

1 of whom are Phygellus and Hermogenes. .... **2 Tm 1:15**

An otherwise unknown Christian from the province of Asia who is said to have deserted Paul (2 Timothy 1:15).

5273. φυγή phugē noun

The act of fleeing, flight.

Cross-Reference:
φεύγω pheugō (5180)

בָּרַח bārach (1300), Flee (Job 27:22).

מָנוֹס mānôṣ (4642), Refuge, place of refuge (Ps 142:4 [141:4], Jer 25:35 [32:35]); flight (Am 2:14).

מְנוּסָה m^enûṣāh (4643), Flight (Is 52:12).

נוּס nûṣ (5308), Flee (2 Sm 18:3, Jer 49:24 [30:13]).

1. φυγή phugē nom sing fem

1 But pray ye that your **flight** be not in the winter, .. Matt 24:20
1 And pray ye that your **flight** be not in the winter. Mark 13:18

This word occurs as early as Homer (Eighth Century B.C.) and is used in two primary ways: "escape or flee," and "exile or banish" (*Liddell-Scott*). In the Septuagint *phugē* most frequently translates *nûṣ*, ("flee, escape") (2 Samuel 18:3) and its related terms *mānôṣ* and *m^enûṣāh*, "a place of refuge" (Psalm 142:4; Isaiah 52:12). The New Testament continues the use of *phugē* as seen in classical Greek and the Septuagint to mean "flight or escape." The word occurs twice in the *Textus Receptus*, at Matthew 24:20 and Mark 13:18. Both texts refer to the act of fleeing during the times of tribulation Jesus foretold.

Strong 5437, Bauer 867, Moulton-Milligan 677, Liddell-Scott 1959, Colin Brown 1:558-59.

5274. φυλακή phulakē noun

Guarding, a guard, prison, a watch.

Cross-Reference:
φυλάσσω phulassō (5278)

אָסִיר 'āṣîr (629), Prison (Jgs 16:21—Codex Alexandrinus only).

אַשְׁמוּרָה 'ashmûrāh (847), Nightwatch (Ps 90:4 [89:4]).

אַשְׁמֹרֶת 'ashmōreth (849), Nightwatch (Ex 14:24, 1 Sm 11:11).

כֶּלֶא kele' (3728), Prison (2 Kgs 17:4, 25:27, Is 42:7).

מַהְפֶּכֶת mahpekheth (4256), Prison (2 Chr 16:10).

מַטָּרָה maṭṭārāh (4446), Guard (Neh 3:25, Jer 32:8 [39:8], 38:13 [45:13]).

מַסְגֵּר maṣgēr (4674), Prison (Ps 142:7 [141:7]).

מְצוּדָה m^etsûdhāh (4848), Custody (Ez 19:9).

מִשְׁמָר mishmār (5110), Custody, guard (Gn 40:3f., Jer 51:12 [28:12]); diligence (Prv 4:23).

מִשְׁמֶרֶת mishmereth (5111), Duty, service (Nm 3:7, Ez 44:14ff.); watch (2 Kgs 11:5ff.).

נָצַר nātsar (5526), Preserve (Prv 20:28).

שָׁמַר shāmar (8490), Watchman (Ps 130:6 [129:6]).

שָׁמְרָה shomrāh (8494), Guard (Ps 141:3 [140:3]).

שְׁמֻרָה sh^emurāh (8495), Eyelid (Ps 77:4 [76:4]).

1. φυλακή phulakē nom sing fem
2. φυλακῆς phulakēs gen sing fem
3. φυλακῇ phulakē dat sing fem
4. φυλακήν phulakēn acc sing fem
5. φυλακαῖς phulakais dat pl fem
6. φυλακάς phulakas acc pl fem

4 and thou be cast into **prison**. .... Matt 5:25
3 and put him in **prison** for Herodias' sake, ... 14:3
3 And he sent, and beheaded John in the **prison**. 14:10
3 fourth **watch** of the night Jesus went unto them, ... 14:25
4 he would not: but went and cast him into **prison**, ... 18:30
3 in what **watch** the thief would come, ... 24:43
3 I was in **prison**, and ye came unto me. 25:36
3 saw we thee sick, or in **prison**, and came unto thee? ... 25:39
3 sick, and in **prison**, and ye visited me not. 25:43
3 or a stranger, or naked, or sick, or in **prison**, ... 25:44
3 and bound him in **prison** for Herodias' sake, ... Mark 6:17
3 and he went and beheaded him in the **prison**, ... 6:27
4 fourth **watch** of the night he cometh unto them, ... 6:48
6 keeping **watch** over their flock by night. .... Luke 2:8
3 this above all, that he shut up John in **prison**. 3:20
3 And if he shall come in the second **watch**, ... 12:38
3 or come in the third **watch**, and find them so, ... 12:38
4 and the officer cast thee into **prison**. 12:58
6 up to the synagogues, and into **prisons**, ... 21:12
4 go with thee, both into **prison**, and to death. 22:33
4 Who ... for murder, was cast into **prison**. 23:19
4 that for sedition and murder was cast into **prison**, ... 23:25
4 For John was not yet cast into **prison**. .... John 3:24
2 But the angel ... by night opened the **prison** doors, .. Acts 5:19
3 and found them not in the **prison**, they returned, ... 5:22
3 whom ye put in **prison** are standing in the temple, ... 5:25
4 haling men and women committed them to **prison**. 8:3
4 he had apprehended him, he put him in **prison**, ... 12:4
3 Peter therefore was kept in **prison**: 12:5
4 and the keepers before the door kept the **prison**. 12:6
4 When they were past the first and ... second **ward**, ... 12:10
2 how the Lord had brought him out of the **prison**. 12:17
4 they cast them into **prison**, ... 16:23
4 thrust them into the inner **prison**, ... 16:24
2 and seeing the **prison** doors open, ... 16:27
4 and have cast us into **prison**; 16:37
2 And they went out of the **prison**, ... 16:40
6 and delivering into **prisons** both men and women. 22:4
5 and many of the saints did I shut up in **prison**, ... 26:10
5 In stripes, in **imprisonments**, in tumults, ... 2 Co 6:5
5 in **prisons** more frequent, in deaths oft. 11:23
2 yea, moreover of bonds and **imprisonment**: .... Heb 11:36
3 he went and preached unto the spirits in **prison**; ..... 1 Pt 3:19
4 the devil shall cast some of you into **prison**, ... Rev 2:10
1 of devils, and the **hold** of every foul spirit, ... 18:2
1 and a **cage** of every unclean and hateful bird. 18:2
2 Satan shall be loosed out of his **prison**, ... 20:7

Classical Greek

This word, which appears as early as Homer (Eighth Century B.C.) and throughout the classical period, essentially has four senses: (1) "guarding" as an action; (2) "a guard" made up of persons; (3) "a prison" as a place of guarding; and (4) "a watch in the night," that is, a division of time (e.g., Herodotus 9:51; cf. *Liddell-Scott*).

Septuagint Usage

In the Septuagint the same wide range of meanings is attested—as evidenced by the various Hebrew words *phulakē* translates. *Phulakē* most often translates various forms of the root verb *shāmar*, "to watch, to guard," notably *mishmār*, "a prison." The papyri also attest this same variety of meaning (see *Moulton-Milligan*).

New Testament Usage

In the New Testament *phulakē* primarily refers to a prison of some sort. It can, however, refer to a division of time—the Roman night watch which was divided into four 3-hour periods from 6 p.m. to 6 a.m. (cf. Matthew 14:25; Mark 6:48). The sense of "guarding" appears in Luke 2:8 where the shepherds guarded their flocks. The meaning "a guard" is attested in Acts 12:10. Here *phulakē* is used to refer to the sentinels guarding the prison where Peter was kept. Perhaps there was more than one guard at the first and second stations, and this is why Luke did not use *phulax* (5277), "a guard." Throughout its history *phulakē* has maintained the same general shades of meaning.

Strong 5438, Bauer 867-68, Moulton-Milligan 677, Kittel 9:241-44, Liddell-Scott 1960, Colin Brown 2:134,136.

5275. φυλακίζω phulakizō verb

To imprison.

Cross-Reference:
φυλάσσω phulassō (5278)

1. φυλακίζων phulakizōn nom sing masc part pres act

1 they know that I imprisoned and beat .... Acts 22:19

This verb is related to *phulakē* (5274), "a prison, a guard," and simply means "to imprison." It occurs in Acts 22:19 in a portion of one of Paul's speeches originally delivered in Aramaic, which was spoken in Jerusalem in the First Century A.D. *Phulakizō* occurs in a periphrastic construction, *ēmēn phulakizōn*, reflecting the underlying Aramaic (Aramaic is fond of this type of sentence structure [Robertson, *Grammar of the Greek New Testament*, p.888]). This particular type of verbal construction stresses continuous activity and demonstrates that Paul's persecution of Christians involved continuously imprisoning them.

Strong 5439, Bauer 868, Liddell-Scott 1960.

5276. φυλακτήριον phulaktērion noun

A phylactery.

Cross-Reference:
φυλάσσω phulassō (5278)

1. φυλακτήρια phulaktēria nom/acc pl neu

1 they make broad their phylacteries, ... Matt 23:5

Classical Greek

This word appears in the extant literature earliest in Herodotus. It is derived from *phulakē* (5274), "guard," and the place suffix *-tērion*. In its development *phulakē* came to have the sense of "a safeguard" as a means of protection. It also came to denote an amulet—a protective charm of some sort. This use is attested in the papyri and appears in Plutarch's *Moralia* (Second Century A.D.) in reference to an amulet of Isis worn around the neck (387b; cf. *Liddell-Scott*). In secular literature of Christ's day it apparently denoted an amulet or good luck charm. The term never appears in the Septuagint.

New Testament Usage

In the New Testament Matthew used it once (23:5) to refer to the *t^ephillin*—the prayer boxes Pharisees wore on their foreheads and wrists (*t^ephillin* is the Aramaic plural of the Hebrew word *t^ephillah*, "prayer"). These boxes contained Scripture verses inscribed with texts from Deuteronomy 5 and 6, 10 and 11, and Exodus 12 and 13 (Gundry, *Matthew*, p.456). The scriptural basis for wearing them came from Exodus 13:16 and Deuteronomy 6:8, and perhaps they were expected to have some protective value. (Tobit 6:6-8 and 8:3 shows that Jewish theology contained belief in certain types of magic charms and formulas.) The Mishnah—the rabbinic oral tradition put into written form about A.D. 200—required male Israelites over 13 to "lay the *telphillin*" at daily morning prayer (Shebuoth 111.8; cf. Davies, "Phylactery," *Interpreter's Dictionary of the Bible*, 3:808). We call these prayer boxes phylacteries today—the Greek word *phulaktērion* having passed into the Vulgate and then into English Bibles via the Geneva Bible of 1557 (ibid.).

Matthew did not purposely misrepresent the Jewish *tephillin* as "amulets," magic good luck charms; rather it appears from Justin (*Dialogue with Trypho* 46:5) and from Jerome's homily on Matthew 23:5 (PL 26:168) that these boxes really were called *phulaktēria* (see Tigay, "On the Term Phylacteries [Matthew 23:5]," p.46). The Aramaic equivalent for *phlaktērion* is *qamîaʿ*. Jesus probably originally used this word in this discourse (ibid., p.49), having substituted it for *tephillin* because of the superstitious veneration that some Jews were associating with them. Their prominent position on the body made them a wonderful proof of "righteousness" and "piety" along with the other outward expressions of godliness. Apparently these Pharisees were increasing the size of their phylacteries to inform everyone more clearly of their piety. Thus the *phulaktēria* "are a type of religious symbol which could be exploited hypocritically" (ibid., p.48); and it is this hypocrisy which Jesus denounced in this discourse against the Pharisees.

STRONG 5440, BAUER 868, MOULTON-MILLIGAN 678, LIDDELL-SCOTT 1960.

5277. φύλαξ phulax noun

A guard, sentinel.

CROSS-REFERENCE:

φυλάσσω phulassō (5278)

צוּר tsûr (6962), Rock (2 Sm 22:47, 23:3).

שָׁמַר shāmar (8490), Keeper, person in charge (Gn 4:9, Est 2:3); watchman (S/S 5:7).

1. **φύλακες phulakes** nom pl masc
2. **φύλακας phulakas** acc pl masc

2 and the **keepers** standing without before the doors: .. Acts 5:23
1 and the **keepers** before the door kept the prison....... 12:6
2 Herod had sought ... he examined the **keepers**,........ 12:19

Phulax is related to the stem *phulak-*, meaning to "guard" or "watch." From Homer (Eighth Century B.C.) onward it referred to a guard or sentinel—the individual given the responsibility to prevent the escape of prisoners or detect any suspicious occurrences (cf. *Liddell-Scott*). This meaning is attested in several papyri between the Third Century B.C. and Second Century A.D. (cf. *Moulton-Milligan*). In its three New Testament occurrences *phulax* continues this use (Acts 5:23; 12:6,19). The responsibility of these guards is graphically shown by their execution when Peter escaped from prison (Acts 12:19). The jailer in Philippi, when he thought his prisoners had escaped, was ready to kill himself rather than face the punishment he knew he would receive (Acts 16:27).

STRONG 5441, BAUER 868, MOULTON-MILLIGAN 678, LIDDELL-SCOTT 1960.

5278. φυλάσσω phulassō verb

Guard, defend, watch over, protect, keep safe; obey, follow; guard against, avoid.

COGNATES:

ἀφοράω aphoraō (865)
γαζοφυλάκιον gazophulakion (1042)
δεσμοφύλαξ desmophulax (1194)
διαφυλάσσω diaphulassō (1308)
φυλακή phulakē (5274)
φυλακίζω phulakizō (5275)
φυλακτήριον phulaktērion (5276)
φύλαξ phulax (5277)

SYNONYMS:

ἀσφαλίζω asphalizō (799)
παρατηρέω paratēreō (3767)
τηρέω tēreō (4931)

זְהִיר zehîr (A2175), Careful (Ezr 4:22—Aramaic).

זָהַר zāhar (2178), Niphal: be warned, take warning (Ps 19:11; [18:11], Ez 33:4,6); hiphil: warn (Ex 33:8).

חָיָה chāyâh (2513), Live; piel: save one's life (Ez 18:27).

מִשְׁמֶרֶת mishmereth (5111), Safekeeping (1 Sm 22:23); guard (1 Chr 9:23).

נָטַר nāṭar (5386), Keep (S/S 1:6).

נָצַר nātsar (5526), Watchman (2 Kgs 17:9); preserve, keep (Prv 2:8, Is 26:3).

עָצַר 'ātsar (6352), Be restricted (Jer 36:5 [43:5]).

עָשָׂה 'āsâh (6449), Observe, do (Dt 5:15, 1 Chr 28:7).

פִּקָּדוֹן piqqādhôn (6736), Reserve (Gn 41:36).

צָפָה tsāphāh (7100), Watchman (Is 52:8).

שָׁמַע shāma' (8471), Listen (1 Kgs 11:38, Prv 19:27).

שָׁמַר shāmar (8490), Qal: observe, keep (Dt 8:1f., Ps 119:167f. [118:67f.], Am 1:11); niphal: be careful, be on one's guard (Gn 31:24, 2 Sm 20:10, Is 7:4); piel: regard (Jon 2:8 [2:9]); hithpael: keep oneself, observe (Ps 18:23 [17:23], Mic 6:16).

1. **φυλάσσουσιν phulassousin** 3pl indic pres act
2. **φυλάσσῃ phulassē** 3sing subj pres act
3. **φυλάσσων phulassōn** nom sing masc part pres act
4. **φυλάσσοντι phulassonti** dat sing masc part pres act
5. **φυλάσσοντες phulassontes** nom pl masc part pres act
6. **φυλάσσειν phulassein** inf pres act
7. **ἐφύλαξα ephulaxa** 1sing indic aor act
8. **ἐφύλαξεν ephulaxen** 3sing indic aor act
9. **ἐφυλάξατε ephulaxate** 2pl indic aor act
10. **φυλάξῃς phulaxēs** 2sing subj aor act
11. **φύλαξον phulaxon** 2sing impr aor act
12. **φυλάξατε phulaxate** 2pl impr aor act
13. **φυλάξαι phulaxai** inf aor act
14. **φυλάξει phulaxei** 3sing indic fut act
15. **φυλάσσου phulassou** 2sing impr pres mid
16. **φυλάσσεσθε phulassesthe** 2pl impr pres mid
17. **φυλασσόμενος phulassomenos** nom sing masc part pres mid
18. **φυλάσσεσθαι phulassesthai** inf pres mid
19. **ἐφυλαξάμην ephulaxamēn** 1sing indic aor mid
20. **φυλάξῃ phulaxē** 3sing subj aor act

19 All these things **have I kept** from my youth up: ... Matt 19:20
19 Master, all these **have I observed** from my youth. Mark 10:20
5 **keeping** watch over their flock by night........... Luke 2:8
17 and he was **kept** bound with chains and in fetters;..... 8:29

2 When a strong man armed **keepeth** his palace, ... Luke 11:21
5 blessed ... that hear the word of God, and **keep** it.... 11:28
16 Take heed, and **beware** of covetousness: 12:15
19 he said, All these **have I kept** from my youth up...... 18:21
14 that hateth his life ... **shall keep** it unto life eternal. John 12:25
20 My sayings, and does not **keep** (NASB) 12:47
7 those that thou gavest me I **have kept**, ... 17:12
9 Who have received the law ... and have not **kept** it. Acts 7:53
6 to four quaternions of soldiers **to keep** him; 12:4
6 they delivered them the decrees for **to keep**, ... 16:4
3 thyself also walkest orderly, and **keepest** the law...... 21:24
18 **keep** themselves from things offered to idols, ... 21:25
3 and **kept** the raiment of them that slew him.......... 22:20
18 **to be kept** in Herod's judgment hall................. 23:35
4 to dwell by himself with a soldier that **kept** him...... 28:16
2 uncircumcision **keep** the righteousness of the law, .. Rom 2:26
1 they themselves who are circumcised **keep** the law; .. Gal 6:13
14 who shall stablish you, and **keep** you from evil..... 2 Th 3:3
10 that thou **observe** these things .... 1 Tm 5:21
11 **keep** that which is committed to thy trust, ... 6:20
13 and am persuaded that he is able **to keep** that ..... 2 Tm 1:12
11 **keep** by the Holy Ghost which dwelleth in us.......... 1:14
15 Of whom be thou **ware** also; 4:15
8 but **saved** Noah the eighth person, a preacher ...... 2 Pt 2:5
16 **beware** lest ye also, being led away with the error 3:17
12 Little children, **keep** yourselves from idols. Amen... 1 Jn 5:21
13 Now unto him that is able **to keep** you from falling, Jude 1:24

Classical Greek

The verb *phulassō* is related to the noun *phulax* (5277), "sentinel, watchman," and indicates the activity of a watchman (Bertram, "phulassō," *Kittel*, 9:236). Another related term is *phulakē* (5274), a "watch" (e.g., Matthew 24:43), especially a "watch of the night." The scope of *phulassō* ranges from "watching over, taking care of," to "keeping" a law or command.

Septuagint Usage

Phulassō enjoys extensive usage (nearly 500 times) in the Septuagint where it replaces as many as 11 Hebrew expressions. The plainly dominant counterparts, however, are the forms of *shāmar* (the qal), "to guard, protect, keep" (around 375 times).

Adam was given the responsibility to "take care of" the Garden of Eden (Genesis 2:15, NIV). In a different understanding, after the Fall, "cherubim (of the Lord) and a flaming sword flashing back and forth (were placed) to *guard* the way to the tree of life" (Genesis 3:24, NIV); that is, they prevented entrance.

In a more figurative sense, "keeping" the way of the Lord, His word, His covenant, or His commandments means to obey Him (Genesis 18:19; Exodus 12:17,24; 19:5; cf. 13:10; cf. Leviticus 18:26,30; Deuteronomy 6:17 and throughout the Old Testament). Elsewhere it may describe "observing" a feast or the Sabbath (e.g., Exodus 23:15; 34:18; Deuteronomy 5:12).

God also "watches over" the righteous. As the Psalmist declares, "O Lord, you will keep us safe" (Psalm 12:7, NIV [LXX 11:7]; cf. 16:1 [15:1]; 25:20 [24:20]). He "protects" us from harm and evil influence (Psalms 140:4 [LXX 139:4]; 141:9 [140:9]). God's role as "Watcher" or "Guardian" may recall His being the Great Shepherd who "guards" His flock (cf. ibid., 9:237; see also Bruce, *New Testament Development of Old Testament Themes*, pp.100-114, for the use of this imagery; e.g., Psalm 23; Jeremiah 31:10).

New Testament Usage

New Testament usage largely accords with the classical and Septuagintal patterns. *Phulassō* may signify "keeping" or "observing" commands, decrees, or feasts (e.g., Matthew 19:20; Mark 10:20; cf. Acts 16:4). It concerns especially "keeping" God's Word by being obedient to His commands (Luke 11:28; cf. John 12:47).

Paul used the expression in his letters to Timothy to encourage him to "guard" (NIV, in the sense of take care of, protect from the threat of false teaching) the "deposit" (NIV) with which he had been entrusted (1 Timothy 6:20; 2 Timothy 1:14). The term "deposit," *parathēkē* (3727), is a metaphor from common life "reflecting the highest kind of sacred obligation in ancient society, namely, being entrusted with some treasured possession for safe-keeping while another is away" (see on this Fee, *Good News Commentary, 1 and 2 Timothy, Titus*, p.118). From another perspective, and perhaps recalling the Old Testament idea of God as a "Guardian," Paul was confident in God's ability to "keep" what he had been entrusted with (2 Thessalonians 3:3; 2 Timothy 1:12; Jude 24; but cf. 1 John 5:21).

Strong 5442, Bauer 868, Moulton-Milligan 678, Kittel 9:236-41, Liddell-Scott 1961, Colin Brown 2:134-35.

5279. φυλή phulē noun

Tribe, nation, people.

Cognates:

συμφυλέτης sumphuletēs (4704)
φύω phuō (5289)

Synonym:

γένος genos (1079)

אֻמָּה 'ummāh (A532), Nation (Dn 3:7,29, 4:1 [3:31]—Aramaic).

בַּיִת bayith (1041), House (Ex 2:1).

גּוֹי gôy (1504), Nation (Ps 72:17 [71:17]).

לְאֹם leʾōm (3947), People (Prv 14:34).

מוֹלֶדֶת môledheth (4274), Relatives (Gn 24:4).

מַטֶּה matteh (4431), Tribe (Nm 1:4, Jos 19:23); rod (Mi 6:9).

מִשְׁפָּחָה mishpāchāh (5121), Relatives, family (Gn 24:40f., 1 Sm 10:21, Zec 12:12ff.).

שֵׁבֶט shēveṯ (8101), Tribe (Dt 1:13, 2 Chr 11:16, Is 19:13).

שְׁבַט shᵉvaṯ (A8103), Tribe (Ezr 6:17—Aramaic).

1. φυλῆς phulēs gen sing fem
2. φυλήν phulēn acc sing fem
3. φυλαί phulai nom pl fem
4. φυλῶν phulōn gen pl fem
5. φυλαῖς phulais dat pl fem
6. φυλάς phulas acc pl fem

6 twelve thrones, judging the twelve **tribes** of Israel. . . Matt 19:28
3 and then shall all the **tribes** of the earth mourn, ... 24:30
1 daughter of Phanuel, of the **tribe** of Aser: . . . . Luke 2:36
6 sit on thrones judging the twelve **tribes** of Israel. 22:30
1 Saul the son of Cis, a man of the **tribe** of Benjamin, Acts 13:21
1 I also am an Israelite, ... of the **tribe** of Benjamin. Rom 11:1
1 of the stock of Israel, of the **tribe** of Benjamin, ... Phlp 3:5
1 For he ... pertaineth to another **tribe**, ... Heb 7:13
2 **tribe** Moses spake nothing concerning priesthood. 7:14
5 to the twelve **tribes** which are scattered abroad, ... Jas 1:1
3 all **kindreds** of the earth shall wail because of him. . . . Rev 1:7
1 behold, the Lion of the **tribe** of Juda, ... 5:5
1 by thy blood out of every **kindred**, and tongue, ... 5:9
1 of all the **tribes** of the children of Israel. 7:4
1 Of the **tribe** of Juda were sealed twelve thousand. 7:5
1 **tribe** of Reuben were sealed twelve thousand. 7:5
1 Of the **tribe** of Gad were sealed twelve thousand. 7:5
1 Of the **tribe** of Aser were sealed twelve thousand. 7:6
1 **tribe** of Nephthalim were sealed twelve thousand. 7:6
1 **tribe** of Manasses were sealed twelve thousand. 7:6
1 **tribe** of Simeon were sealed twelve thousand. 7:7
1 Of the **tribe** of Levi were sealed twelve thousand. 7:7
1 **tribe** of Issachar were sealed twelve thousand. 7:7
1 **tribe** of Zabulon were sealed twelve thousand. 7:8
1 Of the **tribe** of Joseph were sealed twelve thousand. 7:8
1 **tribe** of Benjamin were sealed twelve thousand. 7:8
4 all nations, and **kindreds**, and people, and tongues, ... 7:9
4 the people and **kindreds** and tongues and nations 11:9
2 and power was given him over all **kindreds**, ... 13:7
2 nation, and **kindred**, and tongue, and people, ... 14:6
4 names of the twelve **tribes** of the children of Israel: 21:12

Classical Greek

Phulē, related to *phuō* (5289), "to bring forth, to be born, arise," appears in extant Greek literature as early as Pindar and Herodotus (Fifth Century B.C.; cf. *Liddell-Scott*). In the classical period it primarily denotes a "clan"—a body of people united by ties of blood and descent (Herodotus 5.68; cf. ibid.). It was used frequently in reference to the traditional Doric and Ionic tribes of many Greek city-states. It could also refer to a military contingent furnished by a certain tribe (Herodotus 6.111; cf. *Liddell-Scott*).

Septuagint Usage

Phulē appears more than 400 times in the Septuagint—330 of which have a Hebrew original. Of these, 170 times *maṯṯeh* is translated; 39 times, *mishpāchāh*; and 120 times, *shēveṯ*. In the Septuagint *phulē* becomes a "fixed term for the tribal system of Israel" (Maurer, "phulē," *Kittel*, 9:246).

New Testament Usage

In the New Testament *phulē* appears in reference to the 12 tribes of Israel (Matthew 19:28; Luke 2:36; 22:30; Acts 13:21; Romans 11:1; Philippians 3:5; James 1:1; Revelation 5:5). In a more general use it can denote a "nation" (Matthew 24:30; Revelation 1:7)—a conglomeration of people united by national, rather than blood, ties. *Phulē* is also used several times in the Revelation in the formula "every tribe and language and people and nation" (5:9, NIV; 11:9; 13:7; 14:6)—an expression used to describe all of humanity.

Strong 5443, Bauer 868-69, Moulton-Milligan 678, Kittel 9:245-50, Liddell-Scott 1961, Colin Brown 3:870-71.

5280. φύλλον phullon noun

Leaf, leaves.

עָלֶה ʿāleh (6149), Leaf (Gn 8:11, Job 13:25, Jer 8:13).

1. φύλλα phulla nom/acc pl neu

1 and found nothing thereon, but **leaves** only, ... Matt 21:19
1 of the fig tree; ... and putteth forth **leaves**, ... 24:32
1 And seeing a fig tree afar off having **leaves**, ... Mark 11:13
1 when he came to it, he found nothing but **leaves**; 11:13
1 her branch is yet tender, and putteth forth **leaves**, ... 13:28
1 the **leaves** ... were for the healing of the nations. . . . . Rev 22:2

Phullon appears as early as Homer (Eighth Century B.C.) and generally denotes a "leaf" or "leaves" of any tree. It occurs only six times in the New Testament. Matthew and Mark use it in parallel passages to indicate the leaves of a fig tree. In Matthew 21:19 (and Mark 11:13) the fig tree cursed by Jesus had only leaves (if leaves were present, fruit should have been also). It is the appearance of leaves on a fig tree indicating the arrival of summer to which Jesus pointed to describe His second coming in relation to previously announced apocalyptic signs (Matthew 24:32; Mark 13:28).

It is the leaves of the tree of life that bring healing to the nations (Revelation 22:2). This is not a proof of disease existing in heaven; rather, imagery from the present existence is used to describe the eternal state. On this Mounce writes, "(The) leaves indicate the complete absence of physical and spiritual want" (*New International Commentary on the New Testament, Revelation*, p.387).

Strong 5444, Bauer 869, Moulton-Milligan 678, Liddell-Scott 1962, Colin Brown 3:865.

5281. φύραμα phurama noun

A lump of clay, lump of dough.

מִשְׁאֶרֶת mish'ereth (5049), Kneading trough (Ex 8:3, 12:34).

עֲרִיסָה 'ărîsāh (6420), Coarse meal or dough (Nm 15:20f.).

1. **φύραμα phurama** nom/acc sing neu
2. **φυράματος phuramatos** gen sing neu

2 of the same lump to make one vessel unto honour,.. Rom 9:21
1 For if the firstfruit be holy, the lump is also holy:..... 11:16
1 that a little leaven leaveneth the whole lump?.......1 Co 5:6
1 that ye may be a new lump, as ye are unleavened....... 5:7
1 A little leaven leaveneth the whole lump.............Gal 5:9

This word is used only by Paul in the New Testament. It usually is used figuratively, referring to the people of God. In 1 Corinthians 5:6,7 and Galatians 5:9 Paul warned the believers that a little yeast permeates the whole lump (*phurama*). Here the imagery is of a lump of dough (all of the Septuagintal appearances of *phurama* are in reference to a lump of dough). The *phurama* is the people of God who are to avoid allowing even a small amount of sin (yeast) into their community.

In Romans 11:16 the word occurs in an allusion to Numbers 15:17-21 where the reference is to Israel as God's chosen people. Presumably the firstfruits is the present salvation remnant of verse 5, and the *phurama* is the rest of the unsaved nation. In Romans 9:21 Paul called a lump of clay on the potter's wheel a *phurama*—a use unknown earlier but also found in Plutarch (*Moralia* 811c; cf. *Liddell-Scott*).

STRONG 5445, BAUER 869, MOULTON-MILLIGAN 678-79, LIDDELL-SCOTT 1962, COLIN BROWN 3:917.

5282. φυσικός phusikos adj

Natural, inborn, instinctive.

CROSS-REFERENCE:
φύσις phusis (5285)

1. **φυσικὴν phusikēn** acc sing fem
2. **φυσικά phusika** nom/acc pl neu

1 for even their women did change the natural use.... Rom 1:26
1 the men, leaving the natural use of the woman,.......... 1:27
2 But these, as natural brute beasts,.................. 2 Pt 2:12

Classical Greek

Phusikos is the adjectival form of the noun *phusis* (5285), "nature." *Phusis* had to do with the constitution of something—what a thing really is (Köster, "phusis," *Kittel*, 9:254). *Phusikos* refers to that which is natural—inherent to an object. In classical Greek *phusikos* denotes "that which was caused by nature, inborn, native."

The concept of nature, governed by its own inherent laws, apart from God's immediate control, is foreign to Hebrew thought. Although not found in the Septuagint, *phusikos* does occur in the pseudepigraphic Testament of Dan in reference to the "natural force" of the body (3:4). It also appears in the Epistle of Aristeas referring to the natural way in which men incline their thoughts in a certain direction (cf. *Bauer*).

New Testament Usage

Phusikos occurs three times in the New Testament. In 2 Peter 2:12 (NASB) the apostle described apostate men as "unreasoning animals" (*aloga zōa*) operating on "instinct" (*phusika*). From this it appears that the behavior of animals is *phusikos* behavior—they behave in a "natural" way. Men are to have spiritual and mental faculties that differentiate them from the unreasoning beasts (Jude used *phusikōs* [5283] in a similar way).

In Romans 1:26 and 27 Paul used *phusikos* in the context of sexual relations. It is unnatural—contrary to the basic inborn nature of man—for men and women to engage in homosexual practices. It is important to remember, though, that to Paul what is "natural" is that "which is in accordance with the intentions of the Creator" (Cranfield, *International Critical Commentary, Romans*, 1:125), not merely the product of chance evolutionary factors. Thus, the view that understands homosexuality as the product of prebirth hormonal influences is clearly contrary to Scripture. (There is no hint in this passage that Paul is merely condemning the excesses of pagan religious practices and rituals.) Rather, heterosexuality is "natural"—an inborn quality generated by the Creator.

STRONG 5446, BAUER 869, MOULTON-MILLIGAN 679, KITTEL 9:251-77, LIDDELL-SCOTT 1964, COLIN BROWN 2:656.

5283. φυσικῶς phusikōs adv

Naturally, by instinct.

CROSS-REFERENCE:
φύσις phusis (5285)

1. **φυσικῶς phusikōs**

1 they know not: but what they know naturally,.......Jude 1:10

This word is the adverbial form of the adjective *phusikos* (5282), "natural." It is derived from the Indo-European root *bhu*, "to become, grow," which in Greek is *phuō* (5289) (Köster, "phusis," *Kittel*, 9:252). Its sole New Testament occurrence is in Jude 10. Jude likened the godless men of his letter to unreasoning beasts. Their only understanding comes by instinct—by knowledge inherent in the human nature.

STRONG 5447, BAUER 869, KITTEL 9:251-77, LIDDELL-SCOTT 1964.

5284. φυσιόω phusioō verb

Inflate, puff up; become conceited, put on airs.

CROSS-REFERENCE:
φύσις phusis (5285)

1. **φυσιοῖ phusioi** 3sing indic pres act
2. **φυσιοῦται phusioutai** 3sing indic pres mid
3. **φυσιοῦσθε phusiousthe** 2pl indic pres mid
4. **φυσιούμενος phusioumenos** nom sing masc part pres mid
5. **ἐφυσιώθησαν ephusiōthēsan** 3pl indic aor pass
6. **πεφυσιωμένοι pephusiōmenoi** nom pl masc part perf mid
7. **πεφυσιωμένων pephusiōmenōn** gen pl masc part perf mid

3 of you **be puffed up** for one against another......... 1 Co 4:6
5 Now some **are puffed up**,.............................. 4:18
7 not the speech of them **which are puffed up**,............ 4:19
6 ye are **puffed up**, and have not rather mourned,......... 5:2
1 Knowledge **puffeth up**, but charity edifieth............. 8:1
2 charity vaunteth not itself, is not **puffed up**,........... 13:4
4 vainly **puffed up** by his fleshly mind,................. Col 2:18

Classical Greek

Apparently related to *phusa*, "a pair of bellows," this rare word in classical Greek means "to puff up, to inflate" (*Liddell-Scott*; cf. *Moulton-Milligan*). Evidence suggests *phusioō* is a substitute for the verb *phusaō* which is essentially identical in definition (see *Bauer*). The term does not occur in the Septuagint in either canonical or apocryphal material.

New Testament Usage

Phusioō is a distinctly Pauline word in the New Testament, and six out of its seven appearances occur in his first letter to Corinth. The Pauline usage reflects a narrowing of the definition to a solely figurative sense. As such it means "to be puffed up" in the sense of pride, arrogance, or conceit (e.g., 1 Corinthians 4:6,18,19; 5:2). The term is almost certainly to be interpreted in light of the "boasting" (*kauchaomai* [2714], another word Paul often used) that took place in Corinth (e.g., 1 Corinthians 1:29; 3:21; 4:7).

"Being puffed up" was specifically a spiritual problem from Paul's viewpoint. The problem of spiritual pride or arrogance in Corinth centered around their presumptuous and ungrateful attitudes (cf. 1 Corinthians 4:7). This aberration led to divisions in the community (cf. 1:10-17; 4:6,7), immorality (5:1f.), abuse of the Lord's Supper (chapter 11), abuse of the spiritual gifts (chapters 12–14), as well as numerous other problems.

Such conceit and pride, however, are anything but spiritual. In fact, it seems to be the consequence of a "fleshly mind" (cf. Colossians 2:18). The genuine spiritual life is marked by love (1 Corinthians 13), which "is not *puffed up*" (1 Corinthians 13:4).

STRONG 5448, BAUER 869, MOULTON-MILLIGAN 679, LIDDELL-SCOTT 1964.

5285. φύσις phusis noun

Nature, natural condition, natural order; being, essence, kind, species.

COGNATES:
φυσικός phusikos (5282)
φυσικῶς phusikōs (5283)
φυσιόω phusioō (5284)
φυσίωσις phusiōsis (5286)

1. **φύσις phusis** nom sing fem
2. **φύσεως phuseōs** gen sing fem
3. **φύσει phusei** dat sing fem
4. **φύσιν phusin** acc sing fem

4 the natural use into that which is against **nature**:.... Rom 1:26
3 do **by nature** the things contained in the law,........... 2:14
2 And shall not uncircumcision which is by **nature**,....... 2:27
4 For if God spared not the **natural** branches,........... 11:21
4 cut out of the olive tree which is wild by **nature**,...... 11:24
4 and wert grafted contrary to **nature** into a good....... 11:24
4 which be the **natural** branches,...................... 11:24
1 Doth not even **nature** itself teach you, that,........ 1 Co 11:14
3 are Jews **by nature**, and not sinners of the Gentiles,.. Gal 2:15
3 service unto them which **by nature** are no gods.......... 4:8
3 and were **by nature** the children of wrath,........... Eph 2:3
1 For every kind of beasts, and of birds, (NT)......... Jas 3:7
3 is tamed, and hath been tamed of mankind: (NT)....... 3:7
2 ye might be partakers of the divine **nature**,.......... 2 Pt 1:4

Classical Greek

The word *phusis* comes from an Indo-European root meaning "to become, grow" (Köster, "phusis," *Kittel*, 9:252). It refers to "form, nature," that which impels an object to behave as it did. Thus, among Greek philosophers *phusis* was an object or person's character, not modified or "dependent on conscious direction or education" (Köster, "phusis," *Kittel*, 9:253). *Phusis*, then, could refer to physical descent as opposed to a legally established paternity. *Phusis* could mean "birth" (Herodotus 7.134). *Phusis* was an object's true constitution, "everything which by its origin or by observation of its constitution seems to be a given" (Köster, "phusis," *Kittel*, 9:253). Plato used *phusis* to mean "talent," a natural propensity or ability in some area of endeavor (ibid., 9:261). The basic idea of *phusis* "denoted the growing of the cosmos and of all things contained in it from their own laws" (Burkert, *Greek Religion*, p.312). To the Greek philosopher the created order came to be regarded as ordered by laws which governed its behavior and made it predictable. These laws constituted its *phusis.*

Aristotle understood *phusis* teleologically. The *phusis* of a thing was what this thing was as the end product of its development (Köster, "phusis," *Kittel*, 9:258). All things had "movement"; that is, they were driven by an innate impulse toward some predetermined end. That impulse was *phusis* (Ross, *Aristotle*, pp.66-68). According to Aristotle, all matter (except the heavenly bodies) was made of four elements: earth, water, air, and fire. These four constituted the "eternal stuff"; they were the nature of things (ibid.). Thus, Aristotle held that *phusis* was both the origin and goal of movement and was in union with the divine essence which governed the universe (Köster, "phusis," *Kittel*, 9:259).

The Stoics equated *phusis* with *logos* (3030), "divine reason," the only deity of the Stoics (ibid.). For the Stoic, "according to nature" (*kata phusin*) was equivalent to "according to reason" (*kata logon*) (Köster, *History, Culture, and Religion*, 1:148f.). The goal of a man's life was to live "in accordance with the world design" (Saunders, *Greek and Roman Philosophy*, p.8). To live according to nature was to live according to reason. Since reason was innate, man could be good by nature (Köster, "phusis," *Kittel*, 9:264). *Phusis* administered the universe.

Septuagint Usage

In the Septuagint *phusis* appears only in the apocryphal books; i.e., those originally written in Greek. The reason for its absence in the canonical books is that Hebrew had no term for the Greek concept of nature (ibid., 9:266), that is, a universe governed by laws which inhered in it. In the Apocrypha *phusis* can mean "character, behavior," as in Wisdom of Solomon 7:20 where God gave the writer knowledge of the natures of animals. Elsewhere in this book, water is described as having a fire-quenching nature (19:20). This writer declared that men who are ignorant of God are foolish by *nature* since they did not discover Him when they "investigated the world" (13:1-8). *Phusis* can also mean "creature" (3 Maccabees 3:29).

The Stoic 4 Maccabees uses *phusis* on several occasions. The writer acknowledges that certain attributes of the universe exist by nature. Both body and soul experience pain and pleasure by nature (1:20). Antiochus Epiphanes told Eleazer that nature granted men pork for consumption (5:8). Parental love is innate (by nature) and creates emotions which reason must resist (15:13; 16:3). For this writer the Mosaic law was part of nature; it was given by God and must be obeyed (5:25). Philo also identified the law of Moses with the law of nature (Köster, *History, Culture, and Religion*, 1:280).

New Testament Usage

Phusis occurs 14 times in the New Testament. Its most rudimentary meaning is "nature." It is the Greek root for the English word *physics*, the study of the laws of nature. *Phusikos* (5282) is the adjectival form meaning "natural, instinctive."

While nature is its most basic connotation, various shades of that meaning can be found. When comparing the New Testament usage *Bauer* gives the following range of definitions.

First, *phusis* may refer to one's natural condition as that which is inherited from one's ancestors: "God spared not the *natural* branches" (Romans 11:21); "the olive tree which is wild *by nature*" (Romans 11:24); "uncircumcision which is *by nature*" (Romans 2:27); "graffed contrary to *nature*" (Romans 11:24); "the *natural* branches" (Romans 11:24); "we who are Jews *by nature*" (Galatians 2:15); and "*by nature* the children of wrath" (Ephesians 2:3). In Romans 11:24 *phusis* is that which has grown "naturally" and with no artificial intervention (Köster, "phusis," *Kittel*, 9:271).

Second, *phusis* may refer to the disposition or natural characteristics: "Ye did service unto them which *by nature* are no gods" (Galatians 4:8; *phusei* here is used as a dative of respect [Turner, *Grammar of New Testament Greek*, 3:220]); and "partakers of the divine *nature*" (2 Peter 1:4). Concerning the implications of 2 Peter 1:4 Gunther Harden correctly states, "The thought is evidently not that of a metamorphosis into quasi-deity, for the results of the participation are expressed in positive human qualities. It is rather that to be truly human one needs an enabling which comes from God himself" ("Nature," *Colin Brown*, 2:661).

Third, *phusis* may refer to nature as the regular natural order: "Their women did change the natural use into that which is against *nature*" (Romans 1:26), that is, unnatural intercourse (Plato also held that homosexuality was unnatural [*para phusin*, "beside nature"] since animals do not engage in it [Laws 8.836c]); "when the Gentiles, which have not the law, do by *nature* the things contained in the law" (Romans 2:14); and "Doth not even *nature* itself teach you, that, if a man have long hair, it is a shame unto him?" (1 Corinthians 11:14).

Fourth, *phusis* may refer to the product of nature, the creature, or the natural being: "*every kind* (*phusis*) of beasts, and of birds, and of serpents, and of things in the sea" (James 3:7), thus species. It is not certain whether "mankind (*phusis ta anthrōpinē*)" (James 3:7) belongs in this category or the second.

Most of the above references are located in the Epistle to the Romans where Paul gave a more logical and systematic presentation than in his other writings.

The term continued in use down through the patristic era. It was used to describe theologically the divine nature shared equally by the three Persons of the Trinity.

Strong 5449, Bauer 869-70, Moulton-Milligan 679, Kittel 9:251-77, Liddell-Scott 1964-65, Colin Brown 2:656-62.

5286. φυσίωσις phusiōsis noun

A swelling, pride.

Cross-Reference:

φύσις phusis (5285)

1. **φυσιώσεις phusiōseis** nom pl fem

1 strifes, backbitings, whisperings, **swellings**, tumults: 2 Co 12:20

In early classical Greek this word is a medical term that describes "swelling" or "inflation" of some sort (cf. *Liddell-Scott*). Under the influence of Christianity the word took on a metaphoric sense, "pride, conceit," or "arrogant self-righteousness" (Turner, *Christian Words*, p.346). It occurs only once in the New Testament, in 2 Corinthians 12:20, in a list of vices Paul feared he would find among the believers in Corinth.

Strong 5450, Bauer 870, Liddell-Scott 1965.

5287. φυτεία phuteia noun

A planting, a plant.

Cross-Reference:

φυτεύω phuteuō (5288)

מַטָּע maṭṭāʿ (4439), Place for planting (Ez 17:7, Mi 1:6).

נָטַע nāṭaʿ (5378), Plant (2 Kgs 19:29).

1. **φυτεία phuteia** nom sing fem

1 Every **plant**, which my ... Father hath not planted, Matt 15:13

Phuteia appears as early as Xenophon (Fourth Century B.C.), and in his *Oeconomicus* means "planting"—the act of planting (7:20; cf. *Liddell-Scott*). Its use in the Septuagint also stresses the action (2 Kings 19:29 [LXX 4 Kings 19:29]; Ezekiel 17:7; Micah 1:6). However, by the time of the New Testament the stress had moved to the object of the planting—the plant itself. Thus in Matthew 15:13, its only occurrence, *phuteia* refers to a plant. According to Jesus the Pharisees were plants that God had not planted and would be uprooted.

Strong 5451, Bauer 870, Moulton-Milligan 679, Liddell-Scott 1965, Colin Brown 3:865,868.

5288. φυτεύω phuteuō verb

To plant.

Cognates:

ἔμφυτος emphutos (1705)

φυτεία phuteia (5287)

נָטַע nāṭaʿ (5378), Qal: plant (Dt 28:30, Eccl 2:4f., Jer 29:5 [36:5]); niphal: be planted (Is 40:24).

נֶטַע neṭaʿ (5379), Plant (Is 17:11—Codex Alexandrinus only).

נָצַר nātsar (5526), Tend (Prv 27:18).

עָשָׂה ʿāsâh (6449), Make (Am 9:14—Codex Vaticanus only).

שָׁתַל shāthal (8694), Plant (Pss 1:3, 92:13 [91:13], Ez 19:10).

1. **φυτεύει phuteuei** 3sing indic pres act
2. **φυτεύων phuteuōn** nom sing masc part pres act
3. **ἐφύτευσα ephuteusa** 1sing indic aor act
4. **ἐφύτευσεν ephuteusen** 3sing indic aor act
5. **ἐφύτευον ephuteuon** 3pl indic imperf act
6. **φυτεύθητι phuteuthēti** 2sing impr aor pass
7. **πεφυτευμένην pephuteumenēn** acc sing fem part perf mid

4 which my heavenly Father hath not **planted**,....... Matt 15:13
4 householder, which **planted** a vineyard,................ 21:33
4 A certain man **planted** a vineyard,................ Mark 12:1
7 certain man had a fig tree **planted** in his vineyard; Luke 13:6
6 be thou **planted** in the sea; and it should obey you..... 17:6
5 they bought, they sold, they **planted**, they builded;..... 17:28
4 A certain man **planted** a vineyard,.................... 20:9
3 I have **planted**, Apollos watered;.................. 1 Co 3:6
2 So then neither is he that **planteth** any thing,........... 3:7
2 he that **planteth** and he that watereth are one:.......... 3:8
1 who **planteth** a vineyard, and eateth not ... fruit........ 9:7

Phuteuō is related to the word *phuō* (5289), "to bring forth, to be born." In the classical period it could have both a literal sense, "to plant" vegetation of some sort, and a figurative sense, "to beget" or "to produce" (cf. *Liddell-Scott*). In its 11 New Testament occurrences *phuteuō* is predominantly used in the literal sense, e.g., in Matthew 15:13 Jesus spoke of a plant which had been planted. In all its other occurrences in the Synoptic Gospels and also 1 Corinthians 9:7 it is used literally. In 1 Corinthians 3:6-8 Paul used this word figuratively to describe his work as an evangelist. He had planted spiritual seed among the Corinthians.

Strong 5452, Bauer 870, Moulton-Milligan 679, Liddell-Scott 1965, Colin Brown 3:865,868.

5289. φύω phuō verb

Grow, come up.

Cognates:
- ἀλλόφυλος allophulos (244)
- ἐκφύω ekphuō (1617)
- νεόφυτος neophutos (3367)
- σύμφυτος sumphutos (4705)
- συμφύω sumphuō (4706)
- φυλή phulē (5279)

נָטַע nāṭaʻ (5378), Plant (Jer 31:5 [38:5]—Codex Alexandrinus only).

עָלָה ʻālâh (6148), Go up (Prv 26:9).

פָּרָה pārâh (6759), Bear fruit (Dt 29:18).

צָמַח tsāmach (7048), Grow (Ex 10:5).

1. **φύουσα phuousa** nom sing fem part pres act
2. **φυέν phuen** nom/acc sing neu part aor pass

2 and as soon as it **was sprung up,** it withered away,.. **Luke 8:6**
2 And other fell on good ground, and **sprang up,**......... **8:8**
1 lest any root of bitterness **springing up** trouble you, **Heb 12:15**

This word is related to the Indo-European root *bhu* and is cognate with the Latin root *fu* (found in words like *fetus* and *fecund* [*Liddell-Scott*]). It occurs in Homer and was used extensively in classical Greek to describe any process of genesis or growth (cf. ibid.). *Phuō* appears only three times in the New Testament. Luke used it twice in the Parable of the Sower to describe the growth of the seed (Luke 8:6,8). The writer of Hebrews (12:15) employed *phuō* to warn the believers against allowing a root of bitterness to grow up in their midst.

Strong 5453, Bauer 870, Moulton-Milligan 679, Liddell-Scott 1966-67.

5290. φωλεός phōleos noun

Den, burrow, hole.

1. **φωλεούς phōleous** acc pl masc

1 The foxes have **holes,** and the birds ... have nests;...**Matt 8:20**
1 Foxes have **holes,** and birds of the air have nests;... **Luke 9:58**

Phōleos occurs as early as the time of Aristotle (Fourth Century B.C.) and is cognate with several words whose primary idea is "to lurk." Initially *phōleos* referred to the places where animals lurked and was used of the dens of bears, lions, and serpents (*Liddell-Scott*); thus denoting the place where "lurking" occurred. By the time of the New Testament the word referred simply to the dwelling place—without any sinister connotations. In its two occurrences (Matthew 8:20 and Luke 9:58) *phōleos* denotes the dwelling place of a fox—a foxhole.

Strong 5454, Bauer 870, Moulton-Milligan 679, Liddell-Scott 1967.

5291. φωνέω phōneō verb

Produce a sound or tone, cry aloud, speak loudly, call, summon, address.

Cognates:
- ἀλεκτοροφωνία alektorophōnia (217)
- ἀναφωνέω anaphōneō (398)
- ἄφωνος aphōnos (873)
- ἐπιφωνέω epiphōneō (2003)
- κενοφωνία kenophōnia (2728)
- προσφωνέω prosphōneō (4235)
- συμφωνέω sumphōneō (4707)

Synonyms:
- ἀναβοάω anaboaō (308)
- ἀνακράζω anakrazō (347)
- ἀναφωνέω anaphōneō (398)
- βοάω boaō (987)
- διαλέγομαι dialegomai (1250)
- ἐπιβοάω epiboaō (1901)
- ἐπικαλέω epikaleō (1926)
- ἐπιλέγω epilegō (1935B)
- ἐπιφωνέω epiphōneō (2003)
- ἐπονομάζω eponomazō (2012)
- ἐρεύγομαι ereugomai (2027)
- ἠχέω ēcheō (2255)
- καλέω kaleō (2535)
- κράζω krazō (2869)
- κραυγάζω kraugazō (2878)
- λαλέω laleō (2953)
- λέγω legō (2978)
- μετακαλέομαι metakaleomai (3203)
- μεταπέμπομαι metapempomai (3213)
- ὁμιλέω homileō (3519)
- ὀνομάζω onomazō (3550)
- παρακαλέω parakaleō (3731)
- προσαγορεύω prosagoreuō (4174)
- προσκαλέομαι proskaleomai (4200)
- συγκαλέω sunkaleō (4630)
- φημί phēmi (5183)
- φθέγγομαι phthengomai (5187)
- χρηματίζω chrēmatizō (5372)

הָגָה hāghâh (1965), Make a sound (Ps 115:7 [113:15]).

נָשָׂא nāsâ' (5558), Raise (Is 24:14).

צָפַף tsāphaph (7127), Pilpel: twitter (Is 38:14).

קְרָא q^e^râ' (A7411), Call (Dn 4:14 [4:11], 5:7—Aramaic).

קֹרֵא qōrē' (7412), Partridge (Jer 17:11).

שִׁיר shîr (8301), Polel: sing (Zep 2:14).

תָּקַע tāqa' (8965), Clap, thrust, blow; niphal: be blown (Am 3:6).

1. **φωνεῖ phōnei** 3sing indic pres act
2. **φωνεῖτε phōneite** 2pl indic pres act
3. **φωνοῦσιν phōnousin** 3pl indic pres act
4. **φώνει phōnei** 2sing impr pres act
5. **φωνοῦντες phōnountes** nom pl masc part pres act
6. **ἐφώνησεν ephōnēsen** 3sing indic aor act
7. **ἐφώνησαν ephōnēsan** 3pl indic aor act
8. **φώνησον phōnēson** 2sing impr aor act
9. **φωνήσας phōnēsas** nom sing masc part aor act
10. **φωνήσαντες phōnēsantes** nom pl masc part aor act
11. **φωνῆσαι phōnēsai** inf aor act
12. **φωνήσει phōnēsei** 3sing indic fut act
13. **ἐφώνει ephōnei** 3sing indic imperf act
14. **φωνηθῆναι phōnēthēnai** inf aor pass
15. **φωνήσῃ phōnēsē** 3sing subj aor act
16. **φωνήσατε phōnēsate** 2pl impr aor act
17. **φωνῆσαν phōnēsan** nom/acc sing neu part aor act

6 And Jesus stood still, and **called** them, and said, .. Matt 20:32
11 before the cock **crow**, thou shalt deny me thrice...... 26:34
6 And immediately the cock **crew**...................... 26:74
11 Before the cock **crow**, thou shalt deny me thrice...... 26:75
1 This man **calleth** for Elias.......................... 27:47
17 **cried out** with a loud voice, (NASB) .... Mark 1:26
5 and, standing without, sent unto him, **calling** him...... 3:31
6 and **called** the twelve, and saith unto them,........... 9:35
14 Jesus stood still, and commanded him **to be called**..... 10:49
3 And they **call** the blind man, saying unto him,....... 10:49
1 Be of good comfort, rise; he **calleth** thee............. 10:49
11 before the cock **crow** twice, thou shalt deny me 14:30
6 he went out into the porch; and the cock **crew**........ 14:68
6 And the second time the cock **crew**.................. 14:72
11 Before the cock **crow** twice, thou shalt deny me 14:72
1 when they heard it, said, Behold, he **calleth** Elias..... 15:35
13 he **cried**, He that hath ears to hear, let him hear... Luke 8:8
6 by the hand, and **called**, saying, Maid, arise............ 8:54
4 **call** not thy friends, nor thy brethren,................ 14:12
9 And he **called** him, and said unto him,.............. 16:2
9 And he **cried** and said, Father Abraham,............. 16:24
14 commanded these servants **to be called** unto him,..... 19:15
12 Peter, the cock **shall** not **crow** this day,............. 22:34
6 immediately, while he yet spake, the cock **crew**....... 22:60
11 Before the cock **crow**, thou shalt deny me thrice...... 22:61
9 And when Jesus **had cried** with a loud voice,......... 23:46
11 Before that Philip **called** thee, ... I saw thee........John 1:48
1 the governor of the feast **called** the bridegroom,....... 2:9
8 Go, **call** thy husband, and come hither................ 4:16
7 did not believe ... until they **called** the parents......... 9:18
7 Then again **called** they the man that was blind,........ 9:24
1 and he **calls** his own sheep by name, (NASB)........ 10:3
6 went her way, and **called** Mary her sister secretly,.... 11:28
1 saying, The Master is come, and **calleth** for thee...... 11:28
6 with him when he **called** Lazarus out of his grave,.... 12:17
2 Ye **call** me Master and Lord: and ye say well;....... 13:13
12 cock **shall** not **crow**, till thou hast denied me thrice... 13:38
6 and immediately the cock **crew**...................... 18:27
6 Then Pilate entered ... again, and **called** Jesus,....... 18:33
9 and when he **had called** the saints and widows,..... Acts 9:41
9 he **called** two of his household servants,.......... Acts 10:7
10 And **called**, and asked whether Simon,............... 10:18
6 But Paul **cried** with a loud voice, saying,............. 16:28
6 and **cried** with a loud cry to him................. Rev 14:18

Classical Greek

As the verbal action of *phōnē* (5292), "sound, voice," *phōneō* fundamentally means "to produce a sound or a tone." In classical Greek literature *phōneō* occurs as early as in Homer's (Eighth Century B.C.) and Aristotle's writings. The verb is used primarily of living beings with vocal organs. Animals, therefore, make sounds, as in *Aesop's fable*; and of human beings it can be said they "lift up the voice" or "cause the voice to sound forth," as in Homer's *Iliad* (cf. Betz, "phōneō," *Kittel*, 9:302). *Phōneō* can also carry the meaning of invoking a deity in prayer or "to call to" when used with the dative of person.

Septuagint Usage

Phōneō is rarely used in the Septuagint. It may denote the sounding of an instrument, such as a trumpet (Amos 3:6), or the sounds made by animals (Isaiah 38:14; Zephaniah 2:14). Spirits of the dead are also ascribed the ability to speak or, more descriptively, to "mutter" (Isaiah 8:19; cf. 29:4).

New Testament Usage

Of the approximately 40 instances where *phōneō* is used in the New Testament, none occur in the Epistles and all but 5 are used in the Gospels. As in Septuagint usage, so here the verb means human, angelic, animal, or demonic "speaking, calling," or "crying." Luke and John also use *phōneō* as a synonym for *kaleō* (2535), "to call, summon," e.g., in Luke 16:2; John 2:9; Acts 9:41 (ibid., 9:303). In Mark 10:49 the verb carries an eschatological sense in that the calling which Jesus directed to Bartimeus via others was ultimately the invitation and summons to healing and salvation. John may have had similar connotations in mind in John 11:28 where Martha informed Mary: "The Teacher is here and is *calling* for you" (RSV).

STRONG 5455, BAUER 870, MOULTON-MILLIGAN 679-80, KITTEL 9:301-3, LIDDELL-SCOTT 1967, COLIN BROWN 3:113-14.

5292. φωνή phōnē noun

Sound, tone, voice, call.

CROSS-REFERENCE:

φωνέω phōneō (5291)

אִמְרָה 'imrāh (577), Voice (Is 29:4).

דָּבָר dāvār (1745), Word; speech (Gn 11:1).

הָמוֹן hāmôn (2066), Uproar (1 Sm 4:14—Codex Vaticanus only).

זְעָקָה zeeāqāh (2285), Loud cry (Est 4:1).

לָשׁוֹן lāshôn (4098), Language, tongue (Dt 28:49, Is 54:17).

מִצְוָה mitswāh (4851), Commandment (Dt 28:9).

נְהָמָה nehāmāh (5279), Roar (Is 5:30).

פֶּה peh (6552), Mouth; word (Nm 3:16, 39); sound (Am 6:5).

צְעָקָה tseeāqāh (7095), Loud cry (Gn 27:34).

קוֹל qôl (7249), Sound, voice (Ex 32:18, Ps 93:3f. [92:3f.], Jer 51:54f. [28:54f.]).

קָל gāl (A7315), Sound (Dn 3:7, 10, 7:11—Aramaic).

שָׂפָה sāphāh (8004), Lip; speech (Gn 11:7).

תְּחִנָּה techinnāh (8798), Supplication (1 Kgs 8:30—Codex Alexandrinus only).

תְּרוּעָה terûeāh (8980), Trumpet sound (Lv 25:9); shout (1 Sm 4:5, Ezr 3:13).

1. **φωνή phōnē** nom sing fem
2. **φωνῆς phōnēs** gen sing fem
3. **φωνῇ phōnē** dat sing fem
4. **φωνήν phōnēn** acc sing fem
5. **φωναί phōnai** nom pl fem
6. **φωνῶν phōnōn** gen pl fem
7. **φωναῖς phōnais** dat pl fem
8. **φωνάς phōnas** acc pl fem

1 In Rama was there **a voice** heard, ... **Matt** 2:18
1 The **voice** of one crying in the wilderness, ... 3:3
1 And lo **a voice** from heaven, saying, ... 3:17
4 neither shall any man hear his **voice** in the streets. 12:19
1 and behold **a voice** out of the cloud, which said, ... 17:5
2 send his angels with a great **sound** of a trumpet, ... 24:31
3 about the ninth hour Jesus cried **with** a loud **voice**, ... 27:46
3 Jesus, when he had cried again **with** a loud **voice**, ... 27:50
1 The **voice** of one crying in the wilderness, ... **Mark** 1:3
1 And there came **a voice** from heaven, saying, ... 1:11
3 and cried with a loud **voice**, he came out of him. 1:26
3 And cried with a loud **voice**, and said, ... 5:7
1 and **a voice** came out of the cloud, saying, ... 9:7
3 at the ninth hour Jesus cried **with** a loud **voice**, ... 15:34
4 Jesus cried with a loud **voice**, ... gave up the ghost. 15:37
3 And she spake out **with** a loud **voice**, and said, ... **Luke** 1:42
1 lo, as soon as the **voice** of thy salutation sounded 1:44
1 The **voice** of one crying in the wilderness, ... 3:4
4 and **a voice** came from heaven, which said, ... 3:22
3 and cried out **with** a loud **voice**, ... 4:33
3 fell down before him, and **with** a loud **voice** said, ... 8:28
1 And there came **a voice** out of the cloud, saying, ... 9:35
4 when the **voice** was past, Jesus was found alone. 9:36
4 certain woman of the company lifted up her **voice**, ... 11:27
4 And they lifted up their **voices**, and said, Jesus, ... 17:13
2 turned back, and with a loud **voice** glorified God, ... 17:15
3 began to rejoice and praise God **with** a loud **voice** 19:37
7 And they were instant **with** loud **voices**, ... 23:23
5 **voices** of them and of the chief priests prevailed. 23:23
3 And when Jesus had cried **with** a loud **voice**, ... 23:46
1 I am the **voice** of one crying in the wilderness, ... **John** 1:23
4 and thou hearest the **sound** thereof, ... 3:8
4 because of the bridegroom's **voice**: 3:29
2 the dead shall hear the **voice** of the Son of God: 5:25
2 all that are in the graves shall hear his **voice**, ... 5:28
4 Ye have neither heard his **voice** at any time, ... 5:37
2 and the sheep hear his **voice**: .... **John** 10:3
4 and the sheep follow him: for they know his **voice**. 10:4
4 for they know not the **voice** of strangers. 10:5
2 and they shall hear my **voice**; 10:16
2 My sheep hear my **voice**, and I know them, ... 10:27
3 he cried with a loud **voice**, Lazarus, come forth. 11:43
1 Then came there **a voice** from heaven, saying, ... 12:28
1 **voice** came not because of me, but for your sakes. 12:30
2 Every one that is of the truth heareth my **voice**. 18:37
2 Now when this was **noised** abroad, ... **Acts** 2:6
4 Peter, ... lifted up his **voice**, and said unto them, ... 2:14
4 they lifted up their **voice** to God with one accord, ... 4:24
1 the **voice** of the Lord came unto him, ... 7:31
3 cried out **with** a loud **voice**, and stopped their ears, ... 7:57
3 And he kneeled down, and cried **with** a loud **voice**, ... 7:60
3 For unclean spirits, crying with loud **voice**, ... 8:7
4 and heard **a voice** saying unto him, Saul, Saul, ... 9:4
2 hearing **a voice**, but seeing no man. 9:7
1 And there came **a voice** to him, Rise, Peter; 10:13
1 the **voice** spake unto him again the second time, ... 10:15
2 **a voice** saying unto me, Arise, Peter; slay and eat. 11:7
1 But the **voice** answered me again from heaven, ... 11:9
4 And when she knew Peter's **voice**, ... 12:14
1 saying, It is the **voice** of a god, and not of a man. 12:22
8 nor yet the **voices** of the prophets 13:27
3 Said with a loud **voice**, Stand upright on thy feet. 14:10
4 they lifted up their **voices**, ... 14:11
3 But Paul cried **with** a loud **voice**, saying, ... 16:28
1 all with one **voice** about the space of two hours 19:34
2 and heard **a voice** saying unto me, Saul, Saul, ... 22:7
4 they heard not the **voice** of him that spake to me. 22:9
4 and shouldest hear the **voice** of his mouth. 22:14
4 and then lifted up their **voices**, and said, ... 22:22
2 Except it be for this one **voice**, ... 24:21
4 I heard **a voice** speaking unto me, ... 26:14
3 Festus said with a loud **voice**, Paul, ... 26:24
4 And even things without life giving **sound**, ... **1 Co** 14:7
4 For if the trumpet give an uncertain **sound**, ... 14:8
6 it may be, so many kinds of **voices** in the world, ... 14:10
2 Therefore if I know not the meaning of the **voice**, ... 14:11
4 to change my **voice**; for I stand in doubt of you. ..... **Gal** 4:20
3 with the **voice** of the archangel, ... **1 Th** 4:16
2 Holy Ghost saith, To day if ye will hear his **voice**, ... **Heb** 3:7
2 While it is said, To day if ye will hear his **voice**, ... 3:15
2 as it is said, To day if ye will hear his **voice**, ... 4:7
3 the sound of a trumpet, and the **voice** of words; 12:19
1 Whose **voice** then shook the earth: 12:26
2 came such **a voice** to him from the excellent glory, ... **2 Pt** 1:17
4 And this **voice** which came from heaven we heard, ... 1:18
3 the dumb ass speaking with man's **voice** 2:16
4 heard behind me a great **voice**, as of a trumpet, ... **Rev** 1:10
4 And I turned to see the **voice** that spake with me. 1:12
1 and his **voice** as the sound of many waters. 1:15
1 and his voice as the **sound** of many waters. 1:15
2 if any man hear my **voice**, and open the door, ... 3:20
1 and the first **voice** which I heard 4:1
5 proceeded lightnings and thunderings and **voices**: 4:5
3 I saw a strong angel proclaiming with a loud **voice**, ... 5:2
4 And I beheld, and I heard the **voice** of many angels 5:11
3 Saying **with** a loud **voice**, Worthy is the Lamb 5:12
2 and I heard, as it were the **noise** of thunder, ... 6:1
4 I heard **a voice** in the midst of the four beasts say, ... 6:6
4 I heard the **voice** of the fourth beast say, ... 6:7
3 And they cried **with** a loud **voice**, saying, ... 6:10
3 and he cried **with** a loud **voice** to the four angels, ... 7:2
3 **with** a loud **voice**, saying, Salvation to our God 7:10
5 and cast it into the earth: and there were **voices**, ... 8:5
3 the midst of heaven, saying **with** a loud **voice**, Woe, ... 8:13
6 other **voices** of the trumpet of the three angels, ... 8:13
1 **sound** of their wings was as the sound of chariots 9:9
1 **sound** of chariots of many horses running to battle. 9:9
4 I heard a **voice** from the four horns of the ... altar 9:13
3 cried **with** a loud **voice**, as when a lion roareth: 10:3
8 seven thunders uttered their **voices**. 10:3
8 when the seven thunders had uttered their **voices**, ... 10:4
4 and I heard **a voice** from heaven saying unto me, ... 10:4
2 But in the days of the **voice** of the seventh angel, ... 10:7

1 And the voice which I heard from heaven spake .... Rev 10:8
4 heard a great voice from heaven saying unto them, ... 11:12
5 and there were great voices in heaven, saying, ... 11:15
5 there were lightnings, and voices, and thunderings, ... 11:19
4 And I heard a loud voice saying in heaven, ... 12:10
4 And I heard a voice from heaven, ... 14:2
4 a voice from heaven, as the voice of many waters, ... 14:2
4 and as the voice of a great thunder: 14:2
1 the voice of harpers harping with their harps: 14:2
3 with a loud voice, Fear God, and give glory to him; ... 14:7
3 followed them, saying with a loud voice, ... 14:9
2 And I heard a voice from heaven saying unto me, ... 14:13
3 with a loud voice to him that sat on the cloud, ... 14:15
3 voice to him who had the sharp sickle, (NASB) 14:18
2 And I heard a great voice out of the temple saying 16:1
1 came a great voice out of the temple of heaven, ... 16:17
5 there were voices, and thunders, and lightnings; 16:18
3 he cried mightily with a strong voice, saying, ... 18:2
4 And I heard another voice from heaven, saying, ... 18:4
1 And the voice of harpers, and musicians, ... 18:22
1 the sound of a millstone shall be heard no more 18:22
1 and the voice of the bridegroom and of the bride 18:23
4 And after these things I heard a great voice 19:1
1 And a voice came out of the throne, saying, ... 19:5
4 I heard as it were the voice of a great multitude, ... 19:6
4 a great multitude, and as the voice of many waters, ... 19:6
4 the voice of mighty thunderings, saying, Alleluia: 19:6
3 standing in the sun; and he cried with a loud voice, ... 19:17
2 And I heard a great voice out of heaven saying, ... 21:3

Classical Greek

Phōnē is related to the verb *phēmi* (5183), "I say"; consequently the basic meaning of the noun *phōnē* is the "audible sound produced by living creatures in the throat" (Betz, "phōnē," *Kittel*, 9:278). In classical Greek literature *phōnē* was common already in Homer's writings (Eighth Century B.C.) and had a wide variety of meaning. It was used for the various sounds of animals and could denote the faculty of speech. In particular it referred to statements or sayings made by man or by deity. Most prominently, however, *phōnē* was used for the sound of the human organ of speech, hence the meaning "voice."

Septuagint Usage

In the Septuagint *phōnē* is widely used and most often translates the Hebrew *qôl*. Thus it could signify any kind of audible noise, such as the roar of waterfalls (Psalm 42:7 [LXX 41:7]), the sound of steps (Genesis 3:8), and the gentle whisper of air (1 Kings 19:12 [LXX 3 Kings 19:12]). As in the classical Greek usage it describes the sounds of animals, such as the roaring of a lion (Amos 3:4) as well as the human voice. Significantly, *phōnē* occurs as a representation of God who cannot be seen but whose voice can be heard, e.g., from between the two cherubim above the mercy seat of the ark of the covenant (Numbers 7:89) or in the sound of thunder (e.g., Job 37:4; Isaiah 29:6; cf. Exodus 19:16-20).

New Testament Usage

Phōnē occurs in about 140 instances in the New Testament, most commonly in Luke–Acts, John, and Revelation. The range of meanings in the Old Testament is carried over into the New Testament. It is used for the "sound" of the wind (John 3:8), of instruments (1 Corinthians 14:7,8; Revelation 1:10), and the "voice" of the bridegroom (John 3:29). In a quote from Isaiah 40:3 John the Baptist referred to himself as the "voice" of one who cries out in the desert (John 1:23). On the Day of Pentecost the crowds reacted to the miracle of the outpouring of the Holy Spirit because they heard "this sound" (Acts 2:6, NIV). God's *phōnē* from heaven was heard at the baptism of Jesus (Luke 3:22) and at His transfiguration (Luke 9:35; cf. 2 Peter 1:17,18). That His sheep hear the *phōnē* of the Good Shepherd means they know Him in personal relationship and discipleship (John 10:3,16,27).

STRONG 5456, BAUER 870-71, MOULTON-MILLIGAN 680, KITTEL 9:278-301, LIDDELL-SCOTT 1967-68, COLIN BROWN 3:113-14.

5292B. φῶς phōs noun

Light, source of light.

CROSS-REFERENCE:
φωτίζω phōtizō (5297)

אוֹר 'ôr (214), Light (Gn 1:3ff., Job 18:5f., Is 60:19f.).

אוּר 'ûr (215), Light (Is 50:11).

אוֹרָה 'ôrāh (218), Light; happiness (Est 8:16).

מָאוֹר mā'ôr (4115), Lamp (Ex 27:20, 35:14 [35:16], 39:37 [39:17]).

נֶבְרְשָׁה nevreshāh (A5219), Lampstand (Dn 5:5—Aramaic).

נֹגַהּ nōghahh (5227), Something flaming, light (Is 4:5, 50:10).

נְהִיר nehîr (A5271), Light (Dn 2:22—Aramaic).

נִיר nîr (5403), Fallow ground (Hos 10:12).

נֵר nēr (5552), Lamp (Prv 13:9, 20:27).

1. **φῶς phōs** nom/acc sing neu
2. **φωτός phōtos** gen sing neu
3. **φωτί phōti** dat sing neu
4. **φώτων phōtōn** gen pl neu
5. **φῶτα phōta** nom/acc pl neu

1 The people which sat in darkness saw great light; ... Matt 4:16
1 the region and shadow of death light is sprung up 4:16
1 Ye are the light of the world 5:14
1 Let your light so shine before men, ... 5:16
1 If therefore the light that is in thee be darkness, ... 6:23
3 What I tell you in darkness, that speak ye in light: 10:27
1 and his raiment was white as the light 17:2
1 with the servants, and warmed himself at the fire. Mark 14:54
1 A light to lighten the Gentiles, ... Luke 2:32
1 that they which enter in may see the light 8:16
1 that those who enter may see the light. (NASB) 11:33
1 that the light which is in thee be not darkness 11:35

3 spoken in darkness shall be heard in the **light**; ..... Luke 12:3
2 in their generation wiser than the children of **light**..... 16:8
1 But a certain maid beheld him as he sat by the **fire**, ... 22:56
1 In him was life; and the life was the **light** of men... John 1:4
1 And the **light** shineth in darkness; 1:5
2 to bear witness of the **Light**, ... 1:7
1 He was not that **Light**, but was sent to bear witness 1:8
2 but was sent to bear witness of that **Light**. 1:8
1 That was the true **Light**, which lighteth every man 1:9
1 that **light** is come into the world, ... 3:19
1 and men loved darkness rather than **light**, ... 3:19
1 For every one that doeth evil hateth the **light**, ... 3:20
1 hateth the light, neither cometh to the **light**, ... 3:20
1 But he that doeth truth cometh to the **light**, ... 3:21
3 ye were willing for a season to rejoice in his **light**. 5:35
1 I am the **light** of the world: 8:12
1 but shall have the **light** of life. 8:12
1 I am the **light** of the world. 9:5
1 because he seeth the **light** of this world. 11:9
1 because there is no **light** in him. 11:10
1 Yet a little while is the **light** with you. 12:35
1 Walk while ye have the **light**, ... 12:35
1 While ye have **light**, believe in the light, ... 12:36
1 While ye have light, believe in the **light**, ... 12:36
2 that ye may be the children of **light**. 12:36
1 I am come a **light** into the world, ... 12:46
1 there shined round about him a **light** from heaven: .. Acts 9:3
1 and a **light** shined in the prison: 12:7
1 I have set thee to be a **light** of the Gentiles, ... 13:47
5 Then he called for a **light**, and sprang in, ... 16:29
1 suddenly there shone from heaven a great **light** 22:6
1 And they that were with me saw indeed the **light**, ... 22:9
2 when I could not see for the glory of that **light**, ... 22:11
1 I saw in the way a **light** from heaven, ... 26:13
1 and to turn them from darkness to **light**, ... 26:18
1 and should show **light** unto the people, ... 26:23
1 a **light** of them which are in darkness, ... Rom 2:19
2 and let us put on the armour of **light**. 13:12
1 who commanded the **light** to shine out of darkness, 2 Co 4:6
3 and what communion hath **light** with darkness? 6:14
2 Satan himself is transformed into an angel of **light**. 11:14
1 but now are ye **light** in the Lord: .... Eph 5:8
2 light in the Lord: walk as children of **light**: 5:8
2 for the fruit of the **light** consists in all (NASB) 5:9
2 that are reproved are made manifest by the **light**: 5:13
1 for whatsoever doth make manifest is **light**. 5:13
3 partakers of the inheritance of the saints in **light**: .....Col 1:12
2 Ye are all the children of **light**, ... 1 Th 5:5
1 the **light** which no man can approach unto; .... 1 Tm 6:16
4 and cometh down from the Father of **lights**, ... Jas 1:17
1 out of darkness into his marvellous **light**: .... 1 Pt 2:9
1 that God is **light**, and in him is no darkness at all... 1 Jn 1:5
3 But if we walk in the **light**, as he is in the light, ... 1:7
3 But if we walk in the light, as he is in the **light**, ... 1:7
1 darkness is past, and the true **light** now shineth. 2:8
3 that saith he is in the **light**, and hateth his brother, ... 2:9
3 He that loveth his brother abideth in the **light**, ... 2:10
1 **light** of a candle shall shine no more at all in thee; Rev 18:23
3 them which are saved shall walk in the **light** of it: 21:24
2 not have need of the **light** of a lamp (NASB) 22:5
2 and they need no candle, neither **light** of the sun; 22:5

Classical Greek

Phōs, "light" (originally *phaos* but later contracted), appears on the scene around the time of Homer (Eighth Century B.C.). Its pliable nature expanded it in several directions from this basic definition. Thus it can denote the "brightness" of something; "daylight, starlight," etc. Figuratively, in poetic writings especially, *phōs* stands for the "life" of man. Light further represents intellectual "illumination," or it can stand for physical "sight." Metaphorically it denotes "victory, deliverance," and thus "happiness" (cf. *Liddell-Scott*; Conzelmann, "phōs," *Kittel*, 8:310-313).

Quite naturally *phōs*, "light," stood over against *skotos* (4510), "darkness." These terms were common in the vocabulary of philosophy, religion, ethics, and epistemology (an investigation into the origin, nature, and limits of knowledge). "Light" inevitably denotes "good"; evil deeds were carried out under the cover of darkness or night. As a figure of life itself, *phōs* contrasts the darkness of death. In addition, light illumines; thus it represents knowledge, insight, and understanding. In later "systems"—such as gnosticism, the Qumran community, or later Hellenistic Judaism—the duality between light and darkness became even more exploited in an effort to convey theology (e.g., of Qumran 1QM 13:5,14-16; 1QS 1:9; 2:16; in Hellenistic Judaism Testament of Levi 4:4; 18:3; cf. *Bauer*).

Septuagint Usage

Light plays a prominent role in the Old Testament, functioning both literally (e.g., Judges 16:2; 1 Samuel 25:36 [LXX 1 Kings 25:36]; Isaiah 4:5) and figuratively. Light's significance is implied as early as the creation account in Genesis (1:3). Light replaced the darkness of the primordial, formless earth. The statement, "God saw that the *light* was good" (Genesis 1:4, NIV), anticipates the figurative understanding. Thus, in later writings God is seen in terms of light, which means "life, salvation," and "goodness" (e.g., Psalms 4:6; 36:9 [LXX 35:9]; 56:13 [55:13]; Isaiah 2:5; Sirach 50:29; cf. Exodus 13:21; Psalm 27:1; Daniel 2:22; Habakkuk 3:4). Used of men, light retains its positive character (2 Samuel 23:4 [LXX 2 Kings 23:4]; cf. Isaiah 49:6, Israel as the light to the nations; see also Isaiah 60:3). Later Judaism associated *phōs* with the "light" of Torah (Wisdom of Solomon 18:4) or the "light" of Wisdom (Wisdom of Solomon 7:26; cf. 7:29).

New Testament Usage

The majority of New Testament occurrences of *phōs* are in the Gospels and Acts (nearly 50 times); of these, 23 are found in John's Gospel. Other Johannine writings reflect a similar interest (1 John, six times; Revelation, three). The literal usage can be found (Matthew 17:2; Luke 8:16; 12:3; Revelation 22:5), but even then the figurative nuances cannot always be totally dismissed (e.g., Luke 16:8).

Light is synonymous with spiritual life (Matthew 5:16), and Christians can be the source of this life for the rest of the world (Matthew 5:14). God also is seen in terms of that relationship between light and life. The Light (i.e., Jesus) was the life of men (John 1:4; cf. 8:12). As the Light himself, Jesus entered the world to bring life to those living in darkness (John 3:19; 8:12). God is light (1 John 1:5; cf. James 1:17); if we live and believe in Him—in the light—we have life (John 8:12; cf. 11:10; 12:35,36,46) and we are children of light (John 12:36; cf. Matthew 5:14; 1 Thessalonians 5:5).

Light also means "salvation," especially for those living in darkness (often the Gentiles, e.g., Matthew 4:16; Acts 13:47; 26:17,18; Ephesians 5:8; 1 Peter 2:9; but cf. John 3:19 of all men who love darkness; Acts 26:23 of both Israel and the Gentiles). The "*light* (*phōtismos* [5298]) of the . . . gospel" (2 Corinthians 4:4) penetrates our hearts and grants us insight or "knowledge" for salvation (2 Corinthians 4:6).

Existence in the light has ethical consequences. In order to remain in the light one's conduct must reflect a vibrant relationship with the Light. "Put on the armor of *light*" (Romans 13:12) is synonymous with "clothe yourselves with the Lord Jesus" (Romans 13:14, NIV), and both of these signify an ethical response (cf. 2 Corinthians 6:14; Ephesians 5:9 [the fruit of light which equals goodness, righteousness, and truth]; 1 John 1:7 [fellowship and purity]; 2:10).

STRONG 5457, BAUER 871-72, MOULTON-MILLIGAN 680, KITTEL 9:310-58, LIDDELL-SCOTT 1968, COLIN BROWN 2:490,493,496.

5293. φωστήρ phōstēr noun

Star, luminary; splendor, radiance, light, brilliance, brightness.

CROSS-REFERENCE:
φωτίζω phōtizō (5297)

זֹהַר zōhar (2179), Brightness (Dn 12:3).

מָאוֹר mā'ôr (4115), Celestial light (Gn 1:14,16).

1. φωστήρ phōstēr nom sing masc
2. φωστῆρες phōstēres nom pl masc

2 among whom ye shine as **lights** in the world; .... Phlp 2:15
1 and her **light** was like unto a stone most precious, .. Rev 21:11

Classical Greek and Septuagint Usage

This term is related to the noun *phōs* (5292B), "light," and cannot be found in Greek literature prior to the Septuagint where it means "lights of heaven, stars." In later Greek literature (ca. Second–Third Century A.D.) it means "splendor, radiance." Used metaphorically it describes the "eyes" as an "opening for light" (cf. *Liddell-Scott*).

In the Septuagint the word *phōstēr* occurs four times in the account of creation. In the beginning "God said, Let there be *lights* in the firmament of the heaven to divide the day from the night; and let them be for signs, and for seasons, and for days, and years: . . . God made two great *lights*; the greater *light* to rule the day, and the lesser *light* to rule the night" (Genesis 1:14-16). A parallel passage would be Daniel 12:3: "They that be wise shall shine as the *brightness* of the firmament; and they that turn many to righteousness, as the stars for ever and ever." (See also Wisdom 13:2 and Sirach 43:7.)

New Testament Usage

Phōstēr appears twice in the New Testament. In Philippians 2:15 Paul wrote, "That ye may be blameless and harmless, the sons of God, without rebuke, in the midst of a crooked and perverse nation, among whom ye shine as *lights* in the world." His point is that the contrast between believers and unbelievers should be like daylight and darkness. The world ought to be able to plot their course to God by the shining example of Christians.

In Revelation 21:11 *phōstēr* describes the dazzling radiance of the New Jerusalem coming down from heaven to earth: "Her *light* was like unto a stone most precious, even like a jasper stone, clear as crystal." No city will ever match the splendor of this place.

In each instance the thought of light (as purity), the opposite of darkness (as impurity), is implied.

STRONG 5458, BAUER 872, MOULTON-MILLIGAN 680, KITTEL 9:310-58, LIDDELL-SCOTT 1968, COLIN BROWN 2:490,493.

5294. φωσφόρος phōsphoros adj

Light bearing; the morning star, daystar.

CROSS-REFERENCES:
φέρω pherō (5179)
φωτίζω phōtizō (5297)

1. φωσφόρος phōsphoros nom sing masc

1 and the **day star** arise in your hearts: .... 2 Pt 1:19

Classical Greek

This adjective is related to the noun *phōs* (5292B) meaning "light" or something bearing or giving light. When used substantivally (as a noun) it designates the morning star, that is, the planet Venus. It is also the Greek root for the English word "phosphorous," a substance which glows when activated by radiation. The term has been found in papyri (scrolls made of the papyrus plant) and in the writings of the Jewish philosopher Philo (cf. *Bauer*). From Euripides (Fifth Century B.C.) onward this word can be found in classical Greek. However, it did not find its way into the pages of the Septuagint, the Greek translation of the Old Testament.

New Testament Usage

In the New Testament *phōsphoros* appears only once. In 2 Peter 1:19 the apostle says, "We have also a more sure word of prophecy; whereunto ye do well that ye take heed, as unto a light that shineth in a dark place, until the day dawn, and the *day-star* (the morning star) arise in your hearts." Here its use is figurative of the illumination which will be given to each believer's understanding when Christ returns. The Lord Jesus Christ calls himself "the bright and morning star (*astēr* [786])" in Revelation 22:16. Again, this is found in an eschatological context. He will be the first and brightest star to appear in the dawn, the darkest part of the night.

STRONG 5459, BAUER 872, MOULTON-MILLIGAN 682, KITTEL 9:310-58, LIDDELL-SCOTT 1968, COLIN BROWN 2:490,493,495.

5295. φῶς phōs

See word study at number 5292B.

5296. φωτεινός phōteinos adj

Bright, radiant, luminous, full of light.

COGNATE:
φωτίζω phōtizō (5297)

SYNONYMS:
λαμπρός lampros (2959)
λευκός leukos (2996)

1. φωτεινή phōteinē nom sing fem
2. φωτεινόν phōteinon nom/acc sing neu

2 thy whole body shall be full of **light**. . . . . Matt 6:22
1 behold, a **bright** cloud overshadowed them: 17:5
2 thy whole body also is **full of light**; . . . . Luke 11:34
2 If thy whole body therefore be **full of light**, ... 11:36
2 the whole shall be **full of light**, ... 11:36

This adjective is related to the noun *phōs* (5292B), "light," and can be found in classical Greek from the Fourth Century B.C. meaning "shining, bright" (*Liddell-Scott*). It appears five times in the New Testament, four of which are located in the parallel accounts of Jesus' teaching on the sound eye (Matthew 6:22,23; Luke 11:34-36). Through the eye gate proceeds light or darkness, depending on the person's spiritual outlook.

The other instance is in Matthew's description of the scene on the Mount of Transfiguration where "a *bright* cloud overshadowed them" (17:5). A cloud like this often accompanied the presence of God (cf. Exodus 40:34f.; Numbers 9:15f.; 1 Kings 8:10,11).

STRONG 5460, BAUER 872, MOULTON-MILLIGAN 680, KITTEL 9:310-58, LIDDELL-SCOTT 1968-69, COLIN BROWN 2:490,493.

5297. φωτίζω phōtizō verb

Give light to, light up; bring to light, reveal, make evident; enlighten.

COGNATES:
ἐπιφώσκω epiphōskō (2004)
φῶς phōs (5292B)
φωστήρ phōstēr (5293)
φωσφόρος phōsphoros (5294)
φωτεινός phōteinos (5296)
φωτισμός phōtismos (5298)

SYNONYMS:
ἀστράπτω astraptō (791)
αὐγάζω augazō (820)
ἐπιφαύσκω epiphauskō (2001)
λάμπω lampō (2962)
φαίνω phainō (5154)

אוֹר 'ôr (213), Qal: be light, shine (1 Sm 29:10, Prv 4:18); niphal: be resplendant (Ps 76:4 [75:4]); hiphil: give light (Nm 8:2, Neh 9:12, Ps 119:130 [118:130]).

אוֹר 'ôr (214), Light (Mi 7:8).

יָרָה yārâh (3498), Throw, shoot; hiphil: instruct, teach (2 Kgs 12:2, 17:27f.).

מָאוֹר mā'ôr (4115), Lamp (Nm 4:9).

נָגַהּ nāghahh (5226), Shine; hiphil: illumine (Ps 18:28 [17:28]).

נָהַר nāhar (5281), Be radiant (Ps 34:4 [33:5]).

נִיר nîr (5401), Break up (Hos 10:12).

רָאָה rā'âh (7495), See; hiphil: show (Jgs 13:23—Codex Alexandrinus only).

1. φωτίζει phōtizei 3sing indic pres act
2. φωτίζῃ phōtizē 3sing subj pres act
3. ἐφώτισεν ephōtisen 3sing indic aor act
4. φωτίσαντος phōtisantos gen sing masc part aor act
5. φωτίσαι phōtisai inf aor act
6. φωτίσει phōtisei 3sing indic fut act
7. ἐφωτίσθη ephōtisthē 3sing indic aor pass
8. φωτισθέντες phōtisthentes nom pl masc part aor pass
9. φωτισθέντας phōtisthentas acc pl masc part aor pass

10. πεφωτισμένους pephōtismenous acc pl masc part perf mid

11. φωτιεῖ phōtiei 3sing indic fut act

2 the bright shining of a candle **doth give** thee **light.** Luke 11:36
1 That was the true Light, which **lighteth** every man John 1:9
6 **will bring to light** the hidden things of darkness, ... 1 Co 4:5
10 The eyes of your understanding **being enlightened**; .. Eph 1:18
5 And to **make** all men **see** what is the fellowship 3:9
4 and **hath brought** life and immortality to **light** ..... 2 Tm 1:10
9 is impossible for those who were once **enlightened**, .. Heb 6:4
8 former days, in which, after ye were **illuminated**, ... 10:32
7 angel ... the earth was **lightened** with his glory..... Rev 18:1
3 for the glory of God **did lighten** it, ... 21:23
1 for the Lord God **giveth** them **light**: 22:5

Classical Greek and Septuagint Usage

This term occurs in Greek literature from the time of Aristotle (Fourth Century B.C.) and means "shine, give light" (*Liddell-Scott*). Figuratively its meanings include "enlighten, illuminate, instruct, teach, throw light upon" (ibid.). *Phōtizō* appears about 40 times in the Septuagint where it is almost always used figuratively in the sense of "throw light upon" in order to reveal and make clear. In 2 Kings (LXX 4 Kings) 12:2 and 17:27f. it is used even more specifically to mean "instruct" or "teach."

New Testament Usage

As a verb *phōtizō* can be used intransitively (without a direct object) or transitively (with a direct object). Revelation 22:5 provides an example of the former: "The Lord God *giveth them light.*"

As a transitive verb its meaning in the New Testament ranges from literal to figurative speech. One may actually "give light" to something or someone (Luke 11:36; Revelation 18:1; 21:23; 22:5), or one may "be enlightened" morally or spiritually (John 1:9; Ephesians 1:18; Hebrews 6:4; 10:32).

Lastly, its transitive use may convey the idea of bringing someone or something to light, i.e., to reveal it (1 Corinthians 4:5; Ephesians 3:9; 2 Timothy 1:10).

STRONG 5461, BAUER 872-73, MOULTON-MILLIGAN 680-81, KITTEL 9:310-58, LIDDELL-SCOTT 1969, COLIN BROWN 2:490,493-95.

5298. φωτισμός phōtismos noun

Bright light, illumination, enlightenment; revelation, bringing to light.

CROSS-REFERENCE:

φωτίζω phōtizō (5297)

אוֹר 'ôr (213), Light (Pss 27:1 [26:1], 44:3 [43:3], 139:11 [138:11]).

מָאוֹר mā'ôr (4115), Light (Ps 90:8 [89:8]).

1. φωτισμόν phōtismon acc sing masc

1 lest the **light** of the glorious gospel of Christ, ... 2 Co 4:4
1 to give the **light** of the knowledge of the glory 4:6

Although this term cannot be found in Greek literature prior to the Septuagint, it is used figuratively in the Psalms to refer to the "light" of the Lord (e.g., Psalms 27:1 [LXX 26:1]; 44:3 [43:3]).

Phōtismos is found only twice in the New Testament, both in the apostle Paul's correspondence to the Corinthians. They boasted of having great light or illumination already. He wrote of "the *light* of the glorious gospel of Christ" (2 Corinthians 4:4) and "the *light* of the knowledge of the glory of God in the face of Jesus Christ" (2 Corinthians 4:6).

Both kinds of light have the same source, the divine nature of the Son of God. It is given for the benefit of others. J.H. Bernard explains, "We reflect the light which shines upon us from the Divine Glory, as manifested in Christ" (*Expositor's Greek Testament*, 3:61). The Christian's job is to serve as a mirror so others can see Jesus in his or her life.

STRONG 5462, BAUER 873, MOULTON-MILLIGAN 681, KITTEL 9:310-58, LIDDELL-SCOTT 1969, COLIN BROWN 2:490,493.

χ

5299. χαίρω chairō verb

Rejoice, be glad; welcome, good day, greetings.

COGNATES:

εὐχαριστέω eucharisteō (2149)
συγχαίρω sunchairō (4647)
χαρά chara (5315)
χαριτόω charitoō (5323)

SYNONYMS:

ἀγαλλιάω agalliaō (21)
εὐφραίνω euphrainō (2146)

אָהֵב 'āhēv (154), Love (Prv 17:19).

גִּיל gîl (1559), Rejoice, be glad (Prv 2:14, Jl 2:21, Zec 9:9).

עָלַז 'ālaz (6159), Exult (Ps 96;12 [95:12]).

עַלִּיז 'allîz (6171), Rejoicing person (Is 13:3).

רָנַן rānan (7728), Sing (Zep 3:14).

שׂוּשׂ sûs (7919), Rejoice, be glad (Is 66:14, Lam 1:21, 4:21).

שָׂמַח sāmach (7975), Be glad, rejoice (Ex 4:14, 2 Kgs 11:20, Ez 7:12).

שָׂמֵחַ sāmēach (7976), Joyful, rejoicing (1 Kgs 8:66, 2 Kgs 11:14).

שִׂמְחָה simchāh (7977), Gladness (Jer 7:34).

שָׁלוֹם shālôm (8361), Peace (Is 57:21).

1. **χαίρω chairō** 1sing indic pres act
2. **χαίρει chairei** 3sing indic pres act
3. **χαίρομεν chairomen** 1pl indic pres act
4. **χαίρη chairē** 3sing subj pres act
5. **χαίρωμεν chairōmen** 1pl subj pres act
6. **χαῖρε chaire** 2sing impr pres act
7. **χαίρετε chairete** 2pl impr pres act
8. **χαίρων chairōn** nom sing masc part pres act
9. **χαίροντες chairontes** nom pl masc part pres act
10. **χαιρόντων chairontōn** gen pl masc part pres act
11. **χαίρειν chairein** inf pres act
12. **χαροῦσιν charousin** 3pl indic fut act
13. **ἔχαιρεν echairen** 3sing indic imperf act
14. **ἔχαιρον echairon** 3pl indic imperf act
15. **ἐχάρην echarēn** 1sing indic aor pass
16. **ἐχάρη echarē** 3sing indic aor pass
17. **ἐχάρημεν echarēmen** 1pl indic aor pass
18. **ἐχάρητε echarēte** 2pl indic aor pass
19. **ἐχάρησαν echarēsan** 3pl indic aor pass
20. **χαρῆτε charēte** 2pl subj/impr aor pass
21. **χαρῆναι charēnai** inf aor pass
22. **χαρήσομαι charēsomai** 1sing indic fut pass
23. **χαρήσεται charēsetai** 3sing indic fut pass
24. **χαρήσονται charēsontai** 3pl indic fut pass
25. **χαίρουσιν chairousin** 3pl indic pres act

19 saw the star, ... **rejoiced** with exceeding great joy... Matt 2:10
7 **Rejoice**, and be exceeding glad: ... 5:12
2 I say unto you, **he rejoiceth** more of that sheep, ... 18:13
6 to Jesus, and said, **Hail**, master; and kissed him. ... 26:49
6 and mocked him, saying, **Hail**, King of the Jews! ... 27:29
7 behold, Jesus met them, saying, All **hail**. ... 28:9
19 they **were glad**, and promised to give him money. Mark 14:11
6 And began to salute him, **Hail**, King of the Jews! ... 15:18
24 and many **shall rejoice** at his birth. ... Luke 1:14
6 And the angel came in unto her, and said, **Hail**, ... 1:28
7 **Rejoice** ye in that day, and leap for joy: ... 6:23
7 Notwithstanding in this **rejoice** not, ... 10:20
7 but rather **rejoice**, because your names are written ... 10:20
13 all the people **rejoiced** for all the glorious things ... 13:17
8 found it, he layeth it on his shoulders, **rejoicing**. ... 15:5
21 meet that we should make merry, and **be glad**: ... 15:32
8 and came down, and received him **joyfully**. ... 19:6
9 whole multitude of the disciples began **to rejoice** ... 19:37
19 **were glad**, and covenanted to give him money. ... 22:5
16 when Herod saw Jesus, he was exceeding **glad**: ... 23:8
2 **rejoiceth** greatly ... of the bridegroom's voice: ... John 3:29
4 soweth and he that reapeth **may rejoice** together. ... 4:36
16 and he saw it, and **was glad**. ... 8:56
1 And I **am glad** for your sakes that I was not there, ... 11:15
18 If ye loved me, ye **would rejoice**, ... 14:28
23 the world **shall rejoice**: and ye shall be sorrowful, ... 16:20
23 I will see you again, and your heart **shall rejoice**, ... 16:22
6 And said, **Hail**, King of the Jews! ... 19:3
19 Then were the disciples **glad**, ... they saw the Lord. ... 20:20
9 **rejoicing** that they were counted worthy to suffer ... Acts 5:41
8 and he went on his way **rejoicing**. ... 8:39
16 the grace of God, **was glad**, and exhorted them all, ... 11:23
14 And when the Gentiles heard this, they **were glad**, ... 13:48
11 The apostles and elders and brethren **send greeting** ... 15:23
19 they **rejoiced** for the consolation. ... 15:31
11 most excellent governor Felix sendeth **greeting**. ... 23:26
9 **Rejoicing** in hope; patient in tribulation; ... Rom 12:12
11 **Rejoice** with them that do rejoice, ... 12:15
10 Rejoice with them that do **rejoice**, ... 12:15
1 I **am glad** therefore on your behalf: ... 16:19
9 and they that **rejoice**, as though they rejoiced not; .. 1 Co 7:30
9 and they that rejoice, as though they **rejoiced** not; ... 7:30
2 **Rejoiceth** not in iniquity, ... 13:6
1 I **am glad** of the coming of Stephanas ... 16:17
11 sorrow from them of whom I ought **to rejoice**; ... 2 Co 2:3
9 As sorrowful, yet alway **rejoicing**; ... 6:10

21 so that I **rejoiced** the more........................2 Co 7:7
1 Now I **rejoice**, not that ye were made sorry,........... 7:9
17 exceedingly the more **joyed** we for the joy of Titus,.... 7:13
1 I **rejoice** therefore that I have confidence in you....... 7:16
3 we **are glad**, when we are weak, and ye are strong:... 13:9
7 Finally, brethren, **farewell**. Be perfect,.............. 13:11
1 and I therein **do rejoice**, yea, and will rejoice.......Phlp 1:18
22 and I therein do rejoice, yea, and **will rejoice**.......... 1:18
1 if I be offered ... I **joy**, and rejoice with you all........ 2:17
7 the same cause also do ye **joy**, and rejoice with me.... 2:18
20 that, when ye see him again, ye **may rejoice**,.......... 2:28
7 Finally, my brethren, **rejoice** in the Lord............. 3:1
7 **Rejoice** in the Lord alway:.......................... 4:4
7 and again I say, **Rejoice**............................ 4:4
15 But I **rejoiced** in the Lord greatly,.................... 4:10
1 Who now **rejoice** in my sufferings for you,..........Col 1:24
8 **joying** and beholding your order,..................... 2:5
3 for all the joy wherewith we **joy** for your sakes.... 1 Th 3:9
7 **Rejoice** evermore.................................. 5:16
11 to the twelve tribes ... **greeting**.....................Jas 1:1
7 But **rejoice**, inasmuch as ye are partakers.......... 1 Pt 4:13
20 ye **may be glad** also with exceeding joy................ 4:13
15 I **rejoiced** greatly that I found of thy children...... 2 Jn 1:4
11 receive him not ... neither bid him **God speed**:......... 1:10
11 For he that biddeth him **God speed** is partaker........ 1:11
15 For I **rejoiced** greatly, when the brethren came.....3 Jn 1:3
12 that dwell upon the earth **shall rejoice** over them,..Rev 11:10
5 Let us **be glad** and rejoice, and give honour.......... 19:7

Classical Greek and Septuagint Usage

This term can be found in classical Greek as far back as Homer (Eighth Century B.C.). It is related to *chara* (5315), "joy," and *charis* (5320B), "grace," and means "rejoice at, take pleasure in" (*Liddell-Scott*).

Chairō can be found about 80 times in the Septuagint, translating 8 different Hebrew terms. The word most frequently translated by *chairō* is *sāmach*, "rejoice, be glad, take pleasure in." Often the rejoicing was over something God had done for man (cf. 1 Samuel 19:5 [LXX 1 Kings 19:5]); however, there were times when Israel was exhorted not to "rejoice" because of her unfaithfulness towards God (cf. Hosea 9:1). Throughout the Old Testament obedience brought God's blessing and gave the Israelites reason to rejoice, but when they rebelled against God, it was He who also brought an end to their rejoicing (cf. Jeremiah 7:34).

New Testament Usage

In the New Testament *chairō* means to "rejoice" or "be glad" for many different reasons (e.g., Matthew 2:10; 5:12; Mark 14:11; Luke 15:32; John 3:29; Acts 5:41; Romans 16:19; 2 Corinthians 7:9,16; Philippians 1:18; Colossians 1:24).

However, it also serves as a greeting, such as: "welcome, good day" (Matthew 26:49; Mark 15:18; Luke 1:28; John 19:3; 2 John 10,11) or "good morning" (Matthew 28:9). In the customary form of the First Century A.D. it was used as a salutation at the start of a letter. It should be translated simply "Greetings" (Acts 15:23; 23:26; James 1:1).

STRONG 5463, BAUER 873-74, MOULTON-MILLIGAN 682, KITTEL 9:359-72, LIDDELL-SCOTT 1969-70, COLIN BROWN 2:356-59.

5300. χάλαζα chalaza noun

Hail, hailstone.

אֶלְגָּבִישׁ 'elgāvîsh (422), Hailstone (Ez 38:22).

בָּרָד bāradh (1286), Hail (Is 32:19).

בָּרָד bārādh (1287), Hail, hailstone (Ex 9:18f., Ps 18:12 [17:12], Is 28:2).

1. **χάλαζα chalaza** nom sing fem
2. **χαλάζης chalazēs** gen sing fem

1 there followed **hail** and fire mingled with blood,..... Rev 8:7
1 thunderings, and an earthquake, and great **hail**......... 11:19
1 there fell upon men a great **hail** out of heaven,........ 16:21
2 blasphemed God because of the plague of the **hail**;.... 16:21

The general meaning for this term is "hail." Four occurrences can be located in the New Testament, all in Revelation (8:7; 11:19; 16:21, twice). Each time it is prophesied that this icy precipitation will fall on the unrepentant world during the Tribulation period. It will be associated with electrical storms, "hail, and fire mingled . . . " (cf. Exodus 9:23-28).

STRONG 5464, BAUER 874, MOULTON-MILLIGAN 682, LIDDELL-SCOTT 1970, COLIN BROWN 3:1000,1004.

5301. χαλάω chalaō verb

Let down, lower.

אָרֵךְ 'ārēkh (773), Be long; hiphil: stick out (Is 57:4).

זָחַח zāchach (2199), Niphal: come loose (Ex 39:21 [36:29]).

שָׁלַח shālach (8365), Send, stretch; hiphil: cast down (Jer 38:6 [45:6]).

1. **χαλῶσιν chalōsin** 3pl indic pres act
2. **χαλάσατε chalasate** 2pl impr aor act
3. **χαλάσαντες chalasantes** nom pl masc part aor act
4. **χαλασάντων chalasantōn** gen pl masc part aor act
5. **χαλάσω chalasō** 1sing indic fut act
6. **ἐχαλάσθην echalasthēn** 1sing indic aor pass
7. **χαλῶσι chalōsi** 3pl indic pres act

1 **let down** the bed wherein the sick of the palsy lay...Mark 2:4
2 Launch out into the deep, and **let down** your nets... Luke 5:4
5 nevertheless at thy word I **will let down** the net........ 5:5
3 and let him down by the wall in a basket. (NT)..... Acts 9:25
3 **struck** sail, and so were driven....................... 27:17
4 when they **had let down** the boat into the sea,......... 27:30
6 And through a window in a basket **was I let down** 2 Co 11:33

Classical Greek and Septuagint Usage

This term can be commonly found in classical Greek meaning "slacken, let down," or "let loose" (*Liddell-Scott*). It is usually used in the literal sense of releasing something or someone. Occasionally it is used figuratively of "relaxing" or "letting go of" something intangible such as a principle or personal wish (ibid.). *Chalaō* is used only a few times in the Septuagint, almost always in the sense of physically "letting down" something or someone (e.g., Jeremiah was "let down" into a mire-filled dungeon [Jeremiah 38:6]).

New Testament Usage

Chalaō appears seven times in the New Testament. Once it means to let down a bed, that is, a stretcher (Mark 2:4). Twice it refers to the lowering of fishing nets (Luke 5:4,5). It is used twice to describe Paul's escape from Damascus when he was let down the wall in a basket (Acts 9:25; 2 Corinthians 11:33). Once it means to lower the sails (Acts 27:17). Finally, it means to let down a lifeboat into the sea (Acts 27:30).

STRONG 5465, BAUER 874, MOULTON-MILLIGAN 682, LIDDELL-SCOTT 1971.

5302. Χαλδαῖος Chaldaios name

Chaldean.

1. Χαλδαίων Chaldaiōn gen pl masc

1 Then came he out of the land of the Chaldaeans, ... Acts 7:4

The Chaldeans inhabited a coastal area in what is now southern Iraq. They became the rulers of the Babylonian Empire in its later stages, and so "Chaldean" became a synonym for "Babylonian." The land of the Chaldeans is mentioned in Stephen's speech before the Sanhedrin as the original home of Abraham (Acts 7:4).

5303. χαλεπός chalepos adj

Hard, difficult; fierce, violent; perilous, dangerous.

יָרֵא yārē' (3486), Fear; niphal: something feared (Is 18:2).

1. χαλεποί chalepoi nom pl masc

1 exceeding fierce, so that no man might pass by ...... Matt 8:28
1 that in the last days perilous times shall come....... 2 Tm 3:1

Classical Greek

This term can be found in classical Greek from the Eighth Century B.C. generally meaning "difficult." Frequently it is used of people and emotions, hence "hard to bear or deal with, painful, harsh, grievous" or "troublesome" (cf. *Liddell-Scott*).

Septuagint Usage

The canonical portions of the Septuagint contain *chalepos* only once. In Isaiah 18:2 it describes "a nation scattered and peeled, to a people *terrible* from their beginning hitherto." In context this refers to the Cushites. They will turn from warring to worshiping the Lord.

New Testament Usage

Only two occurrences are found in the New Testament. Matthew, who was an eyewitness, described the two demoniacs in the area of the Gergesenes as "exceeding *fierce*" (Matthew 8:28). Paul the apostle foretold that before the coming of the Lord "*perilous* times shall come" (2 Timothy 3:1). In both cases the situations are so bleak no one will want to experience them (cf. Matthew 8:28). Times will become so difficult and dangerous that people will simply hide, hoping things will get better on their own, since they are powerless to change the situations themselves. Fortunately the believer has the sustaining presence of God with him constantly.

STRONG 5467, BAUER 874, MOULTON-MILLIGAN 682, LIDDELL-SCOTT 1971, COLIN BROWN 1:419-20.

5304. χαλιναγωγέω chalinagōgeō verb

Control, hold in check, guide with a bit and bridle, bridle.

CROSS-REFERENCES:
ἄγω agō (70)
χαλινός chalinos (5305)

1. χαλιναγωγῶν chalinagōgōn nom sing masc part pres act

2. χαλιναγωγῆσαι chalinagōgēsai inf aor act

1 seem to be religious, and bridleth not his tongue, ... Jas 1:26
2 and able also to bridle the whole body................. 3:2

The literal meaning of this term is "guide with or as with bit and bridle." The bridle enabled the owner to signal directions to his animal that normally had no inkling of which way to go; hence, the general meaning of *chalinagōgeō* is "control, hold in check."

Its two New Testament usages are figurative for bridling a person's tongue and body (James 1:26; 3:2). Man's baser nature needs to be and can be controlled by following the leadership of the Holy Spirit and the commands of Scripture.

Strong 5468, Bauer 874, Moulton-Milligan 682, Liddell-Scott 1972.

5305. χαλινός chalinos noun

Bit, bridle.

Cross-Reference:

χαλιναγωγέω chalinagōgeō (5304)

מֶתֶג methegh (5141), Bridle, bit (2 Kgs 19:28, Ps 32:9 [31:9], Is 37:29).

רֶסֶן reşen (7734), Bridle (Job 30:11).

1. χαλινῶν chalinōn gen pl masc

2. χαλινούς chalinous acc pl masc

2 Behold, we put bits in the horses' mouths, ... Jas 3:3
1 and blood came out ... even unto the horse bridles, Rev 14:20

Chalinos specifically refers to a bit, part of the bridle used to guide a horse. Although its predominant use in Greek literature is literal, occasionally it is used figuratively of "anything which curbs, restrains, or compels" (*Liddell-Scott*). In the New Testament it is mentioned in James 3:3: "We put *bits* in the horses' mouths, that they may obey us; and we turn about their whole body."

Chalinos can also refer to the whole "bridle" itself. In Revelation 14:20 the conflict described is so severe that the amount of blood shed will be as high as a horse's bridle (up to its mouth).

Strong 5469, Bauer 874, Moulton-Milligan 682, Liddell-Scott 1972.

5306. χάλκεος chalkeos adj

Brass.

Cross-Reference:

χαλκός chalkos (5311)

נָחוּשׁ nāchûsh (5332), Bronze (Job 6:12—Sixtine Edition only).

נְחוּשָׁה nechûshāh (5333), Bronze (2 Sm 22:35, Ps 18:34 [17:34], Is 48:4).

נְחָשׁ nechāsh (A5359), Bronze (Dn 2:32,39, 7:19—Aramaic).

נְחֹשֶׁת nechōsheth (5361), Bronze (Ex 27:3f., 2 Kgs 25:13f., Jer 52:22).

1. χαλκᾶ chalka nom/acc pl neu

1 idols of gold, and silver, and brass, and stone, ... Rev 9:20

This term means not only "brass" but primarily "copper" or "bronze." It is found only once in the New Testament. In Revelation 9:20 among gold, silver, stone, and wood are mentioned idols of brass (of various qualities, sizes, and shapes) "which neither can see, nor hear, nor walk." In other words, they are completely useless on the Day of Judgment for those who place their confidence in them.

Strong 5470, Bauer 875 (see "chalkous"), Moulton-Milligan 682, Liddell-Scott 1973.

5307. χαλκεύς chalkeus noun

Coppersmith, blacksmith, metalworker.

Cross-Reference:

χαλκός chalkos (5311)

חָרַשׁ chārash (2896), Artificer (Gn 4:22).

חָרָשׁ chārāsh (2900), Ironsmith (2 Chr 24:12).

צָרַף tsāraph (7170), Goldsmith (Neh 3:32, Is 41:7).

1. χαλκεύς chalkeus nom sing masc

1 Alexander the coppersmith did me much evil: ...... 2 Tm 4:14

This term generally signifies a "worker in metal," hence, a "coppersmith, goldsmith," or "blacksmith" (cf. *Liddell-Scott*). This trade in the ancient world often involved the molding of heathen idols (*Bauer*).

The profession is mentioned by name only once in the New Testament: Paul said, "Alexander the *coppersmith* did me much evil" (2 Timothy 4:14). Evidently Alexander was known well enough to be identified in this way. One can only imagine the trouble he may have caused Paul in an effort to protect his trade and income (compare, for example, the incident at Ephesus described in Acts 19:23-41).

Strong 5471, Bauer 874, Moulton-Milligan 683, Liddell-Scott 1973, Colin Brown 2:96.

5308. χαλκηδών chalkēdōn noun

Chalcedony, agate.

Cross-Reference:

χαλκός chalkos (5311)

1. χαλκηδών chalkēdōn nom sing masc

1 the third, a chalcedony; the fourth, an emerald; ..... Rev 21:19

Chalkēdōn is a stone of some value. Although its exact nature is uncertain, some believe it was milky or gray in color. It forms the third foundation of the wall of the New Jerusalem (Revelation 21:19). This is the only occurrence of the term in the New Testament. In the Revised Standard Version of Exodus 28:19 the Hebrew word describing one of the stones on the breastplate is translated as "an agate," although the Septuagint uses another word, *achatēs*.

Strong 5472, Bauer 874, Liddell-Scott 1973, Colin Brown 3:396-97.

5309. χαλκίον chalkion noun

(Copper) vessel, bowl, kettle.

Cross-Reference:

χαλκός chalkos (5311)

סִיר sîr (5707), Pot (2 Chr 35:13).

קַלַּחַת qallachath (7321), Kettle (1 Sm 2:14).

1. χαλκίων chalkiōn gen pl neu

1 as the washing of cups, and pots, brazen vessels, ... Mark 7:4

Chalkion is used in Greek literature to denote various items: copper vessels, cauldrons, kettles, or cymbals. It also refers to copper tickets given to judges that bore the name of the court in which they were to serve. It can even denote a piece of copper money (cf. *Liddell-Scott*).

This term appears in the New Testament only at Mark 7:4 where reference is made to "brazen vessels." The vessels were cooking, mixing, or serving bowls made of copper. Due to the tradition of the elders there were elaborate rituals designed for the purification of eating utensils. Mark referred to them when he said, "Many other things there be, which they have received to hold, as the washing of cups, and pots, *brazen vessels*, and of tables" (Mark 7:4).

Strong 5473, Bauer 874, Moulton-Milligan 683, Liddell-Scott 1973, Colin Brown 2:96.

5310. χαλκολίβανον chalkolibanon noun

Brass (or copper) melted in a furnace and then polished, fine brass, bronze.

Cross-Reference:

χαλκός chalkos (5311)

1. χαλκολιβάνῳ chalkolibanō dat sing neu

1 And his feet like unto fine brass, as if they burned ... Rev 1:15
1 and his feet are like fine brass; 2:18

Chalkolibanon is a metal or alloy of a somewhat uncertain nature. It is mentioned twice in the New Testament. Both times it was the only suitable metal to use as an analogy to describe the beauty and brightness of the feet of the Lord Jesus Christ who appeared to John in apocalyptic glory (Revelation 1:15; 2:18).

It has an alternative spelling, *chalkolibanos*, which is masculine instead of neuter in gender.

Strong 5474, Bauer 875, Liddell-Scott 1974 (see "chalkolibanos").

5311. χαλκός chalkos noun

Copper, brass, bronze; copper coin, money; brass gong.

Cognates:

χάλκεος chalkeos (5306)
χαλκεύς chalkeus (5307)
χαλκηδών chalkēdōn (5308)
χαλκίον chalkion (5309)
χαλκολίβανον chalkolibanon (5310)

Synonyms:

ἀργύριον argurion (688)
κέρμα kerma (2743)
νόμισμα nomisma (3409)
χρῆμα chrēma (5371)

נְחוּשָׁה n^echûshāh (5333), Bronze (Job 28:2, 41:27 [41:18]).

נְחָשׁ n^echāsh (A5359), Bronze (Dn 2:35, 45—Aramaic).

נְחֹשֶׁת n^echōsheth (5361), Bronze (Ex 27:2, 1 Chr 22:3, Jer 52:17).

קַלַּחַת qallachath (7321), Kettle (1 Sm 2:14—Codex Alexandrinus only).

1. χαλκός chalkos nom sing masc
2. χαλκοῦ chalkou gen sing masc
3. χαλκόν chalkon acc sing masc

3 Provide neither gold, ... nor brass in your purses, .. Matt 10:9
3 no scrip, no bread, no money in their purse: .... Mark 6:8
3 how the people cast money into the treasury: 12:41
1 have not charity, I am become as sounding brass, .. 1 Co 13:1
2 precious wood, and of brass, and iron, and marble, .. Rev 18:12

This term denotes copper itself (Revelation 18:12); something made of copper, such as a (brass) gong (1 Corinthians 13:1) or a copper coin; or just money in general (Matthew 10:9; Mark 6:8; 12:41). Often pagan idols were formed out of this metal (cf. *Bauer*).

Strong 5475, Bauer 875, Moulton-Milligan 683, Liddell-Scott 1974, Colin Brown 2:96.

5312. χαμαί chamai adv

On the ground.

אֶרֶץ 'erets (800), Ground (Job 1:20).

1. χαμαί chamai

1 When he had thus spoken, he spat on the ground, ... John 9:6
1 they went backward, and fell to the ground. 18:6

This word is an adverb which refers to place or position, i.e., "on the ground." It may also mean to direct "toward the ground," i.e., earthward. *Chamai* is used in John 9:6: Jesus "spat *on the ground*" to make mud with which He anointed the eyes of a blind man. Obeying Jesus, the blind man then washed the mud from his eyes and came away seeing (verse 7). In John 18:6 the crowd "fell *to the ground*" when Jesus openly admitted His identity to those who sought to arrest Him.

Strong 5476, Bauer 875, Moulton-Milligan 683, Liddell-Scott 1975.

5313. Χαναάν Chanaan name

Canaan.

1. Χαναάν Chanaan fem

1 dearth over all the land of Egypt and **Chanaan**, ... Acts 7:11
1 destroyed seven nations in the land **of Chanaan**, ... 13:19

Canaan is the area which lies west of the River Jordan and extends northward into Phoenicia. In the New Testament it refers to the land which God gave Israel as a possession (Acts 13:19).

5314. Χαναναῖος Chananaios name-adj

Canaanite.

1. Χαναναία Chananaia nom fem

1 a woman **of Canaan** came out of the same coasts, .. Matt 15:22

This term is an adjective used as a noun and refers to a member of the Canaanite race. A Canaanite woman persistently asked Jesus to heal her daughter (Matthew 15:22). In Mark's parallel account (7:26) she is called a "Syrophoenician" (a woman of Syrian Phoenicia).

5315. χαρά chara noun

Joy.

Cognate:

χαίρω chairō (5299)

Synonyms:

ἀγαλλίασις agalliasis (20)
εὐφροσύνη euphrosunē (2148)

גִּיל gîl (1561), Gladness (Jl 1:16).

מָחוֹל māchôl (4369), Dancing (Ps 30:11 [29:11]).

מָשׂוֹשׂ māsôs (5026), Joy (Lam 5:15).

רִנָּה rinnāh (7726), Singing (Is 55:12).

שְׂחֹק sechōq (7926), Laughter (Ps 126:2 [125:2]).

שִׂמְחָה simchāh (7977), Gladness, happiness (1 Chr 29:22, Ps 21;6 [20:6], Jon 4:6).

שָׂשׂוֹן sāsôn (8050), Mirth (Jer 16:9).

1. χαρά chara nom sing fem
2. χαρᾶς charas gen sing fem
3. χαρᾷ chara dat sing fem
4. χαράν charan acc sing fem

4 saw the star, ... rejoiced with exceeding great **joy**.... Matt 2:10
2 heareth the word, and anon with **joy** receiveth it; 13:20
2 for **joy** thereof goeth and selleth all that he hath, ... 13:44
4 enter thou into the **joy** of thy lord.................... 25:21
4 enter thou into the **joy** of thy lord.................... 25:23
2 quickly from the sepulchre with fear and great **joy**; Matt 28:8
2 immediately receive it with **gladness**; .... Mark 4:16
1 And thou shalt have **joy** and gladness; .... Luke 1:14
4 behold, I bring you good tidings of great **joy**, ... 2:10
2 which, when they hear, receive the word with **joy**; 8:13
2 And the seventy returned again with **joy**, saying, ... 10:17
1 I say unto you, that likewise **joy** shall be in heaven 15:7
1 there is **joy** in the presence of the angels of God 15:10
2 while they yet believed not for **joy**, and wondered, ... 24:41
2 and returned to Jerusalem with great **joy**: 24:52
3 rejoiceth greatly ... of the bridegroom's voice: (NT) John 3:29
1 this my **joy** therefore is fulfilled........................ 3:29
1 that my **joy** might remain in you, ... 15:11
1 and that your **joy** might be full........................ 15:11
4 but your sorrow shall be turned into **joy**............... 16:20
4 for **joy** that a man is born into the world.............. 16:21
4 and your **joy** no man taketh from you.................. 16:22
1 ask, and ye shall receive, that your **joy** may be full..... 16:24
4 they might have my **joy** fulfilled in themselves......... 17:13
1 And there was great **joy** in that city.................. Acts 8:8
2 she opened not the gate for **gladness**, but ran in, ... 12:14
2 And the disciples were filled **with joy**, ... 13:52
4 and they caused great **joy** unto all the brethren........ 15:3
2 so that I might finish my course with **joy**, ... 20:24
1 and peace, and **joy** in the Holy Ghost.............. Rom 14:17
2 of hope fill you with all **joy** and peace in believing, ... 15:13
3 I may come unto you with **joy** by the will of God, ... 15:32
2 but are helpers of your **joy**: for by faith ye stand.... 2 Co 1:24
1 that my **joy** is the joy of you all....................... 2:3
3 I am exceeding **joyful** in all our tribulation............. 7:4
3 exceedingly the more joyed we for the **joy** of Titus, ... 7:13
2 the abundance of their **joy** and their deep poverty 8:2
1 But the fruit of the Spirit is love, **joy**, peace, ... Gal 5:22
2 Always in every prayer ... making request with **joy**, .. Phlp 1:4
4 for your furtherance and **joy** of faith; 1:25
4 Fulfil ye my **joy**, that ye be likeminded, ... 2:2
2 Receive him therefore ... with all **gladness**; 2:29
1 dearly beloved and longed for, my **joy** and crown, ... 4:1
2 unto all patience and longsuffering with **joyfulness**; ... Col 1:11
2 received the word ... with **joy** of the Holy Ghost: ... 1 Th 1:6
1 For what is our hope, or **joy**, or crown of rejoicing? 2:19
1 For ye are our glory and **joy**............................ 2:20
3 for all the **joy** wherewith we joy for your sakes 3:9
2 that I may be filled **with joy**; .... 2 Tm 1:4
4 have much **joy** and comfort in your love, (NASB) ... Phlm 1:7
2 and took **joyfully** the spoiling of your goods, ... Heb 10:34
2 who for the **joy** that was set before him 12:2
2 no chastening for the present seemeth to be **joyous**, ... 12:11
2 that they may do it with **joy**, and not with grief: 13:17
4 count it all **joy** when ye fall into divers temptations; .. Jas 1:2
1 turned to mourning, and your **joy** to heaviness.......... 4:9
3 ye rejoice **with joy** unspeakable and full of glory: .... 1 Pt 1:8
1 write we unto you, that your **joy** may be full........ 1 Jn 1:4
1 and speak face to face, that our **joy** may be full..... 2 Jn 1:12
4 I have no greater **joy** than to hear that my children .. 3 Jn 1:4

Classical Greek

Chara (cf. the verb *chairō* [5299]) appears in classical Greek from the Seventh Century B.C. It means "joy, delight" (in an active sense) in something or resulting from some experience. "Joy" marked events of significance such as a king's accession to the throne, weddings, and holidays (cf. *Moulton-Milligan*).

Septuagint Usage

Chara appears as a somewhat inadequate equivalent for seven Hebrew words or constructions. There are only about 20 instances with a Hebrew original. Usually *simchāh*, "joy, hold a festival," or *sāsôn/māsôs*, "joy, exultation," stand behind it. Frequently it is joined with *euphrosunē*

(2148), "gladness" (e.g., Esther 8:17; Proverbs 29:6; Joel 1:16). It does not appear until 1 Chronicles where it is a reference to festal, cultic joy following the installation of Solomon as king (29:22). Joy and celebration followed King Xerxes' (Ahasuerus') edict allowing Jews to assemble and to protect themselves (Esther 8:17; cf. 9:17,18 [no Hebrew]; Zechariah 8:19). God grants joy (Psalm 30:11 [LXX 29:11]); it is an external and internal response (see Conzelmann, "chara," *Kittel*, 9:362f.) to the Lord's triumphing over Israel's enemies (Psalm 126:2 [LXX 125:2]; cf. 21:6 [20:6]). It is also a possession of the righteous (Proverbs 29:6; cf. Wisdom of Solomon 8:16 [of Wisdom's granting joy]; Sirach 1:12).

New Testament Usage

Chara occurs about 60 times in the New Testament. Luke used it slightly more than other writers. As Beyreuther notes: "It is no accident that the words appear particularly where there is express mention of the eschatological fulfillment in Christ, of being in him, and of hope in him .... The whole NT message ... of God's saving work in Christ is a message of joy" ("Joy," *Colin Brown*, 2:357).

Luke's use of *chara*-language reveals a basic assumption that the gospel brings "great joy" (*charan megalēn*; Luke 2:10; cf. 1:14). Joy is the response of those who see God at work through His servant Jesus or through His followers (Luke 10:17; 19:37; Acts 8:8; 15:3; cf. Luke 13:17). Joy characterizes those who put their faith in Him (Luke 8:13), and it is a by-product of repentance (see Jeremias, *New Testament Theology*, p.157f.). Joy also characterizes God's attitude toward the repentant sinner (Luke 15:7,10). Clearly joy is indicative of God's great love for the sinner.

The fulfillment of God's promises and plans brings joy (John 3:29; cf. 1 Thessalonians 2:19f.). As the fulfillment of such anticipation, Jesus himself became the basis for another view of the future which is also characterized by joy (Hebrews 10:34; 1 Peter 1:8). The idea of "perfect" or "completed" joy in the present is a preview of an even greater future joy (e.g., John 15:11; 1 John 1:4; 2 John 12). All of this is possible only because of Christ.

This viewpoint concerning God's plans for the future in turn enables the Christian paradoxically to have joy in times of trial, affliction, suffering, and persecution (Luke 6:23; John 16:20-24; cf. Romans 15:13; 2 Corinthians 7:4; 8:2; 1 Thessalonians 1:6; James 1:2). In fact, Paul pointed out that authentic joy most often occurs precisely under such conditions (Beyreuther, "Joy," *Colin Brown*, 2:359; cf. the similar thought in 2 Maccabees 6:30; 4 Maccabees 10:20).

Joy is moreover a fruit of the Spirit in the life of the believer. The coming of the Spirit, it should be recalled, shows that the new age of the Church has dawned and that the consummation of God's promises is certain. Thus the Spirit is indispensable in terms of the eschatological perspective outlined above (Galatians 5:22; cf. Romans 14:17; 1 Thessalonians 1:6). Joy, therefore, is a reminder and sign of the way believers view the present in light of God's plan for the future.

STRONG 5479, BAUER 875-76, MOULTON-MILLIGAN 683, KITTEL 9:359-72, LIDDELL-SCOTT 1976, COLIN BROWN 2:356-59.

5316. χάραγμα charagma noun

Mark, impression.

COGNATE:

χαρακτήρ charaktēr (5317)

SYNONYMS:

εἶδος eidos (1482)
εἰκών eikōn (1494)
ἰδέα idea (2374)
μορφή morphē (3307)
μόρφωσις morphōsis (3309)
στίγμα stigma (4593)
σχῆμα schēma (4828)
τύπος tupos (5020)

1. **χαράγματος charagmatos** gen sing neu
2. **χαράγματι charagmati** dat sing neu
3. **χάραγμα charagma** nom/acc sing neu
4. **χαράγματα charagmata** nom/acc pl neu

2 or silver, or stone, graven by art and man's device. Acts 17:29
3 a mark in their right hand, or in their foreheads: ....Rev 13:16
3 might buy or sell, save he that had the mark, ... 13:17
3 receive his mark in his forehead, or in his hand, ... 14:9
3 and whosoever receiveth the mark of his name. 14:11
1 over his mark, and over the number of his name, ... 15:2
3 upon the men which had the mark of the beast, ... 16:2
3 them that had received the mark of the beast, ... 19:20
3 neither his image, neither had received his mark 20:4

Classical Greek

In the broadest sense the Greek word *charagma* refers to a stamp, an impression, an engraving, a mark, or a symbol. In this usage it occurs as a noun form of the Greek verb *charassō* which means "to cut to a point or to sharpen" (Martin, "Mark," *Colin Brown*, 2:573).

In the days of the ancient Greek world *charagma* originally denoted the bite of a snake, but as its use developed historically it came to mean an inscription (i.e., on wood, stone, brass, casting dies, minting coins), a writing of any nature, or a stamp of personal identity (e.g., a brand to mark camels). Eventually it denoted an official seal of attestation, validity, and authority (ibid., 2:574; Wilckens, "charagnia," *Kittel*, 9:416).

Septuagint Usage

Charagma does not occur in the canonical portions of the Septuagint. The related term *charassō* appears in the intertestamental writings of 3 Maccabees 2:29 and refers to Jews marked with pagan cult symbols (cf. 1 Kings 15:27 [LXX 3 Kings 15:27]; 2 Kings 17:11 [4 Kings 17:11]). In the Psalms of Solomon 15:8-10 it describes the righteous who are loyal to Israel's heritage as the "marked" for God (Martin, "Mark," *Colin Brown*, 2:574).

New Testament Usage

In the New Testament this word carries contemporary significance in the exegesis of Revelation 13:11-18; in prophetic interpretation *charagma* is referred to as the mark of the beast.

As Revelation 13 unfolds it becomes apparent that this "beast" is the anti-Christ leader who controls world economy and negatively impacts human destiny through the manipulation of this "mark" (*charagma*). Some scholars equate the phrases "mark of the beast" and "name of the beast" (13:17; 14:9,11; 15:2; 16:2; 19:20; 20:4) (Johnson, *Expositor's Bible Commentary*, 12:532).

In this sense *charagma* may be an actual inscription which must appear on the forehead and in the hands of all classes of people if they are to be considered eligible for economic interchange (Revelation 13:17). Other scholars suggest that the "mark" is symbolically describing the loyalty and support given to the anti-Christ by those who "worship the image of the beast" (Revelation 13:15). There is no reliable evidence as to the actual kind or process of this compelled identification, but it is generally accepted that the mark represents a universal signification of the anti-Christ kingdom. It identifies his name and the Greek number of a man—666 (Revelation 13:18).

Turning to Revelation 14:9,10 those who accept *charagma tou therion* (cf. 19:20), the "mark of the beast," incur the wrath of God, but in Revelation 20:4 those who reject it live and reign with Christ. Thus, *charagma* becomes a focal point of eternal destiny in the prophetic interpretation of history.

STRONG 5480, BAUER 876, MOULTON-MILLIGAN 683, KITTEL 9:416-17, LIDDELL-SCOTT 1976, COLIN BROWN 2:573-75.

5317. χαρακτήρ charaktēr noun

Reproduction, exact likeness.

COGNATE:

χάραγμα charagma (5316)

SYNONYM:

εἰκών eikōn (1494)

צָרֶבֶת tsāreveth (7148), Scar (Lv 13:28).

1. χαρακτήρ charaktēr nom sing masc

1 and the express image of his person, ... Heb 1:3

Classical Greek

A derivative of *charassō*, "to cut into," *charaktēr* originally denoted an engraving tool. Later it described the "stamp" or "impression" of something such as the "impression" on a coin or a seal. Gradually *charaktēr* came to be used of the traits inherent in the human personality, especially those features which distinguished one person from another.

Septuagint Usage

Charaktēr occurs three times in the Septuagint, only one of which is a canonical use. In Leviticus 13:28 it translates the Hebrew term *tsāreveth* meaning "a scorching," hence "a scar" (also rendered by *oulē*, "scar," in the Septuagint, e.g., Leviticus 13:23, cf. verses 2,10,19).

Relating more to human personality is the usage in 2 Maccabees 4:10. Jacob, the high priest under Antiochus, was so corrupt he "shifted his countrymen over to the Greek *way of life*" (RSV). Later in 4 Maccabees we read of the "character" of a small child which is "impressed" (*enapesphragizon*) with the "wondrous likeness" (RSV, *homoiotēta thaumasion*), in both mind and form, of its parents (15:4).

New Testament Usage

Charaktēr occurs only once in the New Testament, at Hebrews 1:3. The writer of this Christologically-charged statement declares the Son to be the "express image" or exact representation—like a wax impression is to the seal that makes it—of the Father. Thus in essence, nature, and in every way, the Son is like the Father (cf. verses 1,2). The concept, though not the language, occurs elsewhere (2 Corinthians 4:4; Colossians 1:15).

STRONG 5481, BAUER 876, MOULTON-MILLIGAN 683-84, KITTEL 9:418-23, LIDDELL-SCOTT 1977, COLIN BROWN 2:288-90,292.

5318. χάραξ charax noun

Embankment.

SYNONYM:

φραγμός phragmos (5254)

כַּר kar (3861), Battering ram (Ez 21:22).

מַצָּב mutstsāv (4836), Siegework (Is 29:3).

מָצוֹד mātsôdh (4847), Siegework (Eccl 9:14).

מָצוֹר mātsôr (4857), Siege (Dt 20:19).

סֹלְלָה sōllāh (5745), Siege mound or ramp (Is 37:33, Ez 4:2).

1. χάρακα charaka acc sing masc

1 that thine enemies shall cast **a trench** about thee,.. Luke 19:43

This term is related to the verb *charassō* which means "sharpen to a point." *Charax* first denoted a "pointed stake" that was used to support vines; it also referred to several "stakes" surrounding a vineyard. The term later came to denote a "palisade" which was used as a defensive structure surrounding a city or camp (cf. *Liddell-Scott*). The *charax* mentioned in Luke 19:43 (its only occurrence in the New Testament) served not only as protection for Jerusalem's enemies but as a place where attacks were launched against the city.

STRONG 5482, BAUER 876, MOULTON-MILLIGAN 684, LIDDELL-SCOTT 1977, COLIN BROWN 3:951-52.

5319. χαρίζομαι charizomai verb

Give generously, grant, bestow; remit, forgive, release, pardon.

COGNATE:

χαριτόω charitoō (5323)

SYNONYMS:

ἀποδίδωμι apodidōmi (586)
ἀπολύω apoluō (624)
ἀφίημι aphiēmi (856)
διαδίδωμι diadidōmi (1233)
δίδωμι didōmi (1319)
δωρέομαι dōreomai (1426)
ἐπιδίδωμι epididōmi (1914)
κοινωνέω koinōneō (2814)
παραδίδωμι paradidōmi (3722)

נָתַן nāthan (5598), Give (Est 8:7).

עָשָׂה ʿāsâh (6449), Do; give (Sir 12:3).

1. χαρίζεσθε charizesthe 2pl indic pres mid
2. χαριζόμενοι charizomenoi nom pl masc part pres mid
3. χαρίζεσθαι charizesthai inf pres mid
4. ἐχαρίσθη echaristhē 3sing indic aor pass
5. ἐχαρίσατο echarisato 3sing indic aor mid
6. χαρίσασθε charisasthe 2pl impr aor mid
7. χαρισάμενος charisamenos nom sing masc part aor mid
8. χαρισθέντα charisthenta nom/acc pl neu part aor pass
9. χαρισθῆναι charisthēnai inf aor pass
10. χαρίσασθαι charisasthai inf aor mid
11. κεχάρισμαι kecharismai 1sing indic perf mid
12. κεχάρισται kecharistai 3sing indic perf mid
13. χαρισθήσομαι charisthēsomai 1sing indic fut pass
14. χαρίσεται charisetai 3sing indic fut mid

5 and unto many that were blind he **gave** sight....... Luke 7:21
5 had nothing to pay, he frankly **forgave** them both...... 7:42
5 I suppose that he, to whom he **forgave** most........... 7:43
9 and desired a murderer **to be granted** unto you;.... Acts 3:14
10 no man may **deliver** me unto them.................. 25:11
3 manner of the Romans **to deliver** any man to die,.... 25:16
12 God **hath given** thee all them that sail with thee...... 27:24
14 shall he not with him also **freely give** us all things? Rom 8:32
8 know the things that **are freely given** to us of God. 1 Co 2:12
10 that contrariwise ye ought rather **to forgive** him,.... 2 Co 2:7
1 To whom ye **forgive** any thing, I forgive also:......... 2:10
11 for if I **forgave** any thing, to whom I forgave it,....... 2:10
11 for if I forgave any thing, to whom I **forgave** it,....... 2:10
6 not burdensome to you? **forgive** me this wrong....... 12:13
12 but God **gave** it to Abraham by promise............ Gal 3:18
2 tenderhearted, **forgiving** one another,...............Eph 4:32
5 even as God for Christ's sake **hath forgiven** you........ 4:32
4 For unto you it **is given** in the behalf of Christ,.... Phlp 1:29
5 and **given** him a name which is above every name:.... 2:9
7 **having forgiven** you all trespasses;.................. Col 2:13
2 Forbearing ... and **forgiving** one another,.............. 3:13
5 even as Christ **forgave** you, so also do ye.............. 3:13
13 through your prayers I **shall be given** unto you..... Phlm 1:22

Classical Greek

Charizomai (also appears in the active voice; *charizō* in classical Greek) describes the action of saying or doing something agreeable for or to a person (*Liddell-Scott*), i.e., "to show favor, kindness." It further describes the nature of such actions: "to give graciously, freely, cheerfully." Passively it can refer to "being pleased, gratified" and can also mean "to welcome, accept" some action or gesture (ibid.).

Septuagint Usage

Occurring solely in the middle form in the Septuagint, *charizomai* appears 12 times, but only 1 of these is in canonical material. It translates the common Hebrew term for "give," *nāthan*, and it is used of King Xerxes giving Haman's estate to Esther as a gift (Esther 8:7; cf. 2 Maccabees 1:35). This act was a direct consequence of Esther's being rewarded with "favor" (*charis* [5320B]) by the king (cf. Esther 8:5; Hebrew *chēn*).

Elsewhere in the apocryphal material *charizomai* presents a colorful usage. It variously depicts the gracious action of "giving" alms (Sirach 12:3) or the merciful "granting" of life (as a request made to God, 2 Maccabees 3:31,33; cf. Acts 27:24). It is used of the gift of sleep (3 Maccabees 5:11), clemency (3 Maccabees 7:6), or of the "gift" of dying a martyr's death (4 Maccabees 11:12). Thus *charizomai* in the

Septuagint did not acquire the narrower definition encountered in the New Testament.

New Testament Usage

Charizomai is utilized by only two New Testament writers, Luke and Paul. Luke understood *charizomai* as the demonstration of our Lord's "gracious giving," His "bestowing favor" upon candidates for salvation. It is the outworking of God's "grace" (*charis*). He "grants" sight to the blind (Luke 7:21). Jesus illustrated God's gracious granting of repentance and forgiveness (cf. Luke 7:47f.) with a story about canceled debts (Luke 7:42,43).

Strangely, in Acts *charizomai* loses the theological import it holds in Luke's Gospel. It refers to "granting" a request (Acts 3:14) or to the "giving" over of Paul into custody without legal right (i.e., "freely"; Acts 25:11,16). Even in Acts 27:24, where God "graciously gives" all those on the ship with Paul their lives, any association with the great theological motif of *charis* is remote (cf. 2 Maccabees 3:31ff.), other than God always being a God of "grace."

Paul's 16 instances of *charizomai* clearly connect it to God's graciousness in His giving of Christ on behalf of the world (Romans 8:32; cf. 1 Corinthians 2:12). His grace is freely given and does not depend upon our efforts (Galatians 3:18). Moreover, it concerns *forgiveness*—not only God's forgiveness of the individual, but of the person's forgiveness of others (especially Ephesians 4:32; Colossians 3:13; cf. 2 Corinthians 2:7,10; 12:13; Colossians 2:13). Suffering can even be a favor given by God, for by the same measure of sufferings the believer receives here, will the measure of glory be that he receives in heaven (Romans 8:17; 1 Peter 4:13; cf. Philippians 1:29). (See the article on *charis* [5320B].)

Strong 5483, Bauer 876-77, Moulton-Milligan 684, Kittel 9:372-402, Liddell-Scott 1978, Colin Brown 2:115-16,118-19,122.

5320. χάριν charin prep

Because of, for the sake of, by reason of.

1. χάριν charin

1 **Wherefore I say unto thee, Her sins,** .... Luke 7:47
1 **It was added because of transgressions,** .... Gal 3:19
1 **For this cause I Paul, the prisoner of Jesus Christ** .... Eph 3:1
1 **For this cause I bow my knees unto the Father** 3:14
1 **that it may minister grace unto the hearers** 4:29
1 **to the adversary to speak reproachfully. (NT)** .... 1 Tm 5:14
1 **For this cause left I thee in Crete,** .... Tit 1:5
1 **things which they ought not, for filthy lucre's sake** 1:11
1 **Not as Cain, ... And wherefore slew he him?** .... 1 Jn 3:12
1 **men's persons in admiration because of advantage** .... Jude 1:16

The Greek word *charin* is the singular accusative form of the substantive *charis* (5320B) and can be found in classical Greek, the Septuagint, and in the New Testament to mean "in favor of" or "for the pleasure of."

In its New Testament function Thayer makes the statement that *charin* "takes on completely the nature of a preposition and is joined to the genitive case to mean, for, on account of, for the sake of" (*Greek-English Lexicon*). Grammatically *charin* is always placed after its object (except in 1 John 3:12) and functions as a preposition expressing the idea of "because, therefore, for this reason, in favor of."

In Ephesians 3:1 Paul used the phrase "for this cause (*toutou charin*)" but shaded it with the idea "in favor of" as he made a connecting relationship between Ephesians 2:19 (fellow citizenship), 3:6 (fellow heirs), and 3:7,8 (personal ministry gift of grace and commission to preach the "unsearchable riches of Christ").

Again in Ephesians 3:14 Paul used the same phrase to mean "in favor of" by establishing a spiritual link between his confidence in Christ, which should inspire the Ephesians (Ephesians 3:12,13), and his prayer for them to be strengthened by the power of the Holy Spirit (Ephesians 3:14-16). Further, in Titus 1:5 he implied that he left Titus in Crete "for the reason of" or more specifically a reason "in favor of" giving Titus the responsibility of organizing the church in New Testament order.

Turning to 1 John 3:12 *charin* is transliterated "for the sake of what" (*charin tinos*) with the negative implication of Cain's killing his brother Abel "because (in favor of the fact that) his own works were evil."

Finally, Luke 7:47 records the words of Jesus using *charin* (*hou charin*) to mean "therefore," or in a more literal sense, "of which" or "wherefore." Here, again, the phrase "in favor of" is implied in the idea that because of the committed love exhibited by the woman in anointing the feet of Christ, her sins were forgiven.

Strong 5484, Bauer 877, Moulton-Milligan 684, Liddell-Scott 1979.

5320B. χάρις charis noun

Grace, graciousness, kindness, goodwill; a gift, a favor; thanks, gratitude.

Cognate:

χαριτόω charitoō (5323)

SYNONYMS:

δόμα doma (1384)
δόσις dosis (1388)
δωρεά dōrea (1424)
δώρημα dōrēma (1427)
δῶρον dōron (1428)
κορβᾶν korban (2850)
χάρισμα charisma (5321)

גְּדוּלָּה g^edhûllāh (1449II) Greatness; dignity (Est 6:3).

חָלָק chālāq (2607), Flattering (Ez 12:24).RES

חֵן chēn (2682), Favor, grace (Gn 33:8, 1 Sm 20:3, Zec 4:7).

חֶסֶד cheṣedh (2721), Favor (Est 2:9).

טוֹב ṭôv (3005), Good (Prv 18:22).

רַחַם racham (7641II) Mercy, compassion (Gn 43:14, Dn 1:9).

רָצוֹן rātsôn (7814), What is acceptable, favor (Prv 10:32, 11:27, 12:2).

1. **χάρις charis** nom sing fem
2. **χάριτος charitos** gen sing fem
3. **χάριτι chariti** dat sing fem
4. **χάριν charin** acc sing fem
5. **χάριτας charitas** acc pl fem
6. **χάριτα charita** acc sing fem

4 Fear not, ... for thou hast found **favour** with God.... Luke 1:30
1 and the **grace** of God was upon him.................. 2:40
3 in wisdom ... and in **favour** with God and man.......... 2:52
2 and wondered at the **gracious** words.................. 4:22
1 ye love them which love you, what **thank** have ye?...... 6:32
1 them which do good to you, what **thank** have ye?....... 6:33
1 of whom ye hope to receive, what **thank** have ye?...... 6:34
4 Doth he **thank** that servant because he did............ 17:9
2 begotten of the Father, full **of grace** and truth....... John 1:14
4 have all we received, and **grace** for grace.............. 1:16
2 have all we received, and grace for **grace**.............. 1:16
1 but **grace** and truth came by Jesus Christ.............. 1:17
4 and having **favour** with all the people............... Acts 2:47
1 and great **grace** was upon them all.................... 4:33
2 And Stephen, full of **grace** and power, (NASB)......... 6:8
4 and gave him **favour** and wisdom..................... 7:10
4 Who found **favour** before God,....................... 7:46
4 when he came, and had seen the **grace** of God,....... 11:23
3 persuaded them to continue in the **grace** of God....... 13:43
2 which gave testimony unto the word of his **grace**,...... 14:3
3 had been recommended to the **grace** of God.......... 14:26
2 But we believe that through the **grace** of the Lord..... 15:11
3 being recommended ... unto the **grace** of God......... 15:40
2 helped them ... which had believed through **grace**:..... 18:27
2 to testify the gospel of the **grace** of God............. 20:24
2 and to the word of his **grace**,........................ 20:32
5 and Felix, willing to show the Jews a **pleasure**,........ 24:27
4 And desired **favour** against him,...................... 25:3
4 But Festus, willing to do the Jews a **pleasure**,......... 25:9
4 By whom we have received **grace** and apostleship,... Rom 1:5
1 **Grace** to you and peace from God our Father,.......... 1:7
3 Being justified freely by his **grace**..................... 3:24
4 is the reward not reckoned of **grace**, but of debt........ 4:4
4 Therefore it is of faith, that it might be by **grace**;....... 4:16
4 access by faith into this **grace** wherein we stand,........ 5:2
1 much more the **grace** of God, and the gift by grace,.... 5:15
3 and the gift by **grace**, which is by one man,............ 5:15
2 much more they which receive abundance of **grace**...... 5:17
1 **grace** did much more abound:........................ 5:20
1 even so might **grace** reign through righteousness........ 5:21
1 Shall we continue in sin, that **grace** may abound?....... 6:1
4 for ye are not under the law, but under **grace**........... 6:14
4 not under the law, but under **grace**? God forbid..... Rom 6:15
1 But God **be thanked**,................................ 6:17
1 **Thanks** be to God through Jesus (NASB).............. 7:25
2 is a remnant according to the election **of grace**......... 11:5
3 And if **by grace**, then is it no more of works:......... 11:6
1 otherwise **grace** is no more grace...................... 11:6
1 otherwise grace is no more **grace**...................... 11:6
1 But if it be of works, then is it no more **grace**:........ 11:6
2 For I say, through the **grace** given unto me,........... 12:3
4 differing according to the **grace** that is given to us,.... 12:6
4 because of the **grace** that is given to me of God,...... 15:15
1 The **grace** of our Lord Jesus Christ be with you........ 16:20
1 The **grace** of our Lord Jesus Christ be with you all..... 16:24
1 **Grace** be unto you, and peace, from God........... 1 Co 1:3
3 **grace** of God which is given you by Jesus Christ;....... 1:4
4 According to the **grace** of God which is given.......... 3:10
3 For if I **by grace** be a partaker,...................... 10:30
3 But **by** the **grace** of God I am what I am:............. 15:10
1 and his **grace** which was bestowed upon me........... 15:10
1 yet not I, but the **grace** of God which was with me.... 15:10
1 But **thanks** be to God, which giveth us the victory..... 15:57
4 will I send to bring your **liberality** unto Jerusalem...... 16:3
1 The **grace** of our Lord Jesus Christ be with you........ 16:23
1 **Grace** be to you and peace from God our Father,... 2 Co 1:2
3 not with fleshly wisdom, but by the **grace** of God,...... 1:12
4 that ye might have a second **benefit**;................... 1:15
1 Now **thanks** be unto God,........................... 2:14
1 the abundant **grace** might through the thanksgiving..... 4:15
4 that ye receive not the **grace** of God in vain........... 6:1
4 we do you to wit of the **grace** of God.................. 8:1
4 with much entreaty that we would receive the **gift**,...... 8:4
4 so he would also finish in you the same **grace** also...... 8:6
3 see that ye abound in this **grace** also.................. 8:7
4 For ye know the **grace** of our Lord Jesus Christ,........ 8:9
1 **thanks** be to God, which put the same earnest care..... 8:16
3 also chosen ... to travel with us with this **grace**,......... 8:19
4 God is able to make all **grace** abound toward you;...... 9:8
4 for the exceeding **grace** of God in you................. 9:14
1 **Thanks** be unto God for his unspeakable gift........... 9:15
1 he said unto me, My **grace** is sufficient for thee:....... 12:9
1 The **grace** of the Lord Jesus Christ,.................. 13:14
1 **Grace** be to you and peace from God the Father,.... Gal 1:3
3 from him that called you into the **grace** of Christ....... 1:6
2 it pleased God, who ... called me by his **grace**,......... 1:15
4 perceived the **grace** that was given unto me,........... 2:9
4 I do not frustrate the **grace** of God:................... 2:21
2 are justified by the law; ye are fallen from **grace**........ 5:4
1 **grace** of our Lord Jesus Christ be with your spirit....... 6:18
1 **Grace** be to you, and peace, from God our Father,... Eph 1:2
2 To the praise of the glory of his **grace**,................ 1:6
2 redemption ... according to the riches of his **grace**;...... 1:7
3 **by grace** ye are saved;.............................. 2:5
2 the exceeding riches of his **grace** in his kindness........ 2:7
3 For by **grace** are ye saved through faith;............... 2:8
2 of the **grace** of God which is given me to you-ward:.... 3:2
2 according to the gift of the **grace** of God.............. 3:7
1 Unto me, who am less ... is this **grace** given,........... 3:8
1 **grace** according to the measure of the gift of Christ..... 4:7
1 **Grace** be with all them that love our Lord Jesus........ 6:24
1 **Grace** be unto you, and peace, from God........... Phlp 1:2
2 ye all are partakers of my **grace**....................... 1:7
1 The **grace** of our Lord Jesus Christ be with you all...... 4:23
1 **Grace** be unto you, and peace, from God............ Col 1:2
4 and knew the **grace** of God in truth:.................. 1:6
3 singing with **grace** in your hearts to the Lord.......... 3:16
3 Let your speech be alway with **grace**,.................. 4:6
1 Remember my bonds. **Grace** be with you. Amen........ 4:18
1 **Grace** be unto you, and peace, from God.......... 1 Th 1:1
1 The **grace** of our Lord Jesus Christ be with you......... 5:28
1 **Grace** unto you, and peace, from God our Father... 2 Th 1:2
4 according to the **grace** of our God and the Lord........ 1:12
3 consolation and good hope through **grace**,.............. 2:16
1 The **grace** of our Lord Jesus Christ be with you all...... 3:18
1 **Grace**, mercy, and peace, from God our Father..... 1 Tm 1:2
4 And I **thank** Christ Jesus our Lord,.................... 1:12
1 And the **grace** of our Lord was exceeding abundant..... 1:14
1 **Grace** be with thee. Amen........................... 6:21

1 To Timothy, my dearly beloved son: Grace,........ 2 Tm 1:2
4 I thank God, whom I serve from my forefathers........ 1:3
4 but according to his own purpose and grace,........... 1:9
3 be strong in the grace that is in Christ Jesus.......... 2:1
1 Jesus Christ be with thy spirit. Grace be with you....... 4:22
1 Grace, mercy, and peace, from God the Father....... Tit 1:4
1 For the grace of God that bringeth salvation.......... 2:11
3 That being justified by his grace,...................... 3:7
1 Grace be with you all. Amen.......................... 3:15
1 Grace to you, and peace, from God our Father..... Phlm 1:3
4 For we have great joy and consolation in thy love,...... 1:7
1 grace of our Lord Jesus Christ be with your spirit....... 1:25
3 that he by the grace of God should taste death...... Heb 2:9
2 therefore come boldly unto the throne of grace,........ 4:16
4 and find grace to help in time of need................. 4:16
2 and hath done despite unto the Spirit of grace?....... 10:29
2 Looking diligently lest any man fail of the grace....... 12:15
4 we receiving a kingdom ... let us have grace,.......... 12:28
3 good thing that the heart be established with grace;.... 13:9
1 Grace be with you all. Amen......................... 13:25
4 But he giveth more grace. Wherefore he saith,........ Jas 4:6
4 but giveth grace unto the humble...................... 4:6
1 Grace unto you, and peace, be multiplied...........1 Pt 1:2
2 who prophesied of the grace that should come.......... 1:10
4 the grace that is to be brought unto you............... 1:13
1 For this is thankworthy,.............................. 2:19
1 ye take it patiently, this is acceptable with God......... 2:20
2 and as being heirs together of the grace of life;......... 3:7
2 as good stewards of the manifold grace of God......... 4:10
4 and giveth grace to the humble........................ 5:5
2 But the God of all grace, who hath called us........... 5:10
4 and testifying that this is the true grace of God......... 5:12
1 Grace and peace be multiplied unto you............ 2 Pt 1:2
3 grow in grace, and in the knowledge of our Lord....... 3:18
1 Grace be with you, mercy, and peace, from God.... 2 Jn 1:3
4 turning the grace of our God into lasciviousness,.... Jude 1:4
1 Grace be unto you, and peace, from him which is,... Rev 1:4
1 The grace of our Lord Jesus Christ be with you all..... 22:21

Classical Greek

The noun *charis* is formed from the root *char-* whose derivatives all focus on that which gives pleasure, benefit, and happiness. Thus there is a certain relationship between *charis*, "grace, kindness," and *chara* (5315), "joy." *Charis* evokes joy and delight, often in a totally undeserved and unexpected way. Initially secular Greek did not differentiate between *charis* and *chara* so sharply. They generally had the same basic meaning: *Charis* promotes pleasure and well-being, while *chara* is the joy and happiness experienced as a result of *charis*. Therefore, the fundamental definition of *charis* includes the ideas of "grace, favor, kindness, goodness, beauty, gratitude, pleasure," and so on (see Esser, "Grace," *Colin Brown*, 2:115).

Septuagint Usage

Although there are about 190 instances of *charis* in the Septuagint, less than one-half of these have a Hebrew equivalent (ibid.). In about 115 cases *charis* is a supplementary or explanatory word. Of the nearly 75 places where *charis* has a corresponding Hebrew word, about 60 are translations of *chēn*, usually meaning "grace, favor." Other Hebrew terms rendered by *charis* include *g*^{e}*dûlāh*, *chālāq*, *ches̱edh*, *racham*, and *rātsôn*. Most important are the terms *chēn* and *ches̱edh*. *Chēn* carries many shades of meaning such as "favor, delight, grace." The basic definition of its cognate verb is "to bow toward an insignificant one in kindness." *Ches̱edh* primarily denotes "kindness, steadfast love, covenant love, goodness, favor, mercy," and "grace." The chief meaning of the cognate verb is "to live in a godly manner." In many texts *ches̱edh* equals gentleness and mercy; its range of definition exceeds that of *chēn*. *Ches̱edh* especially is concerned with the faithfulness of God in granting grace through His covenant.

The covenant relationship between Israel and God dominates the Old Testament account of revelation history. The two terms *grace* and *covenant* are related. Through God's initiative the covenant, an agreement founded upon God's grace, became the basis for a relationship between the community of Israel and God. Continually it is God's faithfulness demonstrated in grace that renews the covenant agreement broken by a backsliding people. God's merciful acts of deliverance demonstrate the grace inherent in the covenant arrangement.

The term *chēn* was particularly employed when favor was shown or asked without conditions or stipulations (ibid., 2:116f.). Thus Noah and Moses found "*grace* in the eyes of the LORD" (Genesis 6:8; Exodus 33:12,16). The Psalmist recognizes that his very existence is predicated upon God's being a merciful God who gives grace (Psalms 4:1; 6:2).

Grace often approaches the idea of mercy (ibid.). The Hebrew term *racham*, "compassion, mercy," denotes the kind of grace whose basis rests upon a close relationship between the giver and recipient of grace. Parents, for example, show mercy to their children (Psalm 103:13; Isaiah 49:15; cf. Hosea 1:6). Where *racham* is used of God's "compassion" to Israel, their relationship is probably assumed (Isaiah 49:13; 54:7; Jeremiah 30:18; 31:20).

Ches̱edh captures the more corporate notion of grace and is closely connected to the covenant relationship. "Covenant" (*b*^{e}*rîth*) and "mercy" (*ches̱edh*) join company on numerous occasions (e.g., Deuteronomy 7:12; Psalm 106:45). Here *ches̱edh* denotes the faithfulness members of the covenant community can expect from one another (1 Samuel 20:8; 2 Samuel 9:1,7). God demands the same kind of faithfulness from Israel (Hosea 6:6; Micah 6:8), and *ches̱edh* uniquely conveys this sense of corporate faithfulness to the covenant (Nehemiah 9:17; Jeremiah 3:12; Hosea 2:21-23).

In the most elementary statements about His identity, God describes himself with the language of grace. "The LORD, The LORD God, merciful and *gracious*, long-suffering, and abundant in goodness and truth, keeping mercy for thousands, forgiving iniquity and transgression and sin" (Exodus 34:6,7; cf. Numbers 14:18; Nehemiah 9:17; Psalm 103:8). Grace is the predominant character trait of God in the Old Testament: "For his anger endureth but a moment; in his favor is life" (Psalm 30:5; cf. Exodus 20:6; Isaiah 54:8; 57:15f.).

New Testament Usage

God's grace is again the main theme of the New Testament. *Charis* occurs about 155 times in the New Testament, about 100 of these in the letters of Paul. *Charis* plays a crucial role in the New Testament's presentation of God's relationship to mankind. Grace is the autograph of the decree of God's kingdom; it is governed by grace. Grace also shapes existence in the new age (Luke 4:19). The concept of *charis* is consistently defined in terms of God's "gracious" act of redemption in Christ. His intervention in history for establishing a new covenant as well as His effort to maintain the new covenant are manifestations of His grace. Grace is simultaneously the cause as well as the effect of the saving work of Christ. The main gifts we receive because of grace are the forgiveness of sins, fellowship with God, and eternal life (see Romans 3:24f.; 5:1f.; Ephesians 2:5f.).

Everything that Jesus says and does reveals and actualizes the grace of God; thus, "*grace* and truth came by Jesus Christ" (John 1:17), and "of his fulness have all we received, and *grace* for *grace*" (John 1:16). Jesus' message about the kingdom of God, the central element of His preaching, expresses God's grace. The Kingdom's coming is a sovereign act of grace, an unmerited, undeserved, merciful gift (Matthew 18:14; Luke 2:14; 12:32). The recipients of grace include the unworthy (Matthew 5:5; 11:5; Luke 15:21f.; 18:13,14), the lost (Luke 15), and the sinful (Matthew 9:13). By virtue of the shedding of His blood Jesus established the new covenant; moreover, He secured redemption for pardoned sinners (Matthew 26:28).

Grace is also a central concept in Paul's theology; his entire theology might be termed "a theology of grace" (see Conzelman, "charis," *Kittel*, 9:393). God's grace partially concerns the favor and goodness of God toward sinners which displaces His wrath (Romans 5:2). At the same time, Paul considered grace to pertain also to the merciful act of God in sending His Son as the atonement for humanity's sins (Romans 5:8,9). Because of His grace God justifies the unworthy and undeserving. Through grace in Christ He grants them a share in eternal life (Romans 3:24f.; 5:1f.,15).

Being a Christian means one is a "partaker" of grace (Philippians 1:7). It is in this grace that believers "stand" (Romans 5:2). Grace is the sphere of existence for believers (Romans 1:7; 1 Corinthians 1:3; Colossians 1:2), and they live every aspect of their lives in light of this. They are, as Paul said in Romans 6:14, "under grace." Although they "stand" in grace, they may also "fall" from it (Galatians 5:4).

Grace as a way of salvation stands in radical opposition to any notion that one can be saved by the Law (ibid., 9:394f.). Grace excludes any hope of achieving righteousness through works of the Law or self-redemption (Romans 6:14; Galatians 5:4). Likewise, human praise and wisdom are ineffective for securing salvation, "For by *grace* are ye saved through faith; and that not of yourselves: it is the gift of God: not of works, lest any man should boast" (Ephesians 2:8,9; cf. Titus 3:5). Grace and faith, therefore, complement one another (Romans 4:16; Ephesians 2:8). By faith we accept grace, and by faith the grace is in effect. Grace and faith, then, form an inseparable unity (1 Timothy 1:14).

In one sense it is proper to speak of different levels of grace (Romans 12:6; Ephesians 4:7). God's grace may be manifest expressly through the gifts (*charismata* [see 5321]) given and distributed by the Spirit. Believers also can be strong or weak in their faith (2 Timothy 2:1; cf. John 1:16; 2 Peter 3:18). The effects of grace take place on a multiplicity of levels. One can speak of the "manifold *grace* of God" (1 Peter 4:10; cf. Romans 1:11; 2 Corinthians 1:15). The various gifts of grace and demonstrations of grace are all manifestations of the one grace—the grace of God in Christ. Grace instructs us in holy living and provides the impetus for sanctification (cf. 2 Timothy 2:1; Titus 2:12).

Paul's understanding of grace is echoed elsewhere in the New Testament. The message of God's saving act in Christ is thus described as "the gospel of the *grace* of God" (Acts 20:24) and the "word of his *grace*" (Acts 20:32; cf. 14:3). In this work of grace Christ tastes death (Hebrews 2:9). And at the "throne of *grace*" believers receive "*grace* to help" (Hebrews 4:16). To become a Christian is to experience the grace of God and to hold it fast (Acts 11:23; 13:43).

John did not speak of grace as frequently as the apostle Paul; however, his whole notion of love (*agapē* [26]) includes the concept of grace. Here too the notion of grace involves first and foremost the saving act of God in Christ, just as it did for Paul (John 1:14,16; cf. 1:17). Grace forms the basis for fellowship with God and the forgiveness of sins (1 John 1:6ff.). And again, faith works hand in hand with grace to see that forgiveness realized (John 3:16,36; etc.).

In summary, one could say that *charis* primarily denotes the demonstration of God's grace, favor, kindness toward mankind. This especially relates to the work of Christ as that demonstration. Moreover, it concerns the effects of this gesture of grace: a new relationship with God based upon faith and grace. *Charis* further expresses the manifestations of God's grace that believers continue to receive in the life of the Church (e.g., the *charismata*).

God's act of grace in the giving of His only Son was accomplished for all mankind (Titus 2:11). Nevertheless, grace as a sign of God's delight in humanity can only take place in keeping with the covenant established on Calvary (Romans 3:22-25). Only those who acknowledge and share in the grace of God, manifest in Christ's atoning death, can stand in God's grace (Romans 8:1; Colossians 2:12-14). Outside of fellowship with God, God's wrath is still in effect (Romans 5:1f.; 8:1f.; Ephesians 2:3f.; cf. John 3:36). God's grace and favor are realized only upon the condition of faith (Romans 5:17; cf. 5:1,2; 6:1f.). Apart from accepting by faith the gracious act of God in Christ, one cannot participate in the justification and redemption provided in Christ, which includes the averting of God's inevitable wrath because of sin. Therefore, grace closely parallels favor in the Old Testament, especially as it concerns the covenant relationship between God and His people. Grace rests at the foundation of both covenants and is the sole basis for the forgiveness of sins.

STRONG 5485, BAUER 877-78, MOULTON-MILLIGAN 684-85, KITTEL 9:372-402, LIDDELL-SCOTT 1978-79, COLIN BROWN 2:115-24.

5321. χάρισμα charisma noun

A gift, grace, favor.

COGNATE:

χαριτόω charitoō (5323)

SYNONYMS:

δόμα doma (1384)
δόσις dosis (1388)
δωρεά dōrea (1424)
δώρημα dōrēma (1427)
δῶρον dōron (1428)
κορβᾶν korban (2850)
χάρις charis (5320B)

1. **χάρισμα charisma** nom/acc sing neu
2. **χαρίσματος charismatos** gen sing neu
3. **χαρίσματα charismata** nom/acc pl neu
4. **χαρισμάτων charismatōn** gen pl neu
5. **χαρίσματι charismati** dat sing neu

1 that I may impart unto you some spiritual gift,...... Rom 1:11
1 But not as the offence, so also is the free gift........... 5:15
1 the free gift is of many offences unto justification....... 5:16
1 but the gift of God is eternal life through Jesus......... 6:23
3 gifts and calling of God are without repentance........ 11:29
3 Having then gifts differing according to the grace...... 12:6
5 So that ye come behind in no gift;................ 1 Co 1:7
1 But every man hath his proper gift of God,........... 7:7
4 there are diversities of gifts, but the same Spirit....... 12:4
3 to another the gifts of healing by the same Spirit;..... 12:9
3 after that miracles, then gifts of healings,............ 12:28
3 Have all the gifts of healing?........................ 12:30
3 But covet earnestly the best gifts:.................... 12:31
1 that for the gift bestowed upon us.................. 2 Co 1:11
2 Neglect not the gift that is in thee,................ 1 Tm 4:14
1 in remembrance that thou stir up the gift of God,... 2 Tm 1:6
1 As every man hath received the gift,................ 1 Pt 4:10

Classical Greek and Septuagint Usage

The noun *charisma*, "gift, grace, benefit," is related to the verb *charizomai* (5319), "to show favor." The term is rare in classical Greek and occurs late in Greek antiquity. Although *charisma* is not present in the canonical writings of the Septuagint, it is a variant reading at Sirach 7:33 by Codex Sinaiticus (Alexandrinus and Vaticanus read *charis* [5320B]). It also occurs at Sirach 38:30 in Codex Vaticanus. In the latter it is probably a scribal error (cf. the chosen reading *chrisma*, "anointing," in this case "glazing" [RSV] such as a potter's finishing). Theodotion's first-century B.C. version of the Septuagint reads *charisma* at Psalm 33:22: "May your (God's) *charisma* (Hebrew *chesedh*), O Lord, be upon us, according as we hope in thee." Other editions read *eleos* (1643), "mercy," while the Hebrew original is *chesedh*, "grace, mercy, favor, loving-kindness."

New Testament Usage

Except for one instance in 1 Peter *charisma* is exclusively a member of the Pauline vocabulary. The use of *charisma* apparently falls into two theological contexts. One, it concerns the "gift" of salvation God has given to us in Christ. Two, *charisma* involves the spiritual "gifts" bestowed upon the Church. Below we will address each of these two roles. The common denominator between the two usages is that *charisma* is a "*theo*-logical" term, that is, God is always behind the giving of gifts, whether salvation in Christ or gifts for His Church.

The basis for God's giving salvation in Christ is solely *charis*, "grace." In other words, it is exclusively a "gift" of God. The nature of *charisma* as the demonstration of God's graciousness—or to put it in Old Testament language, the outworking of His *chesedh*—is most fully realized in Christ's delivering mankind from the power of sin and the Law. Romans 5:15-17 demonstrates that the basis of gift (*charisma*) is grace (*charis*). This theme is echoed elsewhere in the letters of Paul (e.g., Romans 3:23,24; 6:14,15; Galatians 2:9; Ephesians 1:6 [*charitoō* (5323)]). (See also Conzelmann, "charisma," *Kittel*, 9:403f.)

Paul freely interchanges the concepts of *charisma* with *dōrea* (1424)/*dōrean* (1425) and *charisma* with *charis*. Thus in Ephesians 2:8 we read that salvation is *ouk ex humōn*, "not of your own (doing)" but it is "the gift" (*dōron*) of God. This classic statement underscores Paul's emphatic stance that grace itself is God's gift (cf. Ephesians 3:7; cf. 4:7 of the gifts [*dōrea*] of Christ; see also 1 Corinthians 12).

Grace is even further reflected in Paul's analogy that the "reward" or "wages" of sin is death, but the gift (*charisma*, "free gift") of God is eternal life (Romans 6:23). The same idea appears earlier in 4:4: "Now when a man works, his wages are not credited to him as a *gift* (*charis*), but as an obligation" (NIV). Again we note the interrelationship between *charis* and *charisma*.

The second usage of *charisma*, which has received so much more attention in recent years, concerns the "gifts" of the Spirit given to the Church. The classic discussion of the *charismata* (plural of *charisma*) is found in 1 Corinthians 12–14. However, we can learn a great deal about the nature and purpose of the *charismata* from other Pauline texts. Below we will look at the broad characteristics of the *charismata*.

Most certainly *charismata* are to be associated with the work of the Spirit in the lives of believers; nonetheless, we observe that Paul regards himself as a "dispenser" of the *charismata*. For example, one reason Paul hopes to see the Romans is that he might impart to them a "spiritual gift" (Romans 1:11). Furthermore, Paul reminded Timothy to "fan into flame the *gift*" he had and which came to him through the laying on of Paul's hands (2 Timothy 1:6, NIV). From 1 Timothy 4:14 it seems as if this impartation involved several elders (cf. Acts 8:17-19; 9:12,17,18; 19:6 where the reception of the Spirit comes through the laying on of hands). The purpose—whatever the means of reception—is to establish and strengthen the Church (Romans 1:11) or in Timothy's case to strengthen him in the face of severe opposition and resistance (cf. 2 Timothy 1:7ff.).

Oddly enough, "spiritual gift" (*charisma pneumatikon*) is a phrase actually found only in Romans 1:11; however, Paul associates the *charismata* with the Spirit. Further, he may be referring to *charismata* in his use of the neuter plural of *pneumatikos* (4012) (e.g., 1 Corinthians 14:1). This, however, is debatable. (Commentators like Barrett, Conzelmann, Reuf [cf. Cranfield on the Romans text] read it as spiritual gifts; however, this is the only time it functions thus [cf. Ephesians 6:12]. Nevertheless it remains the best interpretation.)

Romans 12:6 clearly indicates that just as salvation is a "gift" of God's grace, so too are the *charismata*: "We have different gifts (*charismata*), according to the grace (*charis*) given to us" (NIV). Obviously Paul associated the *charismata* with the manifestations of the Spirit listed in 1 Corinthians 12:7-11. In addition to these more spectacular gifts, Paul included others such as teaching, encouraging, giving, and showing mercy in his "list" of *charismata* given by God on behalf of His Church (Romans 12:7,8).

Unquestionably we would be doing Paul—and the Holy Spirit—a disservice if we were to limit the gifts of the Spirit in terms of either character or number. Moreover, if we restrict the concept of God's granting gifts to His Church to the vocabulary of *charisma*, we would be creating a deficiency in Paul's own understanding. He also speaks of other gifts (*domata*) in Ephesians 4:8—apostle, prophet, evangelist, and pastor-teacher—some of which recur in the 1 Corinthians text. The key word in understanding "gift" in Pauline terms is "give." God is the only "giver" of "gifts" to His Church (Ephesians 4:7-11).

Behind God's giving of gifts always stands the purpose "to prepare God's people for works of service" (Ephesians 4:12, NIV) and to build them up unto unity (Ephesians 4:12,13; cf. 1 Corinthians 12:7, "common good" [NIV]). It is no accident that the imagery of the body as a symbol of unity appears in connection with Paul's discussion of the *charismata* both in Romans (12:4-8) and 1 Corinthians (12:12-31; cf. Ephesians 4:3-13).

Gifts, therefore, are for the Church, even though they may build up the individual recipient. The gifts of the Spirit are not to be exercised selfishly; rather, their intent is most fully realized only in the context of corporate worship and edification. The ministry of the Spirit is ultimately manifest in the *charismata*. We learn from 1 Corinthians 12:4-6 that Paul did not see the *charismata*; *diakoniai* (see 1242), "ministries"; and *energēmata* (see 1739), "workings," as three distinct manifestations from the three members of the Godhead. In fact, this would run counter to Paul's whole point that it is "the same God" who "works all of them in all men" (verse 6, NIV). Rather, the gifts, ministries, and workings of God are all for the benefit of the Church that God may be glorified.

The sole usage outside the letters of Paul, in 1 Peter 4:10, is entirely in keeping with the Pauline usage. Peter views the exercise of gifts (*charisma*) on behalf of others as the responsible Christian position. He does not comment on whether or not the gift is "spiritual." The implication though, is that God is the source, just as He is the source of all grace (cf. 1 Peter 1:2,10,13; 3:7; 4:10; 5:5). He is "the God of all grace" (1 Peter 5:10). Interestingly, through the exercise of a *charisma*, God's grace (*charis*) is ministered in a variety of ways.

Strong 5486, Bauer 878-79, Moulton-Milligan 685, Kittel 9:402-6, Liddell-Scott 1979, Colin Brown 2:115,118-24.

5322. χάρις charis

See word study at number 5320B.

5323. χαριτόω charitoō verb

To give grace, bestow favor.

Cognates:

- ἀχάριστος acharistos (877)
- χαίρω chairō (5299)
- χαρίζομαι charizomai (5319)
- χάρις charis (5320B)
- χάρισμα charisma (5321)

Synonym:

- εὐλογέω eulogeō (2108)

1. ἐχαρίτωσεν echaritōsen 3sing indic aor act
2. κεχαριτωμένη kecharitōmenē nom sing fem part perf mid

2 and said, Hail, thou that art highly favoured,........Luke 1:28
1 wherein he hath made us accepted in the beloved.....Eph 1:6

Classical Greek

In the most technical sense the word *charitoō* means "to endue with grace" (cf. *Liddell-Scott*). However, in order to understand its New Testament usage it is important to note that words formed from the Greek root *char* indicate things which produce well-being. It is essential, then, to understand that from this basic meaning of well-being the individual meanings of *charis* (5320B) are derived as "grace, favor, beauty, thankfulness, gratitude, delight, kindness, expression of favor, good turn, benefit . . . " (Braumann, "Grace," *Colin Brown*, 2:115).

Thus, within this context *charitoō* functions as the verb form in which there is the enduement of *charis*. Subjectively, grace on the part of the giver is bestowed as part of a favor or kindness. Objectively there is a recognition of favors received with the response of gratitude and joy (see Luke 1:30; 2:52; Acts 2:47; 7:10,46; 24:27; 25:9).

Septuagint Usage

Historically *charitoō* is linked to *charis* and gains form from its Old Testament counterpart which denotes the kind expression of one person to another through assistance and help. For example, in Sirach 18:17 it is used in the passive voice meaning "to have grace shown to one, to be highly favored."

Developmentally the general usage of *charis* does not change significantly in the Judaistic tradition of the rabbinic writings or the Septuagint. In Philo, however, *charis* emerges as the power behind God's good gifts and provides the fullest understanding of God's rule as "creator, preserver, world governor and redeemer" (Conzelmann, "charis," *Kittel*, 9:389f.).

New Testament Usage

Turning to the New Testament, Luke portrayed *charis* as the message of salvation in "gracious words" (Luke 4:22; cf. Acts 20:24,32; Colossians 4:6). In this samc rcgard mighty works confirm the gospel (Acts 14:3), and *charis* is subsequently used to depict the Spirit-filled person (ibid., 9:392).

Building on this theme, *charitoō* functions only in connection with divine *charis* and becomes the dynamic force of the gospel that bestows grace, blesses believers, and provides joy regardless of circumstances.

Thus, the apostle Paul utilized *charis* to express the salvation event in terms of making glad by gifts, showing unmerited favor, and providing pardoning power to overcome sin. Hence, in Ephesians 1:6ff. and 2:7 *charitoō* expresses *charis* as the power of blessing and favor that anticipates exaltation as the ultimate outcome of redemption through the blood of Christ (Ephesians 1:7; cf. 2:5; 4:7).

Finally, in the broadest sense *charitoō* refers to the bestowal of God's favor in relationship to the word *charismata* (see 5321). This term is used to designate spiritual gifts. In its most technical sense it means "gifts of holy grace" and refers to these gifts as "enablers" or "equippers" for personal service in the kingdom of God (Ephesians 4:11-13).

STRONG 5487, BAUER 879, MOULTON-MILLIGAN 685, KITTEL 9:372-402, LIDDELL-SCOTT 1980, COLIN BROWN 2:115-16,118-19,122.

5324. Χαῤῥάν Charrhan name

Haran.

1. Χαῤῥάν Charrhan fem

1 in Mesopotamia, before he dwelt in Charran, ... Acts 7:2
1 Then came he out ... and dwelt in Charran: 7:4

According to the speech of Stephen in Acts 7:2,4 Haran was a city in Mesopotamia where Abraham lived for a time before his journey to Canaan (cf. Genesis 11:31f.; 12:4).

5325. χάρτης chartēs noun

Paper.

מְגִלָּה m^{e}ghillāh (4178), Scroll (Jer 36:23 [43:23]).

1. χάρτου chartou gen sing masc

1 I would not write with paper and ink: .... 2 Jn 1:12

The word *chartēs* refers to paper made from papyrus stems that had been cut into strips. This paper was composed of two layers laid at right angles to one another and pressed together to form one unit. Glue was often added to cement the two layers. The paper, when dried, could be used on either side, but usually only the side where the strips were laid horizontally was used. In the New Testament the word *chartēs* is used only in 2 John 12.

STRONG 5489, BAUER 879, MOULTON-MILLIGAN 685, LIDDELL-SCOTT 1980.

5326. χάσμα chasma noun

Pit, ravine.

פַּחַת pachath (6597), Pit (2 Sm 18:17).

1. χάσμα chasma nom/acc sing neu

1 between us and you there is a great gulf fixed: ..... Luke 16:26

The word *chasma* refers to a deep open pit, ravine, or a precipice. It is the root word to the English word *chasm*. It is related to the Greek word *chaskō*, "to yawn." In Luke 16:26 *chasma* is used for the great gulf between "Abraham's bosom" and hell which cannot be passed over.

STRONG 5490, BAUER 879, LIDDELL-SCOTT 1981.

5327. χεῖλος cheilos noun

Lip; brink, edge.

אֵמֶר 'ēmer (571), Word (Prv 6:2).

יָד yādh (3135), Hand (Prv 12;14); bank (Dn 10:4).

לְחִי l^{e}chî (4029), Jaw (Job 41:2 [40:21]).

פֶּה peh (6552), Mouth (Prv 6:2).

שָׂפָה sāphāh (8004), Lip; edge (Ex 26:4).

1. χεῖλος cheilos nom/acc sing neu
2. χειλέων cheileōn gen pl neu
3. χείλεσιν cheilesin dat pl neu
4. χείλη cheilē nom/acc pl neu

3 and honoureth me with their lips; .... Matt 15:8
3 This people honoureth me with their lips, ... Mark 7:6
4 the poison of asps is under their lips: .... Rom 3:13
3 With men of other tongues and other lips .... 1 Co 14:21
1 as the sand which is by the sea shore innumerable. Heb 11:12
2 the fruit of our lips giving thanks to his name. 13:15
4 and his lips that they speak no guile: .... 1 Pt 3:10

The word *cheilos* has two usages in the Greek. One usage is metaphoric, referring to the brink or the edge such as that of a shore or beach. The other refers to the lips of the mouth. In Matthew 15:8; Mark 7:6; Romans 3:13; 1 Corinthians 14:21; Hebrews 13:15; and 1 Peter 3:10 the word means "lip." In Hebrews 11:12 *cheilos* denotes the shore of the sea.

STRONG 5491, BAUER 879, MOULTON-MILLIGAN 686, LIDDELL-SCOTT 1982.

5328. χειμάζω cheimazō verb

To struggle with the elements.

חִיל chîl (2523), Writhe; polel: wound (Prv 26:10).

1. χειμαζομένων cheimazomenōn
gen pl masc part pres mid

1 And we being exceedingly tossed with a tempest, ... Acts 27:18

The word *cheimazō* means "to struggle with the elements" such as a storm or fierce gale (*Liddell-*

Scott). It implies exposure to severe cold such as is common in winter. It is used in Acts 27:18 in connection with the tempest that drove the ship and resulted in shipwreck for the crew that was taking the apostle Paul as a prisoner to Rome.

STRONG 5492, BAUER 879, MOULTON-MILLIGAN 686, LIDDELL-SCOTT 1982.

5329. χειμάῤῥος cheimarrhos noun

Stream, wadi.

אָפִיק 'āphîq (665), Ravine (Ez 36:4).

גַּיְא gê' (1548I), Valley (Ez 36:4—Codex Vaticanus only).

נַחַל nachal (5337), Valley (Dt 3:8); brook, stream (1 Kgs 17:3-7, Am 5:24).

1. χειμάῤῥου cheimarrhou gen sing masc

1 with his disciples over the **brook** Cedron,.......... John 18:1

The word *cheimarros* refers to a stream of water or a brook that exists only during certain times; for example, the runoff of winter snows or during periods of rain (*Liddell-Scott*). It is used in John 18:1 to refer to the Kidron Valley bordering the temple mount of Jerusalem which would fill with water at certain seasonal times but was otherwise dry.

STRONG 5493, BAUER 879, MOULTON-MILLIGAN 686, LIDDELL-SCOTT 1982.

5330. χειμών cheimōn noun

Winter storm, winter.

גֶּשֶׁם geshem (1700), Rain (Ezr 10:9).

סְתָו s^ethāw (5843), Winter (S/S 2:11).

1. χειμών cheimōn nom sing masc

2. χειμῶνος cheimōnos gen sing masc

1 It will be **foul weather** to day:.................... Matt 16:3
2 But pray ye that your flight be not in the **winter**,...... 24:20
2 And pray ye that your flight be not in the **winter**...Mark 13:18
1 the feast of the dedication, and it was **winter**.......John 10:22
2 and no small **tempest** lay on us,.................. Acts 27:20
2 Do thy diligence to come before **winter**............2 Tm 4:21

The word *cheimōn* is used to mean a "winter storm" with its accompanying high winds, torrential rains, snow, sleet, etc. (*Liddell-Scott*). It is also sometimes used to denote bad weather common to the winter months, characterized by dull skies, drizzling rain, and damp cold (ibid.). It may also simply refer to the winter season itself. The word *cheimōn* is used in Matthew 16:3; 24:20; Mark 13:18; John 10:22; Acts 27:20; and 2 Timothy 4:21.

STRONG 5494, BAUER 879, MOULTON-MILLIGAN 686, LIDDELL-SCOTT 1983.

5331. χείρ cheir noun

Hand.

COGNATES:

αὐτόχειρ autocheir (842)
ἀχειροποίητος acheiropoiētos (879)
διαχειρίζομαι diacheirizomai (1309)
ἐπιχειρέω epicheireō (2005)
προχειρίζομαι procheirizomai (4258)
χειραγωγέω cheiragōgeō (5332)
χειραγωγός cheiragōgos (5333)
χειρόγραφον cheirographon (5334)
χειροποίητος cheiropoiētos (5335)
χειροτονέω cheirotoneō (5336)

חֹפֶן chōphen (2756), Handful, hands (Ex 9:8, Lv 16:12, Ez 10:7).

יָד yādh (3135), Hand (Gn 27:22f., 1 Sm 17:37, Jer 38:3 [45:3f.]).

יַד yadh (A3136), Hand (Ezr 5:12, 7:14, Dn 2:45—Aramaic).

כֹּחַ kōach (3699), Power (Nm 14:17—Codex Alexandrinus only).

כַּף kaph (3834), Palm hand (Lv 14:15f., 2 Sm 18:18f., Ez 29:7).

שֹׁעַל shō'al (8545), Hollow of a hand (Is 40:12).

תָּו tāw (8750), Signature (Job 31:35).

1. χείρ cheir nom sing fem
2. χειρός cheiros gen sing fem
3. χειρί cheiri dat sing fem
4. χεῖρα cheira acc sing fem
5. χεῖρες cheires nom pl fem
6. χειρῶν cheirōn gen pl fem
7. χερσίν chersin dat pl fem
8. χεῖρας cheiras acc pl fem

3 Whose fan is in his **hand**,.......................... Matt 3:12
6 and in their **hands** they shall bear thee up,............. 4:6
1 And if thy right **hand** offend thee, cut it off,........... 5:30
4 And Jesus put forth his **hand**, and touched him,........ 8:3
2 And he touched her **hand**, and the fever left her:....... 8:15
4 lay thy **hand** upon her, and she shall live............... 9:18
2 and took her by the **hand**, and the maid arose.......... 9:25
4 there was a man which had his **hand** withered......... 12:10
4 Then saith he to the man, Stretch forth thine **hand**..... 12:13
4 he stretched forth his **hand** toward his disciples,....... 12:49
4 And immediately Jesus stretched forth his **hand**,....... 14:31
8 for they wash not their **hands** when they eat bread..... 15:2
7 but to eat with unwashen **hands** defileth not a man..... 15:20
8 Son ... shall be betrayed into the **hands** of men:....... 17:22
1 Wherefore if thy **hand** or thy foot offend thee,........ 18:8
8 rather than having two **hands** or two feet to be cast.... 18:8
8 that he should put his **hands** on them, and pray:....... 19:13
8 he laid his **hands** on them, and departed thence........ 19:15
8 Bind him **hand** and foot, and take him away,.......... 22:13
4 He that dippeth his **hand** with me in the dish,......... 26:23
8 Son of man is betrayed into the **hands** of sinners....... 26:45
8 Then came they, and laid **hands** on Jesus,............. 26:50
4 which were with Jesus stretched out his **hand**,......... 26:51
8 and washed his **hands** before the multitude, saying,.... 27:24
2 came and took her by the **hand**, and lifted her up;..Mark 1:31

4 moved with compassion, put forth his **hand**, ... Mark 1:41
4 there was a man there which had a withered **hand**. 3:1
4 saith unto the man which had the withered **hand**, ... 3:3
4 he saith unto the man, Stretch forth thine **hand**. 3:5
1 and his **hand** was restored whole as the other. 3:5
8 I pray thee, come and lay thy **hands** on her, ... 5:23
2 he took the damsel by the **hand**, and said unto her, ... 5:41
6 even such mighty works are wrought by his **hands?** 6:2
8 save that he laid his **hands** upon a few sick folk, ... 6:5
7 that is to say, with unwashen, **hands**, ... 7:2
8 except they wash their **hands** oft, eat not, ... 7:3
7 but eat bread with unwashen **hands?** 7:5
4 and they beseech him to put his **hand** upon him. 7:32
2 And he took the blind man by the **hand**, ... 8:23
8 and put his **hands** upon him, ... 8:23
8 After that he put his **hands** again upon his eyes, ... 8:25
2 But Jesus took him by the **hand**, and lifted him up; 9:27
8 The Son of man is delivered into the **hands** of men, ... 9:31
1 And if thy **hand** offend thee, cut it off: 9:43
8 than having two **hands** to go into hell, ... 9:43
8 put his **hands** upon them, and blessed them. 10:16
8 Son of man is betrayed into the **hands** of sinners. 14:41
8 And they laid their **hands** on him, and took him. 14:46
8 they shall lay **hands** on the sick, ... 16:18
1 And the **hand** of the Lord was with him. .... Luke 1:66
2 and from the **hand** of all that hate us; 1:71
2 we being delivered out of the **hand** of our enemies 1:74
3 Whose fan is in his **hand**, and he will thoroughly 3:17
6 And in their **hands** they shall bear thee up, ... 4:11
8 and he laid his **hands** on every one of them, ... 4:40
4 And he put forth his **hand**, and touched him, ... 5:13
7 corn, and did eat, rubbing them in their **hands**. 6:1
1 there was a man whose right **hand** was withered. 6:6
4 and said to the man which had the withered **hand**, ... 6:8
4 he said unto the man, Stretch forth thy **hand**. 6:10
1 and his **hand** was restored whole as the other. 6:10
2 he put them all out, and took her by the **hand**, ... 8:54
8 shall be delivered into the **hands** of men. 9:44
4 No man, having put his **hand** to the plow, ... 9:62
8 And he laid his **hands** on her: 13:13
4 and put a ring on his **hand**, and shoes on his feet: 15:22
8 scribes the same hour sought to lay **hands** on him; 20:19
8 before all these, they shall lay their **hands** on you, ... 21:12
1 the **hand** of him that betrayeth me is with me 22:21
8 ye stretched forth no **hands** against me: 22:53
8 Father, into thy **hands** I commend my spirit: 23:46
8 must be delivered into the **hands** of sinful men, ... 24:7
8 Behold my **hands** and my feet, that it is I myself: 24:39
8 he showed them his **hands** and his feet. 24:40
8 and he lifted up his **hands**, and blessed them. 24:50
3 and hath given all things into his **hand**. .... John 3:35
4 but no man laid **hands** on him, ... 7:30
8 but no man laid **hands** on him. 7:44
2 neither shall any man pluck them out of my **hand**. 10:28
2 is able to pluck them out of my Father's **hand**. 10:29
2 but he escaped out of their **hand**, ... 10:39
8 bound **hand** and foot with graveclothes: 11:44
8 that the Father had given all things into his **hands**, ... 13:3
8 not my feet only, but also my **hands** and my head. 13:9
8 he showed unto them his **hands** and his side. 20:20
7 Except I shall see in his **hands** the print of ... nails, ... 20:25
4 and thrust my **hand** into his side, ... 20:25
8 Reach hither thy finger, and behold my **hands**; 20:27
4 reach hither thy **hand**, and thrust it into my side: 20:27
8 thou shalt stretch forth thy **hands**, ... 21:18
6 and by wicked **hands** have crucified and slain: .... Acts 2:23
2 he took him by the right **hand**, and lifted him up: 3:7
8 they laid **hands** on them, and put them in hold 4:3
1 For to do whatsoever thy **hand** and thy counsel 4:28
4 By stretching forth thine **hand** to heal; 4:30
6 And by the **hands** of the apostles were many signs 5:12
8 And laid their **hands** on the apostles, ... 5:18
8 they laid their **hands** on them. 6:6
2 how that God by his **hand** would deliver them: 7:25
3 and a deliverer by the **hand** of the angel 7:35
6 and rejoiced in the works of their own **hands**. 7:41
1 Hath not my **hand** made all these things? 7:50
8 Then laid they their **hands** on them, ... Acts 8:17
6 through laying on of the apostles' **hands** 8:18
8 that on whomsoever I lay **hands**, ... 8:19
4 Ananias coming in, and putting his **hand** on him, ... 9:12
8 and putting his **hands** on him said, Brother Saul, ... 9:17
4 And he gave her his **hand**, and lifted her up, ... 9:41
1 And the **hand** of the Lord was with them: 11:21
2 and sent it to the elders by the **hands** of Barnabas 11:30
8 Herod the king stretched forth his **hands** 12:1
6 And his chains fell off from his **hands**. 12:7
2 and hath delivered me out of the **hand** of Herod, ... 12:11
3 But he, beckoning unto them with the **hand** 12:17
8 fasted and prayed, and laid their **hands** on them, ... 13:3
1 now, behold, the **hand** of the Lord is upon thee, ... 13:11
3 Paul stood up, and beckoning with his **hand** said, ... 13:16
6 signs and wonders to be done by their **hands**. 14:3
2 And they wrote letters by them (NT) 15:23
6 Neither is worshipped with men's **hands**, ... 17:25
8 And when Paul had laid his **hands** upon them, ... 19:6
6 wrought special miracles by the **hands** of Paul: 19:11
6 that they be no gods, which are made with **hands**: 19:26
4 And Alexander beckoned with the **hand**, ... 19:33
5 these **hands** have ministered unto my necessities, ... 20:34
8 and bound his own **hands** and feet, and said, ... 21:11
8 shall deliver him into the **hands** of the Gentiles. 21:11
8 stirred up all the people, and laid **hands** on him, ... 21:27
3 and beckoned with the **hand** unto the people. 21:40
2 Then the chief captain took him by the **hand**, ... 23:19
6 with ... violence took him away out of our **hands**, ... 24:7
4 Then Paul stretched forth the **hand**, ... 26:1
2 a viper out of the heat, and fastened on his **hand**. 28:3
2 saw the venomous beast hang on his **hand**, ... 28:4
8 and laid his **hands** on him, and healed him. 28:8
8 from Jerusalem into the **hands** of the Romans. 28:17
8 All day long I have stretched forth my **hands** ...... Rom 10:21
7 And labour, working with our own **hands**: .... 1 Co 4:12
1 Because I am not the **hand**, I am not of the body; 12:15
3 And the eye cannot say unto the **hand**, ... 12:21
3 The salutation of me Paul with mine own **hand**. 16:21
8 was I let down by the wall, and escaped his **hands**. 2 Co 11:33
3 was ordained by angels in the **hand** of a mediator. ... Gal 3:19
3 I have written unto you with mine own **hand**. 6:11
7 working with his **hands** the thing which is good, ... Eph 4:28
3 The salutation by the **hand** of me Paul. .... Col 4:18
7 and to work with your own **hands**, ... 1 Th 4:11
3 The salutation of Paul with mine own **hand**, ... 2 Th 3:17
8 lifting up holy **hands**, without wrath and doubting. .. 1 Tm 2:8
6 with the laying on of the **hands** of the presbytery. 4:14
8 Lay **hands** suddenly on no man, ... 5:22
6 which is in thee by the putting on of my **hands**. .... 2 Tm 1:6
3 I Paul have written it with mine own **hand**, ... Phlm 1:19
6 and the heavens are the works of thine **hands**: .... Heb 1:10
6 and didst set him over the works of thy **hands**: 2:7
6 doctrine of baptisms, and of laying on **of hands**, ... 6:2
2 by the **hand** to lead them out of the land of Egypt; 8:9
8 to fall into the **hands** of the living God. 10:31
8 Wherefore lift up the **hands** which hang down, ... 12:12
8 Cleanse your **hands**, ye sinners; .... Jas 4:8
4 under the mighty **hand** of God, ... 1 Pt 5:6
5 have looked upon, and our **hands** have handled, ... 1 Jn 1:1
3 And he had in his right **hand** seven stars: .... Rev 1:16
4 he laid his right **hand** upon me, saying unto me, ... 1:17
3 that sat on him had a pair of balances in his **hand**. 6:5
7 with white robes, and palms in their **hands**; 7:9
2 ascended up before God out of the angel's **hand**. 8:4
6 yet repented not of the works of their **hands**, ... 9:20
3 And he had in his **hand** a little book open: 10:2
4 and upon the earth lifted up his **hand** to heaven, ... 10:5
3 little book which is open in the **hand** of the angel 10:8
2 And I took the little book out of the angel's **hand**, ... 10:10
2 a mark in their right **hand**, or in their foreheads: 13:16
4 receive his mark in his forehead, or in his **hand**, ... 14:9
3 a golden crown, and in his **hand** a sharp sickle. 14:14
3 a golden cup in her **hand** full of abominations 17:4
2 hath avenged the blood of his servants at her **hand**. 19:2
4 having the key ... and a great chain in his **hand**. 20:1
4 his mark upon their foreheads, or in their **hands**; 20:4

Classical Greek

The Greek word *cheir* is a noun that literally denotes the physical "hand" of the human body. This particular word, however, is important for Biblical study in that it takes on a wide range of significance far beyond the designation for a part of the human anatomy.

Practically, it denotes the functional use of the hand in work, defense, and service to others. In addition, strength and energy are connoted as the hand becomes the representative agency of human interaction in daily life.

Ancient Greek writers often referred to the plural form, *cheires*, and coupled it with *dunameis*, "powers." Consequently this particular usage becomes more than just a symbol of power. Rather, "When it is linked with a personal name, it stands as a substitute for the person himself in action" (Laubach, "Hand," *Colin Brown*, 2:148).

Septuagint Usage

The Old Testament also depicts the hand in terms of power. There is *physical* power in work; *political* power in terms of control (Genesis 32:11; Judges 2:14; Jeremiah 27:6ff. [LXX 34:6ff.]); *spiritual* power in God's omnipotent nature (2 Chronicles 20:6; Psalm 89:13 [LXX 88:13]), God's creative action (Isaiah 48:13), God's redemption of Israel (Exodus 7:4; 9:3; 1 Samuel 7:13 [LXX 1 Kings 7:13]), God's righteous discipline (1 Samuel 5:6 [1 Kings 5:6]), God's nurturing care (Ezra 7:6; Job 5:18; Psalm 145:16 [LXX 144:16]; Isaiah 49:16), and God's providential oversight (Isaiah 51:16).

Figuratively the Old Testament is very descriptive in its portrayal of the right hand being more active than the left because of its strength and effectiveness (Exodus 15:6,12; Psalm 118:15ff. [LXX 117:15ff.]; Isaiah 41:13). Further, the hand expresses the full spectrum of emotions (Numbers 24:10; Psalms 28:2 [LXX 27:2]; 47:1 [46:1]; Jeremiah 2:37; Ezekiel 6:11) and represents the very flow of the energy of God in the practice of laying on of hands for blessing, healing, and worship practices (Genesis 48:14; Leviticus 1:4; 3:2,8,13; 4:4,15,24,29,33; 8:14,22; 2 Kings 13:16 [LXX 4 Kings 13:16]).

Developmentally the Dead Sea Scrolls refer to the hand of God in terms of victory over enemies, comfort in prayer, and guidance in a righteous life (Lohse, "cheir," *Kittel*, 9:427); yet, in contrast, Hellenistic Judaism and the rabbinic writings are very restrained in any usage or anthropomorphic descriptions of God with the exceptions of direct quotations from the Old Testament.

New Testament Usage

Turning to the New Testament, *cheir* is used idiomatically ("by the *hand* of; at the hand of") to signify an acting agency (Acts 5:12; 7:35; 14:3; 17:25; Galatians 3:19; Revelation 19:2). It is employed metaphorically to illustrate the power of God (Luke 1:66; 23:46; John 10:28,29; Acts 11:21; 13:11; Hebrews 1:10; 2:7; 10:31). It is utilized spiritually in the laying on of hands for healing (Mark 5:23; 7:32; 8:23,25, etc.), blessing (Matthew 19:13; Mark 10:16; Luke 24:50); impartation of the Holy Spirit (Acts 8:17; 19:6; Hebrews 6:2), and enabling for anointed ministry (Acts 6:6; 13:1-3; 1 Timothy 1:18; 4:14; 2 Timothy 1:6).

Finally, *cheir* is applied to the ministry of Christ and depicts His embodiment of divine power in His acts of creation (Hebrews 1:10), salvation (Acts 4:28), judgment (Hebrews 10:31), providential care (Luke 1:66; 23:46; John 10:29), wonder-working ministry (Acts 4:30; 11:21), and strengthening support (1 Peter 5:6).

STRONG 5495, BAUER 879-80, MOULTON-MILLIGAN 686-87, KITTEL 9:424-34, LIDDELL-SCOTT 1983-84, COLIN BROWN 2:148-50.

5332. χειραγωγέω cheiragōgeō verb

To lead by the hand.

CROSS-REFERENCES:

ἀγωνίζομαι agōnizomai (74)
χείρ cheir (5331)

1. χειραγωγοῦντες cheiragōgountes nom pl masc part pres act

2. χειραγωγούμενος cheiragōgoumenos nom sing masc part pres mid

1 he saw no man: but they **led him by the hand,** .... Acts 9:8
2 **being led by the hand** of them that were with me, ... 22:11

The word *cheiragōgeō* is a verb which means "to lead by the hand" (*Liddell-Scott*). In the literal sense it means to guide by holding the hand and towing one along. For example, the men traveling with Saul led him by the hand after he was blinded (Acts 9:8). It is also used in Acts 22:11.

STRONG 5496, BAUER 880, MOULTON-MILLIGAN 687, KITTEL 9:435, LIDDELL-SCOTT 1984.

5333. χειραγωγός cheiragōgos noun

One who leads by the hand.

Cross-References:
ἀγωνίζομαι agōnizomai (74)
χείρ cheir (5331)

1. χειραγωγούς cheiragōgous acc pl masc

1 went about seeking **some to lead him by the hand**....Acts 13:11

The word *cheiragōgos* refers to one who leads by the hand or directs another's movements by leading him by the hand. It is used in Acts 13:11 as the person who would lead the blinded Elymas, i.e., "some(one) to lead him by the hand."

Strong 5497, Bauer 880, Moulton-Milligan 687, Kittel 9:435, Liddell-Scott 1984.

5334. χειρόγραφον cheirographon noun

Record of indebtedness, bond.

Cross-References:
γράφω graphō (1119)
χείρ cheir (5331)

1. χειρόγραφον cheirographon nom/acc sing neu

1 the **handwriting** of ordinances that was against us,.... Col 2:14

Classical Greek

This noun is related to the verb *cheirographeō*, a compound of *cheir* (5331), "hand," and *graphō* (1119) "to write"; it denotes "a written report." It especially carries the sense of a "written agreement, a 'note of indebtedness,' a bond" (cf. *Liddell-Scott*; *Moulton-Milligan*).

Septuagint Usage

The word only occurs in apocryphal writings in the Septuagint. It is read at Tobit 5:3 where Tobias gives his son some kind of "receipt" (RSV) for the silver he left with Gabael (cf. Tobit 4:20). This bond would apparently allow Tobias' son to retrieve the money on his father's behalf. Upon receiving the "receipt" from Raphael, Gabael indeed gives him the money (Tobit 9:5). (*Cheirographon* is also attested three additional times in Codex Sinaiticus [5:3, twice; 9:2].)

New Testament Usage

The single instance of *cheirographon* in the New Testament occurs in Colossians 2:14 where it probably picks up on the Jewish belief that God kept an account of an individual's "indebtedness" (with regard to sin). According to this belief, God would later call for payment; in other words, He would exact a penalty (cf. Lohse, "cheir," *Kittel*, 9:435).

Lohse reports that there is "no thought of the myth which the fathers later introduced . . . that the document . . . is a compact with the devil" by which man relinquishes his life to Satan in exchange for services (ibid., 9:436). Rather, as Lohse correctly points out, the cancellation of the "written code" (NIV) concerns God's forgiving our sins through Christ (Colossians 2:13) (ibid.).

All of humanity throughout the ages is indebted to God. God could have elected to collect His debt and to administer judgment and penalty to those living outside of His originally intended relationship (cf. especially Deuteronomy 27:14-26; 30:15-20 of Jewish obligation to God). Instead of penalty, however, God chose to "forgive" those who turn to Him (cf. the parable in Matthew 18:23ff.) and to cancel their debt by nailing it to the cross.

Strong 5498, Bauer 880, Moulton-Milligan 687, Kittel 9:435-36, Liddell-Scott 1985.

5335. χειροποίητος cheiropoiētos adj

Made by human hands.

Cross-References:
ποιέω poieō (4020)
χείρ cheir (5331)
אֱלִיל 'ělîl (462), Idol (Lv 26:1, Is 2:18, 19:1).

1. χειροποίητον cheiropoiēton acc sing masc
2. χειροποιήτοις cheiropoiētois dat pl masc
3. χειροποιήτου cheiropoiētou gen sing fem
4. χειροποίητα cheiropoiēta nom/acc pl neu

1 I will destroy this temple that is **made with hands,** Mark 14:58
2 dwelleth not in temples **made with hands;**........... Acts 7:48
2 dwelleth not in temples **made with hands;**............. 17:24
3 the Circumcision in the flesh **made by hands;**.........Eph 2:11
3 and more perfect tabernacle, not **made with hands,**... Heb 9:11
4 not entered into the holy places **made with hands,**....... 9:24

Classical Greek

Cheiropoiētos is a compound form of the noun *cheir* (5331), "hand," and the verb *poieō* (4020), "to do, make." In classical Greek and elsewhere it means "made with hands" or "artificial." It stands in contrast to something "natural" (*autophuēs*), and it can suggest something done intentionally (*Liddell-Scott*).

Septuagint Usage

Of its 14 appearances in the Septuagint, only 6 have a Hebrew original (cf. Leviticus 26:30; Isaiah 16:12; 46:6 where it is doubtful). Where the Hebrew is certain it is always *'ělîl*, a term meaning "worthless." When used of pagan gods in a contemptuous sense it implies that they do not exist (*Concise Hebrew and Aramaic Lexicon*, "'ělîl").

Cheiropoiētos consistently denotes the "man-made" idols erected by humans (Leviticus 26:1;

Isaiah 2:18; 10:11). This understanding carries over into later Jewish writings as well (e.g., Judith 8:18; Wisdom of Solomon 14:8).

New Testament Usage

Although *cheiropoiētos* occurs only six times in the New Testament, the fact that four different writers use it indicates it was in common circulation at that time. The Septuagint appears to be a major factor for the understanding of the term in the New Testament. This is clearly seen in Mark 14:58; Acts 7:48; 17:24; Hebrews 9:11; and 9:24. Each of these texts emphasizes that the one true God dwells not in man-made temples or tabernacles but in heaven (Acts 7:48,49; Hebrews 9:24; cf. 1 Kings 8:27). As creator of all things God does not need to have a sanctuary fashioned by man (Acts 17:24). He exists on a plane above the created order itself (Hebrews 9:11).

Because of the plain association of *cheiropoiētos* with pagan idols in the Septuagint, the false witnesses against Jesus are almost certainly implying that Jesus had called the temple an idolatrous shrine (Mark 14:58). Interestingly Mark does not record the incident itself, but we learn from John that Jesus had made a statement similar to that. However, Jesus' reference to a temple "not made with hands" (*acheiropoiētos* [879]) did not refer to another temple but to His body; at least that is how John understands it (John 2:21f.; cf. 2 Corinthians 5:1).

Cheiropoiētos is also applied to the man-made rite of circumcision. The idea here is how ineffective such human efforts are for establishing a covenant relationship with God. Only through Christ can we be truly circumcised before God (Colossians 2:11). God had always expected Israel to be circumcised in their hearts as well as their flesh (e.g., Leviticus 26:41; Deuteronomy 30:6; Jeremiah 4:4; 9:26; cf. Jeremiah 31:31-33; Acts 7:51).

STRONG 5499, BAUER 880-81, MOULTON-MILLIGAN 687, KITTEL 9:436, LIDDELL-SCOTT 1985.

5336. χειροτονέω cheirotoneō verb

Choose, select, elect by raising the hand.

COGNATES:

προχειροτονέω procheirotoneō (4259)
χείρ cheir (5331)

SYNONYMS:

αἱρετίζω hairetizō (139)
αἱρέω haireō (141)
ἐκλέγομαι eklegomai (1573)
ἐπιλέγω epilegō (1935B)
καθίστημι kathistēmi (2497)
ὁρίζω horizō (3587)
προχειρίζομαι procheirizomai (4258)
τάσσω tassō (4872)
τίθημι tithēmi (4935)

1. χειροτονήσαντες cheirotonēsantes nom pl masc part aor act

2. χειροτονηθείς cheirotonētheis nom sing masc part aor pass

3. χειροτονηθέντα cheirotonēthenta acc sing masc part aor pass

1 they **had ordained** them elders in every church,..... Acts 14:23
2 but who was also **chosen** of the churches to travel... 2 Co 8:19

Classical Greek

In classical Greek writings *cheirotoneō* is used to describe how votes were cast in an assembly, i.e., by the raising of a hand or by a show of hands (*Liddell-Scott*). As early as the Fifth Century B.C. the term meant to "select" or "nominate" (Lohse, "cheirotoneō," *Kittel*, 9:437). Later, additional meanings were also implied, such as "electing" or "appointing." The verb does not appear in the Septuagint. It was used, however, in the writings of later church fathers and described the ordination process of bishops and deacons (cf. *Moulton-Milligan*).

New Testament Usage

Cheirotoneō occurs twice in the New Testament: at Acts 14:23 and 2 Corinthians 8:19. The first passage describes how Paul and Barnabas "appointed, chose," or perhaps "nominated" elders to serve in the Galatian churches of Lystra, Iconium, and Antioch. After they had prayed and fasted, the "electees" were *committed* to the Lord (see *paratithēmi* [3769], "entrusted into the care or protection" of God [cf. *Bauer*]).

In 2 Corinthians 8:19 *cheirotoneō* shows that the churches selected one trustworthy individual to accompany Paul back to Jerusalem in order to deliver monies collected for the poor saints there. Later writings of the Church also reveal that individuals were selected for specific tasks by the community of believers (Lohse, "cheirotoneō," *Kittel*, 9:437).

STRONG 5500, BAUER 881, MOULTON-MILLIGAN 687, KITTEL 9:437, LIDDELL-SCOTT 1986, COLIN BROWN 1:478.

5337. χείρων cheirōn adj

A worse evil, more severe.

1. χείρων cheirōn comp nom sing masc/fem

2. χείρονος cheironos comp gen sing fem

3. χεῖρον cheiron comp nom/acc sing neu
4. χείρονα cheirona comp nom/acc pl neu

3 and the rent is made **worse**.........................Matt 9:16
4 and the last state of that man is **worse** than the first... 12:45
1 so the last error shall be **worse** than the first.......... 27:64
3 and the rent is made **worse**........................ Mark 2:21
3 but rather grew **worse**,................................ 5:26
4 and the last state of that man is **worse** than the first.Luke 11:26
3 sin no more, lest a **worse** thing come unto thee......John 5:14
1 hath denied the faith, and is **worse** than an infidel...1 Tm 5:8
3 evil men and seducers shall wax **worse** and worse,.. 2 Tm 3:13
2 Of how much **sorer** punishment, suppose ye,....... Heb 10:29
4 latter end is **worse** with them than the beginning.....2 Pt 2:20

The word *cheirōn* is an adjective used to compare degrees of evil, such as a worsening spiritual or physical condition. It is used in Hebrews 10:29 to illustrate the severity of punishment for those who continue to sin deliberately after having accepted Christ. It is used elsewhere in the New Testament to denote the degree of evil of certain men. It is sometimes rendered "sorer" in the KJV.

STRONG 5501, BAUER 881, MOULTON-MILLIGAN 688, LIDDELL-SCOTT 1986.

5338. χερούβ cheroub noun

An angel, cherub.

כְּרוּב kerûv (3872), Cherub (Ex 25:19 [25:18], Ez 28:14, 41:18).

1. χερουβίμ cheroubim nom pl masc
2. χερουβίν cheroubin nom pl masc
3. χερουβείν cheroubein nom pl masc

1 the **cherubims** of glory shadowing the mercyseat;.....Heb 9:5

The word *cheroub* is the singular form of the word *cheroubim* (Hebrew *kerûbîm*). As a part of the ark of the covenant the *cheroubim* were represented as two-winged living creatures. Together with the mercy seat they comprised a unified whole, symbolizing Christ's union with redeemed humanity. In Hebrews 9:5 the plural *cheroubim* is used to signify beings which glorify God in all His majesty as manifested in the Holy of Holies. Some manuscripts contain either *cheroubein* or *cheroubin* as the plural.

STRONG 5502, BAUER 881, MOULTON-MILLIGAN 688 (see "cheroubein"), KITTEL 9:438-39 (see "cheroubin"), COLIN BROWN 1:279-80.

5339. χήρα chēra noun

Widow.

אַלְמָנָה 'almānāh (496), Widow (Dt 10:18, Job 22:9, Jer 7:6).

אַלְמָנוּת 'almānûth (497), Widowhood (2 Sm 20:3).

גַּלְמוּד galmûdh (1606), Barren (Is 49:21).

1. χήρα chēra nom sing fem
2. χήραν chēran acc sing fem
3. χῆραι chērai nom pl fem
4. χηρῶν chērōn gen pl fem
5. χήραις chērais dat pl fem
6. χήρας chēras acc pl fem

4 hypocrites! for ye devour **widows'** houses,..........Matt 23:14
4 Which devour **widows'** houses,.....................Mark 12:40
1 And there came a certain poor **widow**,................ 12:42
1 That this poor **widow** hath cast more in,............. 12:43
1 she was **a widow** of about fourscore and four years, Luke 2:37
3 many **widows** were in Israel in the days of Elias,........ 4:25
2 a city of Sidon, unto a woman that was a **widow**........ 4:26
1 the only son of his mother, and she was **a widow**:....... 7:12
1 And there was **a widow** in that city;.................. 18:3
2 Yet because this **widow** troubleth me,................. 18:5
4 Which devour **widows'** houses,........................ 20:47
2 a certain poor **widow** casting in thither two mites...... 21:2
1 this poor **widow** hath cast in more than they all:....... 21:3
3 because their **widows** were neglected................Acts 6:1
3 and all the **widows** stood by him weeping,.............. 9:39
6 and when he had called the saints and **widows**,......... 9:41
5 I say therefore to the unmarried and **widows**,....... 1 Co 7:8
6 Honour **widows** that are widows indeed............1 Tm 5:3
6 Honour widows that are **widows** indeed................. 5:3
1 But if any **widow** have children or nephews,............ 5:4
1 Now she that is **a widow** indeed, and desolate,.......... 5:5
1 Let not **a widow** be taken into the number............. 5:9
6 But the younger **widows** refuse:........................ 5:11
6 If any man or woman that believeth have **widows**,...... 5:16
5 that it may relieve them that are **widows** indeed......... 5:16
6 visit the fatherless and **widows** in their affliction,..... Jas 1:27
1 queen, and am no **widow**, and shall see no sorrow...Rev 18:7

Classical Greek

In Greek literature as early as Homer (ca. Eighth Century B.C.), *chēra* has denoted "a widow." In many places it is linked with the word *orphanos* (3600), "orphan," and conveys the idea of being destitute or needy. *Chēra* is the feminine noun form of a related adjective *chēros* which means "deprived" (e.g., the widow is a woman "deprived" of a husband). Stahlin reports that in the pagan world the greatest fear among women was that of becoming a widow. Many women preferred to die at their spouse's grave rather than continue life without a husband ("chēra," *Kittel*, 9:442). Losing a husband to death meant that a woman often lost her sole sustainer and protector. Also in the Roman Empire, women who remarried lost certain rights and were generally less respected in the community (ibid., 9:443).

Septuagint Usage

The word *chēra* appears about 60 times in the Septuagint and nearly always translates the Hebrew term *'almānāh*. Occasionally the word describes a woman who was separated from her husband or a woman without a husband (e.g., 2 Samuel 20:3 [LXX 2 Kings 20:3]), but in the majority of its occurrences it simply means "a widow."

In the Old Testament, widows were grouped together with other disadvantaged classes such as strangers, orphans, and the poor (see Exodus 22:21f.; Isaiah 1:23; 10:2; Jeremiah 5:28). In His mercy, God made special provisions for their protection and preservation (Leviticus 22:13; Deuteronomy 10:18). For example, a portion of tithes taken on the third year were designated for helping the widow (Deuteronomy 14:28f.); field gleanings were to be left for her (Deuteronomy 24:19ff.); and the levirate marriage was to take effect when a widow was also without a male child (see Deuteronomy 25:5-10). In addition, the Lord himself promised to uphold and defend her (Deuteronomy 10:18; Proverbs 15:25).

Yet despite God's injunctions that Israel show compassion on the widow and maintain her rights, the Scriptures reveal that the plight of the widow was particularly difficult. The Bible describes how widows were exploited and generally abused (Isaiah 1:23; Ezekiel 22:7). It is not surprising, therefore, that widowhood was seen by many to be a reproach (Isaiah 4:1). As a result, the term "widow" was figuratively applied to the exiled nation of Israel (Isaiah 54:4) and to Jerusalem at the time of her captivity (Lamentations 1:1).

New Testament Usage

In the New Testament the widow remains a picture of neediness, destitution, and poverty. The Gospel of Mark (12:42f.), for example, describes a poor widow who cast all she had, "two mites," into the treasury at the temple. Luke's gospel in particular singles out the plight of widows in the time of Jesus. Luke 7:11-15 relates the story of a grieving widow whose only son had just died. The Lord recognized her desperate situation and out of His great compassion raised the young man from the dead. Chapter 18 tells the parable of a persistent widow seeking justice against an adversary. Luke also described the widow who cast two mites into the collection box (21:2f.). In addition, all three Synoptic Gospels record one of Jesus' strongest rebukes against the scribes and Pharisees who "devour *widows'* houses, and for a show make long prayers: the same shall receive greater damnation" (Luke 20:47; cf. Matthew 23:14; Mark 12:40).

God's concern for widows is recorded outside the Gospels as well. Acts 6:1-6 shows how the Early Church took special care to solve a problem which affected widows. The result was that both Jewish and Greek widows received enough food to meet their needs. Elsewhere, James 1:27 presents a clear definition of what God views as "pure religion": it includes visiting orphans and widows in their affliction.

One final section of the New Testament, 1 Timothy 5:3-16, provides significant detail that relates to widows. These passages specify the obligations that the church and family have with respect to their care. Paul differentiates between three categories of widows: (1) those with children or grandchildren (verses 4,8,16); (2) those who are young and in a position to remarry (verses 11-15); (3) those who are "widows indeed," i.e., not having a family to support them (verses 5-7,16). The first group is to be cared for by their own family. In fact, a believer who does not care for a widowed parent (or grandparent) has "denied the faith, and is worse than an infidel" (verse 8). The second group, young widows, are encouraged to remarry so as not to "cast off their first faith" and become "busybodies" (cf. verses 12,13; see also 1 Corinthians 7:8). The third category defines "true" widows whose needs the Church must meet, provided certain conditions exist: they have no family to support them, they are over 60 years old, and they continue in good works (verses 9,10).

While widows throughout history have been a disadvantaged class, the Scriptures show that God has special compassion for them. Both the Old and New Testament reveal His love and concern for them. It was not His intention for the nation of Israel to neglect their needs, and it is not His will for the Church to overlook their plight either.

STRONG 5503, BAUER 881, MOULTON-MILLIGAN 688, KITTEL 9:440-65, LIDDELL-SCOTT 1990, COLIN BROWN 3:1073-76.

5340. χθές chthes adv

Yesterday.

1. χθές chthes

1 Yesterday at the seventh hour the fever left him..... John 4:52
1 as thou diddest the Egyptian yesterday?............ Acts 7:28
1 the same yesterday, and to day, and for ever....... Heb 13:8

The word *chthes* means "yesterday" and is possibly an old Ionic form of the Attic term *echthes* which also means "yesterday" (cf. *Liddell-Scott*). It occurs in John 4:52; Acts 7:28; Hebrews 13:8.

STRONG 5504, BAUER 881, MOULTON-MILLIGAN 688, LIDDELL-SCOTT 1991.

5341. χιλίαρχος chiliarchos noun

A commander.

Cross-References:

ἀρχή archē (741)
χιλιάς chilias (5342)

אַלּוּף 'allûph (444), Leader (Zec 9:7, 12:5f.).

1. **χιλίαρχος chiliarchos** nom sing masc
2. **χιλιάρχῳ chiliarchō** dat sing masc
3. **χιλίαρχον chiliarchon** acc sing masc
4. **χιλίαρχοι chiliarchoi** nom pl masc
5. **χιλιάρχων chiliarchōn** gen pl masc
6. **χιλιάρχοις chiliarchois** dat pl masc

6 lords, **high captains,** and chief estates of Galilee;....Mark 6:21
1 and the **captain** and officers of the Jews took Jesus, John 18:12
2 tidings came unto the **chief captain** of the band,.... Acts 21:31
3 when they saw the **chief captain** and the soldiers,...... 21:32
1 Then the **chief captain** came near, and took him,...... 21:33
2 he said unto the **chief captain,** May I speak........... 21:37
1 The **chief captain** commanded him to be brought...... 22:24
2 he went and told the **chief captain,**.................. 22:26
1 Then the **chief captain** came, and said unto him,....... 22:27
1 And the **chief captain** answered,...................... 22:28
1 and the **chief captain** also was afraid,................ 22:29
1 the **chief captain,** fearing lest Paul should............ 23:10
2 ye with the council signify to the **chief captain**......... 23:15
3 Bring this young man unto the **chief captain:**.......... 23:17
3 he took him, and brought him to the **chief captain,**.... 23:18
1 Then the **chief captain** took him by the hand,.......... 23:19
1 So the **chief captain** then let the young man depart,.... 23:22
1 But the **chief captain** Lysias came upon us,............ 24:7
1 When Lysias the **chief captain** shall come down,....... 24:22
6 the **chief captains,** and principal men of the city,....... 25:23
4 and the rich men, and the **chief captains,**............ Rev 6:15
5 the flesh of kings, and the flesh of **captains,**........... 19:18

The word *chiliarchos* refers to a commander of 1,000 soldiers. It is used to indicate the commander of the Roman garrison in Jerusalem (Acts 21:33), the captain of the temple guard (John 18:12), and in general any military commander or captain in command of a large number of troops (cf. Mark 6:21; Acts 21:31,37; Revelation 6:15; 19:18).

Strong 5506, Bauer 882, Moulton-Milligan 688, Liddell-Scott 1992, Colin Brown 2:699.

5342. χιλιάς chilias noun

One thousand.

Cognates:

δισχίλιοι dischilioi (1360)
ἑπτακισχίλιοι heptakischilioi (2018)
χιλίαρχος chiliarchos (5341)
χίλιοι chilioi (5343)

1. **χιλιάδες chiliades** nom pl fem
2. **χιλιάδων chiliadōn** gen pl fem
3. **χιλιάσιν chiliasin** dat pl fem

3 with ten **thousand** to meet him that cometh against Luke 14:31
2 that cometh against him with twenty **thousand?**........ 14:31
1 the number of the men was about five **thousand.**.... Acts 4:4
1 and fell in one day three and twenty **thousand.**.....1 Co 10:8
1 times ten thousand, and **thousands** of thousands;..... Rev 5:11
2 times ten thousand, and thousands of **thousands;**........ 5:11
1 sealed an hundred and forty and four **thousand**......... 7:4
1 Of the tribe of Juda were sealed twelve **thousand.**...... 7:5
1 tribe of Reuben were sealed twelve **thousand.**........... 7:5
1 Of the tribe of Gad were sealed twelve **thousand.**....... 7:5
1 Of the tribe of Aser were sealed twelve **thousand.**...... 7:6
1 tribe of Nephthalim were sealed twelve **thousand.**....... 7:6
1 tribe of Manasses were sealed twelve **thousand.**......... 7:6
1 tribe of Simeon were sealed twelve **thousand.**........... 7:7
1 Of the tribe of Levi were sealed twelve **thousand.**....... 7:7
1 tribe of Issachar were sealed twelve **thousand.**.......... 7:7
1 tribe of Zabulon were sealed twelve **thousand.**.......... 7:8
1 Of the tribe of Joseph were sealed twelve **thousand.**..... 7:8
1 tribe of Benjamin were sealed twelve **thousand.**......... 7:8
1 in the earthquake were slain ... seven **thousand:**....... 11:13
1 and with him an hundred forty and four **thousand,**..... 14:1
1 but the hundred and forty and four **thousand,**......... 14:3
2 he measured the city ... twelve **thousand** furlongs....... 21:16

The word *chilias* is a noun meaning "a (group of a) thousand." It is always plural in the New Testament; for example: "ten thousand" (Luke 14:31); "five thousand" (Acts 4:4); "twenty-three thousand" (1 Corinthians 10:8). The remaining 18 uses are in Revelation. Coupled with the appropriate prefixes it can come to mean 2,000; 3,000; 4,000. This is how it is found in the New Testament where *dischilioi* (1360) means 2,000 (Mark 5:13); *trischilioi* (4993) means 3,000 (Acts 2:41); *tetrakischilioi* (4919) means 4,000 (Matthew 15:38; 16:10; Mark 8:9,20; Acts 21:38).

Strong 5505, Bauer 882, Moulton-Milligan 688, Kittel 9:466-71, Liddell-Scott 1992, Colin Brown 2:697-700,703.

5343. χίλιοι chilioi num

One thousand.

Cross-Reference:

χιλιάς chilias (5342)

1. **χιλίων chiliōn** card gen masc/fem/neu
2. **χιλίας chilias** card acc fem
3. **χίλια chilia** card nom/acc neu

3 that one day is with the Lord as **a thousand** years,...2 Pt 3:8
3 and **a thousand** years as one day...................... 3:8
2 **a thousand** two hundred and threescore days,....... Rev 11:3
2 **a thousand** two hundred and threescore days.......... 12:6
1 the space of **a thousand** and six hundred furlongs...... 14:20
3 and Satan, and bound him **a thousand** years,.......... 20:2
3 till the **thousand** years should be fulfilled:............. 20:3
3 lived and reigned with Christ **a thousand** years......... 20:4
3 not again until the **thousand** years were finished....... 20:5
3 and shall reign with him **a thousand** years............. 20:6
3 And when the **thousand** years are expired,............. 20:7

Classical Greek and Septuagint Usage

This adjective can be found in classical Greek from the time of Homer (ca. Eighth Century B.C.) and means "a thousand." Herodotus used it of "a thousand" horses (*Liddell-Scott*). As a demonstration of his love for God, Solomon offered "a *thousand* burnt offerings" to the Lord (1 Kings 3:4 [LXX 3 Kings 3:4]).

New Testament Usage

In the New Testament Peter used *chilioi* to describe the timeless dimension of God where "one day is with the Lord as a *thousand* years, and a *thousand* years as one day" (2 Peter 3:8). In Revelation 11:3 the "two witnesses," empowered by God, will "prophesy a *thousand* two hundred and threescore days," the same length of time that God promised to sustain the "woman" in the "wilderness" (Revelation 12:6). *Chilioi* is also used in reference to the "*thousand* years" Satan will be bound while the redeemed reign with Christ (Revelation 20:2-7).

STRONG 5507, BAUER 882, KITTEL 9:466-71, LIDDELL-SCOTT 1992, COLIN BROWN 2:697,699-700,703-4.

5344. Χίος Chios name

Chios.

1. Χίου Chiou gen fem

1 and came the next day over against **Chios**;......... Acts 20:15

A Greek island in the eastern Aegean Sea. It was a port of call for Paul and his companions on his final journey to Jerusalem (Acts 20:15).

5345. χιτών chitōn noun

Tunic, inner garment.

SYNONYMS:
ἔνδυμα enduma (1726)
ἐσθής esthēs (2049B)
ἱμάτιον himation (2416)
ἱματισμός himatismos (2417)
σκέπασμα skepasma (4484)

בֶּגֶד beghedh (933), Garment, clothes (Ex 35:19, 1 Kgs 21:27 [20:27], Is 36:22).

כְּתֹנֶת kuttōneth (3930I), Robe, garment (Gn 37:31ff., 2 Sm 13:18, S/S 5:3).

מַד madh (4196), Garment (Lv 6:10).

מְעִיל m$^{e'}$îl (4752), Robe (Is 61:10).

1. χιτών chitōn nom sing masc
2. χιτῶνα chitōna acc sing masc
3. χιτῶνας chitōnas acc pl masc

2 sue thee ... and take away thy **coat**,................ Matt 5:40
3 Nor scrip for your journey, neither two **coats**,......... 10:10
3 be shod with sandals; and not put on two **coats**..... Mark 6:9
3 Then the high priest rent his **clothes**, and saith,........ 14:63
3 He that hath two **coats**, let him impart to him that.. Luke 3:11
2 taketh ... thy cloak forbid not to take thy **coat** also...... 6:29
3 neither money; neither have two **coats** apiece........... 9:3
2 took his garments, ... and also his **coat**:............ John 19:23
1 now the **coat** was without seam,...................... 19:23
3 the **coats** and garments which Dorcas made,......... Acts 9:39
2 hating even the **garment** spotted by the flesh........ Jude 1:23

The Greek word *chitōn* denotes a specialized article of clothing. Historically, Homer, the Septuagint, and the New Testament all generally refer to the *chitōn* as a man's tunic (*Liddell-Scott*). However, in the New Testament the word is used more specifically of an undergarment or inner shirt that was worn next to the skin.

In this regard *chitōn* (an inner garment) is to be distinguished from *phelones*—an all-purpose coat for comfort in inclement weather; *himation* (2416)—a robe-like outer garment thrown over the *chitōn* and often used to mean clothing, apparel, or raiment; *esthēs* (2049B)—an especially valuable garment described as "shining" and "white" in both Luke and John; and *stolē* (4600)—the long outer garment which probably indicated social standing as in the case of the priests and scribes.

In the New Testament Matthew 5:40 states, "If someone wants to sue you and take your tunic (*chitōn*), let him have your cloak (*himation*) as well" (NIV). It is interesting that in Luke 6:29 the order is reversed which is probably best explained from the contextual circumstances of each respective passage.

For instance, in Matthew 5:40 Christ was referring to a legal process in which the claimant legally was supposed to request the inner garment which was less costly. However, as an act of Christian grace the defendant was to be willing to relinquish the more valuable outer garment also. In contrast, in Luke 6:29 an affront of violence is implied with no reference to law. According to Vine, in this case the outer garment would be the first to be seized (*Expository Dictionary*, "Clothing").

In John 19:23 the soldiers participated in the crucifixion event by taking Christ's garments (the *himation* in the plural) and the coat or tunic (the *chitōn* or inner garment) which was without seam. The point is that the outer garments were easily divided into four parts, but because it had no seam the *chitōn* (inner garment) could not appropriately be divided by splitting and was thus put up for the casting of lots.

In Mark 14:63 the high priest tore his clothes (*chitōn*) when Jesus acknowledged that He was the Christ. Here there is the connotation of outrage and horror in that the priest rent his inner garments as an expression of deep indignation (see Fortune, "Rending of Clothes," *International Standard Bible Encyclopedia*, 1:725).

In Jude 23 the garment defiled by the flesh is the *chitōn*, and the word is appropriately applied in that the inner garment naturally is the closest to the body and metaphorically is "stained by corrupted flesh" (NIV). Thus the wickedness of men is so complete that even their garments are polluted by their sinful nature.

STRONG 5509, BAUER 882, MOULTON-MILLIGAN 688, LIDDELL-SCOTT 1993.

5346. χιών chiōn noun

Snow.

שֶׁלֶג shelegh (8345), Snow (Nm 12:10, Job 6:16, Jer 18:14).

תְּלַג t^elagh (A8846), Snow (Dn 7:9—Aramaic).

1. **χιών chiōn** nom sing fem

1 was like lightning, and his raiment white as **snow**:.. Matt 28:3
1 raiment became shining, exceeding white as **snow**;... Mark 9:3
1 his hairs were white like wool, as white as **snow**;..... Rev 1:14

Chiōn, "snow," occurs three times in the New Testament. In each case it is used metaphorically to describe the "whiteness" of something, e.g., the angel's raiment (Matthew 28:3), the Lord's hair (Revelation 1:14), and the Lord's raiment (Mark 9:3, some manuscripts).

STRONG 5510, BAUER 882, MOULTON-MILLIGAN 688, LIDDELL-SCOTT 1993, COLIN BROWN 3:1000,1004.

5347. χλαμύς chlamus noun

Cloak.

1. **χλαμύδα chlamuda** acc sing fem

1 they stripped him, and put on him a scarlet **robe**... Matt 27:28
1 they took the **robe** off from him,.................... 27:31

The word *chlamus* denotes "a cloak" or "vest-type garment" but is often translated "robe" (Matthew 27:28,31). It was commonly worn over an undergarment, the *chitōn* (5345), by rulers, officials, and military officers as a symbol of authority. In Matthew 27:28,31 Christ was dressed in the *chlamus* by Pilate's soldiers in mockery of His kingship. The color described in Mark and John as "purple" was an indefinite color and could just as easily have been called "scarlet" as it is in Matthew. It symbolized royal or magisterial rank.

STRONG 5511, BAUER 882, MOULTON-MILLIGAN 688-89, LIDDELL-SCOTT 1993.

5348. χλευάζω chleuazō verb

Make mockery of, ridicule.

1. **χλευάζοντες chleuazontes** nom pl masc part pres act
2. **ἐχλεύαζον echleuazon** 3pl indic imperf act

1 Others **mocking** said, ... men are full of new wine.... Acts 2:13
2 of the resurrection of the dead, some **mocked**:......... 17:32

Chleuazō, meaning "to mock" or "ridicule," is related to *chleuē*, "joke" or "jest." Its two New Testament occurrences describe the mocking of those who observed the phenomena on the Day of Pentecost (Acts 2:13) and the Athenian philosophers' response to Paul's testimony about the resurrection of the dead (Acts 17:32).

STRONG 5512, BAUER 882, MOULTON-MILLIGAN 689, LIDDELL-SCOTT 1994.

5349. χλιαρός chliaros adj

Lukewarm, tepid.

1. **χλιαρός chliaros** nom sing masc

1 thou art **lukewarm**, and neither cold nor hot,........ Rev 3:16

This word can be found in classical Greek from the Fifth Century B.C. meaning "warm." In its only New Testament occurrence (Revelation 3:16) *chliaros* metaphorically indicates the condition of the Laodicean church. They were only moderately committed to Christ.

STRONG 5513, BAUER 882, MOULTON-MILLIGAN 689, KITTEL 2:876-77, LIDDELL-SCOTT 1994, COLIN BROWN 1:317-19.

5350. Χλόη Chloē name

Chloe.

1. **Χλόης Chloēs** gen fem

1 by them which are of the house of **Chloe**,........... 1 Co 1:11

Quarrels among the Christians of Corinth were reported to Paul by "Chloe's people" (1 Corinthians 1:11, RSV), that is, members of her household. Her identity is otherwise unknown.

5351. χλωρός chlōros adj

Light green, yellow-green, pale.

חָצִיר chātsîr (2785), Grass (Prv 27:25).

יָרוֹק yārôq (3501), Something green (Job 39:8).

יָרָק yārāq (3536), Green herb (2 Kgs 19:26).

יֶרֶק yereq (3537), Green plant, grass (Gn 1:30, Nm 22:4, Is 15:6).

לָבָן lāvān (3968), White (Gn 30:37).

לַח lach (4026), Fresh, green (Gn 30:37, Ez 17:24, 20:47).

עֵשֶׂב 'ēsev (6448), Grass (Dt 29:23).

שִׂיחַ sîach (7944), Shrub (Gn 2:5).

1. χλωρός chlōros nom sing masc
2. χλωρῷ chlōrō dat sing masc
3. χλωρόν chlōron nom/acc sing neu

2 sit down by companies upon the green grass........ Mark 6:39
1 And I looked, and behold a pale horse:............. Rev 6:8
1 and all green grass was burnt up....................... 8:7
3 the grass of the earth, neither any green thing,......... 9:4

Chlōros denotes anything "pale, light green," or "yellowish." It is related to the Greek woman's name *Chōlē* (5350) meaning "tender" (1 Corinthians 1:11).

Classical Greek and Septuagint Usage
Classical Greek and later literature use *chlōros* in the literal sense of "light green" with reference to plants. It can be used adjectivally for "fresh" branches, sticks, and vegetation or the countenance of an ill person (e.g., of Sappho's "pale" appearance in death [*Liddell-Scott*]). *Chlōros* can also be used to describe a number of things that are green or yellow, e.g., sand, a yolk, the sea, etc. (ibid.). The Septuagint uses *chlōros* to refer to vegetation in the pre-Flood era. Before the Flood the "plant" was in the field (Genesis 2:5). (See *Bauer*.)

New Testament Usage
The New Testament usage of *chlōros* is similar to classical and Septuagint meanings. Mark 6:39 uses *chlōros* with reference to the "green" grass in Palestine. Furthermore, Revelation 8:7 and 9:4 use *chlōros* to denote the judgments upon the "green" grass in the entire earth.

The New Testament also uses *chlōros* adjectivally. The "pale" (yellowish or jaundiced) horse (Revelation 6:8) whose rider is "Death" denotes fatal illness resulting from divine judgment. According to Mounce, "It is the color of a corpse . . . the pallor of death . . . the blanched appearance of a person struck with terror" (see *New International Commentary on the New Testament, Revelation*, p.156).

STRONG 5515, BAUER 882, MOULTON-MILLIGAN 689, LIDDELL-SCOTT 1995.

5352. χξς' chxw' num
Six hundred-sixty-six.

1. χξς' chxw' card

1 and his number is Six hundred threescore and six.... Rev 13:18

Chxw, appearing only once in the New Testament (Revelation 13:18), is an abbreviated form of the combined words *hexakosioi* (1796), "600," *hexēkonta* (1818), "60," and *hex* (1787), "6." Greeks and Hebrews both employed letters of the alphabet as numbers, e.g., *a*=1; *b*=2; *g*=3, etc. In this case *ch*=600; *x*=60, and *w* (digamma, a letter obsolete in writing by this time) = 6; hence, the translation "666."

Biblical scholars agree how *chxw* should be translated, but they debate how it should be understood. The issue is further clouded by the existence of a variant reading which yields the number *616* (Codex C). Cullman believes that this number may have been original (*The State in the New Testament*, p.80; Barclay, however, adamantly disagrees; see "Great Themes of the New Testament," p.295). The number of a triangle in Pythagorean language is 616. Ford notes that the number may have been changed in the time of Irenaeus (late Second Century A.D.) to conform it to Marcus Aurelius (A.D. 156–180) whose name adds up to 666 (*The Anchor Bible*, 38:216).

Interpretations of this number generally fall into two categories. First, some scholars interpret 666 figuratively or symbolically. They teach that the Old Testament presents *six* as the number of man and of incompleteness. Man was created on the sixth day (Genesis 1:26ff.), but God completed His work by the seventh day (Genesis 2:3). Thus, 666 is the number which "falls short of perfection in each of its digits" (Mounce, *New International Commentary on the New Testament, Revelation*, p.265). According to some the number *666* points to a trinity of evil. "This evil trinity 666 apes the Holy Trinity 777, but always falls short and fails" (Torrance, *The Apocalypse Today*, p.105). Others base their interpretation on the number *8*, which they refer to as the number of the devil. By adding the numbers *1* to *8*, one gets 36; by adding the numbers *1* to *36* one gets 666 (see Cullman, *The State in the New Testament*, p.81; Rühle, "arithmeō," *Kittel*, 1:464).

Second, some scholars understand 666 as a use of gematria (adding the numerical equivalents of the letters of a name to produce a secret number). According to Mounce, "Gematria was widely used in apocalyptic (literature) because of its symbolic and enigmatic quality. It served as a precaution against the charge of sedition" (*New International Commentary on the New Testament, Revelation*, p.264). An example of gematria can be found in the *Sibylline Oracles* 1:344ff. In this passage the name of Jesus (*Iēsous*) is made to equal 888. (For other examples of gematria in Jewish literature see *Encyclopedia Judaica*, "Gematria," 7:370-372; cf. Sibylline Oracles 1:137-146; and Barclay, "Great Themes of the New Testament"; and *The Epistle of Barnabas* 9.7.8).

Gematria was also used in popular writings and in religion. Greek gods were given secret numbers based on the total of the letters of their names. One graffitto found in Pompeii reads: "I love her whose name is 545" (Deissmann, *Light from the Ancient East*, p.277). Thus, some identify 666 with a notable persecutor of the church—"a Jesus in heretical disguise" (*Bauer*), Domitian, Trajan, or even Nero. When all totaled, more than 100 interpretations emerge within the historical school alone (Thompson, "Antichrist," *International Standard Bible Encyclopedia*, 1:139ff.). However interpreted, the Book of Revelation says that the "beast" (described throughout chapter 13) will require everyone, "small and great, rich and poor, free and slave, to receive a mark on his right hand or on his forehead" (13:16, NIV). Unless they have this mark, they will not be allowed to buy or sell (verse 17).

STRONG 5516, BAUER 882-83.

5353. χοϊκός choikos adj

Earthy, earthborn, made of soil or dust.

CROSS-REFERENCE:

χοῦς chous (5365)

1. **χοϊκός choikos** nom sing masc
2. **χοϊκοῦ choikou** gen sing masc
3. **χοϊκοί choikoi** nom pl masc

1 The first man is of the earth, **earthy:** .... 1 Co 15:47
1 As is the **earthy**, such are they also that are earthy: ... 15:48
3 As is the earthy, such are they also that are **earthy:** 15:48
2 And as we have borne the image of the **earthy**, ... 15:49

Occurring only three times in the New Testament, *choikos* means "earthy, earthborn." The term may have been coined by Paul (Schweizer, "choikos," *Kittel*, 9:472). In 1 Corinthians 15:47-49 Paul called Adam, the first man, *choikos* on the basis of Genesis 2:7. According to Schweizer, Paul is contrasting the first man, Adam, with the second man "from heaven, Christ . . . Each man founds a race of men, earthly on the one side and heavenly on the other" (ibid., 9:477f.). According to Fee (*New International Commentary on the New Testament, 1 Corinthians*, p.791-795), the emphasis in these verses is not on Christ's incarnation but on His resurrection. The first man was of the earth and made of dust (*choikos*); the second man was of heaven, i.e., His life is "heavenly." In the present life the believer, like Adam, retains an earthly body; at the resurrection he, like Christ, will assume a heavenly body. In the present life the believer must not try to assume a heavenly body but, rather, should seek to conform his life to the behavior and character of the man of heaven, Jesus Christ (verse 49).

STRONG 5517, BAUER 883, MOULTON-MILLIGAN 689, KITTEL 9:472-79, LIDDELL-SCOTT 1996, COLIN BROWN 1:520.

5354. χοῖνιξ choinix noun

One quart.

SYNONYMS:

κόρος koros (2857)
μέτρον metron (3228)
σάτον saton (4424)

1. **χοῖνιξ choinix** nom sing fem
2. **χοίνικες choinikes** nom pl fem

1 A **measure** of wheat for a penny, ... Rev 6:6
2 and three **measures** of barley for a penny; 6:6

Homer, inscriptions, and the papyri use *choinix* to indicate approximately "one quart" of dry goods especially. The writings of Herodotus (Fifth Century B.C.) indicate *choinix* as an acceptable daily allowance of corn for one man serving in Xerxes' army (cf. *Liddell-Scott*). (See *Bauer*.) Revelation 6:6 (NIV) indicates this small amount of grain as being worth "a day's wages" (*denarios*) in the Tribulation period. This, then, points to both the lack of food and the costliness of daily sustenance during that period of time.

STRONG 5518, BAUER 883, MOULTON-MILLIGAN 689, LIDDELL-SCOTT 1996.

5355. χοῖρος choiros noun

Swine, young pig.

1. **χοῖροι choiroi** nom pl masc
2. **χοίρων choirōn** gen pl masc
3. **χοίρους choirous** acc pl masc

2 neither cast ye your pearls before **swine**, ... Matt 7:6
2 an herd of many **swine** feeding. 8:30
2 suffer us to go away into the herd of **swine**. 8:31

2 they went into the herd of swine:.................. Matt 8:32
2 the whole herd of swine ran violently down............ 8:32
2 unto the mountains a great herd of swine feeding....Mark 5:11
3 Send us into the swine, that we may enter.............. 5:12
3 and entered into the swine:............................ 5:13
3 And they that fed the swine fled,...................... 5:14
2 and also concerning the swine.......................... 5:16
2 And there was there an herd of many swine........ Luke 8:32
3 devils out of the man, and entered into the swine:...... 8:33
3 and he sent him into his fields to feed swine........... 15:15
1 filled ... belly with the husks that the swine did eat:... 15:16

Occurring 14 times in the New Testament, in the Synoptic Gospels only, *choiros* can be translated "swine"—a meaning also found in Josephus (First Century A.D.) and Plutarch (First and Second Centuries A.D.; cf. *Bauer*).

"Swine" were detestable creatures being classified with the dog (cf. Luke 8:32ff.; 15:15). They were considered unclean according to the laws of purification (Leviticus 11:7). As well, the ancient Canaanites sacrificed and ate them before the gods (Redditt, "Swine," *International Standard Bible Encyclopedia*, 4:673). Despite their being a popular sacrificial animal among the Greeks at special events, the Old Testament paints them as destructive, undesirable creatures (Psalm 80:13; Proverbs 11:22).

The New Testament references to "swine" reflect the Jewish idea that swine were "unclean." Swine were considered to be worthless by the Jews and an appropriate place for demons to reside once they had been cast out of humans (Matthew 8:32; Mark 5:11-16; Luke 8:32f.). In Matthew 7:6 Jesus may have been quoting a popular proverb concerning discrimination when He said, "Do not throw your pearls to *pigs*" (NIV; cf. Proverbs 9:7-9).

Strong 5519, Bauer 883, Moulton-Milligan 689, Liddell-Scott 1996, Colin Brown 1:117.

5356. χολάω cholaō verb

Be angry.

Synonyms:

θυμόω thumoō (2350)
ὀργίζομαι orgizomai (3573)
παροξύνω paroxunō (3809)

1. χολᾶτε cholate 2pl indic pres act

1 Moses should not be broken; are ye angry at me,... John 7:23

Occurring only once in the New Testament the Greek verb *cholaō* is related to the noun *cholē* (5357), "gall, bile," and means "to be full of black bile, to be melancholy mad" (*Liddell-Scott*). *Cholaō* is not found in the Septuagint, but a related form, *choloomai*, "to be angry, rage," is used in 3 Maccabees 3:1. John 7:23 uses *cholaō* where it describes how Jesus was asking His hearers why they should be "angry" at Him for His conduct on the Sabbath (John 7:23).

Strong 5520, Bauer 883, Moulton-Milligan 689, Liddell-Scott 1996.

5357. χολή cholē noun

Gall.

Synonym:

ἄψινθος apsinthos (887)

לַעֲנָה laʿănāh (4081), Wormwood (Prv 5:4, Lam 3:15).

מְרֵרָה m^e^rērāh (5008), Gall (Job 16:13 [16:14]).

מְרֹרָה m^e^rōrāh (5009), Venom (Job 20:14).

רֹאשׁ rō'sh (7514), Poison, gall (Dt 32:32, Ps 69:21 [68:21], Jer 8:14).

1. χολῆς cholēs gen sing fem

2. χολήν cholēn acc sing fem

1 They gave him vinegar to drink mingled with gall: Matt 27:34
2 I perceive that thou art in the gall of bitterness,..... Acts 8:23

Classical Greek

Cholē can be found in classical Greek from the Eighth Century B.C. meaning "gall, bile." Metaphorically it had the meaning of "giving one a disgust for a thing." For example, it was the custom of mothers to put gall on their nipples in order to wean a child (*Liddell-Scott*).

Septuagint Usage

The Septuagint uses *cholē* to translate the Hebrew word *rō'sh*, "head." In some instances where *cholē* translates *rō'sh* the NIV translates it as "poison" or "poisonous" (see Deuteronomy 29:18; 32:32; Jeremiah 8:14; 9:15). *Cholē* is also used to translate two additional Hebrew words: *laʿănāh*, which literally means "wormwood" but figuratively means "bitterness," and *m^e^rōrāh* which means "bitter things, gall," or "poison."

New Testament Usage

In the New Testament *cholē* appears twice, once literally and once metaphorically. In Matthew 27:34 Christ was offered "vinegar . . . mingled with *gall*." It was customary to mix wine with *cholē* to form a sedative. This opium mixed with wine caused a deep sleep, a sustained state of unconsciousness. The recipient became oblivious to his surroundings, and his pain was quickly numbed. (See Leedy, "Plants," *Zondervan's Pictorial Bible Dictionary*, p.663.) Christ refused this sedative so He might fully "taste death for every man" (Hebrews 2:9).

Cholē is also used metaphorically in Acts 8:23 to describe Simon the sorcerer's life. He possessed a sinful and intoxicating attitude toward God that was dreadfully distasteful (Acts 8:23; cf. 8:21).

Strong 5521, Bauer 883, Moulton-Milligan 689, Liddell-Scott 1997, Colin Brown 2:27-28.

5358. Χοραζίν Chorazin name

Chorazin.

1. Χωραζίν Chōrazin fem
2. Χοραζίν Chorazin fem

2 Woe unto thee, Chorazin! ... unto thee, Bethsaida! Matt 11:21
1 Woe unto thee, Chorazin! ... unto thee, Bethsaida! Luke 10:13

A city of Galilee condemned by Jesus for its failure to repent in response to His miraculous ministry (Matthew 11:21; Luke 10:13). It no longer exists.

5359. χορηγέω chorēgeō verb

Lavishly supply for, provide for, totally underwrite.

Cognates:
ἐπιχορηγέω epichorēgeō (2007)
ἐπιχορηγία epichorēgia (2008)

Synonyms:
ἐπιχορηγέω epichorēgeō (2007)
προστίθημι prostithēmi (4227)

זוּן zûn (2191), Hithpeel: feed on (Dn 4:12 [4:9]—Aramaic).

כּוּל kûl (3677), Pilpel: provide (1 Kgs 4:7,27).

1. χορηγεῖ chorēgei 3sing indic pres act
2. χορηγήσαι chorēgēsai 3sing opt aor act
3. χορηγήσει chorēgēsei 3sing indic fut act

2 both minister bread for your food,................. 2 Co 9:10
1 let him do it as of the ability which God giveth:..... 1 Pt 4:11

Classical Greek and Septuagint Usage

This term can be found in classical Greek meaning "to lead a chorus." Metaphorically it can mean "to minister to, furnish abundantly with" (*Liddell-Scott*). *Chorēgeō* means "to lead a chorus." In Athenian drama wealthy men in the community would be chosen to administrate the production of plays. This man, the *chorēgos*, was responsible for all the costs involved: clothing, props, trainers, etc. Often the *chorēgos* would spend a fortune to produce the play which would win the prize. From the role of the *chorēgos* as the provider of the needs for production, *chorēgeō* developed the metaphoric meanings "to supply, to furnish, to minister." (For further information see Durant, *The Story of Civilization, The Life of Greece*, pp.377-383; Parke, *Festivals of the Athenians*, pp.125-136.) *Chorēgeō* is also used in the Septuagint meaning "furnish, supply." For example, Solomon's 12 governors "provided" food for the king's household (1 Kings 4:7 [LXX 3 Kings 4:7]).

New Testament Usage

The New Testament uses the term only twice. First Peter 4:11 states that Christians should minister according to the "ability which God provides." God is both the supplier and source of all ministry. In 2 Corinthians 9:10 the cheerful giver is promised that God will "abundantly provide" him with seed (resources, RSV).

Strong 5524, Bauer 883, Moulton-Milligan 689-90, Liddell-Scott 1998.

5360. χορός choros noun

Dancing, company of dancers, chorus, troop, dance.

הִלּוּלִים hillûlîm (2043), Festival (Jgs 9:27—Codex Alexandrinus only).

חֶבֶל chevel (2346), Group (1 Sm 10:5,10).

מָחוֹל māchôl (4369), Dancing (Pss 149:3, 150:4, Lam 5:15).

מְחֹלָה m^echōlāh (4383), Dancing (Ex 15:20, Jgs 11:34, S/S 6:13 [7:1]).

1. χορῶν chorōn gen pl masc

1 nigh to the house, he heard music and dancing..... Luke 15:25

Classical Greek

Choros can be found in classical Greek from the Eighth Century B.C. meaning "dance." It is usually used of corporate dance such as that done by a group in a public religious ceremony (*Liddell-Scott*). *Choros* is also used for a "troop or band of dancers" or even a "place for dancing" (ibid.).

Septuagint Usage

In the Septuagint *choros* usually translates the Hebrew terms *māchôl* and *m^echōlāh*, "circle-dance," both derivatives of *chûl*, "dance." Usually the "dance" mentioned in the Old Testament involved a procession that expressed praise of God; for example, dancing preceded men returning from some victory (Exodus 15:20; Judges 11:34). Dancing for reasons other than religious celebrations was not commonly practiced among the Jews as it was by the Greeks and Egyptians (Johnston, "Dance," *International Standard Bible Encyclopedia*, 1:857f.). Dancing for after-dinner entertainment, including participation of scantily clad professional dancers, was considered appropriate for idolatrous celebrations. This type of dancing was contrasted with David's legitimate celebration of the return of the ark of the covenant (2 Samuel 6:12-19; cf. ibid.).

New Testament Usage

Choros occurs only once in the New Testament. In the Parable of the Lost Son Jesus told of how there was "music and *dancing*" at his return home (Luke 15:25). This was *not* the same dancing seductively performed by Salome (Matthew 14:6) but was a public expression of deep joy; it has much more in common with David's dance before the ark.

STRONG 5525, BAUER 883, MOULTON-MILLIGAN 690, LIDDELL-SCOTT 1999.

5361. χορτάζω chortazō verb

Satisfy, satiate hunger, fill.

COGNATE:
χόρτος chortos (5363)

SYNONYMS:
βόσκω boskō (999)
ἐκτρέφω ektrephō (1611)
τρέφω trephō (4982)
ψωμίζω psōmizō (5430)

שָׂבֵעַ sāvēaʿ (7881), Qal: be satisfied, be filled (Pss 17:15 [16:15], 104:13 [103:13], Lam 3:30); hiphil: satisfy, feed (Job 38:27, Ps 81:16 [80:16], Jer 5:7).

1. **χορτάσαι chortasai** inf aor act
2. **χορτάζεσθε chortazesthe** 2pl impr pres mid
3. **χορτάζεσθαι chortazesthai** inf pres mid
4. **ἐχορτάσθητε echortasthēte** 2pl indic aor pass
5. **ἐχορτάσθησαν echortasthēsan** 3pl indic aor pass
6. **χορτασθῆναι chortasthēnai** inf aor pass
7. **χορτασθήσεσθε chortasthēsesthe** 2pl indic fut pass
8. **χορτασθήσονται chortasthēsontai** 3pl indic fut pass

8 thirst after righteousness: for they **shall be filled**..... Matt 5:6
5 And they did all eat, and were **filled**:................. 14:20
1 so much bread ... as to **fill** so great a multitude?....... 15:33
5 And they did all eat, and were **filled**:................. 15:37
5 And they did all eat, and were **filled**............... Mark 6:42
6 Let the children first **be filled**:......................... 7:27
1 From whence can a man **satisfy** these men............ 8:4
5 So they did eat, and **were filled**:...................... 8:8
7 ye that hunger now: for ye **shall be filled**........... Luke 6:21
5 And they did eat, and were all **filled**:.................. 9:17
6 And desiring **to be fed** with the crumbs which fell...... 16:21
4 because ye did eat of the loaves, and **were filled**..... John 6:26
3 I am instructed both **to be full** and to be hungry,.... Phlp 4:12
2 Depart in peace, be ye warmed and **filled**;........... Jas 2:16
5 and all the fowls **were filled** with their flesh......... Rev 19:21

Classical Greek

In classical Greek literature *chortazō* can be found in reference to feeding or fattening animals (cf. *Liddell-Scott*). When referring to men it was used both literally and figuratively. When used literally it is often synonymous with *esthiō* (2052), "to eat." Figuratively it can mean "satisfied" as with grief (ibid.).

Septuagint Usage

In the Septuagint *chortazō* occurs 14 times, 9 of which are in the Psalms. The Psalmist used it only in reference to man with two exceptions: Psalm 104:13 (LXX 103:13) says the earth is "satisfied," and 104:16 (103:16) refers to a tree being "full." One other time *chortazō* uses the earth or land as its object ("*satisfy* the desolate and waste ground"; Job 38:27). The other references have to do with man (Lamentations 3:15,30 is metaphoric, and Psalms 37:19 [LXX 36:19] and 59:15 [58:15] are literal).

New Testament Usage

In the New Testament it occurs both literally and figuratively and is used with reference to people and animals. Fourteen times it refers to people, 12 times in the Gospels. Matthew 5:6 is the only figurative usage: "Blessed are they which do hunger and thirst after righteousness: for they shall be *filled*" (see Mark 7:27).

Only in Revelation 19:21 are animals the subject: fowls will be "filled" with the flesh of the slain.

STRONG 5526, BAUER 883-84, MOULTON-MILLIGAN 690, LIDDELL-SCOTT 1999-2000, COLIN BROWN 1:743-44.

5362. χόρτασμα chortasma noun

Food, staples, grain, fodder.

CROSS-REFERENCE:
χόρτος chortos (5363)

מִסְפּוֹא mispôʾ (4706), Provender, fodder (Gn 24:32, 42:27, Jgs 19:19).

עֵשֶׂב ʿēsev (6448), Grass (Dt 11:15).

1. **χορτάσματα chortasmata** nom/acc pl neu

1 and our fathers found no **sustenance**............... Acts 7:11

Chortasma can be found in classical Greek denoting "fodder, forage" for cattle or "food" for men (cf. *Liddell-Scott*). In the Septuagint *chortasma* is usually used in reference to "food" for domesticated animals such as camels (Genesis 24:32), cattle (Deuteronomy 11:15), and donkeys (Judges 19:19).

Chortasma occurs only once in the New Testament, at Acts 7:11. When Stephen defended himself before the high priest, he referred to the time of famine when his forefathers "found no *sustenance.*" This "food" could have referred to that eaten by both man and animals, for example, "corn" (cf. Acts 7:12).

STRONG 5527, BAUER 884, MOULTON-MILLIGAN 690, LIDDELL-SCOTT 2000, COLIN BROWN 1:743-44.

5363. χόρτος chortos noun

Grass, hay, fodder.

COGNATES:
χορτάζω chortazō (5361)
χόρτασμα chortasma (5362)

SYNONYM:
βοτάνη botanē (1001)

דֶּשֶׁא deshe' (1940), Tender grass (Is 15:6).

חָצִיר chātsîr (2785), Grass (Job 40:15 [40:10], Ps 103:15 [102:15], Is 44:4).

עֲשַׂב 'ăsav (A6447), Grass (Dn 4:15,32f. [4:12,29f.]—Aramaic).

עֵשֶׂב 'ēsev (6448), Vegetation, new growth (Gn 1:11f., Prv 27:25).

קַשׁ qash (7475), Chaff, stubble (Job 13:25, 41:28 [41:19]).

1. **χόρτος chortos** nom sing masc
2. **χόρτου chortou** gen sing masc
3. **χόρτῳ chortō** dat sing masc
4. **χόρτον chorton** acc sing masc
5. **χόρτους chortous** acc pl masc

4 Wherefore, if God so clothe the **grass** of the field,.. Matt 6:30
1 But when the **blade** was sprung up,.................... 13:26
5 commanded the multitude to sit down on the **grass**,.... 14:19
4 first the **blade**, then the ear, after that the full corn Mark 4:28
3 sit down by companies upon the green **grass**............ 6:39
4 If then God so clothe the **grass**, which is to day... Luke 12:28
1 Now there was much **grass** in the place............ John 6:10
4 gold, silver, precious stones, wood, **hay**, stubble;.... 1 Co 3:12
2 as the flower of the **grass** he shall pass away......... Jas 1:10
4 withereth the **grass**, and the flower thereof falleth,...... 1:11
1 For all flesh is as **grass**,...........................1 Pt 1:24
2 and all the glory of man as the flower of **grass**.......... 1:24
1 The **grass** withereth,................................ 1:24
1 and all green **grass** was burnt up.................... Rev 8:7
4 that they should not hurt the **grass** of the earth,........ 9:4

Occurring 15 times in the New Testament, *chortos* can indicate "grass" in the fields (Matthew 14:19) or grain in a stage of grasslike development, i.e., "the stalk" (Matthew 13:26; Mark 4:28). It also refers to "grass" that is uncultivated (Matthew 6:30; Luke 12:28; 1 Corinthians 3:12).

Grass can be the scene of Christ's miracles (Matthew 14:19; John 6:10), the object in His parables (Mark 4:28), and the victim of God's judgment (Revelation 8:7; 9:4). Man's lifetime is as comparatively short as the blade's duration (James 1:10,11; 1 Peter 1:24) but always the object of God's provision (Luke 12:28).

STRONG 5528, BAUER 884, MOULTON-MILLIGAN 690, LIDDELL-SCOTT 2000, COLIN BROWN 1:743-44; 2:210-11.

5364. Χουζᾶς Chouzas name

Chuza.

1. **Χουζᾶ Chouza** gen masc

1 And Joanna the wife of **Chuza** Herod's steward,..... Luke 8:3

The manager of Herod Antipas' household and husband of Joanna who is named at Luke 8:3 as a follower of Jesus.

5365. χοῦς chous noun

Dust, dirt.

COGNATE:
χοϊκός choikos (5353)

SYNONYM:
γῆ gē (1087)

מָעָה mā'āh (4732), Grain of sand (Is 48:19).

מֹץ mōts (4833), Chaff (Is 41:15—Codex Alexandrinus only).

עָפָר 'āphār (6312), Plaster (Lv 14:41f.); powder, dust (2 Kgs 23:6, Mi 7:17).

1. **χοῦν choun** acc sing masc

1 shake off the **dust** under your feet for a testimony.. Mark 6:11
1 they cast **dust** on their heads, and cried,............Rev 18:19

Classical Greek and Septuagint Usage

In classical Greek *chous* can be found from the Eighth Century B.C. referring to a measure of capacity or meaning "soil excavated or heaped up" (cf. *Liddell-Scott*). Both uses are related to *cheō*, "pour out, shed, scatter." The Septuagint uses *chous* in speaking of the "dust" of the road (Isaiah 49:23).

New Testament Usage

In Mark 6:11 (cf. Isaiah 52:2) "to shake off the dust" from one's feet implies both total displeasure and rejection of those who were spiritually defiled and a clear relinquishment of personal responsibility for their coming judgment.

Chous is used in Revelation 18:19 in reference to acts of mourning over the destruction of Babylon: "And they cast *dust* on their heads, and cried, weeping and wailing." It was a common cultural practice for the heartbroken to bury their faces in the dirt or pour dust on their heads as a public expression of their contrition over death, sin, or loss (cf. Joshua 7:6; Lamentations 2:10).

Strong 5522, Bauer 884, Moulton-Milligan 690, Liddell-Scott 2000, Colin Brown 1:520.

5366. χράομαι chraomai verb

Use, employ; act, behave.

Cognates:

ἀπόχρησις apochrēsis (665)
ἀχρειόω achreioō (882)
καταχράομαι katachraomai (2679)
παραχρῆμα parachrēma (3777)
συγχράομαι sunchraomai (4649)
χρῆμα chrēma (5371)
χρηματίζω chrēmatizō (5372)
χρήσιμος chrēsimos (5374)
χρῆσις chrēsis (5375)
χρηστεύομαι chrēsteuomai (5376)

אָדוֹן 'ādhôn (112), Master (Prv 25:13).

בַּעַל ba'al (1196), Owner (Prv 17:8).

עָשָׂה 'āsāh (6449), Do, deal with (Gn 19:8, Est 3:11, Dn 1:13).

צָלֵחַ tsālēach (7014), Be useful (Jer 13:7).

שָׁאַל shā'al (8068), Qal; ask (1 Sm 2:20); hiphil: give what one asks for (Ex 12:36).

1. **χρώμεθα chrōmetha** 1pl indic pres mid
2. **χρῆται chrētai** 3sing subj pres mid
3. **χρῶ chrō** 2sing impr pres mid
4. **χρώμενοι chrōmenoi** nom pl masc part pres mid
5. **ἐχρησάμην echrēsamēn** 1sing indic aor mid
6. **ἐχρησάμεθα echrēsametha** 1pl indic aor mid
7. **χρήσωμαι chrēsōmai** 1sing subj aor mid
8. **χρῆσαι chrēsai** 2sing impr aor mid
9. **χρησάμενος chrēsamenos** nom sing masc part aor mid
10. **ἐχρῶντο echrōnto** 3pl indic imperf mid
11. **κέχρημαι kechrēmai** 1sing indic perf mid

9 And Julius courteously entreated Paul,............Acts 27:3
10 Which when they had taken up, they used helps,..... 27:17
8 but if thou mayest be made free, use it rather......1 Co 7:21
4 And they that use this world, as not abusing it:....... 7:31
6 we have not used this power; but suffer all things,..... 9:12
5 But I have used none of these things:................. 9:15
5 I therefore was thus minded, did I use lightness?...2 Co 1:17
1 we use great plainness of speech:..................... 3:12
7 lest being present I should use sharpness,............ 13:10
2 know that the law is good, if a man use it lawfully; 1 Tm 1:8
3 but use a little wine for thy stomach's sake............ 5:23

Chraomai occurs most commonly with the dative but occasionally with the accusative; in either case it means "to use" or "to employ." With the dative of characteristic or with an adverb, *chraomai* also means "to act" or "to proceed." With the dative of person it means "to treat" someone in a certain way.

Classical Greek

In classical Greek the verb *chraomai* occurs from Homer (Eighth Century B.C.) on in the sense of "use, employ." It also appears in the fifth-century B.C. writings of Herodotus where it means "act, proceed." The use of *chraomai* meaning "to treat" is not attested until the early Hellenistic period (Third Century B.C.).

Septuagint Usage

The word *chraomai* is rather rare in the Septuagint, but it appears with its full scope of meanings. Thus, "instruction is to them that *use* it a gracious reward" (Proverbs 17:8 [Septuagint only]). Isaiah 28:21 says the Lord's wrath "shall *act* strangely" (author's translation); according to Esther 2:9 King Xerxes "*treated* her (Esther) well" (author's translation; cf. also Genesis 12:16).

New Testament Usage

In the New Testament *chraomai* occurs in the Pauline epistles (four in 1 Corinthians; three in 2 Corinthians; two in 1 Timothy) and twice in Acts (27:3,17). In all four instances in 1 Corinthians the verb has the primary meaning "to use." As an eschatological people, the married who "use" the things of the world must not misuse them (7:31). For the sake of the gospel Paul did not "make use of" the rights pertaining to his ministry (9:12,15). In 1 Corinthians 7:21 the phrase *mallon chrēsai* (literally, "to make the most of") lacks an explicit object; in the context, however, Paul likely had a slave's freedom in mind, as reflected in most translations. In 2 Corinthians 1:17 Paul asked, "Did I *use* lightness?" in reference to the clarity of his purpose for coming. And in Acts 27:3 Luke mentioned how the centurion Julius "entreated" Paul and gave him certain liberties even though he was a prisoner.

Strong 5530, Bauer 884, Moulton-Milligan 690, Liddell-Scott 2001-2.

5367. χρεία chreia noun

Need, necessity, lack; duty, task.

Cognates:

χρή chrē (5369)
χρήζω chrēzō (5370)

חַשְׁחָה chashchāh (A2928), Need (Ezr 7:20—Aramaic).

צֹרֶךְ tsōrekh (7163), What is needed (2 Chr 2:16).

1. **χρείας chreias** gen/acc sing/pl fem
2. **χρεία chreia** nom sing fem
3. **χρείαν chreian** acc sing fem
4. **χρείαις chreiais** dat pl fem

3 I have need to be baptized of thee,.................Matt 3:14
3 your Father knoweth what things ye have need of,...... 6:8
3 They that be whole need not a physician,............. 9:12
3 They need not depart; give ye them to eat............ 14:16

3 ye shall say, The Lord hath **need** of them;......... Matt 21:3
3 what further **need** have we of witnesses?............. 26:65
3 They that are whole have no **need** of the physician, Mark 2:17
3 when he had **need,** and was an hungred,............... 2:25
3 say ye that the Lord hath **need** of him;............... 11:3
3 and saith, What **need** we any further witnesses?....... 14:63
3 They that are whole **need** not a physician;.......... Luke 5:31
3 and healed them that had **need** of healing............. 9:11
2 But one thing is **needful:**............................. 10:42
3 ninety and nine just ... which **need** no repentance...... 15:7
3 Because the Lord hath **need** of him................... 19:31
3 And they said, The Lord hath **need** of him............ 19:34
3 And they said, What **need** we any further witness?..... 22:71
3 And **needed** not that any should testify of man:..... John 2:25
3 He that is washed **needeth** not save to wash his feet,... 13:10
3 Buy those things that we have **need** of................ 13:29
3 and **needest** not that any man should ask thee:........ 16:30
3 parted them to all men, as every man had **need**...... Acts 2:45
3 unto every man according as he had **need**............... 4:35
1 whom we may appoint over this **business**............... 6:3
4 these hands have ministered unto my **necessities,**...... 20:34
3 they laded us with such things as were **necessary**....... 28:10
4 Distributing to the **necessity** of saints;............ Rom 12:13
3 cannot say unto the hand, I have no **need** of thee: 1 Co 12:21
3 again the head to the feet, I have no **need** of you...... 12:21
3 For our comely parts have no **need:**.................... 12:24
3 that he may have to give to him that **needeth**........ Eph 4:28
1 but that which is good to the **use** of edifying,........... 4:29
1 and he that ministered to my **wants**................. Phlp 2:25
3 ye sent once and again unto my **necessity**............... 4:16
3 But my God shall supply all your **need**................. 4:19
3 so that we **need** not to speak any thing............ 1 Th 1:8
3 ye **need** not that I write unto you:..................... 4:9
3 and that ye may have **lack** of nothing.................. 4:12
3 ye have no **need** that I write unto you................. 5:1
1 learn to maintain good works for necessary **uses,**..... Tit 3:14
3 ye have **need** that one teach you again............. Heb 5:12
3 and are become such as have **need** of milk,.............. 5:12
2 what further **need** was there that another priest......... 7:11
3 For ye have **need** of patience,......................... 10:36
3 and ye **need** not that any man teach you:........... 1 Jn 2:27
3 and seeth his brother have **need,**....................... 3:17
3 increased with goods, and have **need** of nothing;..... Rev 3:17
3 And the city had no **need** of the sun,................. 21:23
3 shall be no night there; and they **need** no candle,...... 22:5

Classical Greek

The common meaning of the noun *chreia* is "need, lack, necessity," while "service, office, duty," or "business" are derived concepts. These meanings are attested as early as in the tragic writers of the classical Greek era (e.g., in Aeschylus' *Prometheus,* "will have need of my help") and the derived sense appears in Aristotle's *Politics,* i.e., "the *business* of war and peace" (Lane, "Want," *Colin Brown,* 3:956).

Septuagint Usage

In the Septuagint the noun *chreia* occurs infrequently. The fundamental meaning of need is reflected in 2 Chronicles 2:16, for instance, where Hiram, king of Tyre, assures Solomon of supplying him with all the logs of Lebanon he needed. According to Isaiah 13:17 the Medes have no need of (i.e., do not care for) silver. The derived meaning of *chreia* ("duty, service") is used amply in the apocryphal books (cf. Sirach 35:2 [LXX 32:2]; 1 Maccabees 10:42; 2 Maccabees 8:9).

New Testament Usage

Chreia is used about 50 times in the New Testament; it occurs with the meaning of "need" in the absolute sense, e.g., "seeth his brother have *need*" (1 John 3:17) or "for you say . . . I *need* nothing" (Revelation 3:17, RSV). In the plural *chreia* denotes "needs" or "necessities," as in the exhortation to believers to be contributing to the needs of the saints (Romans 12:13). The noun also occurs frequently with the verb *echō* (2174), "to have," meaning "to be in need of something." Thus "those who are well have no *need* of a physician, but those who are sick" (Luke 5:31, RSV). Speaking of the individual believers in the Corinthian church, Paul argued illustratively that no member of the body of Christ can say of any other member, "I have no *need* of you" (1 Corinthians 12:21, RSV). The only New Testament instance of *chreia* denoting duty or service is found in Acts 6:3 where men are to be chosen "whom we may appoint to this *duty*" (RSV).

Strong 5532, Bauer 884-85, Moulton-Milligan 691, Liddell-Scott 2002-3, Colin Brown 3:956-58.

5367B. χρεοφειλέτης

chreopheiletēs noun

Debtor.

This is a variant spelling of *chreōpheiletēs.* See the word study at number 5368.

5368. χρεωφειλέτης

chreōpheiletēs noun

Debtor.

Cognate:

ὀφείλω opheilō (3648)

Synonym:

ὀφειλέτης opheiletēs (3645)

1. χρεωφειλέται chreōpheiletai nom pl masc
2. χρεωφειλετῶν chreōpheiletōn gen pl masc
3. χρεοφειλέται chreopheiletai nom pl masc
4. χρεοφειλετῶν chreopheiletōn gen pl masc

1 was a certain creditor which had two **debtors:**....... Luke 7:41
2 So he called every one of his lord's **debtors**........... 16:5

Classical Greek and Septuagint Usage

Chreōpheiletēs is composed of *chreōs,* "debt," and *opheiletēs* (3645), "one who owes." Thus, *chreōpheiletēs* indicates "the one who owes a debt." In ancient times a person may take a loan to avert hunger or loss; rarely if ever was a loan issued for commercial enterprise (Hartley, "Debt," *International Standard Bible Encyclopedia*, 1:905f.). And though the Old Testament required mercy in the payment of debts (Exodus 22:25; Deuteronomy 24:6,17; Job 24:3, etc.), by New Testament times the treatment of debtors became harsh under Roman influence (see Matthew 5:25,26; 18:34).

New Testament Usage

The term *chreōpheiletēs* occurs only twice in the New Testament. In Luke 7:41 Jesus used it in the lesson on forgiveness that He taught Simon the Pharisee. In Luke 16:5 Jesus used it again in the Parable of the Dishonest Steward. Both of these occurrences include a sense of mercy on the part of the one who forgave the debt as well as a sense of relief for the one forgiven.

STRONG 5533, BAUER 885, MOULTON-MILLIGAN 691 (see "chreophiletēs"), LIDDELL-SCOTT 2004.

5369. χρή chrē verb

It is necessary.

CROSS-REFERENCE:
χρεία chreia (5367)

1. χρή chrē 3sing indic pres act

1 My brethren, these things **ought** not so to be......... Jas 3:10

This word, meaning "it is necessary" or "it ought," usually occurs with an infinitive or with the infinitive implied. It was a common term in classical Greek literature, but as time passed it was almost totally replaced by its synonym *dei* (1158). In the New Testament *chrē* occurs only once (James 3:10) as compared to *dei* which is used more than 100 times.

STRONG 5534, BAUER 885, MOULTON-MILLIGAN 691, LIDDELL-SCOTT 2004, COLIN BROWN 3:956-58.

5370. χρήζω chrēzō verb

Have need.

CROSS-REFERENCE:
χρεία chreia (5367)

1. χρήζει chrēzei 3sing indic pres act
2. χρήζομεν chrēzomen 1pl indic pres act
3. χρήζετε chrēzete 2pl indic pres act
4. χρήζῃ chrēzē 3sing subj pres act

3 your heavenly Father knoweth that ye **have need**..... Matt 6:32
1 he will rise and give him as many as he **needeth**.... Luke 11:8
3 your Father knoweth that ye **have need of** these........ 12:30
4 her in whatsoever business she **hath need** of you:... Rom 16:2
2 or **need** we, ... epistles of commendation to you,.... 2 Co 3:1

Classical Greek and Septuagint Usage

This term can be found in classical Greek from the Eighth Century B.C. meaning "want, lack, have need of" (cf. *Liddell-Scott*). It is related to the verb *chrē* (5369), "it is necessary, it is required," and can also be found meaning "desire, long for, crave" (ibid.).

Chrēzō occurs only rarely in the Septuagint. In Judges 11:7 this term describes the elders of Gilead being "in distress." They were "in need of" military allies to defend themselves against the Ammonites.

New Testament Usage

In the New Testament *chrēzō* occurs five times, all of which have the meaning "to have need." In the Sermon on the Mount Jesus exhorted His hearers not to worry about clothing, food, or drink, "For the pagans run after all these things, and your heavenly Father knows that you *need* them" (Matthew 6:32, NIV; cf. Luke 12:30). When Jesus taught His disciples to pray *chrēzō* is used in a parable of how a man will be willing to get up in the middle of the night to give his friend "as much as he *needs*" because of his friend's persistent appeal (Luke 11:8, NIV).

Paul used *chrēzō* in his appeal to the believers in Rome, that they would give Phoebe "any help she may *need*" because she had proven her faithfulness to the church in Cenchrea (Greece) and had "been a great help to many people," including Paul (Romans 16:2, NIV). Paul also used *chrēzō* in a rhetorical question to the Corinthians. Aware that his words were likely to be misused by the false teachers at Corinth, he attempted to call attention to their need of authentication while at the same time chiding the Corinthians: "Or do we *need*, like some people, letters of recommendation to you or from you?" (2 Corinthians 3:1, NIV).

STRONG 5535, BAUER 885, MOULTON-MILLIGAN 691, LIDDELL-SCOTT 2004, COLIN BROWN 3:956-58.

5371. χρῆμα chrēma noun

Riches, money.

COGNATE:
χράομαι chraomai (5366)

SYNONYMS:
ἀργύριον argurion (688)
κέρμα kerma (2743)
κτῆμα ktēma (2905)
μαμωνᾶς mamōnas (3098)

νόμισμα nomisma (3409)
πλοῦτος ploutos (4009)
χαλκός chalkos (5311)

דָּבָר dāvār (1745), Word; matter (Neh 11:24).

כֶּסֶף keseph (3826B), Silver (Job 27:17).

מְחִיר m^echîr (4379), Price (Prv 17:16).

נְכָסִים n^ekhāsîm (5420), Riches (Jos 22:8, 2 Chr 1:11f.).

רְכוּשׁ r^ekhûsh (7688), Equipment, riches (Dn 11:13,24,28).

1. **χρῆμα chrēma** nom/acc sing neu
2. **χρήματα chrēmata** nom/acc pl neu
3. **χρημάτων chrēmatōn** gen pl neu
4. **χρήμασιν chrēmasin** dat pl neu

2 How hardly shall they that have **riches** enter...... Mark 10:23
4 how hard is it for them that trust in **riches**........... 10:24
2 How hardly shall they that have **riches** enter.......Luke 18:24
1 Having land, sold it, and brought the **money**,........Acts 4:37
2 the Holy Ghost was given, he offered them **money**,..... 8:18
3 that the gift of God may be purchased with **money**...... 8:20
2 He hoped also that **money** should have been given..... 24:26

Classical Greek

Classical literature uses *chrēma* to indicate "things that are used or needed," such as goods, property, or money (cf. *Liddell-Scott*). It can also be used to express a large quantity or mass such as "a gigantic swarm of locusts" or perhaps "womankind" (ibid.). Frequently *ktēma* (2905), "possession," and *chrēma*, "what one desires or uses," are used synonymously (*Liddell-Scott*).

Septuagint Usage

Chrēma can be found in the Septuagint as a translation of the Hebrew *keseph*, "money"; *n^ekhāsîm*, "riches"; and *r^ekhûsh*, "what is gathered." The majority of its appearances in the Septuagint are in the apocryphal books. There wealth is seen as a reward for following God (Joshua 22:8; 2 Chronicles 1:11,12), although in the hand of a fool money is worthless (Proverbs 17:16). In the noncanonical literature *chrēma* generally means "money, wealth." Simon, son of Mattathias, for instance, spent his own *money* to arm the Jews (1 Maccabees 14:32).

New Testament Usage

The New Testament uses *chrēma* in the singular (Acts 4:37) denoting a "payment," or it uses the plural noun indicating "a collection of wealth" (Matthew 19:22, some manuscripts contain *ktēmata*). "They that have riches" (*hoi ta chrēmata echontes*) find it difficult to become "poor" (Mark 10:23; cf. Matthew 5:3) and so enter the kingdom of God. This is because they "trust in riches" (Mark 10:24), not God. Neither are they "rich toward God" (Luke 12:21). In short, they do not possess riches at all. Their riches possess them.

Strong 5536, Bauer 885, Moulton-Milligan 691-92, Kittel 9:480, Liddell-Scott 2004-5, Colin Brown 2:845; 3:324.

5372. χρηματίζω chrēmatizō verb

Be given a revelation, receive a warning; be named.

Cognates:
χράομαι chraomai (5366)
χρηματισμός chrēmatismos (5373)

Synonyms:
ἐπιλέγω epilegō (1935B)
ἐπονομάζω eponomazō (2012)
καλέω kaleō (2535)
ὀνομάζω onomazō (3550)
προσαγορεύω prosagoreuō (4174)

דָּבַר dāvar (1744), Piel: speak, say (Jer 26:2 [33:2], 29:23 [36:23], 30:2 [37:2]).

שָׁאַג shā'agh (8057), Roar (Jer 25:30 [32:30]).

1. **χρηματίζοντα chrēmatizonta** acc sing masc part pres act
2. **χρηματίσαι chrēmatisai** inf aor act
3. **χρηματίσει chrēmatisei** 3sing indic fut act
4. **ἐχρηματίσθη echrēmatisthē** 3sing indic aor pass
5. **χρηματισθείς chrēmatistheis** nom sing masc part aor pass
6. **χρηματισθέντες chrēmatisthentes** nom pl masc part aor pass
7. **κεχρημάτισται kechrēmatistai** 3sing indic perf mid
8. **κεχρηματισμένον kechrēmatismenon** nom/acc sing neu part perf mid

6 And **being warned** of God in a dream............. Matt 2:12
5 notwithstanding, **being warned of God** in a dream,....... 2:22
8 And it was **revealed** unto him by the Holy Ghost,... Luke 2:26
4 **was warned** from God by an holy angel............Acts 10:22
2 the disciples were **called** Christians first in Antioch..... 11:26
3 she **shall be called** an adulteress:................... Rom 7:3
7 as Moses was **admonished of God**.................. Heb 8:5
5 **being warned of God** of things not seen as yet,......... 11:7
1 turn away from him that **speaketh** from heaven:....... 12:25

Classical Greek

In classical writings this very complex term means, among other things, "to negotiate (often financially), to transact business, to give or (passively) receive a message from an oracle." In some special cases *chrēmatizō* means "to be called, named" (*Liddell-Scott*; see also *Moulton-Milligan*).

Septuagint Usage

There are eight canonical instances of *chrēmatizō* in the Septuagint and two without Hebrew equivalent (1 Kings 18:27 [LXX 3 Kings 18:27]; Job 40:8). All of the canonical occurrences are found in Jeremiah. The most common equivalent Hebrew term is *dāvar* (piel; "to speak, talk, to say something"), but *chrēmatizō* also replaces *shā'agh* ("roar") twice (Jeremiah 25:30 [LXX 32:30], of God's "roaring" in judgment). Elsewhere the classical overtones of *chrēmatizō* as some kind of divine pronouncement may be detected in the prophet Jeremiah (Jeremiah 26:2 [LXX 33:2]; 30:2 [37:2]; 36:2,4 [43:2,4]; cf. 29:23 [36:23]).

New Testament Usage

Writers of the New Testament, though not all, clearly associate *chrēmatizō* with divine "revelation," a "word from God." This draws upon the Septuagintal and classical understandings. It is used of the way God spoke to the Magi and Joseph in dreams (Matthew 2:12,22). Luke used it of Simeon's being "told" by the Spirit that he would not die before he saw Messiah (Luke 2:26). In Acts 10:22 he used it of the angelic message to Cornelius that Peter was to come to him (cf. Noah and Moses whom God spoke to and "warned"; Hebrews 8:5; 11:7; 12:25; see also Brown, "Revelation," *Colin Brown*, 3:324f.).

Otherwise it means "to name, call" in Acts 11:26 where it tells us the believers were first "called" Christians in Antioch. Paul followed that same understanding in Romans 7:3 when he wrote of a woman being "called" an adulteress if she marries another while her husband still lives.

Strong 5537, Bauer 885, Moulton-Milligan 692, Kittel 9:480-82, Liddell-Scott 2005, Colin Brown 3:324-25.

5373. χρηματισμός chrēmatismos noun

Answer of God, divine response; communication, oracle.

Cross-Reference:

χρηματίζω chrēmatizō (5372)

מַשָּׂא massā' (5015), Oracle (Prv 31:1 [24:69]).

1. χρηματισμός chrēmatismos nom sing masc

1 But what saith the answer of God unto him? .... Rom 11:4

Chrēmatismos is a noun related to the Greek verbs *chraomai* (5366), "to make use of, to act," and *chrēmatizō* (5372), "to respond to, to behave toward, to act." Occurring only once in the New Testament (Romans 11:4), its meaning, "the answer of God," is similarly found in 2 Maccabees (2:4) which uses *chrēmatismos* to indicate a revelation that contains a "divine answer" for Jeremiah. The Septuagint uses *chrēmatismos* to translate the Hebrew *massā'*, indicating practical advice (Proverbs 31:1 [LXX 24:69]) or a prophetic "burden" (Isaiah 13:1).

In the New Testament (Romans 11:4) *chrēmatismos* is that act whereby God responds to man by a verbal utterance. God does more than "answer" Elijah (Authorized Version). He responds by revealing himself. In the words of Reicke, "Elijah is thought of, not as an attorney submitting written petitions, nor as a mantic practicing incubation, but as a man of God receiving revelations" (Reicke, "chrēmatismos," *Kittel*, 9:482).

Strong 5538, Bauer 885, Moulton-Milligan 692, Kittel 9:482, Liddell-Scott 2005, Colin Brown 3:324-25.

5374. χρήσιμος chrēsimos adj

Useful, beneficial.

Cross-Reference:

χράομαι chraomai (5366)

בֶּצַע betsa' (1240), Profit (Gn 37:26).

1. χρήσιμον chrēsimon nom/acc sing neu

1 that they strive not about words to no profit, ... 2 Tm 2:14

Classical Greek and Septuagint Usage

This adjective was fairly common in the Greek of the classical period. It was applied to both things and persons to describe them as "useful" or "serviceable." However, it was becoming less used by the time of Koine Greek; it appears 15 times in the Septuagint and only rarely among writers by the First Century A.D. This form of the word is not found at all among the writings of the church fathers after the Second Century.

New Testament Usage

Chrēsimos is found in the New Testament only at 2 Timothy 2:14. In that verse the word is used in a negative construction ("to no profit," i.e., "useful for nothing"). This construction is basically synonymous with *achreios* (881) and *achrēstos* (883), "useless." The implication in this case is that arguing about "words" (here "words" probably refers to ideas or doctrines) is not useful, beneficial, or helpful, but rather is harmful to those involved in such quarreling. *Chrēsimos* is also found in a lengthy addition to one manuscript following Matthew 20:28.

Strong 5539, Bauer 885, Moulton-Milligan 692, Liddell-Scott 2006.

5375. χρῆσις chrēsis noun

Use, employment, function.

CROSS-REFERENCE:
χράομαι chraomai (5366)

שָׁאַל shā'al (8068), Lend (1 Sm 1:28).

1. χρῆσιν chrēsin acc sing fem

1 for even their women did change the natural use.... Rom 1:26
1 the men, leaving the natural use of the woman,......... 1:27

Occurring only twice in the Pauline portion of the New Testament (Romans 1:26,27), *chrēsis* means "use" or "employment."

Classical Greek

Such is also the case in classical Greek literature. Xenophon (Fourth Century B.C.) used *chrēsis* with reference to "the uses of war"; Hippocrates (Fifth Century B.C.) used it to mean "practice." In Thucydides (Fifth Century B.C.) it means "power or the means of using"; Pindar (early Fifth Century B.C.), "the response" of an oracle; and Aristotle, a "lending" or "a loan." Most enlightening for New Testament meaning are Aristotle's and Polybius' usages where *chrēsis* is "intimacy" or "acquaintance"; and Isocrates (Fourth Century B.C.) where literally *hai oikoi chrēsis*, "the use of houses," means practically sexual "intercourse" with women. (See *Liddell-Scott.*)

The papyri continue this tradition by using *chrēsis* to refer to the "use" of wine, a "loan" of new wheat, or a house for lifetime "use" (*Moulton-Milligan*).

Septuagint Usage

In the Septuagint *chrēsis* appears several times. In its only canonical appearance the word denotes "a loan"; Samuel was a loan to the Lord. Otherwise, *chrēsis* means "use." Wisdom 15:15 notes that idols have no use for their hands, eyes, or ears. Sirach asks, "What use is man?" (18:8). The use of *chrēsis* in Wisdom of Solomon 15:7 shows that it did not have any inherent negative connotations. The writer describes the work of a potter who makes vessels for clean or "contrary" uses, "but which shall be the *use* of each of these the worker in clay decides" (RSV). Thus *chrēsis* can be either "clean" or "contrary" use.

New Testament Usage

The Pauline use of *chrēsis* (Romans 1:26,27) conveys the idea of physical intimacy; but it is the "employment" or "use" of sexuality (1:26). The wrong use of sexuality is "against nature" (1:26), for it violates the original divine intention. Man is made for woman. Woman is made for man.

This shameful "use" (1:27) dishonors the body (1:24) and has a present and recognizable "penalty" attached to it (1:27). It is the direct result of man hardening his heart toward God (1:20-25,28); the individual who practices such things comes under His direct judgment (1:18,32). Such judgment is evident in the case of Sodom and Gommorah (Genesis 19:1-29).

STRONG 5540, BAUER 885-86, MOULTON-MILLIGAN 692, LIDDELL-SCOTT 2006.

5376. χρηστεύομαι

chrēsteuomai verb

To act kindly.

COGNATES:
εὔχρηστος euchrēstos (2154)
χράομαι chraomai (5366)
χρηστολογία chrēstologia (5377)
χρηστός chrēstos (5378)
χρηστότης chrēstotēs (5379)

1. χρηστεύεται chrēsteuetai 3sing indic pres mid

1 Charity suffereth long, and is kind;................ 1 Co 13:4

Septuagint Usage

The verb *chrēsteuomai* is not found in any secular Greek writings. Though it has been argued that it "is almost certainly a coinage of Christian Greek" (Turner, *Christian Words*, p.247), it is found in Psalms of Solomon 9:6, the Greek text of which may be coincident with early New Testament writings (Wright, *The Old Testament Pseudepigrapha*, 2:640). The verb is related to the noun *chrēstotēs* (5379), "kindness," and the adjective *chrēstos* (5378), "kind." Thus, the verb *chrēsteuomai* refers to the actual performing of a deed of kindness.

New Testament Usage

The only occurrence of this verb in the New Testament is at 1 Corinthians 13:4 where Paul wrote that love (*agapē* [26]) "is kind." It is important, however, that it is the verb that is used here and not the adjective as the KJV might suggest. Paul did not describe love as kind, that is, as only an attitude; rather, he stated that love performs deeds of kindness ("acts kindly"; Louw and Nida, *Greek-English Lexicon*, 1:750). The personification of love as a subject that acts in certain ways is the consistent pattern found in 1 Corinthians 13:4-8.

STRONG 5541, BAUER 886, MOULTON-MILLIGAN 692, KITTEL 9:491-92, LIDDELL-SCOTT 2006, COLIN BROWN 2:105.

5377. χρηστολογία chrēstologia noun

Fair or attractive speech.

CROSS-REFERENCE:
λέγω legō (2978)

1. χρηστολογίας chrēstologias gen sing fem

1 and by **good words** and fair speeches deceive.......Rom 16:18

Classical Greek

The noun *chrēstologia* is a compound Greek word formed from *chrēstos* (5378), "kind, good," and *legō* (2978), "to speak." This noun designates "eloquent and attractive speech involving pleasing rhetorical devices" (Louw and Nida, *Greek-English Lexicon*, 1:393). It is used both positively of the speech of an excellent quality and negatively in an ironic sense similar to the English figure of speech "a smooth talker."

New Testament Usage

It is this negative connotation that is found in Romans 16:18, the only occurrence of *chrēstologia* in the New Testament. Paul warned the recipients to beware of those people who would bring divisions into the Christian community by using "smooth talk and flattery (to) deceive the minds of naive people" (NIV). These people were using their eloquence as "a mask for fraudulent purposes" (Weiss, "chrēstologia," *Kittel*, 9:492).

STRONG 5542, BAUER 886, MOULTON-MILLIGAN 692, KITTEL 9:492, LIDDELL-SCOTT 2007.

5378. χρηστός chrēstos adj

Good, pleasant, easy; useful, reputable; kind, loving.

COGNATE:
χρηστεύομαι chrēsteuomai (5376)

SYNONYMS:
ἀγαθός agathos (18)
καλός kalos (2541)

טָב ṭāv (A2978), Pure (Dn 2:32—Aramaic).

טוֹב ṭôv (3005), Good (Ps 25:8 [24:8], Jer 24:2f.,5, Na 1:7).

יָקָר yāqār (3479), Precious (Ez 28:13).

יָשָׁר yāshār (3596), Upright person (Prv 2:21).

1. χρηστός chrēstos nom sing masc
2. χρηστοί chrēstoi nom pl masc
3. χρηστόν chrēston nom/acc sing neu
4. χρῆσθ' chrēsth' nom/acc pl neu
5. χρηστότερος chrēstoteros comp nom sing masc
6. χρηστά chrēsta nom/acc pl neu

1 For my yoke is **easy**, and my burden is light....... Matt 11:30
5 desireth new: for he saith, The old is **better**......... Luke 5:39
1 for he is **kind** unto the unthankful and to the evil....... 6:35
3 the **goodness** of God leadeth thee to repentance?....Rom 2:4
4 evil communications corrupt **good** manners......... 1 Co 15:33
2 And be ye **kind** one to another, tenderhearted,...... Eph 4:32
1 If so be ye have tasted that the Lord is **gracious**..... 1 Pt 2:3

Classical Greek

Chrēstos is related to the verb *chraomai* (5366), "to need, to use, to borrow," and means "useful, serviceable." As well it can denote something as "good" (not necessarily in the ethical sense). The idea of "good" here includes ethical and moral dimensions; *chrēstos* is associated with bravery, kindness, honesty. It also describes the qualities of being "kind, merciful, generous, etc." (*Liddell-Scott*).

Septuagint Usage

Chrēstos translates three Hebrew words in the Septuagint, although one clearly predominates—*ṭôv* ("good" [as opposed to evil or in terms of value], "friendly, kind, pleasant"). Of the 29 canonical instances of *chrēstos*, 14 occur in the Psalms. The Psalmist particularly ascribes "kindness, mercy, goodness" to the Lord (Psalms 25:8 [LXX 24:8]; 34:8 [33:8]; 69:16 [68:16]; 86:5 [85:5]; 100:5 [99:5]; 109:21 [108:21]; cf. Wisdom of Solomon 15:1; Jeremiah 33:11 [40:11]).

Jeremiah uses *chrēstos* to describe figs as either "good" (that is, suitable for eating) or "bad" (Jeremiah 24:2,3,5). Elsewhere it is used of human kindness (Jeremiah 52:32; 1 Maccabees 6:11; 2 Maccabees 9:19).

New Testament Usage

Chrēstos describes objects as "good" (i.e., "suitable" or "kind, easy"; Matthew 11:30; Luke 5:39). It is a quality expected of the believer (Ephesians 4:32; cf. 1 Corinthians 15:33). But most importantly, God is *chrēstos*, "kind." God's "goodness" is especially manifest in His willingness to forgive the unforgivable (Luke 6:35). The "kindness" demonstrated in His delaying judgment is designed to lead men to repentance (Romans 2:4). Experiencing God's "goodness" should also be an incentive to maintain a holy life (1 Peter 2:3; cf. Ephesians 4:32).

STRONG 5543, BAUER 886, MOULTON-MILLIGAN 693, KITTEL 9:483-89, LIDDELL-SCOTT 2007, COLIN BROWN 2:105-6.

5379. χρηστότης chrēstotēs noun

Goodness, uprightness, kindness, mercy, generosity.

COGNATE:
χρηστεύομαι chrēsteuomai (5376)

SYNONYM:
ἀγαθωσύνη agathōsunē (19)

טוֹב ṭôv (3004), Be pleasing, be good; hiphil: do good (Ps 119:68 [118:68]).

טוֹב ṭôv (3005), Good, well (Pss 14:1 [13:1], 85:12 [84:12], 119:65 [118:65]).

טוּב ṭûv (3008), Goodness (Pss 25:7 [24:7], 31:19 [30:19], 145:7 [144:7]).

טוֹבָה ṭôvāh (3009B), Bounty, goodness (Pss 65:11 [64:11], 68:10 [67:10], 106:5 [105:5]).

1. **χρηστότης chrēstotēs** nom sing fem
2. **χρηστότητος chrēstotētos** gen sing fem
3. **χρηστότητι chrēstotēti** dat sing fem
4. **χρηστότητα chrēstotēta** acc sing fem

2 his **goodness** and forbearance and longsuffering; ..... Rom 2:4
4 there is none that doeth **good**, no, not one............ 3:12
4 Behold ... the **goodness** and severity of God: 11:22
4 which fell, severity; but toward thee, **goodness**, ... 11:22
3 if thou continue in his **goodness**: 11:22
3 by **kindness**, by the Holy Ghost, by love unfeigned, 2 Co 6:6
1 peace, longsuffering, **gentleness**, goodness, faith, ... Gal 5:22
3 the exceeding riches of his grace in his **kindness** ..... Eph 2:7
4 bowels of mercies, **kindness**, humbleness of mind, ... Col 3:12
1 **kindness** and love of God our Saviour ... appeared, ... Tit 3:4

Classical Greek

Chrēstotēs is a noun related to the adjective *chrēstos* (5378) and the verb *chraomai* (5366), "need, use." It means "kindness, goodness, honesty," especially in a behavioral sense. At times *chrēstotēs* is joined with *philanthrōpia* (5200) (literally "love of humanity") as a quality of a ruler. Oddly, *chrēstotēs* is not always positive. Too much *chrēstotēs* in the face of evil might be considered as "soft-hearted" (cf. *Liddell-Scott*; Weiss, "chrēstotēs," *Kittel*, 9:489).

Septuagint Usage

The 16 instances of *chrēstotēs* in the Septuagint's canonical material all occur in Psalms. The Hebrew behind it in every case is a form of *ṯôv*, "good, kind, pleasant," etc. The Psalmist laments the fact that there is no one who does "good" (NIV, Psalms 14:1,3 [LXX 13:1,3]; 53:3 [52:3]); this is particularly applied to his enemies. "Doing good" is to characterize God's people (Psalm 37:3 [LXX 36:3]; cf. 119:66 [118:66]). God's "kindness" is seen most clearly in His forgiveness (Psalm 25:7 [LXX 24:7]) and in His power and desire to rescue those who fear Him (Psalms 31:19 [LXX 30:19]; cf. verse 1; 106:5 [105:5]).

New Testament Usage

Chrēstotēs is exclusively a member of the Pauline vocabulary in the New Testament, where it occurs 10 times. In speaking of all of humanity's nature when compared to God, Paul cited Psalm 14:3 which says no one does good/kindness (cf. Romans 3:12). The exception, of course, is God. The "kindness" of God, the "riches of his grace" (goodness), are demonstrated in Christ. God's act of kindness is solely an act of grace (Ephesians 2:7ff.; Titus 3:4). The marvelous feature of this kindness is that it was done when we were in rebellion to God (Titus 3:3,4).

Chrēstotēs, "kindness, goodness," is also to mark the life of the individual believer. That human beings are capable of "goodness" is not in contradiction to Paul's statement in Romans 2:4 that "no one is *good*." Rather, believers are capable of goodness only because of the Spirit (Galatians 5:22; cf. 2 Corinthians 6:6). Paul urged the Colossians to "clothe themselves" (*enduō* [1730]) with "kindness" (cf. Romans 13:12,14; Galatians 3:27; Ephesians 4:24; Colossians 3:10,12).

Chrēstotēs is similar in meaning to *agathōsunē* (19), "goodness." However, they are not exactly the same (e.g., Galatians 5:22, both words appear describing distinct aspects of beneficence). According to Trench, the sternness Christ displayed when He cleansed the temple was a manifestation of *agathōsunē*, not *chrēstotēs*, "mildness" (*Synonyms of the New Testament*, p.219). *Agathōsunē* could be manifested through rebuke and chastisement as well as gentleness. *Chrēstotēs* primarily involves mildness; *agathōsunē*, moral perfection and holy righteousness, both attributable to God who has goodness (*chrēstotēs*) and severity (Romans 11:22).

STRONG 5544, BAUER 886, MOULTON-MILLIGAN 693, KITTEL 9:489-91, LIDDELL-SCOTT 2007, COLIN BROWN 2:105-7.

5380. χρῖσμα chrisma noun

Anointing oil; anointing, unction.

CROSS-REFERENCE:

χρίω chriō (5383)

מִשְׁחָה mishchāh (5068), Anointing (Ex 29:7, 35:15 [35:19]).

מָשְׁחָה moshchāh (5070), Anointing (Ex 40:15).

מָשִׁיחַ māshîach (5081), Messiah (Dn 9:26).

1. **χρῖσμα chrisma** nom/acc sing neu

1 But ye have an **unction** from the Holy One, ... 1 Jn 2:20
1 But the **anointing** which ye have received of him 2:27
1 as the same **anointing** teacheth you of all things, ... 2:27

Classical Greek and Septuagint Usage

The noun *chrisma* has a considerable range of meaning. In its broadest sense it refers to anything smeared onto something else, for example, coatings of plaster applied to walls (*Liddell-Scott*). Thus, in Sirach 38:30 the "anointing of pots" refers to the glaze applied to pottery before it is fired in order to give it color and finish. It also has the more limited use to denote a "scented ointment," often consisting of a mixture of oil and herbs used for the purpose of anointing either persons or things. *Chrisma* as an anointing oil was distinguished from *muron* (3326), "ointment, perfume," in that *chrisma* was of a thicker consistency. This use of *chrisma* is found several times in the Septuagint text of Exodus referring to the "spiced oil of anointing" used to consecrate both the priests and the tabernacle and its fixtures (see Exodus 29:7; 30:25, etc.).

In addition to the more specialized meaning of *chrisma* as an "anointing oil," the use of the noun was extended to refer to the "state or act of being anointed" (*Moulton-Milligan*) or, more simply, "anointing" or "unction" (*Liddell-Scott*). The word is found in this sense as a translation of the Hebrew *moshchāh* in the Septuagint text of Exodus 40:15. The meaning could also be further extended to refer to "an anointed one," and thus appears as the translation of the Hebrew *māshîach* ("anointed one, Messiah") in Daniel 9:26.

New Testament Usage

Chrisma occurs three times in the New Testament, at 1 John 2:20 and 27 (twice). In each of these cases *chrisma* refers to an anointing that provides the believers with knowledge by teaching them "all things." By drawing on the connection between this effect and Jesus' promise concerning the Paraclete in John 16:7-14 ("the Spirit of truth . . . will guide you into all truth"), it is possible to understand this use of *chrisma* as referring to the anointing with the Holy Spirit (cf. Thayer, *Greek-English Lexicon*; Grundmann, "chrisma," *Kittel*, 9:572; *Bauer*). This anointing and its resulting knowledge were what distinguished those who remained in the Johannine community from those who had left it. *Chrisma* was later used to designate the postbaptismal anointing with oil that symbolized the receiving of the Holy Spirit (see Lampe, *Patristic Greek Lexicon*).

STRONG 5545, BAUER 886, MOULTON-MILLIGAN 693, KITTEL 9:493-580, LIDDELL-SCOTT 2007, COLIN BROWN 1:119,121-23.

5381. Χριστιανός Christianos name

Christian.

1. Χριστιανός Christianos nom sing masc

2. Χριστιανόν Christianon acc sing masc

3. Χριστιανούς Christianous acc pl masc

3 the disciples were called Christians first in Antioch. Acts 11:26
2 Almost thou persuadest me to be a Christian.......... 26:28
1 Yet if any man suffer as a Christian,................ 1 Pt 4:16

Though later also used as an adjective, the word *Christianos* occurs only as a noun within the New Testament. According to Acts 11:26 the designation *Christian* was first applied to the disciples in Syrian Antioch, possibly as early as A.D. 44 (Turner, *Christian Words*, p.66). The formation of the word follows the Latin pattern, frequently copied in the Greek of this period, of attaching an *-ian* suffix to a proper name to designate the followers or adherents of a particular person. Other examples include the Herodians in the New Testament and the Caesariani (imperial slaves) and the Pompeiani.

The origin and significance of this name is a matter of some debate. Bickerman ("The Name of Christians," pp.109-124) argued that the disciples in Antioch developed the name *Christians* to designate themselves as "servants of Christ" (compare *Caesariani* above; see *Moulton-Milligan*). This theory is consistent with a tradition of the Early Church that the name was coined by Euodius, the first bishop of Syrian Antioch. Origen and Cyril of Alexandria argued that the name *Christian* described "one who partakes of Christ's anointing" (see Lampe, *Patristic Greek Lexicon*).

The problem with these theories is that the name *Christian* was at first applied to believers only by nonbelievers. All three uses of *Christianos* in the New Testament fit this pattern. In Acts 11:26 "the disciples were called Christians first in Antioch" by nonbelievers. Agrippa used the name *Christian* for one who believes in Christ in Acts 26:28. And in 1 Peter 4:16 believers were persecuted by nonbelievers because they were *Christianos*. Apart from these uses in the New Testament, the earliest occurrences of *Christian* are to be found in the secular writers Josephus (*Antiquities* 18.3.3), Pliny the Younger (*Epistles* 10.96,97), Tacitus (*Annals* 15.44), and Suetonius (*Life of Nero* 16.2). The first appearances of *Christianos* as a self-designation by a Christian writer are found in the early second-century writings of Ignatius who was bishop of Syrian Antioch.

Even the formation of the word *Christianos* (see the first paragraph above) suggests that it was coined by Gentile nonbelievers who thought *Christ* was a proper name and did not recognize it as a title (Greek *Christ* = Hebrew *Messiah*). Though it is often stated that nonbelievers used the name *Christian* as a term of derision or ridicule (so Cremer, *Lexicon*, p.582; Lampe, *Patristic Greek Lexicon*; and Rengstorf, "Jesus Christ," *Colin Brown*, 2:343), this would not necessarily always have been the case (see Grundmann, "chriō," *Kittel*, 9:537).

Strong 5546, Bauer 886, Moulton-Milligan 693, Kittel 9:493-580, Liddell-Scott 2007, Colin Brown 2:343.

5382. Χριστός Christos name

Christ, anointed, the Anointed One.

1. **Χριστός Christos** nom masc
2. **Χριστοῦ Christou** gen masc
3. **Χριστῷ Christō** dat masc
4. **Χριστόν Christon** acc masc
5. **Χριστέ Christe** voc masc

2 The book of the generation of Jesus **Christ**,......... Matt 1:1
1 of whom was born Jesus, who is called **Christ**........... 1:16
2 unto **Christ** are fourteen generations.................... 1:17
2 Now the birth of Jesus **Christ** was on this wise:......... 1:18
1 he demanded of them where **Christ** should be born...... 2:4
2 John had heard in the prison the works of **Christ**,..... 11:2
1 Thou art the **Christ**, the Son of the living God........ 16:16
1 should tell no man that he was Jesus the **Christ**........ 16:20
1 Jesus **Christ** began to show His disciples (NASB)...... 16:21
2 What think ye of **Christ**? whose son is he?............ 22:42
1 for one is your Master, even **Christ**;................. 23:8
1 for one is your Master, even **Christ**.................. 23:10
1 many shall come in my name, saying, I am **Christ**;..... 24:5
1 if any man shall say unto you, Lo, here is **Christ**,...... 24:23
1 tell us whether thou be the **Christ**, the Son of God..... 26:63
5 Saying, Prophesy unto us, thou **Christ**,................ 26:68
4 Barabbas, or Jesus which is called **Christ**?............ 27:17
4 do then with Jesus which is called **Christ**?............ 27:22
2 The beginning of the gospel of Jesus **Christ**,........ Mark 1:1
1 And Peter answereth ... Thou art the **Christ**............ 8:29
2 give you a cup ... because ye belong to **Christ**,.......... 9:41
1 How say the scribes that **Christ** is the son of David?... 12:35
1 if any man shall say to you, Lo, here is **Christ**;........ 13:21
1 Art thou the **Christ**, the Son of the Blessed?.......... 14:61
1 Let **Christ** the King ... descend now from the cross,.... 15:32
1 is born ... a Saviour, which is **Christ** the Lord....... Luke 2:11
4 before he had seen the Lord's **Christ**.................. 2:26
1 whether he were the **Christ**, or not;..................... 3:15
1 and saying, Thou art **Christ** the Son of God........... 4:41
4 not to speak: for they knew that he was **Christ**.......... 4:41
4 Peter answering said, The **Christ** of God............... 9:20
4 How say they that **Christ** is David's son?.............. 20:41
1 Art thou the **Christ**? tell us. And he said............ 22:67
4 saying that he himself is **Christ** a King................ 23:2
1 if he be **Christ**, the chosen of God.................... 23:35
1 saying, If thou be **Christ**, save thyself and us........... 23:39
4 Ought not **Christ** to have suffered these things,........ 24:26
4 and thus it behoved **Christ** to suffer,.................. 24:46
2 but grace and truth came by Jesus **Christ**........... John 1:17
1 and denied not; but confessed, I am not the **Christ**...... 1:20
1 if thou be not that **Christ**, nor Elias,................... 1:25
1 the Messias, which is, being interpreted, the **Christ**...... 1:41
1 that I said, I am not the **Christ**,...................... 3:28
1 I know that Messias cometh, which is called **Christ**:..... 4:25
1 Come, see a man, ... is not this the **Christ**?............ 4:29
1 and know that this is indeed the **Christ**,................ 4:42
1 we believe and are sure that thou art that **Christ**,....... 6:69
1 know indeed that this is the very **Christ**?........... John 7:26
1 but when **Christ** cometh, no man knoweth.............. 7:27
1 When **Christ** cometh, will he do more miracles......... 7:31
1 Others said, This is the **Christ**......................... 7:41
1 But some said, Shall **Christ** come out of Galilee?....... 7:41
1 That **Christ** cometh of the seed of David,.............. 7:42
4 that if any man did confess that he was **Christ**,......... 9:22
1 If thou be the **Christ**, tell us plainly.................. 10:24
1 I believe that thou art the **Christ**, the Son of God,..... 11:27
1 heard out of the law that **Christ** abideth for ever:...... 12:34
4 true God, and Jesus **Christ**, whom thou hast sent...... 17:3
1 that ye might believe that Jesus is the **Christ**,.......... 20:31
4 he would raise up **Christ** to sit on his throne;....... Acts 2:30
2 before spake of the resurrection of **Christ**,.............. 2:31
4 whom ye have crucified, both Lord and **Christ**.......... 2:36
2 the name of Jesus **Christ** for the remission of sins,...... 2:38
2 In the name of Jesus **Christ** of Nazareth rise up........ 3:6
4 that **Christ** should suffer, he hath so fulfilled........... 3:18
4 And he shall send Jesus **Christ**,....................... 3:20
2 that by the name of Jesus **Christ** of Nazareth,.......... 4:10
2 against the Lord, and against his **Christ**................ 4:26
4 they ceased not to teach and preach Jesus **Christ**........ 5:42
4 city of Samaria, and preached **Christ** unto them......... 8:5
2 the kingdom of God, and the name of Jesus **Christ**,..... 8:12
4 I believe that Jesus **Christ** is the Son of God........... 8:37
4 straightway he preached **Christ** in the synagogues,........ 9:20
1 proving that this is very **Christ**........................ 9:22
1 Jesus **Christ** maketh thee whole:....................... 9:34
2 preaching peace by Jesus **Christ**: he is Lord of all:..... 10:36
2 baptized in the name of Jesus **Christ**. (NASB)......... 10:48
4 unto us, who believed on the Lord Jesus **Christ**;....... 11:17
2 that through the grace of the Lord Jesus **Christ**........ 15:11
2 their lives for the name of our Lord Jesus **Christ**....... 15:26
2 I command thee in the name of Jesus **Christ**.......... 16:18
4 And they said, Believe on the Lord Jesus **Christ**,...... 16:31
4 that **Christ** must needs have suffered,................. 17:3
1 that this Jesus, whom I preach unto you, is **Christ**...... 17:3
4 and testified to the Jews that Jesus was **Christ**......... 18:5
4 showing by the scriptures that Jesus was **Christ**........ 18:28
4 should come after him, that is, on **Christ** Jesus......... 19:4
4 and faith toward our Lord Jesus **Christ**............... 20:21
4 and heard him concerning the faith in **Christ**.......... 24:24
1 That **Christ** should suffer,.......................... 26:23
2 those things which concern the Lord Jesus **Christ**,...... 28:31
2 Paul, a servant of Jesus **Christ**,.................... Rom 1:1
2 from the dead: Jesus **Christ** our Lord. (NIV).......... 1:4
2 Among whom ... ye also the called of Jesus **Christ**:..... 1:6
2 and peace from God ... and the Lord Jesus **Christ**...... 1:7
2 I thank my God through Jesus **Christ** for you all,....... 1:8
2 For I am not ashamed of the gospel of **Christ**:.......... 1:16
2 judge ... by Jesus **Christ** according to my gospel......... 2:16
2 **Christ** unto all and upon all them that believe:......... 3:22
3 through the redemption that is in **Christ** Jesus:......... 3:24
2 peace with God through our Lord Jesus **Christ**:......... 5:1
1 in due time **Christ** died for the ungodly................ 5:6
1 while we were yet sinners, **Christ** died for us............ 5:8
2 we also joy in God through our Lord Jesus **Christ**,...... 5:11
2 Jesus **Christ**, hath abounded unto many................ 5:15
2 shall reign in life by one, Jesus **Christ**................ 5:17
2 unto eternal life by Jesus **Christ** our Lord.............. 5:21
4 into Jesus **Christ** were baptized into his death?......... 6:3
1 that like as **Christ** was raised up from the dead......... 6:4
3 Now if we be dead with **Christ**,....................... 6:8
1 Knowing that **Christ** being raised from the dead........ 6:9
3 but alive unto God through Jesus **Christ** our Lord....... 6:11
3 eternal life through Jesus **Christ** our Lord.............. 6:23
2 are become dead to the law by the body of **Christ**;..... 7:4
2 I thank God through Jesus **Christ** our Lord............. 7:25
3 condemnation to them which are in **Christ** Jesus,....... 8:1
3 For the law of the Spirit of life in **Christ** Jesus......... 8:2
2 Now if any man have not the Spirit of **Christ**,.......... 8:9
1 if **Christ** be in you, the body is dead because of sin;.... 8:10
4 he that raised up **Christ** from the dead shall also........ 8:11
2 heirs of God, and joint-heirs with **Christ**;.............. 8:17
1 Who is he that condemneth? It is **Christ** that died,...... 8:34
2 Who shall separate us from the love of **Christ**?......... 8:35
3 the love of God, which is in **Christ** Jesus our Lord...... 8:39

3 I say the truth in **Christ**, I lie not, ... Rom 9:1
2 myself were accursed from **Christ** for my brethren, ... 9:3
1 and of whom as concerning the flesh **Christ** came, ... 9:5
1 For **Christ** is the end of the law for righteousness 10:4
4 that is, to bring **Christ** down from above: 10:6
4 that is, to bring up **Christ** again from the dead. 10:7
2 and hearing by the word of **Christ**. (NASB) 10:17
3 So we, being many, are one body in **Christ**, ... 12:5
4 But put ye on the Lord Jesus **Christ**, ... 13:14
1 to this end **Christ** both died, and rose, and revived, ... 14:9
2 shall all stand before the judgment seat of **Christ**. 14:10
1 Destroy not him ... for whom **Christ** died. 14:15
3 For he that in these things serveth **Christ** 14:18
1 For even **Christ** pleased not himself; 15:3
4 one toward another according to **Christ** Jesus: 15:5
2 even the Father of our Lord Jesus **Christ**. 15:6
1 as **Christ** also received us to the glory of God. 15:7
4 Now I say that Jesus **Christ** was a minister 15:8
2 That I should be the minister of Jesus **Christ** 15:16
3 therefore whereof I may glory through Jesus **Christ** 15:17
1 those things which **Christ** hath not wrought by me, ... 15:18
2 I have fully preached the gospel of **Christ**. 15:19
1 to preach the gospel, not where **Christ** was named, ... 15:20
2 fulness of the blessing of the gospel of **Christ**. 15:29
2 beseech you, ... for the Lord Jesus **Christ's** sake, ... 15:30
3 Greet Priscilla and Aquila my helpers in **Christ** 16:3
4 who is the firstfruits of Achaia unto **Christ**. 16:5
3 who also were in **Christ** before me. 16:7
3 Salute Urbane, our helper in **Christ**, ... 16:9
3 Salute Apelles approved in **Christ**. 16:10
2 The churches **of Christ** salute you. 16:16
3 they that are such serve not our Lord Jesus **Christ**, ... 16:18
2 The grace of our Lord Jesus **Christ** be with you. 16:20
2 The grace of our Lord Jesus **Christ** be with you all. 16:24
2 and the preaching of Jesus **Christ**, ... 16:25
2 be glory through Jesus **Christ** for ever. Amen. 16:27
2 Paul, called to be an apostle of Jesus **Christ** .... 1 Co 1:1
3 to them that are sanctified in **Christ** Jesus, ... 1:2
2 call upon the name of Jesus **Christ** our Lord, ... 1:2
2 God our Father, and from the Lord Jesus **Christ**. 1:3
3 grace of God which is given you by Jesus **Christ**; 1:4
2 as the testimony of **Christ** was confirmed in you: 1:6
2 waiting for the coming of our Lord Jesus **Christ**: 1:7
2 be blameless in the day of our Lord Jesus **Christ**. 1:8
2 the fellowship of his Son Jesus **Christ** our Lord. 1:9
2 by the name of our Lord Jesus **Christ**, ... 1:10
2 and I of Apollos; and I of Cephas; and I **of Christ**. 1:12
1 Is **Christ** divided? was Paul crucified for you? 1:13
1 For **Christ** sent me not to baptize, but to preach 1:17
2 the cross of **Christ** should be made of none effect. 1:17
4 But we preach **Christ** crucified, ... 1:23
4 **Christ** the power of God, and the wisdom of God. 1:24
3 But of him are ye in **Christ** Jesus, ... 1:30
4 save Jesus **Christ**, and him crucified. 2:2
2 But we have the mind **of Christ**. 2:16
3 but as unto carnal, even as unto babes in **Christ**. 3:1
1 foundation ... that is laid, which is Jesus **Christ**. 3:11
2 And ye are **Christ's**; and Christ is God's. 3:23
1 And ye are Christ's; and **Christ** is God's. 3:23
2 as of the ministers **of Christ**, ... 4:1
4 We are fools for **Christ's** sake, but ye are wise 4:10
3 We are fools ... but ye are wise in **Christ**; 4:10
3 though ye have ten thousand instructors in **Christ**, ... 4:15
3 for in **Christ** Jesus I have begotten you 4:15
3 into remembrance of my ways which be in **Christ**, ... 4:17
2 In the name of our Lord Jesus **Christ**, ... 5:4
2 with the power of our Lord Jesus **Christ**, ... 5:4
1 For even **Christ** our passover is sacrificed for us: 5:7
2 the name of the Lord Jesus **Christ**, (NASB) 6:11
2 that your bodies are the members **of Christ**? 6:15
2 shall I then take the members of **Christ**, ... 6:15
2 he that is called, being free, is **Christ's** servant. 7:22
1 and one Lord Jesus **Christ**, by whom are all things, ... 8:6
1 the weak brother perish, for whom **Christ** died? 8:11
4 wound their weak conscience, ye sin against **Christ**. 8:12
4 have I not seen Jesus **Christ** our Lord? 9:1
2 lest we should hinder the gospel of **Christ**. 9:12
2 I may make the gospel of **Christ** without charge, ... 1 Co 9:18
3 but under the law **to Christ**, ... 9:21
1 that spiritual Rock ... and that Rock was **Christ**. 10:4
4 Neither let us tempt **Christ**, ... 10:9
2 is it not the communion of the blood of **Christ**? 10:16
2 is it not the communion of the body of **Christ**? 10:16
2 Be ye followers of me, even as I also am **of Christ**. 11:1
1 that the head of every man is **Christ**; 11:3
2 and the head **of Christ** is God. 11:3
1 being many, are one body: so also is **Christ**. 12:12
2 are the body **of Christ**, and members in particular. 12:27
1 **Christ** died for our sins according to the scriptures; 15:3
1 if **Christ** be preached that he rose from the dead, ... 15:12
1 if ... be no resurrection ... then is **Christ** not risen: 15:13
1 if **Christ** be not risen, then is our preaching vain, ... 15:14
4 we have testified of God that he raised up **Christ**: 15:15
1 For if the dead rise not, then is not **Christ** raised: 15:16
1 And if **Christ** be not raised, your faith is vain; 15:17
3 also which are fallen asleep in **Christ** are perished. 15:18
3 If in this life only we have hope in **Christ**, ... 15:19
1 But now is **Christ** risen from the dead, ... 15:20
3 even so in **Christ** shall all be made alive. 15:22
1 every man in his own order: **Christ** the firstfruits; 15:23
2 afterward they that are **Christ's** at his coming. 15:23
3 I protest by your rejoicing which I have in **Christ** 15:31
2 the victory through our Lord Jesus **Christ**. 15:57
4 If any man love not the Lord Jesus **Christ**, ... 16:22
2 The grace of our Lord Jesus **Christ** be with you. 16:23
3 My love be with you all in **Christ** Jesus. Amen. 16:24
2 Paul, an apostle of Jesus **Christ** by the will of God, 2 Co 1:1
2 God our Father, and from the Lord Jesus **Christ**. 1:2
2 God, even the Father of our Lord Jesus **Christ**, ... 1:3
2 For as the sufferings of **Christ** abound in us, ... 1:5
2 so our consolation also aboundeth by **Christ**. 1:5
1 For the Son of God, Jesus **Christ**, ... 1:19
4 Now he which stablisheth us with you in **Christ**, ... 1:21
2 for your sakes forgave I it in the person **of Christ**; 2:10
2 when I came to Troas to preach **Christ's** gospel, ... 2:12
3 which always causeth us to triumph in **Christ**, ... 2:14
2 For we are unto God a sweet savour **of Christ**, ... 2:15
3 in the sight of God speak we in **Christ**. 2:17
2 to be the epistle of **Christ** ministered by us, ... 3:3
2 such trust have we through **Christ** to God-ward: 3:4
3 which veil is done away in **Christ**. 3:14
2 lest the light of the glorious gospel of **Christ**, ... 4:4
4 For we preach not ourselves, but **Christ** Jesus 4:5
2 of the glory of God in the face of Jesus **Christ**. 4:6
2 must all appear before the judgment seat of **Christ**; 5:10
2 For the love of **Christ** constraineth us; 5:14
4 yea, though we have known **Christ** after the flesh, ... 5:16
3 if any man be in **Christ**, he is a new creature: 5:17
2 who hath reconciled us to himself by Jesus **Christ**, ... 5:18
3 To wit, that God was in **Christ**, ... 5:19
2 Now then we are ambassadors for **Christ**, ... 5:20
2 we pray you in **Christ's** stead, ... 5:20
3 And what concord hath **Christ** with Belial? 6:15
2 For ye know the grace of our Lord Jesus **Christ**, ... 8:9
2 and the glory of **Christ**. 8:23
2 professed subjection unto the gospel of **Christ**, ... 9:13
2 by the meekness and gentleness of **Christ**, ... 10:1
2 captivity every thought to the obedience of **Christ**; 10:5
2 If any man trust to himself that he is **Christ's**, ... 10:7
2 that, as he is **Christ's**, even so are we Christ's. 10:7
2 that, as he is Christ's, even so are we **Christ's**. 10:7
2 as to you also in preaching the gospel of **Christ**: 10:14
3 that I may present you as a chaste virgin to **Christ**. 11:2
4 from the simplicity that is in **Christ**. 11:3
2 As the truth **of Christ** is in me, ... 11:10
2 transforming themselves into the apostles **of Christ**. 11:13
2 Are they ministers **of Christ**? 11:23
2 The God and Father of our Lord Jesus **Christ**, ... 11:31
3 I knew a man in **Christ** above fourteen years ago, ... 12:2
2 that the power of **Christ** may rest upon me. 12:9
2 in persecutions, in distresses for **Christ's** sake: 12:10
3 we speak before God in **Christ**: 12:19
2 Since ye seek a proof of **Christ** speaking in me, ... 13:3
1 how that Jesus **Christ** is in you, ... 13:5

2 The grace of the Lord Jesus **Christ**, ... 2 Co 13:14
2 neither by man, but by Jesus **Christ**, and God ....Gal 1:1
2 God the Father, and from our Lord Jesus **Christ**, ... 1:3
2 from him that called you into the grace of **Christ** 1:6
2 and would pervert the gospel of **Christ**................. 1:7
2 pleased men, I should not be the servant of **Christ**...... 1:10
2 but by the revelation of Jesus **Christ**.................. 1:12
3 unto the churches of Judaea which were in **Christ**:...... 1:22
3 spy out our liberty which we have in **Christ** Jesus, ... 2:4
2 but by the faith of Jesus **Christ**, ... 2:16
4 even we have believed in Jesus **Christ**, ... 2:16
2 that we might be justified by the faith of **Christ**, ... 2:16
3 But if, while we seek to be justified by **Christ**, ... 2:17
1 is therefore **Christ** the minister of sin? God forbid....... 2:17
3 I am crucified with **Christ**: nevertheless I live; 2:20
1 yet not I, but **Christ** liveth in me:..................... 2:20
1 by the law, then **Christ** is dead in vain................. 2:21
1 Jesus **Christ** hath been evidently set forth, ... 3:1
1 **Christ** hath redeemed us from the curse of the law, ... 3:13
3 come on the Gentiles through Jesus **Christ**; 3:14
1 but as of one, And to thy seed, which is **Christ**......... 3:16
4 confirmed before of God in **Christ**, the law, ... 3:17
2 the promise by faith of Jesus **Christ** might be given 3:22
4 law was our schoolmaster to bring us unto **Christ**, ... 3:24
3 are all the children of God by faith in **Christ** Jesus...... 3:26
4 have been baptized into **Christ** have put on Christ....... 3:27
4 have been baptized into Christ have put on **Christ**....... 3:27
3 for ye are all one in **Christ** Jesus...................... 3:28
2 And if ye be **Christ's**, then are ye Abraham's seed, ... 3:29
2 and if a son, then an heir of God through **Christ**........ 4:7
4 but received me as an angel ... even as **Christ** Jesus..... 4:14
1 I travail in birth again until **Christ** be formed 4:19
1 in the liberty wherewith **Christ** hath made us free, ... 5:1
1 **Christ** shall profit you nothing......................... 5:2
2 **Christ** is become of no effect unto you, ... 5:4
3 in Jesus **Christ** ... circumcision availeth any thing, ... 5:6
2 And they that are **Christ's** have crucified the flesh 5:24
2 and so fulfil the law of **Christ**......................... 6:2
2 should suffer persecution for the cross of **Christ**......... 6:12
2 glory, save in the cross of our Lord Jesus **Christ**, ... 6:14
3 For in **Christ** Jesus neither circumcision availeth 6:15
2 grace of our Lord Jesus **Christ** be with your spirit....... 6:18
2 an apostle of Jesus **Christ** by the will of God, ...Eph 1:1
3 to the saints ... and to the faithful in **Christ** Jesus: 1:1
2 God our Father, and from the Lord Jesus **Christ**........ 1:2
2 the God and Father of our Lord Jesus **Christ**, ... 1:3
3 all spiritual blessings in heavenly places in **Christ**: 1:3
2 the adoption of children by Jesus **Christ** to himself, ... 1:5
3 might gather together in one all things in **Christ**, ... 1:10
3 the praise of his glory, who first trusted in **Christ**....... 1:12
2 That the God of our Lord Jesus **Christ**, ... 1:17
3 Which he wrought in **Christ**, when he raised him 1:20
3 hath quickened us together with **Christ**, ... 2:5
3 made us sit together in heavenly places in **Christ** 2:6
3 of his grace ... toward us through **Christ** Jesus.......... 2:7
3 created in **Christ** Jesus unto good works, ... 2:10
2 That at that time ye were without **Christ**, ... 2:12
3 now in **Christ** Jesus ye who sometimes were far off 2:13
2 are made nigh by the blood of **Christ**.................. 2:13
2 Jesus **Christ** himself being the chief corner stone; 2:20
2 the prisoner of Jesus **Christ** for you Gentiles, ... 3:1
2 understand my knowledge in the mystery of **Christ** 3:4
3 partakers of his promise in **Christ** by the gospel: 3:6
2 should preach ... the unsearchable riches of **Christ**; 3:8
2 hid in God, who created all things by Jesus **Christ**: 3:9
3 which he purposed in **Christ** Jesus our Lord: 3:11
2 unto the Father of our Lord Jesus **Christ**, ... 3:14
4 That **Christ** may dwell in your hearts by faith; 3:17
2 And to know the love of **Christ**, ... 3:19
3 Unto him be glory in the church by **Christ** Jesus 3:21
2 grace according to the measure of the gift of **Christ**..... 4:7
2 for the edifying of the body of **Christ**: 4:12
2 the measure of the stature of the fulness of **Christ**: 4:13
1 which is the head, even **Christ**: 4:15
4 But ye have not so learned **Christ**; 4:20
3 even as God for **Christ's** sake hath forgiven you......... 4:32
1 And walk in love, as **Christ** also hath loved us, ... 5:2
2 hath any inheritance in the kingdom of **Christ**....... Eph 5:5
1 and **Christ** shall give thee light........................ 5:14
2 the Father in the name of our Lord Jesus **Christ**; 5:20
2 to one another in the fear of **Christ**. (NASB) 5:21
1 even as **Christ** is the head of the church: 5:23
3 Therefore as the church is subject unto **Christ**, ... 5:24
1 even as **Christ** also loved the church, ... 5:25
1 just as **Christ** also does (NASB) 5:29
4 but I speak concerning **Christ** and the church........... 5:32
3 in singleness of your heart, as unto **Christ**; 6:5
2 but as the servants of **Christ**, ... 6:6
2 from God the Father and the Lord Jesus **Christ**.......... 6:23
4 that love our Lord Jesus **Christ** in sincerity. Amen...... 6:24
2 Paul and Timotheus, the servants of Jesus **Christ**, ... Phlp 1:1
3 all the saints in **Christ** Jesus which are at Philippi, ... 1:1
2 God our Father, and from the Lord Jesus **Christ**........ 1:2
2 will perform it until the day of Jesus **Christ**: 1:6
2 I long after you all in the bowels of Jesus **Christ**........ 1:8
2 sincere and without offence till the day of **Christ**; 1:10
2 fruits of righteousness, which are by Jesus **Christ**, ... 1:11
3 my bonds in **Christ** are manifest in all the palace, ... 1:13
4 Some ... preach **Christ** even of envy and strife; 1:15
4 The one preach **Christ** of contention, not sincerely, ... 1:16
1 in pretence, or in truth, **Christ** is preached; 1:18
2 and the supply of the Spirit of Jesus **Christ**, ... 1:19
1 so now also **Christ** shall be magnified in my body, ... 1:20
1 For to me to live is **Christ**, and to die is gain........... 1:21
3 having a desire to depart, and to be with **Christ**; 1:23
3 rejoicing may be more abundant in Jesus **Christ** 1:26
2 be as it becometh the gospel of **Christ**: 1:27
2 For unto you it is given in the behalf of **Christ**, ... 1:29
3 any consolation in **Christ**, if any comfort of love, ... 2:1
3 this mind ... which was also in **Christ** Jesus: 2:5
1 **Christ** is Lord, to the glory of God the Father.......... 2:11
2 that I may rejoice in the day of **Christ**, ... 2:16
2 their own, not the things which are Jesus **Christ's**....... 2:21
2 for the work of **Christ** he was nigh unto death, ... 2:30
3 and rejoice in **Christ** Jesus, ... 3:3
4 were gain to me, those I counted loss for **Christ**........ 3:7
2 loss for the excellency of the knowledge of **Christ** 3:8
4 do count them but dung, that I may win **Christ**, ... 3:8
2 but that which is through the faith of **Christ**, ... 3:9
2 for which also I am apprehended of **Christ** Jesus........ 3:12
3 the prize of the high calling of God in **Christ** Jesus...... 3:14
2 that they are the enemies of the cross of **Christ**: 3:18
4 we look for the Saviour, the Lord Jesus **Christ**: 3:20
3 keep your hearts and minds through **Christ** Jesus........ 4:7
3 all things through **Christ** which strengtheneth me........ 4:13
3 according to his riches in glory by **Christ** Jesus.......... 4:19
3 Salute every saint in **Christ** Jesus...................... 4:21
2 The grace of our Lord Jesus **Christ** be with you all...... 4:23
2 Paul, an apostle of Jesus **Christ** by the will of God, .. Col 1:1
3 To the saints and faithful brethren in **Christ** 1:2
2 God our Father and the Lord Jesus **Christ**.............. 1:2
2 to God and the Father of our Lord Jesus **Christ**, ... 1:3
3 Since we heard of your faith in **Christ** Jesus, ... 1:4
2 who is for you a faithful minister of **Christ**; 1:7
2 afflictions of **Christ** in my flesh for his body's sake, ... 1:24
1 which is **Christ** in you, the hope of glory: 1:27
3 we may present every man perfect in **Christ** Jesus: 1:28
2 mystery of God, and of the Father, and of **Christ**; 2:2
4 and the stedfastness of your faith in **Christ**.............. 2:5
4 ye have therefore received **Christ** Jesus the Lord, ... 2:6
4 the rudiments of the world, and not after **Christ**......... 2:8
2 by the circumcision of **Christ**: 2:11
2 but the body is of **Christ**............................. 2:17
3 dead with **Christ** from the rudiments of the world, ... 2:20
3 If ye then be risen with **Christ**, ... 3:1
1 where **Christ** sitteth on the right hand of God.......... 3:1
3 and your life is hid with **Christ** in God................ 3:3
1 When **Christ**, who is our life, shall appear, ... 3:4
1 bond nor free: but **Christ** is all, and in all............. 3:11
1 even as **Christ** forgave you, so also do ye.............. 3:13
2 peace of **Christ** rule in your hearts, (NASB) 3:15
2 Let the word of **Christ** dwell in you richly 3:16
3 receive the reward ... for ye serve the Lord **Christ**....... 3:24
2 to speak the mystery of **Christ**, ... 4:3

2 Epaphras, who is one of you, a servant of Christ, ... Col 4:12
3 is in God the Father and in the Lord Jesus Christ: .. 1 Th 1:1
2 from God our Father, and the Lord Jesus Christ........ 1:1
2 and patience of hope in our Lord Jesus Christ, ... 1:3
2 been burdensome, as the apostles of Christ............. 2:6
3 the churches of God which in Judaea are in Christ 2:14
2 presence of our Lord Jesus Christ at his coming? 2:19
2 and our fellowlabourer in the gospel of Christ, ... 3:2
1 Now God himself ... and our Lord Jesus Christ, ... 3:11
2 coming of our Lord Jesus Christ with all his saints...... 3:13
3 and the dead in Christ shall rise first: 4:16
2 but to obtain salvation by our Lord Jesus Christ, ... 5:9
3 for this is the will of God in Christ Jesus 5:18
2 unto the coming of our Lord Jesus Christ............... 5:23
2 The grace of our Lord Jesus Christ be with you.......... 5:28
3 in God our Father and the Lord Jesus Christ: .... 2 Th 1:1
2 from God our Father and the Lord Jesus Christ.......... 1:2
2 that obey not the gospel of our Lord Jesus Christ: 1:8
2 the name of our Lord Jesus Christ may be glorified 1:12
2 the grace of our God and the Lord Jesus Christ......... 1:12
2 by the coming of our Lord Jesus Christ, ... 2:1
2 as that the day of Christ is at hand.................... 2:2
2 the obtaining of the glory of our Lord Jesus Christ...... 2:14
1 Now our Lord Jesus Christ himself, and God, ... 2:16
2 and into the patient waiting for Christ.................. 3:5
2 command ... in the name of our Lord Jesus Christ, ... 3:6
2 we command and exhort by our Lord Jesus Christ, ... 3:12
2 The grace of our Lord Jesus Christ be with you all...... 3:18
2 Paul, an apostle of Jesus Christ .... 1 Tm 1:1
2 and Lord Jesus Christ, which is our hope; 1:1
2 from God our Father and Jesus Christ our Lord........... 1:2
3 And I thank Christ Jesus our Lord, ... 1:12
3 with faith and love which is in Christ Jesus............. 1:14
1 Christ Jesus came into the world to save sinners; 1:15
1 Jesus Christ might show forth all longsuffering, ... 1:16
1 and one mediator ... the man Christ Jesus; 2:5
3 I speak the truth in Christ, and lie not; 2:7
3 great boldness in the faith which is in Christ Jesus...... 3:13
2 thou shalt be a good minister of Jesus Christ, ... 4:6
2 they have begun to wax wanton against Christ, ... 5:11
2 charge thee before God, and the Lord Jesus Christ, ... 5:21
2 even the words of our Lord Jesus Christ, ... 6:3
2 in the sight of God, ... and before Christ Jesus, ... 6:13
2 until the appearing of our Lord Jesus Christ: 6:14
2 Paul, an apostle of Jesus Christ by the will of God, 2 Tm 1:1
3 according to the promise of life which is in Christ 1:1
2 from God the Father and Christ Jesus our Lord.......... 1:2
3 given us in Christ Jesus before the world began, ... 1:9
2 by the appearing of our Saviour Jesus Christ, ... 1:10
3 in faith and love which is in Christ Jesus............... 1:13
3 be strong in the grace that is in Christ Jesus............ 2:1
2 endure hardness, as a good soldier of Jesus Christ....... 2:3
4 Remember that Jesus Christ of the seed of David 2:8
3 also obtain the salvation which is in Christ Jesus 2:10
2 Let every one that nameth the name of Christ 2:19
3 live godly in Christ Jesus shall suffer persecution........ 3:12
3 through faith which is in Christ Jesus................... 3:15
2 before God, and the Lord Jesus Christ, ... 4:1
1 The Lord Jesus Christ be with thy spirit................ 4:22
2 a servant of God, and an apostle of Jesus Christ, ... Tit 1:1
2 the Father and the Lord Jesus Christ our Saviour....... 1:4
2 of the great God and our Saviour Jesus Christ; 2:13
2 abundantly through Jesus Christ our Saviour; 3:6
2 Paul, a prisoner of Jesus Christ, and Timothy .... Phlm 1:1
2 from God our Father and the Lord Jesus Christ......... 1:3
4 every good thing which is in you in Christ Jesus........ 1:6
3 Wherefore, though I might be much bold in Christ 1:8
2 and now also a prisoner of Jesus Christ................ 1:9
3 refresh my heart in Christ. (NASB) 1:20
3 Epaphras, my fellowprisoner in Christ Jesus; 1:23
2 grace of our Lord Jesus Christ be with your spirit....... 1:25
4 and High Priest of our profession, Christ Jesus; ...... Heb 3:1
1 But Christ as a son over his own house; 3:6
2 For we are made partakers of Christ, ... 3:14
1 So also Christ glorified not himself 5:5
2 leaving the principles of the doctrine of Christ, ... 6:1
1 But Christ being come an high priest 9:11
2 How much more shall the blood of Christ, ... Heb 9:14
1 For Christ is not entered into the holy places made 9:24
1 Christ was once offered to bear the sins of many; 9:28
2 the offering of the body of Jesus Christ once for all.... 10:10
2 Esteeming the reproach of Christ greater riches 11:26
1 Jesus Christ the same yesterday, and to day, ... 13:8
2 Jesus Christ; to whom be glory for ever and ever...... 13:21
2 a servant of God and of the Lord Jesus Christ, ... Jas 1:1
2 have not the faith of our Lord Jesus Christ, ... 2:1
2 Peter, an apostle of Jesus Christ, ... 1 Pt 1:1
2 and sprinkling of the blood of Jesus Christ: 1:2
2 Christ, which according to his abundant mercy 1:3
2 by the resurrection of Jesus Christ from the dead, ... 1:3
2 honour and glory at the appearing of Jesus Christ: 1:7
2 the Spirit of Christ which was in them did signify, ... 1:11
4 it testified beforehand the sufferings of Christ, ... 1:11
2 brought unto you at the revelation of Jesus Christ; 1:13
2 But with the precious blood of Christ, ... 1:19
2 acceptable to God by Jesus Christ...................... 2:5
1 Christ also suffered for us, leaving us an example, ... 2:21
4 but sanctify Christ as Lord in your hearts, (NASB) 3:15
3 falsely accuse your good conversation in Christ.......... 3:16
1 For Christ also hath once suffered for sins, ... 3:18
2 by the resurrection of Jesus Christ: 3:21
2 Forasmuch then as Christ hath suffered for us 4:1
2 in all things may be glorified through Jesus Christ, ... 4:11
2 inasmuch as ye are partakers of Christ's sufferings; 4:13
2 If ye be reproached for the name of Christ, ... 4:14
2 and a witness of the sufferings of Christ, ... 5:1
3 called us unto his eternal glory by Christ Jesus, ... 5:10
3 Peace be with you all that are in Christ Jesus........... 5:14
2 Peter, a servant and an apostle of Jesus Christ, ... 2 Pt 1:1
2 righteousness of God and our Saviour Jesus Christ: 1:1
2 in the knowledge of our Lord Jesus Christ.............. 1:8
2 kingdom of our Lord and Saviour Jesus Christ.......... 1:11
1 even as our Lord Jesus Christ hath showed me.......... 1:14
2 the power and coming of our Lord Jesus Christ, ... 1:16
2 knowledge of the Lord and Saviour Jesus Christ, ... 2:20
2 knowledge of our Lord and Saviour Jesus Christ......... 3:18
2 is with the Father, and with his Son Jesus Christ..... 1 Jn 1:3
2 and the blood of Jesus Christ his Son cleanseth us 1:7
4 we have an advocate ... Jesus Christ the righteous: 2:1
1 is a liar but he that denieth that Jesus is the Christ? 2:22
2 should believe on the name of his Son Jesus Christ, ... 3:23
4 that Jesus Christ is come in the flesh is of God: 4:2
4 confesseth not that Jesus Christ is come in the flesh 4:3
1 believeth that Jesus is the Christ is born of God: 5:1
1 that came by water and blood, even Jesus Christ; 5:6
3 even in his Son Jesus Christ. This is the true God, ... 5:20
2 God the Father, and from the Lord Jesus Christ, ... 2 Jn 1:3
4 confess not that Jesus Christ is come in the flesh........ 1:7
2 and abideth not in the doctrine of Christ, ... 1:9
2 He that abideth in the doctrine of Christ, ... 1:9
2 Jude, the servant of Jesus Christ, ... Jude 1:1
3 and preserved in Jesus Christ, and called: 1:1
4 and our Lord Jesus Christ............................ 1:4
2 of the apostles of our Lord Jesus Christ; 1:17
2 looking for the mercy of our Lord Jesus Christ 1:21
2 through Jesus Christ our Lord, (NASB) 1:25
2 The Revelation of Jesus Christ, which God gave ..... Rev 1:1
2 and of the testimony of Jesus Christ, ... 1:2
2 And from Jesus Christ, who is the faithful witness, ... 1:5
2 and in the kingdom and patience of Jesus Christ, ... 1:9
2 and for the testimony of Jesus Christ.................. 1:9
2 the kingdoms of our Lord, and of his Christ; 11:15
2 kingdom of our God, and the power of his Christ: 12:10
2 and have the testimony of Jesus Christ................ 12:17
2 lived and reigned with Christ a thousand years......... 20:4
2 but they shall be priests of God and of Christ, ... 20:6
2 The grace of our Lord Jesus Christ be with you all..... 22:21

Classical Greek

Christos is a verbal adjective related to the verb *chriō* (5383) which means "to rub, to smear," or "to anoint" when used of fats or oil. It is related also to *chrisma* (5380), the oil used for anointing. *Christos* identifies that which has been thus smeared or anointed. In the New Testament it is used only as a noun, either as an appellative ("the Anointed One, the Christ") or as a personal name ("Jesus Christ" or "Christ") (*Bauer*).

Outside of Biblical literature and tradition *christos* is used only as an adjective, never as a personal title. In classical Greek it is used of anything that was rubbed on externally (*pharmaka christa* or *epichrisma*, "salves, ointments"). Its earliest apparent use as a title is found in Psalms of Solomon 17:36, "And their king shall be *christos kurios*" ("Lord Christ"). (*Moulton-Milligan* suggests emending this to read *christos kuriou*, "the Lord's anointed.")

The Greeks used another word for "anointing," *aleimma* (from *aleiphō* [216]). We see *aleiphō* numerous times in the New Testament in connection with an anointing with oil (Matthew 6:17; Mark 6:13; Luke 7:38,46; John 11:2; 12:3; James 5:14). It is noteworthy that in his Greek translation of the Hebrew Old Testament, Aquila did not use *christos* but *ēleimmenos* as the equivalent to *māshîach*, "Messiah." This is probably because the verbal adjective *christos* was not a favorable word to apply to a person. *Christos*, therefore, had no special religious or sacred sense among the Greeks. In fact, it was more a term of derision than respect (Rengstorf, "Jesus Christ," *Colin Brown*, 2:334,335).

In light of this background it may seem striking that the translators of the Septuagint chose *chriō* as the replacement of the verb *māshach* and the adjective *christos* for *māshîach*. Consequently, we note that the designation *christos* for the Messiah was not originally a Christian understanding. Rather, it was adopted from the Old Testament. Thus the term itself would not have been offensive to Jewish ears. Peter wrote to Jewish Christians in the Diaspora not to be ashamed of being called Christians; instead, they should praise God (1 Peter 4:16).

Septuagint Usage

In the Septuagint *christos* is a translation of the Hebrew *māshîach*, "anointed" or "Messiah," which is related to *māshach*, which also means "to rub, anoint," or "spread" a liquid. The Aramaic form of the same word is *m^eshach*, and in Greek this is transliterated as *messias* (3193). *Mishchāh*, "anointing oil," is also a related term. *Māshach* can be used in rather common contexts: painting a house (Jeremiah 22:14) or smearing oil on a shield (Isaiah 21:5). But it had special theological significance when referring to the anointing of people for special service or office: priest (Exodus 29:7; Leviticus 4:5,16; 6:22; 21:10), prophet (1 Kings 19:16), and king (1 Samuel 2:10; 12:3; 16:6; 24:6; 2 Samuel 12:7; 19:21; etc.). The anointing oil was sprinkled on things but poured on the head of people, leaving the perfumed aroma as an identifying characteristic. The person who experienced such anointing was often called simply "the Lord's anointed" (cf. 1 Samuel 26:9; 2 Samuel 23:1). In the case of David it is clear that he was "anointed by God" before he was anointed by Samuel (1 Samuel 16:6); ideally, the human act was a verification of God's prior action.

Hamilton suggests a fourfold significance to such anointing ("māshach," *Theological Wordbook of the Old Testament*, 1:530): (1) separation unto God, (2) authorization by God, (3) divine enablement, and (4) the coming Deliverer. In regards to this final use he says, "Though this association with the term *māshach* is not as prevalent in the OT as often supposed, the prospect of a righteous, Spirit-filled ruler is increasingly discernible in the OT (cf. Isaiah 9:1-7; 11:1-5; 61:1)" (ibid.). It was probably because of his role as a deliverer of God's people, selected by the Lord for His purpose, that Cyrus, a Gentile emperor, was given the title of "messiah, anointed" (Isaiah 45:1). However, long after Cyrus, God's people were still promised Messiah the prince, the one to fulfill *all* of the Biblical promises (Daniel 9:25,26).

Because the anointed one of the Lord was considered especially holy by virtue of his sacred office, it was dangerous to attempt to harm him (2 Samuel 1:14; 1 Chronicles 16:22; Psalm 105:15). During the time it was ruled by a king, Israel especially applied the title to its ruler (1 Samuel 2:10,35; 16:6; 26:9,11; Psalms 2:2; 18:50). The king in fact was considered to be God's representative on earth; he administered God's kingdom to Israel. The office and authority of the king, therefore, were of divine origin. Nonetheless, the king in Israel was never deified as was the case in many of the neighboring countries.

Israel's hope for salvation was placed upon a personal mediator who, as the Lord's chosen instrument, would save and redeem Israel in the end time. Apparently there were two strains of thought concerning how this would take place. One saw the appearance of a messiah, a solely human figure, who would politically, militarily, and socially deliver Israel from its foes. The other viewpoint saw God as directly intervening in human history. He would come in perfect power and establish His kingdom over all the earth. He would redeem His people, deliver them from exile, and become their ruler (Isaiah 40:10f.; 45:4f.; 52:12; Ezekiel 34:11, and elsewhere). Thus, this view saw God as directly and personally interrupting human history in the end time.

However, these two lines of thought—one that God himself would save and lead His people and the other that He would accomplish this through a human instrument—intersect. Ezekiel 34, for example, clearly depicts a union between the divine and the human. In verses 11 and following the Lord declares that He himself carries out the work of redemption. But in verse 23 it is stated that He does this through His servant David. In verse 24 both lines of thought converge: "I the Lord will be their God, and my servant David a prince among them." In the God-man Jesus we distinctly note this internal unity and relationship.

The person of the Saviour, only gradually drawn in the pages of the Old Testament, was called Messiah according to Judaism, despite the fact that the Old Testament almost never uses this appellation for the future ruler of the kingdom of God. The expression "anointed of the Lord" appears in connection with a future mediator of salvation in Psalm 2:2 and Daniel 9:25f., however. When this mediator of salvation is called Messiah, it is tied to the fact that the king of Israel, as the Lord's anointed, more than anyone else was the instrument of God's kingdom of earth.

The expectation of a future salvation was closely tied to the Davidic kingship. According to 2 Samuel 7:12ff. the Lord promised that David's kingdom would last forever. Nathan's prophecy is thus the starting point of the eschatological hope of a king-deliverer from the line of David. The association between this expectation and the Davidic line appears in passages like Psalm 89:4,5,20f.; Isaiah 11:1; 55:3; Jeremiah 23:5; 30:8f.; 33:15; Ezekiel 34:23; 37:24; and Amos 9:11.

Messianic expectation finds its most beautiful and passionate expression in the Psalms about Israel and its kings (Psalms 2, 20, 21, 45, 72, 110, and 132). These psalms go beyond general comments about kings in Israel. Just as the promises of an eternal kingdom to David anticipate promises of eschatological deliverance and salvation, the institution of king is a prophetic model of the kingship of the Messiah. These psalms are therefore considered messianic.

Psalm 2 describes from an eschatological perspective the struggle between the almighty God and His enemies. The issue here is the final, universal victory of God and His kingdom (cf. Psalm 46; Ezekiel 38; Revelation 20:8f.). In the course of this battle "the anointed one of the Lord" comes on the scene as the one who manifests the kingdom of God on earth (verse 9). The fate of all peoples depends upon their relationship with the anointed of the Lord (verse 12). He is installed as the Son of God (in the theocratic/messianic sense of the term) and given universal dominion. The new aspect here, which differs from former messianic expectations, is that the Messiah will have universal dominion. Furthermore, it is also obvious that the Messiah's accomplishments are in keeping with the will of the Lord himself for the establishment of His kingdom on earth (verses 2 and 3).

The same eschatological perspective of struggle that occurred in Psalm 2 is repeated in Psalm 110. The unique feature here is that Messiah also has a priestly role; He is a priest after the order of Melchizedek (verse 4). Melchizedek was a "priest-king" who joined the duties of both priest and king in one person. This parallels the priestly status—on a universal scope—of the Messiah-King. The priest is responsible for providing atonement for the people and for opening the way to fellowship with God. We find similar priestly roles played by Messiah (Jeremiah 30:21; Zechariah 3:8,9; 6:12,13; and especially Isaiah 53). But Psalms 2 and 110 particularly stress that it is the Messiah as king who through the help of the Lord conquers the enemies of God and administers the kingdom of God on earth.

The most complete picture of Messiah in the Old Testament is perhaps Psalm 72. It provides an almost total summary of all of the messianic prophecies of the Old Testament. This psalm is a prayer for God to send Israel a king from the lineage of David who will mirror God's own merciful intentions. It is a request for a righteous descendant of David, such as the one prophesied by Isaiah (11:2f.; cf. 2 Samuel 23:3f.). The distinct feature of this psalm is that the Messiah-King will gain followers because of His mercy and love (verses 8-14). He is a "prince of peace" who cares for the poor and destitute (verses 4,12-14). Fear of the Lord (verse 5), righteousness (verses 1,2), and peace (verse 3) will blossom.

More than anything else peace is a sign of the Messianic Age (cf. Isaiah 2:4; 9:5,6; 11:9; 65:25; Micah 5:3; Zechariah 9:10). Psalm 72 also mentions the effect of Messiah upon all of existence (verse 16). All peoples are blessed through Messiah (verse 17), just as the blessing of Abraham foretold (Genesis 22:18).

The prophecies of Scripture complete the portrait of Messiah even further. A central thought in Scripture is that Messiah will be victorious over the enemies of the kingdom of God. Many prophecies about Messiah are to be realized in the terrible and inevitable judgment which is to come. Messiah would be born from among the small remnant of people who survive the judgment (Isaiah 7:15f.; 10:20-22). Only a "root" or "stump" will remain of the royal lineage; nevertheless, from this small stump will sprout fruit (Isaiah 11:1; Micah 5:1f.). Texts like those mentioned above, as well as Amos 9:11, depict the appearance of Messiah against the backdrop of the lowest ebb of the Davidic dynasty. Messiah is especially depicted as impoverished and despised (e.g., Isaiah 53; Zechariah 9:9). Amos can call this the restoration of the "fallen tabernacle of David" (cf. Amos 9:11f.).

The writings of the prophets Isaiah and Micah shed even more light on the person of Messiah. From the Immanuel prophecy of Isaiah 7:10-17 we learn that Messiah's appearance belongs to the realm of the miraculous. The name itself says something about the nature of the child. In the child is "God with us." He represents the incarnate presence of God and His help. He himself guarantees that the promises of David are not void (cf. Isaiah 8:9,10). Setting Him apart from all others is His miraculous virgin birth (cf. Matthew 1:18f.). Messiah is equipped with supernatural qualities according to Isaiah 9:6: "Unto us a child is born, unto us a son is given: and the government shall be upon his shoulder: and his name shall be called Wonderful, Counselor, The mighty God, The everlasting Father, The Prince of Peace." Although the Messiah comes from lowly circumstances, His "goings forth have been from of old," from *'ôlām* (Micah 5:2). Long before His birth in Bethlehem, this child assumed a role in salvation history because He is from eternity. Therefore, His future kingdom is also without end (Isaiah 9:7).

The prophecy also indicates that new covenant will reestablish mankind's fellowship with God. He creates this covenant based upon the total forgiveness of sin (Jeremiah 31:31-34). By His forgiving of sins through the Messiah the Lord fulfills the Law in the hearts of men (Jeremiah 31:33; Ezekiel 36:25f.). The well-known Servant Songs (Isaiah 42:1-4; 49:1-7; 50:4-11; 52:13 to 53:12) relate many kingly and prophetic features of the Messiah. But the most important feature is that He is the founder of a new covenant. Through His atoning sacrifice He secures forgiveness of sins for humanity, that is, justification (Isaiah 53:11). Through His act of supreme abasement and humility Messiah wins His universal kingdom (Isaiah 52:13f.). He becomes the instrument of the Lord not only to guide Israel back to God, but to become a "light of the nations" and a Saviour of all (Isaiah 42:1-4; 49:6).

The suffering aspect is especially prominent in the Servant Songs. In the first three songs the suffering closely resembles the suffering which follows the prophetic call. But in the final song it depicts the suffering of the priest who offers His own person in sacrifice to the Lord (Isaiah 53:10) on behalf of the sins of the people (verse 8). The Messiah is a "man of sorrows" (literally, "pains"), inflicted with the wrath of God (verses 6 and 10).

In Daniel 7:13 we are told of the King of salvation who acquires an eternal kingdom over all the universe. He is the embodiment of God's people of the end times, and He is characterized as a heavenly, divine Person. He is described as "one like the Son of man."

Later, in Jewish apocalyptic literature, the title *Son of Man* was a distinctly messianic title (e.g., 1 Enoch; 4 Ezra). The messianic expectation which was linked to the figure of the Son of Man hinted at the notion of a preexistent, heavenly, and divine Messiah. The preexistence of Messiah is further expressed in Micah 5:1, and His heavenly nature, in Isaiah 9:6. The redemption accomplished by this person shatters all the political, military, and material understandings of that day. His salvation occurs on a cosmic-universal scale; it surpasses any simple human concept. Messiah is thus judge of the world as well as the One who brings new life to it.

The two centuries immediately prior to the appearance of Christ were marked by strong messianic expectation. In virtually every level of society it was thought that Messiah would be a national-political king who, like His forefather David, would wield great power. He was expected to redeem Israel from the yoke of the Gentiles (i.e., Rome) and to reestablish the throne of

David's kingdom in the Holy City of Jerusalem. There would not be any question as to when He appeared; His external glory would legitimize Him. This "popular" and earthly figure was completely foreign to Jesus' understanding of His role as Messiah. The New Testament reveals that this contrast caused Jesus tremendous difficulties.

New Testament Usage

That Jesus is indeed the promised Messiah-King of the Old Testament is a fundamental confession of New Testament faith. Jesus is confirmed as Messiah no less than 280 times. The double title *Jesus Christ* is actually a confession: Jesus is the Christ, that is, the Messiah. This was the oldest Christological confession of a Jewish background. From a Gentile perspective, however, the title was so unfamiliar that "Christ" was soon regarded as more of a proper name.

It was the rising expectation of a deliverer for Israel that gave substance to messianic doctrine during the era of Rabbinic Judaism immediately preceding and accompanying the time of Christ. Official Pharisaic belief and practice did not stress the messianic hope; the term occurs only once in the Mishnah (*Sotah* 9:15), written after the life of Jesus. However, the Dead Sea Scrolls reveal how popular the concept was in Qumran, and presumably in much of Judaism. The oldest use of *Messiah* as a name is possibly found in 1QSa 2:12 (Vander Woude, "chriō," *Kittel*, 9:518). The Qumran community may have actually expected three Messiahs, "a great prophet, a great captain and ruler, and a great priest" (Bruce, *Second Thoughts on the Dead Sea Scrolls*, p.84). For certain they expected two: one to fulfill the promises to Phinehas (Numbers 25:12f.) and another to fulfill the covenant with David (2 Samuel 7:11-16). The pseudepigrapha also are rife with references to the Messiah (cf. Jocz, "Messiah," *The Zondervan Pictorial Encyclopedia of the Bible*, 4:202).

Such expectations are evident in the discussions and debates about the identity of the Lord Jesus (Matthew 2:4; 11:2,3; 22:42; 26:63 and Synoptic parallels; John 1:20,25; 4:25,29,42; 7:26-42; 10:24; 12:34). It is the primary contention of Christianity that Jesus of Nazareth is the one and only Christ (John 20:31), His full title being the Lord Jesus Christ (Revelation 22:21).

The word *christos* is used over 500 times in the New Testament, in every book except 3 John. It is never used in a mundane sense, but only to refer to the anticipated Messiah, and then only as a reference to Jesus, either as Jesus Christ, Christ Jesus, or Christ the Lord. Over 70 percent of those uses are in Paul's 13 epistles.

In Gentile lands the title most frequently employed was *kurios* (2935), "Lord." When Paul placed *Christ* in front of the name *Jesus*, it is more in keeping with its being an official designation. The Messiah/Christ title occurs about 60 times in the Gospels. Every other name associated with Messiah is subordinate to this title. Thus we speak of "Christ-ology" as the study of the doctrine and person of Christ. The overall "religion" of the followers of Jesus is also characterized by this title, for they are first of all "Christians" because they confess Jesus is Messiah (Acts 11:26).

The Christ is an historical person, Jesus of Nazareth, a Jew, descendant of David (Matthew 1:16,17; cf. 2 Samuel 7:12-16). He was expected to live and reign forever (Luke 1:32,33; John 12:34). He is the ultimate Deliverer, the Saviour from sin (Luke 2:11). The baptism of Jesus was His historical anointing (Luke 3:22; 4:1,14,18,21; Acts 10:38), matching on earth what God had already ordained in heaven. His resurrection was conclusive evidence (Acts 2:30-36), proving that the suffering and death of the Christ was not foreign to the plan of God despite the universal surprise at it (Luke 24:26; cf. Matthew 16:21,22; Luke 23:35,37).

The Christ is not a disembodied spirit or ideal, moving from person to person. No one else ever has the right to assume that title (Matthew 24:5,23,24). Those who do are antichrists, opponents of and substitutes for the only legitimate One (1 John 4:3). A primary test of orthodoxy is one's view of the Christ, for it is by faith in the historical Lord Jesus Christ alone that one is redeemed from sin and granted eternal life (Acts 4:10-12; 1 John 2:22; 4:2). The early apostles proclaimed boldly to Jew and Gentile alike that Jesus is the Christ (Acts 18:5,28).

Upon close examination the Gospels reveal that Jesus was somewhat reluctant to apply the title *Christ* to himself; nonetheless, He did not reject it (John 10:24). His hesitancy is a result of several factors. For one, official Judaism propagated a view of Messiah as a national-political figure to which Jesus could not subscribe (John 6:15; 18:33f.). Jesus avoided arousing false hopes in those who held such views. In addition, He needed to maintain a peaceable relationship with government authorities because they were always on the lookout for messianic pretenders. Jewish patriots and zealot leaders regularly attempted to throw off the yoke of Roman oppression (Matthew 2:3; Acts 5:36).

Jesus' messianic self-awareness was supported by the prophetic word of revelation. The prophecies about the Suffering Servant of the Lord particularly did so (Isaiah 42:1-4; 49:1-7; 50:4-11; 52:13 to 53:12), as did the figure of the apocalyptic Son of Man (Daniel 7:13f.). During His earthly life Jesus experienced the humiliation reserved for the Servant of the Lord; He gave His life as a ransom for the sin of the world (Matthew 20:28; 26:28; Luke 24:26,27). The disciples themselves only gradually came to realize this (Matthew 16:20f.). They were extremely slow to pick up on Jesus' testimony about His role as Messiah, the Servant of the Lord (Mark 9:31f.).

Jesus' uniting of the figure of Messiah with the Son of Man was a unique act. It was unthinkable that the Son of Man could appear on earth in humiliation—*Son of Man* was a divine title of exaltation in apocalyptic thought! The title *Son of Man* was a riddle to those segments of the population who had not been exposed to the terminology of apocalyptic thought, but Jesus used it to shatter the national-political concept of Messiah of His day.

Jesus' reluctance to apply the title *Messiah* to himself is first and foremost explained as an attempt to preserve the true nature of the salvation He brought. Jesus could not allow himself to be catapulted to messianic status on the basis of the accolades and expectations of the masses. He could only be the Messiah when He had fulfilled His role as the Suffering Servant of God, who through suffering and death atones for sin (Acts 2:36). Consequently, there was a veil of secrecy about the ministry and person of Jesus Christ (Matthew 11:25f.; 21:23-27; Luke 20:41-44). His person and ministry can only be completely explained and understood in light of the fact that He knew himself to be the promised mediator of salvation and the king of deliverance of the Old Testament—the Messiah.

Throughout His ministry Jesus worked to develop His disciples' faith in this kind of Messiah (Matthew 16:15f.). The sum of Jesus' preaching of the nearness of the Kingdom (Matthew 4:17) was indirectly tied to the fact that the promised eschatological king of salvation had actually arrived in His own person and work (Matthew 13:16f.; John 4:25,26). Jesus' preaching of the good news as well as His working of miracles are both to be understood as messianic signs, indicators of the presence of the Messiah's redemption (Matthew 11:1f.). The motif of Jesus' desire for secrecy can be traced throughout Jesus' overall self-testimony and His works.

Toward the end of His ministry at Caesarea Philippi Jesus elicited a messianic confession from His disciples (Matthew 16:13f.; Mark 8:27f.; Luke 9:18f.). As the hour of salvation neared, there was an increased revelation of Jesus' identity. At the triumphant entry into Jerusalem—arranged by Jesus himself—Jesus received public confirmation of His status as Messiah. He was honored as the "Son of David," the long-awaited king of salvation (Matthew 21:1-9; Mark 11:1-10; Luke 19:28-38). During His trial Jesus himself declared His messianic status after He was provoked by the high priest (Matthew 26:63,64; Mark 14:61,62; Luke 22:66-70). Moreover, it is a historical fact that Jesus was crucified as a messianic pretender—the "king of the Jews" (John 19:19).

Jesus' status as Messiah is described in the New Testament in terms of His being preexistent (John 6:62; 8:56-58), His having a heavenly origin (John 3:13), and His being the Son of Man and the Son of God (John 1:1f.; Hebrews 1:1f.). He is the Mediator of all creation (Colossians 1:16f.). In the fullness of time He "put on" flesh (John 1:14; Philippians 2:7). Jesus was born as a descendant of David (Matthew 1:1f.; Romans 1:3). Through His suffering and death He, as high priest, secured our eternal redemption (the main theme of the letter to the Hebrews). As the sacrificial lamb He redeemed us from a meaningless way of life (1 Peter 1:19).

By virtue of Jesus' resurrection and ascension God has exalted Him to the position of both Lord and Christ (Acts 2:33f.; cf. Matthew 28:18f.). As Lord and Messiah He will return in glory from heaven as the judge of the world (Matthew 16:27; 25:31f.; Acts 17:31) as well as the one who renews it (Matthew 19:28; Romans 8:18f.; 2 Peter 3:13; Revelation 21:5). At the return of Jesus God's kingdom will be consummated. What began on earth in the Church will be finalized. According to the Biblical witness, the messianic kingdom comes as a restoration of creation. It is eternal in scope and dominion (Luke 1:33; Hebrews 1:8).

With Paul, *Christ* became a proper name, whether linked with Jesus or standing alone but obviously referring to Jesus. Paul's letters emphasize the soteriological aspects of the Messiah for the Church, which is the body of Christ and is composed of both Jews and Gentiles. He is concerned with spiritual, not political, deliverance. "The author has attached his conception to its historical Jewish basis; he has retained the old term, but has so purged it of its political, and even of its apocalyptic, significance, and given it a purely religious meaning, that 'the Christ' is in his thought chiefly a deliverer from death and from that which is the cause of death" (Burton, *The International Critical Commentary, Galatians*, p.399). Paul's characteristic description of a redeemed individual is that he is a person "in Christ" (*en christos*; e.g., 2 Corinthians 12:2; Ephesians 1:1,3; 2:6,10).

It is not legitimate to say that the title *Christ* has been stripped of any apocalyptic or political content. The final book of the Bible is technically the Revelation of Jesus Christ (1:1). It contains a majestic portrait of the Son of God in His present glory among the churches (1:12-18), but it also reveals Him as the yet coming One who will complete the unfulfilled prophecies regarding the Messiah (1:7; 11:15; 12:10). "The testimony of Jesus is the spirit of prophecy" (19:10); all the prophecies of the Christ have looked toward historical fulfillment in Jesus (at either His first or second coming). That historical Lord Jesus Christ is King of kings, and Lord of lords (19:16), the Alpha and Omega, the beginning and the end (22:13).

Strong 5547, Bauer 887, Moulton-Milligan 693, Kittel 9:493-580, Liddell-Scott 2007, Colin Brown 2:334-35,338-40.

5383. χρίω chriō verb

To anoint; to appoint.

Cognates:

ἐγχρίω enchriō (1465)
ἐπιχρίω epichriō (2009)
χρῖσμα chrisma (5380)

Synonyms:

ἀλείφω aleiphō (216)
ἐπιχρίω epichriō (2009)
μυρίζω murizō (3324)

מָשַׁח māshach (5066), Qal: spread with oil (Ex 29:2); anoint (1 Sm 15:1, Is 61:1); niphal: be anointed (Nm 7:10,84, 1 Chr 14:8).

מָשִׁיחַ māshîach (5081), Something covered with oil (2 Sm 1:21).

סוּךְ sûkh (5665), Anoint (Dt 28:40); hophal: be poured out (Ex 30:32).

1. ἔχρισας echrisas 2sing indic aor act
2. ἔχρισεν echrisen 3sing indic aor act
3. χρίσας chrisas nom sing masc part aor act

2 because he **hath anointed** me to preach the gospel... Luke 4:18
1 thy holy child Jesus, whom thou **hast anointed**,...... Acts 4:27
2 How God **anointed** Jesus of Nazareth................. 10:38
3 with you in Christ, and **hath anointed** us, is God;....2 Co 1:21
2 even thy God, hath **anointed** thee with the oil....... Heb 1:9

Classical Greek

In classical Greek the verb *chriō* has a broad semantic range (cf. the related noun *chrisma* [5380]). It means "to smear something on something else" and could thus designate to "anoint with oil, apply paints or glazes," etc. Even when an author of the Homeric school used *chriō* for the "anointing" of a person by a god by smearing ambrosia on him (*Hymn to Demeter* 237), the word *chriō* itself carried no special religious significance.

Septuagint Usage

The range of meaning of *chriō* in the Septuagint is more limited. It is used for the ritual anointing with oil to consecrate and appoint someone to a special office such as priest or king. Only once (1 Kings 19:16 [LXX 3 Kings 19:16]) is it used for a literal anointing with oil to appoint someone to the office of prophet. Phrases such as "to anoint to the kingship/for the purpose of ruling" are found frequently in the Septuagint.

As a result of this ceremonial anointing, a person received the abilities or rights needed for the execution of the office. This effect led to the figurative use of the verb to indicate any endowment of spiritual gifts or even the very Spirit of God. It is with this figurative meaning that *chriō* most often appears with reference to the prophets. They would describe themselves as "anointed" when they had received the Spirit of God and thereby been "appointed" to the office of prophet (see Isaiah 61:1). These symbolic uses of *chriō* caused it to be distinguished from *aleiphō* (216), "to anoint," which designated the physical act of anointing (see Brunotte, "Anoint," *Colin Brown*, 1:120; Müller, "Anoint," *Colin Brown*, 1:121).

New Testament Usage

This tendency in the Septuagint to distinguish *chriō* from *aleiphō* became the consistent pattern in the New Testament; "*aleiphein* is the mundane and profane, *chriein* the sacred and religious, word" (Trench, *Synonyms of the New Testament*, p.39). In the New Testament *chriō* is always an act performed by God. Further, it always has the figurative meaning "to assign a person to a task, with the implication of supernatural sanctions, blessing and endowment" (Louw and Nida, *Greek-English Lexicon*, 1:484) that had been developed by the Septuagintal usage.

More specifically, the use of *chriō* in the New Testament seems to draw more on its application in the Septuagint to the prophets than to either the priests or kings. Thus, it appears four times in reference to God's consecrating Jesus to and empowering Him for the "office" of Messiah (including Luke 4:18 which cites Isaiah 61:1). This empowerment is accomplished by the "anointing" with the Holy Spirit (Acts 10:38; cf. Luke 4:18).

Chriō occurs once in the New Testament with reference to believers (2 Corinthians 1:21,22). Although it is unclear whether the "us" who were "anointed" or "commissioned" (RSV) included both the apostles and the Corinthian believers (notice the distinction "establishes us with you" earlier in verse 21), the "anointing" was still connected with the reception of the Holy Spirit.

STRONG 5548, BAUER 887, MOULTON-MILLIGAN 693, KITTEL 9:493-580, LIDDELL-SCOTT 2007, COLIN BROWN 1:119-23; 2:334-35,347.

5384. χρονίζω chronizō verb

To delay, linger, spend time, stay somewhere for a long time.

CROSS-REFERENCE:

χρόνος chronos (5385)

אָחַר 'āchar (310), Qal: stay (Gn 32:4); piel: delay, tarry (Dt 23:31, Eccl 5:4 [5:3], Hb 2:3).

בּוֹשׁ bôsh (991), Be ashamed; polel: delay (Ex 32:1).

יָשֵׁן yāshēn (3583), Sleep; niphal: remain a long time (Dt 4:25).

מָהַהּ māhahh (4244), Hithpalpel: take a long time (Sir 14:12).

מָשַׁךְ māshakh (5082), Drag, extend; niphal: be prolonged (Is 13:22 [14:1]).

1. **χρονίζει chronizei** 3sing indic pres act
2. **χρονίζοντος chronizontos** gen sing masc part pres act
3. **χρονίζειν chronizein** inf pres act
4. **χρονιεῖ chroniei** 3sing indic fut act
5. **χρονίσει chronisei** 3sing indic fut act

1 shall say in his heart, My lord delayeth his coming; Matt 24:48
2 While the bridegroom tarried, they all slumbered...... 25:5
3 marvelled that he tarried so long in the temple...... Luke 1:21
1 say in his heart, My lord delayeth his coming;......... 12:45
4 he that shall come will come, and will not tarry.....Heb 10:37

Classical Greek

The Greek verb *chronizō* is related to *chronos* (5385) and means "to wait." Further definitions include "to delay" or "to fail to appear." It can also mean "to spend time" or to "grow old" as of wine (*Liddell-Scott*).

Septuagint Usage

Chronizō occurs approximately 15 times in the canonical Septuagint where it replaces as many as 5 Hebrew words (including various forms of these). The predominant equivalent, however, is a form of *'āchar* (qal and piel), "to delay, hesitate." It is used of someone "staying" somewhere (e.g., Genesis 32:4), but more often it concerns an extended period of time (e.g., Genesis 34:19; Exodus 32:1 [of Moses' stay on Mount Sinai]; Sirach 14:12 [a reminder that death will not "delay"]).

New Testament Usage

Chronizō occurs only five times in the New Testament; of these, two belong to Matthew, two to Luke, and one to the writer of the Book of Hebrews. Apart from Luke's recalling that Zechariah, John the Baptist's father, "delayed" or "stayed a long time" in the temple, the other passages may all have Christological nuances. Even Matthew's parable of the servant who waits for his master's return calls the master *ho kurios* (note the use of the definite article; Matthew 24:48), which might be translated "the Lord." One need not see a one-to-one correspondence with all the characters in the parable to interpret *ho kurios* in this way. The same can be said for the image of the bridegroom in Matthew 25:5 who also delays his coming. Hebrews 10:37 unquestionably points to Jesus as the coming One of God. This writer, however, stated that He (Jesus) will "not delay" His coming.

STRONG 5549, BAUER 887, MOULTON-MILLIGAN 693-94, LIDDELL-SCOTT 2008, COLIN BROWN 3:839,843.

5385. χρόνος chronos noun

Time, season, delay, respite.

COGNATES:

μακροχρόνιος makrochronios (3090)
χρονίζω chronizō (5384)
χρονοτριβέω chronotribeō (5386)

SYNONYMS:

αἰών aiōn (163)
καιρός kairos (2511)
ὥρα hōra (5443)

זְמַן zāman (2248), Pual: something appointed (Neh 13:31).

זְמָן zᵉmān (2249), Time (Eccl 3:1).

זְמַן zᵉman (A2251), Time (Dn 2:16,21, 7:12—Aramaic).

יוֹם yôm (3219), Day (Gn 26:15, Prv 9:11, Jer 38:28 [45:28]).

יוֹם yôm (A3220), Day (Dn 2:44—Aramaic).

עֵת ʿēth (6496), Time (Jer 31:1 [38:1], 49:8 [29:8]).

פַּעַם paʿam (6718), Pace, foot; now (Prv 7:12).

קֵץ qēts (7377), End (Job 6:11).

רֶגַע reghaʿ (7569), Moment (Is 54:7).

תּוֹר tôr (8781), Turn (Est 2:15).

1. **χρόνος chronos** nom sing masc
2. **χρόνου chronou** gen sing masc
3. **χρόνῳ chronō** dat sing masc
4. **χρόνον chronon** acc sing masc
5. **χρόνων chronōn** gen pl masc
6. **χρόνοις chronois** dat pl masc
7. **χρόνους chronous** acc pl masc

4 Herod, ... inquired of them diligently what time ..... Matt 2:7
4 according to the time ... inquired of the wise men....... 2:16
4 After a long time the lord of those servants cometh,... 25:19
4 as long as they have the bridegroom (NT) .... Mark 2:19
1 How long is it ago since this came unto him? 9:21
1 Now Elisabeth's full time came that she should be ... Luke 1:57
2 all the kingdoms of the world in a moment of time...... 4:5
5 which had devils long time, and ware no clothes,....... 8:27
6 For oftentimes it had caught him: 8:29
4 And he would not for a while: but afterward 18:4
7 and went into a far country for a long time........... 20:9
5 wanted to see Him for a long time (NASB) 23:8
4 knew that he had been ... a long time in that case,.. John 5:6
4 Yet a little while am I with you,....................... 7:33
4 Yet a little while is the light with you................. 12:35
4 Have I been so long time with you,................... 14:9
3 wilt thou at this time restore again the kingdom ..... Acts 1:6
7 It is not for you to know the times or the seasons,...... 1:7
3 time that the Lord Jesus went in and out among us,.... 1:21
5 Whom the heaven must receive until the times 3:21
1 But when the time of the promise drew nigh,........... 7:17
1 And when he was full forty years old, (NT) 7:23
3 because that of long time he had bewitched them 8:11
4 And about the time of forty years 13:18
4 Long time therefore abode they speaking boldly 14:3
4 And there they abode long time with the disciples..... 14:28
4 And after they had tarried there a space,.............. 15:33
7 And the times of this ignorance God winked at;....... 17:30
4 they desired him to tarry longer time with them,....... 18:20
4 after he had spent some time there, he departed,...... 18:23
4 but he himself stayed in Asia for a season............. 19:22
4 what manner I have been with you at all seasons,..... 20:18
2 Now when much time was spent,...................... 27:9
4 dominion over a man as long as he liveth? (NT) .... Rom 7:1
6 which was kept secret since the world began, (NT).... 16:25
4 by the law as long as her husband liveth; (NT) ...... 1 Co 7:39
4 but I trust to tarry a while with you,.................. 16:7
4 That the heir, as long as he is a child, (NT) .... Gal 4:1
2 But when the fulness of the time was come,............ 4:4
5 But of the times and the seasons, brethren,......... 1 Th 5:1
5 in Christ Jesus before the world began, (NT) .... 2 Tm 1:9
5 which God, ... promised before the world began; ...... Tit 1:2
4 To day, after so long a time; as it is said,........... Heb 4:7
4 For when for the time ye ought to be teachers,......... 5:12
1 for the time would fail me to tell of Gedeon,.......... 11:32
4 pass the time of your sojourning here in fear:....... 1 Pt 1:17
5 but was manifest in these last times for you,.......... 1:20
4 the rest of his time in the flesh to the lusts of men,..... 4:2
1 For the time past of our life may suffice us 4:3
3 told you there should be mockers in the last time,... Jude 1:18
4 And I gave her space to repent of her fornication;... Rev 2:21
4 that they should rest yet for a little season,.......... Rev 6:11
1 And sware ... that there should be time no longer:..... 10:6
4 and after that he must be loosed a little season........ 20:3

Classical Greek

"Time" is the most simple definition of *chronos*; however, by its very nature, this is an extremely complex concept. *Chronos* can refer to a long period of time, or it may refer to time in the abstract sense. It may describe the passing of time, the effects of time, the duration of time, or a specific point in time. *Chronos* entered into the philosophical and cosmological discussions of antiquity, especially among Greek philosophers (see e.g., Delling, "chronos," *Kittel*, 9:582-585; cf. *Liddell-Scott*). (See also *kairos* [2511] which concerns a specific point in time; thus it refers to "timeliness, the right time, the opportune time.")

To the Greek, time was virtually a "power which inescapably determined his life" (Hahn, "Time," *Colin Brown*, 3:840). Time had both positive and negative roles in the life of the individual. Time could heal and reveal, but it could also take life itself.

In religious systems gods were exempt from the ravages of time; they were unchanging (ibid., 3:841).

Septuagint Usage

The Septuagint translators chose *chronos* much less than they did *kairos*. Although there are as many as 13 different constructions, the most common Hebrew equivalent is *yāmîm* (plural of *yôm*, "day"). It depicts the "times" in which Abraham lived (Genesis 26:1,15). In Deuteronomy 12:19 it again refers to a time frame in which individuals live (cf. Joshua 4:24; 24:31).

In a number of passages *chronos* concerns the "time of the ages" (i.e., "eternity"). Isaiah's famous prophecy of the Messiah's birth (Isaiah 9:1-8) tells of the child whose government and peace will know "no end" (verse 7; cf. Isaiah 33:20). But *chronos* language is also used of the "finality" of judgment (Isaiah 13:20).

Unlike the Greeks, the Hebrews spent little time speculating about the nature and essence of time. For the Jew, time was only important as far as it concerned a particular event in history. Thus time and history are inseparably bound, particularly because God acts in time and history. God, as the controller of time, is eternal.

New Testament Usage

Chronos occurs about 50 times in the New Testament. Of these, 23 are attributed to Luke and 9 to Paul. *Chronos* speaks of the precise "time" of an event (e.g., Matthew 2:7,16; Acts 1:6) or of an extended or shortened period of time (e.g., Mark 9:21; Luke 8:27,29; Acts 1:21; cf. John 7:33). As a point in time it may concern a significant theological event (e.g., Luke 1:57; Acts 1:6; 7:17; Galatians 4:4).

The most crucial event in time was the appearance of Jesus Christ. He introduced the new age and stands at the crossroads of the old and new. Thus Christ stands in the center of time, not in the quantitative sense, but in terms of calling men and women to choose between the old and the new. This especially holds true in Luke (e.g., Luke 16:16; cf. John 1:17). God's gift of Jesus actually took place "before the times of the ages" (2 Timothy 1:9; cf. Titus 1:2), but it is being revealed "in these last times" (1 Peter 1:20; cf. Hebrews 4:7).

STRONG 5550, BAUER 887-88, MOULTON-MILLIGAN 694, KITTEL 9:581-93, LIDDELL-SCOTT 2008-9, COLIN BROWN 3:839-44.

5386. χρονοτριβέω chronotribeō verb

To spend or waste time.

CROSS-REFERENCE:
χρόνος chronos (5385)

1. **χρονοτριβῆσαι chronotribēsai** inf aor act

1 because he would not **spend** the **time** in Asia:...... Acts 20:16

The verb *chronotribeō* is a compound formed from the noun *chronos* (5385), "time," and the verb *tribō*, "rub, wear." Aristotle used it as an example of the proper coining of compound words (*Rhetoric* 3.3.3). *Chronotribeō* can either be a neutral term for the experiencing of the passage of time (so Louw and Nida, *Greek-English Lexicon*, 1:639), or it may have a negative nuance and thus mean "to waste time" (cf. *Bauer*; Hahn, "Time," *Colin Brown*, 3:840). It is difficult to decide whether this negative nuance is intended in the only New Testament use of the word. According to Acts 20:16, Paul's haste to arrive in Jerusalem meant not stopping in Ephesus "because he would not spend (waste?) the time in Asia."

STRONG 5551, BAUER 888, MOULTON-MILLIGAN 694, LIDDELL-SCOTT 2009, COLIN BROWN 3:839-40,843.

5387. χρύσεος chruseos adj

Golden.

CROSS-REFERENCE:
χρυσός chrusos (5392)

1. **χρυσοῦν chrusoun** nom/acc sing masc/neu
2. **χρυσοῦς chrusous** acc pl masc
3. **χρυσῆ chrusē** nom sing fem
4. **χρυσῆν chrusēn** acc sing fem
5. **χρυσῶν chrusōn** gen pl fem
6. **χρυσᾶς chrusas** acc pl fem
7. **χρυσοῦ chrusou** gen sing neu
8. **χρυσᾶ chrusa** nom/acc pl neu
9. **χρυσοῖ chrusoi** nom pl masc
10. **χρυσᾶν chrusan** acc sing fem

8 there are not only vessels **of gold** and of silver,..... 2 Tm 2:20
1 Which had the **golden** censer,........................Heb 9:4
3 wherein was the **golden** pot that had manna,........... 9:4
6 And being turned, I saw seven **golden** candlesticks;.. Rev 1:12
4 and girt about the paps with a **golden** girdle............ 1:13
6 seven stars ... and the seven **golden** candlesticks......... 1:20
5 in the midst of the seven **golden** candlesticks;........... 2:1
2 and they had on their heads crowns **of gold**............ 4:4
6 harps, and **golden** vials full of odours,................. 5:8
1 another angel came ... having a **golden** censer;.......... 8:3
1 upon the **golden** altar which was before the throne...... 8:3
7 four horns of the **golden** altar which is before God,..... 9:13
8 they should not worship devils, and idols **of gold**,....... 9:20
1 Son of man, having on his head a **golden** crown,...... 14:14
6 having their breasts girded with **golden** girdles......... 15:6
6 seven **golden** vials full of the wrath of God,........... 15:7
1 a **golden** cup in her hand full of abominations......... 17:4
1 had a **golden** reed to measure the city,................ 21:15

The adjective *chruseos* is related to the noun *chrusos* (5392), "gold," and is used to describe things as either being made from or adorned with gold, or as having a golden color. It also developed a number of metaphoric uses, such as "the Golden Age" (cf. *Liddell-Scott*), since gold was the most valued metal among the ancients. By the time of the Septuagint, the common pronunciation and spelling had shifted to *chrusous* in favor of following the Attic rules of contraction. This contracted form is the only one found in the New Testament (for occurrences of the uncontracted form in some variant readings to the text of Revelation, see *Bauer*). All 18 uses in the New Testament describe things which are either made or adorned with gold, although the metaphoric nuances certainly contribute to the descriptions, particularly in Revelation.

STRONG 5552, BAUER 888, MOULTON-MILLIGAN 694, LIDDELL-SCOTT 2009, COLIN BROWN 2:95.

5388. χρυσίον chrusion noun

Gold; gold coin; gold ornament or jewelry.

CROSS-REFERENCE:
χρυσός chrusos (5392)

דְּהַב dehav (A1774), Gold (Ezr 7:15f., Dn 2:32,35—Aramaic).

זָהָב zāhāv (2174), Gold (Ex 25:3, 1 Kgs 10:10f., Is 2:7).

חָרוּץ chārûts (2843), Gold (Ps 68:13 [67:13], Prv 3:14, 8:10).

כֶּתֶם kethem (3929), Gold (Job 28:16,19).

פָּז paz (6580), Gold (Is 13:12, Lam 4:2).

1. χρυσίον chrusion nom/acc sing neu
2. χρυσίου chrusiou gen sing neu
3. χρυσίῳ chrusiō dat sing neu
4. χρυσίων chrusiōn gen pl neu

1 Then Peter said, Silver and **gold** have I none; .... Acts 3:6
2 I have coveted no man's silver, or **gold**, or apparel. 20:33
3 not with braided hair and **gold** or pearls (NASB) ... 1 Tm 2:9
3 covenant overlaid round about **with gold**, ... Heb 9:4
2 much more precious than **of gold** that perisheth, ... 1 Pt 1:7
3 with corruptible things, as silver and **gold**, ... 1:18
4 and of wearing **of gold**, or of putting on of apparel; 3:3
1 I counsel thee to buy of me **gold** tried in the fire, ... Rev 3:18
3 adorned **with gold** and precious stones (NASB) 17:4
3 adorned **with gold** and precious stones (NASB) 18:16
1 and the city was pure **gold**, like unto clear glass. 21:18
1 and the street of the city was pure **gold**, ... 21:21

The noun *chrusion* is the diminutive of *chrusos* (5392), "gold," and thus denotes "a piece of gold." However, the two terms had long since become interchangeable by New Testament times. As a result, one word often replaces the other in different parts of the textual tradition (cf. 1 Timothy 2:9). The more general meaning of *chrusion* as "gold" was narrowed by the use of metonymy (naming a thing by one of its attributes) to refer to "gold coinage" (cf. Acts 3:6) and "gold jewelry" (cf. 1 Peter 3:3). "Gold" was also often used as a symbol for "purity" (cf. Revelation 21:18,21).

J.G. Baldwin ("Gold," *Colin Brown*, 2:96) has suggested that "the danger of covetousness and the association of idolatry" is responsible for the negative valuation of gold (*chrusion*) in Acts 20:33 and 1 Peter 1:18,19. This is clearly the case in the Acts reference; it is more probable, however, that the verses in 1 Peter utilize hyperbole. The usually permanent metals gold and silver are said to be "perishable" in comparison to the exceeding value of the "precious blood of Christ" that has redeemed the Christian.

Strong 5553, Bauer 888, Moulton-Milligan 694, Liddell-Scott 2010, Colin Brown 2:95.

5389. χρυσοδακτύλιος chrusodaktulios adj

Gold ring.

Cross-Reference:
χρυσός chrusos (5392)

1. χρυσοδακτύλιος chrusodaktulios nom sing masc

1 come unto your assembly a man **with a gold ring**, ... Jas 2:2

This noun is a compound word formed from *chrusos* (5392), "gold," and *daktulios* (1141), "ring." Such rings "usually contain(ed) the signet of the owner by which he could mark ownership and seal documents" (Louw and Nida, *Greek-English Lexicon*, 1:76). The word first appears in Greek literature at James 2:2, and may well have been coined by James (cf. Davids, *New International Greek Testament Commentary, James*, p.108). The "gold ring" is part of the stylized picture of a wealthy man whose treatment by the Christian congregation is contrasted to their treatment of a poor man. The mention of "gold rings" as a stylistic element representing wealth and social status is also found in Epictetus (*Discourses*, 1.22.18), though he did not use the compound form *chrusodaktulios.*

Strong 5554, Bauer 888, Moulton-Milligan 694, Liddell-Scott 2010.

5390. χρυσόλιθος chrusolithos noun

Chrysolite; yellow topaz.

Cross-References:
λίθος lithos (3010B)
χρυσός chrusos (5392)

תַּרְשִׁישׁ tarshîsh (8997), Beryl (Ex 28:20, Ez 28:13).

1. χρυσόλιθος chrusolithos nom sing masc

1 the seventh, **chrysolyte**; the eighth, beryl; .... Rev 21:20

Classical Greek and Septuagint Usage

The noun *chrusolithos* is a compound word formed from *chrusos* (5392), "gold," and *lithos* (3010B), "stone," and thus describes a "gold-colored stone." The word appears three times in the Septuagint as the translation of the Hebrew *tarshîsh* (Exodus 28:20, parallel 39:13 [LXX 36:20]; cf. Ezekiel 28:13). Three other times the Septuagint simply transliterates *tarshish* (Song of Solomon 5:14; Ezekiel 1:16; Daniel 10:6) and once renders it by *anthrax* (438), "ruby" (Ezekiel 10:9), which appears as the translation of the Hebrew *nōphekh* in Exodus 28:18. On the basis of Pliny the Elder's description of *chrusolithos* (*Natural History* 37.42), it seems that the word referred to what is now known as yellow topaz (see *Bauer*).

New Testament Usage

Chrusolithos occurs in the New Testament only at Revelation 21:20, where it is the gem which adorns the seventh foundation of the wall of the New Jerusalem. The list of gems in these verses is clearly dependent on the gems used in the breastplate of the high priest described in Exodus

28:17-21 (cf. Hillyer, "Rock," *Colin Brown*, 3:396). But while the stones on the high priest's breastplate were engraved with the names of the tribes of Israel, the foundations bear the names of the 12 apostles (Revelation 21:14). No satisfactory basis for discerning the correspondence between these names and the different gems has yet been found. For a balanced discussion of possible symbolic significance for these gems, see Una Jart, "The Precious Stones in the Revelation of St. John xxi.18-21," pp.150-178.

STRONG 5555, BAUER 888, MOULTON-MILLIGAN 694, LIDDELL-SCOTT 2010, COLIN BROWN 3:396-97.

5391. χρυσόπρασος

chrusoprasos noun

Chrysoprase, green quartz.

CROSS-REFERENCE:

χρυσός chrusos (5392)

1. χρυσόπρασος chrusoprasos nom sing masc

1 **the ninth, a topaz; the tenth, a chrysoprasus;** .... **Rev 21:20**

Classical Greek

This noun is a compound word formed from *chrusos* (5392), "gold," and *prason*, "leek, onion," and describes a greenish-gold gemstone. Chrysoprase is a very translucent, fine-grained quartz. It is among the gems discussed by Pliny the Elder (*Natural History* 37.113).

New Testament Usage

Chrusoprasos designates the stone adorning the 10th foundation of the New Jerusalem (Revelation 21:20). It is one of four gemstone names in this list that does not appear in the Septuagint description of the high priest's breastplate in Exodus 28:17-21 (cf. the discussion under *chrusolithos* [5390]). Morris (*Tyndale New Testament Commentaries, Revelation*, p.252) explains the divergences between the two lists by arguing that John made his own translation of the Hebrew and may have had different ideas concerning the correspondence between the Hebrew and Greek names for these stones. *Chrusoprasos* is apparently the rendering of Hebrew *leshem* from Exodus 28:19, which was translated with *ligurion* by the Septuagint (see Charles, *The International Critical Commentary, Revelation*, 2:170).

STRONG 5556, BAUER 888, MOULTON-MILLIGAN 695, LIDDELL-SCOTT 2011, COLIN BROWN 3:396-97.

5392. χρυσός chrusos noun

Gold.

COGNATES:

χρύσεος chruseos (5387)
χρυσίον chrusion (5388)
χρυσοδακτύλιος chrusodaktulios (5389)
χρυσόλιθος chrusolithos (5390)
χρυσόπρασος chrusoprasos (5391)
χρυσόω chrusoō (5393)

דְּהַב d^ehav (A1774), Gold (Dn 2:45—Aramaic).

זָהָב zāhāv (2174), Gold (Ezr 1:6, Prv 17:3, Is 60:9).

חָרוּץ chārûts (2844), Threshing sledge (Job 41:30 [41:21]).

1. χρυσός chrusos nom sing masc
2. χρυσοῦ chrusou gen sing masc
3. χρυσῷ chrusō dat sing masc
4. χρυσόν chruson acc sing masc

4 **gold,** and frankincense, and myrrh.................. Matt 2:11
4 Provide neither **gold,** nor silver, ... in your purses,..... 10:9
3 whosoever shall swear by the **gold** of the temple,...... 23:16
1 the **gold,** or the temple that sanctifieth the **gold?**...... 23:17
4 the gold, or the temple that sanctifieth the **gold?**...... 23:17
3 not to think that the Godhead is like unto **gold,**....Acts 17:29
4 Now if any man build upon this foundation **gold,**....1 Co 3:12
3 not with broided hair, or **gold,** or pearls,........... 1 Tm 2:9
1 Your **gold** and silver is cankered;................... Jas 5:3
3 on their heads were as it were crowns like **gold,**..... Rev 9:7
3 decked with **gold** and precious stones and pearls,...... 17:4
2 The merchandise of **gold,** and silver,.................. 18:12
3 decked with **gold,** and precious stones, and pearls!..... 18:16

Classical Greek

The term *chrusos*, "gold," is an oriental loanword, in part because gold was a far more common commodity in the East. However, after Alexander the Great conquered Persia and confiscated its riches (including gold), it became more common (Baldwin, "Gold," *Colin Brown*, 2:95).

Septuagint Usage

The Septuagint utilizes *chrusos* and its synonym *chrusion* (5388) to replace four different Hebrew words. These words perhaps indicate different levels of metallic purity (ibid.). Like its neighbors, Israel became very sophisticated in the use of precious metals and stones. Gold was especially prized because it could be hammered or molded easily; it was also a cherished ornament. At a very early date gold became a medium of exchange; later, gold coins were introduced. Gold was also used in Israel's religion. The tabernacle and later the temple were both decorated extensively with gold. Gold also acquired symbolic meaning in Israel. It described that which was "durable" and "valuable" (e.g., Proverbs 8:18f.).

New Testament Usage

There are 13 instances of *chrusos* in the New Testament; the diminutive form *chrusion* appears 9 times. The related adjective *chruseos* (5387) occurs 18 times. *Chrusos* is most often used of gold jewelry and gold ornamentation. "Gold that perisheth" is not as precious as the trial of our faith

(1 Peter 1:7). Also the price of our redemption exceeded the value of "silver and gold"—we were bought with the precious blood of the Lamb (1 Peter 1:18). In 1 Corinthians 3:10-12 Paul likened the Christian life to building a house—Christ is the foundation, and various materials symbolize those attributes which could be part of the building. He showed gold as representing the best qualities, followed by less valuable traits, symbolized by "silver, precious stones, wood, hay, stubble." Notice that the six materials mentioned by Paul fall into one of two groups: combustible or incombustible. In these verses Paul exhorted the Corinthians to be certain that the character of their "work" for Jesus be imperishable because God will test the nature of each man's work as fire might test gold, silver, precious stones, wood, hay, and stubble. Inferior, combustible "building materials" (not specified by Paul) will be burned up in the judgment fires.

Strong 5557, Bauer 888, Moulton-Milligan 695, Liddell-Scott 2011, Colin Brown 2:95.

5393. χρυσόω chrusoō verb

To overlay with gold, to gild.

Cross-Reference:

χρυσός chrusos (5392)

חָפָה chāphâh (2750), Piel: overlay (2 Chr 3:7).

צָפָה tsāphâh (7099), Watch, spy; piel: overlay (Ex 25:11 [25:10], 2 Kgs 18:16, 2 Chr 3:10); pual: be overlaid (Ex 26:32).

1. κεχρυσωμένη kechrusōmenē nom sing fem part perf mid

1 **decked with gold and precious stones and pearls,....Rev 17:4**
1 **decked with gold, and precious stones, and pearls!..... 18:16**

The verb *chrusoō* is related to the noun *chrusos* (5392), "gold," and means "to overlay, adorn, or gild with gold." It occurs twice in the New Testament, both times in reference to the opulent wealth of the harlot Babylon. In Revelation 17:4 she is described as being "bedecked with gold and jewels" (RSV), while in 18:16 it refers to "the great city" itself that has been "adorned with gold and precious stones and pearls" (NASB).

Strong 5558, Bauer 889, Moulton-Milligan 695, Liddell-Scott 2012, Colin Brown 2:95.

5394. χρώς chrōs noun

Skin.

בָּשָׂר bāsār (1340), Flesh, skin (Ex 28:42 [28:38], Lv 13:2ff.,13-16).

עוֹר 'ôr (5997), Skin (Lv 13:21).

1. χρωτός chrōtos gen sing masc

1 **So that from his body were brought unto the sick.. Acts 19:12**

The noun *chrōs* is widely attested in classical Greek and is found 16 times in the Septuagint—14 times as the translation of the Hebrew *bāsār*, "flesh" (12 of these in Leviticus 13 with reference to skin diseases), and twice for the Hebrew *'ôr*, "skin." *Chrōs* designates "human skin," and as such is distinguished from *derma* (1186) which usually denotes the skin of an animal, normally with the hair still attached (see Louw and Nida, *Greek-English Lexicon*, 1.75). The only occurrence of *chrōs* in the New Testament is at Acts 19:12. Handkerchiefs and aprons that touched Paul's skin were taken to the sick, and they were healed. The aprons merely came into contact with the surface of Paul's body.

Strong 5559, Bauer 889, Liddell-Scott 2012.

5395. χωλός chōlos adj

Lame.

Synonyms:

ἀνάπηρος anapēros (374C)
κυλλός kullos (2921)
παραλυτικός paralutikos (3746)

פִּסֵּחַ pissēach (6701), Lame (Dt 15:21, 2 Sm 5:6, Mal 1:8).

1. χωλόν chōlon nom/acc sing masc/neu
2. χωλός chōlos nom sing masc
3. χωλοῦ chōlou gen sing masc
4. χωλοί chōloi nom pl masc
5. χωλῶν chōlōn gen pl masc
6. χωλούς chōlous acc pl masc

4 **The blind receive their sight, and the lame walk,... Matt 11:5**
6 **having with them those that were lame,............... 15:30**
6 **the maimed to be whole, the lame to walk,............ 15:31**
1 **better for thee to enter into life halt or maimed,...... 18:8**
4 **the blind and the lame came to him in the temple;.... 21:14**
1 **it is better for thee to enter halt into life,.......... Mark 9:45**
4 **how that the blind see, the lame walk,..............Luke 7:22**
6 **call the poor, the maimed, the lame, the blind:........ 14:13**
6 **poor, and the maimed, and the halt, and the blind..... 14:21**
5 **impotent folk, of blind, halt, withered,..............John 5:3**
2 **And a certain man lame from his mother's womb....Acts 3:2**
3 **And as the lame man which was healed held Peter..... 3:11**
4 **and that were lame, were healed....................... 8:7**
2 **being a cripple from his mother's womb,.............. 14:8**
1 **lest that which is lame be turned out of the way;... Heb 12:13**

The adjective *chōlos* describes a physical "disability that involves the imperfect function of the lower limbs" (Louw and Nida, *Greek-English Lexicon*, 1:273) that might range in severity from causing a limp to an inability to walk. It can also describe impaired functioning of the hands. Though most often used in a literal sense of actual physical handicap, *chōlos* is also used metaphorically to describe other kinds of defects (cf. Hebrews 12:13).

This adjective is used in both the Septuagint and the New Testament to designate the group of people who suffer such afflictions, usually grouped together with "the blind" and other handicapped groups. Since the Law forbade the full cultic participation of people who were physically impaired, the healing of such people and their consequent reintegration into society was symbolic of the glories of the coming kingdom of God in both the Old and New Testaments (cf. Matthew 11:4-6 and Isaiah 35:5,6 which is alluded to there).

STRONG 5560, BAUER 889, MOULTON-MILLIGAN 695, LIDDELL-SCOTT 2014, COLIN BROWN 2:415.

5396. χώρα chōra noun

Region, country, dry land, countryside, field.

SYNONYMS:
- ἀγρός agros (67)
- κλίμα klima (2797)

אֲדָמָה 'ădhāmāh (124), Land (Dn 11:39).

אוּר 'ûr (217), Ur (Gn 11:28,31, 15:7).

אֵיתָן 'êthān (393), Normal state (Ex 14:27).

אֶרֶץ 'erets (800), Land (Gn 10:20, 2 Kgs 18:33, Is 19:19f.).

מְדִינָה m^edhînāh (4224), Province (Ezr 2:1, Est 8:9, Lam 1:1).

מְדִינָה m^edhînāh (A4225), Province (Ezr 5:8, Dn 3:1ff.,30—Aramaic).

מָקוֹם māqôm (4887), Place (Gn 36:40).

שָׂדֶה sādheh (7898), Country (Gn 32:3).

1. **χώρας chōras** gen/acc sing/pl fem
2. **χώρα chōra** nom sing fem
3. **χώρᾳ chōra** dat sing fem
4. **χώραν chōran** acc sing fem
5. **χώραις chōrais** dat pl fem

4 they departed into their own **country** another way... Matt 2:12
3 them which sat in the **region** and shadow of death...... 4:16
4 into the **country** of the Gergesenes,.................... 8:28
2 there went out unto him all the **land** of Judaea,.....Mark 1:5
4 other side ... into the **country** of the Gadarenes......... 5:1
1 he would not send them away out of the **country**........ 5:10
4 and ran about that whole **country** (NASB)............. 6:55
3 And there were in the same **country** shepherds......Luke 2:8
1 of Ituraea and of the **region** of Trachonitis,............ 3:1
4 And they arrived at the **country** of the Gadarenes,...... 8:26
2 **ground** of a ... rich man brought forth plentifully:...... 12:16
4 and took his journey into a far **country**,............... 15:13
4 there arose a mighty famine in that **land**;............. 15:14
1 joined himself to a citizen of that **country**;............ 15:15
4 into a far **country** to receive for himself a kingdom,.... 19:12
5 not them that are in the **countries** enter thereinto...Luke 21:21
1 Lift up your eyes, and look on the **fields**;...........John 4:35
4 went thence unto a **country** near to the wilderness,.... 11:54
1 and many went out of the **country** up to Jerusalem.... 11:55
1 **regions** of Judaea and Samaria, except the apostles...Acts 8:1
3 things which he did both in the **land** of the Jews,...... 10:39
4 their **country** was nourished by the king's country...... 12:20
1 was published throughout all the **region**.............. 13:49
4 gone throughout Phrygia and the **region** of Galatia,.... 16:6
4 and went over all the **country** of Galatia............. 18:23
4 and throughout all the **coasts** of Judaea,.............. 26:20
4 deemed that they drew near to some **country**;......... 27:27
1 the labourers who have reaped down your **fields**,.....Jas 5:4

Classical Greek

The noun *chōra* is a very general term whose meaning and usage remained quite constant in the classical and Koine periods of the Greek language. In classical Greek *chōra* has two primary uses. The first of these denotes any "space in which a thing is" and thus a "place" or "position." This usage can be metaphorically extended to include the "station" or "position" a person held within society. The second usage is a geographical term for "land, country," or "territory" (*Liddell-Scott*).

Septuagint Usage

The geographical sense of the word dominates its use in the Septuagint. In general it means "land, country, region." Job 1:1 says Job lived "in the *land* of Uz." In Numbers 32:1 the Reubenites and Gadites saw the *lands* of Jazer and Gilead.

New Testament Usage

In the New Testament the geographical uses of *chōra* dominate. The most common and the most general use refers to a "region or regions of the earth, normally in relation to some ethnic group or geographical center, but not necessarily constituting a unit of governmental administration" (Louw and Nida, *Greek-English Lexicon*, 1:15). Two special occurrences of this use of *chōra* deserve attention. In Matthew 4:16 the word is used in the phrase "in the region and shadow of death" (see Isaiah 9:1). This use of *chōra* may be "geographical" if it reflects the older "three-story cosmology" where the dead dwelt in a subterranean realm. However, it probably has the more general sense of "place" of the dead following classical usage. The other special use of *chōra* is in Mark 1:5 where it designates the inhabitants of a region by metonymy ("all [the inhabitants of] the land of Judea" went out to see John) (cf. Genesis 41:57).

Secondly, *chōra* is used for "land" as opposed to "sea," and is thus sometimes translated as "shore" or "coast." *Chōra* can also designate rural areas as opposed to a "city" or "village," and in such cases it has the meaning of "countryside."

More specifically, *chōra* can refer to countryside which is either under cultivation or being used as pasture, and thus means "field."

STRONG 5561, BAUER 889, MOULTON-MILLIGAN 695, LIDDELL-SCOTT 2015.

5397. χωρέω chōreō verb

Move forward, progress, proceed, make room; contain, receive.

COGNATES:

ἀναχωρέω anachōreō (400)
ἀποχωρέω apochōreō (666)
ἐκχωρέω ekchōreō (1620)
εὐρύχωρος euruchōros (2130)
περίχωρος perichōros (3926)
στενοχωρέω stenochōreō (4580)
ὑποχωρέω hupochōreō (5136)
χωρίζω chōrizō (5398)
χωρίον chōrion (5399)
χωρίς chōris (5400)
χῶρος chōros (5401)

SYNONYMS:

ἀναλύω analuō (358)
ἀναχωρέω anachōreō (400)
ἀπαλλάσσω apallassō (521)
ἀπέρχομαι aperchomai (562)
ἀποβαίνω apobainō (571)
ἀπολύω apoluō (624)
ἀποχωρέω apochōreō (666)
ἀφίημι aphiēmi (856)
ἀφίστημι aphistēmi (861)
διαχωρίζω diachōrizō (1310)
ἐκβαίνω ekbainō (1530B)
ἐκπορεύω ekporeuō (1594)
ἐξέρχομαι exerchomai (1814)
ἐξιέναι exienai (1821)
μεταίρω metairō (3202)
παράγω paragō (3717)
πορεύομαι poreuomai (4057)
ὑπάγω hupagō (5055)

חָזַק chāzaq (2480), Be strong; hiphil: hold (2 Chr 4:5).

יָכֹל yākhōl (3310), Be able to do something (Gn 13:6—Sixtine Edition only).

כּוּל kûl (3677), Hiphil: hold (1 Kgs 7:26—Codex Alexandrinus only).

נָשָׂא nāsâ' (5558), Support (Gn 13:6).

1. **χωρεῖ chōrei** 3sing indic pres act
2. **χωροῦσιν chōrousin** 3pl indic pres act
3. **χωρείτω chōreitō** 3sing impr pres act
4. **χωροῦσαι chōrousai** nom pl fem part pres act
5. **χωρεῖν chōrein** inf pres act
6. **χωρήσατε chōrēsate** 2pl impr aor act
7. **χωρῆσαι chōrēsai** inf aor act
8. **χωρήσειν chōrēsein** inf fut act

1 entereth in at the mouth goeth into the belly,...... Matt 15:17
2 All men cannot receive this saying,.................. 19:11
5 He that is able to receive it, let him receive it......... 19:12
3 He that is able to receive it, let him receive it.......... 19:12
5 insomuch that there was no room to receive them,.. Mark 2:2
4 containing two or three firkins apiece............... John 2:6
1 kill me, because my word hath no place in you......... 8:37
7 could not contain the books that should be written..... 21:25
6 Receive us; we have wronged no man,.............. 2 Co 7:2
7 but that all should come to repentance............. 2 Pt 3:9

Classical Greek

The verb *chōreō* is well attested in all stages of the Greek language and has a rather broad semantic range. The meanings vary depending on whether the verb is used with (transitive) or without (intransitive) a direct object. Among classical authors, the meaning in intransitive uses was "to make room" for someone or something, usually by moving away from the space which it occupied. Thus, among post-Homeric authors, *chōreō* overlapped with *erchomai* (2048), "go, come," and meant "to move forward, progress." It could be applied to a number of different things, such as the "progress" of food through the digestive tract (cf. Matthew 15:17), the "spread" of information, or even the prosecution of a war (Schmidt, "Fullness," *Colin Brown*, 1:741). In transitive constructions *chōreō* meant "to hold, contain," frequently in reference to the capacity of vessels.

Septuagint Usage

Chōreō is somewhat rare in the Septuagint as compared to other bodies of ancient Greek literature. In books that are translations from the Hebrew Bible it occurs a total of six times as a translation of several different Hebrew words. Both transitive and intransitive uses appear, and the range of meanings is consistent with what is found in classical Greek. However, an important new figurative use is found in Philo who used this verb in transitive constructions to describe the human inability to comprehend divine revelation (*De Specialibus Legibus* 1.44 and *De Posteritate Caini* 143). Later, Plutarch (*De Catone Minore* 64.3) also used *chōreō* in reference to human intellectual capacity.

New Testament Usage

In the New Testament there are no purely figurative uses of *chōreō* when intransitive. John 8:37 is an example of the use of *chōreō* in the sense of "to progress"; that Jesus' word has "no place in you" means that these believing Jews (cf. John 8:31) were not continuing to progress in Jesus' teaching. The sense of "to progress" is probably also present in 2 Peter 3:9 where the delay in the return of the Lord is attributed to God's desire that people "come to repentance" (for an alternative explanation, cf. Schmidt, "Fullness," *Colin Brown*, 1:742).

The transitive meaning of "to hold, contain" is used of vessels in John 2:6 and Mark 2:2. A figurative use of *chōreō* when transitive is found in 2 Corinthians 7:2. Paul admonished the Corinthians to extend their friendship to the apostles by using the spatial metaphor *make room for us* (KJV translates it simply "Receive us"; see Louw and Nida, *Greek-English Lexicon*, 1:448). In Matthew 19:11,12 the figurative meaning "to understand" Jesus' teaching is used, but the figure extends "beyond understanding and points to the capacity to receive and act upon the teaching" (Schmidt, "Fullness," *Colin Brown*, 1:742). Given John's tendency to dramatize the inability of people to understand Jesus' teaching (e.g., Nicodemus in John 3 and the woman at the well in John 4), it would be tempting to include the use of *chōreō* in John 8:37 in this category if the construction were not so clearly intransitive.

Strong 5562, Bauer 889-90, Moulton-Milligan 695, Liddell-Scott 2015, Colin Brown 1:741-42.

5398. χωρίζω chōrizō verb

To divide, separate; to depart; to divorce.

Cognates:

ἀποχωρίζω apochōrizō (667)
διαχωρίζω diachōrizō (1310)
χωρέω chōreō (5397)

Synonyms:

ἀποδιορίζω apodiorizō (587)
ἀποχωρίζω apochōrizō (667)
ἀφορίζω aphorizō (866)
διακρίνω diakrinō (1246)
διαχωρίζω diachōrizō (1310)
κρίνω krinō (2892)
μερίζω merizō (3177)
σχίζω schizō (4829)

בָּדָד bādhādh (945), Alone (Lv 13:46).

בָּדַל bādhal (950), Niphal: separate oneself (Ezr 9:1, Neh 9:2); hiphil: exclude (Neh 13:3).

מוּשׁ mûsh (4318), Depart (Jgs 6:18).

פָּרַד pāradh (6754), Niphal: separate (Prv 18:1).

1. **χωριζέτω chōrizetō** 3sing impr pres act
2. **χωρίσαι chōrisai** inf aor act
3. **χωρίσει chōrisei** 3sing indic fut act
4. **χωρίζεται chōrizetai** 3sing indic pres mid
5. **χωριζέσθω chōrizesthō** 3sing impr pres mid
6. **χωρίζεσθαι chōrizesthai** inf pres mid
7. **ἐχωρίσθη echōristhē** 3sing indic aor pass
8. **χωρισθῇ chōristhē** 3sing subj aor pass
9. **χωρισθείς chōristheis** nom sing masc part aor pass
10. **χωρισθῆναι chōristhēnai** inf aor pass
11. **κεχωρισμένος kechōrismenos** nom sing masc part perf mid

1 God hath joined together, let not man **put asunder**. Matt 19:6
1 God hath joined together, let not man **put asunder**. Mark 10:9
6 commanded them that they should not **depart** ...... Acts 1:4
9 After these things Paul **departed** from Athens, ... 18:1
6 Claudius had commanded all Jews **to depart** 18:2
3 Who **shall separate** us from the love of Christ? ..... Rom 8:35
2 shall be able **to separate** us from the love of God, ... 8:39
10 Let not the wife **depart** from her husband: .... 1 Co 7:10
8 But and if she **depart**, let her remain unmarried, ... 7:11
4 But if the unbelieving **depart**, let him depart. 7:15
5 But if the unbelieving depart, let him **depart**. 7:15
7 For perhaps he therefore **departed** for a season, ... Phlm 1:15
11 harmless, undefiled, **separate** from sinners, ... Heb 7:26

Classical Greek

In classical Greek the verb *chōrizō* is used in the sense of "to separate or divide" between things. By extension, the passive form of the verb is used to designate the separation of a person from or to a new place, and thus meant "to depart." From these two basically spatial ideas, the verb was later applied to the action "to separate in thought, distinguish." *Chōrizō* also had a technical use for the "separation" of husband and wife, and thus meant "to divorce" (*Liddell-Scott*).

Septuagint Usage

Most occurrences of *chōrizō* in the Septuagint are in the passive voice and designate movement from one place to another. The word developed a slightly new nuance when it was used for the post-Exilic "separation" of the Jews from the "foreigners" who then lived in Judea (cf. Ezra 6:21; 9:1; Nehemiah 9:2; 13:3). This "separation" was to be both a spatial as well as a moral separation from pagan beliefs and practices. Although the technical meaning of "to divorce" is not found in the Septuagint, it is attested in Greek papyri from this period (see *Moulton-Milligan* for references).

New Testament Usage

Chōrizō is used in the New Testament in several of these senses. It occurs in middle and passive voices to refer to departures from one place to another (cf. Acts 1:4; Philemon 15). The use in Hebrews 7:26 draws on both this spatial sense in that Jesus is "separated from sinners" by His exaltation into heaven and on the moral nuance found in the Septuagint in that Jesus is "separated from sinners" by His moral attributes (cf. *Bauer*; Harris, "Separate," *Colin Brown*, 3:534).

The meaning of "to separate something from something" is found in Romans 8:35 and 39 where Paul wrote that nothing can "separate us from the love of God, which is in Christ Jesus our Lord." Some lexicons include the use of *chōrizō* in Mark 10:9, parallel Matthew 19:6, "What therefore God hath joined together, let not man put asunder," under this meaning (cf. Thayer, *Greek-English Lexicon*; *Bauer*). But given the context of this saying within a debate concerning divorce, *chōrizō* probably has the technical meaning "to divorce" in these verses (so also Harris, "Separate," *Colin Brown*, 3:534). *Chōrizō* is also used for "to divorce" in 1 Corinthians 7:11,15. Some see in the use of two different words, *aphiēmi* (856) and *chōrizō*, an important distinction in meaning; however, there is no lexical basis for proposing that *aphiēmi* is used in this passage for "legal divorce" whereas *chōrizō* designates simply a separation of marital partners. The two terms are synonymous in their technical applications to divorce (see Louw and Nida, *Greek-English Lexicon*, 1:457). According to Fee, modern interpreters attempt to find a distinction in these words due to "our own urgencies for greater precision." In Greco-Roman culture divorce did not need a document to legalize it. Hence, "divorce" took place whenever a "separation" occurred (*New International Commentary on the New Testament, First Corinthians*, p.293).

STRONG 5563, BAUER 890, LIDDELL-SCOTT 2016, COLIN BROWN 3:534-35.

5399. χωρίον chōrion noun

Field; garden; landed estate.

COGNATE:

χωρέω chōreō (5397)

SYNONYMS:

ἀγρός agros (67)
κτῆμα ktēma (2905)

כֶּרֶם kerem (3884), Vineyard (1 Chr 27:27).

1. χωρίου chōriou gen sing neu
2. χωρίον chōrion nom/acc sing neu
3. χωρία chōria nom/acc pl neu
4. χωρίων chōriōn gen pl neu

2 Jesus with them unto **a place** called Gethsemane, ... Matt 26:36
2 came to **a place** which was named Gethsemane: .... Mark 14:32
1 **parcel of ground** that Jacob gave to his son Joseph... John 4:5
2 purchased **a field** with the reward of iniquity; .... Acts 1:18
2 insomuch as that **field** is called ... field of blood. 1:19
2 Aceldama, that is to say, The **field** of blood. 1:19
4 were possessors of **lands** or houses sold them, ... 4:34
1 and to keep back part of the price of the **land**? 5:3
2 Tell me whether ye sold the **land** for so much? 5:8
3 In the same quarters were **possessions** of the chief 28:7

The noun *chōrion* is the diminutive form of *chōra* (5396), and the terms are often used synonymously. To the degree that they can be distinguished, *chōrion* designates "a definite portion of space viewed as enclosed or complete in itself," and thus is more "circumscribed" than the more "extensive" space designated by *chōra* (Thayer, *Greek-English Lexicon*, "topos"). *Chōrion* is used in the New Testament of a garden (Gethsemane, Mark 14:32, parallel Matthew 26:36), of open fields under cultivation (John 4:5), of a field used as a cemetery (Aceldama, Acts 1:18,19), and of landed estates (Acts 4:34; 5:3,8; 28:7).

STRONG 5564, BAUER 890, MOULTON-MILLIGAN 696, LIDDELL-SCOTT 2016.

5400. χωρίς chōris prep

Separately, without, apart from, besides.

CROSS-REFERENCE:

χωρέω chōreō (5397)

1. χωρίς chōris

1 and **without** a parable spake he not unto them: .... Matt 13:34
1 five thousand men, **beside** women and children. 14:21
1 four thousand men, **beside** women and children. 15:38
1 But **without** a parable spake he not unto them: ..... Mark 4:34
1 is like a man that **without** a foundation built .... Luke 6:49
1 and **without** him was not any thing made .... John 1:3
1 for **without** me ye can do nothing. 15:5
1 but wrapped together in a place **by itself**. 20:7
1 righteousness of God **without** the law is manifested, Rom 3:21
1 is justified by faith **without** the deeds of the law. 3:28
1 whom God imputeth righteousness **without** works, ... 4:6
1 For **without** the law sin was dead. 7:8
1 For I was alive **without** the law once: 7:9
1 and how shall they hear **without** a preacher? 10:14
1 ye are rich, ye have reigned as kings **without** us: .... 1 Co 4:8
1 neither is the man **without** the woman, ... 11:11
1 neither the woman **without** the man, in the Lord. 11:11
1 **Beside** those things that are without, ... 2 Co 11:28
1 in the body, or **apart from** the body (NASB) 12:3
1 That at that time ye were **without** Christ, ... Eph 2:12
1 Do all things **without** murmurings and disputings: .... Phlp 2:14
1 lifting up holy hands, **without** wrath and doubting... 1 Tm 2:8
1 these things **without** preferring one before another, ... 5:21
1 But **without** thy mind would I do nothing; .... Phlm 1:14
1 tempted like as we are, yet **without** sin. .... Heb 4:15
1 And **without** all contradiction the less is blessed 7:7
1 as not **without** an oath he was made priest: 7:20
1 For those priests were made **without** an oath; 7:21
1 priest alone once every year, not **without** blood, ... 9:7
1 neither ... testament was dedicated **without** blood. 9:18
1 and **without** shedding of blood is no remission. 9:22
1 appear the second time **without** sin unto salvation. 9:28
1 died **without** mercy under two or three witnesses: 10:28
1 But **without** faith it is impossible to please him: 11:6
1 that they **without** us should not be made perfect. 11:40
1 be **without** chastisement, ... then are ye bastards, ... 12:8
1 holiness, **without** which no man shall see the Lord: 12:14
1 show me your faith **without** the works, (NASB) ...... Jas 2:18
1 know, ... that faith **without** works is dead? 2:20
1 For as the body **without** the spirit is dead, so faith 2:26
1 so faith **without** works is dead also. 2:26

Chōris is one of the so-called "improper prepositions"; that is, it does not form compound words with verbs. When *chōris* is used as a preposition, it "governs" the genitive case and serves to specify the use of the "genitive of separation" (what some grammarians refer to as the "ablative" case). Its meaning and usage remained virtually unchanged from the classical to the New Testament period.

Only once in the New Testament is *chōris* used as an adverb. In John 20:7 it is used to modify a perfect passive participle: "(having been) wrapped together . . . *by itself*." All other occurrences of *chōris* are prepositions. In one example of its prepositional use, it is found in "postpositive" position, that is, immediately following its object rather than before it (Hebrews 12:14).

As a preposition, *chōris* may take persons, things, or abstract nouns as its object and is usually translated "without." It has a variety of nuances. *Chōris* is used to indicate the relationship of being "outside" the boundaries of a space or group (some texts of 2 Corinthians 12:3) or otherwise being separated from some person (Ephesians 2:12) or thing (James 2:26). It can have the sense of "without the use of" a thing (James 2:20) or "without assistance from" a person (John 1:3). It also is used to show that no relationship exists between two things, or that they are "independent of" each other (Romans 3:28). Finally, it can have the sense of "besides" where the object of *chōris* is either excluded from (Matthew 14:21) or included with (2 Corinthians 11:28) the element(s) under consideration in the clause that it modifies.

Strong 5565, Bauer 890-91, Moulton-Milligan 696, Liddell-Scott 2016.

5401. χῶρος chōros noun

Northwest wind.

Cross-Reference:
χωρέω chōreō (5397)

1. χῶρον chōron acc sing masc

1 and lieth toward the south west and **north west**..... Acts 27:12

The Greek noun *chōros* found at Acts 27:12 is a transliterated form of the Latin *corus/caurus*, "northwest wind." There is some confusion as to whether Luke intended to describe the harbor of Phoenix as being open to the southwest and northwest or to the southeast and northeast. The final clause of Acts 27:12 translates literally as "looking to the southwest wind and the northwest wind." The confusion results from whether the description uses "the directions of the wind either as the direction from which the wind comes or the direction toward which the wind blows" (Louw and Nida, *Greek-English Lexicon*, 1:711). For a discussion of the possibilities and their relationship to the identification of the harbor, see Bruce, *New International Commentary on the New Testament, Acts*, pp.507f.

Strong 5566, Bauer 891, Moulton-Milligan 696, Liddell-Scott 2016.

5402. ψάλλω psallō verb

To sing (a spiritual or sacred song), sing praise.

COGNATE:

ψαλμός psalmos (5403)

SYNONYMS:

ᾄδω adō (102)
ὑμνέω humneō (5053)

זָמַר zāmar (2252), Piel: sing (Jgs 5:3, Pss 18:49 [17:49], 108:1 [107:1]).

נָגַן nāghan (5235), Qal: musician (Ps 68:25 [67:25]—Codex Vaticanus only); piel: play a harp (1 Sm 16:16, 19:9, 2 Kgs 3:15).

1. ψαλλέτω psalletō 3sing impr pres act
2. ψάλλοντες psallontes nom pl masc part pres act
3. ψαλῶ psalō 1sing indic fut act

3 I will confess to thee ... and sing unto thy name.... Rom 15:9
3 I will sing with the spirit,........................ 1 Co 14:15
3 and I will sing with the understanding also........... 14:15
2 singing and making melody in your heart........... Eph 5:19
1 Is any merry? let him sing psalms................... Jas 5:13

Classical Greek

In classical Greek the verb *psallō* means "to pluck, pull" in a very general sense, such as to "pluck out a hair" or "to pull a bowstring." It is also used with a technical meaning "to play a stringed musical instrument" on which the strings were plucked rather than struck with a mallet.

Septuagint Usage

The usage of *psallō* in the Septuagint, however, introduces an expansion of its meaning. Twelve times it is used to translate Hebrew *nāghan*, "to play a stringed instrument," in keeping with its technical use in classical Greek. However, nearly 40 times the Septuagint uses *psallō* to translate Hebrew *zāmar*, "to *make music* in praise of God" (Brown-Driver-Briggs, "zmr," *Hebrew Lexicon*, p.274). This Hebrew word describes music made either by musical instruments or vocally, and thus can also mean "to sing." In some Old Testament contexts it is apparent that *zāmar/psallō* refer to singing that is accompanied by instruments (cf. Psalm 66:4 [LXX 65:4]). As a result, the meaning of *psallō* began to be extended to include "to sing," and by Modern Greek it had come to mean this exclusively (*Bauer*).

New Testament Usage

This gradual shift in meaning presents minor problems for understanding the use of *psallō* in the New Testament. It is widely agreed that the primary meaning in the New Testament is "to sing" with at least the possible nuance of "to sing with instrumental accompaniment" (cf. *Moulton-Milligan*; *Bauer*; and Louw and Nida, *Greek-English Lexicon*, 1:402). Clearly no conclusions can be drawn solely from the lexical meaning of *psallō* as to whether instrumental accompaniment should be included with Christian worship in song. As in the Septuagint, *psallō* is used in the New Testament only of singing directed to God in praise.

STRONG 5567, BAUER 891, MOULTON-MILLIGAN 697, KITTEL 8:489-503, LIDDELL-SCOTT 2018, COLIN BROWN 2:874; 3:670-75.

5403. ψαλμός psalmos noun

Song of praise, psalm.

CROSS-REFERENCE:

ψάλλω psallō (5402)

זָמִיר zāmîr (2244), Song (2 Sm 23:1).

זָמַר zāmar (2252), Piel: sing (Ps 147:1 [146:1]).

זִמְרָה zimrāh (2256), Song (Am 5:23).

מִזְמוֹר mizmôr (4344), Psalm (Pss 5:title, 30:title [29:title], 140:title [139:title]).

נֵבֶל nēvel (5213), Harp (Ps 71:22 [70:22]).

נְגִינָה neghînāh (5234), Song, music (Lam 3:14, 5:14).

נָגַן nāghan (5235), Piel: play on a harp (1 Sm 16:18).

עוּגָב ʿûghāv (5966), Flute (Job 21:12, 30:31).

שִׁגָּיוֹן shiggāyôn (8150), Shiggaion (Ps 7:title).

שִׁיר shîr (8302), Son (Ps 46:title [45:title]).

תְּהִלָּה tehillāh (8747), Psalms (The Book of Psalms:title).

1. ψαλμῷ **psalmō** dat sing masc
2. ψαλμόν **psalmon** acc sing masc
3. ψαλμῶν **psalmōn** gen pl masc
4. ψαλμοῖς **psalmois** dat pl masc

3 And David himself saith in the book **of Psalms**, ... Luke 20:42
4 in the prophets, and in the **psalms**, concerning me. 24:44
3 For it is written in the book **of Psalms**, ... Acts 1:20
1 as it is also written in the second **psalm**, ... 13:33
2 every one of you hath **a psalm**, hath a doctrine, ... 1 Co 14:26
4 **in psalms** and hymns and spiritual songs, ... Eph 5:19
4 teaching and admonishing one another **in psalms** ..... Col 3:16

Classical Greek

In classical Greek *psalmos* refers either to the "sound" of an instrument or to the actual playing ("plucking, twanging" of strings) of an instrument (cf. *Liddell-Scott*). It is related to the verb *psallō*, which denotes the act of playing a (normally) stringed instrument.

Septuagint Usage

Psalmos, the word from which we get the word *psalm*, occurs most often in the Book of Psalms in the Septuagint. Usually it occurs in the title to the psalm, although that is not always the case (e.g., Psalms 110–136 do not have this designation).

Elsewhere it is used of David, of whom it is said he knew how to "play a harp" (NIV; literally "to psalm a psalm"; 1 Samuel 16:18 [LXX 1 Kings 16:18]). "Song," a very appropriate translation for *psalmos*, was usually a song of joy accompanied by instruments (e.g., Judith 16:2; Job 21:12; cf. Job 30:31; Amos 5:23). Still, a "song" need not be joyous to all (Lamentations 3:14). *Psalmos* predominantly translates the Hebrew word *mizmôr*, "song, melody." The meaning of *psalmos* changed under the influence of the verb form of *mizmôr*, *zāmar*, which can mean either "make music" or "sing." *Psallō* was used to translate *zāmar* and assumed the meaning "to sing." In the same way, its cognate *psalmos* took on the meaning "a song."

New Testament Usage

The New Testament writers used *psalmos* in two basic senses: first, it refers to the Old Testament psalms, and second, it refers to "songs" of praise and joy. The related verb *psallō* (5402) is always used in this last understanding ("to sing"). The seven instances of *psalmos* can be broken down into four for Luke and three for Paul (cf. the verb which occurs only four times, three in Paul's writings and once in James).

Only Luke used *psalmos* in the first sense, that is, of an Old Testament psalm. Once he used it in reference to a particular psalm (Acts 13:33), and on two other occasions he referred to the entire "book of Psalms" (Luke 20:42; Acts 1:20). In another instance he used *psalmos* for that part of the Old Testament known as the *Ketubim*, "Writings," as distinct from the Pentateuch and Prophets, the other two major divisions of the Old Testament (Luke 24:44). The Book of Psalms was the first member of the *Ketubim*.

Strong 5568, Bauer 891, Moulton-Milligan 697, Kittel 8:489-503, Liddell-Scott 2018, Colin Brown 2:874; 3:670-71,674-75.

5404. ψευδάδελφος

pseudadelphos noun

False brother.

Cross-References:
ἀδελφός adelphos (79)
ψεύδομαι pseudomai (5409)

1. ψευδαδέλφοις **pseudadelphois** dat pl masc
2. ψευδαδέλφους **pseudadelphous** acc pl masc

1 in perils in the sea, in perils among **false brethren**; 2 Co 11:26
2 because of **false brethren** unawares brought in, ... Gal 2:4

The noun *pseudadelphos* is a compound of *pseudēs* (5406), "false," and *adelphos* (79), "brother." It designates "an individual who pretends to be a close member of a socio-religious group but is not" (Louw and Nida, *Greek-English Lexicon*, 1:127). In the New Testament it is used only of those who present themselves as members of the Christian community but do not truly accept its teachings and standards of godliness. On the basis of Galatians 2:4, some have tried to limit Paul's use of the term strictly to the Judaizers (cf. Turner, *Christian Words*, p.158; and *Bauer*). However, it is more likely that, particularly at 2 Corinthians 11:26, Paul applied the term generally to all persons who were not true members of the community (cf. Polycarp, *Epistle to the Philippians* 6:3). It is only the context of the Galatian controversy with the Judaizers that would seem to limit the scope of the word at Galatians 2:4.

Strong 5569, Bauer 891, Kittel 1:144-46, Liddell-Scott 2019, Colin Brown 1:254,257; 2:472.

5405. ψευδαπόστολος

pseudapostolos noun

False apostle.

Cross-References:
ἀποστέλλω apostellō (643)
ψεύδομαι pseudomai (5409)

1. ψευδαπόστολοι **pseudapostoloi** nom pl masc

1 For such are false apostles, deceitful workers,...... 2 Co 11:13

This term does not appear in any other extant ancient Greek literature except for its one appearance in 2 Corinthians 11:13. Here false apostles are called servants of Satan (verse 15). Such a title demonstrates the serious nature of their false teaching. They apparently were of Jewish origin (verse 22). The exact nature of their error is not clear, but Paul openly condemned them for preaching "another Jesus," "a different spirit," and "a different gospel" (verse 4). The result of their teaching was that the Corinthians were being led away from a "sincere and pure devotion to Christ" (verse 3; NIV). Though they appeared busy in the work of Christ, they were serving themselves (verse 13). Like the one they served, regardless of how pure and wonderful they may have appeared on the outside, they were corrupt.

Strong 5570, Bauer 891, Kittel 1:445-46, Liddell-Scott 2019, Colin Brown 2:472.

5406. ψευδής pseudēs adj

False, lying, liar.

Cross-Reference:

ψεύδομαι pseudomai (5409)

אַכְזָב 'akhzāv (397), Deceptive (Jer 15:18).

כִּדְבָה kidh^e^vāh (A3657), Lie (Dn 2:9—Aramaic).

כָּזָב kāzāv (3695), Lie (Jgs 16:10, Ps 58:3 [57:3], Ez 22:28).

כַּחַשׁ kachash (3704), Deceitfulness, lies (Is 30:9, Hos 10:13, Na 3:1).

שָׁוְא shaw^e'^ (8175), False, lying (Dt 5:20, Ez 13:6-9, Jon 2:8 [2:9]).

שֶׁקֶר sheqer (8632), Something deceitful, something false (1 Kgs 22:22f., Prv 25:14, Jer 14:14).

1. ψευδέσιν pseudesin dat pl masc

2. ψευδεῖς pseudeis acc pl masc

2 And set up false witnesses, which said,.............. Acts 6:13
2 and hast found them liars:.......................... Rev 2:2
1 and sorcerers, and idolaters, and all liars,............. 21:8

Classical Greek

Pseudēs means "false, untrue, lying," and as such it contrasts with *alēthēs* (225), "true." As a substantive it denotes a "liar" or a "falsehood." Actively and transitively *pseudēs* describes a "*deceiving* person"; passively and intransitively it describes a "*deceived* person" (Conzelmann, "pseudos," *Kittel,* 9:595). (See also the articles on *pseudomai* [5409], *pseudos* [5414], *pseustēs* [5418].)

Septuagint Usage

Pseudēs appears some 70 times in the canonical material of the Septuagint. Most often the Hebrew word it replaces is *sheqer,* "lie, falsehood, deception." It describes false witnesses (*pseudomartus* [5412]) who give "false" testimony (Exodus 20:16; Deuteronomy 5:20; cf. Theodotion's version of Susanna 43,49; Proverbs 21:28) or "false, deceptive" prophetic messages (e.g., Jeremiah 14:14,15; 23:25,26,32). God alone is true and in Him alone is life; therefore, apart from God existence itself is "deception" (Psalm 62:9 [LXX 61:9]; Proverbs 19:21-23).

New Testament Usage

Pseudēs occurs only three times in the New Testament: Acts 6:13; Revelation 2:2; 21:8. Like his Lord before him, Stephen fell prey to the "false witness" produced by the Sanhedrin (Acts 6:13; cf. Mark 14:56,57, *pseudomartureō* [5410]; cf. Matthew 26:60). Elsewhere it concerns men who pretended to be apostles but were "false" (Revelation 2:2; cf. 2 Corinthians 11:13). The fate awaiting all "liars" is the lake of fire (Revelation 21:8).

Strong 5571, Bauer 891, Moulton-Milligan 697, Kittel 9:594-603, Liddell-Scott 2020, Colin Brown 2:470-73.

5407. ψευδοδιδάσκαλος pseudodidaskalos noun

False teacher.

Cross-References:

διδάσκω didaskō (1315)
ψεύδομαι pseudomai (5409)

1. ψευδοδιδάσκαλοι pseudodidaskaloi nom pl masc

1 even as there shall be false teachers among you,..... 2 Pt 2:1

Although this term appears only once in the New Testament (2 Peter 2:1) and nowhere else in all of Greek literature, the problem of false teachers, false prophets, and false christs was common in the Early Church. From the very beginning, Jesus warned of those who would arise and lead many away from the Faith (Matthew 24:5,11,23,24). Paul struggled against the false teachers at Corinth (2 Corinthians 11), against the Judaizers at Galatia (Galatians 1:6), against the false teachers at Colossae (Colossians 2:8,16-23), and against the false teachers who disturbed the Thessalonians (2 Thessalonians 2:2,3).

The writer of 2 Peter warned his readers about false teachers who would inevitably seek to carry them away by twisting Scripture (2 Peter 3:16,17) and who, in their greed, would exploit them with false words (2:3). He characterized them as "bold and willful" in their sin (2:10, RSV). Such teachers were "waterless springs and mists driven by a storm" (2:17, RSV). They promised freedom but were themselves slaves to their own sin and passions (2:19).

STRONG 5572, BAUER 891, KITTEL 2:160, LIDDELL-SCOTT 2020, COLIN BROWN 2:472; 3:766,768.

5408. ψευδολόγος pseudologos adj

Liar.

CROSS-REFERENCES:
λόγος logos (3030)
ψεύδομαι pseudomai (5409)

1. ψευδολόγων pseudologōn gen pl masc

1 **Speaking lies in hypocrisy;** .... **1 Tm 4:2**

Appearing in classical literature as early as the Fifth Century B.C. with the meaning "speaking falsely, lying" (*Liddell-Scott*), *pseudologos* occurs only one time in the New Testament. In 1 Timothy 4:2 Paul conveyed to Timothy the Spirit's warning concerning the false teachers that would arise in the last days. Paul called these *pseudologōn*, "liars." As Fee notes, the translation "liar" may mislead the reader into seeing these as individuals who deliberately state what they know is not true. The implication of the word, however, is simply that they speak falsehood rather than truth by saying things about the gospel that are not true (*Good News Commentary, 1 and 2 Timothy, Titus*, p.60).

STRONG 5573, BAUER 891, MOULTON-MILLIGAN 697, LIDDELL-SCOTT 2020, COLIN BROWN 2:472.

5409. ψεύδομαι pseudomai verb

Lie, deceive.

COGNATES:
ἀψευδής apseudēs (886)
ψευδάδελφος pseudadelphos (5404)
ψευδαπόστολος pseudapostolos (5405)
ψευδής pseudēs (5406)
ψευδοδιδάσκαλος pseudodidaskalos (5407)
ψευδολόγος pseudologos (5408)
ψευδομαρτυρέω pseudomartureō (5410)
ψευδομαρτυρία pseudomarturia (5411)
ψευδόμαρτυς pseudomartus (5412)
ψευδοπροφήτης pseudoprophētēs (5413)
ψεῦδος pseudos (5414)
ψευδόχριστος pseudochristos (5415)
ψευδώνυμος pseudōnumos (5416)
ψεῦσμα pseusma (5417)
ψεύστης pseustēs (5418)

בָּדָא bādhâ' (943), Invent (Neh 6:8).
כָּזַב kāzav (3694), Piel: lie (Job 6:28, Prv 14:5, Is 57:11).
כָּחַד kāchadh (3701), Piel: conceal (Job 27:11).
כָּחַשׁ kāchash (3703), Niphal: cower (Dt 33:29); piel: lie (Lv 19:11); cringe (Ps 66:3 [65:3]); fail (Hb 3:17); hithpael: cringe (2 Sm 22:45).

1. ψεύδομαι pseudomai 1sing indic pres mid
2. ψευδόμεθα pseudometha 1pl indic pres mid
3. ψεύδονται pseudontai 3pl indic pres mid
4. ψεύδεσθε pseudesthe 2pl impr pres mid
5. ψευδόμενοι pseudomenoi nom pl masc part pres mid
6. ἐψεύσω epseusō 2sing indic aor mid
7. ψεύσασθαι pseusasthai inf aor mid

5 **and shall say all manner of evil against you falsely,** .. **Matt 5:11**
7 **Satan filled thine heart to lie to the Holy Ghost,** .... **Acts 5:3**
6 **thou hast not lied unto men, but unto God.** **5:4**
1 **I say the truth in Christ, I lie not,** .... **Rom 9:1**
1 **our Lord Jesus Christ, ... knoweth that I lie not.** .... **2 Co 11:31**
1 **behold, before God, I lie not.** .... **Gal 1:20**
4 **Lie not one to another,** .... **Col 3:9**
1 **I speak the truth in Christ, and lie not;** .... **1 Tm 2:7**
7 **in which it was impossible for God to lie,** .... **Heb 6:18**
4 **glory not, and lie not against the truth.** .... **Jas 3:14**
2 **and walk in darkness, we lie, and do not the truth:** .. **1 Jn 1:6**
3 **which say they are Jews, and are not, but do lie;** ..... **Rev 3:9**

Classical Greek

While the literal translation of *pseudomai* in classical Greek is usually the same as Biblical Greek, there is a difference in the implications and in how lying was regarded. While there were popular reasons for not lying (e.g., one's credibility would decrease), deception was permissible for business or political gain. In plays, deception is seen bringing about justice (Conzelmann, "pseudos," *Kittel*, 9:596).

Meanings for *pseudomai* include "err, break a treaty, feign" (ibid., 9:595,596), "pretend, falsify," and "be false." This word can also mean "be cheated, be deceived," etc. (*Liddell-Scott*). With the negation *mē* (3231), *pseudomai* was used in oaths to declare the reliability of the testimony or historical account (*Moulton-Milligan*).

Septuagint Usage

In the Septuagint *pseudomai* can mean "deny" or "disclaim" in addition to the general meanings listed above. Used with *prophētēs* (4254) the word means "false prophet," as in Jeremiah 5:31 and Ezekiel 13:19. Prophets often characterized idolatry as the people being led astray by lies (e.g., Amos 2:4).

Exodus 20:16 states, "You shall not bear false witness against your neighbor" (NASB). In legal disputes the Israelites were forbidden to commit perjury. While there is not a direct prohibition against all lying, there are many cases from which a Biblical prohibition must be deduced in general and not only in legal disputes and trials (see Leviticus 19:11; Becker and Link, "Lie," *Colin Brown*, 2:470,471).

New Testament Usage

In the New Testament Jesus told His disciples not to worry about those who "speak falsely" about them (Matthew 5:11). Peter told Ananias that he *lied* to the Holy Ghost (Acts 5:3f.). In this case Ananias engaged in a deliberate act of falsehood. Titus 1:2 states that God cannot lie (*apsuedēs*). Believers are commanded not to lie since they have put off the old man (Colossians 3:9; James 3:14). Paul stated several times in his letters that he was not lying (Romans 9:1; 2 Corinthians 11:31; Galatians 1:20; 1 Timothy 2:7). In Revelation 3:9 Jesus mentioned certain individuals who claimed to be Jews but were lying. Presumably those who claimed to be Jews really believed they were. Therefore, *pseudomai*, as Jesus used it here, does not necessarily imply a deliberate act of deception but may merely indicate the existence of a falsehood. These "Jews" were deceived about themselves and consequently were lying about their assertions. Thus, *pseudomai* may indicate either the innocent propagation of an untruth or a deliberate act of deception.

STRONG 5574, BAUER 891, MOULTON-MILLIGAN 697, KITTEL 9:594-603, LIDDELL-SCOTT 2020, COLIN BROWN 2:470,472.

5410. ψευδομαρτυρέω

pseudomartureō verb

Bear false witness, give false evidence or testimony.

CROSS-REFERENCES:

μαρτυρέω martureō (3113)
ψεύδομαι pseudomai (5409)

עָנָה ʿānâh (6257), Answer; testify (Ex 20:16, Dt 5:20).

1. ψευδομαρτυρήσῃς pseudomarturēsēs
2sing subj aor act

2. ψευδομαρτυρήσεις pseudomarturēseis
2sing indic fut act

3. ἐψευδομαρτύρουν epseudomarturoun
3pl indic imperf act

2 **Thou shalt not bear false witness,** .... Matt 19:18
1 Do not steal, **Do not bear false witness,** .... Mark 10:19
3 For many **bare false witness against him,** 14:56
3 arose certain, and **bare false witness against him,** 14:57
1 Do not steal, **Do not bear false witness,** .... Luke 18:20
2 **Thou shalt not bear false witness,** .... Rom 13:9

Classical Greek

Pseudomartureō occurs in Greek literature as early as the Fourth Century B.C. It generally means "to be a false witness" or to "bear false witness," usually in a legal context. Thus, it could be translated "to perjure." According to Strathmann, the emphasis of the word is on the act of deception or distortion. It is not contested that the one testifying is a "witness"; rather, he is a *false* witness because he is incorrect in his assertions. Whether he testifies as a *martus* (3116) or a *pseudomartus* (5412) depends on whether or not he tells the truth ("martus," *Kittel*, 4:513).

Septuagint Usage

In the Septuagint *pseudomartureō* appears in the ninth commandment, "Thou shalt not bear false witness . . . " (Exodus 20:16; Deuteronomy 5:20 [LXX 5:17]). In Theodotion's text of Susanna *pseudomartureō* is used of the two elders who had lied about Susanna.

Old Testament Background

The idea of false witness cannot be understood outside of its background in the Old Testament and the legal proceedings of ancient Israel as well as the entire Ancient Near East. According to Childs, "the ninth commandment contains several technical legal terms which point quite clearly to its original significance" (*The Old Testament Library, Exodus*, p.424). The terms *ʿēd shāqer* (Exodus 20:16) and *ʿēd shāwᵉʾ* (Deuteronomy 5:20 [5:17 Masoretic Text]) denote a "lying witness."

In the courts of the Ancient Near East a man would testify against another before an assembly of the elders. This commandment was not originally a general prohibition against lying but a command to protect members of the covenant community from the false accusations of fellow members (ibid.). However, as Childs points out, Leviticus 19:16 shows that early on it became important to protect members of the covenant community from any type of slanderous comments or idle rumors (cf. Hosea 4:2; ibid., p.425).

New Testament Usage

Even though there were Old Testament laws that sought to protect individuals against false witnesses (e.g., the law of two or three witnesses, Numbers 35:30; Deuteronomy 17:6; 19:15), both the Old and New Testaments provide vivid examples of how this system was abused throughout Israel's history. One of the most striking is the trial of Jesus before the high priest and the Jewish Council (Mark 14:56,57). Here the high priest and the Council, seeking to find sufficient reason to execute Jesus, brought many who gave false testimony about Him. The result was not the accumulation of overwhelming evidence but the confusion of many lies.

The other four occurrences of this verb in the New Testament (Matthew 19:18; Mark 10:19; Luke 18:20; Romans 13:9) are direct quotations from the Ten Commandments as found in the Septuagint (Exodus 20:16; Deuteronomy 5:20). The citations from the Gospels show Christ's commitment not to destroy the Law but to fulfill it. These four quotations further demonstrate the Early Church's belief that Christian believers were a continuation of the true Israel, i.e., those who were Jews not simply by circumcision of the flesh but of the Spirit (cf. Romans 2:28,29).

STRONG 5576, BAUER 891-92, MOULTON-MILLIGAN 697, KITTEL 4:513-14, LIDDELL-SCOTT 2020, COLIN BROWN 2:470; 3:1038-39,1041.

5411. ψευδομαρτυρία

pseudomarturia noun

False witness, false testimony.

CROSS-REFERENCES:
μαρτυρέω martureō (3113)
ψεύδομαι pseudomai (5409)

1. **ψευδομαρτυρίαν pseudomarturian** acc sing fem
2. **ψευδομαρτυρίαι pseudomarturiai** nom pl fem

2 For out of the heart proceed ... **false witness**,...... Matt 15:19
1 all the council, sought **false witness** against Jesus,...... 26:59

In classical literature this term appears primarily in legal contexts and is translated "perjury" or "false witness" (*Liddell-Scott*). The word is also used in the Septuagint. (For a discussion of the Old Testament idea of "false witness" see *pseudomartureō* [5410].) Its use in Matthew 29:56 continues the legal sense of false testimony. Those who desired to see Jesus executed purposefully sought out false testimony that could be used to build a case against Him. The only other New Testament occurrence of the word (Matthew 15:19) lists "false witness" as one of the evil emanations of the human heart that defile an individual.

STRONG 5577, BAUER 892, MOULTON-MILLIGAN 697, KITTEL 4:513-14, LIDDELL-SCOTT 2020, COLIN BROWN 2:472; 3:1038-39.

5412. ψευδόμαρτυς

pseudomartus noun

One who gives misrepresenting testimony, a false witness.

CROSS-REFERENCES:
μαρτυρέω martureō (3113)
ψεύδομαι pseudomai (5409)

1. **ψευδομάρτυρες pseudomartures** nom pl masc
2. **ψευδομαρτύρων pseudomarturōn** gen pl masc

2 yea, though many **false witnesses** came,............ Matt 26:60
1 At the last came two **false witnesses**,.................. 26:60
1 Yea, and we are found **false witnesses** of God;..... 1 Co 15:15

Found as early as the Fifth Century B.C. in the writings of Gorgias meaning "false witness" (*Liddell-Scott*), *pseudomartus* is not used in classical literature as frequently as its related noun *pseudomarturia* (5411). It is found in the New Testament in Matthew 26:60 and 1 Corinthians 15:15. Paul wrote that had Christ not been raised from the dead then Paul and the other apostles could be considered guilty of "misrepresenting" God. Fidelity to the revelation and teaching of Christ was a primary concern in the life and ministry of Paul and the other apostles. This concern was evidenced by the numerous occasions on which Paul addressed false teaching and encouraged young ministers such as Timothy to "take heed to yourself and to your teaching" (1 Timothy 4:16, RSV). The false witnesses brought before the Sanhedrin during Jesus' trial presumably related distorted information concerning the teaching and work of Jesus.

BAUER 892, KITTEL 4:513-14, LIDDELL-SCOTT 2020, COLIN BROWN 2:472; 3:1038-39.

5413. ψευδοπροφήτης

pseudoprophētēs noun

False prophet.

CROSS-REFERENCES:
προφητεύω prophēteuō (4253)
ψεύδομαι pseudomai (5409)

נָבִיא nāvî' (5204), Prophet (Jer 26:7f. [33:7f.], 28:1 [35:1], Zec 13:2).

1. **ψευδοπροφήτης pseudoprophētēs** nom sing masc
2. **ψευδοπροφήτου pseudoprophētou** gen sing masc
3. **ψευδοπροφήτην pseudoprophētēn** acc sing masc
4. **ψευδοπροφῆται pseudoprophētai** nom pl masc
5. **ψευδοπροφητῶν pseudoprophētōn** gen pl masc
6. **ψευδοπροφήταις pseudoprophētais** dat pl masc

5 Beware of **false prophets**, ... in sheep's clothing,..... Matt 7:15
4 **false prophets** shall rise, and shall deceive many........ 24:11
4 there shall arise false Christs, and **false prophets**,...... 24:24
4 For false Christs and **false prophets** shall rise,..... Mark 13:22
6 for so did their fathers to the **false prophets**......... Luke 6:26
3 they found a certain sorcerer, **a false prophet**,...... Acts 13:6
4 there were **false prophets** also among the people,.... 2 Pt 2:1
4 many **false prophets** are gone out into the world..... 1 Jn 4:1
2 and out of the mouth of the **false prophet**...........Rev 16:13
1 **false prophet** that wrought miracles before him,........ 19:20
1 where the beast and the **false prophet** are,............. 20:10

Classical Greek

This is a compound formed from the noun *pseudos* (5414), "lie," and the noun *prophētēs* (4254), "prophet." It is exceptionally rare in classical Greek, and only becomes widely used in Christian literature.

Septuagint Usage

It occurs in the canonical portions of the Septuagint 10 times. All but one of these (Zechariah 13:2) appear in the Book of Jeremiah. The Hebrew in every case is *nāvî'*, the common word for "prophet"; however, it can be used in an unfavorable sense (as is obviously the case when translated by *pseudoprophētēs*). The Septuagint translators often make the distinction between the "good" prophet and the "bad" prophet which might not always be clear from the Hebrew. The English text can also reflect that ambiguity (e.g., Zechariah 13:2, a prophetic saying concerning the removal of prophets on the day "a fountain [will be] opened to the house of David").

A similar situation is reflected by the prophet Jeremiah. The English translation "prophet" (rendered *pseudoprophētēs* by the Septuagint) is intelligible only in light of the historical context (e.g., Jeremiah 6:13; 26:7,8,11 [LXX 33:7,8,11]). The word "prophets" here particularly concerns the corrupt prophetic guild of Jeremiah's day.

New Testament Usage

Pseudoprophētēs occurs more frequently in the New Testament (11 times) than in the Old Testament. It is found in the Synoptic Gospels but not in John. Luke notes that one of the signs of the true prophet of the past was his mistreatment by the Israelites; the *false prophets*, on the other hand, were well-treated by them (Luke 6:26).

Consistently, false prophets appear as a "sign of the times," in particular the "end times" (Matthew 24:11,24; Mark 13:22; 2 Peter 2:1; cf. 1 John 4:1). *The* False Prophet is likewise an end-time figure (e.g., Revelation 16:13). He, as an assistant to the Beast, works deluding miracles and signs (19:20; cf. 16:13f.). False prophets in general and the False Prophet in particular both refuse to acknowledge that Jesus is from God (1 John 4:1). In addition, both seek to deceive God's people.

Peter associated false prophets of the past with the false teachers of his day who "secretly introduce destructive heresies" (2 Peter 2:1, NIV). He noted that they even deny the Lord. Greed is another mark of their heresy (2 Peter 2:1-3,14). The destiny of the false prophets/False Prophet is destruction (2 Peter 2:1-13; Revelation 21:8-10).

STRONG 5578, BAUER 892, KITTEL 6:781-861, LIDDELL-SCOTT 2020-21, COLIN BROWN 2:472,474; 3:74,81.

5414. ψεῦδος pseudos noun

Lie, falsehood, lying.

CROSS-REFERENCE:

ψεύδομαι pseudomai (5409)

אַכְזָב 'akhzāv (397), Deceptive (Jer 15:18).

כָּזָב kāzāv (3695), Lie, falsehood (Pss 4:2, 5:6, Is 28:17).

כָּחַשׁ kāchash (3703), Piel: lie (Hos 4:2).

כַּחַשׁ kachash (3704), Leanness (Job 16:8 [16:9]); lie (Hos 11:12).

מִרְמָה mirmāh (4983), Deceit, deception (Dn 8:25, 11:23).

שֶׁקֶר sheqer (8632), Deception, lie (Jer 3:23, 23:14, Mic 2:11).

1. **ψεῦδος pseudos** nom/acc sing neu
2. **ψεύδους pseudous** gen sing neu
3. **ψεύδει pseudei** dat sing neu

1 When he speaketh a lie, he speaketh of his own:.... John 8:44
3 Who changed the truth of God into a lie,........... Rom 1:25
1 Wherefore putting away lying,...................... Eph 4:25
2 with all power and signs and lying wonders,........ 2 Th 2:9
3 strong delusion, that they should believe a lie:.......... 2:11
1 because ye know it, and that no lie is of the truth... 1 Jn 2:21
1 and is truth, and is no lie,........................... 2:27
1 And no lie was found in their mouth; (NASB)..... Rev 14:5
1 whatsoever worketh abomination, or maketh a lie:..... 21:27
1 idolaters, and whosoever loveth and maketh a lie...... 22:15

Classical Greek

The origin of this term and its cognates is uncertain. A noun, *pseudos* denotes "a lie, a falsehood," in contrast to *alētheia* (223), "truth." *Pseudos* occurs in numerous compounds (e.g., *pseudoprophētēs* [5413], "false prophet"). To the ancient Greeks lying was not merely the opposite of truth. In addition, Greeks recognized that oftentimes how things appear does not reflect how they truly are. A person's senses can be deceived. For the Greek, untruth is nonbeing, but error is a "false judgment of reality" (Conzelmann, "pseudos," *Kittel*, 9:595). Thus, philosophers equated truth with reality and being (ibid., p.597); to the Greek "that which is" is true (Boman, *Hebrew Thought Compared with Greek*, p.202).

The Greeks in general regarded lying as ethically improper, particularly perjury as a deliberate act of falsehood. However, lying could be justified for social or political reasons. Aristotle, for instance, argued that a man who deceived for the sake of reputation was (for a boaster) not really that bad. However, he who lied for monetary gain or for no purpose at all was very evil (*Nichomachean Ethics* 1127b. 9-15).

Septuagint Usage

Pseudos often translates the Hebrew word *sheqer,* "falseness," in the Septuagint. The cognate verb, *pseudomai* (5409), most frequently translates the Hebrew word *kāchash,* "to deceive, deny, lie."

Pseudos occurs about 40 times, generally denoting a "falsehood" or a "lie." In Job 16:8 (LXX 16:9) Job states that his *pseudos* has become a testimony and has risen against him. In Hosea 4:2 Hosea complains that there is cursing and *lying* and murder in the land. Sirach 7:12,13 sums up the Jewish attitude toward falsehood: "Do not devise a lie against your brother, nor do the like to a friend. Refuse to utter a lie, for the habit of lying serves no good" (RSV).

Old Testament Background

The dichotomy between the "truth" and a "lie" is vital to the Biblical revelation of God. Fundamental to God's nature is the quality of being truthful (Romans 3:4); thus, He opposes anything false. All truth resides in Him; He is "abundant in . . . truth" (Exodus 34:6). Moreover, His revelation (Psalm 43:3), His law (Psalm 119:142), and His works (Daniel 4:37) are true. The righteous walk in the truth of God, which results in holy fear of God as well as ethical responsibility (Psalm 86:11; Proverbs 8:7). The Lord "desirest truth in the inward parts" (Psalm 51:6). Lies and falsehood are the chief trademarks of God's enemies.

Condemnation of the religious "lie" of the nation of Israel is a common feature of the prophetic message. Likewise, the idolatry of the Gentiles is characterized as a "lie." Their gods are gods of falsehood who lead people astray (Isaiah 44:20). Behind these idols are lying spirits (1 Kings 22:22) which control the false prophets, fortune-tellers, soothsayers, sorcerers, and magicians (Deuteronomy 18:10-12).

God judges harshly those responsible for introducing "falsehood" into the religion of Israel. The true prophets often complained that the people had been led astray by false prophets (Jeremiah 23:14,32; 27:10; 28:15; Ezekiel 13:19; 21:29; 22:28). False prophecy typically is false in that it predicts "prosperity" and "joy" rather than presenting the true condition of the people before God. They cried "peace, peace" to an unrepentant, backslidden people who were facing God's judgment and wrath (Jeremiah 6:14; 14:13f.; Ezekiel 13:10f.; Micah 3:5). The scribes, the authorities on the Law, were accused by Jeremiah of having written their interpretations of the Law with a "lying pen" (Jeremiah 8:8). Similarly, the priesthood was snared by the deceit of the lie (Jeremiah 6:13). God will do away with the "lies" of pagan religions at the time of messianic redemption. The people of God will realize that "surely our (their) fathers have inherited lies, vanity, and things wherein there is no profit" (Jeremiah 16:19).

New Testament Usage

As many as 15 different words contain the stem *pseud-* in the New Testament. Included in this group are: the verb *pseudomai,* "to lie"; the noun *pseudos,* "a lie"; the adjective *pseustēs* (5418), "a liar"; *pseudēs* (5406), "a deceiver"; compounds include *pseudapostolos* (5405), "false apostle" (2 Corinthians 11:13); *pseudadelphos* (5404), "false brother" (2 Corinthians 11:26; Galatians 2:4); *pseudodidaskalos* (5407), "false teacher" (2 Peter 2:1); *pseudomartus* (5412), "false witness" (Matthew 26:60f.; 1 Corinthians 15:15); *pseudomartureō* (5410), "to give false testimony" (Matthew 19:18; Mark 10:19; 14:56f.; Luke 18:20; Romans 13:9); *pseudomarturia* (5411), "false testimony" (Matthew 15:19; 26:59); *pseudoprophētēs* (5413), "false prophet" (Matthew 7:15; 24:11,24; Mark 13:22; Luke 6:26; Acts 13:6; etc.); *pseudochristos* (5415), "false christ" (Matthew 24:24; Mark 13:22); *pseudōnumos* (5416), "falsely named, so-called" (1 Timothy 6:20). Cognates of this stem appear in virtually every book of the New Testament, but they occur more often in the writings of Paul and John.

The contrast and tension between "the truth" and "a lie" reaches its climax in the appearance of Jesus Christ, the Truth (John 1:17; 14:6; 1 John 2:21, "no lie comes from the truth" [NIV]). The conflict initiated in the first coming of Jesus Christ will be settled at His return, although, its outcome has already been decided by the Cross. The "father of the lie" (*pseudos*), the devil, Satan (John 8:44), with his "subjects"—"spiritual wickedness in high places" (Ephesians 6:12)—will be ultimately destroyed. All liars ("maketh a lie" [*pseudos*]) will be cast into the lake of fire (Revelation 21:8).

Satan is the source of all lies (*pseudos,* John 8:44). He himself is the "liar," and he has been so from the beginning. Behind every activity of deception and lying stands his "handiwork."

Evil, satanic spirits underlie all idolatry and paganism (1 Corinthians 10:20). The Gentiles have exchanged the truth of God for a "lie" (*pseudos*, Romans 1:25). The churches receive strong warnings against the poison of the "false apostles, false teachers, and false christs" (see above). During the last days, with the appearance of Antichrist, Satan will promote his lie with "all power and signs and lying wonders" (2 Thessalonians 2:9; cf. verse 11: "that they should believe a lie" [*pseudos*]).

Jesus, however, through His divine insight exposed the lies of Satan and his cohorts through the proclamation of the kingdom of God (Matthew 12:28). Thus believers are preserved from being deceived by these "lies" because they are born "with the word of truth" (James 1:18). They are "of the truth" (1 John 3:19) because they have the "Spirit of truth" residing in them (John 14:17; 15:26; 16:13). They are made holy by the truth (John 17:17). God especially requires that our inner person, our heart, be free of hypocrisy; He detests such deceit (1 Peter 2:1; cf. Matthew 6:2f.). Therefore, the people of God must avoid every kind of hypocrisy—the ultimate lie (Luke 12:1).

Because of this relationship with the truth/Truth, believers are admonished to live and speak the truth in terms of their life-styles. They are to do away with lying (*pseudos*), and to "speak every man truth with his neighbor" (Ephesians 4:25). Holy Writ plainly presents the demands upon those choosing to follow the truth (see "Lie," *Illustrated Bible Dictionary*).

Strong 5579, Bauer 892, Moulton-Milligan 697, Kittel 9:594-603, Liddell-Scott 2021, Colin Brown 2:470,472-74.

5415. ψευδόχριστος

pseudochristos noun

False christ, false messiah.

Cognate:

ψεύδομαι pseudomai (5409)

Synonym:

ἀντίχριστος antichristos (497)

1. ψευδόχριστοι pseudochristoi nom pl masc

1 there shall arise **false Christs**, and false prophets, . . . Matt 24:24
1 For **false Christs** and false prophets shall rise, ... Mark 13:22

This term does not appear in Greek material prior to the Christian period (including the Septuagint). It is formally a compound from *pseudos* (5414), "lie, falsehood," and *christos* (5382), "anointed one," hence, "Christ, Messiah."

Although related to the term *antichristos* (497), "antichrist," false christ is more the opposite of the true Christ. Antichrist, on the other hand, is "against" (anti) or "instead of" Christ. He denies God (1 John 2:22), whereas the false christ tries to assume the place and to falsify the role of the real Christ. This is a fine line and of course the differences between a "false christ" and "antichrist" often become indistinct, for the Antichrist will claim to be the real Christ.

The notion of false christ/messiah can only be understood in light of the true Messiah. A false messiah does not deny the messianic promises. On the contrary, he utilizes the expectations of the true promises to manipulate followers to succumb to his demands. Jesus was speaking of the false messiah when He told of others who came before Him who pretended to be "the Coming One" (John 10:8; cf. Matthew 11:3).

Because Jesus, the true Messiah, was rejected, false messiahs continued to appear even after He had come. Jesus himself cautioned that this would happen both among His contemporaries (Matthew 24:24) as well as among the people of the last days. One such false messiah was Bar Kochba ("Son of Star"), the leader of a Jewish revolt against Rome (A.D. 132–135), who pretended to be the "star of Jacob" of whom Scripture prophesied (Numbers 24:17).

Although first and foremost the Antichrist will be an *opponent* of the true Messiah, it can justifiably be said that to some extent he is a *false* messiah. One example of this is that the "man of sin" elevates himself to a position "above all that is called god"; he sets himself up in the temple as God (2 Thessalonians 2:4). Similarly, he denies Christ while at the same time he assumes the place of Christ by pretending to be the savior of the world.

Nevertheless, the Antichrist of the last days will not pretend to be God's Messiah as the *pseudochristos* does. The most prominent feature of the Antichrist is that he scoffs at God and wants to set himself up in Christ's stead. Thus there are many features shared between Antichrist and the false christ. Whereas the *psuedochristos* will be a snare for the Jew looking for a particular kind of messiah, the Antichrist will be the great seducer who deceives an unbelieving world.

Strong 5580, Bauer 892, Liddell-Scott 2021, Colin Brown 1:124-25; 2:472.

5416. ψευδώνυμος pseudōnumos adj

Falsely called.

Cross-References:
ὄνομα onoma (3549)
ψεύδομαι pseudomai (5409)

1. ψευδωνύμου pseudōnumou gen sing fem

1 and oppositions of science falsely so called:......... 1 Tm 6:20

Classical Greek

Formed from the combination of *pseud-*, "false," and *onoma* (3549), "name," *pseudōnumos* means "falsely named, falsely called." Although the expression occurs in classical writings, it does not appear in the Septuagint. Aeschylus (Fifth Century B.C.) said that the river Hybristes was not *falsely named* (Prometheus Bound 717). In Aeschylus' *The Seven Against Thebes*, the king of Thebes says of his brother who is attacking Thebes, "Justice is falsely named if she helps my brother" (line 670).

New Testament Usage

The sole appearance of *pseudōnumos* in the New Testament comes from the pen of the apostle Paul. Paul wrote to caution Timothy about the false teachers in his midst (1 Timothy 1:3,7; cf. 4:1-3; 6:3). In his closing remarks Paul again reminded Timothy to "guard what has been entrusted to your care" (i.e., the gospel; 6:20, NIV). Those opposing Timothy supposedly had "knowledge"; however, Paul said it was "falsely called" knowledge.

There is no need here to read any kind of Gnostic assault upon the church in Ephesus, for it is not simply an issue of "knowledge" (*gnōsis* [1102]); rather, it involves a larger problem of "unsound doctrine" which includes disputing over the Law, asceticism, licentiousness, greed, and general misconduct (e.g., 1 Timothy 1:7-11; 4:1-3,7; 5:15; 6:3-5). Paul apparently equated this "so-called knowledge" with "godless chatter" (1 Timothy 6:20, NIV), "godless myths and old wives tales" (1 Timothy 4:7, NIV), and "meaningless talk" (1 Timothy 1:6, NIV).

Strong 5581, Bauer 892, Moulton-Milligan 697, Kittel 5:282-83, Liddell-Scott 2021, Colin Brown 2:648,652,655.

5417. ψεῦσμα pseusma noun

Falsehood, untruthfulness.

Cross-Reference:
ψεύδομαι pseudomai (5409)

1. ψεύσματι pseusmati dat sing neu

1 more abounded through my lie unto his glory;...... Rom 3:7

Paul is the only writer in the New Testament to use this word. In Romans 3:7 Paul, speaking "in a human way" (i.e., according to human reasoning), used *pseusma* in a rhetorical question that reflects the antinomianism he was addressing from verse 5 onward. As Murray points out, Paul was not dealing here with the principle that "where sin abounded, grace did much more abound" (Romans 5:20; *New International Commentary on the New Testament, Romans,* p.97). Rather, Paul simply appealed to the fact of universal judgment to answer the question, "How can God be just in judging us if our sin brings His righteousness to light?"

Though categorical assertion of a point to be proved is no argument, this is precisely what we find Paul doing in this passage. Paul's argument illustrates our need to remember that in dealing with the ultimate facts of revelation, argument must be content with categorical affirmation (ibid., p.99).

Strong 5582, Bauer 892, Kittel 9:594-603, Liddell-Scott 2021.

5418. ψεύστης pseustēs noun

Liar.

Cross-Reference:
ψεύδομαι pseudomai (5409)

כָּזָב kāzav (3694), Liar (Ps 116:11 [115:2]).

כָּזָב kāzāv (3695), Liar (Prv 19:22—Codex Alexandrinus and some Sinaiticus texts only).

1. ψεύστης pseustēs nom sing masc
2. ψεύστην pseustēn acc sing masc
3. ψεῦσται pseustai nom pl masc
4. ψεύσταις pseustais dat pl masc

1 for he is a liar, and the father of it................. John 8:44
1 if I should say, I know him not, I shall be a liar........ 8:55
1 God be true, but every man a liar; as it is written,.. Rom 3:4
4 for menstealers, for liars, for perjured persons,..... 1 Tm 1:10
3 Cretians are alway liars, evil beasts, slow bellies...... Tit 1:12
2 we make him a liar, and his word is not in us....... 1 Jn 1:10
1 and keepeth not his commandments, is a liar,........... 2:4
1 is a liar but he that denieth that Jesus is the Christ?.... 2:22
1 and hateth his brother, he is a liar:.................... 4:20
2 he that believeth not God hath made him a liar;........ 5:10

Classical Greek

Pseustēs appears in Greek literature as early as Homer (Eighth Century B.C.) and means a "liar." In Sophocles' *Antigone* a messenger claims to be presenting the truth lest he be found a liar (1195).

Septuagint Usage

Although *pseustēs* only appears four times in the Septuagint, each reference addresses a different aspect of a "liar." The Psalmist wrote that, in comparison to God's trustworthiness, *all* men are liars! (Psalm 116:11 [LXX 115:2]). This thought is echoed in the New Testament by Paul, who declared: "Yea, let God be true, but every man a liar" (Romans 3:4). Proverbs 19:22 states that it is better to be a poor man than a rich liar, and a rich liar aroused hatred and disgust in Sirach (Sirach 25:2). Another occurrence of *pseustēs* reveals that wisdom is far from the thoughts of a liar (Sirach 15:8).

New Testament Usage

In addition to the New Testament passage cited above, *pseustēs* occurs nine other times. The most important of these is John 8:44, where Jesus indicated the very nature of the devil: "He was a murderer from the beginning, and abode not in the truth, because there is no truth in him. When he speaketh a lie, he speaketh of his own: for he is a *liar*, and the father of it." All those who lie are accomplishing the desires of their father, the devil (John 8:44).

The New Testament seems to indicate two categories of liars. The first includes those individuals who claim to have a relationship with God but, in reality, do not know Him. The Jews who opposed Jesus would be found in this category (John 8:55). John wrote that anyone who claims to know God, while disregarding His commands, is a liar (1 John 2:4). This is also true of the person who says he loves God, yet hates his brother (1 John 4:20). The second category involves those who deny the revealed truths of God. In 1 John 2:22 the one who denies that Jesus is the Christ is both a liar and an antichrist. Those who do not believe God, and who deny their own sinful nature, take the dangerous step of declaring God a liar (1 John 1:10; 5:10). Their actions qualify them to be counted among the murderers, the immoral men, the homosexuals, and the perjurers (1 Timothy 1:10). The last occurrence of *pseustēs* is found in Titus 1:12, where the Cretans are said to have a reputation for always being liars.

Strong 5583, Bauer 892, Moulton-Milligan 697, Kittel 9:594-603, Liddell-Scott 2021, Colin Brown 2:470,472.

5419. ψηλαφάω psēlaphaō verb

Handle, touch, feel for something, grope for something.

Synonyms:

ἅπτω haptō (674)
θιγγάνω thinganō (2322)
προσψαύω prospsauō (4237)

גָּשַׁשׁ gāshash (1707), Piel: grope, feel one's way (Is 59:10).

יָמַשׁ yāmash (3346), Hiphil: let feel (Jgs 16:26).

מוּשׁ mûsh (4318), Feel (Gn 27:12, Ps 115:7 [113:15]); remove (Zec 3:10).

מָשַׁשׁ māshash (5135), Touch, feel; piel: grope (Dt 28:29).

1. **ἐψηλάφησαν epsēlaphēsan** 3pl indic aor act
2. **ψηλαφήσειαν psēlaphēseian** 3pl opt aor act
3. **ψηλαφήσατε psēlaphēsate** 2pl impr aor act
4. **ψηλαφωμένῳ psēlaphōmenō** dat sing neu part pres mid

3 **handle me**, and see; for a spirit hath not flesh ..... Luke 24:39
2 if haply they **might feel after him**, and find him, ... Acts 17:27
4 not come unto the mount that **might be touched**, ... Heb 12:18
1 have looked upon, and our hands have **handled**, ... 1 Jn 1:1

Classical Greek

This verb is used in three primary ways in classical literature: (1) of the literal act of touching or handling an object or person; (2) of the act of feeling or groping about for something, such as a blind man might grope or feel about; (3) and in a metaphoric sense of searching after something, or the act of examining or testing (*Liddell-Scott*).

Septuagint Usage

The Septuagint usage of this Greek verb is similar to that found in classical literature. The translators of the Septuagint used *psēlaphaō* to translate four Hebrew words, but primarily, *mûsh* ("touch" or "feel"). However, *psēlaphaō* also translates *gāshash* and its older synonym *māshash* (see Delitzsch, *Commentary on the Old Testament*, 7b:399), both of which mean "grope." In Isaiah 59:10 *psēlaphaō* is used metaphorically in a striking picture of Israel's "impulse to self-preservation" (ibid., 7b:400), i.e., their hopeless search for righteousness and for God.

New Testament Usage

The New Testament continues both the literal and metaphoric uses of *psēlaphaō* seen in classical and Septuagintal material. In Luke 24:39 the disciples were commanded by Jesus to "handle" Him in response to their doubts that He truly had risen as He said. A similar use is found in 1 John 1:1 where the writer is establishing himself as an eyewitness of Jesus and His message, and thereby proves his authority to proclaim this same message. Beyond affirming the writer's authority, some feel that the use of such vivid and sense-oriented verbs may be a polemical point against the Docetists who denied the real, physical incarnation of Christ (Marshall, *New International Commentary on the New Testament, The Epistles of John*, p.101, note 9). Others see the possibility that these words might have been designed to refute the agnostic misuse of the saying from Isaiah 64:4 quoted in 1 Corinthians 2:9: "Eye hath not seen, nor ear heard . . . the things which God hath prepared for them that love him" (Bruce, *The Epistles of John*, p.46, note 3).

Another example of the literal use is found in Hebrews 12:18. Here the writer returns to a motif seen earlier in the book (2:2-4): the contrast between the giving of the Law and the reception of the gospel (Bruce, *New International Commentary on the New Testament, Hebrews*, p.371). While the circumstances surrounding the giving of the Law were awesome, they are here presented as largely physical and temporal, i.e., those things that can be "touched" or experienced with the senses. This is contrasted with the tremendous consequences of both the reception and rejection of the gospel. The second revelation of God is pictured as superior, for this covenant takes place in the spiritual realm and is mediated by Christ.

Finally, in Acts 17:27, Paul used *psēlaphaō* in a way similar to that of Isaiah 59:10. Paul stated that God's purpose in arranging the nations and times was for the benefit of mankind, that they should seek God, in the hope that "they might *feel after* him, and find him." The use of this Greek verb here may contain the idea of man's groping in the darkness or semidarkness when the light of God's full revelation is not available (Bruce, *New International Commentary on the New Testament, Acts*, p.358, note 48).

STRONG 5584, BAUER 892, MOULTON-MILLIGAN 697-98, LIDDELL-SCOTT 2022.

5420. ψηφίζω psēphizō verb

Count, calculate, figure.

COGNATES:

συγκαταψηφίζω sunkatapsēphizō (4636)
συμψηφίζω sumpsēphizō (4711)

SYNONYM:

λογίζομαι logizomai (3023)

סָפַר sāphar (5807), Count; niphal: be counted (1 Kgs 3:8—Codex Alexandrinus only).

1. ψηφίζει psēphizei 3sing indic pres act
2. ψηφισάτω psēphisatō 3sing impr aor act

1 sitteth not down first, and counteth the cost, ... Luke 14:28
2 hath understanding count the number of the beast: .. Rev 13:18

Found only twice in the New Testament (Luke 14:28; Revelation 13:18), this word refers to the process of counting or calculating. In a powerful presentation concerning the high cost of discipleship, Jesus challenged His listeners to consider the implications of following Jesus. Any decision to follow Jesus that does not consider the costs may result in the humiliating discovery that the cost is too great to continue. This humiliation will come not only in this life but in the judgment to come.

In Revelation 13:18 John gave a clue to discovering the identity of the beast by "calculating" the number of the beast. This would be made possible by following the common practice of assigning numbers in Greek/Hebrew to the letters (e.g., *a*=1, *b*=2, *c*=3, etc.). This practice has been duly noted (Beasley-Murray, *New Century Bible Commentary, Revelation*, p.219).

STRONG 5585, BAUER 892, MOULTON-MILLIGAN 698, KITTEL 9:604-7, LIDDELL-SCOTT 2022.

5421. ψῆφος psēphos noun

Pebble, little stone.

SYNONYMS:

λίθος lithos (3010B)
πέτρα petra (3934)

חָצָץ chātsāts (2789), Gravel (Lam 3:16).

חֶשְׁבּוֹן cheshbôn (2918), Assessment (2 Kgs 12:4—Codex Alexandrinus only).

צֹר tsōr (7144), Flint (Ex 4:25).

1. ψῆφον psēphon acc sing fem

1 put to death, I gave my voice against them......... Acts 26:10
1 and will give him a white stone,.................... Rev 2:17
1 white stone, and in the stone a new name written,...... 2:17

Classical Greek

Psēphos may be used for any pebble, but it is most often used for a particular type of pebble or little stone. In classical Greek pebbles were used in board games and in mosaic works of art. *Psēphos* can indicate a precious stone or stones on a seashore (Braumann, "psēphos," *Kittel*, 9:605).

Juries used stones in voting (a white one for acquittal and a black one for conviction). Such was the method at Socrates' trial (*Bauer*). Therefore, the word came to mean "vote" or "number" (*Moulton-Milligan*).

Septuagint Usage

The Septuagint exhibits the same semantic range. Exodus 4:25 speaks of sharp stones. Lamentations 3:16 speaks of little pebbles. Among other places, the voting stone is mentioned in 4 Maccabees 15:26 (Braumann, "psēphos," *Kittel*, 9:605).

Many believe that the Urim and Thummim used by the Israelites were stones, one white and one black, in a leather bag. Etymologically, however, no explanation can be given credence over any other. (For a further treatment see Motyer, "Urim and Thummim," *The New Bible Dictionary.*)

New Testament Usage

Only two verses in the New Testament contain this word. In Acts 26:10 Paul stated that when the saints were sentenced to death, "I gave my voice against them," i.e., he voted against them. Revelation 2:17 notes that the one who overcomes will receive a white stone with a secret name.

Strong 5586, Bauer 892, Moulton-Milligan 698, Kittel 9:604-7, Liddell-Scott 2022-23.

5422. ψιθυρισμός psithurismos noun

A gossip, slanderer.

לַחַשׁ lachash (4043), Charming (Eccl 10:11).

1. ψιθυρισμοί psithurismoi nom pl masc

1 strifes, backbitings, **whisperings,** swellings, tumults: 2 Co 12:20

Psithurismos occurs only in 2 Corinthians 12:20 in the New Testament. It appears amidst a list of vices and destructive attitudes Paul feared he would find in his forthcoming visit to the church at Corinth. This term is related to *psithuristēs* (5423), "a gossip" or "tale-bearer," which is also used only by Paul in a similar list of vices and evil actions (Romans 1:29).

Strong 5587, Bauer 892-93, Liddell-Scott 2023.

5423. ψιθυριστής psithuristēs noun

A gossip, talebearer.

1. ψιθυριστάς psithuristas acc pl masc

1 murder, debate, deceit, malignity; **whisperers,** .... Rom 1:29

Related to *psithurismos* (5422), a "whispering" or "gossiping," *psithuristēs* is found only in the New Testament (Romans 1:29 where it is translated "whisperers" by the KJV). Because of humanity's failure to acknowledge God, He turned them over to a "base mind and to improper conduct" (Romans 1:28, RSV), i.e., He allowed them to carry out their depravity to its fullest. Among the expressions of this depravity is the destructive act of gossiping or slandering others.

Strong 5588, Bauer 893, Moulton-Milligan 698, Liddell-Scott 2023.

5424. ψιχίον psichion noun

Crumb, a small scrap of food.

1. ψιχίων psichiōn gen pl neu

1 yet the dogs eat of the **crumbs** which fall .... Matt 15:27
1 dogs under the table eat of the children's **crumbs**. . . .Mark 7:28
1 And desiring to be fed with the **crumbs** which fell . .Luke 16:21

This diminutive of *psix*, "crumb," is found only in Matthew 15:27, Mark 7:28, and the *Textus Receptus* reading of Luke 16:21. In the account of the Canaanite woman's faith, *psichion* is used in her response to Jesus' seemingly harsh and insensitive statement. Rather than being discouraged by Jesus' initial reply, which was designed to test her faith, the woman responded in faith with a very clever reply. (For an excellent discussion on this encounter, and both the personal and cultural contexts for Jesus' response, see Lane, *New International Commentary on the New Testament, Mark,* pp.261ff. For instance, Jesus' reluctance to act may be connected to His concern for being identified with the many "miracle workers" found in Hellenistic communities.)

Strong 5589, Bauer 893, Moulton-Milligan 698, Liddell-Scott 2025.

5425. ψυχή psuchē noun

Soul, life, mind, heart, person, self.

Cognates:

ἀνάψυξις anapsuxis (401)
ἀναψύχω anapsuchō (402)
ἀποψύχω apopsuchō (668)
ἄψυχος apsuchos (889)
δίψυχος dipsuchos (1368)
ἐκψύχω ekpsuchō (1621)
εὐψυχέω eupsucheō (2155)
ἰσόψυχος isopsuchos (2446)
καταψύχω katapsuchō (2680)
ὀλιγόψυχος oligopsuchos (3505)
σύμψυχος sumpsuchos (4712)
ψυχικός psuchikos (5426)
ψύχω psuchō (5429)

Synonyms:

βίος bios (972)
ζωή zōē (2205)
πνεῦμα pneuma (4011)

אִישׁ 'îsh (382), Man (Lv 17:4).

חַיָּה chayyāh (2517), Appetite (Job 38:39).

חַיִּים chayyîm (2522), Life (Ps 64:1 [63:1]).

לֵב lēv (3949), Heart, mind (2 Kgs 6:11, 2 Chr 7:11, Is 7:2).

נֶפֶשׁ nephesh (5497), Person, soul (Lv 17:10ff., Job 33:20); life (Jer 48:6 [31:6]).

רוּחַ rûach (7593), Spirit (Gn 41:8).

1. **ψυχή psuchē** nom sing fem
2. **ψυχῆς psuchēs** gen sing fem
3. **ψυχῇ psuchē** dat sing fem
4. **ψυχήν psuchēn** acc sing fem
5. **ψυχαί psuchai** nom pl fem
6. **ψυχῶν psuchōn** gen pl fem
7. **ψυχαῖς psuchais** dat pl fem
8. **ψυχάς psuchas** acc pl fem

4 they are dead which sought the young child's **life**.... Matt 2:20
3 Take no thought for your **life**, what ye shall eat,........ 6:25
1 Is not the **life** more than meat,........................ 6:25
4 kill the body, but are not able to kill the **soul**:........ 10:28
4 able to destroy both **soul** and body in hell............ 10:28
4 He that findeth his **life** shall lose it:.................. 10:39
4 and he that loseth his **life** for my sake shall find it..... 10:39
7 and ye shall find rest unto your **souls**................. 11:29
1 my beloved, in whom my **soul** is well pleased:......... 12:18
4 For whosoever will save his **life** shall lose it:.......... 16:25
4 will lose his **life** for my sake shall find it............. 16:25
4 gain the whole world, and lose his own **soul**?.......... 16:26
2 or what shall a man give in exchange for his **soul**?..... 16:26
4 and to give his **life** a ransom for many................ 20:28
3 and with all thy **soul**, and with all thy mind.......... 22:37
1 My **soul** is exceeding sorrowful, even unto death:...... 26:38
4 to save **life**, or to kill? But they held their peace.... Mark 3:4
4 For whosoever will save his **life** shall lose it;........... 8:35
4 but whosoever shall lose his **life** for my sake........... 8:35
4 shall gain the whole world, and lose his own **soul**?...... 8:36
2 Or what shall a man give in exchange for his **soul**?..... 8:37
4 to minister, and to give his **life** a ransom for many..... 10:45
2 with all thy **soul**, and with all thy mind,............... 12:30
2 and with all the **soul**, and with all the strength,........ 12:33
1 My **soul** is exceeding sorrowful unto death:............ 14:34
1 And Mary said, My **soul** doth magnify the Lord,.... Luke 1:46
4 a sword shall pierce through thy own **soul** also,......... 2:35
4 or to do evil? to save **life**, or to destroy it?............ 6:9
4 For whosoever will save his **life** shall lose it:........... 9:24
4 For whosoever will save his **life** shall lose it:........... 9:24
8 the Son of man is not come to destroy men's **lives**,..... 9:56
2 and with all thy **soul**, and with all thy strength,........ 10:27
3 And I will say to my **soul**, Soul, thou hast much....... 12:19
1 And I will say to my soul, **Soul**, thou hast much...... 12:19
4 fool, this night thy **soul** shall be required of thee:...... 12:20
3 no thought for your **life**, what ye shall eat;............ 12:22
1 The **life** is more than meat,.......................... 12:23
4 and his own **life** also, he cannot be my disciple........ 14:26
4 Whosoever shall seek to save his **life** shall lose it;..... 17:33
8 In your patience possess ye your **souls**.................. 21:19
4 the good shepherd giveth his **life** for the sheep..... John 10:11
4 and I lay down my **life** for the sheep................. 10:15
4 my Father love me, because I lay down my **life**,....... 10:17
4 How long dost thou make us to doubt? (NT).......... 10:24
4 He that loveth his **life** shall lose it;.................. 12:25
4 and he that hateth his **life** in this world.............. 12:25
1 Now is my **soul** troubled; and what shall I say?....... 12:27
4 I will lay down my **life** for thy sake................... 13:37
4 Wilt thou lay down thy **life** for my sake?.............. 13:38
4 that a man lay down his **life** for his friends............ 15:13
4 Because thou wilt not leave my **soul** in hell,......... Acts 2:27
1 that his **soul** was not left in hell,...................... 2:31
5 were added unto them about three thousand **souls**....... 2:41
3 And fear came upon every **soul**:...................... 2:43
1 And it shall come to pass, that every **soul**,............. 3:23
1 that believed were of one heart and of one **soul**:........ 4:32
7 all his kindred, threescore and fifteen **souls**............ 7:14
8 and made their **minds** evil affected.................... 14:2
8 Confirming the **souls** of the disciples,................. 14:22
8 troubled you with words, subverting your **souls**,........ 15:24
8 Men that have hazarded their **lives** for the name... Acts 15:26
1 Trouble not yourselves; for his **life** is in him.......... 20:10
4 neither count I my **life** dear unto myself,.............. 20:24
6 voyage will be with hurt ... but also of our **lives**........ 27:10
2 for there shall be no loss of any man's **life**............ 27:22
5 two hundred threescore and sixteen **souls**.............. 27:37
4 upon every **soul** of man that doeth evil,............ Rom 2:9
4 and I am left alone, and they seek my **life**............ 11:3
1 Let every **soul** be subject unto the higher powers....... 13:1
2 Who have for my **life** laid down their own necks:...... 16:4
4 The first man Adam was made a living **soul**;.......1 Co 15:45
4 Moreover I call God for a record upon my **soul**,.... 2 Co 1:23
6 very gladly spend and be spent for you; (NT)......... 12:15
2 doing the will of God from the **heart**;............... Eph 6:6
3 with one **mind** striving together for the faith........ Phlp 1:27
3 he was nigh unto death, not regarding his **life**,.......... 2:30
2 do it **heartily**, as to the Lord, and not unto men;.....Col 3:23
8 not the gospel of God only, but also our own **souls**, 1 Th 2:8
1 spirit and **soul** and body be preserved blameless........ 5:23
2 even to the dividing asunder of **soul** and spirit,...... Heb 4:12
2 Which hope we have as an anchor of the **soul**,......... 6:19
1 my **soul** shall have no pleasure in him................. 10:38
2 but of them that believe to the saving of the **soul**...... 10:39
7 lest ye be wearied and faint in your **minds**............. 12:3
6 submit yourselves: for they watch for your **souls**,...... 13:17
8 engrafted word, which is able to save your **souls**...... Jas 1:21
4 the error of his way shall save a **soul** from death,........ 5:20
6 even the salvation of your **souls**.....................1 Pt 1:9
8 ye have purified your **souls** in obeying the truth........ 1:22
2 from fleshly lusts, which war against the **soul**;.......... 2:11
6 unto the Shepherd and Bishop of your **souls**............ 2:25
5 few, that is, eight **souls** were saved by water............ 3:20
8 commit the keeping of their **souls** to him............... 4:19
4 in seeing and hearing, vexed his righteous **soul**...... 2 Pt 2:8
8 beguiling unstable **souls**:............................ 2:14
4 because he laid down his **life** for us:................1 Jn 3:16
8 we ought to lay down our **lives** for the brethren......... 3:16
1 and be in health, even as thy **soul** prospereth........3 Jn 1:2
4 and to convict all the ungodly (NASB) (NT)........Jude 1:15
8 **souls** of them that were slain for the word of God,...Rev 6:9
8 creatures which were in the sea, and had **life**, died;..... 8:9
4 and they loved not their **lives** unto the death.......... 12:11
1 and every living **soul** died in the sea.................. 16:3
8 horses, and chariots, and slaves, and **souls** of men...... 18:13
2 the fruits that thy **soul** lusted after are departed....... 18:14
8 and I saw the **souls** of them that were beheaded....... 20:4

Classical Greek

Originally *psuchē* denoted "breath" or "breath of life." From this impersonal understanding of *psuchē* as the basis of life in a human being, the range of definition expanded and *psuchē* later came to be regarded as the seat of the individual's conscience. As early as the Sixth Century B.C. *psuchē* was thought of as a distinct element of man's makeup, for which he was responsible (Dihle, "psuchē," *Kittel*, 9:611).

As a philosophical and anthropological term *psuchē* came to represent "life itself" and the "force" of life. It was believed that if the *psuchē* left the body (*sōma* [4835])—which it eventually does—life would cease, the body would die. However, *psuchē* also denoted the inner essence of a human being, the ego, the "self." Finally, *psuchē* indicated the "soul" as over against the body. Thus the soul was considered to be an independent entity that existed apart from the body.

Philosophical speculations about the nature, makeup, and function of the soul traveled in diverse directions; at the same time these speculations often overlapped. Certain philosophers held that the soul was the preexistent, immortal part of man as over against the mortal, temporal body. The attributes of the soul determined the character of the individual. Furthermore, the soul (*psuchē*) was considered to be the seat of understanding, will, feelings, and passions. Thus, the *psuchē* could be understood as an entity completely separate from the body, a conception entirely foreign to the Old Testament. This Greek idea can be seen, however, in certain apocryphal works, particularly 4 Maccabees. In 18:23 the writer spoke of the "immortal souls" of the youths who were martyred. He further discussed the differing effects of pleasure on the soul and body (1:25-27). Wisdom of Solomon expresses the contrast between body and soul found in some Greek philosophers. "A perishable body weighs down the soul" (9:15, RSV). Here the body is seen as a hindrance to the functions of the soul, an idea reminiscent of later gnosticism.

Septuagint Usage

More than 900 occurrences of *psuchē* are counted in the Septuagint (both apocryphal and canonical material). Ordinarily it replaces the Hebrew word *nephesh*, "breath, person, soul" (but cf. Genesis 36:6 where it is rendered by *sōma*, "body"). *Psuchē* also is the equivalent for a number of other Hebrew terms including *lēv*, "heart" (about 25 times); *chayyāh*, "a living being"; *'îsh*, "man"; and *rûach*, "spirit."

Old Testament Background and New Testament Usage

Psuchē can only be properly understood in the New Testament in light of the Old Testament; in general it does not derive its basis from the philosophical realm of Hellenism. By comparing the Old and New Testaments we can detect their harmonious view.

Generally both the Old and the New Testament understand *psuchē* to be the principle of physical life, the spirit of life in both humankind and animals. *Psuchē*, then, is the factor which gives life to the physical matter of creation. Thus the soul is distinct from the body (*beten*; Psalm 31:9) as well as the flesh (*bāsār*; Deuteronomy 12:23). However, the Old Testament rejects the view that the soul can be or becomes separated from the body. The Old Testament "can speak of a dead person as the soul of that person, and mean by this phrase the dead person in his corporeality" (Harder, "Soul," *Colin Brown*, 3:680). The original meaning of *nephesh*, "breath," appears in texts like Genesis 35:18.

On several occasions *nephesh* is synonymous with *chayyîm*, "life" (e.g., Genesis 19:17; Exodus 21:23; Deuteronomy 24:6; Joshua 9:24; 1 Samuel 19:5; 1 Kings 19:14). *Psuchē* denotes on several occasions "physical life" (e.g., Matthew 2:20; 20:28; John 10:11,15; 13:37,38; 15:13; Acts 15:26; Philippians 2:30; 1 Thessalonians 2:8).

Psuchē stands in Scripture as the denotation of the inward part of the human personality or for the various components of this. In any division of the body, soul, and spirit the soul remains a bridge between the other parts (see 1 Thessalonians 5:23; Hebrews 4:12). Here resides the inner consciousness of self. The body is instrumental in contact with earthly reality; the spirit is more concerned with the divine, supernatural realm.

As the seat of human conscience the *psuchē* is the organ of intellectual activity and mental processes (Deuteronomy 4:29; 26:16; and elsewhere). Furthermore, it is the site of emotions such as fear (Genesis 42:21; Romans 2:9), disgust (Numbers 21:5), wrath (Acts 15:24), sorrow (Matthew 26:38), uncertainty (John 10:24), faintheartedness (Hebrews 12:3), joy (John 20:20), love (Matthew 22:37), and other emotions. Finally, the *psuchē* is also the site of the third function of human personality—the will.

Basic inner drives, such as the fulfillment of desires or the satisfying of physical needs, have their source in the *psuchē* of man (Luke 12:19; Revelation 18:14). These drives also include instincts and desires important for the preservation of life itself (Numbers 11:6; Jeremiah 31:25; Psalms 42:2,3; 107:9).

According to some, the Scriptures portray the individual as primarily a bipartite or two-part creation—one part "soul," the other "body" (e.g., Psalm 31:9; Matthew 10:28). The soul is viewed as including also the spirit of man, and moreover, the soul denotes the conscience of man, the individual in relation to God. At death this soul is separated from the physical body. This intermediate state, which occurs prior to the resurrection of the body (Luke 16:23f.; Revelation 6:9f.; 20:4), is not, however, a period of sleep or unconsciousness. The expressions "sleepeth" (John 11:11; Acts 13:36) and "slept" (Matthew 27:52) refer only to the body. Only the physical part of the body remains in the grave, not its soul which continues to exist (Luke 23:43;

2 Corinthians 5:8; Philippians 1:23) until it is reunited with the physical (now spiritual) body at the resurrection.

Other theologians, however, believe that man is a three-part (tripartite) being, that he consists of body, soul, and spirit. Soul and spirit are separate and distinct parts of the total man. This view is based primarily on 1 Thessalonians 5:23 in which Paul said, "May your whole spirit, soul and body be kept blameless at the coming of our Lord Jesus Christ" (NIV).

In contrast to the bipartite or the tripartite views just described, the best option may be what is called a holistic view of man. The idea of soul in this regard also includes the entire human personality. Man does not simply *have* a *psuchē*; he *is* a *psuchē*. Especially in the Old Testament, the physical and the nonphysical parts of the person are viewed as a unity—a soul or a body. Numerous times no distinction between them can be discerned. The creation account records that the man whom God formed from the dust of the earth, into whom He breathed the "breath of life," is called a "living soul" (Genesis 2:7). For the same reasons Scripture on occasion calls the blood the *nephesh* (Deuteronomy 12:23). This is not to say that the blood *contains* the *nephesh* (Leviticus 17:11); rather, it shows that ancient man observed that life ended when the blood left the body. This sheds some light on why the eating of blood (Genesis 9:4) was prohibited.

In the holistic view, man is viewed as a unit with no struggle between his material and immaterial parts. Erickson thus described man as a "conditional unity," the "spiritual and the physical elements are not always distinguishable . . . . The compound is dissoluable, however; the dissolution takes place at death" (*Christian Theology*, p.537). Thus, in this view a man's "spiritual condition cannot be dealt with independently of his physical and psychological condition, and vice versa" (ibid., p.539). Diet is important, as well as mental health. This view also explains why physical health affects mental health and why organic brain disorders or chemical imbalances affect an individual's behavior. Erickson argued that ministry to the individual must involve all aspects of the man (ibid.).

The terms *nephesh* and *psuchē* often denote the whole person (Genesis 46:15,18,22,25-27; Exodus 1:5; Acts 2:43; 3:23). Sometimes *nephesh* appears in place of a personal pronoun; thus in Genesis 17:14 we read: "that soul shall be cut off from his people." Individuals take oaths in their "soul(s)" (Leviticus 5:4). The *psuchē* sins, not only in thought but also in action (Leviticus 4:2,27; Numbers 15:27; Ezekiel 18:4,20). The *psuchē* presents the sacrificial offering (Leviticus 2:1), but it can also violate the Lord's commands (Leviticus 5:15); the *psuchē* (i.e., "person," NIV) who, for example, eats blood or an animal which died an unnatural death, must be cut off from the people (Leviticus 7:27; 17:15).

Thus, the *psuchē* often stands for the entire person. It should be noted that in this sense Scripture places a supreme value upon the *psuchē* of the individual (Matthew 16:26). Christ is the shepherd and overseer of our souls (1 Peter 2:25). His servants are ready to be sacrificed for the believing souls (2 Corinthians 12:15). The leaders and teachers of the Christian church, as Christ's servants, watch over the souls of those in their charge for whom they must give an account (Hebrews 13:17). The goal of every believer is salvation of the soul (1 Peter 1:8,9). Through obeying the truth the *psuchē* is purified (1 Peter 1:22); through the word "planted" (NIV) in believers their souls are saved (James 1:21). Naturally this takes place on the level of faith (Hebrews 10:39). The enemy of the *psuchē* is the sinful nature (1 Peter 2:11). Confronted by the purifying fires of suffering and hardship, the believer commits the preservation of his soul to the faithful Creator (1 Peter 4:19). The Christian hope, made possible through the glorified Christ and His intercession on our behalf, is a firm anchor for the soul (Hebrews 6:18-20).

Just as the *psuchē* can denote the entire human personality, it can also represent God himself. The *psuchē* of the Lord is delighted by the Messiah, the Servant of the Lord (Isaiah 42:1; Matthew 12:18). On the other hand, His *psuchē* has no pleasure in the one who refuses Christ and His salvation (Hebrews 10:38). His *psuchē* abhors idolaters (Leviticus 26:30), and He will be avenged on those who worship idols and commit adultery (Jeremiah 5:7-10,29). God's *psuchē* reacts against any falseness or deceit (Jeremiah 9:8,9) and hates any attempt to worship Him with an evil heart (Isaiah 1:12-16). Because there is nothing higher than to swear oaths by His name, God swears "by himself" (Jeremiah 51:14; Amos 6:8).

The *psuchē* of the Suffering Servant of the Lord endured much pain during His work of atonement (Isaiah 53:11). As fully human (as well as fully divine) Christ experienced in His soul the same anguish, joy, grief, etc. as any human being. He could experience sorrow (Matthew 26:38: "my soul is exceeding sorrowful") or be troubled (John 12:27: "now is my soul troubled"). His soul could be offended (John 11:38), anxious (Matthew 26:38), tempted (Matthew 4:1f.), and angered (Mark 3:5). As every other man, His soul could mourn (Mark 3:5) and weep (John 11:35; Hebrews 5:7), but most of all it could love (John 15:9).

Finally, the statement that humanity is created in the image of God first and foremost concerns the nonphysical attributes of man, those characteristics of a man's soul which correspond to the qualities of God and which make it possible for him to have communion with God.

Strong 5590, Bauer 893-94, Moulton-Milligan 698-99, Kittel 9:608-60, Liddell-Scott 2026-27, Colin Brown 3:676-77,679-88.

5426. ψυχικός psuchikos adj

Pertaining to natural life, natural, unspiritual, physical.

Cross-Reference:
ψυχή psuchē (5425)

1. ψυχικός psuchikos nom sing masc
2. ψυχικοί psuchikoi nom pl masc
3. ψυχική psuchikē nom sing fem
4. ψυχικόν psuchikon nom/acc sing neu

1 But the **natural** man receiveth not ... of the Spirit ... 1 Co 2:14
4 It is sown a **natural** body; ... 15:44
4 There is a **natural** body, and there is a spiritual ... 15:44
4 first which is spiritual, but that which is **natural**; ... 15:46
3 not from above, but is earthly, **sensual**, devilish ... Jas 3:15
2 separate themselves, **sensual**, having not the Spirit ... Jude 1:19

Classical Greek

This adjective is formed from the noun *psuchē* (5425), "soul, life," and means "of the soul." It can stand in contrast to *sōmatikos* (4836), "of the body," and in classical Greek can thus imply something "spiritual" (*Liddell-Scott*). *Moulton-Milligan* suggests that in some cases *psuchikos* means "natural" as over against *pneumatikos* (4012), "spiritual." It can also have the sense "manly, brave" (Dihle, "psuchē," *Kittel*, 9:661).

Septuagint Usage

Psuchikos occurs only once in the Septuagint, in the apocryphal book of 4 Maccabees (1:32). In secular Greek *psuchikos* had a positive reference, denoting the "higher nature" in contrast to that which is "lower" or bodily. It could refer to the "noblest part of man" (Turner, *Christian Words*, p.409). Under the influence of Judaism, however, *psuchikos* took on a negative sense. It came to denote that which is earthly, natural, and human. In Philo the soul became an "earthly component of man" (Schweizer, "psuchē," *Kittel*, 9:661). That which is *psuchikos* is earthly, derived from a natural man.

New Testament Usage

Six instances of *psuchikos* are attested in the New Testament, four of which are attributed to Paul, one to James (3:15), and one to Jude (19). In every case *psuchikos* is used negatively. It is especially seen in conflict with the Spirit and might be best rendered "natural." The "natural" person lacks the Spirit of God and is controlled instead by his/her desire to please self (Jude 19, cf. verse 18). The NIV translates *psuchikos* "unspiritual" in James 3:15. It is correctly contrasting wisdom that comes from heaven—and thus pure, not self-centered—with earthly wisdom which is *psuchikos*, "typical of the natural man."

Paul's usage sheds even more light on our understanding of *psuchikos*. He expressly says that "the *psuchikos* man receiveth not the things of the Spirit of God" (1 Corinthians 2:14). Like James and Jude, then, Paul viewed the natural man as one ruled by his/her own desires. So the spiritual man is the one who, having the Spirit (Jude 19), is taught by the Spirit, understands the Spirit, and lives his life in accordance with the guidance of the Spirit (1 Corinthians 2:10-16). The person without the Spirit cannot even understand the things of the Spirit.

In 1 Corinthians 15 Paul again contrasted the spiritual with the natural. This time, however, he concerned himself with explaining that the body believers will receive at the resurrection is not even of the same order as the natural bodies they now experience. Again the contrast develops between the earthly and the heavenly. The spiritual body (*sōma pneumatikon*) is of a completely different order from the present natural body.

Strong 5591, Bauer 894, Moulton-Milligan 699, Kittel 9:661-63, Liddell-Scott 2027-28, Colin Brown 3:676,684,686-87.

5427. ψῦχος psuchos noun

Cold.

קֹר qōr (7409), Cold (Gn 8:22).
קָרָה qārâh (7424), Cold (Job 37:9, Ps 147:17 [147:6]).

1. ψῦχος psuchos nom/acc sing neu
2. ψύχει psuchei dat sing neu

1 who had made a fire of coals; for it was cold:..... John 18:18
1 the present rain, and because of the cold........... Acts 28:2
2 in fastings often, in cold and nakedness............ 2 Co 11:27

A term that appears in classical literature as early as the Eighth Century B.C., *psuchos* means "cold." It can also denote frost or cold weather in general (*Liddell-Scott*). It occurs only three times in the New Testament (John 18:18; Acts 28:2; 2 Corinthians 11:27), and in each instance it is used as a descriptive term for the weather.

STRONG 5592, BAUER 894, MOULTON-MILLIGAN 699, LIDDELL-SCOTT 2028, COLIN BROWN 1:317-19.

5428. ψυχρός psuchros adj

Cold.

קַר qar (7408), Cold (Prv 25:25).

1. ψυχρός psuchros nom sing masc
2. ψυχροῦ psuchrou gen sing neu

2 a cup of cold water only in the name of a disciple, Matt 10:42
1 know thy works, that thou art neither cold nor hot:.. Rev 3:15
1 I would thou wert cold or hot......................... 3:15
1 thou art lukewarm, and neither cold nor hot,........... 3:16

Classical Greek

In classical Greek *psuchros*, like its related term *psuchos* (5427), functions as an adjective and describes any number of things as "cold" (e.g., water, air, dead things, meat, etc.; *Liddell-Scott*). *Psuchros*, however, is used much more extensively in a metaphoric or figurative way. As such it can describe things as ineffectual or vain, feelings as cold, people as heartless or vain, jokes and literature as flat or insipid (ibid.).

New Testament Usage

In the New Testament *psuchros* also demonstrates both the literal and figurative uses. In Matthew 10:42 *psuchros* is used as a substantive for "cold water." A variant text of Matthew 10:42 (codex D) includes *hudatos* ("water") making *psuchros* an adjective in this case. Jesus told His disciples that doing acts of benevolence for those in need is equivalent to doing them for Christ himself.

The other instances of *psuchros* are in Revelation 3:15,16. Here the word functions figuratively in a judgment against the church of Laodicea and the uselessness of their works.

STRONG 5593, BAUER 894, MOULTON-MILLIGAN 699, KITTEL 2:876-77, LIDDELL-SCOTT 2028, COLIN BROWN 1:317-19.

5429. ψύχω psuchō verb

Grow cold, become cold.

CROSS-REFERENCE:
ψυχή psuchē (5425)

קוּר qûr (7262), Qal: dig (2 Kgs 19:24).

קָרַר qārar (7467), Be cold; hiphil: keep fresh (Jer 6:7).

שָׁטַח shāṭach (8275), Spread out (Jer 8:2).

1. ψυγήσεται psugēsetai 3sing indic fut pass

1 the love of many shall wax cold.................... Matt 24:12

This verb form related to *psuchos* (5427) and *psuchros* (5428) appears frequently in classical literature. Its range of meanings includes: "to make cold, grow cold, to put out a fire, cool, refresh, to chill, to be frigid, to dry, make dry" (*Liddell-Scott*). In the New Testament it appears only in Matthew 24:12. Jesus warned that in the final days before His return, tribulation, false prophets, and the prevalence of wickedness would cause some believers to fall away from the Faith. Their love of God would "grow cold" (NIV).

STRONG 5594, BAUER 894, MOULTON-MILLIGAN 699, LIDDELL-SCOTT 2028-29, COLIN BROWN 1:317-18.

5430. ψωμίζω psōmizō verb

Feed someone, give away.

SYNONYMS:
βόσκω boskō (999)
ἐκτρέφω ektrephō (1611)
τρέφω trephō (4982)
χορτάζω chortazō (5361)

אָכַל 'ākhal (404), Qal: eat (Dt 32:13); hiphil: give something to eat, feed (Nm 11:4, 81:16 [80:16], Ez 3:2).

אֲכַל 'ăkhal (A405), Eat (Dn 4:33 [4:30]—Aramaic).

בָּרָה bārāh (1290), Eat; hiphil: give food to eat (2 Sm 13:5).

טְעֵם ṭ[e']ēm (A3050), Pael: be given something to eat (Dn 4:32 [4:29]—Aramaic).

1. ψώμιζε psōmize 2sing impr pres act
2. ψωμίσω psōmisō 1sing subj aor act

1 Therefore if thine enemy hunger, feed him;........ Rom 12:20
2 And though I bestow all my goods to feed the poor, 1 Co 13:3

Classical Greek

In classical Greek the word *psōmizō* means "feed, nourish." It can also mean to "hand-feed" or to "bait a trap" (*Liddell-Scott*). There are two main uses of *psōmizō*. With an accusative of a person it means to "feed someone"; with an accusative of a thing it means "to give away all one's property, dole out, divide in pieces" (*Bauer*).

Septuagint Usage

Psōmizō occurs 20 times in the Septuagint, mostly for the hiphil (causative) form of *'ākhal* which means literally "cause to eat," or "to feed."

Deuteronomy 8:3,16 notes that God fed the Israelites manna while they were in the wilderness. Psalm 81:16 (LXX 80:16) states that God is the supplier of the harvest. There are instances when *psōmizō* does not mean the blessings of God but simply one person feeding another (2 Samuel 13:5 [LXX 2 Kings 13:5]). In Isaiah 58:14 "feed" is figurative for "bless with." Here God says, "I will . . . *feed* thee with the heritage of Jacob thy father."

New Testament Usage

There are only two instances of this word in the New Testament. In a list of instructions about treatment of one's enemy, Paul stated, "If thine enemy hunger, *feed* him" (Romans 12:20). The overall conclusion of Romans 12:17-20 is recorded in verse 21: "Be not overcome of evil, but overcome evil with good."

After discussing the gifts of the Holy Spirit in 1 Corinthians 12, in chapter 13 Paul emphasizes the importance of love. First Corinthians 13:3 states that although one might dole out all his wealth to feed the poor, if he does not have love it would account for nothing, because it would be for the wrong motive.

Strong 5595, Bauer 894, Moulton-Milligan 699, Liddell-Scott 2029.

5431. ψωμίον psōmion noun

A small piece of bread.

1. ψωμίον psōmion nom/acc sing neu

1 He it is, to whom I shall give a **sop**, ... John 13:26
1 when he had dipped the **sop**, he gave it to Judas 13:26
1 And after the **sop** Satan entered into him. 13:27
1 having received the **sop** went immediately out: 13:30

Psōmion, a diminutive, rarely appears in Greek literature before the Christian Era but occurs quite frequently in documents after the First Century A.D. It is used as a general term for small pieces or morsels of food such as might be fed to animals. It is also used as a substantive for various delicacies and for ordinary bread (*Moulton-Milligan*). In the New Testament it is only used in John 13:26,27,30. Here dipping and giving the small piece of bread to Judas was the sign Jesus used to identify the betrayer.

5432. ψώχω psōchō verb

Rub.

1. ψώχοντες psōchontes nom pl masc part pres act

1 corn, and did eat, **rubbing** them in their hands. ..... Luke 6:1

A very rare verb, possibly a medical term originally, *psōchō* means "to rub" or "to rub to pieces" (Marshall, *New International Greek Testament Commentary*, *Luke*, p.231). The word does not appear in Greek literature before the Christian Era. In the New Testament it occurs only in Luke 6:1. There the term indicates that the disciples were rubbing the heads of wheat with their hands.

Strong 5597, Bauer 894, Moulton-Milligan 700, Liddell-Scott 2029.

5433. ω ō noun
Last letter of the Greek alphabet, omega.

1. ω ō neu
2. ὦ ō neu

2 O faithless and perverse generation, ... Luke 9:41
1 Alpha and Omega, the beginning and the ending, ... Rev 1:8
1 I am Alpha and Omega, the first and the last: 1:11
1 Alpha and Omega, the beginning and the end. 21:6
1 I am Alpha and Omega, ... 22:13

Omega, or *ō*, is the 24th and final letter of the Ionic Greek alphabet. As such, it could represent the "end" or the "last" of something. It could also stand for a number. Depending upon how it was marked *omega* could have numerical value of either 800 or 800,000 (*Liddell-Scott*). The letter is not used symbolically in the Septuagint, although it is in the New Testament.

Except for some minor changes *ō* occurs four times in the New Testament in the formulaic phrase, "I am Alpha and *Omega*" (Revelation 1:8,11; 21:6; 22:13). In every case the idea is symbolic. The Lord God alone is the "Alpha and *Omega*, the beginning and the end, the first and the last." God's majesty, glory, power, and authority are unsurpassed. He is the ultimate Lord of all; He is the great "I AM" (Exodus 3:14; cf. Revelation 1:8).

STRONG 5598, BAUER 895, MOULTON-MILLIGAN 701, KITTEL 1:1-3, LIDDELL-SCOTT 2029.

5434. ὦ ō intrj
"O!".

1. ὦ ō

1 O woman, great is thy faith: .... Matt 15:28
1 O faithless and perverse generation, ... 17:17
1 O faithless generation, how long shall I be .... Mark 9:19
1 O fools, and slow of heart to believe .... Luke 24:25
1 The former treatise have I made, O Theophilus, ... Acts 1:1
1 And said, O full of all subtlety and all mischief, ... 13:10
1 O ye Jews, reason would that I should bear 18:14
1 Sirs, ye should have hearkened unto me, (NT) 27:21
1 Therefore thou art inexcusable, O man, ... Rom 2:1
1 And thinkest thou this, O man, ... Rom 2:3
1 O man, who art thou that repliest against God? 9:20
1 O the depth of the riches both of the wisdom 11:33
1 O foolish Galatians, who hath bewitched you, ... Gal 3:1
1 But thou, O man of God, flee these things; .... 1 Tm 6:11
1 O Timothy, keep that which is committed 6:20
1 But wilt thou know, O vain man, ... Jas 2:20

The last letter of the Greek alphabet, *ō*, is used as an interjection: O! With this sense it may be used with either the circumflex or the acute accent marks. It is used as an interjection in 16 verses in the New Testament (for example, Matthew 15:28; Romans 11:33; James 2:20).

The letter *ō* can introduce a vocative as in Acts 18:14: "If it were a matter of wrong or wicked lewdness, O ye Jews . . . . " It can also indicate surprise: "Jesus answered and said unto her, *O* woman, great is thy faith" (Matthew 15:28). It also appears in expressions of reproof: "But wilt thou know, *O* vain man, that faith without works is dead?" (James 2:20).

STRONG 5599, BAUER 895, MOULTON-MILLIGAN 701, KITTEL 1:1-3, LIDDELL-SCOTT 2029.

5435. Ὠβήδ Obēd name
Obed.

1. Ὠβήδ Obēd masc

1 and Booz begat Obed of Ruth; .... Matt 1:5
1 and Obed begat Jesse; 1:5
1 which was the son of Obed, ... Luke 3:32

The son of Boaz and Ruth and the grandfather of David. He is listed in the genealogy of Jesus (Matthew 1:5; Luke 3:32).

5436. ὧδε hōde adv
Here.

1. ὧδε hōde

1 art thou come hither to torment us before the time? Matt 8:29
1 That in this place is one greater than the temple. 12:6
1 and, behold, a greater than Jonas is here. 12:41

1 and, behold, a greater than Solomon is here........Matt 12:42
1 Give me here John Baptist's head in a charger......... 14:8
1 We have here but five loaves, and two fishes.......... 14:17
1 He said, Bring them hither to me..................... 14:18
1 some standing here, which shall not taste of death,.... 16:28
1 Lord, it is good for us to be here:.................... 17:4
1 if thou wilt, let us make here three tabernacles;....... 17:4
1 Jesus answered ... bring him hither to me............. 17:17
1 Why stand ye here all the day idle?.................. 20:6
1 Friend, how camest thou in hither.................... 22:12
1 shall not be left here one stone upon another,......... 24:2
1 if any man shall say unto you, Lo, here is Christ,...... 24:23
1 Lo, here is Christ, or there; believe it not............ 24:23
1 tarry ye here, and watch with me..................... 26:38
1 He is not here: for he is risen, as he said............. 28:6
1 and are not his sisters here with us?...............Mark 6:3
1 satisfy these ... with bread here in the wilderness?...... 8:4
1 That there be some of them that stand here,........... 9:1
1 Master, it is good for us to be here:................... 9:5
1 and straightway he will send him hither.............. 11:3
1 if any man shall say to you, Lo, here is Christ;........ 13:21
1 Gethsemane: ... Sit ye here, while I shall pray......... 14:32
1 sorrowful unto death: tarry ye here, and watch......... 14:34
1 which was crucified: he is risen; he is not here:........ 16:6
1 done in Capernaum, do also here in thy country.....Luke 4:23
1 and get victuals: for we are here in a desert place....... 9:12
1 I tell you of a truth, there be some standing here,...... 9:27
1 Master, it is good for us to be here:................... 9:33
1 Jesus answering said, ... Bring thy son hither............ 9:41
1 and, behold, a greater than Solomon is here........... 11:31
1 and, behold, a greater than Jonas is here.............. 11:32
1 and bring in hither the poor, and the maimed,......... 14:21
1 but I am dying here with hunger! (NASB)............ 15:17
1 but now he is being comforted here, (NASB).......... 16:25
1 Neither shall they say, Lo here! or, lo there!.......... 17:21
1 See here; or, see there: go not after them,............ 17:23
1 bring hither, and slay them before me................. 19:27
1 And they said, Lord, behold, here are two swords...... 22:38
1 beginning from Galilee to this place.................. 23:5
1 He is not here, but is risen:......................... 24:6
1 There is a lad here, which hath five barley loaves,...John 6:9
1 said unto him, Rabbi, when camest thou hither?........ 6:25
1 if thou hadst been here, my brother had not died...... 11:21
1 if thou hadst been here, my brother had not died...... 11:32
1 Then saith he to Thomas, Reach hither thy finger,...... 20:27
1 And here he hath authority from the chief priests....Acts 9:14
1 and came hither for that intent,........................ 9:21
1 In this case, moreover, it is (NASB)...............1 Co 4:2
1 known unto you all things which are done here.......Col 4:9
1 And here men that die receive tithes;...............Heb 7:8
1 For here have we no continuing city,.................. 13:14
1 Sit thou here in a good place; and say to the poor,...Jas 2:3
1 Stand thou there, or sit here under my footstool:....... 2:3
1 Come up hither, and I will show thee things.........Rev 4:1
1 great voice from heaven saying ... Come up hither..... 11:12
1 Here is the patience and the faith of the saints......... 13:10
1 Here is wisdom. Let him that hath understanding...... 13:18
1 Here is the patience of the saints:.................... 14:12
1 here are they that keep the commandments of God,... 14:12
1 And here is the mind which hath wisdom.............. 17:9

Classical Greek

This demonstrative adverb, related to the demonstrative pronoun *hode* (3455), was used since Homer (Eighth Century B.C.) as an adverb of manner and of place. As an adverb of manner it basically means "in this manner, thus" and "so exceedingly." As an adverb of place it means "hither" or "here."

Septuagint Usage

In the Septuagint *hōde* appears to be used only as an adverb of place. Thus, the Hebrew *kôh* is translated exclusively with *hōde* when it is an adverb of place. Exodus 2:12 notes that Moses looked "*here* and there" (KJV: "*this way* and that way"). In Isaiah 22:16 Isaiah asks, "What hast thou *here*?"

New Testament Usage

In the New Testament it is used only as a demonstrative adverb of place. First, it is used in conjunction with a verb of motion to indicate which place an action occurred, as in Matthew 8:29: " 'What do you want with us, Son of God?' they shouted. 'Have you come *here* to torture us before the appointed time?' " (NIV). Secondly, it is used to indicate the location of someone's or something's existence, as in Matthew 12:6: "But I say to you, that something greater than the temple is *here*" (NASB). Finally, it is used in a sense similar to that just mentioned in Matthew 12:6 but with reference to something intangible, as in Revelation 14:12: "*Here* is the perseverance of the saints who keep the commandments of God and their faith in Jesus" (NASB).

Strong 5602, Bauer 895, Moulton-Milligan 701, Liddell-Scott 2030.

5437. ᾠδή ōdē noun

Song.

Cross-Reference:
ᾄδω adō (102)

הִגָּיוֹן higgāyôn (1970), Higgaion (Ps 9:16); lute (Ps 92:3 [91:3]).

מִזְמוֹר mizmôr (4344), Psalm (Ps 39:title [38:title]).

מַשָּׂא massā' (5015), Singing (1 Chr 15:22,27).

נְגִינָה n^eghînāh (5234), Stringed instruments (Hb 3:19).

שִׁגָּיוֹן shiggāyôn (8150), Shigionoth (Hb 3:1).

שִׁיר shîr (8302), Music, song (2 Chr 7:6, Ps 137:3f. [136:3f.], Am 5:23).

שִׁירָה shîrāh (8303), Song (Ex 15:1, Dt 31:19, 2 Sm 22:1).

1. ᾠδήν ōdēn acc sing fem
2. ᾠδαῖς ōdais dat pl fem

2 in psalms and hymns and spiritual songs,............Eph 5:19
2 in psalms and hymns and spiritual songs,............Col 3:16
1 And they sung a new song, saying,..................Rev 5:9
1 they sung as it were a new song before the throne,.... 14:3
1 and no man could learn that song but................ 14:3
1 And they sing the song of Moses the servant of God,.. 15:3
1 the song of Moses ... and the song of the Lamb,....... 15:3

Classical Greek

In classical Greek the verb *adō* (102) means "to sing" or "to make sounds" such as an animal or some musical instrument might make (e.g., a "flute, lyre," etc.). In a cultic context *adō* denotes worship. The noun *ōdē* signifies "poetry, song, (and) songs of praise." It can also stand for "songs of mourning" as well as "songs of joy" (*Liddell-Scott*). The word does not have an "intrinsically religious significance in non-Biblical Greek" (Bartels, "Song," *Colin Brown*, 3:672).

Septuagint Usage

The verb appears nearly 80 times in the Septuagint, while the noun occurs about 90 times; both replace a series of Hebrew terms with a broad range of definition. *ōdē* has much the same meaning as it had in classical Greek. "Joyful singing" is one sense, as in 2 Samuel 6:5 (LXX 2 Kings 6:5) in which David sings joyfully before the ark. It can also indicate a song of mourning (Amos 8:10). It almost always indicates a religious song and consequently is freely interchangeable with *humnos* (5054) and *psalmos* (5403) (Schlier, "adō," *Kittel*, 1:164). Singing was an integral part of Israel's social and religious life. It was often the accompaniment for instrumental music and dancing (2 Samuel 6:5; 1 Chronicles 16:42). The Old Testament contains numerous examples of social songs (Genesis 31:27; cf. Luke 15:25), royal songs (2 Samuel 19:35; Ecclesiastes 2:8), songs of celebration (Isaiah 5:12), or songs of mourning (2 Samuel 1:17f.; 2 Chronicles 35:25). Trumpets sounded the battle cry and summon Israel to war (Joshua 6:8,9), and songs proclaimed the victory following the battle (Judges 11:34; 1 Samuel 18:6,7). Hymns were sung in response to God's deeds (Exodus 15:20,21; Numbers 21:16-18). Songs were a regular feature of the temple (1 Chronicles 25:1-7) as well as other cultic events (2 Kings 3:15).

New Testament Usage

The verb *adō* appears five times in the New Testament; the noun *ōdē*, seven. The words are always associated with God or Christ. Ephesians 5:19 contains every major word for *song*: *psalmos*, "psalm"; *humnos*, "hymn"; and *ōdē*, "song." The Greek word *ōdē* is further qualified by the adjective *pneumatikos* (4012), "spiritual," that is, "actuated by the Holy Spirit." Thus songs and singing are valid means of worshiping God. Singing was an essential ingredient in the worship of the Early Church along with preaching and the breaking of bread. Hymns vividly expressed Christian joy (James 5:13).

The Book of Revelation has much to say about the song of the eternal, heavenly world. The 24 elders sing a new song, a song about the redeeming blood of the Lamb (Revelation 5:9). This new song is a direct response of praise to the Creator who is worthy to receive praise, honor, and glory (Revelation 4:11; cf. 14:3).

Revelation 15:3 speaks of a multitude which sings "the *song* of Moses the servant of God, and the *song* of the Lamb." The "song of Moses" praises God's redeeming power; the "song of the Lamb" praises Him for the atoning sacrifice of Christ. All of these songs—both the old of Moses and the new of the Lamb—unite in one heavenly symphony to praise and honor God.

Strong 5603, Bauer 895, Moulton-Milligan 701, Kittel 1:164-65, Liddell-Scott 2030, Colin Brown 2:874; 3:672-75.

5438. ὠδίν ōdin noun

Birth pains.

Cross-Reference:
ὠδίνω ōdinō (5439)

חֶבֶל chevel (2346), Snare, cord (2 Sm 22:6, Ps 18:4 [17:4]).

חֲבָל chevel (2347), Destruction (Job 21:17).

חִיל chîl (2523), Polel: calve (Job 39:1).

חִיל chîl (2527), Anguish, pain (Ex 15:14, Jer 6:24, Mic 4:9).

חַלְחָלָה chalchālāh (2580), Anguish (Na 2:10).

יָלַד yāladh (3314), Give birth (Job 39:2).

מַשְׁבֵּר mashbēr (5052), The point of birth (2 Kgs 19:3, Is 37:3).

צִיר tsîr (7006), Pains, pangs (1 Sm 4:19, Is 21:3).

1. **ὠδίν** **ōdin** nom sing fem
2. **ὠδίνων** **ōdinōn** gen pl fem
3. **ὠδῖνας** **ōdinas** acc pl fem

2 All these are the beginning of sorrows............ Matt 24:8
2 these are the beginnings of sorrows.............. Mark 13:8
3 having loosed the **pains** of death:.................. Acts 2:24
1 as travail upon a woman with child;................ 1 Th 5:3

Classical Greek

Literally *ōdin* (earlier form *ōdis*) denotes "birth pains." It can also refer to the result of such pains—"children." Figuratively this extends to any tremendous and inevitable pain, either physical, emotional, spiritual, or otherwise. Or, like the literal use, it can refer to the outcome of such travail, anguish (*Liddell-Scott*). (Cf. the verb *ōdinō* [5439].)

Septuagint Usage

ōdin appears about 30 times in canonical material of the Septuagint; of these there are as many as 6 different Hebrew constructions behind it. The predominant terms replaced, however, are *chēvel/chevel* and *hîl* (in various forms). Moses and the Israelites sing of the Philistines' "anguish"

(NIV; i.e., "terror, dread") when they heard of the Lord's power to deliver His people (Exodus 15:14).

In another figurative use *ōdin* may speak of "cords," as in the phrase "cords of death" (see the NIV's translation of 2 Samuel 22:6 [LXX 2 Kings 22:6] = Psalm 18:5 [17:5]; and Psalm 116:3 [114:3]). However, the Septuagint's reading *ōdin* here may have been due to the confusion of two Hebrew words: *chēvel*, "birth pain," and *chevel*, "cord" (*Liddell-Scott*). Moreover, there is very little evidence elsewhere to support a reading of "cord" (see the data in Bertram, "ōdin," *Kittel*, 9:670; *Bauer*).

New Testament Usage

Four instances of *ōdin* appear in the New Testament; of these, two occur in parallel Synoptic texts (Matthew 24:8; Mark 13:8), one occurs in Acts (2:24), and one appears in Paul's first letter to Thessalonica (5:3) (cf. the verb, three times).

Luke recorded that God freed Jesus (the "firstborn from the dead," Colossians 1:18) from the anguish of death by raising Him from the dead (Acts 2:24). The association of *ōdin* with the pangs of death is attested elsewhere (2 Samuel 22:6; Psalms 18:4; 116:3; Hosea 13:13).

Paul used the image of a woman in labor pains (*ōdin*) to depict the coming of the Lord. He clearly saw this kind of coming as destructive, terrible, and certain, another common Old Testament image (e.g., Psalm 48:6; Isaiah 21:3; Jeremiah 6:24).

The usage in the Gospels of Matthew and Mark should be understood in light of Jewish thought of the day. Rabbinic Judaism, based on Old Testament prophecies, saw birth pangs as accompanying the onset of the Messianic Age. Such "messianic woes" included affliction, cosmic omens, war, etc. (see Bertram, "ōdin," *Kittel*, 9:671f.; *Bauer*). Jesus warned that wars, earthquakes, famines, and so on, are merely the beginning of labor pangs. In other words these signal the onset of last days events. With this in mind it might be in order to see in Revelation 12:2 (the verb *ōdinō*) some messianic overtones (cf. verse 10). The kingdom of God must be brought in through judgment.

Strong 5604, Bauer 895, Moulton-Milligan 701, Kittel 9:667-74, Liddell-Scott 2030, Colin Brown 3:857-59.

5439. ὠδίνω ōdinō verb

Suffer birth pangs.

Cognate:
ὠδίν ōdin (5438)

Synonyms:
αἰών aiōn (163)
καιρός kairos (2511)
χρόνος chronos (5385)

הָרָה hārâh (2106), Pregnant woman (Is 26:17).

חָבַל chāval (2341), Pledge; piel: be in labor (S/S 8:5).

חִיל chîl (2523), Qal: writhe, be in labor (Is 26:18, Jer 4:31, Hb 3:10); polel: give birth (Is 51:2); hophal: be born (Is 66:8).

צָרַר tsārar (7173), Be narrow, tie up; hiphil: be in labor (Jer 49:22 [29:22]).

1. ὠδίνω ōdinō 1sing indic pres act

2. ὠδίνουσα ōdinousa nom sing fem part pres act

1 I travail in birth again until Christ be formed........ Gal 4:19
2 break forth and cry, thou that travailest not:............ 4:27
2 And she being with child cried, travailing in birth,.. Rev 12:2

Classical Greek

At first this ancient word most likely meant to suffer birth pangs during labor. In secular Greek literature it is used in this sense; however, in a broader, almost metaphoric sense it expresses the emergence of pain, travail, and sorrow from any cause (Bertram, "ōdin," Kittel, 9:667).

Septuagint Usage

In the Septuagint *ōdinō* predominately translates *chîl*, "to writhe, be in labor," or "give birth." It is generally used in reference to the act of giving birth, often with emphasis on the pain and anguish involved. For instance, Isaiah 66:7 says, "Before she *goes into labor*, she gives birth; before the pains (*ōdin*) come upon her, she delivers a son" (NIV). The woman avoids the anguish of childbirth expressed by *ōdinō*. Elsewhere *ōdinō* can refer merely the process of childbirth without the emphasis on pain: "Thy mother brought thee forth" (Song of Solomon 8:5).

New Testament Usage

In the New Testament the verb occurs only three times (Galatians 4:19,27; Revelation 12:2), although its related noun appears in four other passages. In Galatians 4:19 Paul described his anguish and concern for the believers as "suffering birth pangs." The pregnant woman in Revelation 12:2 suffers birth pangs.

Strong 5605, Bauer 895, Moulton-Milligan 701, Kittel 9:667-74, Liddell-Scott 2030, Colin Brown 3:857-58.

5440. ὦμος ōmos noun

Shoulder, arm.

כָּתֵף kāthēph (3931II) Shoulder (Ex 28:12, Ez 12:6; support (1 Kgs 7:34).

צַד tsadh (6917), Arm (Is 60:4); hip (Is 66:12).

שְׁכֶם shᵉkhem (8327), Shoulder (Gn 24:15, Jos 4:5, Is 14:25).

1. ὤμους ōmous acc pl masc

1 and lay them on men's **shoulders**; .... Matt 23:4
1 found it, he layeth it on his **shoulders**, rejoicing.... Luke 15:5

The noun *ōmos* refers technically to "the shoulder with the upper arm" (*Liddell-Scott*). In Greek works extending from Homer (Eighth Century B.C.) to the Hellenistic era (e.g., Philo) the term is used to designate either "shoulder" or "arm." The word appears twice in the New Testament (Matthew 23:4; Luke 15:5) and in both instances is usually translated "shoulder" in English versions.

Strong 5606, Bauer 895, Moulton-Milligan 701, Liddell-Scott 2033.

5441. ὠνέομαι ōneomai verb

Buy, purchase.

1. ὠνήσατο ōnēsato 3sing indic aor mid

1 and laid in the sepulchre that Abraham **bought** ...... Acts 7:16

The deponent verb *ōneomai* means "to buy, to purchase." In the classical Greek period the term meant "to deal for, to bargain for." The ordinary meaning "to buy" is prevalent in the nonliterary Greek documents (papyri) (see *Moulton-Milligan*). In the New Testament the word occurs only at Acts 7:16 in the past tense: " . . . the sepulchre that Abraham *bought* for a sum of money . . . . "

Strong 5608, Bauer 895-96, Moulton-Milligan 701-2, Liddell-Scott 2034.

5442. ᾠόν ōon noun

Egg.

בֵּיצִים bêtsîm (1037), Eggs (Dt 22:6, Is 10:14, 59:5).

1. ᾠόν ōon nom/acc sing neu

1 if he shall ask **an egg**, will he offer him a scorpion? Luke 11:12

The term *ōon* is the ordinary Greek word for "egg." It appears in the works of Homer, the Septuagint, the papyri, and the writings of Philo (*Bauer*). It may refer to the eggs of birds, serpents, tortoises, or fish, but more commonly refers to hens' eggs (*Liddell-Scott*). Luke 11:12 contains its only appearance in the New Testament. In a passage extolling the goodness of the Father, Jesus stated that no human father would give a scorpion when asked for a fish, implying that the Heavenly Father would be that much better. According to Pegg a scorpion rolled up with tail tucked in resembled an egg ("A Scorpion for an Egg," p.468). Consequently, the emphasis is upon deception. No human father would deceive his child. It is unnatural. Nor would he try to harm his child in any way. The Heavenly Father, being good, would also never try to harm or deceive His children (see also Fitzmyer, *The Anchor Bible*, 28a:915).

Strong 5609, Bauer 896, Moulton-Milligan 702, Liddell-Scott 2035.

5443. ὥρα hōra noun

A period of time; time of day, hour.

Cross-Reference:
ὡραῖος hōraios (5444)

מֶגֶד meghedh (4162), Choice fruit, choice produce (Dt 33:14,16).

מוֹעֵד môʿēdh (4287), Appointed time (Nm 9:2, Dn 11:35).

נָאָה nā'âh (5171), Be lovely (Is 52:7).

עֵת ʿēth (6496), Time (Ex 18:22, 2 Kgs 7:1, Zec 10:1).

שָׁעָה shāʿāh (A8542), At a certain time, an undetermined amount of time (Dn 3:6, 4:19 [4:16], 5:5—Aramaic).

1. ὥρας hōras gen/acc sing/pl fem
2. ὥρα hōra nom sing fem
3. ὥρᾳ hōra dat sing fem
4. ὥραν hōran acc sing fem
5. ὧραι hōrai nom pl fem
6. ὡρῶν hōrōn gen pl fem

3 And his servant was healed in the selfsame **hour**.....Matt 8:13
1 And the woman was made whole from that **hour**........ 9:22
3 for it shall be given you in that same **hour** 10:19
2 This is a desert place, and the **time** is now past; 14:15
1 her daughter was made whole from that very **hour**..... 15:28
1 and the child was cured from that very **hour**.......... 17:18
3 At the same **time** came the disciples unto Jesus, ... 18:1
4 And he went out about the third **hour**, ... 20:3
4 Again he went out about the sixth and ninth **hour**, ... 20:5
4 And about the eleventh **hour** he went out, ... 20:6
4 that were hired about the eleventh **hour**, ... 20:9
4 Saying, These last have wrought but one **hour**, ... 20:12
1 But of that day and **hour** knoweth no man, ... 24:36
3 for ye know not what **hour** your Lord doth come...... 24:42
3 an **hour** as ye think not the Son of man cometh....... 24:44
3 and in **an hour** that he is not aware of, ... 24:50
4 for ye know neither the day nor the **hour** 25:13
4 What, could ye not watch with me one **hour**? 26:40
2 **hour** is at hand, and the Son of man is betrayed 26:45
3 In that same **hour** said Jesus to the multitudes, ... 26:55
1 Now from the sixth **hour** there was darkness 27:45
1 was darkness over all the land unto the ninth **hour**..... 27:45
4 about the ninth **hour** Jesus cried with a loud voice, ... 27:46
1 And when the day was now far spent, (NT) .... Mark 6:35
2 and now the **time** is far passed: 6:35
1 and now the eventide was come, (NT) 11:11

3 but whatsoever shall be given you in that **hour,** .... Mark 13:11
1 But of that day and that **hour** knoweth no man, ... 13:32
2 if it were possible, the **hour** might pass from him...... 14:35
4 sleepest thou? couldest not thou watch one **hour?** 14:37
2 the **hour** is come; behold, the Son of man is betrayed .. 14:41
2 And it was the third **hour,** and they crucified him...... 15:25
1 And when the sixth **hour** was come, ... 15:33
1 darkness over the whole land until the ninth **hour**...... 15:33
3 at the ninth **hour** Jesus cried with a loud voice, ... 15:34
3 people were praying without at the **time** of incense. Luke 1:10
3 And she coming in that **instant** gave thanks 2:38
3 And in that same **hour** he cured many 7:21
3 In that **hour** Jesus rejoiced in spirit, and said, ... 10:21
3 the Holy Ghost shall teach you in the same **hour** 12:12
3 if the goodman of the house had known what **hour** 12:39
3 Son of man cometh at an **hour** when ye think not...... 12:40
3 and at **an hour** when he is not aware, ... 12:46
3 Just at that **time** some Pharisees came up, (NASB) 13:31
3 And sent his servant at supper **time** to say to them 14:17
3 And the chief priests and the scribes the same **hour** ... 20:19
2 And when the **hour** was come, he sat down, ... 22:14
2 but this is your **hour,** and the power of darkness....... 22:53
1 one **hour** after another confidently affirmed, ... 22:59
2 And it was about the sixth **hour,** 23:44
1 a darkness over all the earth until the ninth **hour**...... 23:44
3 rose up the same **hour,** and returned to Jerusalem, ... 24:33
2 for it was about the tenth **hour**..................... John 1:39
2 mine **hour** is not yet come............................ 2:4
2 and it was about the sixth **hour**...................... 4:6
2 Woman, believe me, the **hour** cometh, ... 4:21
2 But the **hour** cometh, and now is, ... 4:23
4 inquired ... the **hour** when he began to amend.......... 4:52
4 Yesterday at the seventh **hour** the fever left him........ 4:52
3 So the father knew that it was at the same **hour,** 4:53
2 The **hour** is coming, and now is, ... 5:25
2 Marvel not at this: for the **hour** is coming, ... 5:28
4 ye were willing for **a season** to rejoice in his light....... 5:35
2 because his **hour** was not yet come.................... 7:30
2 for his **hour** was not yet come........................ 8:20
5 Are there not twelve **hours** in the day? 11:9
2 **hour** is come, that the Son ... should be glorified....... 12:23
1 what shall I say? Father, save me from this **hour:** 12:27
4 but for this cause came I unto this **hour**.............. 12:27
2 when Jesus knew that his **hour** was come 13:1
2 yea, the **time** cometh, that whosoever killeth you 16:2
2 that when the **time** shall come, ... 16:4
2 hath sorrow, because her **hour** is come: 16:21
2 the **time** cometh, ... no more speak ... in proverbs, ... 16:25
2 Behold, the **hour** cometh, yea, is now come, ... 16:32
2 Father, the **hour** is come; glorify thy Son, ... 17:1
2 about the sixth **hour:** and he saith unto the Jews, ... 19:14
1 from that **hour** ... took her unto his own home......... 19:27
2 seeing it is but the third **hour** of the day............ Acts 2:15
4 at the **hour** of prayer, being the ninth hour............ 3:1
6 And it was about the space of three **hours** after, ... 5:7
4 a vision evidently about the ninth **hour** of the day 10:3
4 upon the housetop to pray about the sixth **hour:** 10:9
1 Four days ago I was fasting until this **hour;** 10:30
4 and at the ninth **hour** I prayed in my house, ... 10:30
3 And he came out the same **hour**...................... 16:18
3 And he took them the same **hour** of the night, ... 16:33
1 all with one voice about the space of two **hours** 19:34
3 And the same **hour** I looked up upon him............ 22:13
1 at the third **hour** of the night; 23:23
2 that now it is high **time** to awake out of sleep: ..... Rom 13:11
1 unto this present **hour** we both hunger, and thirst, ... 1 Co 4:11
4 And why stand we in jeopardy every **hour?** 15:30
4 made you sorry, though it were but for **a season**..... 2 Co 7:8
4 gave place by subjection, no, not for **an hour;** .... Gal 2:5
1 being taken from you for **a short** time in presence, .. 1 Th 2:17
4 For perhaps he therefore departed for **a season,** ..... Phlm 1:15
2 Little children, it is the last **time:** .... 1 Jn 2:18
2 whereby we know that it is the last **time**............... 2:18
4 shalt not know what **hour** I will come upon thee..... Rev 3:3
1 I also will keep thee from the **hour** of temptation, ... 3:10
4 for an **hour,** and a day, and a month, and a year, ... 9:15
3 And the same **hour** was there a great earthquake, ... 11:13
2 glory to him; for the **hour** of his judgment is come: Rev 14:7
2 and reap: for the **time** is come for thee to reap; 14:15
4 but receive power as kings one **hour** with the beast.... 17:12
3 mighty city! for in one **hour** is thy judgment come..... 18:10
3 For in one **hour** so great riches is come to nought..... 18:17
3 for in one **hour** is she made desolate................. 18:19

Classical Greek

The general use of *hōra* in classical Greek is to denote "hour," as in an hour of time. But the term also has a broader reference; it can stand for a whole day or even a year or season. Furthermore, an "hour" might stand for a period of time in life, such as the "hour of youth" or the "hour of old age." In addition *hōra* can denote a particular event in time such as the mealtime hour or the hour of bedtime. When accompanied by the prepositions *en* (1706) and *eis* (1506B) it can mean "in due season" or "at the correct time" (*Liddell-Scott*). The meaning "1 hour," i.e., "60 minutes," occurs only rarely in secular Greek, although *hōra* can denote a short segment of time (Delling, "hōra," *Kittel*, 9:676).

Septuagint Usage

About 50 instances of *hōra* are recorded in the Septuagint. It translates six Hebrew words, but most often it replaces *ʿēth*, "time." In Israel an hour was often something similar to our own understanding; there were sundials for telling time (2 Kings 20:9; Isaiah 38:8). Without sundials the day was divided simply into "day" and "night" and "morning" and "noon" (Psalm 55:17). However, only in passages with no Hebrew text does *hōra* mean "hour" (Delling, "hōra," *Kittel*, 9:677). Three Maccabees 5:14 notes: "Since it was nearly the middle of the tenth *hour*." In the Septuagint *hōra* tends to represent a point in time, i.e., "the fixed time," rather than a period of time.

Like the word "day," hour can also denote a longer or shorter period of time. When it occurs in an eschatological context it might parallel the expression "the day of the Lord." In Daniel 8:17 we read of "the hour of time" (*hōran kairou*) and in Daniel 11:40,45 of the "last hour" (*hōran sunteleias*).

New Testament Usage

Approximately 110 instances of *hōra* appear in the New Testament. The vast majority occur in Acts and the Gospels (over 80); 10 occur in the Book of Revelation. Paul used the term only seven times.

Hōra concerns the divisions of the day in the parable of the workmen in the vineyard (Matthew 20:3,5,6). Thus it can refer to the 12th part of a day. It refers to an extended period of time in 1

John 2:18 but a certain point in time in Matthew 26:45. *Hōra* has much the same semantic range as in the Septuagint and classical Greek. It can denote "the fixed time," a specific time for some activity. The "*hour* of prayer" (Acts 3:1) thus means the time set for prayer, not a 60 minute period of prayer.

One must always keep in mind that Biblical time-markers are given in the language of that day. (Note the use of "day" in this sentence. The English language also uses terms for time demarcation with various meanings.) It is difficult and erroneous to impose precise time frames upon a language relatively unconcerned about that understanding of time.

The related term *hēmiōron* (2236B) occurs in Revelation 8:1. A compound formed from *hēmi* and *hōra*, *hēmiōron* means "a half hour." The text records that heaven will be silent for about half an hour following the opening of the seventh seal. This perhaps reflects a custom common to the worship pattern of that day. During the offering of incense there was a period of about a half hour of silence (Luke 1:10). During that time—at the *hōra* of incense—people prayed. A similar image is presented in Revelation 8:1-5 which speaks of offering incense with the prayers of the saints.

STRONG 5610, BAUER 896, MOULTON-MILLIGAN 702, KITTEL 9:675-81, LIDDELL-SCOTT 2035-36, COLIN BROWN 3:845-49.

5444. ὡραῖος hōraios adj

Timely, seasonable; beautiful, pleasant.

COGNATE:

ὥρα hōra (5443)

SYNONYMS:

ἀστεῖος asteios (785)
καλός kalos (2541)

הָדַר hādhar (1991), Be glorious (Is 63:1).

הָדָר hādhār (1994), Goodly (Lv 23:40).

חָמַד chāmadh (2629), Desire, have pleasure in; niphal: be pleasing (Gn 2:9, 3:6 [3:7]).

חֶמְדָּה chemdāh (2631), Desire (1 Sm 9:20).

טוֹב ṭôv (3005), Beautiful, handsome (Gn 26:7, 1 Kgs 1:6).

יָפֶה yāpheh (3413), Beautiful, handsome (Gn 29:17, 39:6, Jer 11:16).

מַחְמָד machmādh (4398), Valuable articles (2 Chr 36:19).

נָאוֶה nā'weh (5173), Lovely, beautiful (S/S 2:14, 4:3, 6:4 [6:3]).

נָוֶה nāweh (5295), Habitation (Lam 2:2); pasture (Jl 1:19f.).

נָעִים nā'im (5456), Pleasant (2 Sm 1:23, S/S 1:16).

1. ὡραῖοι hōraioi nom pl masc
2. ὡραίᾳ hōraia dat sing fem
3. ὡραίαν hōraian acc sing fem

1 which indeed appear **beautiful** outward, ... Matt 23:27
3 the gate of the temple which is called **Beautiful**, ... Acts 3:2
2 sat for alms at the **Beautiful** gate of the temple: 3:10
1 How **beautiful** are the feet of them that preach ..... Rom 10:15

Classical Greek

This adjective has a wide semantic range. Classical usage includes simple meanings such as "beautiful, fair, lovely," and "pleasant." The word can also mean "produced at the right time" (referring to salted or pickled fish and year-old tunas), "harvesttime" (*Liddell-Scott*), "in season," and "ripe" (*Moulton-Milligan*). *Hōraios* also has the meaning of "seasonable, due," or "proper" (*Liddell-Scott*). This word is related to *hōra* (5443) which originally meant "the right, favorable time" (Delling, "hōra," *Kittel*, 9:675). Thus *hōraios* can describe anything that occurs or appears at the "right" time. Hence it describes things which are "pleasant, proper, beautiful."

Septuagint Usage

The largest number of occurrences in the Septuagint are in Genesis, Song of Solomon (five times each), and Sirach (nine times). Genesis 3:6 says that the fruit of the forbidden tree was "pleasant" to the sight. Rachel, Jacob's wife, was described as "beautiful" (Genesis 29:17). In the Song of Solomon the beloved's countenance, her speech, and the city of Jerusalem are considered "comely" or "beautiful" (1:16; 2:14; 4:3; 6:4).

In the Book of Sirach praise is not "seemly" when coming from a sinner (15:9); the judgment and wisdom of old men is "comely" (25:4,5); and the rainbow that God made is "beautiful" (43:11).

New Testament Usage

There are four occurrences of *hōraios* in the New Testament. In each case the King James Version translates the word "beautiful."

In Matthew 23:27 Jesus reviled the Pharisees for their hypocritical behavior. He noted that like monuments on a tomb the Pharisees were beautiful on the outside but inside were full of unclean and vile things. Acts 3:2 and 10 record the name of the gate ("Beautiful") at which the lame man sat whom the Lord healed through the ministry of Peter and John. According to Bruce this gate may be identified with a gate described by Josephus that was made of Corinthian bronze. The workmanship of this gate was so exquisite that it outvalued comparable gates plated with silver or gold (*New International Commentary on the New Testament, Acts,* p.83). Finally, in a quotation of Isaiah 52:7, Romans 10:15 says, "How *beautiful* are the feet of them that preach the gospel of peace."

Strong 5611, Bauer 896-97, Moulton-Milligan 702, Liddell-Scott 2036, Colin Brown 3:845,847.

5445. ὠρύομαι ōruomai verb

Roar, howl.

Synonyms:
ἠχέω ēcheō (2255)
μυκάομαι mukaomai (3317)

יָפָה yāphâh (3412), Be beautiful (S/S 7:1,6).

נָאָה nā'âh (5171), Be comely (S/S 1:10).

נָעֵם nā'ēm (5459), Be pleasant (2 Sm 1:26).

1. ὠρυόμενος ōruomenos
nom sing masc part pres mid

1 the devil, as a **roaring** lion, walketh about,.......... I Pt 5:8

The verb *ōruomai* means "to roar" when it refers to lions and "to howl" when it pertains to hungry dogs or wolves (*Liddell-Scott*). Occasionally it is used to describe the mourning or rejoicing of persons. The term rarely occurs in classical Greek literature but was used more frequently in the Hellenistic period. Its only appearance in the New Testament is in 1 Peter 5:8; here the devil is described as "a *roaring* lion."

Strong 5612, Bauer 897, Moulton-Milligan 702-3, Liddell-Scott 2038.

5445A. ὡς hōs conj

As, like; when, as long as, after, so that.

1. ὡς hōs

1 did **as** the angel of the Lord had bidden him,....... Matt 1:24
1 **as** your heavenly Father is perfect. (NASB)............ 5:48
1 you are not to be **as** the hypocrites; (NASB)........... 6:5
1 Thy will be done in earth, **as** it is in heaven........... 6:10
1 forgive us our debts, **as** we forgive our debtors.......... 6:12
1 fast, do not ... **as** the hypocrites (NASB)............... 6:16
1 Solomon ... was not arrayed **like** one of these........... 6:29
1 For he taught them **as** one having authority,............ 7:29
1 as one having authority, and not **as** the scribes.......... 7:29
1 and **as** thou hast believed, so be it done unto thee...... 8:13
1 I send you forth **as** sheep in the midst of wolves:...... 10:16
1 be ye therefore wise **as** serpents,..................... 10:16
1 wise as serpents, and harmless **as** doves............... 10:16
1 enough for the disciple that he be **as** his master,....... 10:25
1 be as his master, and the servant **as** his lord.......... 10:25
1 and it was restored whole, like **as** the other............ 12:13
1 Then shall the righteous shine forth **as** the sun........ 13:43
1 because they counted him **as** a prophet............... 14:5
1 great is thy faith: be it unto thee even **as** thou wilt..... 15:28
1 and his face did shine **as** the sun,..................... 17:2
1 and his raiment was white **as** the light................. 17:2
1 If ye have faith **as** a grain of mustard seed,........ Matt 17:20
1 ye be converted, and become **as** little children,........ 18:3
1 humble himself **as** this little child,.................... 18:4
1 Shouldest not thou ... even **as** I had pity on thee?..... 18:33
1 Thou shalt love thy neighbour **as** thyself.............. 19:19
1 I will give unto this last, even **as** unto thee........... 20:14
1 we fear the people; for all hold John **as** a prophet..... 21:26
1 because they took him **for** a prophet.................. 21:46
1 but are **as** the angels of God in heaven................ 22:30
1 Thou shalt love thy neighbour **as** thyself.............. 22:39
1 For **as** in those days ... before the flood (NASB)...... 24:38
1 And the disciples did **as** Jesus had appointed them;.... 26:19
1 nevertheless not **as** I will, but as thou wilt............ 26:39
1 nevertheless not as I will, but **as** thou wilt............ 26:39
1 Are ye come out **as** against a thief with swords........ 26:55
1 go your way, make it **as** sure as ye can................ 27:65
1 His countenance was **like** lightning,................... 28:3
1 and his garment as white **as** snow; (NASB).......... 28:3
1 And **as** they went to tell his disciples,................ 28:9
1 they took the money, and did **as** they were taught:.... 28:15
1 **As** it is written in the prophets,.................... Mark 1:2
1 and the Spirit **like** a dove descending (NASB).......... 1:10
1 for he taught them **as** one that had authority,.......... 1:22
1 as one that had authority, and not **as** the scribes........ 1:22
1 and his hand was restored whole **as** the other........... 3:5
1 **as** if a man should cast seed into the ground;........... 4:26
1 spring and grow up, he knoweth not **how**............... 4:27
1 It is **like** a grain of mustard seed,..................... 4:31
1 they took him even **as** he was in the ship............... 4:36
1 they were **about** two thousand;....................... 5:13
1 That it is a prophet, or **as** one of the prophets......... 6:15
1 because they were **as** sheep not having a shepherd:..... 6:34
1 Well hath Esaias prophesied ... **as** it is written,......... 7:6
1 And they that had eaten were **about** four thousand:..... 8:9
1 he looked up, and said, I see men **as** trees, walking..... 8:24
1 raiment became shining, exceeding white **as** snow;...... 9:3
1 How long is it ago since this came unto him? (NT)..... 9:21
1 and, **as** he was wont, he taught them again........... 10:1
1 not receive the kingdom of God **as** a little child,...... 10:15
1 but are **as** the angels which are in heaven............. 12:25
1 **how** in the bush God spake unto him, saying,......... 12:26
1 Thou shalt love thy neighbour **as** thyself.............. 12:31
1 and to love his neighbour **as** himself,................. 12:33
1 the Son of man is **as** a man taking a far journey,...... 13:34
1 Are ye come out, **as** against a thief, with swords....... 14:48
1 **how** Jesus had made the remark (NASB) (NT)........ 14:72
1 **as soon as** the days of his ministration............. Luke 1:23
1 that, **when** Elisabeth heard the salutation of Mary,...... 1:41
1 lo, **as** soon as the voice of thy salutation sounded....... 1:44
1 stayed with her **about** three months, (NASB)........... 1:56
1 **as** the angels were gone away from them............... 2:15
1 she was a widow of **about** fourscore and four years,..... 2:37
1 And **when** they had performed all things.............. 2:39
1 **As** it is written in the book of the words of Esaias...... 3:4
1 descended upon Him ... **like** a dove, (NASB)........... 3:22
1 being **as** was supposed the son of Joseph,.............. 3:23
1 **when** great famine was throughout all the land;......... 4:25
1 **when** he had left speaking, he said unto Simon,......... 5:4
1 **How** he went into the house of God,.................. 6:4
1 and his hand was restored whole **as** the other........... 6:10
1 shall reproach you, and cast out your name **as** evil,..... 6:22
1 but every one that is perfect shall be **as** his master...... 6:40
1 Now **when** he came nigh to the gate of the city,........ 7:12
1 had one only daughter, **about** twelve years of age,...... 8:42
1 touched him, ... **how** she was healed immediately........ 8:47
1 command fire to come down ... even **as** Elias did?...... 9:54
1 behold, I send you forth **as** lambs among wolves........ 10:3
1 I beheld Satan **as** lightning fall from heaven........... 10:18
1 shalt love the Lord ... and thy neighbour **as** thyself..... 10:27
1 **when** he ceased, one of his disciples said unto him,.... 11:1
1 Thy will be done, **as** in heaven, so in earth........... 11:2
1 **as** when the bright shining of a candle doth give....... 11:36
1 for ye are **as** graves which appear not,................ 11:44
1 that Solomon in all his glory was not arrayed **like**..... 12:27
1 **When** thou goest with thine adversary................. 12:58
1 said, Lord, it is done **as** thou hast commanded,........ 14:22
1 make me **as** one of thy hired servants................. 15:19

1 and **as** he came and drew nigh to the house, ... Luke 15:25
1 accused unto him **that** he had wasted his goods........ 16:1
1 If ye had faith **as** a grain of mustard seed,............ 17:6
1 Likewise also **as** it was in the days of Lot;............ 17:28
1 unjust, adulterers, or even **as** this publican............. 18:11
1 not receive the kingdom of God **as** a little child 18:17
1 And **when** Jesus came to the place, he looked up,..... 19:5
1 **when** he was come nigh to Bethphage and Bethany,.... 19:29
1 And **when** he was come near, he beheld the city,...... 19:41
1 **when** he calleth the Lord the God of Abraham,....... 20:37
1 For **as** a snare shall it come on all them that dwell 21:35
1 is greatest among you, let him be **as** the younger;..... 22:26
1 and he that is chief, **as** he that doth serve............. 22:26
1 but I am among you **as** he that serveth................ 22:27
1 that he may sift you **as** wheat:...................... 22:31
1 Be ye come out, **as** against a thief, with swords........ 22:52
1 the word of the Lord, **how** he had said unto him,...... 22:61
1 And **as soon as** it was day, the elders of the people 22:66
1 **as** one that perverteth the people:.................... 23:14
1 **as** they led him away, ... laid hold upon ... Simon,..... 23:26
1 beheld the sepulchre, and **how** his body was laid....... 23:55
1 remember **how** he spake unto you ... in Galilee,....... 24:6
1 **while** he talked with us by the way,................. 24:32
1 and **while** he opened to us the scriptures?............ 24:32
1 **how** he was known of them in breaking of bread....... 24:35
1 the glory **as** of the only begotten of the Father,..... John 1:14
1 the Spirit descending **as** a dove (NASB)............... 1:32
1 for it was **about** the tenth hour....................... 1:39
1 **When** the ruler of the feast had tasted the water........ 2:9
1 Now **when** he was in Jerusalem at the passover,........ 2:23
1 **When** therefore the Lord knew 4:1
1 It was **about** the sixth hour. (NASB).................. 4:6
1 So **when** the Samaritans were come unto him,.......... 4:40
1 men sat down, ... **about** five thousand. (NASB)......... 6:10
1 **When** they were filled, he said unto his disciples,....... 6:12
1 And **when** even was now come,....................... 6:16
1 So when they had rowed **about** five and twenty......... 6:19
1 But **when** his brethren were gone up,.................. 7:10
1 unto the feast, not openly, but **as** it were in secret...... 7:10
1 officers answered, Never man spake **like** this man....... 7:46
1 **So** when they continued asking him,.................. 8:7
1 **When** he had heard therefore that he was sick,........ 11:6
1 nigh unto Jerusalem, **about** fifteen furlongs off:........ 11:18
1 **as soon as** she heard that Jesus was coming,.......... 11:20
1 **As soon as** she heard that, she arose quickly,.......... 11:29
1 Then **when** Mary was come where Jesus was,.......... 11:32
1 **When** Jesus therefore saw her weeping,.............. 11:33
1 Walk **while** you have the light, (NASB)............... 12:35
1 **While** you have light, believe in the light, (NASB)..... 12:36
1 he is cast forth **as** a branch, and is withered;.......... 15:6
1 **As soon** then **as** he had said unto them, I am he,...... 18:6
1 it was **about** the sixth hour. (NASB).................. 19:14
1 **when** they came to Jesus, ... he was dead already,..... 19:33
1 aloes, **about** a hundred pounds (NASB)............... 19:39
1 and **as** she wept, she stooped down,.................. 20:11
1 but as it **were** two hundred cubits,.................... 21:8
1 **As soon** then **as** they were come to land,............. 21:9
1 And **while** they looked stedfastly toward heaven ..... Acts 1:10
1 together were **about** an hundred and twenty,............ 1:15
1 For these are not drunken, **as** ye suppose,.............. 2:15
1 **as though** by our own power or holiness 3:12
1 raise up unto you of your brethren, **like** unto me;....... 3:22
1 the men came to be **about** five thousand. (NASB)...... 4:4
1 And it was **about** the space of three hours after,........ 5:7
1 Now **when** the high priest and the captain............. 5:24
1 and a group of **about** four hundred men (NASB)....... 5:36
1 And **when** he was full forty years old,................. 7:23
1 **like** unto me; him shall ye hear...................... 7:37
1 **as** your fathers did, so do ye......................... 7:51
1 He was led **as** a sheep to the slaughter;............... 8:32
1 and **like** a lamb dumb before his shearer,.............. 8:32
1 And **as** they went on their way,...................... 8:36
1 from his eyes something **like** scales, (NASB)........... 9:18
1 And **after** that many days were fulfilled,............... 9:23
1 And **when** the angel which spake unto Cornelius 10:7
1 **as** it had been a great sheet 10:11
1 Now **while** Peter doubted in himself 10:17
1 And **as** Peter was coming in, Cornelius met him,... Acts 10:25
1 Ye know **how** that it is an unlawful thing............. 10:28
1 **How** God anointed Jesus of Nazareth.................. 10:38
1 the Holy Spirit just **as** we did, (NASB)............... 10:47
1 **as** it had been a great sheet,........................ 11:5
1 the word of the Lord, **how** that he said,.............. 11:16
1 as God gave them the like gift **as** he did unto us,...... 11:17
1 And **about** the time of forty years.................... 13:18
1 **about** the space of four hundred and fifty years,....... 13:20
1 And **as** John fulfilled his course, he said,............. 13:25
1 **when** they had fulfilled all that was written of him,.... 13:29
1 **as** it is also written in the second psalm,............. 13:33
1 And **when** there was an assault made 14:5
1 And **as** they went through the cities,.................. 16:4
1 And **after** he had seen the vision,..................... 16:10
1 And **when** she was baptized, and her household,....... 16:15
1 But **when** the Jews of Thessalonica had knowledge 17:13
1 brethren sent away Paul to go **as** it were to the sea:... 17:14
1 and Timotheus for to come to him **with** all speed,..... 17:15
1 in all things ye are too superstitious. (NT)............ 17:22
1 **as** certain also of your own poets have said,........... 17:28
1 And **when** Silas and Timotheus were come 18:5
1 But **when** divers were hardened, and believed not,..... 19:9
1 **After** these things were ended,....................... 19:21
1 all with one voice about the **space of** two hours........ 19:34
1 And **when** he met with us at Assos, we took him in,... 20:14
1 **when** they were come to him, he said unto them,...... 20:18
1 And **how** I kept back nothing that was profitable 20:20
1 **so** that I might finish my course with joy,............. 20:24
1 **that** after we were gotten from them,................. 21:1
1 And **when** we heard these things,..................... 21:12
1 And **when** the seven days were almost ended,......... 21:27
1 **As** also the high priest doth bear me witness,.......... 22:5
1 **when** I could not see for the glory of that light,....... 22:11
1 And **as** they bound him with thongs,.................. 22:25
1 for **as** thou hast testified of me in Jerusalem,.......... 23:11
1 **as** though ye would inquire something more........... 23:15
1 **as** though they would inquire somewhat of him........ 23:20
1 have I done no wrong, **as** thou very well knowest...... 25:10
1 And **when** they had been there many days,............ 25:14
1 And **when** it was determined that we should sail....... 27:1
1 But **when** the fourteenth night was come,............. 27:27
1 under colour **as** though they would ... cast anchors..... 27:30
1 And **when** the barbarians saw the venomous beast 28:4
1 not **that** I had ought to accuse my nation of........... 28:19
1 that without ceasing I make mention (NT)......... Rom 1:9
1 they knew God, they glorified him not **as** God,......... 1:21
1 why yet am I also judged **as** a sinner?................ 3:7
1 those things which be not **as** though they were.......... 4:17
1 But not **as** the offence, so also is the free gift.......... 5:15
1 And not **as** it was by one that sinned, so is the gift:.... 5:16
1 Therefore **as** by the offence of one judgment........... 5:18
1 Neither yield ye your members **as** instruments.......... 6:13
1 we are accounted **as** sheep for the slaughter............ 8:36
1 **As** he saith also in Osee,............................ 9:25
1 children of Israel be **as** the sand of the sea,........... 9:27
1 we had been **as** Sodoma, ... like unto Gomorrha........ 9:29
1 **as** Sodoma, and been made like unto Gomorrha........ 9:29
1 but **as** it were by the works of the law................ 9:32
1 **How** beautiful are the feet of them that preach........ 10:15
1 **how** he maketh intercession to God against Israel,..... 11:2
1 **how** unsearchable are his judgments,.................. 11:33
1 but to think soberly, according **as** God hath dealt...... 12:3
1 Thou shalt love thy neighbour **as** thyself.............. 13:9
1 **as** in the day;...................................... 13:13
1 **as** putting you in mind, because of the grace.......... 15:15
1 **Whensoever** I take my journey into Spain,............. 15:24
1 could not speak unto you **as** unto spiritual,......... 1 Co 3:1
1 but **as** unto carnal, even as unto babes in Christ........ 3:1
1 but as unto carnal, even **as** unto babes in Christ........ 3:1
1 even **as** the Lord gave to every man?.................. 3:5
1 **as** a wise masterbuilder, I have laid the foundation,..... 3:10
1 but he himself shall be saved; yet so **as** by fire......... 3:15
1 **as** of the ministers of Christ,......................... 4:1
1 dost thou glory, **as** if thou hadst not received it?........ 4:7
1 us the apostles last, **as** it were appointed to death:...... 4:9
1 we are made **as** the filth of the world,................. 4:13

1 but as my beloved sons I warn you................. 1 Co 4:14
1 are puffed up, as though I would not come to you...... 4:18
1 I verily, as absent in body, but present in spirit,........ 5:3
1 have judged already, as though I were present,......... 5:3
1 For I would that all men were even as I myself......... 7:7
1 It is good for them if they abide even as I............. 7:8
1 But as God hath distributed to every man,............. 7:17
1 as the Lord hath called every one, so let him walk...... 7:17
1 as one that hath obtained mercy of the Lord........... 7:25
1 they that have wives be as though they had none;...... 7:29
1 And they that weep, as though they wept not;.......... 7:30
1 and they that rejoice, as though they rejoiced not;...... 7:30
1 and they that buy, as though they possessed not;....... 7:30
1 And they that use this world, as not abusing it:......... 7:31
1 eat it as a thing offered unto an idol;................. 8:7
1 lead about a sister, a wife, as well as other apostles,.... 9:5
1 And unto the Jews I became as a Jew,................. 9:20
1 to them that are under the law, as under the law,....... 9:20
1 To them that are without law, as without law,.......... 9:21
1 To the weak became I as weak,....................... 9:22
1 I therefore so run, not as uncertainly;.................. 9:26
1 so fight I, not as one that beateth the air:.............. 9:26
1 as it is written, The people sat down to eat........... 10:7
1 I speak as to wise men; judge ye what I say........... 10:15
1 And the rest will I set in order when I come........... 11:34
1 away unto these dumb idols, even as ye were led...... 12:2
1 When I was a child, I spake as a child,............... 13:11
1 I understood as a child, I thought as a child:.......... 13:11
1 I understood as a child, I thought as a child:.......... 13:11
1 but of peace, as in all churches of the saints........... 14:33
1 for he worketh the work of the Lord, as I also do..... 16:10
1 as you are sharers of our sufferings, (NASB)........2 Co 1:7
1 For we are not as many,............................. 2:17
1 but as of sincerity, but as of God,.................... 2:17
1 but as of sincerity, but as of God,.................... 2:17
1 or need we, as some others, epistles.................. 3:1
1 of ourselves to think any thing as of ourselves;......... 3:5
1 To wit, that God was in Christ,...................... 5:19
1 as though God did beseech you by us:................. 5:20
1 approving ourselves as the ministers of God,........... 6:4
1 as deceivers, and yet true;............................ 6:8
1 As unknown, and yet well known;..................... 6:9
1 as dying, and, behold, we live;........................ 6:9
1 as chastened, and not killed;......................... 6:9
1 As sorrowful, yet alway rejoicing;..................... 6:10
1 as poor, yet making many rich;....................... 6:10
1 as having nothing, and yet possessing all things......... 6:10
1 I speak as unto my children, be ye also enlarged........ 6:13
1 but as we spake all things to you in truth,............. 7:14
1 how with fear and trembling ye received him........... 7:15
1 as a matter of bounty, and not as of covetousness....... 9:5
1 generous gift, not as one grudgingly (NIV)............. 9:5
1 think of us as if we walked according to the flesh...... 10:2
1 I may not seem as if I would terrify you by letters..... 10:9
1 as though we reached not unto you:................... 10:14
1 as the serpent beguiled Eve through his subtlety,...... 11:3
1 be transformed as the ministers of righteousness;...... 11:15
1 if otherwise, yet as a fool receive me,................. 11:16
1 as it were foolishly, in this confidence of boasting...... 11:17
1 as though we had been weak......................... 11:21
1 as if I were present, the second time;................. 13:2
1 though we be as reprobates.......................... 13:7
1 As we said before, so say I now again,.............. Gal 1:9
1 He saith not, And to seeds, as of many;............... 3:16
1 but as of one, And to thy seed, which is Christ......... 3:16
1 Brethren, I beseech you, be as I am;.................. 4:12
1 for I am as ye are: ye have not injured me at all........ 4:12
1 nor rejected; but received me as an angel of God,...... 4:14
1 but received me as an angel ... even as Christ Jesus..... 4:14
1 Thou shalt love thy neighbour as thyself................ 5:14
1 As we have therefore opportunity, let us do good....... 6:10
1 by nature the children of wrath, even as others.......Eph 2:3
1 as it is now revealed unto his holy apostles............ 3:5
1 Be ye therefore followers of God, as dear children;..... 5:1
1 light in the Lord: walk as children of light:............ 5:8
1 See then that ye walk circumspectly, not as fools,....... 5:15
1 walk circumspectly, not as fools, but as wise,........... 5:15
1 unto your own husbands, as unto the Lord..........Eph 5:22
1 even as Christ is the head of the church:............... 5:23
1 But as the church is subject to Christ, (NASB)......... 5:24
1 ought men to love their wives as their own bodies...... 5:28
1 let every one ... so love his wife even as himself;....... 5:33
1 in singleness of your heart, as unto Christ;............ 6:5
1 Not with eyeservice, as menpleasers;.................. 6:6
1 but as the servants of Christ,......................... 6:6
1 will render service, as to the Lord, (NASB)............ 6:7
1 I may speak boldly, as I ought to speak................ 6:20
1 For God is my record, how greatly I long after you ..Phlp 1:8
1 but that with all boldness, as always,.................. 1:20
1 And being found in fashion as a man,................. 2:8
1 ye have always obeyed, not as in my presence only,..... 2:12
1 among whom ye shine as lights in the world;........... 2:15
1 the proof of him, that, as a son with the father,........ 2:22
1 so soon as I shall see how it will go with me........... 2:23
1 As ye have therefore received Christ Jesus........... Col 2:6
1 why, as though living in the world,.................... 2:20
1 as the elect of God, holy and beloved,................. 3:12
1 unto your own husbands, as it is fit in the Lord......... 3:18
1 not with eyeservice, as menpleasers;................... 3:22
1 do it heartily, as to the Lord, and not unto men;....... 3:23
1 That I may make it manifest, as I ought to speak........ 4:4
1 even so we speak; not as pleasing men, but God,... 1 Th 2:4
1 been burdensome, as the apostles of Christ............ 2:6
1 even as a nurse cherisheth her children:............... 2:7
1 how holily and justly and unblameably................. 2:10
1 As ye know how we exhorted and comforted........... 2:11
1 how we exhorted ... as a father doth his children,....... 2:11
1 that the day of the Lord so cometh as a thief.......... 5:2
1 that that day should overtake you as a thief............ 5:4
1 Therefore let us not sleep, as do others;............... 5:6
1 nor by word, nor by letter as from us,..............2 Th 2:2
1 as that the day of Christ is at hand.................. 2:2
1 so that he as God sitteth in the temple of God,........ 2:4
1 Yet count him not as an enemy,...................... 3:15
1 not as an enemy, but admonish him as a brother........ 3:15
1 Rebuke not an elder, but entreat him as a father;...1 Tm 5:1
1 and the younger men as brethren;..................... 5:1
1 elder women as mothers; the younger as sisters,........ 5:2
1 elder women as mothers; the younger as sisters,........ 5:2
1 that without ceasing I have remembrance of thee ... 2 Tm 1:3
1 endure hardness, as a good soldier of Jesus Christ....... 2:3
1 suffer trouble, as an evil doer, even unto bonds;........ 2:9
1 And their word will eat as doth a canker:.............. 2:17
1 their folly shall be manifest ... as theirs also was........ 3:9
1 ordain elders ... as I had appointed thee:............Tit 1:5
1 a bishop must be blameless, as the steward of God;..... 1:7
1 being such an one as Paul the aged,............... Phlm 1:9
1 thy benefit should not be as it were of necessity,....... 1:14
1 Not now as a servant, but above a servant,............. 1:16
1 If thou count me ... partner, receive him as myself...... 1:17
1 and they all shall wax old as doth a garment;....... Heb 1:11
1 AS A GARMENT ... BE CHANGED. (NASB)......... 1:12
1 as also Moses was faithful in all his house............. 3:2
1 Moses ... was faithful in all his house, as a servant,..... 3:5
1 But Christ as a son over his own house;............... 3:6
1 Harden not your hearts, as in the provocation,......... 3:8
1 So I sware in my wrath, They shall not enter........... 3:11
1 harden not your hearts, as in the provocation........... 3:15
1 as he said, As I have sworn in my wrath,.............. 4:3
1 Which hope we have as an anchor of the soul,......... 6:19
1 as I may so say, Levi also, who receiveth tithes,........ 7:9
1 in the land of promise, as in a strange country,........ 11:9
1 AS THE SAND ... BY THE SEASHORE. (NASB).... 11:12
1 for he endured, as seeing him who is invisible......... 11:27
1 they passed through the Red sea as by dry land:...... 11:29
1 which speaketh unto you as unto children,............ 12:5
1 God dealeth with you as with sons;................... 12:7
1 any fornicator, or profane person, as Esau,............ 12:16
1 things that are shaken, as of things that are made,..... 12:27
1 them that are in bonds, as bound with them;.......... 13:3
1 as being yourselves also in the body.................. 13:3
1 as they that must give account,...................... 13:17
1 as the flower of the grass he shall pass away......... Jas 1:10
1 Thou shalt love thy neighbour as thyself,.............. 2:8

1 and are convinced of the law as transgressors. . . . . Jas 2:9
1 as they that shall be judged by the law of liberty. 2:12
1 and shall eat your flesh as it were fire. 5:3
1 nourished your hearts, as in a day of slaughter. 5:5
1 As obedient children, ... 1 Pt 1:14
1 as of a lamb without blemish and without spot: 1:19
1 For all flesh is as grass, ... 1:24
1 and all the glory of man as the flower of grass. 1:24
1 As newborn babes, desire the sincere milk 2:2
1 also, as lively stones, are built up a spiritual house, ... 2:5
1 beloved, I beseech you as strangers and pilgrims, ... 2:11
1 that, whereas they speak against you as evildoers, ... 2:12
1 whether it be to the king, as supreme; 2:13
1 Or unto governors, as unto them that are sent 2:14
1 As free, and not using your liberty for a cloak 2:16
1 not using your liberty for a cloak of maliciousness, ... 2:16
1 cloak of maliciousness, but as the servants of God. 2:16
1 For ye were as sheep going astray; 2:25
1 Even as Sara obeyed Abraham, calling him lord: 3:6
1 honour unto the wife, as unto the weaker vessel, ... 3:7
1 and as being heirs together of the grace of life; 3:7
1 whereas they speak evil of you, as of evildoers, ... 3:16
1 as good stewards of the manifold grace of God. 4:10
1 let him speak as the oracles of God; 4:11
1 let him do it as of the ability which God giveth: 4:11
1 as though some strange thing happened unto you: 4:12
1 But let none of you suffer as a murderer, ... 4:15
1 or as a busybody in other men's matters. 4:15
1 Yet if any man suffer as a Christian, ... 4:16
1 to him in well doing, as unto a faithful Creator. 4:19
1 Neither as being lords over God's heritage, ... 5:3
1 the devil, as a roaring lion, walketh about, ... 5:8
1 Silvanus, a faithful brother unto you, as I suppose, ... 5:12
1 According as his divine power hath given unto us . . . 2 Pt 1:3
1 as unto a light that shineth in a dark place, ... 1:19
1 even as there shall be false teachers among you, ... 2:1
1 But these, as natural brute beasts, ... 2:12
1 that one day is with the Lord as a thousand years, ... 3:8
1 and a thousand years as one day. 3:8
1 Lord is not slack ... as some men count slackness; 3:9
1 But the day of the Lord will come as a thief 3:10
1 As also in all his epistles, ... 3:16
1 as they do also the other scriptures, ... 3:16
1 But if we walk in the light, as he is in the light, ... 1 Jn 1:7
1 as the same anointing teacheth you of all things, ... 2:27
1 lady, not as though I wrote a new commandment . . . . 2 Jn 1:5
1 Even as Sodom and Gomorrha, and the cities . . . . Jude 1:7
1 but what they know naturally, as brute beasts, ... 1:10
1 heard behind me a great voice, as of a trumpet, ... Rev 1:10
1 head and His hair were white like (NASB) 1:14
1 his hairs were white like wool, as white as snow; 1:14
1 and his eyes were as a flame of fire; 1:14
1 like unto fine brass, as if they burned in a furnace; 1:15
1 and his voice as the sound of many waters. 1:15
1 countenance was as the sun shineth in his strength. 1:16
1 And when I saw him, I fell at his feet as dead. 1:17
1 who hath his eyes like unto a flame of fire, ... 2:18
1 have not known the depths of Satan, as they speak; 2:24
1 as the vessels of a potter shall they be broken 2:27
1 even as I received of my Father. 2:27
1 thou shalt not watch, I will come on thee as a thief, ... 3:3
1 sit with me in my throne, even as I also overcame, ... 3:21
1 was as it were of a trumpet talking with me; 4:1
1 throne there was as it were, a sea of glass (NASB) 4:6
1 and the third beast had a face as a man, ... 4:7
1 stood a Lamb as it had been slain, ... 5:6
1 and I heard, as it were the noise of thunder, ... 6:1
1 I heard as it were a voice (NASB) 6:6
1 their brethren, that should be killed as they were, ... 6:11
1 and the sun became black as sackcloth of hair, ... 6:12
1 and the moon became as blood; 6:12
1 even as a fig tree casteth her untimely figs, ... 6:13
1 departed as a scroll when it is rolled together; 6:14
1 silence in heaven about the space of half an hour. 8:1
1 and as it were a great mountain burning with fire 8:8
1 great star from heaven, burning as it were a lamp, ... 8:10
1 out of the pit, as the smoke of a great furnace; 9:2
1 as the scorpions of the earth have power. . . . . Rev 9:3
1 and their torment was as the torment of a scorpion, ... 9:5
1 on their heads were as it were crowns like gold, ... 9:7
1 and their faces were as the faces of men. 9:7
1 And they had hair as the hair of women, ... 9:8
1 and their teeth were as the teeth of lions. 9:8
1 had breastplates, as it were breastplates of iron; 9:9
1 sound of their wings was as the sound of chariots 9:9
1 the heads of the horses were as the heads of lions; 9:17
1 and his face was as it were the sun, ... 10:1
1 face was as ... the sun, and his feet as pillars of fire: . . . 10:1
1 as he hath declared to his servants the prophets. 10:7
1 but it shall be in thy mouth sweet as honey. 10:9
1 and it was in my mouth sweet as honey: 10:10
1 out of his mouth water as a flood after the woman, ... 12:15
1 and his feet were as the feet of a bear, ... 13:2
1 and his mouth as the mouth of a lion: 13:2
1 saw one of his heads as it were wounded to death; 13:3
1 two horns like a lamb, and he spake as a dragon. 13:11
1 a voice from heaven, as the voice of many waters, ... 14:2
1 and as the voice of a great thunder: 14:2
1 like the sound of harpists playing (NASB) 14:2
1 they sung as it were a new song before the throne, ... 14:3
1 I saw as it were a sea of glass mingled with fire: 15:2
1 the sea; and it became as the blood of a dead man; . . . 16:3
1 three unclean spirits like frogs; (NASB) 16:13
1 I come as a thief. Blessed is he that watcheth, ... 16:15
1 every stone about the weight of a talent: 16:21
1 but receive power as kings one hour with the beast. . . . 17:12
1 Reward her even as she rewarded you, ... 18:6
1 mighty angel took up a stone like a great millstone, . . . 18:21
1 I heard as it were, a loud voice (NASB) 19:1
1 I heard as it were the voice of a great multitude, ... 19:6
1 a great multitude, and as the voice of many waters, ... 19:6
1 and as the voice of mighty thunderings, saying, ... 19:6
1 His eyes were as a flame of fire, ... 19:12
1 the number of whom is as the sand of the sea. 20:8
1 prepared as a bride adorned for her husband. 21:2
1 even like a jasper stone, clear as crystal; 21:11
1 was pure gold, as it were transparent glass. 21:21
1 a pure river of water of life, clear as crystal, ... 22:1
1 to give every man according as his work shall be. 22:12

Hōs is a relative adverb which can also function as a conjunction. Its usage is fairly consistent throughout classical, Septuagint, and Koine Greek.

As a relative adverb *hōs* functions as a particle of comparison, introducing the model for comparison. In 1 Corinthians 3:15 Paul wrote, "He himself will be saved, but only *as* one escaping through the flames" (NIV). The individual on Paul's mind is compared to "one escaping through the flames." *Hōs* introduces the object of comparison.

As a relative adverb *hōs* can be used in ellipses (clauses with words removed). In 1 Corinthians 13:11, for example, Paul declared, "When I was a child, I spake *as* a child." The implication is "as a child *speaks.*" "Speaks" can be left out because of *hōs. Hōs* can also be an exclamation, "How!" (Romans 10:15). Further, it appears with numerals indicating degree or approximation. Mark 5:13 notes that the herd of pigs into which the legion of demons fled was "*about* two thousand in number" (NIV).

As a conjunction *hōs* can have several senses. First, it can be comparative, "as, like." Here *houtōs* (3643) may appear for emphasis. In Acts 23:11 the Lord says to Paul: "As (*hōs*) you have testified about me in Jerusalem, so (*houtōs*) you must also testify in Rome" (NIV). Again *hōs* introduces the clause of comparison. *Hōs* can also introduce an example. In 1 Peter 3:6, when Peter exhorted wives to be submissive, he used Sarah as an example ("*as* Sarah").

As a conjunction *hōs* is also temporal, "when" or "after." John 7:10 says, "However, *after* his brothers had left for the Feast, he went also" (NIV). *Hōs* can also introduce action which is contemporaneous to another action either present or past. In Luke 12:58 Jesus advised His hearers: "*As* you are going with your adversary . . . try hard to be reconciled to him" (NIV). With a present or imperfect tense verb *hōs* introduces action that occurs at the same time as the main action and is translated "when, while, as"; when used with an aorist tense verb *hōs* means "after" (see *Bauer*).

Hōs can also introduce indirect discourse with verbs of speaking or knowing. In Luke 24:6 the angel declared, "Remember *how* (that) he told you . . . " (NIV). Further, *hōs* can be used in a clause denoting purpose. In Acts 20:24 Paul said, "Neither count I my life dear unto myself, *so that* I might finish my course with joy."

Hōs thus has many uses and meanings depending upon the context and grammatical structures in which it appears; the interpreter must look at both before determining the meaning of this versatile particle.

Strong 5613, Bauer 897, Moulton-Milligan 703, Liddell-Scott 2038-40.

5445B. ὡσάν hōsan conj

As if, so to speak.

1. ὡσάν hōsan

1 **as if I would terrify you by my letters. (NASB)**.... **2 Co 10:9**

Hōsan appears in some manuscripts at 2 Corinthians 10:9. In this instance it would be the equivalent of *hōs an*, "as it were." Most scholars accept a reading of two separate words and regard *hōsan* as spurious.

Bauer 899, Liddell-Scott 2040.

5446. ὡσαννά hōsanna intrj

Hosanna.

1. ὡσαννά hōsanna

1 cried, saying, **Hosanna** to the son of David:........**Matt 21:9**
1 in the name of the Lord; **Hosanna** in the highest....... **21:9**
1 and saying, **Hosanna** to the son of David;............. **21:15**
1 cried, saying, **Hosanna**; Blessed is he that cometh..**Mark 11:9**
1 in the name of the Lord: **Hosanna** in the highest....... **11:10**
1 **Hosanna**: Blessed is the King of Israel............**John 12:13**

Hōsanna is a Greek transliteration of the Hebrew word *hôshîᵉah nā'*. The Aramaic word would be *hôshaʻ nā'*. The Hebrew itself comes from a combination of an imperative form of *yesha*, "save," and *nā'* which can be rendered "now" or "please." The resultant word thus means "save now!"

Septuagint Usage

The Septuagint does not read *hōsanna*, but it does reveal some interesting features behind the Hebrew equivalent. *Hôshîʻah nā'*, "hosanna" in English, appears, among other places, in Psalm 118:25 (LXX 117:25). The Septuagint translators replace it with the Greek word *sōson*, the imperative form of the word for "to save" (*sōzō* [4834]). Many translations treat it thus. The psalm is clearly messianic, and Jesus himself appealed to two passages within the psalm's immediate context: the prophecy about the stone rejected by the builders, which becomes the chief cornerstone (Psalm 118:22; cf. Matthew 21:42), and the prophetic element in the cry, "Blessed is he that cometh in the name of the Lord" (cf. Matthew 23:39). The cry of "Hosanna" occurs as a fulfillment of the (Psalm 118:26) prophecy when Jesus entered Jerusalem (cf. Matthew 21:9).

Thus the expression "hosanna!" comes from Psalm 118. This psalm becomes the basis for the famous Egyptian Hallel which includes Psalms 113–118. This must not be mistaken for the Great Hallel which consists of Psalms 120–136. The first-mentioned Hallel was sung on festive occasions throughout Israel's history—18 days and 1 night during the year. The 18 days included the day on which the Passover lamb was slaughtered in the temple, the first day of the Feast of Weeks (Pentecost), during the 8 days of the Feast of Tabernacles, and during the 8 days of the dedication feast of the temple (Hanukkah). The one night on which it was sung was the Passover night when people ate the Passover meal in their homes (Strack-Billerbeck, *Kommentar zum Neuen Testament*, 1:848).

New Testament Usage

Judaism of Jesus' day had adopted *hosanna* as a cultic cry, and it had messianic/eschatological overtones. When the people cried "Hosanna!" to Jesus ("he who comes in the name of the Lord"

[Matthew 23:39, NIV]) as He entered Jerusalem, this was a messianic proclamation. The "Coming One" was already recognized as a messianic title (Zechariah 9:9).

During the Feast of Tabernacles the celebrants sang the Hallel while they waved palm branches. Children took part in this as soon as they were old enough to wave the branches. Children, then, would be familiar with this custom from an early age. This explains why the children later greeted Jesus in the temple with the same shout of messianic recognition. The branches were called "hosannas," and the last day of the feast was known as the "Great Hosanna."

Hōsanna appears six times in the New Testament, all associated with the entrance of Christ into Jerusalem. The messianic expectation of the people was at a peak, and they cried, "Hosanna," in expectation of the fulfillment of the promises to Israel.

STRONG 5614, BAUER 899, MOULTON-MILLIGAN 703, KITTEL 9:682-84, LIDDELL-SCOTT 2040, COLIN BROWN 1:100.

5447. ὡσαύτως hōsautōs adv

Likewise, in the same way.

SYNONYMS:
ὁμοίως homoiōs (3532)
παραπλησίως paraplēsiōs (3759)

יַחְדָּו yachdāw (3267), Alike (Dt 12:22, 15:22).

כֵּן kēn (3772), Same, just as (Ex 7:11, Jos 11:15).

1. ὡσαύτως hōsautōs

1 Again he went out ... and did **likewise**............ Matt 20:5
1 And he came to the second, and said **likewise**......... 21:30
1 he sent other ... and they did unto them **likewise**....... 21:36
1 And **likewise** he that had received two,.............. 25:17
1 neither left he any seed: and the third **likewise**..... Mark 12:21
1 I will not deny thee ... **Likewise** also said they all...... 14:31
1 but, except ye repent, ye shall all **likewise** perish... Luke 13:3
1 repent, you will all **likewise** perish." (NASB).......... 13:5
1 third took her; and **in like manner** the seven also:..... 20:31
1 **Likewise** also the cup after supper, saying,............. 22:20
1 **Likewise** the Spirit also helpeth our infirmities:...... Rom 8:26
1 After the **same manner** also he took the cup,...... 1 Co 11:25
1 **In like manner** also, that women adorn themselves.. 1 Tm 2:9
1 **Likewise** must the deacons be grave,.................. 3:8
1 **Even so** must their wives be grave, not slanderers,...... 3:11
1 **Likewise** also the good works of some are manifest..... 5:25
1 The aged women **likewise**,.......................... Tit 2:3
1 Young men **likewise** exhort to be sober minded......... 2:6

An adverb of manner, this word was originally two words (*ho autos*) in Homeric literature (Eighth Century B.C.). In later literature it became one word and appeared in the form *hōsautōs*.

It appears frequently in the New Testament. It can be used with repetitions of the main verbal idea and is used to replace details concerning what was said or done as explained in a preceding verse or phrase (e.g., Matthew 20:5; 21:30,36). In doing so, this adverb can set up a comparison or contrast of two actions and the results these actions bring (1 Timothy 5:25). At times *hōsautōs* does not refer simply to one verbal idea but to several actions that are viewed as one event. Often this must be supplied from the context (*Bauer*; e.g., 1 Corinthians 11:25; 1 Timothy 3:8,11).

STRONG 5615, BAUER 899, MOULTON-MILLIGAN 703, LIDDELL-SCOTT 2040.

5448. ὡσεί hōsei adv

Like, as, about.

1. ὡσεί hōsei

1 he saw the Spirit of God descending **like** a dove,.... Matt 3:16
1 scattered abroad, **as** sheep having no shepherd......... 9:36
1 they that had eaten were **about** five thousand men,.... 14:21
1 was like lightning, and his raiment white **as** snow:..... 28:3
1 the keepers did shake, and became **as** dead men....... 28:4
1 and the Spirit **like** a dove descending upon him:.... Mark 1:10
1 that did eat ... were **about** five thousand men........... 6:44
1 **as** one dead; insomuch that many said, He is dead...... 9:26
1 And Mary abode with her **about** three months,...... Luke 1:56
1 descended in a bodily shape **like** a dove upon him,..... 3:22
1 Jesus himself began to be **about** thirty years of age,..... 3:23
1 For they were **about** five thousand men................. 9:14
1 in groups of **about** fifty each." (NASB)................ 9:14
1 And it came to pass **about** an eight days after these..... 9:28
1 he was withdrawn from them **about** a stone's cast,..... 22:41
1 and his sweat was **as** it were great drops of blood..... 22:44
1 And **about** the space of one hour after another........ 22:59
1 And it was **about** the sixth hour,..................... 23:44
1 And their words seemed to them **as** idle tales,......... 24:11
1 the Spirit descending from heaven **like** a dove,...... John 1:32
1 and it was **about** the sixth hour........................ 4:6
1 the men sat down, in number **about** five thousand....... 6:10
1 **about** the sixth hour: and he saith unto the Jews,...... 19:14
1 myrrh and aloes, **about** an hundred pound weight...... 19:39
1 a gathering of **about** one hundred (NASB).......... Acts 1:15
1 appeared unto them cloven tongues like **as** of fire,...... 2:3
1 were added unto them **about** three thousand souls....... 2:41
1 the number of the men was **about** five thousand......... 4:4
1 to whom a number of men, **about** four hundred,......... 5:36
1 saw his face **as** it had been the face of an angel......... 6:15
1 there fell from his eyes **as it had been** scales:........... 9:18
1 a vision evidently **about** the ninth hour of the day..... 10:3
1 And all the men were **about** twelve.................. 19:7
1 to God **as** those alive from the dead, (NASB)....... Rom 6:13
1 And **as** a vesture shalt thou fold them up,........... Heb 1:12
1 **as** the sand which is by the sea shore innumerable..... 11:12
1 His head and his hairs were white **like** wool,......... Rev 1:14

This particle of comparison is primarily used in three ways in the New Testament. First, it is used in contexts where some supernatural event is described in tangible terms (Matthew 3:16; Mark 1:10; 9:26; Acts 2:3; 6:15; 9:18; Hebrews 1:12). Second, Paul used it in an ethical/moral challenge to the believers at Rome: that the members of their bodies should not be used for wickedness but should be given to God "*as* instruments of righteousness" (some texts of 6:13). Third, *hōsei* is used in association with numbers and serves as a statement of estimation, "about" (e.g., Matthew 14:21; John 6:10; Acts 2:41; 5:36).

STRONG 5616, BAUER 899, MOULTON-MILLIGAN 703, LIDDELL-SCOTT 2040.

5449. Ὠσηέ Osēe name

Hosea.

1. Ὠσηέ Osēe masc
2. Ὡσηέ Hōsēe masc

1 As he saith also in Osee, ... Rom 9:25

A prophet of the Old Testament whom Paul quoted by name at Romans 9:25f.

5450. ὥσπερ hōsper conj

As, just as.

SYNONYMS:
καθάπερ kathaper (2481)
καθώς kathōs (2503)

1. ὥσπερ hōsper

1 even as your Father which is in heaven is perfect.... Matt 5:48
1 as the hypocrites do in the synagogues 6:2
1 thou shalt not be as the hypocrites are: 6:5
1 use not vain repetitions, as the heathen do: 6:7
1 Moreover when ye fast, be not, as the hypocrites, ... 6:16
1 For as Jonas was three days ... in the whale's belly; ... 12:40
1 As therefore the tares are gathered and burned 13:40
1 let him be unto thee as a heathen man 18:17
1 Even as the Son of man came not to be ministered 20:28
1 For as the lightning cometh out of the east, ... 24:27
1 But as the days of Noe were, so shall also 24:37
1 For as in the days that were before the flood 24:38
1 is as a man travelling into a far country, ... 25:14
1 as a shepherd divideth his sheep from the goats: 25:32
1 For as the lightning, that lighteneth out of .... Luke 17:24
1 God, I thank thee, that I am not as other men are, ... 18:11
1 For as the Father raiseth up the dead, ... John 5:21
1 For as the Father hath life in himself; 5:26
1 a sound from heaven as of a rushing mighty wind, ... Acts 2:2
1 through ignorance ye did ... as did also your rulers...... 3:17
1 Holy Ghost fell on them, as on us at the beginning.... 11:15
1 as by one man sin entered into the world, ... Rom 5:12
1 For as by one man's disobedience many were 5:19
1 That as sin hath reigned unto death, ... 5:21
1 that like as Christ was raised up from the dead 6:4
1 for as ye have yielded your members 6:19
1 For as ye in times past have not believed God, ... 11:30
1 as there be gods many, and lords many, ... 1 Co 8:5
1 as it is written, "The people sat down to eat (NIV) 10:7
1 For as the woman is of the man, ... 11:12
1 For as in Adam all die, even so in Christ shall all 15:22
1 as I have given order to the churches of Galatia, ... 16:1
1 knowing, that as ye are partakers of the sufferings, .. 2 Co 1:7
1 Therefore, as ye abound in every thing, in faith, ... 8:7
1 as a matter of bounty, and not as of covetousness....... 9:5
1 But as then he that was born after the flesh .... Gal 4:29
1 Therefore as the church is subject unto Christ, ... Eph 5:24
1 as travail upon a woman with child; .... 1 Th 5:3
1 ceased from his own works, as God did from his..... Heb 4:10
1 as those high priests, to offer up sacrifice, ... 7:27
1 as the high priest entereth into the holy place 9:25
1 For as the body without the spirit is dead, so faith ... Jas 2:26
1 cried with a loud voice, as when a lion roareth: ..... Rev 10:3

This adverb of manner appears frequently in the New Testament in the protasis (i.e., that to which the main idea is being compared) of a comparison. For example, "*As* Jonah was three days and three nights in the whale's belly; so shall the Son of man be three days and three nights in the heart of the earth" (Matthew 12:40). Sometimes the author seems to leave a thought or comparison incomplete (called an anacoluthon), and the main thought (apodosis) has to be supplied from the context and general flow of thought (e.g., Matthew 25:14; Romans 5:12). In 2 Corinthians 8:7 *hōsper* functions with *hina kai* and the subjunctive to take the place of the imperative (*Bauer*). Also, *hōsper* is used to connect what follows with what has gone before (ibid., e.g., Matthew 6:7; Luke 18:11; Acts 3:17; 1 Corinthians 8:5).

STRONG 5618, BAUER 899, MOULTON-MILLIGAN 703-4, LIDDELL-SCOTT 2040.

5451. ὡσπερεί hōsperei conj

As, as it were.

1. ὡσπερεί hōsperei

1 seen of me also, as of one born out of due time.... 1 Co 15:8

A rare word in New Testament literature, *hōsperei* appears only in 1 Corinthians 15:8 and in a variant reading of 1 Corinthians 4:13. In both instances the word is in a comparison in which Paul was seeking to establish that in and of himself he was nothing. This was in sharp contrast to the "super apostles" who were causing division in Corinth and were experts at promoting themselves and their own cause.

STRONG 5619, BAUER 899, MOULTON-MILLIGAN 704, LIDDELL-SCOTT 2040.

5452. ὥστε hōste conj

Therefore, for this reason, in order that, so that.

1. ὥστε hōste

1 insomuch that the ship was covered with the waves: Matt 8:24
1 so that no man might pass by that way................. 8:28
1 unclean spirits, to cast them out, (NT) 10:1
1 Wherefore it is lawful to do well on the sabbath 12:12
1 insomuch ... blind and dumb both spake and saw...... 12:22
1 great multitudes ... so that he went into a ship, ... 13:2
1 so that the birds of the air come and lodge 13:32
1 insomuch that they were astonished, ... 13:54
1 Insomuch that the multitude wondered, ... 15:31
1 so much bread ... as to fill so great a multitude? 15:33
1 Wherefore they are no more twain, but one flesh...... 19:6
1 Wherefore ye be witnesses unto yourselves, ... 23:31

1 **insomuch** that, if it were possible, ... Matt 24:24
1 against Jesus to put him to death: (NT) 27:1
1 **insomuch** that the governor marvelled greatly.......... 27:14
1 **insomuch** that they questioned among themselves, ... Mark 1:27
1 **insomuch** that Jesus could no more openly enter 1:45
1 **insomuch** that there was no room to receive them, ... 2:2
1 **that** they were all amazed, and glorified God, ... 2:12
1 **Therefore** the Son of man is Lord also 2:28
1 **insomuch** that they pressed upon him 3:10
1 **so that** they could not so much as eat bread............ 3:20
1 **so that** he entered into a ship, and sat in the sea; 4:1
1 **so that** the fowls of the air may lodge 4:32
1 waves beat into the ship, **so that** it was now full......... 4:37
1 as one dead; **insomuch** that many said, He is dead...... 9:26
1 **so then** they are no more twain, but one flesh......... 10:8
1 yet answered nothing; **so that** Pilate marvelled......... 15:5
1 **in order** to throw Him down the cliff. (NASB) ...... Luke 4:29
1 filled both the ships, **so that** they began to sink......... 5:7
1 village of the Samaritans, to make ready (NT) 9:52
1 **insomuch** that they trode one upon another, ... 12:1
1 **so as** to deliver Him up to the rule (NASB) 20:20
1 **that** he gave his only begotten Son, ... John 3:16
1 **insomuch as** that field is called ... field of blood...... Acts 1:19
1 **Insomuch** that they brought forth the sick 5:15
1 and so spake, **that** a great multitude ... believed........ 14:1
1 And the contention was **so** sharp between them, ... 15:39
1 **so that** the foundations of the prison were shaken: 16:26
1 **so that** all they which dwelt in Asia heard the word 19:10
1 **So that** from his body were brought unto the sick 19:12
1 **so that** they fled out of that house naked 19:16
1 **Wherefore,** my brethren, ye also are become dead ... Rom 7:4
1 **that** we should serve in newness of spirit, ... 7:6
1 **Wherefore** the law is holy, ... 7:12
1 **Whosoever** therefore resisteth the power, ... 13:2
1 **so that** from Jerusalem, ... 15:19
1 **So that** ye come behind in no gift; .... 1 Co 1:7
1 **So then** neither is he that planteth any thing, ... 3:7
1 **Therefore** let no man glory in men..................... 3:21
1 **Therefore** judge nothing before the time, ... 4:5
1 **that** one should have his father's wife................. 5:1
1 **Therefore** let us keep the feast, ... 5:8
1 **So then** he that giveth her in marriage doeth well; 7:38
1 **Wherefore** let him that thinketh he standeth 10:12
1 **Wherefore** whosoever shall eat this bread, ... 11:27
1 **Wherefore,** my brethren, when ye come together 11:33
1 have all faith, **so that** I could remove mountains, ... 13:2
1 **Wherefore** tongues are for a sign, ... 14:22
1 **Wherefore,** brethren, covet to prophesy, ... 14:39
1 **Therefore,** my beloved brethren, be ye stedfast, ... 15:58
1 **insomuch** that we despaired even of life: .... 2 Co 1:8
1 **So that** contrariwise ye ought rather to forgive 2:7
1 **so that** the children of Israel could not 3:7
1 **So then** death worketh in us, but life in you............ 4:12
1 **Wherefore** henceforth know we no man 5:16
1 **Therefore** if any man be in Christ, ... 5:17
1 **so that** I rejoiced the more........................... 7:7
1 **insomuch** that Barnabas also was carried away .... Gal 2:13
1 **So then** they which be of faith are blessed 3:9
1 **Wherefore** the law was our schoolmaster 3:24
1 **Wherefore** thou art no more a servant, but a son; 4:7
1 Am I **therefore** become your enemy, ... 4:16
1 **So that** my bonds in Christ are manifest .... Phlp 1:13
1 **Wherefore,** my beloved, as ye have always obeyed, ... 2:12
1 **Therefore,** my brethren, dearly beloved 4:1
1 **So that** ye were ensamples to all that believe .... 1 Th 1:7
1 **so that** we need not to speak any thing................ 1:8
1 **Wherefore** comfort one another with these words........ 4:18
1 **So that** we ourselves glory in you in the churches ... 2 Th 1:4
1 **so that** he as God sitteth in the temple of God, ... 2:4
1 **So that** we may boldly say, The Lord is my helper, Heb 13:6
1 **Wherefore,** my beloved brethren, ... Jas 1:19
1 **that** your faith and hope might be in God........... 1 Pt 1:21
1 **Wherefore** let them that suffer according to 4:19

This term primarily serves two purposes in the New Testament. First, it functions as a particle with the infinitive to indicate an infinitive of result (Mark 2:12; Luke 5:7: "They came and filled both boats so full that [*hōste*] they began to sink" [NIV]). As such, it relies on the context to determine whether an intended result or indirect result is at work. As an indicator of result *hōste* is most often translated "therefore, so that, as a result, so then, so."

Second, *hōste* functions with the indicative, imperative, and subjunctive moods to form independent clauses indicating purpose (Romans 7:4; 1 Corinthians 3:7; Philippians 2:12). In these cases the implication is that what has preceded has served as the means (Louw and Nida, *Greek-English Lexicon,* 1:785). As an indicator of purpose *hōste* overlaps significantly with its use as an indicator of intended result—to the point that the two are nearly indistinguishable (Blass and DeBrunner, *Greek Grammar of the New Testament,* p.198). The most common ways *hōste* is translated in these instances are: "so, then, in order to, therefore."

STRONG 5620, BAUER 899-900, MOULTON-MILLIGAN 704, LIDDELL-SCOTT 2040-41.

5453. ὡς hōs

See word study at number 5445A.

5453B. ὠτάριον ōtarion noun

Ear.

1. ὠτάριον ōtarion nom/acc sing neu

1 slave of the high priest, ... cut off his **ear.** (NASB) Mark 14:47
1 slave, and cut off his right **ear.** (NASB)........... John 18:10

As the diminutive form of *ous* (3638B), "ear," *ōtarion* could mean "a little ear" (see *Liddell-Scott*); however, in later Hellenistic Greek the two terms are basically equivalent. The papyri show cases where *ōtarion* is figuratively translated in reference to the "handle" of a vessel (*Moulton-Milligan*). In its two New Testament occurrences, Mark 14:47 and John 18:10 (the *Textus Receptus* shows *ōtion* [5454]), the word simply means "an ear," specifically, the ear of Malchus which Peter cut off with a sword.

BAUER 900, MOULTON-MILLIGAN 704, KITTEL 5:559, LIDDELL-SCOTT 2041.

5454. ὠτίον ōtion noun

Ear, outer ear.

אֹזֶן 'ōzen (238), Ear (Dt 15:17, Am 3:12); revelation (1 Sm 22:8).

1. ὠτίου ōtiou gen sing neu

2. ὠτίον ōtion nom/acc sing neu

2 and struck a servant ... and smote off his ear....... Matt 26:51
2 smote a servant of the high priest, ... cut off his ear. Mark 14:47
1 And he touched his ear, and healed him........... Luke 22:51
2 smote the ... servant, and cut off his right ear...... John 18:10
2 being his kinsman whose ear Peter cut off,............ 18:26

Classical Greek and Septuagint Usage

A diminutive of *ous* (3638B), "ear," *ōtion* is rarely found in classical Greek where it is used literally of the ear and metaphorically of a small handle or the handle of a kettle. The Septuagint uses *ōtion* to translate the Hebrew word *'ōzen.* While it is used of the literal, physical ear (Deuteronomy 15:17; Amos 3:12; Ecclesiasticus 21:5), it is primarily used as a figurative expression. As such, *ōtion* appears most frequently to denote the revealing or disclosure of something to someone. It is used of God revealing His will and plans to His servants (1 Samuel 9:15 [LXX 1 Kings 9:15]; 2 Samuel 7:27) and of individuals revealing plans to someone (1 Samuel [LXX 1 Kings] 20:2,13; 22:8,17). In the parallel passages of 2 Samuel 22:45 (LXX 2 Kings 22:45) and Psalm 18:44 (17:44) foreigners are said to have "heard of" (*akoēn ōtiou*) David's reputation. In Isaiah 50:5 and 55:3 it is used in expressions denoting the inner preparation necessary to receive the revelation of God's divine will.

New Testament Usage

In the New Testament this word continues the literal usage indicating the outer ear. At Jesus' arrest Peter drew his sword and cut off the ear of the high priest's servant (Matthew 26:51; cf. the parallel passages Mark 14:47 [Textus Receptus]; Luke 22:51; and John 18:10 [p66 Aleph D], 18:26).

STRONG 5621, BAUER 900, MOULTON-MILLIGAN 704, KITTEL 5:558, LIDDELL-SCOTT 2041.

5455. ὠφέλεια ōpheleia noun

Use, gain, profit, benefit, help, aid, advantage.

CROSS-REFERENCE:

ὠφελέω ōpheleō (5456)

בֶּצַע betsa' (1240), Gain, profit (Job 22:3, Ps 30:9 [29:9]).

יָעַל yā'al (3385), hiphil: gain something (Job 21:15).

1. ὠφέλεια ōpheleia nom sing fem

2. ὠφελείας ōpheleias gen sing fem

1 or what profit is there of circumcision?............ Rom 3:1
2 men's persons in admiration because of advantage... Jude 1:16

Classical Greek

The noun *ōpheleia,* "profit, advantage, benefit," is an alternative form of *ophelia* which comes from a stem meaning to "help" or "aid." Another member of this word group is the verb *ōpheleō* (5456), "to give help," and the adjective *ōphelimos* (5457), "useful, usable." Primarily, then, *ōpheleia* means "help, aid, advantage, profit."

Septuagint Usage

Only five canonical instances of *opheleia* appear in the Septuagint. It follows essentially the classical range of definition. It refers to personal "advantage" (e.g., Psalm 30:9 [LXX 29:9]; Job 21:15) or private "benefit" (Job 22:3, NIV and KJV read "pleasure"). The idea of "help" also comes through in some texts (Isaiah 30:5; Jeremiah 46:11 [LXX 26:11]).

New Testament Usage

ōpheleia occurs only twice in the New Testament (Romans 3:1; Jude 16) (cf. the adjective *ōphelimos,* only in the Pastoral Epistles: 1 Timothy 4:8; 2 Timothy 3:16; Titus 3:8). Paul raised the question, "What *advantage* (*ōpheleia*) . . . is there in circumcision?" (Romans 3:1, NIV). His answer may surprise us, for he said, "Much in every way!" Earlier Paul stated that circumcision did have value (*ōpheleō*) but only if the Law were kept (Romans 2:25). Paul was not saying that keeping the Law thus has value; rather, his point is that circumcision is of value *only* if one is obedient. The advantage for the Jew (the circumcised one) is in being the initial recipient of God's revelation through His Word.

The usage in Jude 16 is negative. Here *ōpheleia* emphasizes the self-centeredness of the ungodly. Because these men lack the Spirit, they concern themselves with satisfying their "natural" (*psuchikos* [5426]) desires (verse 19).

STRONG 5622, BAUER 900, MOULTON-MILLIGAN 704, LIDDELL-SCOTT 2041-42.

5456. ὠφελέω ōpheleō verb

To help, aid, be of benefit to.

COGNATES:

ὠφέλεια ōpheleia (5455)
ὠφέλιμος ōphelimos (5457)

SYNONYMS:

ἀμύνομαι amunomai (290)
ἀντέχομαι antechomai (469)
ἀντιλαμβάνομαι antilambanomai (479)
βοηθέω boētheō (990)
ἐλεέω eleeō (1640)
παραγίνομαι paraginomai (3716)

συλλαμβάνω sullambanō (4666)
συμβάλλω sumballō (4671)
συμφέρω sumpherō (4702)
συναντιλαμβάνομαι sunantilambanomai (4729)

יָעַל yāʻal (3385), Hiphil: profit (Prv 10:2, Jer 2:11, Hb 2:18).

נָשָׁא nāshâʼ (5565), Lend (Jer 15:10).

עָזַר ʻāzar (6038), Help (Is 30:7).

שׁוּב shûv (8178), Return; hiphil: refresh (Prv 25:13).

1. **ὠφελεῖ** **ōphelei** 3sing indic pres act
2. **ὠφελεῖτε** **ōpheleite** 2pl indic pres act
3. **ὠφέλησεν** **ōphelēsen** 3sing indic aor act
4. **ὠφελήσω** **ōphelēsō** 1sing indic fut act
5. **ὠφελήσει** **ōphelēsei** 3sing indic fut act
6. **ὠφελοῦμαι** **ōpheloumai** 1sing indic pres mid
7. **ὠφελεῖται** **ōpheleitai** 3sing indic pres mid
8. **ὠφελήθησαν** **ōphelēthēsan** 3pl indic aor pass
9. **ὠφεληθῇς** **ōphelēthēs** 2sing subj aor pass
10. **ὠφεληθεῖσα** **ōphelētheisa** nom sing fem part aor pass
11. **ὠφεληθήσεται** **ōphelēthēsetai** 3sing indic fut pass

9 by whatsoever **thou mightest be profited** by me; ... Matt 15:5
7 For what is a man **profited**, ... 16:26
1 When Pilate saw that he **could prevail nothing**, ... 27:24
10 spent all that she had, and was nothing **bettered**, .. Mark 5:26
9 by whatsoever **thou mightest be profited** by me; 7:11
5 For what **shall it profit** a man, if he shall gain 8:36
7 what is a man **advantaged**, ... gain the whole world, Luke 9:25
1 spirit that quickeneth; the flesh **profiteth** nothing: .. John 6:63
2 Perceive ye how ye **prevail** nothing? 12:19
1 circumcision verily **profiteth**, if thou keep the law: .. Rom 2:25
6 and have not charity, it **profiteth** me nothing. ..... 1 Co 13:3
4 speaking with tongues, what **shall I profit** you, ... 14:6
5 Christ **shall profit** you nothing. .... Gal 5:2
3 but the word preached **did** not **profit** them, ... Heb 4:2
8 not with meats, which **have** not **profited** them 13:9

Classical Greek

This general term for various expressions of help, aid, benefit, or service is found extensively throughout the history of classical Greek. Its range of meanings in the active voice includes "to be of use (or) service, to enrich, to render service"; and in the passive voice "receive help, derive profit/ advantage" from something or someone (*Liddell-Scott*).

Septuagint Usage

In 12 of the 16 occurrences where *ōpheleō* translates a Hebrew term in the Septuagint, this word is *yāʻal.* The use of *ōpheleō* in the Septuagint takes on a tone of judgment in many places. It primarily appears in the books of Isaiah and Jeremiah and is often part of passages that denounce the useless efforts of the Jews to live a meaningful existence outside of the covenant with the Lord. Those to whom God's people turned for help instead of Him are characterized by the term *ōpheleō*: idols and false gods are worthless and of no value (Isaiah 44:9; Habakkuk 2:18); political alliances that are contrary to God's plan are useless (Isaiah 30:5,6); the abilities of the astrologers and sorcerers to deliver Israel from judgment are ridiculed (Isaiah 47:12); the works and righteousness of Israel were judged to be of no benefit (Isaiah 57:12); the false prophets did not benefit God's people (Jeremiah 23:32). Also, Proverbs states that wealth acquired by immoral means is to be considered of no value (Proverbs 10:2), and wealth in general is deemed to be worthless and of no benefit on the day of judgment (Proverbs 11:4).

New Testament Usage

The use of *ōpheleō* in the New Testament continues that which is seen in both classical Greek and the Septuagint. The general nature of the word makes it necessary for the reader to supply from the context the specific identity of what is being valued or gained. For example, in Matthew 16:26 Jesus placed the accumulation of wealth in its eternal perspective (cf. Mark 8:36 and Luke 9:25) by challenging His listeners to see that the only true profit comes through a life of self-denial and discipleship. Similarly it is used of financial gain in Matthew 15:5 and Mark 7:11 where Jesus confronted the traditions of the Jews with the spirit of the Law.

Paul employed *ōpheleō* twice in 1 Corinthians (13:3 and 14:6) where he sought to articulate the absolute necessity of love. One way this love will be expressed is by benefiting those in the body of Christ through the proper use of the gifts.

In terms of spiritual benefit, Paul reminded the Galatians (5:2) that should they again subject themselves to the rite of circumcision as a sign of their acceptance of the Judaizers' message, then Christ would be of no advantage to them; i.e., they would be returning to a salvation based on the efforts of man rather than on the liberating power of Christ. The writer to the Hebrews (4:2) reminded his readers that in order for the promise of entering God's rest to be fulfilled, it must be met with faith on the part of the believer.

STRONG 5623, BAUER 900, MOULTON-MILLIGAN 705, LIDDELL-SCOTT 2041-42.

5457. ὠφέλιμος ōphelimos adj

Beneficial, useful.

COGNATE:
ὠφελέω ōpheleō (5456)

SYNONYM:
εὔχρηστος euchrēstos (2154)

1. ὠφέλιμος ōphelimos nom sing fem
2. ὠφέλιμα ōphelima nom/acc pl neu

1 For bodily exercise **profiteth** little: .... 1 Tm 4:8
1 but godliness is **profitable** unto all things, ... 4:8
1 and is **profitable** for doctrine, for reproof, ... 2 Tm 3:16
2 These things are good and **profitable** unto men. .... Tit 3:8

This adjective is used in classical Greek primarily of objects and infrequently of people. While it does not occur in the Septuagint, its related noun (*ōpheleia* [5455]) and verb (*ōpheleō* [5456]) forms are both better attested in classical, Septuagintal, and Koine Greek.

In the New Testament *ōphelimos* is confined to the Pastoral Epistles. In 1 Timothy 4:8 Paul used it to describe the difference in value between bodily exercise and personal godliness. The first has temporal benefit, but the second is profitable not only for this life but also for eternity. It is used in 2 Timothy 3:16 of Scripture; i.e., it is useful or beneficial because it accomplishes its purposes. And finally, it is found in Titus 3:8 where it describes the good deeds (cf. 3:1-3) that benefit people not only by positively affecting others but by drawing them to the truth of the gospel as well (Fee, *Good News Commentary, 1 and 2 Timothy, and Titus*, p.162).

STRONG 5624, BAUER 900, MOULTON-MILLIGAN 705, LIDDELL-SCOTT 2041-42.

Bibliography

Resource Tools

BAUER (BAGD)
Bauer, Walter, William F. Arndt, and F. Wilbur Gingrich. *A Greek-English Lexicon of the New Testament and other Early Christian Literature.* Rev. ed. by F. Wilbur Gingrich and Frederick W. Danker. Chicago: The University of Chicago Press. 1979.

COLIN BROWN (NIDNTT)
Brown, Colin, ed. *The New International Dictionary of New Testament Theology.* 4 vols. Grand Rapids: Zondervan Publishing House. 1975.

KITTEL (TDNT)
Kittel, G., and G. Friedrich. *Theological Dictionary of the New Testament.* Trans. by G. W. Bromiley. 10 vols. Grand Rapids: William B. Eerdmans Publishing Co. 1972.

LIDDELL–SCOTT (LSJ)
Liddell, H. G., and R. Scott. *A Greek-English Lexicon.* 9th. ed. Ed. by H. Stuart Jones and R. McKenzie. Oxford: Clarendon. 1940.

MOULTON–MILLIGAN (M-M)
Moulton, J.H., and G. Milligan. *The Vocabulary of the Greek Testament Illustrated from the Papyri and Other Non-Literary Sources.* London: Hodder and Stoughton. 1914–1930. Reprint. Grand Rapids: Wm. B. Eerdmans Publishing Company. 1985.

STRONG
Strong, James. *The Exhaustive Concordance of the Bible.* 1890. Reprint. Nashville: Abingdon Press. 1977.

(Parenthetical abbreviations found in Study Bible.)

Modern Greek Texts

Aland, K. et al. in cooperation with the Institute for New Testament Textual Research. *The Greek New Testament.* 2nd ed. London: United Bible Societies. 1968. (Also known as UBS.)

Aland, K. et al. in cooperation with the Institute for New Testament Textual Research. *The Greek New Testament.* 3rd ed. New York: United Bible Societies. 1975. (Also known as UBS.)

Nestle, E., and K. Aland. *Novum Testamentum Graece.* 25th ed. Stuttgart: Wurtembergische Bibelanstalt. 1963. (Also known as Nestle-Aland or NA 25.)

Nestle, E., and K. Aland. et al. *Novum Testamentum Graece.* 26th ed. Stuttgart: Deutsche Bibelstiftung. 1979. (Also known as Nestle-Aland or NA 26.)

General Bibliography

Abbott, T. K. *Ephesians and Colossians. The International Critical Commentary.* Ed. by S. R. Driver, A. Plummer, and C. A. Briggs. Edinburgh: T. and T. Clark. 1968.

Abbott-Smith, G. *A Manual Greek Lexicon of the New Testament.* New York: Charles Scribner's Sons. 1937.

Achtemeier, Paul J. *Harper's Bible Dictionary.* New York: Harper and Row. 1985.

Aharoni, Yohanan, and Michael Avi-Yonah. *The Macmillan Bible Atlas.* Rev. ed. New York: Macmillan and Company. 1977.

Albright, W. F., and C. S. Mann. *Matthew.* Vol. 26 of *The Anchor Bible.* Ed. by William Foxwell Albright and David Noel Freedman. Garden City, NY: Doubleday and Company, Inc. 1971.

Alford, Henry. *Alford's Greek Testament.* 3 vols. Grand Rapids: Baker Book House. 1980.

Allen, W. C. *A Critical and Exegetical Commentary on the Gospel According to St. Matthew. The International Critical Commentary.* Ed. by S. R. Driver, A. Plummer, and C. A. Briggs. Edinburgh: T. and T. Clark. 1912.

Archer, Gleason L. *Encyclopedia of Bible Difficulties.* Grand Rapids: Zondervan Publishing House. 1982.

Austin, M. M., and P. Vidal-Nacquet. *Economic and Social History of Ancient Greece.* Trans. by M. M. Austin. Los Angeles: University of California Press. 1977.

Autenreith, Georg. *A Homeric Dictionary.* Trans. by Robert P. Keep. Norman, OK: University of Oklahoma Press. 1972.

Barclay, William. *The Gospel of John. The Daily Study Bible.* Rev. ed. Philadelphia: The Westminster Press. 1975.

Barclay, William. *The Gospel of Mark. The Daily Study Bible.* Rev. ed. Philadelphia: The Westminster Press. 1975.

Barclay, William. "Great Themes of the New Testament." *Expository Times* 70 (1958): 292–296.

Barclay, William. *New Testament Words.* Philadelphia: The Westminster Press. 1974.

Barrett, C. K. *A Commentary on the Epistle to the Romans. Harper's New Testament Commentaries.* Ed. by Henry Chadwick. New York: Harper and Row. 1957.

Barrett, C. K. *A Commentary on the First Epistle to the Corinthians. Harper's New Testament Commentaries.* Ed. by Henry Chadwick. New York: Harper and Row. 1968.

Barrett, C. K. *The New Testament Background: Selected Documents.* New York: Harper and Row. 1961.

Barth, Karl. *The Epistle to the Romans.* Trans. by Edwyn C. Hoskyns. London: Oxford University Press. 1933.

Barth, Karl. *The Word of God and the Word of Man.* Trans. by Douglas Horton. New York: Harper and Brothers, Publishers. 1957.

Barth, Markus. *Ephesians.* Vols. 24 and 24a of *The Anchor Bible.* Ed. by William Foxwell Albright and David Noel Freedman. Garden City, NY: Doubleday and Company, Inc. 1974.

Bauckham, Richard J. *Jude, 2 Peter.* Vol. 50 of *Word Biblical Commentary.* Ed. by David A. Hubbard, et al. Waco, TX: Word Books. 1983.

Bauer, Walter. *Griechisch-deutesches Worterbuch zu den Schriften des Neuen Testaments und der fruhchristlichen Literatur.* Ed. by Kurt and Barbara Aland. New York: Walter de Gruyter. 1988.

Bauer, Walter, William F. Arndt, and F. Wilbur Gingrich. *A Greek-English Lexicon of the New Testament and other Early Christian Literature*. Rev. ed. by F. Wilbur Gingrich and Frederick W. Danker. Chicago: The University of Chicago Press. 1979.

Baylis, Charles P. "The Woman Caught in Adultery: A Test of Jesus as the Greater Prophet." *Biblio Theca Sacra* 146 (April–June 1989): 171–184.

Beasley-Murray, G. R. *Baptism in the New Testament*. Grand Rapids: William B. Eerdmans Publishing Co. 1973.

Beasley-Murray, G. R. *Revelation. New Century Bible Commentary*. Ed. by Matthew Black. Grand Rapids: William B. Eerdmans Publishing Co. 1981.

Beiderwolf, William Edward. *The Second Coming Bible*. Grand Rapids: Baker Book House. 1972.

Bickerman, E. J. "The Name of Christians." *Harvard Theological Review* 42, no. 2 (April 1949): 109–124.

Bigg, Charles. *A Critical and Exegetical Commentary on the Epistles of St. Peter and St. Jude. The International Critical Commentary*. Ed. by S. R. Driver, A. Plummer, and C. A. Briggs. Edinburgh: T. and T. Clark. 1978.

Black, David Alan. "Ephesian Address." *Grace Theological Journal* 2 (1981): 59–73.

Blass, F. *Philology of the Gospels*. Amsterdam: B. R. Gruner. 1969.

Blass, F., and A. DeBrunner. *A Greek Grammar of the New Testament and Other Early Christian Literature*. Trans. by Robert W. Funk. Chicago: The University of Chicago Press. 1974.

Blum, Edwin A. *2 Peter*. In *Hebrews–Revelation*. Vol. 12 of *The Expositor's Bible Commentary*. Ed. by Frank E. Gaebelein. Grand Rapids: Zondervan Publishing House. 1981.

Bornkamm, Gunther. *Jesus of Nazareth*. Trans. by Irene and Fraser McLuskey. New York: Harper. 1960.

Botterweck, G. Johannes, and Helmer Ringgren, eds. *Theological Dictionary of the Old Testament*. 5 vols. Trans. by Geoffrey Bromiley, et al. Grand Rapids: William B. Eerdmans Publishing Co. 1974.

Bowra, C. M., trans. *Pindar–The Odes*. London: Penguin Books. 1988.

Bromiley, Geoffrey W., ed. *The International Standard Bible Encyclopedia*. 4 vols. Grand Rapids: William B. Eerdmans Publishing Co. 1979.

Brown, Colin, ed. *The New International Dictionary of New Testament Theology*. 4 vols. Grand Rapids: Zondervan Publishing House. 1975.

Brown, Francis, Samuel Driver, and Charles A. Briggs. *The New Brown-Driver-Briggs-Gesenius Hebrew and English Lexicon of the Old Testament*. Peabody, MA: Hendrickson Publishers. 1979.

Brown, Raymond E. *The Epistles of John*. Vol. 30 of *The Anchor Bible*. Ed. by William Foxwell Albright and David Noel Freedman. Garden City, NY: Doubleday and Company, Inc. 1982.

Brown, Raymond E. *The Gospel According to St. John*. Vols. 29 and 29a of *The Anchor Bible*. Ed. by William Foxwell Albright and David Noel Freedman. Garden City, NY: Doubleday and Company, Inc. 1978.

Bruce, A. B. *The Synoptic Gospels*. In *The Synoptic Gospels and John*. Vol. 1 of *The Expositor's Greek Testament*. Ed. by W. Robertson Nicoll. Grand Rapids: William B. Eerdmans Publishing Co. 1951.

Bruce, F. F. *The Acts of the Apostles*. Vol. 5 of *Tyndale New Testament Commentaries*. Ed. by R. V. G. Tasker. Grand Rapids: William B. Eerdmans Publishing Co. 1952.

Bruce, F. F. *The Acts of the Apostles: The Greek Text*. London: The Tyndale Press. 1956.

Bruce, F. F. *The Book of Acts. The New International Commentary on the New Testament.* Ed. by F. F. Bruce. Grand Rapids: William B. Eerdmans Publishing Co. 1979.

Bruce, F. F. *The Epistle to the Hebrews. The New International Commentary on the New Testament.* Ed. by F. F. Bruce. Grand Rapids: William B. Eerdmans Publishing Co. 1964.

Bruce, F. F. *The Epistle of Paul to the Romans.* Vol. 6 of *Tyndale New Testament Commentaries.* Ed. by R. V. G. Tasker. Grand Rapids: William B. Eerdmans Publishing Co. 1963.

Bruce, F. F. *The Epistles to the Colossians, to Philemon, and to the Ephesians. The New International Commentary on the New Testament.* Ed. by F. F. Bruce. Grand Rapids: William B. Eerdmans Publishing Co. 1984.

Bruce, F. F. *The Epistles of John.* Grand Rapids: William B. Eerdmans Publishing Co. 1983.

Bruce, F. F. *1 and 2 Thessalonians. Word Biblical Commentary.* Ed. by David A. Hubbard, et al. Waco, TX: Word Books. 1982.

Bruce, F. F. *Galatians. New International Greek Testament Commentary.* Ed. by I. Howard Marshall and W. Ward Gasque. Grand Rapids: William B. Eerdmans Publishing Co. 1982.

Bruce, F. F. *The Gospel of John: Introduction, Exposition, and Notes.* Grand Rapids: William B. Eerdmans Publishing Co. 1983.

Bruce, F. F. *The Hard Sayings of Jesus. The Jesus Library.* Ed. by Michael Green. Downers Grove, IL: Inter-Varsity Press. 1983.

Bruce, F. F. *New Testament Development of Old Testament Themes.* Grand Rapids: William B. Eerdmans Publishing Co. 1969.

Bruce, F. F. *Paul, Apostle of the Heart Set Free.* Grand Rapids: William B. Eerdmans Publishing Co. 1977.

Bruce, F. F. *Second Thoughts on the Dead Sea Scrolls.* Grand Rapids: William B. Eerdmans Publishing Co. 1964.

Bruce, F. F., gen. ed. *The New International Bible Commentary with the New International Version.* Grand Rapids: Zondervan Publishing House. 1986.

Bruce, F. F., and E. K. Simpson. *Ephesians and Colossians. The New International Commentary on the New Testament.* Ed. by F. F. Bruce. Grand Rapids: William B. Eerdmans Publishing Co. 1975.

Bullinger, Ethelbert W. *A Critical Lexicon and Concordance to the English and Greek New Testament.* 8th ed. London: The Lamp Press, Ltd. 1957.

Bultmann, Rudolf. *The Gospel of John.* Trans. by G. R. Beasley-Murray. Philadelphia: The Westminster Press. 1975.

Bultmann, Rudolf. *Primitive Christianity in its Contemporary Setting.* Trans. by R. H. Fuller. New York: The World Publishing Company. 1972.

Burdick, Donald W. *Oida and Ginōskō in the Pauline Epistles.* In *New Dimensions in New Testament Study.* Ed. by Richard N. Longenecker and Merrill C. Tenney. Grand Rapids: Zondervan Publishing House. 1974.

Burkert, Walter. *Greek Religion.* Trans. by John Raffan. Cambridge: Harvard University Press. 1985.

Burrows, Millar. *The Dead Sea Scrolls.* New York: Viking Press. 1955.

Burton, Ernest De Witt. *A Critical and Exegetical Commentary on the Epistle to the Galatians. The International Critical Commentary.* Ed. by S. R. Driver, A. Plummer, and C. A. Briggs. Edinburgh: T. and T. Clark. 1975.

Buttrick, George Arthur, ed. *The Interpreter's Dictionary of the Bible.* 5 vols. Nashville: Abingdon Press. 1962.

Carcopino, Jerome. *Daily Life in Ancient Rome.* Trans. by E. O. Lorimer. New Haven: Yale University Press. 1940.

Carson, D. A. *Matthew.* In *Matthew, Mark, and Luke.* Vol. 8 of *The Expositor's Bible Commentary.* Ed. by Frank E. Gaebelein. Grand Rapids: Zondervan Publishing House. 1984.

Casson, Lionel. *Ships and Seamanship in the Ancient World.* Princeton: Princeton University Press. 1971.

Chamberlain, William D. *An Exegetical Grammar of the Greek New Testament.* New York: The Macmillan Company. 1952.

Charles, R. H. *The Revelation of St. John.* 2 vols. *The International Critical Commentary.* Ed. by S. R. Driver, A. Plummer, and C. A. Briggs. Edinburgh: T. and T. Clark. 1971.

Childs, Brevard S. *The Book of Exodus. The Old Testament Library.* Ed. by Peter Ackroyd, et al. Philadelphia: The Westminster Press. 1974.

Clark, Stephen B. *Man and Woman in Christ: An Examination of the Roles of Men and Women in the Light of Scripture and the Social Sciences.* Ann Arbor, MI: Servant Books. 1980.

Conzelmann, Hans. *1 Corinthians.* Ed. by George W. McRae, and trans. by James W. Leitch. *Hermeneia.* Ed. by Helmut Koester, et al. Philadelphia: Fortress Press. 1975.

Cook, Barbara. *Ordinary Women, Extraordinary Strength.* Lynnwood: Aglow Publications. 1988.

Corswant, Willy. *A Dictionary of Life in Bible Times.* Trans. by Arthur Heathcote. London: Hodder and Stoughton. 1960.

Craigie, Peter C. *Deuteronomy. The New International Commentary on the Old Testament.* Ed. by R. K. Harrison. Grand Rapids: William B. Eerdmans Publishing Co. 1976.

Cranfield, C. E. B. *The Epistle to the Romans.* 2 vols. *The International Critical Commentary.* Rev. ed. Ed. by J. A. Emerton and C. E. B. Cranfield. Edinburgh: T. and T. Clark. 1979.

Cremer, Hermann. *Biblico-Theolocial Lexicon of New Testament Greek.* 4th ed. Trans. by William Urwick. Edinburgh: T. and T. Clark. 1895.

Cross, F. L. *The Oxford Dictionary of the Christian Church.* Oxford: Oxford University Press. 1974.

Cullman, Oscar. *The State of the New Testament.* London: SCM Press, Ltd. 1957.

Dana, H. E., and Julius R. Mantey. *A Manual of the Greek New Testament.* New York: The Macmillan Co. 1955.

Daube, David. "Jesus and the Samaritan Woman: The Meaning of *Sugchraomai.*" *Journal of Biblical Literature* 69 (1950): 137–147.

Davids, Peter H. *The Epistle of James: A Commentary on the Greek Text. New International Greek Testament Commentary.* Ed. by I. Howard Marshall and W. Ward Gasque. Grand Rapids: William B. Eerdmans Publishing Co. 1982.

Deissmann, G. Adolf. *Bible Studies.* Winona Lake, IN: Alpha Publications. 1979.

Deissmann, G. Adolf. *Light from the Ancient East.* Trans. by Lionel R. M. Strachan. New York: Harper and Brothers. 1922.

Derrett, J. D. M. "Law in the New Testament: The Parable of the Unjust Judge." *New Testament Studies* 18 (January 1972): 178–191.

Dibelius, Martin. *James.* Trans. by Michael A. Williams. *Hermeneia.* Ed. by Helmut Koester, et al. Philadelphia: Fortress Press. 1976.

Dodd, C. H. *The Apostolic Preaching of the Cross.* Grand Rapids: Baker Book House. 1980.

Dodd, C. H. *The Interpretation of the Fourth Gospel.* Cambridge: Cambridge University Press. 1972.

Dods, Marcus. *The Epistle to the Hebrews.* In *Thessalonians–James.* Vol. 4 of *The Expositor's Greek Testament.* Ed. by W. Robertson Nicoll. Grand Rapids: William B. Eerdmans Publishing Co. 1974.

Doerksen, Vernon. *James.* Chicago: Moody Press. 1983.

Douglas, J. D. *The New Bible Dictionary.* 2d ed. Wheaton: Tyndale House Publishers. 1982.

Douglas, J. D., ed. *The Illustrated Bible Dictionary.* 3 vols. Wheaton: Tyndale House Publishers. 1980.

Dunn, James D. G. *Jesus and the Spirit.* Philadelphia: The Westminster Press. 1975.

Dunn, James D. G. *Romans 9–16.* Vol. 38b of *Word Biblical Commentary.* Ed. by David A. Hubbard, et al. Waco, TX: Word Books. 1988.

Durant, Will. *The Life of Greece, Part 2.* Vol. 2 of *The Story of Civilization.* New York: Simon and Schuster. 1966.

Eadie, John. *Ephesians.* Vol. 2 of *The John Eadie Greek Text Commentaries.* Grand Rapids: Baker Book House. 1979.

Earle, Ralph. *Word Meanings in the New Testament.* 6 vols. Grand Rapids: Baker Book House. 1984.

Edersheim, Alfred. *The Life and Times of Jesus the Messiah.* 2 vols. Grand Rapids: William B. Eerdmans Publishing Co. 1972.

Ehrenberg, Victor. *From Solon to Socrates.* London: Methuen and Co., Ltd. 1967.

Eichrodt, Walter. *Theology of the Old Testament.* 2 vols. Trans. by J. A. Baker. Philadelphia: The Westminster Press. 1967.

Ellis, E. Earle. *Paul's Use of the Old Testament.* Grand Rapids: William B. Eerdmans Publishing Co. 1957.

Ellis, E. Earle. *Prophecy and Hermeneutic in Early Christianity.* Grand Rapids: William B. Eerdmans Publishing Co. 1978.

Ellison, H. L. *Matthew.* In *The International Bible Commentary with the New International Version.* Ed. by F. F. Bruce. Grand Rapids: Zondervan Publishing House. 1986.

English, E. Schugler. *Rethinking the Rapture.* Traveller's Rest, SC: Southern Bible Book House. 1954.

Erickson, Millard J. *Christian Theology.* Grand Rapids: Baker Book House. 1986.

Fee, Gordon D. *The First Epistle to the Corinthians. The New International Commentary on the New Testament.* Ed. by F. F. Bruce. Grand Rapids: William B. Eerdmans Publishing Co. 1987.

Fee, Gordon D. *1 and 2 Timothy, Titus. A Good News Commentary.* Ed. by W. Ward Gasque. San Francisco: Harper and Row. 1984.

Finley, M. I. *The Ancient Economy.* Los Angeles: University of California Press. 1973.

Fitzmyer, Joseph A. *The Gospel According to Luke.* Vol. 28 of *The Anchor Bible.* Ed. by William Foxwell Albright and David Noel Freedman. Garden City, NY: Doubleday and Company, Inc. 1982.

Forbes, R. J., ed. *Studies in Ancient Technology.* 9 vols. Leiden: E. J. Brill. 1965.

Ford, J. Massyngberde. *Revelation.* Vol. 38 of *The Anchor Bible.* Ed. by William Foxwell Albright and David Noel Freedman. Garden City, NY: Doubleday and Company, Inc. 1975.

Foulkes, Francis. *The Epistle of Paul to the Ephesians.* Vol. 10 of *Tyndale New Testament Commentaries.* Ed. by R. V. G. Tasker. Grand Rapids: William B. Eerdmans Publishing Co. 1983.

Furnish, Victor Paul. *2 Corinthians.* Vol. 32a of *The Anchor Bible.* Ed. by William Foxwell Albright and David Noel Freedman. Garden City, NY: Doubleday and Company, Inc. 1984.

Gartner, Betril Edgar. *The Temple and the Community in Qumran and the New Testament.* Cambridge: Cambridge University Press. 1965.

Gehman, Henry Snyder, ed. *The New Westminster Dictionary of the Bible.* Philadelphia: The Westminster Press. 1970.

Gemsler, B. *The Rîv or Controversy Pattern in Hebrew Mentality.* In *Wisdom in Israel and in the Ancient Near East.* Ed. by M. Noth and D. W. Thomas. *Supplements to Vetus Testamentum,* vol. 3. Leiden: E. J. Brill. 1969.

Gesenius, Wilhelm. *Gesenius' Hebrew Grammar.* 2d English ed., ed. and rev. by E. Kautzsch and A. E. Cowley. Oxford: Clarendon Press. 1910.

Glover, T. R. *The Conflict of Religions in the Early Roman Empire.* Washington: Canon Press. 1974.

Grant, Robert McQueen. *Gnosticism and Early Christianity.* 2d ed. New York: Columbia University Press. 1966.

Green, Michael. *The Second Epistle of Peter and the Epistle of Jude.* Vol. 18 of *Tyndale New Testament Commentaries.* Ed. by R. V. G. Tasker. Grand Rapids: William B. Eerdmans Publishing Co. 1975.

Green, Samuel G. *Handbook to the Grammar of the Greek Testament.* London: The Religious Tract Society. N.d.

Greenlee, J. Harold. *A Concise Exegetical Grammar of New Testament Greek.* Grand Rapids: William B. Eerdmans Publishing Co. 1963.

Greenlee, J. Harold. *A New Testament Greek Morpheme Lexicon.* Grand Rapids: Zondervan Publishing House. 1983.

Grimm, C. L. Wilibald. *A Greek-English Lexicon of the New Testament.* 4th ed., trans. and rev. by Joseph Henry Thayer. Edinburgh: T. and T. Clark. 1956.

Gundry, Robert. *Matthew: A Commentary on His Literary and Theological Art.* Grand Rapids: William B. Eerdmans Publishing Co. 1982.

Guthrie, Donald. *The Letter to the Hebrews.* Vol. 20 of *Tyndale New Testament Commentaries.* Ed. by R. V. G. Tasker. Grand Rapids: William B. Eerdmans Publishing Co. 1983.

Guthrie, Donald. *The Pastoral Epistles.* Vol. 14 of *Tyndale New Testament Commentaries.* Ed. by R. V. G. Tasker. Grand Rapids: William B. Eerdmans Publishing Co. 1957.

Guthrie, Donald, and J. A. Motyer. *The New Bible Commentary: Revised.* Grand Rapids: William B. Eerdmans Publishing Co. 1981.

Guthrie, W. K. C. *The Greeks and Their Gods.* Boston: Beacon Press. 1949.

Hagner, Donald A. *Hebrews. A Good News Commentary.* Ed. by W. Ward Gasque. San Francisco: Harper and Row. 1983.

Harner, Philip B. *The "I Am" of the Fourth Gospel.* Facet Books: Biblical Series, no. 26. Philadelphia: Fortress Press. 1970.

Harris, R. Laird, Gleason J. Archer, Jr., and Bruce K. Waltke, eds. *Theological Wordbook of the Old Testament.* 2 vols. Chicago: Moody Press. 1980.

Hastings, James, ed. *Dictionary of Christ and the Gospels.* 2 vols. Grand Rapids: Baker Book House. 1973.

Hastings, James, et al., eds. *Dictionary of the Bible.* New York: Charles Scribner's Sons. 1951.

Hatch, Edwin, and Henry A. Redpath, eds. *A Concordance to the Septuagint.* 2 vols. Reprint. Grand Rapids: Baker Book House. 1983.

Hawthorne, Gerald F. *Philippians.* Vol. 43 of *Word Biblical Commentary.* Ed. by David A. Hubbard, et al. Waco, TX: Word Books. 1983.

Hemer, Colin J. *The Letters to the Seven Churches of Asia in Their Local Setting.* Journal for the Study of the New Testament Supplement Series, vol. 11. Ed. by David Hill. Sheffield, England: JSOT Press. 1986.

Hendriksen, William. *Exposition of the Pastoral Epistles. New Testament Commentary.* Grand Rapids: Baker Book House. 1957.

Hengel, Martin. *Judaism and Hellenism.* Trans. by John Bowden. Philadelphia: Fortress Press. 1981.

Hiebert, D. Edmond. *1 Timothy.* Chicago: Moody Press. 1957.

Hiebert, D. Edmond. *The Thessalonian Epistles.* Chicago: Moody Press. 1971.

Hiebert, D. Edmond. *Titus.* In *Ephesians–Philemon.* Vol. 11 of *The Expositor's Bible Commentary.* Ed. by Frank E. Gaebelein. Grand Rapids: Zondervan Publishing House. 1978.

Hirschfeld, Nicolle. "The Ship of St. Paul: Historical Background, Part 1." *Biblical Archeologist* 53 (March 1990): 25–30.

Hobart, William Kirk. *The Medical Language of St. Luke.* Dublin: Hodges, Figgis, and Co. 1882.

Hodge, Charles. *A Commentary on 1 and 2 Corinthians.* Edinburgh: The Banner of Truth Trust. 1974.

Holladay, William L. *A Concise Hebrew and Aramaic Lexicon of the Old Testament.* Grand Rapids: William B. Eerdmans Publishing Co. 1980.

Hopkins, David C. "Life on the Land: The Subsistence Struggles of Early Israel." *Biblical Archeologist* 50 (September 1987): 179–190.

Hort, Fenton John Anthony. *Judaistic Christianity.* Ed. by J. O. F. Murray. Grand Rapids: Baker Book House. 1980.

Horton, Stanley M. *What the Bible Says about the Holy Spirit.* Springfield, MO: Gospel Publishing House. 1976.

Howard, J. Keir. "Neither Male nor Female: An Examination of the Status of Women in the New Testament." *Evangelical Quarterly* 55, no. 1 (1983): 31–42.

Hughes, Philip E. *The Second Epistle to the Corinthians. The New International Commentary on the New Testament.* Ed. by F. F. Bruce. Grand Rapids: William B. Eerdmans Publishing Co. 1962.

Jackson, F. J. Foakes, and Kirsopp Lake. *The Beginnings of Christianity.* 5 vols. London: Macmillan and Company, Limited. 1920.

Jagersma, Henk. *A History of Israel from Alexander the Great to Bar Kochba.* Trans. by John Bowden. Philadelphia: Fortress Press. 1986.

Jart, Una. "The Precious Stones in the Revelation of St. John 21:18-21." *Studia Theologica* 24 (1970): 150–181.

Jeremias, Joachim. *The Eucharistic Words of Jesus.* London: SCM Press. 1966.

Jeremias, Joachim. *Jerusalem in the Time of Jesus.* Philadelphia: Fortress Press. 1987.

Jeremias, Joachim. *New Testament Theology.* New York: Charles Scribner's Sons. 1971.

Jeremias, Joachim. *The Parables of Jesus.* New York: Charles Scribner's Sons. 1963.

Kaseman, Ernst. *Perspectives on Paul.* Trans. by Margaret Kohl. Philadelphia: Fortress Press. 1974.

Kee, H. C. *The Linguistic Background of Shame in the New Testament.* In *On Language, Culture, and Religion: In Honor of Eugene A. Nida.* Ed. by Matthew Black and William A. Smalley. The Hague: Mouton. 1974.

Keil, C. F., and F. Delitzsch. *Isaiah.* Trans. by James Martin. Vol. 7 of *Commentary on the Old Testament.* Grand Rapids: William B. Eerdmans Publishing Co. 1982.

Kelly, J. N. D. *A Commentary on the Epistles of Peter and Jude. Thornapple Commentaries.* Reprint. Grand Rapids: Baker Book House. 1981.

Kent, Homer. *The Pastoral Epistles.* Chicago: Moody Press. 1958.

Kittel, G., and G. Friedrich, eds. *Theological Dictionary of the New Testament.* Trans. by G. W. Bromiley. 10 vols. Grand Rapids: William B. Eerdmans Publishing Co. 1972.

Kitto, H. D. F. *The Greeks.* Middlesex: Penguin Books. 1951.

Klein, Ralph W. *1 Samuel.* Vol. 10 of *Word Biblical Commentary.* Ed. by John D. Watts, et al. Waco, TX: Word Books. 1983.

Knight, George W. "*Authenteō* in Reference to Women in 1 Timothy 2:12." *New Testament Studies* 30 (1984): 143–157.

Knowling, R. J. *The Acts of the Apostles.* In *Acts–1 Corinthians.* Vol. 2 of *The Expositor's Greek Testament.* Ed. by W. Robertson Nicoll. Grand Rapids: William B. Eerdmans Publishing Co. 1974.

Koester, Helmut. *History, Culture and Religion of the Hellenistic Age.* Philadelphia: Fortress Press. 1982.

Kroeger, Catarine C. "Ancient Heresies and a Strange Greek Verb." *The Reformed Journal* 29, no. 3 (1979): 12–15.

Kubo, Sakae. *A Reader's Greek-English Lexicon of the New Testament.* Berrien Springs: Andrews University Press. 1975.

Kummel, Werner Georg. *Introduction to the New Testament.* Rev. ed., ed. by Howard Clark Kee. Nashville: Abingdon Press. 1975.

Ladd, George Eldon. *The Presence of the Future.* Grand Rapids: William B. Eerdmans Publishing Co. 1974.

Lampe, G. W. H. *A Patristic Greek Lexicon.* Oxford: The Clarendon Press. 1961.

Lane, William L. *The Gospel of Mark. The New International Commentary on the New Testament.* Ed. by F. F. Bruce. Grand Rapids: William B. Eerdmans Publishing Co. 1978.

Lenski, R. C. H. *The Interpretation of the Acts of the Apostles.* Minneapolis: Augsburg Publishing House. 1964.

Lenski, R. C. H. *The Interpretation of the Epistles to the Hebrews and James.* Minneapolis: Augsburg Publishing House. 1966.

Lenski, R. C. H. *The Interpretation of the Epistles of St. Peter, St. John, and St. Jude.* Minneapolis: Augsburg Publishing House. 1966.

Lenski, R. C. H. *The Interpretation of St. Paul's Epistles to the Colossians, to the Thessalonians, to Timothy, to Titus, and to Philemon.* Minneapolis: Augsburg Publishing House. 1966.

Lenski, R. C. H. *The Interpretation of St. Paul's First and Second Epistles to the Corinthians.* Minneapolis: Augsburg Publishing House. 1964.

Lichtheim, Miriam. *The Old and Middle Kingdoms.* Vol. 1 of *Ancient Egyptian Literature.* Los Angeles: University of California Press. 1975.

Liddell, H. G., and R. Scott. *A Greek-English Lexicon.* 9th ed., ed. by H. Stuart Jones and R. McKenzie. Oxford: Clarendon Press. 1940.

Liefeld, Walter L. *Luke.* In *Matthew, Mark, and Luke.* Vol. 8 of *The Expositor's Bible Commentary.* Ed. by Frank E. Gaebelein. Grand Rapids: Zondervan Publishing House. 1984.

Lightfoot, J. B. *The Epistle of St. Paul to the Galatians.* Grand Rapids: Zondervan Publishing House. 1974.

Lightfoot, J. B. *Matthew–Mark.* Vol. 2 of *A Commentary on the New Testament from the Talmud and Hebraica.* Grand Rapids: Baker Book House. 1979.

Lightfoot, J. B. *Saint Paul's Epistle to the Philippians.* Grand Rapids: Zondervan Publishing House. 1953.

Lightfoot, J. B. *Saint Paul's Epistles to the Colossians and to Philemon.* New York: The Macmillan Company. 1897.

Lightfoot, R. H. *St. John's Gospel: A Commentary.* Ed. by C. F. Evans. Oxford: Oxford University Press. 1956.

Limet, Henri. "The Cuisine of Ancient Sumer." *Biblical Archeologist* 50 (September 1987): 132–147.

Lockyer, Hebert, ed. *Nelson's Illustrated Bible Dictionary.* Nashville: Thomas Nelson. 1986.

Lohse, Eduard. *Colossians and Philemon.* Ed. by Helmut Koester, and trans. by William R. Poehlmann and Robert J. Karris. *Hermeneia.* Ed. by Helmut Koester, et al. Philadelphia: Fortress Press. 1982.

Longenecker, Richard N. *The Acts of the Apostles.* In *John–Acts.* Vol. 9 of *The Expositor's Bible Commentary.* Ed. by Frank E. Gaebelein. Grand Rapids: Zondervan Publishing House. 1981.

Louw, Johannes P. and Eugene A. Nida, eds. *Greek-English Lexicon of the New Testament Based on Semantic Domains.* 2 vols. New York: United Bible Societies. 1988.

McDonald, H. Dermot. *Commentary on Colossians and Philemon.* Waco, TX: Word Books. 1982.

Machen, J. Gresham. *New Testament Greek for Beginners.* New York: The Macmillan Company. 1957.

Mackie, George M. *Bible Manners and Customs.* New York: Flemming H. Revell Co. N.d.

Malherbe, Abraham J. *Medical Imagery in the Pastoral Epistles.* In *Texts and Testaments.* Ed. by W. E. March. San Antonio: Trinity University Press. 1980.

Marshall, I. Howard. *The Acts of the Apostles.* Vol. 5 of *Tyndale New Testament Commentaries.* Ed. by R. V. G. Tasker. Grand Rapids: William B. Eerdmans Publishing Co. 1980.

Marshall, I. Howard. *The Epistles of John. The New International Commentary on the New Testament.* Ed. by F. F. Bruce. Grand Rapids: William B. Eerdmans Publishing Co. 1982.

Marshall, I. Howard. *The Gospel of Luke. New International Greek Testament Commentary.* Ed. by I. Howard Marshall and W. Ward Gasque. Grand Rapids: William B. Eerdmans Publishing Co. 1978.

Marshall, I. Howard. *The Meaning of Reconciliation.* In *Unity and Diversity in New Testament Theology: Essays in Honor of George E. Ladd.* Ed. by Robert A. Guelich. Grand Rapids: William B. Eerdmans Publishing Co. 1978.

Mayor, Joseph B. *The Epistle of St. James.* Minneapolis: Klock and Klock Christian Publishers. 1977.

Metzger, Bruce M. *Lexical Aids for Students of New Testament Greek.* Princeton: Bruce M. Metzger. 1978.

Metzger, Bruce M. *A Textual Commentary on the Greek New Testament.* London: United Bible Societies. 1971.

Miranda, Jose. *Christianity is Communism.* In *Third World Liberation Theologies.* Ed. by Deane William Ferm. Maryknoll, NY: Orbis Books. 1986.

Moffatt, James. *The Revelation of St. John the Divine.* In *1 Peter–Revelation.* Vol. 5 of *The Expositor's Greek Testament.* Ed. by W. Robertson Nicoll. Grand Rapids: William B. Eerdmans Publishing Co. 1951.

Moo, Douglas J. "1 Timothy 2:11-15: Meaning and Significance." *Trinity Journal* 1, no. 1 (1980): 62-83.

Morris, Leon. *The First and Second Epistles to the Thessalonians. The New International Commentary on the New Testament.* Ed. by F. F. Bruce. Grand Rapids: William B. Eerdmans Publishing Co. 1959.

Morris, Leon. *The Gospel According to John. The New International Commentary on the New Testament.* Ed. by F. F. Bruce. Grand Rapids: William B. Eerdmans Publishing Co. 1973.

Morris, Leon. *Hebrews.* In *Hebrews–Revelation.* Vol. 12 of *The Expositor's Bible Commentary.* Ed. by Frank E. Gaebelein. Grand Rapids: Zondervan Publishing House. 1981.

Morris, Leon. *The Revelation of St. John.* Vol. 20 of *Tyndale New Testament Commentaries.* Ed. by R. V. G. Tasker. Grand Rapids: William B. Eerdmans Publishing Co. 1969.

Morrish, George. *A Concordance of the Septuagint.* Grand Rapids: Zondervan Publishing House. 1976.

Moule, C. F. D. *An Idiom Book of New Testament Greek.* Cambridge: Cambridge University Press. 1986.

Moulton, Harold K. *The Analytical Greek Lexicon Revised.* Grand Rapids: Zondervan Publishing House. 1977.

Moulton, J. H., and W. F. Howard. *Accidence and Word Formation.* Vol. 2 of *Grammar of New Testament Greek.* Edinburgh: T. and T. Clark. 1979.

Moulton, J. H., and G. Milligan. *The Vocabulary of the Greek Testament Illustrated from the Papyri and Other Non-Literary Sources.* London: Hodder and Stoughton. 1914-1930. Reprint. Grand Rapids: William B. Eerdmans Publishing Co. 1985.

Moulton, W. F., et al. *A Concordance to the Greek New Testament.* Edinburgh: T. and T. Clark. 1897.

Mounce, Robert H. *Revelation. The New International Commentary on the New Testament.* Ed. by F. F. Bruce. Grand Rapids: William B. Eerdmans Publishing Co. 1977.

Muhly, James D. *The Bronze Age Setting.* In *The Coming of the Age of Iron.* Ed. by Theodore A. Wertime and James D. Muhly. New Haven: Yale University Press. 1980.

Muller, J. J. *The Epistles of Paul to the Philippians and to Philemon. The New International Commentary on the New Testament.* Ed. by F. F. Bruce. Grand Rapids: William B. Eerdmans Publishing Co. 1955.

Murphy-O'Connor, Jerome. "1 Corinthians 11:2–16 Once Again." *Catholic Biblical Quarterly* 50, no. 2 (April 1988): 265–274.

Murray, John. *The Epistle to the Romans. The New International Commentary on the New Testament.* Ed. by F. F. Bruce. Grand Rapids: William B. Eerdmans Publishing Co. 1965.

Negev, Abraham. "Understanding the Nabateans." *Biblical Archeology Review* 14 (November–December 1988): 26–45.

O'Brien, Peter T. *Colossians and Philemon.* Vol. 44 of *Word Biblical Commentary.* Ed. by David A. Hubbard, et al. Waco, TX: Word Books. 1982.

Oppenheim, Leo A., ed. *The Assyrian Dictionary.* 21 vols. Chicago: The Oriental Institute of the University of Chicago. 1968.

Orr, William F., and James Arthur Walther. *1 Corinthians.* Vol. 26 of *The Anchor Bible.* Ed. by William Foxwell Albright and David Noel Freedman. Garden City, NY: Doubleday and Company, Inc. 1976.

Osiek, Carolyn. *Galatians.* Vol. 22 of *New Testament Message: A Biblical Theological Commentary.* Wilmington: Michael Glazier, Inc. 1980.

Pegg, Herbert. "A Scorpion for an Egg." *Expository Times* 38 (1926–27): 468–469.

Pfeifer, Charles F., and Howard F. Vos. *The Wycliffe Historical Geography of Bible Lands.* Chicago: Moody Press. 1967.

Plummer, Alfred. *A Critical and Exegetical Commentary on the Gospel According to St. Luke. The International Critical Commentary.* Ed. by S. R. Driver, A. Plummer, and C. A. Briggs. Edinburgh: T. and T. Clark. 1969.

Radford, Lewis B. *The Epistle to Colossians and the Epistle to Philemon. Westminster Commentaries.* Ed. by Walter Lock and D. C. Simpson. London: Melhuen and Co. Ltd. 1931.

Ramsay, W. M. "About the Sixth Hour." *The Expositor* 7 (January–June 1893): 216–223.

Rapinsky, Michael. "The Camel in Ancient Arabia." *Antiquity* 49 (1979): 295–298.

Reicke, Bo Ivar. *The New Testament Era: The World of the Bible from 500 B.C. to A.D. 100.* Philadelphia: Fortress Press. 1968.

Reiling, J., and J. L. Swellengvebel. *A Translator's Handbook on the Gospel of Luke.* London: United Bible Society. 1971.

Richards, Lawrence O. *Expository Dictionary of Bible Words.* Grand Rapids: Zondervan Publishing House. 1985.

Ridderbos, Herman J. *Paul: An Outline of His Theology.* Trans. by Rohn Richard deWitt. Grand Rapids: William B. Eerdmans Publishing Co. 1975.

Ridderbos, Herman J. *Studies in Scripture and its Authority.* Grand Rapids: William B. Eerdmans Publishing Co. 1978.

Rienecker, Fritz. *Linguistic Key to the Greek New Testament.* 2 vols. Grand Rapids: Zondervan Publishing House. 1980.

Robertson, Archibald Thomas. *A Grammar of the Greek New Testament in the Light of Historical Research.* Nashville: Broadman Press. 1934.

Robertson, Archibald Thomas. *Word Pictures in the New Testament.* 6 vols. Nashville: Broadman Press. 1931.

Robinson, J. Armitage. *Commentary on Ephesians.* Grand Rapids: Kregel Publications. 1979.

Ropes, James Hardy. *A Critical and Exegetical Commentary on the Epistle of St. James. The International Critical Commentary.* Ed. by S. R. Driver, A. Plummer, and C. A. Briggs. Edinburgh: T. and T. Clark. 1916.

Rose, H. J. *A Handbook of Greek Mythology.* New York: E. P. Dutton and Co., Inc. 1959.

Ross, David. *Aristotle.* London: Methuen and Co., Ltd. 1964.

Roth, Cecil, et al., eds. *Encyclopedia Judaica.* 16 vols. Jerusalem: Keter Publishing House, Ltd. 1971.

Roth, Cecil, and Geoffrey Wigoder, eds. *The New Standard Jewish Encyclopedia.* 5th ed. Garden City, NY: Doubleday and Company, Inc. 1977.

Russell, David S. *The Method and Message of Jewish Apocalyptic.* Philadelphia: The Westminster Press. 1964.

Sanday, William, and Arthur Headlam. *A Critical and Exegetical Commentary on the Epistle to the Romans. The International Critical Commentary.* Ed. by S. R. Driver, A. Plummer, and C. A. Briggs. Edinburgh: T. and T. Clark. 1897.

Saunders, Jason L. *Greek and Roman Philosophy after Aristotle.* New York: The Free Press. 1966.

Scarborough, John. *Facets of Hellenic Life.* Boston: Houghton Mifflin Company. 1976.

Schmithals, Walter. *Paul and the Gnostics.* Trans. by John E. Steely. Nashville: Abingdon Press. 1972.

Scholem, Gershom. "Gemetria." In *Encyclopedia Judaica.* Ed. by Cecil Roth, et al. 16 vols. Jerusalem: Keter Publishing House, Ltd. 1971.

Selwyn, Edward Gordon. *The First Epistle of St. Peter.* Grand Rapids: Baker Book House. 1981.

Sevier, Paul. *Images of the Church in the New Testament.* Philadelphia: The Westminster Press. 1960.

Sherwin-White, Adrian Nicholas. *Roman Society and Roman Law in the New Testament.* Grand Rapids: Baker Book House. 1978.

Sidebottom, E. M. *James, Jude, 2 Peter. The Century Bible.* Ed. by H. H. Rowley and Matthew Black. Grand Rapids: William B. Eerdmans Publishing Co. 1982.

Singer, Isidore, ed. *The Jewish Encyclopedia.* 12 vols. New York: KTAV Publishing House, Inc. N.d.

Smalley, Stephen. *1, 2, 3 John.* Vol. 51 of *Word Biblical Commentary.* Ed. by David A. Hubbard, et al. Waco, TX: Word Books. 1984.

Smith, J. B. *Greek-English Concordance to the New Testament.* Scottsdale, PA: Herald Press. 1974.

Smyth, Herbert Weir. *Greek Grammar.* Cambridge: Harvard University Press. 1984.

Snodgrass, Anthony M. *Iron and Early Metallurgy in the Mediterranean.* In *The Coming of the Age of Iron.* Ed. by Theodore A. Wertime and James D. Muhly. New Haven: Yale University Press. 1980.

Spence, H. D. M., and J. Marshall Lang. *St. Luke.* In *Mark and Luke.* Vol. 16 of *The Pulpit Commentary.* Grand Rapids: William B. Eerdmans Publishing Co. 1950.

Stagg, Frank. *New Testament Theology.* Nashville: Broadman Press. 1962.

Stagg, Frank. *Polarities of Man's Existence in Biblical Perspective.* Philadelphia: The Westminster Press. 1973.

Stein, Robert H. *The Method and Message of Jesus' Teachings.* Philadelphia: The Westminster Press. 1978.

Strack, Hermann L., and Paul Billerbeck. *Kommentar zum Neuen Testament.* 6 vols. Muchen: C. H. Beck'sche Verlagsbuchhandlung. 1974.

Summers, Ray. *Worthy is the Lamb.* Nashville: Broadman Press. 1951.

Temkin, Owsei. *The Falling Sickness.* 2d ed. Baltimore: The Johns Hopkins Press. 1971.

Tenney, Merrill C., ed. *The Zondervan Pictorial Bible Dictionary.* Grand Rapids: Zondervan Publishing House. 1972.

Tenney, Merrill C., ed. *The Zondervan Pictorial Encyclopedia of the Bible.* 5 vols. Grand Rapids: Zondervan Publishing House. 1975.

Thayer, Joseph Henry. *Greek-English Lexicon of the New Testament.* 4th ed. Grand Rapids: Baker Book House. 1979.

Theissen, Henry C. *Introduction to the New Testament.* Grand Rapids: William B. Eerdmans Publishing Co. 1950.

Thrall, Margaret E. *Greek Participles in the New Testament.* Grand Rapids: William B. Eerdmans Publishing Co. 1962.

Tigoy, Jeffrey H. "On the Term Phylacteries." *Harvard Theological Review* 72 (January–April 1979): 45–54.

Torrance, Thomas F. *The Apocalypse Today.* Greenwood, S.C.: The Attic Press, Inc. 1960.

Trench, Richard C. *Synonyms of the New Testament.* 8th ed. Greenwood: The Attic Press, Inc. 1961.

Turner, Nigel. *Christian Words.* Nashville: Thomas Nelson Publishers. 1982.

Turner, Nigel. *Grammatical Insights into the New Testament.* Edinburgh: T. and T. Clark. 1965.

Turner, Nigel. *Style.* Vol. 4 of *A Grammar of New Testament Greek.* Edinburgh: T. and T. Clark. 1976.

Turner, Nigel. *Syntax.* Vol. 3 of *A Grammar of New Testament Greek.* Edinburgh: T. and T. Clark. 1980.

Tyler, Alice F. *Freedom's Ferment.* New York: Harper and Row. 1962.

Vaughan, Curtis. *Colossians.* In *Ephesians–Philemon.* Vol. 11 of *The Expositor's Bible Commentary.* Ed. by Frank E. Gaebelein. Grand Rapids: Zondervan Publishing House. 1978.

Vaughan, Curtis, and Virtus E. Gideon. *A Greek Grammar of the New Testament.* Nashville: Broadman Press. 1979.

Vincent, Marvin R. *The Epistles to the Philippians and to Philemon. The International Critical Commentary.* Ed. by S. R. Driver, A. Plummer, and C. A. Briggs. Edinburgh: T. and T. Clark. 1972.

Vincent, Marvin R. *Word Studies in the New Testament.* 4 vols. Grand Rapids: William B. Eerdmans Publishing Co. 1946.

Vine, W. E. *An Expository Dictionary of New Testament Words.* Nashville: Royal Publishers, Inc. 1952.

Walbank, F. W. *A Historical Commentary on Polybius.* 3 vols. Oxford: Clarendon Press. 1967.

Waldbaum, Jane C. *The First Archaeological Appearance of Iron and the Transition to the Iron Age.* In *The Coming of the Iron Age.* Ed. by Theodore A. Wertime and James D. Muhly. New Haven: Yale University Press. 1980.

Walters, Peter. *The Text of the Septuagint.* Ed. by D. W. Gooding. Cambridge: Cambridge University Press. 1973.

General Reference Sources by Title

This list is provided to make it easier for the reader to find the source material in those instances where only the title of the general reference is cited in text without the editor(s) or compiler(s).

The Analytical Greek Lexicon Revised. Harold K. Moulton. Grand Rapids: Zondervan Publishing House. 1977.

The Assyrian Dictionary. Ed. by A. Leo Oppenheim. 21 vols. Chicago: The Oriental Institute of the University of Chicago. 1968.

Biblico-Theological Lexicon of New Testament Greek. August Hermann Cremer. 4th ed. Trans. by William Urwick. Edinburgh: T. and T. Clark. 1962.

A Concise Hebrew and Aramaic Lexicon of the Old Testament. William L. Holladay. Grand Rapids: William B. Eerdmans Publishing Co. 1980.

A Critical Lexicon and Concordance to the English and Greek New Testament. Ethelbert W. Bullinger. 8th ed. London: The Lamp Press, Ltd. 1957.

A Dictionary of Life in Bible Times. Willy Corswant. Trans. by Arthur Heathcote. London: Hodder and Stoughton. 1960.

Encyclopedia Judaica. Ed. by Cecil Roth, et al. 16 vols. Jerusalem: Keter Publishing House, Ltd. 1971.

Expository Dictionary of Bible Words. Lawrence O. Richards. Grand Rapids: Zondervan Publishing House. 1985.

An Expository Dictionary of New Testament Words. W. E. Vine. Nashville: Royal Publishers, Inc. 1952.

A Greek-English Lexicon. H. G. Liddell and R. Scott. 9th ed. Ed. by H. Stuart Jones and R. McKenzie. Oxford: Oxford University Press. 1940.

Greek-English Lexicon of the New Testament. Joseph Henry Thayer. 4th ed. Grand Rapids: Baker Book House. 1979.

Greek-English Lexicon of the New Testament Based on Semantic Domains. Ed. by Johannes P. Louw and Eugene A. Nida. 2 vols. New York: United Bible Societies. 1988.

A Greek-English Lexicon of the New Testament and Other Early Christian Literature. W. A. Bauer, William F. Arndt, and F. Wilbur Gingrich. 2d ed. Revised and augmented by F. Wilbur Gingrich and Frederick W. Danker. Chicago: The University of Chicago Press. 1979.

A Homeric Dictionary. Georg Autenreith. Trans. by Robert P. Keep. Norman, OK: University of Oklahoma Press. 1972.

The International Standard Bible Encyclopedia. Ed. by Geoffrey W. Bromiley. 4 vols. Grand Rapids: William B. Eerdmans Publishing Co. 1979.

The Interpreter's Dictionary of the Bible. Ed. by George Arthur Buttrick. 5 vols. Nashville: Abingdon Press. 1962.

The Jewish Encyclopedia. Ed. by Isidore Singer. 12 vols. New York: KTAV Publishing House, Inc. N.d.

The New Bible Dictionary. Ed. by J. D. Douglas. 2d ed. Wheaton: Tyndale House Publishers. 1982.

The New International Dictionary of New Testament Theology. Ed. by Colin Brown. 4 vols. Grand Rapids: Zondervan Publishing House. 1975.

The New Standard Jewish Encyclopedia. Ed. by Cecil Roth and Geoffrey Wigoder. 5th ed. Garden City, NY: Doubleday and Company, Inc. 1977.

The New Westminster Dictionary of the Bible. Ed. by Henry Snyder Gehman. Philadelphia: The Westminster Press. 1970.

A Patristic Greek Lexicon. G. W. H. Lampe. Oxford: The Clarendon Press. 1961.

A Reader's Greek-English Lexicon of the New Testament. Sakae Kubo. Berrien Springs: Andrews University Press. 1975.

Theological Dictionary of the New Testament. Ed. by G. Kittel and G. Friedrich. 10 vols. Trans. by G. W. Bromiley. Grand Rapids: William B. Eerdmans Publishing Co. 1964-1977.

Theological Wordbook of the Old Testament. Ed. by R. Laird Harris, Gleason J. Archer, Jr., and Bruce K. Waltke. 2 vols. Chicago: Moody Press. 1980.

The Vocabulary of the Greek Testament Illustrated from the Papyri and Other Non-Literary Sources. J. H. Moulton and G. Milligan. London: Hodder and Stoughton. 1914-1930. Reprint. Grand Rapids: William B. Eerdmans Publishing Co. 1985.

The Zondervan Pictorial Bible Dictionary. Ed. by Merrill C. Tenney. Grand Rapids: Zondervan Publishing House. 1972.

Literature of Antiquity

The "Literature of Antiquity" (8th century B.C. to 16th century A.D.) refers to the noncanonical quotations and references found in one or all of the volumes of the *Greek-English Dictionary.* Also included are the sources where these materials may be found in print, many of which contain English translations.

Aeschylus.*
Agamemnon.
Prometheus Bound.
Septem contra Thebas.

Anaxandrides.

The Apostolic Fathers.*
1 Clement.
The Didache.
The Epistle of Barnabas.
The Epistle to Diognetus.
The Epistle to the Philippians of St. Polycarp.
The Epistles of St. Ignatius.
The Martyrdom of Polycarp.
The Shepherd of Hermas.

Aristophanes.*
Thesmophriazusae.

Aristotle.*
Analytica Priora (Prior Analytics).
The Athenian Constitution.
De Caelo (On the Heavens).
Ethica Nicomachea (Nichomachean Ethics).
Historia Animalium (The History of Animals).
De Longitudine et Brevitate Vitae (On Length and Shortness of Life).
Meteorologica.
Mirabilia (*De Mirabilibus Auscultationibus,* On Marvelous Things Heard).
Politica (*Politics*).
Problemata (Problems).
Rhetorica (Rhetoric).

The Babylonian Talmud. Ed. by I. Epstein. London: The Soncino Press. 1948.

Cicero.*
In Verrem.
Letters to Atticus.

Demosthenes.*
De Corona and De Falsa Legatione.
Orations.

Diodorus Siculus.
Library of History.

Diogenes Laertius.*
Lives of Eminent Philosophers.

Dionysius of Halicarnassus.*
Roman Antiquities.

Epictetus.*
Discourses.

Epicurus. *To Menoeceus.* In *Letters, Principal Doctrines and Vatican Sayings.* Trans. by Russel M. Geer. Indianapolis: The Bobbs-Merrill Company, Inc. 1964.

Euripides.*
Supplices.

Herodotus.*

Hesiod.*
Fragmenta.
Theogony.
Works and Days.

Hippocrates.*
De Fracturis (On Fractures).
Prognostikon (The Book of Prognostics).

Homer.*
Iliad.
Odyssey.

Homeric Hymns.
Hymn to Demeter.

Josephus. *The Complete Works of Flavius Josephus.* Trans. by William Whiston. Grand Rapids: Kregel Publications. 1960.
Against Apion.
Antiquities of the Jews.
Wars of the Jews.

Justin. *Apology.* In *St. Justin Martyr.* Vol. 6, *The Fathers of the Church.* Washington, D.C.: The Catholic University of America Press. 1977.

Lucian.*
Tyrannicida (The Tyrannicide).
Philopseudes (The Lover of Lies).

Lycurgus. In *Minor Attic Orators.**

Marcus Aurelius. *Lucretius, Epictetus, Marcus Aurelius.* Trans. by George Long. *Great Books of the Western World.* Chicago: William Benton, Publisher. 1971.

Methodius. *The Symposium: A Treatise on Chastity.* Trans. by Herbert Musurillo. Vol. 27 of *Ancient Christian Writers.* New York: Newman Press. 1958.

The Mishna: Translated from the Hebrew with Introduction and Brief Explanatory Notes. Trans. by Herbert Danby. Oxford: Oxford University Press. 1933.

Mishnayoth. 7 vols. Ed. by Philip Blackman. New York: Judaica Press, Inc. 1964.

The Old Testament Pseudepigrapha. 2 vols. Ed. by James H. Charlesworth. Garden City, NY: Doubleday and Company, Inc. 1983.

Pausanias.*
Description of Greece.

Philo.*
De Migratione Abrahami (On the Migration of Abraham).
De Mutatione Nonimum (On the Change of Names).
De Opificio Mundi (On the Creation).
Quid Rerum Divinarum Heres (Who Is the Heir of Divine Things?).
De Specialibus Legibus (On the Special Books).
De Somniis (On Dreams).
De Vita Mosis (The Life of Moses).

Philodemus. *Volumnia Rhetorica.* Ed. by Siegfried Sudhaus. 2 vols. Lipsiae: n.p. 1896.

Philostratus.*
Vitae Sophistarum (The Lives of the Sophists).

Pindar.*
The Odes of Pindar.

Plato.*
Euthyphro, Apology, Crito, Phaedo, Phaedrus.
Legum Allegoriae.
Lysis, Symposium, Gorgias.
Philebus.
Republic.
Timaeus, Critias, Clitophon, Menexenus, Epistulae.

Pliny (The Elder).*
Natural History.

Pliny (The Younger).*
Epistles.

Plotinus.*

Plutarch.*
Alexander.
Demetrius.
Moralia.

Polybius.*
The Histories.

Propertius.*

Pseudo-Phocylidea.

Seneca.*
Moral Essays.

Sophocles.*
Antigone.

Suetonius.*
Life of Nero.

Tacitus.*
Annals.

The Talmud of the Land of Israel. Ed. by Jacob Neusner, et al. Chicago: University of Chicago Press. 1988.

Tertullian. *Against Marcion.* In *Latin Christianity: Its Founder Tertullian.* Vol. 3 of *The Ante-Nicene Fathers.* Ed. by Alexander Roberts and James Donaldson. Edinburgh. 1867. Reprint. Grand Rapids: William B. Eerdmans Publishing Co. 1973.

Theophrastus.*
Characteres.

Thucydides.*

Vettius Valens. *Astrologus.* In *The Greek Anthology and Other Ancient Greek Epigrams.* Ed. and trans. by Peter Jay. New York: Oxford Unisversity Press. 1973.

Xenophon.*
Anabasis.
Constitution of the Lacedaimonians. In *Scripta Minora.*
Cyropaedia (*Institutio Cyri.*)
Memorabilia.

**The Loeb Classical Library.* Cambridge: Harvard University Press.

Author Index

The following men and women have contributed research and/or original manuscripts for the word studies in Volumes 11 through 16 of *The Complete Biblical Library*. Numbers may appear under more than one name if an editor has made a significant contribution. Words not appearing in this index were written entirely by Scandinavian or North American staff members. A more specific author index will appear in volume 17.